THE
1987
Elias Baseball
Analyst

THE
1987
Elias Baseball
Analyst

Seymour Siwoff, Steve Hirdt
& Peter Hirdt

COLLIER BOOKS
Macmillan Publishing Company
New York
COLLIER MACMILLAN PUBLISHERS
London

Macmillan Publishing Company
866 Third Avenue, New York, N.Y. 10022
Collier Macmillan Canada, Inc.

''The Library of Congress has cataloged this
serial publication as follows:''.

The . . . Elias baseball analyst.—1985–   —New York:
  Collier Books, c1985–

      v.; 28 cm.

    Annual.
    Re-arrangement of material issued in a series of computerized reports called: The
Player analysis.
    Produced by the Elias Sports Bureau.
    Editors for 1985–   by S. Siwoff, S. Hirdt, and P. Hirdt.

    1. Baseball—United States—Statistics—Periodicals. 2. National League of Profes-
sional Baseball Clubs—Statistics—Periodicals. 3. Baseball—Statistics—
    1. Baseball—United States—Statistics—Periodicals. 2. National League of Peri-
odicals. 4. Baseball—Miscellanea—Periodicals. I. Siwoff,   Seymour. II. Hirdt,
Steve. III. Hirdt, Peter. IV. Elias Sports Bureau. V. Player analysis. VI. Title:
Baseball analyst.
GV877.E44   85-643022
                              796.357'0973—dc19
                                                          AACR 2   MARC-S
ISBN 0-02-028710-0

Contents

ACKNOWLEDGEMENTS

You only need to glance quickly at these pages to realize that a book of this type couldn't be produced by only three authors. We have been blessed with outstanding support from our colleagues, from within the walls of the Elias Sports Bureau and from outside as well. The ultimate publication of each year's *Analyst* is truly the product of the labor of tens, perhaps hundreds of partners whose names could never fit on our cover. (And not just because three of them are named *Labombarda*.)

Foremost among our Elias partners is Tom Hirdt, who for a third consecutive year (an *Elias Baseball Analyst* record) found enough time between New York Rangers home games to supply his hard work, insight, statistical skepticism, and, grudgingly, his wit to our book. From the time Jesse Orosco tossed his World Championship mitt skyward until the final piece of our manuscript left the office, no one worked harder or longer toward making this a book we could be proud of. As in past years, Tommy made an indispensable contribution to the *Analyst*, without which we could not have produced a book of the quality that we and our readers want. If there's any justice, his hard work will be rewarded with a Stanley Cup. Until then, we'd like to offer our sincerest appreciation.

John Chymczuk and John Labombarda headed a staff of researchers that provided diligent, painstaking, and often thankless hours of investigation. That's an occupational hazard for these guys: John C. spends most of his summer—or at least that part of it spent away from the Shea Stadium mezzanine—poring over thousands of play-by-play reports and coordinating their transfer to a computer-readable format; John L. has earned the nickname "Hammer," as in Mike, for his ability to track down box-score errors throughout the season. For their efforts, John and John are thanked roughly once a year. Till next year, thanks, guys.

Thanks also to the rest of the Elias staff. Santo Labombarda and Frank Labombarda supported John C. and older brother John L. in their scrutiny of play-by-plays and box scores, and not just because if they didn't, they'd have to answer to Mr. and Mrs. L. And thanks to Lino "The Refrigerator" Gutierrez, who also assisted them for two years before playing out his option last summer.

While we all slept, Rocky Avakian made sure that our computer didn't. Of course, that meant that Rocky had to keep weird hours as well; weird, that is, for most of us. But not for Rocky, who made sure those disk drives kept spinning around the clock, and spent the Letterman hours poring over *The Baseball Encyclopedia*, *The Baseball Guide*, and so on to boot. Thanks, big guy. We also want to express our gratitude to Jay Chesler and Bob Rosen. Every team needs its veteran foundation; Rocky, Jay, and Bob have more than 80 years of experience at Elias between them, experience that has benefitted all of us.

No less ambitious or effective than our research crew was our crack computer staff. Needless to say, Christopher Thorn could have brought us to our knees at a moment's notice, but was nice enough not to, even when we appropriated more—much more—than our allotment of computer storage and time. And Chris even managed to keep the shop running smoothly in the few hours we left for him. Nice work.

Chris's staff also took a grin-and-bear-it approach to our often overbearing demands. We owe a debt of gratitude to Andrew Thorn, Andrew Serp, Anthony Sorrentino, Paul Mort, and Gil Traub. Dr. Gil, by the way, was our resident mathematical whiz. Suffice it to say that we benefitted not only from his knowledge of statistics, but also from his patient and willing educator's approach. Couldn't have done it without you.

Larry Meisner kept his software purring, and, more importantly, kept his humor when the software gave an occasional growl. Every year, we carry our wish list to Larry, and every year he wipes the slate clean. We think that's neat. And thanks, as always, to Warren Bannerman, who guided our first steps into the world of computers and play-by-plays in the early 1970s, and who always pops up at the right times when our computers need a swift kick in pants. Dick Hata, who works with Larry and Warren, has also provided many years of tireless work for us, and we are in his debt.

Jeff Neuman, our editor, is one in a million. He has worked ceaselessly to improve the *Analyst*, whether that meant playing devil's advocate over some cockamamie statistical idea, suggesting ideas of his own, correcting our grammar, or exercising his Master's in punning. That sounds like an impossible job, but Jeff's a Red Sox fan, so he knows how to deal with adversity. The Oakland A's may not have seen fit to offer even a one-year managerial contract to their Jeff Newman, but ours can sign one of those lifetime jobs whenever he likes.

The rest of the Macmillan team was a great asset as well. Jon Simon provided editorial assistance throughout the year, for which we are grateful. Copy editor Larry Zuckerman took time from running his Boppers, runners-up in the Obsessive-Compulsive Baseball Association, to help us once again. Larry is one contender who never has trouble staying up top from year to year. Neither does Macmillan's own computer staff: Casey Lee, Fred Richardson, Bob Keefe, and Jackie Dickens. Thanks to all.

We'd also like to express our gratitude to Diane Glynn for her help in telling all of you about our book. Thanks especially to Diane's baseball guru emeritus, Michael Barson. Great job.

THE
1987
Elias Baseball
Analyst

I
Introduction

INTRODUCTION

Welcome to the third annual edition of *The Elias Baseball Analyst*. What's new, you ask? Quite a bit, and we'll get to that shortly. But as usual, we'd like to explain briefly what our book is all about for those unfamiliar with our past editions.

Does the world really need another book of baseball statistics? We think that's the wrong question. A better one would be: Will all these numbers really help me enjoy the game more? We think so. For instance, think back to the ninth inning of Game Five of last year's American League Championship Series. Wouldn't you have viewed the game a little differently if you knew that Don Baylor, who started Boston's comeback rally with a home run, had only two hits in 26 previous at bats against California pitcher Mike Witt? And wouldn't you have wanted to know that Baylor is one of the best hitters in baseball in Late-Inning Pressure Situations? Or that Rich Gedman, whose three hits against Witt that day prompted Angels manager Gene Mauch to pull Witt and replace him with Gary Lucas, had only two other hits against Witt in his entire career? Remember when Lucas hit Gedman with a pitch to put the tying run on base? That was the first batter Lucas had hit in four years. Would you have brought in Donnie Moore with the pennant one out away to face Dave Henderson? What if you knew that. . . well, let's not give away the whole store. Check the California Angels essay on page 23. It's facts like these that make the study of baseball a delicious hobby, and that's exactly what we provide in the *Analyst*.

Another anecdote: On opening day last season, Baltimore trailed Cleveland 6–4 in the bottom of the eighth inning. The bases were loaded with two out when Indians manager Pat Corrales called upon his relief ace, Ernie Camacho. Orioles skipper Earl Weaver responded by sending pinch-hitter Rick Dempsey to the plate. Suddenly, the Baltimore press box was buzzing; on page 184 of *The 1986 Elias Baseball Analyst* was written, "Attention Earl: Since 1981, Dempsey is hitless in 16 at bats with two outs and the bases loaded; he has batted .067 (3-for-45) in such situations in the last 11 years." Dempsey popped out to kill the rally, and at the end of the game, confronted with our figures, angrily swore that they had to be wrong. Sorry, Rick, but we always double-check.

A few weeks later, Chicago White Sox rookie Joel Davis had overpowered the Detroit Tigers for five innings, holding them to one hit. At that point, a network telecast of the game presented the following graphic: "Joel Davis/Career earned run average: 2.56 over the first five innings, 8.06 in the sixth inning and later." Davis was rocked for three runs in the sixth and lost the game. After the game, Ken Harrelson, Chicago's general manager at the time, raced over to broadcaster Don Drysdale and asked, "How did you know about Davis? Even we weren't aware of that." Drysdale might have answered, "Page 276 of *The 1986 Elias Baseball Analyst*."

Throughout the season, a copy of the *Analyst* by your side at the ballpark on in front of the television set will consistently add to your excitement and enjoyment of baseball. The more you know, the more you can anticipate. And the more you anticipate, the more you'll enjoy—and be delighted by the game's subtle surprises.

The Elias Sports Bureau has been recording baseball statistics since the dead-ball era. The company's trademark has always been accuracy, a quality honed when statistics were entered by hand on color-coded tally sheets, and one that has made the transition to the era of microchips. About 15 years ago, we began to assemble the structure of a computer system that would digest play-by-play details from every major-league game and assimilate them into various categories for analytical purposes. By 1975, that system was up and running, and following that season we first produced a group of reports called *The Player Analysis*.

Those reports included breakdowns of player and team performance statistics that are essentially the same as those included in this book. For the first time, there was a systematic, ongoing analysis of how each batter and pitcher did with runners in scoring position, or in the late innings or close games, or against opposing left-handers, or in any of many other meaningful situations. The reports were marketed to what we presumed to be the most interested audience—the major-league teams themselves. Some teams weren't interested, but many took advantage of the opportunity to evaluate their players as they'd never to able to before.

The project was an artistic success, but we were also aware that many people following baseball didn't want to know any more about the sport than they already knew. That's all right; one of the beauties of baseball is that it can be enjoyed on many different levels, and the statistical level is certainly a specialized one. But the growing interest in statistics among an ever-increasing segment of the public demanded that we make our material available to as wide an audience as possible. Two years ago, we celebrated the tenth anniversary of our project by publishing the first edition of *The Elias Baseball Analyst*, a book that contained the best of the material we had formerly provided to the teams themselves, as well as many features created especially for the book.

We feel that the 1987 *Analyst* is our best effort yet. As always, we've tackled some interesting questions and come up with answers we're sure will surprise you as much as they surprised us. Who's been the best manager of the past 25 years? Do players hit better when they take the field coming off a hot streak than when they've been battling a slump? Can a starting pitcher like Roger Clemens really be the most valuable player in his league? Can experienced pitchers exploit inexperienced hitters? How important is it to move your base runners ahead with outs? What simple factor affects the head-to-head matchup of batters and pitch-

ers nearly as much as left- and right-handedness? What are the universal effects of artificial turf? What statistic is a great leading indicator of a team poised for a turnaround? (Hint: Don't be surprised if the Dodgers win the Western Division and the Pirates reverse their poor recent form.)

Within these pages you'll find answers to those questions and thousands of others, as well as all the regular features that have appeared in past editions. For example, we've included the "Loves to face, Hates to face" references in the Batter and Pitcher Sections, which list, for each player, opponents who have proved to be particularly easy or difficult for him to handle. The Batter/Pitcher Matchups Section details how some of the game's best players have done head-to-head against every opponent they've faced at least five times.

We've added a new section this year, Ballparks. A page on each stadium provides tables listing the best and worst visiting players for last season, the best over the 12 years since we began our play-by-play project, and—most important of all—a detailed study of the effects of each stadium on the games played there. How much does Fenway Park pad Wade Boggs's batting average? Does the Oakland Coliseum help or hurt Jose Canseco's home run totals? Which stadium is most likely to increase scoring? Decrease extra-base hits? Affect errors? Casey Stengel probably never dreamed you could look *that* up. But we feel sure he'd describe our book with just one word: Amazin!

II
Team Section

Team Section

The Team Section consists of comments and statistics for each of the twenty-six major-league teams. The examples here, and in all of the section introductions, are from the 1985 season.

WON-LOST RECORD BY STARTING POSITION

BALTIMORE 83-78	C	1B	2B	3B	SS	LF	CF	RF	P	DH	Leadoff	Relief	Starts
Don Aase												26-28	
Eric Bell												0-4	
Mike Boddicker									13-19				13-19
Fritz Connally		1-0		12-15						1-0			14-15
Rich Dauer			32-31	4-4									36-35
Storm Davis									16-12			0-3	16-12
Rick Dempsey	57-56												57-56
Ken Dixon									10-8			2-14	10-8
Jim Dwyer						16-20		16-9		0-1	9-6		32-30
Mike Flanagan									7-8				7-8
Dan Ford										10-6	5-5		10-6
Wayne Gross		0-5		30-27						1-3			31-35
John Habyan												1-1	
Brad Havens									0-1			2-5	0-1
Leo Hernandez										0-4			0-4
Phil Huffman									1-0			0-1	1-0
Lee Lacy						51-61				3-1	16-20		54-62
John Lowenstein				1-3						2-2			3-5

The first table following the team comments is the Won-Lost Record by Starting Position chart. This chart lists, for each player on a team, the team's won-lost record in games started by that player at each position, in the leadoff spot in the lineup, and in games in which a pitcher appeared in relief. (This last is included to give some insight into how the manager chose to use his relief staff.) The players are listed in alphabetical order.

Following this table is a series of four charts detailing the performance of each player and pitcher on the team who played at least semiregularly. Included are all players who had at least 200 plate appearances in the season, all pitchers who faced at least 250 batters, and selected individuals who did not meet the standard but were still significant enough to merit inclusion.

Batting Comparisons: Vs. Left-Handers/Right-Handers and Overall/Late Inning-Pressure Situations

		BA	Rank	SA	Rank	HR %	Rank		BA	Rank	SA	Rank	HR %	Rank
Rich Dauer	vs. Lefties	.247	108	.358	117	2.47	81	Overall	.202	155	.264	154	0.96	129
	vs. Righties	.173	158	.205	158	0.00	152	Pressure	.118	--	.118	--	0.00	--
Rick Dempsey	vs. Lefties	.325	16	.529	20	4.46	44	Overall	.254	99	.406	88	3.31	61
	vs. Righties	.200	149	.312	143	2.44	86	Pressure	.171	149	.293	124	2.44	77
Jim Dwyer	vs. Lefties	.000	--	.000	--	0.00	--	Overall	.249	106	.399	95	3.00	73
	vs. Righties	.250	96	.401	77	3.02	69	Pressure	.344	13	.563	10	3.13	56
Wayne Gross	vs. Lefties	.250	--	1.000	--	25.00	--	Overall	.235	134	.424	69	5.07	17
	vs. Righties	.235	118	.413	69	4.69	27	Pressure	.184	143	.316	113	2.63	69
Lee Lacy	vs. Lefties	.313	26	.470	44	3.01	65	Overall	.293	22	.409	82	1.83	105
	vs. Righties	.282	43	.377	94	1.23	122	Pressure	.297	40	.453	44	4.69	38
Fred Lynn	vs. Lefties	.242	121	.379	104	2.61	79	Overall	.263	78	.449	41	5.13	15
	vs. Righties	.275	53	.485	20	6.44	6	Pressure	.231	104	.481	34	7.69	11
Eddie Murray	vs. Lefties	.286	53	.502	25	4.93	34	Overall	.297	16	.523	4	5.32	13
	vs. Righties	.303	14	.534	7	5.53	15	Pressure	.333	15	.682	3	9.09	4
Floyd Rayford	vs. Lefties	.336	7	.650	2	8.57	1	Overall	.306	78	.521	5	5.01	19
	vs. Righties	.288	31	.438	50	2.74	80	Pressure	.268	64	.585	8	7.32	12
Cal Ripken	vs. Lefties	.272	70	.436	69	2.97	67	Overall	.282	39	.469	25	4.05	44
	vs. Righties	.286	37	.484	22	4.55	29	Pressure	.292	43	.528	23	6.94	15
Gary Roenicke	vs. Lefties	.209	146	.453	59	6.98	9	Overall	.218	151	.458	30	6.67	4
	vs. Righties	.245	--	.472	--	5.66	--	Pressure	.043	--	.174	--	4.35	--
Team Average	vs. Lefties	.271	3	.456	1	4.21	1	Overall	.263	8	.430	1	3.88	1
	vs. Righties	.259	7	.417	4	3.71	1	Pressure	.239	11	.423	1	4.66	1
League Average	vs. Lefties	.266		.416		2.91		Overall	.261		.406		2.82	
	vs. Righties	.259		.401		2.78		Pressure	.253		.381		2.74	

Column Headings Information

BA	Batting Average
SA	Slugging Average
OBA	On-Base Average
HR%	Home Run Percentage (home runs per 100 at bats)
BB%	Base-on-Balls Percentage (bases on balls per 100 plate appearances)
SO%	Strikeout Percentage (strikeouts per 100 plate appearances)
RDI%	Percentage of Runners Driven In

Each chart provides a statistical breakdown of player performance in a selected category. For each category, the player's average or percentage is given, along with his ranking within the league. This enables us to see at a glance that while Jim Dwyer ranked 95th in the league in slugging overall in 1985, he ranked tenth in pressure situations (see below). Rankings in each category are listed for the 169 players and 128 pitchers with the most plate appearances or batters faced in the category (plus ties) in the American League, and the top 142 batters and 116 pitchers (plus ties) in the National League. If a player does not qualify under this standard, no ranking is listed. (For a more detailed description of the methods used in determining the number of qualifiers for a given category, see the introduction to the Leaders Section.)

One batter chart lists breakdowns against left-handed and right-handed pitching and overall performance for the season compared with performance in pressure situations (all at bats occurring in the seventh inning or later with the score tied or the batter's team trailing by one, two, or three runs, or four runs with the bases loaded).

The other batter chart lists miscellaneous comparisons for each player, giving his batting average on grass fields and artificial turf; in home games and in road games; with runners in scoring position and with runners in scoring position and two out; on-base average leading off an inning; and the percentage of runners he drove in from third base with less than two out. (For players who played for more than one team in a league, all totals are combined. The "home" totals for Spike Owen, for example, include all games played in Seattle when he was with the Mariners, and all games played in Boston while he was with the Red Sox.)

On each chart, following the individual batter totals, are the team's averages for each category, and the team's ranking within the league. For purposes of comparison, the overall league average is also included.

The first pitcher chart lists breakdowns against left-handed and right-handed batters and performance with bases empty and runners on base.

The other pitcher chart lists miscellaneous comparisons for each pitcher giving his opponents' batting average on grass fields and artificial turf; in home games and in road games; with runners in scoring position and with runners in scoring position and two out; and opponents' on-base average leading off an inning.

On each chart, following the individual pitcher statistics, are the team's averages for each category, and the team's ranking within the league. For purposes of comparison, the overall league average is also included.

For a detailed discussion of the use of opposing batters' records to examine pitching performance, see the introduction to the Pitcher Section.

American League

BALTIMORE ORIOLES

Goodbye Earl—The Sequel

Earl Weaver replaced Hank Bauer as Baltimore's manager in July 1968, and led the Orioles to a 91–71 finish, good for second place in the American League. That was the first of 18 consecutive winning seasons for Baltimore, the second-longest streak in major-league baseball since 1900. That streak ended this past season, coinciding with Weaver's Retirement II.

The Orioles reached the month of September with a 65–65 record and were a stretch run away from extending the streak to 19 seasons. But like a burned-out sprinter reaching the long home stretch at Churchill Downs, Baltimore failed to respond to Weaver's whip and staggered to the finish line. The O's won only eight of their last 32 games, and finished dead last in the American League's Eastern Division, ending the streak that will evermore be known as "The Weaver Years."

You had to admire Baltimore's consistency throughout baseball's divisional era. Few teams in any of the major team sports have ever compiled longer streaks of winning seasons. No NBA team—not even the legendary Boston Celtics—has ever strung together as many as 15 straight winning seasons. The longest pro baseball, football, and hockey streaks, as of January 1, 1987:

New York Yankees	39	1926–64
Montreal Canadiens	32	1951–83
Dallas Cowboys	20	1966–85
Boston Bruins	19	1967–
Baltimore Orioles	**18**	**1968–85**
Chicago Black Hawks	16	1960–76
Oakland Raiders	16	1965–80
Chicago Bears	15	1930–44
[Philadelphia Flyers	14	1972–]

But as we suggested in the 1985 *Analyst*, Baltimore's streak has been acknowledged with respectful nods but never searing passion. The Orioles weren't tagged with a nickname like the Bronx Bombers, America's Team, or the Monsters of the Midway; they haven't developed a managing image like the outlaw Raiders or the intimidating Flyers. But one thing Baltimore has in common with most of those teams is a legendary leader. Weaver can now take his place alongside Joe McCarthy and Casey Stengel, Tom Landry and George Halas, Toe Blake and Harry Sinden. Earl may or may not have been the best manager of the past 25 years (see the

Seattle essay, page 77), but he was clearly among the most successful in baseball history.

While Weaver spends a well-earned retirement hacking golf balls out of the rough and puttering in his garden, the dawn of a new season means that Orioles fans must confront a troublesome question: What does the future hold for a team that's fallen after so long on top? Will Baltimore suffer a longer or deeper period of decline than teams that stumble after only short-term success?

Only twelve other teams since 1900 have compiled winning records in as many as 10 consecutive seasons, and their post-streak form suggests that the Orioles' down time is likely to be shorter and their rebound higher than that of a typical team that has fallen below the .500 mark. As a control group, we examined 68 teams from 1969 through 1980 that compiled losing records in a season (Year X) immediately following a winning season (Year X minus 1), noting their records in the four seasons after the fall (Years $X+1$ through $X+4$). We compared those results to the records of the 12 teams with long streaks of winning records.

The two sets of teams were nearly identical in the seasons in which they fell below .500 (Year X) as well as in the winning season preceding the fall: The control group declined from an average winning percentage of .545 to .463, the winning-streak group dropped from .543 to .464. The subsequent progress of both groups back through the break-even point is contrasted in the following table:

	$X-1$	X	$X+1$	$X+2$	$X+3$	$X+4$
Winning Streak Teams	.543	.464	.494	.490	.519	.531
68-Team Control Group	.545	.463	.499	.496	.498	.509

The same organizations that produced consistent winners over a decade or more were able to revitalize their teams faster and better than their rivals.

That being the case, there's little doubt that Baltimore's front office spent the winter pondering the solution to its most critical problem of the 1986 season: The Orioles had the least productive leadoff spot in the American League. Weaver used nine different starters in the top spot, tying California for the highest total in the league, and started no leadoff batter in as many as 60 games. (See the Won-Lost Record by Starting Position table for the names and numbers.) The composite of all Baltimore leadoff hitters follows, along with the totals for leadoff batters throughout the rest of the league:

	AB	R	H	2B	3B	HR	RBI	BB	SB	BA	SA	OBA
Baltimore	692	84	159	20	6	5	48	57	30	.230	.298	.289
Boston	664	112	198	47	4	7	58	91	7	.298	.413	.382
California	655	117	160	36	2	19	69	87	29	.244	.392	.334
Chicago	632	95	155	27	5	5	43	86	51	.245	.328	.341
Cleveland	667	121	185	34	6	17	81	81	30	.277	.423	.357
Detroit	692	114	187	29	9	22	81	75	20	.270	.434	.342
Kansas City	688	94	186	24	8	10	42	47	40	.270	.372	.323
Milwaukee	680	95	184	27	8	14	73	55	35	.271	.396	.325
Minnesota	697	118	215	35	6	29	91	41	17	.308	.501	.353
New York	674	137	174	35	5	31	81	91	88	.258	.463	.348
Oakland	646	98	168	22	7	5	66	87	29	.260	.339	.348
Seattle	687	91	158	33	6	8	53	54	41	.230	.330	.288
Texas	675	114	176	28	8	18	53	77	36	.261	.406	.336
Toronto	724	96	219	35	7	16	82	31	23	.302	.436	.335
Averages	677	106	180	31	6	15	66	69	34	.266	.396	.336

Baltimore's leadoff hitters finished last in the league in batting average and slugging average, next-to-last by a single point in on-base average, and—most important of all—last in runs. The Orioles scored 38 fewer runs than the league average of 746, more than half of that difference accounted for by the failure of their leadoff batters, who trailed the league average by 22. Baltimore's second-, third-, and fourth-place hitters exceeded the A.L. average for those spots, the RBI category being a notable exception:

	AB	R	H	2B	3B	HR	RBI	BB	SO	BA	SA	OBA
Baltimore	1906	284	554	86	2	65	257	221	237	.291	.440	.363
A.L. Average	1920	278	529	93	12	63	272	210	301	.276	.435	.347

So the blame for the 22-run deficit from the top spot rests squarely on the shoulders of Wiggins and Co., for failure to place themselves in position to score.

Ironically, Weaver's first move upon his return to the Orioles' dugout in 1985 was designed to improve the leadoff position. He dropped Lee Lacy to the second spot in the batting order, even before the arrival of Alan Wiggins a few weeks later. Lacy rarely walked, and Wiggins had the speed of the leadoff hitters of Baltimore's glory years, Don Buford in the early 1970s and Al Bumbry later in the decade. But within a year, Wiggins had played himself off the team. By the end of the 1986 season, Baltimore's leadoff spot was in no better shape than two years earlier, when the Orioles decided not to re-sign Bumbry at age 37 following his poor 1984 season.

It's curious, then, that Baltimore got on the trade scoreboard early in November not by dealing for a leadoff batter, but by shipping Storm Davis to San Diego for catcher Terry Kennedy. The Orioles had already decided not to exercise their option on another season of Rick Dempsey behind the plate—not at last year's price, at least—and the substitution of Kennedy for Dempsey makes for some interesting speculation for those of you who like a heaping bowl of stats with your morning coffee.

Baltimore's starting catchers had the lowest batting average and the fewest RBIs in the majors. Dempsey, who started 101 games, was the main culprit, but the performance of the reserve catchers provided little hope that help was on the way:

Catcher	GS	AB	R	H	2B	3B	HR	RBI	BB	SO	BA	SA	OBA
Dempsey	101	306	40	64	15	1	13	28	42	73	.209	.392	.311
Stefero	39	105	11	23	2	0	1	9	15	21	.219	.267	.314
Others	22	74	2	7	1	0	1	3	1	24	.095	.149	.107
Totals	162	485	53	94	18	1	15	40	58	118	.194	.328	.283
A.L. Average	162	529	56	124	20	2	15	63	48	90	.235	.365	.301

Nevertheless, Dempsey's reputation as one of the best receivers in baseball—not only for his throwing but also for the way he calls a game and handles his pitchers—offset his shortcomings as a hitter. His value to the team was rarely questioned, especially given the sorry state of catchers in the O's organization. The following figures suggest that Dempsey's catcher's mitt, chest protector, and shin guards were worth about 0.31 runs per game to the Orioles' pitching staff. That's about 32 runs over the 920.2 innings he caught last season. At the rate that Baltimore scores and allows runs, that figure can be converted to about three wins. Runs per nine innings scored against Baltimore over the past three seasons, according to who was behind the plate:

Catcher	Innings	Runs	R/9I
Dempsey	2836.1	1411	4.48
Others	1467.0	780	4.79

On the other hand, Kennedy's reputation as a catcher is that he's . . . well, an adequate first baseman. His arm is average, but his delivery reminds one of ABC's special camera: Super Slo-Mo. Last season, Kennedy allowed 103 stolen bases (not including a steal of home) and threw out only 48 runners, or 31 percent, slightly below the N.L. average. And since throwing is the most visible component of a catcher's defensive ability—it's the only component that's been quantified until now—Kennedy's reputation has suffered. But the rate of runs scored against San Diego with Kennedy behind the plate over the past three seasons was significantly lower than that with San Diego's other backstops (principally Bruce Bochy):

Catcher	Innings	Runs	R/9I
Kennedy	3388.2	1471	3.91
Others	966.1	508	4.73

Kennedy appears to have saved Padres pitchers one run for every 11 innings, equivalent to 103 runs per season, or 10 wins. How valuable is that? No player in baseball—not Mattingly or Boggs or Brett or Schmidt—can add as much as 100 runs per season to his team's offensive production. Not nearly. So common sense tells us that some other factors must be at work. Maybe Kennedy caught the better pitchers, while Bochy caught Ed Whitson. (That turns out not to be the case.) Maybe Bochy is such a poor catcher that he distorts the comparison. Nevertheless, if Kennedy made even half the difference to San Diego's staff that these figures suggest, his value as a catcher has been grossly underrated.

What makes Kennedy even more attractive to Baltimore is that his throwing will be less of a liability in the American League, where the stolen base attempt rate was 29 percent lower than in the National League last season. The drift of aging N.L. stars to designated hitter roles in the American League is a widely acknowledged trend; far less attention has been paid to the one-way signs lining the interleague road travelled by catchers. Three catchers who finished the 1985 season in the National League closed the 1986 season with A.L. teams: Rick Cerone, Darrell Porter, and Steve Yeager. None travelled in the opposite direction. (None, that is, except for Mike Heath, whose reputation as a superior receiver in the American League failed to survive four months in the N.L. Exiled from St. Louis, Heath returned to the A.L., his reputation in tatters.) A year earlier, two catchers—Ron Hassey and Glenn Brummer—were passed from the National League to the American League; only Rick Cerone headed in the other direction and, like Heath, for only a brief stay. And the godfather of them all, of course, is Bob Boone, who found new life when he joined California in 1982 at age 34.

Boone has caught more games than any other catcher in the league since then. To think he was exiled from the National League because he reputedly couldn't throw.

On reputation alone, Kennedy seems an improbable successor to Dempsey. On the numbers, he may outperform those limited expectations. And he's certain to improve on those woeful offensive statistics. But even so, without solving the problems at the top of the order, the Orioles will be hard-pressed to score enough to offset their pitching woes. Storm Davis is gone from a staff that ranked tenth in the league in ERA, despite pitching in the fifth-best pitchers park in the league. The O's may not have done Cal Ripken any favors by making him wait so long before giving him the manager's chair.

WON-LOST RECORD BY STARTING POSITION

BALTIMORE 73-89	C	1B	2B	3B	SS	LF	CF	RF	P	DH	Leadoff	Relief	Starts
Don Aase												44-22	
Tony Arnold												1-10	
Eric Bell									1-3				1-3
Juan Beniquez		7-4	.	14-8		13-22	1-2	2-5		6-3	2-0		43-44
Mike Boddicker									18-15				18-15
Juan Bonilla			29-26	7-12							18-19		36-38
Rich Bordi									0-1			20-31	0-1
Storm Davis									10-15				10-15
Rick Dempsey	52-49												52-49
Ken Dixon									15-18			0-2	15-18
Tom Dodd										1-0			1-0
Jim Dwyer						6-0		4-5		8-12		0-1	18-17
Mike Flanagan									12-16				12-16
Ken Gerhart						1-5	3-7				2-4		4-12
Jackie Gutierrez			11-31	3-1							2-6		14-32
John Habyan						1-4							1-4
Brad Havens												10-36	
Rex Hudler													
Odell Jones												2-19	
Ricky Jones			2-4	1-5									3-9
Mike Kinnunen												0-9	
Lee Lacy							57-59				1-2		57-59
Fred Lynn						54-50							54-50
Dennis Martinez												0-4	
Tippy Martinez												4-10	
Scott McGregor									16-17			0-1	16-17
Eddie Murray		51-68								5-11			56-79
Carl Nichols	1-1												1-1
Tom O'Malley				21-27							4-5		21-27
Al Pardo	5-8									1-0			6-8
Kelly Paris				1-2									1-2
Floyd Rayford	4-1		25-33										29-34
Cal Ripken					73-89								73-89
Larry Sheets	1-1	3-1		1-1		8-13		2-7		30-27			45-50
John Shelby						12-13	15-30	8-12			11-24		35-55
Nate Snell												12-22	
John Stefero	10-29											5-8	10-29
Bill Swaggerty												0-1	
Jim Traber		12-16				1-6	0-1			6-15			19-38
Alan Wiggins			31-28								31-28		31-28
Mike Young						32-30		16-21		2-1			48-51

Batting Comparisons: Vs. Left-Handers/Right-Handers and Overall/Late Inning-Pressure Situations

		BA	Rank	SA	Rank	HR %	Rank		BA	Rank	SA	Rank	HR %	Rank
Juan Beniquez	vs. Lefties	.336	11	.453	50	2.34	94	Overall	.300	20	.397	95	1.75	116
	vs. Righties	.279	54	.363	115	1.40	127	Pressure	.393	4	.508	30	3.28	61
Juan Bonilla	vs. Lefties	.233	119	.301	151	0.97	138	Overall	.243	124	.296	162	0.35	160
	vs. Righties	.249	108	.293	159	0.00	158	Pressure	.200	137	.229	158	0.00	109
Rick Dempsey	vs. Lefties	.254	95	.457	46	4.35	35	Overall	.208	164	.379	108	3.98	50
	vs. Righties	.175	170	.323	140	3.70	59	Pressure	.103	169	.103	170	0.00	109
Jim Dwyer	vs. Lefties	.286	--	.429	--	0.00	--	Overall	.244	--	.488	--	5.00	--
	vs. Righties	.242	116	.490	29	5.23	24	Pressure	.227	112	.523	23	6.82	10
Lee Lacy	vs. Lefties	.280	60	.408	82	3.18	71	Overall	.287	32	.391	98	2.24	104
	vs. Righties	.290	34	.383	99	1.80	109	Pressure	.296	48	.380	78	1.41	99
Fred Lynn	vs. Lefties	.271	72	.521	20	7.29	8	Overall	.287	33	.499	12	5.79	10
	vs. Righties	.292	30	.492	26	5.32	23	Pressure	.281	65	.526	20	5.26	27
Eddie Murray	vs. Lefties	.301	36	.493	33	4.41	33	Overall	.305	15	.463	38	3.43	70
	vs. Righties	.306	19	.451	52	3.06	76	Pressure	.222	117	.444	50	5.56	23
Tom O'Malley	vs. Lefties	.227	--	.273	--	0.00	--	Overall	.254	103	.320	152	0.55	155
	vs. Righties	.258	89	.327	138	0.63	148	Pressure	.286	57	.429	56	3.57	50
Floyd Rayford	vs. Lefties	.194	159	.355	119	4.30	37	Overall	.176	169	.310	155	3.81	60
	vs. Righties	.162	--	.274	--	3.42	--	Pressure	.194	144	.258	149	0.00	109
Cal Ripken	vs. Lefties	.360	4	.683	1	7.32	7	Overall	.282	42	.461	40	3.99	49
	vs. Righties	.255	94	.382	100	2.81	88	Pressure	.274	73	.537	15	6.32	17
Larry Sheets	vs. Lefties	.154	--	.308	--	3.85	--	Overall	.272	55	.488	19	5.33	20
	vs. Righties	.282	47	.503	23	5.45	20	Pressure	.182	148	.295	135	2.27	76
John Shelby	vs. Lefties	.231	124	.388	94	3.73	54	Overall	.228	146	.364	128	2.72	92
	vs. Righties	.226	142	.352	123	2.22	100	Pressure	.264	80	.375	82	0.00	109
John Stefero	vs. Lefties	.167	--	.167	--	0.00	--	Overall	.233	--	.300	--	1.67	--
	vs. Righties	.237	124	.307	150	1.75	111	Pressure	.308	34	.346	100	0.00	109
Jim Traber	vs. Lefties	.200	156	.371	103	5.71	22	Overall	.255	102	.472	29	6.13	8
	vs. Righties	.266	74	.492	27	6.21	11	Pressure	.324	28	.324	115	0.00	109
Alan Wiggins	vs. Lefties	.299	40	.313	146	0.00	148	Overall	.251	111	.272	168	0.00	166
	vs. Righties	.233	129	.256	169	0.00	158	Pressure	.182	148	.182	166	0.00	109
Mike Young	vs. Lefties	.272	69	.400	87	2.40	92	Overall	.252	107	.371	120	2.44	100
	vs. Righties	.242	117	.357	119	2.46	93	Pressure	.264	79	.358	95	1.89	82
Team Average	vs. Lefties	.270	4	.431	4	3.73	2	Overall	.258	8	.395	10	3.06	7
	vs. Righties	.253	11	.381	13	2.80	9	Pressure	.253	8	.380	7	2.60	7
League Average	vs. Lefties	.263		.408		2.88		Overall	.262		.408		2.96	
	vs. Righties	.261		.408		2.99		Pressure	.254		.383		2.61	

Additional Miscellaneous Batting Comparisons

	Grass Surface BA	Rank	Artificial Surface BA	Rank	Home Games BA	Rank	Road Games BA	Rank	Runners in Scoring Position BA	Rank	Runners in Scoring Pos and Two Outs BA	Rank	Leading Off Inning OBA	Rank	Runners on 3B with less than 2 Outs RDI %	Rank
Juan Beniquez	.298	18	.310	33	.273	73	.323	8	.316	25	.200	131	.455	3	.593	73
Juan Bonilla	.232	131	.281	68	.197	162	.278	49	.297	43	.214	125	.311	112	.500	122
Rick Dempsey	.199	163	.242	118	.215	152	.201	162	.132	166	.071	172	.400	11	.313	164
Jim Dwyer	.206	156	.458	--	.216	--	.267	--	.220	139	.269	70	.378	--	.571	83
Jackie Gutierrez	.179	168	.273	--	.200	--	.173	--	.083	--	.111	--	.278	--	.571	--
Lee Lacy	.293	25	.261	93	.304	28	.272	57	.200	149	.174	150	.388	19	.615	60
Fred Lynn	.266	62	.355	10	.284	51	.290	35	.279	64	.259	76	.338	74	.750	16
Eddie Murray	.308	12	.288	61	.310	23	.300	22	.366	5	.333	21	.378	26	.733	20
Tom O'Malley	.256	87	.238	--	.226	145	.284	--	.205	148	.318	30	.255	151	.667	--
Floyd Rayford	.202	159	.071	169	.195	--	.164	169	.137	165	.130	166	.215	166	.429	--
Cal Ripken	.265	69	.369	6	.265	92	.298	26	.255	102	.121	167	.402	10	.697	27
Larry Sheets	.279	41	.220	135	.276	70	.268	63	.303	39	.313	34	.363	39	.833	6
John Shelby	.229	133	.218	137	.199	160	.252	94	.265	82	.229	106	.275	143	.522	113
Jim Traber	.250	96	.292	--	.288	42	.218	145	.259	91	.278	61	.302	123	.643	48
Alan Wiggins	.240	118	.302	45	.274	71	.226	139	.286	--	.313	--	.319	102	.571	83
Mike Young	.252	93	.254	100	.269	81	.238	123	.248	111	.182	143	.311	113	.600	65
Team Average	.253	9	.284	2	.254	11	.261	7	.249	12	.216	13	.341	4	.612	3
League Average	.258		.270		.264		.259		.263		.246		.326		.575	

Pitching Comparisons: Vs. Left-Handers/Right-Handers and Runners On/Bases Empty

		BA	Rank	BB %	Rank	SO %	Rank		BA	Rank	BB %	Rank	SO %	Rank
Don Aase	vs. Lefties	.231	29	7.60	34	19.30	20	Runners On	.265	65	11.36	103	20.45	14
	vs. Righties	.236	36	9.04	91	20.48	30	Bases Empty	.203	11	4.97	13	19.25	25
Mike Boddicker	vs. Lefties	.266	64	7.86	42	15.29	41	Runners On	.275	78	5.37	6	22.51	7
	vs. Righties	.243	48	7.99	68	22.25	20	Bases Empty	.240	44	9.76	98	16.02	48
Rich Bordi	vs. Lefties	.308	107	11.22	99	14.29	47	Runners On	.251	47	7.92	47	20.83	12
	vs. Righties	.216	18	7.09	51	20.52	29	Bases Empty	.258	62	9.82	99	14.73	64
Storm Davis	vs. Lefties	.293	95	9.28	65	12.57	65	Runners On	.302	109	5.95	15	14.13	62
	vs. Righties	.257	67	5.57	30	16.72	61	Bases Empty	.256	61	8.51	79	14.95	60
Ken Dixon	vs. Lefties	.242	42	10.55	88	16.06	33	Runners On	.259	56	10.08	86	21.85	10
	vs. Righties	.256	65	8.45	82	22.83	16	Bases Empty	.243	46	9.09	90	17.79	38
Mike Flanagan	vs. Lefties	.248	49	7.80	40	13.48	57	Runners On	.277	88	7.00	29	12.54	78
	vs. Righties	.275	98	9.08	92	12.71	95	Bases Empty	.263	72	10.40	104	13.12	87
Brad Havens	vs. Lefties	.172	2	8.77	57	22.81	8	Runners On	.280	90	10.71	96	18.57	27
	vs. Righties	.296	116	10.56	113	17.22	57	Bases Empty	.221	26	9.09	90	20.13	22
Odell Jones	vs. Lefties	.379	--	18.07	--	14.46	--	Runners On	.303	110	11.02	99	11.02	97
	vs. Righties	.266	82	5.88	31	14.71	78	Bases Empty	.308	--	9.90	--	18.81	--
Scott McGregor	vs. Lefties	.223	21	4.49	4	14.61	46	Runners On	.265	63	5.85	14	11.11	96
	vs. Righties	.283	107	7.10	53	10.00	121	Bases Empty	.274	83	7.03	54	10.84	108
Nate Snell	vs. Lefties	.269	69	7.89	43	7.89	118	Runners On	.272	75	6.38	19	6.38	130
	vs. Righties	.250	54	7.10	54	10.93	112	Bases Empty	.245	48	8.33	77	12.82	91
Team Average	vs. Lefties	.261	6	9.36	7	14.68	2	Runners On	.273	9	8.34	4	16.07	3
	vs. Righties	.264	10	8.24	8	15.99	8	Bases Empty	.255	8	8.95	11	15.00	12
League Average	vs. Lefties	.265		9.67		13.46		Runners On	.269		9.46		14.39	
	vs. Righties	.259		8.19		16.22		Bases Empty	.256		8.31		15.55	

Additional Miscellaneous Pitching Comparisons

	Grass Surface BA	Rank	Artificial Surface BA	Rank	Home Games BA	Rank	Road Games BA	Rank	Runners in Scoring Position BA	Rank	Runners in Scoring Pos and Two Outs BA	Rank	Leading Off Inning OBA	Rank
Don Aase	.231	31	.250	--	.218	27	.254	53	.303	110	.360	126	.203	1
Mike Boddicker	.260	71	.235	29	.246	54	.262	65	.299	106	.308	112	.378	113
Rich Bordi	.260	70	.200	9	.240	48	.277	81	.252	66	.230	57	.404	122
Storm Davis	.272	88	.308	106	.296	112	.249	47	.288	96	.241	67	.364	105
Ken Dixon	.268	82	.174	2	.267	76	.231	16	.236	40	.279	92	.286	27
Mike Flanagan	.281	101	.229	23	.272	80	.268	72	.247	57	.212	45	.339	83
Brad Havens	.239	41	.321	--	.273	81	.212	--	.295	101	.256	77	.254	8
Odell Jones	.327	125	.160	--	.341	--	.275	77	.311	115	.300	108	.455	--
Scott McGregor	.269	83	.284	77	.279	92	.264	68	.258	72	.240	65	.336	80
Nate Snell	.269	84	.214	13	.255	66	.261	62	.246	52	.212	45	.297	38
Team Average	.268	10	.234	1	.267	9	.259	6	.273	9	.270	13	.340	10
League Average	.258		.270		.259		.264		.263		.246		.326	

BOSTON RED SOX

If the Boston Red Sox had a TV series, it would be scheduled against "The Cosby Show." If they formed a rock band, their album would be released the same week as the Springsteen box. If the Red Sox were sprinters, they'd have peaked just in time for the 1980 Olympic boycott—if we can suspend disbelief long enough to imagine the Red Sox as sprinters.

In baseball, as in so much else, timing is everything. Consider this: Boston won the American League pennant three times in the last three decades, and whom did they face in those three World Series? The team with the best record in the National League during the 1960s, the best in the 1970s, and the best in the 1980s:

Year	N.L. Champion	W	L	Pct.
1967	St. Louis Cardinals	101	60	.627
1975	Cincinnati Reds	108	54	.667
1986	New York Mets	108	54	.667

Now, it's true that Boston hasn't won a World Championship since 1918. And that since then, the Sox have reached the Series four times and lost in seven games on all four occasions. But it's a little too easy to dump on the Sox for those losses. (Is there a baseball fan outside Boston who didn't make at least one joke about the Red Sox and the Heimlich Maneuver last winter?) So let's not overlook this point: Some World Series champions wouldn't even have reached the seventh game had they been matched against the powerful National League teams Boston lost to. Those three teams include the two winningest National League teams of the past 25 years, and a Cardinals team that won more games than any other N.L. team of the 1960s despite losing Bob Gibson for nearly two months when he broke his leg.

Still, you can't help but wonder whether such devastating losses as the ones the Red Sox suffered in the final two games of the 1986 Series could induce a damaging aftershock that would plague the team this season. As usual, we looked for historical precedents.

We employed a statistical model to project a team's record in a given season based upon its record in the previous season. (To increase accuracy, this particular model examined only teams coming off exceptional seasons.) We applied this model to 15 teams that either suffered demoralizing postseason losses or wasted huge, seemingly insurmountable regular-season leads. We then compared their records in the following seasons to the records projected by the model, which was as oblivious to any emotional hangovers as Mr. Spock. If the teams approximated their projected performance, we could reject the notion that ego-busting losses adversely affect a team in the following season.

The results: Ten of the fifteen "demoralized" teams failed to reach their projected win totals in the following seasons, six of them falling more than 10 wins short. As a group, the teams fell a whopping 74 wins short of their projected total, an average of five wins per team. Of the ten teams that produced results outside the standard error of the model (six wins), all but two produced fewer wins than expected.

Year	Team	W–L	Actual W–L	Expected W–L	Diff.
1929	Chicago Cubs	98–54	90–64	91–63	−1
1941	Brooklyn Dodgers	100–54	104–50	91–63	+13
1942	Brooklyn Dodgers	104–50	81–72	94–69	−13
1946	Boston Red Sox	104–50	83–71	94–70	−11
1949	Boston Red Sox	96–58	94–60	90–64	+4
1951	Brooklyn Dodgers	97–60	96–57	88–65	+8
1954	Cleveland Indians	111–43	93–61	100–54	−7
1962	Los Angeles Dodgers	102–63	99–63	94–68	+5
1964	Philadelphia Phillies	92–70	85–76	88–73	−3
1966	Los Angeles Dodgers	95–67	73–89	89–73	−16
1975	Boston Red Sox	95–65	83–79	90–72	−7
1978	Boston Red Sox	99–64	91–69	90–70	+1
1982	California Angels	93–69	70–92	89–73	−19
1984	Chicago Cubs	96–65	77–84	92–70	−15
1985	St. Louis Cardinals	101–61	79–82	93–68	−14

Of course, Red Sox fans can be thankful that Boston's management didn't react to the team's postseason disappointment as Connie Mack did after his 1914 Philadelphia A's dominated the American League but suffered a humiliating Series sweep at the hands of the Miracle Braves. In one of the first recorded examples of "I can lose just as easily without them as I can with them," Mack decided not to enter a bidding war for his players with the fledgling Federal League. Mack lost future Hall of Famers Eddie Plank and Chief Bender to the new league, sold Eddie Collins—also enshrined in Cooperstown—over the winter, and auctioned Jack Lapp, Herb Pennock, Jack Barry, Bob Shawkey, and Eddie Murphy as the 1915 season progressed. Guess old Connie showed those bad boys: The A's didn't come within 20 games of a pennant for nine years thereafter.

Of Arms and Men I Sing

By the time you read this, the furor over the selection of Roger Clemens as the Most Valuable Player in the American League last season will probably have died out. But the passion of the controversy that surrounded that selection last November defied all logic. Sometimes, the best way to deal with such fluff is to avoid the sports pages for a few days, close your eyes, and wait for it to go away. The problem is that this particular debate surfaces every November: Should a top-of-the-line starting pitcher be considered for the MVP award, or should the designation be reserved solely for everyday players?

Those who argue that pitchers shouldn't be considered for MVP present one of two arguments: 1) A pitcher cannot make the same contribution in 35 starts that an everyday player can in 162 games; or 2) The pitchers have their own award, the Cy Young.

We'll deal at length with the first argument in a moment, but let's take a closer look at that other argument, that pitchers should be denied eligibility for the MVP award simply because the Cy Young award exists. It's apparent that prior to the birth of the Cy Young award, the voters felt no hesitation about giving a pitcher the MVP award: Four National League starting pitchers were named MVP in the first nine years, from 1931 through 1939. (One A.L. pitcher, Lefty Grove in 1931, was also named MVP during that period.) And though today, thirty years after the inception of the Cy Young, we hear players say, "They've got their own game going. Keep them away from ours," consider the MVP voting in 1956, when Don Newcombe of the Dodgers won the first Cy Young award (presented to only one major-league pitcher until 1967, not one in each league).

The National League MVP voters that year included, among others, Bob Broeg, Jim Enright, Jack Herman, Cliff Kachline, Jack Lang, and Dick Young, all respected baseball writers. They were certainly more attuned in 1956 to the intentions of the Baseball Writers Association regarding the co-existence of the two awards than anyone can presume to be 30 years later. And who did they select as the 1956 N.L. Most Valuable Player? Don Newcombe. The MVP runner-up? Sal Maglie, Newcombe's partner in the Brooklyn Dodgers' starting rotation. Hank Aaron finished third, and fourth place went to yet another starter, Milwaukee's Warren Spahn. Newcombe (8), Maglie (4), and Spahn (1) accumulated more than half of the first-place votes.

In other words, from the start the Cy Young award was meant as *additional* recognition for pitchers, and anyone who maintains that its inception was meant to exclude them from consideration for the Most Valuable Player award flies in the face of documented fact.

But what about the other argument against pitchers winning the MVP: that they cannot contribute to their teams in 35 or so starts what an everyday player contributes on a daily basis throughout the course of a 162-game season. Now there's an argument we can really sink our statistical molars into.

To state the question statistically: An everyday player contributes a certain number of wins or losses to his team over the course of a season. The Yankees won 90 games last season; it's safe to assume that without Don Mattingly, they would have won fewer games. The difference in the number of wins represents Mattingly's value. That's *value* as in *valu-*

able. This can also be measured for starting pitchers: How many fewer games would the Red Sox have won last season if Roger Clemens had never pulled on a Boston uniform? We won't try to answer that specific question, but we'll compare the contributions of the best starting pitchers in baseball to those of the best everyday players to see if the values are comparable.

We selected a group of 10 pitchers to represent the best starters in baseball over the past three seasons. (The method of selection was simple: 164 pitchers made at least 50 starts during that time; only 10 ranked among the top 20 percent in both wins and ERA.) To measure the value of each pitcher, we compared his team's record in games he started over the three years and its record in games started by pitchers from outside its regular starting rotation. This second figure indicates how the team would have performed if it had had to fill the pitcher's spot with a replacement. The difference represents the pitcher's value, expressed in the following table on a per-season basis:

Pitcher	With Pitcher	With Others	Value
Bert Blyleven	59–46	52–83	6.1
Ron Darling	68–34	30–33	6.5
Dwight Gooden	70–29	30–33	7.6
Orel Hershiser	54–35	25–42	6.9
Bob Knepper	61–48	30–37	4.1
Jack Morris	66–39	38–43	5.6
Mike Scott	54–47	30–37	2.9
John Tudor	56–42	17–20	3.7
Fernando Valenzuela	53–50	25–42	4.9
Mike Witt	60–43	41–46	3.8

Let's work through Mike Witt as an example. Over the last three seasons, California had a record of 41–46 in games started by pitchers other than those in its regular starting rotation. That's a .471 winning percentage, or 48.5 wins pro-rated over Witt's 103 starts during that time. The Angels won 60 of Witt's starts, or 11.5 more than would be expected with those other pitchers. Divide that 11.5-win difference by three seasons, and Witt's worth is 3.8 wins per season.

By taking the average single-season value of the 10 pitchers, we conclude that a top-flight starting pitcher is worth approximately 5.2 wins per season to his team.

To approximate the value of an everyday player, we used the same method, comparing his team's record in games the player started to its record in games the player didn't start. The original group consisted of Jesse Barfield, Wade Boggs, George Brett, Kirk Gibson, Pedro Guerrero, Rickey Henderson, Don Mattingly, Eddie Murray, Tim Raines, and Mike Schmidt. Mattingly hasn't missed enough starts since 1984 to provide a meaningful measure, so we replaced him with Jack Clark. And, as noted in somewhat greater detail in the Dodgers essay on page 121, the average contribution of those 10 players is estimated to be 4.6 wins per season, more than a half-win lower than the average of the 10 top starting pitchers. That difference is hardly large enough to conclude that pitchers are *more* valuable than everyday players, but it sure as hell makes it difficult to argue that the opposite is true.

Starting pitchers may work only every fifth day, but, to

paraphrase Ralph Kramden, "When they go to work, they go to work." We're not talking about four or five at bats, maybe a tough chance or two in the field, and an occasional base-running gambit. We're talking about 100 or more pitches, nearly every one of them with a discernible effect on the outcome of the game. Is it any wonder that the figures indicate that over the course of a season, a starting pitcher contributes as much as an everyday starting player?

The final irony of the MVP controversy, of course, is that the award is wholly operated by the Baseball Writers Association of America. They make the rules. They determine which of their members vote. And then they vote. They even have a copyright on the damned thing. Like the Roman emperors, they have it within their power simply to give thumbs up or thumbs down to pitchers. And they've always explicitly stated that pitchers are eligible. But the loudest shouting throughout the Clemens controversy was heard from the BBWAA members themselves. Which makes you wonder whether all the shouting was necessary in the first place.

Up Against the Wall

The mystique surrounding the difficulties of left-handed pitchers at Fenway Park has only been enhanced over the past few years by the remarkable performances of John Tudor and Bob Ojeda once they escaped the shadow of the Green Monster. A brief review of those events: Tudor compiled a record of 39–32 during his five seasons with Boston; in three years since leaving the Sox, he has a 46–26 record. He won the 1985 National League Cy Young award and led the St. Louis Cardinals to a league championship. Ojeda was 44–39 in six years at Boston, 18–5 last season, leading the Mets in wins and ERA in his first season after leaving Boston.

Those developments make for some juicy speculation over what southpaw Bruce Hurst might accomplish for another team. His career record (55–54) is similar to those of Tudor and Ojeda before their escapes, and Hurst's performance in the 1986 World Series only strengthened the impression that he might be one of major-league baseball's outstanding pitchers were it not for the left-field wall looming just behind his glove hand.

The turnarounds of Tudor and Ojeda present compelling evidence that left-handers pitching for the Red Sox labor under a tremendous disadvantage. But two cases, however striking, are not enough to suggest that a one-way ticket out of Boston can turn any left-handed Clark Kent into Superman.

Let's look at Red Sox pitchers during the divisional era to estimate just how many wins Fenway costs a left-hander over the course of a season. Here's how our test works: We found 15 Red Sox southpaws with at least 10 decisions in road games over the past 18 years, from Gary Peters and Ken Brett in 1970 to Hurst last season. Then we found a right-handed "twin"—a pitcher with the same road-game record as each southpaw. For instance, Brett was 5–5 on the road in 1970; he was paired with right-hander Luis Tiant, who had an identical road record in 1972. Sometimes, more than one right-hander had the same road record; we selected the one from the closest year to the left-hander we were looking to match. When no right-hander matched exactly, we chose the one with the most similar record in the closest year.

We assembled two sets of 15 pitchers—one composed entirely of lefties, the others of righties—with equivalent records away from Fenway Park. All things being equal, we would expect the home-game records of each group to be roughly equal as well. But if Fenway presents an obstacle for left-handers, the difference will be apparent in the home-game records between the two groups. And we'll be able to use that difference to measure just how great Fenway's influence is. Here's what the totals look like:

	Home Games		Road Games	
	W–L	Pct.	W–L	Pct.
Left-Handers	92–74	.554	105–89	.541
Right-Handers	125–75	.625	100–84	.543

The groups were virtually identical on the road, but at Fenway southpaws gained only an insignificant home-field advantage, while right-handers flourished. But the margin of difference hardly supports the suggestion that any old Red Sox left-hander can become an All-Star outside Boston's city limits. Think of the numbers like this: The advantage of right-handers at Fenway, .071 in winning percentage, represents only one win for every 14 home-game decisions, or about one win per season.

How, then, do we account for Tudor and Ojeda? The simple answer is that we don't; 17 years' worth of evidence that Fenway is a relatively small disadvantage to a left-hander says we don't have to. The other side has just two spectacular recent cases. This isn't molecular biology; we're not looking to discover natural laws to which there are no exceptions. Our research indicates that Tudor and Ojeda are exceptions to a rule; we don't see any reason to believe they constitute a whole rule themselves.

WON-LOST RECORD BY STARTING POSITION

BOSTON 95-66	C	1B	2B	3B	SS	LF	CF	RF	P	DH	Leadoff	Relief	Starts
Tony Armas							62-45	8-1					70-46
Marty Barrett			95-63								40-30		95-63
Don Baylor		7-6				0-3				88-55			95-64
Wade Boggs				88-60							33-18		88-60
Oil Can Boyd									17-13				17-13
Mike Brown									6-4			1-4	6-4
Bill Buckner		82-56								7-8			89-64
Roger Clemens									27-6				27-6
Steve Crawford												16-24	-
Pat Dodson		1-1											1-1
Dwight Evans								86-63		0-1	21-13		86-64
Wes Gardner											1-0		-
Rich Gedman	72-52												72-52
Mike Greenwell						0-1		0-2		0-1			0-4
Dave Henderson							5-2						5-2
Glenn Hoffman				3-3									3-3
Bruce Hurst									16-9				16-9
Tim Lollar									1-0			8-23	1-0
Steve Lyons							22-9						22-9
Al Nipper									14-12				14-12
Spike Owen			24-17								0-4		24-17
Rey Quinones			33-27										33-27
Jim Rice						95-61				0-1			95-62
Ed Romero			0-1	6-6	35-19						1-1		41-26
Kevin Romine							4-6						4-6
Joe Sambito												28-25	-
Dave Sax	1-1	1-0											2-1
Calvin Schiraldi												16-9	-
Tom Seaver								7-9					7-9
Jeff Sellers								5-8				0-1	5-8
Bob Stanley									0-1			36-29	0-1
Dave Stapleton		4-1	0-2	1-0									5-3
Mike Stenhouse		0-2				0-1		1-0					1-3
Sammy Stewart												9-18	-
Marc Sullivan	22-13												22-13
LaSchelle Tarver							2-4						2-4
Mike Trujillo												0-3	-
Rob Woodward									2-4			1-2	2-4

Batting Comparisons: Vs. Left-Handers/Right-Handers and Overall/Late Inning Pressure Situations

		BA	Rank	SA	Rank	HR %	Rank		BA	Rank	SA	Rank	HR %	Rank
Tony Armas	vs. Lefties	.289	51	.430	65	1.56	121	Overall	.264	83	.409	87	2.59	95
	vs. Righties	.253	101	.401	87	3.03	79	Pressure	.234	103	.255	150	0.00	109
Marty Barrett	vs. Lefties	.322	19	.485	36	2.34	96	Overall	.286	35	.381	106	0.64	152
	vs. Righties	.273	62	.341	129	0.00	158	Pressure	.359	7	.547	12	0.00	109
Don Baylor	vs. Lefties	.230	126	.388	93	3.29	66	Overall	.238	133	.439	58	5.30	21
	vs. Righties	.240	120	.457	47	6.00	13	Pressure	.213	125	.443	51	6.56	14
Wade Boggs	vs. Lefties	.352	6	.489	34	1.65	117	Overall	.357	1	.486	20	1.38	132
	vs. Righties	.359	1	.485	33	1.26	131	Pressure	.433	1	.533	17	0.00	109
Bill Buckner	vs. Lefties	.218	142	.322	143	1.98	106	Overall	.267	74	.421	78	2.86	86
	vs. Righties	.290	35	.468	42	3.28	66	Pressure	.237	102	.305	129	0.00	109
Dwight Evans	vs. Lefties	.228	129	.397	90	4.41	33	Overall	.259	90	.476	26	4.91	27
	vs. Righties	.270	67	.504	22	5.09	28	Pressure	.305	36	.610	7	8.47	4
Rich Gedman	vs. Lefties	.186	163	.347	127	4.24	41	Overall	.258	95	.424	74	3.46	69
	vs. Righties	.282	48	.451	54	3.20	71	Pressure	.294	50	.529	19	5.88	22
Dave Henderson	vs. Lefties	.267	81	.495	31	5.94	20	Overall	.265	78	.459	42	3.87	58
	vs. Righties	.265	75	.446	59	3.14	74	Pressure	.203	135	.453	48	6.25	18
Spike Owen	vs. Lefties	.273	67	.364	111	0.83	142	Overall	.231	141	.309	157	0.19	165
	vs. Righties	.219	153	.292	160	0.00	158	Pressure	.125	168	.172	168	0.00	109
Jim Rice	vs. Lefties	.351	7	.560	11	4.17	43	Overall	.324	6	.490	17	3.24	73
	vs. Righties	.313	45	.464	45	2.89	83	Pressure	.290	53	.435	54	3.23	62
Ed Romero	vs. Lefties	.254	96	.338	134	0.00	148	Overall	.210	163	.283	166	0.86	145
	vs. Righties	.191	168	.259	167	1.23	133	Pressure	.208	--	.333	--	0.00	--
Marc Sullivan	vs. Lefties	.137	173	.196	171	1.96	107	Overall	.193	--	.252	--	0.84	--
	vs. Righties	.235	--	.294	--	0.00	--	Pressure	.000	--	.000	--	0.00	--
Team Average	vs. Lefties	.269	6	.411	6	2.51	12	Overall	.271	3	.415	7	2.62	11
	vs. Righties	.271	3	.416	7	2.66	11	Pressure	.273	4	.411	4	2.44	10
League Average	vs. Lefties	.263		.408		2.88		Overall	.262		.408		2.96	
	vs. Righties	.261		.408		2.99		Pressure	.254		.383		2.61	

Additional Miscellaneous Batting Comparisons

	Grass Surface BA	Rank	Artificial Surface BA	Rank	Home Games BA	Rank	Road Games BA	Rank	Runners in Scoring Position BA	Rank	Runners in Scoring Pos and Two Outs BA	Rank	Leading Off Inning OBA	Rank	Runners on 3B with less than 2 Outs RDI %	Rank
Tony Armas	.258	84	.302	46	.271	78	.256	88	.289	53	.326	26	.317	106	.560	93
Marty Barrett	.287	34	.281	68	.278	63	.294	28	.311	29	.343	18	.343	63	.519	117
Don Baylor	.240	116	.223	131	.233	135	.242	116	.212	145	.165	153	.343	65	.578	81
Wade Boggs	.352	2	.380	4	.357	3	.356	2	.353	6	.361	12	.433	7	.739	18
Bill Buckner	.264	73	.286	62	.258	100	.276	53	.244	114	.270	69	.267	147	.684	34
Dwight Evans	.247	106	.319	27	.253	104	.264	70	.274	70	.328	25	.359	46	.692	30
Rich Gedman	.245	111	.324	21	.214	153	.298	25	.252	106	.279	60	.272	144	.500	122
Dave Henderson	.219	145	.305	41	.286	49	.242	117	.256	100	.216	123	.357	48	.478	140
Spike Owen	.217	148	.245	113	.246	117	.215	147	.198	153	.169	151	.257	149	.611	62
Jim Rice	.317	8	.358	9	.337	6	.310	15	.340	13	.318	31	.326	90	.629	52
Ed Romero	.212	154	.200	--	.176	168	.240	121	.200	149	.163	155	.333	79	.688	31
Marc Sullivan	.208	--	.111	--	.241	--	.148	--	.303	--	.364	7	.195	--	.333	--
Team Average	.269	3	.282	4	.270	4	.271	3	.269	5	.274	1	.330	6	.589	7
League Average	.258		.270		.264		.259		.263		.246		.326		.575	

Pitching Comparisons: Vs. Left-Handers/Right-Handers and Runners On/Bases Empty

		BA	Rank	BB %	Rank	SO %	Rank		BA	Rank	BB %	Rank	SO %	Rank
Oil Can Boyd	vs. Lefties	.278	77	4.08	2	12.66	63	Runners On	.253	50	5.64	11	13.06	68
	vs. Righties	.251	55	6.09	34	16.39	62	Bases Empty	.272	81	4.68	10	15.29	56
Roger Clemens	vs. Lefties	.210	13	7.76	38	19.83	15	Runners On	.202	5	7.08	30	22.10	8
	vs. Righties	.176	5	5.28	24	29.50	3	Bases Empty	.192	5	6.52	44	24.84	5
Steve Crawford	vs. Lefties	.394	129	12.82	111	5.98	127	Runners On	.280	90	11.51	105	12.23	80
	vs. Righties	.240	--	3.05	--	19.08	--	Bases Empty	.340	--	2.75	--	13.76	--
Bruce Hurst	vs. Lefties	.256	57	7.45	31	21.28	11	Runners On	.231	21	5.61	10	24.75	3
	vs. Righties	.256	63	6.86	47	23.44	13	Bases Empty	.274	84	7.89	70	22.01	9
Al Nipper	vs. Lefties	.305	104	7.81	41	10.68	86	Runners On	.294	101	7.59	43	10.56	103
	vs. Righties	.272	94	5.35	27	11.95	103	Bases Empty	.287	104	6.02	35	11.78	100
Joe Sambito	vs. Lefties	.200	--	8.33	--	21.43	--	Runners On	.300	107	7.44	40	16.53	39
	vs. Righties	.368	--	7.76	--	10.34	--	Bases Empty	.296	--	8.86	--	12.66	--
Calvin Schiraldi	vs. Lefties	.170	1	8.49	52	25.47	4	Runners On	.164	--	8.43	--	31.33	--
	vs. Righties	.235	--	6.52	--	30.43	--	Bases Empty	.226	--	6.96	--	25.22	--
Tom Seaver	vs. Lefties	.279	78	8.16	47	13.27	58	Runners On	.262	59	9.46	74	12.93	72
	vs. Righties	.248	51	6.54	41	13.90	85	Bases Empty	.265	76	5.88	33	14.03	76
Jeff Sellers	vs. Lefties	.297	99	10.43	87	10.43	93	Runners On	.306	113	9.76	81	12.20	81
	vs. Righties	.261	75	11.61	119	18.71	41	Bases Empty	.263	71	11.88	116	15.35	53
Bob Stanley	vs. Lefties	.338	121	8.72	56	9.30	101	Runners On	.324	121	8.42	54	14.36	59
	vs. Righties	.310	124	3.61	5	19.59	33	Bases Empty	.321	124	3.05	1	15.24	57
Sammy Stewart	vs. Lefties	.296	96	18.18	125	12.59	64	Runners On	.240*	32	16.99	129	18.30	29
	vs. Righties	.238	39	14.47	126	19.08	36	Bases Empty	.292	110	15.49	122	13.38	85
Team Average	vs. Lefties	.279	13	8.42	2	14.11	5	Runners On	.262	6	8.56	5	16.49	1
	vs. Righties	.255	7	7.17	5	19.52	1	Bases Empty	.270	11	7.14	3	17.27	1
League Average	vs. Lefties	.265		9.67		13.46		Runners On	.269		9.46		14.39	
	vs. Righties	.259		8.19		16.22		Bases Empty	.256		8.31		15.55	

Additional Miscellaneous Pitching Comparisons

	Grass Surface		Artificial Surface		Home Games		Road Games		Runners in Scoring Position		Runners in Scoring Pos and Two Outs		Leading Off Inning	
	BA	Rank	BA	Rank	BA	Rank	BA	Rank	BA	Rank	BA	Rank	OBA	Rank
Oil Can Boyd	.265	77	.261	--	.290	104	.232	20	.243	49	.250	70	.314	55
Roger Clemens	.197	5	.184	4	.203	12	.188	3	.188	6	.185	26	.262	9
Steve Crawford	.326	124	.245	38	.314	122	.301	--	.271	84	.200	30	.347	91
Bruce Hurst	.261	72	.191	7	.235	43	.284	87	.218	22	.194	28	.374	111
Tim Lollar	.312	120	.259	--	.363	--	.250	--	.274	89	.200	--	.308	--
Al Nipper	.288	106	.295	91	.295	110	.284	91	.303	109	.328	117	.357	100
Joe Sambito	.290	109	.368	--	.250	--	.364	--	.300	107	.297	104	.281	--
Tom Seaver	.267	79	.250	44	.274	84	.255	54	.256	70	.267	82	.269	12
Jeff Sellers	.275	94	.326	119	.280	94	.286	93	.316	117	.300	108	.393	119
Bob Stanley	.350	127	.222	16	.362	127	.286	93	.289	98	.184	24	.319	60
Sammy Stewart	.255	56	.306	104	.235	42	.294	104	.225	32	.231	60	.328	68
Team Average	.269	11	.250	2	.276	13	.256	5	.252	4	.238	6	.328	8
League Average	.258		.270		.259		.264		.263		.246		.326	

CALIFORNIA ANGELS

The Angels, with Mike Witt pitching, are trying to protect a 5–2 lead late in the game when Witt allows a two-run homer, cutting the lead to 5–4. Manager Gene Mauch decides that Witt has had enough and goes to his bullpen. With Dave Henderson coming up to bat, Donnie Moore is brought in to pitch. Henderson hits a dramatic home run, and the Angels go on to lose by a run, with Moore the losing pitcher.

Anyone who saw Game Five of the 1986 American League Championship Series will recognize this scenario immediately. But that wasn't the first time that all these things happened; they first took place not on October 12, 1986, but on August 12, 1985, at the Kingdome in Seattle, in a game between the Angels and the Mariners.

In that game, the Angels took a 5–2 lead into the bottom of the eighth, but Barry Bonnell—playing the role in New Haven in which Don Baylor would later star on Broadway—hit a two-out, two-run homer to cut the lead to one run. Moore relieved Witt to face Henderson, and in their first major-league confrontation, Henderson hit a home run to tie the score; Moore went on to lose in the ninth. Nearly identical circumstances prevailed 14 months later. Not even Elvira, Mistress of the Dark, could have concocted such a painful *deja vu* for southern California's fans.

How does one best describe the agony of the Angels' playoff defeat? Perhaps by taking a detailed look through our statistical microscope at that excruciating ninth inning of Game Five of the playoffs, an inning in which the Angels were on the verge of winning the series in both the top and bottom halves.

George Will has observed that "a 162-game season is, like life, a study in cumulation. . . . Past performances give rise to averages, on which managers calculate probabilities about future performance." Then the really good part, in which Will capsulizes the essence of why we love baseball statistics so much: "The more you study, the less surprised you are. But no matter how hard you study, you are still surprised agreeably often, and the surprises that come to the studious are especially delicious." Let's look back at the delicious surprises that occurred in Anaheim Stadium on Sunday, October 12, 1986.

The Angels, leading the series three games to one, took that 5–2 lead into the ninth inning. Bobby Grich's home run off Henderson's glove gave California the lead with two outs in the sixth; Rob Wilfong's pinch-RBI double and a scoring fly ball by Brian Downing padded the lead in the seventh.

Witt had not allowed a run since the second inning, when

Rich Gedman got the first of his four hits, a two-out, two-run homer. In one of the many ironies surrounding this game, Gedman had a terrible career record of hitting Witt; including their meeting in Game One of the playoffs, Gedman was *2-for-24 lifetime against Witt* before Game Five.

In the ninth inning, another player whom Witt had previously mastered jumped up to bite him. Don Baylor brought a record of *2-for-26 with no home runs against Witt* to the plate; he took a two-run homer back to the dugout. Witt then retired Dwight Evans on a foul pop, bringing Gedman to the plate and Mauch to the mound. Exit Witt, enter Gary Lucas, *who had not hit a batter since May 30, 1982.* Lucas then hit Gedman with his first pitch.

That brought up Dave Henderson. During the regular season, in Late-Inning Pressure Situations with two outs and runners on base, Henderson was *1-for-13 with nine strikeouts and no RBIs.* He had hit *no home runs with two outs and runners on base in 71 such plate appearances* during the season. But he came through this time, producing the two-run homer that was to be *his only hit of the series.*

Then, the bottom of the ninth. Bob Boone, *.148, 4-for-27, lifetime versus Bob Stanley,* led off with a single. The 31-year old Ruppert Jones ran for the 38-year old Boone. Gary Pettis sacrificed, bringing up Wilfong with the tying run on second. McNamara had Mauch cornered: Because of the injury to Wally Joyner, the Angels were playing the game one man short to begin with, and only lefties Jack Howell and Jerry Narron remained as potential pinch-hitters. McNamara could bring in his left-handed specialist, Joe Sambito, with the certain knowledge that he would face a left-handed batter; Sambito had *held lefties to a .200 batting average* in 1986. And Sambito had done a good job in similar game situations for McNamara throughout the year: Opponents had only *four hits in 24 at bats in Late-Inning Pressure Situations with runners in scoring position.*

Wilfong's .219 overall batting average for 1986 was deceptive; he was one of the two American League players who *hit at least 100 points higher with runners on base (.281) than with the bases empty (.178).* But in this situation, the more relevant factor seemed to be the lefty-versus-lefty matchup. Wilfong had only 22 at bats against left-handers in 1986, and even though he produced seven hits in those situations, his *career batting average of .176 against lefties,* based on 324 at bats, made things look hellish for the Angels. In addition, even though Wilfong hit *.300 in 1986 in Late-Inning Pressure Situations,* only *two of his 40 at bats in those situations came* *against left-handers.* And here he was, in the granddaddy of all Late-Inning Pressure Situations, facing Sambito for the first time in his career.

One of Will's delicious surprises was about to occur: Wilfong grounded a single to right, and Jones scored with a magnificent belly slide, reaching out to touch the plate. Score tied, 6–6. In comes Steve Crawford, who was greeted by a single by Dick Schofield. First and third, one out. Due up: Downing, DeCinces, Grich. Schiraldi's not warming up. It's up to Crawford.

An intentional walk would set up a potential double-play, which could facilitate a Boston escape; on the other hand, it would also allow a walk to force in the winning run, with a pitcher making his first postseason appearance on the mound. Remember Stan Williams in the 1962 National League pennant playoff against the Giants?

With a runner on third and less than two outs, whom do you face, Downing or DeCinces? Downing *drove in 68 percent of runners in those situations* during the year; DeCinces, *59 percent.* Downing was also a "backwards" hitter in 1986, who *hit significantly higher against right-handers (.282) than against lefties (.240).* Blend in the fact that he already had six RBIs in the series, and that he was *4-for-6 lifetime against Crawford.*

McNamara's decision: intentional walk, even though the next batter, DeCinces, was also no slouch *(4-for-9)* against Crawford. But the results were perfect for Boston; DeCinces flied to short right, Grich hit a soft line drive back to Crawford, and the inning was over. The thrills continued through two more innings, before Henderson's sacrifice fly produced a 7–6 Boston victory, in what was *the second postseason game in major league history—and the second in the same ballpark within 21 hours—to be won by a team that trailed by more than two runs going into the ninth inning.*

Whew!

What's Up Front

Attention, sabermetricians! Are you looking for a quick yardstick to predict the American League's division champions in 1987? Look no farther than the first pitch each team sees this season.

If you used this system last year, you would have gone two-for-two. The Red Sox and the Angels may have been destined to meet in the playoffs as early as their first games of the season: Boston's first batter of the season, Dwight Evans, hit the first pitch thrown to him for a home run. (That drew lots of attention, because Evans was the first batter in *any* game this season, in Detroit.) The next night, Bobby Grich hit the first pitch of the Angels' season for a home run. (That received next to no attention, because it happened in Seattle.)

Grich was used sporadically (13 games) as a leadoff batter throughout the season, as Mauch juggled nine different players in that position. Only one other American League team— the Orioles—used as many starting leadoff batters. For California, Rick Burleson (31 starts), Ruppert Jones (44), and Gary Pettis (62) were the most frequently used leadoff men.

Despite moving his players in and out of the leadoff spot, Mauch received excellent power production from them: California's number-one hitters combined for 19 home runs last season, 10 of those leading off the first inning.

The leadoff homer in the first is a growing phenomenon in baseball; there were 86 such home runs in 1986. That's quite a leap from the established level of first-inning leadoff home runs in recent seasons:

1975	44	1979	57	1983	54
1976	39	1980	42	1984	44
1977	39	*1981	22	1985	57
1978	48	1982	48	1986	86

* 1981 always has an asterisk next to it.

Most of the leadoff home runs were hit in the American League: 58 of the 86 first-inning leadoff homers were hit with baseballs signed by Dr. Bobby Brown. But the National League featured the only game last season in which both teams had a home run supplied by their first batter; when Curt Ford of the Cardinals and Jeff Stone of the Phillies did that on June 20, it marked only the ninth time in major-league history that it had happened.

Rickey Henderson was the individual leader with nine home runs leading off the first inning; add in Don Mattingly's leadoff homer in the final game of the season (he was batting leadoff to maximize his remote chances of beating out Wade Boggs for the batting title) and the Yankees had 10 such home runs. But the Angels, with their strange potpourri of leadoff hitters, matched the Yankees' total to share the major-league lead. Jones hit five of the home runs, Burleson three, and Pettis one, in addition to Grich's season-opener.

The high total of home runs to start a game is likely not one of those statistical aberrations, but rather the by-product of an effort by major-league teams to move players capable of hitting home runs into the leadoff spot. We may all have to reshape our view of what the number-one hitter in the lineup is being asked to do.

Ask that question of 100 baseball fans, and one hundred of them will answer, "Get on base." But if that is the major criterion for a good number-one hitter, managers throughout baseball have failed to put their best foot forward. Here are the on-base averages for each league for 1986, broken down according to batting order position:

American League		National League	
3d position	.350	3d position	.347
4th position	.348	4th position	.343
2d position	.345	6th position	.333
1st position	.336	2d position	.332
5th position	.331	5th position	.331
6th position	.325	1st position	.329
7th position	.315	7th position	.323
8th position	.311	8th position	.318
9th position	.296	9th position	.218
A.L. average	.330	N.L. average	.322

Players batting in the leadoff position actually had a lower composite on-base average than either second-, third-, or fourth-place hitters. In the National League, fifth- and sixth-place hitters also beat out the leadoff hitter in getting on base.

Meanwhile, there were 206 home runs hit by American League batters hitting in the first position last season, an average of 15 per team. (Detailed statistics on the performance of leadoff batters on each American League team may be found in the Baltimore Orioles essay on page 11.) National League teams saw their leadoff batters hit 136 homers, or 11 per team.

Multitalented players like Henderson, Oddibe McDowell, and Lou Whitaker are partly responsible for the trend toward power; but the Angels were able to duplicate the power numbers put up by some of their American League competitors without having any one outstanding individual for the top of the order. But perhaps the most amazing part of the Angels rotation in the first spot in the batting order was not the numbers that it produced, but the lack of attention that it received. Not once during September or October did we hear or see the phrase, "leadoff spot by committee."

WON-LOST RECORD BY STARTING POSITION

CALIFORNIA 92-70	C	1B	2B	3B	SS	LF	CF	RF	P	DH	Leadoff	Relief	Starts
Bob Boone	84-53												84-53
T.R. Bryden												3-13	-
Rick Burleson			1-4	2-1	15-14					18-17	11-20		36-36
John Candelaria									13-3				13-3
Ray Chadwick									2-5				2-5
Mike Cook									0-1			1-3	0-1
Doug Corbett												22-24	
Doug DeCinces				74-54						2-1			76-55
Brian Downing						81-52				3-6	4-1		84-58
Chuck Finley												5-20	
Todd Fischer												2-7	
Ken Forsch												4-6	
Terry Forster												20-21	
Bill Fraser									1-0				1-0
Bobby Grich		5-4	41-31								7-6		46-35
George Hendrick		1-1				1-0	34-32			0-1			36-34
Jack Howell				15-15		1-5	1-0						17-20
Reggie Jackson								2-0		66-45	0-1		68-45
Ruppert Jones						6-8	2-2	53-32			25-19		61-42
Wally Joyner		85-63											85-63
Gary Lucas												15-12	
Urbano Lugo									2-1			1-2	2-1
Kirk McCaskill									21-12			0-1	21-12
Mark McLemore			0-2										0-2
Darrell Miller	1-2					3-3	0-1	1-1		1-0			6-7
Donnie Moore												36-13	
Jerry Narron	7-15									2-0			9-15
Gary Pettis							88-62				42-20		88-62
Gus Polidor			4-0	1-0	0-1								5-1
Ron Romanick									6-12				6-12
Vern Ruhle									1-2			6-7	1-2
Mark Ryal		1-2						1-2					2-4
Dick Schofield					77-55						1-0		77-55
Jim Slaton									6-6			2-0	6-6
Don Sutton									20-14				20-14
Devon White						1-2	1-5	0-3			0-2		2-10
Rob Wilfong			46-33									2-1	46-33
Mike Witt									20-14				20-14

Batting Comparisons: Vs. Left-Handers/Right-Handers and Overall/Late Inning-Pressure Situations

Player		BA	Rank	SA	Rank	HR %	Rank		BA	Rank	SA	Rank	HR %	Rank
Bob Boone	vs. Lefties	.217	144	.276	158	1.32	130	Overall	.222	152	.305	158	1.58	122
	vs. Righties	.224	145	.321	143	1.72	113	Pressure	.208	131	.264	146	1.89	82
Rick Burleson	vs. Lefties	.248	102	.366	107	2.61	81	Overall	.284	39	.391	97	1.85	114
	vs. Righties	.331	5	.424	77	0.85	141	Pressure	.234	103	.298	132	2.13	79
Doug DeCinces	vs. Lefties	.272	70	.486	35	5.20	24	Overall	.256	99	.459	41	5.08	25
	vs. Righties	.248	110	.445	60	5.01	32	Pressure	.286	57	.506	31	6.49	16
Brian Downing	vs. Lefties	.240	109	.443	59	3.83	52	Overall	.267	75	.452	48	3.90	54
	vs. Righties	.282	49	.458	46	3.94	54	Pressure	.246	95	.459	45	4.92	33
Bobby Grich	vs. Lefties	.295	44	.458	45	3.61	56	Overall	.268	68	.412	83	2.88	85
	vs. Righties	.238	122	.361	117	2.04	104	Pressure	.259	83	.315	125	0.00	109
George Hendrick	vs. Lefties	.299	39	.506	25	5.17	25	Overall	.272	56	.473	28	4.95	26
	vs. Righties	.229	--	.422	--	4.59	--	Pressure	.260	82	.340	104	0.00	109
Jack Howell	vs. Lefties	.208	--	.458	--	0.00	--	Overall	.272	--	.470	--	2.65	--
	vs. Righties	.283	44	.472	40	3.15	72	Pressure	.167	158	.300	131	3.33	58
Reggie Jackson	vs. Lefties	.239	110	.282	157	0.00	148	Overall	.241	127	.408	88	4.30	41
	vs. Righties	.241	118	.434	65	5.17	25	Pressure	.182	148	.255	151	1.82	85
Ruppert Jones	vs. Lefties	.178	164	.378	100	4.44	32	Overall	.229	144	.427	68	4.33	40
	vs. Righties	.236	125	.434	65	4.31	45	Pressure	.226	114	.302	130	1.89	82
Wally Joyner	vs. Lefties	.234	117	.354	121	3.13	75	Overall	.290	28	.457	43	3.71	62
	vs. Righties	.317	12	.506	20	3.99	52	Pressure	.329	26	.557	9	3.80	46
Darrell Miller	vs. Lefties	.200	156	.300	152	0.00	148	Overall	.228	--	.298	--	0.00	--
	vs. Righties	.294	--	.294	--	0.00	--	Pressure	.278	--	.278	--	0.00	--
Gary Pettis	vs. Lefties	.278	63	.369	105	1.14	134	Overall	.258	94	.343	141	0.93	143
	vs. Righties	.248	109	.331	135	0.83	142	Pressure	.164	160	.197	162	0.00	109
Dick Schofield	vs. Lefties	.294	45	.454	49	2.45	88	Overall	.249	117	.397	94	2.84	88
	vs. Righties	.224	146	.366	113	3.05	78	Pressure	.197	141	.348	99	3.03	64
Rob Wilfong	vs. Lefties	.318	--	.455	--	0.00	--	Overall	.219	154	.309	156	1.04	140
	vs. Righties	.211	160	.297	155	1.13	135	Pressure	.300	45	.400	67	2.50	71
Team Average	vs. Lefties	.260	10	.404	8	2.88	7	Overall	.255	9	.404	8	3.07	6
	vs. Righties	.253	12	.404	8	3.17	5	Pressure	.239	10	.357	13	2.53	9
League Average	vs. Lefties	.263		.408		2.88		Overall	.262		.408		2.96	
	vs. Righties	.261		.408		2.99		Pressure	.254		.383		2.61	

Additional Miscellaneous Batting Comparisons

	Grass Surface		Artificial Surface		Home Games		Road Games		Runners in Scoring Position		Runners in Scoring Pos and Two Outs		Leading Off Inning		Runners on 3B with less than 2 Outs	
	BA	Rank	BA	Rank	BA	Rank	BA	Rank	BA	Rank	BA	Rank	OBA	Rank	RDI %	Rank
Bob Boone	.225	138	.203	151	.189	167	.252	95	.225	134	.189	137	.333	79	.553	98
Rick Burleson	.266	66	.344	14	.258	99	.305	20	.309	34	.297	43	.341	66	.333	162
Doug DeCinces	.262	75	.213	144	.263	94	.249	104	.274	69	.293	46	.388	20	.595	71
Brian Downing	.276	47	.218	138	.277	67	.257	86	.268	78	.265	73	.395	14	.676	36
Bobby Grich	.282	36	.196	155	.311	22	.236	125	.224	137	.237	96	.353	56	.667	38
George Hendrick	.279	43	.231	--	.289	40	.257	87	.259	87	.222	114	.355	50	.579	78
Jack Howell	.259	80	.314	--	.239	--	.298	--	.355	--	.294	--	.410	--	.800	--
Reggie Jackson	.247	105	.203	150	.277	67	.210	154	.219	140	.151	160	.368	32	.450	147
Ruppert Jones	.230	132	.226	128	.247	112	.213	149	.194	155	.220	120	.341	66	.455	145
Wally Joyner	.292	26	.274	75	.279	60	.301	21	.294	47	.325	27	.303	121	.697	27
Gary Pettis	.249	102	.309	36	.235	129	.278	49	.328	18	.288	50	.322	98	.758	15
Dick Schofield	.246	109	.273	78	.230	141	.267	65	.239	120	.220	120	.380	24	.517	118
Rob Wilfong	.213	152	.250	103	.224	147	.213	150	.276	65	.357	13	.235	162	.565	88
Team Average	.256	7	.249	13	.254	12	.257	9	.260	8	.254	5	.343	3	.596	6
League Average	.258		.270		.264		.259		.263		.246		.326		.575	

Pitching Comparisons: Vs. Left-Handers/Right-Handers and Runners On/Bases Empty

		BA	Rank	BB %	Rank	SO %	Rank		BA	Rank	BB %	Rank	SO %	Rank
John Candelaria	vs. Lefties	.186	--	7.46	--	25.37	--	Runners On	.215	10	7.48	42	19.05	24
	vs. Righties	.210	16	7.05	50	21.48	22	Bases Empty	.200	10	6.88	52	24.31	6
Doug Corbett	vs. Lefties	.271	72	4.76	8	6.35	125	Runners On	.282	93	7.97	48	11.59	87
	vs. Righties	.202	12	8.60	86	15.05	73	Bases Empty	.191	4	6.32	42	11.49	103
Kirk McCaskill	vs. Lefties	.234	34	9.72	73	17.31	27	Runners On	.262	58	7.48	41	20.45	15
	vs. Righties	.222	23	8.28	76	23.27	15	Bases Empty	.207	15	10.13	101	19.61	24
Donnie Moore	vs. Lefties	.212	14	8.02	45	15.43	37	Runners On	.269	69	7.86	46	14.29	60
	vs. Righties	.248	52	6.77	45	21.05	25	Bases Empty	.194	8	7.10	56	21.29	12
Ron Romanick	vs. Lefties	.299	100	9.54	70	6.64	123	Runners On	.305	112	8.33	51	6.48	129
	vs. Righties	.294	113	9.17	94	9.61	125	Bases Empty	.289	107	10.24	102	9.45	118
Don Sutton	vs. Lefties	.224	23	7.66	35	11.94	75	Runners On	.270	71	6.48	20	12.63	76
	vs. Righties	.260	73	3.67	6	15.40	70	Bases Empty	.227	30	5.36	21	14.11	75
Mike Witt	vs. Lefties	.215	15	6.86	25	16.59	30	Runners On	.237	27	7.69	44	16.63	38
	vs. Righties	.230	29	6.76	44	23.42	14	Bases Empty	.212	16	6.29	41	21.11	15
Team Average	vs. Lefties	.244	2	8.71	5	13.59	7	Runners On	.271	8	7.58	1	14.92	6
	vs. Righties	.251	5	7.05	2	17.89	3	Bases Empty	.231	1	8.10	7	16.34	4
League Average	vs. Lefties	.265		9.67		13.46		Runners On	.269		9.46		14.39	
	vs. Righties	.259		8.19		16.22		Bases Empty	.256		8.31		15.55	

Additional Miscellaneous Pitching Comparisons

	Grass Surface BA	Rank	Artificial Surface BA	Rank	Home Games BA	Rank	Road Games BA	Rank	Runners in Scoring Position BA	Rank	Runners in Scoring Pos and Two Outs BA	Rank	Leading Off Inning OBA	Rank
John Candelaria	.189	4	.353	--	.181	3	.232	19	.222	28	.179	20	.271	16
Doug Corbett	.228	26	.250	--	.199	7	.262	64	.299	105	.192	--	.277	21
Chuck Finley	.257	62	.091	--	.229	--	.243	--	.269	--	.333	--	.372	--
Gary Lucas	.254	55	.200	--	.212	22	.333	--	.289	--	.176	--	.262	--
Kirk McCaskill	.219	14	.295	90	.216	25	.239	30	.283	94	.267	84	.311	52
Donnie Moore	.227	24	.234	27	.198	--	.250	49	.246	52	.200	30	.316	56
Ron Romanick	.293	112	.317	126	.305	115	.288	98	.352	126	.375	129	.316	56
Don Sutton	.235	36	.277	71	.230	38	.259	58	.263	76	.266	81	.234	4
Mike Witt	.224	21	.198	8	.208	19	.235	26	.264	80	.310	113	.242	6
Team Average	.245	3	.264	6	.239	3	.256	4	.283	14	.275	14	.296	1
League Average	.258		.270		.259		.264		.263		.246		.326	

CHICAGO WHITE SOX

How weak was Chicago's attack last season? The White Sox not only finished last in the American with 644 runs scored, but they ranked last in both batting average and extra-base hits. No American League team since the California Angels of 1975 and 1976 had ranked last in both those categories.

That's the bad news. The good news is that the White Sox' three and four hitters, the core of a team's offense, compared favorably with the league average:

	AB	R	H	2B	3B	HR	RBI	BB	BA	SA	OBA
Third-Place Hitters	646	82	186	31	3	23	93	46	.288	.452	.334
Fourth-Place Hitters	618	78	168	25	5	26	94	58	.272	.455	.333
White Sox Totals	1264	160	354	56	8	49	187	104	.280	.453	.334
A.L. Averages	1264	180	346	60	6	50	199	145	.274	.449	.349

Harold Baines in the third spot and Greg Walker (with some help from Carlton Fisk and Ron Hassey) in the cleanup position are pretty substantial building blocks for a strong offense. But to get the most out of those heavy hitters, the White Sox will need to fortify the second spot in their batting order. Ozzie Guillen, Wayne Tolleson (traded to the Yankees for Hassey), Tim Hulett, and Fisk all failed to provide Baines and Walker with ample opportunity to pad their RBI totals last season. The following table compares the performance of Chicago's second batting-order position to the league average. The occasional use of Fisk and Daryl Boston behind leadoff hitter John Cangelosi helped Chicago to exceed the league average in RBIs, but White Sox second hitters ranked last in the league in all three averages: batting, slugging, and on-base.

	AB	R	H	2B	3B	HR	RBI	BB	BA	SA	OBA
White Sox Totals	642	70	151	20	7	7	79	48	.235	.321	.286
A.L. Averages	657	98	183	33	6	14	73	65	.279	.407	.345

Incidentally, you may recall that when the White Sox won the 1983 Western Division championship, their midseason turnaround coincided with the elevation of Fisk to the second spot in the order. To refresh your memory, Chicago was 68–27 with Fisk starting and batting second, 10–19 in other games Fisk started. Chicago's record since then indicates that this may have been a coincidence. Over the past three seasons, the White Sox have a record of 11–21 with Fisk starting and batting second, compared to 77–92 with Fisk starting in other spots in the order.

Changing Sox

The first step in Chicago's shakeup took place last June when Tony LaRussa was fired. Three days later, Jim Fregosi made his debut as White Sox manager and the team was never the same. Compare the most frequent starter at each position under LaRussa last season to those used most often by Fregosi:

Pos.	Under LaRussa	Under Fregosi
1B	Greg Walker	Russ Morman
2B	Tim Hulett	Julio Cruz
SS	Ozzie Guillen	Ozzie Guillen
3B	Wayne Tolleson	Tim Hulett
LF	Carlton Fisk	John Cangelosi
CF	John Cangelosi	Daryl Boston
RF	Harold Baines	Harold Baines
C	Joel Skinner	Carlton Fisk
DH	Ron Kittle	Ron Hassey

Three of LaRussa's regular starters were traded to the Yankees (Tolleson, Skinner, and Kittle), three others were moved to different starting positions, and Walker was injured. Only Guillen and Baines were unaffected by the shake-up. Additionally, Fregosi added Steve Carlton, Joe Cowley, and Jose DeLeon to his rotation. And Chicago lowered its ERA from 4.53 under LaRussa to 3.50 during Fregosi's tenure, the second-lowest ERA in the league during that period. That was despite the torrent of criticism aimed at the Sox for signing Carlton after his aborted comeback with San Francisco, criticism generated by vindictive media members paying back the 41-year-old future Hall of Famer for his years of neglect toward them.

Carlton's renaissance—he was 3–1 with a 2.51 ERA over his last seven starts—was hardly predictable, but there have been precedents, including one that the White Sox may have had in mind. A few years earlier, Jerry Koosman had a 4–13 year for Minnesota at age 39, apparently signaling the end of a successful career. Chicago took a chance on Koosman, trading three minor leaguers to the Twins, and Koosman rewarded the Sox with a pair of 11–7 seasons before winning another 20 games for the Phillies in his final two seasons. (For a look at some other pitchers who succeeded at advanced ages, see the Cleveland Indians essay on page 35.)

In the Big Inning

Every manager loves a big inning. And why not? Did you know, for instance, that teams that scored three runs in an inning last season won 83 percent of those games (660 of 798)? Or that the winners in 953 of the 2103 major-league games last season (45 percent) scored more runs in their biggest inning than their opponents scored in the entire game? No wonder Earl Weaver's crusade for the three-run inning resembled a quest for the Holy Grail.

No American League team should have been less suited to putting together a big inning last season than the Chicago White Sox. Start with the fact that the Sox ranked last in the league with a total of 644 runs. Then consider the classic picture of a big-inning team: like Weaver's Orioles teams of the 1970s, lots of power and a minimum of strategy plays like sacrifice bunts and stolen base attempts. Such plays often trade or risk an out for better field position, increasing a team's chance for one run but hurting its chance for a multirun inning. Chicago was one of three American League teams last season sharing a profile unsuited to that big-inning image: below the league average in scoring and home runs, and above the league average in sacrifice bunts (SH) and attempted stolen bases (ASB). The three teams:

Team	Runs	HR	SH	ASB
Chicago	644	121	50	169
Oakland	731	163	56	202
Seattle	718	158	52	169
A.L. Average	746	164	46	159

We're not about to tell you that the White Sox had the most big innings of any team in the American League. Far from it. But what we'd like to do is to impress upon you that the classic picture we just described is not that of a big-inning ball club; there is, in fact, no such profile. Teams we think of as big-inning teams score a lot of runs, but in innings of all denominations, with no special skew towards scoring their runs in bunches.

Let's look at Chicago's pattern of scoring a little more closely. The White Sox had 194 one-run innings last season, to account for 30 percent of their scoring; the average A.L. team scored 31 percent of its runs in one-run innings. The Sox did 45 percent of their scoring in innings of three or more runs, 11 percent in innings of five or more; the league averages were 42 percent and 12 percent. In fact, if you compared the distribution of White Sox scoring innings to a typical American League distribution of 644 runs (Chicago's total for the season), you'd see little difference. And the differences that did occur would suggest that Chicago tended toward multi-run innings, not one-run innings:

		Distribution of Scoring Innings					
Team	Runs	1	2	3	4	5	6+
White Sox	644	194	79	44	23	10	3
A.L. Average	644	197	88	40	19	8	5

Are those figures just a coincidence? Not according to the results of a more detailed survey of major-league teams over four seasons from 1982 through 1985. To try to refine the portrait of a typical big-inning offense, we selected 15 pairs of teams. Each pair of teams scored nearly the same number of runs per game (we allowed a cushion of about five runs over the course of an entire season), but the teams reached their totals in very different ways. For each pair of teams with similar scoring totals, one team had at least 25 more home runs and batted at least 10 batting-average points lower than its partner. For instance, we matched the 1984 White Sox with the 1982 San Diego Padres:

Year	Team	G	R	R/G	AB	H	HR	BA
1982	San Diego Padres	162	675	4.17	5575	1435	81	.257
1984	Chicago White Sox	162	679	4.19	5513	1360	172	.247

Both teams played 162 games. They scored a nearly identical number of runs. The White Sox had a low batting average and a lot of power; the Padres had a higher average and little power. If home runs produced more big innings than an equivalent number of walks, singles, stolen bases, and what have you, then the White Sox should have had fewer one-run innings and more multirun innings than the Padres. The distributions:

		Distribution of Scoring Innings					
Year	Team	1	2	3	4	5	6+
1984	Chicago White Sox	225	89	44	18	7	6
1982	San Diego Padres	228	77	46	16	13	4

San Diego had an insignificantly higher total of one-run innings; they also had four more innings of three runs or more than Chicago. There is no significant difference between the pattern of scoring for these two teams. And that pair of teams was the rule, not the exception. We accumulated totals for the two groups of teams—the batting average group and the home run group—and they were virtually the same:

	Distribution of Scoring Innings					
Team	1	2	3	4	5	6+
Home Run Teams	3300	1525	665	275	118	62
Batting Average Teams	3285	1488	639	288	113	71

A home run is, of course, the quickest way to score three runs—but only after two runners have already reached base. A team that relies on power at the expense of on-base potential has as much difficulty putting together a three-run rally as a team with little power has driving those runners home two or three at a time. As a result, neither type of offense is more likely than the other to score its runs in bunches.

Having reached that conclusion, we designed another study to determine if any particular component of a team's offense was an indicator of big-inning teams. For this survey, we looked for pairs of teams over the past five seasons that scored roughly the same number of runs (within a margin of five). In each pair, one team had to have at least 10 more one-run innings and 10 fewer big innings (three or more runs) than its partner. For example, last season's Boston Red Sox and New York Yankees:

		Distribution of Scoring Innings					
Team	Total	1	2	3	4	5	6+
New York	797	251	127	44	17	8	7
Boston	794	202	108	42	28	14	10

After finding 20 such pairs, we compiled totals in every offensive category for the 20 one-run–inning teams and the 20 big-inning teams. Categories in which the two groups differ substantially should indicate plays that have a marked effect on a team's chances for one-run innings relative to big innings. The following table indicates the average of the season totals for each group of 20 teams:

Group	AB	R	H	2B	3B	HR	SH	SF	HP	BB	SO	SB	CS	GDP
One-run	5540	714	1443	252	35	143	58	48	29	526	872	130	60	118
Three-run	5516	715	1428	242	34	141	59	45	27	549	859	105	53	131

Very few significant differences occurred. The one-run teams had a composite .260 batting average, compared to .259 for the big-inning teams. On-base averages: .325 for one-run teams, .327 for big-inning teams. The slight difference in home runs supports our earlier conclusion that four-baggers are of no importance in this discussion. Even the dreaded sacrifice bunt has no bearing.

The only statistically significant differences occur in doubles, walks, stolen base attempts, double-play ground outs, and (to a lesser degree) strikeouts. Notice that all of those plays except bases on balls are concerned, to some degree, in moving runners from first base to second. Apparently, the belief that risking an out for better position on the bases will diminish a team's opportunity for a big inning is valid. Notice that teams with *more* double-play ground outs are likely to be big-inning teams, because both GIDPs and multirun innings involve holding runners at first base, at least if the advance to second base would involve risking an out. Low strikeout teams tend toward big innings because strikeouts that freeze runners at first base prompt teams to steal bases to move those runners to second. And stolen base attempts produce one-run innings.

You'll recall that we said earlier that there isn't any profile for a big-inning team, and yet we've seemingly just stated one: above average in walks and double-play ground outs, below average in strikeouts, stolen base attempts, and doubles. (Many doubles result from batters "stretching singles," another strategy that risks an out.) What we might have said is that there is no overwhelming profile. Consider that only one American League team over the past five seasons has matched the big-inning profile in all five categories: the 1982 New York Yankees. They scored roughly the same number of runs as one of the two A.L. teams that had a profile that was opposite in all five categories: the 1985 Kansas City Royals. (The other was the 1986 Toronto Blue Jays.)

Those teams, which we might consider the prototypes of one-run and big-inning teams, distributed their scoring innings as expected, but not nearly to the degree that one would expect from such polar opposites:

		Runs in Scoring Innings					
Year	Team	1	2	3	4	5	6+
1982	New York Yankees	203	85	54	22	11	5
1985	Kansas City Royals	227	101	50	14	8	2

In fact, a distribution at least that similar would have about one chance in nine of occurring simply by chance even from teams with identical offensive statistics. So the notion that a team can build a big-inning offense with certain types of players or strategies is, in practical terms, a myth.

WON-LOST RECORD BY STARTING POSITION

CHICAGO 72-90	C	1B	2B	3B	SS	LF	CF	RF	P	DH	Leadoff	Relief	Starts
Juan Agosto												1-8	
Neil Allen									10-7			0-5	10-7
Harold Baines								63-78		0-3			63-81
Floyd Bannister									11-16			1-0	11-16
Bobby Bonilla		11-17				23-9	1-1	0-2					35-29
Daryl Boston							23-29				15-21		23-29
Scott Bradley										1-5			1-5
Ivan Calderon						0-3				2-3			2-6
John Cangelosi						9-13	41-49	2-2			48-57		52-64
Steve Carlton									6-4				6-4
Bryan Clark												0-5	
Dave Cochrane				8-10									8-10
Joe Cowley									13-14			0-1	13-14
Rodney Craig													
Julio Cruz			34-38								0-1		34-38
Joel Davis									9-10				9-10
Bill Dawley												13-33	
Jose DeLeon									5-8				5-8
Richard Dotson									14-20				14-20
Pete Filson									0-1			0-2	0-1
Carlton Fisk	31-34					9-20				12-9			52-63
George Foster						4-7				0-2			4-9
Brian Giles			1-2	1-0									2-2
Ozzie Guillen					66-84								66-84
Jerry Hairston		7-8				2-4				17-11			26-23
Ron Hassey	5-3									13-20			18-23
Marc Hill	1-5												1-5
Tim Hulett			24-33	37-43									61-76
Bob James												27-22	
Ron Karkovice	15-20												15-20
Ron Kittle						5-15				27-34			32-49
Bryan Little			2-5	0-1	0-1								2-7
Steve Lyons			2-1		13-8		1-3	1-6			1-1		17-18
Joel McKeon												12-18	
Russ Morman		20-25											20-25
Gene Nelson									0-1			18-35	0-1
Reid Nichols						7-11	5-5	3-1					15-17
Jack Perconte			11-12										11-12
Luis Salazar										0-2			0-2
Dave Schmidt									0-1			21-27	0-1
Ray Searage												10-19	
Tom Seaver													
Joel Skinner	20-28												20-28
Bob Thigpen												12-8	
Wayne Tolleson			25-35	5-5							7-8		30-40
Greg Walker		34-40								0-1			34-41
Ken Williams							1-3	3-1			1-2		4-4

Batting Comparisons: Vs. Left-Handers/Right-Handers and Overall/Late Inning Pressure Situations

Player	Split	BA	Rank	SA	Rank	HR %	Rank	Situation	BA	Rank	SA	Rank	HR %	Rank
Harold Baines	vs. Lefties	.262	85	.354	120	1.46	124	Overall	.296	23	.465	33	3.68	63
	vs. Righties	.316	13	.527	12	4.95	33	Pressure	.289	54	.530	18	7.23	8
Bobby Bonilla	vs. Lefties	.269	77	.323	142	0.00	148	Overall	.269	65	.355	133	0.85	146
	vs. Righties	.270	68	.376	109	1.42	125	Pressure	.227	112	.250	152	0.00	109
Daryl Boston	vs. Lefties	.250	101	.417	76	2.08	103	Overall	.266	76	.427	69	2.51	99
	vs. Righties	.272	64	.430	69	2.65	91	Pressure	.095	--	.095	--	0.00	--
Ivan Calderon	vs. Lefties	.231	125	.327	139	0.00	148	Overall	.250	--	.341	--	1.22	--
	vs. Righties	.259	--	.348	--	1.79	--	Pressure	.345	18	.414	61	0.00	109
John Cangelosi	vs. Lefties	.216	146	.343	130	1.49	122	Overall	.235	137	.299	161	0.46	157
	vs. Righties	.243	114	.280	164	0.00	158	Pressure	.213	125	.361	90	1.64	90
Julio Cruz	vs. Lefties	.219	139	.233	166	0.00	148	Overall	.215	158	.225	169	0.00	166
	vs. Righties	.213	158	.221	171	0.00	158	Pressure	.190	--	.190	--	0.00	--
Carlton Fisk	vs. Lefties	.223	134	.350	122	3.18	71	Overall	.221	153	.337	143	3.06	80
	vs. Righties	.220	152	.330	137	3.00	80	Pressure	.215	123	.367	86	3.80	46
Ozzie Guillen	vs. Lefties	.257	91	.299	153	0.60	147	Overall	.250	113	.311	154	0.37	159
	vs. Righties	.247	111	.316	144	0.26	157	Pressure	.247	94	.272	142	0.00	109
Jerry Hairston	vs. Lefties	.220	137	.373	102	3.39	61	Overall	.271	60	.404	91	2.22	105
	vs. Righties	.289	38	.416	80	1.81	108	Pressure	.281	64	.359	93	0.00	109
Ron Hassey	vs. Lefties	.297	43	.359	114	0.00	148	Overall	.323	7	.481	22	2.64	94
	vs. Righties	.329	7	.509	18	3.25	68	Pressure	.378	5	.514	27	2.70	67
Tim Hulett	vs. Lefties	.253	98	.443	56	4.64	30	Overall	.231	142	.379	109	3.27	72
	vs. Righties	.218	154	.340	130	2.45	94	Pressure	.182	148	.260	148	1.30	104
Steve Lyons	vs. Lefties	.242	--	.364	--	0.00	--	Overall	.227	148	.300	160	0.40	158
	vs. Righties	.224	144	.290	162	0.47	152	Pressure	.212	127	.212	160	0.00	109
Russ Morman	vs. Lefties	.242	108	.371	104	3.23	68	Overall	.252	--	.358	--	2.52	--
	vs. Righties	.258	--	.351	--	2.06	--	Pressure	.130	167	.130	169	0.00	109
Reid Nichols	vs. Lefties	.233	122	.267	162	0.00	148	Overall	.228	--	.301	--	1.47	--
	vs. Righties	.200	--	.500	--	10.00	--	Pressure	.318	--	.364	--	0.00	--
Greg Walker	vs. Lefties	.236	113	.360	113	2.25	98	Overall	.277	50	.493	15	4.61	31
	vs. Righties	.295	28	.554	5	5.70	15	Pressure	.302	42	.419	59	0.00	109
Team Average	vs. Lefties	.235	14	.340	14	1.95	14	Overall	.247	14	.363	14	2.24	14
	vs. Righties	.254	9	.375	14	2.40	13	Pressure	.226	14	.316	14	1.54	14
League Average	vs. Lefties	.263		.408		2.88		Overall	.262		.408		2.96	
	vs. Righties	.261		.408		2.99		Pressure	.254		.383		2.61	

Additional Miscellaneous Batting Comparisons

Player	Grass Surface BA	Rank	Artificial Surface BA	Rank	Home Games BA	Rank	Road Games BA	Rank	Runners in Scoring Position BA	Rank	Runners in Scoring Pos and Two Outs BA	Rank	Leading Off Inning OBA	Rank	Runners on 3B with less than 2 Outs RDI %	Rank
Harold Baines	.302	16	.262	91	.331	8	.264	69	.289	52	.255	79	.295	128	.644	47
Bobby Bonilla	.286	35	.143	--	.287	48	.254	91	.250	107	.240	89	.450	4	.583	77
Daryl Boston	.278	45	.220	135	.309	24	.225	142	.275	--	.222	114	.355	50	.375	--
Ivan Calderon	.288	--	.214	143	.203	--	.280	46	.220	--	.167	--	.152	169	.400	156
John Cangelosi	.221	142	.306	38	.238	122	.233	129	.235	125	.222	114	.316	108	.542	102
Julio Cruz	.207	155	.250	103	.265	91	.171	167	.320	19	.333	21	.351	59	.667	38
Carlton Fisk	.214	150	.261	93	.207	158	.236	126	.240	117	.193	136	.245	159	.559	95
Ozzie Guillen	.240	119	.304	42	.254	103	.247	107	.315	27	.381	5	.246	158	.516	120
Jerry Hairston	.288	31	.208	147	.308	26	.231	132	.310	31	.179	147	.377	27	.706	22
Ron Hassey	.343	4	.230	126	.329	9	.316	10	.305	36	.280	--	.500	1	.846	4
Tim Hulett	.235	126	.207	149	.247	114	.214	148	.175	161	.136	165	.248	157	.333	162
Steve Lyons	.235	127	.191	157	.250	106	.203	159	.254	103	.238	93	.286	133	.529	105
Russ Morman	.227	136	.355	--	.281	--	.235	127	.263	--	.238	93	.394	--	.500	122
Reid Nichols	.248	--	.130	--	.256	--	.190	--	.333	--	.400	--	.242	--	.438	149
Greg Walker	.272	53	.298	51	.278	63	.275	54	.274	71	.265	73	.337	75	.571	83
Team Average	.248	11	.243	14	.258	9	.236	14	.260	7	.242	8	.317	10	.539	12
League Average	.258		.270		.264		.259		.263		.246		.326		.575	

Pitching Comparisons: Vs. Left-Handers/Right-Handers and Runners On/Bases Empty

		BA	Rank	BB %	Rank	SO %	Rank			BA	Rank	BB %	Rank	SO %	Rank
Neil Allen	vs. Lefties	.232	33	7.69	37	11.54	78	Runners On		.265	66	6.98	28	12.79	74
	vs. Righties	.256	64	8.62	87	12.93	93	Bases Empty		.232	33	8.84	86	11.90	99
Floyd Bannister	vs. Lefties	.204	9	5.66	17	15.09	44	Runners On		.251	46	10.14	87	11.96	84
	vs. Righties	.269	86	7.22	58	13.06	90	Bases Empty		.263	73	4.85	12	14.32	71
Steve Carlton	vs. Lefties	.188	--	5.88	--	23.53	--	Runners On		.276	--	9.00	--	11.00	--
	vs. Righties	.257	66	9.92	103	14.88	76	Bases Empty		.238	36	10.06	100	18.24	36
Joe Cowley	vs. Lefties	.248	48	12.60	109	15.22	43	Runners On		.234	23	13.68	123	17.54	31
	vs. Righties	.194	9	11.25	118	23.79	11	Bases Empty		.216	21	10.81	109	20.15	21
Joel Davis	vs. Lefties	.293	93	12.70	110	10.71	85	Runners On		.339	126	11.28	102	10.26	106
	vs. Righties	.265	81	8.80	90	12.50	97	Bases Empty		.239	37	10.62	105	12.45	94
Bill Dawley	vs. Lefties	.291	91	8.98	60	8.38	110	Runners On		.240	31	8.85	62	13.02	69
	vs. Righties	.218	20	5.46	28	21.85	21	Bases Empty		.254	60	5.16	15	19.25	26
Jose DeLeon	vs. Lefties	.184	3	14.81	120	15.43	37	Runners On		.161	1	9.03	65	23.61	6
	vs. Righties	.174	4	11.04	117	26.38	6	Bases Empty		.193	6	16.02	124	18.78	31
Richard Dotson	vs. Lefties	.265	61	8.24	49	12.47	66	Runners On		.297	104	9.37	72	11.29	93
	vs. Righties	.316	128	7.77	66	13.11	89	Bases Empty		.284	101	7.03	53	13.86	81
Bob James	vs. Lefties	.239	39	12.12	104	13.64	54	Runners On		.271	74	7.14	33	13.64	64
	vs. Righties	.296	--	5.34	--	10.69	--	Bases Empty		.263	--	11.01	--	10.09	--
Gene Nelson	vs. Lefties	.285	86	10.00	78	12.27	70	Runners On		.260	57	9.02	64	14.12	63
	vs. Righties	.259	71	7.09	51	16.04	66	Bases Empty		.282	94	7.73	67	14.59	66
Dave Schmidt	vs. Lefties	.265	62	9.29	66	15.30	40	Runners On		.230	20	8.56	58	19.25	22
	vs. Righties	.263	77	4.74	18	18.48	42	Bases Empty		.292	111	5.31	18	14.98	58
Ray Searage	vs. Lefties	.200	--	11.25	--	25.00	--	Runners On		.180	--	16.96	--	16.96	--
	vs. Righties	.254	60	13.57	124	11.43	110	Bases Empty		.283	--	8.33	--	15.74	--
Team Average	vs. Lefties	.249	3	10.32	12	13.28	8	Runners On		.258	3	10.28	10	14.07	9
	vs. Righties	.253	6	8.29	9	15.68	10	Bases Empty		.245	4	8.32	9	15.08	10
League Average	vs. Lefties	.265		9.67		13.46		Runners On		.269		9.46		14.39	
	vs. Righties	.259		8.19		16.22		Bases Empty		.256		8.31		15.55	

Additional Miscellaneous Pitching Comparisons

	Grass Surface BA	Rank	Artificial Surface BA	Rank	Home Games BA	Rank	Road Games BA	Rank	Runners in Scoring Position BA	Rank	Runners in Scoring Pos and Two Outs BA	Rank	Leading Off Inning OBA	Rank
Neil Allen	.229	28	.339	123	.264	75	.223	12	.282	92	.206	39	.294	34
Floyd Bannister	.258	65	.263	59	.219	29	.311	117	.214	17	.143	5	.299	41
Steve Carlton	.260	68	.226	21	.217	26	.287	97	.289	--	.333	--	.373	110
Joe Cowley	.221	16	.228	22	.200	9	.244	36	.241	47	.273	88	.285	26
Joel Davis	.280	100	.278	72	.279	91	.281	84	.310	114	.353	123	.272	18
Bill Dawley	.237	38	.333	--	.216	24	.276	79	.262	75	.152	11	.284	25
Jose DeLeon	.180	2	.176	3	.185	5	.175	1	.143	1	.192	--	.393	118
Richard Dotson	.281	102	.331	121	.276	87	.303	112	.296	102	.241	66	.347	92
Pete Filson	.412	--	.313	108	.400	--	.250	--	.348	--	.385	--	.133	--
Bob James	.253	52	.367	--	.306	117	.221	10	.247	58	.179	22	.319	--
Gene Nelson	.263	75	.305	101	.280	95	.261	61	.221	25	.226	55	.350	93
Dave Schmidt	.260	69	.286	78	.238	46	.286	95	.229	37	.276	90	.276	20
Ray Searage	.234	34	.231	--	.260	--	.202	--	.161	3	.120	3	.326	--
Team Average	.246	4	.276	11	.240	4	.262	8	.248	3	.234	5	.305	2
League Average	.258		.270		.259		.264		.263		.246		.326	

CLEVELAND INDIANS

The first time Phil Niekro takes the mound this season, he will become the fifth-oldest player ever to pitch in a major-league game. Niekro turns 48 on April Fool's Day, and his continued success at an age at which many players have ceased competing even in Old Timers' games has become one of the baseball stories of the decade, if not of all time.

When Niekro pitched a four-hit shutout on the final day of the 1985 season for the 300th victory of his career, he became the oldest pitcher in the history of major-league baseball not only to pitch a shutout, but simply to complete a start as well. Last season, he surpassed that feat with five more complete games at age 47, though none was a shutout. And he became the oldest pitcher to start 20 games and to win 10 in a season, once again breaking records he himself had established the previous year.

With so many pitchers remaining competitive into their 40s, it's necessary to put Niekro's age into perspective. Six other players at least 40 years old pitched in the majors last season: from youngest to oldest, they were Ken Forsch, Don Sutton, Steve Carlton, Tom Seaver, Joe Niekro, and Tommy John. Niekro is nearly four years older than John. Jose Rijo, now in his fourth season in the majors, was born on the day that Niekro earned his first major-league victory. Dwight Gooden was six months old three days later. Niekro's teammates have included Gus Bell, Eddie Mathews, and Warren Spahn. The first batter he faced in the majors was Jim Davenport.

Niekro has reached an age at which almost anything he does is noteworthy. To honor him, we've compiled a mini-record book of graybeard accomplishments. Each list contains the five oldest pitchers to accomplish a particular feat. Otherwise, for instance, Niekro would have the list of the five oldest pitchers to complete a start all to himself.

Oldest to Pitch in a Game

	Date	Age
Satchel Paige	9/25/65	59 years, 2 months
Jack Quinn	7/7/33	50 years, 2 days
Hoyt Wilhelm	7/10/72	48 years, 11 months
Nick Altrock	9/30/24	48 years, 15 days
Kaiser Wilhelm	8/26/21	47 years, 7 months

Oldest to Win a Game

	Date	Age
Jack Quinn	9/13/32	49 years, 2 months
Phil Niekro	9/5/86	47 years, 5 months
Satchel Paige	9/22/53	47 years, 2 months
Hoyt Wilhelm	9/2/70	47 years, 1 month
Hod Lisenbee	9/7/45	46 years, 11 months

Oldest to Lose a Game

	Date	Age
Jack Quinn	6/28/33	49 years, 11 months
Hoyt Wilhelm	6/24/72	48 years, 11 months
Phil Niekro	9/19/86	47 years, 5 months
Satchel Paige	8/18/53	47 years, 1 month
Hod Lisenbee	6/28/45	46 years, 9 months

Oldest to Complete a Start

	Date	Age
Phil Niekro	9/19/86	47 years, 5 months
Satchel Paige	9/20/52	46 years, 2 months
Jack Quinn	9/2/29	46 years, 1 month
Bobo Newsom	8/31/53	46 years, 20 days
Ted Lyons	5/19/46	45 years, 4 months

Oldest to Pitch a Shutout

	Date	Age
Phil Niekro	10/6/85	46 years, 6 months
Satchel Paige	9/20/52	46 years, 2 months
Jack Quinn	9/15/28	45 years, 2 months
Gaylord Perry	6/17/83	44 years, 9 months
Cy Young	9/22/11	44 years, 6 months

Oldest to Pitch a No-Hitter

	Date	Age
Cy Young	6/30/08	41 years, 3 months
Warren Spahn	4/28/61	40 years, 5 days
Sal Maglie	9/25/56	39 years, 4 months
Bob Keegan	8/20/57	37 year, 16 days
Allie Reynolds	9/28/51	36 years, 7 months

Oldest to Save a Game

	Date	Age
Hoyt Wilhelm	4/17/72	48 years, 9 months
Jim Kaat	9/1/82	43 years, 9 months
Don McMahon	9/15/73	43 years, 8 months
Woodie Fryman	9/24/82	42 years, 5 months
Ron Reed	9/25/84	41 years, 10 months

Oldest to Win 10 Games in a Season

	Date	Age
Phil Niekro	8/24/86	47 years, 4 months
Satchel Paige	9/1/52	46 years, 56 days
Jack Quinn	8/29/29	46 years, 55 days
Gaylord Perry	9/22/82	44 years, 7 days
Red Faber	9/13/31	43 years, 7 days

Oldest to Start 20 Games in a Season

	Date	Age
Phil Niekro	7/24/86	47 years, 3 months
Jack Quinn	8/10/28	45 yeras, 1 month
Gaylord Perry	7/27/83	44 years, 10 months
Warren Spahn	7/22/65	44 years, 2 months
Cy Young	9/6/10	43 years, 5 months

Comebacks and Carryovers

Last season, we read a comment by Joe Carter that piqued our interest. On July 31, Cleveland defeated Detroit 8–7 in a game in which the Indians trailed 7–1 in the fifth inning. After the game, Carter said that it was the type of victory that can boost the level of a team's play for a few days afterward. Sounds like our kind of topic: Can a team really ride the wave of a stirring come-from-behind victory to improve its performance in upcoming games?

We found 17 games last season in which the winning team trailed by as many as five runs as late as the fifth inning. The following table identifies them, and indicates how the winning teams did in their next five games:

Date	Team and Opponent			Next 5 Games		
April 10	N.Y. vs. K.C.	W	W	W	W	L
April 25	Chi. at Det.	W	L	L	W	L
April 26	Cal. at Minn.	W	W	L	W	L
May 14	Phil. vs. Cin.	L	W	L	L	L
June 10	Clev. vs. Oak.	W	W	L	L	L
June 21	S.D. at L.A.	W	L	W	W	L
July 27	Cin. vs. Mtl.	L	L	L	L	L
July 31	Clev. vs. Det.	W	L	W	L	L
Aug. 6	Tex. at Balt.	W	W	W	L	L
Aug. 9	N.Y. at Mtl.	W	W	L	L	W
Aug. 13	Balt. vs. Tor.	W	L	L	L	L
Aug. 13	Cin. vs. S.F.	W	W	L	W	L
Aug. 16	Sea. vs. Minn.	W	W	L	L	L
Aug. 19	K.C. vs. Tex.	L	W	W	L	L
Aug. 26	Det. vs. Oak.	L	L	L	L	W
Sep. 17	Mtl. vs. Pitt.	L	L	W	L	L
Oct. 3	Clev. vs. Sea.	W	W	—	—	—

The five games afterward strongly support Carter's claim. Twelve of the 17 teams won the game immediately following their come-from-behind wins. The totals declined gradually and progressively thereafter: 10 of 17 won the second game, six of 16 the third, five of 16 the fourth, and two of 16 the fifth. Let's put it another way: The teams had a combined record of 22–12 in the two games immediately following the comeback win, 13–35 in the three games thereafter. That's a significant pattern, the kind of result that rarely occurs without a good reason. The odds, in fact, would be 270 to one.

Nevertheless, 17 games is a pretty small sample, so we took a look at the same question for games played during the 1985 season. The results were much different. Here is a summary of how teams fared following big come-from-behind wins (as defined above) over the past two seasons:

Year	W–L	W–L	W–L	W–L	W–L	W–L
1982	15–10	11–14	16–9	12–12	11–13	65–58
1983	10–7	8–9	8–9	10–7	9–8	45–40
1984	10–12	11–11	10–11	9–12	9–12	49–58
1985	7–12	9–10	9–10	12–7	6–13	43–52
1986	12–5	10–7	6–10	5–11	2–14	35–47
Totals	54–46	49–51	49–49	48–49	37–60	237–255

You can look at those results two ways and reach different conclusions depending on your choice. The first alternative: The teams had a combined record of only 103–97 in their first two games after the come-from-behind wins, hardly indicative of the brief surge Carter spoke of. Maybe a team feels an awful lot better taking the field following such a dramatic comeback victory, but that euphoria won't help win the next game.

Alternative two: Consider games two through four to be a valid representation of these teams' collective ability. The first-game record of 54–46 is somewhat better than the combined records in the three games after it (146–149). Enough to conclude that Carter was correct? Only if you want to believe, we suppose; despite Tug McGraw's famous cry, you don't gotta.

But whatever your conclusion on the immediate benefits of a dramatic come-from-behind win, you can't ignore the bizarre result five games after it. We thought it might be attributable to the five-man rotation—that is, that the same pitcher who got belted early in the comeback win repeated that performance in his next start five games later—but that wasn't the case. Is it possible that these teams play on an emotional high for a few games and then crash back to earth, suffering an emotional letdown a few days later when that high isn't reinforced by the results of their games? Hard to say. But in any event, let's all keep our eyes on this trend in 1987.

Little Big Man

Let's play a game. We're going to show you the statistics of two players. We won't tell you who they are. Look at them for a minute and conjure up a mental image of who those figures might belong to:

	AB	R	H	2B	3B	HR	RBI	BB	SO	SB	BA
Player A	500	79	128	18	1	35	97	96	104	1	.256
Player B	500	65	131	19	4	4	39	36	36	25	.262

Now consider these questions: Which player do you think is younger? Which do you think is taller? Faster? More muscular? We think almost everyone would agree that Player A is taller and more muscular, Player B younger and faster.

The two are scaled-down 500-at bat representations of the careers of Harmon Killebrew and Luis Aparicio, the classic hulk and rabbit of the 1960s. At 195 pounds, Killebrew was built like a six-foot block of ice. Aparicio was five-nine and weighed 160 pounds. Their performance statistics describe them as well as their heights and weights do.

Most players follow the patterns dictated by their sizes. We expect John Cangelosi (5'8") to steal more bases than Mike Marshall (6'5"), and Tom Brunansky (6'4") to hit more home runs than Wally Backman (5'9"). There are instances of players who outperform those expectations, but they're unusual enough that they sometimes warrant a nickname to signify it. Jim Wynn, the Astros' all-time home run leader, was tagged the "Toy Cannon" on account of the power he generated from his small frame (5'9", 165 pounds).

And then there's Andy Allanson. Allanson stands six feet, five inches tall. When Cangelosi comes to bat, Big Andy can just about look him in the eye from his catcher's crouch.

Outfitted with his orange chest protector and his scalloped shin guards, Allanson looks like the guest of honor at a Maine lobster bake. I tell ya, he's so big, they gotta use scaffolding to clean his sunglasses.

But seriously, folks, do you know why Allanson's home run on June 23 made headlines? It wasn't only his first of the season. It wasn't only the first of his major-league career. It was the first home run Allanson had ever hit in professional baseball, in his 1,026th at bat.

Let's put that in perspective. Jerry Reuss has one home run in 1,016 major-league at bats. Joe Niekro has one in 973 at bats. Curtis Wilkerson has hit one major-league home run in 1,115 at bats, and he could wear Allanson's short-sleeved shirts with cufflinks. Andy Allanson is Gulliver (no, not Glenn), helpless despite his size.

Compare the results of Allanson's 324 plate appearances last season to a proportional slice of the composite total of all players who stand at least six-four. Allanson's stats more closely resemble those of players no taller than five feet, nine inches. Except that he hit fewer home runs and stole fewer bases than even those Lilliputians:

Player	AB	R	H	2B	3B	HR	RBI	BB	SO	SB	BA
6'4" or Taller	291	38	75	14	1	11	43	27	57	4	.256
Andy Allanson	293	30	66	7	3	1	29	14	36	10	.225
5'9" or Shorter	288	41	77	12	2	5	27	29	41	14	.267

Now all this isn't of much interest to the Indians, who wouldn't care if Allanson looked like Manute Bol as long as he could hit. And for the first month of the 1986 season, Allanson hit about as well as any player in the league. Although he didn't qualify for the batting average leadership, Allanson was hitting .381 through games of May 7; only one qualifier—little Kirby Puckett—had a higher average. (Did Bob Costas and his wife consider naming the baby Big Andy?) But after that it was all downhill for Allanson: a .200 batting average over his next 140 at bats (through July 25), and then total collapse. Allanson had only 14 hits in 90 at bats for the remainder of the season (.156), including hitless streaks of 18 and 22 at bats.

All this ought to concern the rest of the American League, because Cleveland's starting catchers underperformed the American League average last season, and the Indians still led the league in runs scored with 831. Allanson and Chris Bando combined for a .249 batting average in starting roles but fell short of the league standards in almost every other category:

Starting Catchers	AB	R	H	2B	3B	HR	RBI	BB	SO	SB	BA	SA	OBA
Cleveland	519	55	129	16	3	3	54	35	79	10	.249	.308	.295
A.L. Average	529	56	124	20	2	15	63	48	90	3	.235	.365	.301

So look out, American League. Cleveland's attack could be simply awesome this season if big Andy Allanson starts to hit like those other six-foot-five terrors: Dave Winfield, Darryl Strawberry, Bruce Bochy . . .

WON-LOST RECORD BY STARTING POSITION

CLEVELAND	84-78	C	1B	2B	3B	SS	LF	CF	RF	P	DH	Leadoff	Relief	Starts
Andy Allanson		48-43												48-43
Scott Bailes										4-5*			28-24	4-5
Chris Bando		36-35*												36-35
Jay Bell				0-2										2-2
Tony Bernazard				73-70*							2-0	41-40*		73-70
John Butcher										1-7			0-5	1-7
Brett Butler							79-71*					36-35		79-71
Ernie Camacho													30-20*	
Tom Candiotti										20-14			1-1	20-14
Joe Carter			34-27*				19-18	3-2	26-30					82-77
Carmen Castillo							17-14				11-13			28-27
Dave Clark							5-4				4-2			9-6
Jamie Easterly													3-10	
Julio Franco				8-3		66-66*					1-2	0-1		75-71
Mel Hall							57-51*		3-1		0-1			60-53
Neal Heaton										5-7				5-7
Brook Jacoby					80-74*									80-74
Doug Jones													6-5	
Jim Kern													3-13	
Fran Mullins				3-2		2-1								5-3
Phil Niekro										13-19				13-19
Otis Nixon							7-4	2-5	0-1			7-2		9-10
Dickie Noles													11-21	
Bryan Oelkers										2-2			14-17	2-2
Reggie Ritter													0-5	
Dan Rohn			0-1		1-0									1-1
Jose Roman										1-4				1-4
Ken Schrom										22-11			0-1	22-11
Don Schulze										9-4			3-3	9-4
Cory Snyder				4-4	15-11	1-5			33-28		0-1			53-49
Greg Swindell										5-4				5-4
Pat Tabler			50-51								10-7*			60-58
Andre Thornton											56-52			56-52
Ed Williams											56-52			
Frank Wills													12-13*	
Rich Yett										2-1			13-23	2-1

* Also one tie game.

Batting Comparisons: Vs. Left-Handers/Right-Handers and Overall/Late Inning Pressure Situations

		BA	Rank	SA	Rank	HR %	Rank		BA	Rank	SA	Rank	HR %	Rank
Andy Allanson	vs. Lefties	.274	65	.333	137	0.00	148	Overall	.225	150	.280	167	0.34	161
	vs. Righties	.206	165	.258	168	0.48	151	Pressure	.344	19	.469	39	0.00	109
Chris Bando	vs. Lefties	.301	37	.356	117	1.37	127	Overall	.268	71	.327	148	0.79	147
	vs. Righties	.254	96	.315	145	0.55	150	Pressure	.224	116	.265	145	0.00	109
Tony Bernazard	vs. Lefties	.338	10	.510	23	3.31	65	Overall	.301	19	.456	45	3.02	81
	vs. Righties	.287	41	.436	64	2.92	81	Pressure	.239	101	.324	116	0.00	109
Brett Butler	vs. Lefties	.306	32	.413	77	0.63	146	Overall	.278	46	.375	115	0.68	149
	vs. Righties	.267	72	.361	116	0.70	145	Pressure	.347	14	.400	67	1.33	100
Joe Carter	vs. Lefties	.315	24	.530	14	3.87	51	Overall	.302	18	.514	9	4.37	38
	vs. Righties	.297	27	.508	19	4.56	40	Pressure	.295	49	.462	44	2.56	69
Carmen Castillo	vs. Lefties	.248	104	.422	71	4.59	31	Overall	.278	45	.439	59	3.90	52
	vs. Righties	.313	--	.458	--	3.13	--	Pressure	.231	--	.423	--	3.85	--
Julio Franco	vs. Lefties	.341	9	.537	13	3.66	55	Overall	.306	14	.422	76	1.67	119
	vs. Righties	.292	31	.379	102	0.92	140	Pressure	.277	70	.323	117	0.00	109
Mel Hall	vs. Lefties	.154	--	.231	--	0.00	--	Overall	.296	24	.493	14	4.07	47
	vs. Righties	.305	21	.510	17	4.33	44	Pressure	.304	40	.554	10	5.36	26
Brook Jacoby	vs. Lefties	.261	89	.404	85	3.11	76	Overall	.288	30	.441	57	2.92	84
	vs. Righties	.299	26	.455	49	2.84	85	Pressure	.347	14	.467	40	1.33	100
Otis Nixon	vs. Lefties	.270	74	.324	141	0.00	148	Overall	.263	--	.326	--	0.00	--
	vs. Righties	.259	--	.328	--	0.00	--	Pressure	.214	--	.286	--	0.00	--
Cory Snyder	vs. Lefties	.322	18	.585	6	6.78	11	Overall	.272	58	.500	11	5.77	11
	vs. Righties	.252	102	.466	43	5.37	22	Pressure	.305	36	.525	21	5.08	28
Pat Tabler	vs. Lefties	.333	12	.447	54	1.33	129	Overall	.326	5	.433	64	1.27	135
	vs. Righties	.322	10	.427	72	1.24	132	Pressure	.333	23	.500	32	5.00	30
Andre Thornton	vs. Lefties	.236	115	.407	83	4.88	28	Overall	.229	143	.392	96	4.24	43
	vs. Righties	.227	140	.385	96	3.96	53	Pressure	.196	143	.326	113	2.17	78
Team Average	vs. Lefties	.298	1	.451	2	2.92	6	Overall	.284	1	.430	2	2.75	10
	vs. Righties	.279	2	.422	4	2.69	10	Pressure	.287	1	.413	3	2.06	12
League Average	vs. Lefties	.263		.408		2.88		Overall	.262		.408		2.96	
	vs. Righties	.261		.408		2.99		Pressure	.254		.383		2.61	

Additional Miscellaneous Batting Comparisons

	Grass Surface BA	Rank	Artificial Surface BA	Rank	Home Games BA	Rank	Road Games BA	Rank	Runners in Scoring Position BA	Rank	Runners in Scoring Pos and Two Outs BA	Rank	Leading Off Inning OBA	Rank	Runners on 3B with less than 2 Outs RDI %	Rank
Andy Allanson	.221	141	.258	--	.238	121	.212	151	.259	90	.277	63	.318	105	.500	122
Chris Bando	.256	85	.305	39	.288	43	.250	100	.274	71	.286	53	.345	61	.474	141
Tony Bernazard	.305	15	.276	72	.329	10	.272	59	.276	66	.188	139	.354	53	.760	14
Brett Butler	.273	51	.301	47	.272	77	.283	44	.273	74	.274	66	.360	45	.679	35
Joe Carter	.297	21	.327	18	.312	20	.292	32	.290	50	.288	52	.325	91	.569	87
Carmen Castillo	.280	40	.267	--	.317	18	.240	120	.259	91	.286	53	.289	--	.500	122
Julio Franco	.309	11	.284	64	.291	38	.320	9	.301	40	.229	108	.389	18	.625	53
Mel Hall	.288	32	.349	12	.277	69	.314	13	.273	73	.294	45	.371	30	.565	88
Brook Jacoby	.289	29	.283	65	.266	86	.307	17	.310	31	.310	35	.364	37	.520	116
Cory Snyder	.282	37	.229	127	.280	57	.265	68	.259	89	.231	102	.314	109	.560	93
Pat Tabler	.346	3	.221	133	.348	4	.305	19	.303	37	.216	124	.391	16	.600	65
Andre Thornton	.238	123	.167	162	.279	59	.168	168	.275	68	.275	65	.277	141	.696	29
Team Average	.285	1	.277	6	.291	1	.278	1	.284	2	.261	4	.346	2	.598	5
League Average	.258		.270		.264		.259		.263		.246		.326		.575	

Pitching Comparisons: Vs. Left-Handers/Right-Handers and Runners On/Bases Empty

		BA	Rank	BB %	Rank	SO %	Rank		BA	Rank	BB %	Rank	SO %	Rank
Scott Bailes	vs. Lefties	.299	101	8.40	51	12.98	61	Runners On	.270	72	9.20	68	10.34	104
	vs. Righties	.268	85	8.67	88	11.65	107	Bases Empty	.283	98	7.95	72	13.81	82
John Butcher	vs. Lefties	.340	123	7.08	28	6.46	124	Runners On	.347	127	7.17	35	6.04	131
	vs. Righties	.325	129	6.11	35	10.48	116	Bases Empty	.322	125	6.23	38	10.03	113
Ernie Camacho	vs. Lefties	.284	84	13.97	117	11.76	76	Runners On	.247	40	12.02	111	12.02	83
	vs. Righties	.254	--	9.16	--	15.27	--	Bases Empty	.315	--	10.71	--	16.67	--
Tom Candiotti	vs. Lefties	.237	36	10.00	78	13.21	59	Runners On	.222	13	11.84	110	13.06	67
	vs. Righties	.255	61	9.65	99	17.95	47	Bases Empty	.264	75	8.16	75	17.52	41
Phil Niekro	vs. Lefties	.284	83	10.10	83	7.18	122	Runners On	.275	81	10.31	93	8.30	122
	vs. Righties	.290	109	9.86	101	10.09	120	Bases Empty	.296	115	9.70	96	8.71	121
Dickie Noles	vs. Lefties	.296	97	15.20	121	10.40	94	Runners On	.317	116	13.85	124	9.23	116
	vs. Righties	.245	--	8.73	--	15.08	--	Bases Empty	.224	--	9.92	--	16.53	--
Bryan Oelkers	vs. Lefties	.232	31	10.71	89	11.61	77	Runners On	.236	26	12.90	117	9.68	111
	vs. Righties	.279	104	13.59	125	9.71	124	Bases Empty	.286	103	12.27	120	11.04	106
Ken Schrom	vs. Lefties	.293	94	5.58	16	9.09	103	Runners On	.242	34	6.04	16	10.99	98
	vs. Righties	.242	47	5.51	29	10.78	114	Bases Empty	.289	106	5.20	17	9.06	120
Don Schulze	vs. Lefties	.296	98	9.94	77	8.19	116	Runners On	.284	95	8.48	56	9.70	110
	vs. Righties	.240	43	8.50	84	9.50	126	Bases Empty	.251	54	9.71	97	8.25	123
Greg Swindell	vs. Lefties	.154	--	3.70	--	11.11	--	Runners On	.262	--	6.32	--	17.89	--
	vs. Righties	.254	59	6.14	36	18.86	40	Bases Empty	.232	32	5.63	27	18.13	37
Rich Yett	vs. Lefties	.271	71	9.42	68	12.04	72	Runners On	.328	123	13.46	121	11.54	88
	vs. Righties	.279	105	11.95	121	16.98	58	Bases Empty	.236	34	8.25	76	16.49	46
Team Average	vs. Lefties	.279	12	9.65	8	10.22	14	Runners On	.268	7	10.56	12	10.69	14
	vs. Righties	.269	12	9.18	11	12.69	14	Bases Empty	.278	13	8.32	8	12.35	14
League Average	vs. Lefties	.265		9.67		13.46		Runners On	.269		9.46		14.39	
	vs. Righties	.259		8.19		16.22		Bases Empty	.256		8.31		15.55	

Additional Miscellaneous Pitching Comparisons

	Grass Surface BA	Rank	Artificial Surface BA	Rank	Home Games BA	Rank	Road Games BA	Rank	Runners in Scoring Position BA	Rank	Runners in Scoring Pos and Two Outs BA	Rank	Leading Off Inning OBA	Rank
Scott Bailes	.273	91	.308	106	.245	52	.313	118	.342	123	.357	125	.327	67
John Butcher	.350	128	.306	103	.396	128	.308	115	.331	122	.276	90	.425	125
Ernie Camacho	.257	63	.325	118	.303	114	.231	15	.250	59	.178	19	.500	--
Tom Candiotti	.240	42	.272	68	.250	57	.241	32	.228	34	.200	30	.345	88
Phil Niekro	.287	105	.287	82	.277	88	.294	105	.305	111	.333	118	.339	84
Dickie Noles	.255	57	.375	--	.333	--	.226	14	.246	52	.216	48	.354	--
Bryan Oelkers	.262	74	.265	--	.253	62	.276	80	.246	52	.306	111	.391	117
Ken Schrom	.276	96	.240	34	.255	67	.291	102	.215	18	.230	58	.362	101
Don Schulze	.265	76	.271	67	.237	45	.297	107	.302	108	.342	121	.344	87
Greg Swindell	.239	40	.254	50	.248	55	.236	--	.294	--	.364	--	.288	29
Frank Wills	.276	--	.258	--	.256	--	.289	--	.167	--	.179	20	.353	--
Rich Yett	.278	97	.240	--	.312	120	.237	28	.342	124	.333	118	.270	14
Team Average	.274	13	.272	8	.274	12	.273	13	.273	10	.266	11	.355	14
League Average	.258		.270		.259		.264		.263		.246		.326	

DETROIT TIGERS

If they ran the American League the way run the Big Ten Conference, the 1986 Tigers would have been headed for the Rose Bowl. Or, at least, the American League Championship Series.

You know the way it works in the Big Ten, or any other college conference: Each school's football team plays an 11- or 12-game schedule, including at least a few nonconference games against teams from outside its own little group. These latter games don't count toward the race for the conference championship; in the Big Ten, for instance, only games against other conference members determine the title, and with it the right to be thrashed by the Pac-10 winner to open up the New Year. That leaves the possibility that one team could have a better overall record (say 10–1 overall, 7–1 in conference), while another team, with a lesser overall mark but a better Big Ten mark (say, 9–2, 8–0) would be sent to Pasadena.

This brings us to the 1986 Detroit Tigers.

The Tigers had the best record in the American League East in games against their own division. The trouble is, baseball's division titles are not contested under the Big Ten rules; the league presidents insist on counting all games when determining the division titlists. (Whether Bart Giamatti, familiar as he is with Ivy League procedures, will urge a change in this policy remains to be seen. We'll know that something is up if the National League suddenly adopts a 10-game regular season schedule, with no postseason games.)

Here are last year's American League East standings, broken down against East and West opponents:

	Vs. A.L. East					Vs. A.L. West			
	W	L	Pct.	GB		W	L	Pct.	GB
Detroit	45	33	.577	—	Cleveland	52	32	.619	—
Boston	44	33	.571	0.5	Boston	51	33	.607	1
New York	43	35	.551	2	New York	47	37	.560	5
Toronto	42	36	.538	3	Baltimore	45	39	.536	7
Milwaukee	38	39	.494	6.5	Toronto	44	40	.524	8
Cleveland	32	46	.410	13	**Detroit**	42	42	.500	10
Baltimore	28	50	.359	17	Milwaukee	39	45	.464	13

What does that say about the alleged importance of winning games in your own division? It says that it's a bunch of hooey, at least in the American League.

A brief review of the American League's scheduling pattern is in order. (Note: Any readers who, over the years, have memorized all that Leonard Koppett has written on the subject, detailing the various mathematical possibilities in developing a schedule, may skip the next three paragraphs and rejoin our text with the phrase "With more interdivisional games played each year. . . .")

When the American League expanded from 12 to 14 teams in 1977, a schedule was adopted that kept in place the general pattern of interdivisional and intradivisional games that had existed since 1969. In the 12-team league, that meant 18 games against teams from your own division, and 12 against teams from the other, the same pattern that is still used in the National League. With the increase to 14 teams, it meant 15 games between divisional opponents, and either 10 or 11 games, determined on a rotating basis, against nondivisional opponents.

But that pattern lasted just two years. It required too many two-game series and too much travel under unusual circumstances to suit the teams and players, and so for the 1979 season the current arrangement was introduced. Each team faces the other teams in its own division 13 times apiece and plays every team in the other division 12 times. Under this system, teams actually play more games outside their division (84) than within (78).

With more interdivisional games played each year, there is more of a chance for a strong division to dominate a weak one. And one by-product of that scheduling pattern that is emerging rather steadily is that it seems to be more important for American League teams to do well in games outside their division than in games within the walls. It's a lesson that the Tigers have learned the hard way: The same pattern of wins and losses that prevailed in 1986 also occurred in 1985, when the Tigers had their division's best record in games among their own kind, only to see their poor record against the West allow Toronto to top the East. And in 1986, Detroit achieved its 42–42 record against the West with a symmetrical flair: 7–5 against Minnesota and Texas; 6–6 against Chicago, Oakland and Seattle; and 5–7 against California and Kansas City.

In the seven seasons under this plan (excluding 1981), there have been nine occasions in which different teams from the same division won the intradivisional and interdivisional series. In seven of those nine cases, the teams that won the intradivisional series did not win the division title:

	A.L. Division	Best Pct. vs. Own Division	Best Pct. vs. Other Division	Division Winner
1979	West	Angels	Royals	Angels
1980	West	A's	Royals	Royals
1982	East	Orioles	Brewers	Brewers
1982	West	Angels	White Sox	Angels
1983	East	Yankees	Orioles	Orioles
1984	West	Twins	Royals	Royals
1985	East	Tigers	N.Y./Tor.	Blue Jays
1985	West	Angels	Royals	Royals
1986	East	Tigers	Indians	Red Sox

What has made the last two seasons especially bitter medicine for Detroit fans is that in roughing up the East but playing meek with the West, the Tigers have run counter to the current balance of power in the American League. In fact, forget the word *current*; the East's domination of the West seems to be as much a part of A.L. life as Wade Boggs hitting .300, the Yankees changing managers, or Sparky Anderson saying something silly.

The American League East has had the edge on the West in interdivisional games in 16 of the 18 seasons played under the two-division format. And the imbalance seems to be getting worse instead of better: The East has beat up on the West in each of the last nine years, and by larger margins than they did in the early seventies.

Remember that when the league expanded in 1969, it placed both expansion teams—the Royals and the Seattle Pilots—in the West. Thus, the East's lopsided margins over the West in 1969 and in 1970, when the Pilots became the Milwaukee Brewers but remained in the West, were to be expected. The West overcame that handicap to win the series, although by only one game, in 1971. The Brewers moved to the Eastern Division in 1972, when Bob Short moved his Washington Senators to Texas and that team was assigned to the West. The East continued to dominate through most of the early '70s, but the largest margins in of the series, excluding those first two expansion-skewed years, have come in the years since 1978.

No similar pattern exists in the National League. There, things have been on a much more even keel, even though the East has beaten the West in each of the last three seasons—the first time that either N.L. division has won the series three years in a row. In the 18 years of divisional play, each N.L. division has won the season series nine times; moreover, the margins of victory by the dominant division have been much smaller, year to year, than in the American League. In each of the last nine years, not only has the American League East dominated the American League West, but its winning percentage in interdivisional games has been higher than the winning percentage of whatever National League division won that year's season series.

The American League East's domination has come to be accepted readily among baseball people, and though everyone talks about it, no one does anything about it. George Steinbrenner, in his role as A.L. East publicist, is always up front with his claim that the A.L. East is "the toughest division in sports." His proposed methods of dealing with the fact have ranged from changing the schedule back to one in which the majority of each team's games are played within its division, to the introduction of wild card teams into the playoff structure. Thus far, all changes have been resisted. The schedule format remains the same, and baseball remains the only team sport in which a team must win its division to be admitted into postseason play; there are no at-large appointments.

However unprovable Steinbrenner's claim may be, a year-by-year breakdown of the figures leaves no doubt that the A.L. East is at least the toughest division in the American League:

	American League Dominant Division	W–L	Pct.	National League Dominant Division	W–L	Pct.
1969	East	245–187	.567	West	220–212	.509
1970	East	243–189	.563	West	223–208	.517
1971	West	215–214	.501	East	221–210	.513
1972	East	217–215	.502	East	217–215	.502
1973	East	226–206	.523	West	231–201	.534
1974	East	219–213	.507	West	231–201	.534
1975	East	221–206	.518	East	222–209	.515
1976	East	223–209	.516	West	221–211	.512
1977	West	257–247	.510	East	230–202	.532
1978	East	281–220	.561	West	233–198	.541
1979	East	327–259	.558	East	236–194	.549
1980	East	329–255	.563	West	233–199	.539
1981	East	209–180	.537	West	142–123	.536
1982	East	323–265	.549	East	219–213	.507
1983	East	332–256	.565	West	228–204	.528
1984	East	320–267	.545	East	235–197	.544
1985	East	304–283	.518	East	223–208	.517
1986	East	320–268	.544	East	217–214	.503
Totals	East	4800–4150	.536	West	3824–3777	.503

Even if the American League West teams won every one of the 588 games scheduled against East teams in 1987, the East would still have the overall advantage. You like that, George?

Which American League team's regular lineup has been the most stable over the past five seasons?

The Tigers are certainly contenders for the title. Lance Parrish, Lou Whitaker, Alan Trammell, and Chet Lemon have been regulars every year since 1982, when Lemon joined the Tigers from the White Sox. (Lemon played mostly right field that year, switching to center in 1983.) Have any other American League teams matched that consistency?

Yes. Based on the players who made the most starts at each position, the Angels and the Blue Jays have each had four regulars maintain starting positions in each of the past five years: Bob Boone, Doug DeCinces, Brian Downing, and Reggie Jackson (split between right field and DH, but always a regular) with the Angels; Damaso Garcia, Lloyd Moseby, Rance Mulliniks, and Willie Upshaw for the Jays. But if you're just talking about strength at the up-the-middle positions of catcher, second, short, and center, no team in either league can match the Tigers' consistency.

That consistency may be put to the test in 1987. While Lemon was by any definition the Tigers' regular center fielder in 1986, he started only 111 games, his fewest starts in five years with the team. His status on the team bears watching. In Trammell and Whitaker, the Tigers have one of only three double-play combinations in major-league history to last together as regulars for nine straight years. Only Glenn Beckert and Don Kessinger of the Cubs (1965 to 1973) and Davey Lopes and Bill Russell of the Dodgers (1973 to 1981) have put in nine years together. The old American League record of eight straight seasons, which Trammell and Whitaker broke last year, was held by a Tigers combination, Charlie Gehringer and Billy Rogell (1931 to 1938). Though on one hand their positions seem secure, remember how quick Sparky Anderson was to try an untested rookie, Chris Pittaro, at second base two springs ago.

With the loss of Lance Parrish to free agency, Sparky will be forced to do something he has never done before in 17 years as a major-league manager: develop a new starting catcher. Johnny Bench was already established as the incumbent when Anderson became the Reds' manager in 1970, and Bench was still the regular catcher when Sparky was fired after the '78 season. And when Anderson was hired by the Tigers to replace Les Moss in June of 1979, Parrish was already two months into his first full year as regular catcher.

Anderson's teams have always had up-the-middle strength at the everyday positions as a cornerstone of their success. He has done his vaunted tinkering at other positions: Evans, Garbey, Bergman, and Cabell at first; Brookens, Johnson, and Coles at third; Herndon, Collins, and Wilson on the outfield flanks; Rose in left, in right, and at third; Perez and Driessen at first. And always with the pitchers.

But once he had his up-the-middle group assembled (Bench, Dave Concepcion, Joe Morgan, and Cesar Geronimo in Cincinnati; Parrish, Whitaker, Trammell, and Lemon in Detroit), he has been reluctant to change. Now that a change must be made, it will be interesting to see if Sparky limits himself to selecting one new catcher, or if he will add this spot to those where he tries to get a quart out of a couple of pint pots. If only Dwight Lowry would agree to hit 30 homers a year. . . .

WON-LOST RECORD BY STARTING POSITION

DETROIT 87-75	C	1B	2B	3B	SS	LF	CF	RF	P	DH	Leadoff	Relief	Starts
Doug Baker	·	·	1-0	·	3-5	·	·	·	·	·	·	·	4-5
Dave Bergman	·	15-13	·	·	·	·	·	·	·	·	·	·	15-13
Tom Brookens	·	·	9-16	20-11	8-1	·	·	0-1	·	5-6	9-8	·	42-35
Bill Campbell	·	·	·	·	·	·	·	·	·	·	·	14-20	·
Chuck Cary	·	·	·	·	·	·	·	·	·	·	·	4-18	·
Darnell Coles	·	·	·	66-62	·	·	·	1-1	·	4-3	·	·	71-66
Dave Collins	·	·	·	·	·	39-34	4-3	6-3	·	11-12	9-9	·	60-52
Dave Engle	0-1	10-11	·	·	·	·	·	·	·	3-2	·	·	13-14
Darrell Evans	·	55-43	·	0-1	·	·	·	·	·	20-20	·	·	75-64
Bruce Fields	·	·	·	·	·	6-5	·	·	·	·	·	·	6-5
Kirk Gibson	·	·	·	·	·	·	·	62-51	·	1-3	·	·	63-54
Johnny Grubb	·	·	·	·	·	2-2	·	4-3	·	29-17	·	·	35-22
Brian Harper	·	0-1	·	·	·	·	·	1-6	·	1-0	·	·	2-7
Mike Heath	17-10	·	·	·	·	·	·	·	·	·	·	·	17-10
Willie Hernandez	·	·	·	·	·	·	·	·	·	·	·	40-24	·
Larry Herndon	·	·	·	·	·	38-33	·	·	·	·	3-0	·	38-33
Bryan Kelly	·	·	·	·	·	·	·	·	2-2	·	·	1-1	2-2
Eric King	·	·	·	·	·	·	·	·	10-6	·	·	9-8	10-6
Mike Laga	·	5-6	·	·	·	·	·	·	·	1-0	·	·	6-6
Dave LaPoint	·	·	·	·	·	·	·	·	3-5	·	·	1-7	3-5
Jack Lazorko	·	·	·	·	·	·	·	·	·	·	·	0-3	·
Chet Lemon	·	·	·	·	·	·	59-52	·	·	·	·	·	59-52
Dwight Lowry	22-23	·	·	·	·	·	·	·	·	·	·	·	22-23
Scotti Madison	·	·	·	0-1	·	·	·	·	·	0-1	·	·	0-2
Jack Morris	·	·	·	·	·	·	·	·	22-13	·	·	·	22-13
Matt Nokes	3-4	·	·	·	·	·	·	·	·	·	·	·	3-4
Randy O'Neal	·	·	·	·	·	·	·	·	6-5	·	·	9-17	6-5
John Pacella	·	·	·	·	·	·	·	·	·	·	·	1-4	·
Lance Parrish	45-37	·	·	·	·	·	·	·	·	1-4	·	·	46-41
Dan Petry	·	·	·	·	·	·	·	·	7-13	·	·	·	7-13
Bill Scherrer	·	·	·	·	·	·	·	·	·	·	·	1-12	·
Pat Sheridan	·	·	·	·	·	2-1	24-20	11-9	·	·	0-1	·	37-30
Jim Slaton	·	·	·	·	·	·	·	·	·	·	·	7-15	·
Harry Spilman	·	·	1-0	·	·	·	·	·	·	6-4	·	·	7-4
Frank Tanana	·	·	·	·	·	·	·	·	18-13	·	·	0-1	18-13
Walt Terrell	·	·	·	·	·	·	·	·	16-17	·	·	0-1	16-17
Mark Thurmond	·	·	·	·	·	·	·	·	3-1	·	·	8-13	3-1
Tim Tolman	·	2-1	·	·	·	·	·	2-1	·	4-3	·	·	8-5
Alan Trammell	·	·	·	·	76-69	·	·	·	·	1-0	1-4	·	77-69
Lou Whitaker	·	·	77-59	·	·	·	·	·	·	·	65-53	·	77-59

Batting Comparisons: Vs. Left-Handers/Right-Handers and Overall/Late Inning Pressure Situations

		BA	Rank	SA	Rank	HR %	Rank		BA	Rank	SA	Rank	HR %	Rank
Dave Bergman	vs. Lefties	.250	--	.625	--	0.00	--	Overall	.231	--	.315	--	0.77	--
	vs. Righties	.230	135	.295	158	0.82	143	Pressure	.185	147	.296	133	3.70	48
Tom Brookens	vs. Lefties	.298	41	.409	80	1.17	132	Overall	.270	61	.356	132	1.07	138
	vs. Righties	.227	--	.273	--	0.91	--	Pressure	.317	31	.317	121	0.00	109
Darnell Coles	vs. Lefties	.282	59	.400	87	1.76	114	Overall	.273	54	.453	47	3.84	59
	vs. Righties	.268	70	.479	38	4.84	36	Pressure	.222	117	.317	120	3.17	63
Dave Collins	vs. Lefties	.231	123	.343	131	0.93	140	Overall	.270	63	.329	147	0.24	163
	vs. Righties	.283	45	.325	139	0.00	158	Pressure	.258	84	.339	106	1.61	92
Dave Engle	vs. Lefties	.247	105	.338	135	0.00	148	Overall	.256	--	.337	--	0.00	--
	vs. Righties	.333	--	.333	--	0.00	--	Pressure	.125	--	.188	--	0.00	--
Darrell Evans	vs. Lefties	.272	68	.483	38	6.12	16	Overall	.241	128	.442	56	5.72	12
	vs. Righties	.228	139	.425	76	5.56	18	Pressure	.347	13	.708	1	11.11	1
Kirk Gibson	vs. Lefties	.262	84	.421	72	4.27	39	Overall	.268	72	.492	16	6.35	5
	vs. Righties	.271	65	.534	10	7.58	5	Pressure	.359	7	.625	5	7.81	7
Johnny Grubb	vs. Lefties	.214	--	.286	--	0.00	--	Overall	.333	3	.590	1	6.19	7
	vs. Righties	.342	3	.612	1	6.63	8	Pressure	.231	105	.308	127	0.00	109
Mike Heath	vs. Lefties	.316	23	.456	47	3.51	59	Overall	.265	--	.418	--	4.08	--
	vs. Righties	.195	--	.366	--	4.88	--	Pressure	.091	--	.182	--	0.00	--
Larry Herndon	vs. Lefties	.233	121	.365	109	3.17	73	Overall	.247	118	.385	104	2.83	89
	vs. Righties	.277	--	.426	--	2.13	--	Pressure	.214	124	.262	147	0.00	109
Chet Lemon	vs. Lefties	.284	55	.500	29	4.32	36	Overall	.251	112	.407	89	2.98	82
	vs. Righties	.228	137	.344	127	2.07	103	Pressure	.197	141	.273	139	1.52	95
Dwight Lowry	vs. Lefties	.409	--	.545	--	4.55	--	Overall	.307	--	.393	--	2.00	--
	vs. Righties	.289	39	.367	112	1.56	119	Pressure	.353	--	.353	--	0.00	--
Lance Parrish	vs. Lefties	.262	83	.410	78	4.10	46	Overall	.257	96	.483	21	6.73	4
	vs. Righties	.254	97	.527	13	8.29	1	Pressure	.205	133	.205	161	0.00	109
Pat Sheridan	vs. Lefties	.231	--	.231	--	0.00	--	Overall	.237	134	.360	130	2.54	96
	vs. Righties	.238	122	.376	107	2.86	84	Pressure	.130	--	.130	--	0.00	--
Alan Trammell	vs. Lefties	.279	61	.505	26	3.92	49	Overall	.277	48	.469	31	3.66	64
	vs. Righties	.276	59	.449	55	3.51	60	Pressure	.303	41	.455	47	3.03	64
Lou Whitaker	vs. Lefties	.221	136	.325	140	1.84	109	Overall	.269	67	.437	61	3.42	71
	vs. Righties	.287	40	.480	35	4.04	50	Pressure	.282	62	.333	108	0.00	109
Team Average	vs. Lefties	.260	9	.406	7	2.87	8	Overall	.263	6	.424	6	3.59	1
	vs. Righties	.264	6	.433	2	3.96	1	Pressure	.261	6	.380	8	2.90	5
League Average	vs. Lefties	.263		.408		2.88		Overall	.262		.408		2.96	
	vs. Righties	.261		.408		2.99		Pressure	.254		.383		2.61	

Additional Miscellaneous Batting Comparisons

	Grass Surface BA	Rank	Artificial Surface BA	Rank	Home Games BA	Rank	Road Games BA	Rank	Runners in Scoring Position BA	Rank	Runners in Scoring Pos and Two Outs BA	Rank	Leading Off Inning OBA	Rank	Runners on 3B with less than 2 Outs RDI %	Rank
Dave Bergman	.236	125	.208	--	.213	--	.246	--	.172	--	.154	--	.222	--	.429	--
Tom Brookens	.246	108	.400	3	.257	101	.285	43	.215	143	.229	108	.343	63	.818	8
Darnell Coles	.274	50	.267	86	.286	50	.260	82	.289	51	.290	48	.284	134	.556	96
Dave Collins	.266	65	.290	59	.250	106	.287	40	.284	59	.234	98	.340	70	.647	46
Darrell Evans	.241	114	.237	122	.236	127	.245	110	.255	101	.273	67	.320	99	.517	118
Kirk Gibson	.266	64	.280	70	.278	65	.258	83	.256	99	.229	106	.341	68	.528	108
Johnny Grubb	.328	6	.381	--	.366	2	.296	27	.393	1	.364	7	.364	38	.857	3
Larry Herndon	.256	88	.189	--	.234	134	.260	81	.217	142	.240	89	.278	140	.500	122
Chet Lemon	.245	110	.292	57	.237	123	.263	75	.271	76	.240	89	.319	104	.652	45
Dwight Lowry	.300	17	.333	--	.276	--	.338	--	.282	--	.267	--	.364	--	.667	--
Lance Parrish	.253	92	.274	74	.247	116	.266	66	.257	94	.214	125	.337	76	.526	110
Pat Sheridan	.212	153	.316	32	.234	131	.240	121	.263	83	.185	141	.241	160	.364	161
Alan Trammell	.266	67	.337	16	.262	95	.291	33	.284	60	.292	47	.333	79	.481	139
Lou Whitaker	.273	52	.247	110	.248	110	.289	36	.240	117	.315	33	.324	93	.500	122
Team Average	.258	6	.285	1	.254	10	.270	4	.260	9	.253	7	.321	7	.553	10
League Average	.258		.270		.264		.259		.263		.246		.326		.575	

Pitching Comparisons: Vs. Left-Handers/Right-Handers and Runners On/Bases Empty

		BA	Rank	BB %	Rank	SO %	Rank		BA	Rank	BB %	Rank	SO %	Rank
Bill Campbell	vs. Lefties	.221	--	11.96	--	14.13	--	Runners On	.253	--	11.76	--	15.69	--
	vs. Righties	.236	35	7.30	59	17.52	53	Bases Empty	.214	18	7.09	55	16.54	44
Willie Hernandez	vs. Lefties	.206	11	2.97	--	19.80	17	Runners On	.256	54	5.11	4	19.32	21
	vs. Righties	.269	87	6.55	42	20.73	28	Bases Empty	.247	49	6.00	34	21.50	11
Eric King	vs. Lefties	.239	38	9.93	76	12.41	67	Runners On	.228	18	9.52	77	9.92	108
	vs. Righties	.193	7	11.78	120	14.81	77	Bases Empty	.206	13	11.93	117	16.51	45
Dave LaPoint	vs. Lefties	.279	--	8.82	--	8.82	--	Runners On	.352	128	13.01	119	13.01	70
	vs. Righties	.315	127	10.57	114	12.20	100	Bases Empty	.271	79	7.74	68	10.12	112
Jack Morris	vs. Lefties	.223	22	7.47	32	19.79	18	Runners On	.211	8	7.32	39	19.76	20
	vs. Righties	.236	34	7.56	62	21.12	23	Bases Empty	.240	41	7.62	63	20.82	18
Randy O'Neal	vs. Lefties	.225	25	11.72	101	8.20	115	Runners On	.270	73	11.42	104	11.42	91
	vs. Righties	.291	110	5.26	23	17.67	52	Bases Empty	.253	57	6.27	39	14.19	74
Dan Petry	vs. Lefties	.231	30	10.22	86	13.14	60	Runners On	.250	43	10.98	98	10.57	102
	vs. Righties	.308	122	10.16	107	8.13	129	Bases Empty	.283	96	9.49	94	10.95	107
Jim Slaton	vs. Lefties	.287	87	10.00	78	7.39	120	Runners On	.286	96	9.48	76	8.62	119
	vs. Righties	.296	117	6.37	38	9.74	123	Bases Empty	.297	116	6.79	49	8.68	122
Frank Tanana	vs. Lefties	.317	112	5.30	13	9.09	103	Runners On	.248	42	11.14	100	14.37	58
	vs. Righties	.258	68	8.53	85	15.74	67	Bases Empty	.281	93	5.73	31	14.86	62
Walt Terrell	vs. Lefties	.242	43	10.95	94	8.00	117	Runners On	.276	85	9.47	75	7.89	125
	vs. Righties	.249	53	10.38	110	12.42	98	Bases Empty	.223	27	11.52	114	11.71	101
Mark Thurmond	vs. Lefties	.164	--	3.39	--	11.86	--	Runners On	.194	--	11.63	--	8.14	--
	vs. Righties	.263	78	10.00	104	6.67	130	Bases Empty	.259	63	5.69	30	8.13	126
Team Average	vs. Lefties	.239	1	9.25	6	13.10	10	Runners On	.254	1	10.43	11	12.98	13
	vs. Righties	.259	8	9.28	12	15.13	11	Bases Empty	.249	5	8.40	10	15.28	9
League Average	vs. Lefties	.265		9.67		13.46		Runners On	.269		9.46		14.39	
	vs. Righties	.259		8.19		16.22		Bases Empty	.256		8.31		15.55	

Additional Miscellaneous Pitching Comparisons

	Grass Surface BA	Rank	Artificial Surface BA	Rank	Home Games BA	Rank	Road Games BA	Rank	Runners in Scoring Position BA	Rank	Runners in Scoring Pos and Two Outs BA	Rank	Leading Off Inning OBA	Rank
Bill Campbell	.223	19	.280	--	.193	6	.284	--	.224	30	.286	94	.269	13
Chuck Cary	.198	--	.425	129	.233	--	.286	--	.283	--	.263	--	.269	--
Willie Hernandez	.251	50	.256	--	.250	58	.253	52	.258	73	.259	78	.233	3
Eric King	.202	7	.269	66	.156	1	.267	71	.225	31	.143	5	.310	51
Dave LaPoint	.310	119	.294	89	.294	108	.318	120	.353	127	.265	80	.319	60
Jack Morris	.236	37	.204	11	.221	30	.234	25	.193	8	.173	18	.277	22
Randy O'Neal	.256	59	.284	76	.249	56	.269	73	.222	28	.222	51	.298	39
Dan Petry	.276	95	.138	--	.295	109	.232	21	.250	59	.208	40	.379	114
Jim Slaton	.300	116	.250	44	.289	103	.296	106	.270	82	.288	96	.362	103
Frank Tanana	.259	66	.341	125	.259	70	.282	85	.237	42	.293	99	.301	42
Walt Terrell	.233	33	.319	112	.209	20	.284	90	.264	78	.254	72	.330	71
Mark Thurmond	.231	30	.333	--	.223	32	.275	--	.150	--	.118	--	.375	--
Team Average	.247	5	.273	9	.235	2	.267	9	.238	1	.222	2	.311	4
League Average	.258		.270		.259		.264		.263		.246		.326	

KANSAS CITY ROYALS

We offer for your consideration a tale of two men on different career paths. Opposite sides of the same coin, if you will: one bound for glory, the other for obscurity. But anyone who's ever missed a road sign and found himself in an unfamiliar place can attest to the fact that most routes are winding paths that travel to strange places. And if you're not paying attention, you may wind up like these two gents, a long way from where they were headed, and smack in the middle of the twilight zone.

White Power

Our first vignette is a portrait of Frank White, a player remarkable for nothing but a steady glove during his first decade in the majors, an adequate hitter with little power. But over the years, he steadily increased his home run output: 1, 7, 2, 5, 7, 10, 7, 9, 11, and 11 through 1983. The increase was so gradual that few people noticed—after all, do you change your image of a player because he hits nine home runs rather than five? But what started as a trickle has become a gusher.

In 1984, White emerged as a legitimate home run threat, belting a career-high total of 17 home runs. A year later, White cracked the 20 mark for the first time, hitting 22 home runs, and he equalled that total last season. Twenty-two home runs at age 35 isn't that uncommon—not, that is, for a player who spent his late twenties and early thirties hitting 25 to 35 home runs a year. The graph of White's career track looks like the Reebok profit sheet, and this at a point at which those of most other players would remind you of last year's crude oil prices. White's career batting statistics, divided into three stages:

Years	G	AB	R	H	2B	3B	HR	RBI	BB	SB	BA	SA	OBA
73-77	565	1567	180	370	60	17	15	155	77	60	.236	.325	.273
78-83	809	2925	367	789	170	27	55	329	125	87	.270	.403	.306
84-86	429	1608	196	424	84	9	61	209	98	19	.264	.441	.306

Several aspects make White's development unusual: First, the degree to which he has increased his power; second, the duration and consistency with which he has improved; and third, the age at which he became a slugger. Let's examine each of them.

White hit only one home run for every 104 at bats during his first five seasons in the majors. (Fewer than 20 percent of current major-league players with at least 1,000 at bats have career averages of less than one home run per 100 at bats.) Over the past three seasons, however, White has hit one home run per 26 at bats—a substantial increase. White has hit as many home runs over the past two seasons as he did in his first 3,273 at bats in the majors. His rate from 1973 to 1977 is almost identical to that of Tony Fernandez, who has hit 15 homers in 1,518 at bats; from 1984 to 1986, it's been much like that of Alvin Davis (63 homers in 1,624 at bats).

The consistency with which White has progressed is rare. He has matched or exceeded his previous year's home run total in every season since 1981. Only one other player, Toronto's Lloyd Moseby, has a streak as long as White's. And only seven have similar streaks even since 1983, most of them younger, developing players: Wade Boggs, Tony Gwynn, Fred Lynn, Moseby, Pete O'Brien, John Shelby, and Denny Walling.

Finally, White is one of only seven players in major-league history to hit 20 home runs in a season for the first time after their 35th birthdays. White turned 35 on September 4, 1985, and smacked home run number 20 eleven days later to join what is surely one of the most eclectic groups of players you could imagine: Cy Williams, Charlie Gehringer, Luke Easter, Mickey Vernon, John Lowenstein, and Buddy Bell (who did it last season).

Whether White's home run total will continue to rise is debatable. Gehringer, Lowenstein, and Vernon never again reached the 20 mark. But Easter had consecutive seasons of 28, 27, and 31 before he was stopped by a broken foot at age 38. And after Williams hit 26 home runs in 1922, he broke the 20 mark three more times and led the league in home runs twice. In fact, Williams was still playing at age 41 in 1929 when he surrendered the all-time National League home run lead to Rogers Hornsby at about the same time that a guy named Ruth was rewriting the American League record book. The Royals, desperate for power hitting even before Steve Balboni's back trouble, must certainly hope that White has a few more 20-home run seasons left in his bat.

Trouble Down Under

Our second vignette is not a pretty one. It is a story of a loss of faith and how quickly faith can be lost.

Did anyone really foresee last season's demotion of Dan Quisenberry, the American League saves leader in each of the four previous seasons, from Poobah of the Royals bullpen to just another of the drones? Of course, everyone remembers how the trouble started before a national audience during the

1985 postseason. Quis lost Game Two of the American League Championship Series, then blew a ninth-inning lead in Game Four. A week later he allowed an insurance run in the ninth inning of the opening game of the World Series, then received a vote of no confidence from Dick Howser, who allowed Charlie Leibrandt to turn a two-run ninth-inning lead into a two-run deficit the next night while Quisenberry soft-tossed in the bullpen.

Still, it's strange that Quisenberry would unravel so suddenly, that his confidence and that of his manager would erode so totally. After all, we're talking about a disappointing fortnight in a spectacular career. During an era in which the role of bullpen closers was elevated to new heights, Quisenberry was the best of the best. Despite saving only 12 games last season, he still has 40 more saves than any other pitcher during the 1980s.

So what happened? Quisenberry rebounded from his disappointing 1985 postseason with saves in each of his first three opportunities last season. But over the next two weeks, there just weren't any Quisenberry-type situations. The Royals held few late-inning leads, and when they did Howser elected to let his starters close them out. Quis didn't pitch in a save situation from April 21 through May 4. Over the next month, he was batted about in 10 appearances, and he blew his only three save opportunities:

G	W	L	GF	SV	IP	H	R	ER	HR	HB	BB	SO	ERA
10	0	1	5	0	12.2	21	9	8	1	2	4	5	5.68

In one month, Quisenberry undermined the confidence that Howser had developed in him over the better part of a decade. Although he saved his next five opportunities, he was no longer the one stopper in Kansas City's bullpen. Steve Farr and Bud Black were given increasingly more important roles, and Quisenberry didn't pitch in a save situation from June 25 until August 12.

We've chosen some statistics that indicate the decline not only of Quisenberry, but also of the regard in which he was held. As we've pointed out many times in the past, the best way to evaluate a relief pitcher's effectiveness—especially that of a closer who is expected to extinguish rallies and finish the game—is to examine the performance of opposing batters with runners in scoring position, particularly with two outs. Notice in the following table of opponents' batting averages how far Quisenberry fell in those areas last season:

Situation	Career	1985	1986
Late-Inning Pressure Situations	.265	.277	.309
Runners in Scoring Position	.265	.223	.330
Two Outs & Runners in Scoring Pos.	.263	.200	.288
Vs. Left-Handed Batters	.286	.317	.310
Vs. Right-Handed Batters	.233	.236	.275

Quisenberry was never terribly effective against left-handed batters, but last season right-handed hitters handled him as well. The next table shows how Quisenberry's ineffectiveness eroded the confidence of Howser and of his replacement,

Mike Ferraro. Notice that his save percentage (saves compared to opportunites) didn't drop nearly as much as the number of opportunities he was given:

	1984	1985	1986
Relief Appearances	72	84	62
Save Opportunities	53	49	17
Saves	44	40	12
Save Percentage	83	82	71
Start of Inning	38	39	37
Runners On Base	43	7	25
Runners in Scoring Pos.	31	5	19
Game Tied	14	14	9
Royals Up by 1–3 Runs	47	47	14
Other Games	23	23	39

The drastic reduction in save situations was mirrored by the increase in appearances in games the Royals were losing, or games they were winning big. Quis was called on to protect leads of three runs or less only 30 percent as often last season as in either of the two previous seasons. Another sign of the times: During 1984 and 1985, Quisenberry faced a majority of left-handed hitters (55 out of every 100 batters faced). Last season, Quis faced more right-handers than left-handers for the first time since 1982. Whether it's because opposing right-handers found him less puzzling, or because Howser and Ferraro were pulling him from games to keep him from facing left-handed batters, the comparison is another facet of Quisenberry's damaged reputation. It will be interesting to see if he can regain the respect of both opposing hitters and his manager and teammates this season.

The Way of His Errors
For several seasons, Frank White has simmered over errors charged to him in home games on balls that he felt should have been ruled hits. He boiled over last season, following what he considered a particularly unfair error, and threatened to walk off the field if charged with another error that he considered unwarranted. We took a look at the situation and discovered that Royals Stadium does have an inflationary effect on errors. But when we examined its effect on White . . . well, we're getting a little ahead of ourselves.

If you look through the Ballparks section of this book, you'll notice that only one stadium in baseball increases the rate of errors to a greater extent than Royals Stadium, and that's Shea Stadium. But the increase of 7.9 percent in Kansas City actually understates the effect of the stadium, since one of the nearly universal features of ballparks with artificial turf is their tendency to reduce errors. Royals Stadium is an extreme exception. We'll save you the trouble of checking each ballpark page individually; the following table compares the number of errors in each team's home games over the past five years to those committed in its road games. For instance, there have been 668 errors at Royals Stadium during that time, 619 in Royals road games. The difference represents an increase of 7.9 percent, the highest in the American League. Asterisks indicate stadiums with artificial turf:

Team	Home	Road	Diff.	Team	Home	Road	Diff.
* Kansas City	668	619	+7.9%	New York	744	683	+8.9%
Boston	736	696	+5.7%	Atlanta	760	707	+7.5%
Oakland	726	701	+3.6%	Chicago	661	616	+7.3%
Chicago	666	644	+3.4%	San Diego	736	696	+5.7%
Texas	613	602	+1.8%	Los Angeles	767	740	+3.6%
* Minnesota	588	579	+1.6%	San Francisco	764	756	+1.1%
California	640	646	−0.9%	* St. Louis	673	671	+0.3%
* Toronto	638	647	−1.4%	* Philadelphia	694	714	−2.8%
Baltimore	593	602	−1.5%	* Pittsburgh	649	671	−3.3%
Milwaukee	658	668	−1.5%	* Houston	643	699	−8.0%
Detroit	622	632	−1.6%	* Montreal	603	667	−9.6%
Cleveland	694	718	−2.8%	* Cincinnati	622	696	−10.6%
New York	642	670	−4.2%				
* Seattle	634	679	−6.6%				

You can rearrange the combined league data to demonstrate graphically that carpeted fields reduce errors. If you rank all 26 teams together and mark the teams with grass fields with a *G* and those with artificial turf with an *A*, you can see that nearly every synthetic surface ranks in the lower half (indicating a reduction in errors), and only one *A* falls in the top ten. That lonely *A* represents Royals Stadium:

GAGGGGGGGGGAGAGAGGGAAGGAAAA

To fully appreciate the effect of Royals Stadium on errors, we've measured the level of increase only against the other carpeted fields in the American League. Over the past five years, games played among the four A.L. teams with synthetic surfaces (Royals, Twins, Mariners, and Blue Jays) indicate that Royals Stadium increases errors by 15 percent over the level typical for fields with artificial turf.

Since nearly every other carpeted stadium reduces the number of errors, and none increases errors to nearly the extent that Royals Stadium does, it seems logical to assume that the official scorers in Kansas City give a rather broad interpretation to the rule that defines an error. Of course, there are exceptions to similar statistical trends on artificial turf. Most stadiums with rugs increase batting averages, but not Olympic Stadium. Most increase scoring, but not the Astrodome. So why are we sure that the errors at Royals Stadium are attributable to scoring decisions, rather than being an attribute of the playing conditions?

Frankly, we can't be sure. But there is some supporting evidence. Two years ago, the Royals replaced their old Tartan Turf with a new Astro Turf-8 Drainthru playing surface. If either the old or new carpet were responsible for all those errors, we would see a marked difference in the rate of errors between the two rugs. But both carpets produced increases in errors wholly uncharacteristic of any other synthetic surfaces in either league:

Years	Surface	Home	Road	Diff.
1982–84	Tartan Turf	420	384	+9.4%
1985–86	Astro Turf-8	248	235	+5.5%

We'd like to thank Frank White for tipping us off to this tendency. Ironically, though, White's own fielding statistics indicate that he hasn't been victimized. He has committed only 63 errors over the past five seasons. His .984 fielding percentage ranks 11th among the 34 players with at least 250 games at second base during the time. But more to the point, White has committed 36 errors in road games and only 27 at home. And, in general, home-team players are charged with more errors than road-team players anyway (though by a very slim margin).

So what was all the hollering about? Every player feels victimized from time to time by scoring decisions that he deems unfair. But scoring isn't a black and white issue. Many of you are probably familiar with the rule, "If . . . in the scorer's judgment the fielder could have handled the ball with ordinary effort, an error shall be charged." But how many of you realize that that clause represents only a fraction of the entire Rule 10.13 concerning errors, which covers three full pages in the baseball rule book? Or that the scorer's judgment is cited as the bottom line seven times on those pages? Kansas City well may have the strictest scoring in the majors. That's not to say it doesn't have the best as well; different isn't necessarily good or bad on this issue, it's just different.

Turf's Up

Incidentally, you might be interested in some of the other effects of Kansas City's new carpet. That surface, touted as spongier than most artificial turf, was supposed to play more like natural grass. But it appears that the Royals' new wall-to-wall has made the field "turfier" than ever. It's safe to say that if you like plastic baseball, you'll love Royals Stadium.

The effect of synthetic surfaces on doubles and triples is universal. As we described in detail in the Toronto Blue Jays essay, over the past five years every carpeted stadium in the major leagues has increased the rate of doubles and triples compared to singles. It's easy to see why: Balls that take slow, convenient hops on grass outfields race across artificial turf like pinballs. Notice in the following table that there has been no significant difference in scoring on Kansas City's new surface, but that doubles and triples have risen even above the high levels of the old surface:

	Tartan Turf (1982–84)			Astro Turf-8 (1985–86)		
	Home	Road	Diff.	Home	Road	Diff.
Runs per Game	8.89	8.86	+0.3%	8.18	8.20	−0.3%
Batting Avg.	.269	.270	−0.4%	.257	.252	+1.8%
Doubles	819	757	+8.2%	554	462	+19.9%
Triples	165	124	+33.1%	119	66	+80.3%

During an eight-year period from 1975 through 1982, the Royals were the dominant team in the American League's Western Division, winning four division titles and the 1980 league pennant. They didn't have much home run power, but they generated a potent attack with speed and extra-base hitters. The Royals led the league in triples seven times in those eight years, and they led in doubles four times. The figures above indicate that not all that extra-base speed was the team; some of it was the stadium. But it makes you wonder: What would the Royals' jackrabbits of the late 1970s —guys like Otis and Patek—have accomplished on Kansas City's new racetrack of the late 1980s?

WON-LOST RECORD BY STARTING POSITION

KANSAS CITY 76-86	C	1B	2B	3B	SS	LF	CF	RF	P	DH	Leadoff	Relief	Starts
Steve Balboni	·	64-72	·	·	·	·	·	·	·	·	·	·	64-72
Scott Bankhead	·	·	·	·	·	·	·	·	8-9	·	·	4-3	8-9
Terry Bell	·	·	·	·	·	·	·	·	·	·	·	·	·
Buddy Biancalana	·	·	2-1	·	33-31	·	·	·	·	·	·	·	35-32
Bud Black	·	·	·	·	·	·	·	·	1-3	·	·	26-26	1-3
George Brett	·	·	·	54-61	·	·	·	·	·	5-2	·	·	59-63
Mike Brewer	·	·	·	·	·	·	2-2	·	·	·	·	·	2-2
David Cone	·	·	·	·	·	·	·	·	·	·	·	1-10	·
Steve Farr	·	·	·	·	·	·	·	·	·	·	·	27-29	·
Mark Gubicza	·	·	·	·	·	·	·	·	17-7	·	·	1-10	17-7
Alan Hargesheimer	·	·	·	·	·	·	·	·	1-0	·	·	0-4	1-0
Mark Huismann	·	·	·	·	·	·	·	·	·	·	·	2-8	·
Bo Jackson	·	·	·	·	·	·	11-10	·	·	0-1	·	·	11-11
Danny Jackson	·	·	·	·	·	·	·	·	11-16	·	·	1-4	11-16
Rondin Johnson	·	·	3-5	·	·	·	·	·	·	·	·	·	3-5
Lynn Jones	·	·	·	·	·	1-1	0-2	0-5	·	0-1	·	·	1-9
Mike Kingery	·	·	·	·	·	·	6-3	19-25	·	·	1-0	·	25-28
Rudy Law	·	·	·	·	·	16-22	1-0	17-17	·	1-1	10-12	·	35-40
Charlie Leibrandt	·	·	·	·	·	·	·	·	17-17	·	·	0-1	17-17
Dennis Leonard	·	·	·	·	·	·	·	·	12-18	·	·	2-1	12-18
Hal McRae	·	·	·	·	·	·	·	·	·	23-35	·	·	23-35
Darryl Motley	·	·	·	·	·	·	0-1	27-27	·	·	1-1	·	27-28
Jorge Orta	·	·	·	·	·	·	·	·	·	44-39	·	·	44-39
Bill Pecota	·	·	·	4-5	·	·	·	·	·	·	·	·	4-5
Greg Pryor	·	·	3-4	8-15	·	·	·	·	·	·	·	·	11-19
Jamie Quirk	20-18	2-2	·	10-4	·	·	·	·	·	·	·	·	32-24
Dan Quisenberry	·	·	·	·	·	·	·	·	·	·	·	24-38	·
Bret Saberhagen	·	·	·	·	·	·	·	·	9-16	·	·	2-3	9-16
Argenis Salazar	·	·	·	·	43-55	·	·	·	·	·	·	·	43-55
Kevin Seitzer	·	10-12	·	0-1	·	4-0	·	·	·	·	·	·	14-13
Steve Shields	·	·	·	·	·	·	·	·	·	·	·	0-3	·
Lonnie Smith	·	·	·	·	·	55-63	·	·	·	3-7	26-34	·	58-70
Jim Sundberg	56-68	·	·	·	·	·	·	·	·	·	·	·	56-68
Dwight Taylor	·	·	·	·	·	·	·	·	·	·	·	·	·
Frank White	·	·	68-76	·	·	·	·	·	·	·	·	·	68-76
Willie Wilson	·	·	·	·	·	·	69-80	·	·	·	38-39	·	69-80

Batting Comparisons: Vs. Left-Handers/Right-Handers and Overall/Late Inning Pressure Situations

		BA	Rank	SA	Rank	HR %	Rank		BA	Rank	SA	Rank	HR %	Rank
Steve Balboni	vs. Lefties	.276	64	.590	5	8.96	1	Overall	.229	145	.451	49	5.66	15
	vs. Righties	.212	159	.402	86	4.50	42	Pressure	.250	90	.452	49	4.76	35
Buddy Biancalana	vs. Lefties	.258	--	.323	--	0.00	--	Overall	.242	126	.337	144	1.05	139
	vs. Righties	.239	121	.340	131	1.26	130	Pressure	.125	--	.125	--	0.00	--
George Brett	vs. Lefties	.243	107	.385	97	3.38	62	Overall	.290	27	.481	23	3.63	66
	vs. Righties	.314	15	.529	11	3.75	56	Pressure	.246	122	.316	122	1.75	89
Mike Kingery	vs. Lefties	.067	--	.067	--	0.00	--	Overall	.258	92	.388	102	1.44	128
	vs. Righties	.291	33	.441	61	1.68	115	Pressure	.205	132	.359	94	0.00	109
Rudy Law	vs. Lefties	.143	171	.167	173	0.00	148	Overall	.261	86	.388	101	0.33	162
	vs. Righties	.279	53	.423	79	0.38	153	Pressure	.283	61	.457	46	0.00	109
Hal McRae	vs. Lefties	.268	80	.431	64	3.27	67	Overall	.252	109	.378	110	2.52	98
	vs. Righties	.232	131	.312	146	1.60	117	Pressure	.228	111	.351	97	3.51	52
Darryl Motley	vs. Lefties	.237	112	.387	96	3.23	68	Overall	.203	167	.350	135	3.23	74
	vs. Righties	.177	169	.323	141	3.23	70	Pressure	.143	165	.238	155	2.38	73
Jorge Orta	vs. Lefties	.211	--	.211	--	0.00	--	Overall	.277	49	.411	85	2.68	93
	vs. Righties	.281	50	.423	78	2.84	86	Pressure	.309	33	.382	76	0.00	109
Jamie Quirk	vs. Lefties	.091	--	.091	--	0.00	--	Overall	.215	159	.370	122	3.65	65
	vs. Righties	.221	149	.385	97	3.85	55	Pressure	.229	110	.333	108	0.00	109
Argenis Salazar	vs. Lefties	.297	42	.405	84	0.00	148	Overall	.245	122	.326	149	0.00	166
	vs. Righties	.214	156	.278	165	0.00	158	Pressure	.276	126	.310	126	0.00	109
Lonnie Smith	vs. Lefties	.309	29	.443	57	1.34	128	Overall	.287	31	.411	84	1.57	123
	vs. Righties	.279	55	.398	92	1.67	116	Pressure	.231	105	.295	136	1.28	105
Jim Sundberg	vs. Lefties	.191	161	.348	126	4.26	40	Overall	.212	160	.322	151	2.80	90
	vs. Righties	.222	148	.309	148	2.08	102	Pressure	.279	67	.382	75	1.47	98
Frank White	vs. Lefties	.268	78	.349	125	0.67	145	Overall	.272	56	.465	34	3.89	55
	vs. Righties	.273	61	.506	21	5.04	31	Pressure	.304	39	.543	14	6.52	15
Willie Wilson	vs. Lefties	.309	30	.429	66	2.29	97	Overall	.269	64	.366	125	1.43	129
	vs. Righties	.254	95	.342	128	1.10	136	Pressure	.266	78	.330	111	1.06	108
Team Average	vs. Lefties	.250	13	.383	13	2.59	10	Overall	.252	12	.390	12	2.46	12
	vs. Righties	.253	10	.392	10	2.42	12	Pressure	.248	9	.364	10	2.08	11
League Average	vs. Lefties	.263		.408		2.88		Overall	.262		.408		2.96	
	vs. Righties	.261		.408		2.99		Pressure	.254		.383		2.61	

Additional Miscellaneous Batting Comparisons

	Grass Surface BA	Rank	Artificial Surface BA	Rank	Home Games BA	Rank	Road Games BA	Rank	Runners in Scoring Position BA	Rank	Runners in Scoring Pos and Two Outs BA	Rank	Leading Off Inning OBA	Rank	Runners on 3B with less than 2 Outs RDI %	Rank
Steve Balboni	.256	89	.209	146	.203	159	.253	93	.221	138	.210	128	.353	54	.588	75
Buddy Biancalana	.185	--	.265	89	.266	88	.210	--	.195	--	.120	168	.255	152	.667	--
George Brett	.265	68	.310	34	.322	13	.263	76	.315	28	.361	11	.355	52	.545	100
Bo Jackson	.182	--	.217	141	.250	--	.158	--	.294	--	.400	--	.263	--	1.000	--
Mike Kingery	.254	--	.261	95	.278	62	.234	--	.146	164	.143	164	.295	--	.667	--
Rudy Law	.268	61	.255	99	.278	65	.245	109	.375	4	.400	2	.302	122	.611	62
Hal McRae	.229	--	.269	82	.272	76	.235	127	.257	97	.250	83	.353	56	.706	22
Darryl Motley	.218	--	.190	158	.194	164	.211	153	.180	159	.250	83	.255	152	.286	--
Jorge Orta	.284	--	.273	77	.298	33	.250	100	.259	87	.226	112	.282	137	.619	58
Greg Pryor	.194	--	.160	164	.153	--	.200	--	.206	--	.158	--	.125	--	.333	--
Jamie Quirk	.222	--	.212	145	.223	149	.204	158	.184	158	.077	171	.309	116	.889	--
Argenis Salazar	.218	146	.269	80	.236	126	.251	99	.328	17	.233	100	.241	161	.900	2
Kevin Seitzer	.083	--	.403	2	.458	--	.188	--	.320	--	.000	--	.667	--	.667	--
Lonnie Smith	.259	81	.307	37	.317	17	.260	80	.283	61	.265	72	.335	78	.545	100
Jim Sundberg	.205	157	.217	140	.196	163	.227	138	.214	144	.160	156	.310	114	.800	10
Frank White	.215	149	.309	35	.282	54	.263	74	.253	105	.182	143	.320	99	.688	31
Willie Wilson	.272	54	.268	83	.265	90	.273	56	.287	54	.197	133	.269	146	.565	88
Team Average	.238	13	.261	11	.262	8	.243	12	.257	10	.216	14	.306	14	.625	2
League Average	.258		.270		.264		.259		.263		.246		.326		.575	

Pitching Comparisons: Vs. Left-Handers/Right-Handers and Runners On/Bases Empty

		BA	Rank	BB %	Rank	SO %	Rank		BA	Rank	BB %	Rank	SO %	Rank
Scott Bankhead	vs. Lefties	.242	44	7.02	27	18.06	25	Runners On	.255	52	9.72	79	15.28	50
	vs. Righties	.284	108	7.34	60	18.35	43	Bases Empty	.261	68	5.32	19	20.27	20
Bud Black	vs. Lefties	.219	17	7.10	29	17.42	26	Runners On	.206	6	10.17	88	13.14	65
	vs. Righties	.227	26	9.20	96	11.78	106	Bases Empty	.240	43	7.12	58	13.86	80
Steve Farr	vs. Lefties	.222	20	9.21	63	15.35	39	Runners On	.208	7	11.76	108	20.10	19
	vs. Righties	.234	33	8.37	78	22.33	19	Bases Empty	.243	47	6.28	40	17.57	39
Mark Gubicza	vs. Lefties	.247	47	12.56	108	14.25	48	Runners On	.251	45	9.91	85	16.03	43
	vs. Righties	.218	19	9.12	93	16.81	60	Bases Empty	.220	25	11.85	115	14.93	61
Danny Jackson	vs. Lefties	.292	92	9.80	74	16.34	31	Runners On	.262	60	9.04	66	12.99	71
	vs. Righties	.247	49	10.06	105	14.15	82	Bases Empty	.251	52	10.80	108	15.86	51
Charlie Leibrandt	vs. Lefties	.281	79	6.53	24	13.57	55	Runners On	.277	87	8.76	60	11.44	90
	vs. Righties	.264	80	6.44	40	10.44	117	Bases Empty	.262	69	4.79	11	10.82	109
Dennis Leonard	vs. Lefties	.307	105	7.78	39	10.53	91	Runners On	.273	76	6.94	26	16.47	41
	vs. Righties	.240	44	4.43	14	17.71	49	Bases Empty	.276	85	5.68	28	12.00	98
Dan Quisenberry	vs. Lefties	.310	109	10.78	91	8.38	110	Runners On	.299	106	9.33	71	11.92	85
	vs. Righties	.275	99	3.24	4	11.89	104	Bases Empty	.283	97	3.77	7	8.18	125
Bret Saberhagen	vs. Lefties	.253	55	4.60	7	19.44	19	Runners On	.275	79	5.30	5	15.15	52
	vs. Righties	.291	112	4.21	12	13.79	86	Bases Empty	.264	74	3.87	8	18.56	33
Team Average	vs. Lefties	.268	8	8.42	1	14.63	3	Runners On	.261	5	9.18	9	14.49	8
	vs. Righties	.251	4	7.45	6	14.53	13	Bases Empty	.256	9	6.80	1	14.64	13
League Average	vs. Lefties	.265		9.67		13.46		Runners On	.269		9.46		14.39	
	vs. Righties	.259		8.19		16.22		Bases Empty	.256		8.31		15.55	

Additional Miscellaneous Pitching Comparisons

	Grass Surface BA	Rank	Artificial Surface BA	Rank	Home Games BA	Rank	Road Games BA	Rank	Runners in Scoring Position BA	Rank	Runners in Scoring Pos and Two Outs BA	Rank	Leading Off Inning OBA	Rank
Scott Bankhead	.239	--	.268	63	.273	83	.243	34	.230	38	.140	4	.317	58
Bud Black	.224	22	.225	19	.202	11	.248	44	.221	26	.298	107	.321	63
David Cone	.320	--	.304	100	.333	--	.286	--	.282	--	.250	--	.429	--
Steve Farr	.224	20	.231	25	.216	23	.243	33	.191	7	.245	69	.323	66
Mark Gubicza	.245	48	.230	24	.228	37	.244	35	.253	67	.221	50	.321	62
Alan Hargesheimer	.667	--	.320	115	.317	--	.417	--	.375	--	.250	--	.429	--
Danny Jackson	.267	81	.246	39	.246	53	.263	67	.263	76	.210	42	.335	78
Charlie Leibrandt	.239	39	.289	86	.293	107	.245	41	.256	69	.184	25	.292	31
Dennis Leonard	.291	110	.268	64	.264	74	.289	99	.280	91	.197	29	.307	49
Dan Quisenberry	.336	--	.258	53	.254	64	.322	122	.330	121	.288	96	.338	82
Bret Saberhagen	.225	23	.300	97	.288	101	.249	48	.313	116	.296	103	.335	79
Team Average	.255	7	.260	4	.255	6	.261	7	.262	7	.229	4	.321	6
League Average	.258		.270		.259		.264		.263		.246		.326	

MILWAUKEE BREWERS

Sixty-five percent of all American League games last season were won by the team that scored the first run, and in 84 percent of those wins the team that scored first never trailed. The figures were even higher in the National League, where scoring is generally lower and, as a result, the value of a run is greater. National League teams scoring first won 67 percent of the time, never trailing in 86 percent of those wins. Statistics like those make us wonder about the importance of late-game performance. If most games are decided before the seventh-inning stretch, do we all attach too much importance to late-inning performance?

Despite the value of the first run, and the fact that the team leading after seven innings wins more than 90 percent of all games, a team's performance in those last two innings can have an enormous impact on its position in the standings. Let's say, for instance, that all games ended after seven innings. Not even a five-minute sudden-death overtime to break ties. Here's what last season's American League standings would have looked like:

East	W	L	T	Pct.	West	W	L	T	Pct.
Boston	87	61	13	.581	Texas	81	65	16	.549
New York	80	58	24	.568	California	77	69	16	.525
Detroit	79	60	23	.559	Chicago	74	74	14	.500
Cleveland	77	68	18	.528	Oakland	68	83	21	.485
Toronto	71	72	20	.497	Minnesota	66	79	17	.460
Baltimore	65	83	14	.444	Kansas City	61	77	24	.451
Milwaukee	60	82	19	.432	Seattle	62	87	13	.423

The Texas Rangers would have won the Western Division title if all games had ended after seven innings. There would have been no Red Sox-Angels playoff, no Game Five, no winter of agony for Gene Mauch. The Eastern Division race would have been much closer, with only three and a half games separating the top three teams. But it takes an awful lot of 90-second commercials to pay those million-dollar salaries, so it's fair to assume baseball will remain a nine-inning game. And among the teams that benefited most from the late innings last season was the Milwaukee Brewers.

Milwaukee had one of baseball's least noticed but most effective bullpens. Right-hander Mark Clear had been best known for his wildness: In 1984, he became one of a handful of pitchers in baseball history to walk more than a batter an inning over an entire season. Left-hander Dan Plesac was known for . . . well, we're not sure what he was known for, but we know it wasn't relief pitching: In three years of professional baseball prior to 1986, Plesac had made 62 appear-

ances, only one in relief. Nevertheless, the Brewers lost only two of the 59 games last season in which they led after seven innings, the fewest in the majors. Clear and Plesac accounted for 30 of the team's 32 saves, and Milwaukee's relief pitchers ranked fourth in the league with a combined 3.48 ERA.

How many games was Milwaukee's relief pitching worth? Let's figure it this way: the Brewers led 59 games after seven innings. Since teams leading after seven won 90.7 percent of all American League games last season, a typical team would have won 54 of those games (53.5, to be exact). Figure a split of the 19 games in which Milwaukee was tied after seven innings; add 9.5 more wins. Finally, add a fraction (9.3 percent) of the 82 games in which the Brewers trailed after the seventh, for another 7.6 wins. So far, that's 70.6 wins for a typical team, based on Milwaukee's performance through seven innings. Add a win for Milwaukee's victory over Minnesota on May 17, which actually was called after seven, for a grand total of 72 wins. The Brewers won 77 games; we can approximate the value of their late-game heroics at five wins.

We computed that figure for all 14 American League teams, and only one had a greater gain:

	—After Seven Innings—					
	Ahead	Tied	Behind	Expected	Actual	
Team	W–L	W–L	W–L	W–L	W–L	Diff.
California	72–5	12–4	8–61	84–78	92–70	+8
Milwaukee	57–2	10–9	9–73	72–89	77–84	+5
Toronto	65–5	11–9	9–62	81–81	86–76	+5
Boston	82–4	6–7	6–55	91–70	95–66	+4
Kansas City	57–4	15–9	4–72	74–88	76–86	+2
Cleveland	67–8	7–11	9–58	84–78	84–78	0
New York	59–7	11–13	4–54	90–72	90–72	0
Baltimore	58–7	9–5	6–77	74–88	73–89	−1
Texas	72–9	7–9	8–57	88–74	87–75	−1
Detroit	71–8	9–14	7–52	89–73	87–75	−2
Oakland	61–7	8–13	7–66	79–83	76–86	−3
Seattle	54–8	7–6	6–81	71–91	67–95	−4
Minnesota	59–7	7–10	5–73	76–86	71–91	−5
Chicago	60–14	7–7	5–69	81–81	72–90	−9

Of course, pitching is only one factor in the late-inning equation; clutch hitting plays an equal role. But the Brewers thrived in the late innings last season despite the poor performance of their hitters in Late-Inning Pressure Situations, not on account of it. Milwaukee hit .257 in LIP situations, with a .359 slugging average that ranked 12th among the 14 American League teams. Those five wins Milwaukee picked up in the late innings can be attributed primarily to its pitching. And since relief pitchers accounted for 73 percent of the Brewers' pitching after the seventh inning (89 percent in Milwaukee victories), the lion's share of that edge goes to the bullpen.

Clutch Hitting Revisited

Speaking of clutch hitting, we noticed an ironic twist to Milwaukee's off-season acquisition of Greg Brock. Last season, Gorman Thomas of the Brewers batted .100 in Late-Inning Pressure Situations, the lowest mark in the 12-year history of *The Player Analysis* among American League hitters with at least 50 LIP at bats. It would have been the lowest in either league except that Brock hit .058 in Late-Inning Pressure Situations for the Dodgers last season. Over the past three seasons, Thomas, Brock, and another Brewers slugger, Rob Deer, all rank among the bottom 10 in batting average in LIP situations. The highest and lowest over the past three seasons with a minimum of 100 LIP at bats:

Wade Boggs	.378	Gorman Thomas	.128
Tony Gwynn	.356	Ron Kittle	.152
Thad Bosley	.348	Greg Brock	.156
Tony Perez	.347	Reggie Jackson	.170
Don Mattingly	.340	Spike Owen	.180
Chris Brown	.337	Rob Deer	.180
Steve Sax	.335	Rick Dempsey	.183
Tim Raines	.334	Dane Iorg	.187
Tom Paciorek	.333	George Wright	.193
Hubie Brooks	.332	Chris Bando	.193

You don't need a Ph.D. to know you have to pitch carefully to Wade Boggs or Don Mattingly, whether the game is on the line or not. So the lists we find more interesting are those of the players with the greatest differences between their batting averages in Late-Inning Pressure Situations and in unpressured at bats. The names of the players who increase their batting averages the most in Late-Inning Pressure Situations—players who more truly represent what clutch hitting is all about—will surprise you. The best and worst since 1984 with a minimum of 100 LIP at bats:

Player	LIP	Other	Diff.	Player	LIP	Other	Diff.
Tony Perez	.347	.256	.091	Greg Brock	.156	.254	.098
Alex Trevino	.305	.226	.079	Scot Thompson	.208	.306	.098
Tom Paciorek	.333	.255	.078	Tim Flannery	.210	.297	.087
Ernie Whitt	.313	.240	.073	Gorman Thomas	.128	.211	.083
Jim Sundberg	.295	.227	.068	Ron Kittle	.152	.231	.079
Thad Bosley	.348	.282	.067	Reggie Jackson	.170	.249	.079
Ed Romero	.297	.232	.065	George Hendrick	.193	.270	.077
Terry Harper	.303	.238	.064	Mitch Webster	.221	.297	.077
Jack Clark	.327	.268	.059	Spike Owen	.180	.254	.074
Tito Landrum	.296	.239	.057	Chris Chambliss	.208	.281	.073

Since the *Analyst* is the only publication that provides statistics on clutch hitting, it is one of the topics about which we are most frequently asked. Most fans ask for the names of players who thrive under pressure; some ask about those who shrivel in the clutch. But a few have asked whether

clutch hitting is a mirage, whether players hit well under pressure in random patterns. They have suggested that one season's clutch hero will be the next season's choker.

Frankly, we were surprised that anyone would question the validity of clutch hitting. But when several readers mentioned that their questions were prompted by the contention of certain researchers that there was no basis for clutch hitting, the pieces began to fall into place. Think about it for a minute. Do you remember the scene in "The Wizard of Oz" in which Dorothy and her entourage discover that The Wiz is a fraud, manipulating the entire charade from stage left? Once exposed, the wizard tries to save face with one last ploy. "Pay no attention to that man behind the curtain," he shouts.

Well, if you make your living analyzing baseball statistics, but you don't have access to something as important as clutch-hitting statistics, what's the best thing to do? Deny they exist! "Pay no attention to those statistics. They don't mean anything." Well, Wiz, yes they do. We studied the past 12 seasons of clutch hitting statistics and can conclusively report that players who hit better in Late-Inning Pressure Situations over a period of time are more likely to do so in the next season than those who underachieved under pressure during that period.

We began the research last summer by studying the players active during the 1985 season who had exhibited the strongest clutch tendencies, both positive and negative, over the previous 10 seasons. We selected two groups, good clutch hitters and bad clutch hitters, according to their batting averages in Late-Inning Pressure Situations from 1975 through 1984 relative to their performance in unpressured at bats. (Actually, we didn't just choose the players with the greatest difference in batting-average points; we tested each player for the significance of that difference, which accounts not only for the margin between the averages, but also for the number of at bats. A 200-point difference, for example, is meaningless if the player batted only 10 times in LIP situations.) Each group was composed of 30 players.

Then we checked the clutch performance of each player in either group during the 1985 season in comparison to his overall performance. One player in each group compiled identical averages in both Late-Inning Pressure Situations and unpressured situations. The results of the 29 players remaining in each group:

	1985 in Clutch	
1975–84 Tendency	Good	Poor
Good Clutch Hitters	19	10
Poor Clutch Hitters	16	13

In general, the good clutch hitters of the 10-year period hit better in Late-Inning Pressure Situations during the 1985 season than when unpressured. They also hit better under pressure in 1985 than the poor clutch hitters of the 10 previous seasons. The anomalous result was the success that the poor clutch hitters of 1975 through 1984 had in Late-Inning Pressure Situations during the 1985 season. They didn't hit as well as the other group, but a majority of them improved their performances in LIP situations.

One allegedly serious publication seized upon the 1985 data as proof that clutch hitters do not exist. We were quite taken aback that anyone would interpret a single year's performance as proof of anything—evidence, yes; proof, no. We hope that the semiprominent names that constitute its editorial board had the decency to be embarrassed; after all, even a pseudoscience has to have *some* standards.

But as we were saying, the '85 performances—at least by the perennially poor clutch hitters—were out of line with what we had seen in the past. That wasn't the case for the 1986 season, when we made the test a little more rigorous. We studied all players with at least 50 at bats in LIP situations last season, and from them formed groups of 30 players —good and bad clutch hitters—based on their clutch hitting over the three previous seasons. By limiting the lead-in period to three years, we reduced the effect of players who had dramatically improved or declined under pressure over the course of their careers to the extent that their career stats no longer reflected who they were that season. The comparison of that season's LIP and unpressured statistics for those players follows:

Good in Clutch From 1983 to 1985	1986 Stats LIP	Other	Poor in Clutch From 1983 to 1985	1986 Stats LIP	Other
Bill Almon	.197	.230	George Brett	.246	.297
Steve Balboni	.250	.224	Greg Brock	.058	.267
George Bell	.248	.321	Tom Brunansky	.202	.265
Bruce Bochte	.279	.251	Brett Butler	.347	.268
Hubie Brooks	.375	.332	Chris Chambliss	.286	.333
Chris Brown	.329	.315	Glenn Davis	.300	.258
Bill Buckner	.237	.270	Jody Davis	.220	.257
Jack Clark	.255	.232	Bill Doran	.197	.288
Dave Collins	.258	.272	Julio Franco	.277	:309
Cecil Cooper	.271	.256	George Hendrick	.260	.275
Bo Diaz	.346	.258	Kent Hrbek	.256	.269
Mike Easler	.279	.305	Reggie Jackson	.182	.250
Carlton Fisk	.215	.222	Brook Jacoby	.347	.280
Phil Garner	.300	.259	Ron Kittle	.175	.226
Ozzie Guillen	.247	.251	Ray Knight	.353	.289
Bob Horner	.247	.277	Fred Lynn	.281	.288
Garth Iorg	.262	.260	Gary Matthews	.211	.268
Cliff Johnson	.318	.233	Willie McGee	.227	.262
Lee Mazzilli	.196	.274	Paul Molitor	.339	.272
Lloyd Moseby	.225	.258	Jim Morrison	.229	.283
Dale Murphy	.284	.262	Spike Owen	.125	.246
Eddie Murray	.222	.319	Jim Presley	.310	.257
Graig Nettles	.242	.212	Willie Randolph	.288	.275
Jorge Orta	.309	.270	Johnny Ray	.321	.296
Cal Ripken	.274	.284	Jim Rice	.290	.327
Ron Roenicke	.245	.248	Lonnie Smith	.231	.298
Steve Sax	.378	.323	Ozzie Smith	.283	.280
Jim Sundberg	.279	.199	Mike Scioscia	.211	.261
Ernie Whitt	.353	.251	Denny Walling	.296	.315
Robin Yount	.347	.306	Mitch Webster	.245	.300
Averages	.276	.270	Averages	.256	.278

A summary of the results illustrates that both good and bad clutch hitters reproduced those tendencies last season: Of the 30 good clutch hitters, 17 improved under pressure again last season; of the 30 poor clutch hitters, 21 were worse in the clutch last season than under pressure. Combined with the results of our 12 years of study of the issue, even taking into account the anomalous performance by poor clutch hitters in 1985, there can no longer be any doubt: Clutch hitters, both good and bad, do exist.

WON-LOST RECORD BY STARTING POSITION

MILWAUKEE 77-84	C	1B	2B	3B	SS	LF	CF	RF	P	DH	Leadoff	Relief	Starts
Jim Adduci	-	0-3	-	-	-	-	-	-	-	-	-	-	0-3
Mike Birkbeck	-	-	-	-	-	-	-	-	3-1	-	-	-	3-1
Chris Bosio	-	-	-	-	-	-	-	-	1-3	-	-	0-6	1-3
Glenn Braggs	-	-	-	-	-	-	19-27	3-0	3-2	-	1-1	-	26-30
Juan Castillo	-	-	6-7	-	0-4	-	-	-	-	-	-	-	6-11
Rick Cerone	32-34	-	-	-	-	-	-	-	-	-	-	-	32-34
Mark Clear	-	-	-	-	-	-	-	-	-	-	-	28-31	-
Bryan Clutterbuck	-	-	-	-	-	-	-	-	-	-	-	2-18	-
Jaime Cocanower	-	-	-	-	-	-	-	-	0-2	-	-	2-13	0-2
Cecil Cooper	-	46-43	-	-	-	-	-	-	-	21-22	-	-	67-65
Danny Darwin	-	-	-	-	-	-	-	-	4-10	-	-	4-9	4-10
Rob Deer	-	-	2-1	-	-	-	1-0	-	61-68	-	-	-	64-69
Edgar Diaz	-	-	-	1-4	-	-	-	-	-	-	-	-	1-4
Mike Felder	-	-	-	-	-	-	15-12	3-3	3-2	-	0-1	16-16	21-18
Jim Gantner	-	-	62-68	2-1	-	-	-	-	-	-	-	8-10	64-69
Bob Gibson	-	-	-	-	-	-	-	-	0-1	-	-	3-7	0-1
Ted Higuera	-	-	-	-	-	-	-	-	23-11	-	-	-	23-11
Paul Householder	-	-	-	-	-	-	1-5	2-3	2-4	-	3-0	-	8-12
John Henry Johnson	-	-	-	-	-	-	-	-	-	-	-	6-13	-
Steve Kiefer	-	-	-	1-1	-	-	-	-	-	-	-	-	1-1
Mark Knudson	-	-	-	-	-	-	-	-	0-1	-	-	0-3	0-1
Tim Leary	-	-	-	-	-	-	-	-	13-17	-	-	0-3	13-17
Rick Manning	-	-	-	-	-	-	11-8	11-9	5-8	-	-	-	27-25
Bob McClure	-	-	-	-	-	-	-	-	-	-	-	6-7	-
Paul Molitor	-	-	48-43	-	-	2-2	-	-	2-8	-	48-47	-	52-53
Charlie Moore	33-31	-	-	-	-	-	-	-	2-0	0-1	-	-	35-32
Juan Nieves	-	-	-	-	-	-	-	-	17-16	-	-	1-1	17-16
Ben Oglivie	-	-	-	-	-	-	22-26	-	1-0	20-21	-	-	43-47
Dan Plesac	-	-	-	-	-	-	-	-	-	-	-	31-20	-
Randy Ready	-	-	4-2	1-2	-	6-4	-	-	-	0-1	3-4	-	11-9
Ernest Riles	-	-	-	70-68	-	-	-	-	-	-	-	0-3	70-68
Billy Jo Robidoux	-	21-20	-	-	-	-	-	-	-	3-7	-	-	24-27
Bill Schroeder	12-19	7-10	-	-	-	-	-	-	-	6-4	-	-	25-33
Ray Searage	-	-	-	-	-	-	-	-	-	-	-	2-15	-
Dale Sveum	-	-	5-7	26-38	5-7	-	-	-	-	-	-	-	36-52
Gorman Thomas	-	0-6	-	-	-	-	-	-	-	21-15	-	-	21-21
Pete Vuckovich	-	-	-	-	-	-	-	-	2-4	-	-	-	2-4
Bill Wegman	-	-	-	-	-	-	-	-	-	14-18	-	2-1	14-18
Robin Yount	-	1-1	-	-	-	-	-	58-69	-	0-3	2-4	-	59-73

Batting Comparisons: Vs. Left-Handers/Right-Handers and Overall/Late Inning-Pressure Situations

Player		BA	Rank	SA	Rank	HR %	Rank		BA	Rank	SA	Rank	HR %	Rank
Glenn Braggs	vs. Lefties	.293	46	.517	21	5.17	25	Overall	.237	136	.349	136	1.86	112
	vs. Righties	.217	155	.287	163	0.64	147	Pressure	.200	137	.233	157	0.00	109
Rick Cerone	vs. Lefties	.235	116	.338	133	1.47	123	Overall	.259	89	.380	107	1.85	113
	vs. Righties	.270	66	.399	91	2.03	106	Pressure	.189	146	.243	153	0.00	109
Cecil Cooper	vs. Lefties	.285	53	.358	116	2.19	101	Overall	.258	93	.373	118	2.21	106
	vs. Righties	.249	106	.378	105	2.22	100	Pressure	.271	74	.329	112	0.00	109
Rob Deer	vs. Lefties	.279	62	.605	2	8.53	2	Overall	.232	139	.494	13	7.08	1
	vs. Righties	.214	157	.451	53	6.53	9	Pressure	.217	121	.406	63	4.35	39
Mike Felder	vs. Lefties	.409	1	.500	29	0.00	148	Overall	.239	--	.323	--	0.65	--
	vs. Righties	.171	--	.252	--	0.90	--	Pressure	.222	117	.296	133	0.00	109
Jim Gantner	vs. Lefties	.219	140	.250	163	0.00	148	Overall	.274	53	.370	121	1.41	131
	vs. Righties	.293	29	.412	82	1.90	107	Pressure	.298	46	.393	71	2.38	73
Rick Manning	vs. Lefties	.143	--	.257	--	2.86	--	Overall	.254	104	.434	63	3.90	52
	vs. Righties	.276	57	.471	41	4.12	47	Pressure	.240	--	.400	--	4.00	--
Paul Molitor	vs. Lefties	.270	75	.400	87	1.00	137	Overall	.281	43	.426	72	2.06	108
	vs. Righties	.285	42	.433	67	2.37	96	Pressure	.339	22	.484	37	1.61	92
Charlie Moore	vs. Lefties	.283	58	.433	62	1.67	116	Overall	.260	88	.374	116	1.28	134
	vs. Righties	.251	103	.354	120	1.14	134	Pressure	.282	62	.333	108	0.00	109
Ben Oglivie	vs. Lefties	.254	93	.349	124	0.00	148	Overall	.283	40	.390	99	1.45	127
	vs. Righties	.290	37	.399	89	1.77	110	Pressure	.255	88	.382	76	1.82	85
Ernest Riles	vs. Lefties	.207	151	.319	144	2.59	82	Overall	.252	108	.357	131	1.72	118
	vs. Righties	.265	76	.368	111	1.47	124	Pressure	.256	86	.390	73	3.66	49
Billy Jo Robidoux	vs. Lefties	.314	25	.429	66	2.86	77	Overall	.227	149	.287	165	0.55	155
	vs. Righties	.205	166	.253	170	0.00	158	Pressure	.423	2	.500	32	0.00	109
Bill Schroeder	vs. Lefties	.222	135	.403	86	4.17	43	Overall	.212	161	.373	117	3.23	74
	vs. Righties	.207	164	.359	118	2.76	89	Pressure	.152	166	.182	166	0.00	109
Dale Sveum	vs. Lefties	.271	72	.438	60	2.08	103	Overall	.246	121	.366	126	2.21	107
	vs. Righties	.235	126	.335	133	2.26	98	Pressure	.204	134	.222	159	0.00	109
Gorman Thomas	vs. Lefties	.175	165	.361	112	5.15	27	Overall	.187	168	.371	119	5.08	24
	vs. Righties	.193	167	.376	108	5.05	29	Pressure	.100	170	.340	104	8.00	5
Robin Yount	vs. Lefties	.248	103	.355	118	2.48	86	Overall	.312	9	.450	51	1.72	117
	vs. Righties	.332	4	.479	37	1.50	123	Pressure	.347	14	.467	40	1.33	100
Team Average	vs. Lefties	.253	12	.385	11	2.58	11	Overall	.255	10	.385	13	2.33	13
	vs. Righties	.256	7	.385	11	2.24	14	Pressure	.257	7	.359	12	1.68	13
League Average	vs. Lefties	.263		.408		2.88		Overall	.262		.408		2.96	
	vs. Righties	.261		.408		2.99		Pressure	.254		.383		2.61	

Additional Miscellaneous Batting Comparisons

	Grass Surface BA	Rank	Artificial Surface BA	Rank	Home Games BA	Rank	Road Games BA	Rank	Runners in Scoring Position BA	Rank	Runners in Scoring Pos and Two Outs BA	Rank	Leading Off Inning OBA	Rank	Runners on 3B with less than 2 Outs RDI %	Rank
Glenn Braggs	.239	120	.226	--	.314	--	.186	164	.125	167	.154	159	.311	--	.417	151
Rick Cerone	.271	55	.167	--	.267	85	.250	100	.114	169	.045	173	.360	43	.769	12
Cecil Cooper	.250	96	.305	40	.235	128	.279	48	.329	16	.296	44	.277	142	.576	82
Rob Deer	.226	137	.273	78	.227	143	.237	124	.240	116	.151	160	.339	71	.515	121
Mike Felder	.250	96	.091	--	.267	83	.203	--	.286	--	.250	--	.323	95	.857	--
Jim Gantner	.270	59	.297	52	.259	98	.288	37	.200	149	.203	130	.319	101	.654	43
Rick Manning	.256	85	.245	114	.216	150	.282	45	.151	163	.179	147	.259	148	.571	83
Paul Molitor	.295	22	.170	161	.300	32	.263	72	.351	7	.400	2	.313	111	.500	122
Charlie Moore	.279	42	.178	160	.304	30	.220	143	.333	14	.303	39	.143	170	.619	58
Ben Oglivie	.279	44	.303	44	.290	39	.277	52	.316	25	.286	53	.391	17	.913	1
Ernest Riles	.244	112	.295	54	.260	97	.245	113	.190	157	.196	134	.331	82	.414	153
Billy Jo Robidoux	.241	115	.067	--	.188	--	.257	85	.224	136	.185	141	.348	60	.818	8
Bill Schroeder	.203	158	.267	--	.194	165	.241	--	.123	168	.107	169	.458	2	.200	168
Dale Sveum	.238	122	.279	71	.226	144	.266	67	.286	55	.351	14	.256	150	.500	122
Gorman Thomas	.202	160	.165	163	.138	169	.226	141	.178	160	.093	170	.329	87	.421	150
Robin Yount	.308	13	.343	15	.297	34	.327	5	.284	58	.234	98	.379	25	.579	78
Team Average	.256	8	.252	12	.253	13	.257	8	.244	14	.230	11	.319	9	.576	8
League Average	.258		.270		.264		.259		.263		.246		.326		.575	

Pitching Comparisons: Vs. Left-Handers/Right-Handers and Runners On/Bases Empty

		BA	Rank	BB %	Rank	SO %	Rank		BA	Rank	BB %	Rank	SO %	Rank
Mark Clear	vs. Lefties	.189	6	18.66	126	26.12	3	Runners On	.183	3	14.38	126	26.25	2
	vs. Righties	.209	14	6.40	39	29.07	4	Bases Empty	.218	22	8.90	88	29.45	2
Bryan Clutterbuck	vs. Lefties	.379	126	9.40	67	11.97	74	Runners On	.279	89	6.77	25	15.04	54
	vs. Righties	.228	27	3.76	7	18.05	46	Bases Empty	.315	--	5.98	--	15.38	--
Jaime Cocanower	vs. Lefties	.268	66	22.34	129	10.64	87	Runners On	.270	--	12.84	--	10.09	--
	vs. Righties	.233	--	15.32	--	10.81	--	Bases Empty	.222	--	25.00	--	11.46	--
Danny Darwin	vs. Lefties	.259	60	9.85	75	10.95	83	Runners On	.291	100	7.14	33	8.93	117
	vs. Righties	.233	31	3.04	3	19.01	38	Bases Empty	.216	20	6.07	36	19.17	27
Ted Higuera	vs. Lefties	.243	46	4.32	3	22.84	6	Runners On	.240	33	6.08	17	21.90	9
	vs. Righties	.241	46	7.71	65	19.56	34	Bases Empty	.243	45	7.90	71	18.87	29
John Henry Johnson	vs. Lefties	.227	--	4.17	--	20.83	--	Runners On	.211	--	7.00	--	26.00	--
	vs. Righties	.260	72	5.88	31	23.53	12	Bases Empty	.296	--	3.57	--	19.05	--
Tim Leary	vs. Lefties	.282	81	10.10	82	11.30	79	Runners On	.296	103	6.67	24	15.00	55
	vs. Righties	.296	117	2.74	2	15.71	69	Bases Empty	.284	102	6.35	43	12.25	96
Juan Nieves	vs. Lefties	.318	113	9.52	69	20.41	12	Runners On	.323	120	8.79	61	12.14	82
	vs. Righties	.295	115	9.17	94	12.52	96	Bases Empty	.280	91	9.62	95	15.44	52
Dan Plesac	vs. Lefties	.266	--	9.89	--	18.68	--	Runners On	.228	16	8.25	49	18.04	30
	vs. Righties	.233	30	6.99	49	20.28	31	Bases Empty	.253	58	7.10	57	21.86	10
Bill Wegman	vs. Lefties	.268	67	6.17	21	8.94	107	Runners On	.307	114	4.66	2	9.63	113
	vs. Righties	.294	113	3.83	8	10.93	112	Bases Empty	.262	70	5.45	22	9.92	116
Team Average	vs. Lefties	.270	9	9.97	10	13.21	9	Runners On	.275	11	8.26	3	14.93	5
	vs. Righties	.265	11	6.86	1	16.85	6	Bases Empty	.261	10	7.85	6	15.93	5
League Average	vs. Lefties	.265		9.67		13.46		Runners On	.269		9.46		14.39	
	vs. Righties	.259		8.19		16.22		Bases Empty	.256		8.31		15.55	

Additional Miscellaneous Pitching Comparisons

	Grass Surface BA	Rank	Artificial Surface BA	Rank	Home Games BA	Rank	Road Games BA	Rank	Runners in Scoring Position BA	Rank	Runners in Scoring Pos and Two Outs BA	Rank	Leading Off Inning OBA	Rank
Mike Birkbeck	.233	--	.333	122	.242	--	.308	--	.300	--	.143	--	.375	--
Mark Clear	.181	3	.324	--	.175	2	.231	17	.157	2	.154	12	.279	23
Bryan Clutterbuck	.291	111	.324	--	.278	90	.313	119	.260	74	.200	30	.429	126
Jaime Cocanower	.255	58	.208	--	.250	--	.248	42	.286	--	.269	--	.378	--
Danny Darwin	.247	49	.239	31	.252	61	.238	29	.297	104	.295	101	.308	50
Ted Higuera	.233	32	.289	85	.219	28	.265	70	.206	13	.163	13	.289	30
Tim Leary	.296	114	.265	62	.275	85	.303	111	.240	46	.203	36	.370	109
Juan Nieves	.299	115	.303	98	.315	123	.287	96	.326	119	.367	128	.378	112
Dan Plesac	.241	44	.233	26	.260	72	.214	9	.220	24	.145	8	.304	46
Bill Wegman	.278	98	.290	88	.287	99	.270	74	.327	120	.363	127	.313	53
Team Average	.265	9	.280	13	.264	7	.270	11	.261	6	.245	8	.342	11
League Average	.258		.270		.259		.264		.263		.246		.326	

MINNESOTA TWINS

To paraphrase Walter Mondale's favorite debating partner, "Here we go again!"

Just when we figured that the 1986 *Analyst* would set the characteristics of the Metrodome straight once and for all—that while it's a good place for extra-base hits and run scoring, it's *not* an exceptional home run paradise—the roof falls in on us. But as this is one of those domes in which the roof is supported by hot air, we'll unload our supply of same on you even as the dome gently cascades down around us.

First, the facts as we know them. In 1982, when the dome opened, home runs were hit there with above-average frequency, thus inspiring the "Homerdome" nickname. Even then, however, fans paid too much attention to the total number of home runs hit in the Dome, and too little to who was hitting them. The fact is that the Twins, then and now, are a powerful hitting team with a below-average pitching staff, a pair of qualities that would lead to a harvest of homers regardless of the setting.

The relevant yardstick is the comparison between the rate of home runs hit—for and against the Twins—in their home games and the rate in their road games. Those figures for 1982 were 3.45 home runs for every 100 at bats in the Metrodome, and 2.99 per every 100 at bats on the road.

Then, in 1983, the air conditioning was turned on. *Voila!* (As opposed to *Viola!*) For the next three years, homers at the Dome (2.59 per 100 at bats) came at a slower rate than they did in Twins' road games (2.72). We pointed out this discrepancy in the 1985 *Analyst*. We pointed it out again in the 1986 *Analyst*. Nonetheless, the Homerdome label grew more prevalent, even though it was at odds with the facts.

No sooner were the words out of our mouths than the Metrodome yielded 223 home runs in 1986, the most of any major league stadium. The rates: 3.88 homers per 100 at bats in Twins home games, 3.20 per 100 in Twins road games.

Especially in 1986, the words *Minnesota Twins* and *home runs* were inexorably linked. Kirby Puckett hit 31 for the season, but it was his total of 11 in his first 24 games that, more than any other factor, gave rise to countless "The ball is juiced" stories in the first two months of the season. Gary Gaetti belted 34 home runs to lead the team, Kent Hrbek had 29, Tom Brunansky 23, and Roy Smalley 20. And Bert Blyleven's total of 50 homers allowed set a major-league record —but more on that one later.

So where does all of this leave us? Perry Mason was never afraid to look at new evidence; neither are we. Let's see what the evidence supplied by the 1986 statistics does to our case.

A useful addition to the 1987 *Analyst* is the series of tables on the influence of ballparks that begins on page 410. The statistics presented there will help you identify the particular nuances of each major-league stadium; the data is presented both for last season and for the last five seasons combined. (For example, the park that depressed run scoring to the greatest degree last year was Shea Stadium; over the last five seasons, that title is held by the Oakland Coliseum.)

Remember, these calculations come from comparing the totals generated by both teams in games played by a team in its own stadium with the totals generated in that team's road games. The reason for this is simple: If Mike Schmidt, Jesse Barfield, Jose Canseco, and Dave Parker all played for the Astros, simply looking at the total of home runs hit in the Astrodome would give the impression that homers come cheap down there. Only by comparing the home-game and road-game figures, and calculating the rate of increase or decrease, can the true stadium influences be determined.

The Metrodome was the park that most influenced batting average and runs per game last season. The Twins and their opponents together batted .281 in Twins home games, .261 in their road games, the largest disparity in the majors last season. The five parks that most helped batting average and run scoring in 1986:

Batting Average				Runs per Game			
	Home	Road	Diff.		Home	Road	Diff.
Minnesota	.281	.261	7.4%	Minnesota	10.68	8.83	21.0%
Chi. Cubs	.276	.258	7.0%	Chi. Cubs	9.91	8.35	18.7%
Philadelphia	.267	.251	6.2%	Seattle	10.21	8.95	14.0%
Cincinnati	.265	.252	5.0%	Toronto	9.93	9.00	10.3%
St. Louis	.247	.239	3.4%	Philadelphia	9.46	8.58	10.3%

But even last season, with the ball jumping around inside the Dome as if the park were an arcade game, the Metrodome ranked no higher than seventh in the major leagues in generating home runs:

Home Runs per 100 At Bats			
	Home	Road	Diff.
Seattle	3.44	2.45	40.1%
Atlanta	2.70	2.01	34.1%
Baltimore	3.50	2.78	26.1%
Cincinnati	2.82	2.23	26.1%
San Diego	2.87	2.34	22.2%
Chi. Cubs	2.96	2.42	22.5%
Minnesota	3.88	3.20	21.2%

Ponder that for a moment. Do you hear much reference to Memorial Stadium in Baltimore as a home run paradise? Not at all, yet the increase in the rate of home runs there, both last season and over the last five seasons, is greater than in the Metrodome.

How about San Diego? If you asked a hundred baseball people if Jack Murphy Stadium helps or hurts home run hitters, we would be surprised if a majority thought it helps. And yet, over the past five years, only Wrigley Field, Atlanta Stadium, and the Kingdome stand ahead of Murphy in increasing home run production.

In order to introduce you to the types of things that can be learned from the Ballparks section, and to save you a little time in looking them up, here is a summary of the home run tendencies of all the major-league stadiums over the past five years. Again, the figure given is the difference between home run rates for both teams in a team's home and road games.

Help Home Runs		Hurt Home Runs	
Wrigley Field	+40.4%	Astrodome	−44.9%
Atlanta Stadium	+32.3%	Royals Stadium	−25.2%
Kingdome	+28.4%	Busch Stadium	−17.8%
San Diego Stadium	+22.9%	Dodger Stadium	−16.4%
Anaheim Stadium	+19.0%	Oakland Coliseum	−15.6%
Tiger Stadium	+13.9%	Olympic Stadium	−14.8%
Exhibition Stadium	+10.5%	County Stadium	−12.4%
Memorial Stadium	+6.4%	Arlington Stadium	−9.9%
Metrodome	+5.3%	Yankee Stadium	−7.6%
Three Rivers Stadium	+5.1%	Fenway Park	−5.2%
Veterans Stadium	+1.7%	Comiskey Park	−2.8%
Shea Stadium	+1.6%	Candlestick Park	−2.1%
Cleveland Stadium	+1.1%		
Riverfront Stadium	+0.9%		

What this issue boils down to is the difference between a great home run ballpark and a park in which great home run hitters (and home run pitchers) play. The Metrodome's geographical cousin, County Stadium in Milwaukee, was misunderstood for years, because although it is *not* easy to hit home runs there, it was the home field for Aaron and Mathews and Adcock and later for Scott and Oglivie and Thomas. Recognizing that difference is the key to understanding a stadium's influence.

Hrbek, Brunansky, Gaetti, and Puckett have all come into their own since the Metrodome opened; only Hrbek has played a Twins home game outdoors. Accordingly, they have always had their achievements tarnished by a shadow that, upon closer scrutiny, is without substance. Three of them have higher career home run rates in all other stadiums than they have in the Metrodome; the fourth, Hrbek, is only moderately higher at the Dome:

	At Metrodome			Other Stadiums		
	AB	HR	HR%	AB	HR	HR%
Tom Brunansky	1350	59	4.37	1415	74	5.23
Gary Gaetti	1429	50	3.50	1433	57	3.98
Kirby Puckett	974	16	1.64	954	19	1.99
Kent Hrbek	1427	61	4.27	1389	56	4.03

The 5.1 percent influence that the Metrodome has on home runs over the past five years has certainly not worked to the benefit of these prominent Minnesota home run hitters. Notwithstanding the 223 homers hit in the Dome in 1986, it's time for everyone to admit that Brunansky and Co. are not lifeless Thanksgiving Day floats, pumped up into monstrous proportions by the hot air of the Dome. They are legitimate home run threats who produce even better outdoors than in.

And it's time for us all to work together to stamp out that accursed "Homerdome" label once and for all. The next time you hear someone refer to the Homerdome, give him a copy of this book. If he says it again, hit him over the head with it. And if he persists, *call a cop!*

Tracking Indoor Records

Major-league baseball has been played indoors for 22 years in Houston, for 10 years in Seattle, and for five years in Minneapolis. Let's steal a good idea from the track and field people and present the first embryonic *Indoor Baseball Record Book*:

Most Home Runs, Career
97 Jim Wynn (all at Houston)
68 Tom Brunansky (59 at Minn., 9 at Sea.)
67 Kent Hrbek (61 at Minn., 6 at Sea.)
66 Cesar Cedeno (all at Houston)
65 Doug Rader (63 at Hou., 2 at Sea.)

Most Home Runs, Season
18 Lee May, Hou. 1974 (all at Houston)
18 Gary Ward, Minn. 1982 (16 at Minn., 2 at Sea.)
18 Kent Hrbek, Minn. 1986 (18 at Minn.)

Most Home Runs, Game
3 Jim Wynn, Hou. vs. S. F., June 15, 1967
3 Doug DeCinces, Cal. at Sea., Aug. 8, 1982
3 Dan Ford, Balt. at Sea., June 20, 1983
3 Dave Kingman, Oak. at Sea., April 16, 1984
3 Harold Baines, Chi. at Minn., Sept. 17, 1984
3 Gorman Thomas, Sea. vs. Oak., April 11, 1985
3 Jim Presley, Sea. vs. Det., Sept. 1, 1986

Most Hits, Game
5 Accomplished 25 times by 23 players. Done twice by:
  Doug Rader, Hou., Aug. 10, 1968 (1g) & May 25, 1975 (12 inn.)
  Cal Ripken, Balt. at Minn., Sept. 3, 1983 & May 5, 1985

Most Strikeouts, Game
16 Jose Rijo, Oak. at Sea., April 19, 1986
15 J.R. Richard, Hou. vs. Atl., Aug. 3, 1979
15 J.R. Richard, Hou. vs. Cin., Sept. 21, 1979 (11 inn.)
15 Mark Langston, Sea. vs. Clev., June 25, 1986
15 Bert Blyleven, Minn. vs. Oak., Aug. 1, 1986

No-Hit Games
  Don Wilson, Hou. vs. Atl., June 18, 1967 (won 2–0)
  Larry Dierker, Hou. vs. Mtl., July 9, 1976 (won 6–0)
  Ken Forsch, Hou. vs. Atl., Apr. 7, 1979 (won 6–0)
  Nolan Ryan, Hou. vs. L.A., Sept. 26, 1981 (won 5–0)
  Mike Scott, Hou. vs. S. F., Sept. 25, 1986 (won 2–0)

Bert

Pitching for a team that finished with the 13th-best record in a 14-team league, Bert Blyleven went 17–14, completed 16 of his 36 starts, had a 4.01 ERA in a stadium that was the highest run generator in the majors, and struck out 215 batters in 271 2/3 innings. He also allowed 50 home runs, breaking the major-league record of 46 allowed by Robin Roberts in 1956.

One of our favorite quotes of the season came from Roberts, who was interviewed on the occasion of Blyleven's breaking his record. "I don't think it's fair to Blyleven, considering the phenomenal record he's had, that you guys bring it up. When I was playing, we didn't have time to worry about those things."

We second the motion. This is a case in which so much attention has been focused on a minor flaw that it has overshadowed outstanding achievements. Did Thomas Edison forget to send birthday greetings to his friends? Did Hemingway like to jaywalk? Did Dr. Jonas Salk like to park in no-parking zones? Who cares!

Blyleven has a career record of 229–197, a 3.08 earned run average, 54 shutouts and 3,090 strikeouts. In 17 major-league seasons, he has finished below the .500 mark only three times; the significance of that is magnified because in only seven of those seasons has his team finished with a winning record (and two of those winning records were 82–80 and 52–51).

His postseason appearances have been few but impressive; he won two games for the Pirates en route to their 1979 championship and has allowed only three earned runs in 21 postseason innings.

Despite his accomplishments, we fear that these credentials will be dismissed when his name is brought up in the future, and that the knee-jerk response to the name "Bert Blyleven" will be "50 home runs."

To be sure, giving up 50 home runs does not weigh to Blyleven's credit, just as striking out 100 times per season did not weigh to Mickey Mantle's. But the comparison is apt, because just as surely as Mantle's strikeouts were an unwelcome but acceptable by-product of the type of player he was, a high total of home runs allowed is part of the overall package that is Bert Blyleven: around the plate, relying on his curveball, and smart enough to realize that home runs don't necessarily beat you every time.

In judging Blyleven's 1986 season, we consider the most important consideration to be his 17–14 record while his teammates were going 54–77 without him. Unfortunately, the urge to track a record—any record—became the story last season, right down to a Maris-style countdown. In this instance, we think Blyleven took a lot of undeserved heat.

WON-LOST RECORD BY STARTING POSITION

MINNESOTA 71-91	C	1B	2B	3B	SS	LF	CF	RF	P	DH	Leadoff	Relief	Starts
Juan Agosto	·	·	·	·	·	·	·	·	0-1	·	·	5-11	0-1
Allan Anderson	·	·	·	·	·	·	·	·	2-8	·	·	3-8	2-8
Keith Atherton	·	·	·	·	·	·	·	·	·	·	·	19-28	·
Billy Beane	·	·	·	·	·	·	22-24	1-0	·	·	2-1	·	25-25
Bert Blyleven	·	·	·	·	·	·	·	·	20-16	·	·	·	20-16
Tom Brunansky	·	·	·	·	·	·	0-1	64-85	·	1-0	·	·	65-86
Dennis Burtt	·	·	·	·	·	·	·	·	·	·	·	0-3	·
Randy Bush	·	1-1	·	·	·	·	32-43	·	5-5	2-2	·	·	40-51
John Butcher	·	·	·	·	·	·	·	·	1-9	·	·	1-5	1-9
Andre David	·	·	·	·	·	·	·	·	·	·	·	·	·
Mark Davidson	·	·	·	·	·	·	5-6	1-2	2-1	·	0-1	6-2	8-10
Ron Davis	·	·	·	·	·	·	·	·	·	·	·	7-29	·
Alvaro Espinoza	·	·	5-6	·	3-2	·	·	·	·	·	·	·	8-8
Pete Filson	·	·	·	·	·	·	·	·	·	·	·	0-4	·
Ray Fontenot	·	·	·	·	·	·	·	·	·	·	·	4-11	·
George Frazier	·	·	·	·	·	·	·	·	·	·	·	9-6	·
Gary Gaetti	·	·	·	66-88	·	·	1-0	·	·	·	·	·	67-88
Greg Gagne	·	·	·	·	68-84	·	·	·	·	·	1-2	·	68-84
Mickey Hatcher	·	8-9	·	·	·	·	11-18	·	·	12-11	·	·	31-38
Neal Heaton	·	·	·	·	·	·	·	·	6-11	·	·	1-3	6-11
Kent Hrbek	·	62-81	·	·	·	·	·	·	·	1-0	·	·	63-81
Roy Lee Jackson	·	·	·	·	·	·	·	·	·	·	·	5-23	·
Bill Latham	·	·	·	·	·	·	·	·	1-1	·	·	0-5	1-1
Tim Laudner	31-26	·	·	·	·	·	·	·	·	·	·	·	31-26
Steve Lombardozzi	·	·	64-76	·	·	·	·	·	·	·	3-4	·	64-76
Frank Pastore	·	·	·	·	·	·	·	·	0-1	·	·	12-20	0-1
Chris Pittaro	·	·	0-7	·	·	·	·	·	·	·	·	·	0-7
Mark Portugal	·	·	·	·	·	·	·	·	6-9	·	·	4-8	6-9
Kirby Puckett	·	·	·	·	·	·	69-88	·	·	·	57-71	·	69-88
Jeff Reed	20-29	·	·	·	·	·	·	·	·	·	·	·	20-29
Mark Salas	20-36	·	·	·	·	·	·	·	·	2-6	·	·	22-42
Alejandro Sanchez	·	·	·	·	·	·	·	·	·	1-2	·	·	1-2
Roy Smalley	·	·	4-3	·	0-5	·	·	·	·	46-58	2-7	·	50-66
Roy Smith	·	·	·	·	·	·	·	·	·	·	·	1-4	·
Mike Smithson	·	·	·	·	·	·	·	·	14-19	·	·	0-1	14-19
Frank Viola	·	·	·	·	·	·	·	·	21-16	·	·	·	21-16
Ron Washington	·	·	2-2	1-0	·	·	·	·	·	3-8	2-5	·	6-10
Al Woods	·	·	·	·	·	·	·	·	·	1-2	·	·	1-2

Batting Comparisons: Vs. Left-Handers/Right-Handers and Overall/Late Inning Pressure Situations

		BA	Rank	SA	Rank	HR %	Rank		BA	Rank	SA	Rank	HR %	Rank
Billy Beane	vs. Lefties	.261	87	.318	145	1.14	134	Overall	.213	--	.295	--	1.64	--
	vs. Righties	.168	--	.274	--	2.11	--	Pressure	.200	--	.360	--	4.00	--
Tom Brunansky	vs. Lefties	.311	27	.575	8	6.59	13	Overall	.256	97	.423	75	3.88	57
	vs. Righties	.235	128	.364	114	2.82	87	Pressure	.202	136	.357	96	2.38	73
Randy Bush	vs. Lefties	.167	--	.250	--	0.00	--	Overall	.269	66	.420	80	1.96	110
	vs. Righties	.272	63	.426	74	2.03	105	Pressure	.321	29	.464	43	1.79	87
Mark Davidson	vs. Lefties	.154	169	.231	167	0.00	148	Overall	.118	--	.162	--	0.00	--
	vs. Righties	.069	--	.069	--	0.00	--	Pressure	.167	--	.167	--	0.00	--
Gary Gaetti	vs. Lefties	.344	8	.603	3	7.28	9	Overall	.287	34	.518	8	5.70	14
	vs. Righties	.267	71	.490	30	5.17	26	Pressure	.256	87	.400	67	3.33	58
Greg Gagne	vs. Lefties	.230	127	.452	51	4.76	29	Overall	.250	114	.398	93	2.54	96
	vs. Righties	.257	91	.379	103	1.73	112	Pressure	.250	90	.269	143	0.00	109
Mickey Hatcher	vs. Lefties	.364	3	.493	32	1.43	126	Overall	.278	47	.366	126	0.95	142
	vs. Righties	.209	162	.266	166	0.56	149	Pressure	.170	156	.191	165	0.00	109
Kent Hrbek	vs. Lefties	.270	76	.382	98	2.63	80	Overall	.267	73	.478	24	5.27	22
	vs. Righties	.266	73	.515	15	6.28	10	Pressure	.256	85	.397	70	3.85	44
Tim Laudner	vs. Lefties	.261	88	.514	22	6.31	15	Overall	.244	123	.451	50	5.18	23
	vs. Righties	.220	--	.366	--	3.66	-.	Pressure	.200	137	.240	154	0.00	109
Steve Lombardozzi	vs. Lefties	.207	147	.347	128	2.48	86	Overall	.227	147	.347	137	1.77	115
	vs. Righties	.235	127	.346	126	1.51	122	Pressure	.240	99	.420	58	4.00	42
Kirby Puckett	vs. Lefties	.325	15	.524	16	3.61	56	Overall	.328	4	.537	4	4.56	34
	vs. Righties	.329	6	.541	9	4.86	35	Pressure	.293	52	.488	36	6.10	19
Jeff Reed	vs. Lefties	.300	--	.300	--	0.00	--	Overall	.236	--	.321	--	1.21	--
	vs. Righties	.232	130	.323	141	1.29	128	Pressure	.292	--	.458	--	0.00	--
Mark Salas	vs. Lefties	.350	--	.450	--	0.00	--	Overall	.233	138	.384	105	3.10	79
	vs. Righties	.223	147	.378	104	3.36	64	Pressure	.179	153	.286	137	1.79	87
Roy Smalley	vs. Lefties	.138	172	.310	147	3.45	60	Overall	.246	120	.438	60	4.36	39
	vs. Righties	.262	83	.456	48	4.49	43	Pressure	.152	163	.273	139	1.52	95
Ron Washington	vs. Lefties	.220	138	.380	99	4.00	48	Overall	.257	--	.459	--	5.41	--
	vs. Righties	.333	--	.625	--	8.33	--	Pressure	.111	--	.111	--	0.00	--
Team Average	vs. Lefties	.279	2	.456	1	3.84	1	Overall	.261	7	.428	3	3.54	2
	vs. Righties	.255	8	.419	6	3.44	3	Pressure	.232	13	.360	11	2.58	8
League Average	vs. Lefties	.263		.408		2.88		Overall	.262		.408		2.96	
	vs. Righties	.261		.408		2.99		Pressure	.254		.383		2.61	

Additional Miscellaneous Batting Comparisons

	Grass Surface BA	Rank	Artificial Surface BA	Rank	Home Games BA	Rank	Road Games BA	Rank	Runners in Scoring Position BA	Rank	Runners in Scoring Pos and Two Outs BA	Rank	Leading Off Inning OBA	Rank	Runners on 3B with less than 2 Outs RDI %	Rank
Billy Beane	.210	--	.216	142	.190	--	.231	133	.234	--	.143	--	.204	167	.400	156
Tom Brunansky	.238	124	.268	85	.267	84	.246	108	.241	115	.224	113	.313	110	.484	138
Randy Bush	.233	129	.289	60	.304	29	.233	130	.232	130	.200	131	.325	92	.625	53
Mark Davidson	.103	--	.128	168	.128	--	.103	--	.059	--	.000	--	.208	--	.667	--
Gary Gaetti	.364	1	.239	120	.250	106	.323	7	.269	77	.254	82	.316	107	.658	42
Greg Gagne	.255	90	.247	111	.239	119	.261	79	.267	80	.254	81	.291	130	.524	111
Mickey Hatcher	.218	147	.316	31	.314	19	.242	115	.260	85	.205	129	.288	131	.611	62
Kent Hrbek	.264	72	.269	81	.273	72	.261	77	.245	112	.188	139	.400	11	.676	36
Tim Laudner	.272	--	.223	132	.232	138	.255	89	.250	107	.300	41	.351	--	.400	156
Steve Lombardozzi	.196	165	.246	112	.251	105	.202	160	.194	156	.235	97	.307	117	.133	169
Kirby Puckett	.287	33	.352	11	.367	1	.287	39	.319	21	.345	17	.385	23	.500	122
Jeff Reed	.175	--	.256	98	.225	146	.254	--	.143	--	.125	--	.306	119	.500	--
Mark Salas	.250	--	.221	133	.211	156	.252	96	.254	104	.282	58	.218	165	.417	151
Roy Smalley	.222	140	.262	92	.266	89	.228	137	.250	107	.255	79	.304	120	.500	122
Ron Washington	.074	--	.362	8	.356	--	.103	--	.143	--	.143	--	.286	--	.800	--
Team Average	.249	10	.269	10	.272	2	.251	11	.248	13	.235	10	.317	11	.544	11
League Average	.258		.270		.264		.259		.263		.246		.326		.575	

Pitching Comparisons: Vs. Left-Handers/Right-Handers and Runners On/Bases Empty

		BA	Rank	BB %	Rank	SO %	Rank		BA	Rank	BB %	Rank	SO %	Rank
Allan Anderson	vs. Lefties	.337	120	8.25	50	12.37	68	Runners On	.333	124	8.38	53	9.58	114
	vs. Righties	.309	123	8.03	69	14.23	81	Bases Empty	.303	119	7.84	69	17.16	42
Keith Atherton	vs. Lefties	.302	102	13.21	115	13.68	53	Runners On	.277	86	10.66	95	16.80	35
	vs. Righties	.237	37	8.22	72	17.35	54	Bases Empty	.259	65	10.70	106	13.90	78
Bert Blyleven	vs. Lefties	.238	37	5.13	12	20.23	14	Runners On	.246	38	5.41	8	19.06	23
	vs. Righties	.268	84	5.18	22	17.34	56	Bases Empty	.252	56	4.99	14	19.12	28
Ron Davis	vs. Lefties	.390	128	17.31	124	10.58	89	Runners On	.317	117	17.42	130	16.67	37
	vs. Righties	.288	--	11.70	--	20.21	--	Bases Empty	.379	--	9.09	--	12.12	--
Neal Heaton	vs. Lefties	.250	52	6.45	23	12.26	71	Runners On	.228	17	12.06	112	9.65	112
	vs. Righties	.270	89	10.22	108	10.22	119	Bases Empty	.293	112	7.55	62	11.32	105
Roy Lee Jackson	vs. Lefties	.232	31	9.17	62	10.09	97	Runners On	.226	15	7.26	38	11.29	94
	vs. Righties	.273	96	4.29	13	15.00	75	Bases Empty	.282	95	5.60	26	14.40	68
Frank Pastore	vs. Lefties	.243	45	12.20	105	10.57	90	Runners On	.298	105	13.56	122	6.78	128
	vs. Righties	.330	--	9.00	--	5.00	--	Bases Empty	.268	--	7.62	--	9.52	--
Mark Portugal	vs. Lefties	.218	16	12.55	107	16.32	32	Runners On	.236	25	9.73	80	15.04	53
	vs. Righties	.310	125	8.26	74	11.57	109	Bases Empty	.291	109	10.98	110	12.94	90
Mike Smithson	vs. Lefties	.315	110	7.68	36	8.99	105	Runners On	.302	108	5.60	9	11.20	95
	vs. Righties	.260	74	4.62	17	19.08	37	Bases Empty	.287	105	7.19	59	14.37	70
Frank Viola	vs. Lefties	.273	73	4.85	10	12.73	62	Runners On	.247	41	7.76	45	18.95	26
	vs. Righties	.267	83	8.45	81	19.14	35	Bases Empty	.283	99	7.97	73	17.56	40
Team Average	vs. Lefties	.278	10	8.59	3	13.63	6	Runners On	.282	13	8.79	6	13.83	11
	vs. Righties	.283	14	7.61	7	15.95	9	Bases Empty	.280	14	7.39	4	15.90	6
League Average	vs. Lefties	.265		9.67		13.46		Runners On	.269		9.46		14.39	
	vs. Righties	.259		8.19		16.22		Bases Empty	.256		8.31		15.55	

Additional Miscellaneous Pitching Comparisons

	Grass Surface		Artificial Surface		Home Games		Road Games		Runners in Scoring Position		Runners in Scoring Pos and Two Outs		Leading Off Inning	
	BA	Rank	BA	Rank	BA	Rank	BA	Rank	BA	Rank	BA	Rank	OBA	Rank
Juan Agosto	.393	--	.455	130	.391	--	.462	--	.440	--	.409	--	.391	--
Allan Anderson	.294	--	.330	120	.335	125	.290	100	.346	125	.343	122	.379	115
Keith Atherton	.258	--	.275	70	.241	49	.298	109	.274	88	.172	16	.313	53
Bert Blyleven	.222	17	.262	58	.263	73	.231	18	.228	35	.240	64	.296	37
Ron Davis	.384	--	.303	98	.284	--	.395	--	.250	59	.222	51	.448	--
Ray Fontenot	.238	--	.407	128	.422	--	.267	--	.500	--	.500	--	.467	--
George Frazier	.229	--	.234	28	.212	--	.255	--	.226	--	.071	--	.227	--
Neal Heaton	.273	89	.255	51	.258	69	.273	76	.239	45	.261	79	.386	116
Roy Lee Jackson	.267	--	.252	49	.222	31	.299	--	.182	5	.032	1	.333	72
Bill Latham	.600	--	.288	84	.288	--	.600	--	.389	--	.286	--	.188	--
Frank Pastore	.227	--	.319	113	.351	--	.213	--	.294	100	.233	61	.256	--
Mark Portugal	.273	90	.260	55	.267	77	.264	69	.198	10	.171	14	.433	127
Mike Smithson	.289	107	.296	93	.301	113	.285	92	.292	99	.315	116	.352	96
Frank Viola	.241	43	.286	81	.285	97	.251	50	.286	95	.256	76	.333	72
Team Average	.271	12	.286	14	.289	14	.272	12	.282	13	.253	9	.345	12
League Average	.258		.270		.259		.264		.263		.246		.326	

NEW YORK YANKEES

By the end of the 1987 season, Dave Winfield will be 36 years old. The 10-year contract he signed with the Yankees in 1980 will have just three years to run. We're not trying to rush him, but sometime in the foreseeable future we won't have Winfield—the most maligned superstar of the 1980s—to kick around anymore.

Despite 14 outstanding seasons, the last six under the scrutiny of the New York media microscope, Winfield still lacks the general acceptance that most great players have received in the late stages of their careers. Everywhere they go, Pete Rose, Reggie Jackson, and Tom Seaver hear only applause from fans who treat them like grandfathers in need of tender loving care. Winfield's ears ring with boos, even at Yankee Stadium. Winfield has vocal detractors among fans, writers, and his team's own calm, dispassionate owner. Perhaps because of his enormous contract, unprecedented at the time, or his futile performance in the 1981 World Series, or his losing battle with the ghost of Reggie for the hearts of Yankees fans, Winfield has been that rarest of baseball commodities: a superstar disrespected even in his own home town. Like Richie Allen and Dave Kingman—both vastly inferior players by comparison—Winfield has been maligned despite his often spectacular performance.

The time has come to clarify Winfield's standing. So let's take a detailed look at his accomplishments and failures, paying particular attention to the six seasons since he signed his megacontract with New York.

As most of you probably know, George Steinbrenner has often been among Winfield's most vocal critics. Last July, as Winfield battled to escape a season-long slump, Boss George told the press that Winfield hadn't lived up to expectations during his tenure in New York, and specifically that he had been found lacking under pressure. Hmmmm. Let's examine Winfield's performance with the Yankees compared to his last six seasons in San Diego.

Years	G	AB	R	H	2B	3B	HR	RBI	BB	SB	BA	SA	OBA
1975–80	886	3358	533	963	157	34	131	539	411	124	.287	.471	.364
1981–86	847	3290	536	949	174	32	151	608	328	62	.288	.498	.350

The similarity between those six-year periods is uncanny. No one except Steinbrenner can say exactly what he was expecting from Winfield, but the numbers above indicate that Dave is no less the player for New York than he was for San Diego. He has stolen fewer bases and walked less frequently for the Yankees, but significantly increased his extra-base hit and RBI totals. Sounds like a good deal to us.

We can already hear the skeptics. "Of course he drove in more runs. He was batting behind Willie Randolph, Rickey Henderson, and Don Mattingly instead of Enzo Hernandez, Tito Fuentes, and Gene Richards." Forget it. Winfield actually batted with more runners in scoring position during his last six seasons with the Padres than he has in his six years with the Yankees. The reason he has driven in more runs—aside from the fact that he's hit 20 more home runs for New York—has nothing to do with an increase in opportunities. The reason is plain and simple: He has driven in more runs because he's hit better with runners in scoring position.

	1975–80	1981–86
BA with runners in scoring position	.279	.303
RBI opportunities from scoring pos.	1106	1100
Runners driven in from scoring pos.	354	387
Pct. driven in from scoring position	32.0	35.2

Only two players in either league have driven in more runs than Winfield over the past six seasons: Jim Rice and Eddie Murray. Only three full-time starters drove in a higher percentage of runners from scoring position: Murray, Don Mattingly, and Wade Boggs. Incidentally, Winfield's RBI percentage was even higher in Late-Inning Pressure Situations. (Remember that—we'll come back to it later.)

Although consistency is a word rarely connected with Winfield, he is the only player to have 100 or more RBIs in each of the past five seasons. In fact, he's the first player in 20 years to have five consecutive 100-RBI seasons. Thirty players in baseball history have done it, but most played during high-scoring eras. All except four are Hall of Famers: Aaron, Bottomley, Cronin, DiMaggio, Duffy, Foxx, Gehrig, Gehringer, Goslin, Heilmann, Hodges, Bob Johnson, Joe Kelley, Mays, Mize, Musial, Ott, Rosen, Ruth, Simmons, Terry, Thompson, Traynor, Trosky, Williams, and Wilson. And Winfield.

Another thought to keep in mind: Winfield has accomplished all that despite playing in a home ballpark that has certainly suppressed his statistics. Ironically, Winfield had to contend with an uncooperative ballpark during eight years in San Diego as well. (A few years after his departure, the Padres shortened their fences by five to 15 feet, and cut the height of the outfield walls from 18 feet to eight-and-a-half down the lines.) A true measure of Winfield's power is his total of 84 home runs in road games, the most in the American League over the past six seasons.

Shortcomings? He has had some undeniable failures. His 1-for-21 performance in the 1981 World Series, which the Yankees lost to Los Angeles, is his personal ball-and-chain. For an organization that measures success not in wins and losses but in pennant flags waving in the breeze, postseason failure draws life without parole. Unless Winfield has a post-season opportunity to atone for his World Series collapse, it will remain the largest blot on his record. But it's ludicrous to evaluate Winfield on that basis; no player should be viewed as having undone 14 years of excellence in a fortnight. Some of the greatest players in postseason history had bad Series: Babe Ruth was 2-for-17 in 1922; Mickey Mantle was 3-for-25 in 1962; Yogi Berra was a combined 7-for-50 in his first three World Series. But all proved themselves over a period of time. Winfield may never have that opportunity.

On the surface, Winfield's performance in Late-Inning Pressure Situations also supports the claim that he wilts under pressure. His batting average in LIP situations has been lower than his overall mark in each of his six seasons with the Yankees. But as we pointed out earlier—did you remember?—he's driven in a greater percentage of runners from scoring position in LIP Situations than overall, a 38.1 percent mark that ranks 10th among the 300 players with at least 50 opportunities during that period. Does that sound to you like an inability to handle pressure?

The time has come get off Winfield's case, and make the man feel appreciated as his career reaches its golden years. We may not see another like him for a long, long time.

A Sharp Left Turn

For the first time in two decades, the Yankees organization has produced a series of left-handed power hitters, sending Don Mattingly, Mike Pagliarulo, and Dan Pasqua to the Bronx in successive seasons. And these guys are apparently cut from a different cloth from that of Roger Repoz and Steve Whitaker, who burst upon the scene in the 1960s under a blizzard of hype, like Nehru jackets, and were marked down just as quickly.

The three current lefty sluggers hit a total of 75 home runs last season, marking the first time since 1982 that three left-handed Yankees batters each topped 15 home runs. Altogether, New York's left-handed hitters walloped 111 homers (including one by switch-hitter Butch Wynegar facing a right-handed pitcher), their highest single-season total in that department since 1980. That was despite Pasqua's slow start, which banished him to Columbus for the first two months of the season.

Of course we're not talking Ruth, Gehrig, and Dickey here. But for a team with a tradition of power hitters groomed to exploit the cozy right-field porch at Yankee Stadium (including some noteworthy switch-hitters), the development of the young left-handed bulls has some historical significance. Mattingly, Pagliarulo, and Pasqua extend a long line of home-grown talent that includes Ruth, Gehrig, Dickey, Yogi Berra, Mickey Mantle, Joe Pepitone, and Bobby Murcer, as well as some noteworthy adopted sons like Roger Maris, Reggie Jackson, and Graig Nettles.

And what an opportune time to produce a lineup loaded with left-handed power hitters. Last season, for the first time since 1974, right-handed pitchers accounted for more than 70 percent of all starts in the American League. It was also the first time since 1979 that the percentage of starts by right-handed pitchers was greater in the American League than in the National. Note the increasing use of right-handed starters in the A.L. over the past few seasons:

	1977	1978	1979	1980	1981	1982	1983	1984	1985	1986
American League	.70	.67	.69	.65	.64	.64	.62	.66	.66	.71
National League	.68	.66	.69	.65	.79	.76	.75	.70	.69	.65

That trend is of particular interest in the cases of Pagliarulo and Pasqua, who haven't yet demonstrated an ability to handle lefty pitching. In fact, until July 10 last season, left-handed Yankees batters had hit only one home run against a southpaw, and that was by Mattingly. Pagliarulo has a career average of one home run for every 61 at bats vs. left-handers; Pasqua, one per 22 at bats vs. left-handers. Both have career batting averages below .200 against southpaws. But with the progressive decrease in the number of American League starting lefties, why worry?

Youth Will Be Served—On a Platter

Late last summer, we read that NBC broadcaster Tony Kubek attributed the success of many aging American League pitchers to their exploitation of the league's younger hitters. That image—of survivors like Tommy John and Steve Carlton toying with burly, inexperienced hitters like Jose Canseco and Pete Incaviglia—awakened memories of Ali's shuffle, his bolo windup, and his rope-a-dope against hopelessly outclassed opponents. Or of Cousy calmly and deftly dribbling out the clock for a Celtics championship with desperate opponents racing helter-skelter after him.

Great stuff, and an opportunity to explore a topic of particular importance to the Yankees. Last season, pitchers over the age of 35 accounted for 28 percent of New York's innings pitched and 26 percent of its wins, compared to league-wide averages of 11 percent in both categories. (The Yankees' figures would have been higher still had John not spent nearly three months on the disabled list.) Truth be told, we also couldn't resist the opportunity to test Kubek's hypothesis.

We selected a group of American League pitchers who turned 35 before the end of 1986 and pitched at least 40 innings last season. They were Doyle Alexander, Doug Bair, Bert Blyleven, Bill Campbell, Steve Carlton, Mike Flanagan, Ron Guidry, Tommy John, Dennis Leonard, Vern Ruhle, Tom Seaver, Jim Slaton, Don Sutton, Frank Tanana, and Milt Wilcox. We excluded Charlie Hough and the Niekro brothers; their knuckleballs can make even veteran hitters look silly. Then the tricky part—assembling two matched sets of hitters, one composed of inexperienced players, the other of veterans, but otherwise similar. In fact, as close to identical as possible, except for their collective experience.

A line was drawn at 1,000 plate appearances. Players with a career total below that mark were eligibile for the group of inexperienced hitters; all others were eligible for the veteran group. After dividing the American League hitters according to that rule, we matched pairs of players, one from each group, with nearly identical batting averages last season (a margin of two percent was permitted) and a similar number of at bats (within twenty percent). Right-handed batters were matched only with other right-handers. Left-handed hitters formed a common pool with switch-hitters, who bat left-handed about two-thirds of the time. We found 32 such pairs. Some examples:

Inexperienced	BA	AB	H	Experienced	BA	AB	H
Jose Canseco	.240	600	144	Don Baylor	.238	585	139
Wally Joyner	.290	593	172	Pete O'Brien	.290	551	160
Danny Tartabull	.270	511	138	Brian Downing	.267	513	137

The group totals were nearly identical: Each had a composite batting average of .250, and they were separated by eight hits and 37 at bats out of a total pool of more than 25,000 plate appearances among the 64 players involved.

The last step was to examine the collective performance of the veteran pitchers against each of the batters in both groups. The results:

Pitcher	Vs. Inexperienced Opponents			Vs. Experienced Opponents		
	BA	AB	H	BA	AB	H
Doyle Alexander	.233	60	14	.200	70	14
Doug Bair	.308	26	8	.313	16	5
Bert Blyleven	.265	147	39	.189	143	27
Bill Campbell	.179	28	5	.304	23	7
Steve Carlton	.122	49	6	.364	44	16
Mike Flanagan	.264	87	23	.326	92	30
Ron Guidry	.192	104	20	.303	109	33
Tommy John	.238	42	10	.429	28	12
Dennis Leonard	.252	119	30	.300	120	36
Vern Ruhle	.042	24	1	.333	27	9
Tom Seaver	.259	112	29	.180	111	20
Jim Slaton	.255	51	13	.241	58	14
Don Sutton	.222	144	32	.183	93	17
Frank Tanana	.194	98	19	.286	91	26
Milt Wilcox	.286	21	6	.235	34	8
Totals	.229	1112	255	.259	1059	274

Nine of the 15 pitchers were more effective against the younger group than against the experienced hitters. That in itself isn't a significant margin, but notice some of the spreads: Ruhle was nearly 300 points better against the inexperienced hitters; Carlton and John were more than 200 points better. The average difference for the nine pitchers who were better against the young hitters was 130 points; the *largest* individual difference in the other direction was 79 points (vs. Seaver). The totals tell the story more accurately: The younger hitters batted .229, the experienced group .259. And if that doesn't seem like a big spread, consider that that's the difference between the career averages of Ron Kittle and Eric Davis.

In short, when the dust settled, we discovered that Kubek had scored a bulls-eye. This year's Silver Slide Rule goes to the ex-Yankee shortstop.

WON-LOST RECORD BY STARTING POSITION

NEW YORK 90-72	C	1B	2B	3B	SS	LF	CF	RF	P	DH	Leadoff	Relief	Starts
Mike Armstrong	.	.	.	.	.	.	.	.	0-1	.	.	1-5	0-1
Brad Arnsberg	.	.	.	.	.	.	.	.	1-0	.	.	0-1	1-0
Dale Berra	.	.	.	6-10	10-5	.	.	.	.	0-4	.	.	16-19
Henry Cotto	.	.	.	.	.	3-4	7-5	.	.	.	.	.	10-9
Ivan DeJesus	.	.	.	.	0-2	.	.	.	.	.	.	.	0-2
Doug Drabek	.	.	.	.	.	.	.	.	11-10	.	.	.	11-10
Mike Easler	.	.	.	.	.	5-1	.	1-2	.	66-49	.	1-5	72-52
Juan Espino	6-3	.	.	.	.	.	.	.	.	.	.	.	6-3
Mike Fischlin	.	.	7-4	.	9-15	.	.	.	.	.	.	.	16-19
Brian Fisher	.	.	.	.	.	.	.	.	.	.	.	35-27	.
Ken Griffey	.	.	.	.	.	26-15	0-1	.	.	1-0	0-1	.	27-16
Ron Guidry	.	.	.	.	.	.	.	.	14-16	.	.	.	14-16
Ron Hassey	29-19	.	.	.	.	.	.	.	.	1-1	.	.	30-20
Rickey Henderson	.	.	.	.	.	4-4	77-59	.	.	3-2	84-64	.	84-65
Leo Hernandez	.	.	.	3-3	.	.	.	.	.	.	.	.	3-3
Al Holland	.	.	.	.	.	.	.	.	1-0	.	.	9-15	1-0
Tommy John	.	.	.	.	.	.	.	.	6-4	.	.	1-2	6-4
Ron Kittle	.	.	.	.	.	0-1	.	.	.	12-8	.	.	12-9
Bryan Little	.	.	6-7	.	.	.	.	.	.	.	.	.	6-7
Phil Lombardi	0-1	.	.	.	.	7-1	.	.	.	.	.	.	7-2
Don Mattingly	.	90-69	.	0-2	.	.	.	.	.	0-1	1-0	.	90-72
Bobby Meacham	.	.	.	.	32-18	.	.	.	.	.	.	.	32-18
John Montefusco	.	.	.	.	.	.	.	.	.	.	.	1-3	.
Joe Niekro	.	.	.	.	.	.	.	.	14-11	.	.	.	14-11
Scott Nielsen	.	.	.	.	.	.	.	.	5-4	.	.	0-1	5-4
Mike Pagliarulo	.	.	.	78-55	.	.	.	.	.	.	.	.	78-55
Dan Pasqua	.	0-2	.	.	.	31-25	.	6-4	.	2-0	.	.	39-31
Alfonso Pulido	.	.	.	.	.	.	.	.	2-1	.	.	2-5	2-1
Willie Randolph	.	.	77-60	.	.	.	.	.	.	.	0-1	.	77-60
Dennis Rasmussen	.	.	.	.	.	.	.	.	22-9	.	.	.	22-9
Dave Righetti	.	.	.	.	.	.	.	.	.	.	.	60-14	.
Gary Roenicke	.	0-1	.	.	.	8-17	.	1-0	.	3-5	.	.	12-23
Rod Scurry	.	.	.	.	.	.	.	.	.	.	.	13-18	.
Bob Shirley	.	.	.	.	.	.	.	.	1-5	.	.	10-23	1-5
Joel Skinner	28-24	.	.	.	.	.	.	.	.	.	.	.	28-24
Tim Stoddard	.	.	.	.	.	.	.	.	.	.	.	8-16	.
Bob Tewksbury	.	.	.	.	.	.	.	.	12-8	.	.	0-3	12-8
Wayne Tolleson	.	.	0-1	3-2	30-23	.	.	.	.	.	1-1	.	33-26
Claudell Washington	.	.	.	.	.	6-4	6-7	4-2	.	.	4-5	.	16-13
Ed Whitson	.	.	.	.	.	.	.	.	1-3	.	.	4-6	1-3
Dave Winfield	.	.	.	.	.	.	.	78-64	.	2-2	.	.	80-66
Butch Wynegar	27-25	.	.	.	.	.	.	.	.	.	.	.	27-25
Paul Zuvella	.	.	.	.	9-9	.	.	.	.	.	.	.	9-9

Batting Comparisons: Vs. Left-Handers/Right-Handers and Overall/Late Inning Pressure Situations

		BA	Rank	SA	Rank	HR %	Rank		BA	Rank	SA	Rank	HR %	Rank
Dale Berra	vs. Lefties	.254	96	.394	91	2.82	78	Overall	.231	--	.352	--	1.85	--
	vs. Righties	.189	--	.270	--	0.00	--	Pressure	.267	--	.467	--	6.67	--
Henry Cotto	vs. Lefties	.193	160	.228	168	0.00	148	Overall	.213	--	.288	--	1.25	--
	vs. Righties	.261	--	.435	--	4.35	--	Pressure	.000	--	.000	--	0.00	--
Mike Easler	vs. Lefties	.226	131	.302	150	0.94	139	Overall	.302	17	.449	53	2.86	87
	vs. Righties	.323	9	.490	31	3.39	62	Pressure	.279	68	.377	81	0.00	109
Ken Griffey	vs. Lefties	.235	--	.294	--	0.00	--	Overall	.303	16	.475	27	4.55	35
	vs. Righties	.317	11	.512	16	5.49	19	Pressure	.400	3	.567	8	3.33	58
Rickey Henderson	vs. Lefties	.234	117	.443	58	4.17	43	Overall	.263	84	.469	30	4.61	32
	vs. Righties	.276	58	.481	34	4.81	37	Pressure	.347	14	.627	4	6.67	12
Ron Kittle	vs. Lefties	.173	166	.330	138	3.91	50	Overall	.218	155	.420	79	5.59	16
	vs. Righties	.259	87	.503	24	7.11	6	Pressure	.175	155	.316	122	3.51	52
Don Mattingly	vs. Lefties	.358	5	.523	19	2.06	105	Overall	.352	2	.573	2	4.58	33
	vs. Righties	.348	2	.601	2	5.99	14	Pressure	.351	10	.514	27	4.05	41
Bobby Meacham	vs. Lefties	.156	168	.200	170	0.00	148	Overall	.224	--	.280	--	0.00	--
	vs. Righties	.250	104	.310	147	0.00	158	Pressure	.308	--	.308	--	0.00	--
Mike Pagliarulo	vs. Lefties	.196	158	.288	155	1.23	131	Overall	.238	132	.464	35	5.56	17
	vs. Righties	.258	88	.548	7	7.62	4	Pressure	.242	98	.424	57	4.55	37
Dan Pasqua	vs. Lefties	.216	147	.451	52	5.88	21	Overall	.293	25	.525	7	5.71	13
	vs. Righties	.310	17	.541	8	5.68	17	Pressure	.182	148	.432	55	6.82	10
Willie Randolph	vs. Lefties	.311	26	.426	69	2.19	102	Overall	.276	51	.346	138	1.02	141
	vs. Righties	.256	92	.298	154	0.32	155	Pressure	.288	55	.346	100	0.00	109
Gary Roenicke	vs. Lefties	.256	92	.368	106	2.56	83	Overall	.265	--	.368	--	2.21	--
	vs. Righties	.316	--	.368	--	0.00	--	Pressure	.357	--	.357	--	0.00	--
Joel Skinner	vs. Lefties	.215	149	.250	163	0.69	144	Overall	.232	140	.314	153	1.59	121
	vs. Righties	.246	112	.368	110	2.34	97	Pressure	.161	161	.194	163	0.00	109
Wayne Tolleson	vs. Lefties	.284	54	.388	95	1.64	118	Overall	.265	79	.339	142	0.63	153
	vs. Righties	.253	100	.308	149	0.00	158	Pressure	.253	89	.367	86	1.27	106
Dave Winfield	vs. Lefties	.259	90	.523	18	6.09	18	Overall	.262	85	.462	39	4.25	42
	vs. Righties	.264	80	.429	70	3.26	67	Pressure	.240	99	.320	118	1.33	100
Butch Wynegar	vs. Lefties	.236	113	.483	37	6.74	12	Overall	.206	165	.345	139	3.61	67
	vs. Righties	.181	--	.229	--	0.95	--	Pressure	.211	129	.237	156	0.00	109
Team Average	vs. Lefties	.254	11	.397	10	2.73	9	Overall	.271	2	.430	1	3.38	3
	vs. Righties	.281	1	.448	1	3.72	2	Pressure	.278	3	.424	2	3.03	4
League Average	vs. Lefties	.263		.408		2.88		Overall	.262		.408		2.96	
	vs. Righties	.261		.408		2.99		Pressure	.254		.383		2.61	

Additional Miscellaneous Batting Comparisons

	Grass Surface BA	Rank	Artificial Surface BA	Rank	Home Games BA	Rank	Road Games BA	Rank	Runners in Scoring Position BA	Rank	Runners in Scoring Pos and Two Outs BA	Rank	Leading Off Inning OBA	Rank	Runners on 3B with less than 2 Outs RDI %	Rank
Mike Easler	.297	20	.326	19	.288	44	.315	11	.300	41	.222	114	.386	21	.688	31
Ken Griffey	.270	58	.457	--	.244	118	.352	3	.196	154	.111	--	.326	89	.579	78
Rickey Henderson	.253	91	.316	30	.235	130	.290	34	.211	147	.145	163	.365	36	.500	122
Ron Kittle	.200	161	.321	24	.191	166	.241	119	.200	149	.231	102	.330	84	.414	153
Don Mattingly	.335	5	.438	1	.334	7	.367	1	.311	30	.323	29	.421	9	.739	18
Bobby Meacham	.250	96	.080	--	.247	115	.197	--	.160	162	.167	152	.341	--	.300	166
Mike Pagliarulo	.235	128	.256	97	.230	140	.245	110	.234	126	.163	154	.301	126	.536	104
Dan Pasqua	.270	56	.379	5	.271	78	.314	12	.232	129	.212	127	.400	11	.643	48
Willie Randolph	.289	28	.203	152	.311	21	.243	114	.263	83	.290	48	.438	5	.529	105
Gary Roenicke	.263	74	.273	--	.281	--	.250	--	.219	--	.143	--	.243	--	.455	145
Joel Skinner	.232	130	.231	--	.237	124	.226	140	.295	45	.304	37	.253	154	.412	155
Wayne Tolleson	.276	46	.208	148	.261	96	.269	60	.282	62	.264	75	.366	34	.786	11
Dave Winfield	.265	70	.247	109	.272	74	.252	98	.294	46	.256	77	.368	33	.732	21
Butch Wynegar	.220	144	.133	--	.231	139	.178	165	.239	119	.304	37	.292	129	.750	--
Team Average	.271	2	.274	8	.269	6	.274	2	.250	11	.225	12	.350	1	.605	4
League Average	.258		.270		.264		.259		.263		.246		.326		.575	

Pitching Comparisons: Vs. Left-Handers/Right-Handers and Runners On/Bases Empty

		BA	Rank	BB %	Rank	SO %	Rank		BA	Rank	BB %	Rank	SO %	Rank
Doug Drabek	vs. Lefties	.278	76	10.81	92	10.47	92	Runners On	.253	49	9.25	69	11.45	89
	vs. Righties	.223	24	6.79	46	16.98	58	Bases Empty	.251	53	8.68	82	14.97	59
Brian Fisher	vs. Lefties	.316	111	12.50	106	15.91	35	Runners On	.287	98	11.74	107	10.80	100
	vs. Righties	.251	57	6.05	33	15.73	68	Bases Empty	.268	78	5.69	29	20.85	17
Ron Guidry	vs. Lefties	.248	50	5.52	15	22.07	9	Runners On	.276	84	5.38	7	14.87	56
	vs. Righties	.269	88	4.52	15	16.27	63	Bases Empty	.259	64	4.26	9	18.86	30
Tommy John	vs. Lefties	.286	--	8.33	--	8.33	--	Runners On	.200	4	7.09	31	11.81	86
	vs. Righties	.274	97	4.55	16	9.92	122	Bases Empty	.329		3.68	6	7.98	128
Joe Niekro	vs. Lefties	.273	74	13.98	118	8.96	106	Runners On	.323	119	14.17	125	9.84	109
	vs. Righties	.277	102	8.22	72	11.64	108	Bases Empty	.240	40	8.52	81	10.73	110
Scott Nielsen	vs. Lefties	.324	114	7.50	33	5.00	128	Runners On	.280	--	7.87	--	8.99	--
	vs. Righties	.273	--	2.61	--	12.17	--	Bases Empty	.309	122	3.42	5	8.22	124
Dennis Rasmussen	vs. Lefties	.184	3	7.95	44	15.23	42	Runners On	.263	61	8.30	50	17.33	33
	vs. Righties	.225	25	9.28	97	16.17	65	Bases Empty	.194	7	9.41	93	15.31	54
Dave Righetti	vs. Lefties	.304	--	9.88	--	19.75	--	Runners On	.226	14	9.09	67	16.02	44
	vs. Righties	.209	15	7.63	63	18.93	39	Bases Empty	.226	29	6.86	51	22.55	7
Bob Shirley	vs. Lefties	.204	8	5.51	14	22.83	7	Runners On	.326	122	8.70	59	14.49	57
	vs. Righties	.298	120	10.09	106	10.70	115	Bases Empty	.229	31	8.91	89	13.77	83
Tim Stoddard	vs. Lefties	.308	--	12.00	--	8.00	--	Runners On	.211	--	10.09	--	17.43	--
	vs. Righties	.188	6	10.53	112	21.05	25	Bases Empty	.253	--	12.12	--	15.15	--
Bob Tewksbury	vs. Lefties	.252	54	4.58	6	7.39	119	Runners On	.280	92	5.69	12	7.32	126
	vs. Righties	.314	126	6.57	43	10.22	118	Bases Empty	.283	100	5.45	23	9.94	115
Team Average	vs. Lefties	.267	7	9.76	9	12.86	12	Runners On	.274	10	9.07	7	13.22	12
	vs. Righties	.260	9	7.08	3	14.90	12	Bases Empty	.254	7	7.11	2	15.00	11
League Average	vs. Lefties	.265		9.67		13.46		Runners On	.269		9.46		14.39	
	vs. Righties	.259		8.19		16.22		Bases Empty	.256		8.31		15.55	

Additional Miscellaneous Pitching Comparisons

	Grass Surface BA	Rank	Artificial Surface BA	Rank	Home Games BA	Rank	Road Games BA	Rank	Runners in Scoring Position BA	Rank	Runners in Scoring Pos and Two Outs BA	Rank	Leading Off Inning OBA	Rank
Doug Drabek	.253	54	.246	40	.259	71	.244	40	.288	97	.271	86	.329	69
Brian Fisher	.272	87	.305	102	.310	119	.249	46	.274	87	.271	87	.301	43
Ron Guidry	.266	78	.261	57	.284	96	.234	23	.252	65	.267	84	.294	33
Tommy John	.282	103	.250	44	.288	100	.257	56	.148	--	.182	--	.394	120
Joe Niekro	.274	92	.297	94	.306	116	.244	37	.264	79	.275	89	.294	34
Scott Nielsen	.314	121	.200	--	.356	--	.260	60	.310	--	.294	--	.293	32
Dennis Rasmussen	.216	11	.219	15	.204	14	.224	13	.307	113	.255	75	.267	11
Dave Righetti	.223	18	.243	36	.206	16	.244	39	.217	21	.183	23	.295	36
Bob Shirley	.257	61	.500	--	.296	111	.234	24	.282	93	.255	73	.303	45
Tim Stoddard	.243	46	.182	--	.255	--	.197	--	.222	--	.240	--	.375	--
Bob Tewksbury	.283	104	.273	69	.279	93	.284	87	.270	83	.310	114	.333	72
Ed Whitson	.357	--	.283	74	.356	--	.310	--	.298	--	.292	--	.432	--
Team Average	.263	8	.259	3	.274	11	.251	1	.263	8	.258	10	.310	3
League Average	.258		.270		.259		.264		.263		.246		.326	

OAKLAND A'S

Things looked pretty rosy in Oakland late last summer. Although the A's were in the Western Division's basement as late as August 10, Oakland finished the season on a roll, tying Kansas City for third place by defeating the Royals on the final day of the season.

Actually, Oakland's turnaround began just before midseason, about the time the A's hired Tony LaRussa to replace Jackie Moore as manager. LaRussa took over on July 7 with the A's mired in last place, 14 games behind Texas. They bottomed out five days later, but when play resumed following the All-Star break, Oakland was loaded for bear. The A's had a record of 34–56 before the All-Star break, 22 games below .500; they had the third-best mark in the American League over the second half of the season, only a half-game behind California and Detroit:

A.L. East	W–L	Pct.	A.L. West	W–L	Pct.
Detroit	44–31	.587	California	44–31	.587
New York	40–33	.548	**Oakland**	42–30	.583
Toronto	39–33	.542	Texas	40–34	.541
Boston	39–35	.527	Kansas City	36–38	.486
Cleveland	38–39	.494	Minnesota	34–40	.459
Milwaukee	36–39	.480	Chicago	32–44	.421
Baltimore	27–48	.360	Seattle	28–44	.389

How did LaRussa arrange that reversal of form? Well, frankly, he didn't. Much of it was just a matter of luck—bad luck in the first half of the season, good luck in the second. Consider these figures: Oakland was outscored by a total of 39 runs before the All-Star break but finished the first half 22 games under the .500 mark. That's a record you'd expect from a team outscored by more than a run a game. Minnesota allowed 59 more first-half runs than it scored, but had a record only 14 games below .500; Kansas City, outscored by 34 runs—only five fewer than Oakland—was just eight games below even.

While the A's pitching was better after the All-Star break, the difference wasn't nearly enough to suggest such a drastic turnaround. The offense barely improved. Oakland's about-face was reflected mainly in its improvement in one-run games:

	BA	R/G	ERA	1-Run Games	Other Games
Before All-Star Break	.252	4.49	4.52	8–23	26–33
After All-Star Break	.252	4.54	4.05	14–6	28–24

The A's rebound, barely noticed because of their slow start, was of nearly unprecedented proportion in the expansion era. Oakland won 15 more games in the second half (dividing after 81 games) than in the first half last season, equalling the largest difference in the major leagues over the past 25 years. The question for A's fans is, does that kind of improvement in the second half tend to carry over into the next season? Should the A's be more optimistic about the 1987 season than, say, the Montreal Expos? Montreal won two more games than the A's last season, but suffered a second-half collapse after struggling nobly to keep pace with the New York Mets in the first half. The comparative records of the teams, before and after the All-Star break:

	Overall		First Half		Second Half	
Team	W–L	Pct.	W–L	Pct.	W–L	Pct.
Oakland	76–86	.469	34–56	.378	42–30	.583
Montreal	78–83	.484	46–39	.541	32–44	.421

The A's probably expect more out of 1987 than the the Expos do, but our research indicates that neither team should be too optimistic. Over the past quarter-century, teams that played much better in one half of the season than the other rarely improved their records in the next season, regardless of when they played better—early or late. And those that had stronger second halves declined further, on average, than those with stronger first halves.

First, let's look at the teams that seemed to straighten themselves out as the season progressed. From 1962 through 1985, we found 17 teams with second-half winning percentages at least .150 higher (approximately 12 more wins in 81 games) than they had in the first half of the season:

		1st Half	2d Half	Overall		Next Season	
Year	Team	W–L	W–L	W–L	Pct.	W–L	Pct.
1962	Philadelphia	34–47	47–33	81–80	.503	87–75	.537
1964	St. Louis	40–41	53–28	93–69	.574	80–81	.497
1966	Minnesota	38–43	51–30	89–73	.549	91–71	.562
1966	Atlanta	36–45	49–32	85–77	.525	77–85	.475
1969	St. Louis	37–44	50–31	87–75	.537	76–86	.469
1973	Cleveland	28–53	43–38	71–91	.438	77–85	.475
1973	Cincinnati	43–38	56–25	99–63	.611	98–64	.605
1973	Mets	35–46	47–33	82–79	.509	71–91	.438
1974	Yankees	38–43	51–30	89–73	.549	83–77	.519
1974	Pittsburgh	37–44	51–30	88–74	.543	92–69	.571
1975	Baltimore	39–42	51–27	90–69	.566	88–74	.543
1977	Kansas City	44–37	58–23	102–60	.630	92–70	.568
1977	Texas	40–41	54–27	94–68	.580	87–75	.537
1982	San Francisco	37–44	50–31	87–75	.537	79–83	.488
1983	White Sox	42–39	57–24	99–63	.611	74–88	.457
1984	Yankees	36–45	51–30	87–75	.537	97–64	.602
1984	Pittsburgh	31–50	44–37	75–87	.463	57–104	.354

Only five of the 17 teams won more games in the following season. On average, they fell five wins short of their total in the "split" season. Part of that decline might be attributed to the fact that, in general, the teams had good overall records; despite poor first halves, only two had losing records for the entire season. Since, in general, teams collapse toward the center, a majority of teams with winning records suffer modest declines the next season.

But what about the other side of the coin—those teams whose records declined by .150 or more in the second half? Most of them had overall losing records, and so, by the same rule cited above, we'd expect a majority to improve in the following season. Not so: Of 15 teams with that large a second-half collapse, 10 had fewer wins a year later, while an eleventh posted the same record. The group, which had a composite .476 percentage, won an average of three fewer games the next season:

Year	Team	1st Half W–L	2d Half W–L	Overall W–L	Pct.	Next Season W–L	Pct.
1962	Cleveland	47–34	33–48	80–82	.494	79–83	.488
1966	Houston	43–38	29–52	72–90	.444	69–93	.426
1969	Cubs	53–28	39–42	92–70	.568	84–78	.519
1970	Cincinnati	58–23	44–37	102–60	.630	79–83	.488
1971	Cleveland	37–44	23–58	60–102	.370	72–84	.462
1973	Cubs	48–33	29–51	77–84	.478	66–96	.407
1974	Cleveland	45–36	32–49	77–85	.475	79–80	.497
1974	Detroit	43–38	29–52	72–90	.444	57–102	.358
1975	Detroit	35–46	22–56	57–102	.358	74–87	.460
1975	Milwaukee	43–38	25–56	68–94	.420	66–95	.410
1977	Cubs	51–30	30–51	81–81	.500	79–83	.488
1978	Boston	56–25	43–39	99–64	.607	91–69	.569
1978	Oakland	42–39	27–54	69–93	.426	54–108	.333
1982	San Diego	47–34	34–47	81–81	.500	81–81	.500
1983	California	44–37	26–55	70–92	.432	81–81	.500

We don't feel that these statistics guarantee a disappointing 1987 for either Oakland or Montreal. The past 25 years of data offer some compelling evidence, but we also checked all National League teams from 1900 through 1960, trying to find concurring evidence. The results were quite different. We found 38 teams with a difference of at least .150 in winning percentage between the first and second halves, with the dividing line drawn after 77 games:

	Split Season	Next Season	Next Season Better	Worse
Strong First Halves	.484	.522	11	4
Strong Second Halves	.549	.565	13	10

Conclusions: Recent history suggests that teams with very volatile records from one half of a season to the other will decline the next season, regardless of which half was better. But a study of pre-expansion National League teams fails to support that theory. Either way, however, there is no evidence in either survey to indicate that teams that finished strongly over the second half do better the next season than teams that started strong in the first half and limped home from there.

Rookie of the Year of the Rookie

The National Football League touts its quarterback class of 1983, when John Elway, Dan Marino, Ken O'Brien, Jim Kelly, Tony Eason, and Todd Blackledge were all chosen in the first round. Last season's crop of American League rookies was just as impressive, led by Rookie of the Year Jose Canseco, with a noteworthy supporting cast:

Player	AB	R	H	2B	3B	HR	RBI	BB	SB	BA	SA	OBA
Jose Canseco	600	85	144	29	1	33	117	65	15	.240	.457	.318
Pete Incaviglia	540	82	135	21	3	30	88	55	3	.250	.463	.320
Wally Joyner	593	82	172	27	3	22	100	57	5	.290	.457	.348
Ruben Sierra	382	50	101	13	10	16	55	22	7	.264	.476	.302
Cory Snyder	416	58	113	21	1	24	69	16	2	.272	.500	.299
Danny Tartabull	511	76	138	25	6	25	96	61	4	.270	.489	.347

The statistics for the group as a whole bear an uncanny resemblance to the career totals of Lance Parrish, long considered one of the American League's most dangerous hitters. The following table compares Parrish's figures with the totals of the six rookies prorated to reach his career total in plate appearances:

	AB	R	H	2B	3B	HR	RBI	BA	SA	OBA
Rookies (raw totals)	3042	433	803	136	23	150	525	.264	.472	.325
Rookies (prorated)	4202	598	1109	188	32	207	725	.264	.472	.325
Lance Parrish	4273	577	1123	201	23	212	700	.262	.469	.316

Everyone agreed it was tough to pick the leading rookie from that group, and one sore loser stuck out like a sore thumb. After the selection of Canseco, Joyner commented, "No one can tell me Canseco had a better year [than I did]." Well, Wally, the baseball writers told you, and now we're telling you.

For sake of argument, let's consider a two-player race between Canseco and Joyner. (That does require some imagination, since they were the bottom two in slugging average among the six players listed above.) The overall figures are close: Canseco compensated with his power for what he lacked in average; they had identical slugging averages. Canseco drove in more runs than Joyner, and in past seasons, one might have been able to argue that since Wonderful Wally often batted second, he had fewer RBI opportunities than Canseco, who batted third or cleanup for most of the season. But now that we publish those figures each season in the *Analyst*, it's a simple matter to support arguments like that when true and refute them when wrong. This one's wrong—Joyner actually had more opportunities to drive a runner home from scoring position than Canseco did.

Let's take a closer look. Here are the so-called hidden statistics for all the rookie-of-the-year candidates. The following table indicates each player's batting averages with runners on base (ROB), runners in scoring position (SP), two outs and runners on base (2O/ROB), in Late-Inning Pressure Situations (LIP), in Late-Inning Pressure Situations with runners on base (LIP/ROB), the number of opportunities to drive in runners from scoring position (OPP), and the percentage of those runners they drove in (RDI%), that same percentage in Late-Inning Pressure Situations (LIP/RDI%), and the percentage of runners they drove in from third base with less than two outs (3B/ < 2O):

Player	ROB	SP	2O/ ROB	LIP	LIP/ ROB	OPP	RDI%	LIP/ RDI%	3B/ <2O
Canseco	.310	.345	.350	.276	.438	181	34.8	39.3	62.2
Joyner	.320	.294	.350	.329	.278	195	33.8	30.0	69.7
Incaviglia	.231	.236	.229	.302	.333	184	25.5	38.5	58.8
Sierra	.290	.235	.315	.333	.333	126	27.8	12.5	59.1
Snyder	.274	.259	.266	.305	.286	127	30.7	30.0	56.0
Tartabull	.303	.318	.250	.280	.273	163	31.3	33.3	50.0

The remarkable part about those figures is that everyone with the exception of Incaviglia looks even better under such close scrutiny. Canseco and Joyner step prominently to the head of the class, but Jose gets the nod. Comparing those two merely on the basis of batting average gives Joyner an edge, but in key situations, Canseco more than holds his own. He outhit Joyner by 51 points with runners in scoring position, and while Wally holds a substantial edge in Late-Inning Pressure Situations, Canseco batted .438 with runners on in LIP situations, those times when the game was most on the line. Also, you can see that Canseco made more of his RBI opportunities. What's not shown here is that Jose hit 22 home runs with runners on base, the highest total in the majors since 1984, and as many as Wally hit all season, runners on or not.

Joyner, Tartabull, and Snyder would certainly have been rookie award winners in most other seasons. But there's only one winner each year, and in this case the writers chose the best of an outstanding group. To rephrase the old cliche, it's not only too bad somebody had to lose. It's too bad he had to be a sore loser as well.

The Comeback Kid

Did anyone notice the brief but spectacular comeback of Fernando Arroyo? Whaddya mean, you didn't know he was gone? All right, we'll start at the beginning.

Though longtime baseball fans remain skeptical, baseball historians contend that a man named Fernando Arroyo pitched for the Detroit Tigers, Minnesota Twins, and Oakland A's for eight years during the late 1970s and early 1980s. Ask any baseball fan, "Do you remember a pitcher named Arroyo?" They might recall Luis, but none remember Fernando.

Painstaking investigation through some of the seediest sections of Cooperstown produced evidence of an Arroyo who won 24 games. But the trail ends in 1982. Then last season, out of nowhere, this Arroyo—or a man claiming to be Arroyo—resurfaced with the A's. The Oakland management was intrigued but wanted proof that he was who he said he was. After all, not just anyone could pitch for nearly a decade in such anonymity.

Blood types, voice prints, dental records—they all seemed to support the mystery man's claim. Could this be Arroyo? On the evening of August 11, more than 13,000 fans gather at Oakland Coliseum, waiting to see if this man can face the ultimate test. With two out in the top of the ninth inning of a tie game, Oakland manager Tony LaRussa approaches the mound, ostensibly to discuss Seattle's two base runners with pitcher Dave Von Ohlen. Suddenly, LaRussa's right arm goes up, and a hush falls upon the multitude—well, OK, the 13,547, but who's counting?—and Arroyo leaves the bullpen for the pitcher's mound.

Could this be the man, gone so long, who once pitched a perfect game? (All right, so it was against West Palm Beach. And it was only seven innings. You guys. Picky, picky.) Arroyo takes the ball from LaRussa, and with a practiced hand walks Bob Kearney to load the bases. The crowd buzzes.

Now Spike Owen approaches the plate. Arroyo—or the man who calls himself Arroyo—walks Owen, too, forcing in the tie-breaking run. A woman behind home plate shrieks something in Spanish, and her final cry is heard throughout the stadium as she sobs, "Fernando, Fernando." Next up, Domingo Ramos. Only the real Fernando Arroyo would walk Domingo Ramos with the bases loaded. Ramos walks, another run scores, and bedlam breaks loose in the stands.

Distracted by the frenzy, no one is quite sure what happened next. But the facts are these: The man—Arroyo?—left the field. He was not seen again, that night or for the rest of the summer. His season's work was perfection itself: Three batters, three walks; two runs permitted and a loss ensured. Spike Owen, an accessory, was traded by the Mariners within a week for, among others, another mystery man, Trujillo. More than that we can't tell you.

To commemorate his extraordinary 1986 season, we announce the inauguration of the Fernando Arroyo Award, in honor of those who have achieved a perfect year. The 1986 nominees: Lee Smith, who batted five times last season and struck out five times; Harold Reynolds, who came to bat with 121 runners on first base and didn't drive in a single one; Jim Deshaies, who batted seven times with the bases loaded and struck out every time; and Bob Knepper, who batted with 16 runners on third base without bringing one in. Choose carefully. Fernando would want it that way.

WON-LOST RECORD BY STARTING POSITION

OAKLAND 76-86	C	1B	2B	3B	SS	LF	CF	RF	P	DH	Leadoff	Relief	Starts
Darrel Akerfelds	·	·	·	·	·	·	·	·	·	·	·	0-2	·
Joaquin Andujar	·	·	·	·	·	·	·	·	13-13	·	·	1-1	13-13
Fernando Arroyo	·	·	·	·	·	·	·	·	·	·	·	0-1	·
Keith Atherton	·	·	·	·	·	·	·	·	·	·	·	5-8	·
Doug Bair	·	·	·	·	·	·	·	·	·	·	·	11-20	·
Dusty Baker	·	0-1	·	·	·	10-23	12-7	·	·	8-7	·	·	30-38
Bill Bathe	11-23	·	·	·	·	·	·	·	·	·	·	·	11-23
Tim Birtsas	·	·	·	·	·	·	·	·	·	·	·	0-2	*
Bruce Bochte	·	47-59	·	·	·	·	·	·	·	·	·	·	47-59
Jose Canseco	·	·	·	·	·	57-57	·	15-26	·	0-1	·	·	72-84
Chris Codiroli	·	·	·	·	·	·	·	·	7-9	·	·	·	7-9
Mike Davis	·	·	·	·	·	·	13-19	44-52	·	·	3-3	·	57-71
Tom Dozier	·	·	·	·	·	·	·	·	·	·	·	0-4	·
Mike Gallego	·	·	7-5	·	·	·	·	·	·	·	·	·	7-5
Alfredo Griffin	·	·	·	·	76-86	·	·	·	·	·	20-13	·	76-86
Wayne Gross	·	·	·	·	·	·	·	·	·	·	·	·	·
Moose Haas	·	·	·	·	·	·	·	·	9-3	·	·	·	9-3
Steve Henderson	·	·	·	·	·	5-2	·	·	·	·	·	·	5-2
Donnie Hill	·	·	24-29	13-16	·	·	·	·	·	1-0	1-3	·	38-45
Jay Howell	·	·	·	·	·	·	·	·	·	·	·	24-14	·
Stan Javier	·	·	·	·	·	0-1	12-21	·	·	·	1-2	·	12-22
Dave Kingman	·	1-1	·	·	·	·	·	·	·	66-73	·	·	67-74
Bill Krueger	·	·	·	·	·	·	·	·	2-1	·	·	3-5	2-1
Rick Langford	·	·	·	·	·	·	·	·	1-10	·	·	1-4	1-10
Carney Lansford	·	27-25	·	42-52	·	·	·	·	·	1-2	·	·	70-79
Dave Leiper	·	·	·	·	·	·	·	·	·	·	·	9-24	·
Mark McGwire	·	·	10-5	·	·	·	·	·	·	·	·	·	10-5
Bill Mooneyham	·	·	·	·	·	·	·	·	1-5	·	·	17-22	1-5
Dwayne Murphy	·	·	·	·	·	·	50-43	·	·	·	·	·	50-43
Rob Nelson	·	1-0	·	·	·	·	·	·	·	0-1	·	·	1-1
Steve Ontiveros	·	·	·	·	·	·	·	·	·	·	·	21-25	·
Ricky Peters	·	·	·	·	·	2-1	1-0	·	·	·	1-0	·	3-1
Tony Phillips	·	·	39-48	11-13	·	·	0-3	·	·	0-1	50-65	·	50-65
Eric Plunk	·	·	·	·	·	·	·	·	6-9	·	·	0-11	6-9
Jose Rijo	·	·	·	·	·	·	·	·	11-15	·	·	4-9	11-15
Rick Rodriguez	·	·	·	·	·	·	·	·	1-2	·	·	·	1-2
Lenn Sakata	·	·	6-4	·	·	·	·	·	·	·	·	·	6-4
Terry Steinbach	0-3	·	·	·	·	·	·	·	·	·	·	·	0-3
Dave Stewart	·	·	·	·	·	·	·	·	10-7	·	·	2-10	10-7
Mickey Tettleton	37-40	·	·	·	·	·	·	·	·	·	·	·	37-40
Rusty Tillman	·	·	·	·	·	2-2	5-1	·	·	·	·	·	7-3
Dave Von Ohlen	·	·	·	·	·	·	·	·	·	·	·	13-11	·
Jerry Willard	28-20	·	·	·	·	·	·	·	·	0-1	·	·	28-21
Curt Young	·	·	·	·	·	·	·	·	15-12	·	·	1-1	15-12

Batting Comparisons: Vs. Left-Handers/Right-Handers and Overall/Late Inning Pressure Situations

		BA	Rank	SA	Rank	HR %	Rank		BA	Rank	SA	Rank	HR %	Rank
Dusty Baker	vs. Lefties	.227	130	.309	148	1.82	110	Overall	.240	131	.322	150	1.65	120
	vs. Righties	.250	104	.333	134	1.52	120	Pressure	.211	129	.316	122	2.63	68
Bill Bathe	vs. Lefties	.204	155	.408	81	6.12	16	Overall	.184	--	.359	--	4.85	--
	vs. Righties	.167	--	.315	--	3.70	--	Pressure	.083	--	.083	--	0.00	--
Bruce Bochte	vs. Lefties	.216	147	.216	169	0.00	148	Overall	.256	101	.337	145	1.47	125
	vs. Righties	.261	84	.354	121	1.69	114	Pressure	.279	68	.361	90	1.64	90
Jose Canseco	vs. Lefties	.283	57	.476	39	4.28	38	Overall	.240	130	.457	44	5.50	19
	vs. Righties	.220	150	.448	56	6.05	12	Pressure	.276	71	.402	66	1.15	107
Mike Davis	vs. Lefties	.300	38	.475	40	3.33	63	Overall	.268	70	.454	46	3.89	56
	vs. Righties	.257	90	.447	58	4.07	49	Pressure	.164	159	.342	102	4.11	40
Alfredo Griffin	vs. Lefties	.251	100	.295	154	0.00	148	Overall	.285	37	.364	129	0.67	150
	vs. Righties	.302	24	.401	88	1.03	138	Pressure	.307	35	.523	23	3.41	55
Donnie Hill	vs. Lefties	.271	71	.364	110	0.71	143	Overall	.283	41	.378	111	1.18	136
	vs. Righties	.291	32	.387	95	1.51	121	Pressure	.270	75	.349	98	1.59	94
Stan Javier	vs. Lefties	.160	167	.240	165	0.00	148	Overall	.202	--	.272	--	0.00	--
	vs. Righties	.234	--	.297	--	0.00	--	Pressure	.250	--	.333	--	0.00	--
Dave Kingman	vs. Lefties	.217	143	.503	28	8.00	4	Overall	.210	162	.431	66	6.24	6
	vs. Righties	.207	163	.399	90	5.44	21	Pressure	.169	157	.361	89	6.02	21
Carney Lansford	vs. Lefties	.307	31	.460	44	3.17	73	Overall	.284	38	.421	77	3.21	76
	vs. Righties	.274	60	.403	85	3.23	69	Pressure	.190	145	.405	64	5.06	29
Dwayne Murphy	vs. Lefties	.223	133	.287	156	1.06	136	Overall	.252	106	.386	103	2.74	91
	vs. Righties	.264	79	.426	75	3.40	61	Pressure	.250	90	.341	103	0.00	109
Tony Phillips	vs. Lefties	.321	20	.455	48	2.24	99	Overall	.256	98	.345	140	1.13	137
	vs. Righties	.228	138	.296	156	0.65	146	Pressure	.269	76	.373	85	1.49	97
Mickey Tettleton	vs. Lefties	.262	86	.524	17	7.14	10	Overall	.204	166	.389	100	4.74	30
	vs. Righties	.165	171	.299	153	3.15	72	Pressure	.179	153	.393	71	7.14	9
Jerry Willard	vs. Lefties	.348	--	.391	--	0.00	--	Overall	.267	--	.385	--	2.48	--
	vs. Righties	.254	98	.384	98	2.90	82	Pressure	.333	23	.375	82	0.00	109
Team Average	vs. Lefties	.260	8	.403	9	3.04	5	Overall	.252	13	.390	11	3.00	8
	vs. Righties	.248	14	.385	12	2.98	8	Pressure	.235	12	.375	9	2.88	6
League Average	vs. Lefties	.263		.408		2.88		Overall	.262		.408		2.96	
	vs. Righties	.261		.408		2.99		Pressure	.254		.383		2.61	

Additional Miscellaneous Batting Comparisons

	Grass Surface BA	Rank	Artificial Surface BA	Rank	Home Games BA	Rank	Road Games BA	Rank	Runners in Scoring Position BA	Rank	Runners in Scoring Pos and Two Outs BA	Rank	Leading Off Inning OBA	Rank	Runners on 3B with less than 2 Outs RDI %	Rank
Dusty Baker	.238	121	.245	114	.223	148	.254	92	.273	74	.276	64	.324	94	.308	165
Bruce Bochte	.259	78	.233	124	.247	111	.263	73	.257	94	.237	95	.370	31	.550	99
Jose Canseco	.228	134	.298	50	.213	154	.268	62	.345	9	.364	7	.279	139	.622	56
Mike Davis	.251	94	.366	7	.266	87	.269	60	.238	121	.220	120	.385	22	.458	144
Alfredo Griffin	.282	38	.299	49	.281	55	.288	38	.229	131	.230	105	.365	35	.564	92
Donnie Hill	.275	48	.322	23	.293	36	.275	55	.266	81	.302	40	.361	42	.600	65
Dave Kingman	.199	164	.274	76	.212	155	.208	156	.248	110	.229	108	.219	164	.395	160
Carney Lansford	.291	27	.250	103	.319	16	.249	103	.286	55	.244	88	.338	73	.704	24
Dwayne Murphy	.251	95	.259	96	.256	102	.248	106	.244	113	.195	135	.338	72	.524	111
Tony Phillips	.248	104	.291	58	.234	133	.278	51	.350	8	.366	6	.355	49	.500	122
Mickey Tettleton	.191	166	.245	114	.198	161	.210	155	.218	141	.250	83	.353	56	.556	--
Jerry Willard	.261	77	.316	--	.287	45	.243	--	.225	133	.333	21	.435	6	.556	--
Team Average	.246	12	.282	3	.253	14	.251	10	.269	4	.266	3	.330	5	.527	13
League Average	.258		.270		.264		.259		.263		.246		.326		.575	

Pitching Comparisons: Vs. Left-Handers/Right-Handers and Runners On/Bases Empty

		BA	Rank	BB %	Rank	SO %	Rank		BA	Rank	BB %	Rank	SO %	Rank
Joaquin Andujar	vs. Lefties	.254	56	8.53	53	8.24	113	Runners On	.238	29	12.76	115	10.29	105
	vs. Righties	.222	22	8.79	89	14.33	80	Bases Empty	.239	39	6.19	37	11.63	102
Chris Codiroli	vs. Lefties	.259	59	10.14	84	9.22	102	Runners On	.245	37	11.70	106	8.19	123
	vs. Righties	.240	42	8.47	83	12.17	101	Bases Empty	.253	59	7.66	66	12.34	95
Moose Haas	vs. Lefties	.283	82	9.63	71	8.89	108	Runners On	.179	--	11.61	--	12.50	--
	vs. Righties	.164	3	3.87	9	18.06	45	Bases Empty	.240	42	3.37	4	14.61	65
Jay Howell	vs. Lefties	.330	116	13.16	112	14.04	51	Runners On	.287	97	10.17	88	15.25	51
	vs. Righties	.200	--	6.90	--	22.41	--	Bases Empty	.238	--	9.82	--	21.43	--
Rick Langford	vs. Lefties	.337	119	6.19	22	10.62	88	Runners On	.388	--	10.31	--	8.25	--
	vs. Righties	.270	90	7.97	67	13.04	91	Bases Empty	.248	50	5.19	16	14.29	72
Bill Mooneyham	vs. Lefties	.270	70	16.31	123	12.02	73	Runners On	.243	36	12.99	118	18.50	28
	vs. Righties	.271	92	13.00	123	21.08	24	Bases Empty	.305	121	16.83	125	13.86	79
Steve Ontiveros	vs. Lefties	.303	103	11.04	97	15.58	36	Runners On	.252	48	9.80	83	16.99	34
	vs. Righties	.229	28	5.30	25	19.87	32	Bases Empty	.277	86	6.58	45	18.42	34
Eric Plunk	vs. Lefties	.226	26	19.21	127	14.90	45	Runners On	.242	35	16.12	127	16.53	39
	vs. Righties	.199	10	18.72	129	22.55	17	Bases Empty	.190	3	21.36	128	19.66	23
Jose Rijo	vs. Lefties	.241	41	14.73	119	17.01	29	Runners On	.273	77	13.44	120	20.16	18
	vs. Righties	.233	32	9.89	102	25.13	9	Bases Empty	.212	17	11.98	118	20.87	16
Dave Stewart	vs. Lefties	.236	35	10.87	93	13.98	52	Runners On	.214	9	11.79	109	15.71	46
	vs. Righties	.247	50	9.32	98	17.70	50	Bases Empty	.261	67	8.79	83	15.93	50
Curt Young	vs. Lefties	.219	18	6.06	20	18.18	24	Runners On	.256	53	7.12	32	14.24	61
	vs. Righties	.240	45	7.11	55	13.01	92	Bases Empty	.223	28	6.75	47	13.91	77
Team Average	vs. Lefties	.257	5	12.23	14	12.99	11	Runners On	.255	2	11.94	13	14.57	7
	vs. Righties	.238	1	9.45	13	16.92	5	Bases Empty	.240	3	9.77	13	15.52	8
League Average	vs. Lefties	.265		9.67		13.46		Runners On	.269		9.46		14.39	
	vs. Righties	.259		8.19		16.22		Bases Empty	.256		8.31		15.55	

Additional Miscellaneous Pitching Comparisons

	Grass Surface		Artificial Surface		Home Games		Road Games		Runners in Scoring Position		Runners in Scoring Pos and Two Outs		Leading Off Inning	
	BA	Rank	BA	Rank	BA	Rank	BA	Rank	BA	Rank	BA	Rank	OBA	Rank
Joaquin Andujar	.230	29	.297	94	.232	41	.248	45	.198	11	.151	9	.333	72
Chris Codiroli	.258	64	.148	--	.226	35	.275	78	.209	15	.209	41	.306	48
Moose Haas	.253	53	.132	1	.242	--	.204	6	.196	--	.143	--	.270	14
Jay Howell	.301	118	.083	--	.286	--	.233	--	.333	--	.160	--	.295	--
Rick Langford	.274	93	.611	--	.204	--	.371	128	.463	--	.375	--	.267	10
Bill Mooneyham	.261	73	.341	124	.244	50	.298	108	.215	19	.222	51	.424	124
Steve Ontiveros	.260	67	.297	--	.201	10	.331	123	.265	81	.298	105	.400	121
Eric Plunk	.212	8	.224	18	.223	33	.204	7	.255	68	.212	44	.344	86
Jose Rijo	.218	13	.306	105	.205	15	.263	66	.272	86	.229	56	.302	44
Dave Stewart	.245	47	.226	20	.226	36	.261	63	.215	20	.200	30	.329	70
Curt Young	.229	27	.299	96	.199	8	.290	101	.245	51	.213	47	.304	47
Team Average	.244	1	.264	5	.226	1	.269	10	.253	5	.222	1	.322	7
League Average	.258		.270		.259		.264		.263		.246		.326	

SEATTLE MARINERS

When the Seattle Mariners took the field on Friday, May 9 for their first game under manager Dick Williams, they were in sixth place in the American League's Western Division, six games behind the California Angels. By the time the weekend was over, the Mariners had slipped into last place. And five months later, when the season ended, Seattle was still in the basement. Those who took little interest in Seattle's season would be tempted to conclude that Williams had no impact on the Mariners, that his Midas touch, exhibited in reversing the fortunes of the Boston Red Sox in the late 1960s, the Montreal Expos a decade later, and the San Diego Padres a few years after that, had vanished. Maybe yes, maybe no, but the impression that Williams had little effect on Seattle's fortunes, for better or worse, is dead wrong.

No team with the exception of the Chicago White Sox underwent more drastic changes during the 1986 season than the Mariners. Little by little, Williams restructured Seattle's starting lineup, starting rotation, and bullpen, until the team barely resembled the cast of characters he had inherited from Chuck Cottier.

Williams's first move was to recall Harold Reynolds from Calgary to fill the vacancy created at second base when Danny Tartabull was disabled. Upon his return, Tartabull was shifted not only to right field, replacing Al Cowens, but also from the leadoff spot to the middle of the Mariners' batting order. Dave Henderson lost his center field job to John Moses (also recalled from Calgary), who became Seattle's new leadoff batter.

By mid-June, Williams was ready with another round of changes. Out went catcher Steve Yeager (who had shared the position with Bob Kearney) and designated hitter Gorman Thomas; in came Scott Bradley, acquired from the White Sox, and Ken Phelps, promoted from left-handed pinch-hitter to starter. Phelps and Alvin Davis split the first base and DH chores between them.

The final change occurred when Seattle had an opportunity to acquire Boston's promising shortstop Rey Quinones for Henderson and Spike Owen. Within three months, Williams had reworked the Seattle starting lineup as follows:

Pos.	Under Cottier	Under Williams
1B	Alvin Davis	Ken Phelps
2B	Danny Tartabull	Harold Reynolds
SS	Spike Owen	Rey Quinones
3B	Jim Presley	Jim Presley
LF	Phil Bradley	Phil Bradley
CF	Dave Henderson	John Moses
RF	Ivan Calderon	Danny Tartabull
C	Bob Kearney	Scott Bradley
DH	Gorman Thomas	Alvin Davis

Williams juggled the starting rotation a little as well, keeping the nucleus of Mark Langston, Mike Moore, and Mike Morgan, but replacing Milt Wilcox with Bill Swift and leaving no stone unturned in a vain search for a fifth starter. Pete Ladd had been the bullpen closer under Cottier; Williams handed that role to a former ace of Seattle's starting staff, left-hander Matt Young, and added Mark Huismann from the Kansas City Royals to bolster Ladd from the right side.

So it's true that Williams was unable to move Seattle into a challenging position in the Western Division pennant race last season. But no one can say Williams did not leave his mark on the team. He infused the lineup with younger blood, cutting dinosaurs like Cowens, Thomas, and Wilcox, not just from starting positions but from the team. Nevertheless, managers are paid not to change teams, but to change them for the better. So the crucial question is: How will Team Williams respond in 1987?

The Measure of a Manager

We're going to try to answer that question by raising two others: How good a manager is Dick Williams? And to what extent can any manager alter his team's performance?

Despite the importance of the manager's role, no reliable method has been developed to evaluate his performance. Since all teams are not created equal, we can't judge managers with poor or mediocre teams by the same standards we apply to those who perennially run first-division squads. But how do you quantify a manager's performance—his tactical decisions, the evaluation and use of his personnel, his ability to draw every ounce of ability from 24 different personalities? Until now, no one has; we've been left with only a vague consensus of who the best managers are, and with no way to compare them to one another or to measure their value against a typical Brand X skipper.

Over the past year, we developed a mathematical model for evaluating a team's records over its past few seasons, identifying the general trend of improvement or deterioration, and forecasting that team's performance in the next season. The model turned out to be quite a reliable predictor of a team's performance, nailing half the teams within six wins of their final mark, a third of them within half that margin. (This is not as easy as it sounds. Try making your own predictions of each team's record this season and see how close you come.) But there didn't seem to be an awful lot to do with it. It wasn't until we tossed around the idea of measuring managers' contributions that we realized the model's potential. Think about it: What a manager ultimately does is raise or lower his team's performance above or below its expected level. And if you know what to expect, you can judge the result accordingly. A simple example: Based on the recent past, the Minnesota Marshmallows are expected to finish the season with a 75–87 record. Manager Billy Martin leads them to a .500 season (81–81). He has improved the Marshmallows' performance by six wins. And when you look at a longer period of time, so that what you're measuring is a manager's contribution over his whole career, the accuracy of the model increases dramatically. For managers with 1,000 games managed, the system should be accurate within 10 wins (.010 in winning percentage) half the time; for those with 2,500 games, 70 percent should be that accurate.

We know that over the course of one season, lots of things can happen. Pedro Guerrero can twist his leg like a pretzel in spring training; Jose Canseco can emerge from the womb fully formed and ready to battle for the league lead in home runs and runs batted in; a team might add Catfish Hunter or Goose Gossage or both through the free agent market. Players retire, they're traded, or they have career years or wretched seasons. These and a thousand other things can warp an expected level of performance based only on a team's recent history. Nevertheless, time tends to balance fortune and misfortune, and even a casual baseball fan is accustomed to overlooking occasional glitches. If, for example, Wade Boggs were to hit .200 for the first month of the season, we'd say, "Well, it's only 100 at bats. By the end of the season, he'll be hitting his usual .350 or better." Luck evens out.

Because of the limits of 162 games as a sample upon which to base these evaluations, we have restricted our study to managers with at least 1,000 games of experience over the past 25 years. Sure, Tommy Lasorda's Dodgers were plagued by injuries last season, and maybe his performance shouldn't be judged according to a preseason forecasting model that knew nothing about them. But he's the same manager who benefited when his team acquired Rick Honeycutt a few years ago when Honeycutt was leading the American League in ERA. And while he expected better seasons in 1986 from Greg Brock and Jerry Reuss, Steve Sax and Fernando Valenzuela had years beyond even Lasorda's Dodger blue expectations. Over a period of six years (a manager needs that and a little more to meet our 1,000-game minimum), it's almost certain that the good trades and the bad, the career years and the debilitating injuries, the surprises and the disappoint-

ments all tend to even out. And if they don't, and you're looking for a reason why they didn't, the manager's office might not be a bad place to begin that search.

Our system shows that over the past 25 years, only six managers have added at least four wins per season: Bobby Cox, Billy Martin, Danny Ozark, Harry Walker, Earl Weaver, and Dick Williams. And among that group, one emerges as the best of the past quarter-century: Billy Martin.

The following table includes all who have managed at least 1,000 games since 1962, listing their records during that period alongside the expected records of their teams, based on the model's season-by-season projections. (The first two seasons for any franchise have been excluded, so Gene Mauch's totals, for instance, do not include his first two seasons in Montreal.) The differences between the actual and expected records are listed as well, and that difference is expressed not only in total wins, but also in winning percentage and in wins per 162 games:

Manager	Actual Won	Actual Lost	Expected Won	Expected Lost	—Difference— Total	Pct.	W/162G
Billy Martin	1218	990	1127	1081	90.70	.041	6.7
Bobby Cox	621	615	582	654	38.92	.031	5.1
Dick Williams	1470	1335	1390	1415	80.34	.029	4.6
Danny Ozark	618	542	588	572	29.87	.026	4.2
Harry Walker	579	537	551	565	28.37	.025	4.1
Earl Weaver	1480	1060	1416	1124	63.93	.025	4.1
Sparky Anderson	1513	1121	1449	1185	63.81	.024	3.9
Hank Bauer	559	477	536	500	22.67	.022	3.5
Walter Alston	1343	1077	1296	1124	47.36	.020	3.2
Herman Franks	605	521	583	543	22.00	.020	3.2
Danny Murtaugh	757	641	731	667	26.06	.019	3.0
Gene Mauch	1596	1550	1539	1607	57.19	.018	2.9
Whitey Herzog	989	847	966	870	22.84	.012	2.0
Gil Hodges	660	754	649	765	11.28	.008	1.3
Tony LaRussa	567	544	558	553	8.55	.008	1.2
Tommy Lasorda	855	718	845	728	9.60	.006	1.0
Bill Virdon	995	921	985	931	10.07	.005	0.9
Leo Durocher	633	621	631	623	2.47	.002	0.3
Alvin Dark	909	885	906	888	2.83	.002	0.3
Red Schoendienst	1028	944	1035	937	−6.63	−.003	−0.5
Ralph Houk	1510	1478	1520	1468	−10.50	−.004	−0.6
John McNamara	927	952	934	945	−6.99	−.004	−0.6
Don Zimmer	620	601	627	594	−7.03	−.006	−0.9
Chuck Tanner	1271	1262	1292	1241	−21.47	−.008	−1.4
Dave Bristol	593	667	611	649	−18.29	−.015	−2.4
Darrell Johnson	352	388	364	376	−12.12	−.016	−2.7
Pat Corrales	541	578	562	557	−20.77	−.019	−3.0
Bill Rigney	681	721	711	691	−29.86	−.021	−3.5
Joe Torre	543	649	576	616	−32.82	−.028	−4.5

Of course, we're not dealing with an exact measurement here. As explained above, there is an expected margin of error, so that managers rated within .010 of each other in winning percentage are virtually inseparable. In addition, the value of a manager like Earl Weaver, who spent his entire career with a single team, is difficult to estimate. We evaluate Weaver's performance by comparing Baltimore's record in a given season to a prediction based on its records in recent seasons. But those past records are already colored by Weaver's talent. So he is, in a real sense, constantly being compared to himself, a difficult burden even for Earl. Weaver never had the advantage that Martin and Williams have had several times in their careers: namely, cleaning up someone else's mess. And if you don't think that can be an enormous edge, consider the career of Ronald Reagan. The fact that Weaver ranks among the elite under those circumstances is amazing.

Martin took over losing situations in Minnesota and Detroit, and disasters in Texas and Oakland; Williams took command of sinking ships in Boston, Montreal, and San Diego. Of course, other managers have failed even in "can't-lose" instances such as those (notice Dave Bristol's records in the following table), but Weaver, Anderson, and some others never had the statistical benefit of carrying teams up the ladder on their backs.

To better rate these managers on even terms, we've split their performances into seasons in which they were expected to manage contending teams (an expected winning percentage of .500 or better) and those in which their teams were expected to have losing seasons. (A manager who takes over a team during the season is considered to be managing a non-contender for the remainder of the season.)

Bobby Cox is the standout manager with front-runners, but that result represents only two seasons and its significance is clearly compromised by the small sample size. Danny Ozark placed second to Cox with expected winners, and that's a shocker. Ozark was roundly criticized for a lack of strategic expertise during his successful six-year tenure with Philadelphia. But one of his former players told us that no manager got more out of his players than Ozark, if only because he was so well liked and respected. Our figures suggest, in this case, that tactics may be only a small part of a manager's contribution toward victory.

But Martin, a clear leader when all seasons are considered, falls to fourth, at the top of a virtual four-way tie with Weaver, Williams, and Anderson, when we exclude the seasons in which he managed teams that did not figure to contend. Notice that he moved those losing teams up by more than 10 games over the course of a 162-game schedule. We're not saying that those seasons were invalid tests of Martin's managerial ability; only that given the same opportunities, Weaver and others might have performed just as well.

Dick Williams ranks third overall among the group of 1,000-game managers, and third behind Martin and Walter Alston with teams expected to have losing seasons, adding an average of five wins per season to those teams. His successful turnarounds in Boston, Montreal, and San Diego are obviously what made him attractive to Seattle's management last season. And though Williams failed to improve the Mariners' lot over the final five months of 1986, it should be pointed out that with the three teams mentioned above, Williams didn't take over in midseason, but started with a clean slate in spring training.

With that in mind, our forecasting model predicts a record of 74–88 for Seattle this season. The presence of Williams would suggest that another five wins can be expected, improving the Mariners' forecast to 79–83. But the Mariners might need all of that Williams touch just to make up for the loss of Matt Young and Danny Tartabull. Williams arrived in spring training needing to fill several holes he thought he had plugged last season, and what should have been a promising season now looks like yet another reconstruction project.

Manager	Expected Winning Teams				Expected Losing Teams			
	Yrs.	Diff.	Pct.	W/162G	Yrs.	Diff.	Pct.	W/162G
Walter Alston	13	33.43	.016	2.6	2	13.93	.043	7.0
Sparky Anderson	16	61.76	.024	4.0	1	2.05	.020	3.2
Hank Bauer	5	14.24	.020	3.2	2	8.43	.020	3.3
Dave Bristol	3	9.02	.019	3.0	7	−27.31	−.035	−5.7
Pat Corrales	4	−9.57	−.020	−3.2	5	−11.20	−.018	−2.9
Bobby Cox	2	21.88	.068	11.0	6	17.04	.019	3.0
Alvin Dark	6	−0.71	−.001	−0.1	6	3.54	.004	0.7
Leo Durocher	6	3.12	.003	0.6	3	−0.65	−.003	−0.6
Herman Franks	5	13.57	.017	2.7	2	8.43	.026	4.2
Whitey Herzog	9	15.80	.011	1.8	4	7.04	.019	3.0
Gil Hodges	2	−7.94	−.025	−4.0	7	19.22	.018	2.9
Ralph Houk	11	1.33	.001	0.1	8	−11.83	−.009	−1.5
Darrell Johnson	3	5.15	.013	2.0	3	−17.27	−.052	−8.4
Tony LaRussa	5	3.58	.005	0.8	4	4.97	.012	2.0
Tommy Lasorda	10	9.77	.006	1.0	1	insufficient data*		
Billy Martin	9	35.50	.026	4.2	8	55.20	.065	10.6
Gene Mauch	9	−3.30	−.003	−0.4	14	60.49	.033	5.3
John McNamara	8	−5.52	−.005	−0.8	6	−1.47	−.002	−0.3
Danny Murtaugh	7	30.75	.027	4.4	3	−4.69	−.018	−2.9
Danny Ozark	4	18.63	.030	4.9	4	11.24	.021	3.4
Bill Rigney	3	−5.45	−.014	−2.3	7	−24.41	−.024	−3.9
R. Schoendienst	12	−5.78	−.003	−0.5	1	insufficient data**		
Chuck Tanner	10	−14.74	−.009	−1.5	7	−6.73	−.004	−0.6
Joe Torre	2	−3.23	−.010	−1.6	6	−29.59	−.034	−5.5
Bill Virdon	9	−2.96	−.002	−0.4	5	13.03	.019	3.1
Harry Walker	4	10.12	.019	3.1	4	18.25	.031	5.0
Earl Weaver	15	60.51	.026	4.2	2	3.42	.018	3.0
Dick Williams	8	29.92	.025	4.0	11	50.42	.031	5.1
Don Zimmer	5	6.36	.009	1.4	4	−13.39	−.028	−4.5

* 4 games in 1976
** 37 games in 1980

WON-LOST RECORD BY STARTING POSITION

SEATTLE 67-95	C	1B	2B	3B	SS	LF	CF	RF	P	DH	Leadoff	Relief	Starts
Jim Beattie									0-7			0-2	0-7
Karl Best												5-21	
Barry Bonnell		0-3				3-4				1-0			4-7
Phil Bradley						57-77	2-3				2-3		59-80
Scott Bradley	21-28									1-1			22-29
Mickey Brantley							9-16				6-9		9-16
Mike Brown									0-2			0-4	0-2
Ivan Calderon						0-1	1-1	9-20					10-22
Al Cowens						0-1	6-10			0-1			6-12
Alvin Davis		43-56								11-21			54-77
Steve Fireovid									0-1			2-7	0-1
Lee Guetterman									2-2			7-30	2-2
Dave Henderson							13-28	13-16		13-9			39-53
Dave Hengel						0-5		0-2		2-6			2-13
Mark Huismann									0-1			13-22	0-1
Ross Jones			1-1	1-1									2-2
Bob Kearney	24-36												24-36
Pete Ladd												22-30	
Mark Langston									16-20				16-20
Paul Mirabella												2-6	
Mike Moore									19-18			1-0	19-18
Mike Morgan									13-20			1-3	13-20
John Moses		0-3				42-47				1-1	30-37		43-51
Rickey Nelson										0-1			0-1
Edwin Nunez									1-0			0-13	1-0
Spike Owen					48-64						5-9		48-64
Ken Phelps		24-29								24-26			48-55
Jim Presley				63-91									63-91
Rey Quinones					12-23						1-5		12-23
Domingo Ramos			1-5	2-3	6-7						0-2		9-15
Jerry Reed									4-0			2-5	4-0
Harold Reynolds			54-71								16-22		54-71
Bill Swift									5-12			1-11	5-12
Danny Tartabull			12-19	1-0		7-7		39-47		0-3	7-8		59-76
Gorman Thomas										14-26			14-26
Mike Trujillo									2-2			2-5	2-2
Dave Valle	3-6	0-4											3-10
Milt Wilcox									3-7			0-3	3-7
Steve Yeager	19-25												19-25
Matt Young									2-3			31-29	2-3

Batting Comparisons: Vs. Left-Handers/Right-Handers and Overall/Late Inning Pressure Situations

		BA	Rank	SA	Rank	HR %	Rank		BA	Rank	SA	Rank	HR %	Rank
Phil Bradley	vs. Lefties	.325	14	.421	73	1.59	120	Overall	.310	11	.445	55	2.28	102
	vs. Righties	.305	22	.453	51	2.50	92	Pressure	.284	60	.378	79	0.00	109
Scott Bradley	vs. Lefties	.214	--	.357	--	0.00	--	Overall	.300	21	.432	65	2.27	103
	vs. Righties	.306	20	.437	62	2.43	95	Pressure	.351	10	.378	79	0.00	109
Alvin Davis	vs. Lefties	.246	106	.270	161	0.00	148	Overall	.271	59	.426	71	3.76	61
	vs. Righties	.280	51	.479	36	5.04	30	Pressure	.222	117	.403	65	5.56	23
Bob Kearney	vs. Lefties	.267	82	.427	68	2.67	79	Overall	.240	129	.377	112	2.94	83
	vs. Righties	.225	143	.349	124	3.10	75	Pressure	.296	47	.407	62	0.00	109
John Moses	vs. Lefties	.291	48	.418	74	1.82	110	Overall	.256	100	.333	146	0.75	148
	vs. Righties	.242	115	.301	152	0.35	154	Pressure	.231	105	.269	143	0.00	109
Ken Phelps	vs. Lefties	.237	111	.390	92	1.69	115	Overall	.247	119	.526	6	6.98	2
	vs. Righties	.249	107	.554	6	8.07	3	Pressure	.216	122	.510	29	7.84	6
Jim Presley	vs. Lefties	.323	17	.506	24	3.80	53	Overall	.265	80	.463	37	4.38	37
	vs. Righties	.245	113	.448	57	4.59	39	Pressure	.310	32	.655	2	9.20	3
Rey Quinones	vs. Lefties	.214	150	.272	160	0.00	148	Overall	.218	157	.295	163	0.64	151
	vs. Righties	.220	151	.306	151	0.96	139	Pressure	.083	171	.083	171	0.00	109
Harold Reynolds	vs. Lefties	.205	153	.274	159	0.85	141	Overall	.222	141	.290	164	0.22	164
	vs. Righties	.229	136	.296	157	0.00	158	Pressure	.154	162	.192	164	0.00	109
Danny Tartabull	vs. Lefties	.304	34	.464	43	2.40	92	Overall	.270	62	.489	18	4.89	28
	vs. Righties	.259	86	.497	25	5.70	15	Pressure	.280	66	.467	40	4.00	42
Steve Yeager	vs. Lefties	.268	79	.366	108	2.44	89	Overall	.208	--	.269	--	1.54	--
	vs. Righties	.180	--	.225	--	1.12	--	Pressure	.333	--	.333	--	0.00	--
Team Average	vs. Lefties	.263	7	.385	12	2.10	13	Overall	.253	11	.399	9	2.87	9
	vs. Righties	.250	13	.403	9	3.13	6	Pressure	.235	11	.391	6	3.61	2
League Average	vs. Lefties	.263		.408		2.88		Overall	.262		.408		2.96	
	vs. Righties	.261		.408		2.99		Pressure	.254		.383		2.61	

Additional Miscellaneous Batting Comparisons

	Grass Surface BA	Rank	Artificial Surface BA	Rank	Home Games BA	Rank	Road Games BA	Rank	Runners in Scoring Position BA	Rank	Runners in Scoring Pos and Two Outs BA	Rank	Leading Off Inning OBA	Rank	Runners on 3B with less than 2 Outs RDI %	Rank
Phil Bradley	.264	71	.333	17	.324	12	.293	30	.257	98	.286	53	.426	8	.522	113
Scott Bradley	.271	--	.319	28	.347	5	.245	112	.306	35	.316	32	.358	47	.636	50
Mickey Brantley	.236	--	.149	166	.171	--	.213	--	.150	--	.200	--	.341	--	.000	--
Al Cowens	.167	--	.192	156	.206	--	.167	--	.217	--	.333	--	.167	--	.667	--
Alvin Davis	.225	139	.299	48	.281	56	.261	78	.295	44	.238	93	.362	40	.600	65
Bob Kearney	.192	--	.267	87	.295	35	.193	163	.224	135	.269	70	.229	163	.231	167
John Moses	.266	63	.251	102	.232	137	.285	42	.317	23	.324	28	.323	97	.615	60
Ken Phelps	.178	169	.292	56	.287	45	.206	157	.268	79	.178	149	.374	29	.625	53
Jim Presley	.214	151	.293	55	.307	27	.219	144	.294	47	.278	61	.301	124	.528	108
Rey Quinones	.250	96	.157	165	.234	132	.201	161	.238	122	.156	157	.283	136	.471	142
Domingo Ramos	.094	--	.224	129	.191	--	.173	--	.154	--	.214	--	.231	--	.111	--
Harold Reynolds	.184	167	.247	108	.227	142	.218	146	.211	146	.155	158	.301	125	.636	50
Danny Tartabull	.274	49	.268	83	.272	75	.267	64	.318	22	.288	51	.309	115	.500	122
Steve Yeager	.185	--	.224	130	.217	--	.200	--	.300	--	.313	--	.242	--	1.000	--
Team Average	.225	14	.270	9	.267	7	.239	13	.262	6	.239	9	.320	8	.507	14
League Average	.258		.270		.264		.259		.263		.246		.326		.575	

Pitching Comparisons: Vs. Left-Handers/Right-Handers and Runners On/Bases Empty

		BA	Rank	BB %	Rank	SO %	Rank		BA	Rank	BB %	Rank	SO %	Rank
Mike G. Brown	vs. Lefties	.336	118	11.18	98	9.32	100	Runners On	.269	70	10.46	94	15.69	47
	vs. Righties	.291	111	10.40	111	15.03	74	Bases Empty	.348	128	11.05	111	9.39	119
Lee Guetterman	vs. Lefties	.333	117	8.62	54	8.62	109	Runners On	.372	130	9.38	73	8.85	118
	vs. Righties	.354	130	8.44	80	11.81	105	Bases Empty	.320	123	7.45	60	13.04	89
Mark Huismann	vs. Lefties	.308	106	4.81	9	10.10	96	Runners On	.235	24	6.49	21	16.76	36
	vs. Righties	.204	13	7.50	61	25.50	8	Bases Empty	.278	90	5.83	32	18.39	35
Pete Ladd	vs. Lefties	.290	89	9.17	61	18.33	23	Runners On	.238	30	6.94	27	17.36	32
	vs. Righties	.238	38	4.02	11	17.82	48	Bases Empty	.277	86	5.33	20	18.67	32
Mark Langston	vs. Lefties	.184	5	8.70	55	27.17	2	Runners On	.275	83	10.87	97	18.98	25
	vs. Righties	.271	91	12.26	122	22.34	18	Bases Empty	.239	38	12.24	119	26.53	4
Mike Moore	vs. Lefties	.282	80	10.96	95	9.63	99	Runners On	.275	80	8.37	52	10.82	99
	vs. Righties	.263	78	5.16	21	16.21	64	Bases Empty	.271	80	8.09	74	14.20	73
Mike Morgan	vs. Lefties	.274	75	9.68	72	11.29	80	Runners On	.269	68	8.94	63	12.39	79
	vs. Righties	.298	119	8.35	77	13.19	88	Bases Empty	.300	118	9.13	92	12.04	97
Bill Swift	vs. Lefties	.384	127	12.04	103	7.36	121	Runners On	.333	124	9.89	84	12.55	77
	vs. Righties	.239	41	8.09	71	14.04	84	Bases Empty	.305	120	10.70	107	8.12	127
Mike Trujillo	vs. Lefties	.229	28	15.38	122	11.11	81	Runners On	.278	--	7.32	--	10.98	--
	vs. Righties	.224	--	3.75	--	12.50	--	Bases Empty	.190	--	13.04	--	12.17	--
Milt Wilcox	vs. Lefties	.374	125	13.19	113	8.33	112	Runners On	.304	111	10.17	88	8.47	121
	vs. Righties	.272	--	7.83	--	12.17	--	Bases Empty	.347	127	11.35	112	11.35	104
Matt Young	vs. Lefties	.209	12	8.84	59	23.81	5	Runners On	.254	51	8.46	55	20.22	16
	vs. Righties	.302	121	10.61	115	15.11	72	Bases Empty	.298	117	12.37	121	14.52	67
Team Average	vs. Lefties	.288	14	10.13	11	12.45	13	Runners On	.288	14	9.17	8	14.05	10
	vs. Righties	.279	13	8.52	10	16.74	7	Bases Empty	.278	12	9.27	12	15.60	7
League Average	vs. Lefties	.265		9.67		13.46		Runners On	.269		9.46		14.39	
	vs. Righties	.259		8.19		16.22		Bases Empty	.256		8.31		15.55	

Additional Miscellaneous Pitching Comparisons

	Grass Surface BA	Rank	Artificial Surface BA	Rank	Home Games BA	Rank	Road Games BA	Rank	Runners in Scoring Position BA	Rank	Runners in Scoring Pos and Two Outs BA	Rank	Leading Off Inning OBA	Rank
Jim Beattie	.379	--	.321	116	.318	--	.367	--	.280	--	.200	--	.390	--
Karl Best	.342	--	.222	16	.209	--	.348	--	.298	--	.310	114	.250	--
Mike G. Brown	.340	126	.241	35	.323	124	.292	--	.250	59	.341	120	.468	129
Lee Guetterman	.327	--	.359	127	.353	126	.340	125	.374	129	.303	110	.442	128
Mark Huismann	.262	--	.257	52	.258	68	.259	59	.204	12	.151	9	.318	59
Pete Ladd	.243	--	.264	61	.240	47	.282	86	.231	39	.079	2	.356	99
Mark Langston	.270	86	.244	37	.252	60	.259	57	.271	85	.204	37	.351	95
Mike Moore	.279	99	.269	65	.273	81	.273	75	.229	36	.238	63	.362	102
Mike Morgan	.267	80	.295	92	.292	106	.280	83	.257	71	.225	54	.354	97
Edwin Nunez	.342	--	.240	32	.238	--	.326	--	.440	--	.385	--	.100	--
Jerry Reed	.359	--	.240	32	.244	--	.321	--	.219	--	.200	--	.235	--
Bill Swift	.320	122	.318	111	.308	118	.332	124	.353	127	.283	93	.350	94
Mike Trujillo	.240	--	.216	14	.223	33	.233	--	.233	--	.227	--	.319	--
Milt Wilcox	.342	--	.320	114	.267	--	.364	127	.315	--	.355	124	.362	103
Matt Young	.323	--	.247	42	.245	51	.311	116	.247	56	.286	94	.345	89
Team Average	.291	14	.278	12	.273	10	.293	14	.274	11	.242	7	.348	13
League Average	.258		.270		.259		.264		.263		.246		.326	

TEXAS RANGERS

Over the past few seasons, many organizations have rushed their best young prospects to the majors at increasingly younger ages, and with little minor-league experience—in some cases with none. The Texas Rangers are a prime example. At the end of August last season, Texas had six players— a quarter of its active roster—ranked among the 25 youngest players in the majors. Edwin Correa and Ruben Sierra were the two youngest major leaguers of the 1986 season; the others were Mitch Williams (10th youngest), Bobby Witt (17th), Pete Incaviglia (21st), and Mike Loynd (22nd). Loynd pitched for Florida State in the College World Series in June, and then for the Rangers in July following a five-game apprenticeship at Tulsa. Incaviglia joined the Rangers without any minor-league experience, after a much-publicized holdout following his career at Oklahoma State. Witt pitched only 35 innings in the minors, following an amateur career at the University of Oklahoma and with the 1984 U.S. Olympic team. Williams, Sierra, and Correa each had several seasons of pro experience, but only because they signed pro contracts while their peers were standing in line for tickets to "Porky's II"; Correa won five of seven decisions for Sarasota in 1982 at sweet sixteen.

Two seasons ago, the Rangers had one of the oldest starting rotations in the majors. Charlie Hough, Burt Hooton, and Frank Tanana (for half the season) formed its backbone, and despite the presence of several younger pitchers (Mike Mason, for example), Texas was one of only four teams in either league whose starters averaged more than 30 years of age. But last season, with Tanana, Hooton, and Dickie Noles gone, and such young pitchers as Correa, Jose Guzman, Loynd, and Witt in their place, only two teams in the majors had a lower average.

The following table lists the average age of starting pitchers for American League teams in each of the past two seasons, weighted by games started. (A brief digression for the ground rules: Throughout this essay, ages will be computed as of July 1 for the year in question, and averages will be weighted. For example, Charlie Hough started 33 games last season, while Mike Loynd started eight. Hough's age will account for a proportionately larger segment of Texas's team age.)

Team	1986	1985	Diff.
Milwaukee	25.88	30.00	−4.12
Texas	26.42	30.38	−3.96
Kansas City	27.10	25.03	+2.07
Seattle	27.26	26.21	+1.05
Oakland	27.73	29.96	−2.23
Boston	27.56	26.72	+0.84
Toronto	28.43	29.01	−0.58
Detroit	28.87	29.03	−0.16
Baltimore	28.90	28.47	+0.43
Minnesota	29.04	28.76	+0.28
Chicago	29.29	29.60	−0.31
California	30.38	28.33	+2.05
Cleveland	31.42	27.70	+3.72
New York	31.73	33.52	−1.81

Texas had the second-youngest starting rotation in the league last season despite 33 starts by 38-year-old Charlie Hough. This mixture of extreme youth and extreme age— baseball age, that is—was mirrored throughout the squad. Only six major leaguers played last season for managers younger than they were; four of them played for Valentine, the youngest manager in the majors: Toby Harrah, Hough, Bobby Jones, and Tom Paciorek.

The young pitchers had an enormous impact on the Rangers' performance. Rookies started more than 100 games and accounted for nearly that many decisions. The composite statistics of Texas's rookies follow; their totals were the highest in the American League in every category listed below except home runs (Milwaukee allowed 78), and their ERA ranked sixth in the league:

W	L	ERA	GS	CG	SV	IP	H	HR	BB	SO
46	50	4.36	101	6	16	775.2	720	74	464	643

The addition of Sierra and Incaviglia last season and of Oddibe McDowell a year earlier significantly reduced the average age of the Rangers' lineup as well. Weighted by plate appearances, that average declined sharply last season to 27.86 years, nearly two years lower than it had been a year earlier. When the average is weighted by performance categories like home runs and runs batted in, the difference between 1985 and 1986 is even greater, indicating not only that Texas added young players, but that those players made substantial contributions:

Category	—Average Age—		
	1986	1985	Diff.
Home Runs	27.53	29.96	−2.43
Runs Batted In	28.20	30.43	−2.23
Plate Appearances	27.86	29.76	−1.90

The trend toward younger players isn't confined to one or two teams; it's a major-league–wide phenomenon. The average age of major-league rookies—everyday players, that is—has dropped steadily since the early 1980s, a period during which the average age of experienced players has remained fairly constant despite the prevailing economic conditions. It's fair to assume that the average age of veterans would have increased were it not for the growing reluctance of many teams to pay half-million-dollar salaries to utility players. The following averages are weighted by plate appearances:

Group	1986	1985	1984	1983	1982
Rookies	23.88	24.05	24.16	24.27	24.36
Veterans	29.89	29.93	29.83	29.80	29.95

Rookie pitchers have also arrived in the majors at increasingly younger ages over the past five years, dropping from an average of 24.90 in 1982 to 24.23 years last season while the average age of veteran pitchers during that period was rising marginally from 29.52 to 29.58 years. The increasing use of younger rookies resulted last season in one of the greatest rookie crops in baseball history. Sierra and Incaviglia would have been legitimate contenders for rookie of the year in many seasons; Correa and Witt might have been considered in some years. But they were all just afterthoughts compared to players like Jose Canseco, Wally Joyner, and Danny Tartabull. Canseco and Incaviglia were only the third pair of rookies in major-league history to hit 30 home runs in the same season. (Tony Oliva and Jim Ray Hart did it in 1964, Earl Williams and Willie Montanez in 1971.) Compare the combined rookie totals for last season with those of the four previous years:

Year	AB	R	H	2B	3B	HR	RBI	SB	BA	SA	OBA
1986	16237	2060	3999	686	109	400	1841	387	.246	.375	.311
1985	13458	1720	3298	531	120	252	1235	383	.245	.358	.302
1984	17023	2115	4220	689	134	309	1701	489	.247	.358	.309
1983	15823	1957	3821	621	150	332	1702	378	.241	.362	.304
1982	20234	2457	5061	789	147	385	1988	512	.250	.360	.306

Year	W	L	Pct.	ERA	GS	CG	SV	IP	H	BB	SO
1986	326	352	.480	4.26	663	45	128	6056.0	6042	2650	3961
1985	268	256	.511	4.22	503	41	115	5118.0	5054	2048	2982
1984	276	288	.489	3.94	585	68	66	5306.2	5222	1991	3428
1983	310	333	.482	3.85	662	104	113	6182.2	6074	2355	3328
1982	246	273	.473	3.96	503	48	104	5024.1	5011	1922	2825

It's long been held by baseball people that their sport is one of such subtleties that it requires a lengthy apprenticeship—a course in what Red Barber once called "the vicissitudes of baseball." The Rangers appear to have adopted a policy of rushing their best young players into the majors, challenging the conventional wisdom. It will be interesting to watch this trend toward younger players over the next few seasons.

Clearly, there is a bottom limit to the age at which a player can be successful not only in baseball, but in any sport. But despite the remarkable achievements in other sports by athletes who haven't even reached drinking age—Mike Tyson, Wayne Gretzky, Boris Becker, Nadia Comaneci, Steve Cauthen—many in baseball still contend that their sport is different, and that their ballplayers aren't born, they're made, and not overnight. There are already signs that baseball is fast approaching its limit: Notice that the ERA of rookie pitchers has risen sharply in the past two seasons. If teams continue to promote their prospects more rapidly, we'll soon find out just what that limit is.

Gettin' Wasted in the Heat

Last summer, many Rangers fans expressed concern over the collapse of the Texas pitching staff following the All-Star break. On July 6, Texas ranked fourth in the American League with an ERA of 3.96 and led the Western Division by a game and a half over California. In their next 36 games, Rangers pitchers compiled a 5.15 ERA. Texas nearly managed to split those games, posting a 17–19 record on the strength of an offense that averaged more than five runs per game, but by August 16 the Rangers trailed California by two and a half games.

Some fans speculated that it might be normal for young pitchers to experience a serious midseason slump. After all, many young pitchers are unaccustomed to the length of the major-league schedule, while others who thrive on their first pass through the league fail to survive their second. That reasoning sounded good at the time, but we think the inexperience of the Rangers pitchers was a red herring. The real culprit was what we described in the 1985 Analyst as the June swoon, Texas-style.

Although the Cubs and Giants may be better known for their summer slumps, no team deserves that reputation more than the Rangers. Many contend that the Rangers swoon from the effects of the heat of the Texas summer, and our figures do nothing to refute that claim. When statisticians study trends, they often use what's called the Cox and Stuart trend test. Here's how it works: We've divided each Rangers season (with the exclusion of the strike-shortened 1972 and 1981 seasons) into five-game segments and accumulated their record over the years in each of those segments. For example, Texas won two of its first five games in every season from 1973 through 1976, one of its first five in 1977, and so on. Through the 1986 season, the Rangers' overall record in games 1 through 5—discounting the bastard seasons—is 34 wins and 31 losses. The table below shows how the Rangers have fared over those 13 seasons in each five-game bundle:

Game #	W–L	Game #	W–L	Better Record
1–5	34–31	81–85	23–42	1st half
6–10	29–36	86–90	25–40	1st half
11–15	32–33	91–95	26–39	1st half
16–20	35–30	96–100	31–34	1st half
21–25	29–36	101–105	28–37	1st half
26–30	30–35	106–110	34–31	2d half
31–35	28–37	111–115	33–32	2d half
36–40	30–35	116–120	24–41	1st half
41–45	30–35	121–125	26–39	1st half
46–50	31–34	126–130	31–34	same record
51–55	34–31	131–135	28–37	1st half
56–60	29–36	136–140	29–36	same record
61–65	33–32	141–145	30–35	1st half
66–70	39–26	146–150	40–25	2d half
71–75	32–33	151–155	31–34	1st half
76–80	29–36	156–160	40–25	2d half

If a trend exists, it can be spotted by splitting the won-lost records into two sets at midseason and comparing the record in each first-half segment to the corresponding mark in the second half. If Texas plays increasingly worse as the season progresses, the records in the first half should be better in most cases than those of the matching segments in the second half. The results: 10 first-half records were better than their second-half partners, four were worse, two were the same. The Rangers had worse records in each of the first five segments of the second half—which occur during the middle month of summer—than in the corresponding first-half segments. Two of the four pairs in which the second-half record was better occurred during the closing weeks of the season; those are being compared with the hottest weeks of the first half, and anyway, nobody said Arlington ain't a great place to spend the autumn.

Oh, yes, the collapse of the pitching staff. When we took a closer look at Texas's midseason slumps, we found that typically they have been attributable more to pitching problems than to the offense. The following table shows by month the average number of runs per game scored by and against the Rangers during their first 14 seasons in Texas:

	For	Against
April	4.19	4.17
May	4.01	4.49
June	4.27	4.16
July	3.95	4.54
August	4.14	4.38
Sept./Oct.	4.05	4.20
Averages	4.10	4.33

During the disastrous months of July and August, the Rangers scored an average of 4.05 runs per game, only 1.6 percent lower than during the other months, when they averaged 4.12 runs per game. But they allowed an average of 4.46 runs per game in those two months, 4.5 percent higher than their average of 4.26 at other times. So, yes, the Rangers did suffer their traditional summer swoon in 1986; and, yes, the pitching was to blame. But the reason was not inexperience; over the years, Gaylord Perry, Ferguson Jenkins, and Charlie Hough have encountered the same problem that befell Correa, Witt, and the others this season: It's hard to throw 100 pitches in 100-degree heat.

WON-LOST RECORD BY STARTING POSITION

TEXAS 87-75	C	1B	2B	3B	SS	LF	CF	RF	P	DH	Leadoff	Relief	Starts
Bob Brower	-	-	-	-	-	1-0	0-1	-	-	-	-	-	1-1
Curt Brown	-	-	-	-	-	-	-	-	1-0	-	-	-	1-0
Jerry Browne	-	-	4-1	-	-	-	-	-	-	-	-	-	4-1
Steve Buechele	-	-	16-14	60-49	-	0-1	-	-	-	-	-	-	76-64
Ed Correa	-	-	-	-	-	-	-	-	14-18	-	-	-	14-18
Scott Fletcher	-	-	4-5	-	72-58	-	-	-	-	-	11-14	-	76-63
Jose Guzman	-	-	-	-	-	-	-	-	12-17	-	-	-	12-17
Toby Harrah	-	-	41-42	-	-	-	-	-	-	-	2-1	-	41-42
Greg Harris	-	-	-	-	-	-	-	-	-	-	-	40-33	-
Dwayne Henry	-	-	-	-	-	-	-	-	-	-	-	4-15	-
Charlie Hough	-	-	-	-	-	-	-	-	19-14	-	-	-	19-14
Pete Incaviglia	-	-	-	-	-	0-1	-	67-44	-	16-21	-	-	83-66
Bobby Jones	-	1-1	-	-	-	1-2	-	-	-	-	-	-	2-3
Jeff Kunkel	-	-	-	-	2-2	-	-	-	-	-	-	-	2-2
Mike Loynd	-	-	-	-	-	-	-	-	5-3	-	-	1-0	5-3
Mickey Mahler	-	-	-	-	-	-	-	-	3-2	-	-	5-19	3-2
Mike Mason	-	-	-	-	-	-	-	-	14-8	-	-	1-4	14-8
Oddibe McDowell	-	-	-	-	-	-	74-62	-	-	-	73-60	-	74-62
Orlando Mercado	20-11	-	-	-	-	-	-	-	-	-	-	-	20-11
Ron Meridith	-	-	-	-	-	-	-	-	-	-	-	2-3	-
Dale Mohorcic	-	-	-	-	-	-	-	-	-	-	-	27-31	-
Pete O'Brien	-	77-67	-	-	-	-	-	-	-	-	-	-	77-67
Tom Paciorek	-	9-7	-	7-6	-	7-8	-	0-1	-	4-2	-	-	27-24
Larry Parrish	-	-	15-15	-	-	-	-	-	-	52-45	-	-	67-60
Geno Petralli	14-7	-	-	3-3	-	-	-	-	-	-	-	-	17-10
Darrell Porter	11-12	-	-	-	-	-	-	-	-	12-7	-	-	23-19
Dave Rozema	-	-	-	-	-	-	-	-	-	-	-	1-5	-
Jeff Russell	-	-	-	-	-	-	-	-	-	-	-	14-23	-
Ruben Sierra	-	-	-	-	-	26-13	6-10	17-21	-	-	-	-	49-44
Don Slaught	42-43	-	-	-	-	-	-	-	-	2-0	-	-	44-43
Mike Stanley	0-2	-	-	2-2	-	1-0	-	-	-	-	-	-	3-4
Gary Ward	-	-	-	-	-	48-49	3-1	-	-	-	1-0	-	52-50
Curtis Wilkerson	-	-	22-13	-	13-15	-	-	-	-	-	1-0	-	35-28
Mitch Williams	-	-	-	-	-	-	-	-	-	-	-	37-43	-
Bobby Witt	-	-	-	-	-	-	-	-	18-13	-	-	-	18-13
George Wright	-	-	-	-	-	3-1	4-1	3-9	-	-	-	-	10-11
Ricky Wright	-	-	-	-	-	-	-	-	1-0	-	-	6-14	1-0

Batting Comparisons: Vs. Left-Handers/Right-Handers and Overall/Late Inning Pressure Situations

		BA	Rank	SA	Rank	HR %	Rank		BA	Rank	SA	Rank	HR %	Rank
Steve Buechele	vs. Lefties	.273	66	.446	55	3.60	58	Overall	.243	125	.410	86	3.90	51
	vs. Righties	.230	133	.394	93	4.04	51	Pressure	.305	36	.475	38	3.39	56
Scott Fletcher	vs. Lefties	.291	47	.423	70	1.14	133	Overall	.300	21	.400	92	0.57	154
	vs. Righties	.304	23	.389	94	0.28	156	Pressure	.212	127	.273	139	0.00	109
Toby Harrah	vs. Lefties	.233	119	.417	75	1.94	108	Overall	.218	156	.367	124	2.42	101
	vs. Righties	.210	161	.339	132	2.69	90	Pressure	.231	105	.385	74	2.56	69
Pete Incaviglia	vs. Lefties	.306	32	.600	4	7.50	5	Overall	.250	114	.463	36	5.56	17
	vs. Righties	.226	141	.405	84	4.74	38	Pressure	.302	44	.492	35	4.76	35
Oddibe McDowell	vs. Lefties	.219	140	.336	136	2.34	94	Overall	.266	77	.427	70	3.15	78
	vs. Righties	.279	52	.453	50	3.38	63	Pressure	.269	76	.418	60	2.99	66
Pete O'Brien	vs. Lefties	.309	28	.448	53	2.42	91	Overall	.290	26	.468	32	4.17	45
	vs. Righties	.282	46	.477	39	4.92	34	Pressure	.329	27	.548	11	5.48	25
Tom Paciorek	vs. Lefties	.288	52	.344	129	1.60	119	Overall	.286	36	.376	113	1.88	111
	vs. Righties	.284	--	.420	--	2.27	--	Pressure	.344	19	.375	82	0.00	109
Larry Parrish	vs. Lefties	.254	94	.569	9	8.46	3	Overall	.276	52	.509	10	6.03	9
	vs. Righties	.284	43	.485	32	5.09	27	Pressure	.246	95	.443	51	4.92	33
Gene Petralli	vs. Lefties	.182	--	.182	--	0.00	--	Overall	.255	--	.409	--	1.46	--
	vs. Righties	.262	82	.429	71	1.59	118	Pressure	.304	--	.652	--	8.70	--
Darrell Porter	vs. Lefties	.000	--	.000	--	0.00	--	Overall	.265	--	.535	--	7.74	--
	vs. Righties	.277	56	.561	4	6.11	2	Pressure	.138	166	.276	138	3.45	54
Ruben Sierra	vs. Lefties	.253	99	.434	61	4.04	47	Overall	.264	81	.476	25	4.19	44
	vs. Righties	.269	69	.491	28	4.24	46	Pressure	.333	23	.617	6	5.00	30
Don Slaught	vs. Lefties	.303	35	.504	27	4.20	42	Overall	.264	82	.449	52	4.14	46
	vs. Righties	.241	119	.415	81	4.10	48	Pressure	.302	42	.628	3	9.30	2
Gary Ward	vs. Lefties	.317	22	.467	42	2.50	85	Overall	.316	8	.405	90	1.32	133
	vs. Righties	.315	14	.377	106	0.77	144	Pressure	.339	21	.536	16	3.57	50
Curtis Wilkerson	vs. Lefties	.111	--	.111	--	0.00	--	Overall	.237	134	.305	159	0.00	166
	vs. Righties	.254	99	.330	136	0.00	158	Pressure	.200	--	.200	--	0.00	--
Team Average	vs. Lefties	.274	3	.443	3	3.45	3	Overall	.267	5	.428	4	3.33	4
	vs. Righties	.265	5	.421	5	3.28	4	Pressure	.278	2	.452	1	3.68	1
League Average	vs. Lefties	.263		.408		2.88		Overall	.262		.408		2.96	
	vs. Righties	.261		.408		2.99		Pressure	.254		.383		2.61	

Additional Miscellaneous Batting Comparisons

	Grass Surface BA	Rank	Artificial Surface BA	Rank	Home Games BA	Rank	Road Games BA	Rank	Runners in Scoring Position BA	Rank	Runners in Scoring Pos and Two Outs BA	Rank	Leading Off Inning OBA	Rank	Runners on 3B with less than 2 Outs RDI %	Rank
Steve Buechele	.243	113	.244	117	.237	125	.249	105	.232	128	.180	146	.288	131	.824	7
Scott Fletcher	.312	9	.241	119	.308	25	.292	31	.286	55	.240	89	.360	43	.741	17
Toby Harrah	.221	143	.200	154	.207	157	.228	136	.333	14	.231	102	.271	145	.846	4
Pete Incaviglia	.258	83	.203	153	.287	47	.211	152	.236	123	.222	114	.306	118	.588	75
Oddibe McDowell	.258	82	.304	42	.279	58	.252	97	.292	49	.255	78	.323	96	.444	148
Pete O'Brien	.289	30	.296	53	.268	82	.311	14	.344	10	.349	15	.330	83	.704	24
Tom Paciorek	.270	56	.323	22	.233	--	.325	6	.303	38	.286	53	.362	41	.667	38
Larry Parrish	.280	39	.250	103	.289	40	.264	71	.393	2	.392	4	.328	88	.654	43
Darrell Porter	.240	117	.385	--	.299	--	.239	--	.220	--	.227	111	.344	--	.250	--
Ruben Sierra	.249	101	.318	29	.238	120	.286	41	.235	124	.250	83	.250	155	.591	74
Don Slaught	.269	60	.239	120	.302	31	.230	134	.299	42	.343	19	.281	138	.500	122
Gary Ward	.311	10	.347	13	.321	14	.310	16	.378	3	.333	21	.394	15	.600	65
Curtis Wilkerson	.227	135	.286	62	.233	136	.242	118	.260	86	.250	83	.283	135	.600	65
Team Average	.265	4	.280	5	.269	5	.266	6	.293	1	.272	2	.313	13	.626	1
League Average	.258		.270		.264		.259		.263		.246		.326		.575	

Pitching Comparisons: Vs. Left-Handers/Right-Handers and Runners On/Bases Empty

		BA	Rank	BB %	Rank	SO %	Rank		BA	Rank	BB %	Rank	SO %	Rank
Ed Correa	vs. Lefties	.224	24	13.20	114	19.05	21	Runners On	.246	39	12.69	114	21.39	11
	vs. Righties	.221	21	15.33	127	23.82	10	Bases Empty	.203	12	15.50	123	21.28	14
Jose Guzman	vs. Lefties	.309	108	8.15	46	11.03	82	Runners On	.290	99	11.15	101	9.29	115
	vs. Righties	.272	95	7.65	64	12.06	102	Bases Empty	.294	113	5.53	24	13.13	86
Greg Harris	vs. Lefties	.251	53	11.32	100	14.15	49	Runners On	.237	28	9.27	70	20.56	13
	vs. Righties	.251	56	7.20	57	26.00	7	Bases Empty	.267	77	8.88	87	20.56	19
Charlie Hough	vs. Lefties	.204	10	8.83	58	16.02	34	Runners On	.250	43	10.17	91	13.08	66
	vs. Righties	.239	40	9.77	100	14.44	79	Bases Empty	.206	14	8.79	84	16.45	47
Mike Mason	vs. Lefties	.266	63	5.88	19	10.78	84	Runners On	.264	62	7.20	36	15.53	48
	vs. Righties	.255	62	10.31	109	15.26	71	Bases Empty	.252	55	11.46	113	13.62	84
Dale Mohorcic	vs. Lefties	.285	85	8.21	48	8.21	114	Runners On	.268	67	6.10	18	7.93	124
	vs. Righties	.276	100	2.09	1	9.42	127	Bases Empty	.290	108	3.11	2	9.94	114
Jeff Russell	vs. Lefties	.290	90	11.97	102	14.08	50	Runners On	.275	82	9.55	78	15.29	49
	vs. Righties	.212	17	7.14	56	17.35	55	Bases Empty	.218	23	8.84	85	16.57	43
Mitch Williams	vs. Lefties	.203	7	13.29	116	20.28	13	Runners On	.219	11	16.74	128	20.17	17
	vs. Righties	.202	11	20.55	130	20.89	27	Bases Empty	.184	2	19.80	127	21.29	13
Bobby Witt	vs. Lefties	.248	51	21.03	128	19.80	16	Runners On	.231	22	19.67	131	24.59	4
	vs. Righties	.193	8	17.17	128	28.01	5	Bases Empty	.215	19	18.93	126	22.40	8
Team Average	vs. Lefties	.256	4	11.84	13	15.38	1	Runners On	.259	4	12.21	14	16.34	2
	vs. Righties	.243	2	11.52	14	17.90	2	Bases Empty	.240	2	11.19	14	17.16	2
League Average	vs. Lefties	.265		9.67		13.46		Runners On	.269		9.46		14.39	
	vs. Righties	.259		8.19		16.22		Bases Empty	.256		8.31		15.55	

Additional Miscellaneous Pitching Comparisons

	Grass Surface BA	Rank	Artificial Surface BA	Rank	Home Games BA	Rank	Road Games BA	Rank	Runners in Scoring Position BA	Rank	Runners in Scoring Pos and Two Outs BA	Rank	Leading Off Inning OBA	Rank
Ed Correa	.214	9	.260	56	.207	17	.234	22	.206	14	.210	43	.354	98
Jose Guzman	.294	113	.286	78	.288	102	.300	110	.242	48	.200	30	.337	81
Greg Harris	.251	51	.250	44	.251	59	.251	51	.227	33	.236	62	.322	64
Charlie Hough	.217	12	.238	30	.236	44	.208	8	.274	90	.230	58	.239	5
Mike Loynd	.274	--	.391	--	.254	65	.395	--	.255	--	.320	--	.362	--
Mike Mason	.234	35	.346	126	.231	40	.284	89	.244	50	.143	5	.370	108
Dale Mohorcic	.270	85	.317	109	.253	63	.305	113	.236	41	.244	68	.369	107
Jeff Russell	.243	45	.250	44	.252	--	.240	31	.238	43	.298	105	.286	27
Mitch Williams	.200	6	.213	12	.211	21	.193	4	.179	4	.172	17	.368	106
Bobby Witt	.227	25	.190	6	.207	18	.244	37	.222	27	.220	49	.412	123
Team Average	.244	2	.273	10	.245	5	.253	2	.241	2	.228	3	.335	9
League Average	.258		.270		.259		.264		.263		.246		.326	

TORONTO BLUE JAYS

Despite the attention paid over the past few seasons to the effects that different stadiums have on games played there, myths have arisen with little basis in fact. For example, most baseball executives, players, writers, broadcasters, fans, household pets, and garden-variety insects have come to call Minnesota's Metrodome "The Homerdome," considering it to be one of baseball's best home run parks. As we've shown in this year's *Analyst* (and last year's, and the year before that's), it just isn't so. On the other hand, Shea Stadium, considered a tough park for home runs, ranks 12th among the 26 stadiums, only four notches below the Metrodome.

So that you can tell the difference between fact and fiction, we've included in this year's *Analyst* the results of some extensive research on the various effects of each of the major-league stadiums. One example is the effect of artificial turf on extra-base hits. Kansas City and Cleveland tied for the American League lead with 45 triples last season, a seemingly trivial piece of information, but actually the most visible evidence of the proliferation of extra-base hits at carpeted stadiums. That snapped the Toronto's streak of leading the American League in triples for three consecutive seasons, but extended a more significant streak: although there are only four A.L. teams with stadiums with artificial turf, one of those teams has led the league in triples in each of the past 12 seasons. The streak started before there was a franchise in Toronto or Seattle and before there was a Metrodome, at a time when the only stadium in the American League with artificial turf was Royals Stadium.

Synthetic playing surfaces inflate not only the number of triples but the number of doubles as well. We've reworked the data from the Ballparks section to show how enormous the impact is. For each stadium, we computed the ratio of doubles and triples to all hits except home runs. That figure tells how many of the hits that stay in the ballpark go for extra bases. In practical terms, we're measuring the tendency of balls that would be singles on grass fields to scoot between the outfielders in left- and right-center, or down the line past futile dives by first and third basemen.

For example, there were 987 singles, 297 doubles, and 33 triples hit at Exhibition Stadium last season. Doubles and triples accounted for 25.1 percent of those 1,317 hits in the park. (Inside-the-park home runs are an annoyance of no importance that we're going to ignore.) Four stadiums had higher percentages: Veterans Stadium, the Metrodome, Three Rivers Stadium, and the Kingdome, none of which have grass fields. We then compared each percentage to that

in the road games of the stadium's occupant. For example, the extra-base percentage in Toronto's road games, by both the Blue Jays and their opponents, was 21.2; we can conclude that Exhibition Stadium inflated the ratio by approximately 18 percent last season. We performed those calculations for all ballparks over the past five seasons. Not only was Exhibition Stadium's impact the largest, but seven of the next eight positions were also held by fields with artificial turf. Asterisks indicate turfed fields:

Stadium	Home Games	Road Games	Diff.
* Exhibition Stadium	26.0	20.7	+ 26.0%
* Metrodome	25.4	21.2	+ 19.5%
Fenway Park	24.5	20.9	+ 17.3%
* Riverfront Stadium	23.6	20.2	+ 16.3%
* Veterans Stadium	23.8	20.6	+ 15.4%
* Busch Stadium	23.5	20.7	+ 13.3%
* Royals Stadium	24.2	21.7	+ 11.8%
* Olympic Stadium	24.1	22.0	+ 9.5%
* Three Rivers Stadium	23.5	22.0	+ 6.6%
Comiskey Park	23.2	22.3	+ 4.0%
* Kingdome	23.2	22.4	+ 3.6%
Wrigley Field	22.6	22.4	+ 0.9%
County Stadium	21.6	21.4	+ 0.8%
* Astrodome	21.2	21.1	+ 0.3%
Atlanta Stadium	19.3	19.8	− 2.3%
Arlington Stadium	20.8	22.2	− 6.3%
Yankee Stadium	21.2	23.0	− 7.9%
Candlestick Park	19.6	21.3	− 8.2%
Cleveland Stadium	19.9	22.0	− 9.6%
Shea Stadium	19.3	21.3	− 9.6%
San Diego Stadium	19.0	21.2	− 10.5%
Tiger Stadium	20.8	23.7	− 12.0%
Anaheim Stadium	20.0	22.7	− 12.0%
Memorial Stadium	19.4	22.3	− 12.7%
Oakland Coliseum	18.9	23.6	− 19.8%
Dodger Stadium	15.9	22.7	− 30.0%

All 10 fields with synthetic surfaces show an increase in extra-base hits compared to singles, making this one of the truly universal ballpark effects. It also lends a new perspective to the unusual contours of Fenway Park, the only grass-covered stadium that can compete with the slick, plastic fields of the seventies and eighties in the race for the extra base. Fenway's Green Monster has traditionally been thought to aid the home run hitters who could pop balls into the screen; in fact, over the past five seasons, it has caused a *decrease* in homers, while aiding doubles and triples substantially.

There are two other areas on which artificial turf has an enormous and nearly universal impact. In the Kansas City essay we've covered the sharp reduction in errors produced by fake grass. (Royals Stadium is the exception to that rule.) The other area is stolen-base percentage, with every carpeted field except Three Rivers Stadium showing an increase over the past five seasons:

Stadium	Home Games	Road Games	Diff.
* Exhibition Stadium	.710	.630	+ 12.7%
* Royals Stadium	.707	.642	+ 10.1%
* Olympic Stadium	.746	.683	+ 9.2%
* Astrodome	.724	.668	+ 8.5%
* Kingdome	.667	.622	+ 7.2%
* Metrodome	.657	.621	+ 5.8%
Tiger Stadium	.638	.624	+ 2.3%
Oakland Coliseum	.686	.672	+ 2.1%
* Riverfront Stadium	.695	.686	+ 1.4%
Dodger Stadium	.648	.640	+ 1.2%
* Busch Stadium	.722	.717	+ 0.7%
* Veterans Stadium	.723	.719	+ 0.6%
County Stadium	.649	.647	+ 0.4%
Candlestick Park	.659	.662	− 0.4%
Arlington Stadium	.664	.678	− 2.0%
* Three Rivers Stadium	.623	.637	− 2.2%
San Diego Stadium	.675	.692	− 2.5%
Comiskey Park	.685	.703	− 2.5%
Wrigley Field	.663	.686	− 3.4%
Memorial Stadium	.659	.692	− 4.8%
Cleveland Stadium	.648	.690	− 6.2%
Atlanta Stadium	.631	.681	− 7.4%
Shea Stadium	.678	.733	− 7.4%
Anaheim Stadium	.581	.635	− 8.5%
Yankee Stadium	.653	.721	− 9.5%
Fenway Park	.599	.662	− 9.6%

Of the ten leading base stealers of the past three seasons, eight had higher percentages on artificial turf: Vince Coleman (86.0 percent to 79.6 percent), Tim Raines (88.7 to 87.8), Juan Samuel (78.6 to 76.0), Gary Pettis (82.8 to 79.3), Lonnie Smith (79.8 to 75.0), Willie Wilson (85.1 to 80.9), Gary Redus (82.6 to 70.0), and Alan Wiggins (77.4 to 73.5). Only Rickey Henderson (85.7 to 71.4) and Brett Butler (71.6 to 60.6) had higher marks on grass fields.

Triple Threat

With spring training for the 1990 season just three World Series away, the time has come to consider whether Jesse Barfield, George Bell, and Lloyd Moseby are the best outfield of the 1980s. All three combine speed with power, and they provide the Blue Jays with the best outer wall of defense in the American League, if not the majors. Over the past three seasons, the Blue Jays have barely been a winning team with *any* of their three regular outfielders out of the lineup. Toronto's record with Barfield, Bell, and Moseby all starting, compared to other games:

	All Three Starting			Other Games		
Year	W	L	Pct.	W	L	Pct.
1984	39	20	.661	50	53	.485
1985	87	53	.621	12	9	.571
1986	63	59	.516	23	17	.575
Totals	189	132	.589	85	79	.518

Those figures seem to indicate that last season was the poorest of the three seasons that Barfield, Bell, and Moseby played together, but even a quick look at their statistics proves otherwise. All three reached career highs in home runs: Barfield cracked the 40 mark, Bell the 30 mark, and Moseby the 20 mark, all for the first time. Bell also set a career high with a .309 batting average, and Barfield missed his personal record by a single hit. Moseby more or less reproduced his 1985 season. In fact, if you combine the statistics of the starting outfielders in every game last season, Toronto outclasses the rest of the American League by kilometers. The outfields are ranked below by home runs, but Toronto ranked second in batting average as well:

Team	AB	R	H	2B	3B	HR	RBI	BB	SB	BA	SA	OBA
Toronto	1890	308	540	100	12	94	309	175	46	.286	.501	.348
New York	1844	322	500	95	9	82	267	240	104	.271	.466	.356
Texas	1846	286	509	70	20	67	232	164	59	.276	.444	.336
Minnesota	1879	261	522	89	15	64	227	141	42	.278	.443	.331
Oakland	1754	247	426	82	7	64	237	197	54	.243	.407	.320
Baltimore	1823	255	485	71	5	61	225	166	27	.266	.411	.328
Cleveland	1852	301	541	87	22	61	259	150	65	.292	.462	.346
Milwaukee	1788	242	477	79	20	59	225	192	40	.267	.432	.338
Boston	1776	256	494	106	10	58	282	197	8	.278	.447	.351
Detroit	1711	234	446	68	10	53	210	183	71	.261	.405	.336
Seattle	1866	266	502	87	15	52	221	197	53	.269	.415	.341
California	1726	289	445	83	12	51	237	235	68	.258	.408	.349
Chicago	1818	218	463	76	11	37	199	181	64	.255	.370	.324
Kansas City	1906	244	497	85	24	30	164	131	81	.261	.378	.315
Averages	1820	266	489	84	14	60	235	182	56	.269	.428	.337

As we mentioned earlier, Barfield, Bell, and Moseby are also considered the best defensive outfield in the American League. Over the past three seasons, Barfield has led the majors in outfield assists, and Bell is tied for third in the league. The A.L. leaders since 1984: Barfield (51), Kirby Puckett (43), Bell and Brett Butler (41), Tom Brunansky (37), Jim Rice (36), Gary Pettis (33), Harold Baines (31), Dave Henderson and Gary Ward (30).

The following table shows the number of runs scored per nine innings against the Blue Jays over the past three years with each outfielder in his regular position, as well as the rate scored against Toronto with other players at that position. The difference should be a general guide to the value of each player on defense:

		With Regular			With Others			
Pos.	Player	Innings	Runs	R/9I	Innings	Runs	R/9I	Diff.
LF	Bell	3225.2	1440	4.02	1162.1	577	4.47	+ 0.45
CF	Moseby	3968.2	1831	4.15	419.1	186	3.99	− 0.16
RF	Barfield	3233.1	1447	4.03	1154.2	570	4.44	+ 0.42

Barfield's reputation as the best right fielder since Roberto Clemente is supported by these figures, which indicate that he saved Toronto about 50 runs per season with his glove—about as much as he contributed with his bat. Moseby, generally considered a superior center fielder, appears here to be a defensive liability, but two factors make that conclusion questionable. First, Moseby has played all but 419 innings over the past three seasons, so we don't have a large enough sample to compute a valid average for his backups. Second, Toronto's reserve center fielders over the past three seasons—Mitch Webster, Ron Shepherd, and Barfield—are all excellent fielders. Only by comparison to them, we imagine, would Moseby suffer.

The real surprise is Bell. The least talked-about of Toronto's outfielders gets a Barfield-sized number for his defense. We know these figures are, at best, general estimates of defensive ability. But with all the talk about making Bell a designated hitter, we can't help feeling that the publicity for Barfield and Moseby has blinded everyone to the fact that Toronto's perimeter defense is three deep, not two.

Another three years like the last three would certainly mark Toronto's outfield as the best in baseball for the 1980s. Then again, a decade ago, people were saying the same things about Andre Dawson, Ellis Valentine, and Warren Cromartie, Montreal's outfield of the 1970s.

The Pen Is Mightier

The Blue Jays compiled their worst record since 1982, when they last finished below the .500 mark, but last season may prove an important turning point for the club: Toronto finally solved its decade-long bullpen problem.

The team's efforts to improve the pen have been mighty and well documented: After taking a flier on Randy Moffitt in 1983 and spending big bucks on Dennis Lamp a year later, the Jays went for broke when they acquired Bill Caudill and Gary Lavelle in separate trades prior to the 1985 season for Dave Collins, Alfredo Griffin, Jim Gott, and two minor leaguers (including Augie Schmidt, whom Toronto selected ahead of Dwight Gooden in the 1982 free agent draft). The Jays lost the battle and won the war; despite the ineffectiveness of Caudill and Lavelle, they won the 1985 division title. But with a new war to fight in 1986, Toronto was still stuck without a reliable short man when Tom Henke, the Terminator who looked so strong in September 1985, compiled an April ERA that looked more like Thomas a Beckett's birthdate.

Enter Mark Eichhorn. The most unlikely savior imaginable for Toronto's bullpen, Eichhorn was invited to the Blue Jays camp as a nonroster player. He had made only 41 relief appearances in seven years in professional baseball, and didn't have a single career save. But with a new sidearm motion that gave left-handed hitters trouble and right-handers nightmares, Eichhorn was the most effective rookie reliever in the majors last season, Todd Worrell notwithstanding. Eichhorn became only the second pitcher in the 1980s to make at least 50 relief appearances, strike out at least a batter an inning, and allow no more than one base runner per inning. It would be hard to imagine a greater contrast between two pitching styles than between Eichhorn's junk and the Goose's heat:

Year	Player	G	IP	H	BB	HB	BR	SO
1982	Rich Gossage	56	93.0	63	28	0	91	102
1986	Mark Eichhorn	69	157.0	105	45	7	157	166

Eichhorn's sidearm delivery was deadly to opposing right-handed hitters. His ratio of seven strikeouts per walk versus right-handers was the highest in *Player Analysis* history among pitchers with at least 100 strikeouts. The following table shows the statistics of five leading sidearm pitchers last season. The difference in batting average for left- and right-handed batters is more exaggerated against the sidearmers than versus right-handed pitchers in general, but even greater differences occur in extra-base hit percentage (XBH divided by at bats) and strikeout-to-walk ratio. Against left-handed batters, the sidearmers are about as effective as the rest of the right-handed pitchers in the majors. But against right-handed batters, the sidearmers are far better:

	Vs. Left-Handers			Vs. Right-Handers		
Pitcher	BA	XBH%	SO/BB	BA	XBH%	SO/BB
Mark Eichhorn	.259	.108	1.86	.135	.024	7.00
Gene Garber	.246	.051	1.86	.273	.052	5.00
Dan Quisenberry	.310	.041	0.78	.275	.035	3.67
Kent Tekulve	.254	.041	0.86	.227	.046	4.09
Frank Williams	.232	.014	0.78	.198	.000	2.17
Averages	.262	.061	1.35	.211	.033	4.61
All Right-Handers	.265	.079	1.33	.248	.077	2.32

How did Eichhorn, and a rejuvenated Henke, affect the overall performance of the Toronto bullpen? In last season's *Analyst*, we presented a table that showed each American League team's record from 1982 through 1985 in games in which it led after seven innings. We've rerun that table here, along with each team's performance last season. Notice that Toronto, which ranked last over the four-year period, moved to the top half of the league last season, blowing only half as many late leads as in the past:

Leading After Seven Innings

	1982–1985				1986		
Team	W	L	Pct.	Team	W	L	Pct.
Seattle	220	17	.928	Milwaukee	57	2	.966
Chicago	286	23	.926	Boston	82	4	.953
Kansas City	282	23	.925	New York	75	5	.938
New York	277	25	.917	California	72	5	.935
Detroit	290	28	.912	Kansas City	57	4	.934
Boston	268	26	.912	Toronto	65	5	.929
Minnesota	241	24	.909	Detroit	71	8	.899
Baltimore	281	33	.895	Oakland	61	7	.897
California	268	33	.890	Minnesota	59	7	.894
Oakland	220	28	.887	Cleveland	67	8	.893
Milwaukee	247	33	.882	Baltimore	58	7	.892
Texas	212	29	.880	Texas	72	9	.889
Cleveland	216	33	.867	Seattle	54	8	.871
Toronto	264	48	.846	Chicago	60	14	.811
Totals	3572	403	.899	Totals	910	93	.907

Three of Toronto's five such losses last season occurred within a six-day period in August while the Blue Jays were trying to claw their way through the American League's Eastern Division, gaining ground on everyone but division-leading Boston. Toronto can look back at that lost week and think what might have been. After all, despite those three losses, the Jays closed Boston's lead to just three-and-a-half games at the start of September. But Toronto also learned that a strong bullpen can hold a good team together for a run at the pennant even in an off year for the rest of the pitching staff. And the experience gained by Eichhorn and Henke last season may make an even bigger difference in 1987. We suspect we won't have to discuss Toronto's perennial bullpen problems again next year.

WON-LOST RECORD BY STARTING POSITION

TORONTO 86-76	C	1B	2B	3B	SS	LF	CF	RF	P	DH	Leadoff	Relief	Starts
Jim Acker									1-4			4-14	1-4
Doyle Alexander									10-7				10-7
Luis Aquino												3-4	
Jesse Barfield							4-7	78-67					82-74
George Bell						77-69*				7-4			84-73
Bill Caudill												11-28*	
John Cerutti									12-8			10-4	12-8
Jim Clancy									18-16				18-16
Stan Clarke												0-10	
Steve Davis												1-2	
Mark Eichhorn												33-35*	
Tony Fernandez					85-76*						59-47*		85-76
Cecil Fielder		4-1								6-9			10-10
Damaso Garcia			54-48							2-3	15-13		56-51
Don Gordon												3-11	
Kelly Gruber			1-4	12-15				1-1	1-1				15-21
Jeff Hearron	4-3												4-3
Tom Henke												46-17	
Garth Iorg			19-16	22-19*									41-35
Cliff Johnson		0-1								47-41*			47-42
Joe Johnson									9-5*			0-1	9-5
Jimmy Key									20-15		1-0		20-15
Dennis Lamp									0-2			11-26*	0-2
Rick Leach		5-1				8-5		6-5		19-14			38-25
Manny Lee			12-8*		1-0								13-8
Mickey Mahler												0-2	
Buck Martinez	22-24*												22-24
Fred McGriff										1-1			1-1
Lloyd Moseby							76-67*			0-2	11-16		76-69
Rance Mulliniks				52-42						2-1			54-43
Ron Musselman												1-5	
Ron Shepherd						1-2	6-2	1-3*		1-0			9-7
Dave Stieb									16-18			1-2	16-18
Willie Upshaw		77-73*									1-0		77-73
Duane Ward									0-1			0-1	0-1
Ernie Whitt	60-49												60-49

* Also one tie game.

Batting Comparisons: Vs. Left-Handers/Right-Handers and Overall/Late Inning Pressure Situations

		BA	Rank	SA	Rank	HR %	Rank		BA	Rank	SA	Rank	HR %	Rank
Jesse Barfield	vs. Lefties	.284	56	.527	15	6.08	19	Overall	.289	29	.559	3	6.79	3
	vs. Righties	.290	36	.569	3	7.03	7	Pressure	.286	57	.524	22	6.67	12
George Bell	vs. Lefties	.330	13	.553	12	5.59	23	Overall	.309	13	.532	5	4.84	29
	vs. Righties	.301	25	.524	14	4.55	41	Pressure	.248	93	.438	53	3.81	45
Tony Fernandez	vs. Lefties	.317	21	.468	41	2.44	89	Overall	.310	10	.428	67	1.46	126
	vs. Righties	.307	18	.411	83	1.04	137	Pressure	.363	6	.520	25	1.96	80
Cecil Fielder	vs. Lefties	.150	170	.175	172	0.00	148	Overall	.157	--	.325	--	4.82	--
	vs. Righties	.163	--	.465	--	9.30	--	Pressure	.000	--	.000	--	0.00	--
Damaso Garcia	vs. Lefties	.324	16	.432	63	1.44	125	Overall	.281	44	.375	114	1.42	130
	vs. Righties	.260	85	.347	125	1.40	126	Pressure	.294	50	.338	107	0.00	109
Kelly Gruber	vs. Lefties	.217	145	.350	123	3.33	63	Overall	.196	--	.343	--	3.50	--
	vs. Righties	.181	--	.337	--	3.61	--	Pressure	.130	--	.130	--	0.00	--
Garth Iorg	vs. Lefties	.289	50	.410	79	1.81	113	Overall	.260	87	.352	134	0.92	144
	vs. Righties	.230	133	.292	161	0.00	158	Pressure	.262	81	.308	127	0.00	109
Cliff Johnson	vs. Lefties	.290	49	.579	7	7.48	6	Overall	.250	114	.426	73	4.46	36
	vs. Righties	.231	132	.354	122	3.06	77	Pressure	.318	30	.545	13	6.06	20
Rick Leach	vs. Lefties	.130	--	.130	--	0.00	--	Overall	.309	12	.435	62	2.03	109
	vs. Righties	.327	8	.466	44	2.24	99	Pressure	.288	55	.365	88	1.92	81
Buck Martinez	vs. Lefties	.191	162	.309	148	1.82	110	Overall	.181	--	.269	--	1.25	--
	vs. Righties	.160	--	.180	--	0.00	--	Pressure	.350	12	.500	32	5.00	30
Lloyd Moseby	vs. Lefties	.229	128	.378	101	3.19	70	Overall	.253	105	.418	81	3.57	68
	vs. Righties	.264	77	.436	63	3.74	57	Pressure	.225	115	.360	92	3.37	57
Rance Mulliniks	vs. Lefties	.200	--	.250	--	0.00	--	Overall	.259	91	.417	82	3.16	77
	vs. Righties	.262	81	.427	73	3.35	65	Pressure	.200	137	.325	114	2.50	71
Ron Shepherd	vs. Lefties	.205	153	.359	115	2.56	83	Overall	.203	--	.348	--	2.90	--
	vs. Righties	.200	--	.333	--	3.33	--	Pressure	.154	--	.385	--	7.69	--
Willie Upshaw	vs. Lefties	.223	132	.341	132	2.23	100	Overall	.251	110	.368	123	1.57	124
	vs. Righties	.264	78	.381	101	1.27	129	Pressure	.231	105	.319	119	2.20	77
Ernie Whitt	vs. Lefties	.370	2	.565	10	6.52	14	Overall	.268	69	.448	54	4.05	48
	vs. Righties	.255	93	.433	68	3.72	58	Pressure	.353	9	.515	26	4.41	38
Team Average	vs. Lefties	.270	5	.427	5	3.28	4	Overall	.269	4	.427	5	3.17	5
	vs. Righties	.269	4	.426	3	3.12	7	Pressure	.268	5	.405	5	3.09	3
League Average	vs. Lefties	.263		.408		2.88		Overall	.262		.408		2.96	
	vs. Righties	.261		.408		2.99		Pressure	.254		.383		2.61	

Additional Miscellaneous Batting Comparisons

	Grass Surface BA	Rank	Artificial Surface BA	Rank	Home Games BA	Rank	Road Games BA	Rank	Runners in Scoring Position BA	Rank	Runners in Scoring Pos and Two Outs BA	Rank	Leading Off Inning OBA	Rank	Runners on 3B with less than 2 Outs RDI %	Rank
Jesse Barfield	.298	19	.282	66	.278	61	.299	24	.276	67	.233	101	.353	55	.538	103
George Bell	.294	23	.319	26	.327	11	.293	29	.316	24	.337	20	.329	85	.486	137
Tony Fernandez	.294	24	.320	25	.320	15	.300	23	.342	12	.404	1	.336	77	.621	57
Cecil Fielder	.179	--	.136	167	.083	--	.186	--	.160	--	.133	--	.286	--	.400	--
Damaso Garcia	.306	14	.262	90	.282	53	.280	46	.280	63	.222	114	.250	155	.667	38
Kelly Gruber	.211	--	.181	159	.183	--	.208	--	.167	--	.143	--	.185	--	.500	--
Garth Iorg	.326	7	.217	139	.216	151	.306	18	.319	20	.362	10	.319	103	.529	105
Cliff Johnson	.200	161	.282	67	.270	80	.228	135	.258	93	.348	16	.376	28	.556	96
Rick Leach	.277	--	.325	20	.292	37	.328	4	.343	11	.273	67	.203	168	.765	13
Manny Lee	.171	--	.233	125	.244	--	.162	--	.190	--	.222	--	.417	--	.429	--
Buck Martinez	.104	--	.237	123	.188	--	.176	166	.136	--	.111	--	.200	--	.400	156
Lloyd Moseby	.261	76	.248	107	.248	109	.258	84	.257	96	.145	162	.329	85	.700	26
Rance Mulliniks	.246	107	.266	88	.284	52	.233	131	.310	33	.308	36	.344	62	.522	113
Willie Upshaw	.248	103	.254	101	.247	113	.255	90	.227	132	.188	138	.340	69	.594	72
Ernie Whitt	.259	79	.275	73	.265	93	.272	58	.234	127	.182	143	.295	127	.467	143
Team Average	.263	5	.274	7	.271	3	.268	5	.271	3	.254	6	.316	12	.564	9
League Average	.258		.270		.264		.259		.263		.246		.326		.575	

Pitching Comparisons: Vs. Left-Handers/Right-Handers and Runners On/Bases Empty

		BA	Rank	BB %	Rank	SO %	Rank			BA	Rank	BB %	Rank	SO %	Rank
Jim Acker	vs. Lefties	.340	122	11.02	96	6.30	126	Runners On		.265	64	10.24	92	10.24	107
	vs. Righties	.229	--	6.06	--	18.18	--	Bases Empty		.295	114	6.82	50	14.39	69
Doyle Alexander	vs. Lefties	.268	65	4.51	5	10.25	95	Runners On		.294	102	2.20	1	15.93	45
	vs. Righties	.278	103	3.98	10	17.70	51	Bases Empty		.259	66	5.56	25	12.50	92
John Cerutti	vs. Lefties	.240	40	5.04	11	17.27	28	Runners On		.257	55	6.61	23	16.34	42
	vs. Righties	.277	101	8.39	79	13.63	87	Bases Empty		.277	86	8.36	78	13.09	88
Jim Clancy	vs. Lefties	.229	27	7.38	30	13.52	56	Runners On		.283	94	5.70	13	11.40	92
	vs. Righties	.258	69	6.35	37	14.12	83	Bases Empty		.219	24	7.65	65	15.30	55
Mark Eichhorn	vs. Lefties	.259	58	10.03	81	18.69	22	Runners On		.183	2	12.41	113	24.45	5
	vs. Righties	.135	1	4.95	20	34.67	1	Bases Empty		.198	9	3.25	3	29.29	3
Tom Henke	vs. Lefties	.220	19	10.15	85	31.47	1	Runners On		.222	12	9.78	82	27.72	1
	vs. Righties	.158	2	6.94	48	32.37	2	Bases Empty		.164	1	7.53	61	36.02	1
Joe Johnson	vs. Lefties	.288	88	6.90	26	12.32	69	Runners On		.355	129	5.00	3	10.71	101
	vs. Righties	.272	93	4.85	19	8.48	128	Bases Empty		.237	35	6.58	45	10.53	111
Jimmy Key	vs. Lefties	.268	68	5.74	18	21.53	10	Runners On		.229	19	6.53	22	12.79	73
	vs. Righties	.253	58	8.27	75	12.80	94	Bases Empty		.274	82	8.51	80	15.97	49
Dennis Lamp	vs. Lefties	.349	124	9.22	64	4.96	129	Runners On		.382	131	7.24	37	8.55	120
	vs. Righties	.280	106	5.32	26	12.23	99	Bases Empty		.248	51	6.78	48	9.60	117
Mickey Mahler	vs. Lefties	.382	--	8.64	--	6.17	--	Runners On		.310	115	12.86	116	7.14	127
	vs. Righties	.258	70	10.84	116	11.33	111	Bases Empty		.277	89	7.64	64	12.50	92
Dave Stieb	vs. Lefties	.329	115	10.74	90	9.92	98	Runners On		.317	118	8.52	57	12.65	75
	vs. Righties	.262	76	8.05	70	18.16	44	Bases Empty		.281	92	10.24	102	14.76	63
Team Average	vs. Lefties	.278	11	8.66	4	14.51	4	Runners On		.277	12	7.73	2	15.21	4
	vs. Righties	.248	3	7.10	4	17.13	4	Bases Empty		.250	6	7.81	5	16.60	3
League Average	vs. Lefties	.265		9.67		13.46		Runners On		.269		9.46		14.39	
	vs. Righties	.259		8.19		16.22		Bases Empty		.256		8.31		15.55	

Additional Miscellaneous Pitching Comparisons

	Grass Surface BA	Rank	Artificial Surface BA	Rank	Home Games BA	Rank	Road Games BA	Rank	Runners in Scoring Position BA	Rank	Runners in Scoring Pos and Two Outs BA	Rank	Leading Off Inning OBA	Rank
Jim Acker	.264	--	.289	87	.313	121	.248	42	.239	44	.290	98	.333	72
Doyle Alexander	.319	--	.246	41	.231	39	.320	121	.250	59	.204	38	.274	19
Bill Caudill	.265	--	.247	43	.216	--	.294	--	.295	--	.227	--	.300	--
John Cerutti	.256	60	.279	73	.286	98	.256	55	.250	59	.250	70	.347	90
Jim Clancy	.220	15	.259	54	.271	79	.223	11	.297	103	.295	102	.298	40
Mark Eichhorn	.176	1	.201	10	.204	13	.179	2	.194	9	.171	15	.250	7
Don Gordon	.286	--	.323	117	.315	--	.306	--	.393	--	.357	--	.333	--
Tom Henke	.201	--	.185	5	.182	4	.200	5	.219	23	.255	74	.208	2
Joe Johnson	.301	117	.264	60	.268	78	.292	103	.345	--	.250	--	.271	16
Jimmy Key	.215	10	.286	78	.276	86	.236	27	.213	16	.188	27	.341	85
Dennis Lamp	.351	--	.283	75	.278	89	.348	126	.434	130	.472	130	.284	24
Mickey Mahler	.290	108	.313	--	.314	--	.278	82	.324	118	.267	82	.323	65
Dave Stieb	.324	123	.287	83	.292	105	.306	114	.306	112	.294	100	.335	77
Team Average	.254	6	.265	7	.266	8	.256	3	.275	12	.267	12	.311	5
League Average	.258		.270		.259		.264		.263		.246		.326	

National League

ATLANTA BRAVES

You are the manager of the Atlanta Braves. Rafael Ramirez has been your everyday starter at shortstop all season long, but has gone into a slump recently: He's got only two hits in 17 at bats over the past five games. Do you write his name on tonight's lineup card hoping that he'll hit his way out? Or do you give him that day of rest you've been planning for him anyway? Maybe you should sit Ramirez on the bench for a few days, and look at one of those younger players who hasn't been getting much playing time. Whatever your choice, it's a decision every manager faces almost daily throughout the course of the season.

Underlying the decision is a common-sense assumption that players on hot streaks are more likely to hit well in a given game than those approaching that game in a slump. No player has demonstrated that principle better in recent years than Ramirez. Look at the statistics for the past three seasons; Ramirez has hit for more than twice the batting average coming off brief hot streaks than off cold spells:

	After Hot Streaks				After Cold Spells			
Year	G	AB	H	Avg.	G	AB	H	Avg.
1984	13	59	20	.339	12	50	9	.180
1985	8	34	11	.324	10	41	6	.146
1986	5	18	6	.333	10	35	5	.143
Totals	26	111	37	.333	32	126	20	.159

To qualify as a hot streak, Ramirez must have hit .400 or better over his previous five games, and that streak must have covered no more than one week; a cold spell requires that Ramirez hit .125 or worse over a five-game period within seven days. The incentive for Chuck Tanner to keep an eye on Ramirez's performance was simple: When Ramirez was going well coming up to a given game, he hit like Tony Gwynn; when he was going sour, he hit like Steve Trout.

The evidence we've gathered through an extensive analysis of streaks and slumps over the past three seasons indicates beyond the shadow of a doubt that the conventional wisdom is completely wrong. There are two basic conclusions to be drawn from the study. First, a player is just as likely to hit well in a game that follows a slump as he is following a hot week of hitting. Conversely, he is no more likely to take the collar when he's been slumping in recent games than when he's been tattooing the ball. A corollary: Teammates of equal ability are equally likely to have a good game even if one has been hot during the preceding week and the other is in a slump.

Second, there is essentially no such creature as a "streaky hitter." In any season, some players will tend to put good games back to back, sometimes even over periods of a week or more; others consistently follow bad games with good ones and vice versa, rarely putting together streaks of several good games. But the streaky players of one season are as likely to be steady players in the following season as they are to have a second consecutive streaky season. Ramirez notwithstanding, only a handful of players can be considered streaky in each of the past three seasons—we'll name names later—and we can attribute that to chance in the same way we still trust that a nickel is unbiased if we occasionally toss three consecutive heads or tails. It just happens that way sometimes.

Let's go back and take a closer look at our first conclusion: Players are no more likely to hit better when they approach a game on a hot streak than when they have experienced a recent slump. A brief review of the rules: A hot streak consists of five games over a period of no more than seven days during which a player hits .400 or better; a slump is considered to be a set of five games within one week during which a player hits .125 or below.

We examined the 127 players with at least 502 plate appearances during the 1986 season. By using this group of everyday players, we eliminated the bias we might have encountered when players were benched for lack of hitting before their slumps reached the required length. Our study group is composed of everyday players who were rarely benched on account of three or four poor games.

Eight of the players produced what we considered invalid data. To gather a valid sample, we required that a player have at least five games following hot streaks, and at least five after slumps. Several failed to meet those criteria. Steve Jeltz, for example, played only one game last season in which he was deemed "hot" over his five previous games.

Of the remaining 119 players under study, 59 had higher batting averages in the games following hot streaks, and 60 had higher averages in games following slumps. We also accumulated the per-game averages for each player. For instance (referring to Ramirez's 1986 totals above), 18 at bats and six hits in five post-hot streak games yielded averages of 3.6 at bats and 1.2 hits per game following a hot streak. We compiled totals of those averages for the 119 players, and the results follow:

	AB	H	Avg.
Following hot streaks	454.19	120.22	.265
Following cold spells	445.39	121.16	.272

We repeated the study for the 1985 season. Once again, after excluding players with an insufficient number of streaks or slumps from our group of players with 502 plate appearances, we were left with 119 regulars. This time, 60 had higher averages following hot streaks; 59 had higher averages following slumps. Take a moment and think about this: over a two-year period, 238 players qualified, and exactly half hit better when they had experienced recent hot streaks, the other half when they were coming off slumps. The conclusion couldn't be more obvious.

When we applied the same technique to the 1984 season, the results were a little different. We found 107 batters who met our eligibility tests: 42 players hit better following hot streaks, 65 following slumps. That would be a significant variance if it were the only data we had observed, but when combined with the past two seasons, the difference is entirely within the expected random variation for a sample of its size:

	1984	1985	1986	Total
Higher avg. after streaks	42	60	59	161
Higher avg. after slumps	65	59	60	184

We also examined player performance following streaks and slumps of different lengths. When we used a 10-game period (within 15 days) to determine the occurrence of streaks and slumps, more than 60 percent of the players hit significantly better coming off slumps than they did following hot streaks, a result that would occur by chance only once in 1,900 trials:

	1984	1985	1986	Total
Higher avg. after streaks	42	31	34	107
Higher avg. after slumps	57	46	62	165

The conclusion can be drawn here that few everyday players have bats that remain dormant for as long as 10 games. And few can keep a torrid streak going for that period of time, either. (Incidentally, for the 10-game definition, we reduced the average needed to qualify for a streak to .375 and raised that needed for a slump to .150.) But what of these results, obtained when we shortened our definition to cover only a player's *three* previous games (over no more than five days)? There can be no doubt that, in general, players hit significantly better when they have slumped over the three previous games than when they have hit well during that period:

	1984	1985	1986	Total
Higher avg. after streaks	48	55	51	154
Higher avg. after slumps	72	72	76	220

To review the results presented so far: Players hit equally well in games preceded by a five-game hot streak and games preceded by a five-game slump. There is no reason to expect a typical player to continue a roll, good or bad. But when we changed the length of the lead-in period, that is, when we examined performance in a game in relation to the previous three games or the previous 10 games, slumping players out-hit hot players by a significant margin. The unmistakable (though absurd) conclusion is that it is better to rest your regulars when they're hot than when they're cold. The more logical way to use this is to realize that resting a regular because he's cold is no more effective than deciding, say, to rest him every Thursday.

But what of our other contention, that streakiness is not a trait a player carries with him over several seasons? You've undoubtedly read or heard over the years about players like Steve Garvey and Keith Hernandez being consistent hitters without peaks and valleys, and others, Don Baylor and Dave Winfield for instance, swinging from one extreme to the other throughout the season, first hot, then cold, and rarely in between. Despite all that talk, there is no evidence to suggest that players cluster their good and bad games in anything but a random pattern—not only during a particular season, but throughout their careers as well.

There are certain individual traits that players demonstrate year after year, traits that can be traced through the players' statistics. Power hitting, for instance. Players like Jesse Barfield, Dave Kingman, Mike Schmidt, and Glenn Davis, the home run leaders of 1986, will unquestionably hit more home runs in 1987 than players like Vince Coleman, Ozzie Smith, Spike Owen, and Ozzie Guillen. Other qualities, like contact hitting (as seen through a player's strikeout percentage), speed (through stolen bases), and clutch hitting (through a study of performance in Late-Inning Pressure Situations), all tend to reproduce themselves. But not streakiness.

In terms of our research, let's consider what would constitute a streaky hitter or an unstreaky one, whom we will refer to as "steady" or "consistent." The streaky hitters are those who hit well following five-game hot spurts but poorly after five poor games, extending short streaks or slumps into longer ones in a form of baseball inertia. Of course, all streaks, whether good or bad, end at some point; but there are players in a given season who consistently curtail theirs before they get rolling: a good game, three bad ones, two good ones, a bad one, and so on. These are the consistent hitters, who rarely have extended streaks in either direction. The table below compares the 1986 performances of the five streakiest and steadiest hitters in the majors: their overall batting averages, their averages in the first game following hot and cold streaks, and their longest hitting streak of the season. Notice that, on average, the streaky hitters had a longest hitting streak of 11 games (compared to seven for the consistent hitters) despite an overall batting average 31 points lower than the steady group:

Streaky	All	Hot	Not	Streak	Steady	All	Hot	Not	Streak
Cangelosi	.235	.348	.140	13	DeCinces	.256	.158	.364	6
Da. Evans	.241	.314	.176	8	Griffin	.285	.159	.364	11
Lombardozzi	.227	.379	.211	12	Oberkfell	.270	.143	.303	5
Ramirez	.240	.333	.143	12	Pettis	.258	.143	.286	7
Wallach	.233	.290	.152	9	Strawberry	.259	.128	.298	8
Averages	.235	.331	.167	11	Averages	.266	.146	.314	7

But will one season's streaky hitters reproduce that trait in the next season? Let's consider only those players who qualified as streaky according to our study of the 1985 season— that is, all players who hit better off a hot streak than they did following a slump. Were those players any streakier in 1986 than the players who were considered steady (i.e. *unstreaky*) in 1985? Not at all: Among those who had enough streaks and slumps for a valid measurement, 25 hit better in 1986 following hot streaks, and 26 hit better following slumps. How about the steadiest hitters of 1985, those who hit better in games following a poor five-game lead-in? Among that group, 20 qualifiers hit better in 1986 following hot streaks, and 23 hit better following slumps.

Now, just because a certain tendency isn't apparent within a general population doesn't mean that certain segments of the population don't exhibit that trait. So we decided to look at more tightly defined groups. Starting with a group of 161 players who had at least 250 at bats in each of the past three seasons, we extracted two subgroups. The first was composed of all players who were streaky in both 1984 and 1985; the second of those who were steady in both seasons. We then examined the 1986 game-by-game statistics for both groups of players during the 1986 season. If streaky and unstreaky players existed, this would be the acid test:

	Streaky Players	Steady Players
Higher avg. after streaks in 1986	9	11
Higher avg. after slumps in 1986	9	16

The results tend slightly in the direction of repetitiveness: at least the steady players of both 1984 and 1985 were less streaky last season than the streaky players of the two-year trial period. But let's not lose sight of the fact that the 18 supposed streaky players split their 1986 performance right down the middle: Nine were better off hot streaks, nine off slumps.

We also studied several other distinct subgroups of players to see if one was more prone to streaks than others. For instance, it was suggested that free swingers might be more likely to suffer extended slumps than contact hitters. Or that rookies would tend to be streakier than other players. Neither suggestion appears to be true.

In the following table, players are considered free swingers for a given season if they had averages of more than one strikeout for every six plate appearances; contact hitters had averages of fewer than one strikeout per 10 plate appearances. Rookies are determined according to the official baseball criteria. All groups are limited to players with at least 502 plate appearances for the season in question. (Remember: Players who hit better following hot streaks than after slumps are considered streaky.) The three-year totals follow:

	Contact Hitters	Free Swingers	Rookies
Higher avg. after streaks	33	53	5
Higher avg. after slumps	35	47	10

Given the weight of evidence, we'll conclude that streakiness is not a predictable or recurring trait, and take another look this season. In case you'd like to keep score at home, here are lists of the players with the same tendencies in each of the past three seasons:

Streaky Hitters: George Bell (.306 after 5-game streaks, .286 after slumps), Jose Cruz (.345, .263), Steve Garvey (.313, .229), Brook Jacoby (.326, .275), Dale Murphy (.292, .265), Graig Nettles (.247, .216), Rafael Ramirez (.333, .159), Cal Ripken (.310, .300), and Andre Thornton (.243, .222).

Steady Hitters: Juan Beniquez (.258, .301), George Brett (.313, .375), Doug DeCinces (.179, .296), Dwight Evans (.271, .306), Julio Franco (.316, .411), Gary Gaetti (.220, .266), Rich Gedman (.254, .341), Tom Herr (.282, .311), Dave Kingman (.190, .271), Willie McGee (.303, .333), Willie Randolph (.222, .281), Darryl Strawberry (.168, .263), Alan Trammell (.273, .306), Andy Van Slyke (.167, .411), Frank White (.223, .307), and Willie Wilson (.251, .299).

We could be wrong, but it's our guess that the first group will be no streakier in 1987 than the second.

WON-LOST RECORD BY STARTING POSITION

ATLANTA 72-89	C	1B	2B	3B	SS	LF	CF	RF	P	Leadoff	Relief	Starts
Jim Acker												
Doyle Alexander									4-10		0-7	4-10
Paul Assenmacher									8-9		0-1	8-9
Bruce Benedict	19-30										29-32	19-30
Chris Chambliss		6-6										6-6
Jeff Dedmon												
Gene Garber											22-35	
Ken Griffey											36-25	
Albert Hall						30-43						30-43
Terry Harper								7-7		7-7		7-7
						23-32	1-9					24-41
Bob Horner		61-76										61-76
Glenn Hubbard			65-74									65-74
Joe Johnson									8-7			8-7
Brad Komminsk				0-1							0-2	0-1
Rick Mahler									18-21		1-0	18-21
Craig McMurtry									1-4		11-24	1-4
Omar Moreno						9-6	4-3	28-28		34-32		41-37
Darryl Motley							0-3			0-2		0-3
Dale Murphy							68-86	3-2				71-88
Ken Oberkfell			6-13	57-62								63-75
Ed Olwine											8-29	
David Palmer									19-16			19-16
Gerald Perry		0-1				9-7						9-8
Charlie Puleo									1-2		0-2	1-2
Rafael Ramirez			14-26	41-41						0-2		55-67
Paul Runge			1-2									1-2
Billy Sample						1-1		18-23		16-22		19-24
Steve Shields											1-5	
Ted Simmons	2-4	5-6		1-0								8-10
Zane Smith									12-20		7-4	12-20
Cliff Speck												
Bruce Sutter									1-0		1-11	1-0
Andre Thomas					31-48						8-8	31-48
Ozzie Virgil	51-55									0-8		51-55
Duane Ward											1-9	
Claudell Washington								15-17		15-16		15-17

Batting Comparisons: Vs. Left-Handers/Right-Handers and Overall/Late Inning Pressure Situations

Player	Split	BA	Rank	SA	Rank	HR %	Rank	Situation	BA	Rank	SA	Rank	HR %	Rank
Bruce Benedict	vs. Lefties	.269	63	.403	62	0.00	119	Overall	.225	--	.300	--	0.00	--
	vs. Righties	.194	--	.226	--	0.00	--	Pressure	.125	--	.188	--	0.00	--
Chris Chambliss	vs. Lefties	.267	--	.333	--	0.00	--	Overall	.311	--	.426	--	1.64	--
	vs. Righties	.318	13	.439	50	1.87	85	Pressure	.286	45	.393	67	1.79	81
Ken Griffey	vs. Lefties	.259	75	.447	43	3.53	33	Overall	.308	12	.503	8	4.11	26
	vs. Righties	.329	11	.527	5	4.35	29	Pressure	.404	1	.702	1	8.77	1
Terry Harper	vs. Lefties	.271	57	.361	85	1.50	94	Overall	.257	77	.392	77	3.02	50
	vs. Righties	.242	94	.424	57	4.55	25	Pressure	.370	8	.609	5	4.35	26
Bob Horner	vs. Lefties	.313	23	.500	22	4.22	27	Overall	.273	47	.472	21	5.22	10
	vs. Righties	.254	83	.459	27	5.70	6	Pressure	.247	84	.329	93	1.37	94
Glenn Hubbard	vs. Lefties	.220	116	.291	120	0.79	111	Overall	.230	120	.304	128	0.98	115
	vs. Righties	.235	103	.310	118	1.07	107	Pressure	.220	105	.280	112	0.00	102
Omar Moreno	vs. Lefties	.146	--	.220	--	0.00	--	Overall	.234	114	.351	105	1.11	109
	vs. Righties	.245	91	.368	86	1.26	101	Pressure	.196	124	.314	98	1.96	71
Dale Murphy	vs. Lefties	.280	48	.508	20	4.66	19	Overall	.265	60	.477	18	4.72	15
	vs. Righties	.259	67	.463	23	4.75	19	Pressure	.284	49	.632	4	7.37	2
Ken Oberkfell	vs. Lefties	.233	102	.310	117	1.55	88	Overall	.270	53	.360	99	0.99	113
	vs. Righties	.283	34	.377	79	0.80	118	Pressure	.250	76	.325	94	1.25	96
Rafael Ramirez	vs. Lefties	.207	127	.263	133	1.12	104	Overall	.240	106	.335	114	1.61	93
	vs. Righties	.259	68	.375	80	1.89	83	Pressure	.250	76	.381	74	2.38	56
Billy Sample	vs. Lefties	.289	41	.430	52	2.82	52	Overall	.285	24	.430	44	3.00	51
	vs. Righties	.276	--	.431	--	3.45	--	Pressure	.333	--	.500	--	0.00	--
Ted Simmons	vs. Lefties	.256	--	.487	--	5.13	--	Overall	.252	--	.386	--	3.15	--
	vs. Righties	.250	--	.341	--	2.27	--	Pressure	.170	135	.226	133	1.89	79
Andres Thomas	vs. Lefties	.266	67	.388	69	1.44	96	Overall	.251	89	.372	90	1.86	86
	vs. Righties	.239	99	.359	98	2.17	72	Pressure	.240	96	.340	89	2.00	70
Ozzie Virgil	vs. Lefties	.262	72	.355	88	1.87	75	Overall	.223	130	.373	88	4.18	23
	vs. Righties	.206	130	.381	77	5.16	11	Pressure	.250	76	.313	99	1.56	90
Claudell Washington	vs. Lefties	.265	--	.353	--	0.00	--	Overall	.270	--	.460	--	3.65	--
	vs. Righties	.272	45	.495	8	4.85	16	Pressure	.167	--	.292	--	4.17	--
Team Average	vs. Lefties	.247	10	.367	10	2.11	8	Overall	.250	10	.381	6	2.56	5
	vs. Righties	.252	7	.388	5	2.78	3	Pressure	.261	6	.399	3	2.76	4
League Average	vs. Lefties	.257		.384		2.28		Overall	.253		.380		2.32	
	vs. Righties	.251		.378		2.34		Pressure	.257		.376		2.31	

Additional Miscellaneous Batting Comparisons

	Grass Surface BA	Rank	Artificial Surface BA	Rank	Home Games BA	Rank	Road Games BA	Rank	Runners in Scoring Position BA	Rank	Runners in Scoring Pos and Two Outs BA	Rank	Leading Off Inning OBA	Rank	Runners on 3B with less than 2 Outs RDI %	Rank
Bruce Benedict	.220	121	.242	--	.226	123	.224	--	.176	--	.353	--	.288	101	.500	--
Chris Chambliss	.275	51	.381	--	.288	--	.333	--	.258	--	.313	--	.381	--	.600	--
Ken Griffey	.322	11	.262	--	.342	3	.270	41	.182	134	.231	82	.413	9	.333	--
Terry Harper	.280	46	.211	123	.300	27	.226	115	.261	65	.351	11	.319	76	.429	--
Bob Horner	.279	47	.250	80	.306	23	.237	97	.294	37	.169	123	.333	56	.727	14
Glenn Hubbard	.243	94	.192	135	.246	103	.215	122	.273	52	.265	56	.273	115	.435	128
Omar Moreno	.252	78	.169	142	.282	58	.185	138	.222	112	.245	71	.277	113	.375	--
Dale Murphy	.274	54	.242	95	.268	75	.263	57	.295	35	.310	28	.345	45	.400	135
Ken Oberkfell	.279	48	.244	93	.284	53	.255	68	.297	33	.255	63	.254	129	.684	23
Rafael Ramirez	.233	108	.260	65	.235	115	.244	88	.135	143	.103	140	.330	61	.500	101
Billy Sample	.275	52	.310	--	.280	63	.290	18	.175	--	.056	--	.291	98	.455	123
Ted Simmons	.173	140	.391	--	.164	--	.319	--	.205	121	.238	77	.438	--	.643	35
Andres Thomas	.209	130	.340	7	.200	139	.287	22	.232	102	.317	25	.254	129	.412	134
Ozzie Virgil	.234	106	.191	136	.265	85	.185	139	.231	103	.293	36	.303	88	.520	98
Claudell Washington	.293	33	.211	--	.239	--	.303	--	.280	--	.333	--	.323	72	.571	--
Team Average	.252	8	.245	11	.260	7	.241	9	.240	10	.239	6	.301	11	.540	10
League Average	.254		.253		.260		.247		.252		.235		.316		.562	

Pitching Comparisons: Vs. Left-Handers/Right-Handers and Runners On/Bases Empty

		BA	Rank	BB %	Rank	SO %	Rank		BA	Rank	BB %	Rank	SO %	Rank
Jim Acker	vs. Lefties	.302	100	6.94	27	8.98	107	Runners On	.268	68	8.38	30	10.06	97
	vs. Righties	.231	36	5.73	22	9.55	109	Bases Empty	.278	96	4.93	16	8.52	115
Doyle Alexander	vs. Lefties	.295	95	6.33	19	16.46	46	Runners On	.280	85	4.72	2	15.09	55
	vs. Righties	.281	96	0.77	1	13.51	82	Bases Empty	.292	109	2.46	2	14.79	71
Paul Assenmacher	vs. Lefties	.268	74	10.53	69	20.00	24	Runners On	.252	46	10.22	62	18.25	28
	vs. Righties	.228	32	8.33	65	19.27	35	Bases Empty	.232	28	8.00	65	20.67	15
Jeff Dedmon	vs. Lefties	.248	55	9.68	63	12.90	73	Runners On	.227	22	10.60	67	12.44	80
	vs. Righties	.237	47	8.82	73	14.29	73	Bases Empty	.257	68	7.73	59	14.98	67
Gene Garber	vs. Lefties	.246	52	9.09	49	16.88	40	Runners On	.253	48	8.98	38	17.37	34
	vs. Righties	.273	89	3.64	6	18.18	42	Bases Empty	.267	81	3.29	6	17.76	39
Joe Johnson	vs. Lefties	.306	105	10.55	72	16.51	45	Runners On	.300	98	9.29	44	12.57	79
	vs. Righties	.269	86	6.98	45	7.56	113	Bases Empty	.280	99	8.70	81	12.56	93
Rick Mahler	vs. Lefties	.335	114	9.71	64	11.93	83	Runners On	.320	111	12.69	95	10.72	93
	vs. Righties	.260	77	8.10	62	14.29	73	Bases Empty	.288	106	6.18	26	14.69	74
Craig McMurtry	vs. Lefties	.313	108	15.17	112	10.67	96	Runners On	.245	40	14.13	108	13.59	72
	vs. Righties	.222	23	8.99	76	17.42	48	Bases Empty	.286	103	9.88	92	14.53	77
David Palmer	vs. Lefties	.234	41	13.73	102	19.96	27	Runners On	.236	32	11.20	73	19.20	24
	vs. Righties	.234	40	8.98	75	18.20	41	Bases Empty	.233	30	11.67	108	19.07	25
Zane Smith	vs. Lefties	.226	28	5.47	12	25.78	8	Runners On	.276	82	11.16	71	17.34	35
	vs. Righties	.284	98	12.88	108	13.93	79	Bases Empty	.275	92	12.39	110	14.10	82
Team Average	vs. Lefties	.279	11	10.08	9	15.61	5	Runners On	.267	8	10.81	10	14.69	7
	vs. Righties	.256	10	8.85	11	14.89	10	Bases Empty	.266	11	8.21	8	15.66	8
League Average	vs. Lefties	.257		9.83		14.90		Runners On	.260		10.11		15.02	
	vs. Righties	.251		8.19		16.33		Bases Empty	.248		7.89		16.30	

Additional Miscellaneous Pitching Comparisons

	Grass Surface BA	Rank	Artificial Surface BA	Rank	Home Games BA	Rank	Road Games BA	Rank	Runners in Scoring Position BA	Rank	Runners in Scoring Pos and Two Outs BA	Rank	Leading Off Inning OBA	Rank
Jim Acker	.252	61	.341	115	.242	55	.309	104	.250	55	.205	37	.381	105
Doyle Alexander	.286	94	.292	100	.293	101	.281	89	.270	77	.308	101	.246	8
Paul Assenmacher	.234	37	.262	--	.178	2	.314	107	.247	51	.194	31	.313	57
Jeff Dedmon	.239	42	.258	--	.266	85	.209	11	.207	19	.167	16	.345	91
Gene Garber	.269	74	.237	--	.261	79	.259	65	.276	83	.319	108	.306	50
Joe Johnson	.294	107	.275	--	.288	97	.291	97	.265	73	.233	58	.308	51
Rick Mahler	.286	96	.343	116	.284	95	.317	110	.303	101	.277	86	.310	54
Craig McMurtry	.305	111	.157	2	.310	109	.210	12	.243	46	.288	89	.436	117
Ed Olwine	.197	5	.231	--	.234	--	.185	--	.184	--	.167	16	.295	--
David Palmer	.244	49	.210	13	.245	57	.224	19	.233	35	.228	51	.327	71
Zane Smith	.281	87	.248	44	.264	83	.293	100	.288	97	.269	81	.335	80
Cliff Speck	.213	11	.375	--	.182	--	.264	--	.143	--	.214	--	.333	--
Team Average	.266	10	.267	10	.262	9	.271	11	.260	9	.252	9	.326	9
League Average	.254		.253		.247		.260		.252		.235		.316	

CHICAGO CUBS

The home-field advantage isn't nearly as strong in baseball as in the other major sports. Home teams won 54 percent of all major-league baseball games over the past five seasons, compared to 58 percent in the National Football League, 60 percent (of games played to a decision) in the National Hockey League, and 64 percent in the National Basketball Association. And the advantage isn't as strong in the National League (53 percent) as it is in the American League (55 percent). But one of the joys of baseball is that even a slight edge is meaningful over a six-month season. The proof: Road teams have won more National League games than home teams in only three seasons since 1900 (1917, 1923, and 1972), and never by a margin of more than 11 wins.

It's no surprise, then, that only two National League teams had better records on the road than at home last season: Montreal and Pittsburgh. Nor that over the past five years, every one of the 26 major-league teams fared better in its home ballpark than in road games.

During that period, the Chicago Cubs had the greatest home-field advantage in the National League. Only one team, the San Francisco Giants, has a worse record than the Cubs in road games since 1982, but Chicago ranks seventh in the league at home. Here's a look at the records, with the teams ranked according to the difference between their home and road marks:

Team	Home Games			Road Games			Diff.
	W–L	Pct.	Rank	W–L	Pct.	Rank	
Chicago	215–187	.535	7	172–232	.426	11	.109
Philadelphia	230–174	.569	1	191–214	.472	7	.098
San Diego	225–180	.556	6	186–219	.459	8	.096
San Francisco	207–198	.511	8	170–235	.420	12	.091
Houston	228–178	.562	3T	193–211	.478	6	.084
New York	228–178	.562	3T	201–203	.498	3	.064
Los Angeles	225–179	.557	5	201–205	.495	4	.062
St. Louis	230–175	.568	2	205–199	.507	1	.060
Pittsburgh	190–214	.470	12	174–231	.430	10	.041
Cincinnati	198–207	.489	11	182–222	.450	9	.038
Atlanta	199–205	.493	10	196–209	.484	5	.009
Montreal	205–199	.507	9	203–200	.504	2	.004

It seems natural that Chicago would top that list. After all, Wrigley Field is the most idiosyncratic outdoor ballpark in the league. It's by far the oldest; opened in 1914, it housed the Chicago Whales of the Federal League for two years before the Cubs took over, and was in operation for 46 years by the time the league's second-oldest current stadium, Candlestick Park, opened for business. It's been the only stadium in the majors without lighting since 1948. The outfield walls are covered with ivy, and the winds are legendary for turning pop flies into home runs; a glance through our new Ballparks section, starting on page 409, shows that Wrigley increases home runs by approximately 40 percent, the largest increase of any park in either league.

It stands to reason that the Cubs would build a team to exploit Wrigley's many idiosyncrasies. And you'd expect such a team to be at a disadvantage on the road, especially at the cookie-cutter synthetic stadiums around the league. But as we demonstrated in the Houston Astros essay in last year's *Analyst*, custom-crafting a roster to your ballpark is not nearly as significant a factor as you might think. (We took a look at the records of teams that play on artificial turf and those that play on grass, and found no special home-field advantage against teams from the opposite surface. In fact, over the previous 10 seasons, teams actually did better at home against opponents with the *same* home surface.)

Before we go any further, let's take a look at the American League home and away records for the past five seasons, again ranked by difference:

Team	Home Games			Road Games			Diff.
	W–L	Pct.	Rank	W–L	Pct.	Rank	
Minnesota	212–195	.521	11	146–256	.363	14	.158
Kansas City	240–165	.593	3	180–224	.446	8	.147
Oakland	212–193	.523	10	159–245	.394	11	.130
Texas	204–198	.507	12	155–250	.383	13	.125
Chicago	232–171	.576	5	184–222	.453	7	.122
New York	243–160	.603	1	200–205	.494	6	.109
Milwaukee	219–185	.542	9	177–225	.440	9	.102
Seattle	197–211	.483	14	154–247	.384	12	.099
Cleveland	201–202	.499	13	166–240	.409	10	.090
Toronto	237–166	.588	4	204–201	.504	3	.084
Detroit	241–165	.594	2	208–194	.517	1	.076
Baltimore	229–173	.570	6	204–202	.502	4	.067
California	223–181	.552	7	202–203	.499	5	.053
Boston	222–181	.551	8	207–198	.511	2	.040

There's quite a shocker at the bottom of that list: Fenway Park, the most idiosyncratic ballpark in the American League, and the nearest twin to Wrigley Field in both age and charm, has yielded the smallest home-field advantage of any park in the league. The Red Sox, it appears, have achieved their recent success without a team terribly well crafted for their park.

The whole issue of building for your home park has drawn an enormous amount of attention in the last five years or so—so much that we would expect to find a considerable increase in the home-field advantage over that time. It hasn't happened, either on a team-by-team or league-wide basis. In fact, the opposite has occurred. The chart below ranks National League teams by their home-field advantage (HFA) over three distinct five-year periods:

1972–76		1977–81		1982–86	
Team	HFA	Team	HFA	Team	HFA
Pittsburgh	.085	Houston	.197	Chicago	.109
Philadelphia	.085	Philadelphia	.149	Philadelphia	.098
Houston	.073	Montreal	.135	San Diego	.096
Chicago	.072	Chicago	.133	San Francisco	.091
San Francisco	.062	Pittsburgh	.132	Houston	.084
St. Louis	.056	Los Angeles	.130	New York	.064
Los Angeles	.056	Atlanta	.127	Los Angeles	.062
San Diego	.055	San Diego	.112	St. Louis	.060
Atlanta	.040	San Francisco	.090	Pittsburgh	.041
Montreal	.038	St. Louis	.088	Cincinnati	.038
Cincinnati	.023	Cincinnati	.048	Atlanta	.009
New York	.021	New York	.045	Montreal	.004

Despite the sudden increase in New York's home-field advantage and the decrease over the years of Pittsburgh's, there is enough similarity to suggest that certain stadiums do consistently produce a greater edge for their occupants than others, but that the edge has declined sharply. The Cubs' home-field edge, the largest over the past five years, would have ranked *ninth* in the period from 1977–81. If everyone's trying to build for their park, they're not doing it terribly well. And we didn't find any skew toward what one would think would be the obvious factors that might improve the advantage: grass vs. plastic, indoor vs. outdoor, symmetric vs. asymmetric, hitters parks vs. pitchers parks vs. balanced parks—nothing. In either league. So why all the fuss?

One explanation may come from an historical curiosity. The studies done elsewhere that have stressed the need to build for your home park came out of the mid-1970s, a time of unusually high home-field edges across the board. From 1975 to 1980, the National League's home edge averaged .109. The only comparable period in N.L. history was from 1925 to 1935, when the won-lost differential fell below .100 just twice; no other six-year period has averaged above .100. Some members of the baseball research community may have overreacted to the unusual conditions of this period, which was one of adjustment to the changes in the game brought on by the proliferation of those cookie-cutter synthetic stadiums we mentioned earlier.

Lowballing the Opposition

One way the Cubs can take advantage of Wrigley Field is to acquire pitchers who keep the ball down in the strike zone. Out of harm's way, so to speak. As we mentioned earlier, 40 percent more home runs have been hit at Wrigley than in Cubs road games over the past five years, and pitchers who avoid the home run ball have a decided advantage there.

That advantage isn't apparent if you simply divide the pitchers into ground-ballers and fly-ballers according to whether their ratios of ground outs to air outs fell above or below the team average (1.26 last season). Consider the home and road records of last year's Cubs pitchers: The ground-ball pitchers included Ron Davis, Frank DiPino, Ray Fontenot, Dave Gumpert, Drew Hall, Greg Maddux, Jamie Moyer, Dick Ruthven, and Steve Trout; the fly-ball pitchers were Jay Baller, Dennis Eckersley, George Frazier, Guy Hoffman, Matt Keough, Ed Lynch, Scott Sanderson, Lee Smith, and Rick Sutcliffe.

1986 season only	Home Games		Road Games		
	W–L	Pct.	W–L	Pct.	Diff.
Ground-ball pitchers	12–11	.522	10–17	.370	.151
Fly-ball pitchers	30–27	.526	18–35	.340	.187

Nor is the trend apparent if we extend the same study over the past five seasons. The two groups had equivalent road-game records during that time, but the fly-ball pitchers were better at Wrigley Field:

1982–86	Home Games		Road Games		
	W–L	Pct.	W–L	Pct.	Diff.
Ground-ball pitchers	81–75	.519	70–96	.422	.098
Fly-ball pitchers	134–112	.545	102–136	.429	.116

But if we consider only pitchers with a *strong* tendency toward ground balls and compare their records to those of all other pitchers, the difference in performance becomes clear. For the following table, ground-ball pitchers are those with a ground outs-to-air outs ratio of 2.00 or more in the season in question (Steve Trout from 1983 through 1986, Chuck Rainey in 1983, and Ray Fontenot in 1985):

1982–86	Home Games		Road Games		
	W–L	Pct.	W–L	Pct.	Diff.
Ground-ball pitchers	32–22	.593	25–36	.410	.183
Other pitchers	183–165	.526	147–196	.429	.097

The "other" group had the edge on the road, but the ground-ball pitchers were far more successful at Wrigley. To further support the theory that extreme ground-ball pitchers have an advantage over fly-ball pitchers in home-run parks, we did the same study for the Atlanta Braves. Atlanta Stadium has the second-largest home run differential in the majors over the past five seasons. The ground-ball pitchers include Rick Camp in 1983, Zane Smith in 1985 and 1986, and David Palmer in 1986:

1982–86	Home Games		Road Games		
	W–L	Pct.	W–L	Pct.	Diff.
Ground-ball pitchers	20–19	.513	18–26	.409	.104
Other pitchers	178–187	.488	178–183	.493	−.005

Atlanta's other pitchers had no advantage pitching at home. In fact, their winning percentage was slightly higher in road games than in home games. But the pitchers with ground outs-to-air outs ratios of 2.00 or more were significantly better at Atlanta Stadium than in road games. So though there doesn't seem to be an advantage for pitchers with slight tendencies toward ground balls, those with the strongest tendencies have an enormous edge.

The Braves have developed a pitching staff loaded with just

that type of pitcher. In addition to Palmer and Smith, their three most-used relievers, Paul Assenmacher, Jeff Dedmon, and Gene Garber, all had ratios above 2.00 last season. Jim Acker (2.11) and Rick Mahler (1.58) are also career ground-ballers. The Cubs have yet to make a concentrated effort to acquire low-ball pitchers; of the current staff, only Trout has had a consistently high ratio throughout his career. The ground-ball leaders for the 1986 season among pitchers who faced at least 250 batters:

Starters		Relievers	
National League			
Bryn Smith, Mtl.	2.52	Roger McDowell, N.Y.	3.47
John Denny, Cin.	2.38	Randy Niemann, N.Y.	2.95
Zane Smith, Atl.	2.29	Jim Winn, Pitt.	2.75
Bruce Ruffin, Phil.	2.26	Doug Sisk, N.Y.	2.70
Rick Reuschel, Pitt.	2.20	Ray Fontenot, Chi.	2.60
Steve Trout, Chi.	2.17	Jeff Dedmon, Atl.	2.56
David Palmer, Atl.	2.10	Gene Garber, Atl.	2.40
Chris Welsh, Cin.	2.03	Greg Minton, S.F.	2.37
Mike LaCoss, S.F.	1.93	Paul Assenmacher, Atl.	2.23
Orel Hershiser, L.A.	1.79	Charlie Kerfeld, Hou.	2.17
American League			
Bob Tewksbury, N.Y.	1.92	Doug Corbett, Cal.	2.76
Danny Jackson, K.C.	1.70	Terry Forster, Cal.	2.14
Dan Petry, Det.	1.60	Nate Snell, Balt.	2.12
Richard Dotson, Chi.	1.49	Bob Stanley, Bos.	2.11
Mike Morgan, Sea.	1.48	Dale Mohorcic, Tex.	2.09
Mike Moore, Sea.	1.44	Dan Quisenberry, K.C.	2.07
Mike Flanagan, Balt.	1.43	Bill Mooneyham, Oak.	2.07
Mike Witt, Cal.	1.41	Mark Eichhorn, Tor.	2.05
Jose Guzman, Tex.	1.41	Dennis Lamp, Tor.	2.03
Storm Davis, Balt.	1.41	Matt Young, Sea.	1.90

Chicago not only plays in one of baseball's most peculiar settings; the team itself seems to march to its own beat as well. Two unconventional strategies employed by manager Gene Michael are found in his lineup construction and base-running philosophy.

Chicago ranked 16th in the majors with 680 runs last season, but had the most powerful seventh slot in either league. Cubs hitting in the seventh batting-order position hit 27 home runs with 94 runs batted in—both major-league highs—and had a slugging average of .454, second in the majors only to the Seattle Mariners (.467). The composite statistics of Chicago's seventh-place hitters:

	AB	R	H	2B	3B	HR	RBI	BB	SO	BA	SA	OBA
Chicago	579	73	151	27	2	27	94	58	116	.261	.454	.325
N.L. Avg.	578	63	145	29	2	15	72	61	106	.251	.386	.323

The success of the Cubs' seventh hitters is all the more unusual because it wasn't predominantly the work of one individual. Ron Cey was the most frequent seventh hitter on the team, but even he accounted for only 23 percent of those plate appearances. Jody Davis (21%), Manny Trillo (12%), Shawon Dunston (8%), Brian Dayett (8%), Gary Matthews (7%), Jerry Mumphrey (5%), and Chris Speier (5%) all batted seventh in the order at least 30 times. And some of the less-used of those players made substantial contributions to the overall totals: Matthews and Dayett batted .333 and hit eight home runs there in only 97 at bats.

Since the strength of the seventh position was a team effort, we think that it derived its power in large part from Chicago's similarly strong eight slot. Most teams—especially National League teams—have exceptionally weak eighth spots, and as a result, opposing pitchers are probably inclined to pitch more selectively to those teams' seventh-place hitters. But Shawon Dunston accounted for 50 percent of Chicago's eighth-place appearances, and with help from Bob Dernier (19%), Chris Speier (11%), and a cast of thousands, the Cubs had more home runs and extra-base hits than any eighth position in either league:

	AB	R	H	2B	3B	HR	RBI	BB	SO	BA	SA	OBA
Chicago	578	71	149	36	2	20	73	38	114	.258	.431	.306
N.L. Avg.	554	55	131	22	3	8	57	65	98	.237	.326	.318

No less unusual than Chicago's lower batting-order strength was its approach to running the bases. We analyzed how often Cubs base runners advanced two or more bases on singles and found that only 27 percent of Chicago runners took an extra base, the lowest average in the National League. The Cubs' conservative style had nothing to do with playing for the big inning at Wrigley Field, either; they advanced two bases on 27.5 percent of singles at home, 27.4 percent on the road.

Actually, we weren't that interested in the low overall figure—somebody's got to finish last—but the internal breakdown of those situations was, well, a little weird. Most National League teams advance an extra base on singles slightly more often when they lead than when they are behind, and slightly more often still when the game is tied. We emphasize the word *slightly*. But the Cubs burned the base paths in tie games and were stuck in mud at other times:

	Winning	Tied	Losing	Overall
Chicago	25.3%	41.0%	22.3%	27.4%
N.L. Avg.	33.3%	35.6%	30.3%	32.8%

What's noteworthy about the pattern is its similarity to the base-running style of the 1981–82 New York Yankees, also managed predominantly by Gene Michael. New York was more aggressive when it led than the 1986 Cubs were, but used the same conservative approach when it trailed:

	Winning	Tied	Losing	Overall
1981–82 New York	35.5%	36.7%	23.7%	31.1%
1981–82 A.L. Avg.	35.5%	34.7%	29.1%	32.9%

Michael's conservative style when losing seems not to have hurt the Cubs, however. They won 32 games last season in which they trailed at some point, to rank eighth in the National League; not an inspiring performance, perhaps, but an improvement on their overall standing of 11th in the league. What we were wondering, though, is just how Michael enforces his preference for playing one base at a time when trailing? Fines? Threats? Forced viewing of the '84 LCS?

WON-LOST RECORD BY STARTING POSITION

CHICAGO 70-90	C	1B	2B	3B	SS	LF	CF	RF	P	Leadoff	Relief	Starts
Jay Baller											17-19	
Thad Bosley						4-5	0-2			0-1		4-7
Ron Cey				32-43								32-43
Steve Christmas	0-1	1-0										1-1
Jody Davis	59-82											59-82
Ron Davis											2-15	
Brian Dayett						1-3	6-5					7-8
Bob Dernier							32-50			19-30		32-50
Frank DiPino											9-21	
Shawon Dunston					66-82					22-20		66-82
Leon Durham		54-79										54-79
Dennis Eckersley									10-22		0-1	10-22
Ray Fontenot											11-31	
Terry Francona		6-4				0-3	2-1					8-8
George Frazier											7-28	
Dave Gumpert											12-26	
Drew Hall									2-2		1-0	2-2
Guy Hoffman									5-3		10-14	5-3
Matt Keough									0-2		5-12	0-2
Steve Lake	3-1											3-1
Dave Lopes				13-16		5-5		1-1		8-12		19-22
Ed Lynch									5-8		6-4	5-8
Greg Maddux									2-3		0-1	2-3
Mike Martin	2-2											2-2
Dave Martinez						11-14				5-8		11-14
Gary Matthews						46-58						46-58
Keith Moreland	6-4	3-6		9-10				49-64				67-84
Jamie Moyer									10-6			10-6
Jerry Mumphrey						6-9	19-23	3-10		5-12		28-42
Rafael Palmeiro						8-7	3-0					11-7
Dick Ruthven											1-5	
Ryne Sandberg			67-86									67-86
Scott Sanderson									13-15		8-1	13-15
Lee Smith											46-20	
Chris Speier		1-3	6-8	4-8								11-19
Rick Sutcliffe									9-18			9-18
Manny Trillo		6-1	2-1	10-13							0-1	18-15
Steve Trout									14-11		1-11	14-11
Chico Walker						8-3	6-7			11-7		14-10

Batting Comparisons: Vs. Left-Handers/Right-Handers and Overall/Late Inning Pressure Situations

		BA	Rank	SA	Rank	HR %	Rank		BA	Rank	SA	Rank	HR %	Rank
Thad Bosley	vs. Lefties	.571	--	.714	--	0.00	--	Overall	.275	--	.350	--	0.83	--
	vs. Righties	.257	74	.327	112	0.88	116	Pressure	.311	27	.426	50	1.64	84
Ron Cey	vs. Lefties	.325	15	.638	3	6.25	11	Overall	.273	45	.508	5	5.08	11
	vs. Righties	.250	85	.449	37	4.55	25	Pressure	.244	91	.400	62	2.22	60
Jody Davis	vs. Lefties	.233	100	.353	90	2.26	65	Overall	.250	90	.428	46	3.98	28
	vs. Righties	.256	78	.453	34	4.56	24	Pressure	.220	105	.410	55	5.00	18
Bob Dernier	vs. Lefties	.305	32	.429	53	1.90	74	Overall	.225	126	.312	122	1.23	106
	vs. Righties	.187	140	.256	137	0.91	114	Pressure	.192	126	.308	103	1.92	74
Shawon Dunston	vs. Lefties	.231	104	.423	54	3.85	29	Overall	.250	93	.411	62	2.93	52
	vs. Righties	.256	75	.407	67	2.59	60	Pressure	.215	109	.393	68	3.74	36
Leon Durham	vs. Lefties	.227	109	.367	83	2.34	62	Overall	.262	65	.452	24	4.13	24
	vs. Righties	.275	41	.483	17	4.78	18	Pressure	.244	92	.453	33	5.81	7
Terry Francona	vs. Lefties	.143	--	.143	--	0.00	--	Overall	.250	--	.323	--	1.61	--
	vs. Righties	.256	76	.333	109	1.71	90	Pressure	.235	--	.353	--	2.94	--
Gary Matthews	vs. Lefties	.352	4	.600	6	5.71	14	Overall	.259	70	.478	15	5.68	6
	vs. Righties	.223	121	.430	55	5.66	7	Pressure	.211	113	.316	97	3.51	40
Keith Moreland	vs. Lefties	.306	30	.449	42	3.40	36	Overall	.271	50	.384	82	2.05	78
	vs. Righties	.260	65	.362	89	1.59	95	Pressure	.314	26	.514	12	4.76	22
Jerry Mumphrey	vs. Lefties	.197	131	.213	141	0.00	119	Overall	.304	14	.401	74	1.62	92
	vs. Righties	.331	7	.448	39	2.02	80	Pressure	.211	111	.296	107	2.82	48
Ryne Sandberg	vs. Lefties	.264	70	.377	78	2.52	58	Overall	.284	26	.411	61	2.23	70
	vs. Righties	.291	26	.423	58	2.14	76	Pressure	.255	72	.306	104	0.00	102
Chris Speier	vs. Lefties	.244	--	.444	--	4.44	--	Overall	.284	--	.452	--	3.87	--
	vs. Righties	.300	21	.455	32	3.64	43	Pressure	.300	34	.350	84	0.00	102
Manny Trillo	vs. Lefties	.328	14	.431	49	0.00	119	Overall	.296	--	.382	--	0.66	--
	vs. Righties	.277	--	.351	--	1.06	--	Pressure	.200	--	.333	--	3.33	--
Team Average	vs. Lefties	.261	4	.407	3	2.86	3	Overall	.256	3	.398	3	2.82	1
	vs. Righties	.255	3	.394	3	2.80	1	Pressure	.245	10	.387	7	3.13	1
League Average	vs. Lefties	.257		.384		2.28		Overall	.253		.380		2.32	
	vs. Righties	.251		.378		2.34		Pressure	.257		.376		2.31	

Additional Miscellaneous Batting Comparisons

	Grass Surface BA	Rank	Artificial Surface BA	Rank	Home Games BA	Rank	Road Games BA	Rank	Runners in Scoring Position BA	Rank	Runners in Scoring Pos and Two Outs BA	Rank	Leading Off Inning OBA	Rank	Runners on 3B with less than 2 Outs RDI %	Rank
Thad Bosley	.271	60	.286	--	.323	--	.224	--	.257	--	.000	--	.361	--	.833	--
Ron Cey	.266	64	.297	--	.241	108	.311	9	.310	23	.276	46	.443	3	.500	101
Jody Davis	.239	102	.278	40	.267	80	.233	103	.248	79	.197	109	.349	41	.516	99
Bob Dernier	.248	82	.182	139	.255	96	.198	131	.203	124	.206	102	.294	95	.444	124
Shawon Dunston	.260	68	.221	111	.262	88	.236	99	.270	55	.224	87	.254	128	.545	86
Leon Durham	.281	45	.215	120	.283	54	.234	101	.245	83	.222	89	.318	78	.632	40
Terry Francona	.205	134	.361	--	.178	--	.291	--	.227	--	.400	--	.314	--	.500	--
Dave Martinez	.113	145	.214	--	.136	--	.143	--	.174	--	.125	--	.206	--	.500	--
Gary Matthews	.274	55	.219	115	.286	49	.232	104	.205	123	.242	73	.375	24	.550	82
Keith Moreland	.288	37	.231	106	.293	40	.249	79	.252	74	.244	72	.351	40	.700	17
Jerry Mumphrey	.328	8	.230	--	.361	1	.253	73	.284	45	.265	56	.427	8	.563	77
Ryne Sandberg	.281	44	.291	25	.302	25	.265	54	.303	26	.284	40	.257	125	.594	62
Chris Speier	.283	41	.286	--	.309	--	.264	--	.333	--	.267	--	.243	--	1.000	--
Manny Trillo	.292	35	.302	--	.308	--	.287	21	.333	14	.240	74	.361	--	.857	--
Team Average	.260	3	.248	10	.272	1	.240	10	.256	5	.228	8	.323	4	.582	4
League Average	.254		.253		.260		.247		.252		.235		.316		.562	

Pitching Comparisons: Vs. Left-Handers/Right-Handers and Runners On/Bases Empty

		BA	Rank	BB %	Rank	SO %	Rank		BA	Rank	BB %	Rank	SO %	Rank
Jay Baller	vs. Lefties	.259	65	13.49	100	16.67	41	Runners On	.308	--	14.66	--	12.93	--
	vs. Righties	.291	--	9.02	--	17.21	--	Bases Empty	.250	56	8.33	75	20.45	17
Frank DiPino	vs. Lefties	.172	6	6.80	23	22.33	13	Runners On	.275	80	7.23	15	15.66	48
	vs. Righties	.279	93	9.50	84	19.42	34	Bases Empty	.220	18	10.06	95	24.58	8
Dennis Eckersley	vs. Lefties	.301	98	6.88	26	11.61	89	Runners On	.294	95	6.89	12	14.33	64
	vs. Righties	.266	84	2.77	2	20.91	23	Bases Empty	.279	97	3.61	7	17.03	44
Ray Fontenot	vs. Lefties	.274	77	7.32	31	21.95	15	Runners On	.287	--	9.09	--	10.91	--
	vs. Righties	.262	81	9.43	83	3.77	116	Bases Empty	.250	56	8.40	76	9.16	112
George Frazier	vs. Lefties	.281	83	13.59	101	12.62	76	Runners On	.311	107	12.80	97	15.20	54
	vs. Righties	.333	--	14.29	--	20.00	--	Bases Empty	.310	--	15.25	--	18.64	--
Dave Gumpert	vs. Lefties	.354	116	5.71	14	8.57	110	Runners On	.293	94	10.95	69	18.98	25
	vs. Righties	.202	11	14.29	115	23.38	8	Bases Empty	.239	--	10.66	--	15.57	--
Guy Hoffman	vs. Lefties	.246	--	15.00	--	13.75	--	Runners On	.287	91	10.12	59	10.12	96
	vs. Righties	.299	105	6.14	26	13.00	87	Bases Empty	.290	108	6.35	31	15.87	56
Ed Lynch	vs. Lefties	.302	101	5.98	17	11.11	94	Runners On	.299	96	7.32	17	12.20	82
	vs. Righties	.249	62	4.95	14	17.58	46	Bases Empty	.267	79	4.37	10	15.08	65
Jamie Moyer	vs. Lefties	.300	--	16.33	--	10.20	--	Runners On	.312	108	9.64	49	9.64	102
	vs. Righties	.313	112	9.83	87	11.56	97	Bases Empty	.310	114	11.62	107	13.13	87
Scott Sanderson	vs. Lefties	.260	66	4.99	8	15.22	58	Runners On	.255	53	5.19	4	16.30	43
	vs. Righties	.249	63	5.70	21	20.89	24	Bases Empty	.255	66	5.39	20	18.74	29
Lee Smith	vs. Lefties	.221	24	15.71	114	25.24	10	Runners On	.191	6	14.36	109	25.53	2
	vs. Righties	.208	13	5.56	19	24.69	5	Bases Empty	.237	36	8.15	70	24.46	9
Rick Sutcliffe	vs. Lefties	.245	49	12.09	89	17.67	36	Runners On	.266	67	15.64	113	14.72	59
	vs. Righties	.261	79	13.17	111	.13.77	81	Bases Empty	.242	45	10.27	97	16.89	48
Steve Trout	vs. Lefties	.356	117	3.64	3	7.27	113	Runners On	.310	103	12.83	98	9.62	103
	vs. Righties	.287	99	12.31	106	10.15	106	Bases Empty	.288	107	9.24	87	9.78	109
Team Average	vs. Lefties	.277	10	9.12	3	14.74	7	Runners On	.288	12	10.48	9	13.80	11
	vs. Righties	.280	12	8.77	10	15.87	8	Bases Empty	.271	12	7.61	3	16.72	6
League Average	vs. Lefties	.257		9.83		14.90		Runners On	.260		10.11		15.02	
	vs. Righties	.251		8.19		16.33		Bases Empty	.248		7.89		16.30	

Additional Miscellaneous Pitching Comparisons

	Grass Surface BA	Rank	Artificial Surface BA	Rank	Home Games BA	Rank	Road Games BA	Rank	Runners in Scoring Position BA	Rank	Runners in Scoring Pos and Two Outs BA	Rank	Leading Off Inning OBA	Rank
Jay Baller	.288	98	.258	62	.296	--	.262	68	.317	109	.290	90	.404	--
Frank DiPino	.286	94	.214	15	.233	44	.258	62	.241	45	.316	106	.312	55
Dennis Eckersley	.289	103	.274	86	.298	104	.276	81	.284	93	.240	65	.288	30
Ray Fontenot	.255	64	.302	--	.237	49	.300	--	.270	76	.257	72	.278	23
George Frazier	.281	88	.375	--	.284	--	.328	111	.266	74	.267	79	.385	--
Dave Gumpert	.247	54	.359	--	.264	82	.273	--	.373	117	.333	110	.320	--
Guy Hoffman	.289	101	.287	96	.270	88	.313	106	.305	104	.308	101	.390	110
Ed Lynch	.289	104	.250	47	.322	113	.217	15	.359	116	.389	116	.292	32
Greg Maddux	.405	--	.309	111	.455	--	.312	--	.333	--	.350	--	.438	--
Jamie Moyer	.317	113	.291	--	.318	111	.297	--	.245	49	.231	54	.391	112
Scott Sanderson	.252	62	.268	77	.232	42	.282	92	.272	80	.175	21	.293	33
Lee Smith	.205	7	.247	--	.219	27	.208	10	.226	27	.255	71	.329	73
Rick Sutcliffe	.251	59	.256	60	.261	78	.240	35	.271	78	.247	69	.337	82
Steve Trout	.292	106	.310	112	.305	107	.291	98	.304	102	.277	85	.376	103
Team Average	.276	12	.285	12	.280	12	.277	12	.289	12	.271	12	.339	12
League Average	.254		.253		.247		.260		.252		.235		.316	

CINCINNATI REDS

No team has made preseason predictions more difficult for so many baseball fans over the past few seasons than the Cincinnati Reds. Two years ago, following a third consecutive season below sea level, Cincinnati exploded with 89 wins and a second-place finish in the National League West. surpassing the hopes of even the most loyal Reds fans. Last season, with the city poised for its first division title in a decade, the Reds failed to find their stride until midseason, occupying the division's cellar until the Fourth of July.

But we've done some studies that show that Cincinnati's backslide last season was actually quite typical. One of the nice things about analyzing baseball statistics is that you've got nearly 100 years of numbers to work with, including 16 or more teams and hundreds of players each season. We get a kick out of what's known as technical stock market analysis, stuff like, "The market's due to surge. Up volume exceeded down volume by a 10-to-one ratio yesterday. There have been only eight of those days in the past, and a sharp rise followed six of them." Do these guys really expect us to risk our cash based on a 75 percent success rate in only eight cases? They've got to be kidding. You could toss coins and do better than six of eight heads if you had a minute or two to spare. But in baseball, there's strength in numbers; when you spot a pattern like the Reds' vertical leap after several dormant seasons, you can usually find quite a few teams that have made similar moves in the past, and project Cincinnati's future in accordance with the paths those teams followed. And besides, when we're wrong, no one goes belly-up.

So we searched the history of the National League for teams that crossed over the .500 level after at least three years on the dark side and found 34 such cases from 1900 through 1984. Based on the subsequent records of those teams, we expected the Reds to suffer a decline last season: Only 11 of those 34 teams—one of eight over the past 20 years—improved further in the season following their rise above the .500 mark.

That's not a particularly surprising result. Despite the euphoria that progress brings, teams that advance one season are likely to regress the next. Teams that increase their winning percentages from one season to the next give back about one-third of the gain the following season. For example, we found 185 National League teams from 1900 through 1984 that gained up to .050 in winning percentage from one season to the next; on average, they gained .025, and lost .008 the next year.

But as we mentioned, Cincinnati was an exceptional case.

The Reds did follow the pattern outlined above—surpassing the break-even level after at least three years below—but they did it in dramatic style. Their leap carried them from a 70–92 (.432) mark in 1984 to a 89–72 mark (.553) a year later. The move from below the .450 mark to above .550 had been accomplished by only six other National League teams since 1900. And that select group marches to its own beat. On average, those teams jumped from a .412 winning percentage to a .587 mark the next season, a gain of 175 points. Normally, they would be expected to return nearly 60 points of that, falling to roughly .522 the next season. But four of those six teams increased their percentage even further the next year, and another experienced only a slight decline. On average, the teams gained an additional nine points the year after the sharp increase:

Year	Team	Year X−1	Year X	Year X+1
1903	New York Giants	.353	.604	.693
1945	Brooklyn Dodgers	.409	.565	.615
1953	Boston/Milwaukee Braves	.418	.597	.578
1961	Cincinnati Reds	.435	.604	.605
1984	Chicago Cubs	.438	.596	.478
1984	New York Mets	.420	.556	.605
	Averages	.412	.587	.596

Exceptional teams produce exceptional results. But as we cautioned earlier, a prediction based on only a few precedents is about as reliable as the back end of a five-day weather forecast. It must be balanced with the findings of other surveys that carry the weight of a large sample. That approach would have worked quite nicely for Cincinnati last season. Had the Reds added those nine points of winning percentage, they would have finished the season with a record of 91–71, five wins better than their actual mark. But if you tempered that optimistic forecast with a pessimism gleaned from the survey of teams with three losing seasons before posting a winning record, you might have hit the nail right on the head.

The two 1984 teams in the table above provide a stark contrast with important ramifications for Cincinnati. The Cubs and Mets became the first teams in baseball history to rise from the bottom two spots in their division or league to the top two in a single season. And although they appeared headed for a decade-long battle for the Eastern Division's top rung, Chicago headed south a year later and has fashioned consecutive losing seasons since its dramatic one-year rise.

In retrospect, the difference between the two teams should

have been clear even in 1984: Chicago had the second-oldest starting lineup in the National League, New York the second youngest. A year later, with New York trying to prevent a Chicago repeat, the Mets added some experienced and talented players—Gary Carter, Howard Johnson, and a full season of Ray Knight—along with still more young players like Len Dykstra and Roger McDowell. The Cubs, unable to afford the luxury of adding experienced pennant insurance to an already graying team, and without much support coming from its minor-league operation, could do little but watch their players grow a year older. They played their only ace in spring training, replacing shortstop Larry Bowa with Shawon Dunston, but were trumped: Dunston couldn't handle the position, and Bowa returned a month into the season. The average ages of the Mets and Cubs:

	New York		Chicago	
	1984	1985	1984	1985
Non-Pitchers	27.19	29.00	30.10	30.82
Pitchers	25.63	25.09	29.34	29.17

Like the 1984 Cubs, the 1985 Cincinnati club was one of the oldest in the National League. Although only the Mets' pitching staff had an average age lower than that of the Reds' pitchers (26.75), Cincinnati had the oldest starting lineup in either league, with an average of 32.48 years. (Incidentally, all these averages are weighted by plate appearances.) Maybe it was the memory of Chicago's collapse, maybe it just was common sense, but last season Cincinnati reduced its average by nearly a full year. The average age of everyday National League players for the past two seasons:

Team	1986	1985	Diff.
Cincinnati	31.50	32.48	−0.98
Chicago	30.39	30.83	−0.44
Houston	30.27	30.25	+0.02
Atlanta	30.07	28.47	+1.60
San Diego	29.80	30.33	−0.53
New York	28.84	29.00	−0.16
Los Angeles	28.58	28.01	+0.57
Philadelphia	28.31	28.13	+0.18
Montreal	27.95	28.25	−0.30
St. Louis	27.84	27.97	−0.13
Pittsburgh	27.36	28.58	−1.22
San Francisco	26.98	28.31	−1.33

Although Cincinnati still had the highest average in the National League last season, the imminent emergence of players like Barry Larkin, Kal Daniels, and Tracy Jones along with the continued development of Eric Davis, the reduced role of Dave Concepcion, the retirement of Tony Perez, and the presumed retirement of Pete Rose all guarantee that the Reds won't head that list again this season. Rather than going for broke in a stubborn commitment to aging players—a philosophy that has worked only for George Allen and the Washington Redskins—the Reds have backed off momentarily, regrouped, and now appear ready to make another run at the Western Division title, with the reassurance that if they fail this season, there's another season after that, and another after that, and another . . .

It Ain't Over . . .

Cincinnati and San Francisco tied for the title of major-league comeback kings last season. Both the Reds and the Giants won 16 games in which they trailed after six innings, the highest total in either league. Modest totals for league leaders, or so they seem when you consider all the late-game turnarounds during the 1986 playoffs and World Series. But despite those come-from-behind postseason heroics, a late-game lead is almost as good as gold, and the records of all major-league teams last season in games in which they trailed after the sixth inning prove the point:

Team	W	L	Pct.	Team	W	L	Pct.
Cincinnati	16	58	.216	Baltimore	13	70	.157
San Francisco	16	60	.211	Cleveland	12	56	.176
Montreal	14	54	.206	Texas	12	57	.174
San Diego	14	63	.182	Milwaukee	12	70	.146
New York	12	39	.235	Boston	11	53	.172
Houston	11	48	.186	Toronto	11	55	.167
Atlanta	11	64	.147	Oakland	11	64	.147
Chicago	10	65	.133	Chicago	10	67	.130
Philadelphia	8	53	.131	Kansas City	10	71	.123
Pittsburgh	7	71	.090	California	9	55	.141
Los Angeles	6	52	.103	New York	7	53	.117
St. Louis	4	58	.065	Minnesota	6	67	.082
				Seattle	6	74	.075
N.L. Totals	129	685	.158	Detroit	5	56	.082
				A.L. Totals	135	868	.135

Teams leading after six innings won 85 percent of the time last season, and that mark rose to 90 percent for teams leading after seven, 95 percent for those leading after eight. We've been citing figures like these for several years now, but clearly they tell only part of the story. Obviously, teams leading after six innings by three runs have a much better chance of winning (92 percent) than those leading by a single run (70 percent). So we've developed a set of tables of late-game situations, a different table for one-run leads, two-run leads, on so on, and the percentages of come-from-behind wins resulting from those situations in the major leagues last season:

One-run leads	After 6th	Middle of 7th	After 7th	Middle of 8th	After 8th	Middle of 9th
Home team leading	29.3%	17.4%	19.8%	9.9%	13.3%	—
Road team leading	30.6%	33.2%	23.7%	29.4%	15.3%	20.5%

Two-run leads	After 6th	Middle of 7th	After 7th	Middle of 8th	After 8th	Middle of 9th
Home team leading	16.8%	10.6%	14.0%	7.0%	9.4%	—
Road team leading	19.0%	21.7%	14.7%	16.3%	6.2%	6.4%

Three-run leads	After 6th	Middle of 7th	After 7th	Middle of 8th	After 8th	Middle of 9th
Home team leading	5.2%	2.1%	3.0%	0.7%	1.2%	—
Road team leading	10.6%	11.8%	6.9%	5.9%	1.4%	2.5%

Four-plus-run leads	After 6th	Middle of 7th	After 7th	Middle of 8th	After 8th	Middle of 9th
Home team leading	2.3%	1.0%	1.3%	0.6%	0.7%	—
Road team leading	2.9%	5.2%	1.9%	2.8%	0.7%	0.6%

The value of these tables is best shown by examining in further detail the general statement that home teams won only 5 percent of all games in which they trailed after eight innings. They won more than 10 times as often when their deficit going to the ninth inning was a single run as when they trailed by three runs. And the road team was three times more likely to win when leading by two runs going to the bottom of the ninth than when leading by one—quite an impressive payoff for a single insurance run.

Armed with that load of data, let's reexamine Cincinnati's accomplishments. Although Cincinnati won 16 games in which it trailed after six innings, the deficit was one run in nine of those games. Still, nine other major-league teams had no more comeback wins than that from seventh-inning deficits of any margin. And the Reds also won seven other games in which they trailed after six, when the margin was two runs or more. The only team to overcome more deficits of two or more runs was the San Diego Padres, with eight. San Francisco, tied with Cincinnati for the major-league lead in the table above, had a breakdown similar to the Reds', and one in line with league averages. The margin of deficit after the sixth inning in their come-from-behind victories:

Team	1 Run	2 Runs	3 + Runs
Cincinnati	9	3	4
San Francisco	8	3	3
Major-League Totals	158	67	39
	60%	25%	15%

But maybe the award for the best comeback team last season belongs to a team that won only nine games in which they trailed after six innings, the California Angels. We produced a list of the nine least likely comebacks of the season, wins in situations indicated in the tables above by figures of less than 1.5 percent. Not only was California the only team to appear twice, but the Angels grabbed two of the top three spots:

Date	Teams and Final Score	Situation
Aug. 29	Cal. (13) vs. Det. (12)	Trailed 12–5 in middle of ninth.
June 18	Minn. (10) vs. Chi. (9)	Trailed 9–5 in middle of ninth.
Apr. 26	Cal. (7) at Minn. (6)	Trailed 6–1 after the eighth.
Oct. 2	Cin. (6) at Atl. (4)	Trailed 4–0 after the eighth.
Sept. 3	S.D. (7) at Phil. (5)	Trailed 5–1 after the eighth.
Aug. 6	Tex. (13) at Balt. (11)	Trailed 11–6 after the seventh.
June 29	Phil. (8) at St.L. (7)	Trailed 7–4 after the eighth.
June 12	Chi. (8) at Sea. (4)	Trailed 4–0 after the seventh.
Aug. 9	N.Y. (10) at Mtl. (8)	Trailed 6–1 after the seventh.

And, in view of our findings, let's review the comebacks during last year's playoffs and World Series. California overcame a 3–0 deficit in the middle of the ninth in Game Four of the American League Championship Series to defeat the Red Sox in extra innings. Home teams won four of 162 regular-season games in which they trailed by three runs after eight-and-a-half innings.

Boston won Game Five of the A.L.C.S., in which it trailed by three runs after eight innings. New York won Game Six of the N.L.C.S. after trailing 3–0 going to the top of the ninth. Road teams won only two of 142 games last season in which they trailed by three runs after eight innings.

Finally, New York won Game Six of the World Series by overcoming a two-run deficit in the middle of the 10th inning. Only three of sixty-four home teams won extra-inning games last season in which they trailed during overtime by more than one run.

WON-LOST RECORD BY STARTING POSITION

CINCINNATI 86-76	C	1B	2B	3B	SS	LF	CF	RF	P	Leadoff	Relief	Starts
Buddy Bell	-	-	-	82-68	-	-	-	-	-	-	-	82-68
Tom Browning	-	-	-	-	-	-	-	-	19-20	-	5-2	19-20
Sal Butera	19-12	-	-	-	-	-	-	-	-	-	0-1	19-12
Dave Concepcion	-	2-1	5-4	1-6	27-31	-	-	-	-	-	-	35-42
Kal Daniels	-	-	-	-	-	22-20	-	-	-	16-10	-	22-20
Eric Davis	-	-	-	-	-	23-19	31-31	4-1	-	6-13	-	58-51
John Denny	-	-	-	-	-	-	-	-	16-11	-	-	16-11
Bo Diaz	66-63	-	-	-	-	-	-	-	-	-	-	66-63
Nick Esasky	-	25-24	-	-	-	22-19	-	-	-	-	-	47-43
John Franco	-	-	-	-	-	-	-	-	-	-	46-28	-
Bill Gullickson	-	-	-	-	-	-	-	-	20-17	-	-	20-17
Tracy Jones	-	-	-	-	-	6-10	-	-	-	3-5	-	6-10
Tito Landrum	-	-	-	-	-	-	-	-	-	-	-	-
Barry Larkin	-	-	2-0	-	21-13	-	-	-	-	14-8	-	23-13
Eddie Milner	-	-	-	-	-	-	55-43	-	-	29-29	-	55-43
Rob Murphy	-	-	-	-	-	-	-	-	-	-	18-16	-
Paul O'Neill	-	-	-	-	-	-	-	-	-	-	0-3	-
Ron Oester	-	-	77-71	-	-	-	-	-	-	3-1	-	77-71
Dave Parker	-	-	-	-	-	-	-	82-75	-	-	-	82-75
Tony Perez	29-20	-	-	-	-	-	-	-	-	-	-	29-20
Ted Power	-	-	-	-	-	-	-	-	8-2	-	11-35	8-2
Joe Price	-	-	-	-	-	-	-	-	0-2	-	6-17	0-2
Ron Robinson	-	-	-	-	-	-	-	-	-	-	43-27	-
Pete Rose	-	30-31	-	-	-	-	-	-	-	-	-	30-31
Wade Rowdon	-	-	2-1	3-2	1-5	3-1	-	-	-	1-0	-	9-9
Tom Runnells	-	-	-	-	-	-	-	-	-	-	-	-
Mike Smith	-	-	-	-	-	-	-	-	1-0	-	-	1-0
Mario Soto	-	-	-	-	-	-	-	-	8-12	-	0-1	8-12
Kurt Stillwell	-	-	-	-	37-27	-	-	-	-	14-9	-	37-27
Scott Terry	-	-	-	-	-	-	-	-	1-1	-	6-19	1-1
Dave Van Gorder	1-1	-	-	-	-	-	-	-	-	-	-	1-1
Max Venable	-	-	-	-	-	10-7	0-2	-	-	0-1	-	10-9
Chris Welsh	-	-	-	-	-	-	-	-	13-11	-	-	13-11
Carl Willis	-	-	-	-	-	-	-	-	-	-	11-18	-

Batting Comparisons: Vs. Left-Handers/Right-Handers and Overall/Late Inning Pressure Situations

		BA	Rank	SA	Rank	HR %	Rank		BA	Rank	SA	Rank	HR %	Rank
Buddy Bell	vs. Lefties	.270	60	.471	29	4.60	20	Overall	.278	33	.445	33	3.52	40
	vs. Righties	.282	37	.434	53	3.05	49	Pressure	.298	38	.429	47	2.38	56
Dave Concepcion	vs. Lefties	.337	7	.455	37	0.99	107	Overall	.260	69	.344	111	0.96	117
	vs. Righties	.224	117	.290	123	0.95	111	Pressure	.311	27	.459	30	1.64	84
Kal Daniels	vs. Lefties	.188	--	.219	--	0.00	--	Overall	.320	5	.519	4	3.31	44
	vs. Righties	.349	1	.584	2	4.03	35	Pressure	.321	--	.679	--	7.14	--
Eric Davis	vs. Lefties	.319	18	.590	8	7.64	3	Overall	.277	38	.523	3	6.51	2
	vs. Righties	.255	80	.487	14	5.90	4	Pressure	.303	33	.470	28	4.55	24
Bo Diaz	vs. Lefties	.271	57	.398	64	2.26	65	Overall	.272	48	.380	85	2.11	74
	vs. Righties	.273	44	.372	82	2.05	78	Pressure	.346	15	.513	13	5.13	16
Nick Esasky	vs. Lefties	.237	96	.458	35	4.24	26	Overall	.230	121	.403	69	3.64	37
	vs. Righties	.226	111	.373	81	3.30	45	Pressure	.178	130	.378	76	6.67	3
Tracy Jones	vs. Lefties	.317	19	.444	44	3.17	41	Overall	.349	--	.453	--	2.33	--
	vs. Righties	.435	--	.478	--	0.00	--	Pressure	.391	--	.478	--	0.00	--
Barry Larkin	vs. Lefties	.340	--	.480	--	4.00	--	Overall	.283	--	.403	--	1.89	--
	vs. Righties	.257	72	.367	87	0.92	113	Pressure	.500	--	.556	--	0.00	--
Eddie Milner	vs. Lefties	.224	111	.276	128	0.00	119	Overall	.259	71	.446	30	3.54	39
	vs. Righties	.265	51	.473	21	4.10	33	Pressure	.192	126	.385	71	3.85	33
Ron Oester	vs. Lefties	.184	136	.243	138	0.74	112	Overall	.258	73	.356	102	1.53	95
	vs. Righties	.284	33	.395	70	1.81	86	Pressure	.290	41	.398	65	2.15	63
Dave Parker	vs. Lefties	.302	36	.513	15	4.31	23	Overall	.273	46	.477	17	4.87	14
	vs. Righties	.257	73	.457	30	5.19	10	Pressure	.271	58	.500	17	5.21	14
Tony Perez	vs. Lefties	.270	62	.348	93	0.87	108	Overall	.255	82	.355	104	1.00	112
	vs. Righties	.235	--	.365	--	1.18	--	Pressure	.385	4	.462	29	0.00	102
Pete Rose	vs. Lefties	.273	--	.364	--	0.00	--	Overall	.219	132	.270	137	0.00	136
	vs. Righties	.214	125	.260	135	0.00	131	Pressure	.217	--	.348	--	0.00	--
Kurt Stillwell	vs. Lefties	.244	92	.279	125	0.00	119	Overall	.229	122	.258	140	0.00	136
	vs. Righties	.223	120	.249	139	0.00	131	Pressure	.208	117	.229	132	0.00	102
Max Venable	vs. Lefties	.125	--	.125	--	0.00	--	Overall	.211	--	.313	--	1.36	--
	vs. Righties	.221	122	.336	108	1.53	96	Pressure	.211	113	.237	128	0.00	102
Team Average	vs. Lefties	.264	2	.403	4	2.70	4	Overall	.254	6	.387	5	2.60	4
	vs. Righties	.249	9	.380	7	2.56	6	Pressure	.273	2	.411	1	2.85	3
League Average	vs. Lefties	.257		.384		2.28		Overall	.253		.380		2.32	
	vs. Righties	.251		.378		2.34		Pressure	.257		.376		2.31	

Additional Miscellaneous Batting Comparisons

	Grass Surface BA	Rank	Artificial Surface BA	Rank	Home Games BA	Rank	Road Games BA	Rank	Runners in Scoring Position BA	Rank	Runners in Scoring Pos and Two Outs BA	Rank	Leading Off Inning OBA	Rank	Runners on 3B with less than 2 Outs RDI %	Rank
Buddy Bell	.250	79	.291	27	.308	22	.250	76	.243	88	.208	99	.376	23	.621	46
Sal Butera	.450	--	.194	133	.203	--	.295	--	.257	--	.267	--	.314	--	.600	52
Dave Concepcion	.275	53	.254	77	.274	66	.250	76	.205	121	.231	82	.288	103	.600	52
Kal Daniels	.351	--	.313	14	.309	21	.338	--	.235	--	.250	--	.429	7	.571	--
Eric Davis	.277	49	.277	41	.264	86	.289	19	.282	48	.319	23	.345	46	.357	139
Bo Diaz	.310	15	.252	79	.286	50	.260	60	.286	41	.267	52	.288	102	.548	84
Nick Esasky	.247	83	.223	110	.226	121	.234	102	.167	138	.146	129	.367	29	.458	121
Tracy Jones	.000	--	.395	1	.303	--	.377	--	.318	--	.273	--	.405	--	.800	--
Barry Larkin	.348	--	.257	67	.280	--	.286	--	.350	--	.238	77	.290	99	.636	37
Eddie Milner	.271	59	.254	73	.288	45	.231	107	.238	93	.270	48	.270	119	.500	101
Ron Oester	.245	89	.263	54	.280	61	.237	98	.266	60	.265	54	.315	83	.577	73
Dave Parker	.284	40	.268	50	.268	76	.278	34	.344	11	.419	3	.327	69	.565	75
Tony Perez	.244	93	.262	58	.250	99	.260	61	.288	39	.194	111	.220	--	.789	4
Pete Rose	.231	--	.215	119	.256	94	.181	140	.348	10	.444	2	.245	134	.429	--
Kurt Stillwell	.212	127	.239	98	.219	129	.242	91	.295	34	.282	41	.256	126	.375	138
Max Venable	.250	--	.184	138	.197	--	.224	--	.143	142	.095	142	.265	--	.600	52
Team Average	.258	6	.252	7	.259	8	.248	7	.256	4	.254	2	.307	10	.531	12
League Average	.254		.253		.260		.247		.252		.235		.316		.562	

Pitching Comparisons: Vs. Left-Handers/Right-Handers and Runners On/Bases Empty

		BA	Rank	BB %	Rank	SO %	Rank		BA	Rank	BB %	Rank	SO %	Rank
Tom Browning	vs. Lefties	.241	45	10.97	75	14.84	63	Runners On	.271	73	7.79	25	10.91	92
	vs. Righties	.246	60	6.16	27	14.40	71	Bases Empty	.231	26	6.34	29	16.64	50
John Denny	vs. Lefties	.318	109	8.79	46	10.44	98	Runners On	.265	64	8.60	34	13.69	71
	vs. Righties	.227	28	6.54	34	20.98	21	Bases Empty	.277	93	6.95	44	17.27	40
John Franco	vs. Lefties	.211	16	3.70	5	16.05	49	Runners On	.238	33	12.23	90	20.96	10
	vs. Righties	.251	66	11.78	102	20.40	28	Bases Empty	.247	51	8.00	65	18.00	35
Bill Gullickson	vs. Lefties	.275	80	7.36	33	10.57	97	Runners On	.268	70	4.40	1	11.25	90
	vs. Righties	.252	70	4.34	10	13.43	83	Bases Empty	.262	73	6.94	43	12.40	95
Rob Murphy	vs. Lefties	.133	--	6.00	--	26.00	--	Runners On	.128	--	12.50	--	18.75	--
	vs. Righties	.163	3	12.41	107	15.86	58	Bases Empty	.178	--	9.09	--	18.18	--
Ted Power	vs. Lefties	.262	68	10.90	74	15.41	55	Runners On	.240	34	11.48	81	20.08	15
	vs. Righties	.229	34	8.49	68	19.93	31	Bases Empty	.249	55	8.19	72	15.70	59
Joe Price	vs. Lefties	.227	--	6.25	--	22.92	--	Runners On	.315	--	10.48	--	14.29	--
	vs. Righties	.317	114	13.01	109	13.01	86	Bases Empty	.269	--	12.36	--	16.85	--
Ron Robinson	vs. Lefties	.294	93	14.10	108	14.54	66	Runners On	.243	37	12.32	94	19.91	16
	vs. Righties	.220	20	4.23	9	32.31	2	Bases Empty	.260	72	6.16	25	27.17	3
Mario Soto	vs. Lefties	.300	96	12.64	96	11.90	85	Runners On	.275	81	12.75	96	16.67	37
	vs. Righties	.254	72	6.25	28	18.23	40	Bases Empty	.283	100	7.78	60	12.84	90
Scott Terry	vs. Lefties	.343	115	10.57	73	12.20	81	Runners On	.333	112	11.36	78	10.61	94
	vs. Righties	.259	--	14.07	--	12.59	--	Bases Empty	.266	--	13.49	--	14.29	--
Chris Welsh	vs. Lefties	.226	29	7.53	35	11.83	86	Runners On	.310	104	4.81	3	8.52	110
	vs. Righties	.315	113	6.53	33	5.74	115	Bases Empty	.294	110	8.23	73	5.18	116
Carl Willis	vs. Lefties	.333	112	14.29	109	5.49	117	Runners On	.232	28	16.54	115	7.09	114
	vs. Righties	.246	59	13.38	112	13.38	84	Bases Empty	.330	--	10.38	--	14.15	--
Team Average	vs. Lefties	.281	12	9.71	5	12.70	11	Runners On	.267	9	9.29	3	14.12	9
	vs. Righties	.254	8	7.61	3	16.07	7	Bases Empty	.261	9	7.68	4	15.36	9
League Average	vs. Lefties	.257		9.83		14.90		Runners On	.260		10.11		15.02	
	vs. Righties	.251		8.19		16.33		Bases Empty	.248		7.89		16.30	

Additional Miscellaneous Pitching Comparisons

	Grass Surface BA	Rank	Artificial Surface BA	Rank	Home Games BA	Rank	Road Games BA	Rank	Runners in Scoring Position BA	Rank	Runners in Scoring Pos and Two Outs BA	Rank	Leading Off Inning OBA	Rank
Tom Browning	.238	41	.249	46	.237	48	.251	48	.272	79	.253	70	.277	22
John Denny	.259	67	.277	91	.278	92	.266	74	.230	33	.162	14	.372	101
John Franco	.215	13	.254	57	.250	68	.234	25	.230	32	.267	79	.256	13
Bill Gullickson	.266	71	.263	69	.277	90	.251	46	.245	48	.222	46	.296	40
Rob Murphy	.136	--	.161	3	.143	--	.169	--	.122	--	.045	--	.318	--
Ted Power	.245	50	.245	46	.259	75	.229	22	.240	42	.232	57	.333	76
Joe Price	.310	--	.290	97	.253	--	.330	--	.340	--	.292	--	.415	--
Ron Robinson	.277	82	.243	38	.247	61	.261	66	.214	23	.182	22	.313	60
Mario Soto	.248	55	.294	103	.327	114	.236	29	.278	84	.280	88	.339	84
Scott Terry	.292	--	.303	110	.320	112	.274	--	.281	88	.290	90	.418	116
Chris Welsh	.330	115	.295	105	.289	98	.317	109	.309	106	.315	105	.352	94
Carl Willis	.203	--	.313	113	.310	--	.247	--	.286	96	.292	--	.460	--
Team Average	.254	5	.268	11	.271	11	.257	5	.255	8	.240	7	.331	11
League Average	.254		.253		.247		.260		.252		.235		.316	

HOUSTON ASTROS

Some teams, like the 1986 New York Mets, win championships simply by the overwhelming talent of their players. Others, like last season's Houston Astros, enter the season as contenders in search of an edge to put them over the top. One of Houston's important edges last season—like Baltimore's in 1983 and Toronto's in 1985—was the performance of its platoon players: Craig Reynolds and Dickie Thon at shortstop, but especially Denny Walling and Phil Garner at third.

Considering how often recent division winners have used two-player platoons to fill a position, it's surprising how few National League teams employed that strategy last season. Of course, the league was filled with platooned players, usually left-handed hitters who only faced southpaw pitching occasionally, like San Diego's Marvell Wynne. But they shared their positions with a wide variety of righty counterparts. Only the four pairs of players listed below (along with their number of starts against each type of pitching) shared positions for the entire season on that basis:

Team	Pos.	Left-Hander	Vs. LHP	Vs. RHP	Right-Hander	Vs. LHP	Vs. RHP
Houston	3B	Walling	1	80	Garner	61	12
Houston	SS	Reynolds	2	76	Thon	58	18
New York	2B	Backman	2	90	Teufel	60	10
San Diego	2B	Flannery	4	80	Roberts	42	23

Houston's shortstop platoon of Reynolds and Thon merely allowed the Astros to spread some mediocrity a little thinner. But the third-base platoon of Walling and Garner performed far better than the National League average for third basemen. The following table compares the performance of Astros third basemen in games started last season to the league standard at the position:

Starter	GS	AB	R	H	2B	3B	HR	RBI	BB	SB	BA	SA	OBA
Garner	76	276	40	77	13	2	8	34	23	10	.279	.428	.333
Walling	81	306	44	88	18	1	11	46	24	1	.288	.461	.335
Others	5	20	1	4	1	0	0	1	2	0	.200	.250	.273
Totals	162	602	85	169	32	3	19	81	49	11	.281	.439	.332
N.L. Avg.	162	659	76	156	28	3	17	79	60	10	.267	.413	.337

Just how much of an edge does the flexibility of the platoon give Houston? Let's compare the combined performance of the Astros' third basemen to projected full-season statistics for both Garner and Walling. What we've done is to project Walling's performance against left-handed pitchers last season over Garner's 216 plate appearances versus southpaws,

and Garner's statistics against right-handed pitchers over Walling's 358 plate appearances against them. Here's what Garner and Walling might have accomplished had they been forced to play every day, against pitching from both sides:

Player	PA	AB	H	2B	3B	HR	RRF	BB	SO	BA	SA	OBA
Garner	574	523	130	21	3	14	68	47	85	.249	.380	.310
Walling	574	520	145	25	1	13	79	50	45	.279	.406	.340
Platoon	574	516	164	32	4	19	84	50	47	.318	.506	.375

A postseason postscript: Houston's platoons made for some choice second-guessing during the playoffs. Reynolds's shaky fielding prompted Tim McCarver, among others, to wonder whether Dickie Thon shouldn't have been at shortstop against Darling and Gooden as well as against Ojeda and Fernandez. Thon's home run in Game Four fueled that discussion as well. But over the past three seasons, Houston has allowed fewer runs per nine innings with Reynolds in the field than with Thon. Here's how the two platoons size up defensively since 1984:

Shortstop	Innings	Runs	R/9I	3d Baseman	Innings	Runs	R/9I
Reynolds	2689.1	1141	3.82	Walling	1519.2	604	3.58
Thon	1347.2	616	4.11	Garner	2235.0	1025	4.13

Those figures also shed some light on a seemingly strange move that Hal Lanier made in Game Five at Shea Stadium. Jesse Orosco had relieved Dwight Gooden to start the 11th inning. Walling was due up for Houston, and Lanier chose to let him bat against the left-hander rather than pinch-hit Garner. Right move, wrong time: Walling is clearly a better fielder than Garner (see the stats above), an important consideration in extra innings, but after Orosco struck him out, the Mets started their winning 12th-inning rally with Wally Backman's hot smash off Walling's glove. Which just goes to prove that you can have all the stats in the world on your side, but the game still has to be played out on the field, and no stat can tell you unfailingly what's going to happen.

Road Warriors

Houston's postseason appearance seems finally to have tipped off casual baseball fans to what has been clear to some for several seasons: that the Astros no longer win on bunt singles, sacrifice bunts, stolen bases, and good pitching. They have become the most powerful team in the National League, a trait masked by the Astrodome.

In the 1985 edition of the *Analyst*, we noted that Houston ranked second in the National League in 1984 with 61 home runs in road games, a truer measure of a team's power than its overall total since it eliminates the effect of its home park. Well, the Astros led the league last season, to take the league lead in road-game home runs over the past three seasons:

Road-Game Home Runs		Home-Game Home Runs	
Houston	211	Chicago	273
Los Angeles	208	Philadelphia	237
Philadelphia	205	San Diego	204
New York	198	Atlanta	195
Montreal	192	Cincinnati	191
Atlanta	180	New York	191
San Francisco	178	San Francisco	163
Cincinnati	173	Los Angeles	153
Chicago	168	Pittsburgh	136
Pittsburgh	153	Montreal	132
San Diego	150	**Houston**	114
St. Louis	128	St. Louis	92

Of course, Houston has an edge in road-game home runs: they're the only team that doesn't play any road games at the Astrodome. But after all those years of being penalized—statistically speaking, at least—for playing in the Dome, let's cut 'em some slack.

The Mike Shall Inherit
(Well, Aren't You Tired of *Great Scott*?)

The selection of Mike Scott as the 1986 National League Cy Young Award winner culminates the swiftest and most improbable turnaround in recent memory. Scott was traded to Houston by the Mets following a dismal 1982 season in which he lost 13 of 20 decisions and compiled a 5.14 ERA. His market value at the time was nil; New York was able to extract only Danny Heep, who appeared doomed to a career of Triple-A batting titles. Scott posted a 10–6 record in his first season with Houston but regressed to 5–11 in 1984. Then a miracle occurred:

	GS	CG	SHO	W	L	Pct.	ERA	IP	H	BB	SO
Through 1984	113	5	3	29	44	.397	4.45	663	736	211	307
Since 1985	72	11	7	36	18	.667	2.69	497	376	152	443

How it happened no one knows for certain. Scott and his mentor, Roger Craig, say split-fingered fast ball; Gary Carter and Leon Durham say sandpaper. Regardless, the transformation has been amazing. Scott completed one of every 23 starts prior to 1985, but has finished one of seven since then. He allowed 10.00 hits and 4.17 strikeouts per nine innings before; he has more strikeouts than hits allowed since, and it isn't even close.

Perhaps the best way to appreciate Scott's about-face is to look at the pitchers who most closely approximated his career totals after the 1984 season. We warn you—it's not a pretty sight. Five pitchers active in 1984 had at least 50 career starts with winning percentages within .025 and ERAs

within 0.25 of Scott's at the conclusion of the season. Their totals at that time:

Pitcher	W–L	Pct.	ERA
Jim Gott	21–30	.412	4.45
Renie Martin	24–35	.407	4.26
Dickie Noles	25–38	.397	4.42
Bob Owchinko	36–60	.375	4.30
Charlie Puleo	16–23	.410	4.56
Totals	122–186	.396	4.38

As you can see, the group was about as successful as Scott through 1984. Its combined winning percentage was nearly identical to Scott's. And how did those five pitchers do over the past two seasons? Well, Martin never pitched again in the majors. Owchinko and Puleo pitched 39 1/3 innings between them. Gott and Noles each won seven of 17 decisions, with a combined ERA of 4.63. And they're all, no doubt, beating a path to Roger Craig's door.

Astronotes

Some random notes on Scott's no-hitter against San Francisco on September 25, the game in which Houston clinched the Western Division title:

It was the eighth no-hitter by a Houston pitcher, the highest total by any team since the National League expanded to Texas in 1962. The only other team in either league with as many as five no-hitters during that 25-year period is the Los Angeles/California Angels, who have thrown seven. It was the Angels who benefited most from Nolan Ryan's five no-hitters: he pitched four for California, only one for the Astros. Houston's eight no-hitters were thrown by seven different pitchers:

May 17, 1963	Don Nottebart, vs. Philadelphia
April 23, 1964	Ken Johnson, vs. Cincinnati (lost 1–0)
June 18, 1967	Don Wilson, vs. Atlanta
May 1, 1969	Don Wilson at Cincinnati
July 9, 1976	Larry Dierker, vs. Montreal
April 7, 1979	Ken Forsch, vs. Atlanta
September 26, 1981	Nolan Ryan, vs. Los Angeles
September 25, 1986	Mike Scott, vs. San Francisco

Scott pitched six hitless innings in his next start before the ghost of Johnny VanderMeer, in the guise of Will Clark, snapped Scott's bid at immortality with a leadoff double in the seventh inning. Coincidentally, Clark had made the final out in Scott's masterpiece a week earlier. Scott's six innings of hitless work was the strongest challenge to VanderMeer's legendary feat since 1973, when—you guessed it—Nolan Ryan no-hit Detroit on July 15, and then held Baltimore hitless for seven innings before Mark Belanger singled in the eighth.

Astrologers, take note: Scott shares his birthday with three other no-hit pitchers: Ray Caldwell, Virgil Trucks, and Sal Maglie, all born on April 26. No other day of the year has as many as three representatives on the all-time no-hit list.

The acid test: The only other major leaguers active in 1986 born on April 26 were Steve Lombardozzi, Louis Thornton, and Curtis Wilkerson. If one of those guys pitches a no-hitter, remember you heard it here first.

Speaking of hexes, we don't want to put the whammy on Nolan Ryan, who turned 40 over the past winter, but only one pitcher in baseball history has struck out more than 200 batters in a season after his 40th birthday. (Phil Niekro—who else?—fanned 208 batters in 1979.) Nevertheless, with 194 strikeouts last season, despite missing nearly 10 starts due to elbow problems, Ryan shows no signs of slowing down.

Ryan is the all-time major-league leader with an average of 9.35 strikeouts per nine innings. And over the past five seasons, from age 35 to age 39, Ryan fell only 13 strikeouts short of fanning a batter an inning. It seems only natural that a pitcher's strikeout rate should deteriorate beyond his 35th birthday. But we studied the nine-inning rates of the all-time strikeout leaders and found that most didn't hit "the wall" until age 40. Notice that Steve Carlton struck out 8.22 batters per nine innings from age 35 to 39, a marked increase over his career average. Actually, Ryan was one of a minority of four pitchers with lower rates in their late 30s than in their early 30s:

Autumn's Spectators

One of our lasting memories of Houston's loss in the fifth game of the 1980 National League Championship Series is that of Jose Cruz sitting in the Astros dugout after the game ended, head hung almost to his knees. Cruz slowly raised his head and turned toward the television camera, the tracks of his tears sparkling in the TV light like rivulets of ice.

Although there were no similar pictures of Cruz in Houston's dugout following their loss to the Mets last October, he must have retreated to the comfort of the locker room for some private grief. And who could blame him?

In last year's *Analyst*, we acknowledged that Cruz was baseball's most underrated player by acclamation. Away from the glare of national exposure in either a media center or postseason activity, Cruz's accomplishments long went unnoticed. But last season, after his career took a slight southbound turn, Cruz at last appeared headed toward a World Series. At least until Houston's relief pitchers collapsed under the strain of postseason pressure.

And so Cruz remains the active player to have appeared in the most regular-season contests without ever participating in a World Series. The career and active leaders (through 1986) in games played among those who never played in the Series (not including games played prior to its inception):

Pitcher	20–24	25–29	30–34	35–39	40–up	Career
Nolan Ryan	8.64	10.05	9.19	8.89	—	9.35
Steve Carlton	7.15	7.03	6.70	8.22	5.63	7.19
Tom Seaver	6.54	8.39	7.21	5.09	5.14	6.85
Gaylord Perry	5.45	6.74	5.98	6.21	4.83	5.94
Walter Johnson	6.33	5.58	4.39	4.50	—	5.33
Don Sutton	7.10	6.64	5.77	5.84	4.64	6.17
Phil Niekro	—	5.11	5.70	6.08	5.31	5.60
Ferguson Jenkins	4.63	6.94	5.66	5.57	—	6.38
Bob Gibson	6.49	7.65	7.78	6.21	—	7.22
Bert Blyleven	7.42	6.75	6.33	7.12	—	6.97

All-Time Leaders		Active Leaders	
Ernie Banks	2,528	Jose Cruz	2,189
Billy Williams	2,488	Toby Harrah	2,155
Rod Carew	2,469	Buddy Bell	2,133
Luke Appling	2,422	Chris Speier	2,039
Mickey Vernon	2,409	Cesar Cedeno	2,006
Ron Santo	2,243	Dave Kingman	1,941
Joe Torre	2,209	Enos Cabell	1,688
Tony Taylor	2,195	Brian Downing	1,586
Jose Cruz	2,189	Al Cowens	1,584
Toby Harrah	2,155	Roy Smalley	1,543

Cruz should have no trouble vaulting into sixth place on the all-time list this season—unless, of course, his teammates screw things up for him and put him in the Series. We suspect this is one list whose leadership he'd gladly relinquish.

WON-LOST RECORD BY STARTING POSITION

HOUSTON 96-66	C	1B	2B	3B	SS	LF	CF	RF	P	Leadoff	Relief	Starts
Larry Andersen	-	-	-	-	-	-	-	-	-	-	18-20	-
Alan Ashby	59-27	-	-	-	-	-	-	-	-	-	-	59-27
Mark Bailey	23-22	-	-	-	-	-	-	-	-	-	-	23-22
Kevin Bass	-	-	-	-	-	23-14	69-48	-	-	0-1	-	92-62
Eric Bullock	-	-	-	-	-	3-3	-	-	-	0-2	-	3-3
Jeff Calhoun	-	-	-	-	-	-	-	-	-	-	6-14	-
Jose Cruz	-	-	-	-	-	81-50	-	-	-	-	-	81-50
Danny Darwin	-	-	-	-	-	-	-	-	6-2	-	3-1	6-2
Glenn Davis	-	93-63	-	-	-	-	-	-	-	-	-	93-63
Jim Deshaies	-	-	-	-	-	-	-	-	18-8	-	-	18-8
Frank DiPino	-	-	-	-	-	-	-	-	-	-	12-19	-
Bill Doran	-	-	87-56	-	-	-	-	-	-	68-47	-	87-56
Dan Driessen	-	3-1	-	-	-	-	-	-	-	-	-	3-1
Tom Funk	-	-	-	-	-	-	-	-	-	-	2-6	-
Ty Gainey	-	-	-	-	-	7-4	0-1	-	-	-	-	7-5
Phil Garner	·	-	0-4	43-33	-	-	-	-	-	-	-	43-37
Billy Hatcher	-	-	-	-	-	4-3	52-36	4-2	-	26-11	-	60-41
Manny Hernandez	-	-	-	-	-	-	-	-	1-3	-	1-4	1-3
Matt Keough	-	-	-	-	-	-	-	-	3-2	-	3-2	3-2
Charlie Kerfeld	-	-	-	-	-	-	-	-	-	-	38-23	-
Bob Knepper	-	-	-	-	-	-	-	-	23-15	-	2-0	23-15
Mark Knudson	-	-	-	-	-	-	-	-	2-5	-	1-1	2-5
Dave Lopes	-	-	2-2	-	-	5-4	6-2	1-0	-	1-4	-	14-8
Aurelio Lopez	-	-	-	-	-	-	-	-	-	-	23-22	-
Mike Madden	-	-	-	-	-	-	-	-	2-4	-	1-6	2-4
Louie Meadows	-	-	-	-	-	-	-	-	-	-	-	-
John Mizerock	13-17	-	-	-	-	-	-	-	-	-	-	13-17
Rafael Montalvo	-	-	-	-	-	-	-	-	-	-	0-1	-
Jim Pankovits	-	-	9-6	-	-	0-2	-	-	-	-	-	9-8
Bert Pena	-	-	-	0-1	3-5	-	-	-	-	-	-	3-6
Terry Puhl	-	-	-	-	-	0-2	-	22-15	-	-	-	22-17
Craig Reynolds	-	-	-	-	48-30	-	-	-	-	-	-	48-30
Nolan Ryan	-	-	-	-	-	-	-	-	17-13	-	-	17-13
Mike Scott	-	-	-	-	-	-	-	-	24-13	-	0-1	24-13
Dave Smith	-	-	-	-	-	-	-	-	-	-	42-12	-
Julio Solano	-	-	-	-	-	-	-	-	0-1	-	6-9	0-1
Dickie Thon	-	-	-	-	45-31	-	-	-	-	-	-	45-31
Tony Walker	-	-	-	-	-	8-10	-	-	-	1-1	-	8-10
Denny Walling	-	0-2	-	51-30	-	3-2	-	-	-	-	-	54-34
Robbie Wine	1-0	-	-	-	-	-	-	-	-	-	-	1-0

Batting Comparisons: Vs. Left-Handers/Right-Handers and Overall/Late Inning-Pressure Situations

		BA	Rank	SA	Rank	HR %	Rank			BA	Rank	SA	Rank	HR %	Rank
Alan Ashby	vs. Lefties	.276	52	.388	71	1.72	83		Overall	.257	75	.371	91	2.22	71
	vs. Righties	.246	90	.362	93	2.51	61		Pressure	.245	90	.347	87	2.04	68
Mark Bailey	vs. Lefties	.172	139	.234	140	1.56	86		Overall	.176	--	.288	--	2.61	--
	vs. Righties	.180	--	.326	--	3.37	--		Pressure	.152	--	.303	--	3.03	--
Kevin Bass	vs. Lefties	.323	17	.540	11	4.84	18		Overall	.311	9	.486	10	3.38	43
	vs. Righties	.303	19	.446	41	2.33	68		Pressure	.303	32	.438	44	3.37	41
Jose Cruz	vs. Lefties	.284	45	.392	67	1.03	105		Overall	.278	34	.403	70	2.09	77
	vs. Righties	.274	43	.411	64	2.81	52		Pressure	.243	93	.400	62	4.29	29
Glenn Davis	vs. Lefties	.270	59	.512	17	5.69	15		Overall	.265	62	.493	9	5.40	9
	vs. Righties	.262	60	.482	18	5.23	9		Pressure	.300	34	.500	17	5.56	10
Bill Doran	vs. Lefties	.304	34	.407	60	1.40	98		Overall	.276	40	.373	89	1.09	110
	vs. Righties	.259	66	.351	103	0.89	115		Pressure	.197	121	.296	107	1.41	93
Phil Garner	vs. Lefties	.292	39	.469	31	3.13	44		Overall	.265	61	.415	59	2.88	53
	vs. Righties	.223	118	.331	111	2.48	63		Pressure	.300	34	.500	17	4.00	31
Billy Hatcher	vs. Lefties	.286	42	.390	68	1.43	97		Overall	.258	74	.356	103	1.43	98
	vs. Righties	.230	108	.321	114	1.44	98		Pressure	.308	30	.404	58	1.92	74
Dave Lopes	vs. Lefties	.255	80	.394	66	3.19	40		Overall	.275	42	.420	55	2.75	56
	vs. Righties	.286	32	.435	52	2.48	62		Pressure	.320	25	.500	17	4.00	31
Jim Pankovits	vs. Lefties	.267	66	.333	101	0.00	119		Overall	.283	--	.381	--	0.88	--
	vs. Righties	.302	--	.434	--	1.89	--		Pressure	.300	--	.423	--	3.85	--
Terry Puhl	vs. Lefties	.304	--	.348	--	0.00	--		Overall	.244	--	.355	--	1.74	--
	vs. Righties	.235	102	.356	100	2.01	81		Pressure	.171	133	.200	136	0.00	102
Craig Reynolds	vs. Lefties	.143	--	.171	--	0.00	--		Overall	.249	95	.348	106	1.92	84
	vs. Righties	.263	57	.371	84	2.16	73		Pressure	.288	43	.404	58	1.92	74
Dickie Thon	vs. Lefties	.243	93	.305	119	0.56	116		Overall	.248	96	.335	115	1.08	111
	vs. Righties	.257	--	.386	--	1.98	--		Pressure	.424	--	.606	--	6.06	--
Tony Walker	vs. Lefties	.264	70	.453	39	3.77	32		Overall	.222	--	.367	--	2.22	--
	vs. Righties	.162	--	.243	--	0.00	--		Pressure	.100	--	.100	--	0.00	--
Denny Walling	vs. Lefties	.190	134	.207	142	0.00	119		Overall	.312	8	.479	14	3.40	41
	vs. Righties	.333	5	.528	4	4.01	36		Pressure	.296	39	.408	56	2.82	48
Team Average	vs. Lefties	.260	7	.380	8	2.08	9		Overall	.255	4	.381	7	2.30	8
	vs. Righties	.252	6	.381	6	2.44	7		Pressure	.272	3	.397	4	2.94	2
League Average	vs. Lefties	.257		.384		2.28			Overall	.253		.380		2.32	
	vs. Righties	.251		.378		2.34			Pressure	.257		.376		2.31	

Additional Miscellaneous Batting Comparisons

	Grass Surface BA	Rank	Artificial Surface BA	Rank	Home Games BA	Rank	Road Games BA	Rank	Runners in Scoring Position BA	Rank	Runners in Scoring Pos and Two Outs BA	Rank	Leading Off Inning OBA	Rank	Runners on 3B with less than 2 Outs RDI %	Rank
Alan Ashby	.245	90	.262	56	.252	98	.263	58	.244	84	.224	86	.292	96	.615	49
Mark Bailey	.109	--	.206	126	.200	--	.154	--	.122	144	.143	--	.297	--	.400	--
Kevin Bass	.300	24	.316	11	.314	13	.308	12	.311	22	.268	51	.329	64	.600	52
Jose Cruz	.220	122	.302	18	.298	32	.256	65	.389	2	.400	4	.261	124	.655	29
Glenn Davis	.231	110	.279	39	.298	30	.232	106	.265	61	.256	62	.317	79	.595	61
Bill Doran	.246	88	.290	30	.274	66	.279	32	.242	91	.265	54	.370	27	.647	33
Phil Garner	.272	57	.262	56	.265	84	.265	51	.221	115	.314	26	.329	65	.476	114
Billy Hatcher	.250	79	.261	62	.257	93	.259	63	.222	112	.206	102	.331	59	.588	65
Dave Lopes	.300	24	.238	99	.311	15	.241	93	.254	71	.333	16	.439	5	.526	95
Terry Puhl	.220	--	.257	67	.214	--	.265	54	.190	130	.136	131	.294	--	.500	--
Craig Reynolds	.200	136	.276	42	.319	9	.189	135	.355	7	.370	6	.159	144	.550	82
Mike Scott	.048	--	.149	143	.106	--	.146	--	.158	--	.250	--	.200	--	.333	--
Dickie Thon	.203	--	.263	55	.250	99	.246	84	.212	117	.188	116	.394	16	.545	86
Denny Walling	.345	3	.298	22	.295	37	.328	5	.250	75	.289	38	.346	44	.652	31
Team Average	.239	11	.262	2	.262	5	.249	5	.254	6	.251	4	.308	9	.551	9
League Average	.254		.253		.260		.247		.252		.235		.316		.562	

Pitching Comparisons: Vs. Left-Handers/Right-Handers and Runners On/Bases Empty

		BA	Rank	BB %	Rank	SO %	Rank		BA	Rank	BB %	Rank	SO %	Rank
Larry Andersen	vs. Lefties	.305	104	9.59	61	15.07	61	Runners On	.279	84	9.09	40	11.76	85
	vs. Righties	.288	100	6.78	40	11.30	100	Bases Empty	.315	115	6.62	36	14.71	73
Danny Darwin	vs. Lefties	.304	103	5.56	13	15.74	52	Runners On	.195	--	5.49	--	17.58	--
	vs. Righties	.178	--	2.63	--	20.18	--	Bases Empty	.268	84	3.05	5	18.32	32
Jim Deshaies	vs. Lefties	.241	46	12.00	87	20.00	24	Runners On	.180	1	10.08	56	20.17	14
	vs. Righties	.232	37	9.42	82	21.64	17	Bases Empty	.268	83	9.70	90	22.16	13
Matt Keough	vs. Lefties	.246	50	9.16	53	12.21	80	Runners On	.253	47	14.05	107	14.05	68
	vs. Righties	.246	--	12.77	--	19.86	--	Bases Empty	.241	42	8.61	78	17.88	37
Charlie Kerfeld	vs. Lefties	.247	54	11.24	82	15.73	53	Runners On	.222	20	13.26	101	18.78	26
	vs. Righties	.184	4	10.38	94	23.11	9	Bases Empty	.206	10	8.61	79	20.57	16
Bob Knepper	vs. Lefties	.227	33	3.68	4	22.09	14	Runners On	.244	39	8.23	28	11.14	91
	vs. Righties	.244	56	6.29	30	12.02	93	Bases Empty	.240	41	4.38	11	15.16	64
Mark Knudson	vs. Lefties	.292	91	9.00	48	10.00	102	Runners On	.294	--	13.25	--	10.84	--
	vs. Righties	.265	--	6.59	--	10.99	--	Bases Empty	.269	--	3.70	--	10.19	--
Aurelio Lopez	vs. Lefties	.183	7	9.36	57	15.79	51	Runners On	.231	27	8.82	35	16.18	45
	vs. Righties	.265	83	6.00	25	11.33	99	Bases Empty	.215	15	7.03	45	11.89	100
Mike Madden	vs. Lefties	.267	--	10.53	--	18.42	--	Runners On	.257	--	14.13	--	15.22	--
	vs. Righties	.305	110	12.24	105	15.65	60	Bases Empty	.333	--	9.68	--	17.20	--
Nolan Ryan	vs. Lefties	.184	9	13.77	103	24.52	11	Runners On	.214	16	13.31	102	24.82	3
	vs. Righties	.191	6	8.74	72	28.69	3	Bases Empty	.173	3	9.98	94	27.72	2
Mike Scott	vs. Lefties	.215	21	8.70	43	19.72	28	Runners On	.181	2	7.47	18	33.60	1
	vs. Righties	.156	2	4.58	11	38.84	1	Bases Empty	.189	6	6.38	32	26.09	5
Dave Smith	vs. Lefties	.167	5	8.11	40	16.22	48	Runners On	.196	--	7.21	--	20.72	--
	vs. Righties	.237	--	11.61	--	25.00	--	Bases Empty	.204	--	12.50	--	20.54	--
Team Average	vs. Lefties	.225	1	9.75	6	18.02	1	Runners On	.226	1	10.07	6	18.86	1
	vs. Righties	.226	1	8.05	7	20.10	1	Bases Empty	.225	1	7.73	5	19.61	1
League Average	vs. Lefties	.257		9.83		14.90		Runners On	.260		10.11		15.02	
	vs. Righties	.251		8.19		16.33		Bases Empty	.248		7.89		16.30	

Additional Miscellaneous Pitching Comparisons

	Grass Surface BA	Rank	Artificial Surface BA	Rank	Home Games BA	Rank	Road Games BA	Rank	Runners in Scoring Position BA	Rank	Runners in Scoring Pos and Two Outs BA	Rank	Leading Off Inning OBA	Rank
Larry Andersen	.381	117	.250	47	.244	56	.338	113	.308	105	.320	109	.415	115
Jeff Calhoun	.333	--	.247	42	.233	--	.333	--	.367	--	.444	--	.192	--
Danny Darwin	.214	12	.261	67	.315	--	.199	8	.239	--	.296	--	.241	7
Jim Deshaies	.270	79	.225	23	.229	32	.241	36	.140	1	.125	5	.342	87
Matt Keough	.250	58	.240	34	.309	--	.220	17	.196	--	.240	66	.391	111
Charlie Kerfeld	.256	66	.190	8	.188	9	.234	26	.158	3	.125	5	.295	38
Bob Knepper	.227	24	.249	45	.248	65	.235	28	.229	31	.170	18	.288	29
Mark Knudson	.313	--	.259	64	.279	--	.279	--	.279	--	.304	--	.295	--
Aurelio Lopez	.259	68	.206	11	.259	76	.187	4	.243	47	.293	94	.221	4
Mike Madden	.346	--	.274	85	.333	--	.274	--	.273	--	.150	--	.395	--
Nolan Ryan	.225	21	.176	4	.151	1	.239	32	.239	41	.214	41	.273	21
Mike Scott	.191	4	.185	7	.179	4	.196	6	.159	4	.119	3	.261	16
Dave Smith	.184	--	.210	12	.202	--	.198	7	.172	--	.107	--	.311	--
Julio Solano	.351	--	.292	99	.273	--	.338	--	.255	--	.200	--	.424	--
Team Average	.244	3	.218	1	.218	2	.233	1	.216	1	.201	2	.297	2
League Average	.254		.253		.247		.260		.252		.235		.316	

LOS ANGELES DODGERS

Throughout the spring of 1986, Tommy Lasorda crowed over the middle of the Dodgers' batting order. According to Lasorda, no team had better three-four-five hitters than Los Angeles: Bill Madlock, Pedro Guerrero, and Mike Marshall.

All that ended on April 3, when Guerrero ruptured the tendon that held his left kneecap in place. The heart of the Dodgers' batting order would be lost to the team for most of the season, and, as *The Sporting News* reported, "in one crushing moment, the Dodgers went from odds-on favorites to rule the National League West . . . to a club in trouble." Vice President Al Campanis thought things might not be quite that dire. He observed, "We still have a good club, but it's certainly better when Pete's in there."

Taken at face value, the results seem to indicate that Campanis was whistling in the dark. The Dodgers matched their poorest record of the past 40 years (they had a 73–89 mark, as in 1967), and escaped the ignominy of their second last-place finish since 1905 only because the Atlanta Braves were swept by the Houston Astros in a three-game season-ending series. Los Angeles scored only 637 runs to rank ninth in the league, and at the core of the problem was the meat of the order. The National League totals for three-four-five hitters:

Team	AB	R	H	2B	3B	HR	RBI	BB	SO	BA	SA	OBA
Atlanta	1845	247	501	87	10	78	238	204	302	.272	.456	.343
Chicago	1877	242	507	91	7	57	235	181	262	.270	.417	.331
Cincinnati	1893	283	508	85	11	75	300	216	329	.268	.444	.342
Houston	1874	277	520	98	10	67	269	170	232	.277	.448	.340
Los Angeles	1902	237	481	71	2	69	257	158	345	.253	.401	.313
Montreal	1903	249	546	109	19	56	278	177	297	.287	.452	.349
New York	1860	308	511	93	10	76	332	258	322	.275	.458	.363
Philadelphia	1878	304	535	111	11	69	307	213	308	.285	.466	.359
Pittsburgh	1869	249	513	107	9	49	258	202	234	.274	.420	.344
St. Louis	1852	222	451	85	15	33	225	219	313	.244	.359	.324
San Diego	1883	239	502	79	10	62	279	183	274	.267	.418	.329
San Francisco	1884	253	522	99	12	45	261	186	302	.277	.414	.344
Averages	1877	259	507	93	11	61	270	197	293	.271	.429	.340

The Dodgers ranked next-to-last in batting average and slugging average and last in on-base average—quite a humbling experience for what Lasorda had considered to be the National League's best. And while Madlock and Marshall both spent time on the disabled list last season, the key to the downfall of the Dodgers offense was the loss of Guerrero.

Still, it's hard to imagine that the loss of a single player—even a player of Guerrero's talent—could be responsible for such a dramatic team turnaround. Our skepticism prompted us to design a study to measure the value of a superstar.

Similar published studies have tended to disintegrate under their own weight. They have been limited not only by dealing in obscure measures of a player's value, but also by following a convoluted and dubious path from that figure to an expression of the number of wins a player contributed. Guerrero, for instance, would be assigned a certain value for every hit, every home run, every walk, every putout and assist, every error—everything. Those values would be rolled up into something that would be called, let's say, his "run factor," or some other puffed-up term; that figure was translated into the number of runs Guerrero contributed; then, the runs were translated into wins. Even assuming that the original "run factor" had validity—and in many cases that required a fanatic's leap of faith—the margin of error grew at each stage, undermining the final result.

Our method: Go right to the source. If you want to know how many wins a player contributes, forget about hits, walks, assists, and so on; *look at wins.* We looked at the record of each player's team in games he started and compared it to the team's performance without him in the starting lineup. Clean and simple. No estimates of how much a home run is worth, or, even worse, how much a putout or an assist is worth; just a pure measurement of each player's contribution in bottom-line terms: wins and losses.

Over a single season, the margin of error is too large to produce meaningful results. So we studied the figures for a five-year period (1982–86), and further minimized the error margin by examining 20 players. The errors that might occur for a single player, reduced when studied over five years, are further absorbed or balanced by others in the group.

The players included aren't intended to constitute a definitive list of the best in the majors since 1982. Some players—Cal Ripken, for example—were excluded because they simply didn't miss enough starts over the years to produce a functional set of figures. (The Orioles haven't won a game without Ripken in the lineup since '82, but that may be an overstatement of his value.) On the whole, we were guided by the question: Would the loss of this player create an enormous hardship for his team? There are certainly players other than those listed below who could have been used, but we have no problem using these players as our test group. The results:

Player	In Lineup W–L	Pct.	Not in Lineup W–L	Pct.	Diff.
Jesse Barfield	325–262	.554	116–106	.523	.031
Wade Boggs	371–329	.530	58–51	.532	–.002
George Brett	341–299	.533	79–91	.465	.068
Gary Carter	407–319	.561	45–38	.542	.018
Jack Clark	272–259	.512	140–138	.504	.009
Andre Dawson	353–336	.512	55–63	.466	.046
Kirk Gibson	324–249	.565	126–100	.558	.008
Pedro Guerrero	317–271	.539	109–113	.491	.048
Rickey Henderson	353–351	.501	53–52	.505	–.003
Keith Hernandez	431–318	.575	33–26	.559	.016
Kent Hrbek	321–397	.447	38–54	.413	.034
Eddie Murray	402–347	.537	31–29	.517	.020
Tim Raines	383–373	.507	25–26	.490	.016
Jim Rice	404–348	.537	25–32	.439	.099
Ryne Sandberg	371–397	.483	16–22	.421	.062
Mike Schmidt	391–359	.521	30–29	.508	.013
Ozzie Smith	389–330	.541	46–44	.511	.030
Darryl Strawberry	305–235	.565	74–82	.474	.090
Dave Winfield	403–324	.554	41–41	.500	.054
Robin Yount	349–363	.490	48–47	.505	–.015

From that table, we computed the average contribution (that is, the average of the "Diff." column): Teams had winning percentages .032 higher with those players in their starting lineups than without them. Multiply that figure by 162 games to compute the number of wins that a superstar adds over the course of a full season: 5.21 wins. But remember, few players play every game. And in any given season, there are likely to be some, like Guerrero and Clark last year, who miss a substantial number of games. As a result, the estimate of 5.21 wins is a seldom-achieved ideal.

We made a more realistic estimate with a method that is best explained by an example. Let's work through Guerrero's figures. Over the past five years, the Dodgers have a winning percentage .048 higher with Guerrero in the lineup than without him. During that period, Guerrero started an average of 117.6 games per season. That total multiplied by the difference in winning percentage indicates that Guerrero was worth 5.7 wins per season. When the corresponding figure is calculated for each player in the group, the average contribution is estimated to be 4.56 wins per season—less than one win per month, and substantially lower than you might have expected.

That figure seems especially low in light of the Dodgers' collapse following the injury to Guerrero. But think about this: Los Angeles scored 44 fewer runs last season than a year earlier, but allowed 100 more runs in 1986 than in 1985. The loss of Guerrero certainly damaged the Dodgers' offense, but the failure of L.A.'s pitching was obviously more responsible for the team's downfall. Our conclusion: Had Guerrero not been injured, Los Angeles would have won only about five more games. The team's collapse was due in larger part to the decline of its pitching staff.

So the bad news for the Dodgers is that they can expect to add only five wins or so on account of Guerrero's return this season. But we've got some good news for them as well: Teams that lose a lot of one-run games usually show a vast

improvement in their overall record the next season. That's good for the Dodgers, because only seven National League teams since 1900 have lost more one-run games than the Dodgers lost last season.

It's only natural that Los Angeles couldn't overcome the weight of those one-run losses: None of the top 10 one-run losers in league history managed a winning record. Only two winning teams in modern National League history had as many as 34 one-run losses: the 1928 Brooklyn Dodgers (77–76) and the 1982 Montreal Expos (86–76).

But the following season is another matter entirely. We examined the performance of the 24 National League teams (from 1900 through 1985) that lost more than 35 one-run games, and the results were astounding:

Year	Team	One-Run Losses	W–L	Pct.	Following Season W–L	Pct.	Diff.
1971	Houston	43	79–83	.488	84–69	.549	+5
1916	Cincinnati	41	60–93	.392	78–76	.506	+18
1946	Cincinnati	41	67–87	.435	73–81	.474	+6
1975	Houston	41	64–97	.398	80–82	.494	+16
1917	Pittsburgh	40	51–103	.331	65–60	.520	+14
1907	Cincinnati	39	66–87	.431	73–81	.474	+7
1962	New York	39	40–120	.250	51–111	.315	+11
1912	Brooklyn	38	58–95	.379	65–84	.436	+7
1946	New York	38	61–93	.396	81–73	.526	+20
1985	Pittsburgh	38	57–104	.354	64–98	.395	+7
1986	**Los Angeles**	38	73–89	.451	—	—	—
1916	Chicago	37	67–86	.438	74–80	.481	+7
1968	New York	37	73–89	.451	100–62	.617	+27
1970	San Diego	37	63–99	.389	61–100	.379	–2
1976	St. Louis	37	72–90	.444	83–79	.512	+11
1986	Pittsburgh	37	64–98	.395	—	—	—
1908	Brooklyn	36	53–101	.344	55–98	.359	+2
1913	Brooklyn	36	65–84	.436	75–79	.487	+10
1937	Cincinnati	36	56–98	.364	82–68	.547	+26
1968	Pittsburgh	33	80–82	.494	88–74	.543	+8
1974	Chicago	36	66–96	.407	75–87	.463	+9
1974	New York	36	71–91	.438	82–80	.506	+11
1978	Montreal	36	76–86	.469	95–65	.594	+19
1980	San Diego	36	73–89	.451	41–69	.373	–13
1984	Montreal	36	78–83	.484	84–77	.522	+6
1985	San Francisco	36	62–100	.383	83–79	.512	+21

All but two of the teams improved their overall records a year later, half of them by 10 wins or more. The group average was an improvement of 10.5 wins. Teams below the .500 mark generally show some improvement, but certainly not to the degree we see here. In fact, from 1900 through 1985, 26 National League teams compiled winning percentages between .406 and .416 (the average of this group was .411); they improved to an average of only .413 the next season.

Who would have predicted the rise of the Miracle Mets of 1969? No one we know did, but you might have if you'd noticed that they lost 37 one-run games in 1968. Last season's Giants surprised everyone by posting a winning record following their 100-loss season a year earlier. Everyone, that is, except those who understood the significance of those 36 one-run losses in 1985. The one-run decision is the key to anticipating some of baseball's greatest and most unpredictable turnarounds, an item that should not escape the notice of fans of either the Dodgers or the Pirates.

Incidentally, teams that win a lot of one-run games are as likely to suffer a sharp decline as one-run losers are to show a marked improvement. Following are the National League teams that won more than 35 one-run games in a season, and their performance a year later:

Year	Team	One-Run Wins	W–L	Pct.	Following Season W–L	Pct.	Diff.
1978	San Francisco	42	89–73	.549	71–91	.438	−18
1940	Cincinnati	41	100–53	.654	88–66	.571	−12
1969	New York	41	100–62	.617	83–79	.512	−17
1979	Houston	39	89–73	.549	93–70	.571	+4
1985	Cincinnati	39	89–72	.553	86–76	.531	−3
1982	San Francisco	38	87–75	.537	79–83	.488	−8
1907	Chicago	37	107–45	.704	99–55	.643	−8
1944	Cincinnati	37	89–65	.578	61–93	.396	−28
1968	Philadelphia	37	76–86	.469	63–99	.389	−13
1976	Los Angeles	37	92–70	.568	98–64	.605	+6
1959	Pittsburgh	36	78–76	.506	95–59	.617	+17

Eight of the 11 teams lost ground the next season, five by more than 10 games. The group average was 7.2 fewer wins,

despite the presence of the 1959 Pirates, who won 36 one-run contests among their total of 78 wins and then proceeded to win 95 games and the World Series a year later.

So there seems little doubt that Los Angeles will bounce back strongly in 1986 from its dismal 1985 season. The return of Guerrero, the expected return to form of its pitching staff, and the rebound expected following last season's 38 one-run losses suggest that the Dodgers could easily tack on 20 wins to their total of 73 last season. And that should be enough to take the Western Division title. Especially since the National League co-leader with 34 one-run wins last season was

One-Run Wins		One-Run Losses	
Houston	34	**Los Angeles**	38
Montreal	34	Pittsburgh	37
Philadelphia	34	St. Louis	32
San Diego	32	San Diego	31
San Francisco	30	San Francisco	30
Chicago	29	Montreal	28
New York	29	Chicago	28
Los Angeles	28	Houston	27
St. Louis	28	Cincinnati	26
Atlanta	26	Philadelphia	25
Cincinnati	26	Atlanta	24
Pittsburgh	16	New York	20

WON-LOST RECORD BY STARTING POSITION

LOS ANGELES 73-89	C	1B	2B	3B	SS	LF	CF	RF	P	Leadoff	Relief	Starts
Ed Amelung									1-0			1-0
Dave Anderson			1-1	13-11	11-20					0-2		25-32
Joe Beckwith											1-14	
Greg Brock		39-45										39-45
Ralph Bryant								7-14				7-14
Enos Cabell		20-24		1-5		0-1		6-7				27-37
Cesar Cedeno						8-9	1-2					9-11
Carlos Diaz											3-16	
Mariano Duncan					54-52					28-28		54-52
Jack Fimple	2-2											2-2
Balvino Galvez											1-9	
Jose Gonzalez							8-16					8-16
Pedro Guerrero		1-3				4-5						5-8
Jeff Hamilton				8-22	0-1							8-23
Orel Hershiser									18-17		2-0	18-17
Brian Holton									0-3		2-7	0-3
Rick Honeycutt									14-14		2-2	14-14
Ken Howell											32-30	
Ken Landreaux						4-4	24-29	0-1				28-34
Bill Madlock		0-1		51-50								51-51
Mike Marshall								39-47				39-47
Len Matuszek		9-13				16-14						25-27
Tom Niedenfuer											25-35	
Alejandro Pena									4-6		2-12	4-6
Dennis Powell									1-5		5-16	1-5
Jerry Reuss									3-10		1-5	3-10
Bill Russell			2-4	0-1	5-9	4-8		5-4				16-26
Steve Sax			70-84							45-58		70-84
Mike Scioscia	51-57											51-57
Larry See		3-3										3-3
Craig Shipley				3-7								3-7
Franklin Stubbs		1-0				33-43	7-12	9-6				50-61
Alex Trevino	20-30											20-30
Fernando Valenzuela									21-13		2-3	21-13
Ed Vande Berg											9-51	
Bob Welch									12-21		0-2	12-21
Terry Whitfield						0-1						0-1
Reggie Williams						4-4	33-30	6-10		0-1		43-44

Batting Comparisons: Vs. Left-Handers/Right-Handers and Overall/Late Inning Pressure Situations

Player		BA	Rank	SA	Rank	HR %	Rank		BA	Rank	SA	Rank	HR %	Rank
Dave Anderson	vs. Lefties	.240	94	.267	131	0.00	119	Overall	.245	104	.301	130	0.46	128
	vs. Righties	.248	86	.319	115	0.71	121	Pressure	.310	29	.405	57	0.00	102
Greg Brock	vs. Lefties	.102	143	.153	143	0.00	119	Overall	.234	115	.422	50	4.92	12
	vs. Righties	.263	55	.481	19	6.02	3	Pressure	.058	142	.077	142	0.00	102
Enos Cabell	vs. Lefties	.284	44	.371	81	1.02	106	Overall	.256	78	.318	120	0.72	123
	vs. Righties	.188	--	.188	--	0.00	--	Pressure	.326	21	.413	54	2.17	61
Cesar Cedeno	vs. Lefties	.258	77	.323	112	0.00	119	Overall	.231	--	.282	--	0.00	--
	vs. Righties	.125	--	.125	--	0.00	--	Pressure	.071	--	.071	--	0.00	--
Mariano Duncan	vs. Lefties	.260	74	.347	94	2.31	63	Overall	.229	123	.305	127	1.97	81
	vs. Righties	.205	131	.274	132	1.71	90	Pressure	.357	11	.429	47	1.79	81
Jose Gonzalez	vs. Lefties	.259	76	.431	49	3.45	35	Overall	.215	--	.355	--	2.15	--
	vs. Righties	.143	--	.229	--	0.00	--	Pressure	.250	--	.375	--	0.00	--
Jeff Hamilton	vs. Lefties	.273	55	.382	75	1.82	79	Overall	.224	--	.361	--	3.40	--
	vs. Righties	.196	--	.348	--	4.35	--	Pressure	.269	--	.538	--	7.69	--
Ken Landreaux	vs. Lefties	.267	--	.333	--	0.00	--	Overall	.261	67	.364	96	1.41	99
	vs. Righties	.261	62	.370	85	1.68	92	Pressure	.200	120	.236	129	0.00	102
Bill Madlock	vs. Lefties	.312	24	.482	24	4.26	24	Overall	.280	31	.404	68	2.64	60
	vs. Righties	.261	62	.357	99	1.68	92	Pressure	.242	94	.339	90	1.61	87
Mike Marshall	vs. Lefties	.248	85	.512	18	6.98	4	Overall	.233	116	.439	38	5.76	3
	vs. Righties	.224	116	.393	72	4.98	13	Pressure	.245	86	.377	77	3.77	35
Len Matuszek	vs. Lefties	.154	--	.154	--	0.00	--	Overall	.261	68	.432	41	4.52	19
	vs. Righties	.269	48	.452	35	4.84	17	Pressure	.206	--	.412	--	5.88	--
Bill Russell	vs. Lefties	.325	16	.368	82	0.00	119	Overall	.250	90	.301	130	0.00	136
	vs. Righties	.167	142	.225	141	0.00	131	Pressure	.246	85	.279	114	0.00	102
Steve Sax	vs. Lefties	.329	11	.467	32	1.33	100	Overall	.332	3	.441	36	0.95	118
	vs. Righties	.333	5	.426	56	0.74	120	Pressure	.378	5	.531	9	3.06	44
Mike Scioscia	vs. Lefties	.234	99	.308	118	1.87	75	Overall	.251	87	.345	110	1.34	103
	vs. Righties	.258	69	.360	96	1.12	105	Pressure	.211	111	.254	122	0.00	102
Franklin Stubbs	vs. Lefties	.227	108	.381	76	4.12	28	Overall	.226	125	.421	51	5.48	8
	vs. Righties	.226	112	.433	54	5.88	5	Pressure	.281	52	.491	24	5.26	13
Alex Trevino	vs. Lefties	.232	103	.328	109	1.60	85	Overall	.262	66	.386	80	1.98	80
	vs. Righties	.312	--	.481	--	2.60	--	Pressure	.298	37	.447	38	2.13	64
Reggie Williams	vs. Lefties	.294	37	.388	70	0.59	115	Overall	.277	37	.376	87	1.32	104
	vs. Righties	.256	79	.361	95	2.26	70	Pressure	.269	61	.423	52	1.92	74
Team Average	vs. Lefties	.264	3	.373	9	1.91	10	Overall	.251	9	.370	11	2.38	7
	vs. Righties	.243	11	.368	10	2.66	5	Pressure	.253	8	.360	9	2.00	9
League Average	vs. Lefties	.257		.384		2.28		Overall	.253		.380		2.32	
	vs. Righties	.251		.378		2.34		Pressure	.257		.376		2.31	

Additional Miscellaneous Batting Comparisons

Player	Grass Surface BA	Rank	Artificial Surface BA	Rank	Home Games BA	Rank	Road Games BA	Rank	Runners in Scoring Position BA	Rank	Runners in Scoring Pos and Two Outs BA	Rank	Leading Off Inning OBA	Rank	Runners on 3B with less than 2 Outs RDI %	Rank
Dave Anderson	.276	50	.167	--	.289	44	.210	125	.214	116	.080	144	.268	120	.571	74
Greg Brock	.222	118	.267	51	.236	113	.232	104	.237	94	.200	105	.329	62	.500	101
Enos Cabell	.269	62	.215	--	.271	72	.241	93	.233	98	.125	136	.268	121	.688	20
Mariano Duncan	.222	119	.260	--	.220	127	.238	96	.212	117	.212	97	.221	139	.474	115
Jose Gonzalez	.214	126	.217	--	.214	--	.216	--	.125	--	.000	--	.240	--	.667	--
Jeff Hamilton	.239	100	.176	--	.282	--	.171	--	.303	--	.143	--	.118	--	.778	5
Ken Landreaux	.244	92	.308	15	.236	112	.282	28	.231	103	.190	114	.358	34	.688	20
Bill Madlock	.282	42	.274	45	.263	87	.295	17	.319	18	.297	33	.305	86	.880	1
Mike Marshall	.257	74	.145	--	.240	109	.225	117	.244	86	.229	84	.286	105	.545	86
Len Matuszek	.295	27	.200	--	.315	12	.218	121	.286	41	.222	89	.233	137	.556	79
Bill Russell	.247	85	.259	--	.236	111	.264	56	.227	106	.143	130	.286	105	.778	5
Steve Sax	.309	17	.387	2	.310	19	.352	1	.342	12	.309	30	.365	31	.667	25
Mike Scioscia	.253	77	.247	85	.249	102	.254	72	.145	141	.091	143	.337	55	.625	43
Franklin Stubbs	.216	124	.250	80	.262	89	.196	132	.180	135	.153	128	.272	116	.524	97
Alex Trevino	.270	61	.241	--	.268	77	.256	67	.254	70	.348	12	.465	--	.333	140
Fernando Valenzuela	.230	111	.200	--	.250	--	.197	--	.167	--	.143	--	.240	--	.400	135
Reggie Williams	.290	36	.247	86	.272	71	.283	26	.271	53	.323	22	.348	42	.471	116
Team Average	.250	9	.254	4	.253	9	.249	4	.236	12	.208	11	.297	12	.584	3
League Average	.254		.253		.260		.247		.252		.235		.316		.562	

Pitching Comparisons: Vs. Left-Handers/Right-Handers and Runners On/Bases Empty

		BA	Rank	BB %	Rank	SO %	Rank		BA	Rank	BB %	Rank	SO %	Rank
Orel Hershiser	vs. Lefties	.252	59	9.32	56	13.69	70	Runners On	.247	42	11.97	87	14.79	58
	vs. Righties	.233	38	8.01	60	17.53	47	Bases Empty	.240	40	6.23	27	16.01	53
Rick Honeycutt	vs. Lefties	.238	43	2.73	1	20.91	19	Runners On	.282	86	8.89	36	12.59	78
	vs. Righties	.251	67	6.97	44	12.77	88	Bases Empty	.231	27	4.74	13	14.90	68
Ken Howell	vs. Lefties	.238	44	16.60	116	21.70	16	Runners On	.227	23	17.47	116	22.27	8
	vs. Righties	.240	50	11.88	103	26.24	4	Bases Empty	.250	56	11.06	103	25.48	6
Tom Niedenfuer	vs. Lefties	.284	87	12.36	91	16.29	47	Runners On	.263	59	11.60	83	16.57	39
	vs. Righties	.276	90	4.19	8	15.57	62	Bases Empty	.297	113	4.88	14	15.24	63
Alejandro Pena	vs. Lefties	.310	107	10.98	76	14.63	64	Runners On	.273	77	9.27	42	19.21	23
	vs. Righties	.225	26	8.28	64	15.17	64	Bases Empty	.268	82	10.13	96	10.76	105
Dennis Powell	vs. Lefties	.197	--	4.23	--	15.49	--	Runners On	.255	49	8.33	29	7.50	113
	vs. Righties	.301	107	10.95	98	9.95	107	Bases Empty	.285	102	9.87	91	14.47	78
Jerry Reuss	vs. Lefties	.220	--	3.45	--	12.07	--	Runners On	.339	114	9.29	43	4.29	116
	vs. Righties	.331	116	5.49	18	8.06	112	Bases Empty	.296	112	2.09	1	12.04	98
Fernando Valenzuela	vs. Lefties	.246	51	5.31	11	20.29	22	Runners On	.255	51	7.52	20	17.48	33
	vs. Righties	.222	22	8.27	63	22.35	13	Bases Empty	.207	11	7.85	62	25.08	7
Ed Vande Berg	vs. Lefties	.275	79	9.89	65	14.29	68	Runners On	.261	58	11.24	74	12.92	77
	vs. Righties	.296	104	10.26	92	12.39	90	Bases Empty	.323	116	8.84	83	12.93	88
Bob Welch	vs. Lefties	.265	71	5.74	15	15.30	57	Runners On	.244	38	7.73	23	19.81	18
	vs. Righties	.235	43	5.46	17	22.49	12	Bases Empty	.256	67	4.06	9	17.81	38
Team Average	vs. Lefties	.263	7	8.64	2	16.15	3	Runners On	.263	5	10.09	7	15.82	4
	vs. Righties	.252	6	7.70	5	17.43	4	Bases Empty	.252	7	6.42	1	17.86	3
League Average	vs. Lefties	.257		9.83		14.90		Runners On	.260		10.11		15.02	
	vs. Righties	.251		8.19		16.33		Bases Empty	.248		7.89		16.30	

Additional Miscellaneous Pitching Comparisons

	Grass Surface		Artificial Surface		Home Games		Road Games		Runners in Scoring Position		Runners in Scoring Pos and Two Outs		Leading Off Inning	
	BA	Rank	BA	Rank	BA	Rank	BA	Rank	BA	Rank	BA	Rank	OBA	Rank
Orel Hershiser	.240	43	.252	52	.231	38	.257	61	.226	26	.265	78	.294	35
Rick Honeycutt	.249	57	.250	47	.247	63	.252	50	.319	110	.293	95	.225	5
Ken Howell	.234	36	.253	54	.218	24	.264	71	.252	62	.196	32	.309	53
Tom Niedenfuer	.275	80	.296	--	.253	70	.314	108	.283	90	.300	98	.314	62
Alejandro Pena	.253	63	.293	101	.181	5	.347	114	.282	89	.314	104	.384	106
Dennis Powell	.280	86	.253	--	.352	--	.249	44	.259	68	.227	--	.388	109
Jerry Reuss	.286	97	.409	--	.301	105	.331	112	.375	118	.429	117	.321	65
Fernando Valenzuela	.232	34	.212	14	.216	20	.236	31	.254	65	.259	75	.246	10
Ed Vande Berg	.289	100	.293	102	.303	106	.279	85	.263	70	.222	46	.369	99
Bob Welch	.246	52	.275	87	.247	62	.256	57	.240	43	.218	44	.313	59
Team Average	.254	6	.264	9	.247	7	.266	8	.266	11	.262	11	.295	1
League Average	.254		.253		.247		.260		.252		.235		.316	

MONTREAL EXPOS

Someone once observed that if you have one foot in the fireplace and the other in a bucket of ice, a statistician will tell you that you're comfortable.

You get a similar feeling when you look at the Expos' offensive statistics from 1986, a season in which they finished 78–83, in fourth place in their division. The Expos' figures in the key "percentage" categories were virtually identical to the league average figures:

	Batting	Slugging	On-Base
Expos	.254	.379	.322
N.L. Avg.	.253	.380	.322

But when they combined those three elements, the bottom line was not the equal of the sum of the parts: Montreal scored only 637 runs for the season, compared to the league average of 675. And when looking for reasons why, our examination led us back to the fireplace and the bucket of ice.

The Expos' composite averages were compiled by two groups of players separated by a chasm the size of the Olympic Stadium deficit. Those two groups were defined very well by the batting order positions in which they performed.

Of course, every team expects that the players at the top of its batting order will outperform those at the lower end. It's in recognition of their unequal level of offensive talent that the manager has put them in that order on his lineup card. But with the Expos, the difference was more extreme than that of any other team in the National League.

To start, here are the figures on the Montreal offense, broken down according to position in the batting order:

	PA	AB	R	H	2B	3B	HR	RBI	BB	BA	SA	OBA
1st	754	679	95	189	37	8	9	49	69	.278	.396	.344
2d	736	658	90	170	30	15	6	49	63	.258	.377	.326
3d	723	640	92	198	36	9	21	87	69	.309	.492	.376
4th	705	642	90	202	42	7	19	103	51	.315	.491	.367
5th	690	621	67	146	31	3	16	88	57	.235	.372	.303
6th	671	590	62	151	24	1	12	61	66	.256	.361	.336
7th	651	573	66	133	27	3	8	59	65	.232	.332	.311
8th	630	556	46	126	19	3	14	68	60	.227	.347	.301
9th	614	549	29	86	9	1	5	38	37	.157	.204	.211
Totals	6174	5508	637	1401	255	50	110	602	537	.254	.379	.322

If you eliminate the ninth spot (more on pitchers' batting later in this essay) and contrast the first through fourth spots with the fifth through eighth spots, you get this:

	PA	AB	R	H	2B	3B	HR	RBI	BB	BA	SA	OBA
1st–4th	2918	2619	367	759	145	39	55	288	252	.290	.438	.353
5th–8th	2642	2340	241	556	101	10	50	276	248	.238	.353	.313

Tim Raines, Mitch Webster, Andre Dawson, and Hubie Brooks were the most frequently used players in the top four batting order spots for the Expos. Three of them finished the season among the top 15 National League batters; the other, Brooks, was leading the league in hitting at .340 when an injury cut short his season and left him shy of the requisite 502 plate appearances.

Just how large the gap is between the Expos' haves and have-nots is underscored by a look at the twelve National League teams, their statistics broken down the same way as the Expos'. Here are the key categories, with the teams listed according to the margin, in batting average points, by which a team's top four positions outperformed its bottom four:

		Batting	Slugging	On-Base
Montreal	1st–4th	.290 (+52)	.438 (+85)	.353 (+40)
	5th–8th	.238	.353	.313
New York	1st–4th	.297 (+45)	.450 (+56)	.377 (+50)
	5th–8th	.252	.394	.327
Philadelphia	1st–4th	.274 (+27)	.445 (+64)	.347 (+19)
	5th–8th	.247	.381	.328
San Diego	1st–4th	.283 (+25)	.416 (+27)	.340 (+17)
	5th–8th	.258	.389	.323
Los Angeles	1st–4th	.265 (+15)	.387 (+7)	.325 (+7)
	5th–8th	.250	.380	.318
Atlanta	1st–4th	.263 (+14)	.418 (+54)	.327 (−3)
	5th–8th	.249	.364	.330
Cincinnati	1st–4th	.268 (+8)	.435 (+58)	.343 (+14)
	5th–8th	.260	.377	.329
San Francisco	1st–4th	.265 (+7)	.389 (+8)	.326 (−12)
	5th–8th	.258	.381	.338
Houston	1st–4th	.267 (+3)	.400 (+3)	.336 (+3)
	5th–8th	.264	.397	.333
Chicago	1st–4th	.264 (−1)	.390 (−51)	.325 (−4)
	5th–8th	.265	.441	.329
St. Louis	1st–4th	.243 (−4)	.336 (−5)	.321 (+2)
	5th–8th	.247	.341	.319
Pittsburgh	1st–4th	.254 (−9)	.387 (+2)	.332 (+1)
	5th–8th	.263	.385	.331
N.L. Average	1st–4th	.270 (+16)	.408 (+26)	.338 (+12)
	5th–8th	.254	.382	.326

Only the Mets outhit the Expos collectively in the first four spots in the batting order; only the Mets and Phillies had higher slugging averages through the same positions.

On the downside, the Expos' bottom four spots (ninth position excluded) had the lowest batting average in the league, and the second-lowest slugging average next to the Cardinals. Montreal and St. Louis were also the only teams in the league that failed to get 70 runs scored from any of the five through eight spots. The Expos had the largest gap between the top four and bottom four in both batting average and slugging average; their margins were more than triple the league-average increments in both of those categories.

The four players who usually batted in the five through eight spots in the batting order were third baseman Tim Wallach, who had a bad year (a career-low .233, 18 home runs, 71 RBI), the second baseman (usually Vance Law), the first baseman, and the catcher.

With Mike Fitzgerald and Tom Nieto as their catchers, the Expos had expectations for offense from the position that could safely be described as modest. That's exactly what they got, as we can see by comparing the totals for Montreal's starting catchers with the National League average for the same:

Starting Catchers	Batting	Slugging	On-Base
Expos	.228	.350	.297
N.L. Avg.	.248	.379	.327

Coming up 20 to 30 points short across the board last season, the Expos continue to lag at the position that was their offensive and defensive strength during the Carter administration. But perhaps more troubling in 1986 was the lack of production from first base.

Andres Galarraga went into the season as the potential regular, and his position looked even more secure after the team decided to release Jason Thompson in late June. (That large gulping noise was the sound of the Expos eating Thompson's salary.) It's a baseball truism that having a big bopper at first base is the cornerstone of an offense, and so it was again in the National League in 1986: More runs were driven in by starting first basemen than by players at any other position.

But Galarraga was injured soon after Thompson left and wound up with only three at bats in the period from July 10 to September 3. That meant that the Expos had to rely on Wayne Krenchicki and Wallace Johnson who, in 60 starts between them at first base, managed just one home run and 16 RBIs. The average National League starting first baseman would drive in 31 runs in 60 games. The Expos, just at that one position in the lineup and in that 37 percent of the season during which Krenchicki and Johnson started at first base, lost 15 runs batted in. That's a big chunk in a short period of time toward that 38-run shortfall between Montreal's 637 runs and the league average of 675.

A healthy Galarraga and a turnaround from Wallach seem to be essential for the Expos to improve themselves in 1987. Even those elements, however, may not be enough to offset the loss of Andre Dawson and/or Tim Raines from the solid "front four."

Eeeh Gahds, *Pitchers* as Pinch-Hitters???

When each of the major-league teams decided to carry only 24 players on its active roster for the 1986 season, there followed a lengthy hullabaloo that filled the newspapers and radio talk shows for the better part of three months. The furor centered around two issues: first, were the owners actually saving any money by trimming one player off their rosters? And second, was the competitive side of the game influenced, or was a manager handicapped, by having one fewer player?

The financial issue is for others to decide. However, the silliest "analysis" of the situation, one that was often repeated, was that the amount of savings was minimal or nonexistent, since each of the 25th men excluded from the active roster would earn no more than the major-league minimum of $60,000 per season. Exactly who decided that all such players would be making that little escaped us somehow, but it is certainly untrue, and any calculations using such an assumption are deeply flawed. A player like Rusty Staub, whose defensive limitations made his retention on the shortened roster untenable, would certainly not have been making the minimum. But it's not our point here to get into a financial discussion; Lord knows you can get enough of that elsewhere.

Let's look at the competitive side of the game. Did the truncated rosters have an effect on managerial strategy? Certainly. Did that give some teams an unfair advantage over others? Certainly not.

Much of the steam in this controversy was given off by National League managers; most were one position-player short of the company they had had on the bench in previous years. This translated into one fewer pinch-hitter, whether for actual or potential use. But there is nothing inherently unfair about that, their claims to the contrary. (The early season saw constant knee-jerk managerial criticism of the 24-player roster, especially if the manager involved had just lost an extra-inning game in which he had gone deep into his available reserves. The Mets lost only three games in April; after two of them, Davey Johnson muttered something the reduced roster.)

The most visible mark of the shortened rosters was the use of pitchers as pinch-hitters in the National League. It happened 50 times last season, compared with only six times in 1985. Few if any of those occasions went by without a media observation on the impact of the shortened roster, that here was the silly spectacle of managers being forced to use pitchers as pinch-hitters.

Hogwash! Pitchers have been used as pinch-hitters throughout baseball history, although the practice had been in lamentable decline—as has pitchers' batting, period—in recent years. *The Baseball Encyclopedia* is sprinkled with the exploits of pinch-hitting pitchers. Even though pinch-hitters were rather uncommon in his day, Walter Johnson accumulated 110 pinch-hit at bats in his 21-year career. The first major leaguer to get 100 pinch-hits, Red Lucas, was a pitcher for the Reds and Pirates in the 1920s and '30s.

Schoolboy Rowe, Red Ruffing, Don Newcombe, and more recently Don Drysdale, Gary Peters, Bob Gibson, and Ken Brett all served as regular pinch-hitters in at least one season during their careers. (Drysdale was once asked if he got paid extra for his pinch-hitting. He answered, "No, and it worked against me, because Walter Alston used to make me hang around until the end of each game; Koufax got to go home early!")

In 1953, Tommy Byrne, a left-handed batting and throwing pitcher, lived out the all-time pitchers' fantasy. In the ninth inning of a game against the Yankees—his former team—with New York leading 3–1, with two outs and the bases loaded, Byrne was tabbed by White Sox manager Paul Richards to pinch-hit for Vern Stephens, a right-handed batter with more than 200 home runs, against right-handed sidearmer Ewell Blackwell. Byrne delivered a game-winning grand-slam home run, a blow that left such an impression on Casey Stengel that the Yankees reacquired Byrne, perhaps as much for his bat as for his arm. (The moment must have been seared in Stengel's memory, because he continued to use Byrne as a pinch-hitter even though that homer was his only hit in 51 pinch-hit at bats—24 of them under Stengel—from 1952 to 1956.)

Against the backdrop of the great-hitting pitchers of the past, the accomplishments of the 1986 crop of pinch-hitting pitchers are quite modest. By far the most successful of them was Dan Schatzeder, who started the season with Montreal before being traded to Philadelphia in late July. In 14 games as what *The Sporting News* used to call "an emergency swinger," Schatzeder went 5-for-12 with two doubles and two walks. The rest of the league's pinch-hitting pitchers went a combined 3-for-29, with no extra-base hits and two walks (both by New York's Rick Aguilera). Fernando Valenzuela had two of the hits, and Rick Rhoden the other.

For fans who like traditional, nine-man baseball, the whole business of pitchers being used as pinch-hitters was a small payback for 14 years of watching designated hitters in the American League. It also added something new to the game; tell us that there wasn't a Dodger fan who didn't get a rise out of seeing Fernando coming out of the dugout swinging a couple of bats.

In a broader sense, it's just possible that the 24-man roster will make for a more interesting game. In this age of specialization, the sight of left-handed first basemen playing third or outfielders in the infield is entertaining; the spectacle of pitchers such as Todd Worrell, Jesse Orosco, and Roger McDowell playing the outfield, as each did last season, is even more intriguing. In a season that includes more than 19,000 innings, baseball fans do not demand a Mattingly-versus-Clemens matchup day in and day out, inning after inning. Aberrations from the norm, when sprinkled throughout a season, are not unwelcome; they are the spices that make for a flavorful meal. Although seemingly on the decline in baseball, they are still more commonplace there than in other major sports. They are an essential part of the attraction of the game; long may they wave.

WON-LOST RECORD BY STARTING POSITION

MONTREAL 78-83	C	1B	2B	3B	SS	LF	CF	RF	P	Leadoff	Relief	Starts
Dann Bilardello	23-32											23-32
Hubie Brooks					46-34							46-34
Curt Brown									1-1		0-6	1-1
Tim Burke											34-32	
Casey Candaele			10-12							10-12		10-12
Andre Dawson								58-66				58-66
Mike Fitzgerald	37-23											37-23
Tom Foley			9-10	4-5	11-11							24-26
Andres Galarraga		40-39								4-11		40-39
Rene Gonzales				0-4	0-3							0-7
Joe Hesketh									10-5			10-5
Randy Hunt	7-10											7-10
Wallace Johnson		11-10								8-6		11-10
Wayne Krenchicki		14-25		10-5								24-30
Vance Law		4-3	42-45	1-0							0-3	47-48
Dennis Martinez									6-9		0-4	6-9
Bob McClure											22-30	
Andy McGaffigan									6-8		13-22	6-8
Billy Moore		0-1										0-1
Al Newman			17-16		3-7					6-4		20-23
Tom Nieto	8-12											8-12
Bob Owchinko									2-1			2-1
Jeff Parrett											3-9	
Tim Raines						71-75				35-35		71-75
Jeff Reardon											46-16	
George Riley											3-7	
Luis Rivera					18-28					5-5		18-28
Bert Roberge											3-18	
Dan Schatzeder									0-1		9-20	0-1
Bob Sebra									5-8		1-3	5-8
Bryn Smith									16-14			16-14
Randy St. Claire											5-6	
Wil Tejada	3-6											3-6
Jason Thompson		9-5										9-5
Jay Tibbs									14-17		1-3	14-17
Dave Tomlin											0-7	
Sergio Valdez									1-4			1-4
Tim Wallach				61-66								61-66
Mitch Webster						2-1	52-62	17-9		8-4		71-72
Herm Winningham						1-0	18-12	0-4		2-4		19-16
Jim Wohlford			2-3			2-4		2-3		0-1		6-10
George Wright						2-3	8-9	1-1		0-1		11-13
Floyd Youmans									17-15		0-1	17-15

Batting Comparisons: Vs. Left-Handers/Right-Handers and Overall/Late Inning Pressure Situations

Player	Split	BA	Rank	SA	Rank	HR %	Rank		BA	Rank	SA	Rank	HR %	Rank
Dann Bilardello	vs. Lefties	.175	--	.175	--	0.00	--	Overall	.194	142	.283	134	2.09	76
	vs. Righties	.199	136	.311	117	2.65	59	Pressure	.200	--	.240	--	0.00	--
Hubie Brooks	vs. Lefties	.365	2	.682	2	5.88	12	Overall	.340	1	.569	1	4.58	17
	vs. Righties	.330	8	.525	6	4.07	34	Pressure	.375	6	.571	8	3.57	38
Andre Dawson	vs. Lefties	.331	10	.625	4	6.88	5	Overall	.284	25	.478	16	4.03	27
	vs. Righties	.262	58	.408	66	2.68	56	Pressure	.330	17	.454	32	2.06	67
Mike Fitzgerald	vs. Lefties	.227	107	.333	101	1.52	93	Overall	.282	27	.440	37	2.87	54
	vs. Righties	.308	17	.490	13	3.50	44	Pressure	.268	62	.390	70	2.44	55
Tom Foley	vs. Lefties	.290	--	.323	--	0.00	--	Overall	.266	58	.357	100	0.38	131
	vs. Righties	.263	56	.362	91	0.43	126	Pressure	.291	40	.364	81	0.00	102
Andres Galarraga	vs. Lefties	.333	8	.475	28	3.33	37	Overall	.271	51	.405	67	3.12	46
	vs. Righties	.234	104	.363	88	2.99	51	Pressure	.277	55	.446	39	3.08	43
Wayne Krenchicki	vs. Lefties	.000	--	.000	--	0.00	--	Overall	.240	107	.312	121	0.90	121
	vs. Righties	.248	88	.322	113	0.93	112	Pressure	.176	131	.235	130	1.96	71
Vance Law	vs. Lefties	.252	83	.417	57	3.15	43	Overall	.225	127	.325	118	1.39	101
	vs. Righties	.210	128	.275	129	0.43	127	Pressure	.250	76	.368	79	1.47	91
Al Newman	vs. Lefties	.220	--	.317	--	2.44	--	Overall	.200	141	.232	142	0.54	125
	vs. Righties	.194	138	.208	142	0.00	131	Pressure	.205	118	.256	120	0.00	102
Tim Raines	vs. Lefties	.315	22	.453	38	2.21	68	Overall	.334	2	.476	20	1.55	94
	vs. Righties	.343	2	.486	15	1.25	102	Pressure	.374	7	.505	16	2.02	69
Luis Rivera	vs. Lefties	.246	87	.333	101	0.00	119	Overall	.205	--	.283	--	0.00	--
	vs. Righties	.175	--	.247	--	0.00	--	Pressure	.367	--	.433	--	0.00	--
Tim Wallach	vs. Lefties	.215	120	.356	87	2.22	67	Overall	.233	116	.396	75	3.75	34
	vs. Righties	.241	97	.412	62	4.35	29	Pressure	.247	83	.358	82	2.47	54
Mitch Webster	vs. Lefties	.337	6	.513	16	2.51	59	Overall	.290	18	.431	42	1.39	101
	vs. Righties	.265	49	.387	73	0.80	119	Pressure	.245	89	.304	105	0.98	100
Herm Winningham	vs. Lefties	.308	--	.423	--	3.85	--	Overall	.216	138	.346	108	2.16	73
	vs. Righties	.201	133	.333	109	1.89	84	Pressure	.268	62	.366	80	0.00	102
Jim Wohlford	vs. Lefties	.306	31	.458	34	1.39	99	Overall	.266	--	.383	--	1.06	--
	vs. Righties	.136	--	.136	--	0.00	--	Pressure	.222	103	.250	123	0.00	102
Team Average	vs. Lefties	.269	1	.414	2	2.44	6	Overall	.254	5	.379	8	2.00	11
	vs. Righties	.248	10	.364	11	1.81	11	Pressure	.272	4	.375	8	1.58	10
League Average	vs. Lefties	.257		.384		2.28		Overall	.253		.380		2.32	
	vs. Righties	.251		.378		2.34		Pressure	.257		.376		2.31	

Additional Miscellaneous Batting Comparisons

Player	Grass Surface BA	Rank	Artificial Surface BA	Rank	Home Games BA	Rank	Road Games BA	Rank	Runners in Scoring Position BA	Rank	Runners in Scoring Pos and Two Outs BA	Rank	Leading Off Inning OBA	Rank	Runners on 3B with less than 2 Outs RDI %	Rank
Dann Bilardello	.153	--	.212	122	.226	--	.168	142	.192	129	.115	139	.302	91	.429	--
Hubie Brooks	.330	7	.345	4	.350	2	.331	3	.283	46	.250	66	.370	26	.586	67
Casey Candaele	.222	--	.232	104	.274	--	.167	--	.167	--	.250	--	.286	105	.512	100
Andre Dawson	.294	29	.280	37	.296	35	.273	38	.261	65	.333	14	.388	18	.778	5
Mike Fitzgerald	.302	--	.274	44	.278	64	.286	24	.203	124	.184	118	.316	81	.667	25
Tom Foley	.318	--	.249	84	.242	107	.287	23	.261	65	.327	19	.376	22	.267	143
Andres Galarraga	.233	109	.285	33	.286	51	.256	66	.261	65	.385	--	.457	1	.500	--
Wallace Johnson	.323	--	.271	47	.277	--	.290	--	.296	--	.385	--	.279	--	.625	43
Wayne Krenchicki	.257	--	.232	103	.231	117	.246	84	.232	101	.200	105	.276	114	.591	63
Vance Law	.152	144	.255	72	.260	92	.191	134	.268	57	.214	95	.194	142	.625	--
Al Newman	.188	--	.203	127	.190	140	.208	126	.200	--	.211	--	.404	10	.655	29
Tim Raines	.335	5	.334	8	.326	7	.342	2	.331	16	.255	63	.327	69	.429	--
Luis Rivera	.190	--	.210	124	.207	138	.203	--	.154	--	.190	114	.347	43	.581	72
Tim Wallach	.204	135	.245	90	.226	122	.240	95	.224	109	.262	59	.368	28	.591	63
Mitch Webster	.351	1	.269	49	.265	83	.314	8	.250	75	.222	89	.322	75	.200	--
Herm Winningham	.162	--	.230	108	.153	143	.270	42	.167	--	.130	134	.353	--	.857	--
Jim Wohlford	.333	--	.247	88	.269	--	.262	--	.167	--	.077	--	.353	--	.714	--
George Wright	.229	--	.171	141	.140	--	.224	--	.167	--	.143	--	.265	--		
Team Average	.259	5	.253	6	.250	12	.258	3	.243	9	.226	9	.329	2	.553	7
League Average	.254		.253		.260		.247		.252		.235		.316		.562	

Pitching Comparisons: Vs. Left-Handers/Right-Handers and Runners On/Bases Empty

		BA	Rank	BB %	Rank	SO %	Rank		BA	Rank	BB %	Rank	SO %	Rank
Tim Burke	vs. Lefties	.302	102	12.86	97	15.35	56	Runners On	.273	78	13.84	104	15.63	49
	vs. Righties	.218	18	7.14	49	21.43	18	Bases Empty	.252	62	6.61	35	20.70	14
Joe Hesketh	vs. Lefties	.250	--	11.76	--	23.53	--	Runners On	.310	105	10.07	55	16.78	36
	vs. Righties	.288	101	8.04	61	17.68	45	Bases Empty	.265	77	7.51	51	19.72	22
Dennis Martinez	vs. Lefties	.244	47	7.39	34	15.22	59	Runners On	.255	54	11.86	86	14.12	67
	vs. Righties	.311	111	5.91	24	15.05	66	Bases Empty	.286	103	2.93	4	15.90	55
Bob McClure	vs. Lefties	.184	8	7.06	29	21.18	17	Runners On	.257	--	7.02	--	16.67	--
	vs. Righties	.257	76	9.88	88	13.95	78	Bases Empty	.213	13	10.49	99	16.08	52
Andy McGaffigan	vs. Lefties	.204	15	11.73	86	16.61	43	Runners On	.203	10	10.80	68	16.40	41
	vs. Righties	.244	53	6.88	42	19.20	37	Bases Empty	.237	37	8.41	77	18.92	28
Jeff Reardon	vs. Lefties	.250	56	10.10	67	15.66	54	Runners On	.219	17	8.52	33	19.89	17
	vs. Righties	.252	69	3.53	5	21.18	19	Bases Empty	.278	94	5.73	23	16.67	49
Bob Sebra	vs. Lefties	.231	36	9.09	49	15.00	62	Runners On	.235	31	8.50	32	14.38	63
	vs. Righties	.250	65	3.18	3	21.02	20	Bases Empty	.242	43	5.36	19	19.64	23
Bryn Smith	vs. Lefties	.286	88	8.73	79	12.23	79	Runners On	.259	56	8.08	27	13.93	69
	vs. Righties	.207	12	6.59	35	14.04	77	Bases Empty	.246	49	7.59	54	12.28	97
Jay Tibbs	vs. Lefties	.274	78	8.86	47	12.82	74	Runners On	.290	93	10.19	61	14.51	62
	vs. Righties	.235	44	8.70	71	16.85	50	Bases Empty	.235	35	7.82	61	14.80	70
Floyd Youmans	vs. Lefties	.188	13	15.28	113	21.03	18	Runners On	.222	19	9.81	51	22.34	6
	vs. Righties	.189	5	10.22	91	23.94	6	Bases Empty	.166	1	15.24	116	22.30	12
Team Average	vs. Lefties	.249	4	10.66	11	15.78	4	Runners On	.260	4	9.75	4	16.22	3
	vs. Righties	.243	4	7.57	2	18.08	3	Bases Empty	.236	3	8.63	12	17.48	4
League Average	vs. Lefties	.257		9.83		14.90		Runners On	.260		10.11		15.02	
	vs. Righties	.251		8.19		16.33		Bases Empty	.248		7.89		16.30	

Additional Miscellaneous Pitching Comparisons

	Grass Surface BA	Rank	Artificial Surface BA	Rank	Home Games BA	Rank	Road Games BA	Rank	Runners in Scoring Position BA	Rank	Runners in Scoring Pos and Two Outs BA	Rank	Leading Off Inning OBA	Rank
Tim Burke	.222	17	.279	93	.236	46	.283	96	.228	30	.189	27	.337	81
Joe Hesketh	.171	--	.314	114	.328	116	.228	21	.337	112	.317	107	.279	24
Dennis Martinez	.284	92	.271	80	.294	103	.251	47	.290	98	.356	113	.283	27
Bob McClure	.167	--	.253	55	.246	59	.219	16	.286	--	.241	68	.286	28
Andy McGaffigan	.240	44	.215	16	.198	12	.241	39	.215	24	.230	52	.313	57
Jeff Reardon	.194	--	.265	73	.282	94	.214	13	.208	20	.152	12	.338	83
Bert Roberge	.360	--	.276	89	.240	--	.339	--	.366	--	.263	--	.346	--
Bob Sebra	.228	--	.242	37	.231	37	.247	42	.216	25	.233	58	.283	26
Bryn Smith	.270	77	.242	35	.246	60	.256	58	.258	67	.292	93	.325	69
Jay Tibbs	.303	109	.248	43	.235	45	.283	93	.275	82	.233	61	.294	37
Floyd Youmans	.201	6	.184	6	.183	6	.194	5	.200	16	.202	34	.298	41
Team Average	.245	4	.246	3	.243	4	.249	2	.251	4	.242	8	.304	4
League Average	.254		.253		.247		.260		.252		.235		.316	

NEW YORK METS

The National League Championship Series and World Series showed that the 1986 New York Mets were one of the most dramatic teams in baseball history. The regular season merely proved they were one of the most talented. By almost any measure, New York's domination of the National League's Eastern Division last season equalled or surpassed that of many of the great teams of the recent past. New York's final record of 108–54 was the best in either league since Cincinnati compiled an identical record in 1975. The Mets led the National League in both batting average (.263) and earned run average (3.11), something no team in either league had accomplished since the 1971 Baltimore Orioles, no National League team since the 1958 Milwaukee Braves.

But no measure of New York's 1986 season illustrates its domination as well as its margin of 21.5 games over the second-place Philadelphia Phillies. That was the second-largest gap in modern major-league history, exceeded only by the 27.5-game bulge of the 1902 Pittsburgh Pirates. (That's right, the Kitty Bransfield-Wid Conroy team.) Say what you will about Philadelphia, St. Louis, and the rest of the division providing less than sensational opposition; you certainly won't be the first to say it. The fact remains that it's awfully difficult to look good chasing a runaway champion. Twice a Prince, a stakes winner, looked like Rusty Staub while chasing Secretariat in the 1973 Belmont Stakes. The largest victory margins in either league since 1900:

Year	Team	W	L	Pct.	Lead
1902	Pittsburgh Pirates	103	36	.741	27.5
1986	**New York Mets**	108	54	.667	21.5
1906	Chicago Cubs	116	36	.763	20
1975	Cincinnati Reds	108	54	.667	20
1983	Chicago White Sox	99	63	.611	20
1936	New York Yankees	102	51	.667	19.5
1927	New York Yankees	110	44	.714	19
1969	Baltimore Orioles	109	53	.673	19
1929	Philadelphia A's	104	46	.693	18
1943	St. Louis Cardinals	105	49	.682	18

The Mets look a little less awesome if you judge them according to their run differential. New York outscored its opponents by 205 runs last season. That's the biggest gap since the Big Red Machine edged its opponents by 224 runs in 1976, but six teams were plus 200 or more runs during the 1970s, including another team in 1976 (Philadelphia). Over the 87 seasons since 1900, 65 teams have had greater run margins than last season's Mets, with the all-time benchmark

being the 376-run differential by (who else?) the 1927 Yankees.

What's most remarkable about the Mets is their perseverance. Consider the team's records over the past six seasons: 41–62 (.398) in 1981, followed by 65–97 (.401), 68–94 (.420), 90–72 (.556), 98–64 (.605), and 108–54 (.667). That's an improvement in every season since 1982, when the Mets crossed over the line of futility at the .400 mark.

The law of diminishing returns applies as surely in baseball as anywhere else. There's a limit on how many seasons a team can continue to improve its record before it turns south again. And common sense tells us that the Mets can't continue their streak much longer; after all, no matter which direction you're traveling in, it's tough to improve on a 108–54 record.

The Mets have already surpassed the point in years at which all but a few other teams have reversed direction. The only other National League team to increase its winning percentage for five years in a row was the Brooklyn Dodgers, who moved from .405 in 1937 to .675 in 1942. (By the way, dem Bums regressed all the way to .409 by 1944 before stringing together 13 consecutive seasons of .545 or better preceding their move to the West Coast.) Two American League teams had streaks of six consecutive upward moves, the modern major-league high: the Cleveland Indians of 1915 through 1920, and the Philadelphia A's of 1920 through 1925. The start of Cleveland's advance corresponded to its acquisition of Tris Speaker; the start of Philadelphia's could be tied to its recovery from Connie Mack's great fire sale of 1915, when he sold most of his pennant-winning 1914 team. And that's it; only three other teams in baseball history have progressed as relentlessly as the Mets of the 1980s.

What does all this tell us about the Mets' future? Certainly that New York has advanced about as far as possible without taking a step back. But a closer look at teams that have consistently improved over a period of several years indicates that they suffer declines proportional to their lofty positions; the bigger they are, the harder they fall. The following table represents the results of a study of National League teams from 1900 through 1985. We've included every team whose record was worse than the previous season, and then divided them by the number of consecutive seasons that each team had improved before the fall. The first line, no seasons of improvement, shows teams that declined for a second consecutive season; those teams won an average of 8.3 games fewer (based on the 162-game schedule) than the year before:

Years	Teams	Average Decline
0	147	.051 (8.1 wins)
1	119	.054 (8.7 wins)
2	60	.066 (10.8 wins)
3	22	.062 (10.1 wins)
4+	8	.090 (14.5 wins)

The size of the decline increases, albeit irregularly, as the lead-in period of consecutive improving seasons grows; the graph takes a precipitous drop for teams that had improved their records for four or more consecutive seasons before the fall. The Mets, as we mentioned, have already made five consecutive upward moves. That's the bad news for Mets fans.

Landing the Big One

The good news is that New York could fall 15 wins from its 1986 record and still post a 93–69 mark, good enough to win the division eight times in the last 14 years. The even better news is that the Mets have refused to surrender to the inevitable. Working on the assumption that there's room for improvement on any team that wins fewer than 162 games, New York traded for Kevin McReynolds over the winter.

McReynolds was one of baseball's best-kept secrets last season. He hit 26 home runs with 96 RBIs. Only three National League players had higher totals in both categories: Glenn Davis, Dale Murphy, and Mike Schmidt. And of the three only Schmidt, the league's Most Valuable Player, had a higher batting average than McReynolds's .288 mark.

Championship teams rarely make major moves. Of course, the Yankees of 1977 and 1978 were active in the free-agent market, signing Goose Gossage and Rawly Eastwick the first year, Luis Tiant and Tommy John the next. They also swung deals for Jim Spencer, Andy Messersmith, Juan Beniquez, and Dave Righetti during those winters. But since then, only one championship team has acquired an everyday starting player during the offseason: the 1980 Philadelphia Phillies, who traded Bob Walk for Gary Matthews. One other, the 1984 Detroit Tigers, made a significant addition to its starting rotation (Walt Terrell, obtained from the Mets for Howard Johnson). Maybe that inactivity explains why no team has won consecutive titles since the free-spending Yankees of the late 1970s.

And although it's unusual for a team to make a major transaction during the offseason following a World Series victory, it's unprecedented for a World Series winner to acquire a player of McReynolds's caliber. We took a look at the offseason acquisitions of every team following a World Series victory and found that none had hit as many home runs in the preceding season as McReynolds hit last season. Only one, Eddie Robinson in 1953, had as many RBIs. (Another, Sherry Magee, drove in 103 runs in 1914, before RBIs were compiled on an official basis.) The following table lists the all-time leaders in those categories among offseason pick-ups by championship teams (RBIs are included only since they became an official statistic in 1920):

Year	Player	From	To	HR
1986	Kevin McReynolds	Padres	Mets	26
1953	Eddie Robinson	Athletics	Yankees	22
1980	Gary Matthews	Braves	Phillies	19
1977	Jim Spencer	White Sox	Yankees	18
1935	Al Simmons	White Sox	Tigers	16
1974	Billy Williams	Cubs	Athletics	16
1914	Sherry Magee	Phillies	Braves	15
1983	Wayne Gross	Athletics	Orioles	12
1930	Phil Todt	Red Sox	Athletics	11
1945	Eddie Lake	Red Sox	Tigers	11
1969	Joe Foy	Royals	Mets	11

Year	Player	From	To	RBI
1953	Eddie Robinson	Athletics	Yankees	102
1986	Kevin McReynolds	Padres	Mets	96
1935	Al Simmons	White Sox	Tigers	79
1980	Gary Matthews	Braves	Phillies	75
1969	Joe Foy	Royals	Mets	71
1977	Jim Spencer	White Sox	Yankees	69
1974	Billy Williams	Cubs	Athletics	68
1921	Dave Robertson	Pirates	Giants	62
1930	Phil Todt	Red Sox	Athletics	62
1933	George Watkins	Cardinals	Giants	62

Most of the traded players listed above were past their primes. Williams was 36, Robinson and Simmons 33. In fact, all but three were past 30 at the time of the trades; of those three, Eddie Lake and Phil Todt were 29. McReynolds turned 27 a few hours after Jesse Orosco struck out Kevin Bass to win the National League pennant for the Mets; the only listed player younger than that at the time of his trade was—yes, Mets fans—Joe Foy. (Still doesn't make him worth Amos Otis.)

Incidentally, reliable starting pitchers have joined championship teams as infrequently as everyday players. We compiled a list of all pitchers who met these criteria: 1) they joined a team during the offseason following its World Series victory; 2) they won at least 10 starts the previous season; and 3) they had a winning record the previous season. The list: Tommy John (joined Yankees following 1978 title), Luis Tiant (1978 Yankees), Bob Purkey (1964 Cardinals), Stan Williams (1962 Yankees), Ed Lopat (1947 Yankees), Pat Malone (1934 Cardinals, and traded again before ever pitching for St. Louis), and Slim Love (1918 Boston).

The attitude of Frank Cashen, Joe McIlvaine, and the rest of the Mets organization is admirable. They actively pursued one of the National League's best young players and hooked him using some promising young talent for bait. Of course, that's nothing new for the Mets; a year earlier, they added Bob Ojeda in a trade that seemed superfluous to some, parting with promising minor-league pitchers Wes Gardner and Calvin Schiraldi. And what happened? Ojeda was their biggest winner during the 1986 season, and Schiraldi their savior in the Series. Now perhaps New York's aggressive pursuit and capture of McReynolds will prove that teams can still win consecutive championships, if they maintain a strong will to win.

Slam the Door

The mention of Schiraldi reminds us that last year's post-season proved the old axiom that the game isn't over until the last out is made. In fact, three times in five days during the playoffs, teams that trailed by two or more runs going into the ninth inning rallied for victories, something that had never been done in the 648 previous games in postseason history. (Hold the mail! If you haven't heard by now, Bobby Thomson's homer was technically hit in a regular-season game. It's right there in his record in *The Baseball Encyclopedia*. You could look it up.) And that illustrates the importance of slamming the door shut on your opponent, whether it's in a series, a game, or an inning.

Few teams in recent history have nailed down the final out of an inning as well as the 1986 Mets, especially when there was a scoring threat. Opposing batters hit .188 with two outs and runners in scoring position, the lowest mark in the National League last season, and the second lowest since 1975. The Mets also led the league in that category in 1985 with a .206 mark. A year earlier, Montreal set the *Player Analysis* record with a .180 average. Since the common denominator for those three teams is such a humble fellow, we're forced to point out that that player is The Kid himself, Gary Carter. The 10 lowest opponents' batting averages with two outs and runners in scoring position in the 12-year history of *The Player Analysis*:

Year	Team	AB	H	BA
1984	Montreal Expos	596	107	.180
1986	**New York Mets**	638	120	.188
1981	Los Angeles Dodgers	387	74	.191
1977	Oakland A's	624	123	.197
1986	Houston Astros	632	127	.201
1981	New York Yankees	366	74	.202
1984	Pittsburgh Pirates	607	123	.203
1975	Cincinnati Reds	603	123	.204
1976	Cleveland Indians	634	130	.205
1981	Houston Astros	419	86	.205

Last season, batters opposing the Mets' four most frequent starters and two main relievers batted .167 in those situations (.129 vs. Darling, .148 vs. McDowell, .149 vs. Gooden, .188 vs. Fernandez, .192 vs. Orosco, and .202 vs. Ojeda). Is it just a coincidence that Carter's arrival in New York coincided with the increased effectiveness of Mets pitchers with two outs and runners in scoring position? We can't say for sure, but look at the performance of batters against Montreal and New York in those situations over the past three seasons. When Carter left Montreal, the Expos average jumped; when he joined New York, the Mets average declined:

Team	—1984—			—1985—			—1986—		
	2O/SP	Overall	Diff.	2O/SP	Overall	Diff.	2O/SP	Overall	Diff.
Montreal	.180	.249	−69	.241	.247	−6	.242	.246	−4
New York	.236	.252	−16	.206	.237	−31	.188	.236	−37
N.L. Avg.	.236	.255	−19	.235	.252	−17	.235	.253	−18

Of course, the Mets pitching has improved in general since Carter arrived in 1985, with the development of Darling and Gooden and the addition of Aguilera and Ojeda. But notice that New York's opposing batters have compiled lower averages with two outs and runners in scoring position under Carter even when judged according to the difference between that mark and their overall averages. And Montreal's opponents' averages have risen by that measure as well. Whether Carter is responsible is unclear. But just raising the issue will sure make watching his pitch selection more interesting this season, especially with two outs and the tying run a single away.

WON-LOST RECORD BY STARTING POSITION

NEW YORK 108-54	C	1B	2B	3B	SS	LF	CF	RF	P	Leadoff	Relief	Starts
Rick Aguilera												
Rick Anderson									12-8		2-6	12-8
Wally Backman			63-29							2-3	4-6	2-3
Bruce Berenyi									4-3		1-6	63-29
Gary Carter	79-42	5-2				1-0			1-1			4-3
												86-45
Tim Corcoran		1-0										
Ron Darling									26-8			1-0
Len Dykstra							66-32			64-32		26-8
Kevin Elster					6-3							66-32
Sid Fernandez									20-11		1-0	6-3
												20-11
George Foster					40-22							
John Gibbons	5-0											40-22
Dwight Gooden									21-12			5-0
Ed Hearn	22-12											21-12
Danny Heep						25-14	7-4					22-12
												32-18
Keith Hernandez		97-49										97-49
Stan Jefferson							4-1			2-1		
Howard Johnson				17-12	14-8	1-0						4-1
Ray Knight			89-41									32-20
Terry Leach											3-3	89-41
Ed Lynch												
Barry Lyons	2-0									0-1		
Dave Magadan		2-2										2-0
Lee Mazzilli		2-1				2-4	0-1					2-2
Roger McDowell											57-18	4-6
John Mitchell												
Kevin Mitchell		1-0		2-1	11-9	20-6	5-1	13-8		0-1	1-2	0-1
Randy Myers										6-1		52-25
Randy Niemann										4-6		
Bob Ojeda								1-0			11-19	1-0
									22-8		1-1	22-8
Jesse Orosco											42-16	
Rafael Santana					77-34							42-16
Doug Sisk												77-34
Darryl Strawberry											12-29	
Tim Teufel			45-25					87-40				87-40
												45-25
Mookie Wilson						19-8	33-20			36-20		52-28

Batting Comparisons: Vs. Left-Handers/Right-Handers and Overall/Late Inning Pressure Situations

Player		BA	Rank	SA	Rank	HR %	Rank		BA	Rank	SA	Rank	HR %	Rank
Wally Backman	vs. Lefties	.192	133	.250	135	0.00	119	Overall	.320	6	.385	81	0.26	133
	vs. Righties	.340	3	.406	68	0.30	128	Pressure	.364	9	.382	73	0.00	102
Gary Carter	vs. Lefties	.275	54	.480	25	5.85	13	Overall	.255	81	.439	39	4.90	13
	vs. Righties	.245	92	.417	60	4.39	28	Pressure	.348	14	.449	35	2.90	47
Len Dykstra	vs. Lefties	.233	101	.291	121	0.00	119	Overall	.295	17	.445	31	1.86	87
	vs. Righties	.314	14	.494	9	2.44	64	Pressure	.328	20	.393	66	0.00	102
George Foster	vs. Lefties	.221	115	.442	45	6.73	8	Overall	.227	124	.429	45	5.58	7
	vs. Righties	.233	106	.419	59	4.65	21	Pressure	.171	--	.200	--	0.00	--
Ed Hearn	vs. Lefties	.234	98	.328	107	3.13	44	Overall	.265	--	.390	--	2.94	--
	vs. Righties	.292	--	.444	--	2.78	--	Pressure	.263	--	.316	--	0.00	--
Danny Heep	vs. Lefties	.083	--	.083	--	0.00	--	Overall	.282	28	.421	53	2.56	62
	vs. Righties	.295	22	.443	47	2.73	54	Pressure	.265	--	.294	--	0.00	--
Keith Hernandez	vs. Lefties	.312	25	.422	55	1.83	77	Overall	.310	10	.446	29	2.36	67
	vs. Righties	.309	16	.462	24	2.70	55	Pressure	.270	59	.392	69	2.70	50
Howard Johnson	vs. Lefties	.213	122	.404	61	4.26	24	Overall	.245	103	.445	32	4.55	18
	vs. Righties	.254	81	.457	31	4.62	23	Pressure	.245	86	.453	34	5.66	8
Ray Knight	vs. Lefties	.379	1	.601	5	4.55	21	Overall	.298	16	.424	48	2.26	68
	vs. Righties	.243	93	.302	122	0.69	122	Pressure	.353	12	.574	7	4.41	25
Lee Mazzilli	vs. Lefties	.173	138	.269	129	1.92	73	Overall	.245	--	.351	--	1.99	--
	vs. Righties	.283	36	.394	71	2.02	79	Pressure	.196	123	.250	123	1.79	81
Kevin Mitchell	vs. Lefties	.307	29	.503	21	3.52	34	Overall	.277	36	.466	23	3.66	36
	vs. Righties	.233	106	.411	63	3.88	39	Pressure	.286	45	.510	14	6.12	6
Rafael Santana	vs. Lefties	.245	90	.288	122	0.61	114	Overall	.218	135	.254	141	0.25	134
	vs. Righties	.199	135	.229	140	0.00	131	Pressure	.127	140	.182	138	0.00	102
Darryl Strawberry	vs. Lefties	.209	125	.353	91	2.67	56	Overall	.259	72	.507	6	5.68	5
	vs. Righties	.292	25	.608	1	7.64	1	Pressure	.270	59	.500	17	5.41	12
Tim Teufel	vs. Lefties	.245	91	.372	79	1.53	91	Overall	.247	98	.369	94	1.43	97
	vs. Righties	.253	--	.361	--	1.20	--	Pressure	.273	57	.432	46	2.27	59
Mookie Wilson	vs. Lefties	.291	40	.418	56	1.53	91	Overall	.289	20	.430	43	2.36	66
	vs. Righties	.286	29	.443	45	3.24	46	Pressure	.274	56	.403	60	1.61	87
Team Average	vs. Lefties	.260	6	.395	6	2.55	5	Overall	.263	1	.401	1	2.66	3
	vs. Righties	.265	1	.405	1	2.73	4	Messure	.277	1	.403	2	2.54	6
League Average	vs. Lefties	.257		.384		2.28		Overall	.253		.380		2.32	
	vs. Righties	.251		.378		2.34		Pressure	.257		.376		2.31	

Additional Miscellaneous Batting Comparisons

	Grass Surface BA	Rank	Artificial Surface BA	Rank	Home Games BA	Rank	Road Games BA	Rank	Runners in Scoring Position BA	Rank	Runners in Scoring Pos and Two Outs BA	Rank	Leading Off Inning OBA	Rank	Runners on 3B with less than 2 Outs RDI %	Rank
Wally Backman	.308	19	.346	3	.311	16	.329	4	.226	107	.333	16	.397	13	.615	49
Gary Carter	.263	66	.242	96	.268	79	.244	87	.282	47	.240	74	.331	58	.646	34
Len Dykstra	.309	16	.262	60	.322	8	.268	44	.350	9	.333	16	.392	17	.500	101
George Foster	.207	131	.275	--	.208	135	.248	81	.250	75	.233	81	.339	52	.462	120
Ed Hearn	.257	73	.296	--	.250	--	.278	--	.103	--	.143	--	.361	--	.500	--
Danny Heep	.263	67	.328	--	.298	33	.267	45	.404	1	.370	6	.239	136	.636	37
Keith Hernandez	.320	12	.291	29	.310	20	.311	10	.299	30	.218	93	.330	60	.548	85
Howard Johnson	.242	99	.254	--	.217	130	.266	48	.362	6	.348	12	.196	141	.636	37
Ray Knight	.301	23	.294	24	.289	42	.306	13	.354	8	.396	5	.342	50	.618	48
Lee Mazzilli	.247	84	.243	94	.288	47	.197	--	.244	86	.250	--	.389	--	.667	25
Kevin Mitchell	.282	43	.266	52	.302	24	.253	74	.275	51	.325	20	.284	109	.333	140
Rafael Santana	.218	123	.220	113	.188	141	.246	83	.189	131	.163	124	.228	138	.652	31
Darryl Strawberry	.265	65	.247	87	.227	120	.284	25	.261	64	.205	104	.344	47	.541	91
Tim Teufel	.242	97	.259	66	.236	113	.259	62	.234	96	.235	80	.292	97	.563	77
Mookie Wilson	.313	14	.235	101	.289	43	.288	20	.368	5	.324	21	.316	81	.667	25
Team Average	.267	1	.254	5	.262	4	.264	1	.272	1	.254	3	.316	6	.551	8
League Average	.254		.253		.260		.247		.252		.235		.316		.562	

Pitching Comparisons: Vs. Left-Handers/Right-Handers and Runners On/Bases Empty

		BA	Rank	BB %	Rank	SO %	Rank		BA	Rank	BB %	Rank	SO %	Rank
Rick Aguilera	vs. Lefties	.290	90	6.55	21	11.72	88	Runners On	.264	63	5.49	5	15.69	47
	vs. Righties	.238	49	5.40	16	22.22	15	Bases Empty	.262	74	6.29	28	18.29	33
Rick Anderson	vs. Lefties	.215	22	6.80	23	7.77	112	Runners On	.261	--	8.54	--	8.54	--
	vs. Righties	.275	--	4.08	--	13.27	--	Bases Empty	.235	--	3.36	--	11.76	--
Bruce Berenyi	vs. Lefties	.319	110	16.85	117	14.61	65	Runners On	.349	--	10.31	--	18.56	--
	vs. Righties	.282	--	7.37	--	17.89	--	Bases Empty	.243	--	13.79	--	13.79	--
Ron Darling	vs. Lefties	.227	31	7.90	37	18.85	31	Runners On	.207	13	8.95	37	18.42	27
	vs. Righties	.245	57	9.02	77	19.27	36	Bases Empty	.250	59	8.01	67	19.42	24
Sid Fernandez	vs. Lefties	.224	27	15.00	111	27.50	4	Runners On	.213	14	10.38	64	22.95	4
	vs. Righties	.215	16	9.93	89	22.72	11	Bases Empty	.218	16	10.84	102	23.72	10
Dwight Gooden	vs. Lefties	.211	17	8.45	42	18.75	32	Runners On	.203	11	8.01	26	20.37	12
	vs. Righties	.221	21	7.01	47	20.79	25	Bases Empty	.223	21	7.72	58	19.04	26
Roger McDowell	vs. Lefties	.247	53	12.08	88	9.06	106	Runners On	.265	64	7.26	16	9.40	106
	vs. Righties	.211	14	3.86	7	15.83	59	Bases Empty	.200	7	8.62	80	14.83	69
Bob Ojeda	vs. Lefties	.150	3	6.67	22	20.00	24	Runners On	.204	12	5.87	7	17.60	32
	vs. Righties	.242	51	5.86	23	16.51	53	Bases Empty	.247	52	6.04	24	16.57	51
Jesse Orosco	vs. Lefties	.187	12	6.17	18	29.63	2	Runners On	.183	3	10.06	54	19.55	21
	vs. Righties	.227	30	11.67	101	14.79	69	Bases Empty	.254	64	10.69	100	16.98	45
Doug Sisk	vs. Lefties	.265	70	12.50	94	9.56	103	Runners On	.299	96	9.64	48	10.24	95
	vs. Righties	.295	103	7.95	58	10.23	105	Bases Empty	.264	75	10.27	97	9.59	111
Team Average	vs. Lefties	.232	2	9.33	4	16.50	2	Runners On	.230	2	8.56	1	17.04	2
	vs. Righties	.239	3	7.55	1	18.27	2	Bases Empty	.241	5	8.02	6	17.98	2
League Average	vs. Lefties	.257		9.83		14.90		Runners On	.260		10.11		15.02	
	vs. Righties	.251		8.19		16.33		Bases Empty	.248		7.89		16.30	

Additional Miscellaneous Pitching Comparisons

	Grass Surface BA	Rank	Artificial Surface BA	Rank	Home Games BA	Rank	Road Games BA	Rank	Runners in Scoring Position BA	Rank	Runners in Scoring Pos and Two Outs BA	Rank	Leading Off Inning OBA	Rank
Rick Aguilera	.268	72	.250	47	.259	77	.267	75	.250	55	.258	74	.315	63
Rick Anderson	.266	70	.171	--	.257	--	.227	--	.216	--	.167	--	.320	--
Bruce Berenyi	.300	108	.294	--	.295	--	.306	--	.333	--	.250	--	.425	--
Ron Darling	.230	30	.243	39	.219	26	.249	44	.199	15	.129	8	.333	76
Sid Fernandez	.211	9	.227	24	.178	3	.254	54	.204	17	.188	26	.299	42
Dwight Gooden	.209	8	.231	26	.183	7	.243	41	.167	6	.149	11	.332	75
Roger McDowell	.221	16	.246	41	.183	8	.267	76	.264	71	.148	10	.272	20
Randy Niemann	.278	84	.400	--	.293	--	.328	--	.345	--	.200	--	.297	--
Bob Ojeda	.226	23	.236	32	.224	30	.236	30	.206	18	.202	35	.295	38
Jesse Orosco	.249	56	.153	1	.275	89	.166	1	.172	7	.192	30	.323	68
Doug Sisk	.283	90	.280	--	.209	17	.347	115	.304	103	.262	77	.377	104
Team Average	.235	2	.240	2	.218	1	.254	3	.220	2	.188	1	.321	8
League Average	.254		.253		.247		.260		.252		.235		.316	

PHILADELPHIA PHILLIES

"Hi. You may not know our faces, and we'll bet that you don't know many of our names, either! Oh, you may know Schmitty, but we've changed since we were regulars on post-season TV, with six appearances in eight years. Pete, Little Joe, and Doggy left us a couple of years ago. Then Tug. Now even Lefty is gone. But we did have the third-best record in the National League last season. Even so, we know we're going to go down in history bearing this:

1986 PHILADELPHIA PHILLIES
21.5 GAMES BEHIND METS
LARGEST 2ND-PLACE DEFICIT IN
DIVISION HISTORY"

Being a footnote to history is one way to assure baseball immortality. Just ask Tracy Stallard, who gave up an historic home run, or Tom House, who caught one. But within the limited meaning of the word *success* imposed by the Mets runaway, 1986 was also a successful season for the Phillies and manager John Felske.

Felske took over the team in 1985, and for a time it seemed as if he would be presiding at a wake. Just two years removed from the National League championship, the Phillies fell to a 75–87 record and fifth place, their worst performance in a dozen years. They batted only .245 as a team and scored 53 fewer runs than the previous year. Some observers were surprised when Felske was invited back for a second year.

But the joke was on the doomsayers. The Phillies' 86–75 record last season was not only the best of the rest after the Mets and the Astros, but their offense, given up for dead a year earlier, made like Lazarus. Their run production increased from 667 to 739, second in the league, as a result of an increase in almost every component category:

	Runs	H	2B	3B	HR	SB	BB	SO	BA	SA	OBA
1985	667	1343	238	47	141	122	527	1095	.245	.383	.312
1986	739	1386	266	39	154	153	589	1154	.253	.400	.327

Yes, even the strikeouts increased, as the Phillies easily extended their own major-league record of 1,000-strikeout seasons to 10.

By their offseason acquisitions of Gary Redus from the Reds and Milt Thompson from the Braves, the Phillies seemed intent on getting more out of the top of their batting order than they had in 1985. That's exactly what they got:

The top of the order was so successful early in games that the Phillies wound up leading the majors in first-inning runs. These runs accounted for about one-sixth of their total output for the season, the highest such percentage in baseball. Here are all the teams that scored 100 or more first-inning runs, along with the league averages:

	1st Inning Runs	Total Runs	Pct. of Total
Philadelphia	122	739	16.5
N.Y. Yankees	116	797	14.6
Boston	110	794	13.9
Cleveland	107	831	12.9
Oakland	104	731	14.2
Los Angeles	103	638	16.1
N.Y. Mets	103	783	13.2
Montreal	102	637	16.0
Minnesota	100	741	13.5
N.L. Average	87	675	12.8
A.L. Average	89	746	11.9

A brief digression: The Phillies were the only National League team among the top five, even though the A.L. average for first-inning runs is only marginally higher than the N.L.'s. This led us to compare runs scored by innings in each league, in an effort to isolate the effects of the designated hitter. It turns out that the rates are very similar in the innings in which the pitcher is least likely to bat—the first, obviously, and the ninth, when more often than not a team is behind if it is batting at all. The margins are greatest in the second and third innings when, in the National League, the pitcher is almost always assured of coming to the plate:

	1	2	3	4	5	6	7	8	9
A.L. Average	89	79	87	86	85	81	87	84	55
N.L. Average	87	61	69	81	73	79	72	78	56

Now back to the Phillies. Given the trades of the previous offseason and the first-inning run production in 1986, one would assume that Redus and/or Thompson had banner years. Wrong! Redus was disabled for nearly 10 weeks before the All-Star Game, and Thompson was so-so all year long (.251 batting, .341 slugging, and .311 on-base averages).

In fact, Felske tinkered throughout the season with the top three spots in his batting order. To give you an idea of the extent of his maneuvering, here are all the players who started in those three positions:

Batting First: Redus (78 games), Jeff Stone (39), Thompson (28), Ron Roenicke (9), Greg Gross (4), Chris James (3).

Batting Second: Juan Samuel (44), Thompson (41), Roenicke (22), Rick Schu (20), Stone (19), Luis Aguayo (4), Gross (4), Darren Daulton (3), Von Hayes (2), James (1), Greg Legg (1).

Batting Third: Samuel (76), Hayes (64), Roenicke (17), Schu (3), Gross (1).

The actual plot convolutions were even more complex. Welcome to another episode of "Felske and the Restless."

Gary was usually the leadoff man, when healthy, although he spent part of September batting sixth, while Milt and Chris batted first. When Gary was hurt early in the season, Milt was his first understudy, although when Milt faltered in June, Jeff was recalled and filled in until Gary returned, except for the games when Ron filled in for the fill-in.

Meanwhile, the second spot was full of mischief. Milt started the season there but was replaced by Rick at the end of April, and then by a shifting cast of characters through most of May. Ron took over as the semiregular on May 31, but by mid-June the job was up for grabs again, with Juan taking over in early July. But after the All-Star break, we saw the return of Jeff, as Juan moved to the number-three spot, with occasional returns to number two. Milt, who had been injured, returned in mid-August and took over his old number-two spot, since Gary, healthy again, was number one. But Milt eventually had to share time with Juan, who was in the two hole regularly through most of September.

While all this was going on, Juan started the season batting third, only to go on the disabled list the first weekend. Von filled in until Juan returned in early May; Juan held the job until the start of July, when Juan moved to number two and the peripatetic Ron took over batting third. But not for long. Juan was back after the break, only to give way eventually to Von, who mercifully held the job from from August 17 till season's end. Well, almost season's end; Rick was there the last day.

Through all of those trials and tribulations, the Phillies came through consistently in the first inning. And the key guys were not the table-setters but the cleanup crew, Mike Schmidt and Von Hayes.

Schmidt was the cleanup hitter in all 152 games he started. To say that Schmidt had a good year is, of course, an understatement. He led the league in home runs, runs batted in, and slugging average, the third time that he's hit that trifecta. Only Babe Ruth and Ted Williams have done that at least three times. (Ruth actually did it six.) Schmidt won the MVP award in each of those three years.

Hayes, in his fourth season in Philadelphia, put up the numbers that should shut up those "Five for One" chanters once and for all. He started at four different positions in the field and in five different positions in the batting order, settling into first base and the number-three slot in August and September. He achieved career-highs in the Triple Crown categories with 19, 98, and .305, while stealing 24 bases and scoring 107 runs.

And as good as these two were overall, they were murderous when they came up in the first inning:

	PA	AB	H	2B	3B	HR	RRF	BA	SA	OBA
Schmidt, 1st inning	105	83	32	6	0	9	36	.386	.783	.495
Schmidt, other innings	552	469	128	23	1	28	89	.273	.505	.370
Hayes, 1st inning	103	92	34	9	0	2	21	.370	.533	.422
Hayes, other innings	587	518	152	37	2	17	80	.293	.471	.422

The big numbers from Schmidt and Hayes offset less than spectacular contributions from Redus, Thompson, and Stone. Redus batted .247 for the season, with a .343 on-base average, and once again demonstrated an uncanny ability to hit balls into the air, rather than trying to take advantage of his speed and the artificial turf by banging them off the carpet. His ground outs-to-air outs ratio of 0.61—based on 67 ground outs and 113 air outs—continued his curious career pattern of hitting everything in the air. His habit of uppercutting the ball was a source of trouble between Redus and his former manager, Pete Rose of the Reds, and gave us a glimpse of Rose's remarkable powers of baseball observation.

During the summer of 1985, following 11 years of coding the batter-by-batter description of every major-league game, feeding the information into our computers, editing and correcting the raw material, and writing a new set of programs to digest the matter, we were ready to determine which player, of anyone in the majors since 1975 with 1,000 plate appearances, had the highest and lowest ratios of ground outs-to-air outs. As luck would have it, our travels took us to Cincinnati the week after we had finished these calculations.

In talking with Rose before the game at Riverfront that night, the conversation got around to statistics—no surprise there. We mentioned to Pete that we had just finished our work on this new one, and asked him if he could identify the single player in baseball over the preceding 10 years who had the highest rate of making outs in the air, rather than on the ground. No one outside our office, not even Price Waterhouse's accountants, knew the identity of the player.

"Is he a regular?" Rose asked.

We explained the 1,000-plate appearance minimum.

Pete thought for no more than five seconds before answering, "Gary Redus."

Silence. It was a little bit like thinking that you're the first to climb a mountain, but when you reach the summit you find some old Coke cans scattered about. Pete was absolutely right; we went away convinced that he must know *everyone's* statistics, not just his own.

Now, two years later, Redus still tops that list. His career rate of 0.60 ground outs-per-air out puts him at the head of a "top 10" that also includes Jim Dwyer, Ken Phelps, Gene Tenace, Joe Morgan, Steve Balboni, Andre Thornton, Darrell Evans, Don Baylor, and Tim Hulett. That's something of a strange mix. Morgan and Baylor (early in his career) had speed, but none of the others did. Most of them were long ball threats. And most of them drew a lot of walks.

To show how Redus compares with the rest of that group, here are his career statistics, matched with the composite of the other players, with that composite scaled to the same amount of career plate apperarances that Redus has had:

	PA	AB	R	H	2B	3B	HR	RBI	BB	SO	SB	BA	SA	OBA
Redus	1762	1516	284	376	80	22	42	141	219	333	171	.248	.413	.344
Others	1762	1480	229	380	65	9	60	216	242	231	44	.257	.435	.364

We can see here how Redus differs from his fly-ball cousins. If you throw out the runs and RBIs, which are dependent on batting-order position, you see that Redus has more speed, and more double/triple power, but that he has less home run power and makes far less contact than the other uppercut hitters. And he has drawn fewer walks than the composite of the other nine—not, all in all, exactly what you're looking for in a leadoff man, which is what he's been in 300 of his 376 major-league starts.

Where does this leave us? Back with Felske's lineup tinkering. Redus and Samuel are the pivotal players in the batting order, whose roles seemed the least defined at season's end. One will likely bat ahead of Hayes and Schmidt, the other behind them. It might be worthwhile to give Redus the first shot behind those two, if for no other reason than his difficulties at the plate when leading off innings (.227 batting, .367 slugging, and .306 on-base averages, against .261, .477, and .368 in all other at bats). Given his propensity for hitting the ball in the air, getting Redus out of the top spot of the order may let him bloom as a power hitter. Every once in a while, you have to go with the flow, even if the river takes a wandering route.

Swish! (Continued)

Remember last April when the Seattle Mariners were striking out at a rate of better than nine times per game? When they struck out 20 times one night and 16 times the next night at Fenway Park? When they sent everyone running to the record books to find out that the record for striking out in one season is 1,203 by the 1968 Mets?

Well, which team in the majors do you think struck out the most times last season?

Of course. The Phillies.

To any real Phillie phanatic, the ultimate outcome was as predictable as the results of a Steve Carlton press conference, even when the Phillies were 91 behind Seattle at the end of April, 49 behind at the end of July, or six behind at the end of September, with four games remaining for each team. The running totals:

	April	May	June	July	Aug.	Sept.
Mariners	202	407	584	750	931	1,123
Phillies	111	322	517	701	904	1,117

The true faithful didn't even doubt the eventual outcome when, on October 1, the Mariners struck out nine times at Chicago while the Phillies game with the Cubs was rained out and would not be rescheduled. That left the Mariners with a 15-strikeout advantage with three games remaining for each team.

Piece of cake. The Phillies went out and whiffed 12 times against the Expos on Friday night, while Seattle had just three. Then on Saturday, seeing Seattle strike out eight times in an afternoon game at Cleveland, the Phils knew what had to be done. Their night game lasted 14 innings, and they struck out 15 times—including five in extra innings—to take a one-strikeout lead.

Sunday dawned. The Mariners would be facing knuckleballer Tom Candiotti. The Phillies would go against one of Chris Berman's favorites, Bob "Ice Station" Sebra. To the Phillies, he was Sandy Koufax, as Sebra fanned nine in seven innings, and Bob McClure added another. Candiotti fanned only five, and the Phillies won, 1,154 to 1,148.

Who says that all of the baseball drama last October was crammed into the postseason?

WON-LOST RECORD BY STARTING POSITION

PHILADELPHIA 86-75	C	1B	2B	3B	SS	LF	CF	RF	P	Leadoff	Relief	Starts
Luis Aguayo			7-9		7-7							14-16
Larry Andersen											2-8	
Steve Bedrosian											48-20	
Jeff Bittiger									2-1			2-1
Steve Carlton									6-10			6-10
Don Carman									9-5		16-20	9-5
Rocky Childress											0-2	
Darren Daulton	21-23											21-23
Tom Foley					5-9							5-9
Marvin Freeman									3-0			3-0
Tom Gorman										1-7		
Greg Gross		0-1				2-4	2-1			1-3	0-1	4-6
Kevin Gross									19-17		0-1	19-17
Von Hayes		71-56				9-14	3-2	0-1				83-73
Charles Hudson									9-14		3-7	9-14
Tom Hume									1-0	19-28		1-0
Mike Jackson										2-7		
Chris James						1-2	3-4			2-1		4-6
Steve Jeltz				73-59								73-59
Joe Lefebvre							1-2					1-2
Greg Legg			2-0		1-0							3-0
Randy Lerch											1-3	
Garry Maddox						0-1						0-1
Mike Maddux									6-10			6-10
Francisco Melendez												
Shane Rawley									14-9			14-9
Gary Redus						48-37						48-37
Ronn Reynolds	20-15									44-34		20-15
Ron Roenicke						5-3	34-23	4-0		5-4		43-26
Dave Rucker											6-13	
Bruce Ruffin									15-6			15-6
John Russell	45-37											45-37
Juan Samuel			77-66									77-66
Dan Schatzeder											10-15	
Mike Schmidt		15-18		67-52								82-70
Rick Schu				19-23								19-23
Dave Stewart											1-7	
Jeff Stone						21-15	8-14			21-18		29-29
Kent Tekulve											34-39	
Milt Thompson						38-31				13-15		38-31
Fred Toliver									2-3			2-3
Glenn Wilson								79-71				79-71

Batting Comparisons: Vs. Left-Handers/Right-Handers and Overall/Late Inning Pressure Situations

		BA	Rank	SA	Rank	HR %	Rank		BA	Rank	SA	Rank	HR %	Rank
Luis Aguayo	vs. Lefties	.169	141	.282	124	2.82	52	Overall	.211	--	.361	--	3.01	--
	vs. Righties	.258	--	.452	--	3.23	--	Pressure	.296	--	.370	--	0.00	--
Darren Daulton	vs. Lefties	.235	--	.294	--	0.00	--	Overall	.225	--	.428	--	5.80	--
	vs. Righties	.223	118	.446	40	6.61	2	Pressure	.115	--	.154	--	0.00	--
Greg Gross	vs. Lefties	.167	--	.167	--	0.00	--	Overall	.248	--	.297	--	0.00	--
	vs. Righties	.265	--	.325	--	0.00	--	Pressure	.143	139	.167	140	0.00	102
Von Hayes	vs. Lefties	.231	104	.328	106	1.54	89	Overall	.305	13	.480	13	3.11	47
	vs. Righties	.340	--	.552	3	3.86	40	Pressure	.284	48	.422	53	2.94	45
Steve Jeltz	vs. Lefties	.221	114	.257	134	0.00	119	Overall	.219	134	.262	139	0.00	136
	vs. Righties	.217	123	.264	134	0.00	131	Pressure	.262	65	.295	109	0.00	102
Gary Redus	vs. Lefties	.248	86	.385	73	1.83	77	Overall	.247	100	.432	40	3.24	45
	vs. Righties	.247	89	.455	32	3.90	38	Pressure	.231	97	.385	71	1.92	74
Ron Roenicke	vs. Lefties	.308	26	.439	46	2.80	54	Overall	.247	99	.356	101	1.82	88
	vs. Righties	.208	129	.304	121	1.19	104	Pressure	.245	86	.283	110	0.00	102
John Russell	vs. Lefties	.254	81	.451	41	3.28	39	Overall	.241	105	.444	34	4.13	25
	vs. Righties	.233	105	.440	49	4.66	20	Pressure	.217	108	.400	62	5.00	18
Juan Samuel	vs. Lefties	.256	79	.456	36	2.78	55	Overall	.266	59	.448	27	2.71	58
	vs. Righties	.270	46	.445	43	2.68	58	Pressure	.258	70	.441	43	4.30	28
Mike Schmidt	vs. Lefties	.357	3	.707	1	9.55	1	Overall	.290	19	.547	2	6.70	1
	vs. Righties	.263	54	.484	16	5.57	8	Pressure	.286	45	.495	23	5.49	11
Rick Schu	vs. Lefties	.279	49	.452	40	3.85	29	Overall	.274	43	.447	28	3.85	31
	vs. Righties	.269	47	.442	48	3.85	41	Pressure	.147	--	.235	--	2.94	--
Jeff Stone	vs. Lefties	.317	19	.476	27	3.17	41	Overall	.277	38	.406	66	2.41	65
	vs. Righties	.263	53	.382	75	2.15	74	Pressure	.279	53	.442	42	4.65	23
Milt Thompson	vs. Lefties	.220	--	.240	--	0.00	--	Overall	.251	88	.341	113	2.01	79
	vs. Righties	.257	71	.361	94	2.41	66	Pressure	.261	67	.283	111	0.00	102
Glenn Wilson	vs. Lefties	.222	113	.335	100	2.16	70	Overall	.271	52	.413	60	2.57	61
	vs. Righties	.293	24	.449	38	2.76	53	Pressure	.260	69	.302	106	0.00	102
Team Average	vs. Lefties	.251	9	.395	5	2.86	2	Overall	.253	8	.400	2	2.81	2
	vs. Righties	.254	4	.402	2	2.78	2	Pressure	.251	9	.360	10	2.24	8
League Average	vs. Lefties	.257		.384		2.28		Overall	.253		.380		2.32	
	vs. Righties	.251		.378		2.34		Pressure	.257		.376		2.31	

Additional Miscellaneous Batting Comparisons

	Grass Surface BA	Rank	Artificial Surface BA	Rank	Home Games BA	Rank	Road Games BA	Rank	Runners in Scoring Position BA	Rank	Runners in Scoring Pos and Two Outs BA	Rank	Leading Off Inning OBA	Rank	Runners on 3B with less than 2 Outs RDI %	Rank
Luis Aguayo	.182	--	.220	112	.245	--	.188	--	.250	--	.214	--	.400	--	.750	--
Darren Daulton	.182	--	.245	91	.231	--	.219	--	.194	128	.176	122	.244	--	.625	--
Greg Gross	.250	--	.247	88	.302	--	.207	--	.231	--	.154	--	.355	--	.800	--
Von Hayes	.347	2	.289	32	.314	13	.296	16	.339	13	.346	14	.444	2	.622	45
Steve Jeltz	.227	113	.216	118	.217	131	.221	120	.223	110	.206	101	.327	68	.643	35
Gary Redus	.211	129	.257	69	.288	46	.206	127	.253	72	.267	52	.306	85	.333	140
Ron Roenicke	.229	112	.254	76	.268	78	.226	116	.298	31	.314	26	.338	54	.619	47
John Russell	.230	--	.244	92	.283	55	.199	130	.284	44	.340	15	.250	132	.588	65
Juan Samuel	.293	32	.256	70	.266	81	.266	49	.267	58	.279	43	.305	87	.500	101
Mike Schmidt	.287	39	.291	26	.298	29	.282	27	.315	20	.358	9	.340	51	.613	51
Rick Schu	.212	127	.303	17	.270	73	.278	34	.189	132	.258	61	.350	--	.571	--
Jeff Stone	.247	86	.291	28	.319	10	.243	90	.222	112	.111	--	.283	110	.417	132
Milt Thompson	.224	115	.262	59	.273	69	.228	111	.288	39	.308	32	.302	90	.800	3
Glenn Wilson	.221	120	.290	31	.302	26	.241	92	.297	32	.247	69	.308	84	.688	20
Team Average	.243	10	.256	3	.271	2	.236	11	.264	3	.265	1	.315	7	.591	1
League Average	.254		.253		.260		.247		.252		.235		.316		.562	

Pitching Comparisons: Vs. Left-Handers/Right-Handers and Runners On/Bases Empty

		BA	Rank	BB %	Rank	SO %	Rank		BA	Rank	BB %	Rank	SO %	Rank
Steve Bedrosian	vs. Lefties	.213	19	11.17	80	20.87	20	Runners On	.234	30	10.36	63	20.21	13
	vs. Righties	.252	68	6.29	29	22.29	14	Bases Empty	.230	25	7.45	50	22.87	11
Don Carman	vs. Lefties	.233	39	5.05	9	18.18	33	Runners On	.213	15	12.27	92	19.55	22
	vs. Righties	.235	42	10.54	96	17.94	44	Bases Empty	.247	53	7.69	57	16.92	47
Kevin Gross	vs. Lefties	.272	75	11.42	85	13.70	69	Runners On	.264	62	9.33	45	15.33	53
	vs. Righties	.244	55	5.62	20	16.39	54	Bases Empty	.257	69	8.81	82	14.41	79
Charles Hudson	vs. Lefties	.282	85	10.53	69	11.91	84	Runners On	.320	110	5.86	6	14.29	65
	vs. Righties	.302	109	7.22	50	14.08	76	Bases Empty	.269	86	11.51	104	11.78	101
Tom Hume	vs. Lefties	.250	56	10.00	66	11.36	92	Runners On	.233	29	10.10	58	16.35	42
	vs. Righties	.255	73	6.59	36	14.29	73	Bases Empty	.271	90	6.70	39	8.76	114
Mike Maddux	vs. Lefties	.254	64	11.36	84	12.27	77	Runners On	.305	102	9.82	52	13.50	74
	vs. Righties	.336	--	6.87	--	12.98	--	Bases Empty	.269	87	9.57	89	11.70	103
Shane Rawley	vs. Lefties	.288	89	3.61	2	18.07	34	Runners On	.270	72	8.45	31	11.27	89
	vs. Righties	.267	85	7.97	59	9.83	108	Bases Empty	.270	89	6.68	38	10.54	107
Bruce Ruffin	vs. Lefties	.138	2	9.09	49	27.27	5	Runners On	.250	44	7.63	22	10.04	98
	vs. Righties	.271	87	7.03	48	8.98	111	Bases Empty	.252	60	7.12	46	12.82	91
Dan Schatzeder	vs. Lefties	.300	97	8.08	39	13.13	72	Runners On	.257	55	11.66	84	8.59	109
	vs. Righties	.223	25	9.78	85	12.32	91	Bases Empty	.235	32	7.55	52	15.57	60
Kent Tekulve	vs. Lefties	.254	62	6.48	20	5.56	116	Runners On	.230	26	9.05	39	12.38	81
	vs. Righties	.227	29	4.78	13	19.57	33	Bases Empty	.248	54	2.54	3	13.14	86
Team Average	vs. Lefties	.264	9	10.25	10	13.50	9	Runners On	.264	7	9.79	5	14.36	8
	vs. Righties	.265	11	7.94	6	14.33	11	Bases Empty	.265	10	8.07	7	13.70	11
League Average	vs. Lefties	.257		9.83		14.90		Runners On	.260		10.11		15.02	
	vs. Righties	.251		8.19		16.33		Bases Empty	.248		7.89		16.30	

Additional Miscellaneous Pitching Comparisons

	Grass Surface BA	Rank	Artificial Surface BA	Rank	Home Games BA	Rank	Road Games BA	Rank	Runners in Scoring Position BA	Rank	Runners in Scoring Pos and Two Outs BA	Rank	Leading Off Inning OBA	Rank
Steve Bedrosian	.269	76	.218	18	.194	11	.259	64	.163	5	.184	25	.333	76
Don Carman	.211	10	.242	36	.245	58	.224	18	.232	34	.234	62	.343	89
Kevin Gross	.278	83	.253	56	.251	69	.271	77	.270	75	.274	84	.335	79
Charles Hudson	.342	116	.277	92	.290	99	.292	99	.336	111	.343	112	.323	67
Tom Hume	.338	--	.227	25	.230	34	.280	87	.238	40	.271	82	.299	44
Mike Maddux	.254	--	.295	106	.314	110	.257	59	.346	115	.294	96	.412	114
Shane Rawley	.316	112	.259	65	.277	91	.264	72	.246	50	.183	24	.327	71
Bruce Ruffin	.224	19	.260	66	.248	66	.256	56	.227	28	.182	22	.265	17
Dan Schatzeder	.315	--	.224	22	.216	21	.283	94	.247	53	.233	58	.259	14
Kent Tekulve	.246	51	.237	33	.249	67	.231	24	.185	9	.175	20	.255	12
Team Average	.272	11	.262	8	.263	10	.267	9	.255	7	.257	10	.328	10
League Average	.254		.253		.247		.260		.252		.235		.316	

PITTSBURGH PIRATES

The years from 1837 to 1861 probably saw the lowest ebb of presidential timber in American history. During that span of 24 years, eight men became president, and no one was elected to a second term: Van Buren, Harrison, Tyler, Polk, Taylor, Fillmore, Pierce, and Buchanan. That group holds the record for most consecutive presidential administrations without any second terms. (Of course, not all of them lived long enough to run again.)

The same sort of turnover is going on today at the top of the baseball standings. There hasn't been a repeat World Series champion since the New York Yankees of 1977–78. In fact, in the nine years starting with 1978, nine different teams have won the World Series, without even a nonconsecutive repeater (a Grover Cleveland, if you will) during that span. That, too, is a record. Perhaps more amazingly, only one team in the last five years has repeated so much as a division title (Kansas City, in 1984 and 1985). No National League team has repeated as a division winner since the Phillies and Dodgers both did it in 1977 and 1978.

Given all of this volatility at the top of the standings, how have things been going down at the bottom? You recall that in 1985, there were three 100-game losers in the major leagues (Cleveland, Pittsburgh, San Francisco) for the first time in 20 years; the other last-place team, Texas, fell one loss short. Three of those four teams bounced back to win more than half of their games in 1986. The one that didn't was the Pirates.

The Pirates finished in the National League East cellar last season for the third straight time. Despite the upward mobility demonstrated by the Indians, Rangers, and Giants last season, repeating at the bottom of the standings has been much more common in recent history than has repeating at the top. During the last five seasons, in which only the '85 Royals repeated as division champs, seven teams have repeated as division chumps. Baseball's basement was even graced with an unusual measure of class in 1986 when the Orioles moved in, just three years removed from winning the World Series.

But we're not saying that if you've seen one last place team, you've seen them all. There's a pecking order even in the slums of the standings, one that is visible in the newspapers every day. Only one team will have fewer wins, more losses, and redder faces than any other in the major leagues in any given season. And for the last two years, that team has been the Pirates.

It's a little odd, but in researching this essay we were struck by how little attention is paid to which is the worst team in baseball in any given year. Imagine that you have before you a group of fans who follow baseball in the summer and football in the fall with equal interest. We don't have a doubt that more people could say with assurance that the Bucs had the poorest record in the NFL last season than could tell you that the Bucs had the corresponding distinction in major-league baseball.

There are probably two reasons for this. First, teams like the Indianapolis Colts can go a number of weeks into a season without winning a game, bringing into play a phenomenon best described as the aura of the streak. (That aura, which we'll discuss at length some other time, can be briefly described as interest in some otherwise meaningless event merely because it has happens to extend or break a streak of some kind. If a backup shortstop started a game for 25 of the 26 teams, hardly anyone would notice; it would be front-page news in Baltimore.)

The other major factor, of course, is the prominence of the player chosen number one in the NFL's college draft, the silver lining in a last-place finish. Baseball rules offer a corresponding bonus to the last-place finisher, the right to pick first in the summer amateur draft (although it's not exactly the same as the NFL, as the first pick is given to the worst team by league on an alternating basis.) But the difference in visibility between college football on the one hand and college or high school baseball on the other makes all the difference in the world in the focus on the number-one pick. Fans in the Tampa area have been thinking about Vinny Testaverde for months; Pittsburgh fans may not even get to see the Pirates' number-one selection for three or four years.

With this as a backdrop, we were curious about the business of the team with the poorest record in baseball each year. No standard reference books contain a single list of the annual worst teams in baseball. And since we look upon this book as a companion to the existing reference books such as *The Baseball Encyclopedia*, *The Book of Baseball Records*, and *The Baseball Guide*, we decided to print that list here.

For clarity, we decided to use the familiar current name of each team ("Dodgers" for the 1905 Brooklyn team, even though the team was then called the "Superbas") rather than city names, where practical; the 1901 Milwaukee team became the St. Louis Browns in 1902. "Senators" refers to whatever team was being called the Senators at the time.

1900	Giants	1930	Phillies/Red Sox	1960	Athletics
1901	Milwaukee AL	1931	White Sox	1961	Phillies
1902	Giants	1932	Red Sox	1962	Mets
1903	Cards/Senators	1933	Browns	1963	Mets
1904	Senators	1934	Reds	1964	Mets
1905	Dodgers	1935	Braves	1965	Mets
1906	Red Sox	1936	Athletics	1966	Cubs
1907	Senators	1937	Browns	1967	Mets
1908	Cardinals	1938	Phillies	1968	Senators
1909	Senators	1939	Browns	1969	Expos/Padres
1910	Browns	1940	Phillies	1970	White Sox
1911	Braves	1941	Phillies	1971	Indians
1912	Yankees	1942	Phillies	1972	Rangers
1913	Cardinals	1943	Athletics	1973	Rangers
1914	Indians	1944	Phillies	1974	Padres
1915	Athletics	1945	Phillies	1975	Tigers
1916	Athletics	1946	Athletics	1976	Expos
1917	Pirates	1947	Browns	1977	Blue Jays
1918	Cardinals	1948	White Sox	1978	Mariners
1919	Athletics	1949	Senators	1979	Blue Jays
1920	Athletics	1950	Athletics	1980	Mariners
1921	Phillies	1951	Browns	1981	Blue Jays
1922	Braves	1952	Pirates	1982	Twins
1923	Phillies	1953	Pirates	1983	Mariners
1924	Braves	1954	Athletics	1984	Giants
1925	Red Sox	1955	Senators	1985	Pirates
1926	Red Sox	1956	Athletics	1986	Pirates
1927	Phillies/Red Sox	1957	Senators		
1928	Phillies	1958	Senators		
1929	Braves	1959	Senators		

The Phillies have had the worst record in baseball 12 times, all compressed into the 41 years from 1921 to 1961. The Athletics come next with 11, while the Senators/Twins club has 10. All 16 of the original franchises have been the worst team at least once, although the Cubs, Reds, Dodgers, Tigers and Yankees only once apiece. Among expansion franchises, only the Astros, Angels, Royals, and Brewers haven't been on the bottom.

Frankly, we expected to find the Pirates better represented. Maybe it's just that we've heard so many Joe Garagiola and Ralph Kiner stories over the years about the trials of the Pittsburgh teams of the early fifties, but we were surprised that those Pirates had the worst record for only two years—a mark that has been equalled by the Pirates of current vintage. And only once in the years before 1952 had the Pirates finished dead last, in 1917.

No team since Texas in 1972–73 had finished last in baseball two consecutive years before the current Buccos. No team has done it three straight years since the Mets spent four consecutive years as baseball's worst team, the longest run in major-league history, from 1962 to 1965.

But what are the prospects for the current Pirates? Will they go for the hat trick in '87 or climb out of the cellar? To answer that question, let's look back at last year's team.

The Pirates got to their final 64–98 record with an extraordinary breakdown of runs scored and allowed. They scored 663 runs, to rank sixth in the National League, and allowed 700 runs, to rank seventh. No great shakes, but far from the kind of numbers that should make a team the worst in baseball. Five National League teams, and five more in the

American, had poorer run differentials than the Pirates' minus-37:

	Scored	Allowed	Diff.	W–L
Atlanta	615	719	−104	72–89
Chi. Cubs	680	781	−101	70–90
San Diego	656	723	−67	74–88
Montreal	637	688	−51	78–83
Los Angeles	638	679	−41	73–89
Seattle	718	835	−117	67–95
Minnesota	741	839	−98	71–91
Milwaukee	667	734	−67	77–84
Chi. White Sox	644	699	−55	72–90
Baltimore	708	760	−52	73–89

In fact, going back to our list of dead-last teams in the major leagues since 1900, no team in this century that had the worst record in the majors in any given year had a run differential as narrow as the 1986 Pirates did. The average run differential for those teams was —233, making the Pirates' —37 figure all the more astounding. Here are the narrowest differences from the group:

		Scored	Allowed	Diff.	W–L
1986	**Pirates**	663	700	−37	64–98
1918	Cardinals	454	534	−80	51–78
1959	Senators	619	701	−82	63–91
1900	Giants	713	823	−110	60–78
1944	Phillies	539	658	−119	61–92
1984	Giants	682	807	−125	66–96
1917	Pirates	464	594	−130	51–103
1981	Blue Jays	329	466	−137	37–69
1985	Pirates	568	708	−140	57–104
1960	Athletics	615	756	−141	58–96
1968	Senators	524	665	−141	65–96

Note that three of these teams played fewer than 140 games in their season's work, and so didn't have as great a chance as the modern 162-game teams to accumulate large differentials. Notice also that the Pirates not only head the list with their 1986 team, but their 1985 team also made the top 10, as did the worst team of 1984, the Giants.

How the Pirates managed to contort a record 34 games under .500 out of a minus-37 run differential is a mystery only until you look at the records of teams in games decided by one run. The Pirates' 16–37 record in one-run games was the 10th worst in modern National League history:

		One-Run Games		Other Games	
		W–L	Pct.	W–L	Pct.
1935	Braves	7–31	.184	31–84	.270
1936	Phillies	12–34	.261	42–66	.389
1952	Pirates	13–35	.271	29–77	.274
1953	Giants	9–24	.273	61–60	.504
1913	Dodgers	14–36	.280	51–48	.515
1937	Reds	14–36	.280	42–62	.404
1975	Astros	16–41	.281	48–56	.462
1981	Padres	12–30	.286	29–39	.426
1912	Dodgers	16–38	.296	42–57	.424
1986	**Pirates**	16–37	.302	48–61	.440

As we noted in the Dodgers essay, losing a lot of one-run games in a season is usually the precursor of a sizeable gain in the standings the next year. And to that we can add a longer-range forecast: There have been five teams since the end of World War II that finished with the worst record in baseball for two straight seasons. Among that group, the average bounce-back time until their next winning season was 3.4 years. But four of those five teams went on to the World Series within seven years. We find that quick jump from being the worst team in baseball to playing in the Fall Classic rather remarkable:

Team	Years With Worst Record	Next Winning Record	Next World Series
Phillies	1944–45	1949	1950
Pirates	1952–53	1958	1960
Senators/Twins	1957–59	1962	1965
Mets	1962–65	1969	1969
Rangers	1972–73	1974	—

This stuff doesn't come with guarantees. But our statistical tea leaves point to some very hopeful signs for a franchise that's badly in need of some good news.

From the Home Office in Scottsdale, Arizona

For fans of "Late Night with David Letterman," 10 reasons why Pirates fans should not consider 1986 a total loss:

10. The Pirates did beat the Mets once in 18 tries.

9. Sid Bream set a National League record for assists by a first baseman.

8. Bobby Bonilla's back!

7. R.J. Reynolds's home run off Dwight Gooden leading off the season raised a lot of hopes.

6. Stan Fansler made his eagerly awaited major-league debut.

5. Johnny Ray led the majors in reaching base on catcher's interference.

4. Chuck Berry refused to play at only one postgame concert.

3. Chuck Noll was not asked to leave any of Jim Leyland's press conferences.

2. Jose DeLeon will probably never lose another game for the Pirates.

1. It was Jim Morrison's best year since the release of "Touch Me."

WON-LOST RECORD BY STARTING POSITION

PITTSBURGH 64-98	C	1B	2B	3B	SS	LF	CF	RF	P	Leadoff	Relief	Starts
Bill Almon				6-6	0-1	8-19		1-0		1-10		15-26
Rafael Belliard			5-10		37-48					1-2		42-58
Mike Bielecki									12-15		0-4	12-15
Barry Bonds							43-65			34-43		43-65
Bobby Bonilla		1-2		0-4		7-10	0-4	12-7				20-27
Sid Bream		55-82										55-82
Mike Brown								23-40				23-40
Pat Clements											18-47	
Trench Davis							2-2			2-1		2-2
Jose DeLeon									0-1		2-6	0-1
Mike Diaz		6-11				16-19						22-30
Benny Distefano							0-5					0-5
Stan Fansler									2-3			2-3
Cecilio Guante											16-36	
Barry Jones											7-19	
Steve Kemp						2-1						2-1
Sam Khalifa			0-2		17-33							17-35
Bob Kipper									8-11		1-0	8-11
Ray Krawczyk											2-10	
Lee Mazzilli		1-2				5-5	0-2			0-1		6-9
Larry McWilliams									3-12		8-26	3-12
Jim Morrison				57-88								57-88
Joe Orsulak						0-6	17-17	18-33		12-30		35-56
Junior Ortiz	12-16											12-16
Bob Patterson									2-3		2-4	2-3
Hipolito Pena									0-1		1-8	0-1
Tony Pena	52-81	1-1										53-82
Johnny Ray			59-85									59-85
Rich Renteria				1-0								1-0
Rick Reuschel									13-21		2-7	13-21
R.J. Reynolds						26-38	2-8	10-13		11-10		38-59
Rick Rhoden									17-17		0-7	17-17
Don Robinson											21-29	
Ruben Rodriguez	0-1											0-1
Rich Sauveur									1-2			1-2
John Smiley											1-11	
Bob Walk									6-9		12-17	6-9
U.L. Washington			0-1		10-16					3-1		10-17
Jim Winn									0-3		15-32	0-3

Batting Comparisons: Vs. Left-Handers/Right-Handers and Overall/Late Inning Pressure Situations

		BA	Rank	SA	Rank	HR %	Rank		BA	Rank	SA	Rank	HR %	Rank
Bill Almon	vs. Lefties	.198	130	.322	113	2.48	61	Overall	.219	133	.383	83	3.57	38
	vs. Righties	.253	--	.480	--	5.33	--	Pressure	.197	122	.311	100	3.28	42
Rafael Belliard	vs. Lefties	.246	89	.246	137	0.00	119	Overall	.233	118	.262	138	0.00	136
	vs. Righties	.225	115	.273	133	0.00	131	Pressure	.217	--	.261	--	0.00	--
Barry Bonds	vs. Lefties	.219	118	.371	80	1.99	72	Overall	.223	131	.416	57	3.87	30
	vs. Righties	.225	114	.443	46	4.96	14	Pressure	.171	133	.271	116	1.43	92
Bobby Bonilla	vs. Lefties	.270	61	.337	99	0.00	119	Overall	.240	108	.307	125	0.52	126
	vs. Righties	.214	126	.282	127	0.97	110	Pressure	.162	137	.270	117	2.70	50
Sid Bream	vs. Lefties	.224	112	.349	92	1.32	101	Overall	.268	56	.450	26	3.07	49
	vs. Righties	.286	29	.492	10	3.78	42	Pressure	.219	107	.333	91	2.08	65
Mike C. Brown	vs. Lefties	.197	132	.239	139	0.85	110	Overall	.218	136	.296	132	1.65	91
	vs. Righties	.238	100	.349	104	2.38	67	Pressure	.261	67	.348	85	2.17	61
Mike Diaz	vs. Lefties	.267	65	.511	19	6.87	6	Overall	.268	57	.483	11	5.74	4
	vs. Righties	.269	--	.436	--	3.85	--	Pressure	.392	3	.529	10	1.96	71
Sammy Khalifa	vs. Lefties	.266	68	.328	107	0.00	119	Overall	.185	--	.225	--	0.00	--
	vs. Righties	.126	--	.149	--	0.00	--	Pressure	.071	--	.143	--	0.00	--
Jim Morrison	vs. Lefties	.266	68	.438	47	3.13	44	Overall	.274	44	.482	12	4.28	22
	vs. Righties	.278	38	.507	7	4.93	15	Pressure	.229	99	.448	37	5.21	14
Joe Orsulak	vs. Lefties	.260	--	.320	--	0.00	--	Overall	.249	94	.342	112	0.50	127
	vs. Righties	.248	87	.345	106	0.57	125	Pressure	.212	110	.258	119	0.00	102
Tony Pena	vs. Lefties	.333	8	.471	29	2.30	64	Overall	.288	21	.406	65	1.96	82
	vs. Righties	.265	52	.372	83	1.79	87	Pressure	.252	75	.279	113	0.00	102
Johnny Ray	vs. Lefties	.261	73	.311	116	0.45	118	Overall	.301	15	.394	76	1.21	107
	vs. Righties	.325	12	.445	42	1.68	92	Pressure	.321	24	.443	40	1.89	79
R.J. Reynolds	vs. Lefties	.219	117	.286	123	0.00	119	Overall	.269	55	.420	54	2.24	69
	vs. Righties	.286	52	.468	22	3.03	50	Pressure	.210	115	.321	96	1.23	97
U.L. Washington	vs. Lefties	.216	--	.270	--	0.00	--	Overall	.200	--	.259	--	0.00	--
	vs. Righties	.194	139	.255	138	0.00	131	Pressure	.191	128	.234	131	0.00	102
Team Average	vs. Lefties	.245	12	.345	11	1.51	11	Overall	.250	11	.374	10	2.03	10
	vs. Righties	.253	5	.389	4	2.32	8	Pressure	.229	12	.321	12	1.58	10
League Average	vs. Lefties	.257		.384		2.28		Overall	.253		.380		2.32	
	vs. Righties	.251		.378		2.34		Pressure	.257		.376		2.31	

Additional Miscellaneous Batting Comparisons

	Grass Surface BA	Rank	Artificial Surface BA	Rank	Home Games BA	Rank	Road Games BA	Rank	Runners in Scoring Position BA	Rank	Runners in Scoring Pos and Two Outs BA	Rank	Leading Off Inning OBA	Rank	Runners on 3B with less than 2 Outs RDI %	Rank
Bill Almon	.135	--	.250	80	.213	132	.227	--	.275	50	.313	--	.254	129	.583	68
Rafael Belliard	.305	21	.201	128	.208	135	.255	70	.244	84	.250	66	.329	65	.458	121
Barry Bonds	.234	105	.219	114	.242	106	.203	128	.208	119	.154	127	.343	48	.545	86
Bobby Bonilla	.344	--	.219	115	.250	99	.230	109	.262	63	.143	--	.250	--	.500	101
Sid Bream	.235	103	.280	38	.282	57	.254	71	.294	36	.212	97	.322	74	.846	2
Mike C. Brown	.243	95	.207	125	.208	137	.230	108	.188	133	.207	100	.298	92	.733	13
Mike Diaz	.224	--	.285	35	.253	97	.281	30	.233	97	.185	117	.244	--	.600	52
Sammy Khalifa	.159	--	.196	130	.182	--	.189	--	.057	--	.100	141	.375	--	.400	--
Jim Morrison	.296	26	.266	53	.297	34	.250	76	.302	28	.279	44	.358	35	.535	93
Joe Orsulak	.336	4	.216	117	.224	124	.271	40	.208	119	.179	120	.352	38	.500	101
Junior Ortiz	.323	--	.342	5	.380	--	.300	--	.419	--	.462	--	.474	--	.500	--
Tony Pena	.255	76	.300	19	.298	31	.278	33	.223	111	.191	113	.383	19	.444	124
Johnny Ray	.308	18	.298	21	.285	52	.317	7	.286	41	.224	87	.394	15	.690	19
R.J. Reynolds	.307	20	.253	78	.283	56	.255	69	.248	80	.262	58	.398	12	.632	40
U.L. Washington	.211	--	.196	131	.151	--	.232	--	.250	--	.273	--	.255	127	.500	101
Team Average	.256	7	.248	9	.253	10	.248	6	.243	8	.213	10	.332	1	.579	5
League Average	.254		.253		.260		.247		.252		.235		.316		.562	

Pitching Comparisons: Vs. Left-Handers/Right-Handers
and Runners On/Bases Empty

		BA	Rank	BB %	Rank	SO %	Rank		BA	Rank	BB %	Rank	SO %	Rank
Mike Bielecki	vs. Lefties	.261	67	10.34	68	8.91	108	Runners On	.271	74	12.30	93	15.53	51
	vs. Righties	.262	80	14.73	116	16.30	55	Bases Empty	.254	65	12.57	111	9.78	110
Pat Clements	vs. Lefties	.284	86	16.09	115	11.49	91	Runners On	.243	36	15.44	112	11.76	85
	vs. Righties	.236	46	10.65	97	12.43	89	Bases Empty	.259	--	9.17	--	12.50	--
Cecilio Guante	vs. Lefties	.185	10	12.41	93	17.52	37	Runners On	.268	69	7.74	24	21.94	9
	vs. Righties	.253	71	6.35	31	20.63	26	Bases Empty	.185	5	9.94	93	16.96	46
Bob Kipper	vs. Lefties	.268	--	1.35	--	20.27	--	Runners On	.272	76	7.00	13	13.00	76
	vs. Righties	.272	88	7.82	57	15.64	61	Bases Empty	.271	91	6.76	40	18.58	30
Larry McWilliams	vs. Lefties	.213	18	7.87	36	26.97	6	Runners On	.317	109	10.42	65	14.58	60
	vs. Righties	.280	94	9.21	79	12.28	92	Bases Empty	.233	29	7.87	63	14.75	72
Rick Reuschel	vs. Lefties	.307	106	7.35	32	9.09	105	Runners On	.264	61	6.64	10	12.09	83
	vs. Righties	.236	45	4.60	12	18.89	38	Bases Empty	.283	101	5.71	22	14.57	76
Rick Rhoden	vs. Lefties	.230	35	8.20	41	12.12	82	Runners On	.226	21	9.26	41	17.99	29
	vs. Righties	.225	27	6.61	38	20.04	29	Bases Empty	.229	24	6.44	33	14.29	80
Don Robinson	vs. Lefties	.186	11	11.19	81	20.15	23	Runners On	.240	34	7.48	19	17.69	30
	vs. Righties	.278	92	7.45	53	16.15	57	Bases Empty	.235	34	10.81	101	18.24	34
Bob Walk	vs. Lefties	.254	63	12.91	98	11.26	93	Runners On	.248	43	13.15	100	13.55	73
	vs. Righties	.248	61	8.62	70	15.17	64	Bases Empty	.253	63	9.09	86	12.90	89
Jim Winn	vs. Lefties	.295	94	11.26	83	19.21	29	Runners On	.303	100	13.79	103	16.67	37
	vs. Righties	.234	39	9.29	80	18.14	43	Bases Empty	.223	22	6.90	42	20.20	18
Team Average	vs. Lefties	.256	6	9.99	8	13.08	10	Runners On	.268	11	10.34	8	14.88	6
	vs. Righties	.254	9	8.60	8	16.26	6	Bases Empty	.245	6	8.28	10	14.92	10
League Average	vs. Lefties	.257		9.83		14.90		Runners On	.260		10.11		15.02	
	vs. Righties	.251		8.19		16.33		Bases Empty	.248		7.89		16.30	

Additional Miscellaneous Pitching Comparisons

	Grass Surface		Artificial Surface		Home Games		Road Games		Runners in Scoring Position		Runners in Scoring Pos and Two Outs		Leading Off Inning	
	BA	Rank	BA	Rank	BA	Rank	BA	Rank	BA	Rank	BA	Rank	OBA	Rank
Mike Bielecki	.232	33	.273	84	.247	64	.277	83	.247	52	.230	53	.350	93
Pat Clements	.242	--	.255	58	.224	31	.274	80	.279	86	.231	54	.356	96
Cecilio Guante	.289	102	.199	9	.199	13	.256	55	.236	38	.222	46	.279	25
Barry Jones	.130	--	.232	28	.231	--	.193	--	.250	--	.250	--	.243	--
Bob Kipper	.269	74	.272	82	.294	102	.250	45	.235	37	.278	87	.331	74
Larry McWilliams	.284	91	.263	68	.279	93	.257	60	.314	108	.302	99	.312	56
Bob Patterson	.517	--	.276	90	.274	--	.404	--	.315	--	.316	--	.447	--
Rick Reuschel	.292	105	.269	78	.266	86	.282	91	.235	36	.189	29	.370	100
Rick Rhoden	.251	60	.221	20	.218	23	.240	34	.238	39	.237	64	.260	15
Don Robinson	.275	--	.223	21	.236	47	.239	33	.192	11	.111	2	.375	102
Bob Walk	.229	29	.258	63	.239	52	.262	69	.228	29	.212	40	.367	98
Jim Winn	.222	17	.273	83	.253	71	.261	67	.284	94	.273	83	.190	1
Team Average	.265	9	.251	5	.247	8	.263	7	.253	5	.232	5	.317	6
League Average	.254		.253		.247		.260		.252		.235		.316	

ST. LOUIS CARDINALS

With one out, Willie McGee singles and steals second base. Tom Herr grounds out to the second baseman; McGee advances to third. Jack Clark drives a sacrifice fly to center field, scoring McGee. Invariably, the announcer concludes, "Tommy Herr made that run possible by going the opposite way to move Willie McGee to third base. Whitey Herzog will mark that one down in his book."

It's one of those worn cliches, the kind that all too often has little to do with reality. After all, how often does the sequence evolve as ideally as we constructed it above? Those who subscribe to Earl Weaver's "Big Bang" theory, who are constantly on the prowl for the three-run inning, might scorn the idea of building single runs in such a feeble manner. But guess what? Those plays do add up, and they have an noticeable impact on a team's performance over the course of a season. And though there wasn't much that St. Louis did well last season, the Cardinals did advance 532 bases on outs to lead the majors for the third consecutive season. And they did it with the highest total by any team since 1983.

If the whole is greater than the sum of its parts, maybe you're not looking at all the parts. Think of a team's singles, home runs, walks, stolen bases, and so on as its parts, and the number of runs the team scores as its whole; you'll frequently find teams with nearly identical parts and very different wholes. Look at the 1986 season totals for the Montreal Expos and San Francisco Giants. They are nearly identical right down the line, except for differences in doubles and stolen bases that should cancel each other out. But the Giants scored 61 more runs:

Team	AB	R	H	2B	3B	HR	BB	SB	BA	SA	OBA
Montreal	5508	637	1401	255	50	110	537	193	.254	.379	.322
San Francisco	5501	698	1394	269	29	114	536	148	.253	.375	.322

The Giants made a greater whole out of their parts than the Expos did. One factor in San Francisco's efficiency was its timely hitting: the Giants batted 13 points higher than the Expos with runners on base, 24 points higher with runners in scoring position. Another was that San Francisco advanced 486 bases on outs to rank second in the National League; Montreal ranked next-to-last with 396.

The following table shows the number of runs scored by each National League team last season and how that total differed from an estimate based on the various building blocks: hits, walks, and so on. (The estimates are computed using the linear weights system, a statistical tool with which

some of you may be familiar.) The final column indicates the number of bases that each team's runners advanced on outs. Notice the overwhelming bias: Teams that ranked high in base-advances invariably exceeded their expected run totals; teams that ranked low in advances failed to reach their expected totals.

Team	Est.	Actual	Diff.	Bases	(Rank)
Atlanta	640	615	−25	398	(10)
Chicago	693	680	−13	409	(9)
Cincinnati	716	732	+16	447	(5)
Houston	672	654	−18	439	(7)
Los Angeles	638	638	0	478	(3)
Montreal	675	637	−38	396	(11)
New York	765	783	+18	446	(6)
Philadelphia	729	739	+10	418	(8)
Pittsburgh	661	663	+2	476	(4)
St. Louis	587	601	+14	532	(1)
San Diego	666	656	−10	395	(12)
San Francisco	654	698	+44	486	(2)

Think of the teams that exceeded their estimates as overachievers. We'll mark them in the following table with a plus sign. Teams that fell short of their expected run totals are underachievers, signified with minus signs. (Los Angeles, which matched its expected total, is marked with an equal sign.) When the National League teams are ranked, from one through twelve, in order of the number of bases they advanced on outs, the high end (teams with the most advances) is heavy with the overachievers, the low end loaded with the underachievers:

1	2	3	4	5	6	7	8	9	10	11	12
+	+	=	+	+	+	−	+	−	−	−	−

We repeated the test for the 1984 and 1985 seasons, and the results were similar. The 1985 statistics showed a slight correspondence; the 1984 figures were nearly as biased as those for last season:

Year	1	2	3	4	5	6	7	8	9	10	11	12
1984	+	+	+	−	+	−	+	−	−	−	−	−
1985	+	−	−	+	+	+	−	+	−	−	−	+

So we tried another test. (Hell, we were just as skeptical about the value of moving runners along as the rest of you "Big Bang" proponents.) We found 42 pairs of teams over the past five seasons that we considered statistical twins: that is, they had slugging averages and on-base averages within one-half of one percent of each other. For instance, the 1983 San Diego Padres and the 1982 Cincinnati Reds:

Year	Team	SA	OBA
1983	San Diego Padres	.3506	.3105
1982	Cincinnati Reds	.3499	.3104

All other things being equal, teams with nearly identical slugging and on-base averages should score roughly the same number of runs. But in this case, all other things weren't equal. The Padres advanced 538 bases on outs (the highest single-season total in either league during the 1980s); Cincinnati advanced 437 bases, slightly below the N.L. average. The Padres outscored the Reds by more than 100 runs, 653 to 545.

Not all 42 pairs of teams produced such extreme results, but the pair of teams above indicates the general conclusion we were able to draw. Remember, we found 42 pairs of teams with nearly identical slugging and on-base averages. In 28 of 42 cases, the twin that advanced more bases on outs scored more runs—on average, 14 runs. Clearly, those ground balls to the right side aren't wasted.

Now that you know how important it is to advance runners, here's a list of the guys who did it best, the unsung heroes who moved their teammates along the base paths while making outs. The leaders for the 1986 season:

National League		American League	
Pendleton, St. L.	63	Buckner, Bos.	89
Herr, St. L.	62	Mattingly, N.Y.	77
Ray, Pitt.	62	Butler, Clev.	63
Smith, St. L.	55	Griffin, Oak.	61
Bell, Cin.	54	Joyner, Cal.	60
McReynolds, S.D.	51	Boone, Cal.	56
Oester, Cin.	51	Fletcher, Tex.	56
Pena, Pitt.	51	Fernandez, Tor.	55
Clark, S.F.	50	Gantner, Mil.	55
Thompson, S.F.	50	O'Brien, Tex.	55

So for all you Cardinals fans who spent last season screaming, "What the hell is that guy Pendleton doing?", now you know.

Unrequited Glove

Shortly after the All-Star break last season, the New York papers were filled with rumors of trade talks between the Yankees and the St. Louis Cardinals involving Dave Winfield and Ozzie Smith. Steinbrenner was into some heavy Winfield-trashing at the time. Winfield had been benched briefly —reportedly on the owner's orders—and Steinbrenner was exploring the possibility of filling New York's hole at shortstop with Ozzie, using Winfield as his bait. Or so the story goes.

The possibility of such a trade aroused tremendous interest in New York. One newspaper went so far as to poll its readers: Ozzie for Winfield, yes or no. Now, it's rare that two stars of such magnitude are swapped even-up. But at the heart of the excitement, we think, is the question of the value of the game's premier fielder. Could Ozzie Smith, perhaps the greatest fielder in baseball history at such a crucial position, contribute enough with his glove to compensate for the loss of a bat like Winfield's? We thought that question was right up our alley.

Over the past few years, several researchers have studied fielding statistics, claiming to have produced definitive answers to questions like: who the best fielders are; how many runs they save their teams; how many wins or losses they add; the cost of an error; the value of an assist; the range a player covers; where Judge Crater is; which came first, the chicken or the egg; and so on. But a quick glance at their methodology is all that's needed to convince even the most avid numerophile that the results are worthless. One analyst writes, "Assists are doubly weighted because more fielding skill is generally required to get one than to record a putout." As you can see, we're not talking scientific method here. Why not triply weighted? Or one-and-a-half-ly weighted? Another abstract thinker constructed a point system with arbitrary assignments like, "For catchers, the 40-point consideration is opposition stolen bases per game.... The 20-point consideration is fielding average ..." and so on, with a different arbitrary scale for each position. And after all that, he multiplies the point values by still another arbitrary value—a different one for each position—to approximate the number of wins each player contributes. Galileo this isn't.

Our method is straightforward: We've compared the rate of runs scored against the Cardinals with Smith in the field to the rate when Smith wasn't there. After all, the true measure of a fielder's ability is reflected on the scoreboard. If, over a period of time, a flashy fielder like Smith fails to save runs for his team, he's really nothing more than a sideshow.

We'll be the first to admit that there are a few problems with this method—problems that we've resolved. Let's review them.

Objection: Smith might be playing behind better pitchers than the Cardinals' other shortstops. If that's the case, the rate of runs with Ozzie at shortstop should be lower than that with other shortstops playing, regardless of his fielding ability.

Resolution: Smith has been an everyday player throughout his career in St. Louis, not the type to take the odd day off. If he was healthy, he played. As a result, the pitchers on the mound behind Smith were equivalent to those behind the Cardinals' other shortstops. (And anyway, if he plays for a smart manager—Whitey certainly thinks he does—wouldn't that manager prefer to use Smith when the lesser pitchers who really needed him there were on the mound? If there were to be any bias, it ought to be in the other direction.)

Objection: One year isn't enough to create a meaningful comparison.

Resolution: We agree, so we'll analyze five years' worth of stats, dating back to Ozzie's arrival in St. Louis.

Objection: Ozzie's backups might not represent a typical shortstop. And if St. Louis's reserves were poor fielders and we judged Smith by comparison to them, Ozzie would appear to be more valuable than he really is.

Resolution: Over the past five years, the Cardinals have had a wide assortment of shortstops behind Ozzie. They've ranged from Jose Oquendo, considered by some to be second in fielding ability only to the Wiz; to players like Ivan DeJesus and Chris Speier, everyday shortstops before reaching St. Louis; to perennial utility players like Mike Ramsey and Jimmy Sexton. Just for laughs, even Jamie Quirk was in there a few times. A typical group, we think.

By measuring the runs scored against St. Louis with and without Smith, we can accurately measure the value of Ozzie's defense. Not an evaluation steeped in Byzantine logic and arbitrary assumptions, or based on fielding statistics that nearly everyone in baseball agrees are misleading, but an evaluation based simply on the single measure that best expresses a player's contribution: runs. Ozzie may be a wizard, but if his talent has no effect on the scoreboard, we'll take Tony Fernandez. So over the past five years, the runs scored against the Cardinals, with and without Ozzie Smith at shortstop:

	Smith at Shortstop			Others at Shortstop		
Year	Innings	Runs	R/9I	Innings	Runs	R/9I
1982	1267.0	536	3.81	198.1	73	3.31
1983	1353.2	652	4.33	107.0	58	4.88
1984	1065.1	475	4.01	383.2	170	3.99
1985	1410.0	545	3.48	54.0	27	4.50
1986	1285.0	524	3.67	181.1	87	4.32
Totals	6381.0	2732	3.85	924.1	415	4.04

The Cardinals have allowed 3.85 runs per nine innings with Ozzie in the field, compared to 4.04 with other shortstops. That's a difference of 0.19 runs per nine innings, or one run for every 48 innings. During that time, Ozzie has played an average of 1,276 innings per season, indicating that he has saved the Cardinals an average of 27 runs per season. That's worth slightly less than three wins a year: For a low-scoring team like St. Louis, every 9.5-run swing makes a difference of one win.

How does that compare with the contribution of a player like Winfield? We'll spare you the details here, but in the Los Angeles Dodgers essay (page 121), we've demonstrated that a typical superstar player is worth about 4.6 wins per season, or nearly two wins more than Smith adds with his glove. What's more, the Boston Red Sox essay (page 17), presents evidence that the best starting pitchers can contribute even more (5.2 wins). So watching Ozzie play shortstop might be more fun than seeing Winfield flail away at bat. But apparently the *New York Post* readers were on the mark when they turned thumbs down on Smith for Winfield.

WON-LOST RECORD BY STARTING POSITION

ST. LOUIS 79-82	C	1B	2B	3B	SS	LF	CF	RF	P	Leadoff	Relief	Starts
Greg Bargar	-	-	-	-	-	-	-	-	-	-	4-18	-
Joe Boever	-	-	-	-	-	-	-	-	-	-	2-9	-
Ray Burris	-	-	-	-	-	-	-	-	4-6	-	1-12	4-6
Jack Clark	-	29-35	-	-	-	-	-	-	-	-	-	29-35
Vince Coleman	-	-	-	-	-	59-69	12-5	-	-	71-74	-	71-74
Tim Conroy	-	-	-	-	-	-	-	-	7-14	-	1-3	7-14
Danny Cox	-	-	-	-	-	-	-	-	15-17	-	-	15-17
Ken Dayley	-	-	-	-	-	-	-	-	-	-	13-18	-
Bill Earley	-	-	-	-	-	-	-	-	-	-	0-3	-
Curt Ford	-	-	-	-	-	-	13-8	-	19-9	-	3-2	32-17
Bob Forsch	-	-	-	-	-	-	-	-	16-17	-	1-0	16-17
Mike Heath	21-30	-	-	-	-	-	-	-	-	-	-	21-30
Tom Herr	-	-	72-78	-	-	-	-	-	-	1-0	-	72-78
Ricky Horton	-	-	-	-	-	-	-	-	5-4	-	16-17	5-4
Clint Hurdle	1-2	19-11	-	0-1	2-0	-	2-2	-	-	-	-	24-16
Kurt Kepshire	-	-	-	-	-	-	-	-	0-1	-	0-1	0-1
Alan Knicely	-	7-16	-	-	-	-	-	-	-	-	-	7-16
Mike Laga	-	6-5	-	-	-	-	-	-	-	-	-	6-5
Jeff Lahti	-	-	-	-	-	-	-	-	-	-	1-3	-
Steve Lake	7-7	-	-	-	-	-	-	-	-	-	-	7-7
Tito Landrum	-	-	-	2-2	-	-	14-30	-	-	-	-	16-32
Mike LaValliere	50-43	-	-	-	-	-	-	-	-	-	-	50-43
Tom Lawless	-	-	0-1	2-1	-	1-0	-	-	-	0-1	-	3-2
Jim Lindeman	-	5-8	-	-	0-1	-	-	-	-	-	-	5-9
Fred Manrique	-	-	-	0-3	-	-	-	-	-	-	-	0-3
Greg Mathews	-	-	-	-	-	-	-	-	12-10	-	0-1	12-10
Willie McGee	-	-	-	-	-	-	56-65	-	-	3-4	-	56-65
John Morris	-	-	-	-	-	1-1	2-1	9-9	-	0-1	-	12-11
Jose Oquendo	-	-	7-3	-	7-10	-	-	-	-	-	-	14-13
Rick Ownbey	-	-	-	-	-	-	-	-	2-1	-	1-13	2-1
Terry Pendleton	-	-	-	77-77	-	-	-	-	-	-	-	77-77
Pat Perry	-	-	-	-	-	-	-	-	-	-	15-31	-
Ozzie Smith	-	-	-	-	72-72	-	-	-	-	1-0	-	72-72
Ray Soff	-	-	-	-	-	-	-	-	-	-	13-17	-
John Tudor	-	-	-	-	-	-	-	-	18-12	-	-	18-12
Andy Van Slyke	-	13-7	-	-	-	1-0	9-11	35-32	-	-	-	58-50
Jerry White	-	-	-	-	-	0-1	-	-	-	-	-	0-1
Todd Worrell	-	-	-	-	-	-	-	-	-	-	50-24	-

Batting Comparisons: Vs. Left-Handers/Right-Handers and Overall/Late Inning-Pressure Situations

		BA	Rank	SA	Rank	HR %	Rank		BA	Rank	SA	Rank	HR %	Rank
Jack Clark	vs. Lefties	.303	35	.596	7	6.74	7	Overall	.237	111	.422	49	3.88	29
	vs. Righties	.196	137	.315	116	2.10	77	Pressure	.255	74	.455	31	3.64	37
Vince Coleman	vs. Lefties	.238	95	.278	126	0.00	119	Overall	.232	119	.280	136	0.00	136
	vs. Righties	.228	109	.282	128	0.00	131	Pressure	.250	76	.323	95	0.00	102
Curt Ford	vs. Lefties	.207	--	.276	--	0.00	--	Overall	.248	97	.364	95	0.93	119
	vs. Righties	.254	82	.378	78	1.08	106	Pressure	.333	16	.487	26	0.00	102
Mike Heath	vs. Lefties	.215	119	.380	77	3.31	38	Overall	.205	140	.321	119	2.11	75
	vs. Righties	.188	--	.217	--	0.00	--	Pressure	.118	141	.147	141	0.00	102
Tom Herr	vs. Lefties	.315	21	.402	63	0.46	117	Overall	.252	85	.331	117	0.36	132
	vs. Righties	.212	127	.285	125	0.29	129	Pressure	.176	131	.216	134	0.98	100
Clint Hurdle	vs. Lefties	.143	--	.214	--	0.00	--	Overall	.195	--	.299	--	1.95	--
	vs. Righties	.200	134	.307	119	2.14	75	Pressure	.226	--	.290	--	0.00	--
Alan Knicely	vs. Lefties	.250	84	.344	96	1.56	86	Overall	.195	--	.268	--	1.22	--
	vs. Righties	.000	--	.000	--	0.00	--	Pressure	.286	--	.571	--	7.14	--
Tito Landrum	vs. Lefties	.181	137	.263	132	1.17	102	Overall	.210	139	.283	133	0.98	116
	vs. Righties	.353	--	.382	--	0.00	--	Pressure	.262	66	.357	83	2.38	56
Mike Lavalliere	vs. Lefties	.211	123	.333	101	1.75	82	Overall	.234	113	.310	123	0.99	114
	vs. Righties	.240	98	.305	120	0.81	117	Pressure	.250	76	.442	41	3.85	33
Willie McGee	vs. Lefties	.246	88	.387	72	2.51	59	Overall	.256	79	.370	92	1.41	100
	vs. Righties	.262	59	.359	97	0.67	123	Pressure	.227	100	.250	123	0.00	102
Jose Oquendo	vs. Lefties	.364	--	.432	--	0.00	--	Overall	.297	--	.341	--	0.00	--
	vs. Righties	.266	--	.298	--	0.00	--	Pressure	.250	76	.250	123	0.00	102
Terry Pendleton	vs. Lefties	.278	50	.364	84	0.00	119	Overall	.239	109	.306	126	0.17	135
	vs. Righties	.217	124	.274	131	0.27	130	Pressure	.210	116	.276	115	0.00	102
Ozzie Smith	vs. Lefties	.276	52	.315	115	0.00	119	Overall	.280	29	.333	116	0.00	136
	vs. Righties	.283	35	.344	107	0.00	131	Pressure	.283	50	.348	85	0.00	102
Andy Van Slyke	vs. Lefties	.207	126	.353	89	0.86	109	Overall	.270	54	.452	25	3.11	48
	vs. Righties	.295	23	.490	12	3.97	37	Pressure	.288	44	.500	17	5.00	18
Team Average	vs. Lefties	.246	11	.343	12	1.27	12	Overall	.236	12	.327	12	1.08	12
	vs. Righties	.230	12	.316	12	0.96	12	Pressure	.231	11	.327	11	1.46	12
League Average	vs. Lefties	.257		.384		2.28		Overall	.253		.380		2.32	
	vs. Righties	.251		.378		2.34		Pressure	.257		.376		2.31	

Additional Miscellaneous Batting Comparisons

	Grass Surface BA	Rank	Artificial Surface BA	Rank	Home Games BA	Rank	Road Games BA	Rank	Runners in Scoring Position BA	Rank	Runners in Scoring Pos and Two Outs BA	Rank	Leading Off Inning OBA	Rank	Runners on 3B with less than 2 Outs RDI %	Rank
Jack Clark	.164	--	.260	64	.274	68	.200	129	.169	137	.133	132	.342	49	.400	135
Vince Coleman	.158	143	.254	75	.269	74	.189	136	.200	126	.159	126	.317	80	.583	68
Curt Ford	.122	--	.285	34	.277	65	.225	118	.267	58	.293	36	.296	94	.583	68
Bob Forsch	.095	--	.200	--	.195	--	.143	--	.207	--	.167	--	.294	--	.444	124
Mike Heath	.105	--	.230	107	.212	133	.198	--	.224	108	.240	74	.271	117	.571	--
Tom Herr	.205	132	.269	48	.260	91	.245	86	.242	89	.197	110	.297	93	.479	113
Clint Hurdle	.200	--	.193	134	.145	--	.235	100	.152	140	.130	134	.378	20	.500	--
Tito Landrum	.155	--	.231	105	.209	134	.211	124	.232	99	.133	132	.267	122	.750	10
Mike Lavalliere	.239	101	.233	102	.220	126	.248	80	.268	56	.275	47	.357	36	.526	95
Willie McGee	.205	133	.273	46	.280	60	.227	112	.252	73	.236	79	.328	67	.467	117
Jose Oquendo	.275	--	.306	16	.311	--	.286	--	.355	--	.300	--	.250	--	.727	14
Terry Pendleton	.185	138	.255	71	.255	95	.223	119	.232	99	.213	96	.290	100	.767	8
Ozzie Smith	.222	116	.299	20	.287	48	.273	37	.307	24	.246	70	.440	4	.759	9
Andy Van Slyke	.259	70	.275	43	.280	62	.261	59	.279	49	.295	34	.351	39	.464	119
Team Average	.193	12	.250	8	.251	11	.222	12	.237	11	.200	12	.320	5	.584	2
League Average	.254		.253		.260		.247		.252		.235		.316		.562	

Pitching Comparisons: Vs. Left-Handers/Right-Handers and Runners On/Bases Empty

		BA	Rank	BB %	Rank	SO %	Rank		BA	Rank	BB %	Rank	SO %	Rank
Ray Burris	vs. Lefties	.294	92	9.38	58	6.25	115	Runners On	.340	115	10.43	66	9.82	100
	vs. Righties	.281	97	8.46	67	11.94	95	Bases Empty	.244	48	7.58	53	9.09	113
Tim Conroy	vs. Lefties	.213	19	13.21	99	12.26	78	Runners On	.286	90	10.09	57	9.17	108
	vs. Righties	.290	102	10.32	93	16.22	56	Bases Empty	.266	78	11.53	105	20.00	20
Danny Cox	vs. Lefties	.233	38	6.99	28	10.17	100	Runners On	.255	50	5.99	8	11.38	88
	vs. Righties	.235	41	6.60	37	14.67	70	Bases Empty	.221	20	7.31	48	12.80	92
Bob Forsch	vs. Lefties	.264	69	9.40	59	10.26	99	Runners On	.255	52	11.17	72	9.46	105
	vs. Righties	.230	35	5.10	15	11.89	96	Bases Empty	.242	46	4.92	15	12.03	99
Ricky Horton	vs. Lefties	.222	25	4.65	14	15.12	60	Runners On	.246	41	11.43	79	9.29	107
	vs. Righties	.216	17	7.31	51	11.96	94	Bases Empty	.203	9	4.05	8	14.57	75
Greg Mathews	vs. Lefties	.253	60	6.86	25	11.76	87	Runners On	.269	71	6.78	11	9.75	101
	vs. Righties	.260	78	7.57	55	11.25	101	Bases Empty	.252	60	7.89	64	12.39	96
Pat Perry	vs. Lefties	.268	--	5.33	--	9.33	--	Runners On	.333	112	12.10	89	5.65	115
	vs. Righties	.227	30	14.08	113	10.33	104	Bases Empty	.172	2	11.59	106	13.41	84
John Tudor	vs. Lefties	.189	14	3.95	6	25.66	9	Runners On	.283	88	7.12	14	14.89	57
	vs. Righties	.256	75	6.46	32	9.35	110	Bases Empty	.225	23	5.44	21	10.70	106
Todd Worrell	vs. Lefties	.265	72	12.26	90	16.98	39	Runners On	.185	4	1.25	76	16.25	44
	vs. Righties	.196	8	6.88	41	16.97	49	Bases Empty	.280	98	7.37	49	17.89	36
Team Average	vs. Lefties	.253	5	8.61	1	12.56	12	Runners On	.268	10	9.05	2	11.51	12
	vs. Righties	.249	5	7.68	4	12.55	12	Bases Empty	.239	4	7.27	2	13.28	12
League Average	vs. Lefties	.257		9.83		14.90		Runners On	.260		10.11		15.02	
	vs. Righties	.251		8.19		16.33		Bases Empty	.248		7.89		16.30	

Additional Miscellaneous Pitching Comparisons

	Grass Surface BA	Rank	Artificial Surface BA	Rank	Home Games BA	Rank	Road Games BA	Rank	Runners in Scoring Position BA	Rank	Runners in Scoring Pos and Two Outs BA	Rank	Leading Off Inning OBA	Rank
Ray Burris	.344	--	.272	81	.269	87	.303	103	.295	99	.364	115	.325	70
Tim Conroy	.225	20	.287	95	.285	96	.263	70	.261	69	.225	49	.322	66
Danny Cox	.243	48	.231	27	.215	19	.258	63	.249	54	.208	38	.294	34
Ken Dayley	.292	--	.267	75	.263	--	.288	--	.265	--	.136	--	.297	--
Bob Forsch	.280	85	.235	30	.232	41	.264	73	.285	95	.257	72	.271	18
Ricky Horton	.173	1	.234	29	.231	36	.207	9	.254	72	.235	63	.216	3
Greg Mathews	.247	53	.264	70	.232	40	.274	78	.264	72	.218	45	.340	85
Rick Ownbey	.290	--	.296	108	.275	--	.319	--	.355	--	.389	--	.400	--
Pat Perry	.173	--	.256	61	.306	108	.184	2	.345	114	.167	--	.246	9
Ray Soff	.269	--	.252	51	.254	--	.256	--	.220	--	.167	--	.351	--
John Tudor	.268	73	.236	31	.238	50	.252	51	.274	81	.262	76	.301	47
Todd Worrell	.255	65	.220	19	.218	24	.242	40	.180	8	.147	9	.388	108
Team Average	.256	7	.249	4	.244	5	.257	6	.266	10	.234	6	.303	3
League Average	.254		.253		.247		.260		.252		.235		.316	

SAN DIEGO PADRES

In last year's *Analyst*, we presented an entirely new basis for managerial decision-making: proof that pitchers who induce ground outs rather than fly outs are more effective against hitters who tend toward ground outs. Conversely, pitchers who allow a lot of fly outs are more effective against fly-ball hitters than ground-ball hitters. The reaction within baseball was hardly overwhelming. Having studied the question for another year, however, we're more certain than ever that these tendencies provide an edge for managers who exploit them. Teams that choose to construct lineups and make pitching changes and pinch-hitting decisions without regard to the ground out/fly out patterns forfeit that edge.

The question is crucial to the Padres, because their pitching staff is stocked with fly-ball types, and their lineup with ground-ball hitters. Opposing teams can gain an advantage on San Diego by loading their lineups with ground-ball hitters and starting pitchers who throw a lot of grounders. The ratio of ground outs to air outs for each team in the National League last season, for and against, follows (the higher the value, the greater the tendency toward ground outs):

Batting		Pitching	
St. Louis	1.36	Atlanta	1.78
San Diego	1.31	Pittsburgh	1.39
Pittsburgh	1.30	Los Angeles	1.29
Cincinnati	1.29	Montreal	1.28
Los Angeles	1.26	Chicago	1.26
New York	1.26	San Francisco	1.23
Atlanta	1.22	New York	1.21
Philadelphia	1.18	Cincinnati	1.18
San Francisco	1.15	Philadelphia	1.12
Houston	1.14	St. Louis	1.09
Montreal	1.12	Houston	1.05
Chicago	1.12	**San Diego**	1.01

Because many of you may not have seen last year's study, while others who did may have been skeptical, we'll once again present the evidence. That will also allow us to update our research; the original study dealt with 10 seasons from 1975 through 1984. And we'll take the opportunity to present the study in a style that we hope will be more convincing to the skeptics among you.

To accomplish that, we selected matched pairs of batters from the 1986 season: For each hitter in the ground-ball group, we chose a fly-ball hitter with a nearly identical batting average (within 2 percent) and a similar number of at bats (within 20 percent). The matching player had to be from the same league. Right-handed batters were paired only with other right-handers; left-handed hitters and switch-hitters (who bat left-handed twice as often as right-handed) formed a common pool. For example, we matched Dave Lopes with Ron Cey. Both are right-handed hitters in the National League. Lopes batted .275, with 70 hits in 255 at bats; Cey had one more at bat and an equal number of hits. Lopes was a ground-ball hitter (a ratio of 1.54 ground outs per air out), Cey a fly-ball hitter (0.91). There were 35 pairs of players whose batting average and at bat totals were close enough for the comparison, and while not every one matched as neatly as Lopes and Cey, all were quite similar. The totals bear that out:

	AB	H	BA
Ground-Ball Hitters	14550	3952	.272
Fly-Ball Hitters	14728	4012	.272

We selected groups of pitchers in the same way, matching them by league, "handedness," opposing batting average, and the number of batters they faced. Each of the 38 matched pairs included a ground-out pitcher and a fly-out pitcher. Once again the totals were nearly identical:

	AB	H	BA
Ground-Ball Pitchers	21373	5457	.255
Fly-Ball Pitchers	20882	5341	.256

Next, we culled the head-to-head matchups from last season among all the batters and pitchers included in either group, computing totals for each player. The individual averages for the batters against each group of pitchers appear below. Notice that both representatives from the '86 Padres, Tony Gwynn and Kevin McReynolds, follow the rule to an extreme degree: Gwynn, a ground-ball hitter, had a higher average against fly-ball pitchers; McReynolds, a fly-ball hitter, mashed ground-ball pitchers. Kevin Mitchell, acquired over the winter from the Mets, bucks the trend. "GBP" indicates ground-ball pitchers; "FBP" indicates fly-ball pitchers. The ground-ball hitters are in alphabetical order; the fly-ball hitters are listed beside their paired player:

Ground-Ball Hitters	Vs. GBP	Vs. FBP	Fly-Ball Hitters	Vs. GBP	Vs. FBP
Andy Allanson	.289	.283	Steve Lyons	.265	.160
Rafael Belliard	.194	.279	Mike Marshall	.162	.229
Wade Boggs	.330	.475	Don Mattingly	.372	.331
Phil Bradley	.260	.430	Robin Yount	.364	.333
Glenn Braggs	.471	.163	Dusty Baker	.321	.241
Tom Brookens	.220	.283	George Hendrick	.309	.327
Randy Bush	.262	.256	Ernie Whitt	.211	.228
Rick Cerone	.311	.143	Charlie Moore	.225	.176
Dave Collins	.333	.340	Kirk Gibson	.321	.244
Curt Ford	.400	.182	Howard Johnson	.222	.174
Julio Franco	.290	.250	George Bell	.354	.299
Jim Gantner	.200	.271	Alvin Davis	.262	.286
Damaso Garcia	.265	.290	Larry Parrish	.246	.212
Ozzie Guillen	.337	.220	Roy Smalley	.233	.206
Tony Gwynn	.261	.348	Tim Raines	.313	.344
Billy Hatcher	.048	.333	Gary Carter	.186	.197
Kent Hrbek	.253	.286	Mike Davis	.284	.221
Pete Incaviglia	.233	.258	Greg Gagne	.200	.224
Steve Jeltz	.154	.356	Jose Uribe	.164	.204
Dave Lopes	.167	.190	Ron Cey	.171	.278
Fred Lynn	.352	.189	George Brett	.232	.278
Omar Moreno	.156	.250	Greg Brock	.263	.056
Dale Murphy	.225	.234	Glenn Davis	.298	.338
Eddie Murray	.237	.367	Tony Bernazard	.317	.250
Tony Pena	.264	.226	Kevin McReynolds	.446	.241
Gary Pettis	.221	.293	Cecil Cooper	.218	.302
R.J. Reynolds	.255	.262	Andy Van Slyke	.271	.250
Ernest Riles	.245	.217	Willie Upshaw	.283	.229
Bill Russell	.100	.105	Tony Perez	.400	.000
Argenis Salazar	.327	.179	Larry Herndon	.264	.245
Larry Sheets	.255	.244	Greg Walker	.257	.262
Milt Thompson	.220	.205	Craig Reynolds	.276	.240
Reggie Williams	.296	.242	Kevin Mitchell	.300	.361
Dave Winfield	.262	.316	Rickey Henderson	.216	.252
Mike Young	.221	.200	Ken Phelps	.170	.220

Twenty of the 35 ground-ball hitters had higher batting averages against the selected fly-ball pitchers than the ground-ball pitchers; 19 of 35 fly-ball hitters had higher averages against the ground-ball pitchers. Neither total is conclusive on its own, but the composite group batting averages are. Since the two groups of batters had such similar overall batting averages, and the same was true of the groups of pitchers, the differences in the summarized averages listed below can be attributed only to the advantage a pitcher derives when facing a batter of similar type:

Batter	Pitcher	AB	H	BA
Ground-Ball	Ground-Ball	2253	587	.261
Fly-Ball	Ground-Ball	2275	627	.276
Ground-Ball	Fly-Ball	2329	638	.274
Fly-Ball	Fly-Ball	2247	575	.256

Like all generalities, the rule applies to many players but not all. But that's true even of the universally practiced rule for platooning left-handed and right-handed batters. The average difference of 17 batting-average points between favorable and unfavorable ground out/fly out situations is nearly as large as that found by dividing players according to left-handed and right-handed hitters and pitchers (20 points).

And the differences found by applying the same method to the 1985 season—19 points—is closer still:

Batter	Pitcher	AB	H	BA
Ground-Ball	Ground-Ball	2918	740	.254
Fly-Ball	Ground-Ball	2502	692	.277
Ground-Ball	Fly-Ball	2408	640	.266
Fly-Ball	Fly-Ball	2942	740	.252

A final thought: It's not only San Diego's opponents that need to be aware of the ground out/fly out factor. Any team that platoons some of its starters—which is to say all 26 major-league teams—needs to study the issue, since many players have biases as strong with regard to out distributions as according to left- or right-handedness. San Diego is no exception.

For example, John Kruk, a left-handed ground-ball hitter, was used primarily against right-handed pitchers last season. He started only 15 games against southpaws and batted only 93 times against them. Although there was a noticeable difference in his performance against left- and right-handed pitchers (in extra-base power more than batting average), the difference was even greater with regard to our distributions:

Opp. Pitcher	BA	SA	OBA	Opp. Pitcher	BA	SA	OBA
Left-Handers	.304	.342	.402	Ground-Ballers	.248	.315	.337
Right-Handers	.312	.457	.403	Fly-Ballers	.380	.550	.477

Clearly, Kruk should start against all fly-ball pitchers, left-handed or right-handed. A manager who twists his line-up to rest a player like Kruk against southpaws might be sitting one of his most valuable bats on the bench.

For those of you who'd like to keep track of this factor throughout the season, these were most extreme ground-ball and fly-ball hitters for each league in 1986:

National League ground-ball hitters: Wally Backman, 2.75; Milt Thompson, 2.74; Willie McGee, 2.60; Kal Daniels, 2.30; R.J. Reynolds, 2.25; Steve Jeltz, 2.10; Herm Winningham, 2.09; Steve Sax, 1.98; Rafael Belliard, 1.94; John Kruk, 1.92.

National League fly-ball hitters: Howard Johnson, 0.59; Gary Redus, 0.61; Nick Esasky, 0.62; Andy Van Slyke, 0.66; Franklin Stubbs, 0.66; Craig Reynolds, 0.73; Mike Schmidt, 0.73; Jim Morrison, 0.73; Glenn Hubbard, 0.77; Mitch Webster, 0.78.

American League ground-ball hitters: Gary Pettis, 2.24; Phil Bradley, 1.94; Rance Mulliniks, 1.88; Juan Bonilla, 1.86; Rick Manning, 1.84; Buddy Biancalana, 1.81; Tom O'Malley, 1.67; John Moses, 1.64; Wade Boggs, 1.62; Carmen Castillo, 1.58.

American League fly-ball hitters: Darrell Evans, 0.51; Rob Deer, 0.61; Joe Carter, 0.62; Tom Brunansky, 0.63; Steve Balboni, 0.63; Tim Hulett, 0.66; Alan Trammell, 0.66; Bill Schroeder, 0.67; George Bell, 0.67; Don Baylor, 0.68.

The Harder They Fall

The volatility of the standings from year to year throughout the 1980s has been well documented. We'd like to discuss here one particular aspect of this volatility, one that hasn't been previously identified: the collapse of recent World Series losers.

Consider the case of the Padres, one typical of what's happened to the last few teams to lose the Series. San Diego posted consecutive 81–81 records in 1982 and 1983 before winning the National League title in 1984. The future looked bright as San Diego headed into the second half of the decade. But San Diego finished only four games above the .500 mark in 1985 and fell to a disastrous 74–88 mark last season. Just two years after winning the pennant, the Padres are a team in disarray.

It's hard to say what should have been expected of the Padres. Although no one thought San Diego was a super team, one capable of a string of pennants, a collapse like this was totally unforeseen. So let's examine other recent teams with records similar to San Diego's in 1983 and 1984, and see how they fared in the following seasons. We found eight such teams over the past 25 years, their records within two wins of the Padres' marks for the years in question, Year 1 and Year 2 in the following table:

Years	Team	Year 1	Year 2	Following Seasons	
1983–84	San Diego	81–81	92–70	83–79	74–88
1982–83	Detroit	83–79	92–70	104–58	84–77
1979–80	Los Angeles	79–83	92–71	63–47	88–74
1971–72	White Sox	79–83	87–67	77–85	80–80
1970–71	Detroit	79–83	91–71	86–70	85–77
1969–70	Yankees	80–81	93–69	82–80	79–76
1968–69	Atlanta	81–81	93–69	76–86	82–80
1964–65	Pittsburgh	80–82	92–70	81–81	80–82

The eight teams comparable to the 1983–84 Padres had average winning percentages of .540 and .526 in the next two seasons, compared to San Diego's .512 and .457 marks, and none sunk as low as the Padres' 74–88 mark. Was it a coincidence that San Diego nosedived after its World Series loss, or was there a cause and effect?

We performed the same test on other recent Series losers, and the results were similar. We found 16 teams over the past 25 years with records in consecutive seasons similar to those of the 1982 and 1983 Philadelphia Phillies, the two seasons leading up to their loss to Baltimore in the '83 Series. The 16 had average winning percentages of .548 and .559 in the next two seasons; the Phillies had records of 81–81 (.500) in 1984 and 75–87 (.463) in 1985. Going back another season, to the

Milwaukee Brewers of 1981 and 1982, we could find only two teams of the expansion era that matched the Brewers' performance in those two seasons: the St. Louis Cardinals of 1963 and '64, and the Baltimore Orioles of 1981 and '82:

Years	Team	Year 1	Year 2	Following Seasons	
1981–82	Milwaukee	62–47	95–67	87–75	67–94
1981–82	Baltimore	59–46	94–68	98–64	85–77
1963–64	St. Louis	93–69	93–69	80–81	83–79

Like the 1985 Padres, Milwaukee kept pace the first year after its World Series loss (to St. Louis in 1982), but went into the tank after that. Quicker declines were posted by the 1982 Yankees (79–83 after their '81 Series loss) and, of course, last year's Cardinals (79–82).

No World Series loser during the 1980s has finished higher than third in the standings the following season; this is very different from the pattern in the 1970s, when only one team that lost in the Series failed to finish third or higher the next season. The position of World Series losers in the next season's standings:

	1st	2d	3d	4th	5th	6th	7th
1980s	0	0	2	1	2	0	0
1970s	3	2	4	1	0	0	0

This trend is borne out further by the performance of teams that lost in the League Championship Series in the '70s and '80s. As the chart below shows, while 13 playoff losers in the '70s finished first or second the following year, only two have managed to do so thus far in the '80s:

	1st	2d	3d	4th	5th	6th	7th
1980s	1	1	3	3	4	0	0
1970s	8	5	3	1	2	1	0

Normally, we wouldn't be so quick to conclude that a World Series loss drains a team of its potential, the statistical evidence notwithstanding. It does seem awfully melodramatic to attribute the decline to a year-long, postloss malaise, or to some vague team-wide character flaw that also contributed to the Series loss. But in the Boston Red Sox essay, we uncovered a strong negative impact of particularly demoralizing losses, whether regular- or postseason. The decline following a postseason loss appears to be an extension of that trend, and a most striking example of the year-to-year change that characterizes today's baseball environment.

WON-LOST RECORD BY STARTING POSITION

SAN DIEGO 74-88	C	1B	2B	3B	SS	LF	CF	RF	P	Leadoff	Relief	Starts
Randy Asadoor	·	·	·	7-8	·	·	·	·	·	·	·	7-8
Bruce Bochy	13-17	·	·	·	·	·	·	·	·	·	·	13-17
Greg Booker	·	·	·	·	·	·	·	·	·	·	3-6	·
Dave Dravecky	·	·	·	·	·	·	·	·	13-13	·	4-5	13-13
Tim Flannery	·	·	35-49	5-2	2-2	·	·	·	·	26-35	·	42-53
Steve Garvey	·	64-74	·	·	·	·	·	·	·	·	·	64-74
Rich Gossage	·	·	·	·	·	·	·	·	·	·	32-13	·
Gary Green	·	·	·	·	5-7	·	·	·	·	·	·	5-7
Tony Gwynn	·	·	·	·	·	·	73-85	·	·	2-2	·	73-85
Andy Hawkins	·	·	·	·	·	·	·	·	18-17	·	1-1	18-17
Ray Hayward	·	·	·	·	·	·	·	·	1-2	·	1-0	1-2
LaMarr Hoyt	·	·	·	·	·	·	·	·	13-12	·	3-7	13-12
Dane Iorg	·	2-2	·	0-2	·	1-0	·	·	·	·	0-2	3-4
Jimmy Jones	·	·	·	·	·	·	·	·	2-1	·	·	2-1
Terry Kennedy	54-60	·	·	·	·	·	·	·	·	·	·	54-60
John Kruk	·	1-2	·	·	·	26-36	0-3	·	·	1-2	·	27-41
Dave LaPoint	·	·	·	·	·	·	·	·	1-3	·	1-19	1-3
Craig Lefferts	·	·	·	·	·	·	·	·	·	·	35-48	·
Carmelo Martinez	·	0-4	·	·	·	25-31	·	·	·	·	·	25-35
Lance McCullers	·	·	·	·	·	·	·	·	2-5	·	29-34	2-5
Kevin McReynolds	·	·	·	·	·	22-21	46-57	1-0	·	·	·	69-78
Graig Nettles	·	·	·	45-54	·	·	·	·	·	·	·	45-54
Mark Parent	0-3	·	·	·	·	·	·	·	·	·	·	0-3
Tim Pyznarski	·	7-6	·	·	·	·	·	·	·	·	·	7-6
Randy Ready	·	·	·	0-1	·	·	·	·	·	·	·	0-1
Bip Roberts	·	·	33-32	·	·	·	·	·	·	19-16	·	33-32
Jerry Royster	·	·	6-7	16-19	5-7	·	·	·	·	13-18	·	27-33
Benito Santiago	7-8	·	·	·	·	·	·	·	·	·	·	7-8
Eric Show	·	·	·	·	·	·	·	·	11-11	·	0-2	11-11
Bob Stoddard	·	·	·	·	·	·	·	·	·	·	4-14	·
Tim Stoddard	·	·	·	·	·	·	·	·	·	·	6-24	·
Garry Templeton	·	·	·	·	62-72	·	·	·	·	·	·	62-72
Mark Thurmond	·	·	·	·	·	·	·	·	8-7	·	0-2	8-7
Ed Vosberg	·	·	·	·	·	·	·	·	2-1	·	1-1	2-1
Gene Walter	·	·	·	·	·	·	·	·	·	·	20-37	·
Mark Wasinger	·	·	1-2	·	·	·	·	·	·	·	·	1-2
Ed Whitson	·	·	·	·	·	·	·	·	1-11	·	1-4	1-11
Ed Wojna	·	·	·	·	·	·	·	·	2-5	·	·	2-5
Marvell Wynne	·	·	·	·	·	28-31	·	·	·	13-15	·	28-31

Batting Comparisons: Vs. Left-Handers/Right-Handers and Overall/Late Inning-Pressure Situations

Player	vs	BA	Rank	SA	Rank	HR %	Rank		BA	Rank	SA	Rank	HR %	Rank
Bruce Bochy	vs. Lefties	.253	82	.579	10	8.42	2	Overall	.252	--	.512	--	6.30	--
	vs. Righties	.250	--	.313	--	0.00	--	Pressure	.321	--	.607	--	7.14	--
Tim Flannery	vs. Lefties	.143	142	.250	135	1.79	80	Overall	.280	30	.345	109	0.82	122
	vs. Righties	.304	18	.362	90	0.64	124	Pressure	.194	125	.242	127	1.61	87
Steve Garvey	vs. Lefties	.283	46	.527	12	6.52	9	Overall	.255	83	.408	64	3.77	32
	vs. Righties	.241	96	.349	105	2.41	65	Pressure	.258	71	.330	92	1.03	99
Tony Gwynn	vs. Lefties	.328	13	.523	13	2.98	48	Overall	.329	4	.467	22	2.18	72
	vs. Righties	.329	10	.435	51	1.72	89	Pressure	.359	10	.515	11	2.91	46
Terry Kennedy	vs. Lefties	.229	106	.396	65	3.13	44	Overall	.264	63	.403	71	2.78	55
	vs. Righties	.274	42	.405	69	2.68	56	Pressure	.325	22	.488	25	2.50	52
John Kruk	vs. Lefties	.304	33	.342	98	0.00	119	Overall	.309	11	.424	47	1.44	96
	vs. Righties	.312	15	.457	28	2.01	82	Pressure	.306	31	.347	87	0.00	102
Carmelo Martinez	vs. Lefties	.282	47	.518	14	6.36	10	Overall	.238	110	.389	78	3.69	35
	vs. Righties	.201	132	.284	126	1.49	97	Pressure	.226	101	.434	45	5.66	8
Kevin McReynolds	vs. Lefties	.339	5	.589	9	5.21	17	Overall	.288	22	.504	7	4.64	16
	vs. Righties	.261		.459	26	4.35	29	Pressure	.255	72	.449	36	5.10	17
Graig Nettles	vs. Lefties	.170	140	.358	86	5.66	16	Overall	.218	137	.379	86	4.52	20
	vs. Righties	.226	113	.382	74	4.32	32	Pressure	.242	94	.403	60	4.84	21
Bip Roberts	vs. Lefties	.203	128	.268	130	0.72	113	Overall	.253	84	.303	129	0.41	129
	vs. Righties	.320	--	.350	--	0.00	--	Pressure	.207	--	.207	--	0.00	--
Jerry Royster	vs. Lefties	.273	55	.385	74	1.60	84	Overall	.257	76	.362	97	1.95	83
	vs. Righties	.214	--	.300	--	2.86	--	Pressure	.224	102	.265	118	0.00	102
Garry Templeton	vs. Lefties	.257	78	.343	97	1.14	103	Overall	·.247	100	.308	124	0.39	130
	vs. Righties	.242	95	.290	124	0.00	131	Pressure	.324	22	.380	75	0.00	102
Marvell Wynne	vs. Lefties	.186	135	.329	105	2.86	51	Overall	.264	63	.417	56	2.43	64
	vs. Righties	.289	27	.445	44	2.29	69	Pressure	.290	42	.478	27	4.35	26
Team Average	vs. Lefties	.261	5	.421	1	3.28	1	Overall	.261	2	.388	4	2.47	6
	vs. Righties	.262	2	.371	9	2.04	10	Pressure	.268	5	.392	6	2.59	5
League Average	vs. Lefties	.257		.384		2.28		Overall	.253		.380		2.32	
	vs. Righties	.251		.378		2.34		Pressure	.257		.376		2.31	

Additional Miscellaneous Batting Comparisons

	Grass Surface BA	Rank	Artificial Surface BA	Rank	Home Games BA	Rank	Road Games BA	Rank	Runners in Scoring Position BA	Rank	Runners in Scoring Pos and Two Outs BA	Rank	Leading Off Inning OBA	Rank	Runners on 3B with less than 2 Outs RDI %	Rank
Bruce Bochy	.222	116	.357	--	.246	--	.258	--	.233	--	.200	105	.500	--	.417	132
Tim Flannery	.287	38	.260	63	.295	36	.265	53	.263	62	.178	121	.396	14	.600	52
Steve Garvey	.244	91	.284	36	.244	105	.266	46	.247	81	.276	45	.323	71	.528	94
Tony Gwynn	.333	6	.315	12	.341	4	.317	6	.327	17	.261	60	.403	11	.556	79
Dane Iorg	.192	137	.321	--	.156	--	.279	--	.185	--	.077	--	.435	--	.800	--
Terry Kennedy	.272	56	.241	97	.280	59	.248	82	.303	26	.352	10	.287	104	.467	117
John Kruk	.294	28	.341	6	.311	18	.309	11	.315	19	.484	1	.355	37	.600	52
Carmelo Martinez	.215	125	.321	--	.179	142	.298	15	.158	139	.037	145	.433	6	.429	130
Kevin McReynolds	.271	58	.333	9	.293	39	.282	29	.270	54	.286	39	.359	33	.564	76
Graig Nettles	.233	107	.178	140	.265	82	.176	141	.228	105	.182	119	.250	132	.750	10
Bip Roberts	.257	75	.241	--	.237	110	.268	43	.250	--	.300	--	.207	140	.556	79
Jerry Royster	.260	69	.250	80	.246	104	.266	46	.245	82	.269	49	.286	105	.600	52
Garry Templeton	.242	98	.262	60	.230	118	.266	50	.258	69	.254	65	.264	123	.500	101
Marvell Wynne	.293	34	.167	--	.311	17	.189	137	.235	95	.125	136	.302	89	.600	52
Team Average	.259	4	.268	1	.260	6	.262	2	.252	7	.236	7	.323	3	.532	11
League Average	.254		.253		.260		.247		.252		.235		.316		.562	

Pitching Comparisons: Vs. Left-Handers/Right-Handers and Runners On/Bases Empty

		BA	Rank	BB %	Rank	SO %	Rank		BA	Rank	BB %	Rank	SO %	Rank
Dave Dravecky	vs. Lefties	.226	29	5.21	10	20.83	21	Runners On	.227	23	9.85	53	9.47	104
	vs. Righties	.250	64	8.43	66	11.53	98	Bases Empty	.257	70	6.78	41	15.01	66
Rich Gossage	vs. Lefties	.281	84	9.66	62	17.93	35	Runners On	.272	75	6.54	9	20.92	11
	vs. Righties	.264	--	4.41	--	27.21	--	Bases Empty	.274	--	7.81	--	24.22	--
Andy Hawkins	vs. Lefties	.323	111	9.19	54	12.69	75	Runners On	.274	79	9.72	50	11.76	85
	vs. Righties	.214	15	7.37	52	13.17	85	Bases Empty	.265	76	7.20	47	13.81	83
LaMarr Hoyt	vs. Lefties	.273	76	12.36	91	9.55	104	Runners On	.263	60	11.50	82	11.82	84
	vs. Righties	.280	95	7.00	46	14.87	67	Bases Empty	.286	105	8.29	74	12.44	94
Dave LaPoint	vs. Lefties	.193	--	8.06	--	12.90	--	Runners On	.301	99	11.29	77	14.52	61
	vs. Righties	.301	108	8.96	74	15.57	63	Bases Empty	.257	70	6.67	37	15.33	61
Craig Lefferts	vs. Lefties	.222	25	5.94	16	23.76	12	Runners On	.266	66	11.74	85	15.02	56
	vs. Righties	.263	82	11.01	99	13.91	80	Bases Empty	.243	47	8.15	71	17.17	43
Lance McCullers	vs. Lefties	.278	82	12.50	94	10.71	95	Runners On	.188	5	13.91	105	16.09	46
	vs. Righties	.154	1	8.52	69	22.96	10	Bases Empty	.234	31	8.13	69	17.19	42
Eric Show	vs. Lefties	.250	56	13.89	105	13.58	71	Runners On	.191	7	11.45	80	15.42	52
	vs. Righties	.193	7	9.80	86	20.41	27	Bases Empty	.247	50	12.57	112	17.25	41
Mark Thurmond	vs. Lefties	.310	--	12.24	--	22.45	--	Runners On	.389	116	12.00	88	8.00	111
	vs. Righties	.328	115	7.53	54	7.53	114	Bases Empty	.278	95	5.06	18	11.24	104
Gene Walter	vs. Lefties	.151	4	14.81	110	29.63	2	Runners On	.279	83	11.11	70	19.70	19
	vs. Righties	.276	91	10.51	95	16.56	52	Bases Empty	.219	17	12.05	109	20.09	19
Ed Whitson	vs. Lefties	.244	48	11.06	77	11.56	90	Runners On	.310	105	13.07	99	13.07	75
	vs. Righties	.350	--	10.87	--	16.67	--	Bases Empty	.269	87	9.24	87	14.13	81
Ed Wojna	vs. Lefties	.333	112	10.53	69	8.42	111	Runners On	.244	--	8.60	--	7.53	--
	vs. Righties	.192	--	7.41	--	13.58	--	Bases Empty	.293	--	9.64	--	14.46	--
Team Average	vs. Lefties	.264	8	11.34	12	14.40	8	Runners On	.263	6	11.42	11	13.87	10
	vs. Righties	.253	7	8.73	9	15.46	9	Bases Empty	.254	8	8.45	11	15.97	7
League Average	vs. Lefties	.257		9.83		14.90		Runners On	.260		10.11		15.02	
	vs. Righties	.251		8.19		16.33		Bases Empty	.248		7.89		16.30	

Additional Miscellaneous Pitching Comparisons

	Grass Surface BA	Rank	Artificial Surface BA	Rank	Home Games BA	Rank	Road Games BA	Rank	Runners in Scoring Position BA	Rank	Runners in Scoring Pos and Two Outs BA	Rank	Leading Off Inning OBA	Rank
Dave Dravecky	.238	40	.264	71	.241	54	.252	49	.194	12	.211	39	.294	35
Rich Gossage	.270	78	.289	--	.291	100	.245	--	.250	55	.231	54	.321	--
Andy Hawkins	.259	69	.301	109	.261	80	.276	82	.283	92	.241	67	.348	92
LaMarr Hoyt	.277	81	.275	88	.254	72	.301	102	.241	44	.189	28	.366	97
Dave LaPoint	.281	89	.267	75	.255	73	.293	101	.339	113	.217	--	.302	48
Craig Lefferts	.242	46	.294	104	.232	39	.278	84	.255	66	.217	43	.289	31
Lance McCullers	.229	28	.182	5	.218	22	.214	13	.188	10	.153	13	.300	45
Eric Show	.232	32	.205	10	.222	24	.229	23	.145	2	.055	1	.319	64
Tim Stoddard	.186	3	.280	--	.176	--	.230	--	.283	91	.310	103	.250	--
Mark Thurmond	.323	114	.345	--	.266	84	.390	116	.408	119	.457	118	.342	87
Gene Walter	.238	39	.265	72	.238	51	.254	53	.250	55	.173	19	.355	95
Ed Whitson	.285	93	.291	98	.262	81	.311	105	.300	100	.297	97	.299	43
Ed Wojna	.288	98	.205	--	.213	--	.317	--	.269	--	.105	--	.366	--
Team Average	.256	8	.261	7	.245	6	.271	10	.253	6	.212	3	.320	7
League Average	.254		.253		.247		.260		.252		.235		.316	

SAN FRANCISCO GIANTS

Remember the off-season of 1985–86, after Bob Lurie vowed that the Giants would play the '86 season in downtown San Francisco, in San Jose, on Fisherman's Wharf, in Ghirardelli Square, on Alcatraz—anywhere except Candlestick Park? The team was coming off the first 100-loss season in its 103-year history, and its fortunes may never have looked more bleak.

If someone had approached you during that winter and told you that in 1986 the team would stay in San Francisco and play at Candlestick; that Jeff Leonard, the 1985 team RBI leader, would miss the last two months of the season with an injury; that the team's home run and RBI leader would be Candy Maldonado, a player who would start in only 88 games; that rookies would play regularly at first and second base, having jumped from A and AA leagues respectively; and that the team leader in saves would have 10; then chances are that you would have put the team down for another 100-loss season.

But no. Stuck at the 'Stick, the Giants became only the ninth team in the history of the major leagues to finish over .500 the year after losing 100 games. And they did it the hard way, fighting off injuries to Leonard, Will Clark, and Chris Brown, surviving a flirtation with Steve Carlton, and inducing 10 wins apiece from Vida Blue and Mike LaCoss.

And, despite everything, the fact is that San Francisco's final record wasn't even as good as it should have been.

The teams that preceded the Giants in the 100L/.500+ Club do not exactly evoke memories of the Gillette Cavalcade of Sports. By definition, these 100-game losers were among the most miserable teams of all time. Each is listed here with its won-lost record for its 100-loss season (Year 1), its comeback season (Year 2), and its subsequent season (Year 3); also listed for each team is its next first-place finish (league pennant or division title):

		Year 1 W–L	Year 2 W–L	Year 3 W–L	Next First
1904	Phillies	52–100	83–69	71–82	1915
1917	Pirates	51–103	65–60	71–68	1925
1946	Athletics	49–105	78–76	84–70	1971
1961	Phillies	47–107	81–80	87–75	1976
1962	Cubs	59–103	82–80	76–86	1984
1966	Cubs	59–103	87–74	84–78	1984
1973	Rangers	57–105	84–76	79–83	None
1979	Athletics	54–108	83–79	64–45	1981
1985	**Giants**	62–100	83–79	—	—

Three of the eight teams that turned the trick improved their won-lost record again the following season. One of them, the 1981 A's, even won a division title (albeit one tainted by the split season). However, that Oakland team was the exception rather than the rule. Of the seven other teams, six had to wait an average of 15 years after their turnaround season before they won their next league pennant or division title, and the seventh, Texas, is still waiting.

But the extent of the Giants' improvement from 1985 to 1986 actually goes beyond their won-lost record. Judging by the runs they scored and allowed, the Giants could have been expected to finish with an even better record in 1986. Only five teams in baseball—four of them division champions—had a better run differential than the Giants last year:

	Scored	Allowed	Differential	W–L
Mets	783	578	+205	108–54
Angels	786	684	+102	92–70
Red Sox	794	696	+98	95–66
Astros	654	569	+85	96–66
Tigers	798	714	+84	87–75
Giants	698	618	+80	83–79

The Giants' average margin of victory in 1986 was 3.4 runs per game; that was second highest in the National League to Pittsburgh's 3.7. They won only 51 of 111 games in which the final margin was three runs or less, but they were 14–4 in games decided by six runs or more. The fact that the Giants were outscored by six or more runs in only four games last season is especially noteworthy; only one National League team in the past 60 years lost fewer games by margins that large. (Philadelphia lost three such games in 1976.)

Let's take a minute to inspect that record of 14–4 in games decided by six runs or more. It's usually a mark of a very good team to do that well in blowout games. Besides the '86 Giants, there have been 22 other National League teams since the beginning of divisional play that have had records 10 games over .500 in games decided by six runs or more. (The Mets, with a 20–8 record, were the only other N.L. team in that group in 1986.) Of those 22 teams, 17 won division titles, and only one team, the 80–82 Astros in 1984, had an overall record worse than 10 games above .500.

In the 20 years prior to the introduction of divisional play (1949 to 1968), there were 22 other National League teams with records 10 games over .500 in six-run games. Again, they were mostly winning teams, with only three of the 22 having overall records of less than 10 games above .500. Counting the '84 Astros, that gives us four teams to look at that exhibited the same characteristics as the '86 Giants: great in blowout games, mediocre in other games. Here are their records, along with how they did the next season:

		Overall	Blowout	Other	Next Year
1954	Phillies	75–79	22–7	53–72	77–77
1955	Reds	75–79	18–8	57–71	91–63
1962	Cardinals	84–78	20–8	64–70	93–69
1984	Astros	80–82	18–8	62–74	83–79

Each of these mediocre teams bettered its won-lost record the year after its domination of blowout games, two of them moderately and two significantly. Will the Giants be able to repeat the pattern? First let's take a look at their offense.

In 1985, the Giants scored only 556 runs; in the course of one season, they added 142 runs to their offense. That's an amazing increase. Remember all of the talk about a lively ball during the early portion of 1986? Well, the final totals for the season showed that run-scoring in the National League was up by a total of 197 runs over the previous year; of that total of 197 runs, 142 were accounted for by the Giants. But the even more unusual part about that increase is not so much that they did it, but that they did it without an increase in the team's home run total.

Teams have increased their run scoring in the past, some by even greater margins than the Giants did, but these increases have almost always been due, at least in part, to a surge in home-run hitting. To take a quick but typical example, let's look at the last three National League teams to increase their scoring from one season to the next by as many runs as the '86 Giants (strike seasons of 1972 and 1981 are excluded). All three of these teams had healthy increases in their home run totals, which explained in great measure their overall scoring increases:

	Seasons	Runs	HR
Dodgers	1976–77	608–769	91–191
Cardinals	1969–70	595–744	90–113
Padres	1969–70	468–681	99–172

But the Giants in 1986 actually hit one home run fewer (114) than they had in 1985 (115). Only two National League teams in this century had a year-to-year increase in runs scored as large as the Giants' in a season in which their home run output declined:

	Seasons	Runs	HR
Cardinals	1908–09	372–583	17–15
Cubs	1934–35	705–847	101–88
Giants	1985–86	556–698	115–114

It's not hard to envision the Giants producing as many runs in 1987 as they did in 1986. Neither Brown, Clark, Leonard, nor Maldonado had as many as 420 at bats last season; if healthy, they should all surpass that total this year.

But the more troublesome area that will determine the team's eventual success is the state of its starting pitching.

By any standard, Mike Krukow's 20-win season took baseball by surprise last season. It's unlikely to be duplicated, for a number of reasons. First, consider that of 20 pitchers who won at least 20 games in a season from 1980 to 1985, only one, Joaquin Andujar in 1984, was tough enough to repeat the feat the next season. Second, he was one of only four National League starters (minimum: 25 starts) to be supported by his teammates with more than five runs per start; teammate LaCoss was another, getting a good head start toward his 10 wins. Finally, in Krukow the Giants had a pitcher in his 30s who had never before won even 15 games and who had not had a winning record in any of his three previous seasons. How many pitchers with that checkered profile do you think have produced a 20-win season?

Since 1900, the answer is four, and none in the last 23 years. Luke Hamlin and Dutch Leonard both did it in 1939; Roger Wolff did it in 1945; and Ray Herbert provided White Sox fans with a pleasant surprise in 1962. And none of those pitchers was as old in his 20-game season as the 34-year-old Krukow. The four had a combined 41–45 record the year after their unexpected 20-game seasons, and none of them came close to the 20-mark again.

Beyond Krukow's 20–9 record last season, the rest of the Giants starters combined to go 34–51 (.400). Only Krukow, Blue, and LaCoss started 20 or more games, as Roger Craig wrote the names of 13 different starting pitchers into the lineup, the most by any National League team. One who may bear watching is Kelly Downs, a 26-year-old right-hander whom the Giants acquired from Philadelphia for Renie Martin and Al Oliver in 1984. Called up to the Giants in late July, he took a month to get his feet wet, then went 4–0 with a 1.82 ERA over his last eight starts. And besides, how can you not like a pitcher with a name like an Irish racetrack?

Another Eddie Murray?

Chris Brown has been in the majors a little over two years and has had to put up with a lot of jokes about his seeming susceptibility to injury. But when it comes to production in key situations, his numbers leave his detractors with lockjaw. Brown is the classic clutch performer: Every time the pressure of the situation gets turned up a notch, his performance follows suit. Here are the figures (Brown's 84-at bat 1984 season is included in the career averages):

	1985	1986	Career
Overall average	.271	.317	.293
Runners on base	.313	.378	.342
Runners in scoring position	.337	.370	.355
Runners on base/2 outs	.392	.348	.359
Scoring position/2 outs	.373	.364	.362
Bases loaded	4-for-7	4-for-6	8-for-14
Late-Inning Pressure	.351	.329	.337

Of course Brown is still early in his career, but those numbers are very impressive. He hasn't accumulated enough time in the majors yet to be ranked in the Career Leaders section that starts on page 369, but among veteran players over the past 12 years, only Wade Boggs and Rod Carew have higher career batting averages with runners on base, and only Boggs has hit better with runners in scoring position. And no one—not Boggs, Carew, George Brett, or anyone else—can match Brown's .359 batting average with runners on base and two outs, or his .362 mark with runners in scoring position and two outs.

Some of Brown's other career figures also defy the conventional baseball wisdom. He hits better on grass fields (.302) than on artificial turf (.264); and most noteworthy for a right-handed batter, his career batting average against right-handers (.307) is 49 points higher than it is against left-handers (.258). Here's the case of a guy playing in the right place and time: If he had been born 20 years earlier, all of this stuff would have gone undetected, and Brown would have been underappreciated. Imagine—Chris Brown underappreciated.

Little-Ball North

Roger Craig's return to managing last season—we know, he actually managed the Giants for the last 18 games of 1985—was both successful and surprising. But at least one element of his managerial strategy was familiar and predictable: his love of the sacrifice bunt.

When Craig was hired by the Giants, he was hailed as the man who molded Sparky Anderson's pitching staff in the Tigers' championship season of 1984. Actually, the master of the split-fingered fastball had served three major-league teams as pitching coach over a span of nine seasons. But sandwiched between those various stints as coach were two years as manager of the San Diego Padres, in 1978 and 1979.

In 1978, the managerial duties were thrust upon Craig on March 21 when, in the midst of spring training, Alvin Dark was fired. Craig worked a minor miracle, leading a team that had lost 93 games the previous season to an 84–78 record, the first winning season in its history. The next season, that gain was completely negated, and the Pads lost 93 again. Craig was fired; replaced, in fact, by the team's radio announcer, Jerry Coleman.

In those two years—one good, one bad—Craig demonstrated his affinity for the bunt. The Padres sacrificed 114 times, second most in the league, in 1978; the next year, they had the most, 113. (The league averages those years were 81 and 79, respectively.) Neither time nor a tour of the American League has swayed Craig from his convictions. The Giants, who were a bunting team under Jim Davenport in 1985 with 93 sacrifices, increased their total to 101 in 1986, second in the league to the Cardinals' 108.

What is particularly intriguing about Craig's pattern, however, is not merely the total of bunts, but who he has doing the bunting. His tendency to bunt throughout the batting order is shown in this table, giving the distribution of the 869 sacrifice bunts in the National League in 1986, according to team and batting order position:

	1	2	3	4	5	6	7	8	9	Total
St. Louis	3	9	8	0	3	9	4	8	64	108
San Francisco	12	13	6	3	1	6	12	6	42	101
Los Angeles	7	6	2	4	2	9	4	12	35	81
Atlanta	7	10	0	0	5	4	6	5	42	79
New York	6	17	0	0	0	2	2	2	46	75
Pittsburgh	3	13	1	1	1	0	1	14	34	68
Philadelphia	3	12	1	1	1	0	1	4	43	66
San Diego	8	4	5	2	1	4	5	3	34	66
Cincinnati	6	3	0	0	3	5	3	5	40	65
Chicago	4	2	2	2	1	3	3	8	29	54
Houston	3	11	0	0	1	1	3	2	32	53
Montreal	3	5	2	0	1	4	5	8	25	53
N.L. Totals	65	105	27	13	20	47	49	77	466	869

Craig, more than any other manager in the league, uses his players throughout the batting order to bunt runners along. No other leadoff position had more than eight sacrifices; the Giants had 12. The league average in the second spot was 8.8; the Giants had 13. They even had nine sacrifices from their three and four hitters, the most in the league. To put it another way, the Giants' ninth position accounted for only 41.6 percent of their sacrifices, the lowest percentage in the league. And even though the Cardinals outsacrificed the Giants by a margin of seven bunts for the season, they concentrated 59 percent of their sacrifices in the nine spot, reflecting a sharp difference in overall strategy.

The pattern is slightly different in the American League, as we would expect given the presence of the designated hitter to replace so many of those pitchers' bunts. Here is the team-by-team breakdown for all 14 American League teams:

	1	2	3	4	5	6	7	8	9	Total
California	11	24	5	0	6	8	14	15	8	91
Cleveland	9	11	1	0	0	3	6	4	22	56
Oakland	12	7	1	0	0	0	10	13	13	56
Milwaukee	6	7	3	2	5	5	6	9	10	53
Detroit	4	19	2	1	2	4	3	6	11	52
Seattle	6	5	4	2	1	3	8	10	13	52
Chicago	9	12	0	0	1	4	10	5	9	50
Boston	6	15	0	0	0	3	5	5	12	44
Minnesota	7	4	0	1	2	2	6	8	14	44
New York	0	13	1	3	2	0	2	2	13	36
Baltimore	8	4	0	0	2	1	3	6	9	33
Texas	1	11	0	0	0	2	3	8	6	31
Kansas City	3	3	0	1	0	1	2	3	11	24
Toronto	3	2	2	0	1	3	4	4	5	24
A.L. Totals	85	137	19	10	22	39	80	98	156	646

American League teams bunt slightly more at the top and again in the seven and eight spots; National League teams bunt more from three to six (though the numbers here are small enough that this might just reflect the use of double-switches in the N.L.). The most similar A.L. distribution to San Francisco's is that of Gene Mauch's Angels, baseball's perennial champions of "little ball."

Is there a Craig-Mauch connection? Both came out of the Dodgers system, but by the time Craig started in the minors in 1950, Mauch had been traded away. The closest they ever came was in 1959, when they were both in the American Association: Mauch as manager of Minneapolis, and Craig across the river as a 5–17 pitcher with St. Paul. Could the ghost of John McGraw have hovered over the Twin Cities that summer, instilling in those below his beloved principles of Inside Baseball? And if so, how did Chuck Tanner, an outfielder with Minneapolis that year, avoid its influence—a lead-lined helmet, perhaps?

WON-LOST RECORD BY STARTING POSITION

SAN FRANCISCO 83-79	C	1B	2B	3B	SS	LF	CF	RF	P	Leadoff	Relief	Starts
Mike Aldrete		15-12				16-11		0-1		2-3		31-24
Juan Berenguer									2-2		14-28	2-2
Vida Blue									15-13			15-13
Randy Bockus											1-4	-
Bob Brenly	40-38	5-10		17-19						0-1		62-67
Chris Brown				56-55								56-55
Steve Carlton									3-3			3-3
Will Clark		52-47										52-47
Chili Davis						20-23	55-47			6-3		75-70
Mark Davis									1-1		29-36	1-1
Kelly Downs									6-8		0-1	6-8
Dan Driessen		1-1										1-1
Scott Garrelts									1-1		3-4	1-1
Dan Gladden							43-39			43-39		43-39
Jim Gott									7-11		24-11	7-11
Mark Grant									1-1		0-3	1-1
Brad Gulden	0-2											0-2
Chuck Hensley									0-1		0-2	0-1
Chris Jones											6-5	-
Mike Krukow									23-11		1-0	23-11
Randy Kutcher			0-1		2-2		17-16			17-16		19-19
Mike LaCoss									16-15		3-3	16-15
Rick Lancelotti		0-1										0-1
Bill Laskey											6-14	-
Jeffrey Leonard						44-40						44-40
Candy Maldonado						12-20	3-1	25-27		7-8		40-48
Roger Mason									6-5			6-5
Bob Melvin	39-37	0-1										39-38
Greg Minton											16-32	-
Terry Mulholland									2-8		1-4	2-8
Phil Ouellette	4-2											4-2
Luis Quinones			2-2	9-4	2-3							13-9
Jeff Robinson									1-0		32-31	1-0
Harry Spilman		9-7										9-7
Rob Thompson			75-71									75-71
Jose Uribe					79-74							79-74
Brad Wellman										0-1		-
Frank Williams											12-24	-
Mike Woodard			6-6							5-6		6-6
Joel Youngblood		1-1		1-0		11-8		3-3		3-2		16-12

Batting Comparisons: Vs. Left-Handers/Right-Handers and Overall/Late Inning-Pressure Situations

		BA	Rank	SA	Rank	HR %	Rank		BA	Rank	SA	Rank	HR %	Rank
Mike Aldrete	vs. Lefties	.192	--	.231	--	0.00	--	Overall	.250	90	.389	79	0.93	120
	vs. Righties	.258	70	.411	64	1.05	108	Pressure	.350	13	.575	6	2.50	52
Bob Brenly	vs. Lefties	.268	64	.484	23	3.82	31	Overall	.246	102	.403	72	3.39	42
	vs. Righties	.235	101	.362	92	3.17	48	Pressure	.222	103	.311	102	1.11	98
Chris Brown	vs. Lefties	.292	51	.431	51	2.19	69	Overall	.317	7	.421	52	1.68	90
	vs. Righties	.330	9	.416	61	1.43	99	Pressure	.329	19	.425	51	1.37	94
Will Clark	vs. Lefties	.308	27	.415	58	1.54	89	Overall	.287	23	.444	35	2.70	59
	vs. Righties	.277	39	.457	29	3.24	47	Pressure	.397	2	.679	2	6.41	4
Chili Davis	vs. Lefties	.226	110	.345	95	2.98	49	Overall	.278	35	.416	58	2.47	63
	vs. Righties	.302	20	.450	36	2.23	71	Pressure	.278	54	.505	15	4.12	30
Dan Gladden	vs. Lefties	.276	51	.325	110	0.00	119	Overall	.276	46	.362	98	1.14	108
	vs. Righties	.276	40	.382	76	1.75	88	Pressure	.164	136	.179	139	0.00	102
Randy Kutcher	vs. Lefties	.203	128	.319	114	1.45	95	Overall	.237	112	.409	63	3.76	33
	vs. Righties	.256	76	.462	25	5.13	12	Pressure	.205	118	.256	120	0.00	102
Jeff Leonard	vs. Lefties	.328	12	.437	48	2.52	57	Overall	.279	32	.381	84	1.76	89
	vs. Righties	.252	84	.351	102	1.35	100	Pressure	.268	64	.429	47	3.57	38
Candy Maldonado	vs. Lefties	.235	97	.477	26	4.55	21	Overall	.252	86	.477	19	4.44	21
	vs. Righties	.260	64	.476	20	4.40	27	Pressure	.330	17	.639	3	6.19	5
Bob Melvin	vs. Lefties	.308	27	.462	33	2.88	50	Overall	.224	128	.347	107	1.87	85
	vs. Righties	.171	141	.274	130	1.22	103	Pressure	.150	138	.200	136	0.00	102
Rob Thompson	vs. Lefties	.286	42	.411	59	1.79	80	Overall	.271	49	.370	93	1.28	105
	vs. Righties	.265	50	.352	101	1.05	109	Pressure	.281	51	.375	78	2.08	65
Jose Uribe	vs. Lefties	.214	121	.324	111	2.07	71	Overall	.223	129	.280	135	0.66	124
	vs. Righties	.227	110	.260	136	0.00	131	Pressure	.188	129	.208	135	0.00	102
Joel Youngblood	vs. Lefties	.211	123	.276	127	0.00	119	Overall	.255	80	.402	73	2.72	57
	vs. Righties	.287	28	.491	11	4.63	22	Pressure	.230	98	.311	100	1.64	84
Team Average	vs. Lefties	.257	8	.383	7	2.14	7	Overall	.253	7	.375	9	2.07	9
	vs. Righties	.252	8	.371	8	2.04	9	Pressure	.259	7	.395	5	2.36	7
League Average	vs. Lefties	.257		.384		2.28		Overall	.253		.380		2.32	
	vs. Righties	.251		.378		2.34		Pressure	.257		.376		2.31	

Additional Miscellaneous Batting Comparisons

	Grass Surface BA	Rank	Artificial Surface BA	Rank	Home Games BA	Rank	Road Games BA	Rank	Runners in Scoring Position BA	Rank	Runners in Scoring Pos and Two Outs BA	Rank	Leading Off Inning OBA	Rank	Runners on 3B with less than 2 Outs RDI %	Rank
Mike Aldrete	.267	63	.196	--	.299	28	.192	133	.239	92	.229	84	.333	56	.727	14
Bob Brenly	.243	96	.254	74	.234	116	.257	64	.260	68	.220	92	.366	30	.483	112
Chris Brown	.325	9	.295	23	.333	6	.298	14	.370	4	.364	8	.278	112	.630	42
Will Clark	.315	13	.196	131	.336	5	.229	110	.196	127	.200	105	.374	25	.444	124
Chili Davis	.294	30	.229	109	.291	41	.265	52	.312	21	.282	42	.323	73	.676	24
Dan Gladden	.257	72	.324	10	.272	70	.280	31	.250	75	.162	125	.377	21	.750	10
Mike Krukow	.169	141	.059	--	.140	--	.154	--	.250	--	.231	--	.200	--	.500	101
Randy Kutcher	.227	114	.278	--	.261	90	.213	123	.167	--	.192	112	.329	63	.333	--
Jeff Leonard	.305	22	.200	129	.315	11	.243	89	.301	29	.295	34	.319	77	.538	92
Candy Maldonado	.259	71	.236	100	.228	119	.274	36	.306	25	.309	30	.193	143	.700	17
Bob Melvin	.176	139	.315	13	.220	125	.226	114	.173	136	.119	138	.241	135	.429	130
Luis Quinones	.167	142	.214	--	.196	--	.167	--	.192	--	.267	--	.217	--	.400	--
Harry Spilman	.324	10	.174	--	.371	--	.237	--	.441	--	.333	--	.313	--	.750	--
Rob Thompson	.294	30	.214	121	.294	38	.252	75	.242	90	.216	94	.364	32	.545	86
Jose Uribe	.234	104	.190	137	.219	128	.226	113	.289	38	.319	23	.339	53	.435	128
Mike Woodard	.250	79	.286	--	.255	--	.250	--	.375	--	.375	--	.353	--	.667	--
Joel Youngblood	.246	87	.278	--	.234	--	.271	39	.389	2	.310	28	.283	111	.583	68
Team Average	.260	2	.233	12	.265	3	.242	8	.267	2	.243	5	.313	8	.561	6
League Average	.254		.253		.260		.247		.252		.235		.316		.562	

Pitching Comparisons: Vs. Left-Handers/Right-Handers and Runners On/Bases Empty

		BA	Rank	BB %	Rank	SO %	Rank		BA	Rank	BB %	Rank	SO %	Rank
Juan Berenguer	vs. Lefties	.254	61	13.92	106	25.95	7	Runners On	.286	89	14.71	111	17.65	31
	vs. Righties	.229	33	14.10	114	19.87	32	Bases Empty	.209	12	13.48	115	26.97	4
Vida Blue	vs. Lefties	.216	23	9.09	49	19.19	30	Runners On	.202	9	9.54	47	14.13	66
	vs. Righties	.243	52	12.06	104	14.36	72	Bases Empty	.267	79	13.16	113	15.79	57
Steve Carlton	vs. Lefties	.292	--	10.67	--	16.00	--	Runners On	.305	101	15.92	114	13.88	70
	vs. Righties	.300	106	11.57	100	14.85	68	Bases Empty	.294	111	7.64	56	15.97	54
Mark Davis	vs. Lefties	.131	1	9.47	60	37.89	1	Runners On	.250	44	14.01	106	22.29	7
	vs. Righties	.244	54	10.12	90	21.86	16	Bases Empty	.185	4	6.49	34	29.73	1
Kelly Downs	vs. Lefties	.234	40	9.28	55	15.98	50	Runners On	.191	7	10.18	60	15.57	50
	vs. Righties	.238	48	6.74	39	18.54	39	Bases Empty	.268	85	6.34	30	18.54	31
Scott Garrelts	vs. Lefties	.237	42	11.11	78	14.47	67	Runners On	.220	18	12.26	91	19.68	20
	vs. Righties	.223	24	9.39	81	20.91	22	Bases Empty	.238	38	8.85	84	15.72	58
Mike Krukow	vs. Lefties	.227	32	7.17	30	16.61	44	Runners On	.228	25	7.57	21	16.49	40
	vs. Righties	.219	19	3.37	4	20.00	30	Bases Empty	.221	19	4.38	12	18.96	27
Mike LaCoss	vs. Lefties	.228	34	8.77	45	10.02	101	Runners On	.282	87	9.39	46	7.88	112
	vs. Righties	.255	73	7.71	56	10.47	103	Bases Empty	.215	14	7.62	55	11.72	102
Roger Mason	vs. Lefties	.266	73	14.00	107	16.67	41	Runners On	.266	--	14.41	--	17.80	--
	vs. Righties	.229	--	8.04	--	16.07	--	Bases Empty	.238	39	9.03	85	15.28	62
Greg Minton	vs. Lefties	.302	99	13.82	104	6.58	114	Runners On	.260	57	14.38	110	10.00	99
	vs. Righties	.200	10	9.03	78	16.67	51	Bases Empty	.242	44	8.09	68	13.24	85
Terry Mulholland	vs. Lefties	.273	--	18.18	--	12.73	--	Runners On	.273	--	15.32	--	11.71	--
	vs. Righties	.245	58	13.16	110	10.53	102	Bases Empty	.235	33	13.43	114	10.45	108
Jeff Robinson	vs. Lefties	.278	81	8.00	38	17.50	38	Runners On	.290	92	11.24	75	22.49	5
	vs. Righties	.196	9	6.93	43	23.81	7	Bases Empty	.201	8	4.96	17	19.85	21
Frank Williams	vs. Lefties	.232	37	11.11	78	8.64	109	Runners On	.197	--	11.36	--	14.77	--
	vs. Righties	.198	--	10.62	--	23.01	--	Bases Empty	.223	--	10.38	--	18.87	--
Team Average	vs. Lefties	.240	3	9.98	7	15.38	6	Runners On	.247	3	11.59	12	15.22	5
	vs. Righties	.233	2	9.46	12	17.05	5	Bases Empty	.229	2	8.28	9	17.08	5
League Average	vs. Lefties	.257		9.83		14.90		Runners On	.260		10.11		15.02	
	vs. Righties	.251		8.19		16.33		Bases Empty	.248		7.89		16.30	

Additional Miscellaneous Pitching Comparisons

	Grass Surface BA	Rank	Artificial Surface BA	Rank	Home Games BA	Rank	Road Games BA	Rank	Runners in Scoring Position BA	Rank	Runners in Scoring Pos and Two Outs BA	Rank	Leading Off Inning OBA	Rank
Juan Berenguer	.235	38	.252	53	.258	74	.227	20	.250	55	.200	33	.250	11
Vida Blue	.227	26	.266	74	.230	35	.253	52	.213	22	.215	42	.344	90
Steve Carlton	.303	110	.295	107	.327	115	.274	79	.254	64	.356	114	.342	86
Mark Davis	.219	14	.192	--	.241	53	.186	3	.250	55	.333	110	.237	6
Kelly Downs	.233	35	.243	--	.229	32	.241	37	.195	13	.292	92	.308	51
Scott Garrelts	.221	15	.280	94	.191	10	.280	86	.213	21	.164	15	.314	61
Mike Krukow	.225	22	.217	17	.206	16	.241	38	.196	14	.123	4	.271	19
Mike LaCoss	.229	27	.270	79	.202	15	.281	90	.312	107	.303	100	.300	46
Roger Mason	.231	31	.314	--	.222	28	.280	88	.278	84	.261	--	.397	113
Greg Minton	.242	45	.274	--	.212	18	.283	94	.250	55	.204	36	.305	49
Terry Mulholland	.242	47	.289	--	.200	14	.312	--	.232	--	.125	5	.387	107
Jeff Robinson	.227	25	.256	59	.233	43	.234	27	.280	87	.225	49	.212	2
Frank Williams	.181	2	.286	--	.118	--	.278	--	.220	--	.188	--	.349	--
Team Average	.231	1	.253	6	.219	3	.254	4	.236	3	.220	4	.308	5
League Average	.254		.253		.247		.260		.252		.235		.316	
League Average	.254		.253		.247		.260		.252		.235		.316	

III
Batter Section

Batter Section

The Batter Section is an alphabetical listing of every player who had at least 200 plate appearances in either the American or the National League last season. Also included are key players who did not meet the 200-plate-appearance requirement. Players are listed alphabetically within each league, followed by the totals for each team and the league as a whole.

Column Headings Information

Tony Armas   Bats Right
Boston Red Sox   AB H 2B 3B HR RRF BB SO BA SA OBA

AB	At Bats
H	Hits
2B	Doubles
3B	Triples
HR	Home Runs
RRF	Runs Responsible For (See below)
BB	Bases on Balls
SO	Strikeouts
BA	Batting Average
SA	Slugging Average
OBA	On-Base Average

For each player, information is provided in eleven offensive categories. The only one that may be unfamiliar is RRF, *Runs Responsible For*. RRF includes official runs batted in, but also includes all other plays on which runners score following a batter's action, even if no RBI is officially given. (Examples include a runner scoring from third on a ground-ball double play, a runner scoring as a result of a fielder's error on a batted ball, or a batter hitting a triple and scoring on an error on the same play. Runs scored on such plays as a wild pitch or an error resulting from a pickoff attempt are not credited to the batter.)

Season Summary Information

Season	493	129	29	1	27	91	38	68	.262	.489	.341
vs. Left-Handed Pitchers	188	53	9	0	9	38	18	27	.282	.473	.366
vs. Right-Handed Pitchers	305	76	20	1	18	53	20	41	.249	.498	.326
Home	223	55	11	0	10	43	18	38	.247	.430	.325
Road	270	74	18	1	17	48	20	30	.274	.537	.354
Grass	409	106	26	0	21	79	33	57	.259	.477	.336
Artificial Turf	84	23	3	1	6	12	5	11	.274	.548	.365
April	74	16	6	0	3	7	0	9	.216	.419	.244
May	75	21	4	0	6	12	10	12	.280	.573	.386
June	87	23	3	0	7	24	11	9	.264	.540	.360
July	88	22	6	0	3	11	6	10	.250	.420	.316
August	98	25	4	1	5	21	7	14	.255	.469	.333
Sept./Oct.	71	22	6	0	3	16	4	14	.310	.521	.402

Each player's seasonal performance is broken down into a variety of special categories. The first line for each player gives his totals for the whole season. This is followed by breakdowns of his performance against left- and right-handed pitchers, in home and road games, on grass fields and on artificial turf, and in each month. (For players who played for more than one team within a league, all totals are combined. The "home" totals for Spike Owen, for example, include all games he played in Seattle while with the Mariners, and all games played in Boston while with the Red Sox.)

Leading Off Inn.	107	25	5	0	6	6	8	16	.234	.449	.311
Runners On	272	72	18	0	13	77	20	39	.265	.474	.343
Runners/Scor. Pos.	140	35	9	0	3	51	13	15	.250	.379	.337
Runners On/2 Out	133	29	6	0	5	26	11	19	.218	.376	.325
Scor. Pos./2 Out	60	11	2	0	0	12	7	7	.183	.217	.319

Following these breakdowns, each batter's performance is divided into specific game situations. Totals are given for each batter when he led off an inning and when he batted with runners on base. These are followed by his performance with runners in scoring position (on second or third base, or both), with runners on base and two out, and with runners in scoring position and two out.

Late Inning Pressure	90	23	6	1	3	13	5	13	.256	.444	.299
Bases Empty	42	12	5	1	2	2	1	7	.286	.595	.318
Runners On	48	11	1	0	1	11	4	6	.229	.313	.283
Runners/Scor. Pos.	26	7	1	0	1	11	3	2	.269	.423	.333

The next group shows the batter's performance in late-inning pressure situations: any plate appearances occurring in the seventh inning or later with the score tied or with the batter's team trailing by one, two, or three runs (or four runs if the bases are loaded).

Each player's totals are listed for all late-inning pressure situations, then broken out for his performance when leading off an inning, with runners on base, and with runners in scoring position.

DRIVING IN RUNS	From 1B	From 2B	From 3B	Scoring Position
Total	6/138	14/80	21/57	35/137
Percentage	4%	18%	37%	26%
Driving In Runners from 3B with Less than Two Out:			15/30	50%

The next section, labeled "Driving In Runs," is a measure of the player's ability to drive in runners from each base. For every base, two numbers are listed: the first is the number of RRFs credited to the batter for bringing home runners from that base; the second is the total number of opportunities the batter faced for that situation. (For example, the notation "14/31" under runners on second would mean that the player batted 31 times with runners on second and drove home 14 of the runners.) Plate appearances that result in a base on balls, hit batsman, sacrifice bunt, or an award of first base through catcher's interference are not treated as "opportunities" if they do not result in a run.

If there is more than one runner on base, the batter is charged with an "opportunity" to drive in each base runner. A single with the bases loaded that scores only the runner from third is an opportunity and an RRF for the "From 3B" line, but an unsuccessful opportunity for the "From 2B" and "From 1B" lines. (The exception to this is when a base on balls, hit batsman, sacrifice bunt, or award through interference results in a run. A walk with the bases loaded would result in an RRF and an opportunity for the "From 3B" line, but would not be charged as an unsuccessful opportunity for the other two.)

Also given is the percentage of successful opportunities; runners driven in from scoring position (combining the "From 3B" and "From 2B" totals); and a line summarizing the batter's performance driving in runners from third with less than two out.

Following the "Driving In Runs" information are comments for each player. Included are the pitchers each batter loves to face and hates to face. The statistics listed for each individual match-up are from regular season games since 1975.

American League

Andy Allanson
Cleveland Indians — Bats Right

	AB	H	2B	3B	HR	RRF	BB	SO	BA	SA	OBA
Season	293	66	7	3	1	31	14	36	.225	.280	.260
vs. Left-Handers	84	23	3	1	0	9	4	12	.274	.333	.307
vs. Right-Handers	209	43	4	2	1	22	10	24	.206	.258	.241
Home	147	35	3	2	0	16	6	13	.238	.286	.268
Road	146	31	4	1	1	15	8	23	.212	.274	.252
Grass	262	58	5	3	0	28	12	31	.221	.263	.255
Artificial Turf	31	8	2	0	1	3	2	5	.258	.419	.294
April	49	19	0	1	0	7	1	2	.388	.429	.392
May	64	13	3	1	0	5	3	7	.203	.281	.250
June	53	11	2	1	1	9	3	11	.208	.340	.241
July	42	9	0	0	0	6	5	2	.214	.214	.292
August	47	6	1	0	0	1		10	.128	.149	.146
Sept./Oct.	38	8	1	0	0	4	1	4	.211	.237	.231
Leading Off Inn.	63	18	1	0	0		2	3	.286	.302	.318
Runners On	144	38	4	3	1	31	4	20	.264	.354	.276
Runners/Scor. Pos.	85	22	0	3	1	30	2	9	.259	.365	.264
Runners On/2 Out	68	18	1	3	0	15	1	8	.265	.368	.275
Scor. Pos./2 Out	47	13	0	3	0	15	1	3	.277	.404	.292
Late Inning Pressure	32	11	2	1	0	3	3	3	.344	.469	.400
Leading Off	7	4	0	0	0	0	0		.571	.571	.571
Runners On	14	5	2	1	0	3	1	2	.357	.643	.400
Runners/Scor. Pos.	5	2	0	1	0	3	1	0	.400	.800	.500

DRIVING IN RUNS	From 1B	From 2B	From 3B	Scoring Position
Totals	3/96	14/68	13/35	27/103
Percentage	3%	21%	37%	26%
Driving In Runners from 3B with Less than Two Out:			8/16	50%

Loves to face: Mike Flanagan (3-for-3)
Hates to face: Oil Can Boyd (0-for-9)
Batted 133 points higher in Late-Inning Pressure Situations (.344) than in nonpressure situations (.211), 2d-largest difference in A.L. last season (minimum: 25 LIP AB).... Collected 11 of his 29 RBI in nine games vs. Milwaukee.... Batted .250 in day games, .209 at night.... Only A.L. rookie catcher to start majority (91) of his team's games.... Caught 55 percent of innings for Tribe last season; Bando caught 45 percent. Indians were only major-league team that had just two players catch last season.... Lowest fielding percentage (.960) among major-league catchers (minimum: 50 games), and most errors (20) by catcher in A.L. since Thurman Munson committed 23 in 1975.

Tony Armas
Boston Red Sox — Bats Right

	AB	H	2B	3B	HR	RRF	BB	SO	BA·	SA	OBA
Season	425	112	21	4	11	61	24	77	.264	.409	.305
vs. Left-Handers	128	37	10	1	2	16	6	17	.289	.430	.319
vs. Right-Handers	297	75	11	3	9	45	18	60	.253	.401	.299
Home	210	57	14	2	5	38	17	31	.271	.429	.328
Road	215	55	7	2	6	23	7	46	.256	.391	.281
Grass	372	96	18	3	10	53	23	70	.258	.403	.304
Artificial Turf	53	16	3	1	1	8	1	7	.302	.453	.309
April	62	13	3	0	1	2	4	16	.210	.306	.269
May	43	11	1	0	0	5	2	10	.256	.279	.289
June	61	20	4	1	2	9	8	14	.328	.525	.406
July	40	11	2	1	1	5	0	8	.275	.450	.275
August	113	30	5	2	7	25	8	16	.265	.531	.317
Sept./Oct.	106	27	6	0	0	15	2	13	.255	.311	.266
Leading Off Inn.	98	29	3	2	4	4	3	17	.296	.490	.317
Runners On	188	53	12	2	5	55	13	33	.282	.447	.328
Runners/Scor. Pos.	97	28	6	1	3	47	9	13	.289	.464	.343
Runners On/2 Out	73	25	6	1	3	27	7	8	.342	.575	.407
Scor. Pos./2 Out	43	14	4	1	2	23	6	5	.326	.605	.408
Late Inning Pressure	47	11	1	0	0	2	2	16	.234	.255	.265
Leading Off	10	5	1	0	0	0	0		.500	.600	.500
Runners On	20	2	0	0	0	2	1	9	.100	.100	.143
Runners/Scor. Pos.	12	2	0	0	0	2	1	2	.167	.167	.231

DRIVING IN RUNS	From 1B	From 2B	From 3B	Scoring Position
Totals	11/151	19/81	20/41	39/122
Percentage	7%	23%	49%	32%
Driving In Runners from 3B with Less than Two Out:			14/25	56%

Loves to face: Roy Lee Jackson (.524, 11-for-21, 3 HR)
Hates to face: Stoddards (Bob 0-for-7; Tim .067, 1-for-15)
Last year's 24 walks and 11 home runs finally lifted his career total of walks (230) above his home run total (224).... Of those 230 walks, however, 39 are intentional.... Only player in majors whose batting average has been in .260s in each of last three seasons.... Career batting average of .165 at Tiger Stadium, his lowest at any A.L. ballpark.... Ten home runs in 122 career at bats at the Metrodome.... Had batted under .200 in Late-Inning Pressure Situations in each season from 1983 to 1985.... Since joining Red Sox in 1983, has hit for a higher average at Fenway (.275) than in road games (.230), but has hit the majority of his home runs on the road (59 of 113).

Harold Baines
Chicago White Sox — Bats Left

	AB	H	2B	3B	HR	RRF	BB	SO	BA	SA	OBA
Season	570	169	29	2	21	92	38	89	.296	.465	.338
vs. Left-Handers	206	54	8	1	3	19	10	38	.262	.354	.297
vs. Right-Handers	364	115	21	1	18	73	28	51	.316	.527	.361
Home	275	91	16	2	8	52	21	35	.331	.491	.372
Road	295	78	13	0	13	40	17	54	.264	.441	.306
Grass	486	147	22	2	19	82	35	78	.302	.473	.347
Artificial Turf	84	22	7	0	2	10	3	11	.262	.417	.287
April	75	19	1	0	5	14	3	15	.253	.467	.282
May	106	35	5	0	3	15	8	12	.330	.462	.370
June	105	34	7	1	2	22	12	12	.324	.467	.383
July	97	27	8	1	3	12	9	18	.278	.474	.340
August	99	29	1	0	7	16	2	16	.293	.515	.311
Sept./Oct.	88	25	7	0	1	13	4	16	.284	.398	.315
Leading Off Inn.	100	26	7	0	1	1	5	15	.260	.360	.295
Runners On	242	78	11	1	8	79	19	38	.322	.475	.361
Runners/Scor. Pos.	142	41	7	1	5	71	15	22	.289	.458	.339
Runners On/2 Out	80	21	2	0	4	25	8	12	.263	.438	.330
Scor. Pos./2 Out	55	14	2	0	3	23	7	9	.255	.455	.339
Late Inning Pressure	83	24	2	0	6	16	8	17	.289	.530	.352
Leading Off	21	4	0	0	0	0	2	5	.190	.190	.261
Runners On	34	10	0	0	2	12	5	7	.294	.471	.385
Runners/Scor. Pos.	17	6	0	0	1	10	4	3	.353	.529	.476

DRIVING IN RUNS	From 1B	From 2B	From 3B	Scoring Position
Totals	10/164	25/104	36/68	61/172
Percentage	6%	24%	53%	35%
Driving In Runners from 3B with Less than Two Out:			29/45	64%

Loves to face: Edwin Nunez (.571, 4-for-7, 2 HR)
Hates to face: Dennis Leonard (0-for-15)
First White Sox player to have five straight 20-home run seasons; no other player in team history has had more than three.... Has hit 66 career home runs at Comiskey Park; he's in a race against time and the wrecker's ball to become the first player to hit 100 career home runs there: Bill Melton holds the record with 90.... Hit six 9th-inning homers last season, tying Balboni and Barfield for major-league lead.... Only one home run in 143 career at bats at Cleveland Stadium.... Six home runs and 15 RBI in 12 games vs. Detroit last season.... Has batted for a higher average with runners on base than with bases empty in each of the last four seasons.

Dusty Baker
Oakland As — Bats Right

	AB	H	2B	3B	HR	RRF	BB	SO	BA	SA	OBA
Season	242	58	8	0	4	22	27	37	.240	.322	.314
vs. Left-Handers	110	25	3	0	2	12	13	16	.227	.309	.306
vs. Right-Handers	132	33	5	0	2	10	14	21	.250	.333	.320
Home	112	25	2	0	1	9	15	15	.223	.268	.313
Road	130	33	6	0	3	13	12	22	.254	.369	.315
Grass	193	46	5	0	4	18	23	25	.238	.326	.318
Artificial Turf	49	12	3	0	0	4	4	12	.245	.306	.296
April	51	12	0	0	2	7	5	5	.235	.353	.304
May	38	7	0	0	0	1	3	6	.184	.184	.244
June	55	18	2	0	0	4	5	10	.327	.364	.377
July	39	7	0	0	2	5	8	6	.179	.333	.319
August	28	5	3	0	0	1	2	7	.179	.286	.226
Sept./Oct.	31	9	3	0	0	4	4	3	.290	.387	.371
Leading Off Inn.	60	14	4	0	0	0	8	7	.233	.300	.324
Runners On	104	27	2	0	2	20	16	19	.260	.337	.352
Runners/Scor. Pos.	55	15	1	0	1	17	9	7	.273	.345	.364
Runners On/2 Out	43	11	0	0	0	8	8	6	.256	.256	.373
Scor. Pos./2 Out	29	8	0	0	0	8	6		.276	.276	.364
Late Inning Pressure	38	8	1	0	1	4	5	6	.211	.316	.295
Leading Off	6	2	1	0	0	0	2	2	.333	.500	.500
Runners On	18	3	0	0	0	3	3	1	.167	.167	.273
Runners/Scor. Pos.	11	2	0	0	0	3	1	0	.182	.182	.231

DRIVING IN RUNS	From 1B	From 2B	From 3B	Scoring Position
Totals	2/84	8/41	8/24	16/65
Percentage	2%	20%	33%	25%
Driving In Runners from 3B with Less than Two Out:			4/13	31%

Loves to face: Al Nipper (.800, 4-for-5)
Hates to face: Willie Hernandez (1-for-14)
Name the three current major-league ballparks in which he has never homered. Answer below.... Hit four home runs last season, all against the Brewers.... Started 36 of 53 games in which Oakland faced a starting left-hander, 32 of 109 against right-handers.... Batting average vs. left-handed pitchers (.227) was his lowest in last 12 years.... Two hits in his last 23 at bats with bases loaded.... Some names from his first big-league box score (Sept. 7, 1968): Lee Thomas, John Buzhardt, Tito Francona.... Did anyone out there correctly guess Tiger Stadium, the Metrodome, and Yankee Stadium?

Steve Balboni
Kansas City Royals   Bats Right

	AB	H	2B	3B	HR	RRF	BB	SO	BA	SA	OBA
Season	512	117	25	1	29	91	43	146	.229	.451	.286
vs. Left-Handers	134	37	6	0	12	30	20	37	.276	.590	.370
vs. Right-Handers	378	80	19	1	17	61	23	109	.212	.402	.255
Home	251	51	14	1	10	40	23	75	.203	.386	.264
Road	261	66	11	0	19	51	20	71	.253	.513	.309
Grass	215	55	9	0	18	46	18	53	.256	.549	.316
Artificial Turf	297	62	16	1	11	45	25	93	.209	.380	.265
April	73	18	3	0	3	5	5	16	.247	.411	.295
May	95	17	3	0	4	12	13	30	.179	.337	.284
June	105	23	8	0	8	28	9	35	.219	.524	.271
July	97	26	6	0	5	17	8	19	.268	.485	.321
August	110	29	3	1	8	24	4	33	.264	.527	.289
Sept./Oct.	32	4	2	0	1	5	4	13	.125	.281	.216
Leading Off Inn.	120	34	6	1	11	11	12	30	.283	.625	.353
Runners On	233	53	13	0	11	73	16	62	.227	.425	.271
Runners/Scor. Pos.	145	32	5	0	7	59	13	41	.221	.400	.274
Runners On/2 Out	99	22	5	0	4	25	7	26	.222	.394	.274
Scor. Pos./2 Out	62	13	1	0	3	20	6	17	.210	.371	.279
Late Inning Pressure	84	21	5	0	4	17	3	19	.250	.452	.278
Leading Off	25	5	0	0	2	2	1	7	.200	.440	.259
Runners On	41	12	4	0	1	14	2	9	.293	.463	.311
Runners/Scor. Pos.	21	6	1	0	0	9	2	5	.286	.333	.320

DRIVING IN RUNS	From 1B	From 2B	From 3B	Scoring Position
Totals	15/176	22/118	25/60	47/178
Percentage	9%	19%	42%	26%
Driving In Runners from 3B with Less than Two Out:		20/34	59%	

Loves to face: Walt Terrell (.571, 8-for-14, 2 HR)
Hates to face: Jose Rijo (.091, 1-for-11, 8 SO)

In three seasons with Royals, has hit 56 home runs on road (18 or more in each season), only 37 at Kansas City.... Hit six 9th-inning homers last season, tying for major-league lead. ... Walked four times with bases loaded last season.... Nine home runs in 69 career at bats at Anaheim Stadium.... Batted .295, with 12 home runs in 146 at bats in day games; .202, with 17 home runs in 366 at bats at night.... Career batting average of .219 (7-for-32, 3 home runs) with bases loaded.... Career rate of one walk every 8.3 plate appearances vs. left-handed pitchers, one every 16.6 PA vs. right-handers.... Led major-league first basemen in errors for second time in past three years.

Chris Bando
Cleveland Indians   Bats Left and Right

	AB	H	2B	3B	HR	RRF	BB	SO	BA	SA	OBA
Season	254	68	9	0	2	27	22	49	.268	.327	.325
vs. Left-Handers	73	22	1	0	1	6	0	8	.301	.356	.301
vs. Right-Handers	181	46	8	0	1	21	22	41	.254	.315	.333
Home	118	34	5	0	1	14	6	19	.288	.356	.315
Road	136	34	4	0	1	13	16	30	.250	.301	.333
Grass	195	50	8	0	1	22	19	35	.256	.313	.321
Artificial Turf	59	18	1	0	1	5	3	14	.305	.373	.339
April	18	8	1	0	0	3	0	1	.444	.500	.444
May	27	8	1	0	1	6	5	7	.296	.444	.406
June	35	8	0	0	0	6	5	7	.229	.229	.270
July	42	9	2	0	0	7	5	7	.214	.262	.294
August	62	19	3	0	0	4	6	15	.306	.355	.368
Sept./Oct.	70	16	2	0	1	7	4	14	.229	.300	.270
Leading Off Inn.	52	14	2	0	0		6	16	.269	.308	.345
Runners On	119	34	6	0	1	26	11	15	.286	.361	.338
Runners/Scor. Pos.	73	20	4	0	1	25	9	11	.274	.370	.341
Runners On/2 Out	44	11	3	0	0	10	6	8	.250	.340	.340
Scor. Pos./2 Out	28	8	3	0	0	10	6	6	.286	.393	.412
Late Inning Pressure	49	11	2	0	0	4	3	16	.224	.265	.264
Leading Off	15	3	1	0	0	0	2	7	.200	.267	.294
Runners On	19	3	0	0	0	4	2	1	.158	.158	.190
Runners/Scor. Pos.	12	3	0	0	0	4	1	0	.250	.250	.286

DRIVING IN RUNS	From 1B	From 2B	From 3B	Scoring Position
Totals	3/86	8/60	14/30	22/90
Percentage	3%	13%	47%	24%
Driving In Runners from 3B with Less than Two Out:		9/19	47%	

Loves to face: Tom Seaver (.714, 5-for-7, 1 HR)
Hates to face: Don Sutton (.091, 1-for-11)

Started 53 of 114 games in which Indians faced a right-handed starter; 19 of 49 vs. left-handers. ... One hit in 16 at bats vs. Oakland last season, .174 career record against brother Sal's old team. ... Career batting average of .195 in Late-Inning Pressure Situations, .244 in nonpressure situations. ... Career breakdown: .245 with bases empty, .227 with runners on base, .214 with runners in scoring position, .190 (4-for-21) with the bases loaded. ... Only stolen base of major-league career came on Aug. 24, 1984, against Boyd-Gedman battery; he's been caught five times.... Has been hit by a pitch only once in 1150 plate appearances: by Gene Nelson, in July 1986.

Jesse Barfield
Toronto Blue Jays   Bats Right

	AB	H	2B	3B	HR	RRF	BB	SO	BA	SA	OBA
Season	589	170	35	2	40	113	69	146	.289	.559	.368
vs. Left-Handers	148	42	9	0	9	29	27	41	.284	.527	.397
vs. Right-Handers	441	128	26	2	31	84	42	105	.290	.569	.358
Home	291	81	22	1	16	55	42	70	.278	.526	.371
Road	298	89	13	1	24	58	27	76	.299	.591	.365
Grass	235	70	11	1	16	44	24	59	.298	.557	.370
Artificial Turf	354	100	24	1	24	69	45	87	.282	.559	.367
April	75	19	6	0	2	6	4	25	.253	.413	.300
May	105	29	4	0	9	26	12	16	.276	.571	.358
June	110	35	7	1	8	28	10	20	.318	.618	.379
July	91	31	7	1	7	17	17	23	.341	.670	.455
August	93	30	7	0	4	20	16	26	.323	.527	.418
Sept./Oct.	115	26	4	0	10	16	10	36	.226	.522	.288
Leading Off Inn.	135	38	6	0	11	11	14	36	.281	.570	.353
Runners On	254	74	19	0	13	86	38	61	.291	.520	.381
Runners/Scor. Pos.	156	43	9	0	7	68	32	36	.276	.468	.389
Runners On/2 Out	103	25	3	0	7	32	16	25	.243	.476	.345
Scor. Pos./2 Out	73	17	3	0	4	26	13	17	.233	.438	.349
Late Inning Pressure	105	30	4	0	7	21	10	32	.286	.524	.345
Leading Off	28	8	0	0	3	3	3	11	.286	.607	.355
Runners On	38	12	4	0	2	16	4	12	.316	.579	.372
Runners/Scor. Pos.	26	7	1	0	2	13	3	9	.269	.538	.333

DRIVING IN RUNS	From 1B	From 2B	From 3B	Scoring Position
Totals	20/175	22/117	31/66	53/183
Percentage	11%	19%	47%	29%
Driving In Runners from 3B with Less than Two Out:		21/39	54%	

Loves to face: Eric King (.500, 4-for-8, 2 HR)
Hates to face: Roger Clemens (.077, 1-for-13)

First player on either of the Canadian teams to lead his league in home runs.... Led major leagues in home runs (31) and extra-base hits (59) vs. right-handed pitchers. ... Yearly batting average vs. right-handed pitchers since 1982: .223, .244, .248, .277, .290.... Hit six 9th-inning homers last season, tying Baines and Balboni for major-league lead. ... One of six A.L. players to connect against every opposing club in 1986.... First major-league outfielder with 20 or more assists two years in a row since Johnny Callison in 1962–63; last A.L. outfielder to do it: Joe DiMaggio, 1937–38.... Career rate of 12.3 assists per 100 games is highest among active outfielders (minimum: 500 games).

Marty Barrett
Boston Red Sox   Bats Right

	AB	H	2B	3B	HR	RRF	BB	SO	BA	SA	OBA
Season	625	179	39	4	4	66	65	31	.286	.381	.353
vs. Left-Handers	171	55	12	2	4	23	29	7	.322	.485	.418
vs. Right-Handers	454	124	27	2	0	43	36	24	.273	.341	.326
Home	302	84	18	0	4	34	33	19	.278	.377	.350
Road	323	95	21	4	0	32	32	12	.294	.384	.355
Grass	529	152	30	3	4	53	54	28	.278	.378	.353
Artificial Turf	96	27	9	1	0	13	11	3	.281	.396	.352
April	63	19	4	1	1	6	8	1	.302	.444	.380
May	115	32	8	2	0	14	10	6	.278	.383	.331
June	112	32	8	0	0	6	9	5	.286	.357	.339
July	106	29	4	0	1	6	8	8	.274	.340	.325
August	115	36	11	0	1	18	14	7	.313	.435	.382
Sept./Oct.	114	31	4	1	1	16	16	6	.272	.351	.366
Leading Off Inn.	186	56	14	1	1		11	7	.301	.403	.343
Runners On	242	70	15	2	3	65	36	12	.289	.405	.376
Runners/Scor. Pos.	135	42	11	2	1	60	21	11	.311	.444	.394
Runners On/2 Out	95	29	7	2	1	35	15	5	.305	.453	.400
Scor. Pos./2 Out	67	23	6	2	1	35	10	5	.343	.537	.429
Late Inning Pressure	64	23	10	1	0	13	9	2	.359	.547	.438
Leading Off	14	6	3	0	0	0	2	0	.429	.643	.467
Runners On	32	12	6	1	0	13	4	2	.375	.625	.444
Runners/Scor. Pos.	19	8	5	1	0	13	2	2	.421	.789	.476

DRIVING IN RUNS	From 1B	From 2B	From 3B	Scoring Position
Totals	7/174	30/111	24/53	54/164
Percentage	4%	27%	45%	33%
Driving In Runners from 3B with Less than Two Out:		14/27	52%	

Loves to face: Ken Schrom (.800, 4-for-5)
Hates to face: Bret Saberhagen (.091, 1-for-11)

Career batting average of .312 with two out and runners in scoring position, 6th highest over past 12 years among players with 50 or more hits in such situations; only Boggs, Puckett, Hisle, Munson, and Al Oliver are ahead of him.... Respect his power against lefties at Fenway: He had four home runs in 84 at bats in such circumstances, none in 541 at bats otherwise.... Tied for major league lead with 18 sacrifice bunts. ... Struck out twice in one game by same pitcher only three times last year: twice by Phil Niekro, once by McCaskill.... Has struck out only 21 times in 607 regular-season plate appearances vs. left-handers; no left-handed pitcher has ever fanned him twice in one game.

Don Baylor

Bats Right

Boston Red Sox	AB	H	2B	3B	HR	RRF	BB	SO	BA	SA	OBA
Season	585	139	23	1	31	100	62	111	.238	.439	.344
vs. Left-Handers	152	35	7	1	5	18	24	27	.230	.388	.359
vs. Right-Handers	433	104	16	0	26	82	38	84	.240	.457	.338
Home	279	65	13	0	9	49	40	46	.233	.376	.370
Road	306	74	10	1	22	51	22	65	.242	.497	.317
Grass	491	118	20	1	26	88	59	89	.240	.444	.357
Artificial Turf	94	21	3	0	5	12	3	22	.223	.415	.267
April	71	17	0	0	4	12	10	9	.239	.408	.333
May	105	27	7	0	6	26	10	19	.257	.495	.360
June	95	24	5	1	5	17	9	20	.253	.484	.379
July	96	22	3	0	4	13	7	20	.229	.385	.299
August	107	22	2	0	7	14	14	20	.206	.421	.325
Sept./Oct.	111	27	6	0	5	18	12	23	.243	.432	.356
Leading Off Inn.	116	28	2	0	9	9	11	28	.241	.491	.343
Runners On	289	64	13	0	15	84	34	47	.221	.422	.345
Runners/Scor. Pos.	170	36	9	0	7	68	28	29	.212	.388	.356
Runners On/2 Out	127	21	4	0	5	24	16	26	.165	.315	.307
Scor. Pos./2 Out	85	14	3	0	2	18	14	17	.165	.271	.330
Late Inning Pressure	61	13	2	0	4	17	4	13	.213	.443	.324
Leading Off	13	3	0	0	0	0	0	2	.231	.231	.286
Runners On	30	8	2	0	3	16	4	7	.267	.633	.405
Runners/Scor. Pos.	22	4	1	0	1	12	3	6	.182	.364	.308

DRIVING IN RUNS	From 1B	From 2B	From 3B	Scoring Position
Totals	12/225	26/138	31/71	57/209
Percentage	5%	19%	44%	27%
Driving In Runners from 3B with Less than Two Out:			26/45	58%

Loves to face: Tom Candiotti (.545, 6-for-11, 3 HR)
Hates to face: Mike Witt (.053, 1-for-19)
One of four A.L. players with 20 or more home runs and 80 or more RBI in each of past five seasons; others: Baines, Rice, Ripken. . . . Needs eight sacrifice flies to tie Brooks Robinson's A.L. record of 114. . . . Hank Aaron holds the major-league mark (121). . . . Career total of hit by pitch (227) is 16 shy of Ron Hunt's all-time mark (243). Has been hit over 100 times more than any other active player (Chet Lemon's next at 124); Jim Beattie has hit him the most (five times). . . . 1986 batting average in Late-Inning Pressure Situations was his lowest in past 12 years; LIP batting average since 1975 is .296. . . . Has batted .398 (41-for-103) with bases loaded over the last eight seasons.

George Bell

Bats Right

Toronto Blue Jays	AB	H	2B	3B	HR	RRF	BB	SO	BA	SA	OBA
Season	641	198	38	6	31	112	41	62	.309	.532	.349
vs. Left-Handers	179	59	10	0	10	27	10	18	.330	.553	.363
vs. Right-Handers	462	139	28	6	21	85	31	44	.301	.524	.344
Home	300	98	17	5	15	59	24	22	.327	.567	.375
Road	341	100	21	1	16	53	17	40	.293	.501	.326
Grass	265	78	14	0	11	40	13	34	.294	.472	.327
Artificial Turf	376	120	24	6	20	72	28	28	.319	.574	.364
April	72	26	5	0	4	19	4	7	.361	.597	.390
May	113	35	5	3	3	17	10	11	.310	.487	.363
June	117	35	6	1	7	21	6	6	.299	.547	.325
July	104	33	6	1	9	24	10	13	.317	.654	.374
August	117	40	10	0	4	18	10	6	.342	.530	.398
Sept./Oct.	118	29	6	1	4	13	1	19	.246	.415	.258
Leading Off Inn.	161	49	9	1	8	8	5	22	.304	.522	.329
Runners On	306	97	19	3	11	92	22	24	.317	.507	.356
Runners/Scor. Pos.	174	55	13	1	8	78	19	15	.316	.540	.372
Runners On/2 Out	144	47	9	2	5	43	9	8	.326	.521	.366
Scor. Pos./2 Out	86	29	6	1	4	37	8	6	.337	.570	.394
Late Inning Pressure	105	26	4	2	4	21	4	10	.248	.438	.273
Leading Off	26	5	3	0	1	1	0	3	.192	.423	.192
Runners On	49	17	1	1	2	19	2	5	.347	.531	.365
Runners/Scor. Pos.	28	9	0	0	2	16	2	4	.321	.536	.355

DRIVING IN RUNS	From 1B	From 2B	From 3B	Scoring Position
Totals	19/210	31/136	31/67	62/203
Percentage	9%	23%	46%	31%
Driving In Runners from 3B with Less than Two Out:			17/35	49%

Loves to face: Neal Heaton (.409, 9-for-22)
Hates to face: Mark Clear (0-for-10)
One of two players with at least 25 homers, 85 RBIs, and a .275 average in each of last three seasons; other: Mike Schmidt. . . . Led the majors in hits with two outs and runners on. . . . Career breakdown in Late-Inning Pressure Situations: .351 with runners on base, .261 with bases empty. . . . Career batting average of .212 (21-for-99) at Yankee Stadium, the only A.L. ballpark in which he has not homered. . . . One of six A.L. players to homer against every opposing club in 1986. . . . Had 17 assists last season, 2d in A.L. behind Jesse Barfield's 20. . . . Temporary custodian of the Willie Aikens Cup: most career plate appearances (2286) among active players without a sacrifice bunt.

Juan Beniquez

Bats Right

Baltimore Orioles	AB	H	2B	3B	HR	RRF	BB	SO	BA	SA	OBA
Season	343	103	15	0	6	39	40	49	.300	.397	.372
vs. Left-Handers	128	43	6	0	3	16	16	15	.336	.453	.412
vs. Right-Handers	215	60	9	0	3	23	24	34	.279	.363	.348
Home	154	42	2	0	4	19	18	24	.273	.364	.349
Road	189	61	13	0	2	20	22	25	.323	.423	.392
Grass	285	85	11	0	6	32	32	42	.298	.400	.366
Artificial Turf	58	18	4	0	0	7	8	7	.310	.379	.403
April	22	7	1	0	0	2	5	3	.318	.364	.429
May	63	19	2	0	1	3	7	9	.302	.381	.366
June	62	21	2	0	3	8	6	7	.339	.516	.391
July	82	21	3	0	2	11	8	14	.256	.366	.337
August	46	13	3	0	0	8	6	6	.283	.348	.377
Sept./Oct.	68	22	4	0	0	7	8	10	.324	.382	.380
Leading Off Inn.	75	27	7	0	1	1	12	12	.360	.493	.455
Runners On	160	47	6	0	2	35	18	25	.294	.369	.360
Runners/Scor. Pos.	76	24	3	0	0	31	11	14	.316	.355	.389
Runners On/2 Out	49	11	1	0	0	6	6	8	.224	.245	.321
Scor. Pos./2 Out	30	6	1	0	0	6	3	4	.200	.233	.294
Late Inning Pressure	61	24	1	0	2	11	4	7	.393	.508	.426
Leading Off	13	6	1	0	0	0	1	1	.462	.538	.533
Runners On	31	13	0	0	1	10	0	5	.419	.516	.394
Runners/Scor. Pos.	16	7	0	0	0	8	0	3	.438	.438	.389

DRIVING IN RUNS	From 1B	From 2B	From 3B	Scoring Position
Totals	4/137	12/70	17/37	29/107
Percentage	3%	17%	46%	27%
Driving In Runners from 3B with Less than Two Out:			16/27	59%

Loves to face: Mike Mason (.563, 9-for-16)
Hates to face: Ted Higuera (.091, 1-for-11)
Batting average of .311 over last four seasons is highest by any right-handed batter in major leagues (minimum: 100 AB). . . . One of three major leaguers to bat over .300 in each of those four seasons (others: Boggs and Gwynn), but the only one to hit .300 or better *vs. left-handers* in each of those years (minimum: 100 AB). . . . Royals are his 7th A.L. team, tying record shared by Ken Brett, Woody Held, Eddie Robinson, and Ken Sanders; has never played in N.L.; modern major-league record is 10 clubs, by Bob Miller, Tommy Davis, and Brett. . . . Batted .302 in day games, .213 at night. . . . Six hits in 13 at bats with bases loaded last season, 15-for-36 over last four years.

Tony Bernazard

Bats Left and Right

Cleveland Indians	AB	H	2B	3B	HR	RRF	BB	SO	BA	SA	OBA
Season	562	169	28	4	17	74	53	77	.301	.456	.362
vs. Left-Handers	151	51	11	0	5	21	19	17	.338	.510	.419
vs. Right-Handers	411	118	17	4	12	53	34	60	.287	.436	.341
Home	286	94	12	3	9	41	26	37	.329	.486	.384
Road	276	75	16	1	8	33	27	40	.272	.424	.341
Grass	486	148	25	4	14	63	44	65	.305	.459	.363
Artificial Turf	76	21	3	0	3	11	9	12	.276	.434	.356
April	65	18	1	1	1	6	5	9	.277	.369	.333
May	89	28	6	1	1	9	10	13	.315	.438	.382
June	93	31	6	0	3	14	9	12	.333	.495	.388
July	110	33	4	0	5	16	13	10	.300	.473	.376
August	117	36	7	1	3	17	11	20	.308	.462	.374
Sept./Oct.	88	23	4	1	4	12	5	13	.261	.466	.302
Leading Off Inn.	190	57	12	3	7	7	15	25	.300	.505	.354
Runners On	225	70	14	0	5	62	23	26	.311	.440	.371
Runners/Scor. Pos.	134	37	7	0	3	55	20	15	.276	.396	.360
Runners On/2 Out	90	23	3	0	2	17	12	9	.256	.356	.356
Scor. Pos./2 Out	64	12	1	0	1	14	10	8	.188	.250	.307
Late Inning Pressure	71	17	6	0	0	3	7	15	.239	.324	.316
Leading Off	16	2	0	0	0	0	0	2	.125	.125	.176
Runners On	30	10	5	0	0	3	5	3	.333	.500	.429
Runners/Scor. Pos.	15	3	2	0	0	3	4	1	.200	.333	.368

DRIVING IN RUNS	From 1B	From 2B	From 3B	Scoring Position
Totals	6/154	26/110	25/52	51/162
Percentage	4%	24%	48%	31%
Driving In Runners from 3B with Less than Two Out:			19/25	76%

Loves to face: Mike Moore (.450, 9-for-20, 2 HR)
Hates to face: Mark Clear (.063, 1-for-16)
1986 batting average was 44 points higher than his career average entering season; yearly averages since 1984: .221, .274, .301. . . . Batted .299 in 144 games as a starter, but with help from backups, Indians were only A.L. team whose starting second basemen batted over .300. . . . Has batted .296 at home, .241 on road in three seasons with Indians. . . . Has homered in every A.L. ballpark except Arlington Stadium (107 career AB). . . . Since coming to Cleveland, has only one hit in 23 at bats in Late-Inning Pressure Situations with runners in scoring position and two outs, lowest average (.043) of any A.L. player with 20 or more at bats in such situations over last three years; N.L. low: Jeffrey Leonard, 0-for-27.

Buddy Biancalana

Kansas City Royals — Bats Left and Right

	AB	H	2B	3B	HR	RRF	BB	SO	BA	SA	OBA
Season	190	46	4	4	2	9	15	50	.242	.337	.298
vs. Left-Handers	31	8	0	1	0	1	3	7	.258	.323	.324
vs. Right-Handers	159	38	4	3	2	8	12	43	.239	.340	.292
Home	109	29	2	3	0	5	12	29	.266	.339	.339
Road	81	17	2	1	2	4	3	21	.210	.333	.238
Grass	54	10	0	1	2	4	3	16	.185	.333	.228
Artificial Turf	136	36	4	3	0	5	12	34	.265	.338	.324
April	8	1	0	0	0	0	0	1	.125	.125	.125
May	8	3	0	0	0	1	0	2	.375	.375	.375
June	47	14	0	1	2	2	5	13	.298	.468	.365
July	15	2	0	0	0	0	1	5	.133	.133	.188
August	32	8	0	0	0	1	7	13	.250	.250	.385
Sept./Oct.	80	18	4	3	0	5	2	16	.225	.350	.244
Leading Off Inn.	47	9	0	0	1	1	4	11	.191	.255	.255
Runners On	72	15	2	2	0	7	3	19	.208	.292	.240
Runners/Scor. Pos.	41	8	0	1	0	6	1	13	.195	.244	.214
Runners On/2 Out	37	6	1	1	0	2	1	11	.162	.243	.184
Scor. Pos./2 Out	25	3	0	0	0	1	1	9	.120	.120	.154
Late Inning Pressure	8	1	0	0	.0	0	1	5	.125	.125	.222
Leading Off	3	0	0	0	0	0	1	1	.000	.000	.250
Runners On	2	0	0	0	0	0	0	2	.000	.000	.000
Runners/Scor. Pos.	1	0	0	0	0	0	0	1	.000	.000	.000

DRIVING IN RUNS	From 1B	From 2B	From 3B	Scoring Position
Totals	2/50	2/32	3/12	5/44
Percentage	4%	6%	25%	11%
Driving In Runners from 3B with Less than Two Out:		2/3		67%

Loves to face: Al Nipper (.750, 3-for-4, 1 HR)
Hates to face: Walt Terrell (0-for-8)

Three homers in 26 career at bats in Anaheim; two in 453 career at bats everywhere else. . . . Career batting average of .232 vs. left-handers, only .208 from his power side vs. right-handers (his five HR were all hit off right-handers). . . . Reached 100 career hit plateau last Sept. 30, and is already two to the good on the path to 200. . . . Career batting average of .179 (5-for-28) in Late-Inning Pressure Situations; 0-for-7 in LIP situations with runners on base. . . . And then there were two: he now has a hit in every A.L. ballpark except Tiger Stadium and Yankee Stadium. . . . Over past three seasons, Royals have allowed 3.97 runs per nine innings with him at shortstop, 4.21 with others.

Bruce Bochte

Oakland As — Bats Left

	AB	H	2B	3B	HR	RRF	BB	SO	BA	SA	OBA
Season	407	104	13	1	6	47	65	68	.256	.337	.357
vs. Left-Handers	51	11	0	0	0	5	5	9	.216	.216	.286
vs. Right-Handers	356	93	13	1	6	42	60	59	.261	.354	.367
Home	198	49	5	1	3	25	36	32	.247	.328	.362
Road	209	55	8	0	3	22	29	36	.263	.344	.353
Grass	347	90	10	1	5	41	56	55	.259	.337	.361
Artificial Turf	60	14	3	0	1	6	9	13	.233	.333	.333
April	54	13	2	0	1	8	9	8	.241	.333	.349
May	63	14	2	0	3	5	11	10	.222	.397	.333
June	87	23	3	0	1	10	13	16	.264	.333	.360
July	54	20	3	0	0	7	10	10	.370	.426	.469
August	72	18	1	1	1	8	11	9	.250	.333	.349
Sept./Oct.	77	16	2	0	0	9	11	15	.208	.234	.307
Leading Off Inn.	87	24	4	0	1	1	13	14	.276	.356	.370
Runners On	172	47	3	1	1	42	31	30	.273	.320	.382
Runners/Scor. Pos.	101	26	2	0	0	39	26	20	.257	.277	.406
Runners On/2 Out	87	21	1	1	0	21	14	19	.241	.276	.347
Scor. Pos./2 Out	59	14	1	0	0	20	12	12	.237	.254	.366
Late Inning Pressure	61	17	2	0	1	4	13	12	.279	.361	.405
Leading Off	16	6	2	0	0	0	4	3	.375	.500	.500
Runners On	18	7	0	0	0	3	3	3	.389	.389	.476
Runners/Scor. Pos.	9	3	0	0	0	3	2	1	.333	.333	.455

DRIVING IN RUNS	From 1B	From 2B	From 3B	Scoring Position
Totals	4/120	20/80	17/39	37/119
Percentage	3%	25%	44%	31%
Driving In Runners from 3B with Less than Two Out:		11/20		55%

Loves to face: Dennis Leonard (.387, 24-for-62, 3 HR)
Hates to face: Bud Black (0-for-9)

Has never played on a team with a winning record in 12 seasons in major leagues; best mark: 77–85 by A's in '84 and '85. . . . Overall batting average was the lowest of his 12-year career. . . . Started 104 of 109 games in which A's faced a right-hander, but made only two starts vs. left-handers. . . . Batting average with runners on base has been higher than with bases empty in each of last seven seasons. . . . Yearly batting averages with runners in scoring position since 1982: .375 (did not play in 1983), .320, .300, .257. . . . Career total of 144 at bats at Exhibition Stadium, most among active players without a home run there, and the only A.L. ballpark in which Bochte hasn't homered.

Wade Boggs

Boston Red Sox — Bats Left

	AB	H	2B	3B	HR	RRF	BB	SO	BA	SA	OBA
Season	580	207	47	2	8	73	105	44	.357	.486	.453
vs. Left-Handers	182	64	12	2	3	27	22	18	.352	.489	.420
vs. Right-Handers	398	143	35	0	5	46	83	26	.359	.485	.467
Home	277	99	29	0	3	38	51	24	.357	.495	.456
Road	303	108	18	2	5	35	54	20	.356	.479	.450
Grass	488	172	42	0	8	65	89	40	.352	.488	.449
Artificial Turf	92	35	5	2	0	8	16	4	.380	.478	.472
April	72	22	7	0	2	13	17	5	.306	.486	.438
May	102	48	9	0	3	22	24	5	.471	.647	.567
June	77	26	5	0	0	5	10	13	.338	.403	.414
July	97	24	6	0	0	7	17	13	.247	.309	.357
August	119	42	8	2	2	15	19	4	.353	.504	.436
Sept./Oct.	113	45	12	0	1	11	18	4	.398	.531	.481
Leading Off Inn.	152	55	11	2	1	1	19	6	.362	.480	.433
Runners On	227	86	21	0	4	69	60	21	.379	.524	.502
Runners/Scor. Pos.	119	42	9	0	1	59	43	13	.353	.454	.512
Runners On/2 Out	92	34	8	0	2	36	28	9	.370	.522	.517
Scor. Pos./2 Out	61	22	5	0	1	32	25	7	.361	.492	.547
Late Inning Pressure	60	26	6	0	0	11	10	5	.433	.533	.500
Leading Off	19	8	1	0	0	0	1	0	.421	.474	.450
Runners On	21	9	3	0	0	11	9	3	.429	.571	.563
Runners/Scor. Pos.	11	5	1	0	0	10	7	2	.455	.545	.600

DRIVING IN RUNS	From 1B	From 2B	From 3B	Scoring Position
Totals	9/167	27/103	29/49	56/152
Percentage	5%	26%	59%	37%
Driving In Runners from 3B with Less than Two Out:		17/23		74%

Loves to face: Phil Niekro (.478, 11-for-23)
Hates to face: Dan Quisenberry (.105, 2-for-19)

Leading batters of all time (minimum: 2500 at bats): Ty Cobb, .367; Rogers Hornsby, .358; Joe Jackson, .356; Wade Boggs, .352. First change on that list since Hornsby retired in 1937. . . . Career batting average of .398 vs. right-handed pitchers at Fenway Park; overall career breakdown: .370 vs. right-handers, .311 vs. left-handers. . . . A .393 career hitter in Late-Inning Pressure Situations with runners on base. . . . Began successful quest for batting title by striking out in each of first three at bats of '86 season, vs. Jack Morris. That was his only three-strikeout game of season. . . . Has started in all nine lineup positions in his major-league career; six games batting ninth in 1982, and one game batting cleanup in 1983.

Bobby Bonilla

Chicago White Sox — Bats Left and Right

	AB	H	2B	3B	HR	RRF	BB	SO	BA	SA	OBA
Season	234	63	10	2	2	26	33	49	.269	.355	.361
vs. Left-Handers	93	25	5	0	0	10	9	12	.269	.323	.330
vs. Right-Handers	141	38	5	2	2	16	24	37	.270	.376	.380
Home	108	31	4	2	2	22	16	19	.287	.417	.381
Road	126	32	6	0	0	4	17	30	.254	.302	.343
Grass	206	59	8	2	2	24	28	39	.286	.374	.373
Artificial Turf	28	4	2	0	0	2	5	10	.143	.214	.273
April	46	14	2	1	0	4	5	8	.304	.391	.365
May	86	19	3	0	1	7	11	14	.221	.291	.316
June	68	20	4	1	1	13	15	19	.294	.426	.422
July	34	10	1	0	0	2	2	8	.294	.324	.333
August	0	0	0	0	0	0	0	0	—	—	—
Sept./Oct.	0	0	0	0	0	0	0	0	—	—	—
Leading Off Inn.	50	17	2	0	0	0	9	9	.340	.380	.450
Runners On	96	28	6	1	2	26	11	19	.292	.438	.361
Runners/Scor. Pos.	60	15	4	0	1	23	7	14	.250	.367	.324
Runners On/2 Out	33	9	2	0	1	10	4	8	.273	.424	.351
Scor. Pos./2 Out	25	6	2	0	0	8	3	7	.240	.320	.321
Late Inning Pressure	44	10	1	0	0	2	6	13	.227	.250	.320
Leading Off	9	3	1	0	0	0	2	2	.333	.444	.455
Runners On	17	4	0	0	0	2	2	4	.235	.235	.235
Runners/Scor. Pos.	12	2	0	0	0	2	0	4	.167	.167	.167

DRIVING IN RUNS	From 1B	From 2B	From 3B	Scoring Position
Totals	4/80	10/45	10/24	20/69
Percentage	5%	22%	42%	29%
Driving In Runners from 3B with Less than Two Out:		7/12		58%

Loves to face: Dennis Eckersley (.667, 2-for-3)
Hates to face: Jim Deshaies (0-for-6)

Figures above are for A.L. only; see also N.L. Batters Section. . . . Started 64 games for White Sox, half of them in left field; Chicago was 23–9 (.719) with him starting in left, 49–81 (.377) otherwise. . . . Bonilla's 32 starts in left were actually the most by any of the nine players whom Chicago used as starters there; that's the lowest total of games started by a team leader at any of the 208 team fielding positions (pitcher excluded) in the majors last season. . . . Bonilla batted .292 in his left-field starts; the eight other guys who LaRussa and Fregosi played out there batted a collective .212 with only 32 RBI in 130 games.

Juan Bonilla

Baltimore Orioles — Bats Right

	AB	H	2B	3B	HR	RRF	BB	SO	BA	SA	OBA
Season	284	69	10	1	1	20	25	21	.243	.296	.311
vs. Left-Handers	103	24	4	0	1	8	9	8	.233	.301	.295
vs. Right-Handers	181	45	6	1	0	12	16	13	.249	.293	.320
Home	122	24	4	0	0	8	12	9	.197	.230	.279
Road	162	45	6	1	1	12	13	12	.278	.346	.335
Grass	220	51	7	1	0	13	18	18	.232	.273	.296
Artificial Turf	64	18	3	0	1	7	7	3	.281	.375	.361
April	38	11	4	0	0	4	6	3	.289	.395	.386
May	15	3	0	0	1	2	2	1	.200	.400	.294
June	44	12	1	0	0	2	3	2	.273	.295	.319
July	90	25	3	1	0	6	3	8	.278	.333	.316
August	65	11	1	0	0	4	9	4	.169	.185	.270
Sept./Oct.	32	7	1	0	0	2	2	3	.219	.250	.286
Leading Off Inn.	92	19	3	0	1	1	13	7	.207	.272	.311
Runners On	114	33	4	1	0	19	7	8	.289	.342	.341
Runners/Scor. Pos.	64	19	1	1	0	19	6	6	.297	.344	.366
Runners On/2 Out	45	12	2	1	0	8	2	5	.267	.356	.313
Scor. Pos./2 Out	28	6	1	1	0	8	1	4	.214	.321	.267
Late Inning Pressure	35	7	1	0	0	3	2	4	.200	.229	.243
Leading Off	13	1	0	0	0	0	0	3	.077	.077	.077
Runners On	12	5	1	0	0	3	2	1	.417	.500	.500
Runners/Scor. Pos.	5	3	1	0	0	3	1	0	.600	.800	.667

DRIVING IN RUNS	From 1B	From 2B	From 3B	Scoring Position
Totals	1/81	9/54	9/26	18/80
Percentage	1%	17%	35%	23%
Driving In Runners from 3B with Less than Two Out:			6/12	50%

Loves to face: Phil Niekro (.361, 13-for-36, 1 HR)
Hates to face: Joe Niekro (.095, 2-for-21)
Grounded into 14 double plays in only 55 double-play situations (runner on first, less than two outs), highest rate in A.L. (minimum: five opportunities). ... Only player in majors to start 50 or more games at second base last season, and not have any stolen-base attempts. ... Orioles had winning record with either Bonilla (29–26) or Alan Wiggins (31–28) at second base; but they were 11–31 with Jackie Gutierrez and 2–4 with Rickie Jones. ... Orioles' starting second basemen drove in only 29 runs, fewest in majors by starters at any position (pitchers excluded). ... Career batting average of .228 with runners in scoring position. ... August batting average was 6th lowest in A.L. (minimum: 50 AB).

Bob Boone

California Angels — Bats Right

	AB	H	2B	3B	HR	RRF	BB	SO	BA	SA	OBA
Season	442	98	12	2	7	54	43	30	.222	.305	.287
vs. Left-Handers	152	33	3	0	2	20	17	9	.217	.276	.292
vs. Right-Handers	290	65	9	2	5	34	26	21	.224	.321	.284
Home	212	40	6	2	1	19	23	17	.189	.250	.264
Road	230	58	6	0	6	35	20	13	.252	.357	.310
Grass	373	84	11	2	6	47	39	27	.225	.314	.294
Artificial Turf	69	14	1	0	1	7	4	3	.203	.261	.247
April	62	14	0	0	2	4	4	5	.226	.323	.273
May	72	15	0	0	0	10	9	3	.208	.208	.289
June	82	15	3	1	1	5	6	6	.183	.280	.239
July	67	15	4	0	1	11	6	2	.224	.328	.273
August	81	21	3	0	3	15	9	7	.259	.407	.333
Sept./Oct.	78	18	2	1	0	9	9	7	.231	.282	.310
Leading Off Inn.	94	24	4	0	3	3	11	5	.255	.394	.333
Runners On	212	50	6	0	3	50	19	15	.236	.307	.291
Runners/Scor. Pos.	138	31	1	0	3	48	14	11	.225	.297	.285
Runners On/2 Out	76	17	2	0	2	16	7	3	.224	.329	.289
Scor. Pos./2 Out	53	10	0	0	2	15	6	1	.189	.302	.271
Late Inning Pressure	53	11	0	0	1	6	5	1	.208	.264	.276
Leading Off	12	2	0	0	1	0	1	1	.167	.167	.231
Runners On	23	6	0	0	1	6	1	0	.261	.391	.292
Runners/Scor. Pos.	16	4	0	0	1	6	1	0	.250	.438	.294

DRIVING IN RUNS	From 1B	From 2B	From 3B	Scoring Position
Totals	6/135	15/113	26/56	41/169
Percentage	4%	13%	46%	24%
Driving In Runners from 3B with Less than Two Out:			21/38	55%

Loves to face: Dennis Lamp (.378, 17-for-45, 3 HR)
Hates to face: Mike Mason (0-for-12)
Led A.L. catchers in games played (144) for 5th straight season; record of eight was set by Yogi Berra, 1950–57. ... With Boone catching, opponents stole 41 bases and were caught 42 times; with Narron or Miller catching, opponents had 20 steals, 13 caught. ... Grand slam homer on July 31 was his only hit of season in 13 at bats with bases loaded; two hits in his last 26 at bats with bases loaded. ... Higher batting average in day games than in night games in 10 of last 12 years; 12-year averages: batting .283, slugging .400 in daylight; .237 and .330 at night. ... Has the most sacrifice bunts of any major leaguer over the past five years (67).

Daryl Boston

Chicago White Sox — Bats Left

	AB	H	2B	3B	HR	RRF	BB	SO	BA	SA	OBA
Season	199	53	11	3	5	22	21	33	.266	.427	.335
vs. Left-Handers	48	12	3	1	1	5	6	12	.250	.417	.333
vs. Right-Handers	151	41	8	2	4	17	15	21	.272	.430	.335
Home	97	30	7	2	1	9	14	14	.309	.454	.393
Road	102	23	4	1	4	13	7	19	.225	.402	.275
Grass	158	44	9	2	3	17	17	23	.278	.418	.347
Artificial Turf	41	9	2	1	2	5	4	10	.220	.463	.289
April	0	0	0	0	0	0	0	0	—	—	—
May	0	0	0	0	0	0	0	0	—	—	—
June	0	0	0	0	0	0	0	0	—	—	—
July	0	0	0	0	0	0	0	0	—	—	—
August	102	34	6	2	3	15	10	13	.333	.520	.389
Sept./Oct.	97	19	5	1	2	7	11	20	.196	.330	.278
Leading Off Inn.	72	23	6	0	2	2	4	14	.319	.486	.355
Runners On	68	17	3	3	2	19	9	8	.250	.471	.333
Runners/Scor. Pos.	40	11	2	3	1	17	8	4	.275	.550	.388
Runners On/2 Out	29	4	1	1	1	7	5	2	.138	.345	.265
Scor. Pos./2 Out	18	4	1	1	1	7	5	1	.222	.556	.391
Late Inning Pressure	21	2	0	0	0	1	0	8	.095	.095	.136
Leading Off	6	0	0	0	0	0	1	5	.000	.000	.143
Runners On	9	1	0	0	0	1	0	1	.111	.111	.111
Runners/Scor. Pos.	4	0	0	0	0	0	0	0	.000	.000	.000

DRIVING IN RUNS	From 1B	From 2B	From 3B	Scoring Position
Totals	2/45	8/32	7/18	15/50
Percentage	4%	25%	39%	30%
Driving In Runners from 3B with Less than Two Out:			3/8	38%

Loves to face: Bill Swift (4-for-8)
Hates to face: Mike Moore (0-for-9)
Recalled from Buffalo on July 30, and started 52 of Chicago's last 62 games in center field, including 10 games against left-handed starters. ... Batted .293 with 16 RBI in 16 games batting second in White Sox lineup, highest batting average by anyone who hit second for Sox all season; Chicago's two-hole hitters batted composite .235, worst in majors. ... Career batting average of .134 in Late-Inning Pressure Situations. ... Only career home run off a left-handed pitcher: Aug. 12, 1986, vs. Mark Thurmond. ... How does Boston do against Boston? Career average of .346 (9-for-26). ... For Reggie Cleveland fans: Your guy was 6–6 vs. Cleveland, 99–100 vs. everyone else.

Phil Bradley

Seattle Mariners — Bats Right

	AB	H	2B	3B	HR	RRF	BB	SO	BA	SA	OBA
Season	526	163	27	4	12	51	77	134	.310	.445	.405
vs. Left-Handers	126	41	4	1	2	10	19	25	.325	.421	.418
vs. Right-Handers	400	122	23	3	10	41	58	109	.305	.453	.400
Home	287	93	20	3	5	30	43	64	.324	.467	.417
Road	239	70	7	1	7	21	34	70	.293	.418	.390
Grass	178	47	3	1	6	16	30	55	.264	.393	.382
Artificial Turf	348	116	24	3	6	35	47	79	.333	.471	.416
April	79	17	5	0	3	10	28	.215	.278	.303
May	79	22	4	1	2	4	15	17	.278	.430	.400
June	70	20	2	1	4	12	9	19	.286	.514	.367
July	93	33	3	0	1	12	14	21	.355	.419	.445
August	106	37	8	1	3	11	15	24	.349	.528	.444
Sept./Oct.	99	34	5	1	2	9	14	25	.343	.475	.431
Leading Off Inn.	100	34	8	0	3	3	14	31	.340	.510	.426
Runners On	192	59	10	2	3	39	30	46	.307	.396	.410
Runners/Scor. Pos.	113	29	7	2	1	36	18	28	.257	.381	.358
Runners On/2 Out	59	21	3	1	1	17	9	14	.356	.492	.465
Scor. Pos./2 Out	42	12	1	1	1	15	8	11	.286	.429	.412
Late Inning Pressure	74	21	3	2	0	10	8	23	.284	.378	.376
Leading Off	19	6	1	0	0	1	9	.316	.368	.381
Runners On	27	9	2	2	0	10	4	7	.333	.556	.455
Runners/Scor. Pos.	17	6	1	2	0	9	3	5	.353	.647	.450

DRIVING IN RUNS	From 1B	From 2B	From 3B	Scoring Position
Totals	7/108	15/84	16/44	31/128
Percentage	6%	18%	36%	24%
Driving In Runners from 3B with Less than Two Out:			12/23	52%

Loves to face: Dan Petry (.438, 7-for-16)
Hates to face: Jack Morris (.067, 1-for-15)
Right-handed hitter who, for first time in 1986, batted higher vs. left-handers than vs. righties; still, he has hit over .300 vs. right-handers in each of four years in majors. Career breakdown: batting .317, slugging .463 vs. right-handers, .264 and .396 vs. left-handers. ... Batted .247 with seven RBI in 44 games before going on disabled list in late May; batted .337 with 43 RBI in 99 games after returning on June 12. ... July batting average was 3d highest in A.L. (minimum: 75 AB). ... Has homered in every A.L. ballpark except Fenway Park (46 career AB). ... Career batting average of .391 with bases loaded: 9-for-23, with three triples and a home run.

Scott Bradley

White Sox/Mariners   Bats Left

	AB	H	2B	3B	HR	RRF	BB	SO	BA	SA	OBA
Season	220	66	8	3	5	29	13	7	.300	.432	.347
vs. Left-Handers	14	3	0	1	0	0	0	0	.214	.357	.267
vs. Right-Handers	206	63	8	2	5	29	13	7	.306	.437	.353
Home	118	41	7	2	4	17	9	5	.347	.542	.398
Road	102	25	1	1	1	12	4	2	.245	.304	.288
Grass	85	23	0	1	1	10	5	1	.271	.329	.304
Artificial Turf	135	43	8	2	4	19	8	6	.319	.496	.374
April	0	0	0	0	0	0	0	0	—	—	—
May	12	3	0	0	0	0	0	0	.250	.250	.308
June	17	5	1	0	0	3	1	0	.294	.353	.368
July	58	18	1	2	2	13	3	1	.310	.500	.333
August	64	21	3	1	2	6	4	2	.328	.500	.368
Sept./Oct.	69	19	3	0	1	7	5	4	.275	.362	.342
Leading Off Inn.	52	18	0	1	0	0	0	1	.346	.385	.358
Runners On	100	28	2	1	3	27	9	3	.280	.410	.339
Runners/Scor. Pos.	49	15	2	0	1	22	7	1	.306	.408	.379
Runners On/2 Out	31	8	0	1	0	8	6	1	.258	.323	.378
Scor. Pos./2 Out	19	6	0	0	0	7	5	1	.316	.316	.458
Late Inning Pressure	37	13	1	0	0	4	4	2	.351	.378	.429
Leading Off	14	3	0	0	0	0	0	0	.214	.214	.214
Runners On	11	6	0	0	0	4	4	0	.545	.545	.688
Runners/Scor. Pos.	6	4	0	0	0	4	3	0	.667	.667	.778

DRIVING IN RUNS	From 1B	From 2B	From 3B	Scoring Position
Totals	5/87	9/42	10/20	19/62
Percentage	6%	21%	50%	31%
Driving In Runners from 3B with Less than Two Out:			7/11	64%

Loves to face: Mark Eichhorn (.667, 2-for-3)
Hates to face: Dave Stieb (0-for-9)
A young player who has been platooned in his brief career in majors: 91 percent of his 314 plate appearances have come against right-handers. Even allowing for that, his total of only 13 strikeouts, one every 24.2 plate appearances, is impressive: It's the best among all active players with at least 100 times up; among players with more extensive careers, Buckner (one every 22.8) and Gwynn (one every 20.2) are the best.... Career breakdown: .258 with runners on base, .290 with bases empty.... Grounded into 13 double plays in 65 opportunities, 6th-highest rate in A.L. (minimum: 5 opportunites).... Career batting average of .345 (38-for-110, four home runs) at the Kingdome.

Glenn Braggs

Milwaukee Brewers   Bats Right

	AB	H	2B	3B	HR	RRF	BB	SO	BA	SA	OBA
Season	215	51	8	2	4	19	11	47	.237	.349	.274
vs. Left-Handers	58	17	4	0	3	10	2	13	.293	.517	.313
vs. Right-Handers	157	34	4	2	1	9	9	34	.217	.287	.259
Home	86	27	4	1	2	8	7	13	.314	.453	.368
Road	129	24	4	1	2	11	4	34	.186	.279	.207
Grass	184	44	6	2	4	17	11	39	.239	.359	.281
Artificial Turf	31	7	2	0	0	2	0	8	.226	.290	.226
April	0	0	0	0	0	0	0	0	—	—	—
May	0	0	0	0	0	0	0	0	—	—	—
June	0	0	0	0	0	0	0	0	—	—	—
July	43	12	4	0	0	4	1	8	.279	.372	.295
August	91	21	2	0	3	7	5	18	.231	.352	.265
Sept./Oct.	81	18	2	2	1	8	5	21	.222	.333	.273
Leading Off Inn.	45	14	1	2	2	0	0	7	.311	.556	.311
Runners On	86	17	2	0	1	16	6	19	.198	.256	.242
Runners/Scor. Pos.	48	6	2	0	0	14	4	10	.125	.167	.182
Runners On/2 Out	35	4	1	0	0	7	1	3	.114	.143	.139
Scor. Pos./2 Out	26	4	1	0	0	7	1	1	.154	.192	.185
Late Inning Pressure	30	6	1	0	0	0	4	6	.200	.233	.294
Leading Off	6	1	0	0	0	0	0	0	.167	.167	.167
Runners On	7	2	0	0	0	0	3	2	.286	.286	.500
Runners/Scor. Pos.	4	0	0	0	0	0	2	1	.000	.000	.333

DRIVING IN RUNS	From 1B	From 2B	From 3B	Scoring Position
Totals	2/69	7/41	6/21	13/62
Percentage	3%	17%	29%	21%
Driving In Runners from 3B with Less than Two Out:			5/12	42%

Loves to face: Mike Mason (2-for-2, 2 HR)
Hates to face: Jim Clancy (0-for-6)
Recalled from Vancouver at All-Star break, when Mike Felder was sent down; started 56 of Brewers' 75 games after the break.... Committed 12 errors in 56 games in outfield last season; his .910 fielding percentage was the worst for a major-league outfielder (minimum: 50 games) since Oscar Brown (.899 for 1973 Braves), and lowest in A.L. since Daddy Wags Wagner (.895 for 1968 Indians).... Hit four home runs last season, three of them in seven games against Texas.... Born October 17, 1962; his "Day You Were Born" newspaper has all the details of Ralph Terry's 1–0 win over the Giants in the final game of the 1962 World Series the previous day.

George Brett

Kansas City Royals   Bats Left

	AB	H	2B	3B	HR	RRF	BB	SO	BA	SA	OBA
Season	441	128	28	4	16	74	80	45	.290	.481	.401
vs. Left-Handers	148	36	4	1	5	19	19	24	.243	.385	.329
vs. Right-Handers	293	92	24	3	11	55	61	21	.314	.529	.435
Home	205	66	16	4	8	41	36	15	.322	.556	.418
Road	236	62	12	0	8	33	44	30	.263	.415	.386
Grass	196	52	11	0	7	28	36	25	.265	.429	.383
Artificial Turf	245	76	17	4	9	46	44	20	.310	.522	.415
April	58	14	4	1	4	9	21	6	.241	.552	.451
May	99	24	7	0	2	13	22	11	.242	.374	.377
June	107	38	5	0	2	17	16	7	.355	.458	.448
July	46	10	3	1	2	6	7	5	.217	.457	.321
August	99	36	8	2	5	22	12	13	.364	.636	.425
Sept./Oct.	32	6	1	0	1	7	2	3	.188	.313	.235
Leading Off Inn.	93	22	3	0	6	6	16	11	.237	.462	.355
Runners On	206	63	10	2	7	65	44	20	.306	.476	.424
Runners/Scor. Pos.	111	35	6	0	2	51	33	12	.315	.423	.463
Runners On/2 Out	70	21	3	1	2	21	22	6	.300	.457	.473
Scor. Pos./2 Out	36	13	2	0	1	18	16	2	.361	.500	.566
Late Inning Pressure	57	14	1	0	1	6	9	8	.246	.316	.358
Leading Off	17	3	0	0	0	0	2	3	.176	.176	.300
Runners On	21	6	1	0	1	6	4	2	.286	.476	.400
Runners/Scor. Pos.	11	3	1	0	1	6	2	1	.273	.636	.385

DRIVING IN RUNS	From 1B	From 2B	From 3B	Scoring Position
Totals	11/152	20/80	27/49	47/129
Percentage	7%	25%	55%	36%
Driving In Runners from 3B with Less than Two Out:			18/33	55%

Loves to face: Keith Atherton (.800, 4-for-5, 1 HR)
Hates to face: Curt Young (.091, 1-for-11)
One of four active players (minimum: 500 plate appearances) with .300 batting average and .500 slugging average; others: Pedro Guerrero, Don Mattingly, Jim Rice.... Batting as low as .232 as late as May 28; average climbed steadily and crested at .301 on Aug. 27, his only day above .300 after April 17.... Has had more walks than strikeouts in every season since 1975.... Over past 12 years, has batted .326 in Late-Inning Pressure Situations; .342 in those situations with runners on base and two outs (50-for-146).... With bases loaded over past three years: 11-for-24 overall, 8-for-13 with two outs.

Tom Brookens

Detroit Tigers   Bats Right

	AB	H	2B	3B	HR	RRF	BB	SO	BA	SA	OBA
Season	281	76	11	2	3	27	20	42	.270	.356	.319
vs. Left-Handers	171	51	9	2	2	12	10	20	.298	.409	.337
vs. Right-Handers	110	25	2	0	1	15	10	22	.227	.273	.292
Home	144	37	6	1	2	12	9	27	.257	.354	.299
Road	137	39	5	1	1	15	11	15	.285	.358	.340
Grass	236	58	8	2	3	25	18	36	.246	.335	.300
Artificial Turf	45	18	3	0	0	2	2	6	.400	.467	.426
April	17	5	1	1	0	4	1	2	.294	.471	.333
May	38	14	1	0	0	3	4	3	.368	.395	.417
June	70	20	5	0	1	9	6	6	.286	.400	.338
July	58	9	1	0	0	3	5	15	.155	.172	.234
August	38	12	0	0	1	7	1	5	.316	.395	.333
Sept./Oct.	60	16	3	1	1	1	3	11	.267	.400	.302
Leading Off Inn.	88	23	3	1	0	0	11	16	.261	.318	.343
Runners On	111	30	5	1	2	26	6	13	.270	.387	.308
Runners/Scor. Pos.	65	14	3	1	1	24	4	8	.215	.338	.264
Runners On/2 Out	50	14	1	1	1	13	3	7	.280	.400	.321
Scor. Pos./2 Out	35	8	1	1	1	13	3	4	.229	.400	.289
Late Inning Pressure	41	13	0	0	2	4	9	.317	.317	.370
Leading Off	13	5	0	0	0	0	0	2	.385	.385	.385
Runners On	15	3	0	0	0	3	3	2	.200	.200	.316
Runners/Scor. Pos.	7	1	0	0	0	2	2	2	.143	.143	.300

DRIVING IN RUNS	From 1B	From 2B	From 3B	Scoring Position
Totals	2/75	9/55	13/21	22/76
Percentage	3%	16%	62%	29%
Driving In Runners from 3B with Less than Two Out:			9/11	82%

Loves to face: Tim Birtsas (.667, 4-for-6)
Hates to face: Chris Codiroli (.063, 1-for-16)
Surprising career batting and slugging averages (.282 and .418) against left-handers; those figures are roughly comparable to the career figures (against all pitchers) of hitters like Steve Henderson, Garry Maddox, and Tom Paciorek.... Started 53 of 55 games in which Tigers faced a left-handed starter; 24 of 107 against right-handed starters.... Batted .270 overall for his highest average since 1980, ending run of five straight years in which he batted below .250, yet had at least 200 at bats.... Survived a July in which he had lowest batting average in A.L. (minimum: 50 AB), dropping his overall average from .312 to .262.... Played a career-high 31 games at second base.

Tom Brunansky

Minnesota Twins — Bats Right

Minnesota Twins	AB	H	2B	3B	HR	RRF	BB	SO	BA	SA	OBA
Season	593	152	28	1	23	82	53	98	.256	.423	.315
vs. Left-Handers	167	52	9	1	11	30	12	22	.311	.575	.354
vs. Right-Handers	426	100	19	0	12	52	41	76	.235	.364	.300
Home	296	79	16	1	15	51	26	43	.267	.480	.324
Road	297	73	12	0	8	31	27	55	.246	.367	.306
Grass	223	53	8	0	5	17	22	42	.238	.341	.306
Artificial Turf	370	99	20	1	18	65	31	56	.268	.473	.320
April	82	23	2	0	4	13	4	14	.280	.451	.310
May	109	34	7	1	7	19	8	19	.312	.587	.361
June	111	31	7	0	6	19	10	20	.279	.505	.333
July	101	22	2	0	1	9	5	11	.218	.267	.255
August	100	23	6	0	2	8	15	14	.230	.350	.325
Sept./Oct.	90	19	4	0	3	14	11	20	.211	.356	.294
Leading Off Inn.	144	41	3	0	5	5	6	17	.285	.410	.313
Runners On	282	67	10	0	11	70	28	53	.238	.390	.302
Runners/Scor. Pos.	145	35	2	0	3	50	19	28	.241	.317	.316
Runners On/2 Out	123	28	4	0	4	27	15	26	.228	.358	.312
Scor. Pos./2 Out	67	15	0	0	1	19	11	15	.224	.269	.333
Late Inning Pressure	84	17	7	0	2	11	8	17	.202	.357	.263
Leading Off	16	3	1	0	0	0	0	1	.188	.250	.188
Runners On	39	7	4	0	1	10	5	11	.179	.359	.255
Runners/Scor. Pos.	18	3	2	0	0	7	2	6	.167	.278	.217

DRIVING IN RUNS	From 1B	From 2B	From 3B	Scoring Position
Totals	13/212	23/116	21/55	44/171
Percentage	6%	20%	38%	26%
Driving In Runners from 3B with Less than Two Out:			15/31	48%

Loves to face: Bruce Hurst (.609, 14-for-23, 1 HR)
Hates to face: Don Aase (0-for-10)
One of 10 players to have hit 20 or more home runs in each of past five seasons. . . . Career batting average of .211 in Late-Inning Pressure Situations, but a strong .211: It breaks down to .286 with runners in scoring position, .190 in all other situations. . . . Improved average vs. left-handers from a career-low .214 in 1985 to a career-high .311 in 1986. . . . Don't give him any of this Homerdome stuff: His career rate is one home run every 22.9 at bats at the Metrodome, one every 19.1 at bats at all other parks combined. . . . Has hit 82 home runs over past three years, but none in 36 at bats with bases loaded during that time.

Bill Buckner

Boston Red Sox — Bats Left

Boston Red Sox	AB	H	2B	3B	HR	RRF	BB	SO	BA	SA	OBA
Season	629	168	39	2	18	104	40	25	.267	.421	.311
vs. Left-Handers	202	44	7	1	4	30	8	10	.218	.322	.257
vs. Right-Handers	427	124	32	1	14	74	32	15	.290	.468	.336
Home	299	77	18	2	8	46	19	13	.258	.411	.303
Road	330	91	21	0	10	58	21	12	.276	.430	.318
Grass	538	142	35	2	16	91	35	19	.264	.426	.308
Artificial Turf	91	26	4	0	2	13	5	6	.286	.396	.333
April	79	17	8	1	1	7	4	6	.215	.380	.259
May	110	29	6	0	3	20	10	3	.264	.400	.325
June	113	26	3	1	4	13	4	2	.230	.381	.254
July	105	29	9	0	2	16	3	8	.276	.419	.294
August	114	33	9	0	4	24	10	2	.289	.368	.352
Sept./Oct.	108	34	4	0	8	24	9	4	.315	.574	.364
Leading Off Inn.	102	25	5	1	3	3	3	2	.245	.402	.267
Runners On	342	94	24	0	7	93	30	15	.275	.406	.332
Runners/Scor. Pos.	193	47	13	0	2	79	19	9	.244	.342	.306
Runners On/2 Out	113	33	10	0	0	30	11	4	.292	.381	.370
Scor. Pos./2 Out	74	20	7	0	0	29	8	3	.270	.365	.357
Late Inning Pressure	59	14	4	0	0	8	7	1	.237	.305	.343
Leading Off	13	1	0	0	0	0	0	0	.077	.077	.077
Runners On	34	13	4	0	0	7	7	1	.382	.500	.500
Runners/Scor. Pos.	17	5	1	0	0	7	6	1	.294	.353	.500

DRIVING IN RUNS	From 1B	From 2B	From 3B	Scoring Position
Totals	16/270	32/169	38/73	70/242
Percentage	6%	19%	52%	29%
Driving In Runners from 3B with Less than Two Out:			26/38	68%

Loves to face: Nate Snell (.600, 6-for-10, 2 HR)
Hates to face: Joe Cowley (.043, 1-for-23)
Has never struck out three times in one game. Struck out twice (and had a two-strike count against him in a third at bat) vs. Candelaria in Game Three of 1986 A.L.C.S. Career rate of one strikeout every 22.8 plate appearances is best among active players (minimum: 500 PA). . . . Possible addition to list of four-decade players: He's the youngest active player to have played in the 1960s—one at bat, a pinch-hit appearance against Gaylord Perry in 1969. Other candidates: Vida Blue, Rick Dempsey, Jerry Reuss, Ted Simmons. . . . Batted 26 times with bases loaded last season, most in majors (7-for-25, one walk, one strikeout). . . . Has homered in every current major-league ballpark except Arlington Stadium (66 career at bats).

Steve Buechele

Texas Rangers — Bats Right

Texas Rangers	AB	H	2B	3B	HR	RRF	BB	SO	BA	SA	OBA
Season	461	112	19	2	18	55	35	98	.243	.410	.302
vs. Left-Handers	139	38	7	1	5	18	16	35	.273	.446	.346
vs. Right-Handers	322	74	12	1	13	37	19	63	.230	.394	.282
Home	224	53	8	0	6	18	15	44	.237	.353	.292
Road	237	59	11	2	12	37	20	54	.249	.464	.310
Grass	379	92	12	2	14	45	29	78	.243	.396	.303
Artificial Turf	82	20	7	0	4	10	6	20	.244	.476	.295
April	57	15	2	0	4	6	5	10	.263	.509	.323
May	77	18	3	0	4	10	4	14	.234	.429	.272
June	92	27	5	0	4	10	7	22	.293	.478	.350
July	75	13	2	0	1	6	5	17	.173	.240	.244
August	76	19	3	1	2	15	11	13	.250	.395	.352
Sept./Oct.	84	20	4	1	3	8	3	22	.238	.417	.261
Leading Off Inn.	128	34	5	0	8	8	2	27	.266	.492	.288
Runners On	169	40	5	1	3	40	14	38	.237	.331	.294
Runners/Scor. Pos.	99	23	2	0	2	35	11	20	.232	.313	.301
Runners On/2 Out	78	18	3	1	1	13	7	20	.231	.333	.302
Scor. Pos./2 Out	50	9	2	0	1	12	5	12	.180	.280	.255
Late Inning Pressure	59	18	4	0	2	4	2	9	.305	.475	.333
Leading Off	21	9	3	0	1	1	0	3	.429	.714	.455
Runners On	14	2	0	0	0	2	1	3	.143	.143	.188
Runners/Scor. Pos.	7	2	0	0	0	2	1	2	.286	.286	.333

DRIVING IN RUNS	From 1B	From 2B	From 3B	Scoring Position
Totals	6/122	13/77	18/37	31/114
Percentage	5%	17%	49%	27%
Driving In Runners from 3B with Less than Two Out:			14/17	82%

Loves to face: Charlie Leibrandt (.438, 7-for-16)
Hates to face: Oil Can Boyd (0-for-10)
Mr. Consistency: batting average fell below .250 on July 26, and for rest of season it remained within narrow range of .240 to .249. . . . Never batted above 7th in any of his 140 starts; hit 11 home runs from 8th spot in order, tying Dunston and Schofield for most in majors. . . . Career breakdown: one home run every 23.4 at bats with bases empty; one every 43.0 at bats with men on base. . . . Career batting average of .271 vs. left-handers, .219 vs. right-handers. . . . Drove in 82.4 percent (14-of-17) of runners from third base with less than two outs, 6th-best percentage in A.L. (minimum: 10 RRF). . . . Good thing he plays for the Rangers, not the Cubs: He batted .188 in day games, .258 at night.

Rick Burleson

California Angels — Bats Right

California Angels	AB	H	2B	3B	HR	RRF	BB	SO	BA	SA	OBA
Season	271	77	14	0	5	29	33	32	.284	.391	.363
vs. Left-Handers	153	38	6	0	4	17	18	20	.248	.366	.326
vs. Right-Handers	118	39	8	0	1	12	15	12	.331	.424	.410
Home	120	31	8	0	2	11	16	16	.258	.375	.343
Road	151	46	6	0	3	18	17	16	.305	.404	.379
Grass	207	55	10	0	3	21	23	28	.266	.357	.338
Artificial Turf	64	22	4	0	2	8	10	4	.344	.500	.440
April	53	19	6	0	1	7	9	6	.358	.528	.460
May	52	11	2	0	0	3	4	10	.212	.250	.268
June	28	9	2	0	0	2	3	3	.321	.393	.375
July	39	15	0	0	3	7	4	5	.385	.615	.442
August	45	11	1	0	1	2	4	3	.244	.333	.306
Sept./Oct.	54	12	3	0	0	8	9	5	.222	.278	.333
Leading Off Inn.	79	21	4	0	3	3	9	12	.266	.430	.341
Runners On	112	35	4	0	0	24	18	13	.313	.348	.409
Runners/Scor. Pos.	68	21	3	0	0	24	13	9	.309	.353	.415
Runners On/2 Out	57	17	1	0	0	13	9	9	.298	.316	.394
Scor. Pos./2 Out	37	11	1	0	0	13	6	7	.297	.324	.395
Late Inning Pressure	47	11	0	0	1	5	6	10	.234	.298	.327
Leading Off	13	3	0	0	0	0	1	3	.231	.231	.286
Runners On	18	5	0	0	0	4	4	5	.278	.278	.417
Runners/Scor. Pos.	10	3	0	0	0	4	4	3	.300	.300	.467

DRIVING IN RUNS	From 1B	From 2B	From 3B	Scoring Position
Totals	0/75	16/53	8/29	24/82
Percentage	0%	30%	28%	29%
Driving In Runners from 3B with Less than Two Out:			4/12	33%

Loves to face: Jimmy Key (.571, 4-for-7, 1 HR)
Hates to face: Dan Quisenberry (.067, 1-for-15, 14 ground outs)
Started 44 of 52 games in which Angels faced a left-hander last season; 28 of 110 against right-handers. . . . Very little platoon difference during career; since 1975: batting .277, slugging .373 vs. left-handers; .273 and .357 vs. right-handers. . . . Batted .457 (16-for-35) vs. Blue Jays last season; he'll get one more game against them this year than last. . . . Did not drive in a runner from first base in 75 chances last season; he's 1-for-266 over the past five years. . . . Played more games last season (93) than in the previous four calendar years combined (51). Ted Williams didn't even do that when he missed three full years to fight a war!

Randy Bush

Minnesota Twins   Bats Left

	AB	H	2B	3B	HR	RRF	BB	SO	BA	SA	OBA
Season	357	96	19	7	7	45	39	63	.269	.420	.347
vs. Left-Handers	12	2	1	0	0	1	2	3	.167	.250	.286
vs. Right-Handers	345	94	18	7	7	44	37	60	.272	.426	.349
Home	181	55	12	5	6	33	18	29	.304	.525	.376
Road	176	41	7	2	1	12	21	34	.233	.313	.317
Grass	129	30	4	2	1	9	17	27	.233	.318	.324
Artificial Turf	228	66	15	5	6	36	22	36	.289	.478	.360
April	47	12	0	1	2	7	8	9	.255	.426	.375
May	51	12	5	2	1	7	9	9	.235	.471	.350
June	65	17	4	2	3	15	4	10	.262	.523	.300
July	64	18	2	0	0	1	6	12	.281	.313	.343
August	71	20	6	1	0	8	4	12	.282	.394	.329
Sept./Oct.	59	17	2	1	1	7	8	11	.288	.407	.391
Leading Off Inn.	71	19	2	0	2	2	4	9	.268	.380	.325
Runners On	165	48	9	4	4	42	16	26	.291	.467	.355
Runners/Scor. Pos.	95	22	7	1	2	34	8	16	.232	.389	.295
Runners On/2 Out	63	15	3	0	0	10	8	11	.238	.286	.324
Scor. Pos./2 Out	45	9	2	0	0	9	5	8	.200	.244	.280
Late Inning Pressure	56	18	5	0	1	8	9	10	.321	.464	.415
Leading Off	13	2	0	0	0	0	0	2	.154	.154	.154
Runners On	28	9	1	0	1	8	4	3	.321	.464	.406
Runners/Scor. Pos.	17	5	0	0	1	7	2	2	.294	.471	.368

DRIVING IN RUNS	From 1B	From 2B	From 3B	Scoring Position
Totals	10/113	15/78	13/29	28/107
Percentage	9%	19%	45%	26%
Driving In Runners from 3B with Less than Two Out:		10/16		63%

Loves to face: Bob James (2-for-2, 1 HR)
Hates to face: Al Nipper (.077, 1-for-13)
Batted .433 (13-for-30) as pinch-hitter last season, best in A.L. (minimum: 20 AB); he had been 4-for-32 in that job in 1985. . . . Batted .300 in 38 games batting in 5th spot; .224 in 45 games batting 2d. . . Has homered in every A.L. ballpark except Anaheim Stadium (50 career at bats). . . . Two hits off left-handed pitchers in 1986 matched his single-season career high; he's 5-for-45, without a home run, lifetime against southpaws. . . . Career breakdown: .272 with runners on base, .224 with bases empty. . . . Has the same career batting average (.246) in day games and night games, about what you would expect from someone who plays most of his games under artificial lighting to begin with.

Brett Butler

Cleveland Indians   Bats Left

	AB	H	2B	3B	HR	RRF	BB	SO	BA	SA	OBA
Season	587	163	17	14	4	56	70	65	.278	.375	.356
vs. Left-Handers	160	49	6	4	1	19	21	29	.306	.413	.390
vs. Right-Handers	427	114	11	10	3	37	49	36	.267	.361	.342
Home	276	75	4	9	0	16	39	34	.272	.351	.360
Road	311	88	13	5	4	40	31	31	.283	.395	.352
Grass	494	135	13	13	2	43	59	54	.273	.364	.349
Artificial Turf	93	28	4	1	2	13	11	11	.301	.430	.389
April	66	16	5	1	1	4	11	4	.242	.394	.351
May	98	23	3	1	0	13	17	10	.235	.286	.342
June	106	25	3	3	0	8	9	11	.236	.321	.296
July	85	27	3	3	1	9	13	12	.318	.459	.408
August	106	24	0	1	1	7	7	16	.226	.274	.278
Sept./Oct.	126	48	3	5	1	15	13	12	.381	.508	.444
Leading Off Inn.	168	47	9	6	2	2	21	22	.280	.440	.360
Runners On	228	63	7	3	0	52	35	23	.276	.333	.370
Runners/Scor. Pos.	143	39	7	3	0	51	26	14	.273	.364	.377
Runners On/2 Out	96	23	4	3	0	24	18	11	.240	.344	.360
Scor. Pos./2 Out	73	20	4	3	0	24	13	9	.274	.411	.384
Late Inning Pressure	75	26	1	0	1	14	5	7	.347	.400	.383
Leading Off	11	1	0	0	0	2	2	2	.091	.091	.231
Runners On	33	13	1	0	0	13	2	2	.394	.424	.417
Runners/Scor. Pos.	20	11	1	0	0	13	1	2	.550	.600	.545

DRIVING IN RUNS	From 1B	From 2B	From 3B	Scoring Position
Totals	6/154	19/117	27/56	46/173
Percentage	4%	16%	48%	27%
Driving In Runners from 3B with Less than Two Out:		19/28		68%

Loves to face: Dan Quisenberry (.778, 7-for-9)
Hates to face: Ken Dixon (.059, 1-for-17)
Top home run ballparks: Atlanta Stadium, four; Yankee Stadium, three; Cleveland Stadium and the Metrodome, two each. Career batting average of .361 (26-for-72), and several brilliant catches, in the Bronx. . . . Finished second in A.L. with 17 sacrifice bunts. . . . Batting .405 (17-for-42) with bases loaded since 1984. . . . Has higher career average vs. left-handers (.304) than vs. right-handers (.268); has batted higher against lefties in each of last three seasons. . . . Could eventually be all-time fielding champ among outfielders: Has lifetime fielding average of .99308 in 722 games; major-league record for outfielder (1000 games required) is .99338 by Terry Puhl.

John Cangelosi

Chicago White Sox   Bats Left and Right

	AB	H	2B	3B	HR	RRF	BB	SO	BA	SA	OBA
Season	438	103	16	3	2	35	71	61	.235	.299	.349
vs. Left-Handers	134	29	9	1	2	11	26	21	.216	.343	.350
vs. Right-Handers	304	74	7	2	0	24	45	40	.243	.280	.349
Home	202	48	7	3	1	16	42	27	.238	.317	.384
Road	236	55	9	0	1	19	29	34	.233	.284	.317
Grass	366	81	12	3	2	27	65	53	.221	.287	.347
Artificial Turf	72	22	4	0	0	8	6	8	.306	.361	.363
April	58	14	2	0	1	2	17	8	.241	.328	.416
May	82	19	1	0	0	4	10	7	.232	.244	.315
June	90	24	7	0	0	11	24	13	.267	.344	.441
July	96	26	4	2	1	9	8	19	.271	.385	.340
August	69	12	1	1	0	4	6	10	.174	.217	.240
Sept./Oct.	43	8	1	0	0	5	6	4	.186	.209	.280
Leading Off Inn.	191	46	6	0	0	19	29	9	.241	.293	.316
Runners On	140	35	5	0	1	34	37	15	.250	.307	.412
Runners/Scor. Pos.	81	19	3	0	0	31	22	12	.235	.272	.402
Runners On/2 Out	57	13	1	0	0	13	10	6	.228	.246	.362
Scor. Pos./2 Out	36	8	0	0	0	12	8	5	.222	.222	.391
Late Inning Pressure	61	13	2	2	1	5	8	10	.213	.361	.304
Leading Off	24	6	1	1	0	0	1	5	.250	.375	.280
Runners On	18	3	0	0	0	4	6	1	.167	.167	.375
Runners/Scor. Pos.	9	2	0	0	0	4	5	1	.222	.222	.500

DRIVING IN RUNS	From 1B	From 2B	From 3B	Scoring Position
Totals	3/102	13/63	17/43	30/106
Percentage	3%	21%	40%	28%
Driving In Runners from 3B with Less than Two Out:		13/24		54%

Loves to face: Scott Nielsen (3-for-3)
Hates to face: Bret Saberhagen (0-for-7)
Started 98 of Chicago's first 112 games last season, but only eight of the next 37; then he started 10 of last 13, and became first A.L. rookie to steal 50 bases in season. Old record: 49 by Rollie Zeider of 1910 White Sox. . . . Led major-league rookies with 71 walks last season. . . . Leading hitter among active players in Metrodome (minimum: 20 at bats); he's 12-for-28 (.429) there. . . . Stole six bases in six attempts vs. Oakland last season, only five out of 10 against Minnesota. . . . Had .243 batting average and .310 slugging average while batting in leadoff position last season, well shy of league averages of .266 and .396; but Cangelosi's on-base average of .348 was above A.L. average of .336.

Jose Canseco

Oakland As   Bats Right

	AB	H	2B	3B	HR	RRF	BB	SO	BA	SA	OBA
Season	600	144	29	1	33	120	65	175	.240	.457	.318
vs. Left-Handers	187	53	12	0	8	36	13	44	.283	.476	.325
vs. Right-Handers	413	91	17	1	25	84	52	131	.220	.448	.315
Home	301	64	10	0	14	56	34	82	.213	.385	.296
Road	299	80	19	1	19	64	31	93	.268	.528	.340
Grass	496	113	19	1	28	97	57	143	.228	.440	.312
Artificial Turf	104	31	10	0	5	23	8	32	.298	.538	.348
April	75	20	2	0	5	19	16	26	.267	.493	.396
May	109	30	5	0	10	28	13	36	.275	.596	.355
June	108	26	10	0	4	20	15	30	.241	.444	.331
July	101	27	1	0	4	19	7	30	.267	.396	.309
August	101	17	6	1	4	16	4	31	.168	.366	.211
Sept./Oct.	106	24	5	0	6	18	10	22	.226	.443	.314
Leading Off Inn.	132	26	6	0	3	3	14	45	.197	.311	.279
Runners On	271	84	15	0	22	109	26	62	.310	.609	.368
Runners/Scor. Pos.	148	51	9	0	10	80	19	33	.345	.608	.408
Runners On/2 Out	103	36	9	0	4	37	8	19	.350	.553	.412
Scor. Pos./2 Out	66	24	4	0	1	26	6	12	.364	.470	.440
Late Inning Pressure	87	24	8	0	1	17	8	28	.276	.402	.337
Leading Off	24	3	0	0	0	0	1	6	.125	.125	.160
Runners On	32	14	7	0	0	16	5	9	.438	.656	.487
Runners/Scor. Pos.	21	10	3	0	0	12	4	5	.476	.619	.519

DRIVING IN RUNS	From 1B	From 2B	From 3B	Scoring Position
Totals	24/225	29/115	34/66	63/181
Percentage	11%	25%	52%	35%
Driving In Runners from 3B with Less than Two Out:		23/37		62%

Loves to face: Dave Stieb (.750, 3-for-4, 2 HR)
Hates to face: Joe Cowley (.077, 1-for-13, 8 SO)
This says he deserved Rookie Award: Batted 128 points higher with runners on base than with bases empty, largest difference in A.L. (minimum: 100 AB both ways). Twenty-two of 33 homers came with runners on base; that total of 22 tied Dave Parker for major-league lead. . . . Hairline fracture of little finger suffered when hit by a Scott Bankhead pitch on Sept. 27 may have cost him the Oakland RBI record; he missed two games following injury, and failed to drive in a run in final five games after returning, finishing season with 117 RBI, one short of Oakland record shared by Reggie and Kong. . . . Homered against every A.L. team except Kansas City last season.

Joe Carter

Cleveland Indians — Bats Right

	AB	H	2B	3B	HR	RRF	BB	SO	BA	SA	OBA
Season	663	200	36	9	29	127	32	95	.302	.514	.335
vs. Left-Handers	181	57	10	4	7	35	12	36	.315	.530	.354
vs. Right-Handers	482	143	26	5	22	92	20	59	.297	.508	.327
Home	324	101	16	5	14	53	19	46	.312	.522	.350
Road	339	99	20	4	15	74	13	49	.292	.507	.320
Grass	556	165	29	7	24	101	27	81	.297	.504	.331
Artificial Turf	107	35	7	2	5	26	5	14	.327	.570	.357
April	72	18	1	0	4	11	5	14	.250	.431	.299
May	102	30	4	1	3	21	6	17	.294	.441	.324
June	109	38	8	1	5	24	4	13	.349	.578	.383
July	112	37	7	1	4	17	6	11	.330	.518	.367
August	133	34	6	2	8	22	4	16	.256	.511	.281
Sept./Oct.	135	43	10	4	5	32	7	24	.319	.563	.349
Leading Off Inn.	120	35	5	0	6	6	5	14	.292	.483	.325
Runners On	320	93	15	4	14	112	15	53	.291	.494	.321
Runners/Scor. Pos.	193	56	9	1	6	88	14	34	.290	.440	.335
Runners On/2 Out	114	31	6	1	7	42	5	22	.272	.526	.303
Scor. Pos./2 Out	80	23	5	1	5	37	5	16	.288	.563	.329
Late Inning Pressure	78	23	3	2	2	17	3	17	.295	.462	.325
Leading Off	14	2	0	0	0	0	1	4	.143	.143	.200
Runners On	45	13	2	0	1	16	2	11	.289	.400	.327
Runners/Scor. Pos.	28	9	1	0	1	15	2	9	.321	.464	.375

DRIVING IN RUNS	From 1B	From 2B	From 3B	Scoring Position
Totals	26/224	28/129	43/95	71/224
Percentage	12%	22%	45%	32%
Driving In Runners from 3B with Less than Two Out:		33/58		57%

Loves to face: Mark Knudson (3-for-3, 2 HR)
Hates to face: Roger Clemens (0-for-12)
First Indians player to lead majors in RBI (121) since Al Rosen in 1953. . . . Drove in 26 runners from first base last season, most in majors. . . . Only major leaguer to have three five-hit games last season. . . . Has batted over .300 all three years with Indians in Late-Inning Pressure Situations with runners in scoring position; career average in such situations: .344. . . . Has homered in every ballpark in A.L. except Comiskey Park (38 career at bats). . . . Look out, Lou Gehrig: Carter has three grand slam home runs in 28 career at bats with bases loaded. . . . Rick Sutcliffe certainly was a steal for the Cubs, huh?

Carmen Castillo

Cleveland Indians — Bats Right

	AB	H	2B	3B	HR	RRF	BB	SO	BA	SA	OBA
Season	205	57	9	0	8	33	9	48	.278	.439	.310
vs. Left-Handers	109	27	4	0	5	17	7	29	.248	.422	.293
vs. Right-Handers	96	30	5	0	3	16	2	19	.313	.458	.330
Home	101	32	7	0	4	20	4	21	.317	.505	.346
Road	104	25	2	0	4	13	5	27	.240	.375	.275
Grass	175	49	8	0	6	27	7	39	.280	.429	.310
Artificial Turf	30	8	1	0	2	6	2	9	.267	.500	.313
April	29	7	1	0	1	5	0	6	.241	.379	.241
May	33	7	1	0	0	2	2	5	.212	.242	.257
June	39	14	1	0	3	9	3	10	.359	.615	.409
July	35	10	3	0	0	4	0	10	.286	.371	.286
August	36	8	0	0	2	5	1	4	.222	.389	.243
Sept./Oct.	33	11	3	0	2	8	3	13	.333	.606	.389
Leading Off Inn.	36	9	2	0	1	1	2	9	.250	.389	.289
Runners On	104	31	5	0	6	31	5	23	.298	.519	.327
Runners/Scor. Pos.	58	15	5	0	0	19	3	17	.259	.345	.290
Runners On/2 Out	43	15	2	0	3	11	2	13	.349	.605	.378
Scor. Pos./2 Out	21	6	2	0	0	5	2	11	.286	.381	.348
Late Inning Pressure	26	6	2	0	1	6	1	7	.231	.423	.259
Leading Off	6	0	0	0	0	0	0	0	.000	.000	.000
Runners On	11	5	2	0	1	6	1	5	.455	.909	.500
Runners/Scor. Pos.	8	3	2	0	0	4	1	5	.375	.625	.444

DRIVING IN RUNS	From 1B	From 2B	From 3B	Scoring Position
Totals	6/73	11/49	8/18	19/67
Percentage	8%	22%	44%	28%
Driving In Runners from 3B with Less than Two Out:		6/12		50%

Loves to face: Tommy John (.667, 4-for-6, 1 HR)
Hates to face: Bob Shirley (0-for-8, 8 air outs)
Started 36 of 49 games in which Indians faced a left-handed starter last season; 19 of 114 against right-handers. . . . Batted .323 in 31 games as starting right fielder; .263 in 24 starts as designated hitter; and .143 (3-for-21) as pinch-hitter. That left him with career pinch-hitting mark of .132 (7-for-53). . . . Likes Cleveland Stadium: a career .278 hitter and .483 slugger there, compared with .229 and .376 elsewhere. . . . Career batting average of .375 (14-for-40, five home runs) at the Kingdome. . . . Batted .222 in day games, .303 at night. . . . Grounded into nine double plays in 44 double-play situations, 5th-highest rate in A.L. (minimum: five opportunites).

Rick Cerone

Milwaukee Brewers — Bats Right

	AB	H	2B	3B	HR	RRF	BB	SO	BA	SA	OBA
Season	216	56	14	0	4	21	15	28	.259	.380	.304
vs. Left-Handers	68	16	4	0	1	6	4	7	.235	.338	.274
vs. Right-Handers	148	40	10	0	3	15	11	21	.270	.399	.317
Home	120	32	9	0	3	14	6	10	.267	.417	.295
Road	96	24	5	0	1	7	9	18	.250	.333	.315
Grass	192	52	13	0	4	20	14	25	.271	.401	.316
Artificial Turf	24	4	1	0	0	1	1	3	.167	.208	.200
April	38	6	1	0	0	2	2	7	.158	.184	.220
May	37	9	2	0	2	6	1	6	.243	.459	.256
June	38	10	5	0	0	2	2	4	.263	.395	.300
July	28	6	2	0	0	4	1	1	.214	.286	.303
August	51	15	1	0	1	7	2	7	.294	.373	.309
Sept./Oct.	24	10	3	0	1	3	4	3	.417	.667	.483
Leading Off Inn.	46	14	6	0	1	1	4	6	.304	.500	.360
Runners On	84	17	6	0	0	17	8	11	.202	.274	.265
Runners/Scor. Pos.	44	5	1	0	0	14	5	6	.114	.136	.200
Runners On/2 Out	34	6	3	0	0	3	5	6	.176	.265	.282
Scor. Pos./2 Out	22	1	1	0	0	2	3	4	.045	.091	.160
Late Inning Pressure	37	7	2	0	0	2	2	4	.189	.243	.231
Leading Off	11	2	0	0	0	0	0	1	.182	.182	.182
Runners On	13	3	2	0	0	2	2	1	.231	.385	.333
Runners/Scor. Pos.	9	1	0	0	0	1	1	0	.111	.111	.200

DRIVING IN RUNS	From 1B	From 2B	From 3B	Scoring Position
Totals	3/62	3/36	11/22	14/58
Percentage	5%	8%	50%	24%
Driving In Runners from 3B with Less than Two Out:		10/13		77%

Loves to face: Ron Guidry (.421, 8-for-19)
Hates to face: Joaquin Andujar (.083, 1-for-12)
One of two A.L. players with 50 or more hits, but no three-hit games last season; other: Hal McRae. . . . Career batting average of .305 (36-for-118) at Fenway Park. . . . Hit four home runs in 1986, three of them against Minnesota. . . . Career breakdown: .252 with runners on base, .226 with bases empty. . . . Received a lot of attention for robust hitting with the bases loaded—sort of an early day Pat Tabler—in 1980, his good year: He was 5-for-14 with bases loaded that year, but 4-for-28 since then. . . . Has hit for a higher average against right-handers than against left-handers in each of the last four seasons, despite hitting only .236 vs. righties over that span.

Darnell Coles

Detroit Tigers — Bats Right

	AB	H	2B	3B	HR	RRF	BB	SO	BA	SA	OBA
Season	521	142	30	2	20	86	45	84	.273	.453	.333
vs. Left-Handers	170	48	11	0	3	28	18	20	.282	.400	.346
vs. Right-Handers	351	94	19	2	17	58	27	64	.268	.479	.326
Home	252	72	10	0	12	48	25	47	.286	.468	.346
Road	269	70	20	2	8	38	20	37	.260	.439	.320
Grass	435	119	26	1	17	71	38	71	.274	.455	.332
Artificial Turf	86	23	4	1	3	15	7	13	.267	.442	.337
April	70	19	4	0	2	9	2	8	.271	.414	.292
May	95	31	8	1	6	20	9	15	.326	.621	.398
June	54	14	3	0	1	9	5	10	.259	.370	.317
July	93	18	3	0	3	13	8	25	.194	.323	.267
August	106	30	7	0	4	16	6	13	.283	.462	.325
Sept./Oct.	103	30	5	1	4	19	15	13	.291	.476	.372
Leading Off Inn.	124	28	7	1	3	3	8	20	.226	.371	.284
Runners On	222	64	16	0	8	74	13	27	.288	.468	.322
Runners/Scor. Pos.	121	35	9	0	2	59	8	15	.289	.413	.319
Runners On/2 Out	103	29	9	0	2	30	5	13	.282	.427	.321
Scor. Pos./2 Out	62	18	4	0	0	24	4	8	.290	.355	.333
Late Inning Pressure	63	14	0	0	2	6	8	18	.222	.317	.301
Leading Off	20	6	0	0	1	1	3	5	.300	.450	.391
Runners On	25	4	0	0	0	4	2	6	.160	.160	.207
Runners/Scor. Pos.	14	2	0	0	0	4	2	4	.143	.143	.222

DRIVING IN RUNS	From 1B	From 2B	From 3B	Scoring Position
Totals	14/174	24/107	28/64	52/171
Percentage	8%	22%	44%	30%
Driving In Runners from 3B with Less than Two Out:		20/36		56%

Loves to face: Jim Clancy (.500, 7-for-14)
Hates to face: Jimmy Key (.083, 1-for-12)
Had six extra-base hits (five doubles, one home run) with bases loaded last season to lead majors. In all, batted .348 (8-for-23) with bags full. . . . Batted 96 points higher in night games (.301) than in day games (.205), 5th-largest difference in A.L. (minimum: 50 AB each). . . . Career batting average of .217 at the Kingdome, his old address. . . . Career batting average of .189 in Late-Inning Pressure Situations, .261 in non pressure situations. . . . Sparky had him all over the batting order last season, starting in every slot except leadoff and 8th; most frequently batted 6th (56 starts) or 5th (32 starts).

Batters: American League

Dave Collins

Detroit Tigers — Bats Left and Right

	AB	H	2B	3B	HR	RRF	BB	SO	BA	SA	OBA
Season	419	113	18	2	1	28	44	49	.270	.329	.340
vs. Left-Handers	108	25	7	1	1	12	4	8	.231	.343	.261
vs. Right-Handers	311	88	11	1	0	16	40	41	.283	.325	.366
Home	196	49	10	1	0	11	23	24	.250	.311	.326
Road	223	64	8	1	1	17	21	25	.287	.345	.354
Grass	350	93	15	2	0	21	36	38	.266	.320	.334
Artificial Turf	69	20	3	0	1	7	8	11	.290	.377	.372
April	53	18	2	1	0	8	9	6	.340	.415	.444
May	82	22	6	0	0	3	8	9	.268	.341	.333
June	76	19	5	0	0	2	8	9	.250	.316	.321
July	76	24	1	0	1	7	7	6	.316	.368	.381
August	98	24	4	1	0	5	9	11	.245	.306	.303
Sept./Oct.	34	6	0	0	0	3	3	8	.176	.176	.243
Leading Off Inn.	90	22	3	0	0	0	13	11	.244	.278	.340
Runners On	173	45	6	1	1	28	17	19	.260	.324	.326
Runners/Scor. Pos.	95	27	4	0	0	24	13	12	.284	.326	.364
Runners On/2 Out	77	19	3	0	1	10	5	7	.247	.325	.301
Scor. Pos./2 Out	47	11	2	0	0	7	5	4	.234	.277	.308
Late Inning Pressure	62	16	2	0	1	6	6	6	.258	.339	.324
Leading Off	15	5	0	0	0	0	1	2	.333	.333	.375
Runners On	26	7	1	0	1	6	3	3	.269	.423	.345
Runners/Scor. Pos.	13	3	0	0	0	4	2	3	.231	.231	.333

DRIVING IN RUNS

	From 1B	From 2B	From 3B	Scoring Position
Totals	3/132	12/79	12/34	24/113
Percentage	2%	15%	35%	21%
Driving In Runners from 3B with Less than Two Out:			11/17	65%

Loves to face: Gene Garber (.500, 7-for-14)
Hates to face: Nolan Ryan (.154, 4-for-26, 13 SO)

Expos are his 8th major-league team, and his 6th in the past seven years. . . . Seven of his 12 years in the majors have been spent with teams with artificial-turf home fields; he has hit .284 in those seasons, .261 in seasons in which his home turf was grass. . . . 26 of 32 career home runs have been hit from left side of plate; other than that, there's little to choose in his career batting averages: .276 left-handed, .271 right-handed. . . . Yearly batting averages in Late-Inning Pressure Situations since 1983: .348, .329, .265, .258. . . . Career batting average of .317 with runners in scoring position in LIP situations.

Cecil Cooper

Milwaukee Brewers — Bats Left

	AB	H	2B	3B	HR	RRF	BB	SO	BA	SA	OBA
Season	542	140	24	1	12	76	41	87	.258	.373	.310
vs. Left-Handers	137	39	1	0	3	23	11	28	.285	.358	.342
vs. Right-Handers	405	101	23	1	9	53	30	59	.249	.378	.298
Home	255	60	9	1	6	33	21	46	.235	.349	.294
Road	287	80	15	0	6	43	20	41	.279	.394	.324
Grass	460	115	21	1	11	68	33	76	.250	.372	.299
Artificial Turf	82	25	3	0	1	8	8	11	.305	.378	.367
April	38	7	3	0	1	8	6	13	.184	.342	.289
May	116	34	4	1	4	24	9	20	.293	.448	.349
June	89	21	3	0	2	10	3	15	.236	.337	.261
July	80	21	6	0	0	11	9	13	.263	.338	.337
August	106	29	5	0	4	14	8	14	.274	.434	.319
Sept./Oct.	113	28	3	0	1	9	6	12	.248	.301	.283
Leading Off Inn.	106	25	3	1	2	2	6	22	.236	.340	.277
Runners On	264	78	14	0	7	71	21	27	.295	.428	.345
Runners/Scor. Pos.	149	49	7	0	5	63	15	19	.329	.477	.385
Runners On/2 Out	82	22	5	0	2	26	8	11	.268	.402	.341
Scor. Pos./2 Out	54	16	4	0	1	23	6	9	.296	.426	.377
Late Inning Pressure	70	19	2	1	0	8	6	17	.271	.329	.325
Leading Off	17	6	1	0	1	0	0	4	.353	.529	.353
Runners On	32	10	1	0	0	8	4	6	.313	.344	.372
Runners/Scor. Pos.	17	6	0	0	0	8	4	6	.353	.353	.455

DRIVING IN RUNS

	From 1B	From 2B	From 3B	Scoring Position
Totals	11/179	26/116	27/54	53/170
Percentage	6%	22%	50%	31%
Driving In Runners from 3B with Less than Two Out:			19/33	58%

Loves to face: Jack Morris (.341, 29-for-85, 4 HR)
Hates to face: Mike Brown (.071, 1-for-14)

Had career batting average of .29979 going into 1986 season-ending doubleheader at Toronto; 2-for-3 in opener put him at .29994; pinch-hit single off Eichhorn in 9th inning of second game lifted him over .300, to .30004. . . . That left him as one of five players active in 1986 with both a .300 career average and 2000 hits; others: Brett, Parker, Rice, and Rose. . . . Has hit for a higher average against left-handers than against right-handers in each of the last three seasons. Batting average vs. right-handed pitchers was his lowest in the 12 years. . . . Batted .098 (2-for-41) vs. Boston last season, but still has .313 career average against his old club.

Julio Cruz

Chicago White Sox — Bats Left and Right

	AB	H	2B	3B	HR	RRF	BB	SO	BA	SA	OBA
Season	209	45	2	0	0	19	42	28	.215	.225	.343
vs. Left-Handers	73	16	1	0	0	7	10	12	.219	.233	.310
vs. Right-Handers	136	29	1	0	0	12	32	16	.213	.221	.359
Home	98	26	0	0	0	15	25	10	.265	.265	.408
Road	111	19	2	0	0	4	17	18	.171	.189	.279
Grass	169	35	1	0	0	19	37	22	.207	.213	.344
Artificial Turf	40	10	1	0	0	0	5	6	.250	.275	.333
April	13	1	0	0	0	0	1	3	.077	.077	.143
May	20	3	0	0	0	0	4	3	.150	.150	.292
June	73	24	1	0	0	11	17	8	.329	.342	.451
July	50	9	0	0	0	4	10	9	.180	.180	.317
August	53	8	1	0	0	4	10	5	.151	.170	.277
Sept./Oct.	0	0	0	0	0	0	0	0	—	—	—
Leading Off Inn.	49	12	0	0	0	0	8	6	.245	.245	.351
Runners On	88	21	0	0	0	19	17	13	.239	.239	.352
Runners/Scor. Pos.	50	16	0	0	0	19	11	8	.320	.320	.422
Runners On/2 Out	39	9	0	0	0	8	6	5	.231	.231	.333
Scor. Pos./2 Out	24	8	0	0	0	8	4	5	.333	.333	.429
Late Inning Pressure	21	4	0	0	0	1	4	3	.190	.190	.308
Leading Off	10	2	0	0	0	0	1	0	.200	.200	.273
Runners On	4	1	0	0	0	1	2	1	.250	.250	.429
Runners/Scor. Pos.	1	0	0	0	0	1	1	1	.000	.000	.333

DRIVING IN RUNS

	From 1B	From 2B	From 3B	Scoring Position
Totals	0/62	6/37	13/26	19/63
Percentage	0%	16%	50%	30%
Driving In Runners from 3B with Less than Two Out:			8/12	67%

Loves to face: Frank Tanana (.386, 17-for-44, 2 HR)
Hates to face: Mark Clear (.063, 1-for-16)

Had 127 plate appearances in home games without an extra-base hit; that's the most by anyone over the last 12 years. . . . No XBH in 88 at bats with runners on base, either. . . . This was on the heels of 1985, when he had 118 plate appearances against right-handed pitchers without an extra-base hit; that, too, was a major-league high since 1975. . . . Batting average in August was lowest in A.L. (minimum: 50 AB). . . . Gorman Thomas and George Wright are only players active (if that's the word) in 1986 who, over 1985-86 span, had lower batting average than Cruz's .205. . . . Chicago played .472 ball with Cruz starting at second base; .422 with other starters there.

Alvin Davis

Seattle Mariners — Bats Left

	AB	H	2B	3B	HR	RRF	BB	SO	BA	SA	OBA
Season	479	130	18	1	18	75	76	68	.271	.426	.373
vs. Left-Handers	122	30	3	0	0	16	25	24	.246	.270	.376
vs. Right-Handers	357	100	15	1	18	59	51	44	.280	.479	.372
Home	249	70	9	1	14	50	40	29	.281	.494	.385
Road	230	60	9	0	4	25	36	39	.261	.352	.361
Grass	178	40	5	0	4	16	25	32	.225	.320	.320
Artificial Turf	301	90	13	1	14	59	51	36	.299	.488	.404
April	58	12	1	1	5	9	8	12	.207	.517	.303
May	100	35	6	0	4	22	23	14	.350	.530	.472
June	79	20	6	0	2	13	7	7	.253	.405	.381
July	41	14	0	0	1	5	6	4	.341	.415	.438
August	98	29	3	0	5	16	8	15	.296	.480	.355
Sept./Oct.	103	20	2	0	1	10	14	16	.194	.243	.294
Leading Off Inn.	93	26	4	0	1	1	11	11	.280	.355	.362
Runners On	230	64	10	1	5	62	42	34	.278	.396	.389
Runners/Scor. Pos.	132	39	6	0	2	52	35	17	.295	.386	.441
Runners On/2 Out	73	20	1	0	2	16	21	10	.274	.370	.436
Scor. Pos./2 Out	42	10	1	0	0	12	19	6	.238	.262	.475
Late Inning Pressure	72	16	1	0	4	5	11	11	.222	.403	.325
Leading Off	28	7	1	0	0	0	2	4	.250	.286	.300
Runners On	21	4	0	0	0	1	6	4	.190	.190	.370
Runners/Scor. Pos.	9	2	0	0	0	1	6	0	.222	.222	.533

DRIVING IN RUNS

	From 1B	From 2B	From 3B	Scoring Position
Totals	10/159	23/105	24/50	47/155
Percentage	6%	22%	48%	30%
Driving In Runners from 3B with Less than Two Out:			21/35	60%

Loves to face: Dan Petry (.556, 10-for-18, 1 HR)
Hates to face: Ron Romanick (.056, 1-for-18, 1 HR)

Has hit more homers at the Kingdome than he has in road games in each of his three seasons in majors; career: 40 at home, 23 on road. . . . Favorite place on road: Fenway Park, where his career average is .348 (16-for-46), with three home runs. . . . One of only two A.L. players in the Seventy Club: 70 or more RBI, 70 or more walks and a .270+ batting average in each of last three years; the other: Eddie Murray. . . . Career vs. right-handers: .291, one home run every 20.7 at bats; vs. left-handers: .260, one every 56.0 at bats. . . . Last home run off a southpaw: Sept. 15, 1985, off Royals' Mike Jones. . . . Lowest fielding percentage (.986) of any first baseman in majors in 1986 (minimum: 100 games).

Mike Davis

Oakland As — Bats Left

	AB	H	2B	3B	HR	RRF	BB	SO	BA	SA	OBA
Season	489	131	28	3	19	57	34	91	.268	.454	.314
vs. Left-Handers	120	36	5	2	4	19	6	30	.300	.475	.339
vs. Right-Handers	369	95	23	1	15	38	28	61	.257	.447	.306
Home	244	65	14	2	11	29	28	40	.266	.475	.338
Road	245	66	14	1	8	28	6	51	.269	.433	.287
Grass	418	105	21	2	15	42	32	79	.251	.419	.302
Artificial Turf	71	26	7	1	4	15	2	12	.366	.662	.387
April	47	11	3	0	0	4	2	6	.234	.298	.260
May	88	22	8	0	4	11	8	22	.250	.477	.309
June	92	24	6	0	5	14	9	17	.261	.489	.320
July	83	22	1	1	2	7	4	12	.265	.373	.307
August	77	22	5	0	6	8	5	18	.286	.584	.329
Sept./Oct.	102	30	5	2	2	13	6	16	.294	.441	.330
Leading Off Inn.	104	37	8	1	7	7	5	15	.356	.654	.385
Runners On	196	52	10	2	4	42	16	37	.265	.398	.317
Runners/Scor. Pos.	105	25	6	1	1	33	9	21	.238	.343	.292
Runners On/2 Out	77	18	2	0	0	10	9	16	.234	.260	.314
Scor. Pos./2 Out	50	11	2	0	0	10	7	10	.220	.260	.316
Late Inning Pressure	73	12	1	1	3	6	3	18	.164	.342	.195
Leading Off	15	5	1	0	1	1	0	3	.333	.600	.333
Runners On	30	5	1	1	0	3	3	10	.167	.267	.235
Runners/Scor. Pos.	16	2	1	0	0	2	2	5	.125	.188	.211

DRIVING IN RUNS	From 1B	From 2B	From 3B	Scoring Position
Totals	9/154	12/84	17/49	29/133
Percentage	6%	14%	35%	22%
Driving In Runners from 3B with Less than Two Out:			11/24	46%

Loves to face: Mark Eichhorn (.583, 7-for-12, 3 HR)
Hates to face: Scott McGregor (0-for-12)
Calm before Storm: hit two homers off Baltimore's Davis on Aug. 29; that's the first two-homer game Storm's allowed. . . . Tied Jim Gantner for A.L.'s biggest oh-fer with bases loaded last season: 0-for-10 (with four strikeouts). . . . Career batting average with runners in scoring position: .324 with less than two outs, .207 with two outs. . . . Started 26 of 53 games in which Oakland faced a left-handed starter last year. Evidence says that he has learned to hit left-handers; annual batting averages vs. lefties since 1984: .205, .271, .300. . . . Career average of .260 on grass fields, .307 on artificial surfaces. . . . Has homered in every A.L. ballpark except Yankee Stadium (64 career AB).

Doug DeCinces

California Angels — Bats Right

	AB	H	2B	3B	HR	RRF	BB	SO	BA	SA	OBA
Season	512	131	20	3	26	99	52	74	.256	.459	.325
vs. Left-Handers	173	47	8	1	9	36	21	24	.272	.486	.345
vs. Right-Handers	339	84	12	2	17	63	31	50	.248	.445	.314
Home	259	68	8	0	14	51	25	39	.263	.456	.328
Road	253	63	12	3	12	48	27	35	.249	.462	.322
Grass	451	118	17	3	23	91	43	66	.262	.466	.327
Artificial Turf	61	13	3	0	3	8	9	8	.213	.410	.306
April	80	19	3	1	3	13	7	7	.238	.413	.303
May	95	20	3	0	2	12	11	11	.211	.305	.292
June	73	21	4	0	5	18	9	14	.288	.548	.361
July	72	19	5	0	2	15	4	13	.264	.417	.299
August	95	32	4	1	9	25	12	7	.337	.684	.407
Sept./Oct.	97	20	1	1	5	16	9	22	.206	.392	.280
Leading Off Inn.	83	23	2	1	6	6	14	7	.277	.542	.388
Runners On	268	73	8	2	12	85	23	39	.272	.451	.328
Runners/Scor. Pos.	164	45	6	2	4	68	20	26	.274	.409	.349
Runners On/2 Out	106	31	2	1	5	35	14	14	.292	.472	.380
Scor. Pos./2 Out	75	22	2	1	1	27	13	11	.293	.387	.404
Late Inning Pressure	77	22	2	0	5	14	8	12	.286	.506	.353
Leading Off	13	4	0	0	1	1	3	3	.308	.538	.438
Runners On	43	14	1	0	3	12	2	8	.326	.558	.356
Runners/Scor. Pos.	23	4	0	0	0	5	2	7	.174	.174	.240

DRIVING IN RUNS	From 1B	From 2B	From 3B	Scoring Position
Totals	12/198	32/134	29/65	61/199
Percentage	6%	24%	45%	31%
Driving In Runners from 3B with Less than Two Out:			22/37	59%

Loves to face: Joe Niekro (.667, 4-for-6, 3 HR)
Hates to face: Dave Stewart (.056, 1-for-18)
Has hit 114 home runs over past five years; which third basemen have hit more? Brett? 105. Gaetti? 105. Wallach? 105. Cey? 108. Horner? 109. Only Schmidt (181) stands ahead of him. . . . Batting .368 (42-for-114) with bases loaded over past nine years, but would have traded all of that for just one long fly ball with bases loaded in ninth inning of Game Five of A.L.C.S. . . . Did not go three consecutive games without a hit from July 1985 to August 1986. . . . Drove in 17 runs in 13 games vs. Oakland last season. . . . Only 1.73 assists per nine innings last season, 2d-lowest average among A.L. third basemen (minimum: 500 innings).

Rob Deer

Milwaukee Brewers — Bats Right

	AB	H	2B	3B	HR	RRF	BB	SO	BA	SA	OBA
Season	466	108	17	3	33	89	72	179	.232	.494	.336
vs. Left-Handers	129	36	5	2	11	28	31	40	.279	.605	.416
vs. Right-Handers	337	72	12	1	22	61	41	139	.214	.451	.303
Home	238	54	7	1	19	51	37	91	.227	.504	.329
Road	228	54	10	2	14	38	35	88	.237	.482	.345
Grass	411	93	15	2	27	76	64	158	.226	.470	.333
Artificial Turf	55	15	2	1	6	13	8	21	.273	.673	.365
April	48	10	1	0	4	9	6	18	.208	.479	.309
May	74	19	3	1	5	15	15	28	.257	.527	.389
June	73	14	0	1	4	12	6	33	.192	.479	.247
July	74	19	4	0	6	18	11	23	.257	.554	.356
August	105	26	4	0	11	30	16	36	.248	.600	.347
Sept./Oct.	92	20	5	1	3	5	18	41	.217	.391	.345
Leading Off Inn.	106	24	3	0	6	18	32		.226	.425	.339
Runners On	228	57	11	1	18	74	36	89	.250	.544	.351
Runners/Scor. Pos.	125	30	4	1	8	53	22	43	.240	.480	.351
Runners On/2 Out	95	15	4	1	5	23	24	42	.158	.379	.328
Scor. Pos./2 Out	53	8	2	1	2	16	16	22	.151	.340	.348
Late Inning Pressure	69	15	2	1	3	7	6	28	.217	.406	.289
Leading Off	21	7	1	0	0	0	3	3	.333	.381	.417
Runners On	30	5	1	0	2	6	1	16	.167	.400	.219
Runners/Scor. Pos.	17	3	1	0	1	4	0	6	.176	.412	.222

DRIVING IN RUNS	From 1B	From 2B	From 3B	Scoring Position
Totals	16/177	16/86	24/61	40/147
Percentage	9%	19%	39%	27%
Driving In Runners from 3B with Less than Two Out:			17/33	52%

Loves to face: Charlie Hough (3-for-3, 1 HR)
Hates to face: Frank Tanana (.100, 1-for-10, 5 SO)
Baseball fans, identify Dean Freeland and Eric Pilkington. Time's up; they're the two pitchers obtained by the Giants for Deer in December 1985. . . . One home run every 14.1 at bats last season, 2d-best rate in the majors (minimum: 10 HR). . . . Career vs. left-handers: .256, one home run every 11.1 at bats, one strikeout every 3.7 plate appearances; vs. right-handers: .201, one HR every 17.4 AB, one whiff every 2.7 PA. . . . Has batted 23 times in Late-Inning Pressure Situations with runners on and two outs: He's 2-for-19, with four walks and 13 strikeouts. . . . One advantage to all those strikeouts: grounded into only four double plays in 116 double-play situations, 2d-lowest rate in A.L. (minimum: 40 opportunities).

Rick Dempsey

Baltimore Orioles — Bats Right

	AB	H	2B	3B	HR	RRF	BB	SO	BA	SA	OBA
Season	327	68	15	1	13	29	45	78	.208	.379	.309
vs. Left-Handers	138	35	8	1	6	15	22	21	.254	.457	.356
vs. Right-Handers	189	33	7	0	7	14	23	57	.175	.323	.274
Home	158	34	5	0	7	15	25	35	.215	.380	.326
Road	169	34	10	1	6	14	20	43	.201	.379	.293
Grass	261	52	10	1	11	24	38	60	.199	.372	.308
Artificial Turf	66	16	5	0	2	5	7	18	.242	.409	.315
April	54	12	4	0	3	5	6	11	.222	.463	.300
May	61	13	1	0	3	8	6	13	.213	.377	.294
June	55	10	2	0	2	5	9	16	.182	.327	.308
July	68	19	5	1	3	6	12	16	.279	.515	.395
August	49	4	2	0	0	2	7	14	.082	.122	.196
Sept./Oct.	40	10	1	0	2	3	5	8	.250	.425	.333
Leading Off Inn.	66	21	4	0	6	6	9	14	.318	.652	.400
Runners On	147	18	4	0	3	19	18	36	.122	.211	.228
Runners/Scor. Pos.	91	12	3	0	3	19	10	18	.132	.264	.233
Runners On/2 Out	63	5	0	0	2	7	10	12	.079	.175	.216
Scor. Pos./2 Out	42	3	0	0	2	7	7	5	.071	.214	.220
Late Inning Pressure	39	4	0	0	0	1	7	9	.103	.103	.239
Leading Off	7	1	0	0	0	0	1	2	.143	.143	.333
Runners On	18	1	0	0	0	1	2	2	.056	.056	.150
Runners/Scor. Pos.	11	1	0	0	0	1	2	1	.091	.091	.231

DRIVING IN RUNS	From 1B	From 2B	From 3B	Scoring Position
Totals	2/101	7/79	7/40	14/119
Percentage	2%	9%	18%	12%
Driving In Runners from 3B with Less than Two Out:			5/16	31%

Loves to face: Jamie Easterly (.455, 5-for-11, 2 HR)
Hates to face: Scott Bailes (0-for-7)
Who besides Dempsey was the last to lead Orioles in games caught? Answer below. . . . Has played in each of last 18 A.L. seasons; one year away from A.L. record for consecutive seasons by catcher, set by Luke Sewell (1921–39); Sewell also caught six games in 1942, for 20 seasons overall. . . . Percentage of runners driven in from scoring position (11.8%, 14-of-119) was lowest in majors last season (minimum: 50 opportunities), and percentage from third base with less than two outs (31.3, 5-of-16) was 3d worst in A.L. (minimum: 15 opp.). . . . Batted 155 points lower with runners on than with bases empty, largest difference in majors (minimum: 100 AB both ways). . . . Answer: Dave Duncan, 1976.

Brian Downing

California Angels   Bats Right

	AB	H	2B	3B	HR	RRF	BB	SO	BA	SA	OBA
Season	513	137	27	4	20	98	90	84	.267	.452	.389
vs. Left-Handers	183	44	14	1	7	32	42	34	.240	.443	.385
vs. Right-Handers	330	93	13	3	13	66	48	50	.282	.458	.390
Home	260	72	10	3	13	54	47	37	.277	.488	.392
Road	253	65	17	1	7	44	43	47	.257	.415	.385
Grass	435	120	20	3	18	82	79	73	.276	.460	.397
Artificial Turf	78	17	7	1	2	16	11	11	.218	.410	.340
April	75	21	5	1	5	19	11	14	.280	.573	.385
May	90	28	8	1	0	7	18	15	.311	.422	.441
June	85	26	4	1	4	18	14	10	.306	.518	.416
July	89	18	0	1	3	14	16	13	.202	.326	.336
August	85	18	4	0	2	16	15	16	.212	.329	.343
Sept./Oct.	89	26	6	0	6	24	16	16	.292	.562	.409
Leading Off Inn.	105	30	6	1	4	4	12	16	.286	.476	.395
Runners On	243	67	13	2	13	90	53	37	.276	.506	.403
Runners/Scor. Pos.	149	40	9	2	7	76	32	23	.268	.497	.391
Runners On/2 Out	102	27	8	0	4	35	28	16	.265	.461	.427
Scor. Pos./2 Out	68	18	5	0	3	31	17	12	.265	.471	.419
Late Inning Pressure	61	15	2	1	3	12	14	11	.246	.459	.410
Leading Off	12	3	1	0	1	1	3	2	.250	.583	.438
Runners On	30	7	1	0	2	10	6	5	.233	.467	.361
Runners/Scor. Pos.	18	5	1	0	1	8	4	3	.278	.500	.409

DRIVING IN RUNS	From 1B	From 2B	From 3B	Scoring Position
Totals	15/175	27/117	34/71	61/188
Percentage	9%	23%	48%	32%
Driving In Runners from 3B with Less than Two Out:		25/37		68%

Loves to face: Chris Codiroli (.458, 11-for-24, 3 HR)
Hates to face: Ted Higuera (0-for-12)
Memo to A.L. managers: Don't load the bases for this guy: Nine hits with bases loaded (in 17 AB) last season were the most in A.L. . . . Has hit six grand slams over the last six seasons. . . . Has been hit by a pitch with bases loaded four times in last 12 years, the most by anyone over that span, not even counting his clutch HBP off Schiraldi in A.L.C.S. Game Four. . . . Homered against every opposing A.L. club except Toronto last season. . . . Yearly batting averages vs. left-handed pitchers since 1982: .318, .294, .293, .262, .240. . . . Career fielding percentage as outfielder is .995, highest among active players with 500 games. To qualify for all-time record (.993, Terry Puhl), you need 1000 games; Downing has 743.

Mike Easler

New York Yankees   Bats Left

	AB	H	2B	3B	HR	RRF	BB	SO	BA	SA	OBA
Season	490	148	26	2	14	84	49	87	.302	.449	.362
vs. Left-Handers	106	24	3	1	1	8	4	31	.226	.302	.252
vs. Right-Handers	384	124	23	1	13	76	45	56	.323	.490	.390
Home	233	67	16	1	6	37	24	42	.288	.442	.349
Road	257	81	10	1	8	47	25	45	.315	.455	.375
Grass	404	120	24	1	12	65	36	63	.297	.450	.351
Artificial Turf	86	28	2	1	2	19	13	24	.326	.442	.414
April	63	16	4	0	1	12	4	6	.254	.365	.299
May	75	26	4	1	3	14	9	14	.347	.547	.412
June	107	40	8	0	2	18	8	15	.374	.505	.410
July	93	27	4	0	2	9	15	21	.290	.398	.389
August	82	16	4	1	3	17	7	19	.195	.378	.253
Sept./Oct.	70	23	2	0	3	14	6	12	.329	.486	.382
Leading Off Inn.	106	36	6	0	7	7	8	13	.340	.594	.386
Runners On	241	75	13	1	5	75	30	41	.311	.436	.380
Runners/Scor. Pos.	130	39	7	0	2	64	24	25	.300	.400	.396
Runners On/2 Out	106	29	4	0	3	29	12	27	.274	.396	.347
Scor. Pos./2 Out	63	14	2	0	1	24	10	18	.222	.302	.329
Late Inning Pressure	61	17	4	1	0	8	11	15	.279	.377	.389
Leading Off	18	3	2	0	0	0	2	3	.167	.278	.250
Runners On	26	8	1	0	0	8	7	7	.308	.346	.455
Runners/Scor. Pos.	11	5	1	0	0	8	6	3	.455	.545	.647

DRIVING IN RUNS	From 1B	From 2B	From 3B	Scoring Position
Totals	11/184	30/96	29/63	59/159
Percentage	6%	31%	46%	37%
Driving In Runners from 3B with Less than Two Out:		22/32		69%

Loves to face: Doyle Alexander (.484, 15-for-31, 3 HR)
Hates to face: Bill Campbell (.067, 1-for-15)
Can a full-time designated hitter find happiness by returning to the National League? In 1982 Al Oliver led N.L. in batting and RBIs after spending the 1981 season as A.L.'s premier DH. . . . Made four errors in 31 games in outfield over last two years; last played first base in 1984 (29 games for Boston). . . . Batted 97 points higher vs. right-handed pitchers than against left-handed pitchers, largest difference in A.L. (minimum: 100 AB vs. each). . . . Started all but one of 109 games in which Yankees faced a right-handed starter last season, but only 16 of 53 against lefties. . . . Batting average of .374 in June was 5th highest in major leagues (minimum: 75 AB).

Darrell Evans

Detroit Tigers   Bats Left

	AB	H	2B	3B	HR	RRF	BB	SO	BA	SA	OBA
Season	507	122	15	0	29	86	91	105	.241	.442	.356
vs. Left-Handers	147	40	4	0	9	32	23	39	.272	.483	.374
vs. Right-Handers	360	82	11	0	20	54	68	66	.228	.425	.349
Home	246	58	8	0	15	47	43	48	.236	.451	.351
Road	261	64	7	0	14	39	48	57	.245	.433	.361
Grass	431	104	13	0	26	75	75	89	.241	.452	.354
Artificial Turf	76	18	2	0	3	11	16	16	.237	.382	.370
April	59	14	1	0	5	8	8	11	.237	.508	.328
May	94	20	4	0	4	12	14	16	.213	.383	.315
June	67	20	3	0	3	18	13	11	.299	.478	.407
July	86	23	3	0	4	15	17	14	.267	.442	.394
August	101	27	2	0	10	22	18	25	.267	.584	.378
Sept./Oct.	100	18	2	0	3	11	21	28	.180	.290	.320
Leading Off Inn.	107	22	0	0	5	5	17	21	.206	.346	.320
Runners On	229	58	9	0	10	67	51	54	.253	.424	.387
Runners/Scor. Pos.	141	36	6	0	7	59	33	33	.255	.447	.392
Runners On/2 Out	118	29	7	0	3	30	24	28	.246	.381	.373
Scor. Pos./2 Out	77	21	5	0	2	27	18	19	.273	.416	.411
Late Inning Pressure	72	25	2	0	8	24	14	13	.347	.708	.453
Leading Off	18	5	0	0	3	3	4	4	.278	.778	.409
Runners On	32	15	1	0	2	18	8	4	.469	.688	.575
Runners/Scor. Pos.	17	9	1	0	2	18	5	1	.529	.941	.636

DRIVING IN RUNS	From 1B	From 2B	From 3B	Scoring Position
Totals	9/160	22/106	26/69	48/175
Percentage	6%	21%	38%	27%
Driving In Runners from 3B with Less than Two Out:		15/29		52%

Loves to face: Tim Lollar (.385, 10-for-26, 4 HR)
Hates to face: Al Nipper (.071, 1-for-14)
Leads A.L. with 69 home runs over past two years; Schmidt, with 70, leads N.L. . . . Eight home runs in Late-Inning Pressure Situations tied him with Jim Presley for major-league lead. . . . Eight home runs in 63 career at bats at the Metrodome. . . . One of six A.L. players to hit a home run against every opposing club in 1986. . . . One of three major-league players with two grand slam homers in each of last two seasons (others: Eddie Murray, Dave Parker); seven hits in 18 at bats with bases loaded last season. . . . Had higher fielding percentage at first base (.998) than Don Mattingly (.996), but played in only 105 games there, three shy of minimum needed to qualify as leader.

Dwight Evans

Boston Red Sox   Bats Right

	AB	H	2B	3B	HR	RRF	BB	SO	BA	SA	OBA
Season	529	137	33	2	26	97	97	117	.259	.476	.376
vs. Left-Handers	136	31	5	0	6	23	29	25	.228	.397	.363
vs. Right-Handers	393	106	28	2	20	74	68	92	.270	.504	.381
Home	241	61	18	1	8	41	51	42	.253	.436	.384
Road	288	76	15	1	18	56	46	75	.264	.510	.370
Grass	438	108	26	2	21	80	83	94	.247	.459	.369
Artificial Turf	91	29	7	0	5	17	14	23	.319	.560	.411
April	73	19	4	1	2	9	14	8	.260	.425	.382
May	92	18	11	0	1	7	18	22	.196	.348	.327
June	95	26	2	1	6	26	15	20	.274	.505	.366
July	90	26	5	0	5	22	13	24	.289	.511	.385
August	89	26	6	0	5	18	18	19	.292	.528	.413
Sept./Oct.	90	22	5	0	7	15	19	24	.244	.533	.386
Leading Off Inn.	142	35	12	0	5	5	23	36	.246	.437	.359
Runners On	235	66	18	1	12	83	44	51	.281	.519	.388
Runners/Scor. Pos.	135	37	7	1	4	62	32	28	.274	.430	.402
Runners On/2 Out	98	28	6	1	5	42	21	21	.286	.520	.412
Scor. Pos./2 Out	67	22	5	1	2	35	16	15	.328	.522	.458
Late Inning Pressure	59	18	3	0	5	11	13	8	.305	.610	.431
Leading Off	20	6	2	0	3	3	2	3	.300	.850	.364
Runners On	20	6	1	0	1	7	5	3	.300	.500	.440
Runners/Scor. Pos.	13	4	1	0	1	7	3	3	.308	.615	.438

DRIVING IN RUNS	From 1B	From 2B	From 3B	Scoring Position
Totals	19/190	20/118	32/58	52/176
Percentage	10%	17%	55%	30%
Driving In Runners from 3B with Less than Two Out:		18/26		69%

Loves to face: Ernie Camacho (.714, 5-for-7, 2 HR)
Hates to face: Bill Swaggerty (0-for-8)
First player in history to hit the first pitch of a major-league season's first game for a home run. . . . Has hit 163 home runs over last six years, tied for 2d in A.L. with Tony Armas, one behind Eddie Murray. . . . Evans has also walked the most times (574) by any A.L. player over that span. . . . Hit home runs off Gooden and Darling in World Series. . . . Homered against every opposing A.L. club except Cleveland last season. . . . Batting average vs. left-handers was his lowest in last 12 years, as he batted higher vs. right-handers than vs. left-handers for first time since 1977. . . . McNamara used him as leadoff batter for first 34 games, of which Sox won 21, but during which Evans hit only .250 with three home runs.

Tony Fernandez
Toronto Blue Jays — Bats Left and Right

	AB	H	2B	3B	HR	RRF	BB	SO	BA	SA	OBA
Season	687	213	33	9	10	67	27	52	.310	.428	.338
vs. Left-Handers	205	65	12	2	5	31	9	21	.317	.468	.347
vs. Right-Handers	482	148	21	7	5	36	18	31	.307	.411	.334
Home	337	108	14	5	4	25	11	21	.320	.427	.345
Road	350	105	19	4	6	42	16	31	.300	.429	.332
Grass	272	80	14	2	5	31	13	26	.294	.415	.328
Artificial Turf	415	133	19	7	5	36	14	26	.320	.436	.345
April	83	22	2	1	0	4	5	8	.265	.313	.307
May	109	30	5	1	1	7	8	9	.275	.367	.319
June	122	47	7	3	3	17	6	4	.385	.566	.414
July	120	38	10	2	1	15	2	7	.317	.458	.331
August	125	39	7	1	3	17	4	11	.312	.456	.348
Sept./Oct.	128	37	2	1	2	7	2	13	.289	.367	.298
Leading Off Inn.	236	72	12	1	4	4	8	18	.305	.415	.336
Runners On	232	76	15	4	5	62	8	13	.328	.491	.347
Runners/Scor. Pos.	117	40	10	3	0	49	6	8	.342	.479	.362
Runners On/2 Out	99	34	7	1	2	26	4	5	.343	.495	.369
Scor. Pos./2 Out	52	21	5	1	0	21	3	4	.404	.538	.436
Late Inning Pressure	102	37	6	2	2	13	2	4	.363	.520	.375
Leading Off	30	11	2	0	0	0	1	2	.367	.433	.387
Runners On	45	14	4	2	1	12	0	0	.311	.556	.311
Runners/Scor. Pos.	23	5	1	1	0	8	0	0	.217	.348	.217

DRIVING IN RUNS	From 1B	From 2B	From 3B	Scoring Position
Totals	11/182	16/93	30/48	46/141
Percentage	6%	17%	63%	33%
Driving In Runners from 3B with Less than Two Out:	18/29			62%

Loves to face: Ken Schrom (.438, 7-for-16, 1 HR)
Hates to face: Jack Morris (.045, 1-for-22)
Had 212 of his 213 hits while playing shortstop, the most hits by a shortstop in this century (Cecil Travis had 218 hits for 1941 Senators, but only 197 of them came while playing at short). . . . Toronto won all 10 games in which he hit a home run last season. . . . Had 65 multiple-hit games last season, 3d most in A.L. . . . Batting average of .385 in June was 2d highest in majors (minimum: 75 AB). . . . Career average of .2955 batting right-handed, .2950 batting left-handed. . . . Played 163 games at shortstop last season, but didn't even *tie* the major-league record. Maury Wills played 165 in 1962, including three-game pennant playoff vs. Giants. (At least Fernandez got the American League record.)

Carlton Fisk
Chicago White Sox — Bats Right

	AB	H	2B	3B	HR	RRF	BB	SO	BA	SA	OBA
Season	457	101	11	0	14	66	22	92	.221	.337	.263
vs. Left-Handers	157	35	5	0	5	23	7	35	.223	.350	.253
vs. Right-Handers	300	66	6	0	9	43	15	57	.220	.330	.268
Home	232	48	4	0	5	29	8	43	.207	.289	.236
Road	225	53	7	0	9	37	14	49	.236	.387	.290
Grass	388	83	8	0	9	45	17	74	.214	.304	.250
Artificial Turf	69	18	3	0	5	21	5	18	.261	.522	.329
April	72	14	4	0	2	16	3	18	.194	.333	.241
May	99	23	1	0	2	16	12	23	.232	.303	.325
June	97	24	3	0	3	24	6	23	.247	.371	.296
July	49	4	0	0	0	1	1	8	.082	.082	.100
August	84	21	1	0	5	11	0	14	.250	.440	.250
Sept./Oct.	56	15	2	0	2	8	0	6	.268	.411	.268
Leading Off Inn.	98	18	3	0	5		6	18	.184	.367	.245
Runners On	210	52	4	0	7	59	14	40	.248	.367	.296
Runners/Scor. Pos.	121	29	2	0	5	55	10	24	.240	.380	.295
Runners On/2 Out	86	16	2	0	5	27	8	15	.186	.384	.255
Scor. Pos./2 Out	57	11	1	0	4	25	6	9	.193	.421	.270
Late Inning Pressure	79	17	3	0	3	18	3	19	.215	.367	.247
Leading Off	21	1	0	0	0	0	2	5	.048	.048	.130
Runners On	34	11	2	0	3	18	1	8	.324	.647	.342
Runners/Scor. Pos.	25	9	2	0	2	16	1	5	.360	.680	.379

DRIVING IN RUNS	From 1B	From 2B	From 3B	Scoring Position
Totals	8/155	16/93	28/62	44/155
Percentage	5%	17%	45%	28%
Driving In Runners from 3B with Less than Two Out:	19/34			56%

Loves to face: Mark Langston (.455, 5-for-11, 2 HR)
Hates to face: Ken Schrom (.056, 1-for-18)
Red Sox fans: Who pitched for the Sox when Fisk made his major-league debut, Sept. 18, 1969? Hint: he, too, was a rookie in '69, with a 12–2 record. Answer below. . . . Did not drive in a run in 19 consecutive games from June 30 to Aug. 2, the longest RBI drought of his career; he started 16 of those 19 games. . . . Did he have a clause in his contract based on "official at bats," or what? He did not have a walk—or a hit-by-pitch, or a sacrifice bunt or fly—in any of his 165 plate appearances after July 22. . . . Participated in a triple play for first time in major-league career last June 15. . . . Has hit for a higher average with runners on base than with bases empty in six of the last seven seasons. . . . Answer: Mike Nagy.

Scott Fletcher
Texas Rangers — Bats Right

	AB	H	2B	3B	HR	RRF	BB	SO	BA	SA	OBA
Season	530	159	34	5	3	53	47	59	.300	.400	.360
vs. Left-Handers	175	51	13	2	2	21	15	17	.291	.423	.347
vs. Right-Handers	355	108	21	3	1	32	32	42	.304	.389	.365
Home	253	78	15	3	2	28	19	27	.308	.415	.360
Road	277	81	19	2	1	25	28	32	.292	.386	.359
Grass	443	138	27	4	3	43	37	48	.312	.411	.365
Artificial Turf	87	21	7	1	0	10	10	11	.241	.345	.333
April	51	14	2	1	0	3	6	6	.275	.353	.362
May	78	24	4	2	0	10	8	10	.308	.410	.379
June	91	26	5	2	0	7	8	12	.286	.385	.340
July	104	41	13	0	2	12	7	3	.394	.577	.430
August	107	30	5	0	0	16	9	13	.280	.327	.336
Sept./Oct.	99	24	5	0	1	5	9	15	.242	.323	.312
Leading Off Inn.	116	36	7	0	1	1	9	13	.310	.397	.360
Runners On	195	60	14	1	1	49	16	21	.308	.405	.364
Runners/Scor. Pos.	112	32	8	0	0	43	10	12	.286	.357	.346
Runners On/2 Out	70	18	5	0	1	16	4	6	.257	.371	.307
Scor. Pos./2 Out	50	12	4	0	0	13	2	6	.240	.320	.283
Late Inning Pressure	66	14	4	0	0	8	4	13	.212	.273	.264
Leading Off	18	3	0	0	0	0	1	4	.167	.167	.211
Runners On	32	9	4	0	0	8	2	7	.281	.406	.333
Runners/Scor. Pos.	19	4	1	0	0	7	1	4	.211	.263	.238

DRIVING IN RUNS	From 1B	From 2B	From 3B	Scoring Position
Totals	7/132	16/85	25/44	41/129
Percentage	5%	19%	57%	32%
Driving In Runners from 3B with Less than Two Out:	20/27			74%

Loves to face: Ted Higuera (.563, 9-for-16, 1 HR)
Hates to face: Roger Clemens (0-for-11)
Batted over .300 for most of the season but slipped to .294 by the end of September. It took a five-hit game and some selective benching during the season's final week to ensure a .300 season. . . . There were 22 .300 hitters in majors last season (minimum: 502 PA). Only one had a career average of less than .250 entering the season—Fletcher; and only two were never walked intentionally—Fletcher and Tony Bernazard. . . . July batting average was highest in the majors (minimum: 75 AB). . . . Overall average has improved in each of the last three seasons, while his average with runners in scoring position has dropped: .360, .306, .286. Career average of .303 with runners in scoring position.

Julio Franco
Cleveland Indians — Bats Right

	AB	H	2B	3B	HR	RRF	BB	SO	BA	SA	OBA
Season	599	183	30	5	10	81	32	66	.306	.422	.338
vs. Left-Handers	164	56	12	1	6	25	8	10	.341	.537	.370
vs. Right-Handers	435	127	18	4	4	56	24	56	.292	.379	.326
Home	302	88	15	3	4	40	13	29	.291	.401	.318
Road	297	95	15	2	6	41	19	37	.320	.444	.358
Grass	525	162	29	5	9	71	27	53	.309	.434	.341
Artificial Turf	74	21	1	0	1	10	5	13	.284	.338	.321
April	77	18	6	0	2	10	7	11	.234	.390	.298
May	114	30	2	1	2	13	5	18	.263	.351	.292
June	91	28	5	1	0	8	7	12	.308	.385	.354
July	101	32	5	1	0	12	5	9	.317	.386	.349
August	115	36	9	0	4	21	3	13	.313	.496	.331
Sept./Oct.	101	39	3	2	2	17	5	3	.386	.515	.404
Leading Off Inn.	123	46	7	1	1		3	12	.374	.472	.389
Runners On	278	83	12	3	4	75	16	25	.299	.406	.331
Runners/Scor. Pos.	156	47	9	3	1	66	12	16	.301	.417	.341
Runners On/2 Out	104	28	2	0	1	21	10	9	.269	.365	.333
Scor. Pos./2 Out	70	16	2	0	1	19	9	7	.229	.343	.316
Late Inning Pressure	65	18	3	0	0	7	6	9	.277	.323	.338
Leading Off	15	3	0	0	0	0	0	1	.200	.267	.200
Runners On	36	10	2	0	0	7	3	4	.278	.333	.333
Runners/Scor. Pos.	23	6	1	0	0	7	1	4	.261	.304	.292

DRIVING IN RUNS	From 1B	From 2B	From 3B	Scoring Position
Totals	13/194	24/111	33/70	57/181
Percentage	7%	22%	47%	31%
Driving In Runners from 3B with Less than Two Out:	25/40			63%

Loves to face: Richard Dotson (.500, 11-for-22)
Hates to face: Dan Quisenberry (0-for-14)
Led majors by grounding into 28 double plays last season, although he had only the 4th-highest rate in A.L. (28 in 133 double-play situations). Has grounded into 20 or more double plays in each of last four years; no other player in majors has even done it in the last two. . . . Batted .451 (23-for-51) vs. Milwaukee last season, raising career average against Brewers to .342. . . . Batting average after Sept. 1 was 4th highest in majors (minimum: 75 AB). . . . Career batting average of .308 with runners in scoring position. . . . Yearly batting averages vs. right-handers since 1983: .249, .268, .289, .292; career breakdown: .317 vs. left-handers, .276 vs. right-handers.

Gary Gaetti

Minnesota Twins — Bats Right

	AB	H	2B	3B	HR	RRF	BB	SO	BA	SA	OBA
Season	596	171	34	1	34	112	52	108	.287	.518	.347
vs. Left-Handers	151	52	6	0	11	34	18	22	.344	.603	.409
vs. Right-Handers	445	119	28	1	23	78	34	86	.267	.490	.325
Home	296	74	16	1	16	58	25	56	.250	.473	.311
Road	300	97	18	0	18	54	27	52	.323	.563	.383
Grass	228	83	16	0	16	41	22	40	.364	.645	.421
Artificial Turf	368	88	18	1	18	71	30	68	.239	.440	.300
April	78	22	4	0	3	7	4	11	.282	.449	.317
May	99	29	6	0	9	19	13	15	.293	.626	.377
June	100	23	8	0	5	19	11	22	.230	.460	.304
July	101	26	5	1	4	16	8	19	.257	.446	.312
August	112	36	7	0	6	29	10	20	.321	.545	.376
Sept./Oct.	106	35	4	0	7	22	6	21	.330	.566	.383
Leading Off Inn.	129	36	6	0	8	8	6	19	.279	.512	.316
Runners On	267	76	14	0	16	94	28	50	.285	.517	.352
Runners/Scor. Pos.	156	42	8	0	9	77	19	30	.269	.494	.344
Runners On/2 Out	109	34	7	0	7	39	12	17	.312	.569	.380
Scor. Pos./2 Out	71	18	4	0	4	30	8	12	.254	.479	.329
Late Inning Pressure	90	23	4	0	3	7	11	24	.256	.400	.343
Leading Off	30	6	1	0	1	1	1	7	.200	.333	.250
Runners On	34	9	0	0	2	6	7	10	.265	.441	.390
Runners/Scor. Pos.	18	1	0	0	0	2	4	6	.056	.056	.227

DRIVING IN RUNS	From 1B	From 2B	From 3B	Scoring Position
Totals	18/209	27/122	32/65	59/187
Percentage	9%	22%	49%	32%
Driving In Runners from 3B with Less than Two Out:		25/38		66%

Loves to face: Greg Swindell (.714, 5-for-7, 1 HR)
Hates to face: Bret Saberhagen (0-for-10)
Only A.L. player to go 4-for-4 in three different games last season; Jim Morrison did it in N.L. . . . Also only A.L. player who had 10 or more stolen bases, yet was caught (15) more often than he succeeded (14). . . . One of six A.L. players to hit a home run against every opposing club in 1986. . . . Batted .322 with 21 home runs in 85 games batting anywhere from 2d to 5th in lineup; batted .245 with 12 homers in 64 games batting 6th. . . . Has hit more career home runs in road games (56) than he has at the Metrodome (51). . . . Overall batting average was his highest at any level of pro ball. . . . Led A.L. third basemen with 2.22 assists per nine innings last season (minimum: 500 innings).

Greg Gagne

Minnesota Twins — Bats Right

	AB	H	2B	3B	HR	RRF	BB	SO	BA	SA	OBA
Season	472	118	22	6	12	59	30	108	.250	.398	.301
vs. Left-Handers	126	29	8	1	6	20	9	36	.230	.452	.277
vs. Right-Handers	346	89	14	5	6	39	21	72	.257	.379	.310
Home	238	57	10	4	10	34	17	52	.239	.441	.295
Road	234	61	12	2	2	25	13	56	.261	.355	.308
Grass	184	47	10	2	2	16	10	45	.255	.364	.302
Artificial Turf	288	71	12	4	10	43	20	63	.247	.420	.301
April	67	15	2	1	1	6	2	18	.224	.328	.246
May	86	26	5	2	2	8	8	18	.302	.477	.354
June	83	17	2	0	0	9	5	19	.205	.229	.258
July	70	16	5	1	1	9	5	13	.229	.371	.308
August	82	21	6	1	3	17	6	21	.256	.463	.311
Sept./Oct.	84	23	2	1	5	10	4	19	.274	.500	.315
Leading Off Inn.	108	25	6	2	3	3	8	23	.231	.407	.291
Runners On	191	50	10	2	4	50	13	45	.262	.398	.311
Runners/Scor. Pos.	105	28	7	2	3	45	11	27	.267	.457	.328
Runners On/2 Out	87	22	5	1	2	26	4	23	.253	.402	.293
Scor. Pos./2 Out	59	15	5	1	1	23	3	17	.254	.424	.302
Late Inning Pressure	52	13	1	0	0	6	6	13	.250	.269	.339
Leading Off	15	3	0	0	0	1	0	4	.200	.200	.250
Runners On	18	7	1	0	0	6	1	5	.389	.444	.421
Runners/Scor. Pos.	9	4	1	0	0	6	1	1	.444	.556	.500

DRIVING IN RUNS	From 1B	From 2B	From 3B	Scoring Position
Totals	9/141	19/83	18/44	37/127
Percentage	6%	23%	41%	29%
Driving In Runners from 3B with Less than Two Out:		11/21		52%

Loves to face: John Cerutti (.750, 3-for-4, 2 doubles)
Hates to face: Danny Jackson (.059, 1-for-17)
Batted 9th in starting lineup 109 times last year, most by any player in majors. . . . A decent offensive player, achieving moderate plateaus of 12 homers, 12 steals, .250 average; only one regular A.L. shortstop matched him in all three categories: Alan Trammell. . . . Only 2.64 assists per nine innings last season, 2d-lowest average among major-league shortstops, and a sharp drop from 3.08 in 1985. . . . One hit in 14 career at bats with bases loaded. . . . Career breakdown: .228 with bases empty, .247 with runners on base, .277 with runners in scoring position. . . . Grounded into only four double plays in 99 double-play situations, 3d-lowest rate in A.L. (minimum: 40 opportunities).

Jim Gantner

Milwaukee Brewers — Bats Left

	AB	H	2B	3B	HR	RRF	BB	SO	BA	SA	OBA
Season	497	136	25	1	7	41	26	50	.274	.370	.313
vs. Left-Handers	128	28	4	0	0	9	6	12	.219	.250	.268
vs. Right-Handers	369	108	21	1	7	32	20	38	.293	.412	.329
Home	247	64	14	1	4	27	15	24	.259	.372	.301
Road	250	72	11	0	3	14	11	26	.288	.368	.326
Grass	423	114	21	1	6	37	25	42	.270	.366	.311
Artificial Turf	74	22	4	0	1	4	1	8	.297	.392	.329
April	57	18	3	1	1	6	4	4	.316	.456	.371
May	83	22	6	0	1	5	9	7	.265	.373	.347
June	95	22	3	0	1	6	3	7	.232	.295	.263
July	81	27	5	0	2	9	4	10	.333	.469	.375
August	91	26	5	0	1	7	5	12	.286	.374	.310
Sept./Oct.	90	21	3	0	1	8	1	10	.233	.300	.239
Leading Off Inn.	137	41	8	0	3	3	3	8	.299	.423	.319
Runners On	193	44	9	0	1	35	15	24	.228	.290	.284
Runners/Scor. Pos.	110	22	4	0	1	34	13	9	.200	.264	.286
Runners On/2 Out	86	19	4	0	1	12	7	11	.221	.302	.302
Scor. Pos./2 Out	59	12	2	0	1	12	6	5	.203	.288	.309
Late Inning Pressure	84	25	2	0	2	7	6	10	.298	.393	.344
Leading Off	23	7	0	0	1	1	0	1	.304	.435	.304
Runners On	33	8	1	0	0	5	5	5	.242	.273	.342
Runners/Scor. Pos.	23	7	1	0	0	5	3	2	.304	.348	.385

DRIVING IN RUNS	From 1B	From 2B	From 3B	Scoring Position
Totals	2/154	13/92	19/47	32/139
Percentage	1%	14%	40%	23%
Driving In Runners from 3B with Less than Two Out:		17/26		65%

Loves to face: Don Schulze (.833, 5-for-6, 2 HR)
Hates to face: Roger Clemens (0-for-16)
Could become all-time major-league fielding champion at second base this season. In 917 games at second, Gantner's career fielding percentage is .9847; the all-time leader (with 1000 games needed to qualify) is Jerry Lumpe, at .9844. Based on his usual chances per game, Gantner should break the record if he commits fewer than eight errors over his next 83 games. . . . Tied Mike Davis for A.L.'s biggest oh-fer with bases loaded last season: 0-for-10. . . . Only two of 40 career home runs are vs. left-handers: (Frank Viola and Ed Vande Berg in 1983). . . . Career: .269 on grass fields, .310 on phony phields, but Royals Stadium is only current A.L. park in which he has not homered (162 at bats).

Damaso Garcia

Toronto Blue Jays — Bats Right

	AB	H	2B	3B	HR	RRF	BB	SO	BA	SA	OBA
Season	424	119	22	0	6	48	13	32	.281	.375	.306
vs. Left-Handers	139	45	9	0	2	15	2	14	.324	.432	.336
vs. Right-Handers	285	74	13	0	4	33	11	18	.260	.347	.292
Home	174	49	10	0	3	28	3	17	.282	.391	.300
Road	250	70	12	0	3	20	10	15	.280	.364	.311
Grass	180	55	11	0	2	11	7	11	.306	.400	.339
Artificial Turf	244	64	11	0	4	37	6	21	.262	.357	.282
April	43	9	1	0	0	2	2	3	.209	.233	.261
May	105	28	5	0	1	15	7	7	.267	.343	.319
June	81	28	9	0	1	9	0	7	.346	.494	.346
July	91	26	4	0	2	13	3	7	.286	.396	.305
August	66	18	2	0	2	9	1	3	.273	.394	.284
Sept./Oct.	38	10	1	0	0	0	0	5	.263	.289	.282
Leading Off Inn.	116	26	3	0	2	2	3	9	.224	.302	.250
Runners On	171	50	11	0	3	45	5	12	.292	.409	.315
Runners/Scor. Pos.	93	26	6	0	1	40	5	7	.280	.376	.307
Runners On/2 Out	82	19	4	0	2	21	2	6	.232	.354	.259
Scor. Pos./2 Out	54	12	2	0	1	18	1	4	.222	.315	.250
Late Inning Pressure	68	20	3	0	3	1	5	.294	.338	.304	
Leading Off	15	3	0	0	0	0	0	0	.200	.200	.200
Runners On	30	7	1	0	0	3	1	3	.233	.267	.258
Runners/Scor. Pos.	17	3	1	0	0	2	1	3	.176	.235	.222

DRIVING IN RUNS	From 1B	From 2B	From 3B	Scoring Position
Totals	5/125	16/68	21/47	37/115
Percentage	4%	24%	45%	32%
Driving In Runners from 3B with Less than Two Out:		14/21		67%

Loves to face: Bob Ojeda (.545, 12-for-22)
Hates to face: Tim Conroy (.188, 3-for-16, 6 SO)
Career total of 124 at bats at the Metrodome, the most by any player, active or inactive, living or dead, with no homers there. . . . Jimy Williams started him in every batting order position except cleanup last year. . . . Batted leadoff exclusively from May 8 to June 7, but batted only .233 in those 28 games and was dropped down. . . . Most frequently batted 9th, where he hit .305 in 50 games (48 starts); Tony Fernandez also hit over .300 in the 9th spot (.333 in 26 games), but other Toronto players batted only .202 there. . . . His batting average has decreased in every season since 1982: .310, .307, .284, .282, .281; he's several years away from the Mendoza Line.

Rich Gedman

Boston Red Sox — Bats Left

	AB	H	2B	3B	HR	RRF	BB	SO	BA	SA	OBA
Season	462	119	29	0	16	67	37	61	.258	.424	.315
vs. Left-Handers	118	22	4	0	5	15	3	18	.186	.347	.210
vs. Right-Handers	344	97	25	0	11	52	34	43	.282	.451	.349
Home	224	48	13	0	2	28	21	34	.214	.299	.284
Road	238	71	16	0	14	39	16	27	.298	.542	.345
Grass	388	95	22	0	12	57	32	48	.245	.394	.306
Artificial Turf	74	24	7	0	4	10	5	13	.324	.581	.363
April	66	20	4	0	2	8	3	3	.303	.424	.333
May	79	19	5	0	1	6	8	11	.241	.342	.310
June	72	19	4	0	1	10	7	12	.264	.361	.321
July	79	19	5	0	4	16	2	13	.241	.456	.279
August	85	19	5	0	4	12	11	10	.224	.424	.320
Sept./Oct.	81	23	6	0	4	15	6	12	.284	.506	.330
Leading Off Inn.	98	23	5	0	4	4	4	14	.235	.408	.272
Runners On	221	58	20	0	6	57	27	24	.262	.434	.339
Runners/Scor. Pos.	115	29	11	0	5	52	20	14	.252	.478	.350
Runners On/2 Out	104	29	10	0	4	31	18	10	.279	.490	.385
Scor. Pos./2 Out	61	17	5	0	4	29	13	7	.279	.557	.405
Late Inning Pressure	68	20	4	0	4	13	6	10	.294	.529	.360
Leading Off	13	2	1	0	0	0	0	1	.154	.231	.154
Runners On	38	12	2	0	3	12	4	5	.316	.605	.381
Runners/Scor. Pos.	18	6	1	0	2	10	4	4	.333	.722	.455

DRIVING IN RUNS	From 1B	From 2B	From 3B	Scoring Position
Totals	10/179	20/101	21/51	41/152
Percentage	6%	20%	41%	27%
Driving In Runners from 3B with Less than Two Out:			11/22	50%

Loves to face: Frank Tanana (.385, 5-for-13, 2 HR)
Hates to face: Phil Niekro (.053, 1-for-19)
Also hates to face Sid Fernandez. . . . Opponents stole 55 bases while he was catching last season, while 55 were caught stealing; with Sullivan and Sax catching, opponents had 24 steals, 7 caught stealings. . . . Career breakdown at Fenway Park: .316 vs. right-handers, .149 vs. left-handers. Has never hit a home run at Fenway off a left-handed pitcher (208 plate appearances). . . . Started 24 of 46 games during regular season in which Sox faced a lefty starter; started every postseason game, irrespective of the opposing starter. . . . Batted 96 points higher vs. right-handed pitchers than against left-handed pitchers, 2d-largest difference in A.L. (minimum: 100 AB vs. each). . . . Led A.L. catchers with 14 passed balls last season.

Kirk Gibson

Detroit Tigers — Bats Left

	AB	H	2B	3B	HR	RRF	BB	SO	BA	SA	OBA
Season	441	118	11	2	28	91	68	107	.268	.492	.371
vs. Left-Handers	164	43	5	0	7	31	20	44	.262	.421	.360
vs. Right-Handers	277	75	6	2	21	60	48	63	.271	.534	.378
Home	216	60	2	1	15	50	32	50	.278	.505	.378
Road	225	58	9	1	13	41	36	57	.258	.480	.365
Grass	391	104	9	1	25	82	60	99	.266	.486	.372
Artificial Turf	50	14	2	1	3	9	8	8	.280	.540	.367
April	39	14	2	1	2	10	9	7	.359	.615	.479
May	0	0	0	0	0	0	0	0	—	—	—
June	101	26	1	1	8	22	21	25	.257	.525	.400
July	108	29	4	0	7	24	16	31	.269	.500	.359
August	105	22	1	0	3	12	16	26	.210	.305	.325
Sept./Oct.	88	27	3	0	8	23	6	18	.307	.614	.354
Leading Off Inn.	82	22	2	0	3	3	9	13	.268	.402	.341
Runners On	204	56	5	0	19	82	36	50	.275	.578	.387
Runners/Scor. Pos.	125	32	5	0	10	64	23	34	.256	.536	.374
Runners On/2 Out	66	17	1	0	6	25	15	13	.258	.545	.410
Scor. Pos./2 Out	48	11	1	0	4	21	10	11	.229	.500	.383
Late Inning Pressure	64	23	2	0	5	17	7	15	.359	.625	.446
Leading Off	22	9	0	0	2	2	1	3	.409	.682	.435
Runners On	28	10	1	0	3	15	4	9	.357	.714	.486
Runners/Scor. Pos.	19	7	1	0	2	13	2	6	.368	.737	.478

DRIVING IN RUNS	From 1B	From 2B	From 3B	Scoring Position
Totals	14/138	23/91	26/62	49/153
Percentage	10%	25%	42%	32%
Driving In Runners from 3B with Less than Two Out:			19/36	53%

Loves to face: Steve Ontiveros (.800, 4-for-5, 2 HR)
Hates to face: Jose Rijo (0-for-11, 5 SO)
126 career home runs, but no grand slams; only active player with more homers, but no slams: Claudell Washington, 130. . . . One other weirdo: This guy has only 15 assists in 641 career games in the outfield, a rate of 2.34 per 100 games, which is the lowest among active players who have played at least 500 games in the outfield; number two on the list is Don Baylor (3.29). . . . Gibson and Darryl Strawberry are the only players with 25 or more steals and 25 or more home runs in each of last three seasons. . . . Has batted for a higher average with runners on base than with bases empty in each of the last four seasons. . . . Batting average vs. left-handed pitchers was his highest since he batted .366 against southpaws in 1981.

Bobby Grich

California Angels — Bats Right

	AB	H	2B	3B	HR	RRF	BB	SO	BA	SA	OBA
Season	313	84	18	0	9	31	39	54	.268	.412	.354
vs. Left-Handers	166	49	9	0	6	17	20	21	.295	.458	.369
vs. Right-Handers	147	35	9	0	3	14	19	33	.238	.361	.337
Home	135	42	10	0	5	17	12	18	.311	.496	.372
Road	178	42	8	0	4	14	27	36	.236	.348	.341
Grass	262	74	16	0	7	26	32	47	.282	.424	.364
Artificial Turf	51	10	2	0	2	5	7	7	.196	.353	.305
April	27	5	1	0	2	3	3	3	.185	.444	.290
May	56	19	1	0	0	1	4	9	.339	.357	.383
June	40	6	2	0	1	6	2	6	.150	.275	.190
July	57	19	1	0	4	11	9	11	.333	.561	.433
August	64	20	7	0	1	3	10	13	.313	.469	.413
Sept./Oct.	69	15	6	0	1	7	11	12	.217	.348	.321
Leading Off Inn.	93	27	6	0	4	4	9	17	.290	.484	.353
Runners On	124	28	5	0	2	24	19	20	.226	.315	.331
Runners/Scor. Pos.	67	15	3	0	2	24	14	12	.224	.358	.354
Runners On/2 Out	57	12	4	0	2	14	9	10	.211	.386	.328
Scor. Pos./2 Out	38	9	2	0	2	14	7	8	.237	.447	.356
Late Inning Pressure	54	14	3	0	1	5	5	11	.259	.315	.322
Leading Off	14	3	0	0	0	0	1	6	.214	.214	.267
Runners On	26	7	3	0	0	5	2	3	.269	.385	.321
Runners/Scor. Pos.	17	4	2	0	0	5	1	2	.235	.353	.278

DRIVING IN RUNS	From 1B	From 2B	From 3B	Scoring Position
Totals	2/89	9/54	11/29	20/83
Percentage	2%	17%	38%	24%
Driving In Runners from 3B with Less than Two Out:			8/12	67%

Loved to face: Vern Ruhle (.526, 10-for-19, 2 HR)
Hated to face: John Tudor (.053, 1-for-19)
A five-time loser in A.L. Championship Series; the only time that his team won a postseason series was in 1971, when he was a late addition to the Orioles' postseason roster and did not appear in either the A.L.C.S. or the World Series. . . . Hit the home run off Henderson's glove in Game Five of 1986 playoffs, but failed against Crawford in ninth inning with bases loaded and two outs. . . . Career fielding percentage at second base (.9840) is .0004 short of Jerry Lumpe's major-league record. . . . Yearly batting averages with runners on base since 1983: .306, .296, .255, .226. . . . You can win a lot of bar bets on this one: he's the Angels' all-time leader in home runs (154) and RBI (557).

Ken Griffey

New York Yankees — Bats Left

	AB	H	2B	3B	HR	RRF	BB	SO	BA	SA	OBA
Season	198	60	7	0	9	28	15	24	.303	.475	.349
vs. Left-Handers	34	8	2	0	0	3	0	9	.235	.294	.257
vs. Right-Handers	164	52	5	0	9	25	15	15	.317	.512	.366
Home	90	22	3	0	5	11	8	11	.244	.444	.306
Road	108	38	4	0	4	17	7	13	.352	.500	.383
Grass	163	44	4	0	9	22	14	20	.270	.460	.328
Artificial Turf	35	16	3	0	0	6	1	4	.457	.543	.447
April	65	21	2	0	2	9	7	4	.323	.446	.384
May	64	14	2	0	2	6	4	12	.219	.344	.261
June	69	25	3	0	5	13	4	8	.362	.623	.395
July	0	0	0	0	0	0	0	0	—	—	—
August	0	0	0	0	0	0	0	0	—	—	—
Sept./Oct.	0	0	0	0	0	0	0	0	—	—	—
Leading Off Inn.	44	13	0	0	3	3	2	3	.295	.500	.326
Runners On	91	25	4	0	1	20	7	12	.275	.352	.314
Runners/Scor. Pos.	56	11	2	0	0	18	4	10	.196	.232	.234
Runners On/2 Out	27	3	0	0	0	2	3	4	.111	.111	.200
Scor. Pos./2 Out	18	2	0	0	0	2	2	3	.111	.111	.200
Late Inning Pressure	30	12	2	0	1	7	0	2	.400	.567	.400
Leading Off	7	2	0	0	0	0	0	1	.286	.286	.286
Runners On	14	6	1	0	1	7	0	0	.429	.714	.429
Runners/Scor. Pos.	6	3	1	0	0	5	0	0	.500	.667	.500

DRIVING IN RUNS	From 1B	From 2B	From 3B	Scoring Position
Totals	1/59	6/46	12/28	18/74
Percentage	2%	13%	43%	24%
Driving In Runners from 3B with Less than Two Out:			11/19	58%

Loves to face: Greg Minton (.667, 8-for-12)
Hates to face: Bob Ojeda (.143, 3-for-21)
Figures above are for A.L. only; see also the N.L. Batters section. . . . Another guy he hates to face: former teammate Bob Shirley, against whom Griffey has hit .174 (8-for-46) with 18 strikeouts. . . . Hit two pinch-hit home runs for Yankees last season, both against California. . . . Batted .285 in his five-year stay with Yankees, but ended with a flourish: He hit safely in his last nine games in pinstripes; oddly, he then began his Braves career with a nine-game hitting streak. . . . Hit his first major-league homer on Sept. 9, 1973, off Roric Harrison, the man who a year earlier became the last A.L. pitcher to hit a home run in a regular-season game.

Alfredo Griffin

Oakland As — Bats Left and Right

	AB	H	2B	3B	HR	RRF	BB	SO	BA	SA	OBA
Season	594	169	23	6	4	55	35	52	.285	.364	.323
vs. Left-Handers	207	52	7	1	0	9	8	24	.251	.295	.279
vs. Right-Handers	387	117	16	5	4	46	27	28	.302	.401	.346
Home	302	85	10	1	1	27	17	26	.281	.331	.319
Road	292	84	13	5	3	28	18	26	.288	.397	.328
Grass	497	140	19	5	3	47	30	44	.282	.358	.323
Artificial Turf	97	29	4	1	1	8	5	8	.299	.392	.327
April	75	21	3	0	0	4	7	6	.280	.320	.341
May	97	31	6	0	0	10	4	6	.320	.381	.346
June	99	27	4	2	1	10	9	7	.273	.384	.330
July	96	25	3	0	1	10	7	9	.260	.323	.308
August	112	31	3	1	1	10	3	9	.277	.348	.296
Sept./Oct.	115	34	4	3	1	11	5	15	.296	.409	.325
Leading Off Inn.	156	50	8	1	2	11	11	16	.321	.423	.365
Runners On	246	70	6	3	1	52	13	18	.285	.346	.313
Runners/Scor. Pos.	144	33	2	1	1	48	10	11	.229	.278	.269
Runners On/2 Out	107	28	4	1	1	21	5	8	.262	.346	.295
Scor. Pos./2 Out	74	17	2	0	1	19	4	4	.230	.297	.269
Late Inning Pressure	88	27	4	3	3	13	6	10	.307	.523	.351
Leading Off	31	10	1	0	2	2	1	0	.323	.548	.344
Runners On	31	9	1	2	1	11	4	5	.290	.548	.371
Runners/Scor. Pos.	18	4	0	1	1	9	2	3	.222	.500	.300

DRIVING IN RUNS	From 1B	From 2B	From 3B	Scoring Position
Totals	5/171	17/109	29/68	46/177
Percentage	3%	16%	43%	26%
Driving In Runners from 3B with Less than Two Out:		22/39		56%

Loves to face: Bud Black (.571, 12-for-21)
Hates to face: John Henry Johnson (.053, 1-for-19)
Unlikely weekend: Saturday, July 26: walked twice in one game for first time since Aug. 4, 1983 (so what if one was intentional); Sunday, July 27: walked to force in the only run of a 15-inning game. . . . Oakland's shortstop for all but 24 innings of the 1986 season. Only Ripken missed less time in the field. . . . No home runs in 539 at bats in Late-Inning Pressure Situations up through 1985, but hit three in 88 at bats in those situations last year. . . . Grounded into only five double plays in 117 double-play situations, 5th-lowest rate in A.L. (minimum: 40 opportunities). . . . Batted .262 in 45 games batting first or second, but hit .296 in 116 games batting 7th, 8th, or 9th (1-for-4 in one game batting 6th).

Johnny Grubb

Detroit Tigers — Bats Left

	AB	H	2B	3B	HR	RRF	BB	SO	BA	SA	OBA
Season	210	70	13	1	13	53	28	28	.333	.590	.412
vs. Left-Handers	14	3	1	0	0	1	1	2	.214	.286	.267
vs. Right-Handers	196	67	12	1	13	52	27	26	.342	.612	.421
Home	112	41	6	1	8	33	14	13	.366	.652	.438
Road	98	29	7	0	5	20	14	15	.296	.520	.383
Grass	189	62	11	1	11	45	23	22	.328	.571	.403
Artificial Turf	21	8	2	0	2	8	5	6	.381	.762	.481
April	0	0	0	0	0	0	0	0	———	———	———
May	21	7	1	1	0	6	3	2	.333	.476	.417
June	8	2	0	0	1	1	1	2	.250	.625	.333
July	56	20	2	0	7	24	4	12	.357	.768	.397
August	78	27	8	0	4	17	11	7	.346	.603	.427
Sept./Oct.	47	14	2	0	1	5	9	5	.298	.404	.414
Leading Off Inn.	50	15	4	0	3	4	7	7	.300	.560	.364
Runners On	93	36	7	1	4	44	13	12	.387	.613	.455
Runners/Scor. Pos.	56	22	3	0	3	38	8	8	.393	.607	.456
Runners On/2 Out	54	21	3	0	2	21	7	5	.389	.556	.459
Scor. Pos./2 Out	33	12	2	0	1	18	4	5	.364	.515	.432
Late Inning Pressure	26	6	2	0	0	5	3	7	.231	.308	.310
Leading Off	4	1	0	0	0	0	0	0	.250	.250	.250
Runners On	13	3	1	0	0	5	1	4	.231	.308	.286
Runners/Scor. Pos.	9	3	1	0	0	5	1	1	.333	.444	.400

DRIVING IN RUNS	From 1B	From 2B	From 3B	Scoring Position
Totals	9/65	12/43	19/31	31/74
Percentage	14%	28%	61%	42%
Driving In Runners from 3B with Less than Two Out:		12/14		86%

Loves to face: Joe Niekro (.500, 5-for-10, 2 HR)
Hates to face: Pete Vuckovich (0-for-11)
Made 57 starts last season, his highest total in four years with Tigers; started 46 of Detroit's last 50 games vs. right-handed starters. . . . Drove in 85.7 percent (12-of-14) of runners from third base with less than two outs, 2d-best percentage in A.L. (minimum: 10 RRF). . . . Drove in 41.9 percent (31-of-74) of runners from scoring position, highest rate in majors among players (minimum: 25 RRF). . . . Career batting average (.396, 38-for-96, 7 home runs) at Fenway Park. . . . August batting average was 6th highest in A.L. (minimum: 75 AB). . . . Career batting average of .369 (24-for-65) with bases loaded. . . . Batted in 35 double-play situations last season, and did not ground into one.

Ozzie Guillen

Chicago White Sox — Bats Left

	AB	H	2B	3B	HR	RRF	BB	SO	BA	SA	OBA
Season	547	137	19	4	2	51	12	52	.250	.311	.265
vs. Left-Handers	167	43	4	0	1	13	6	20	.257	.299	.283
vs. Right-Handers	380	94	15	4	1	38	6	32	.247	.316	.258
Home	272	69	9	1	1	26	5	23	.254	.305	.264
Road	275	68	10	3	1	25	7	29	.247	.316	.267
Grass	455	109	15	4	1	40	12	47	.240	.297	.258
Artificial Turf	92	28	4	0	1	11	0	5	.304	.380	.301
April	49	12	2	1	0	7	2	1	.245	.327	.275
May	96	21	2	1	1	7	2	9	.219	.292	.232
June	85	23	4	1	1	15	2	9	.271	.376	.287
July	103	28	5	0	0	6	3	8	.272	.320	.284
August	98	23	2	0	0	7	1	11	.235	.255	.250
Sept./Oct.	116	30	4	1	0	9	2	14	.259	.310	.269
Leading Off Inn.	128	30	3	1	0	0	2	18	.234	.273	.246
Runners On	229	70	12	3	0	49	4	15	.306	.384	.311
Runners/Scor. Pos.	130	41	6	3	0	49	2	7	.315	.408	.314
Runners On/2 Out	96	36	5	3	0	25	1	5	.375	.490	.381
Scor. Pos./2 Out	63	24	3	3	0	25	0	2	.381	.524	.381
Late Inning Pressure	81	20	0	0	0	10	0	10	.247	.272	.238
Leading Off	16	6	0	0	0	0	0	2	.375	.375	.375
Runners On	28	9	0	1	0	10	0	2	.321	.393	.290
Runners/Scor. Pos.	14	6	0	1	0	10	0	1	.429	.571	.353

DRIVING IN RUNS	From 1B	From 2B	From 3B	Scoring Position
Totals	3/157	18/103	28/57	46/160
Percentage	2%	17%	49%	29%
Driving In Runners from 3B with Less than Two Out:		16/31		52%

Loves to face: Jay Howell (.800, 4-for-5)
Hates to face: Walt Terrell (0-for-14)
Has never had an extra-base hit in 42 at bats at the Extra-Base Hitdome in Minneapolis, most among active players. . . . Committed six errors in 78 home games, 16 errors in 81 road games. . . . In two seasons in A.L., has led off 35 innings in Late-Inning Pressure Situations, and has batted .515 (17-for-33) with two walks, an on-base average of .543! This from a man whose overall career on-base average is a modest .278; modest, nothing, that's downright Doris Dayish. . . . Averaged one walk every 48.1 plate appearances in 1986, successfully defending his title as "Toughest to Walk," and with Garcia and Griffin around, it's hard to lead the G's, let alone the rest of the alphabet.

Jerry Hairston

Chicago White Sox — Bats Left and Right

	AB	H	2B	3B	HR	RRF	BB	SO	BA	SA	OBA
Season	225	61	15	0	5	28	26	26	.271	.404	.348
vs. Left-Handers	59	13	3	0	2	5	3	11	.220	.373	.270
vs. Right-Handers	166	48	12	0	3	23	23	15	.289	.416	.374
Home	117	36	8	0	3	18	16	12	.308	.453	.391
Road	108	25	7	0	2	10	10	14	.231	.352	.300
Grass	177	51	11	0	5	24	22	20	.288	.435	.365
Artificial Turf	48	10	4	0	0	4	4	6	.208	.292	.283
April	21	7	0	0	2	5	1	2	.333	.619	.348
May	39	7	1	0	0	4	6	6	.179	.205	.289
June	30	10	4	0	0	4	7	4	.333	.467	.474
July	31	12	4	0	0	7	1	4	.387	.516	.406
August	47	12	3	0	1	1	3	4	.255	.383	.300
Sept./Oct.	57	13	3	0	2	7	8	6	.228	.386	.323
Leading Off Inn.	53	15	7	0	2	2	8	2	.283	.528	.377
Runners On	96	30	5	0	2	25	12	14	.313	.427	.391
Runners/Scor. Pos.	58	18	3	0	2	23	9	8	.310	.466	.406
Runners On/2 Out	39	7	2	0	1	7	9	7	.179	.308	.333
Scor. Pos./2 Out	28	5	1	0	1	6	8	5	.179	.321	.361
Late Inning Pressure	64	18	5	0	0	8	5	7	.281	.359	.338
Leading Off	15	4	3	0	0	0	0	2	.267	.467	.267
Runners On	28	11	1	0	0	8	5	3	.393	.429	.486
Runners/Scor. Pos.	20	8	1	0	0	8	5	2	.400	.450	.519

DRIVING IN RUNS	From 1B	From 2B	From 3B	Scoring Position
Totals	3/66	6/38	14/29	20/67
Percentage	5%	16%	48%	30%
Driving In Runners from 3B with Less than Two Out:		12/17		71%

Loves to face: Dan Petry (.467, 7-for-15, 3 HR)
Hates to face: Mike Witt (0-for-14)
Batted .304 (14-for-46) as a pinch-hitter last season, 6th best in A.L. (minimum: 20 AB). . . . Career breakdown: .305 with runners on base, .225 with bases empty. . . . Batting average of only .226 (on-base average: .314) when leading off innings in Late-Inning Pressure Situations over past 12 years; Hey Freg, let Guillen hit for himself in those spots! . . . Has started only two double plays from outfield in his career, but last June 15, he started a *triple play* from left field. It's not exactly the mark of a Gold Glover; more like a Golden Retriever, in fact: The last three left fielders to start triple plays in the majors were Jim Spencer (1972), Rico Carty (1969), and Alex Johnson (1964). Woof!

Mel Hall
Cleveland Indians — Bats Left

	AB	H	2B	3B	HR	RRF	BB	SO	BA	SA	OBA
Season	442	131	29	2	18	81	33	65	.296	.493	.346
vs. Left-Handers	26	4	2	0	0	3	3	5	.154	.231	.241
vs. Right-Handers	416	127	27	2	18	78	30	60	.305	.510	.353
Home	206	57	13	1	8	33	12	25	.277	.466	.318
Road	236	74	16	1	10	48	21	40	.314	.517	.369
Grass	379	109	22	1	15	68	23	55	.288	.470	.329
Artificial Turf	63	22	7	1	3	13	10	10	.349	.635	.438
April	41	7	3	0	2	10	4	10	.171	.390	.239
May	63	18	7	1	3	8	6	9	.286	.571	.357
June	90	34	5	0	7	23	7	12	.378	.667	.423
July	83	21	2	0	5	22	9	15	.253	.458	.326
August	85	27	4	1	0	10	2	10	.318	.388	.330
Sept./Oct.	80	24	8	0	1	8	5	9	.300	.438	.345
Leading Off Inn.	93	32	7	0	3	3	4	14	.344	.516	.371
Runners On	209	53	17	1	9	72	18	30	.254	.474	.312
Runners/Scor. Pos.	128	35	11	1	5	61	13	17	.273	.492	.333
Runners On/2 Out	104	28	8	1	5	37	9	14	.269	.510	.327
Scor. Pos./2 Out	68	20	6	1	4	35	5	8	.294	.588	.342
Late Inning Pressure	56	17	5	0	3	11	6	5	.304	.554	.365
Leading Off	13	6	3	0	1	1	0	0	.462	.923	.462
Runners On	29	6	1	0	1	9	3	4	.207	.345	.273
Runners/Scor. Pos.	20	5	1	0	1	9	3	3	.250	.450	.333

DRIVING IN RUNS	From 1B	From 2B	From 3B	Scoring Position
Totals	13/145	24/96	25/48	49/144
Percentage	9%	25%	52%	34%
Driving In Runners from 3B with Less than Two Out:		13/23	57%	

Loves to face: Dave Stewart (.444, 4-for-9, 2 HR)
Hates to face: Mark Portugal (0-for-8)

From the "What More Do You Want Me To Do" Department: Hall started on opening day against Mike Flanagan and doubled in his only at bat against him (he was routed early); that was his only start against a lefty all season. (Started 113 of 114 games in which Indians faced a right-hander).... Career breakdown: .121, no home runs in 149 at bats vs. left-handers; .300, 47 homers vs. right-handers.... Batted 81 points lower with runners on than with bases empty, 2d-largest gap in A.L. (minimum: 100 AB both ways).... June batting average of .378 was 3d highest in majors (minimum: 75 AB).... Batted .286 in day games with Cubs; .341 in day games with Indians.

Toby Harrah
Texas Rangers — Bats Right

	AB	H	2B	3B	HR	RRF	BB	SO	BA	SA	OBA
Season	289	63	18	2	7	41	44	53	.218	.367	.322
vs. Left-Handers	103	24	9	2	2	14	26	16	.233	.417	.385
vs. Right-Handers	186	39	9	0	5	27	18	37	.210	.339	.284
Home	140	29	7	0	3	18	20	27	.207	.321	.305
Road	149	34	11	2	4	23	24	26	.228	.409	.339
Grass	249	55	16	1	6	37	37	46	.221	.365	.321
Artificial Turf	40	8	2	1	1	4	7	7	.200	.375	.333
April	41	9	2	0	1	10	3	6	.220	.341	.267
May	73	14	5	0	1	8	16	16	.192	.301	.344
June	39	8	2	1	0	3	2	8	.205	.308	.244
July	33	6	3	0	0	2	1	7	.182	.273	.206
August	71	21	4	1	5	14	15	10	.296	.592	.420
Sept./Oct.	32	5	2	0	0	4	7	6	.156	.219	.300
Leading Off Inn.	76	14	4	0	2	2	9	18	.184	.316	.271
Runners On	112	31	9	1	5	35	24	15	.277	.402	.404
Runners/Scor. Pos.	69	23	8	0	3	34	14	10	.333	.493	.437
Runners On/2 Out	59	12	4	1	0	12	12	8	.203	.305	.347
Scor. Pos./2 Out	39	9	3	0	0	11	7	8	.231	.308	.348
Late Inning Pressure	39	9	3	0	1	6	6	7	.231	.385	.340
Leading Off	12	5	2	0	1	1	0	2	.417	.833	.417
Runners On	16	3	0	0	0	5	4	2	.188	.188	.364
Runners/Scor. Pos.	11	3	0	0	0	5	3	1	.273	.273	.400

DRIVING IN RUNS	From 1B	From 2B	From 3B	Scoring Position
Totals	3/78	15/55	16/29	31/84
Percentage	4%	27%	55%	37%
Driving In Runners from 3B with Less than Two Out:		11/13	85%	

Loved to face: Bruce Hurst (.364, 12-for-33, 3 HR)
Hated to face: Dave Righetti (.083, 2-for-24)

From 1978 to 1986, played for three first-division teams (Texas, 1978 and 1986; New York, 1984) and had composite batting average of .223 for those seasons. While playing for 2d-division teams during that span, he batted .280. Maybe it's no coincidence that he played more games (2155) than any A.L. player active in 1986 without ever being in a World Series.... Drove in 52.5 percent (21-of-40) of runners from scoring position with less than two outs last season, best rate in A.L. (minimum: 15 runs driven in in such situations).... Averaged 2.56 assists per nine innings last season, lowest among A.L. second basemen (minimum: 500 innings).

Ron Hassey
Yankees/White Sox — Bats Left

	AB	H	2B	3B	HR	RRF	BB	SO	BA	SA	OBA
Season	341	110	25	1	9	52	46	27	.323	.481	.406
vs. Left-Handers	64	19	4	0	0	10	6	6	.297	.359	.361
vs. Right-Handers	277	91	21	1	9	42	40	21	.329	.509	.416
Home	167	55	13	1	5	27	26	13	.329	.509	.421
Road	174	55	12	0	4	25	20	14	.316	.454	.390
Grass	280	96	25	1	8	45	38	20	.343	.525	.424
Artificial Turf	61	14	0	0	1	7	8	7	.230	.279	.319
April	42	9	3	0	1	7	7	5	.214	.357	.340
May	36	7	0	0	1	4	6	6	.194	.278	.310
June	65	30	10	0	3	14	7	4	.462	.754	.514
July	51	11	1	0	1	5	5	1	.216	.294	.293
August	59	21	6	0	2	10	7	7	.356	.559	.424
Sept./Oct.	88	32	5	1	1	12	14	4	.364	.477	.452
Leading Off Inn.	66	26	8	0	4	4	14	6	.394	.697	.500
Runners On	169	53	12	0	4	47	19	16	.314	.456	.382
Runners/Scor. Pos.	95	29	10	0	1	39	15	10	.305	.442	.398
Runners On/2 Out	84	25	5	0	4	27	14	9	.298	.500	.398
Scor. Pos./2 Out	50	14	4	0	1	20	11	6	.280	.420	.410
Late Inning Pressure	37	14	2	0	1	7	5	4	.378	.514	.452
Leading Off	5	1	1	0	0	0	0	0	.200	.400	.200
Runners On	15	8	1	0	1	7	4	2	.533	.800	.632
Runners/Scor. Pos.	9	4	1	0	0	5	4	2	.444	.556	.615

DRIVING IN RUNS	From 1B	From 2B	From 3B	Scoring Position
Totals	9/122	17/67	17/41	34/108
Percentage	7%	25%	41%	31%
Driving In Runners from 3B with Less than Two Out:		11/13	85%	

Loves to face: Dave Stewart (.750, 6-for-8, 1 HR)
Hates to face: John Butcher (0-for-12)

That .297 average against left-handers last season was no fluke: career mark is .275 in 396 at bats against them.... Drove in 84.6 percent (11-of-13) of runners from third base with less than two outs, tied for 3d-best rate in A.L. (minimum: 10 RRF).... Has homered in every A.L. ballpark except the Kingdome. He's never even had an extra-base hit in 82 at bats there, the most by any player with no XBH.... Batted .373 as a DH last season.... Batted .400 (40-for-100) vs. teams with winning records.... Batting average after Sept. 1 was 4th highest in A.L. (minimum: 75 AB).... Grounded into 15 double plays in 65 double-play situations, 3d-highest rate in A.L. (minimum: 5 opportunities).

Mickey Hatcher
Minnesota Twins — Bats Right

	AB	H	2B	3B	HR	RRF	BB	SO	BA	SA	OBA
Season	317	88	13	3	3	34	19	26	.278	.366	.315
vs. Left-Handers	140	51	10	1	2	19	11	9	.364	.493	.405
vs. Right-Handers	177	37	3	2	1	15	8	17	.209	.266	.241
Home	156	49	7	3	1	17	9	12	.314	.417	.345
Road	161	39	6	0	2	17	10	14	.242	.317	.285
Grass	124	27	5	0	2	12	9	11	.218	.306	.269
Artificial Turf	193	61	8	3	1	22	10	15	.316	.404	.345
April	41	3	1	0	0	2	1	3	.073	.098	.070
May	52	19	4	0	0	5	2	4	.365	.442	.382
June	62	17	1	1	0	7	5	5	.274	.323	.328
July	46	10	2	0	1	4	4	5	.217	.326	.280
August	54	19	4	0	1	13	5	6	.352	.481	.407
Sept./Oct.	62	20	1	2	1	3	2	3	.323	.452	.348
Leading Off Inn.	63	16	2	1	1		3	5	.254	.365	.288
Runners On	129	37	7	1	2	33	8	10	.287	.403	.319
Runners/Scor. Pos.	73	19	5	0	2	31	6	6	.260	.411	.301
Runners On/2 Out	53	14	2	1	1	16	5	5	.264	.396	.328
Scor. Pos./2 Out	39	8	2	0	1	14	4	4	.205	.333	.279
Late Inning Pressure	47	8	1	0	0	4	2	6	.170	.191	.204
Leading Off	10	0	0	0	0	0	0	3	.000	.000	.000
Runners On	20	4	0	0	0	4	1	1	.200	.200	.238
Runners/Scor. Pos.	11	4	0	0	0	4	1	0	.364	.364	.417

DRIVING IN RUNS	From 1B	From 2B	From 3B	Scoring Position
Totals	3/91	10/59	18/34	28/93
Percentage	3%	17%	53%	30%
Driving In Runners from 3B with Less than Two Out:		11/18	61%	

Loves to face: Don Sutton (.500, 8-for-16, 1 HR)
Hates to face: Curt Young (.071, 1-for-14)

Batted 155 points higher vs. left-handed pitchers than he did against right-handed pitchers, largest such gap in A.L. (minimum: 100 AB vs. each); batting average vs. lefties was a career high, average vs. righties a career low.... Batted .321 in day games, .256 at night.... Has struck out only 182 times in 2706 career plate appearances; Pete Incaviglia had 185 in 606 last season.... Struck out twice in a game only once last season; Walt Terrell got him, May 3.... Career batting average of .356 (16-for-45) with bases loaded.... Batting average with runners in scoring position was his lowest since 1980.... Has hit .311 in five years at the Metrodome.

Dave Henderson

Mariners/Red Sox   Bats Right

	AB	H	2B	3B	HR	RRF	BB	SO	BA	SA	OBA
Season	388	103	22	4	15	49	39	110	.265	.459	.335
vs. Left-Handers	101	27	3	1	6	15	10	18	.267	.495	.336
vs. Right-Handers	287	76	19	3	9	34	29	92	.265	.446	.334
Home	206	59	11	3	10	30	18	61	.286	.515	.345
Road	182	44	11	1	5	19	21	49	.242	.396	.324
Grass	178	39	11	0	4	17	19	51	.219	.348	.298
Artificial Turf	210	64	11	4	11	32	20	59	.305	.552	.366
April	53	6	2	0	2	5	12	23	.113	.264	.277
May	91	27	2	1	5	12	7	20	.297	.505	.343
June	92	26	7	1	4	18	7	28	.283	.511	.340
July	69	24	5	2	2	8	8	17	.348	.565	.416
August	46	13	4	0	1	2	5	12	.283	.435	.365
Sept./Oct.	37	7	2	0	1	4	0	10	.189	.324	.189
Leading Off Inn.	88	25	5	1	3	3	10	24	.284	.466	.357
Runners On	165	41	11	2	5	39	16	53	.248	.430	.317
Runners/Scor. Pos.	90	23	5	1	2	31	13	26	.256	.400	.352
Runners On/2 Out	63	13	1	1	0	10	8	25	.206	.254	.296
Scor. Pos./2 Out	37	8	1	0	0	9	7	15	.216	.243	.341
Late Inning Pressure	64	13	2	1	4	9	8	21	.203	.453	.301
Leading Off	8	2	1	0	0	0	3	2	.250	.375	.455
Runners On	35	5	1	0	2	7	3	15	.143	.343	.231
Runners/Scor. Pos.	19	4	1	0	2	7	3	6	.211	.579	.348

DRIVING IN RUNS	From 1B	From 2B	From 3B	Scoring Position
Totals	8/121	12/72	14/35	26/107
Percentage	7%	17%	40%	24%
Driving In Runners from 3B with Less than Two Out:		11/23		48%

Loves to face: Brad Havens (.636, 7-for-11, 2 HR)
Hates to face: Bert Blyleven (.056, 1-for-18)
Surprised by that playoff home run? Read the Angels essay for some further background. ... Actually, Henderson has hit a home run every 27.18 at bats in his career in majors; that's a better rate than guys like Jody Davis and Dave Parker (both 27.23), Kevin McReynolds (27.5), Tim Wallach (27.6), and Larry Parrish (27.8). ... Of course, Henderson did have the edge of playing in the Kingdome for six years; he's the all-time leading home run hitter there (48). ... Career batting average of .140, with no home runs in 67 plate appearances, in Late-Inning Pressure Situations with runners on base and two outs. In regular-season play, of course!

Rickey Henderson

New York Yankees   Bats Right

	AB	H	2B	3B	HR	RRF	BB	SO	BA	SA	OBA
Season	608	160	31	5	28	75	89	81	.263	.469	.358
vs. Left-Handers	192	45	10	3	8	18	42	27	.234	.443	.370
vs. Right-Handers	416	115	21	2	20	57	47	54	.276	.481	.352
Home	298	70	16	3	13	33	43	38	.235	.440	.332
Road	310	90	15	2	15	42	46	43	.290	.497	.383
Grass	510	129	24	4	20	60	70	68	.253	.433	.344
Artificial Turf	98	31	7	1	8	15	19	13	.316	.653	.427
April	80	21	4	1	2	11	15	14	.263	.413	.379
May	116	31	6	1	7	16	11	18	.267	.517	.331
June	116	38	10	0	6	18	16	15	.328	.569	.414
July	86	20	6	1	3	12	21	10	.233	.430	.380
August	110	22	3	1	6	12	11	13	.200	.409	.276
Sept./Oct.	100	28	2	1	4	6	15	11	.280	.440	.374
Leading Off Inn.	258	70	13	2	15	15	36	33	.271	.512	.365
Runners On	214	53	14	2	8	55	30	23	.248	.444	.337
Runners/Scor. Pos.	133	28	7	0	5	44	22	14	.211	.376	.318
Runners On/2 Out	90	17	6	0	1	14	8	14	.189	.289	.255
Scor. Pos./2 Out	62	9	2	0	1	13	7	10	.145	.226	.232
Late Inning Pressure	75	26	4	1	5	14	8	6	.347	.627	.412
Leading Off	19	5	1	0	1	1	0	0	.263	.474	.333
Runners On	33	11	3	1	0	9	5	2	.333	.485	.410
Runners/Scor. Pos.	18	5	1	0	0	7	4	1	.278	.333	.391

DRIVING IN RUNS	From 1B	From 2B	From 3B	Scoring Position
Totals	10/147	18/106	19/55	37/161
Percentage	7%	17%	35%	23%
Driving In Runners from 3B with Less than Two Out:		13/26		50%

Loves to face: Bryan Oelkers (5-for-5)
Hates to face: Tom Candiotti (.071, 1-for-14)
Stands 7th in career stolen bases (660) since the modern stolen-base rule was adopted in 1898; could overtake Morgan (689), Wagner (703), Carey (738), and Collins (743) this season. Then come Cobb (892) and Brock (938). ... His 15 home runs leading off innings last season tied the most by anyone in majors over past 12 years; Dave Lopes hit 15 in 1979, and Brian Downing did it in 1982. ... Has homered in every A.L. ballpark except Fenway Park (156 career at bats). ... Batting averages with runners in scoring position (.211) and vs. left-handed pitchers (.234) were both career lows. ... Has not had a sacrifice bunt in two years; Yankees were only team in majors last season whose leadoff batters had no sacrifice bunts.

George Hendrick

California Angels   Bats Right

	AB	H	2B	3B	HR	RRF	BB	SO	BA	SA	OBA
Season	283	77	13	1	14	49	26	41	.272	.473	.332
vs. Left-Handers	174	52	7	1	9	31	16	17	.299	.506	.352
vs. Right-Handers	109	25	6	0	5	18	10	24	.229	.422	.300
Home	135	39	6	0	8	27	12	19	.289	.511	.344
Road	148	38	7	1	6	22	14	22	.257	.439	.321
Grass	244	68	13	1	11	42	26	33	.279	.475	.347
Artificial Turf	39	9	0	0	3	7	0	8	.231	.462	.231
April	26	11	1	0	4	7	3	2	.423	.923	.483
May	75	17	4	1	2	9	3	13	.227	.387	.263
June	48	10	0	0	1	7	7	12	.208	.271	.309
July	29	8	2	0	1	6	2	5	.276	.448	.389
August	52	17	3	0	2	12	5	7	.327	.500	.386
Sept./Oct.	53	14	3	0	4	8	2	5	.264	.547	.286
Leading Off Inn.	72	23	6	0	4	4	9	9	.319	.569	.355
Runners On	129	31	5	0	4	39	17	18	.240	.372	.322
Runners/Scor. Pos.	81	21	3	0	3	37	12	15	.259	.407	.344
Runners On/2 Out	68	14	2	0	2	21	7	10	.206	.324	.280
Scor. Pos./2 Out	45	10	2	0	1	19	4	9	.222	.333	.286
Late Inning Pressure	50	13	2	1	0	8	3	9	.260	.340	.296
Leading Off	14	4	1	0	0	0	0	1	.286	.357	.286
Runners On	27	8	1	0	0	8	2	6	.296	.333	.333
Runners/Scor. Pos.	17	4	1	0	0	8	2	6	.235	.294	.300

DRIVING IN RUNS	From 1B	From 2B	From 3B	Scoring Position
Totals	3/101	15/56	17/40	32/96
Percentage	3%	27%	43%	33%
Driving In Runners from 3B with Less than Two Out:		11/19		58%

Loves to face: Mark Langston (.600, 9-for-15, 3 HR)
Hates to face: Dennis Rasmussen (0-for-7)
Has a .283 overall batting average over past 12 years: It's .283 with runners on base, .283 with the bases empty, and .283 with runners in scoring position. But with runners on base and two outs, he's a wild and crazy guy: .285. ... Started all 52 games in which Angels faced a left-handed starter last season; made 18 starts in 110 games vs. right-handers. Batting average vs. right-handers was his lowest in last 12 years; yearly averages vs. righties since 1983: .303, .271, .240, .229. ... How old is George? He made his major-league debut against the *Washington Senators*, on June 4, 1971, in a game that went 21 innings; Hendrick, who pinch-hit for Mike Epstein in the 11th, got his first major-league hit in the 20th inning.

Larry Herndon

Detroit Tigers   Bats Right

	AB	H	2B	3B	HR	RRF	BB	SO	BA	SA	OBA
Season	283	70	13	1	8	37	27	40	.247	.385	.310
vs. Left-Handers	189	44	7	0	6	27	20	22	.233	.365	.302
vs. Right-Handers	94	26	6	1	2	10	7	18	.277	.426	.327
Home	137	32	5	0	4	14	11	22	.234	.358	.289
Road	146	38	8	1	4	23	16	18	.260	.411	.329
Grass	246	63	11	1	7	33	25	36	.256	.394	.321
Artificial Turf	37	7	2	0	1	4	2	4	.189	.324	.231
April	61	17	3	1	0	3	2	10	.279	.361	.313
May	50	9	3	0	2	7	6	10	.180	.360	.263
June	55	13	3	0	2	7	3	7	.236	.400	.276
July	35	13	3	0	0	5	3	4	.371	.457	.410
August	29	4	0	0	1	5	8	5	.138	.241	.316
Sept./Oct.	53	14	1	0	3	10	5	4	.264	.453	.317
Leading Off Inn.	67	15	0	0	2	2	5	9	.224	.313	.278
Runners On	136	32	7	1	6	35	13	21	.235	.434	.292
Runners/Scor. Pos.	69	15	4	1	2	25	7	12	.217	.391	.272
Runners On/2 Out	54	11	4	0	1	9	5	8	.204	.333	.271
Scor. Pos./2 Out	25	6	3	0	0	6	2	5	.240	.360	.296
Late Inning Pressure	42	9	2	0	4	4	4	4	.214	.262	.283
Leading Off	11	2	0	0	0	0	0	3	.182	.182	.182
Runners On	23	6	2	0	0	4	3	1	.261	.348	.346
Runners/Scor. Pos.	11	4	1	0	0	3	1	1	.364	.455	.417

DRIVING IN RUNS	From 1B	From 2B	From 3B	Scoring Position
Totals	8/104	9/54	12/30	21/84
Percentage	8%	17%	40%	25%
Driving In Runners from 3B with Less than Two Out:		10/20		50%

Loves to face: John Candelaria (.439, 18-for-41, 3 HR)
Hates to face: Mike Mason (0-for-12)
Career average of .402 (43-for-107) at Yankee Stadium; he's only active player over .400 in the Bronx (minimum: 25 at bats). ... Batted only .231 (6-for-26) as a pinch-hitter last season, but was one of two major leaguers to hit three pinch-hit home runs (other: Jim Dwyer). Herndon led A.L. with 12 RBIs as a pinch-hitter. Tigers won all eight games in which he hit a home run last season. ... Batting average in May was 6th lowest in A.L. (minimum: 50 AB). ... Started all 55 games in which Tigers faced a left-handed starter, but only 16 of 107 vs. right-handers. So what numbers does he produce? A career-high .277 vs. right-handers, and a career-low .233 vs. left-handers. It was that kind of year for Sparky.

Donnie Hill
Oakland As — Bats Left and Right

	AB	H	2B	3B	HR	RRF	BB	SO	BA	SA	OBA
Season	339	96	16	2	4	30	23	38	.283	.378	.329
vs. Left-Handers	140	38	8	1	1	9	10	16	.271	.364	.320
vs. Right-Handers	199	58	8	1	3	21	13	22	.291	.387	.335
Home	157	46	7	1	0	9	11	21	.293	.350	.339
Road	182	50	9	1	4	21	12	17	.275	.401	.320
Grass	280	77	13	1	2	21	20	31	.275	.350	.323
Artificial Turf	59	19	3	1	2	9	3	7	.322	.508	.355
April	23	9	1	0	2	6	2	3	.391	.696	.440
May	68	20	3	0	0	5	4	4	.294	.338	.333
June	62	17	4	0	0	1	4	10	.274	.339	.318
July	55	15	4	0	0	4	0	4	.273	.345	.273
August	69	19	4	1	1	8	7	7	.275	.406	.342
Sept./Oct.	62	16	0	1	1	6	6	10	.258	.339	.324
Leading Off Inn.	66	20	4	1	1	6	1	7	.303	.439	.361
Runners On	161	42	5	0	3	28	12	13	.261	.348	.312
Runners/Scor. Pos.	94	25	1	0	2	25	10	9	.266	.340	.337
Runners On/2 Out	70	21	1	0	2	15	4	3	.300	.400	.338
Scor. Pos./2 Out	43	13	0	0	1	13	3	2	.302	.372	.348
Late Inning Pressure	63	17	2	0	1	4	1	3	.270	.349	.281
Leading Off	9	3	0	0	0	0	0	0	.333	.333	.333
Runners On	36	8	1	0	1	4	0	1	.222	.333	.222
Runners/Scor. Pos.	19	5	0	0	1	4	0	1	.263	.421	.263

DRIVING IN RUNS	From 1B	From 2B	From 3B	Scoring Position
Totals	4/115	7/71	14/31	21/102
Percentage	3%	10%	45%	21%
Driving In Runners from 3B with Less than Two Out:			9/15	60%

Loves to face: Bob Shirley (.714, 5-for-7)
Hates to face: Mark Langston (.071, 1-for-14)

Only active player with more than 1000 plate appearances (1156) who has never been hit by a pitch.... Batted 100 points higher in day games (.338) than in night games (.238), 3d-largest difference in A.L. last season (minimum: 50 AB each).... Career breakdown: .258 with bases empty, .291 with runners on base, .304 with runners in scoring position, .317 with runners in scoring position and two outs.... Supplied passable offense (.302 with four home runs, 23 RBI) in 53 starts at second base last season, but hit .265 with only six RBI in 29 starts at third.... Had not started a major-league game at third until June 17, when Jackie Moore put him there. It wasn't enough: Moore was fired 10 days later.

Kent Hrbek
Minnesota Twins — Bats Left

	AB	H	2B	3B	HR	RRF	BB	SO	BA	SA	OBA
Season	550	147	27	1	29	94	71	81	.267	.478	.353
vs. Left-Handers	152	41	5	0	4	28	14	33	.270	.382	.333
vs. Right-Handers	398	106	22	1	25	66	57	48	.266	.515	.361
Home	278	76	15	1	18	58	36	43	.273	.529	.359
Road	272	71	12	0	11	36	35	38	.261	.426	.347
Grass	197	52	11	0	9	29	26	26	.264	.457	.352
Artificial Turf	353	95	16	1	20	65	45	55	.269	.490	.354
April	76	24	7	0	1	9	15	8	.316	.447	.424
May	92	24	4	0	8	20	13	14	.261	.565	.352
June	95	38	5	1	8	27	13	12	.400	.726	.452
July	89	16	4	0	6	15	8	12	.180	.427	.255
August	97	22	0	0	4	11	13	16	.227	.351	.315
Sept./Oct.	101	23	7	0	2	12	9	19	.228	.356	.295
Leading Off Inn.	86	26	4	0	6	13	10		.302	.558	.400
Runners On	260	76	12	1	12	77	30	32	.292	.485	.363
Runners/Scor. Pos.	139	34	7	0	2	53	21	21	.245	.338	.333
Runners On/2 Out	82	22	3	0	4	20	15	11	.268	.451	.388
Scor. Pos./2 Out	48	9	2	0	0	11	12	7	.188	.229	.350
Late Inning Pressure	78	20	2	0	3	11	9	13	.256	.397	.341
Leading Off	25	5	0	0	0		2	3	.200	.200	.259
Runners On	31	8	1	0	0	8	3	5	.258	.290	.324
Runners/Scor. Pos.	16	6	1	0	0	8	3	3	.375	.438	.474

DRIVING IN RUNS	From 1B	From 2B	From 3B	Scoring Position
Totals	15/194	23/108	27/52	50/160
Percentage	8%	21%	52%	31%
Driving In Runners from 3B with Less than Two Out:			25/37	68%

Loves to face: Dan Quisenberry (.588, 10-for-17, 2 HR)
Hates to face: Gene Nelson (.059, 1-for-17)

A first-rate pressure performer: .281 overall career average, but .293 in Late-Inning Pressure Situations; .330 in those situations with runners in scoring position, and .400 (14-for-35) in those spots with runners in scoring position and two outs.... One of five major leaguers over past 12 years to have driven in more than 35 percent of runners from scoring position. Top five: Mattingly, 37.5; Boggs, 35.8; Munson, 35.2; Dane Iorg (*sic*), 35.2; Hrbek, 35.1.... Career batting average of .314 at the Metrodome, .263 in road games; 14 of his 15 triples have been hit in the Metrodome.... Batting average of .400 in June was highest in majors (minimum: 75 AB).

Tim Hulett
Chicago White Sox — Bats Right

	AB	H	2B	3B	HR	RRF	BB	SO	BA	SA	OBA
Season	520	120	16	5	17	45	21	91	.231	.379	.260
vs. Left-Handers	194	49	6	2	9	17	13	34	.253	.443	.297
vs. Right-Handers	326	71	10	3	8	28	8	57	.218	.340	.237
Home	263	65	8	3	7	20	14	48	.247	.380	.286
Road	257	55	8	2	10	25	7	43	.214	.377	.233
Grass	438	103	10	5	17	41	18	76	.235	.397	.263
Artificial Turf	82	17	6	0	0	4	3	15	.207	.280	.233
April	36	8	1	0	0	2	5	8	.222	.250	.317
May	90	26	6	3	2	10	2	13	.289	.489	.304
June	82	20	4	2	2	7	7	13	.244	.415	.300
July	79	23	0	0	6	12	1	11	.291	.519	.293
August	116	23	2	0	5	7	4	18	.198	.345	.225
Sept./Oct.	117	20	3	0	2	7	2	28	.171	.248	.190
Leading Off Inn.	118	24	4	2	3	3	7	19	.203	.347	.248
Runners On	232	48	4	0	6	34	8	45	.207	.302	.230
Runners/Scor. Pos.	120	21	1	0	2	26	3	31	.175	.233	.189
Runners On/2 Out	94	15	0	0	0	9	2	15	.160	.160	.177
Scor. Pos./2 Out	59	8	0	0	0	9	1	11	.136	.136	.150
Late Inning Pressure	77	14	1	1	1	6	2	19	.182	.260	.213
Leading Off	18	5	1	0	0	0	0	3	.278	.333	.278
Runners On	36	5	0	0	1	6	1	9	.139	.222	.162
Runners/Scor. Pos.	18	3	0	0	1	6	0	5	.167	.333	.167

DRIVING IN RUNS	From 1B	From 2B	From 3B	Scoring Position
Totals	6/168	6/92	16/57	22/149
Percentage	4%	7%	28%	15%
Driving In Runners from 3B with Less than Two Out:			8/24	33%

Loves to face: Neal Heaton (.389, 7-for-18, 1 HR)
Hates to face: Dave Stieb (0-for-12)

Had 94 at bats with runners on base and two outs, and did not get an extra-base hit; that's the most at bats without an extra-base hit in that situation since we started keeping track in 1975.... Wasn't so great with less than two outs, either: he knocked in only 33.3 percent (8-of-24) of runners from third base with less than two outs, 4th-worst rate in A.L. (minimum: 15 opportunities).... Career breakdown: .258 with bases empty, .227 with runners on base, .207 with runners in scoring position, .191 with runners in scoring position and two outs.... Batted 111 points higher in day games (.309) than in night games (.198), 2d-largest difference in A.L. (minimum: 50 AB each).

Pete Incaviglia
Texas Rangers — Bats Right

	AB	H	2B	3B	HR	RRF	BB	SO	BA	SA	OBA
Season	540	135	21	2	30	90	55	185	.250	.463	.320
vs. Left-Handers	160	49	7	2	12	32	18	55	.306	.600	.374
vs. Right-Handers	380	86	14	0	18	58	37	130	.226	.405	.297
Home	275	79	13	1	17	51	27	94	.287	.527	.353
Road	265	56	8	1	13	39	28	91	.211	.396	.286
Grass	461	119	19	2	27	83	48	154	.258	.484	.329
Artificial Turf	79	16	2	0	3	7	7	31	.203	.342	.264
April	63	10	3	0	3	8	6	21	.159	.349	.239
May	87	31	6	2	6	19	7	31	.356	.678	.404
June	94	24	3	0	4	16	12	34	.255	.415	.330
July	96	24	3	0	4	15	7	31	.250	.406	.305
August	99	22	3	0	3	10	12	33	.222	.343	.313
Sept./Oct.	101	24	3	0	10	22	11	35	.238	.564	.313
Leading Off Inn.	116	30	8	0	5	5	7	38	.259	.457	.306
Runners On	264	61	7	2	13	73	32	91	.231	.420	.311
Runners/Scor. Pos.	144	34	5	1	9	62	19	53	.236	.472	.316
Runners On/2 Out	140	32	1	1	6	27	14	54	.229	.379	.299
Scor. Pos./2 Out	81	18	1	0	6	26	8	35	.222	.457	.292
Late Inning Pressure	63	19	3	0	3	14	10	20	.302	.492	.400
Leading Off	6	1	1	0	0	0	1	2	.167	.333	.286
Runners On	30	10	1	0	2	13	6	8	.333	.567	.447
Runners/Scor. Pos.	18	7	1	0	2	13	4	5	.389	.778	.500

DRIVING IN RUNS	From 1B	From 2B	From 3B	Scoring Position
Totals	13/191	19/112	28/72	47/184
Percentage	7%	17%	39%	26%
Driving In Runners from 3B with Less than Two Out:			20/34	59%

Loves to face: Lee Guetterman (.667, 4-for-6)
Hates to face: Oil Can Boyd (0-for-11, 8 SO)

Struck out 25 times in 40 plate appearances vs. Boston, but Oil Can didn't even lead the league in striking him out: Frank Viola got him nine times in 14 plate appearances.... Tough in the clutch: Had 185 strikeouts, four short of Bobby Bonds's major-league record, with two games to play; did not strike out in seven times up in those two games.... Batting average with runners in scoring position is not that low considering he suffered through a 3-for-49 slump, including a hitless streak of 18 at bats, in such situations.... Lowest fielding percentage (.921) among major-league outfielders (minimum: 100 games); made 14 errors.... It's hard to believe that he won't be a DH one day, but he hit only .199 in 37 games in that role last season.

Garth Iorg

Toronto Blue Jays — Bats Right

	AB	H	2B	3B	HR	RRF	BB	SO	BA	SA	OBA
Season	327	85	19	1	3	45	20	47	.260	.352	.303
vs. Left-Handers	166	48	11	0	3	31	13	20	.289	.410	.339
vs. Right-Handers	161	37	8	1	0	14	7	27	.230	.292	.265
Home	167	36	10	1	1	18	8	29	.216	.305	.256
Road	160	49	9	0	2	27	12	18	.306	.400	.351
Grass	129	42	8	0	2	23	10	14	.326	.434	.369
Artificial Turf	198	43	11	1	1	22	10	33	.217	.298	.258
April	36	9	0	0	0	4	3	8	.250	.250	.308
May	32	10	1	0	0	0	1	6	.313	.344	.333
June	58	14	1	0	2	15	2	9	.241	.362	.270
July	46	8	2	0	0	3	6	8	.174	.217	.269
August	92	23	4	1	1	16	5	8	.250	.348	.289
Sept./Oct.	63	21	11	0	0	7	3	8	.333	.508	.364
Leading Off Inn.	65	18	6	0	0	0	4	8	.277	.369	.319
Runners On	154	45	7	1	2	44	10	14	.292	.390	.331
Runners/Scor. Pos.	94	30	5	1	2	42	8	8	.319	.457	.365
Runners On/2 Out	68	22	5	0	2	26	6	6	.324	.485	.378
Scor. Pos./2 Out	47	17	4	0	2	25	6	3	.362	.574	.434
Late Inning Pressure	65	17	3	0	0	4	7	10	.262	.308	.333
Leading Off	12	4	1	0	0	0	2	1	.333	.417	.429
Runners On	28	8	1	0	0	4	3	1	.286	.321	.355
Runners/Scor. Pos.	13	4	1	0	0	4	3	0	.308	.385	.438

DRIVING IN RUNS	From 1B	From 2B	From 3B	Scoring Position
Totals	6/111	20/79	16/37	36/116
Percentage	5%	25%	43%	31%
Driving In Runners from 3B with Less than Two Out:		9/17		53%

Loves to face: John Henry Johnson (.714, 5-for-7, 2 triples)
Hates to face: Dennis Rasmussen (1-for-11)
Over past three seasons, Toronto has allowed 3.99 runs per nine innings with Iorg at 3d, 4.20 with Mulliniks.... What's left to say about the Iorg brothers as clutch hitters? To those new to the *Analyst*, a brief recap. First, Garth: A .265 overall hitter with a career .315 batting average in Late-Inning Pressure Situations (10th in majors over past 12 years), and .329 in LIP situations with runners in scoring position, including .393 (11-for-28) with two outs.... Now Dane: A .276 career hitter who has driven in 35.2 percent of runners from scoring position, 4th best in majors over past 12 years.... The Waners themselves would have had a hard time matching those clutch figures.

Bo Jackson

Kansas City Royals — Bats Right

	AB	H	2B	3B	HR	RRF	BB	SO	BA	SA	OBA
Season	82	17	2	1	2	9	7	34	.207	.329	.286
vs. Left-Handers	21	2	0	1	0	1	2	12	.095	.190	.174
vs. Right-Handers	61	15	2	0	2	8	5	22	.246	.377	.324
Home	44	11	0	0	1	4	1	17	.250	.318	.298
Road	38	6	2	1	1	5	6	17	.158	.342	.273
Grass	22	4	1	0	1	2	3	8	.182	.364	.280
Artificial Turf	60	13	1	1	1	7	4	26	.217	.317	.288
April	0	0	0	0	0	0	0	0	—	—	—
May	0	0	0	0	0	0	0	0	—	—	—
June	0	0	0	0	0	0	0	0	—	—	—
July	0	0	0	0	0	0	0	0	—	—	—
August	0	0	0	0	0	0	0	0	—	—	—
Sept./Oct.	82	17	2	1	2	9	7	34	.207	.329	.286
Leading Off Inn.	17	3	0	0	1	1	2	5	.176	.353	.263
Runners On	33	9	1	1	1	8	4	15	.273	.455	.385
Runners/Scor. Pos.	17	5	1	1	0	6	2	9	.294	.471	.429
Runners On/2 Out	12	4	0	1	1	5	1	7	.333	.750	.429
Scor. Pos./2 Out	5	2	0	1	0	3	1	3	.400	.800	.571
Late Inning Pressure	14	1	0	0	1	2	5	5	.071	.286	.188
Leading Off	2	0	0	0	0	0	0	0	.000	.000	.000
Runners On	7	1	0	0	1	2	0	4	.143	.571	.333
Runners/Scor. Pos.	4	0	0	0	0	2	0	3	.000	.000	.333

DRIVING IN RUNS	From 1B	From 2B	From 3B	Scoring Position
Totals	2/25	3/17	2/3	5/20
Percentage	8%	18%	67%	25%
Driving In Runners from 3B with Less than Two Out:		1/1		100%

Loves to face: Mike Morgan (.833, 5-for-6)
Hates to face: Mark Langston (0-for-4, 3 SO)
Buccaneers finished 27th among the 28 NFL teams in points (14.9 per game) and yards (272.6 per game), and have won only two games in three of the last four seasons.... Bucs were unable to drive length of the field: They scored a touchdown on only 5 of 75 drives begun at or inside their own 20 yard-line (6.7 percent, compared to league average of 11.2 percent; Miami led league with 27 percent). ... Hold it, how did that *Elias Football Analyst* stuff creep in here? Computer snafu.... Back to baseball: What do Reggie and Bo have in common? We mean besides constantly referring to themselves in the third person, like Nixon.... Both were among a handful of A.L. outfielders (five in all) to have a fielding percentage below .900.

Reggie Jackson

California Angels — Bats Left

	AB	H	2B	3B	HR	RRF	BB	SO	BA	SA	OBA
Season	419	101	12	2	18	59	92	115	.241	.408	.379
vs. Left-Handers	71	17	3	0	0	5	11	24	.239	.282	.349
vs. Right-Handers	348	84	9	2	18	54	81	91	.241	.434	.385
Home	195	54	6	2	11	32	51	54	.277	.497	.426
Road	224	47	6	0	7	27	41	61	.210	.330	.336
Grass	360	89	9	2	15	49	83	98	.247	.408	.390
Artificial Turf	59	12	3	0	3	10	9	17	.203	.407	.309
April	54	22	3	0	5	13	10	15	.407	.741	.500
May	68	16	1	0	2	6	11	23	.235	.338	.342
June	69	20	2	0	0	9	22	16	.290	.319	.468
July	79	15	3	2	2	8	20	26	.190	.354	.354
August	76	12	2	0	2	5	15	19	.158	.263	.297
Sept./Oct.	73	16	1	0	7	18	14	16	.219	.521	.341
Leading Off Inn.	92	20	1	0	4	4	21	19	.217	.359	.368
Runners On	216	54	8	1	9	50	54	62	.250	.421	.398
Runners/Scor. Pos.	114	25	3	1	3	36	54	31	.219	.342	.403
Runners On/2 Out	96	18	2	0	4	21	28	35	.188	.333	.371
Scor. Pos./2 Out	53	8	0	0	1	13	20	21	.151	.208	.384
Late Inning Pressure	55	10	1	0	1	4	13	18	.182	.255	.338
Leading Off	14	3	0	0	0	0	2	2	.214	.214	.313
Runners On	30	4	1	0	1	4	5	11	.133	.267	.257
Runners/Scor. Pos.	9	1	0	0	0	2	5	3	.111	.111	.429

DRIVING IN RUNS	From 1B	From 2B	From 3B	Scoring Position
Totals	12/164	16/101	13/38	29/139
Percentage	7%	16%	34%	21%
Driving In Runners from 3B with Less than Two Out:		9/20		45%

Loves to face: Joaquin Andujar (.714, 5-for-7, 1 HR)
Hates to face: Phil Niekro (.059, 1-for-17)
Appeared in six postseason games last season, boosting his career total to 77, the most by anyone in history; old mark of 75 (all in World Series) was held by Yogi Berra.... Has hit eight of his 11 career grand slams off left-handed pitchers.... Still feared, especially by right-handed pitchers: Reggie had highest walk ratio in majors among players with 502 PA (517 PA, 92 walks).... Last home run against a left-hander: Aug. 17, 1985 off Bill Krueger.... Starts 1987 season with nice, round total of 2500 career strikeouts; Willie Stargell is eating his dust at 1936.... Has batted under .200 in Late-Inning Pressure Situations in each of the last three seasons.

Brook Jacoby

Cleveland Indians — Bats Right

	AB	H	2B	3B	HR	RRF	BB	SO	BA	SA	OBA
Season	583	168	30	4	17	85	56	137	.288	.441	.350
vs. Left-Handers	161	42	6	1	5	24	19	34	.261	.404	.339
vs. Right-Handers	422	126	24	3	12	61	37	103	.299	.455	.354
Home	274	73	11	2	10	47	30	68	.266	.431	.338
Road	309	95	19	2	7	38	26	69	.307	.450	.361
Grass	491	142	22	3	17	77	48	117	.289	.450	.352
Artificial Turf	92	26	8	1	0	8	8	20	.283	.391	.340
April	73	24	5	1	2	11	7	20	.329	.507	.388
May	102	24	3	0	3	16	11	24	.235	.353	.310
June	100	26	5	1	4	16	7	23	.260	.450	.308
July	88	23	5	0	2	14	10	22	.261	.386	.333
August	104	29	4	1	2	10	13	28	.279	.394	.359
Sept./Oct.	116	42	8	1	4	18	8	20	.362	.552	.403
Leading Off Inn.	137	41	4	1	6	6	14	28	.299	.474	.364
Runners On	270	87	15	3	8	76	25	64	.322	.489	.378
Runners/Scor. Pos.	145	45	8	2	6	67	19	41	.310	.517	.388
Runners On/2 Out	107	37	5	1	3	33	12	23	.346	.495	.412
Scor. Pos./2 Out	71	22	3	1	2	29	11	20	.310	.465	.402
Late Inning Pressure	75	26	4	1	1	9	7	17	.347	.467	.402
Leading Off	22	6	0	0	0	1	5	3	.273	.273	.304
Runners On	26	11	1	1	0	8	4	7	.423	.538	.500
Runners/Scor. Pos.	16	8	1	1	0	8	4	3	.500	.688	.600

DRIVING IN RUNS	From 1B	From 2B	From 3B	Scoring Position
Totals	12/190	33/110	22/55	55/165
Percentage	6%	30%	40%	33%
Driving In Runners from 3B with Less than Two Out:		13/25		52%

Loves to face: Rick Langford (.714, 5-for-7, 2 HR)
Hates to face: Bret Saberhagen (.053, 1-for-19)
Hit .360 in 46 games batting 8th in order, and .260 in 112 games elsewhere in lineup. Cleveland's 8th-place hitters hit an astonishing .326 last season; there are 234 team-batting-order positions in majors, and only one, the Yankees' 3d-place hitters (.331), batted higher than the guys that Cleveland had hitting 8th.... Batting average after Sept. 1 was 8th highest in majors (minimum: 75 AB), but only 3d highest on his team: Franco (.386) and Butler (.381) had higher averages over the final five weeks of the season.... Career breakdown: .290 with runners on base, .261 with bases empty.... Yearly batting averages in Late-Inning Pressure Situations since 1984: .167, .229, .347.

Cliff Johnson
Toronto Blue Jays — Bats Right

	AB	H	2B	3B	HR	RRF	BB	SO	BA	SA	OBA
Season	336	84	12	1	15	59	52	57	.250	.426	.355
vs. Left-Handers	107	31	7	0	8	25	20	11	.290	.579	.408
vs. Right-Handers	229	53	5	1	7	34	32	46	.231	.354	.330
Home	174	47	6	0	11	37	25	28	.270	.494	.365
Road	162	37	6	1	4	22	27	29	.228	.352	.346
Grass	130	26	4	1	4	17	25	22	.200	.338	.338
Artificial Turf	206	58	8	0	11	42	27	35	.282	.481	.367
April	41	14	4	0	1	10	7	9	.341	.512	.438
May	77	21	1	1	5	15	13	11	.273	.506	.380
June	88	25	5	0	4	17	6	18	.284	.477	.333
July	23	4	0	0	1	5	6	6	.174	.304	.345
August	74	17	0	0	3	10	15	8	.230	.351	.374
Sept./Oct.	33	3	2	0	1	2	5	5	.091	.242	.211
Leading Off Inn.	74	21	2	1	2	2	10	13	.284	.419	.376
Runners On	150	41	5	0	8	52	24	22	.273	.467	.376
Runners/Scor. Pos.	93	24	3	0	3	40	16	13	.258	.387	.360
Runners On/2 Out	67	17	2	0	0	20	11	15	.254	.284	.375
Scor. Pos./2 Out	46	16	2	0	0	20	10	9	.348	.391	.464
Late Inning Pressure	66	21	1	1	4	19	7	10	.318	.545	.384
Leading Off	17	6	0	1	1	1	2	5	.353	.647	.421
Runners On	29	10	1	0	1	16	3	4	.345	.481	.406
Runners/Scor. Pos.	19	9	1	0	0	14	3	2	.474	.526	.545

DRIVING IN RUNS	From 1B	From 2B	From 3B	Scoring Position
Totals	9/103	17/70	18/38	35/108
Percentage	9%	24%	47%	32%
Driving In Runners from 3B with Less than Two Out:			10/18	56%

Loves to face: John Candelaria (.500, 6-for-12, 1 HR)
Hates to face: Mark Clear (0-for-14, 5 SO)
Which is highest: Johnson's career total of triples, stolen bases, or sacrifice bunts? Answer below. . . . Has played for seven teams and 12 managers; the first: Houston and Leo Durocher in 1972. . . . It just doesn't seem right that his lowest career batting average at any A.L. park would be at Fenway (.209), but the numbers don't lie. . . . Batting average with runners in scoring position and two outs was his highest in last 12 years. . . . Has batted .350 with the bases loaded (28-for-80) over the past 10 years, although his last grand slam came in 1980. . . . Answer: 10 triples, nine stolen bases, four sacrifice bunts. Five of the steals came in the strike season—remember "Billy Ball"?

Ruppert Jones
California Angels — Bats Left

	AB	H	2B	3B	HR	RRF	BB	SO	BA	SA	OBA
Season	393	90	21	3	17	53	64	87	.229	.427	.339
vs. Left-Handers	45	8	3	0	2	8	8	10	.178	.378	.296
vs. Right-Handers	348	82	18	3	15	45	56	77	.236	.434	.345
Home	182	45	12	0	10	25	37	40	.247	.478	.380
Road	211	45	9	3	7	28	27	47	.213	.384	.302
Grass	331	76	20	2	13	44	57	74	.230	.420	.344
Artificial Turf	62	14	1	1	4	9	7	13	.226	.468	.314
April	53	11	2	0	2	9	12	10	.208	.358	.348
May	57	16	10	0	0	8	12	12	.281	.456	.406
June	72	19	2	3	6	14	10	18	.264	.625	.357
July	82	16	6	0	3	8	10	20	.195	.378	.290
August	73	16	0	0	4	5	8	16	.219	.384	.305
Sept./Oct.	56	12	1	0	2	9	12	11	.214	.339	.348
Leading Off Inn.	118	31	6	1	7	7	13	24	.263	.508	.341
Runners On	154	36	8	2	7	43	32	42	.234	.448	.366
Runners/Scor. Pos.	103	20	6	2	5	39	21	34	.194	.437	.333
Runners On/2 Out	63	16	2	2	3	21	10	21	.254	.524	.365
Scor. Pos./2 Out	50	11	4	2	2	19	9	19	.220	.500	.350
Late Inning Pressure	53	12	1	0	1	5	11	13	.226	.302	.369
Leading Off	11	1	0	0	0	0	4	4	.091	.091	.375
Runners On	21	6	1	0	1	5	6	5	.286	.476	.444
Runners/Scor. Pos.	13	3	1	0	0	3	3	3	.231	.308	.375

DRIVING IN RUNS	From 1B	From 2B	From 3B	Scoring Position
Totals	5/104	14/81	17/43	31/124
Percentage	5%	17%	40%	25%
Driving In Runners from 3B with Less than Two Out:			10/22	45%

Loves to face: Mark Eichhorn (.800, 4-for-5, 1 HR)
Hates to face: Charlie Hough (1-for-16)
One of six players in history with two extra-inning grand slam homers. Others: Fred Williams, Roger Maris, Tommy Davis, Cookie Rojas, and Jim Presley; in Rupe's case, they're the only two grand slams of his career. . . . Has homered in every current A.L. stadium except Memorial Stadium in Baltimore (116 career at bats there). . . . Started 101 of 110 games in which Angels faced a right-hander; started twice against lefties. . . . Career breakdown: .265 vs. right-handers, .210 vs. left-handers; has not hit above .200 against lefties since the 1982 season (.231). . . . One of three players chosen by Mariners in 1976 expansion draft who were still in majors in 1986; others: Dave Collins and Julio Cruz.

Wally Joyner
California Angels — Bats Left

	AB	H	2B	3B	HR	RRF	BB	SO	BA	SA	OBA
Season	593	172	27	3	22	102	57	58	.290	.457	.348
vs. Left-Handers	192	45	3	1	6	24	14	24	.234	.354	.289
vs. Right-Handers	401	127	24	2	16	78	43	34	.317	.506	.375
Home	294	82	10	1	11	41	33	27	.279	.432	.347
Road	299	90	17	2	11	61	24	31	.301	.482	.348
Grass	520	152	22	3	18	85	48	47	.292	.450	.349
Artificial Turf	73	20	5	0	4	17	9	11	.274	.507	.341
April	87	29	5	0	6	18	6	8	.333	.598	.379
May	110	31	1	0	10	25	8	15	.282	.564	.325
June	101	30	5	1	3	17	7	9	.297	.455	.336
July	108	38	5	2	2	16	11	11	.352	.491	.410
August	99	23	6	0	1	15	12	9	.232	.323	.307
Sept./Oct.	88	21	5	0	0	11	13	6	.239	.295	.330
Leading Off Inn.	102	26	2	0	5	5	7	13	.255	.422	.303
Runners On	275	88	12	2	9	89	35	25	.320	.476	.382
Runners/Scor. Pos.	160	47	6	1	2	71	23	19	.294	.381	.359
Runners On/2 Out	103	36	4	0	3	36	15	10	.350	.476	.432
Scor. Pos./2 Out	77	25	3	0	1	31	10	9	.325	.403	.402
Late Inning Pressure	79	26	5	2	3	13	10	12	.329	.557	.404
Leading Off	15	4	0	0	0	0	2	3	.267	.267	.353
Runners On	36	10	1	1	2	12	8	6	.278	.528	.409
Runners/Scor. Pos.	18	4	0	1	0	7	5	4	.222	.333	.391

DRIVING IN RUNS	From 1B	From 2B	From 3B	Scoring Position
Totals	14/197	29/127	37/68	66/195
Percentage	7%	23%	54%	34%
Driving In Runners from 3B with Less than Two Out:			23/33	70%

Loves to face: Al Nipper (.833, 5-for-6, 2 HR)
Hates to face: Joe Niekro (1-for-11)
22 home runs were the most by a first baseman for Angels since Don Mincher hit 25 in 1967. He also became the first man to play 150 or more games at first base in the team's 26-year history. . . . One of two major leaguers to have 20 or more home runs and 10+ sacrifice bunts last season; other: Alan Trammell. . . . Batted 82 points higher vs. right-handed pitchers than vs. left-handers, 5th-largest such difference in A.L. (minimum: 100 AB vs. each). . . . Angels had a record of 17–3 in games in which he homered. . . . July batting average was 5th highest in A.L. (minimum: 75 AB), but he hit only .235 after that. . . . First rookie to hit a home run in A.L. Championship Series.

Bob Kearney
Seattle Mariners — Bats Right

	AB	H	2B	3B	HR	RRF	BB	SO	BA	SA	OBA
Season	204	49	10	0	6	25	12	35	.240	.377	.281
vs. Left-Handers	75	20	6	0	2	8	2	15	.267	.427	.282
vs. Right-Handers	129	29	4	0	4	17	10	20	.225	.349	.281
Home	95	28	7	0	4	16	8	16	.295	.495	.346
Road	109	21	3	0	2	9	4	19	.193	.275	.221
Grass	73	14	2	0	1	4	4	10	.192	.260	.234
Artificial Turf	131	35	8	0	5	21	8	25	.267	.443	.307
April	24	4	1	0	0	0	1	6	.167	.208	.200
May	37	7	2	0	0	4	2	6	.189	.243	.225
June	62	17	2	0	3	10	3	6	.274	.452	.308
July	20	5	2	0	0	1	1	5	.250	.350	.286
August	31	13	3	0	3	8	4	4	.419	.806	.486
Sept./Oct.	30	3	0	0	0	2	1	8	.100	.100	.129
Leading Off Inn.	47	10	3	0	0	0	1	10	.213	.277	.229
Runners On	87	21	3	0	5	24	5	12	.241	.448	.280
Runners/Scor. Pos.	49	11	2	0	2	17	4	7	.224	.388	.278
Runners On/2 Out	36	9	1	0	3	14	2	6	.250	.528	.289
Scor. Pos./2 Out	26	7	1	0	1	10	1	4	.269	.423	.296
Late Inning Pressure	27	8	3	0	0	2	4	5	.296	.407	.387
Leading Off	4	0	0	0	0	0	1	0	.000	.000	.200
Runners On	10	3	1	0	0	2	1	3	.300	.400	.364
Runners/Scor. Pos.	6	2	1	0	0	2	1	2	.333	.500	.429

DRIVING IN RUNS	From 1B	From 2B	From 3B	Scoring Position
Totals	5/59	7/38	7/23	14/61
Percentage	8%	18%	30%	23%
Driving In Runners from 3B with Less than Two Out:			3/13	23%

Loves to face: Moose Haas (.615, 8-for-13, 5 doubles)
Hates to face: Bruce Hurst (0-for-15)
Over last two years, has delivered only 19.4 percent (6-of-31) of runners from third base with less than two outs, lowest rate in majors among players with at least 20 chances (A.L. average over 1985–86: 58.1 percent). . . . Career batting average of .120 (3-for-25, no extra-base hits, no walks) with bases loaded. . . . Starting catcher in 60 games last season, most on the team; Mariners were one of six A.L. teams on which no catcher started the majority of team's games. . . . Born October 3, 1956, the day of Jackie Robinson's last home run, in the opening game of the World Series. (Yes, Virginia, World Series did once start in the first week of October.)

Mike Kingery

Kansas City Royals — Bats Left

	AB	H	2B	3B	HR	RRF	BB	SO	BA	SA	OBA
Season	209	54	8	5	3	15	12	30	.258	.388	.296
vs. Left-Handers	30	2	0	0	0	2	2	8	.067	.067	.121
vs. Right-Handers	179	52	8	5	3	13	10	22	.291	.441	.326
Home	115	32	5	3	1	7	6	12	.278	.400	.309
Road	94	22	3	2	2	8	6	18	.234	.372	.280
Grass	67	17	3	2	1	5	5	10	.254	.403	.306
Artificial Turf	142	37	5	3	2	10	7	20	.261	.380	.291
April	0	0	0	0	0	0	0	0	—	—	—
May	0	0	0	0	0	0	0	0	—	—	—
June	0	0	0	0	0	0	0	0	—	—	—
July	71	20	3	2	1	4	5	7	.282	.423	.325
August	77	16	3	1	1	3	3	15	.208	.312	.238
Sept./Oct.	61	18	2	2	1	8	4	8	.295	.443	.333
Leading Off Inn.	40	9	2	4	1	1	4	9	.225	.550	.295
Runners On	85	22	2	0	1	13	5	10	.259	.318	.293
Runners/Scor. Pos.	48	7	1	0	0	11	3	5	.146	.167	.189
Runners On/2 Out	31	8	0	0	0	2	4	5	.258	.258	.343
Scor. Pos./2 Out	21	3	0	0	0	2	2	4	.143	.143	.217
Late Inning Pressure	39	8	2	2	0	1	1	7	.205	.359	.225
Leading Off	11	4	1	2	0	0	1	1	.364	.818	.417
Runners On	14	2	0	0	0	0	0	3	.143	.143	.143
Runners/Scor. Pos.	7	0	0	0	0	0	0	1	.000	.000	.000

DRIVING IN RUNS	From 1B	From 2B	From 3B	Scoring Position
Totals	1/56	5/38	6/13	11/51
Percentage	2%	13%	46%	22%
Driving In Runners from 3B with Less than Two Out:		6/9		67%

Loves to face: Chris Bosio (4-for-4, 1 HR)
Hates to face: Bert Blyleven (0-for-8, 4 SO)
Started 49 of Royals' last 59 games vs. right-handers; also made four starts vs. left-handers. . . . Two hits vs. lefties both came in routs; he's 0-for-20 vs. left-handers when batting with no more than three runs separating teams. . . . Ended season with 0-for-17 streak vs. lefties. . . . A.L. starting right fielders hit more home runs and drove in more runs than starters at any other position; Royals' right-field starters had a last-place sweep of Triple Crown categories: composite batting average of .221, 12 home runs and 55 RBI (averages for 13 other teams: .270, 28 HR, 94 RBI). . . . Kingery had 44 starts there; his partners in crime: Darryl Motley (54 starts), Rudy Law (34), Bo Jackson (21), Lynn Jones (five), Mike Brewer (four).

Dave Kingman

Oakland As — Bats Right

	AB	H	2B	3B	HR	RRF	BB	SO	BA	SA	OBA
Season	561	118	19	0	35	96	33	126	.210	.431	.255
vs. Left-Handers	175	38	8	0	14	31	13	45	.217	.503	.274
vs. Right-Handers	386	80	11	0	21	65	20	81	.207	.399	.246
Home	297	63	8	0	15	45	14	68	.212	.391	.244
Road	264	55	11	0	20	51	19	58	.208	.477	.266
Grass	477	95	16	0	24	68	28	113	.199	.384	.244
Artificial Turf	84	23	3	0	11	28	5	13	.274	.702	.315
April	57	9	0	0	2	10	3	15	.158	.263	.197
May	105	25	1	0	9	20	3	30	.238	.505	.277
June	106	20	5	0	6	22	9	21	.189	.406	.248
July	96	19	3	0	5	14	5	18	.198	.385	.238
August	98	28	6	0	8	18	7	19	.286	.592	.330
Sept./Oct.	99	17	4	0	5	12	6	23	.172	.364	.215
Leading Off Inn.	128	21	5	0	4	4	7	30	.164	.297	.219
Runners On	256	52	9	0	10	71	13	56	.223	.375	.256
Runners/Scor. Pos.	149	37	7	0	7	64	10	33	.248	.436	.287
Runners On/2 Out	117	23	3	0	5	30	10	27	.197	.350	.260
Scor. Pos./2 Out	70	16	3	0	3	26	8	17	.229	.400	.308
Late Inning Pressure	83	14	1	0	5	10	5	16	.169	.361	.213
Leading Off	21	2	0	0	1	1	1	1	.095	.238	.136
Runners On	30	4	0	0	2	7	2	9	.133	.333	.182
Runners/Scor. Pos.	16	2	0	0	1	5	2	4	.125	.313	.211

DRIVING IN RUNS	From 1B	From 2B	From 3B	Scoring Position
Totals	11/193	23/110	27/78	50/188
Percentage	6%	21%	35%	27%
Driving In Runners from 3B with Less than Two Out:		17/43		40%

Loves to face: Matt Young (.667, 6-for-9, 4 HR)
Hates to face: Ron Romanick (.042, 1-for-24)
Led A.L. with 14 home runs off left-handed pitchers. . . . Has 100 home runs over past three years, most in A.L.; Schmidt (106) and Murphy (102) have 100 in N.L. . . . Has homered in every current major-league ballpark except Memorial Stadium (60 career at bats) and County Stadium (65). . . . Has hit 13 home runs in 76 at bats at Fenway Park, and 12 in 79 at the Kingdome. . . . Drove in 15 runs in 10 games vs. Seattle last season. . . . Hit one grand slam last year, bringing career total to 16, tied with Ruth and Aaron for 5th place all time; leaders: Gehrig, 23; McCovey, 18; Foxx and Williams, 17. . . . Kingman's first grand slam came in his first start in majors, on July 31, 1971, off Dave Giusti—even before his first strikeout!

Ron Kittle

White Sox/Yankees — Bats Right

	AB	H	2B	3B	HR	RRF	BB	SO	BA	SA	OBA
Season	376	82	13	0	21	60	35	110	.218	.420	.284
vs. Left-Handers	179	31	7	0	7	20	20	60	.173	.330	.257
vs. Right-Handers	197	51	6	0	14	40	15	50	.259	.503	.309
Home	173	33	6	0	6	23	19	57	.191	.329	.271
Road	203	49	7	0	15	37	16	53	.241	.498	.296
Grass	320	64	8	0	15	47	29	102	.200	.366	.267
Artificial Turf	56	18	5	0	6	13	6	8	.321	.732	.387
April	65	15	2	0	6	14	1	22	.231	.538	.239
May	73	14	4	0	0	9	8	19	.192	.247	.267
June	89	16	4	0	7	16	11	29	.180	.461	.275
July	72	18	1	0	4	9	9	20	.250	.431	.341
August	22	5	2	0	0	2	1	9	.227	.318	.250
Sept./Oct.	55	14	0	0	4	10	5	11	.255	.473	.311
Leading Off Inn.	83	18	3	0	4	4	12	26	.217	.398	.330
Runners On	186	42	6	0	10	49	17	60	.226	.419	.280
Runners/Scor. Pos.	100	20	4	0	3	35	11	34	.200	.330	.261
Runners On/2 Out	70	15	3	0	3	18	9	26	.214	.386	.304
Scor. Pos./2 Out	39	9	2	0	1	14	6	13	.231	.359	.333
Late Inning Pressure	57	10	2	0	2	9	3	15	.175	.316	.222
Leading Off	8	2	1	0	0	0	1	2	.250	.375	.333
Runners On	35	7	1	0	1	8	1	8	.200	.314	.211
Runners/Scor. Pos.	14	2	0	0	0	6	1	3	.143	.143	.176

DRIVING IN RUNS	From 1B	From 2B	From 3B	Scoring Position
Totals	9/145	11/75	19/46	30/121
Percentage	6%	15%	41%	25%
Driving In Runners from 3B with Less than Two Out:		12/29		41%

Loves to face: Mike Mason (.545, 6-for-11, 3 HR)
Hates to face: Mike Boddicker (0-for-12, 6 SO)
Has hit 114 home runs over the past four seasons, tied with Jim Rice for most in A.L. during that time. . . . Batted 86 points higher vs. right-handed pitchers than against left-handed pitchers, largest "backward" difference by any right-handed batter in A.L. (minimum: 100 AB vs. each). . . . Has homered in every A.L. ballpark except Memorial Stadium (65 career at bats). . . . Career home run rate is one every 15.4 at bats, but in Late-Inning Pressure Situations, it's one every 40.3 at bats; lifetime batting average of .169 in LIP situations. . . . 43 career plate appearances with bases full: .244 (10-for-41), no walks, no home runs. . . . He's on George Bell's trail, with 1966 career plate appearances and no sacrifice bunts.

Lee Lacy

Baltimore Orioles — Bats Right

	AB	H	2B	3B	HR	RRF	BB	SO	BA	SA	OBA
Season	491	141	18	0	11	48	37	71	.287	.391	.334
vs. Left-Handers	157	44	5	0	5	14	13	14	.280	.408	.333
vs. Right-Handers	334	97	13	0	6	34	24	57	.290	.383	.334
Home	230	70	8	0	5	19	18	34	.304	.404	.353
Road	261	71	10	0	6	29	19	37	.272	.379	.317
Grass	399	117	13	0	10	38	29	55	.293	.401	.337
Artificial Turf	92	24	5	0	1	10	8	16	.261	.348	.320
April	69	23	4	0	0	7	2	9	.333	.391	.347
May	88	21	4	0	2	12	6	13	.239	.352	.278
June	100	27	3	0	4	10	6	18	.270	.420	.311
July	99	29	2	0	3	11	11	13	.293	.404	.360
August	104	32	3	0	2	7	9	14	.308	.394	.363
Sept./Oct.	31	9	2	0	0	1	3	4	.290	.355	.353
Leading Off Inn.	100	37	6	0	4	4	3	11	.370	.550	.388
Runners On	198	51	5	0	4	41	13	30	.258	.343	.296
Runners/Scor. Pos.	105	21	2	0	3	37	10	17	.200	.305	.258
Runners On/2 Out	71	13	3	0	0	11	6	14	.183	.225	.247
Scor. Pos./2 Out	46	8	2	0	0	10	6	10	.174	.217	.269
Late Inning Pressure	71	21	3	0	1	4	4	10	.296	.380	.333
Leading Off	17	7	1	0	0	0	1	2	.412	.471	.444
Runners On	36	7	0	0	0	3	2	6	.194	.194	.237
Runners/Scor. Pos.	24	3	0	0	0	3	2	4	.125	.125	.192

DRIVING IN RUNS	From 1B	From 2B	From 3B	Scoring Position
Totals	5/141	13/86	19/45	32/131
Percentage	4%	15%	42%	24%
Driving In Runners from 3B with Less than Two Out:		16/26		62%

Loves to face: Frank Viola (.429, 9-for-21, 2 HR)
Hates to face: Walt Terrell (0-for-12, 6 SO)
Has turned into a quasi-everyday player right before our very eyes: The last three years were the first three in his 15-year career in which he had 500 plate appearances. . . . Last year was first time since 1981 that he batted below .300 against left-handed pitchers. . . . Has played for Walter Alston, Tommy Lasorda, Chuck Tanner, and Earl Weaver, among others. . . . Became a fixture in number-two batting slot after Weaver replaced Joe Altobelli in 1985; in '86, Lacy batted second in 115 games, most in A.L., with 76 runs scored in those games. That contribution was pivotal, because Orioles' leadoff batters had 2d-lowest on-base average in majors (.289) and scored fewest runs in A.L. (84).

Carney Lansford

Oakland As — Bats Right

	AB	H	2B	3B	HR	RRF	BB	SO	BA	SA	OBA
Season	591	168	16	4	19	72	39	51	.284	.421	.332
vs. Left-Handers	189	58	7	2	6	15	15	14	.307	.460	.364
vs. Right-Handers	402	110	9	2	13	57	24	37	.274	.403	.317
Home	298	95	11	3	10	48	24	20	.319	.477	.369
Road	293	73	5	1	9	24	15	31	.249	.365	.294
Grass	495	144	15	3	16	63	33	41	.291	.430	.338
Artificial Turf	96	24	1	1	3	9	6	10	.250	.375	.305
April	80	24	3	1	0	10	5	5	.300	.363	.341
May	98	27	2	0	5	12	5	8	.276	.449	.311
June	100	28	2	0	2	6	8	8	.280	.360	.345
July	99	28	2	2	3	14	5	11	.283	.434	.321
August	102	28	2	1	6	18	4	10	.275	.490	.308
Sept./Oct.	112	33	5	0	3	12	12	9	.295	.420	.363
Leading Off Inn.	139	43	5	1	7	7	6	11	.309	.511	.338
Runners On	242	72	4	2	7	60	20	21	.298	.417	.352
Runners/Scor. Pos.	140	40	2	2	5	56	16	8	.286	.436	.360
Runners On/2 Out	100	27	2	2	2	25	8	7	.270	.390	.330
Scor. Pos./2 Out	78	19	2	2	1	23	5	4	.244	.359	.298
Late Inning Pressure	79	15	1	2	4	12	7	13	.190	.405	.256
Leading Off	26	5	1	0	3	3	1	2	.192	.577	.222
Runners On	28	7	0	2	1	9	4	5	.250	.500	.344
Runners/Scor. Pos.	16	5	0	2	1	9	4	1	.313	.750	.450

DRIVING IN RUNS	From 1B	From 2B	From 3B	Scoring Position
Totals	6/175	21/109	26/61	47/170
Percentage	3%	19%	43%	28%
Driving In Runners from 3B with Less than Two Out:		19/27		70%

Loves to face: Scott Bankhead (.800, 4-for-5, 1 HR)
Hates to face: Tim Stoddard (0-for-10)

Only right-handed batter to win A.L. batting crown in the last 15 seasons, and from the looks of things, maybe the next 15 as well. ... Had not gone hitless in three consecutive games in over a year when he slumped in late July, collecting one hit over a nine-game span. ... Had 16 bases-loaded at bats without a strikeout last season, most in majors, but had only two hits. ... Averaged only 1.60 assists per nine innings at third last season, fewest in majors (minimum: 500 innings). ... Has batted higher in home games than in road games in each of the last seven seasons. The curious part is that he has played on three different home fields with wildly differing influences: Anaheim, Fenway, and Oakland.

Tim Laudner

Minnesota Twins — Bats Right

	AB	H	2B	3B	HR	RRF	BB	SO	BA	SA	OBA
Season	193	47	10	0	10	29	24	56	.244	.451	.333
vs. Left-Handers	111	29	7	0	7	17	19	30	.261	.514	.379
vs. Right-Handers	82	18	3	0	3	12	5	26	.220	.366	.267
Home	95	22	4	0	9	19	10	31	.232	.558	.321
Road	98	25	6	0	1	10	14	25	.255	.347	.345
Grass	81	22	5	0	1	10	12	22	.272	.370	.362
Artificial Turf	112	25	5	0	9	19	12	34	.223	.509	.313
April	4	2	1	0	1	2	2	2	.500	1.500	.667
May	44	11	3	0	3	10	10	12	.250	.523	.386
June	28	8	2	0	2	7	4	10	.286	.571	.375
July	42	10	1	0	1	2	2	13	.238	.333	.289
August	41	8	1	0	1	4	1	11	.195	.293	.233
Sept./Oct.	34	8	2	0	2	4	5	8	.235	.471	.333
Leading Off Inn.	31	7	0	0	1		4	11	.226	.323	.351
Runners On	91	20	7	0	1	20	11	26	.220	.330	.298
Runners/Scor. Pos.	56	14	5	0	1	19	7	18	.250	.393	.323
Runners On/2 Out	43	13	4	0	1	11	6	11	.302	.465	.388
Scor. Pos./2 Out	30	9	2	0	1	10	5	8	.300	.467	.400
Late Inning Pressure	25	5	1	0	0	2	3	10	.200	.240	.276
Leading Off	4	0	0	0	0	0	0	1	.000	.000	.000
Runners On	12	4	1	0	0	2	2	6	.333	.417	.400
Runners/Scor. Pos.	6	1	0	0	0	1	2	4	.167	.167	.333

DRIVING IN RUNS	From 1B	From 2B	From 3B	Scoring Position
Totals	3/69	8/46	8/27	16/73
Percentage	4%	17%	30%	22%
Driving In Runners from 3B with Less than Two Out:		4/10		40%

Loves to face: Tommy John (.467, 7-for-15, 1 HR)
Hates to face: Jack Morris (.071, 1-for-14)

Caesar said, "All Gaul is divided into three parts." So was the Twins' catching job last season. ... Laudner's part consisted of 57 starts; Mark Salas had 56, Jeff Reed, 49. ... Team was 31–26 with Laudner starting, 40–65 with the others. ... Don't dismiss this guy so easily: He has homered once every 27.0 at bats in majors, a rate better than Jody Davis's (27.3), for instance. (We know, one of them plays in a home run paradise—Davis.) ... Career vs. left-handers: .259, one home run every 19.8 at bats; career vs. right-handers: .199, one HR every 37.8 at bats. ... A.L. pitchers, he's your way out of a tough inning. Laudner is a lifetime 0-for-15 with bases loaded and two outs; no walks, either.

Rudy Law

Kansas City Royals — Bats Left

	AB	H	2B	3B	HR	RRF	BB	SO	BA	SA	OBA
Season	307	80	26	5	1	39	29	22	.261	.388	.327
vs. Left-Handers	42	6	1	0	0	8	0	1	.143	.167	.143
vs. Right-Handers	265	74	25	5	1	31	29	21	.279	.423	.354
Home	144	40	14	2	1	21	16	5	.278	.424	.358
Road	163	40	12	3	0	18	13	17	.245	.356	.299
Grass	123	33	8	3	0	14	10	13	.268	.382	.321
Artificial Turf	184	47	18	2	1	25	19	9	.255	.391	.332
April	64	16	7	1	0	7	7	1	.250	.391	.333
May	87	27	8	2	1	11	7	11	.310	.483	.358
June	84	22	6	1	0	16	9	5	.262	.357	.340
July	11	0	0	0	0	0	1	2	.000	.000	.083
August	0	0	0	0	0	0	0	0	—	—	—
Sept./Oct.	61	15	5	1	0	5	5	3	.246	.361	.303
Leading Off Inn.	77	17	6	1	0	1	9	3	.221	.325	.302
Runners On	135	41	14	2	1	38	9	12	.304	.459	.354
Runners/Scor. Pos.	80	30	13	0	0	34	8	8	.375	.538	.433
Runners On/2 Out	46	13	4	0	0	14	4	4	.283	.370	.353
Scor. Pos./2 Out	30	12	4	0	0	14	3	3	.400	.533	.455
Late Inning Pressure	46	13	4	2	0	5	3	5	.283	.457	.320
Leading Off	11	3	1	0	0	0	0	0	.273	.364	.273
Runners On	19	6	2	1	0	5	1	4	.316	.526	.333
Runners/Scor. Pos.	14	3	1	0	0	4	1	4	.214	.286	.250

DRIVING IN RUNS	From 1B	From 2B	From 3B	Scoring Position
Totals	3/86	18/64	16/29	34/93
Percentage	3%	28%	55%	37%
Driving In Runners from 3B with Less than Two Out:		11/18		61%

Loves to face: Dickie Noles (.583, 7-for-12, 1 HR)
Hates to face: Dan Petry (.100, 2-for-20)

You know how managers look for a guy guaranteed to knock in 100 runs each season? Here's someone who'll get you 30; he's been locked into the 30s in each of his five years in A.L.: 32, 34, 37, 36, 36; no other active player has even been in the 30s in each of the last four years, only Mike Fitzgerald in the last three. ... Has batted over .300 with runners in scoring position in four of last five seasons; his 1986 average was a career high. ... Career average of .469 (15-for-32) with bases loaded; over past 12 years, only Pat Tabler (.522) is higher (minimum: 15 hits with BL). ... Neither Rudy (77 AB) nor Vance Law (49 AB) has ever had an extra-base hit in Royals Stadium.

Rick Leach

Toronto Blue Jays — Bats Left

	AB	H	2B	3B	HR	RRF	BB	SO	BA	SA	OBA
Season	246	76	14	1	5	42	13	24	.309	.435	.335
vs. Left-Handers	23	3	0	0	0	0	0	3	.130	.130	.130
vs. Right-Handers	223	73	14	1	5	42	13	21	.327	.466	.354
Home	130	38	7	0	4	25	5	11	.292	.438	.316
Road	116	38	7	1	1	17	8	13	.328	.431	.354
Grass	83	23	5	0	0	10	7	11	.277	.337	.319
Artificial Turf	163	53	9	1	5	32	6	13	.325	.485	.343
April	21	7	0	0	0	5	1	1	.333	.333	.364
May	36	13	4	0	1	5	0	5	.361	.556	.333
June	35	10	2	0	1	7	1	0	.286	.429	.306
July	57	15	5	1	0	4	6	5	.263	.386	.328
August	41	13	2	0	2	11	4	5	.317	.512	.362
Sept./Oct.	56	18	1	0	1	10	1	8	.321	.393	.328
Leading Off Inn.	58	11	0	0	2		1	5	.190	.328	.203
Runners On	122	43	7	0	3	40	5	13	.352	.484	.358
Runners/Scor. Pos.	70	24	3	0	2	37	4	9	.343	.471	.346
Runners On/2 Out	53	16	0	1	1	13	3	8	.302	.415	.339
Scor. Pos./2 Out	33	9	1	0	1	12	2	4	.273	.394	.314
Late Inning Pressure	52	15	1	0	1	10	5	7	.288	.365	.339
Leading Off	13	2	0	0	0	1	0	2	.154	.154	.214
Runners On	25	10	0	0	1	10	2	2	.400	.520	.414
Runners/Scor. Pos.	12	5	0	0	1	10	2	2	.417	.667	.438

DRIVING IN RUNS	From 1B	From 2B	From 3B	Scoring Position
Totals	4/95	17/56	16/30	33/86
Percentage	4%	30%	53%	38%
Driving In Runners from 3B with Less than Two Out:		13/17		76%

Loves to face: Pete Vuckovich (.467, 7-for-15)
Hates to face: Dennis Leonard (.077, 1-for-13)

Batted .323 (10-for-31) as a pinch-hitter last season, 3d best in A.L. (minimum: 20 AB). ... Pitched one game with Toronto in 1984, and Jerry Willard is thankful—he homered off Leach, the only one he's ever hit off a left-handed "pitcher." ... Has .350 batting average and five extra-base hits (three doubles, two triples) in 20 career at bats with bases loaded. ... Those 23 at bats vs. left-handers may not seem like much, but it's the most he's ever had in one season; 9-for-54 against lefties in his career, looking for his first extra-base hit.

Chet Lemon

Detroit Tigers   Bats Right

	AB	H	2B	3B	HR	RRF	BB	SO	BA	SA	OBA
Season	403	101	21	3	12	55	39	53	.251	.407	.326
vs. Left-Handers	162	46	10	2	7	21	15	17	.284	.500	.346
vs. Right-Handers	241	55	11	1	5	34	24	36	.228	.344	.313
Home	190	45	9	2	7	25	19	21	.237	.416	.318
Road	213	56	12	1	5	30	20	32	.263	.399	.333
Grass	355	87	17	3	12	50	30	47	.245	.411	.313
Artificial Turf	48	14	4	0	0	5	9	6	.292	.375	.414
April	63	14	3	0	2	9	6	12	.222	.365	.290
May	56	24	5	1	1	9	3	5	.429	.607	.459
June	57	6	3	0	0	2	5	5	.105	.158	.190
July	67	16	4	0	0	7	5	11	.239	.299	.312
August	77	21	3	0	4	14	5	9	.273	.468	.325
Sept./Oct.	83	20	3	2	5	14	15	11	.241	.506	.366
Leading Off Inn.	104	27	10	0	3	3	8	15	.260	.442	.319
Runners On	187	53	8	1	6	49	20	25	.283	.433	.358
Runners/Scor. Pos.	96	26	2	1	3	41	13	12	.271	.406	.357
Runners On/2 Out	84	23	6	0	3	23	8	15	.274	.452	.351
Scor. Pos./2 Out	50	12	2	0	1	17	7	7	.240	.340	.345
Late Inning Pressure	66	13	2	0	1	7	5	9	.197	.273	.254
Leading Off	16	4	0	0	1	1	1	2	.250	.438	.294
Runners On	36	8	2	0	0	6	2	4	.222	.278	.263
Runners/Scor. Pos.	17	4	0	0	0	5	1	1	.235	.235	.278

DRIVING IN RUNS	From 1B	From 2B	From 3B	Scoring Position
Totals	8/151	17/78	18/41	35/119
Percentage	5%	22%	44%	29%
Driving In Runs from 3B with Less than Two Out:		15/23		65%

Loves to face: Curt Young (.462, 6-for-13, 3 HR)
Hates to face: Juan Nieves (0-for-11)

Had his fewest plate appearances (other than strike season) since 1978, and batting average was his lowest since 1976.... Started 111 games in center field last season, as Tigers received almost exactly average production from their starting center fielders. Detroit averages: batting .261, slugging .406, on-base .337; league averages for center-field starters: .266, .406, .337.... Over last three seasons, has batted .334 vs. left-handers, .233 vs. right-handers.... Career batting average of .370 (40-for-108) at the Metrodome.... One of three active players with 100 stolen-base attempts but more caught stealing (67) than steals (53); others: Buddy Bell and Charlie Moore.

Steve Lombardozzi

Minnesota Twins   Bats Right

	AB	H	2B	3B	HR	RRF	BB	SO	BA	SA	OBA
Season	453	103	20	5	8	34	52	76	.227	.347	.308
vs. Left-Handers	121	25	8	0	3	17	14	17	.207	.347	.289
vs. Right-Handers	332	78	12	5	5	17	38	59	.235	.346	.315
Home	235	59	14	3	6	24	28	37	.251	.413	.333
Road	218	44	6	2	2	10	24	39	.202	.275	.281
Grass	168	33	4	2	2	10	19	33	.196	.280	.278
Artificial Turf	285	70	16	3	6	24	33	43	.246	.386	.326
April	49	11	3	0	1	4	3	10	.224	.347	.269
May	79	20	4	2	5	17	14	14	.253	.544	.366
June	97	30	5	3	0	4	12	10	.309	.423	.385
July	68	13	5	0	1	2	8	12	.191	.309	.286
August	85	14	2	0	0	3	10	15	.165	.188	.286
Sept./Oct.	75	15	1	0	1	4	5	15	.200	.253	.250
Leading Off Inn.	129	34	7	2	4	4	7	18	.264	.442	.307
Runners On	175	37	7	1	3	29	31	35	.211	.314	.330
Runners/Scor. Pos.	93	18	5	0	3	27	22	22	.194	.344	.348
Runners On/2 Out	89	22	5	0	1	17	15	15	.247	.337	.356
Scor. Pos./2 Out	51	12	4	0	1	17	10	10	.235	.373	.361
Late Inning Pressure	50	12	1	2	5	5	6	12	.240	.420	.309
Leading Off	14	3	0	0	1	1	1	3	.214	.429	.267
Runners On	18	6	0	1	1	4	1	1	.333	.611	.368
Runners/Scor. Pos.	6	2	0	0	1	3	1	1	.333	.833	.429

DRIVING IN RUNS	From 1B	From 2B	From 3B	Scoring Position
Totals	6/123	13/75	7/34	20/109
Percentage	5%	17%	21%	18%
Driving In Runners from 3B with Less than Two Out:		2/15		13%

Loves to face: Richard Dotson (.667, 4-for-6, 1 HR)
Hates to face: Danny Jackson (0-for-10)

Most of us have a soft spot in our hearts for baseball played outdoors, on God's grass, in daylight. Then there are the Lombardozzis of the world: He batted .145 (8-for-55) with two RBI in 20 games under those conditions last season.... Led A.L. second basemen in fielding (.991), only the 2d Twins' second baseman ever to do that; other: Rob Wilfong, 1980.... Had the worst rate (13.3 percent, 2-of-15) of runners driven in from third base with less than two outs by any player in any season since 1975 (minimum: 15 opportunities).... August batting average was 4th lowest in A.L. (minimum 50 AB); had only five RBI in 58 games from Aug. 2 until end of season—four of them on grand slam homer on Oct. 3.

Fred Lynn

Baltimore Orioles   Bats Left

	AB	H	2B	3B	HR	RRF	BB	SO	BA	SA	OBA
Season	397	114	13	1	23	67	53	59	.287	.499	.371
vs. Left-Handers	96	26	3	0	7	21	7	24	.271	.521	.333
vs. Right-Handers	301	88	10	1	16	46	46	35	.292	.492	.382
Home	197	56	6	0	13	38	28	28	.284	.513	.371
Road	200	58	7	1	10	29	25	31	.290	.485	.370
Grass	304	81	10	0	15	48	42	46	.266	.447	.356
Artificial Turf	93	33	3	1	8	19	11	13	.355	.667	.419
April	68	22	3	0	1	9	7	7	.324	.412	.377
May	86	28	1	1	5	16	13	11	.326	.535	.410
June	26	6	0	0	2	5	4	7	.231	.462	.333
July	101	29	6	0	9	22	9	17	.287	.614	.351
August	73	20	1	0	4	12	16	12	.274	.452	.407
Sept./Oct.	43	9	2	0	2	3	4	5	.209	.395	.277
Leading Off Inn.	68	15	1	0	4	4	12	7	.221	.412	.338
Runners On	185	55	5	0	12	56	25	26	.297	.519	.380
Runners/Scor. Pos.	86	24	3	0	7	46	11	14	.279	.558	.353
Runners On/2 Out	46	12	1	0	4	14	9	11	.261	.543	.382
Scor. Pos./2 Out	27	7	1	0	3	12	7	5	.259	.630	.412
Late Inning Pressure	57	16	3	1	3	10	9	18	.281	.526	.388
Leading Off	15	0	0	0	0	0	2	5	.000	.000	.118
Runners On	27	11	1	0	3	10	3	7	.407	.778	.484
Runners/Scor. Pos.	13	5	1	0	1	6	1	4	.385	.692	.429

DRIVING IN RUNS	From 1B	From 2B	From 3B	Scoring Position
Totals	11/146	11/67	22/36	33/103
Percentage	8%	16%	61%	32%
Driving In Runners from 3B with Less than Two Out:		18/24		75%

Loves to face: Roy Smith (2-for-2, 2 HR)
Hates to face: Dave Stewart (0-for-10)

Missed quite a bit of time last season—yes, even for him: His total of 456 plate appearances was his lowest in any full season in majors, excluding 1981.... Orioles were 54–50 (.519) in Lynn's 104 starts; 19–39 (.328) when he didn't start.... One of 10 players in majors with 20 home runs in each of past five years: 21, 22, 23, 23, 23.... Batting average with runners in scoring position and two outs has been under .200 in four of last six seasons.... Interesting contrast in Late-Inning Pressure Situations: batted .407 last season (11-for-27), with three home runs, with runners in scoring position; was 0-for-15, with two walks, when leading off innings.

Steve Lyons

Red Sox/White Sox   Bats Left

	AB	H	2B	3B	HR	RRF	BB	SO	BA	SA	OBA
Season	247	56	9	3	1	21	19	47	.227	.300	.280
vs. Left-Handers	33	8	0	2	0	4	1	11	.242	.364	.257
vs. Right-Handers	214	48	9	1	1	17	18	36	.224	.290	.284
Home	124	31	3	3	1	14	12	16	.250	.347	.317
Road	123	25	6	0	0	7	7	31	.203	.252	.242
Grass	200	47	5	3	1	18	18	34	.235	.305	.297
Artificial Turf	47	9	4	0	0	3	1	13	.191	.277	.204
April	12	3	0	1	0	2	1	3	.250	.417	.308
May	79	21	5	1	1	12	7	13	.266	.392	.322
June	33	7	2	0	0	4	4	7	.212	.273	.289
July	60	13	2	0	0	4	3	16	.217	.250	.258
August	1	0	0	0	0	0	0	0	.000	.000	.000
Sept./Oct.	62	12	0	1	0	2	4	8	.194	.226	.242
Leading Off Inn.	52	12	4	0	0	4	4	8	.231	.308	.286
Runners On	108	25	2	2	0	20	9	26	.231	.287	.281
Runners/Scor. Pos.	59	15	1	1	0	19	5	18	.254	.305	.294
Runners On/2 Out	49	11	0	1	0	7	6	16	.224	.265	.309
Scor. Pos./2 Out	30	9	0	1	0	7	4	10	.300	.367	.382
Late Inning Pressure	33	7	0	0	0	1	4	5	.212	.212	.297
Leading Off	9	2	0	0	0	0	1	1	.222	.222	.300
Runners On	12	2	0	0	0	1	1	2	.167	.167	.286
Runners/Scor. Pos.	4	1	0	0	0	1	1	1	.250	.250	.400

DRIVING IN RUNS	From 1B	From 2B	From 3B	Scoring Position
Totals	2/79	6/48	12/28	18/76
Percentage	3%	13%	43%	24%
Driving In Runners from 3B with Less than Two Out:		9/17		53%

Loves to face: John Butcher (.800, 4-for-5)
Hates to face: Chris Codiroli (0-for-9)

Left-handed hitter who has hit lefties (26-for-100) better than righties (.247) in two seasons in majors.... Started 31 times for Red Sox, all in center field; his 35 starts for White Sox were all over the map, but mainly in left (21).... One of four outfielders on Chisox who started at least one game at all three outfield positions last season; others: Bobby Bonilla, John Cangelosi, Reid Nichols. Brewers were only other team in majors with as many interchangeable outfielders.... Born June 3, 1960; one other player in majors in 1986 shares his birthday, and he also shares his surname: Mets catcher Barry Lyons. Barry was born in Biloxi, Steve in Tacoma; we don't think they're twins.

Rick Manning
Bats Left

Milwaukee Brewers	AB	H	2B	3B	HR	RRF	BB	SO	BA	SA	OBA
Season	205	52	7	3	8	30	17	20	.254	.434	.310
vs. Left-Handers	35	5	1	0	1	8	3	5	.143	.257	.200
vs. Right-Handers	170	47	6	3	7	22	14	15	.276	.471	.333
Home	88	19	5	0	4	16	9	10	.216	.409	.286
Road	117	33	2	3	4	14	8	10	.282	.453	.328
Grass	156	40	6	3	7	25	11	14	.256	.468	.308
Artificial Turf	49	12	1	0	1	5	6	6	.245	.327	.316
April	5	2	0	0	0	0	0	0	.400	.400	.400
May	47	9	0	2	0	4	3	3	.191	.277	.250
June	19	6	0	0	1	4	0	1	.316	.474	.316
July	28	7	2	0	0	2	2	5	.250	.321	.300
August	44	19	3	1	3	6	4	3	.432	.750	.479
Sept./Oct.	62	9	2	0	4	14	8	8	.145	.371	.236
Leading Off Inn.	52	12	3	3	1	1	2	2	.231	.462	.259
Runners On	92	21	2	0	4	26	8	10	.228	.380	.282
Runners/Scor. Pos.	53	8	0	0	2	21	7	7	.151	.264	.238
Runners On/2 Out	41	7	0	0	1	8	3	4	.171	.244	.227
Scor. Pos./2 Out	28	5	0	0	1	8	2	4	.179	.286	.233
Late Inning Pressure	25	6	1	0	1	4	2	4	.240	.400	.286
Leading Off	7	2	1	0	0	0	1	1	.286	.429	.375
Runners On	11	1	0	0	0	3	0	2	.091	.091	.083
Runners/Scor. Pos.	7	1	0	0	0	3	0	1	.143	.143	.125

DRIVING IN RUNS	From 1B	From 2B	From 3B	Scoring Position
Totals	4/71	7/41	11/30	18/71
Percentage	6%	17%	37%	25%
Driving In Runners from 3B with Less than Two Out:			8/14	57%

Loves to face: Mike Smithson (.379, 11-for-29, 5 doubles)
Hates to face: Don Aase (.111, 2-for-18)
Had the fewest starts (52) and plate appearances (227) of his 12-year career, which made a career-best-tying eight home runs noteworthy. . . . Has driven in 109 runs in 395 games with Brewers, three fewer than the man whom Milwaukee essentially traded for him, Gorman Thomas, had the year before the trade. . . . Batting average with runners in scoring position was the lowest of his career. . . . Career breakdown: .224 vs. left-handers, .273 vs. right-handers. . . . Career batting average of .220 with two out and runners in scoring position. . . . One of three A.L. outfielders with 10 starts at each outfield position; others: John Shelby, Ruben Sierra.

Don Mattingly
Bats Left

New York Yankees	AB	H	2B	3B	HR	RRF	BB	SO	BA	SA	OBA
Season	677	238	53	2	31	123	53	35	.352	.573	.394
vs. Left-Handers	243	87	23	1	5	47	17	13	.358	.523	.398
vs. Right-Handers	434	151	30	1	26	76	36	22	.348	.601	.392
Home	320	107	23	0	17	63	28	16	.334	.566	.383
Road	357	131	30	2	14	60	25	19	.367	.580	.404
Grass	565	189	38	1	26	99	46	30	.335	.543	.381
Artificial Turf	112	49	15	1	5	24	7	5	.438	.723	.463
April	82	22	4	0	1	21	9	2	.268	.354	.341
May	117	44	12	0	6	23	10	8	.376	.632	.412
June	123	43	7	0	6	18	7	5	.350	.553	.379
July	110	37	12	1	6	18	6	8	.336	.627	.368
August	117	38	7	0	6	20	9	5	.325	.538	.375
Sept./Oct.	128	54	11	1	6	23	12	7	.422	.664	.465
Leading Off Inn.	116	46	9	1	6	6	5	8	.397	.647	.421
Runners On	317	104	25	0	12	104	31	17	.328	.521	.377
Runners/Scor. Pos.	164	51	16	0	9	95	23	12	.311	.573	.376
Runners On/2 Out	95	34	6	0	3	29	15	5	.358	.516	.445
Scor. Pos./2 Out	62	20	4	0	3	28	12	5	.323	.532	.432
Late Inning Pressure	74	26	3	0	3	18	9	2	.351	.514	.417
Leading Off	19	4	1	0	0	0	2	2	.211	.263	.286
Runners On	36	15	2	0	3	18	5	0	.417	.722	.476
Runners/Scor. Pos.	22	9	1	0	2	16	5	0	.409	.727	.500

DRIVING IN RUNS	From 1B	From 2B	From 3B	Scoring Position
Totals	14/232	35/131	43/74	78/205
Percentage	6%	27%	58%	38%
Driving In Runners from 3B with Less than Two Out:			34/46	74%

Loves to face: Don Aase (.833, 5-for-6, 2 HR)
Hates to face: Storm Davis (.105, 2-for-19)
Has driven in 37.5 percent of runners in scoring position in career, highest rate in majors over past 12 years. . . . Career batting average on road is .337, highest among active players (Boggs: .326 career on road). . . . Led majors with 87 hits off left-handers. Only one left-handed batter in the last 12 years has had more, and he was also a New York first baseman. Keith Hernandez? Nope, Chris Chambliss: 88 in 1976 and 93 in '78. . . . First 30 home-run hitter since Ted Kluszewski and Yogi Berra (both in 1956) with less than 40 strikeouts. Joe DiMaggio did it seven times. . . . Mattingly has 200 hits, 20 HR, and 100 RBI in each of last three seasons. Something to aim for: Chuck Klein had a 5-year streak (1929–33).

Oddibe McDowell
Bats Left

Texas Rangers	AB	H	2B	3B	HR	RRF	BB	SO	BA	SA	OBA
Season	572	152	24	7	18	51	65	112	.266	.427	.341
vs. Left-Handers	128	28	4	1	3	11	14	32	.219	.336	.296
vs. Right-Handers	444	124	20	6	15	40	51	80	.279	.453	.353
Home	290	81	13	5	8	30	27	62	.279	.441	.340
Road	282	71	11	2	10	21	38	50	.252	.411	.342
Grass	480	124	18	5	14	44	56	93	.258	.404	.336
Artificial Turf	92	28	6	2	4	7	9	19	.304	.543	.366
April	70	19	6	0	3	9	13	12	.271	.486	.386
May	103	25	4	0	3	9	10	21	.243	.369	.310
June	100	31	3	4	5	10	10	18	.310	.570	.373
July	99	24	3	1	2	8	9	21	.242	.354	.303
August	99	29	6	1	3	7	10	23	.293	.465	.364
Sept./Oct.	101	24	2	1	2	8	13	17	.238	.337	.322
Leading Off Inn.	235	61	10	5	11	11	22	48	.260	.485	.323
Runners On	182	56	7	1	3	36	21	34	.308	.407	.379
Runners/Scor. Pos.	96	28	5	1	2	32	14	24	.292	.427	.375
Runners On/2 Out	75	19	3	0	1	14	8	17	.253	.293	.325
Scor. Pos./2 Out	47	12	3	0	0	14	7	12	.255	.319	.352
Late Inning Pressure	67	18	2	1	2	10	15	18	.269	.418	.402
Leading Off	16	5	0	1	1	1	2	3	.313	.625	.389
Runners On	30	7	2	0	1	9	7	9	.233	.400	.378
Runners/Scor. Pos.	16	4	1	0	1	8	4	7	.250	.500	.400

DRIVING IN RUNS	From 1B	From 2B	From 3B	Scoring Position
Totals	5/131	15/73	11/34	26/107
Percentage	4%	21%	32%	24%
Driving In Runners from 3B with Less than Two Out:			8/18	44%

Loves to face: Bob Tewksbury (.556, 5-for-9)
Hates to face: Walt Terrell (.056, 1-for-18)
One hit in 34 at bats vs. Detroit last season; career batting average of .094 at Tiger Stadium. . . . Failed to start 26 games last season; in 22 of the 26 games, a left-hander was starting against Texas. . . . Career vs. left-handers: .231, one HR every 41.8 at bats; career vs. right-handers: .263, one HR every 24.2 at bats. . . . Hit 16 home runs while batting in leadoff position, but that was good for only 4th place in A.L. behind Rickey Henderson (28), Kirby Puckett (25), and Lou Whitaker (19). . . . In two seasons, has driven in only 22.5 percent of runners from scoring position (1985–86 A.L. average: 28.5 percent); in Late-Inning Pressure Situations, McDowell's rate is only 16.7 percent.

Hal McRae
Bats Right

Kansas City Royals	AB	H	2B	3B	HR	RRF	BB	SO	BA	SA	OBA
Season	278	70	14	0	7	40	18	39	.252	.378	.298
vs. Left-Handers	153	41	10	0	5	24	13	21	.268	.431	.325
vs. Right-Handers	125	29	4	0	2	16	5	18	.232	.312	.263
Home	125	34	8	0	1	21	10	17	.272	.360	.331
Road	153	36	6	0	6	19	8	22	.235	.392	.270
Grass	118	27	3	0	6	15	6	17	.229	.407	.264
Artificial Turf	160	43	11	0	1	25	12	22	.269	.356	.322
April	53	10	4	0	1	10	4	5	.189	.321	.237
May	46	13	3	0	1	11	3	9	.283	.413	.327
June	41	11	5	0	1	6	2	7	.268	.463	.302
July	52	17	0	0	1	7	4	7	.327	.385	.375
August	52	12	1	0	2	4	4	9	.231	.365	.286
Sept./Oct.	34	7	1	0	1	2	1	2	.206	.324	.250
Leading Off Inn.	66	22	5	0	3	2	6	6	.333	.545	.353
Runners On	141	34	6	0	4	37	13	20	.241	.369	.306
Runners/Scor. Pos.	70	18	5	0	0	29	10	9	.257	.329	.349
Runners On/2 Out	62	13	2	0	1	13	8	11	.210	.290	.300
Scor. Pos./2 Out	36	9	2	0	0	11	5	5	.250	.306	.341
Late Inning Pressure	57	13	1	0	2	6	5	8	.228	.351	.290
Leading Off	14	6	1	0	1	1	1	1	.429	.714	.467
Runners On	28	5	0	0	1	5	3	3	.179	.286	.258
Runners/Scor. Pos.	13	1	0	0	0	3	3	1	.077	.077	.250

DRIVING IN RUNS	From 1B	From 2B	From 3B	Scoring Position
Totals	6/117	10/53	17/29	27/82
Percentage	5%	19%	59%	33%
Driving In Runners from 3B with Less than Two Out:			12/17	71%

Loves to face: Mike Flanagan (.429, 27-for-63, 3 HR)
Hates to face: Willie Hernandez (.091, 1-for-11, 1 HR)
Had 70 hits last season, the most by anyone in majors who didn't have a 3-hit game. . . . Turned 40 on July 10; the only older non-pitcher active in A.L. last season was Reggie, who has McRae by nearly two months. . . . Batted .319 (15-for-47) as a pinch-hitter last season, 4th best in A.L. (minimum: 20 AB). Led league with 54 pinch-hit games. . . . Major-league debut: July 11, 1968, playing second base and going 2-for-4 off Gaylord Perry. He had been recalled to replace military-bound second baseman Tommy Helms. Why didn't Reds simply switch Pete Rose back to second from outfield, as they often did in those years? Because, believe it or not, Rose was on the disabled list at the time!

Paul Molitor
Milwaukee Brewers   Bats Right

	AB	H	2B	3B	HR	RRF	BB	SO	BA	SA	OBA
Season	437	123	24	6	9	55	40	81	.281	.426	.340
vs. Left-Handers	100	27	6	2	1	8	7	23	.270	.400	.318
vs. Right-Handers	337	96	18	4	8	47	33	58	.285	.433	.346
Home	213	64	9	4	5	34	16	34	.300	.451	.345
Road	224	59	15	2	4	21	24	47	.263	.402	.335
Grass	390	115	22	6	9	55	38	69	.295	.451	.355
Artificial Turf	47	8	2	0	0	0	2	12	.170	.213	.204
April	69	18	8	1	0	9	13	17	.261	.406	.378
May	38	13	0	1	3	9	6	5	.342	.632	.422
June	13	3	0	0	0	0	0	3	.231	.231	.231
July	74	21	6	0	1	6	4	14	.284	.405	.321
August	126	34	5	1	4	20	11	20	.270	.421	.326
Sept./Oct.	117	34	5	3	1	11	6	22	.291	.410	.323
Leading Off Inn.	169	46	7	3	5	5	10	38	.272	.438	.313
Runners On	155	48	9	2	3	49	21	25	.310	.452	.385
Runners/Scor. Pos.	94	33	4	1	3	45	14	19	.351	.511	.423
Runners On/2 Out	77	28	5	0	2	27	9	10	.364	.506	.430
Scor. Pos./2 Out	50	20	1	0	2	24	7	8	.400	.540	.474
Late Inning Pressure	62	21	6	0	1	10	4	7	.339	.484	.368
Leading Off	12	4	1	0	1	1	1	1	.333	.667	.385
Runners On	30	8	3	0	0	9	2	4	.267	.367	.294
Runners/Scor. Pos.	17	6	1	0	0	8	2	3	.353	.412	.381

DRIVING IN RUNS	From 1B	From 2B	From 3B	Scoring Position
Totals	5/103	18/70	23/43	41/113
Percentage	5%	26%	53%	36%
Driving In Runners from 3B with Less than Two Out:			10/20	50%

Loves to face: Neal Heaton (.500, 8-for-16)
Hates to face: Tim Stoddard (0-for-18)

Placed on disabled list three different times within 40 days last season: He was out from May 10 to May 30, from June 2 to June 17, and from June 19 to July 8. . . . Batted 119 points higher in night games (.322) than in day games (.203), 2d-largest difference in the majors (minimum: 50 AB each). Prior to 1986, he had batted higher in day games than in night games for six consecutive seasons. . . . Walked four times with bases loaded last season. . . . Has batted .300 or better with runners on base in each of the last three seasons. . . . Higher average vs. right-handers than against lefties for the first time since his rookie season. Career breakdown: .312 vs. left-handers, .281 vs. right-handers.

Charlie Moore
Milwaukee Brewers   Bats Right

	AB	H	2B	3B	HR	RRF	BB	SO	BA	SA	OBA
Season	235	61	12	3	3	40	21	38	.260	.374	.317
vs. Left-Handers	60	17	2	2	1	11	5	7	.283	.433	.354
vs. Right-Handers	175	44	10	1	2	29	16	31	.251	.354	.311
Home	112	34	6	2	2	24	10	12	.304	.446	.352
Road	123	27	6	1	1	16	11	26	.220	.309	.284
Grass	190	53	10	2	3	30	17	27	.279	.400	.333
Artificial Turf	45	8	2	1	0	10	4	11	.178	.267	.245
April	20	6	1	1	0	3	4	4	.300	.450	.417
May	52	15	3	1	1	14	5	10	.288	.442	.351
June	48	14	1	1	1	6	4	6	.292	.417	.340
July	33	10	3	0	0	7	3	2	.303	.394	.361
August	32	5	1	0	0	5	3	7	.156	.188	.222
Sept./Oct.	50	11	3	0	1	5	2	9	.220	.340	.245
Leading Off Inn.	47	5	0	0	1	1	2	11	.106	.170	.143
Runners On	109	30	6	3	0	37	14	14	.275	.385	.349
Runners/Scor. Pos.	69	23	5	2	0	35	12	7	.333	.464	.417
Runners On/2 Out	46	13	2	2	0	16	10	6	.283	.413	.411
Scor. Pos./2 Out	33	10	1	2	0	15	9	3	.303	.455	.452
Late Inning Pressure	39	11	0	1	0	6	3	9	.282	.333	.333
Leading Off	13	2	0	0	0	0	0	3	.154	.154	.154
Runners On	19	8	0	1	0	6	2	4	.421	.526	.476
Runners/Scor. Pos.	12	5	0	0	0	5	2	2	.417	.417	.500

DRIVING IN RUNS	From 1B	From 2B	From 3B	Scoring Position
Totals	4/77	14/55	19/32	33/87
Percentage	5%	25%	59%	38%
Driving In Runners from 3B with Less than Two Out:			13/21	62%

Loves to face: Bob Stanley (.472, 17-for-36)
Hates to face: Bill Krueger (.071, 1-for-14)

Batted 168 points higher in day games (.352) than in night games (.185), largest such difference in majors (minimum: 50 AB each). . . . Drove in 37.9 percent of runners from scoring position last season to rank 8th in A.L. among at least semiregulars; Brewers had three players among top 20 (others: Molitor and Oglivie). . . . Batting average with runners in scoring position was his highest in the 12 years we've been charting these things. . . . Played 326 games in outfield, caught only 34 games, 1982–84; 174 games caught and 7 in the outfield, 1985–86. . . . One of three active players with 100 stolen base attempts but more caught stealing (67) than steals (53); others: Buddy Bell and Chet Lemon.

Lloyd Moseby
Toronto Blue Jays   Bats Left

	AB	H	2B	3B	HR	RRF	BB	SO	BA	SA	OBA
Season	589	149	24	5	21	88	64	122	.253	.418	.329
vs. Left-Handers	188	43	6	2	6	25	10	37	.229	.378	.277
vs. Right-Handers	401	106	18	3	15	63	54	85	.264	.436	.352
Home	290	72	14	0	11	44	38	67	.248	.410	.337
Road	299	77	10	5	10	44	26	55	.258	.425	.320
Grass	222	58	9	4	6	31	21	43	.261	.419	.328
Artificial Turf	367	91	15	1	15	57	43	79	.248	.417	.329
April	86	26	2	1	3	9	5	17	.302	.453	.341
May	113	36	6	1	4	19	16	20	.319	.496	.417
June	99	26	5	1	5	17	17	22	.263	.485	.370
July	100	17	1	1	2	11	9	20	.170	.260	.239
August	97	30	7	1	6	20	14	17	.309	.588	.389
Sept./Oct.	94	14	3	0	1	12	3	21	.149	.213	.186
Leading Off Inn.	149	37	4	1	5	5	17	33	.248	.389	.329
Runners On	235	68	12	2	9	76	20	40	.289	.472	.341
Runners/Scor. Pos.	136	35	5	1	4	62	14	27	.257	.397	.321
Runners On/2 Out	78	18	4	1	2	16	5	11	.231	.385	.286
Scor. Pos./2 Out	55	8	2	1	0	12	4	8	.145	.218	.217
Late Inning Pressure	89	20	3	0	3	11	10	22	.225	.360	.317
Leading Off	25	6	1	0	0	0	3	5	.240	.280	.345
Runners On	37	9	2	0	1	9	5	8	.243	.378	.348
Runners/Scor. Pos.	21	5	1	0	1	9	3	4	.238	.429	.357

DRIVING IN RUNS	From 1B	From 2B	From 3B	Scoring Position
Totals	13/162	22/106	32/65	54/171
Percentage	8%	21%	49%	32%
Driving In Runners from 3B with Less than Two Out:			28/40	70%

Loves to face: Joe Niekro (3-for-3, 1 HR)
Hates to face: Dave Stewart (.091, 1-for-11)

One of two players in majors with 30 stolen bases and 70 RBI in each of last three years. Other: Ryne Sandberg. . . . Overall batting average of .315 in 1983, has declined in each season since: .260, .259, .253. . . . Batting .538 (14-for-26) with bases loaded over past three seasons, including 6-for-12 performance last year. . . . Batting average in July was 2d lowest in A.L. (minimum: 50 AB). . . . Higher batting average on grass than on artificial surfaces for the first time in his seven major-league seasons. . . . Has hit 43 triples over the last five seasons to rank third in A.L. behind Willie Wilson (60) and Brett Butler (50).

John Moses
Seattle Mariners   Bats Left and Right

	AB	H	2B	3B	HR	RRF	BB	SO	BA	SA	OBA
Season	399	102	16	3	3	35	34	65	.256	.333	.311
vs. Left-Handers	110	32	6	1	2	8	12	13	.291	.418	.361
vs. Right-Handers	289	70	10	2	1	27	22	52	.242	.301	.292
Home	220	51	8	3	2	18	21	37	.232	.323	.298
Road	179	51	8	0	1	17	13	28	.285	.346	.328
Grass	124	33	3	0	1	10	8	18	.266	.315	.306
Artificial Turf	275	69	13	3	2	25	26	47	.251	.342	.314
April	0	0	0	0	0	0	0	0	—	—	—
May	19	3	0	1	0	2	4	3	.158	.263	.304
June	112	32	2	1	1	14	10	16	.286	.348	.341
July	101	28	6	1	0	12	12	19	.277	.356	.351
August	73	17	2	0	0	2	3	12	.233	.260	.263
Sept./Oct.	94	22	6	0	2	5	5	15	.234	.362	.267
Leading Off Inn.	144	37	7	1	0	0	14	21	.257	.319	.323
Runners On	131	38	5	1	0	32	9	21	.290	.344	.326
Runners/Scor. Pos.	82	26	4	1	0	32	5	13	.317	.390	.341
Runners On/2 Out	57	16	0	0	0	15	2	9	.281	.281	.305
Scor. Pos./2 Out	37	12	0	0	0	15	2	7	.324	.324	.359
Late Inning Pressure	52	12	2	0	0	5	8	14	.231	.269	.328
Leading Off	18	4	0	0	0	2	2	4	.222	.222	.300
Runners On	19	6	0	0	0	5	3	4	.316	.421	.391
Runners/Scor. Pos.	13	4	1	0	0	5	1	2	.308	.385	.333

DRIVING IN RUNS	From 1B	From 2B	From 3B	Scoring Position
Totals	0/77	13/70	18/32	31/102
Percentage	0%	19%	56%	30%
Driving In Runners from 3B with Less than Two Out:			8/13	62%

Loves to face: Dan Quisenberry (.625, 5-for-8)
Hates to face: Charlie Hough (.077, 1-for-13)

Recalled from Calgary May 26 and started 94 of Mariners' 118 games from then until season's end, including 89 starts in center field. . . . Mariners were 42–47 (.472) with Moses starting in center; no big deal, except that Seattle was 25–48 (.342) with other guys out there. . . . Had .304 on-base average when batting in leadoff position; as a team, Seattle's leadoff batters had .288 on-base average, lowest by any team in majors. . . . Has played in both majors and minors in each of last five years. . . . Career breakdown: .233 with bases empty, .279 with runners on base, .287 with runners in scoring position.

Darryl Motley

Kansas City Royals — Bats Right

	AB	H	2B	3B	HR	RRF	BB	SO	BA	SA	OBA
Season	217	44	9	1	7	21	11	31	.203	.350	.241
vs. Left-Handers	93	22	3	1	3	11	5	11	.237	.387	.276
vs. Right-Handers	124	22	6	0	4	10	6	20	.177	.323	.215
Home	103	20	5	0	3	9	6	9	.194	.330	.239
Road	114	24	4	1	4	12	5	22	.211	.368	.244
Grass	101	22	4	1	3	11	5	20	.218	.366	.255
Artificial Turf	116	22	5	0	4	10	6	11	.190	.336	.230
April	62	14	3	1	3	9	2	9	.226	.452	.250
May	82	15	5	0	2	4	5	15	.183	.317	.230
June	9	1	0	0	0	0	2	0	.111	.111	.273
July	21	1	0	0	0	0	0	1	.048	.048	.048
August	38	10	1	0	2	8	2	6	.263	.447	.300
Sept./Oct.	5	3	0	0	0	0	0	0	.600	.600	.600
Leading Off Inn.	49	11	4	0	3	3	2	7	.224	.490	.228
Runners On	98	20	3	0	2	16	3	16	.204	.296	.228
Runners/Scor. Pos.	50	9	2	0	2	15	2	7	.180	.340	.212
Runners On/2 Out	38	11	2	0	1	9	2	4	.289	.421	.325
Scor. Pos./2 Out	24	6	2	0	1	9	1	2	.250	.458	.280
Late Inning Pressure	42	6	1	0	1	1	2	6	.143	.238	.182
Leading Off	9	3	1	0	1	1	1	0	.333	.778	.400
Runners On	19	1	0	0	0	0	1	4	.053	.053	.100
Runners/Scor. Pos.	9	0	0	0	0	0	1	1	.000	.000	.100

DRIVING IN RUNS	From 1B	From 2B	From 3B	Scoring Position
Totals	4/78	7/41	3/17	10/58
Percentage	5%	17%	18%	17%
Driving In Runners from 3B with Less than Two Out:		2/7		29%

Loves to face: Bob Ojeda (.500, 5-for-10)
Hates to face: Danny Darwin (.091, 1-for-11)
Figures above are for A.L. only. . . . Career average of 1.13 RRFs per bases-loaded plate appearance, 2d highest in majors over past 12 years to Murray's 1.15 (minimum: 30 RRFs with BL). Motley is 13-for-27, 2 HRs, 34 RRFs, one walk, 2 sacrifice flies. . . . Four hits in last five at bats as a pinch-hitter for Royals, but did not pinch-hit after trade to Atlanta. . . . Batted under .200 (combined leagues) against right-handed pitchers for the second straight year. . . . Led Royals with 54 starts in right field last season; he hit seven home runs in those starts, compared with five by other K.C. right-field starters. That total of 12 was lowest by any A.L. team.

Rance Mulliniks

Toronto Blue Jays — Bats Left

	AB	H	2B	3B	HR	RRF	BB	SO	BA	SA	OBA
Season	348	90	22	0	11	46	43	60	.259	.417	.340
vs. Left-Handers	20	4	1	0	0	1	0	4	.200	.250	.200
vs. Right-Handers	328	86	21	0	11	45	43	56	.262	.427	.348
Home	176	50	14	0	5	23	23	30	.284	.449	.370
Road	172	40	8	0	6	23	20	30	.233	.384	.309
Grass	130	32	6	0	6	19	14	22	.246	.431	.315
Artificial Turf	218	58	16	0	5	27	29	38	.266	.408	.355
April	52	11	3	0	1	6	9	9	.212	.327	.328
May	86	23	5	0	3	13	11	11	.267	.430	.347
June	73	23	3	0	4	11	9	12	.315	.521	.386
July	68	17	6	0	3	15	10	14	.250	.471	.346
August	12	2	1	0	0	1	0	4	.167	.250	.167
Sept./Oct.	57	14	4	0	0	0	4	10	.246	.316	.306
Leading Off Inn.	57	15	3	0	1	1	6	9	.263	.368	.344
Runners On	146	40	9	0	5	40	22	22	.274	.438	.365
Runners/Scor. Pos.	84	26	6	0	3	33	16	17	.310	.488	.412
Runners On/2 Out	44	14	2	0	2	13	12	9	.318	.500	.464
Scor. Pos./2 Out	26	8	1	0	1	10	11	5	.308	.462	.514
Late Inning Pressure	40	8	2	0	1	2	6	5	.200	.325	.304
Leading Off	9	3	1	0	0	0	2		.333	.444	.333
Runners On	18	4	1	0	0	1	5	2	.222	.278	.391
Runners/Scor. Pos.	10	2	1	0	0	1	3	1	.200	.300	.385

DRIVING IN RUNS	From 1B	From 2B	From 3B	Scoring Position
Totals	8/94	12/62	15/32	27/94
Percentage	9%	19%	47%	29%
Driving In Runners from 3B with Less than Two Out:		12/23		52%

Loves to face: Mike Brown (.800, 4-for-5, 2 HR)
Hates to face: Al Nipper (.059, 1-for-17)
Jays' third-base platoon was effective again last year: starters produced 17 HR and 80 RBI while batting .264 (A.L. average at third: 20 HR, 81 RBI, .267). . . . Between 310 and 370 at bats in all five seasons with Toronto. Only Rick Dempsey has also been in the 300s in each of the past five years. . . . One of two players whose batting average has dropped 25 points in each of past two seasons (minimum: 300 AB in each). The other: Dave Kingman. . . . Ranked third among A.L. third basemen with 2.09 assists per nine innings (minimum: 500 innings). . . . Has batted higher with runners on than with bases empty in each of last seven seasons, and over .300 with runners in scoring position in each of last three seasons.

Dwayne Murphy

Oakland As — Bats Left

	AB	H	2B	3B	HR	RRF	BB	SO	BA	SA	OBA
Season	329	83	11	3	9	42	56	80	.252	.386	.364
vs. Left-Handers	94	21	1	1	1	14	14	23	.223	.287	.324
vs. Right-Handers	235	62	10	2	8	28	42	57	.264	.426	.379
Home	168	43	3	2	5	19	32	39	.256	.387	.379
Road	161	40	8	1	4	23	24	41	.248	.385	.347
Grass	275	69	9	3	8	31	44	65	.251	.393	.356
Artificial Turf	54	14	2	0	1	11	12	15	.259	.352	.400
April	73	18	2	0	1	11	17	15	.247	.315	.394
May	18	4	1	1	1	3	2	5	.222	.556	.300
June	0	0	0	0	0	0	0	0	—		
July	69	17	2	1	1	7	10	19	.246	.348	.346
August	96	23	3	0	3	11	17	21	.240	.365	.357
Sept./Oct.	73	21	3	1	3	10	10	20	.288	.479	.373
Leading Off Inn.	58	13	3	0	1	1	10	11	.224	.328	.338
Runners On	147	39	5	3	3	36	29	32	.265	.401	.385
Runners/Scor. Pos.	86	21	2	3	1	29	16	20	.244	.372	.349
Runners On/2 Out	57	13	3	1	0	12	14	13	.228	.316	.380
Scor. Pos./2 Out	41	8	1	1	0	10	8	9	.195	.268	.327
Late Inning Pressure	44	11	2	1	0	3	9	9	.250	.341	.389
Leading Off	9	3	1	0	0	0	2	0	.333	.444	.455
Runners On	21	4	0	1	0	3	6	4	.190	.286	.370
Runners/Scor. Pos.	13	3	0	1	0	3	2	2	.231	.385	.333

DRIVING IN RUNS	From 1B	From 2B	From 3B	Scoring Position
Totals	7/104	12/61	14/39	26/100
Percentage	7%	20%	36%	26%
Driving In Runners from 3B with Less than Two Out:		11/21		52%

Loves to face: Mike Brown (.583, 7-for-12, 1 HR)
Hates to face: Kirk McCaskill (.071, 1-for-14)
Only major leaguer who has had at least 400 plate appearances in each of last six years without even hitting .260 once during that time; reached the 400 mark exactly in 1986, despite being on disabled list from May 12 to July 5. . . . Batting averages for 1986 against left-handers and right-handers closely resemble his career figures: .221 vs. left-handers, .262 vs. right-handers. . . . Career batting average of only .207 in Late-Inning Pressure Situations with runners in scoring position. . . . Ambivalent about domes: .311 batting average at the Kingdome is his highest at any park, .217 mark at the Metrodome is his lowest.

Eddie Murray

Baltimore Orioles — Bats Left and Right

	AB	H	2B	3B	HR	RRF	BB	SO	BA	SA	OBA
Season	495	151	25	1	17	86	78	49	.305	.463	.396
vs. Left-Handers	136	41	8	0	6	25	13	13	.301	.493	.360
vs. Right-Handers	359	110	17	1	11	61	65	36	.306	.451	.409
Home	242	75	10	1	9	48	31	24	.310	.471	.387
Road	253	76	15	0	8	38	47	25	.300	.455	.405
Grass	422	130	22	1	15	78	71	42	.308	.472	.404
Artificial Turf	73	21	3	0	2	8	7	7	.288	.411	.350
April	75	20	2	0	4	13	11	12	.267	.453	.360
May	89	30	4	0	3	24	17	10	.337	.483	.427
June	102	27	5	0	4	16	16	10	.265	.431	.361
July	23	8	0	0	0	3	1	3	.348	.348	.423
August	87	29	4	0	2	11	11	6	.333	.448	.408
Sept./Oct.	119	37	10	1	4	22	20	10	.311	.513	.410
Leading Off Inn.	126	34	6	0	3	3	22	11	.270	.389	.378
Runners On	245	79	13	0	11	80	32	22	.322	.510	.394
Runners/Scor. Pos.	123	45	9	0	7	70	21	11	.366	.610	.443
Runners On/2 Out	113	36	6	0	5	33	12	14	.319	.504	.384
Scor. Pos./2 Out	54	18	3	0	4	29	7	8	.333	.611	.410
Late Inning Pressure	72	16	4	0	4	10	12	8	.222	.444	.329
Leading Off	21	3	1	0	0	0	4	2	.143	.190	.280
Runners On	28	6	0	0	2	8	3	2	.214	.429	.258
Runners/Scor. Pos.	14	2	0	0	0	4	1	1	.143	.143	.188

DRIVING IN RUNS	From 1B	From 2B	From 3B	Scoring Position
Totals	13/198	20/88	36/59	56/147
Percentage	7%	23%	61%	38%
Driving In Runners from 3B with Less than Two Out:		22/30		73%

Loves to face: Mike Brown, again (.750, 3-for-4, 2 HR)
Hates to face: Eric King (0-for-12)
Has hit grand slam home runs in each of past six seasons; A.L. record is seven, by Vern Stephens, 1944–50. Major league record (nine) is held by Willie McCovey (1964–72). Other long streaks: seven, Gil Hodges (1949–55); six, Lou Gehrig (1927–32), and Willie Stargell (1969–74). . . . Career batting average of .447 (59-for-132) with bases loaded. Has batted over .400 with bases full in each of the last seven seasons. . . . First time in 10-year career that Murray failed to hit 20 home runs. Only player to hit 20 in each of past 10 seasons: Mike Schmidt. . . . Career averages in Late-Inning Pressure Situations: .364 with runners on base, .383 with runners in scoring position.

Pete O'Brien

Texas Rangers — Bats Left

	AB	H	2B	3B	HR	RRF	BB	SO	BA	SA	OBA
Season	551	160	23	3	23	99	87	66	.290	.468	.385
vs. Left-Handers	165	51	11	0	4	28	19	28	.309	.448	.380
vs. Right-Handers	386	109	12	3	19	71	68	38	.282	.477	.387
Home	265	71	13	0	11	45	37	34	.268	.442	.356
Road	286	89	10	3	12	54	50	32	.311	.493	.411
Grass	453	131	20	2	19	83	74	56	.289	.468	.387
Artificial Turf	98	29	3	1	4	16	13	10	.296	.469	.378
April	66	26	7	1	5	16	9	8	.394	.758	.467
May	98	25	5	0	1	12	11	13	.255	.337	.330
June	84	22	2	1	2	15	14	9	.262	.381	.360
July	99	26	1	1	4	16	12	9	.263	.414	.342
August	108	34	5	0	8	27	13	14	.315	.583	.385
Sept./Oct.	96	27	3	0	3	13	28	13	.281	.406	.444
Leading Off Inn.	106	31	4	1	5	5	6	10	.292	.491	.330
Runners On	249	75	12	2	12	88	47	26	.301	.510	.408
Runners/Scor. Pos.	131	45	8	1	5	69	37	17	.344	.534	.480
Runners On/2 Out	64	18	4	0	2	27	21	7	.281	.438	.459
Scor. Pos./2 Out	43	15	4	0	1	24	17	5	.349	.512	.533
Late Inning Pressure	73	24	4	0	4	10	14	8	.329	.548	.437
Leading Off	26	9	1	0	3	3	1	4	.346	.731	.370
Runners On	24	6	1	0	1	7	8	3	.250	.417	.438
Runners/Scor. Pos.	12	4	1	0	1	7	6	2	.333	.667	.556

DRIVING IN RUNS	From 1B	From 2B	From 3B	Scoring Position
Totals	21/186	27/100	27/44	54/144
Percentage	11%	27%	61%	38%
Driving In Runners from 3B with Less than Two Out:	19/27			70%

Loves to face: Frank Wills (.455, 5-for-11, 2 HR)
Hates to face: Willie Hernandez (0-for-16)
Compare overall season totals of .290, 23 homers, 90 RBI with Wally Joyner's .290, 22 homers and 100 RBI; close, but Joyner had the better year on basis of RBI, right? Wrong! Sure, Joyner had 10 more RBI, but he batted with 51 more runners in scoring position than did O'Brien, whose batting average with runners in scoring position was 6th highest among A.L. players who qualified for batting title. . . . Has homered in every A.L. ballpark except Yankee Stadium (77 career at bats). . . . Yearly batting averages vs. left-handers since 1984: .213, .225, .309. Career average of one HR every 70.4 at bats vs. lefties, one HR every 24.3 at bats vs. right-handers.

Ben Oglivie

Milwaukee Brewers — Bats Left

	AB	H	2B	3B	HR	RRF	BB	SO	BA	SA	OBA
Season	346	98	20	1	5	54	30	33	.283	.390	.334
vs. Left-Handers	63	16	6	0	0	9	4	8	.254	.349	.294
vs. Right-Handers	283	82	14	1	5	45	26	25	.290	.399	.343
Home	169	49	13	0	2	28	15	16	.290	.402	.340
Road	177	49	7	1	3	26	15	17	.277	.379	.328
Grass	280	78	20	1	3	42	28	27	.279	.389	.340
Artificial Turf	66	20	0	0	2	12	2	6	.303	.394	.310
April	7	1	0	0	0	1	1	1	.143	.143	.222
May	85	29	6	0	2	15	8	1	.341	.482	.394
June	106	33	7	0	1	22	5	6	.311	.406	.394
July	47	11	3	0	0	1	6	8	.234	.298	.321
August	60	15	3	1	1	9	8	11	.250	.383	.329
Sept./Oct.	41	9	1	0	1	6	2	6	.220	.317	.244
Leading Off Inn.	81	28	2	0	2	2	6	6	.346	.444	.391
Runners On	169	48	12	1	3	52	14	21	.284	.420	.326
Runners/Scor. Pos.	95	30	8	1	3	45	12	12	.316	.421	.316
Runners On/2 Out	80	22	7	1	2	18	7	10	.275	.463	.333
Scor. Pos./2 Out	42	12	4	1	0	13	6	5	.286	.429	.375
Late Inning Pressure	55	14	2	1	1	5	5	7	.255	.382	.311
Leading Off	11	6	1	0	1	1	5	7	.545	.909	.583
Runners On	24	2	0	1	0	4	3	5	.083	.167	.179
Runners/Scor. Pos.	14	2	0	1	0	4	2	2	.143	.286	.235

DRIVING IN RUNS	From 1B	From 2B	From 3B	Scoring Position
Totals	8/123	16/74	25/37	41/111
Percentage	7%	22%	68%	37%
Driving In Runners from 3B with Less than Two Out:	21/23			91%

Loves to face: Oil Can Boyd (.500, 8-for-16, 1 HR)
Hates to face: Dave Schmidt (0-for-14)
Drove in 21 of 23 runners from third base with less than two outs last season, a rate of 91.3 percent; that's the highest in majors over past 12 years (minimum: 15 runners driven in). . . . Started 81 of 123 games in which Brewers faced a right-handed starter; nine of 38 against lefties. . . . Last homer off a left-hander: Aug. 2, 1985, vs. Frank Tanana. . . . Has hit 40 home runs in 1559 at bats over last four years; hit 41 in 592 at bats in 1980. . . . His strikeout rate has decreased along with his home runs: fanned once every 11.6 plate appearances last year, lowest rate of his career. . . . Hit his first major-league home run on May 14, 1972, off a Hall of Famer, Catfish Hunter.

Tom O'Malley

Baltimore Orioles — Bats Left

	AB	H	2B	3B	HR	RRF	BB	SO	BA	SA	OBA
Season	181	46	9	0	1	18	17	21	.254	.320	.317
vs. Left-Handers	22	5	1	0	0	3	2	2	.227	.273	.292
vs. Right-Handers	159	41	8	0	1	15	15	19	.258	.327	.320
Home	93	21	3	0	1	5	7	12	.226	.290	.280
Road	88	25	6	0	0	13	10	9	.284	.352	.354
Grass	160	41	8	0	1	16	13	16	.256	.325	.312
Artificial Turf	21	5	1	0	0	2	4	5	.238	.286	.346
April	0	0	0	0	0	0	0	0	——		
May	0	0	0	0	0	0	0	0	——		
June	77	21	4	0	1	11	5	9	.273	.364	.317
July	65	17	4	0	0	5	9	6	.262	.323	.347
August	39	8	1	0	0	2	3	6	.205	.231	.262
Sept./Oct.	0	0	0	0	0	0	0	0	——		
Leading Off Inn.	45	10	2	0	1	1	2	3	.222	.333	.255
Runners On	67	15	3	0	0	17	10	10	.224	.269	.321
Runners/Scor. Pos.	44	9	3	0	0	17	8	6	.205	.273	.321
Runners On/2 Out	26	8	2	0	0	11	4	3	.308	.385	.400
Scor. Pos./2 Out	22	7	2	0	0	11	3	2	.318	.409	.400
Late Inning Pressure	28	8	1	0	1	3	2	6	.286	.429	.323
Leading Off	7	2	0	0	1	1	1	0	.286	.714	.375
Runners On	10	2	0	0	0	2	1	3	.200	.200	.250
Runners/Scor. Pos.	5	1	0	0	0	2	1	1	.200	.200	.286

DRIVING IN RUNS	From 1B	From 2B	From 3B	Scoring Position
Totals	1/48	6/37	10/18	16/55
Percentage	2%	16%	56%	29%
Driving In Runners from 3B with Less than Two Out:	6/9			67%

Loves to face: Joaquin Andujar (.600, 6-for-10)
Hates to face: Walt Terrell (0-for-8)
Recalled from Rochester, June 3; sent back, Aug. 20. . . . Made 48 starts at third base during that time, one of the eight starting third basemen that Weaver shuffled through last season (most by any team in majors); the ugly eight combined for a .223 batting average, .308 slugging average, and only 45 RBI, each of those figures representing a major-league low. . . . Career batting average of .223 with runners in scoring position. . . . Eight of nine career home runs have been hit against right-handed pitchers. His only one against a lefty: Aug. 18, 1983 off Dan Schatzeder. . . . The name *O'Malley* still haunts New York: This one has four hits (including a home run) in seven career at bats at Yankee Stadium.

Jorge Orta

Kansas City Royals — Bats Left

	AB	H	2B	3B	HR	RRF	BB	SO	BA	SA	OBA
Season	336	93	14	2	9	47	23	34	.277	.411	.321
vs. Left-Handers	19	4	0	0	0	3	1	4	.211	.211	.250
vs. Right-Handers	317	89	14	2	9	44	22	30	.281	.423	.326
Home	188	56	12	1	5	27	13	18	.298	.452	.343
Road	148	37	2	1	4	20	10	16	.250	.358	.294
Grass	109	31	1	1	3	17	8	6	.284	.394	.328
Artificial Turf	227	62	13	1	6	30	15	28	.273	.419	.318
April	14	5	1	0	1	0	5	2	.357	.571	.438
May	56	14	3	0	1	6	8	2	.250	.357	.333
June	85	30	4	0	1	14	2	5	.353	.435	.368
July	64	15	3	1	3	4	4	7	.234	.453	.279
August	70	19	3	0	2	10	7	6	.271	.400	.338
Sept./Oct.	47	10	0	0	2	8	0	10	.213	.340	.213
Leading Off Inn.	66	15	5	0	1	1	5	6	.227	.348	.282
Runners On	181	58	7	1	5	43	10	18	.320	.453	.352
Runners/Scor. Pos.	108	28	3	0	4	38	6	14	.259	.398	.293
Runners On/2 Out	81	24	2	0	2	14	2	8	.296	.395	.313
Scor. Pos./2 Out	53	12	0	0	2	13	1	6	.226	.340	.241
Late Inning Pressure	55	17	4	0	0	4	5	6	.309	.382	.367
Leading Off	10	2	1	0	0	0	0	1	.200	.300	.200
Runners On	31	12	0	0	0	4	2	3	.387	.452	.424
Runners/Scor. Pos.	15	3	0	0	0	3	1	2	.200	.200	.250

DRIVING IN RUNS	From 1B	From 2B	From 3B	Scoring Position
Totals	4/131	17/81	17/42	34/123
Percentage	3%	21%	40%	28%
Driving In Runners from 3B with Less than Two Out:	13/21			62%

Loves to face: Gene Nelson (.455, 5-for-11)
Hates to face: Ron Guidry (.143 3-for-21)
Regained the job as Royals' DH against right-handed pitchers that he had lost to Hal McRae over latter part of 1985 season: started 83 of 120 games in which Royals faced a right-hander last season. . . . Batted .311 in day games, .264 at night. . . . June batting average was 6th highest in A.L. (minimum: 75 AB). . . . Batting average with runners on base was his highest in the 12 years that we've been keeping track. . . . Last extra-base hit against a left-handed pitcher: Sept. 27, 1981 (a homer off Bob Ojeda); 12-for-55 vs. lefties over last five years.

Spike Owen
Mariners/Red Sox — Bats Left and Right

	AB	H	2B	3B	HR	RRF	BB	SO	BA	SA	OBA
Season	528	122	24	7	1	50	51	51	.231	.309	.300
vs. Left-Handers	121	33	6	1	1	16	12	15	.273	.364	.341
vs. Right-Handers	407	89	18	6	0	34	39	36	.219	.292	.287
Home	268	66	17	6	0	30	31	28	.246	.354	.328
Road	260	56	7	1	1	20	20	23	.215	.262	.270
Grass	267	58	7	1	1	21	30	25	.217	.262	.297
Artificial Turf	261	64	17	6	0	29	21	26	.245	.356	.303
April	66	16	3	1	0	2	5	7	.242	.318	.296
May	87	20	8	3	0	5	11	11	.230	.391	.323
June	103	30	5	2	0	14	3	10	.291	.379	.308
July	88	24	5	0	0	15	8	9	.273	.330	.330
August	98	16	2	0	1	7	10	5	.163	.214	.241
Sept./Oct.	86	16	1	1	0	7	14	9	.186	.221	.304
Leading Off Inn.	124	23	4	2	0	0	12	16	.185	.250	.257
Runners On	222	57	11	4	0	49	23	23	.257	.342	.325
Runners/Scor. Pos.	121	24	1	1	0	40	12	14	.198	.223	.270
Runners On/2 Out	96	23	6	1	0	15	17	12	.240	.323	.354
Scor. Pos./2 Out	59	10	1	1	0	12	10	11	.169	.186	.290
Late Inning Pressure	64	8	3	0	0	4	6	10	.125	.172	.200
Leading Off	14	2	1	0	0	0	1	5	.143	.214	.200
Runners On	27	3	1	0	0	4	4	2	.111	.148	.226
Runners/Scor. Pos.	19	1	0	0	0	3	2	1	.053	.053	.143

DRIVING IN RUNS	From 1B	From 2B	From 3B	Scoring Position
Totals	10/158	11/88	28/72	39/160
Percentage	6%	13%	39%	24%
Driving In Runners from 3B with Less than Two Out:		22/36		61%

Loves to face: Dave Schmidt (.636, 7-for-11, 1 HR)
Hates to face: Tom Candiotti (.056, 1-for-18)

Tied modern major league record by scoring six runs in a game on Aug. 21; shares mark with Mel Ott, Johnny Pesky, and Frank Torre. . . . Strikeout victim number 19 when former and future teammate Roger Clemens struck out 20 on April 29. . . . No extra-base hits in 60 at bats at Anaheim Stadium, most among active players; during playoffs, went 1-for-8 at Anaheim, 8-for-13 at Fenway. . . . Career batting average of .165 in Late-Inning Pressure Situations. . . . Ranked 2d among A.L. shortstops with 3.18 assists per nine innings (minimum: 500 innings). . . . Just one year, but Red Sox allowed only 3.93 runs per nine innings with Owen at short last season, 4.33 with Romero, and 4.84 with Quinones.

Tom Paciorek
Texas Rangers — Bats Right

	AB	H	2B	3B	HR	RRF	BB	SO	BA	SA	OBA
Season	213	61	7	0	4	24	3	41	.286	.376	.305
vs. Left-Handers	125	36	1	0	2	11	3	25	.288	.344	.310
vs. Right-Handers	88	25	6	0	2	13	0	16	.284	.420	.297
Home	90	21	3	0	0	6	1	20	.233	.267	.250
Road	123	40	4	0	4	18	2	21	.325	.455	.344
Grass	148	40	3	0	2	13	2	31	.270	.331	.289
Artificial Turf	65	21	4	0	2	11	1	10	.323	.477	.338
April	19	6	2	0	0	1	0	3	.316	.421	.350
May	52	16	1	0	0	6	0	8	.308	.327	.308
June	47	14	2	0	2	6	0	10	.298	.468	.327
July	26	5	0	0	1	1	1	3	.192	.308	.222
August	32	8	0	0	0	3	1	5	.250	.250	.273
Sept./Oct.	37	12	2	0	1	7	1	12	.324	.459	.333
Leading Off Inn.	45	15	1	0	3	3	2	5	.333	.556	.362
Runners On	96	26	1	0	0	20	1	20	.271	.281	.297
Runners/Scor. Pos.	66	20	1	0	0	19	1	14	.303	.318	.319
Runners On/2 Out	40	9	0	0	0	9	1	10	.225	.225	.244
Scor. Pos./2 Out	28	8	0	0	0	8	1	7	.286	.286	.310
Late Inning Pressure	32	11	1	0	0	0	0	5	.344	.375	.344
Leading Off	9	3	0	0	0	0	0	1	.333	.333	.333
Runners On	18	6	0	0	0	6	0	3	.333	.333	.333
Runners/Scor. Pos.	12	5	0	0	0	5	0	2	.417	.417	.417

DRIVING IN RUNS	From 1B	From 2B	From 3B	Scoring Position
Totals	1/61	5/48	14/29	19/77
Percentage	2%	10%	48%	25%
Driving In Runners from 3B with Less than Two Out:		8/12		67%

Loves to face: Don Aase (.538, 7-for-13)
Hates to face: John Candelaria (.111, 2-for-18, 8 SO)

Has played in major leagues for all or part of 17 seasons; only once has he batted enough times to qualify for a batting title, and that was in strike-interrupted 1981, when the qualifications were reduced proportionate to the games canceled. . . . Started 51 games last season (37 of them when a left-hander opposed Texas), including 13 at third base, where he had never before started. . . . One of six players in majors last season (four of them on Texas) who was older than his manager. . . . Batted over .340 in Late-Inning Pressure Situations for sixth time in last 11 years. . . . Hit four Late-Inning Pressure home runs with White Sox in 1982, but none in 183 at bats since 1983.

Mike Pagliarulo
New York Yankees — Bats Left

	AB	H	2B	3B	HR	RRF	BB	SO	BA	SA	OBA
Season	504	120	24	3	28	73	54	120	.238	.464	.316
vs. Left-Handers	163	32	9	0	2	12	11	54	.196	.288	.254
vs. Right-Handers	341	88	15	3	26	61	43	66	.258	.548	.344
Home	243	56	8	2	14	31	31	64	.230	.453	.325
Road	261	64	16	1	14	42	23	56	.245	.475	.307
Grass	422	99	21	2	24	58	51	101	.234	.464	.322
Artificial Turf	82	21	3	1	4	15	3	19	.256	.463	.279
April	61	13	4	0	3	7	10	17	.213	.426	.319
May	83	19	4	0	6	13	9	20	.229	.494	.312
June	107	30	9	0	7	18	9	26	.280	.561	.333
July	83	27	2	0	7	20	5	11	.325	.602	.371
August	76	16	2	3	5	12	10	18	.211	.513	.310
Sept./Oct.	94	15	3	0	0	3	11	29	.160	.191	.255
Leading Off Inn.	111	25	3	1	11	11	12	30	.225	.568	.301
Runners On	230	55	10	1	10	55	30	55	.239	.422	.330
Runners/Scor. Pos.	124	29	6	1	7	48	22	33	.234	.468	.349
Runners On/2 Out	80	15	4	0	3	14	12	23	.188	.350	.293
Scor. Pos./2 Out	49	8	3	0	3	13	9	14	.163	.367	.293
Late Inning Pressure	66	16	3	0	3	8	6	20	.242	.424	.315
Leading Off	18	4	0	0	3	3	3	7	.222	.722	.333
Runners On	28	7	1	0	0	5	3	8	.250	.286	.344
Runners/Scor. Pos.	11	4	1	0	0	3	2	5	.364	.455	.500

DRIVING IN RUNS	From 1B	From 2B	From 3B	Scoring Position
Totals	8/185	15/92	22/53	37/145
Percentage	4%	16%	42%	26%
Driving In Runners from 3B with Less than Two Out:		15/28		54%

Loves to face: John Butcher (.500, 4-for-8, 2 HR)
Hates to face: Bert Blyleven (.053, 1-for-19)

Massachusetts native has a career batting average of only .156 (7-for-47, one HR) at Fenway Park, his lowest at any A.L. ballyard. . . . Did not hit a home run in his final 99 at bats last season, and drove in only two runs in his final 28 games. . . . Ranked second among A.L. third basemen with 2.09 assists per nine innings (minimum: 500 innings). . . . Yearly batting averages in majors: .239, .239, .238. . . . Career vs. right-handers: .252, one home run every 16.8 at bats; vs. left-handers: .193, one every 61.0 at bats. . . . Despite appearance of having a "Stadium stroke," has actually hit more home runs in road games (28) than he has at Yankee Stadium (26).

Lance Parrish
Detroit Tigers — Bats Right

	AB	H	2B	3B	HR	RRF	BB	SO	BA	SA	OBA
Season	327	84	6	1	22	64	38	83	.257	.483	.340
vs. Left-Handers	122	32	1	1	5	20	13	23	.262	.410	.328
vs. Right-Handers	205	52	5	0	17	44	25	60	.254	.527	.347
Home	158	39	2	0	8	29	20	29	.247	.411	.341
Road	169	45	4	1	14	35	18	54	.266	.550	.340
Grass	265	67	5	1	16	51	33	55	.253	.460	.343
Artificial Turf	62	17	1	0	6	13	5	28	.274	.581	.329
April	71	11	1	0	2	10	8	21	.155	.254	.241
May	92	29	2	1	8	22	13	27	.315	.620	.411
June	95	25	3	0	7	21	11	20	.263	.516	.339
July	69	19	0	0	5	11	6	15	.275	.493	.346
August	0	0	0	0	0	0	0	0	—	—	—
Sept./Oct.	0	0	0	0	0	0	0	0	—	—	—
Leading Off Inn.	78	19	2	0	6	6	11	19	.244	.500	.337
Runners On	158	39	4	0	8	50	17	40	.247	.424	.330
Runners/Scor. Pos.	101	26	3	0	4	41	11	28	.257	.406	.345
Runners On/2 Out	80	17	4	0	2	26	7	20	.213	.488	.284
Scor. Pos./2 Out	56	12	3	0	4	21	6	16	.214	.482	.302
Late Inning Pressure	44	9	0	0	0	2	11	15	.205	.205	.357
Leading Off	7	1	0	0	0	0	2	4	.143	.143	.333
Runners On	23	4	0	0	0	2	5	7	.174	.174	.310
Runners/Scor. Pos.	12	2	0	0	0	2	3	5	.167	.167	.313

DRIVING IN RUNS	From 1B	From 2B	From 3B	Scoring Position
Totals	9/105	19/73	14/44	33/117
Percentage	9%	26%	32%	28%
Driving In Runners from 3B with Less than Two Out:		10/19		53%

Loves to face: Ron Romanick (.714, 5-for-7, 1 HR)
Hates to face: Dennis Rasmussen (.118, 2-for-17)

Had a Kingmanesque distribution of extra-base hits last season: six doubles, one triple, 22 home runs; this phenomenon is named in honor of the man who took it to these heights: 442 home runs, but only 240 doubles and 25 triples. . . . Batted 98 points higher in night games (.286) than in day games (.188), 4th-largest difference in A.L. (minimum: 50 AB each). . . . Yearly batting averages in Late-Inning Pressure Situations since 1983: .270, .221, .210, .205. . . . Career batting average of .154 (6-for-39) with bases loaded and two outs. . . . A good double-play threat, no? No! He grounded into only three in 70 double-play situations last season, 6th-lowest rate in A.L. (minimum: 40 opportunities).

Larry Parrish
Texas Rangers — Bats Right

	AB	H	2B	3B	HR	RRF	BB	SO	BA	SA	OBA
Season	464	128	22	1	28	99	52	114	.276	.509	.347
vs. Left-Handers	130	33	6	1	11	29	20	33	.254	.569	.351
vs. Right-Handers	334	95	16	0	17	70	32	81	.284	.485	.346
Home	225	65	11	1	14	49	25	53	.289	.533	.354
Road	239	63	11	0	14	50	27	61	.264	.485	.341
Grass	396	111	19	1	24	82	46	96	.280	.515	.353
Artificial Turf	68	17	3	0	4	17	6	18	.250	.471	.311
April	66	17	3	1	3	17	7	19	.258	.470	.320
May	61	16	3	0	5	15	8	17	.262	.557	.348
June	44	8	0	0	3	5	1	14	.182	.386	.200
July	90	31	8	0	4	23	14	15	.344	.567	.430
August	105	33	7	0	6	19	4	25	.314	.552	.342
Sept./Oct.	98	23	1	0	7	20	18	24	.235	.459	.350
Leading Off Inn.	106	26	6	0	7	7	12	24	.245	.500	.328
Runners On	206	63	9	1	10	81	25	46	.306	.505	.374
Runners/Scor. Pos.	107	42	7	1	5	69	17	24	.393	.617	.458
Runners On/2 Out	80	26	4	0	2	33	13	13	.325	.450	.426
Scor. Pos./2 Out	51	20	4	0	0	29	9	7	.392	.471	.492
Late Inning Pressure	61	15	3	0	3	10	8	19	.246	.443	.333
Leading Off	17	6	1	0	2	2	0	6	.353	.765	.353
Runners On	29	8	2	0	0	7	5	6	.276	.345	.382
Runners/Scor. Pos.	16	5	2	0	0	7	3	2	.313	.438	.421

DRIVING IN RUNS	From 1B	From 2B	From 3B	Scoring Position
Totals	15/169	31/89	25/46	56/135
Percentage	9%	35%	54%	41%
Driving In Runners from 3B with Less than Two Out:		17/26		65%

Loves to face: Oil Can Boyd (.500, 7-for-14, 3 HR)
Hates to face: Willie Hernandez (.067, 1-for-15)
If RBI were an equal opportunity statistic, this fellow would have led the majors in 1986. He drove in 41.5 percent (56-of-135) of runners from scoring position, highest rate in majors (minimum: 502 total PA).... Batting average with runners in scoring position was a career high, a full 100 points higher than his career average. ... But a bases-loaded situation had the effect of Kryptonite on this clutch-hitting Superman: His hit off Steve Ontiveros with bases full on Oct. 1 was his first bases-loaded hit since June 13, 1984, ending an 0-for-20 streak.... Career batting average of .187 at Tiger Stadium; at least when he plays there in 1987, he'll be the only Parrish around.

Gary Pettis
California Angels — Bats Left and Right

	AB	H	2B	3B	HR	RRF	BB	SO	BA	SA	OBA
Season	539	139	23	4	5	61	69	132	.258	.343	.339
vs. Left-Handers	176	49	6	2	2	23	14	35	.278	.369	.328
vs. Right-Handers	363	90	17	2	3	38	55	97	.248	.331	.344
Home	251	59	7	1	1	20	32	63	.235	.283	.320
Road	288	80	16	3	4	41	37	69	.278	.396	.356
Grass	458	114	18	2	5	51	59	113	.249	.330	.331
Artificial Turf	81	25	5	2	0	10	10	19	.309	.420	.385
April	77	16	3	0	0	6	6	17	.208	.247	.262
May	77	20	2	0	2	13	2	18	.260	.364	.272
June	97	26	4	1	0	6	17	26	.268	.330	.377
July	92	24	4	1	1	13	13	25	.261	.359	.349
August	97	26	4	0	0	7	15	21	.268	.309	.366
Sept./Oct.	99	27	6	2	2	16	16	25	.273	.434	.371
Leading Off Inn.	184	47	5	2	1	1	18	45	.255	.321	.322
Runners On	197	58	11	1	3	59	35	46	.294	.406	.392
Runners/Scor. Pos.	116	38	9	1	3	58	22	31	.328	.500	.420
Runners On/2 Out	90	23	3	0	2	20	16	25	.256	.356	.368
Scor. Pos./2 Out	59	17	3	0	2	20	11	16	.288	.441	.400
Late Inning Pressure	61	10	2	0	0	5	4	17	.164	.197	.209
Leading Off	22	2	0	0	0	0	1	5	.091	.091	.130
Runners On	19	4	2	0	0	5	1	4	.211	.316	.227
Runners/Scor. Pos.	9	3	2	0	0	5	1	2	.333	.556	.333

DRIVING IN RUNS	From 1B	From 2B	From 3B	Scoring Position
Totals	3/135	21/92	32/57	53/149
Percentage	2%	23%	56%	36%
Driving In Runners from 3B with Less than Two Out:		25/33		76%

Loves to face: Joaquin Andujar (.500, 6-for-12, 1 HR)
Hates to face: Mike Boddicker (.071, 1-for-14)
Led majors with five bases-loaded walks last season. ... Career average of .500 (10-for-20) in Late-Inning Pressure Situations with two outs and runners in scoring position, best in majors over past 12 years (minimum: 10 hits).... Career batting average of .295 with runners in scoring position. ... Had never hit a home run in 471 at bats against left-handed pitchers until he took Mike Mason deep last Sept. 26; six days later, he hit his second home run off a lefty. The pitcher? Mike Mason. ... He's vice president of the Ground Out Association: His career rate of 2.31 ground outs for every air out is 2d highest in majors over past 12 years to President Wally Backman's.

Dan Pasqua
New York Yankees — Bats Left

	AB	H	2B	3B	HR	RRF	BB	SO	BA	SA	OBA
Season	280	82	17	0	16	45	47	78	.293	.525	.399
vs. Left-Handers	51	11	3	0	3	10	6	20	.216	.451	.322
vs. Right-Handers	229	71	14	0	13	35	41	58	.310	.541	.415
Home	140	38	10	0	9	24	29	37	.271	.536	.396
Road	140	44	7	0	7	21	18	41	.314	.514	.401
Grass	222	60	13	0	12	33	40	62	.270	.491	.386
Artificial Turf	58	22	4	0	4	12	7	16	.379	.655	.448
April	0	0	0	0	0	0	0	0	—	—	—
May	30	9	2	0	3	6	9	10	.300	.667	.462
June	48	13	2	0	1	4	5	12	.271	.375	.340
July	42	15	2	0	4	10	5	11	.357	.690	.438
August	87	26	4	0	5	12	15	22	.299	.517	.398
Sept./Oct.	73	19	7	0	3	13	13	23	.260	.479	.386
Leading Off Inn.	57	18	1	0	7	7	6	17	.316	.702	.400
Runners On	141	40	10	0	4	33	29	44	.284	.440	.404
Runners/Scor. Pos.	82	19	5	0	3	31	13	28	.232	.402	.333
Runners On/2 Out	58	16	1	0	3	13	15	20	.276	.448	.425
Scor. Pos./2 Out	33	7	0	0	2	11	9	13	.212	.394	.381
Late Inning Pressure	44	8	2	0	3	6	10	14	.182	.432	.333
Leading Off	11	3	0	0	3	3	0	4	.273	1.091	.273
Runners On	21	2	1	0	0	3	9	9	.095	.143	.367
Runners/Scor. Pos.	13	1	1	0	0	3	5	5	.077	.154	.333

DRIVING IN RUNS	From 1B	From 2B	From 3B	Scoring Position
Totals	4/96	13/69	12/23	25/92
Percentage	4%	19%	52%	27%
Driving In Runners from 3B with Less than Two Out:		9/14		64%

Loves to face: Mike Moore (.600, 6-for-10, 1 HR)
Hates to face: Kirk McCaskill (0-for-6, 4 SO)
Started season in Columbus, recalled on May 20; started 62 of team's last 83 games vs. right-handers, and made eight starts vs. lefties. ... Has 428 at bats in two seasons, averaging one home run every 17.1 at bats (nearly Frank Robinson's career rate); at Yankee Stadium, it's one every 14.2 at bats (a Harmon Killebrew rate); and at home against right-handers, it's one every 12.9 at bats (not quite Babe Ruth). ... Batted .318 (7-for-22) as a pinch-hitter last season, 5th best in A.L. (minimum: 20 AB). ... Batted .182 in Late-Inning Pressure Situations, .314 in nonpressure situations. ... Hit the last home run allowed by Tom Seaver last year (Sept. 13)—maybe the last ever off Tom Terrific.

Ken Phelps
Seattle Mariners — Bats Left

	AB	H	2B	3B	HR	RRF	BB	SO	BA	SA	OBA
Season	344	85	16	4	24	65	88	96	.247	.526	.406
vs. Left-Handers	59	14	4	1	1	13	10	18	.237	.390	.373
vs. Right-Handers	285	71	12	3	23	52	78	78	.249	.554	.413
Home	174	50	8	3	15	41	47	42	.287	.626	.445
Road	170	35	8	1	9	24	41	54	.206	.424	.364
Grass	135	24	3	0	6	12	31	43	.178	.333	.339
Artificial Turf	209	61	13	4	18	53	57	53	.292	.651	.447
April	20	3	0	0	2	3	6	9	.150	.450	.346
May	33	10	0	1	3	5	11	9	.303	.818	.477
June	68	17	5	0	4	11	16	15	.250	.500	.400
July	70	18	5	0	5	13	23	21	.257	.543	.448
August	86	19	3	1	3	15	15	25	.221	.384	.346
Sept./Oct.	67	18	3	2	5	15	17	17	.269	.597	.419
Leading Off Inn.	83	21	5	0	6	6	15	22	.253	.530	.374
Runners On	152	39	7	3	11	52	55	49	.257	.559	.453
Runners/Scor. Pos.	82	22	6	2	7	42	35	26	.268	.646	.475
Runners On/2 Out	76	14	3	1	4	21	23	26	.184	.408	.374
Scor. Pos./2 Out	45	8	2	1	2	16	14	17	.178	.400	.373
Late Inning Pressure	51	11	3	0	4	8	13	17	.216	.510	.394
Leading Off	5	2	1	0	0	0	3	1	.400	.600	.625
Runners On	22	4	0	0	2	6	8	10	.182	.455	.438
Runners/Scor. Pos.	11	3	0	0	1	4	7	6	.273	.545	.556

DRIVING IN RUNS	From 1B	From 2B	From 3B	Scoring Position
Totals	11/109	18/63	12/34	30/97
Percentage	10%	29%	35%	31%
Driving In Runners from 3B with Less than Two Out:		10/16		63%

Loves to face: Jim Clancy (.429, 6-for-14, 3 HR)
Hates to face: Jack Morris (0-for-20, 12 SO)
Career rate of one home run every 12.7 at bats vs. right-handed pitchers, best in majors over past 12 years (minimum: 40 HR vs. RHP), with large lead over No. 2, Mike Schmidt (one HR every 14.5 at bats vs. RHP). ... One home run every 14.3 at bats last season, 3d-best rate in majors (minimum: 10 HR). ... One walk every 5.0 plate appearances last season, highest rate in majors (minimum: 200 PA). ... One of six A.L. players to homer against every opposing club in 1986. ... Hit into a triple play and participated in a triple play last season, first to do that since Ed Mathews in 1955; some others who have done it: Irv Noren, Eddie Waitkus, George Sisler, Harry Steinfeldt, and Cy Seymour (no, not the coauthor).

Tony Phillips

Oakland As — Bats Left and Right

	AB	H	2B	3B	HR	RRF	BB	SO	BA	SA	OBA
Season	441	113	14	5	5	55	76	82	.256	.345	.367
vs. Left-Handers	134	43	5	2	3	20	29	22	.321	.455	.443
vs. Right-Handers	307	70	9	3	2	35	47	60	.228	.296	.331
Home	214	50	8	1	3	33	42	39	.234	.322	.362
Road	227	63	6	4	2	22	34	43	.278	.366	.373
Grass	355	88	12	3	4	45	60	63	.248	.332	.358
Artificial Turf	86	25	2	2	1	10	16	19	.291	.395	.404
April	73	23	3	0	0	6	17	16	.315	.356	.457
May	118	34	4	2	2	18	12	17	.288	.407	.359
June	112	21	1	2	0	11	18	21	.188	.232	.300
July	99	25	5	0	3	14	19	17	.253	.394	.367
August	39	10	1	1	0	6	10	11	.256	.333	.400
Sept./Oct.	0	0	0	0	0	0	0	0	—	—	—
Leading Off Inn.	178	42	5	1	3	3	32	33	.236	.326	.355
Runners On	154	49	9	3	0	50	27	26	.318	.416	.419
Runners/Scor. Pos.	100	35	7	3	0	49	20	16	.350	.480	.447
Runners On/2 Out	60	19	2	1	0	19	15	9	.317	.383	.461
Scor. Pos./2 Out	41	15	2	1	0	19	13	7	.366	.463	.519
Late Inning Pressure	67	18	2	1	1	9	16	10	.269	.373	.405
Leading Off	15	4	0	0	0	0	4	3	.267	.267	.421
Runners On	29	9	2	1	0	8	9	2	.310	.448	.462
Runners/Scor. Pos.	17	5	1	1	0	8	4	2	.294	.471	.409

DRIVING IN RUNS	From 1B	From 2B	From 3B	Scoring Position
Totals	4/99	24/76	22/46	46/122
Percentage	4%	32%	48%	38%
Driving In Runners from 3B with Less than Two Out:		13/23		57%

Loves to face: Dave Stieb (.455, 4-for-11)
Hates to face: Kirk McCaskill (0-for-7, 4 SO)
Tied major-league record for second basemen with 12 assists in game on July 6. Led A.L. second basemen with 3.52 assists per nine innings last season (minimum: 500 innings). . . . Grounded into only two double plays in 76 double-play situations, lowest rate in A.L. (minimum: 40 opportunities). . . . Yearly batting averages vs. right-handers have declined since 1983 (.277, .245, .233, .228); he's been over .300 against lefties in each of last three years. . . . Shuttled between second and third, with three starts in center field, until June 13; from then until Aug. 13, when he was injured, he started every game at second. . . . Averaged .66 runs per game in leadoff position; other Oakland leadoff men averaged .47.

Darrell Porter

Texas Rangers — Bats Left

	AB	H	2B	3B	HR	RRF	BB	SO	BA	SA	OBA
Season	155	41	6	0	12	29	22	51	.265	.535	.360
vs. Left-Handers	7	0	0	0	0	0	2	5	.000	.000	.222
vs. Right-Handers	148	41	6	0	12	29	20	46	.277	.561	.367
Home	67	20	2	0	6	16	10	20	.299	.597	.397
Road	88	21	4	0	6	13	12	31	.239	.489	.330
Grass	129	31	3	0	10	22	16	44	.240	.496	.329
Artificial Turf	26	10	3	0	2	7	6	7	.385	.731	.500
April	21	5	1	0	2	2	0	8	.238	.571	.273
May	44	13	1	0	3	6	7	12	.295	.523	.392
June	2	0	0	0	0	0	1	0	.000	.000	.333
July	4	1	0	0	0	1	1	1	.250	.250	.400
August	31	6	1	0	2	5	4	13	.194	.419	.286
Sept./Oct.	53	16	3	0	5	15	9	17	.302	.642	.403
Leading Off Inn.	29	8	0	0	3	3	3	7	.276	.586	.344
Runners On	74	20	3	0	5	22	11	24	.270	.514	.365
Runners/Scor. Pos.	41	9	2	0	3	17	5	13	.220	.488	.304
Runners On/2 Out	43	11	1	0	3	12	6	14	.256	.488	.347
Scor. Pos./2 Out	22	5	1	0	2	10	3	6	.227	.545	.320
Late Inning Pressure	29	4	1	0	1	2	4	14	.138	.276	.242
Leading Off	1	0	0	0	0	0	0	1	.000	.000	.000
Runners On	11	2	1	0	0	1	2	6	.182	.273	.308
Runners/Scor. Pos.	4	0	0	0	0	0	1	3	.000	.000	.000

DRIVING IN RUNS	From 1B	From 2B	From 3B	Scoring Position
Totals	5/55	6/32	6/19	12/51
Percentage	9%	19%	32%	24%
Driving In Runners from 3B with Less than Two Out:		2/8		25%

Loves to face: Charles Hudson (.450, 9-for-20, 1 HR)
Hates to face: Floyd Bannister (0-for-17)
Averaged one home run every 12.9 at bats last season, best rate in majors among players with 10 or more home runs. Related fact: only seven at bats vs. left-handed pitchers. . . . Started 23 games at catcher, 19 at DH; batted .317, with five home runs and 15 RBI, as the DH, a job he held against right-handed pitchers through most of September. . . . Yearly batting averages vs. right-handers since 1984: .216, .228, .277. . . . Batted 156 points lower in Late-Inning Pressure Situations (.138) than in nonpressure situations (.294), 4th-largest such gap in majors last years (minimum: 25 LIP AB). . . . Batting average with runners in scoring position was his lowest since 1976.

Jim Presley

Seattle Mariners — Bats Right

	AB	H	2B	3B	HR	RRF	BB	SO	BA	SA	OBA
Season	616	163	33	4	27	108	32	172	.265	.463	.303
vs. Left-Handers	158	51	9	1	6	23	11	49	.323	.506	.367
vs. Right-Handers	458	112	24	3	21	85	21	123	.245	.448	.281
Home	319	98	25	2	16	60	18	84	.307	.549	.348
Road	297	65	8	2	11	48	14	88	.219	.370	.254
Grass	220	47	5	1	11	38	13	60	.214	.395	.258
Artificial Turf	396	116	28	3	16	70	19	112	.293	.500	.328
April	78	16	2	0	2	9	3	30	.205	.308	.244
May	108	33	9	0	4	19	2	29	.306	.500	.318
June	107	34	8	1	10	29	10	23	.318	.692	.392
July	109	23	6	2	3	12	1	31	.211	.385	.216
August	99	28	4	1	2	16	9	22	.283	.404	.336
Sept./Oct.	115	29	4	0	6	23	7	37	.252	.443	.290
Leading Off Inn.	130	35	10	1	6	6	4	24	.269	.500	.301
Runners On	293	81	15	2	13	94	17	83	.276	.474	.315
Runners/Scor. Pos.	160	47	9	2	7	77	10	50	.294	.506	.326
Runners On/2 Out	115	33	5	1	7	47	10	30	.287	.530	.349
Scor. Pos./2 Out	72	20	2	1	4	37	6	23	.278	.500	.333
Late Inning Pressure	87	27	6	0	8	24	6	23	.310	.655	.354
Leading Off	24	3	2	0	0	0	0	6	.125	.208	.125
Runners On	34	13	3	0	5	21	4	10	.382	.912	.439
Runners/Scor. Pos.	19	8	1	0	4	18	2	4	.421	1.105	.435

DRIVING IN RUNS	From 1B	From 2B	From 3B	Scoring Position
Totals	17/221	30/115	34/78	64/193
Percentage	8%	26%	44%	33%
Driving In Runners from 3B with Less than Two Out:		19/36		53%

Loves to face: Jeff Russell (3-for-3, 2 HR)
Hates to face: Tom Candiotti (0-for-11, 7 SO)
One of six players in history with two extra-inning grand slam homers (see Ruppert Jones), but he's the only man to do it twice in one season: a 10th-inning slam in Seattle's season opener last year, and an 11th-inning slam in the first game after the All-Star break. . . . Had seven hits in 18 at bats with bases loaded last season. . . . Total of five homers with runners on base in Late-Inning Pressure Situations was most in majors last season and one short of *The Player Analysis* record of six held by Tony Armas (1982) and Bob Horner (1985). . . . Led majors with 43 extra-base hits in home games. . . . Seven home runs in 63 career at bats at Arlington Stadium.

Kirby Puckett

Minnesota Twins — Bats Right

	AB	H	2B	3B	HR	RRF	BB	SO	BA	SA	OBA
Season	680	223	37	6	31	96	34	99	.328	.537	.366
vs. Left-Handers	166	54	11	2	6	19	9	26	.325	.524	.364
vs. Right-Handers	514	169	26	4	25	77	25	73	.329	.541	.367
Home	346	127	21	6	14	51	16	53	.367	.584	.405
Road	334	96	16	0	17	45	18	46	.287	.488	.326
Grass	254	73	14	0	13	39	13	38	.287	.496	.322
Artificial Turf	426	150	23	6	18	57	21	61	.352	.561	.392
April	91	36	6	1	8	16	4	10	.396	.747	.433
May	116	40	5	0	7	22	8	12	.345	.569	.392
June	123	37	6	1	0	6	4	16	.301	.366	.333
July	108	35	8	2	6	17	5	18	.324	.602	.354
August	115	41	8	1	5	15	9	21	.357	.574	.408
Sept./Oct.	127	34	4	1	5	20	4	22	.268	.433	.295
Leading Off Inn.	253	87	12	2	10	10	13	29	.344	.526	.385
Runners On	234	78	9	4	13	78	11	33	.333	.573	.366
Runners/Scor. Pos.	135	43	7	1	7	62	8	24	.319	.541	.357
Runners On/2 Out	93	32	4	1	7	38	3	17	.344	.634	.367
Scor. Pos./2 Out	58	20	4	0	4	31	3	13	.345	.621	.377
Late Inning Pressure	82	24	1	0	5	12	4	13	.293	.488	.341
Leading Off	22	8	0	0	2	2	0	2	.364	.636	.391
Runners On	34	8	0	0	3	10	2	5	.235	.500	.278
Runners/Scor. Pos.	19	4	0	0	2	8	1	3	.211	.526	.250

DRIVING IN RUNS	From 1B	From 2B	From 3B	Scoring Position
Totals	16/156	28/109	21/47	49/156
Percentage	10%	26%	45%	31%
Driving In Runners from 3B with Less than Two Out:		12/24		50%

Loves to face: Jaime Cocanower (.636, 7-for-11)
Hates to face: Bill Wegman (0-for-10, 4 SO)
Only player ever to have a 30-home run season after having a 500-at bat, no home run season earlier in his career; Puckett had no homers in 557 at bats in 1984. . . . Career average of .333 vs. left-handed pitchers is highest in majors over past 12 years (minimum: 150 hits vs. LHP). Has career average of .378 vs. left-handers at the Metrodome. . . . Led the A.L. batting race with a .348 average on morning of Sept. 8 but went 4-for-40 over next 10 games to fall 17 points back by Sept. 20. . . . Had 66 multiple-hit games last season, 2d in majors to Mattingly's 79. . . . Career batting average of .340 at the Metrodome, .268 in road games. . . . Has hit 19 of his 35 career homers on the road.

Rey Quinones
Red Sox/Mariners   Bats Right

	AB	H	2B	3B	HR	RRF	BB	SO	BA	SA	OBA
Season	312	68	16	1	2	22	24	57	.218	.295	.279
vs. Left-Handers	103	22	6	0	0	7	8	22	.214	.272	.274
vs. Right-Handers	209	46	10	1	2	15	16	35	.220	.306	.281
Home	158	37	12	0	2	12	11	25	.234	.348	.284
Road	154	31	4	1	0	10	13	32	.201	.240	.273
Grass	204	51	11	1	2	20	19	37	.250	.343	.320
Artificial Turf	108	17	5	0	0	2	5	20	.157	.204	.195
April	0	0	0	0	0	0	0	0	—	—	—
May	37	8	2	0	0	4	11	7	.216	.270	.420
June	67	14	1	1	1	7	2	7	.209	.299	.229
July	70	20	7	0	1	4	4	10	.286	.429	.324
August	57	11	3	0	0	2	4	10	.193	.246	.254
Sept./Oct.	81	15	3	0	0	5	3	23	.185	.222	.214
Leading Off Inn.	85	19	3	0	0	0	7	17	.224	.259	.283
Runners On	139	33	9	1	1	21	6	25	.237	.338	.275
Runners/Scor. Pos.	80	19	6	1	0	17	3	13	.238	.338	.267
Runners On/2 Out	68	13	2	0	0	6	2	14	.191	.221	.225
Scor. Pos./2 Out	45	7	2	0	0	6	1	8	.156	.200	.191
Late Inning Pressure	36	3	0	0	0	3	3	12	.083	.083	.175
Leading Off	6	1	0	0	0	0	2	2	.167	.167	.375
Runners On	18	1	0	0	0	0	0	6	.056	.056	.105
Runners/Scor. Pos.	9	0	0	0	0	0	0	1	.000	.000	.100

DRIVING IN RUNS

	From 1B	From 2B	From 3B	Scoring Position
Totals	3/90	7/64	10/34	17/98
Percentage	3%	11%	29%	17%
Driving In Runners from 3B with Less than Two Out:		8/17		47%

Loves to face: Dave Righetti (.667, 2-for-3)
Hates to face: Steve Carlton (0-for-6, 3 SO)
Had lowest fielding percentage (.942) among major-league shortstops last season (minimum: 50 games). . . . Made 12 errors in 32 games on artificial turf; 12 errors in 66 games on grass fields. . . . Here's something that will surely *not* be a part of Quinones's 1989 arbitration presentation: Red Sox played .550 ball with Quinones as starting shortstop, .614 with other starting shortstops; Mariners were a .343 team with Quinones starting, .433 with others. . . . Batted 152 points lower in Late-Inning Pressure Situations (.083) than in nonpressure situations (.236), 5th-largest such difference in majors last season (minimum: 25 LIP AB).

Jamie Quirk
Kansas City Royals   Bats Left

	AB	H	2B	3B	HR	RRF	BB	SO	BA	SA	OBA
Season	219	47	10	0	8	26	17	41	.215	.370	.273
vs. Left-Handers	11	1	0	0	0	1	0	3	.091	.091	.091
vs. Right-Handers	208	46	10	0	8	25	17	38	.221	.385	.284
Home	121	27	8	0	5	15	10	20	.223	.413	.288
Road	98	20	2	0	3	11	7	21	.204	.316	.255
Grass	63	14	1	0	3	10	6	12	.222	.381	.290
Artificial Turf	156	33	9	0	5	16	11	29	.212	.365	.266
April	9	2	0	0	1	2	0	1	.222	.556	.200
May	29	7	3	0	0	0	5	5	.241	.345	.353
June	39	7	1	0	1	3	3	9	.179	.282	.256
July	30	6	1	0	0	3	2	6	.200	.233	.250
August	27	5	1	0	1	7	2	6	.185	.333	.241
Sept./Oct.	85	20	4	0	5	13	5	14	.235	.459	.278
Leading Off Inn.	52	14	5	0	0	0	3	9	.269	.365	.309
Runners On	93	23	3	0	5	23	9	15	.247	.441	.311
Runners/Scor. Pos.	49	9	1	0	3	18	7	7	.184	.388	.281
Runners On/2 Out	45	8	0	0	2	5	4	9	.178	.311	.245
Scor. Pos./2 Out	26	2	0	0	1	3	4	5	.077	.192	.200
Late Inning Pressure	48	11	5	0	0	3	4	6	.229	.333	.288
Leading Off	9	4	2	0	0	0	1	2	.444	.667	.500
Runners On	21	4	1	0	0	3	3	2	.190	.238	.292
Runners/Scor. Pos.	10	2	1	0	0	3	3	0	.200	.300	.385

DRIVING IN RUNS

	From 1B	From 2B	From 3B	Scoring Position
Totals	4/65	5/38	9/24	14/62
Percentage	6%	13%	38%	23%
Driving In Runners from 3B with Less than Two Out:		8/9		89%

Loves to face: Moose Haas (.545, 6-for-11)
Hates to face: Mike Morgan (.083, 1-for-12)
Eight home runs last season boosted his career total to 23; that's seven short of the all-time record for homers by a player whose name starts with Q: Joe Quinn had 30 from 1884 to 1901. . . . If Quirk passes Quinn, will Q-Tips come after him for an endorsement? . . . It's been a revival of sorts for Quinn: This item comes on the heels of his prominence last summer, when Craig Shipley became the 2d Australian-born player to reach the majors. The first? Joe Quinn. . . . All 23 of Quirk's homers have come off right-handed pitchers; four of his eight last season were hit against Oakland. . . . Career batting average of .162 (23-for-142) with runners in scoring position and two outs.

Willie Randolph
New York Yankees   Bats Right

	AB	H	2B	3B	HR	RRF	BB	SO	BA	SA	OBA
Season	492	136	15	2	5	55	94	49	.276	.346	.393
vs. Left-Handers	183	57	7	1	4	15	25	14	.311	.426	.392
vs. Right-Handers	309	79	8	1	1	40	69	35	.256	.298	.393
Home	241	75	9	2	2	27	61	20	.311	.390	.451
Road	251	61	6	0	3	28	33	29	.243	.303	.332
Grass	418	121	14	2	4	48	85	40	.289	.361	.410
Artificial Turf	74	15	1	0	1	7	9	9	.203	.257	.291
April	72	23	3	0	0	7	15	8	.319	.361	.437
May	96	29	4	1	0	15	28	10	.302	.365	.460
June	99	21	4	0	1	12	15	15	.212	.283	.316
July	87	19	1	1	0	7	15	6	.218	.253	.337
August	75	22	1	0	2	3	12	7	.293	.387	.391
Sept./Oct.	63	22	2	0	2	11	9	3	.349	.476	.432
Leading Off Inn.	93	30	3	1	2	2	18	5	.323	.441	.438
Runners On	199	55	6	0	0	50	40	16	.276	.307	.396
Runners/Scor. Pos.	133	35	3	0	0	49	29	10	.263	.286	.386
Runners On/2 Out	84	22	1	0	0	21	20	8	.262	.274	.404
Scor. Pos./2 Out	62	18	1	0	0	21	14	4	.290	.306	.421
Late Inning Pressure	52	15	1	0	0	11	11	8	.288	.346	.415
Leading Off	11	3	0	0	0	3	2	2	.273	.273	.429
Runners On	25	9	1	0	0	11	5	3	.360	.400	.469
Runners/Scor. Pos.	16	6	1	0	0	11	3	2	.375	.438	.450

DRIVING IN RUNS

	From 1B	From 2B	From 3B	Scoring Position
Totals	2/117	20/99	28/64	48/163
Percentage	2%	20%	44%	29%
Driving In Runners from 3B with Less than Two Out:		18/34		53%

Loves to face: Bruce Hurst (.404, 21-for-52)
Hates to face: Bill Swift (.091, 1-for-11)
One of two players to hit between .275 and .300, in each of last five years; the other: Mookie Wilson. . . . One of three batters in majors to hit .300 or better vs. left-handed pitchers in each of the past three seasons (minimum: 100 AB); others: Juan Beniquez and Kirby Puckett. . . . Has also batted over .300 leading off innings in each of those three seasons. . . . Batting average in Late-Inning Pressure Situations was lower than his overall average in eight consecutive seasons from 1978 to 1985. . . . Home batting average was a career high. . . . Who do you like in a bases-loaded situation, Randolph or Mattingly? Randolph career: .361 (35-for-97), 10 extra-base hits; Mattingly: .255 (12-for-47), 1 XBH (a double).

Floyd Rayford
Baltimore Orioles   Bats Right

	AB	H	2B	3B	HR	RRF	BB	SO	BA	SA	OBA
Season	210	37	4	0	8	19	15	50	.176	.310	.231
vs. Left-Handers	93	18	3	0	4	8	7	24	.194	.355	.250
vs. Right-Handers	117	19	1	0	4	11	8	26	.162	.274	.216
Home	82	16	3	0	5	12	10	22	.195	.415	.283
Road	128	21	1	0	3	7	5	28	.164	.242	.195
Grass	168	34	4	0	7	17	13	37	.202	.351	.260
Artificial Turf	42	3	0	0	1	2	2	13	.071	.143	.114
April	25	5	0	0	1	2	1	7	.200	.320	.231
May	53	5	1	0	0	3	4	12	.094	.113	.158
June	26	6	1	0	0	0	0	6	.231	.269	.231
July	22	2	0	0	1	1	3	10	.091	.227	.200
August	27	5	2	0	0	3	0	7	.185	.259	.185
Sept./Oct.	57	14	0	0	6	10	7	8	.246	.561	.328
Leading Off Inn.	61	10	0	0	3	3	4	13	.164	.311	.215
Runners On	93	15	3	0	3	14	3	26	.161	.290	.188
Runners/Scor. Pos.	51	7	2	0	2	12	2	14	.137	.294	.170
Runners On/2 Out	33	4	0	0	1	4	0	10	.121	.212	.121
Scor. Pos./2 Out	23	3	0	0	1	4	0	4	.130	.261	.130
Late Inning Pressure	31	6	0	0	4	4	2	9	.194	.258	.242
Leading Off	9	2	0	0	0	0	0	2	.222	.222	.222
Runners On	12	3	0	0	0	4	1	7	.250	.417	.308
Runners/Scor. Pos.	9	2	2	0	0	4	0	5	.222	.444	.222

DRIVING IN RUNS

	From 1B	From 2B	From 3B	Scoring Position
Totals	2/67	4/45	5/18	9/63
Percentage	3%	9%	28%	14%
Driving In Runners from 3B with Less than Two Out:		3/7		43%

Loves to face: Oil Can Boyd (.529, 9-for-17, 2 HR)
Hates to face: Mike Witt (.083, 1-for-12, 4 SO)
Only player in majors to drop from .300 batting average in 1985 to sub-.200 mark in '86 (minimum: 100 PA in each season); his '86 average (.176) was lowest in majors (minimum: 125 PA). . . . Drove in only 14.3 percent of runners from scoring position (9-of-63), 2d-lowest rate in majors (minimum: 50 opportunities); teammate Rick Dempsey had the lowest. . . . Career batting average of .441 (15-of-34) at Fenway Park. . . . Career vs. left-handers: .277, one home run every 19.3 at bats; vs. right-handers: .220, one every 42.3 at bats. . . . The last player to hit a three-run homer for Earl; he did it on Sept. 9, which tells you a little about the team's offense in the closing weeks of 1986.

Harold Reynolds

Seattle Mariners — Bats Left and Right

	AB	H	2B	3B	HR	RRF	BB	SO	BA	SA	OBA
Season	445	99	19	4	1	25	29	42	.222	.290	.275
vs. Left-Handers	117	24	5	0	1	10	6	13	.205	.274	.250
vs. Right-Handers	328	75	14	4	0	15	23	29	.229	.296	.283
Home	220	50	12	4	1	13	16	19	.227	.332	.283
Road	225	49	7	0	0	12	13	23	.218	.249	.267
Grass	174	32	4	0	0	6	10	20	.184	.207	.232
Artificial Turf	271	67	15	4	1	19	19	22	.247	.343	.301
April	0	0	0	0	0	0	0	0	——		
May	64	15	6	0	0	5	4	8	.234	.328	.279
June	110	24	4	0	0	3	5	12	.218	.255	.271
July	89	18	3	1	0	8	7	4	.202	.258	.260
August	83	15	3	0	0	3	7	7	.181	.217	.244
Sept./Oct.	99	27	3	3	1	6	6	11	.273	.394	.314
Leading Off Inn.	135	33	5	3	0	0	9	17	.244	.326	.301
Runners On	172	35	6	1	0	24	11	15	.203	.250	.251
Runners/Scor. Pos.	90	19	4	1	0	24	7	6	.211	.278	.268
Runners On/2 Out	90	12	1	0	0	11	2	6	.133	.144	.152
Scor. Pos./2 Out	58	9	1	0	0	11	1	5	.155	.172	.169
Late Inning Pressure	52	8	0	0	0	1	7	5	.154	.192	.267
Leading Off	15	3	0	0	0	0	2	1	.200	.200	.294
Runners On	17	3	0	1	0	1	2	1	.176	.294	.263
Runners/Scor. Pos.	9	2	0	1	0	1	2	0	.222	.444	.364

DRIVING IN RUNS	From 1B	From 2B	From 3B	Scoring Position
Totals	0/121	12/75	12/34	24/109
Percentage	0%	16%	35%	22%
Driving In Runners from 3B with Less than Two Out:		7/11	64%	

Loves to face: Mike Boddicker (.500, 6-for-12)
Hates to face: Ken Dixon (.091, 1-for-11)

Recalled from Calgary May 14, five days after Dick Williams took over as Mariners manager. Regular leadoff batter until June 25, but had hit only .225, with 18 runs scored in 35 games, and was dropped to 9th, where he stayed with few exceptions thereafter. . . . Tied major-league record for second basemen with 12 assists in game on Aug. 27; ranked second among A.L. second basemen with 3.42 assists per nine innings (minimum: 500 innings). . . . Has played in both majors and minors in each of last four years. . . . Career batting average of .127 (8-for-63, one RRF) in Late-Inning Pressure Situations. . . . His only career home run was hit at the Kingdome off Pete Filson.

Jim Rice

Boston Red Sox — Bats Right

	AB	H	2B	3B	HR	RRF	BB	SO	BA	SA	OBA
Season	618	200	39	2	20	111	62	78	.324	.490	.384
vs. Left-Handers	168	59	14	0	7	39	19	14	.351	.560	.413
vs. Right-Handers	450	141	25	2	13	72	43	64	.313	.464	.373
Home	312	105	25	2	10	49	28	35	.337	.526	.387
Road	306	95	14	0	10	62	34	43	.310	.454	.381
Grass	523	166	32	2	17	96	53	65	.317	.484	.378
Artificial Turf	95	34	7	0	3	15	9	13	.358	.526	.419
April	77	20	5	0	3	15	6	4	.260	.442	.313
May	114	42	8	0	2	23	15	15	.368	.491	.430
June	106	36	11	0	2	16	9	19	.340	.500	.385
July	88	29	5	2	2	9	7	8	.330	.500	.379
August	117	36	5	0	4	21	13	21	.308	.453	.378
Sept./Oct.	116	37	5	0	7	27	14	11	.319	.543	.393
Leading Off Inn.	158	42	9	0	4	4	13	18	.266	.399	.326
Runners On	307	104	20	0	11	102	37	39	.339	.511	.403
Runners/Scor. Pos.	203	69	12	0	9	98	29	31	.340	.532	.409
Runners On/2 Out	134	43	7	0	4	37	22	20	.321	.463	.420
Scor. Pos./2 Out	85	27	5	0	2	33	16	14	.318	.447	.426
Late Inning Pressure	62	18	3	0	2	8	10	13	.290	.435	.397
Leading Off	16	6	1	0	1	1	1	3	.375	.625	.412
Runners On	27	7	1	0	1	7	9	5	.259	.407	.459
Runners/Scor. Pos.	20	5	1	0	0	5	9	5	.250	.300	.500

DRIVING IN RUNS	From 1B	From 2B	From 3B	Scoring Position
Totals	5/213	33/148	53/102	86/250
Percentage	2%	22%	52%	34%
Driving In Runners from 3B with Less than Two Out:		39/62	63%	

Loves to face: Chris Codiroli (.423, 11-for-26, 3 HR)
Hates to face: Ernie Camacho (0-for-12)

Only player in majors with 20 home runs and 100 RBI in each of last four years. . . . Thank you, Wade, Marty, and Bucks: Rice had 250 "opportunities" in scoring position when he batted, most in majors last season, and 3d-highest total over past 12 years. . . . Has batted over .300 with runners in scoring position in each of last five seasons, nine of last 10. . . . Career batting average vs. left-handers (.319) is 2d highest in majors over past 12 years (minimum: 150 hits vs. LHP). . . . Did not drive in a run in the 1986 World Series, the first time that a team's regular-season RBI leader has been held without an RBI in a seven-game Series since way back in 1985, when Tommy Herr did it.

Earnest Riles

Milwaukee Brewers — Bats Left

	AB	H	2B	3B	HR	RRF	BB	SO	BA	SA	OBA
Season	524	132	24	2	9	48	54	80	.252	.357	.321
vs. Left-Handers	116	24	2	1	3	13	9	22	.207	.319	.270
vs. Right-Handers	408	108	22	1	6	35	45	58	.265	.368	.336
Home	246	64	9	2	2	17	29	31	.260	.337	.337
Road	278	68	15	0	7	31	25	49	.245	.374	.307
Grass	446	109	20	2	8	41	48	68	.244	.352	.318
Artificial Turf	78	23	4	0	1	7	6	12	.295	.385	.341
April	70	15	0	1	2	8	4	16	.214	.329	.257
May	108	31	5	0	2	14	10	12	.287	.389	.342
June	90	25	5	0	1	4	14	11	.278	.367	.381
July	95	21	4	1	1	8	10	17	.221	.316	.295
August	81	20	3	0	2	5	9	12	.247	.358	.322
Sept./Oct.	80	20	7	0	1	9	7	12	.250	.375	.307
Leading Off Inn.	124	33	10	0	0	0	12	17	.266	.347	.331
Runners On	217	55	7	0	8	47	24	27	.253	.396	.327
Runners/Scor. Pos.	126	24	1	0	4	37	17	20	.190	.294	.281
Runners On/2 Out	85	22	3	0	5	20	12	11	.259	.471	.351
Scor. Pos./2 Out	56	11	0	0	3	15	10	9	.196	.357	.318
Late Inning Pressure	82	21	2	0	3	13	7	12	.256	.390	.319
Leading Off	20	4	1	0	0	0	3	3	.200	.250	.304
Runners On	31	10	0	0	2	12	4	4	.323	.516	.405
Runners/Scor. Pos.	15	6	0	0	1	8	3	3	.400	.600	.474

DRIVING IN RUNS	From 1B	From 2B	From 3B	Scoring Position
Totals	9/160	17/108	13/47	30/155
Percentage	6%	16%	28%	19%
Driving In Runners from 3B with Less than Two Out:		12/29	41%	

Loves to face: Mike Smithson (.526, 10-for-19)
Hates to face: Mike Boddicker (.059, 1-for-17)

Started in every position in batting order except 3d and 4th; most frequent position: 2d, where he was written in 35 times. . . . Averaged 2.38 assists per nine innings, lowest in majors among shortstops (minimum: 500 innings). . . . Had one hit in 14 at bats with bases loaded last season. . . . Career breakdown: .283 vs. right-handers, .226 vs. left-handers; .294 with four home runs at County Stadium, .242 with 10 on road. . . . Batting average with runners in scoring position fell off by 102 points from .292 mark in 1985. . . . One of three active nonpitchers with 1000 plate appearances who has never been intentionally walked; the other two: Wayne Tolleson and Curtis Wilkerson.

Cal Ripken

Baltimore Orioles — Bats Right

	AB	H	2B	3B	HR	RRF	BB	SO	BA	SA	OBA
Season	627	177	35	1	25	86	70	60	.282	.461	.355
vs. Left-Handers	164	59	17	0	12	25	20	12	.360	.683	.428
vs. Right-Handers	463	118	18	1	13	61	50	48	.255	.382	.329
Home	291	77	18	0	10	40	36	35	.265	.430	.344
Road	336	100	17	1	15	46	34	25	.298	.488	.365
Grass	524	139	27	1	18	65	60	51	.265	.424	.341
Artificial Turf	103	38	8	0	7	21	10	9	.369	.650	.426
April	77	19	4	0	3	15	10	11	.247	.416	.330
May	91	23	6	0	4	14	15	11	.253	.451	.367
June	106	33	8	1	2	8	12	8	.311	.462	.381
July	103	39	8	0	7	22	16	10	.379	.660	.459
August	116	29	3	0	5	14	12	10	.250	.405	.282
Sept./Oct.	134	34	6	0	4	13	5	10	.254	.388	.282
Leading Off Inn.	119	43	7	0	8	8	8	10	.361	.622	.402
Runners On	303	79	18	0	9	70	37	30	.261	.409	.339
Runners/Scor. Pos.	149	38	8	0	5	55	25	14	.255	.369	.354
Runners On/2 Out	111	23	5	0	4	16	18	13	.207	.360	.323
Scor. Pos./2 Out	58	7	2	0	1	10	16	10	.121	.207	.311
Late Inning Pressure	95	26	7	0	6	23	6	9	.274	.537	.314
Leading Off	20	6	1	0	3	3	1	2	.300	.800	.333
Runners On	42	14	5	0	2	19	3	3	.333	.595	.370
Runners/Scor. Pos.	21	10	4	0	1	16	3	1	.476	.810	.520

DRIVING IN RUNS	From 1B	From 2B	From 3B	Scoring Position
Totals	13/238	21/119	27/58	48/177
Percentage	5%	18%	47%	27%
Driving In Runners from 3B with Less than Two Out:		23/33	70%	

Loves to face: Jack Morris (.341, 14-for-41, 3 HR)
Hates to face: Tom Candiotti (.067, 1-for-15)

Batted 105 points higher vs. left-handed pitchers than against right-handers, 2d-largest difference in A.L. (minimum: 100 AB vs. each). . . . Only A.L. player in history to have two five-hit games indoors (one in each dome); career batting average of .392 at the Metrodome, .346 at the Kingdome. . . . One of six A.L. players to hit a home run against every opposing club in 1986. . . . Career batting average of .338 leading off innings. . . . Career batting average of .396 (36-for-91) in Late-Inning Pressure Situations with runners in scoring position. . . . News Flash: Ripken did *not* lead A.L. shortstops in games played last season; sure, he had 162, but Tony Fernandez played in 163, including the replay of a tied game.

Billy Jo Robidoux

Milwaukee Brewers — Bats Left

	AB	H	2B	3B	HR	RRF	BB	SO	BA	SA	OBA
Season	181	41	8	0	1	23	33	36	.227	.287	.344
vs. Left-Handers	35	11	1	0	1	7	6	10	.314	.429	.405
vs. Right-Handers	146	30	7	0	0	16	27	26	.205	.253	.329
Home	80	15	4	0	0	4	17	12	.188	.238	.330
Road	101	26	4	0	1	19	16	24	.257	.327	.356
Grass	166	40	8	0	1	23	31	33	.241	.307	.359
Artificial Turf	15	1	0	0	0	0	2	3	.067	.067	.176
April	63	21	5	0	1	13	15	15	.333	.460	.456
May	44	10	3	0	0	7	8	5	.227	.295	.346
June	41	7	0	0	0	2	6	5	.171	.171	.277
July	1	0	0	0	0	0	2	0	.000	.000	.667
August	0	0	0	0	0	0	0	0	---	---	---
Sept./Oct.	32	3	0	0	0	1	2	11	.094	.094	.147
Leading Off Inn.	37	7	2	0	0	0	9	4	.189	.243	.348
Runners On	95	25	4	0	1	23	18	17	.263	.337	.377
Runners/Scor. Pos.	58	13	4	0	1	23	11	10	.224	.345	.343
Runners On/2 Out	40	8	0	0	0	6	10	6	.200	.200	.360
Scor. Pos./2 Out	27	5	0	0	0	6	7	4	.185	.185	.353
Late Inning Pressure	26	11	2	0	0	4	9	3	.423	.500	.571
Leading Off	8	4	1	0	0	0	2	0	.500	.625	.600
Runners On	12	4	0	0	0	4	4	0	.333	.333	.500
Runners/Scor. Pos.	8	2	0	0	0	4	1	0	.250	.250	.333

DRIVING IN RUNS	From 1B	From 2B	From 3B	Scoring Position
Totals	2/67	8/42	12/23	20/65
Percentage	3%	19%	52%	31%
Driving In Runners from 3B with Less than Two Out:			9/11	82%

Loves to face: Bruce Hurst (.667, 2-for-3, 2 HR)
Hates to face: Jim Clancy (0-for-11)

Has hit just .216 in 232 major-league at bats, but about as impressive a .216 as you can have: batted 230 points higher in Late-Inning Pressure Situations (.423) than in nonpressure situations (.194), largest difference in majors last season (minimum: 25 LIP at bats); has career averages of .254 with runners on base, .175 with bases empty. . . . All four major-league home runs have been hit away from County Stadium, where he has batted only .180. . . . Yes, he is a left-handed batter: career average of .302 vs. left-handers, .196 vs. right-handers. Only career homer against a right-hander: Sept. 19, 1985, off Mike Boddicker.

Ed Romero

Boston Red Sox — Bats Right

	AB	H	2B	3B	HR	RRF	BB	SO	BA	SA	OBA
Season	233	49	11	0	2	27	18	16	.210	.283	.270
vs. Left-Handers	71	18	6	0	0	8	7	5	.254	.338	.316
vs. Right-Handers	162	31	5	0	2	19	11	11	.191	.259	.249
Home	108	19	6	0	2	13	8	5	.176	.287	.231
Road	125	30	5	0	0	14	10	11	.240	.280	.302
Grass	198	42	10	0	2	24	16	13	.212	.293	.271
Artificial Turf	35	7	1	0	0	3	2	3	.200	.229	.263
April	48	12	5	0	0	6	5	3	.250	.354	.333
May	43	9	0	0	0	7	3	4	.209	.209	.271
June	51	11	2	0	0	6	3	3	.216	.255	.255
July	19	2	1	0	0	1	1	3	.105	.158	.150
August	46	11	2	0	1	6	3	2	.239	.348	.280
Sept./Oct.	26	4	1	0	1	1	3	1	.154	.308	.241
Leading Off Inn.	53	15	3	0	1	1	3	8	.283	.396	.333
Runners On	101	20	4	0	1	26	10	5	.198	.267	.270
Runners/Scor. Pos.	75	15	3	0	1	26	6	4	.200	.280	.250
Runners On/2 Out	53	8	1	0	1	11	4	4	.151	.226	.211
Scor. Pos./2 Out	43	7	1	0	1	11	3	4	.163	.256	.217
Late Inning Pressure	24	5	3	0	0	2	1	2	.208	.333	.240
Leading Off	10	2	1	0	0	0	0	2	.200	.300	.200
Runners On	9	2	2	0	0	2	1	0	.222	.444	.300
Runners/Scor. Pos.	7	1	1	0	0	2	1	0	.143	.286	.143

DRIVING IN RUNS	From 1B	From 2B	From 3B	Scoring Position
Totals	2/65	5/53	18/43	23/96
Percentage	3%	9%	42%	24%
Driving In Runners from 3B with Less than Two Out:			11/16	69%

Loves to face: Ron Guidry (.355, 11-for-31)
Hates to face: Dave Righetti (.091, 1-for-11)

Started 54 games at shortstop last season, but only one between Spike Owen's first game with team (Aug. 19) and the division clinching on Sept. 28. . . . Boston's starting shortstops batted a combined .221 last season, lowest in A.L.; breakdown: Quinones, .238 in 60 starts; Romero, .225 in 54; Owen, .183 in 41; Hoffman, .263 in six. . . . Career batting average of .311 in Late-Inning Pressure Situations, .241 in nonpressure situations. . . . Career breakdown: .236 with bases empty, .266 with runners on base, .271 with runners in scoring position. . . . Hit two home runs in a season for first time in his career; his homer off Bill Campbell on Aug. 15 was his first off a right-hander since 1980.

Mark Salas

Minnesota Twins — Bats Left

	AB	H	2B	3B	HR	RRF	BB	SO	BA	SA	OBA
Season	258	60	7	4	8	35	18	32	.233	.384	.282
vs. Left-Handers	20	7	0	1	0	7	1	3	.350	.450	.381
vs. Right-Handers	238	53	7	3	8	28	17	29	.223	.378	.274
Home	123	26	4	2	5	15	9	16	.211	.398	.263
Road	135	34	3	2	3	20	9	16	.252	.370	.299
Grass	104	26	2	0	2	14	9	10	.250	.327	.310
Artificial Turf	154	34	5	4	6	21	9	22	.221	.422	.262
April	70	16	1	1	4	14	6	7	.229	.443	.286
May	33	8	0	0	1	7	4	3	.242	.333	.316
June	30	8	0	0	1	4	4	7	.267	.367	.371
July	39	7	1	1	0	0	3	5	.179	.256	.238
August	38	7	1	2	0	6	0	4	.184	.316	.179
Sept./Oct.	48	14	4	0	2	4	1	6	.292	.500	.306
Leading Off Inn.	51	8	0	0	1	1	4	2	.157	.216	.218
Runners On	108	29	2	2	4	31	10	16	.269	.435	.328
Runners/Scor. Pos.	63	16	0	1	4	29	7	10	.254	.476	.315
Runners On/2 Out	58	14	0	1	2	18	4	10	.241	.379	.302
Scor. Pos./2 Out	39	11	0	0	2	18	3	7	.282	.487	.333
Late Inning Pressure	56	10	1	1	1	6	2	12	.179	.286	.207
Leading Off	13	3	0	0	0	1	1	3	.231	.231	.286
Runners On	22	2	0	0	0	5	1	5	.091	.182	.130
Runners/Scor. Pos.	13	2	0	1	0	5	1	3	.154	.308	.214

DRIVING IN RUNS	From 1B	From 2B	From 3B	Scoring Position
Totals	5/79	12/53	10/27	22/80
Percentage	6%	23%	37%	28%
Driving In Runners from 3B with Less than Two Out:			5/12	42%

Loves to face: Charlie Hough (.524, 11-for-21, 2 HR)
Hates to face: Greg Harris (0-for-7)

Started 56 games at catcher, all against right-handers, but caught less as season went on. Distribution of starts behind plate against right-handed starters: April–May: Salas, 28, Jeff Reed, five, Tim Laudner, three; June–October: Reed, 44, Salas, 28, Laudner, nine. . . . For season, Salas caught 35.7 percent of innings, Laudner, 33.7 percent, Reed, 30.6 percent; Salas and Laudner are eligible for the runoff. . . . Batted 113 points higher at night (.267) than in day games (.154), 3d-largest difference in majors (minimum: 50 AB each). . . . Career breakdown: .298 with runners on base, .242 with bases empty. . . . Hit only two home runs after June 19; both came on Sept. 11 against Charlie Hough.

Argenis Salazar

Kansas City Royals — Bats Right

	AB	H	2B	3B	HR	RRF	BB	SO	BA	SA	OBA
Season	298	73	20	2	0	25	7	47	.245	.326	.266
vs. Left-Handers	111	33	10	1	0	11	0	10	.297	.405	.297
vs. Right-Handers	187	40	10	1	0	14	7	37	.214	.278	.249
Home	127	30	6	1	0	9	1	18	.236	.299	.254
Road	171	43	14	1	0	16	6	29	.251	.345	.275
Grass	142	31	9	0	0	9	4	24	.218	.282	.238
Artificial Turf	156	42	11	2	0	16	3	23	.269	.365	.292
April	43	9	3	0	0	2	3	4	.209	.279	.261
May	77	22	4	0	0	7	2	11	.286	.338	.321
June	46	10	3	1	0	3	0	8	.217	.326	.217
July	66	14	6	0	0	3	1	14	.212	.303	.224
August	56	15	3	1	0	7	1	9	.268	.357	.276
Sept./Oct.	10	3	1	0	0	3	0	1	.300	.400	.300
Leading Off Inn.	78	18	6	0	0	1	1	7	.231	.308	.241
Runners On	118	33	7	1	0	25	2	23	.280	.356	.289
Runners/Scor. Pos.	64	21	6	1	0	24	1	11	.328	.453	.333
Runners On/2 Out	48	12	4	1	0	10	1	9	.250	.375	.265
Scor. Pos./2 Out	30	7	3	1	0	9	0	4	.233	.400	.233
Late Inning Pressure	29	8	1	0	0	2	0	2	.276	.310	.276
Leading Off	6	0	0	0	0	0	0	0	.000	.000	.000
Runners On	10	5	1	0	0	2	0	1	.500	.600	.500
Runners/Scor. Pos.	3	3	1	0	0	2	0	0	1.000	1.333	1.000

DRIVING IN RUNS	From 1B	From 2B	From 3B	Scoring Position
Totals	5/88	10/58	10/16	20/74
Percentage	6%	17%	63%	27%
Driving In Runners from 3B with Less than Two Out:			9/10	90%

Loves to face: Ted Higuera (.357, 5-for-14)
Hates to face: Jack Morris (0-for-4, 3 SO)

Winner of Joe Nuxhall Timing Award: one year too early for Mets championship, one year too late for Royals. (Nuxhall was in Reds organization from 1944 to 1966 except for one year—1961, when they won their only pennant in a generation). . . . Royals allowed 4.13 runs per nine innings with Salazar at shortstop, 4.37 with Buddy B. . . . St. Louis selected Salazar out of free-agent pool (from Expos system) as compensation for Braves' signing of Bruce Sutter in 1984. Who got best of that deal? Candidates: Braves (got Sutter), Cards (lost Sutter), Expos (lost Salazar), Mets (lost Jose Oquendo, traded to Cards for Salazar), Royals (got Salazar). Our 1-900-lines will log your votes.

Dick Schofield

California Angels — Bats Right

	AB	H	2B	3B	HR	RRF	BB	SO	BA	SA	OBA
Season	458	114	17	6	13	58	48	55	.249	.397	.321
vs. Left-Handers	163	48	8	3	4	19	28	20	.294	.454	.397
vs. Right-Handers	295	66	9	3	9	39	20	35	.224	.366	.276
Home	226	52	5	2	7	28	30	32	.230	.363	.322
Road	232	62	12	4	6	30	18	23	.267	.431	.321
Grass	403	99	12	6	11	51	45	52	.246	.387	.322
Artificial Turf	55	15	5	0	2	7	3	3	.273	.473	.311
April	31	7	2	0	3	5	1	4	.226	.581	.250
May	87	24	4	0	2	14	9	13	.276	.391	.347
June	80	15	3	1	1	6	12	8	.188	.288	.298
July	74	19	2	1	2	7	9	4	.257	.392	.341
August	91	25	2	2	4	19	6	13	.275	.473	.320
Sept./Oct.	95	24	4	2	1	7	11	13	.253	.368	.324
Leading Off Inn.	99	32	5	2	6	6	9	10	.323	.596	.380
Runners On	201	45	7	2	4	49	24	28	.224	.338	.301
Runners/Scor. Pos.	113	27	4	1	4	47	17	19	.239	.398	.321
Runners On/2 Out	88	14	2	1	2	15	6	14	.159	.273	.221
Scor. Pos./2 Out	50	11	2	1	2	15	4	11	.220	.420	.278
Late Inning Pressure	66	13	2	1	2	9	7	7	.197	.348	.270
Leading Off	19	5	0	1	1	1	2	1	.263	.526	.333
Runners On	20	4	1	0	1	8	4	4	.200	.400	.320
Runners/Scor. Pos.	11	2	1	0	1	8	3	3	.182	.545	.333

DRIVING IN RUNS	From 1B	From 2B	From 3B	Scoring Position
Totals	7/142	18/98	20/51	38/149
Percentage	5%	18%	39%	26%
Driving In Runners from 3B with Less than Two Out:		15/29		52%

Loves to face: Willie Hernandez (.625, 5-for-8, 1 HR)
Hates to face: Mike Smithson (0-for-15)
Started 132 games, during which Angels were 22 games above .500; in the 30 games that he didn't start, team was 15–15. . . . Hit 11 home runs from 8th spot in the batting order, tied with Dunston and Buechele for most in majors. . . . Career batting average of .193 when any base occupied, but .280 (7-for-25, three home runs) when they're *all* occupied. . . . Has now outhomered his father, 28 to 21, although his dad played 19 years in majors. Have both Schofields hit home runs off any particular pitcher? No, but there's still hope since Schofield, Sr., hit a 12th-inning game-winner off Phil Niekro in 1968. (Of course, we could also see a comeback by John Tsitouris. . . .)

Bill Schroeder

Milwaukee Brewers — Bats Right

	AB	H	2B	3B	HR	RRF	BB	SO	BA	SA	OBA
Season	217	46	14	0	7	21	9	59	.212	.373	.262
vs. Left-Handers	72	16	4	0	3	8	3	25	.222	.403	.263
vs. Right-Handers	145	30	10	0	4	13	6	34	.207	.359	.261
Home	134	26	6	0	2	7	5	35	.194	.284	.245
Road	83	20	8	0	5	14	4	24	.241	.518	.289
Grass	187	38	12	0	4	14	8	50	.203	.332	.250
Artificial Turf	30	8	2	0	3	7	1	9	.267	.633	.333
April	0	0	0	0	0	0	0	0	—	—	—
May	48	14	4	0	1	6	4	14	.292	.438	.352
June	41	6	2	0	0	1	1	12	.146	.195	.186
July	44	7	2	0	2	4	0	10	.159	.341	.196
August	23	5	2	0	0	0	1	7	.217	.304	.250
Sept./Oct.	61	14	4	0	4	11	3	16	.230	.492	.288
Leading Off Inn.	44	18	8	0	0	0	3	8	.409	.591	.458
Runners On	102	18	3	0	5	19	3	29	.176	.353	.220
Runners/Scor. Pos.	57	7	1	0	3	14	2	16	.123	.298	.164
Runners On/2 Out	47	7	1	0	2	8	2	15	.149	.298	.216
Scor. Pos./2 Out	28	3	0	0	2	7	1	8	.107	.321	.167
Late Inning Pressure	33	5	1	0	1	3	1	10	.152	.182	.222
Leading Off	6	1	1	0	0	0	2	1	.167	.333	.375
Runners On	18	3	0	0	0	1	1	5	.167	.167	.211
Runners/Scor. Pos.	11	1	0	0	0	1	0	3	.091	.091	.091

DRIVING IN RUNS	From 1B	From 2B	From 3B	Scoring Position
Totals	4/76	4/43	6/27	10/70
Percentage	5%	9%	22%	14%
Driving In Runners from 3B with Less than Two Out:		3/15		20%

Loves to face: Juan Agosto (4-for-4, 1 HR)
Hates to face: Bert Blyleven (0-for-10)
Drove in only 20 percent (3-of-15) of runners from third base with less than two outs, 2d-lowest rate in A.L. (minimum: 15 opportunities). . . . Career breakdown: .256 with bases empty, .199 with runners on base, .140 with runners in scoring position, 3-for-22 with bases loaded. . . . Has as many career home runs as walks (32). . . . Maybe they should just let him hit, and forget the defense: batted only .171 in 31 games as starting catcher, and just .222 in 17 games starting at first base, but hit .297 in 10 games as starting DH. . . . Seems to attract the baseball: has been hit by 11 pitches in just 752 plate appearances; only one other active player with fewer than 1000 times up has been hit 10 times (Luis Aguayo).

Larry Sheets

Baltimore Orioles — Bats Left

	AB	H	2B	3B	HR	RRF	BB	SO	BA	SA	OBA
Season	338	92	17	1	18	63	21	56	.272	.488	.317
vs. Left-Handers	26	4	1	0	1	4	2	8	.154	.308	.207
vs. Right-Handers	312	88	16	1	17	59	19	48	.282	.503	.326
Home	181	50	10	0	10	36	6	31	.276	.497	.302
Road	157	42	7	1	8	27	15	25	.268	.478	.333
Grass	297	83	16	1	17	60	20	47	.279	.512	.325
Artificial Turf	41	9	1	0	1	3	1	9	.220	.317	.256
April	29	10	1	1	1	5	1	0	.345	.552	.367
May	70	21	4	0	5	20	4	14	.300	.571	.347
June	65	20	4	0	3	15	7	9	.308	.508	.375
July	37	10	2	0	1	4	1	4	.270	.405	.300
August	76	19	4	0	7	15	5	18	.250	.579	.296
Sept./Oct.	61	12	2	0	1	4	3	11	.197	.279	.231
Leading Off Inn.	74	23	5	0	1	1	5	12	.311	.419	.363
Runners On	158	44	6	1	14	59	12	22	.278	.595	.329
Runners/Scor. Pos.	76	23	6	1	5	41	8	12	.303	.605	.368
Runners On/2 Out	61	17	5	0	3	19	4	10	.279	.508	.333
Scor. Pos./2 Out	32	10	2	0	1	15	2	6	.313	.563	.371
Late Inning Pressure	44	8	2	0	1	5	5	13	.182	.295	.280
Leading Off	11	2	0	0	0	0	0	2	.182	.182	.250
Runners On	20	2	1	0	0	4	3	5	.100	.150	.217
Runners/Scor. Pos.	11	2	1	0	0	4	2	3	.182	.273	.308

DRIVING IN RUNS	From 1B	From 2B	From 3B	Scoring Position
Totals	11/132	20/69	14/26	34/95
Percentage	8%	29%	54%	36%
Driving In Runners from 3B with Less than Two Out:		10/12		83%

Loves to face: Ron Romanick (.500, 6-for-12, 1 HR)
Hates to face: Al Nipper (.091, 1-for-11)
Started 57 games as DH and 38 in the field, scattered among the five positions nearest the foul lines. . . . Started three games against left-handers last season, the first of his career; two hits vs. left-handers on June 8 (single off Bob Shirley, home run off Tommy John) equalled his previous career total. Career batting average of .136 (6-for-44) against southpaws. . . . Drove in 83 percent (10-of-12) of runners from third base with less than two out, 5th-best percentage in A.L. (minimum: 10 RRF). . . . Seven hits in 18 career at bats with bases loaded. . . . Career batting average of .219 in Late-Inning Pressure Situations, .280 in nonpressure situations.

John Shelby

Baltimore Orioles — Bats Left and Right

	AB	H	2B	3B	HR	RRF	BB	SO	BA	SA	OBA
Season	404	92	14	4	11	53	18	75	.228	.364	.263
vs. Left-Handers	134	31	4	1	5	13	5	22	.231	.388	.264
vs. Right-Handers	270	61	10	3	6	40	13	53	.226	.352	.262
Home	186	37	6	0	5	18	6	39	.199	.312	.226
Road	218	55	8	4	6	35	12	36	.252	.408	.294
Grass	349	80	13	2	10	47	15	70	.229	.364	.262
Artificial Turf	55	12	1	2	1	6	3	5	.218	.364	.271
April	53	11	4	0	0	4	3	14	.208	.283	.250
May	48	8	0	1	1	3	1	9	.167	.271	.184
June	91	24	2	0	4	15	4	19	.264	.418	.295
July	58	10	2	2	1	12	2	6	.172	.328	.222
August	51	13	1	1	1	4	6	12	.255	.373	.333
Sept./Oct.	103	26	5	0	4	15	2	15	.252	.417	.264
Leading Off Inn.	132	32	1	0	6	6	6	23	.242	.386	.275
Runners On	165	40	10	3	2	43	5	30	.242	.376	.270
Runners/Scor. Pos.	98	26	7	1	1	37	4	17	.265	.388	.302
Runners On/2 Out	82	18	4	2	1	21	4	11	.220	.354	.256
Scor. Pos./2 Out	48	11	2	0	1	17	4	4	.229	.333	.288
Late Inning Pressure	72	19	6	1	0	7	2	12	.264	.375	.284
Leading Off	24	7	1	0	0	0	0	2	.292	.333	.292
Runners On	28	7	3	1	0	7	1	6	.250	.429	.276
Runners/Scor. Pos.	20	6	2	1	0	7	1	4	.300	.500	.333

DRIVING IN RUNS	From 1B	From 2B	From 3B	Scoring Position
Totals	7/117	16/76	18/46	34/122
Percentage	6%	21%	39%	28%
Driving In Runners from 3B with Less than Two Out:		12/23		52%

Loves to face: Ted Higuera (.571, 8-for-14)
Hates to face: Dennis Rasmussen (.071, 1-for-14)
Only player in majors last season who made 20 starts at each outfield position. . . . Orioles' leadoff batter in 35 games last season, mostly late in season; team was 11–24, and Shelby batted .242 with a .273 on-base average in those games. . . . Batting average in July was 3d-lowest in A.L. (minimum: 50 AB). . . . Home/road batting average each of last four seasons: .224/.283, .190/.226, .245/.320, .199/.252; career: .218 at home, .259 on road. . . . Career batting average of .375 (12-for-32) with bases loaded. . . . Grounded into only three double plays in 67 double-play situations, 8th-lowest rate in A.L. (minimum: 40 opportunities). . . .

Pat Sheridan

Detroit Tigers   **Bats Left**

	AB	H	2B	3B	HR	RRF	BB	SO	BA	SA	OBA
Season	236	56	9	1	6	20	21	57	.237	.360	.300
vs. Left-Handers	26	6	0	0	0	0	1	10	.231	.231	.286
vs. Right-Handers	210	50	9	1	6	20	20	47	.238	.376	.302
Home	111	26	5	0	3	10	11	24	.234	.360	.303
Road	125	30	4	1	3	10	10	33	.240	.360	.297
Grass	179	38	7	0	3	14	20	45	.212	.302	.289
Artificial Turf	57	18	2	1	3	6	1	12	.316	.544	.339
April	12	1	1	0	0	2	1	0	.083	.167	.154
May	65	9	3	0	2	3	3	18	.138	.277	.176
June	58	18	1	0	3	7	6	14	.310	.483	.369
July	35	9	2	1	0	2	2	7	.257	.371	.297
August	32	8	1	0	0	1	5	11	.250	.281	.351
Sept./Oct.	34	11	1	0	1	5	4	7	.324	.441	.400
Leading Off Inn.	51	10	1	0	2	3	3	14	.196	.333	.241
Runners On	106	25	4	0	1	15	10	26	.236	.302	.297
Runners/Scor. Pos.	57	15	2	0	1	15	9	19	.263	.351	.353
Runners On/2 Out	49	11	1	0	0	5	6	12	.224	.245	.309
Scor. Pos./2 Out	27	5	0	0	0	5	6	11	.185	.185	.333
Late Inning Pressure	23	3	0	0	0	1	1	5	.130	.130	.167
Leading Off	10	2	0	0	0	0	0	3	.200	.200	.200
Runners On	5	1	0	0	0	0	0	0	.200	.200	.200
Runners/Scor. Pos.	1	0	0	0	0	0	0	0	.000	.000	.000

DRIVING IN RUNS	From 1B	From 2B	From 3B	Scoring Position
Totals	1/79	8/49	5/19	13/68
Percentage	1%	16%	26%	19%
Driving In Runners from 3B with Less than Two Out:		4/11		36%

Loves to face: Dave Stieb (.444, 12-for-27)
Hates to face: Mike Witt (.095, 2-for-21)
Started season at Nashville, recalled on April 25; did not immediately impress the hometown fans: batting average in May was 2d lowest in majors (minimum: 50 AB). . . . From time that he was recalled until season's end, started 62 of 97 games in which Tigers faced a right-handed starter, plus five against lefties. . . . Has hit 23 of his 24 career home runs against right-handed pitchers. Only homer off a southpaw: April 10, 1984, off Scott McGregor. Career breakdown: .270 vs. right-handers, .195 vs. left-handers. . . . One man who likes the Bay Area baseball status quo: owns a career batting average of .463 (19-for-41) at Oakland Coliseum.

Ruben Sierra

Texas Rangers   **Bats Left and Right**

	AB	H	2B	3B	HR	RRF	BB	SO	BA	SA	OBA
Season	382	101	13	10	16	57	22	65	.264	.476	.302
vs. Left-Handers	99	25	4	1	4	15	4	11	.253	.434	.269
vs. Right-Handers	283	76	9	9	12	42	18	54	.269	.491	.315
Home	172	41	2	6	8	32	5	38	.238	.459	.256
Road	210	60	11	4	8	25	17	27	.286	.490	.339
Grass	297	74	7	8	11	43	16	53	.249	.438	.286
Artificial Turf	85	27	6	2	5	14	6	12	.318	.612	.359
April	0	0	0	0	0	0	0	0	——		
May	0	0	0	0	0	0	0	0	——		
June	109	21	4	1	4	8	4	25	.193	.358	.228
July	58	14	1	4	2	8	5	8	.241	.500	.297
August	91	30	6	4	3	18	7	12	.330	.582	.374
Sept./Oct.	124	36	2	1	7	23	6	20	.290	.492	.316
Leading Off Inn.	81	18	4	1	1	1	3	12	.222	.333	.250
Runners On	169	49	4	4	6	47	14	26	.290	.467	.335
Runners/Scor. Pos.	102	24	0	4	4	42	7	17	.235	.431	.272
Runners On/2 Out	73	23	2	2	4	23	7	14	.315	.562	.375
Scor. Pos./2 Out	52	13	0	2	2	18	5	10	.250	.442	.316
Late Inning Pressure	60	20	4	2	3	7	2	11	.333	.617	.355
Leading Off	15	3	0	0	0	1	3		.200	.200	.250
Runners On	27	9	1	1	1	5	0	4	.333	.556	.333
Runners/Scor. Pos.	12	2	0	1	0	2	0	1	.167	.333	.167

DRIVING IN RUNS	From 1B	From 2B	From 3B	Scoring Position
Totals	5/125	16/88	19/38	35/126
Percentage	4%	18%	50%	28%
Driving In Runners from 3B with Less than Two Out:		13/22		59%

Loves to face: Bill Swift (.667, 4-for-6, 1 HR)
Hates to face: Eric Plunk (0-for-7)
Recalled from Oklahoma City on June 1; from then until end of season, played in 113 of 115 Texas games, starting in 93. . . . Slugging average of .476 was 3d highest among A.L. rookies, higher than Incaviglia's (.463), Joyner's (.457), or Canseco's (.457). . . . Set Texas Rangers' club record with 10 triples. . . . Only A.L. player in double figures in doubles, triples and home runs last season; Juan Samuel was only one in N.L. . . . Batted .333 in Late-Inning Pressure Situations, .252 in nonpressure situations. . . . Three hits in six at bats with bases loaded. . . . One of three A.L. outfielders with 10 starts at each outfield position; others: Rick Manning, John Shelby.

Joel Skinner

White Sox/Yankees   **Bats Right**

	AB	H	2B	3B	HR	RRF	BB	SO	BA	SA	OBA
Season	315	73	9	1	5	37	16	83	.232	.314	.269
vs. Left-Handers	144	31	2	0	1	16	7	36	.215	.250	.252
vs. Right-Handers	171	42	7	1	4	21	9	47	.246	.368	.284
Home	169	40	5	0	1	17	8	44	.237	.284	.274
Road	146	33	4	1	4	20	8	39	.226	.349	.265
Grass	276	64	9	1	3	33	16	71	.232	.304	.275
Artificial Turf	39	9	0	0	2	4	0	12	.231	.385	.231
April	41	7	0	1	0	4	2	11	.171	.220	.222
May	25	5	0	0	1	3	1	4	.200	.320	.231
June	39	9	3	0	0	5	3	12	.231	.308	.286
July	47	10	2	0	3	8	3	17	.213	.447	.260
August	68	13	1	0	1	4	2	25	.191	.250	.211
Sept./Oct.	95	29	3	0	0	13	5	14	.305	.337	.340
Leading Off Inn.	73	14	2	0	1	1	5	18	.192	.260	.253
Runners On	135	30	6	0	4	36	7	33	.222	.356	.257
Runners/Scor. Pos.	61	18	3	0	3	33	3	14	.295	.492	.318
Runners On/2 Out	55	14	2	0	0	9	2	10	.255	.291	.281
Scor. Pos./2 Out	23	7	1	0	0	9	2	5	.304	.348	.360
Late Inning Pressure	31	5	1	0	0	1	1	12	.161	.194	.188
Leading Off	10	3	1	0	0	0	1	3	.300	.400	.364
Runners On	9	0	0	0	0	1	0	5	.000	.000	.000
Runners/Scor. Pos.	4	0	0	0	0	1	0	2	.000	.000	.000

DRIVING IN RUNS	From 1B	From 2B	From 3B	Scoring Position
Totals	5/105	16/44	11/30	27/74
Percentage	5%	36%	37%	36%
Driving In Runners from 3B with Less than Two Out:		7/17		41%

Loves to face: Scott McGregor (.462, 6-for-13, 1 HR)
Hates to face: Mike Boddicker (0-for-11, 5 SO)
Career batting average of .173 at Comiskey Park, .300 at Yankee Stadium. . . . Career breakdown: .229 vs. left-handers, .248 vs. right-handers. Only one home run in 188 career at bats against southpaws: July 13 off Scott McGregor. . . . Hitless in 11 career at bats with runners on base in Late-Inning Pressure Situations. . . . No Yankees catcher started even one-third of the team's games behind the plate last season; Skinner and Butch Wynegar had 52 starts apiece to lead the team, followed by Ron Hassey (48), Juan Espino (nine), and Phil Lombardi (one). . . . Yankees have had 14 catchers over the last seven seasons, including Mike O'Berry, Bruce Robinson, Dennis Werth, Bobby Ramos, and Barry Foote.

Don Slaught

Texas Rangers   **Bats Right**

	AB	H	2B	3B	HR	RRF	BB	SO	BA	SA	OBA
Season	314	83	17	1	13	47	16	59	.264	.449	.308
vs. Left-Handers	119	36	7	1	5	20	4	24	.303	.504	.323
vs. Right-Handers	195	47	10	0	8	27	12	35	.241	.415	.299
Home	149	45	11	0	5	20	9	26	.302	.477	.348
Road	165	38	6	1	8	27	7	33	.230	.424	.271
Grass	268	72	14	1	10	39	13	50	.269	.440	.310
Artificial Turf	46	11	3	0	3	8	3	9	.239	.500	.294
April	51	18	4	0	5	16	3	6	.353	.725	.404
May	41	9	1	1	2	7	1	8	.220	.439	.273
June	0	0	0	0	0	0	0	0	——		
July	71	19	6	0	4	9	3	14	.268	.521	.297
August	84	21	5	0	0	6	4	18	.250	.310	.292
Sept./Oct.	67	16	1	0	2	9	5	13	.239	.343	.284
Leading Off Inn.	60	14	6	0	0	0	4	15	.233	.333	.281
Runners On	131	41	5	1	5	39	6	16	.313	.481	.354
Runners/Scor. Pos.	77	23	3	1	2	33	1	10	.299	.442	.313
Runners On/2 Out	57	18	1	1	3	18	2	7	.316	.526	.361
Scor. Pos./2 Out	35	12	0	1	2	16	0	3	.343	.571	.378
Late Inning Pressure	43	13	2	0	4	10	3	10	.302	.628	.362
Leading Off	11	1	1	0	0	0	0	3	.091	.182	.091
Runners On	15	6	1	0	1	7	2	3	.400	.667	.471
Runners/Scor. Pos.	10	4	1	0	0	5	0	3	.400	.500	.400

DRIVING IN RUNS	From 1B	From 2B	From 3B	Scoring Position
Totals	5/96	16/62	13/30	29/92
Percentage	5%	26%	43%	32%
Driving In Runners from 3B with Less than Two Out:		8/16		50%

Loves to face: Tommy John (.583, 7-for-12, 1 HR)
Hates to face: Oil Can Boyd (.100, 1-for-10, HBP)
Batting .293 when beaned by Oil Can Boyd on May 17; hit .252 after his return (July 4). . . . Hitless in three at bats vs. Boyd (with 2 SO) after the beaning. . . . Nine of his 13 home runs came in the 7th inning or later, including two in overtime. . . . Career total of 51 at bats at Fenway Park, a *Player Analysis* high for players without an extra-base hit there. . . . Has batted over .300 in Late-Inning Pressure Situations in three of the last four seasons. . . . Batting average vs. right-handed pitchers was his lowest of 5-year career. Lifetime marks: .308 vs. left-handers, .262 vs. right-handers. . . . Rangers pitchers have allowed an average of 4.96 runs per nine innings with Slaught catching over past two seasons, 4.49 with other catchers.

Roy Smalley

Minnesota Twins	AB	H	2B	3B	HR	RRF	BB	SO	BA	SA	OBA
Season	459	113	20	4	20	58	68	80	.246	.438	.342
vs. Left-Handers	58	8	4	0	2	7	9	12	.138	.310	.250
vs. Right-Handers	401	105	16	4	18	51	59	68	.262	.456	.356
Home	222	59	11	3	9	29	36	40	.266	.464	.368
Road	237	54	9	1	11	29	32	40	.228	.414	.317
Grass	180	40	7	1	7	21	25	31	.222	.389	.314
Artificial Turf	279	73	13	3	13	37	43	49	.262	.470	.360
April	74	21	5	1	3	11	10	9	.284	.500	.369
May	64	16	4	0	5	9	10	12	.250	.547	.351
June	83	21	3	2	6	12	6	14	.253	.554	.303
July	80	20	6	0	2	9	17	17	.250	.400	.374
August	102	21	1	1	4	11	11	16	.206	.353	.283
Sept./Oct.	56	14	1	0	0	6	14	12	.250	.268	.400
Leading Off Inn.	113	26	4	0	5	5	12	15	.230	.398	.304
Runners On	196	51	10	1	5	43	38	37	.260	.398	.377
Runners/Scor. Pos.	100	25	5	1	2	34	25	25	.250	.380	.394
Runners On/2 Out	84	21	4	0	2	23	21	18	.250	.369	.400
Scor. Pos./2 Out	55	14	1	0	1	19	16	15	.255	.327	.423
Late Inning Pressure	66	10	3	1	1	6	10	16	.152	.273	.263
Leading Off	12	1	0	0	0	0	3	1	.083	.083	.267
Runners On	28	6	2	1	0	5	5	6	.214	.357	.333
Runners/Scor. Pos.	16	4	1	1	0	5	3	3	.250	.438	.368

DRIVING IN RUNS	From 1B	From 2B	From 3B	Scoring Position
Totals	9/147	17/81	12/33	29/114
Percentage	6%	21%	36%	25%
Driving In Runners from 3B with Less than Two Out:		5/10		50%

Loves to face: Gene Nelson (.462, 6-for-13, 1 HR)
Hates to face: Joe Cowley (0-for-13)
Career batting average of .190 at Royals Stadium. . . . Career batting average of .225 in Late-Inning Pressure Situations, .262 in nonpressure situations. . . . Has hit 35 of his last 37 home runs from the left side of the plate. Has batted under .200 right-handed in two of the last three seasons. . . . One of three A.L. players to hit below .250 in Late-Inning Pressure Situations in each of the past three seasons (minimum: 50 AB in each). The others: Reggie Jackson and Tom Brunansky. . . . Hitless in his last 13 at bats with two outs and the bases loaded. . . . Played only 125 innings in the field last season, almost evenly divided between third base and shortstop. Starting DH in 104 games.

Lonnie Smith

Kansas City Royals	AB	H	2B	3B	HR	RRF	BB	SO	BA	SA	OBA
Season	508	146	25	7	8	49	46	78	.287	.411	.357
vs. Left-Handers	149	46	6	4	2	16	12	19	.309	.443	.360
vs. Right-Handers	359	100	19	3	6	33	34	59	.279	.398	.356
Home	243	77	14	4	2	22	24	30	.317	.432	.390
Road	265	69	11	3	6	27	22	48	.260	.392	.327
Grass	205	53	8	2	5	18	17	38	.259	.390	.329
Artificial Turf	303	93	17	5	3	31	29	40	.307	.426	.376
April	20	4	0	0	0	0	1	5	.200	.200	.273
May	57	11	0	1	0	5	7	9	.193	.228	.292
June	106	31	6	3	3	19	16	18	.292	.491	.394
July	105	30	6	0	3	8	11	14	.286	.429	.364
August	117	34	4	0	0	5	6	21	.291	.325	.336
Sept./Oct.	103	36	9	3	2	12	5	11	.350	.553	.385
Leading Off Inn.	148	43	7	0	1	1	9	23	.291	.358	.335
Runners On	187	57	8	5	2	43	17	32	.305	.433	.374
Runners/Scor. Pos.	99	28	1	3	1	34	13	20	.283	.384	.371
Runners On/2 Out	75	22	2	2	1	18	8	17	.293	.413	.369
Scor. Pos./2 Out	49	13	0	2	1	15	5	14	.265	.408	.333
Late Inning Pressure	78	18	0	1	1	7	5	9	.231	.295	.302
Leading Off	23	3	0	0	0	0	1	3	.130	.130	.167
Runners On	33	11	0	1	0	6	2	5	.333	.394	.405
Runners/Scor. Pos.	24	8	0	1	0	6	1	4	.333	.417	.360

DRIVING IN RUNS	From 1B	From 2B	From 3B	Scoring Position
Totals	10/135	14/74	17/44	31/118
Percentage	7%	19%	39%	26%
Driving In Runners from 3B with Less than Two Out:		12/22		55%

Loves to face: Rick Rhoden (.333, 15-for-45, 3 HR)
Hates to face: Jose DeLeon (.118, 2-for-17, 7 SO)
Always willing to take one for the team: Smith has been hit with a pitch to force in a run three times in his career (58 PA with bases loaded). In the 12-year history of *The Player Analysis*, only Brian Downing has done it more often (4). . . . Has batted better than .300 with runners on base in five of past seven seasons. . . . One of five players to bat .250 or lower in Late-Inning Pressure Situations in each of the past four seasons (minimum: 50 LIP AB in each). . . . Career batting average of .420 (21 for 50, 3 HR) at Anaheim Stadium. . . . Over past three seasons, Cardinals and Royals allowed an average of 4.22 runs per nine innings with Smith in left field, 3.71 with other left fielders.

Cory Snyder

Cleveland Indians	AB	H	2B	3B	HR	RRF	BB	SO	BA	SA	OBA
Season	416	113	21	1	24	73	16	123	.272	.500	.299
vs. Left-Handers	118	38	7	0	8	24	2	31	.322	.585	.333
vs. Right-Handers	298	75	14	1	16	49	14	92	.252	.466	.285
Home	186	52	9	1	12	34	8	60	.280	.532	.309
Road	230	61	12	0	12	39	8	63	.265	.474	.290
Grass	333	94	14	1	22	60	16	98	.282	.529	.315
Artificial Turf	83	19	7	0	2	13	0	25	.229	.386	.229
April	0	0	0	0	0	0	0	0	—	—	—
May	0	0	0	0	0	0	0	0	—	—	—
June	62	17	5	1	5	11	1	20	.274	.629	.286
July	89	25	3	0	4	13	4	23	.281	.449	.312
August	132	35	4	0	8	19	5	35	.265	.477	.292
Sept./Oct.	133	36	9	0	7	30	6	45	.271	.496	.302
Leading Off Inn.	99	27	3	1	3	3	6	22	.273	.414	.314
Runners On	190	52	10	0	11	60	6	62	.274	.500	.296
Runners/Scor. Pos.	112	29	5	0	5	47	5	39	.259	.438	.291
Runners On/2 Out	79	21	3	0	4	23	1	28	.266	.456	.275
Scor. Pos./2 Out	52	12	2	0	2	19	1	21	.231	.385	.245
Late Inning Pressure	59	18	4	0	3	9	3	17	.305	.525	.339
Leading Off	16	6	0	0	1	1	1	5	.375	.563	.412
Runners On	28	8	2	0	0	6	1	8	.286	.357	.310
Runners/Scor. Pos.	19	6	1	0	0	6	0	6	.316	.368	.316

DRIVING IN RUNS	From 1B	From 2B	From 3B	Scoring Position
Totals	10/137	18/77	21/50	39/127
Percentage	7%	23%	42%	31%
Driving In Runners from 3B with Less than Two Out:		14/25		56%

Loves to face: Don Sutton (.500, 3-for-6, 2 HR)
Hates to face: Ron Guidry (0-for-6, 4 SO)
One of two 20-home run hitters in majors last season with more home runs (24) than walks (16). The other: Dave Kingman. Snyder was the only 20-home run hitter without an intentional pass. . . . Rookie of year if not for late start: Debuted on June 13, tied for 3d in A.L. in RBIs (51), 4th in home runs (16) after the All-Star break. Compare to Canseco (10 HR, 39 RBI) and Joyner (2 HR, 28 RBI). . . . Homered against every opposing A.L. club except the White Sox. . . . Ratio of 15.5 strikeouts per walk vs. left-handed pitchers was highest in A.L. in 12-year history of *The Player Analysis* (minimum: 100 PA). . . . Only player in majors to start at least 25 games at shortstop and in the outfield last season.

Jim Sundberg

Kansas City Royals	AB	H	2B	3B	HR	RRF	BB	SO	BA	SA	OBA
Season	429	91	9	1	12	46	57	91	.212	.322	.303
vs. Left-Handers	141	27	2	1	6	15	16	36	.191	.348	.272
vs. Right-Handers	288	64	7	0	6	31	41	55	.222	.309	.317
Home	209	41	4	0	5	28	25	47	.196	.287	.278
Road	220	50	5	1	7	18	32	44	.227	.355	.325
Grass	171	35	5	0	5	14	25	34	.205	.322	.306
Artificial Turf	258	56	4	1	7	32	32	57	.217	.322	.300
April	62	10	0	0	0	5	3	12	.161	.161	.200
May	83	23	6	0	2	11	13	14	.277	.422	.367
June	68	13	1	0	0	2	6	14	.191	.206	.257
July	66	12	0	0	3	9	13	13	.182	.318	.313
August	73	14	1	0	3	6	18	16	.192	.329	.352
Sept./Oct.	77	19	1	1	4	13	4	22	.247	.442	.284
Leading Off Inn.	90	21	5	1	4	4	10	17	.233	.444	.310
Runners On	184	42	2	0	6	40	27	46	.228	.337	.322
Runners/Scor. Pos.	103	22	1	0	5	37	18	24	.214	.369	.323
Runners On/2 Out	88	20	1	0	2	16	11	21	.227	.307	.313
Scor. Pos./2 Out	50	8	0	0	1	13	9	13	.160	.220	.288
Late Inning Pressure	68	19	2	1	1	8	10	14	.279	.382	.367
Leading Off	14	5	1	1	0	1	3	3	.357	.571	.400
Runners On	26	7	1	0	1	8	6	6	.269	.423	.394
Runners/Scor. Pos.	15	4	0	0	1	7	3	3	.267	.467	.368

DRIVING IN RUNS	From 1B	From 2B	From 3B	Scoring Position
Totals	6/131	9/85	19/36	28/121
Percentage	5%	11%	53%	23%
Driving In Runners from 3B with Less than Two Out:		12/15		80%

Loves to face: Mike Morgan (.588, 10-for-17, 1 HR)
Hates to face: Mark Langston (.067, 1-for-15, 6 SO)
Ranks 7th in major-league history with 1741 games caught. Within reach this season: Johnny Bench (1744), Ted Simmons (1747), Gabby Hartnett (1790), Rick Ferrell (1805), and possibly Bob Boone (1808). All-time leader Al Lopez (1918) is safe from him for now. . . . During two seasons with Kansas City, Royals pitchers allowed an average of 4.05 runs per nine innings with Sundberg behind the plate, 4.12 with other catchers. . . . Batting average peaked at .240 on May 15. . . . Mirrored leaguewide trend: set career highs in home runs and strikeouts. . . . Has batted .184 in day games over past four seasons, lowest in majors during that time (minimum: 250 AB), compared to .240 in night games.

Dale Sveum
Milwaukee Brewers   Bats Left and Right

	AB	H	2B	3B	HR	RRF	BB	SO	BA	SA	OBA
Season	317	78	13	2	7	37	32	63	.246	.366	.316
vs. Left-Handers	96	26	8	1	2	12	14	15	.271	.438	.366
vs. Right-Handers	221	52	5	1	5	25	18	48	.235	.335	.293
Home	159	36	7	0	4	17	20	29	.226	.346	.317
Road	158	42	6	2	3	20	12	34	.266	.386	.316
Grass	256	61	9	1	7	28	27	52	.238	.363	.312
Artificial Turf	61	17	4	1	0	9	5	11	.279	.377	.333
April	0	0	0	0	0	0	0	0	——	——	——
May	65	25	6	1	1	12	4	14	.385	.554	.420
June	97	19	3	0	2	8	6	16	.196	.289	.240
July	56	17	2	0	1	7	9	14	.304	.393	.400
August	42	8	1	1	1	1	6	5	.190	.333	.292
Sept./Oct.	57	9	1	0	2	9	7	14	.158	.281	.262
Leading Off Inn.	73	15	0	0	3	3	5	17	.205	.329	.256
Runners On	138	36	11	1	1	31	16	27	.261	.377	.340
Runners/Scor. Pos.	77	22	8	0	0	27	8	14	.286	.390	.356
Runners On/2 Out	62	17	8	0	0	18	6	15	.274	.403	.348
Scor. Pos./2 Out	37	13	7	0	0	17	5	8	.351	.541	.442
Late Inning Pressure	54	11	1	0	0	5	5	13	.204	.222	.271
Leading Off	14	1	0	0	0	0	1	4	.071	.071	.133
Runners On	21	6	0	0	0	3	3	4	.286	.286	.375
Runners/Scor. Pos.	14	5	0	0	0	5	2	2	.357	.357	.438

DRIVING IN RUNS	From 1B	From 2B	From 3B	Scoring Position
Totals	6/104	12/64	12/30	24/94
Percentage	6%	19%	40%	26%
Driving In Runners from 3B with Less than Two Out:	7/14			50%

Loves to face: Danny Jackson (.500, 4-for-8)
Hates to face: John Cerutti (0-for-6)
Led majors with 26 errors at third base, despite only 65 games played there; .865 fielding percentage was lowest by a 3d baseman since 1902 (minimum: 50 games), and 4th lowest since 1900, behind "Piano Legs" Hickman (.842 in 1900), "Sunset" Jimmy Burke (.860 in 1901) and Herman "Germany" Schaefer (.865 in 1902).... Brewers allowed 5.21 runs per nine innings with Sveum at third, 4.22 otherwise.... Only player in A.L. last season to start at least 10 games at second base, third base, and shortstop. Jerry Royster did it in N.L.... Batted .388, hitting safely in 20 of his first 22 games in majors; hit half that (.194) thereafter.... Batted .285 against teams with records below .500, .208 vs. winning teams.

Pat Tabler
Cleveland Indians   Bats Right

	AB	H	2B	3B	HR	RRF	BB	SO	BA	SA	OBA
Season	473	154	29	2	6	53	29	75	.326	.433	.368
vs. Left-Handers	150	50	11	0	2	18	13	18	.333	.447	.387
vs. Right-Handers	323	104	18	2	4	35	16	57	.322	.427	.359
Home	227	79	12	0	5	31	15	34	.348	.467	.389
Road	246	75	17	2	1	22	14	41	.305	.402	.347
Grass	396	137	25	0	6	48	26	65	.346	.455	.388
Artificial Turf	77	17	4	2	0	5	3	10	.221	.325	.259
April	70	26	9	0	2	7	7	8	.371	.586	.429
May	108	28	6	1	1	11	4	22	.259	.361	.296
June	20	3	0	0	0	1	1	6	.150	.150	.190
July	60	14	2	0	1	5	2	10	.233	.317	.258
August	108	50	6	0	1	13	11	15	.463	.546	.513
Sept./Oct.	107	33	6	1	1	16	4	14	.308	.411	.339
Leading Off Inn.	91	35	6	0	0	0	1	12	.385	.451	.391
Runners On	203	66	11	1	3	50	16	32	.325	.433	.381
Runners/Scor. Pos.	122	37	7	0	2	46	8	20	.303	.410	.348
Runners On/2 Out	79	21	6	1	0	15	8	16	.266	.367	.333
Scor. Pos./2 Out	51	11	5	0	0	13	4	10	.216	.314	.273
Late Inning Pressure	60	20	1	0	3	12	6	13	.333	.500	.412
Leading Off	12	1	0	0	0	0	0	5	.083	.083	.083
Runners On	23	10	1	0	2	11	3	3	.435	.739	.536
Runners/Scor. Pos.	16	5	0	0	1	8	0	2	.313	.500	.313

DRIVING IN RUNS	From 1B	From 2B	From 3B	Scoring Position
Totals	4/130	21/96	22/47	43/143
Percentage	3%	22%	47%	30%
Driving In Runners from 3B with Less than Two Out:	15/25			60%

Loves to face: Bob Shirley (.438, 7-for-16)
Hates to face: Steve Crawford (0-for-7, 3 SO)
Only 2-for-10 with bases loaded last season, but is still at .522 lifetime (24-for-46), highest in majors over past 12 years.... Has batted over .300 with runners on base in each of the last four seasons.... He's also one of five players to have hit over .300 with runners in scoring position in each of the last four seasons (minimum: 100 SP at bats).... Career batting average of .372 (29-for-78) at Yankee Stadium.... Eleven of his last 12 home runs have been hit at Cleveland Stadium.... Led A.L. with a .373 batting average against teams with winning records last season.... Led majors in batting during August.... Best trade of 1980s? Dark horse candidate: Tabler from the White Sox for Jerry Dybzinski.

Danny Tartabull
Seattle Mariners   Bats Right

	AB	H	2B	3B	HR	RRF	BB	SO	BA	SA	OBA
Season	511	138	25	6	25	97	61	157	.270	.489	.347
vs. Left-Handers	125	38	9	1	3	17	17	37	.304	.464	.385
vs. Right-Handers	386	100	16	5	22	80	44	120	.259	.497	.335
Home	268	73	14	4	13	48	26	83	.272	.500	.338
Road	243	65	11	2	12	49	35	74	.267	.477	.357
Grass	175	48	6	2	9	39	26	56	.274	.486	.366
Artificial Turf	336	90	19	4	16	58	35	101	.268	.491	.337
April	68	16	4	0	4	16	12	28	.235	.471	.350
May	56	15	2	3	3	9	6	20	.268	.571	.333
June	90	28	5	0	4	13	10	20	.311	.500	.376
July	99	29	3	1	5	26	6	24	.293	.495	.330
August	91	21	5	0	7	19	10	33	.231	.516	.307
Sept./Oct.	107	29	6	2	2	14	17	30	.271	.421	.376
Leading Off Inn.	125	29	6	2	4	4	14	36	.232	.408	.309
Runners On	234	71	13	4	16	88	32	74	.303	.598	.385
Runners/Scor. Pos.	129	41	7	3	9	70	15	40	.318	.628	.385
Runners On/2 Out	104	26	5	2	7	39	19	38	.250	.538	.366
Scor. Pos./2 Out	66	19	4	2	5	34	10	24	.288	.636	.382
Late Inning Pressure	75	21	3	1	3	12	7	28	.280	.467	.341
Leading Off	21	6	0	0	1	1	1	7	.286	.429	.318
Runners On	33	9	1	1	2	11	4	13	.273	.545	.351
Runners/Scor. Pos.	16	6	0	1	2	10	2	7	.375	.875	.444

DRIVING IN RUNS	From 1B	From 2B	From 3B	Scoring Position
Totals	21/186	27/101	24/62	51/163
Percentage	11%	27%	39%	31%
Driving In Runners from 3B with Less than Two Out:	16/32			50%

Loves to face: Floyd Bannister (.714, 5-for-7)
Hates to face: Mike Boddicker (0-for-7, 6 SO)
Struck out eight times with bases loaded last season, one short of *The Player Analysis* record of Mike Schmidt (1975). Good results when he made contact though, batting .333 (6-for-18, two HR) with bases full.... Had two streaks of 10 or more games with strikeouts after the All-Star break, and another of eight in a row.... Only player in majors to start 25 games at second base and at any other position.... Led A.L. in RBIs during the month of July.... Two hits in 19 career at bats at Oakland Coliseum. Both were home runs.... Has driven in 25 of 214 runners from first base (11.7 percent), highest average in 12-year *Player Analysis* history (minimum: 10 RRF).

Mickey Tettleton
Oakland As   Bats Left and Right

	AB	H	2B	3B	HR	RRF	BB	SO	BA	SA	OBA
Season	211	43	9	0	10	37	39	51	.204	.389	.325
vs. Left-Handers	84	22	4	0	6	18	15	21	.262	.524	.370
vs. Right-Handers	127	21	5	0	4	19	24	30	.165	.299	.297
Home	106	21	4	0	4	12	20	22	.198	.349	.326
Road	105	22	5	0	6	25	19	29	.210	.429	.325
Grass	162	31	7	0	8	26	28	37	.191	.383	.309
Artificial Turf	49	12	2	0	2	11	11	14	.245	.408	.377
April	44	6	2	0	0	3	7	5	.136	.182	.255
May	9	1	0	0	1	3	2	4	.111	.444	.333
June	30	10	2	0	1	6	2	7	.333	.500	.375
July	33	6	1	0	0	4	7	11	.182	.212	.333
August	53	13	3	0	4	14	10	15	.245	.528	.375
Sept./Oct.	42	7	1	0	4	7	11	9	.167	.476	.333
Leading Off Inn.	41	8	0	0	6	6	10	6	.195	.634	.353
Runners On	102	23	8	0	2	29	18	22	.225	.363	.336
Runners/Scor. Pos.	55	12	4	0	2	25	14	15	.218	.400	.365
Runners On/2 Out	40	10	3	0	2	13	8	7	.250	.475	.375
Scor. Pos./2 Out	20	5	1	0	2	11	7	5	.250	.600	.444
Late Inning Pressure	28	5	0	0	2	4	6	6	.179	.393	.233
Leading Off	4	2	0	0	2	2	0	0	.500	2.000	.500
Runners On	15	3	0	0	0	2	2	3	.200	.200	.294
Runners/Scor. Pos.	7	1	0	0	0	2	2	1	.143	.143	.333

DRIVING IN RUNS	From 1B	From 2B	From 3B	Scoring Position
Totals	5/74	7/39	15/29	22/68
Percentage	7%	18%	52%	32%
Driving In Runners from 3B with Less than Two Out:	10/20			50%

Loves to face: Greg Harris (.667, 2-for-3, 1 HR)
Hates to face: Bert Blyleven (0-for-8, 4 SO)
Hitless in three at bats with bases loaded last season (running career mark to 0-for-10), but drove in four runs with walks.... One hit in 20 career at bats at the Metrodome.... Career total of 14 home runs, only two with runners on base.... Career batting average of .211 with runners in scoring position, including .184 with two outs.... Switch-hitter with balanced career batting averages (.235 vs. left-handers, .238 vs. right-handers) despite last season's imbalance. More power from right side: one home run per 22.4 at bats, compared to one per 53.2 AB batting left-handed.... Other career batting averages: .266 in day games, .211 in night games.

Gorman Thomas

Bats Right

Mariners/Brewers	AB	H	2B	3B	HR	RRF	BB	SO	BA	SA	OBA
Season	315	59	8	1	16	37	58	105	.187	.371	.316
vs. Left-Handers	97	17	3	0	5	10	25	26	.175	.361	.344
vs. Right-Handers	218	42	5	1	11	27	33	79	.193	.376	.302
Home	138	19	3	0	7	12	24	51	.138	.312	.270
Road	177	40	5	1	9	25	34	54	.226	.418	.351
Grass	188	38	5	1	9	20	43	61	.202	.383	.351
Artificial Turf	127	21	3	0	7	17	15	44	.165	.354	.259
April	64	14	1	0	5	11	12	26	.219	.469	.351
May	73	14	3	0	4	11	8	19	.192	.397	.272
June	33	5	0	0	1	4	7	10	.152	.242	.300
July	34	8	2	0	2	4	6	11	.235	.471	.350
August	76	13	1	0	3	6	16	27	.171	.303	.315
Sept./Oct.	35	5	1	1	1	1	9	12	.143	.314	.318
Leading Off Inn.	67	16	4	0	5	5	8	17	.239	.522	.329
Runners On	159	24	2	0	4	25	27	49	.151	.239	.274
Runners/Scor. Pos.	90	16	2	0	3	23	22	25	.178	.300	.339
Runners On/2 Out	79	7	0	0	0	4	13	31	.089	.089	.217
Scor. Pos./2 Out	43	4	0	0	0	4	11	15	.093	.093	.278
Late Inning Pressure	50	5	0	0	4	5	10	18	.100	.340	.250
Leading Off	9	2	0	0	1	1	1	1	.222	.556	.300
Runners On	25	1	0	0	1	2	4	9	.040	.160	.172
Runners/Scor. Pos.	11	0	0	0	0	0	4	4	.000	.000	.267

DRIVING IN RUNS	From 1B	From 2B	From 3B	Scoring Position
Totals	3/116	7/73	11/34	18/107
Percentage	3%	10%	32%	17%
Driving In Runners from 3B with Less than Two Out:		8/19		42%

Loves to face: Bruce Hurst (.391, 9-for-23, 4 HR)
Hates to face: Mike Morgan (.125, 2-for-16, 8 SO)
One of only five active players with five 30-HR seasons. The others: Mike Schmidt (12), Reggie Jackson (7), Dave Kingman (7), and Dale Murphy (5). . . . Bad enough that he batted .089 (7-for-79) with two outs and runners on base, but all seven hits were singles. . . . Over the 12 years of *The Player Analysis*, Thomas has batted .168 (17-for-101, four HR) with bases loaded. . . . Over the last three seasons Thomas has batted .043 (3-for-69) with runners on base in Late-Inning Pressure Situations. Last season he stranded all 14 runners he found in scoring position in LIP situations. . . . One of two players to hit below .230 in each of the past four seasons (minimum: 100 AB in each). The other: Steve Yeager.

Andre Thornton

Bats Right

Cleveland Indians	AB	H	2B	3B	HR	RRF	BB	SO	BA	SA	OBA
Season	401	92	14	0	17	67	65	67	.229	.392	.333
vs. Left-Handers	123	29	3	0	6	21	22	22	.236	.407	.356
vs. Right-Handers	278	63	11	0	11	46	43	45	.227	.385	.322
Home	222	62	8	0	12	46	29	31	.279	.477	.357
Road	179	30	6	0	5	21	36	36	.168	.285	.305
Grass	353	84	12	0	15	60	60	59	.238	.399	.344
Artificial Turf	48	8	2	0	2	7	5	8	.167	.333	.245
April	70	12	2	0	2	7	11	14	.171	.286	.289
May	92	19	4	0	5	12	16	13	.207	.413	.321
June	80	21	3	0	4	14	14	10	.263	.450	.368
July	74	20	2	0	3	20	9	17	.270	.419	.333
August	79	18	1	0	3	10	15	13	.228	.354	.347
Sept./Oct.	6	2	2	0	0	4	0	0	.333	.667	.333
Leading Off Inn.	115	21	0	0	5	5	15	21	.183	.348	.277
Runners On	194	47	7	0	7	57	30	34	.242	.387	.335
Runners/Scor. Pos.	102	28	4	0	5	50	21	19	.275	.461	.374
Runners On/2 Out	95	20	2	0	4	21	16	18	.211	.358	.324
Scor. Pos./2 Out	51	14	2	0	4	21	10	10	.275	.549	.393
Late Inning Pressure	46	9	3	0	1	7	10	7	.196	.326	.333
Leading Off	16	1	1	0	0	0	5	2	.063	.125	.286
Runners On	21	6	2	0	1	7	3	5	.286	.524	.360
Runners/Scor. Pos.	11	1	0	0	0	3	3	4	.091	.091	.267

DRIVING IN RUNS	From 1B	From 2B	From 3B	Scoring Position
Totals	9/137	19/85	22/40	41/125
Percentage	7%	22%	55%	33%
Driving In Runners from 3B with Less than Two Out:		16/23		70%

Loves to face: Chris Codiroli (6-for-6, 1 HR)
Hates to face: Charlie Leibrandt (0-for-14)
Batted 45 consecutive times without a runner in scoring position from May 15 through May 26, unusual for any player, but this is the cleanup hitter on the major leagues' batting average and scoring leader. . . . Four hits, including one home run, in five at bats with bases loaded last season. . . . Career total of 253 home runs ranks 2d among active players with more walks than strikeouts. The leader: Darrell Evans (347). . . . Yearly batting averages in Late-Inning Pressure Situations since 1983: .304, .298, .224, .196. . . . Six hits with two home runs in 14 pinch-hit at bats over past two seasons. . . . Has played only 57 games in the field during the 1980s, and not an inning since 1984.

Wayne Tolleson

Bats Left and Right

White Sox/Yankees	AB	H	2B	3B	HR	RRF	BB	SO	BA	SA	OBA
Season	475	126	16	5	3	43	52	76	.265	.339	.338
vs. Left-Handers	183	52	4	3	3	19	19	35	.284	.388	.350
vs. Right-Handers	292	74	12	2	0	24	33	41	.253	.308	.330
Home	230	60	8	3	1	24	24	33	.261	.335	.328
Road	245	66	8	2	2	19	28	43	.269	.343	.347
Grass	398	110	13	5	2	38	46	58	.276	.349	.350
Artificial Turf	77	16	3	0	1	5	6	18	.208	.286	.274
April	69	18	3	2	1	11	13	8	.261	.406	.373
May	92	23	1	1	1	5	12	22	.250	.315	.333
June	58	10	2	0	1	6	7	7	.172	.259	.262
July	44	16	1	0	0	7	6	6	.364	.386	.431
August	106	27	3	1	0	4	7	17	.255	.302	.298
Sept./Oct.	106	32	6	1	0	10	7	16	.302	.377	.357
Leading Off Inn.	118	33	2	3	1	1	16	22	.280	.373	.366
Runners On	187	50	9	2	2	42	21	25	.267	.369	.338
Runners/Scor. Pos.	103	29	6	1	1	38	12	13	.282	.388	.350
Runners On/2 Out	85	22	4	1	0	15	9	14	.259	.329	.330
Scor. Pos./2 Out	53	14	3	0	0	14	5	9	.264	.321	.328
Late Inning Pressure	79	20	2	2	1	4	12	20	.253	.367	.348
Leading Off	19	7	0	2	0	0	2	3	.368	.579	.429
Runners On	26	6	1	0	1	4	5	10	.231	.385	.344
Runners/Scor. Pos.	15	2	0	0	0	2	4	6	.133	.133	.300

DRIVING IN RUNS	From 1B	From 2B	From 3B	Scoring Position
Totals	6/136	14/81	20/45	34/126
Percentage	4%	17%	44%	27%
Driving In Runners from 3B with Less than Two Out:		11/14		79%

Loves to face: Mike Flanagan (.533, 8-for-15, 1 HR)
Hates to face: Mark Langston (1-for-15, 6 SO)
Most plate appearances (1903) of any active player without an intentional walk. If, for any reason, he cannot fulfill requirements of this title, next in line is Curtis Wilkerson (1203). . . . Led A.L. shortstops with 3.23 assists per nine innings last season (minimum: 500 innings). . . . Career breakdown: .272 with bases empty, .227 with runners on base, .203 with runners in scoring position. . . . Batting average with runners in scoring position was a career high. . . . Career batting average of .304 at Yankee Stadium is his highest at any A.L. ballpark. . . . Switch-hitter with higher career average from right side (.266 to .249), and only one home run in 1,139 career at bats vs. right-handers.

Jim Traber

Bats Left

Baltimore Orioles	AB	H	2B	3B	HR	RRF	BB	SO	BA	SA	OBA
Season	212	54	7	0	13	44	18	31	.255	.472	.321
vs. Left-Handers	35	7	0	0	2	9	3	6	.200	.371	.302
vs. Right-Handers	177	47	7	0	11	35	15	25	.266	.492	.325
Home	111	32	3	0	9	25	13	16	.288	.559	.375
Road	101	22	4	0	4	19	5	15	.218	.376	.259
Grass	188	47	6	0	11	39	18	29	.250	.457	.321
Artificial Turf	24	7	1	0	2	5	0	2	.292	.583	.320
April	0	0	0	0	0	0	0	0	—	—	—
May	0	0	0	0	0	0	0	0	—	—	—
June	0	0	0	0	0	0	0	0	—	—	—
July	43	14	2	0	5	15	4	5	.326	.721	.388
August	104	29	3	0	6	20	7	13	.279	.481	.331
Sept./Oct.	65	11	2	0	2	9	7	13	.169	.292	.260
Leading Off Inn.	47	10	3	0	1	1	4	8	.213	.340	.302
Runners On	105	32	0	0	8	39	9	12	.305	.552	.361
Runners/Scor. Pos.	58	15	1	0	3	28	7	6	.259	.431	.324
Runners On/2 Out	56	14	1	0	5	21	4	7	.250	.536	.311
Scor. Pos./2 Out	36	10	1	0	3	17	4	3	.278	.556	.350
Late Inning Pressure	37	12	0	0	0	6	2	6	.324	.324	.357
Leading Off	8	3	0	0	0	0	0	2	.375	.375	.375
Runners On	16	7	0	0	0	6	1	2	.438	.438	.450
Runners/Scor. Pos.	7	3	0	0	0	6	0	1	.429	.429	.400

DRIVING IN RUNS	From 1B	From 2B	From 3B	Scoring Position
Totals	9/86	8/51	14/26	22/77
Percentage	10%	16%	54%	29%
Driving In Runners from 3B with Less than Two Out:		9/14		64%

Loves to face: Bret Saberhagen (2-for-2, 2 HR)
Hates to face: Kirk McCaskill (0-for-5)
With 13 home runs in 212 at bats, it was Traber who had the best home run rate of any major-league rookie with 10 home runs last season: one every 16.3 at bats. In fact, Oakland slugger Jose Canseco finished *fifth*. The top 10: Traber, 16.3; Cory Snyder, 17.3; Mike Diaz, 17.4; Pete Incaviglia, 18.0; Canseco, 18.2; Danny Tartabull, 20.4; Ruben Sierra, 23.9; Barry Bonds, 25.8; Wally Joyner, 27.0; Kevin Mitchell, 27.3. . . . Six hits in 13 career at bats at Cleveland Stadium. . . . Stole 79 bases in five minor-league seasons, but you know Earl: Traber hasn't so much as attempted a steal in 75 games for O's.

Alan Trammell

Detroit Tigers — Bats Right

	AB	H	2B	3B	HR	RRF	BB	SO	BA	SA	OBA
Season	574	159	33	7	21	77	59	57	.277	.469	.347
vs. Left-Handers	204	57	16	3	8	24	19	19	.279	.505	.344
vs. Right-Handers	370	102	17	4	13	53	40	38	.276	.449	.349
Home	282	74	13	3	8	36	28	35	.262	.415	.335
Road	292	85	20	4	13	41	31	22	.291	.521	.359
Grass	482	128	26	7	17	61	52	52	.266	.454	.340
Artificial Turf	92	31	7	0	4	16	7	5	.337	.543	.386
April	66	16	6	2	3	10	4	8	.242	.530	.286
May	82	21	3	0	0	6	7	8	.256	.293	.315
June	113	27	5	0	2	14	7	11	.239	.336	.281
July	101	30	6	1	4	11	18	10	.297	.495	.415
August	118	36	6	3	6	21	10	11	.305	.559	.362
Sept./Oct.	94	29	7	1	6	15	13	9	.309	.596	.394
Leading Off Inn.	100	30	5	2	8	8	5	9	.300	.630	.333
Runners On	240	60	12	1	6	62	34	23	.250	.383	.345
Runners/Scor. Pos.	141	40	7	0	4	55	26	12	.284	.418	.390
Runners On/2 Out	106	29	7	1	3	31	17	10	.274	.443	.379
Scor. Pos./2 Out	72	21	5	0	3	28	12	6	.292	.486	.400
Late Inning Pressure	66	20	4	0	2	11	8	10	.303	.455	.395
Leading Off	17	8	1	0	1	0	0	0	.471	.706	.471
Runners On	33	11	2	0	1	10	6	5	.333	.485	.450
Runners/Scor. Pos.	20	6	1	0	0	8	4	4	.300	.350	.417

DRIVING IN RUNS	From 1B	From 2B	From 3B	Scoring Position
Totals	7/170	30/117	19/49	49/166
Percentage	4%	26%	39%	30%
Driving In Runners from 3B with Less than Two Out:		13/27		48%

Loves to face: Charlie Leibrandt (.500, 8-for-16, 2 HR)
Hates to face: Mike Mason (.067, 1-for-15)
Career total of 1258 games played at shortstop, and hasn't played even an inning at any other position. . . . Has hit 62 home runs over past four seasons, compared to 26 in four previous years. . . . Has homered in every A.L. ballpark except Comiskey Park (174 career AB). . . . Career batting average of .275 on grass fields; .316 on artificial surfaces, including .345 over past four seasons (2d highest in majors during that time, 250 AB minimum). . . . Career batting average of .363 (33-for-91) with bases loaded. . . . One of four A.L. players to steal at least 10 bases in every season since 1979. The others: Rickey Henderson, Willie Randolph, and Willie Wilson.

Willie Upshaw

Toronto Blue Jays — Bats Left

	AB	H	2B	3B	HR	RRF	BB	SO	BA	SA	OBA
Season	573	144	28	6	9	62	78	87	.251	.368	.341
vs. Left-Handers	179	40	7	1	4	19	17	38	.223	.341	.291
vs. Right-Handers	394	104	21	5	5	43	61	49	.264	.381	.362
Home	267	66	16	3	3	34	43	46	.247	.363	.350
Road	306	78	12	3	6	28	35	41	.255	.373	.332
Grass	238	59	8	2	5	21	31	31	.248	.361	.336
Artificial Turf	335	85	20	4	4	41	47	56	.254	.373	.345
April	70	21	3	1	1	12	15	12	.300	.414	.419
May	99	27	5	1	0	10	13	11	.273	.343	.363
June	91	21	5	1	1	10	16	20	.231	.341	.346
July	103	26	6	3	1	8	9	12	.252	.398	.316
August	115	26	8	0	3	10	12	20	.226	.374	.299
Sept./Oct.	95	23	1	0	3	12	13	12	.242	.347	.327
Leading Off Inn.	126	33	6	0	3	4	14	18	.262	.381	.340
Runners On	250	62	9	4	4	56	31	40	.248	.364	.329
Runners/Scor. Pos.	141	32	3	1	2	47	20	24	.227	.305	.315
Runners On/2 Out	108	22	3	2	3	25	12	23	.204	.352	.283
Scor. Pos./2 Out	69	13	1	1	1	19	7	13	.188	.275	.263
Late Inning Pressure	91	21	2	0	2	9	12	16	.231	.319	.317
Leading Off	29	6	1	0	0	0	3	4	.207	.241	.281
Runners On	33	8	1	0	1	8	5	7	.242	.364	.333
Runners/Scor. Pos.	18	4	0	0	0	6	4	4	.222	.222	.348

DRIVING IN RUNS	From 1B	From 2B	From 3B	Scoring Position
Totals	11/177	14/93	27/70	41/163
Percentage	6%	15%	39%	25%
Driving In Runners from 3B with Less than Two Out:		19/32		59%

Loves to face: Dan Petry (.452, 14-for-31, 3 HR)
Hates to face: Willie Hernandez (0-for-12)
Tied major-league record for first basemen with three errors in an inning on July 1. . . . Batted .220 in day games, .270 in night games last season. . . . Batting average with runners in scoring position was his worst of any full year in the majors. . . . Grounded into only five double plays in 122 opportunities, 4th-lowest rate in A.L. (minimum: 40 opportunities). . . . Has a career batting average better than .300 at Arlington Stadium only (.302). . . . Has batted for a higher average with bases empty than with runners on base in five of the last six seasons. . . . Career breakdown: .265 vs. left-handers, .269 vs. right-handers. . . . If Seaver doesn't play again, Upshaw was his 3640th, and last, strikeout victim (Sept. 19).

Greg Walker

Chicago White Sox — Bats Left

	AB	H	2B	3B	HR	RRF	BB	SO	BA	SA	OBA
Season	282	78	10	6	13	57	29	44	.277	.493	.345
vs. Left-Handers	89	21	3	1	2	14	11	17	.236	.360	.324
vs. Right-Handers	193	57	7	5	11	43	18	27	.295	.554	.355
Home	151	42	8	5	6	29	21	22	.278	.517	.366
Road	131	36	2	1	7	28	8	22	.275	.466	.319
Grass	235	64	8	5	11	49	26	36	.272	.489	.346
Artificial Turf	47	14	2	1	2	8	3	8	.298	.511	.340
April	22	8	2	1	2	4	2	3	.364	.818	.462
May	62	20	4	1	2	9	8	14	.323	.516	.408
June	98	19	3	1	5	25	10	17	.194	.398	.273
July	93	29	1	3	3	19	6	7	.312	.484	.347
August	7	2	0	0	1	2	1	3	.286	.714	.375
Sept./Oct.	0	0	0	0	0	0	0	0	—	—	—
Leading Off Inn.	80	23	2	4	3	3	6	17	.288	.525	.337
Runners On	123	33	6	1	7	51	16	17	.268	.504	.345
Runners/Scor. Pos.	73	20	2	0	6	46	12	9	.274	.548	.364
Runners On/2 Out	55	16	2	0	4	21	8	7	.291	.564	.381
Scor. Pos./2 Out	34	9	0	0	3	17	7	4	.265	.529	.390
Late Inning Pressure	43	13	3	1	0	6	0	10	.302	.419	.295
Leading Off	19	5	1	1	0	0	0	6	.263	.421	.263
Runners On	11	6	1	0	0	6	0	2	.545	.636	.500
Runners/Scor. Pos.	6	5	1	0	0	6	0	0	.833	1.000	.714

DRIVING IN RUNS	From 1B	From 2B	From 3B	Scoring Position
Totals	8/92	15/54	21/39	36/93
Percentage	9%	28%	54%	39%
Driving In Runners from 3B with Less than Two Out:		12/21		57%

Loves to face: Moose Haas (.438, 7-for-16, 3 HR)
Hates to face: Bruce Hurst (0-for-9, 4 SO)
Batted 98 points higher in day games (.345) than in night games (.247), 4th-largest difference in A.L. (minimum: 50 AB each). . . . Batted 103 points higher against teams with losing records (.331) than vs. teams with records above the .500 mark (.228). . . . Career average of .221 (one HR per 49.9 AB) vs. left-handers, .292 (one HR per 19.2 AB) vs. right-handers. . . . Had not committed an error in 34 consecutive games when his season ended on Aug. 2. . . . Yearly fielding percentages since 1984: .995, .994, .993. . . . Born October 6, 1959, the day the White Sox last won a World Series game: Bob Shaw's 1–0 win over Sandy Koufax in Game Five at the Coliseum, before the largest crowd in Series history, 92,706.

Gary Ward

Texas Rangers — Bats Right

	AB	H	2B	3B	HR	RRF	BB	SO	BA	SA	OBA
Season	380	120	15	2	5	51	31	72	.316	.405	.372
vs. Left-Handers	120	38	7	1	3	20	14	23	.317	.467	.388
vs. Right-Handers	260	82	8	1	2	31	17	49	.315	.377	.364
Home	193	62	8	1	3	24	13	34	.321	.420	.370
Road	187	58	7	1	2	27	18	38	.310	.390	.373
Grass	331	103	13	1	4	36	28	65	.311	.393	.370
Artificial Turf	49	17	2	1	1	15	3	7	.347	.490	.382
April	63	18	2	0	1	10	7	13	.286	.365	.357
May	81	21	4	0	1	9	11	15	.259	.346	.355
June	81	27	5	2	1	16	3	14	.333	.481	.368
July	70	25	2	0	1	4	5	10	.357	.429	.408
August	74	24	2	0	1	11	4	17	.324	.392	.354
Sept./Oct.	11	5	0	0	0	1	1	3	.455	.455	.500
Leading Off Inn.	100	34	4	0	1	1	9	17	.340	.410	.394
Runners On	150	51	8	2	3	49	13	29	.340	.480	.395
Runners/Scor. Pos.	82	31	7	2	1	44	8	21	.378	.549	.430
Runners On/2 Out	69	22	2	1	2	22	4	18	.319	.464	.365
Scor. Pos./2 Out	42	14	2	1	1	20	3	13	.333	.500	.391
Late Inning Pressure	56	19	1	2	2	10	5	11	.339	.536	.393
Leading Off	15	5	0	0	1	1	1	3	.333	.533	.375
Runners On	22	7	0	2	0	8	3	4	.318	.500	.400
Runners/Scor. Pos.	13	5	0	2	0	8	3	4	.385	.692	.500

DRIVING IN RUNS	From 1B	From 2B	From 3B	Scoring Position
Totals	7/112	23/61	16/36	39/97
Percentage	6%	38%	44%	40%
Driving In Runners from 3B with Less than Two Out:		9/15		60%

Loves to face: Chris Codiroli (.481, 13-for-27, 2 HR)
Hates to face: Dan Quisenberry (.150, 3-for-20)
One of four major leaguers to drive in better than 40 percent of base runners from scoring position last year. Top four: Johnny Grubb, 41.9; Larry Parrish, 41.5; Ray Knight, 40.3; Ward, 40.2. . . . Batting average against right-handers was a career high. . . . Batted .376 against teams with losing records last season, .261 vs. teams above the .500 mark. . . . After being signed by Yankees, said his opposite-field batting style was suited to Yankee Stadium. Well, he could've fooled us: Career batting average of .198 there (with 3 HR in 111 AB) is his lowest at any A.L. ballpark. . . . Has batted over .300 against left-handers in six of his eight seasons in the majors. . . . Career batting average of .303 with runners in scoring position.

Claudell Washington
New York Yankees — Bats Left

	AB	H	2B	3B	HR	RRF	BB	SO	BA	SA	OBA
Season	135	32	5	0	6	17	7	33	.237	.407	.285
vs. Left-Handers	14	3	1	0	0	0	1	2	.214	.286	.267
vs. Right-Handers	121	29	4	0	6	17	6	31	.240	.421	.287
Home	55	13	2	0	4	10	2	14	.236	.491	.263
Road	80	19	3	0	2	7	5	19	.238	.350	.299
Grass	108	29	4	0	6	16	4	27	.269	.472	.307
Artificial Turf	27	3	1	0	0	1	3	6	.111	.148	.200
April	0	0	0	0	0	0	0	0	—	—	—
May	0	0	0	0	0	0	0	0	—	—	—
June	4	1	0	0	0	0	0	1	.250	.250	.250
July	65	18	4	0	5	12	2	14	.277	.569	.299
August	42	6	0	0	0	2	3	11	.143	.143	.217
Sept./Oct.	24	7	1	0	1	3	2	7	.292	.458	.370
Leading Off Inn.	30	2	0	0	2	2	3	10	.067	.267	.152
Runners On	53	14	3	0	1	12	3	11	.264	.377	.316
Runners/Scor. Pos.	34	8	1	0	1	11	2	7	.235	.353	.297
Runners On/2 Out	27	7	1	0	1	7	1	4	.259	.407	.286
Scor. Pos./2 Out	20	6	1	0	1	7	1	2	.300	.500	.333
Late Inning Pressure	18	4	0	0	1	1	1	5	.222	.389	.263
Leading Off	4	0	0	0	0	0	0	2	.000	.000	.000
Runners On	7	1	0	0	0	0	1	3	.143	.143	.250
Runners/Scor. Pos.	2	0	0	0	0	0	0	1	.000	.000	.000

DRIVING IN RUNS	From 1B	From 2B	From 3B	Scoring Position
Totals	1/35	6/30	3/9	9/39
Percentage	3%	20%	33%	23%
Driving In Runners from 3B with Less than Two Out:		1/2		50%

Loves to face: Ron Darling (.467, 7-for-15, 3 HR)
Hates to face: Nolan Ryan (.159, 13-for-82, 34 SO)
Figures above are for A.L. only.... Has 130 career home runs, but no grand slams; that's the most home runs by any active player who is slamless. Batted 111 points higher in night games (.282) than in day games (.171), 7th-largest difference in the majors (minimum: 50 AB each).... Started only one game vs. a southpaw after joining the Yankees.... Last home run off a lefty: Sept. 30, 1985, off Frank DiPino.... Yearly batting averages in Late-Inning Pressure Situations since 1983: .377, .328, .213, .190.... Batting average of .118 (13-for-110) with the bases loaded over the last ten years.... Four hits in seven at bats as a rookie in 1974 World Series, has been on two L.C.S. losers since (1975 A's, 1982 Braves).

Lou Whitaker
Detroit Tigers — Bats Left

	AB	H	2B	3B	HR	RRF	BB	SO	BA	SA	OBA
Season	584	157	26	6	20	75	63	70	.269	.437	.338
vs. Left-Handers	163	36	4	2	3	21	15	33	.221	.325	.283
vs. Right-Handers	421	121	22	4	17	54	48	37	.287	.480	.359
Home	286	71	11	5	8	40	37	37	.248	.406	.334
Road	298	86	15	1	12	35	26	33	.289	.464	.341
Grass	499	136	22	6	14	64	54	59	.273	.425	.341
Artificial Turf	85	21	4	0	6	11	9	11	.247	.506	.319
April	65	18	4	1	0	5	3	8	.277	.369	.304
May	103	30	7	1	5	16	10	10	.291	.524	.354
June	118	29	5	2	4	14	12	17	.246	.424	.313
July	99	26	2	1	3	5	9	11	.263	.394	.324
August	110	30	5	1	5	26	18	13	.273	.473	.369
Sept./Oct.	89	24	3	0	3	9	11	11	.270	.404	.350
Leading Off Inn.	199	51	10	3	8	8	20	23	.256	.457	.324
Runners On	225	67	9	2	10	65	28	30	.298	.489	.370
Runners/Scor. Pos.	121	29	3	2	2	48	17	18	.240	.347	.324
Runners On/2 Out	82	28	5	0	4	28	11	9	.341	.549	.419
Scor. Pos./2 Out	54	17	2	0	2	23	8	4	.315	.463	.403
Late Inning Pressure	78	22	4	0	0	4	8	12	.282	.333	.341
Leading Off	13	4	1	0	0	0	3	1	.308	.385	.438
Runners On	34	9	1	0	0	4	5	6	.265	.294	.341
Runners/Scor. Pos.	12	2	0	0	0	4	5	2	.167	.167	.368

DRIVING IN RUNS	From 1B	From 2B	From 3B	Scoring Position
Totals	12/156	22/96	21/53	43/149
Percentage	8%	23%	40%	29%
Driving In Runners from 3B with Less than Two Out:		14/28		50%

Loves to face: Dave Stewart (.875, 7-for-8)
Hates to face: Bob Shirley (0-for-10)
Tigers' regular second baseman for nine consecutive years. Last man to do that was Charlie Gehringer, Detroit's regular second baseman from 1926 through 1941.... Tigers allowed an average of 4.41 runs per nine innings with Whitaker at second base last season, 4.67 with Brookens, 4.91 with Baker.... Homered against every opposing A.L. club except Texas last season.... Grounded into three double plays in 1985, 20 GIDPs in 1986.... Yearly batting averages since 1984: .289, .279, .269. Looks like a .259 season in 1987.... Career batting average of .355 (33-for-93, 1 HR) with bases loaded.... Has never played a game in the field at any position other than second base (1264 games).

Frank White
Kansas City Royals — Bats Right

	AB	H	2B	3B	HR	RRF	BB	SO	BA	SA	OBA
Season	566	154	37	3	22	86	43	88	.272	.465	.322
vs. Left-Handers	149	40	7	1	1	11	17	21	.268	.349	.337
vs. Right-Handers	417	114	30	2	21	75	26	67	.273	.506	.316
Home	277	78	18	2	12	55	21	38	.282	.491	.329
Road	289	76	19	1	10	31	22	50	.263	.439	.315
Grass	223	48	11	0	8	21	20	45	.215	.372	.280
Artificial Turf	343	106	26	3	14	65	23	43	.309	.525	.349
April	77	22	6	1	1	11	2	13	.286	.429	.300
May	108	29	7	0	5	19	6	19	.269	.472	.304
June	97	28	5	1	2	12	7	11	.289	.423	.340
July	89	20	4	0	5	16	13	14	.225	.438	.314
August	100	27	8	0	5	20	11	18	.270	.500	.342
Sept./Oct.	95	28	7	1	4	8	4	13	.295	.516	.327
Leading Off Inn.	138	36	8	1	6	6	10	24	.261	.464	.320
Runners On	261	72	16	1	8	72	23	40	.276	.437	.326
Runners/Scor. Pos.	162	41	10	1	4	62	17	23	.253	.401	.312
Runners On/2 Out	130	31	5	0	4	23	11	20	.238	.369	.298
Scor. Pos./2 Out	88	16	3	0	2	19	9	15	.182	.284	.258
Late Inning Pressure	92	28	4	0	6	17	6	17	.304	.543	.343
Leading Off	23	8	3	0	3	3	3	3	.348	.870	.423
Runners On	44	12	0	0	3	14	2	10	.273	.477	.298
Runners/Scor. Pos.	23	6	0	0	2	12	2	3	.261	.522	.308

DRIVING IN RUNS	From 1B	From 2B	From 3B	Scoring Position
Totals	12/195	27/124	25/65	52/189
Percentage	6%	22%	38%	28%
Driving In Runners from 3B with Less than Two Out:		22/32		69%

Loves to face: Mike Morgan (.591, 13-for-22, 1 HR)
Hates to face: Roger Clemens (.059, 1-for-17)
One of two major leaguers to match or exceed his previous year's home run total in every season since 1981. The other: Lloyd Moseby.... Royals had a record of 19–2 in games in which he homered. ... Had hit 53 of 109 career home runs against left-handers through the 1985 season. Only 1986 home run vs. a left-hander was Aug. 17 off Ron Guidry.... Has hit a grand slam home run in each of the last three seasons.... Played one game at shortstop (first since 1977) and one game at third base (first since 1975) last season. Only four men have started opening day at second base for the Royals in their 18-year history: White (1976–86), Cookie Rojas (1971–75), Luis Alcaraz (1970), and Jerry Adair (1969).

Ernie Whitt
Toronto Blue Jays — Bats Left

	AB	H	2B	3B	HR	RRF	BB	SO	BA	SA	OBA
Season	395	106	19	2	16	58	35	39	.268	.448	.326
vs. Left-Handers	46	17	0	0	3	7	2	8	.370	.565	.396
vs. Right-Handers	349	89	19	2	13	51	33	31	.255	.433	.317
Home	189	50	12	2	7	27	22	21	.265	.460	.341
Road	206	56	7	0	9	31	13	18	.272	.437	.311
Grass	162	42	4	0	8	22	12	12	.259	.432	.307
Artificial Turf	233	64	15	2	8	36	23	27	.275	.459	.339
April	12	0	0	0	0	0	0	1	.000	.000	.000
May	82	17	3	0	4	15	11	7	.207	.390	.298
June	68	20	4	0	4	11	7	1	.294	.529	.360
July	79	19	3	1	2	10	6	8	.241	.380	.294
August	82	26	6	1	3	15	3	14	.317	.524	.337
Sept./Oct.	72	24	3	0	3	7	8	8	.333	.500	.395
Leading Off Inn.	82	20	5	0	5	5	6	8	.244	.500	.295
Runners On	193	57	9	1	6	48	19	21	.295	.446	.353
Runners/Scor. Pos.	107	25	6	0	2	38	12	14	.234	.346	.303
Runners On/2 Out	69	19	3	0	2	13	12	6	.275	.406	.383
Scor. Pos./2 Out	44	8	2	0	1	11	10	3	.182	.295	.333
Late Inning Pressure	68	24	0	0	3	9	3	5	.353	.515	.375
Leading Off	21	6	0	0	3	3	2	1	.286	.714	.348
Runners On	20	9	0	0	0	6	1	2	.450	.450	.455
Runners/Scor. Pos.	12	5	0	0	0	6	0	1	.417	.417	.385

DRIVING IN RUNS	From 1B	From 2B	From 3B	Scoring Position
Totals	9/143	15/79	18/51	33/130
Percentage	6%	19%	35%	25%
Driving In Runners from 3B with Less than Two Out:		14/30		47%

Loves to face: Richard Dotson (.361, 13-for-36, 4 HR)
Hates to face: Don Aase (0-for-10)
Batted .538 (14-for-26) vs. Yankees last season. Career batting average of .342 (25-for-73, 3 HR) at Yankee Stadium.... Batting average with runners on base was a career high.... Five hits in 13 at bats with bases loaded last season.... Has batted over .300 in Late-Inning Pressure Situations in three of the last four seasons.... Yearly batting averages vs. left-handed pitchers since 1982: .143 (35 AB), .114 (35 AB), .160 (25 AB), .213 (75 AB), .370 (46 AB).... Blue Jays allowed an average of 4.36 runs per nine innings with Whitt calling the signals, 4.65 with Buck Martinez, and 4.89 with Jeff Hearron.... Made major-league debut with the Red Sox on Sept. 12, 1976. His first big-league batterymate? Luis Tiant.

Alan Wiggins

Bats Left and Right

Baltimore Orioles

	AB	H	2B	3B	HR	RRF	BB	SO	BA	SA	OBA
Season	239	60	3	1	0	12	22	20	.251	.272	.309
vs. Left-Handers	67	20	1	0	0	3	4	5	.299	.313	.333
vs. Right-Handers	172	40	2	1	0	9	18	15	.233	.256	.301
Home	124	34	2	1	0	6	14	7	.274	.306	.345
Road	115	26	1	0	0	6	8	13	.226	.235	.270
Grass	196	47	2	1	0	8	19	15	.240	.260	.304
Artificial Turf	43	13	1	0	0	4	3	5	.302	.326	.333
April	62	12	2	0	0	3	4	6	.194	.226	.239
May	90	32	1	1	0	7	11	4	.356	.389	.417
June	69	12	0	0	0	1	7	8	.174	.174	.247
July	18	4	0	0	0	1	0	2	.222	.222	.222
August	0	0	0	0	0	0	0	0	—	—	—
Sept./Oct.	0	0	0	0	0	0	0	0	—	—	—
Leading Off Inn.	104	25	1	1	0	0	12	11	.240	.269	.319
Runners On	69	18	2	0	0	12	7	3	.261	.290	.313
Runners/Scor. Pos.	35	10	1	0	0	12	4	2	.286	.314	.326
Runners On/2 Out	32	7	1	0	0	3	4	2	.219	.250	.306
Scor. Pos./2 Out	16	5	1	0	0	3	4	1	.313	.375	.450
Late Inning Pressure	33	6	0	0	0	1	2	4	.182	.182	.229
Leading Off	5	2	0	0	0	0	0	0	.400	.400	.400
Runners On	15	3	0	0	0	1	1	2	.200	.200	.250
Runners/Scor. Pos.	5	0	0	0	0	1	0	1	.000	.000	.000

DRIVING IN RUNS	From 1B	From 2B	From 3B	Scoring Position
Totals	0/55	2/31	10/20	12/51
Percentage	0%	6%	50%	24%
Driving In Runners from 3B with Less than Two Out:		8/14		57%

Loves to face: Tommy John (.833, 5-for-6)
Hates to face: Joaquin Andujar (.130, 3-for-23)
Has not homered in 537 A.L. at bats, but two of his four N.L. home runs were hit off current Angels pitchers: Gary Lucas and John Candelaria. Last home run: Aug. 20, 1984, off Sid Fernandez. . . . Averaged 2.65 assists per nine innings last season, 2d lowest among A.L. second basemen (minimum: 500 innings). . . . Led the majors with most double-play opportunities (38) without grounding into one. . . . Batted .315 vs. teams with losing records, .198 against teams above the .500 mark. . . . Career breakdown: .302 vs. left-handers, .245 vs. right-handers. Has never homered against a right-handed pitcher. . . . One hit in 14 career at bats at Fenway Park. . . . Has never struck out with bases loaded (28 career PA).

Rob Wilfong

Bats Left

California Angels

	AB	H	2B	3B	HR	RRF	BB	SO	BA	SA	OBA
Season	288	63	11	3	3	35	16	34	.219	.309	.263
vs. Left-Handers	22	7	1	1	0	3	0	5	.318	.455	.318
vs. Right-Handers	266	56	10	2	3	32	16	29	.211	.297	.259
Home	152	34	6	0	3	21	9	18	.224	.322	.270
Road	136	29	5	3	0	14	7	16	.213	.294	.255
Grass	244	52	9	1	3	29	12	29	.213	.295	.252
Artificial Turf	44	11	2	2	0	6	4	5	.250	.386	.320
April	55	14	4	2	0	7	3	3	.255	.400	.293
May	51	14	0	0	2	6	5	8	.275	.392	.339
June	59	14	3	0	0	11	2	10	.237	.288	.270
July	41	9	2	1	0	7	3	5	.220	.317	.267
August	39	7	2	0	0	1	1	1	.179	.231	.200
Sept./Oct.	43	5	0	0	1	3	2	7	.116	.186	.174
Leading Off Inn.	79	14	0	0	1	1	5	8	.177	.241	.235
Runners On	114	32	4	2	0	32	5	17	.281	.351	.311
Runners/Scor. Pos.	76	21	2	2	0	31	5	14	.276	.355	.321
Runners On/2 Out	42	13	3	1	0	13	2	8	.310	.429	.356
Scor. Pos./2 Out	28	10	2	1	0	12	2	5	.357	.500	.419
Late Inning Pressure	40	12	1	0	1	5	1	3	.300	.400	.317
Leading Off	10	3	1	0	0	0	0	0	.300	.400	.300
Runners On	16	6	0	0	0	4	1	3	.375	.375	.412
Runners/Scor. Pos.	8	2	0	0	0	4	1	2	.250	.250	.333

DRIVING IN RUNS	From 1B	From 2B	From 3B	Scoring Position
Totals	2/85	13/62	17/35	30/97
Percentage	2%	21%	49%	31%
Driving In Runners from 3B with Less than Two Out:		13/23		57%

Loves to face: Bill Wegman (.556, 5-for-9, 1 HR)
Hates to face: Don Aase (.067, 1-for-15)
Batted 103 points higher with runners on base than with bases empty, 2d-largest difference in A.L. (minimum: 100 AB both ways). . . . Career breakdown: .235 with bases empty, .269 with runners on base, .278 with runners in scoring position. . . . Career batting average of .306 (19-for-62) with bases loaded. . . . Don't be fooled by that .318 average in 22 at bats vs. lefties last season. Career batting average of .176 vs. left-handers, .259 vs. right-handers. . . . Last home run against a southpaw was June 22, 1985, off Chisox' Bob Fallon. . . . Likes the Kingdome (.320 career), not the Metrodome (.175 career). . . . Ranked 3d among A.L. second basemen with 3.34 assists per nine innings last season (minimum: 500 innings).

Curtis Wilkerson

Bats Left and Right

Texas Rangers

	AB	H	2B	3B	HR	RRF	BB	SO	BA	SA	OBA
Season	236	56	10	3	0	16	11	42	.237	.305	.273
vs. Left-Handers	27	3	0	0	0	1	2	5	.111	.111	.172
vs. Right-Handers	209	53	10	3	0	15	9	37	.254	.330	.286
Home	116	27	4	3	0	10	6	17	.233	.319	.274
Road	120	29	6	0	0	6	5	25	.242	.292	.272
Grass	194	44	8	3	0	14	9	32	.227	.299	.263
Artificial Turf	42	12	2	0	0	2	2	10	.286	.333	.318
April	46	8	1	0	0	2	3	7	.174	.196	.224
May	43	12	3	0	0	3	1	8	.279	.349	.295
June	69	19	3	0	0	5	2	13	.275	.319	.301
July	42	7	1	2	0	4	2	7	.167	.286	.205
August	21	9	2	1	0	1	2	3	.429	.619	.478
Sept./Oct.	15	1	0	0	0	1	1	4	.067	.067	.125
Leading Off Inn.	55	12	1	1	0	0	4	15	.218	.273	.283
Runners On	83	21	4	2	0	16	4	12	.253	.349	.284
Runners/Scor. Pos.	50	13	3	1	0	15	3	9	.260	.360	.296
Runners On/2 Out	39	11	3	1	0	7	2	6	.282	.410	.317
Scor. Pos./2 Out	24	6	2	0	0	6	2	5	.250	.333	.308
Late Inning Pressure	20	4	0	0	0	0	0	5	.200	.200	.238
Leading Off	5	0	0	0	0	0	0	3	.000	.000	.167
Runners On	4	1	0	0	0	0	0	0	.250	.250	.250
Runners/Scor. Pos.	2	1	0	0	0	0	0	0	.500	.500	.500

DRIVING IN RUNS	From 1B	From 2B	From 3B	Scoring Position
Totals	2/55	4/36	10/20	14/56
Percentage	4%	11%	50%	25%
Driving In Runners from 3B with Less than Two Out:		6/10		60%

Loves to face: Kirk McCaskill (.438, 7-for-16)
Hates to face: Don Sutton (0-for-15)
Career batting average of .228 vs. left-handers, .246 vs. right-handers. Ratio of 4.67 strikeouts per walk batting left-handed, 1.56 batting right-handed. . . . Total of 1203 career plate appearances, 2d most among active major leaguers who have never been intentionally walked. . . . Games started, year by year since 1984: 144, 111, 63. . . . Batted .174 in day games, .263 in night games last season. . . . Batting average with runners in scoring position was a career high, despite his lowest overall average since 1983. . . . One of eight players with an on-base average below .300 in each of the last three seasons (minimum: 200 PA). . . . Has hit only one major-league home run: Sept. 8, 1984, off John Butcher.

Willie Wilson

Bats Left and Right

Kansas City Royals

	AB	H	2B	3B	HR	RRF	BB	SO	BA	SA	OBA
Season	631	170	20	7	9	46	31	97	.269	.366	.313
vs. Left-Handers	175	54	5	2	4	13	4	33	.309	.429	.328
vs. Right-Handers	456	116	15	5	5	33	27	64	.254	.342	.307
Home	309	82	8	6	5	20	20	40	.265	.379	.322
Road	322	88	12	1	4	26	11	57	.273	.354	.303
Grass	239	65	9	1	2	18	11	48	.272	.343	.310
Artificial Turf	392	105	11	6	7	28	20	49	.268	.380	.314
April	76	16	1	0	1	8	2	12	.211	.263	.247
May	118	33	3	0	3	11	8	17	.280	.381	.336
June	113	31	3	4	0	5	10	19	.274	.372	.339
July	105	25	5	2	1	8	6	16	.238	.352	.292
August	109	32	4	0	1	6	2	15	.294	.358	.319
Sept./Oct.	110	33	4	1	3	8	3	18	.300	.436	.319
Leading Off Inn.	187	43	5	2	4	4	8	31	.230	.342	.269
Runners On	235	63	8	2	2	39	13	29	.268	.345	.308
Runners/Scor. Pos.	136	39	2	2	1	37	7	17	.287	.353	.324
Runners On/2 Out	96	24	0	1	0	14	8	9	.250	.323	.308
Scor. Pos./2 Out	66	13	1	0	0	12	5	8	.197	.212	.254
Late Inning Pressure	94	25	1	1	1	7	5	19	.266	.330	.303
Leading Off	18	3	0	0	0	2	4	.167	.167	.250
Runners On	44	9	1	1	0	6	1	9	.205	.273	.222
Runners/Scor. Pos.	29	6	0	1	0	6	1	7	.207	.276	.233

DRIVING IN RUNS	From 1B	From 2B	From 3B	Scoring Position
Totals	2/164	16/103	18/51	34/154
Percentage	1%	16%	35%	22%
Driving In Runners from 3B with Less than Two Out:		13/23		57%

Loves to face: John Candelaria (.714, 5-for-7)
Hates to face: Tom Candiotti (.125, 2-for-16, 5 SO)
Has stolen 30 or more bases in 9 consecutive seasons. Only four players in major-league history have 30 or more steals in 10 straight years: Brock (14), Cobb (12), Wagner (11), and Campaneris (10). . . . Career total of 187 at bats at the Oakland Coliseum, the highest total for players without a home run there over past 12 seasons. Same is true of his 173 career at bats at Fenway Park. . . . Has a higher career batting average on grass fields (.302) than on artificial turf (.293). . . . Set career-high marks in home runs (9) and strikeouts (97). . . . Career batting average of .226 (14-for-62, 1 HR) with the bases loaded. . . . Lowest overall batting average since 1978 dropped his career average below .300, to .297.

Dave Winfield

New York Yankees — Bats Right

	AB	H	2B	3B	HR	RRF	BB	SO	BA	SA	OBA
Season	565	148	31	5	24	106	77	106	.262	.462	.349
vs. Left-Handers	197	51	10	3	12	41	37	29	.259	.523	.373
vs. Right-Handers	368	97	21	2	12	65	40	77	.264	.429	.336
Home	279	76	15	3	12	57	40	46	.272	.477	.362
Road	286	72	16	2	12	49	37	60	.252	.448	.336
Grass	476	126	28	5	22	98	68	87	.265	.483	.355
Artificial Turf	89	22	3	0	2	8	9	19	.247	.348	.316
April	73	20	6	1	1	10	17	15	.274	.425	.411
May	95	20	5	1	6	21	16	18	.211	.474	.316
June	99	21	3	1	5	16	16	22	.212	.414	.322
July	77	26	6	1	4	20	7	12	.338	.597	.400
August	104	30	5	0	3	13	11	16	.288	.423	.357
Sept./Oct.	117	31	6	1	5	26	10	23	.265	.462	.320
Leading Off Inn.	117	31	8	0	4	4	18	23	.265	.436	.368
Runners On	293	79	13	5	14	96	41	48	.270	.491	.355
Runners/Scor. Pos.	170	50	8	2	6	76	27	35	.294	.471	.379
Runners On/2 Out	136	31	7	1	5	38	21	24	.228	.404	.331
Scor. Pos./2 Out	86	22	4	0	2	30	15	24	.256	.372	.366
Late Inning Pressure	75	18	3	0	1	6	7	16	.240	.320	.298
Leading Off	17	8	1	0	0	0	1	4	.471	.529	.500
Runners On	30	5	0	0	0	5	3	4	.167	.167	.229
Runners/Scor. Pos.	20	4	0	0	0	5	2	2	.200	.200	.250

DRIVING IN RUNS	From 1B	From 2B	From 3B	Scoring Position
Totals	16/217	26/125	40/78	66/203
Percentage	7%	21%	51%	33%
Driving In Runners from 3B with Less than Two Out:			30/41	73%

Loves to face: Mike Moore (.667, 8-for-12, 1 HR)
Hates to face: Moose Haas (.118, 2-for-17)

Walked four times with bases loaded last season.... Career batting average of .186 at County Stadium.... Batted .307 in day games, .239 at night.... Has batted for a higher average in unpressured situations than in Late-Inning Pressure Situations in each of his six seasons with New York.... Career average of 1.29 walks per strikeout vs. left-handers, one for every 0.62 strikeouts vs. right-handers. Despite that, he has hit for a higher average against right-handers than southpaws in four of the last five seasons (1983 being the exception).... Born Oct. 3, 1951, the day of Bobby Thomson's pennant-winning home run.... For more on Winfield, see the Yankees essay.

Butch Wynegar

New York Yankees — Bats Left and Right

	AB	H	2B	3B	HR	RRF	BB	SO	BA	SA	OBA
Season	194	40	4	1	7	29	30	21	.206	.345	.310
vs. Left-Handers	89	21	2	1	6	20	11	11	.236	.483	.317
vs. Right-Handers	105	19	2	0	1	9	19	10	.181	.229	.304
Home	104	24	2	1	3	16	13	8	.231	.356	.314
Road	90	16	2	0	4	13	17	13	.178	.333	.306
Grass	164	36	4	1	4	23	25	16	.220	.329	.319
Artificial Turf	30	4	0	0	3	6	5	5	.133	.433	.257
April	32	6	1	0	2	7	4	4	.188	.406	.278
May	64	12	1	0	3	12	16	6	.188	.344	.333
June	47	13	0	0	1	5	4	5	.277	.340	.327
July	51	9	2	1	1	5	8	6	.176	.314	.283
August	0	0	0	0	0	0	0	0	—	—	—
Sept./Oct.	0	0	0	0	0	0	0	0	—	—	—
Leading Off Inn.	42	8	1	0	1	1	6	5	.190	.286	.292
Runners On	88	17	1	0	4	26	21	11	.193	.341	.342
Runners/Scor. Pos.	46	11	0	0	2	26	15	6	.239	.500	.413
Runners On/2 Out	41	9	0	0	2	13	9	6	.220	.366	.360
Scor. Pos./2 Out	23	7	0	0	2	13	7	2	.304	.565	.467
Late Inning Pressure	38	8	1	0	0	4	4	7	.211	.237	.286
Leading Off	15	3	1	0	0	0	2	2	.200	.267	.294
Runners On	13	3	0	0	0	4	2	3	.231	.231	.333
Runners/Scor. Pos.	8	3	0	0	0	4	2	1	.375	.375	.500

DRIVING IN RUNS	From 1B	From 2B	From 3B	Scoring Position
Totals	4/75	7/38	11/20	18/58
Percentage	5%	18%	55%	31%
Driving In Runners from 3B with Less than Two Out:			6/8	75%

Loves to face: Juan Agosto (.556, 5-for-9, 1 HR)
Hates to face: Mark Langston (0-for-11)

Yankees won all seven games in which he hit home runs.... Batting average in July was 5th lowest in A.L. (minimum: 50 AB).... Yearly batting averages since 1983: .296, .267, .223, .206.... Hit 10 home runs in each of his first two seasons with the Twins, but has not reached double figures since.... Career batting average of .246 at Yankee Stadium, .247 at Anaheim Stadium.... Has homered in every A.L. ballpark except Fenway Park (168 career AB).... Only player to hit better with two outs and runners on than overall in each of the last six seasons.

Mike Young

Baltimore Orioles — Bats Left and Right

	AB	H	2B	3B	HR	RRF	BB	SO	BA	SA	OBA
Season	369	93	15	1	9	43	49	90	.252	.371	.342
vs. Left-Handers	125	34	5	1	3	15	16	26	.272	.400	.357
vs. Right-Handers	244	59	10	0	6	28	33	64	.242	.357	.335
Home	167	45	9	0	5	17	22	35	.269	.413	.359
Road	202	48	6	1	4	26	27	55	.238	.337	.328
Grass	310	78	11	0	9	35	39	69	.252	.374	.339
Artificial Turf	59	15	4	1	0	8	10	21	.254	.356	.357
April	51	14	3	0	0	5	12	13	.275	.333	.413
May	74	19	7	0	1	7	15	18	.257	.392	.389
June	82	19	1	0	4	14	8	24	.232	.390	.297
July	51	9	1	1	0	5	6	14	.176	.235	.259
August	7	1	0	0	1	1	0	1	.143	.571	.143
Sept./Oct.	104	31	3	0	3	11	8	20	.298	.413	.357
Leading Off Inn.	67	16	1	0	2	2	4	13	.239	.343	.311
Runners On	195	52	8	0	2	36	26	44	.267	.338	.348
Runners/Scor. Pos.	113	28	4	0	1	34	12	27	.248	.310	.313
Runners On/2 Out	83	16	2	0	1	14	8	26	.193	.253	.264
Scor. Pos./2 Out	55	10	1	0	1	14	7	18	.182	.255	.274
Late Inning Pressure	53	14	2	0	1	8	9	11	.264	.358	.365
Leading Off	11	1	1	0	0	0	0	2	.091	.182	.091
Runners On	30	11	1	0	1	8	5	4	.367	.500	.444
Runners/Scor. Pos.	20	6	1	0	1	8	4	4	.300	.500	.400

DRIVING IN RUNS	From 1B	From 2B	From 3B	Scoring Position
Totals	1/149	14/94	19/45	33/139
Percentage	1%	15%	42%	24%
Driving In Runners from 3B with Less than Two Out:			12/20	60%

Loves to face: Bruce Hurst (.455, 5-for-11, 3 HR)
Hates to face: Jay Howell (0-for-8, 5 SO)

Has hit home runs in every current A.L. ballpark except its two domed stadiums, the Metrodome (50 career AB) and the Kingdome (51 AB).... Career batting average of .400 (14-for-35, 1 HR) with bases loaded.... Career batting average of .201 with two outs and runners in scoring position.... Rotisserie-league advice: grab Young around midseason. Batting average was 5th lowest in A.L. during month of July (minimum: 50 AB); didn't hit his first home run last season until his 82d at bat.... Good second-half hitter: .244 for career (one HR per 33 AB) before the All-Star break; .267 (one HR per 19 AB) after.... Only A.L. player to hit more than 25 home runs in 1985 (he had 28), and fewer than 10 last season.

Robin Yount

Milwaukee Brewers — Bats Right

	AB	H	2B	3B	HR	RRF	BB	SO	BA	SA	OBA
Season	522	163	31	7	9	49	62	73	.312	.450	.388
vs. Left-Handers	121	30	2	1	3	11	18	18	.248	.355	.343
vs. Right-Handers	401	133	29	6	6	38	44	55	.332	.479	.402
Home	259	77	12	6	4	24	28	37	.297	.436	.370
Road	263	86	19	1	5	25	34	36	.327	.464	.406
Grass	452	139	20	6	7	44	52	64	.308	.425	.382
Artificial Turf	70	24	11	1	2	5	10	9	.343	.614	.425
April	71	29	4	1	1	7	6	9	.408	.535	.462
May	69	23	5	0	1	6	8	10	.333	.449	.403
June	85	27	8	1	1	5	15	12	.318	.471	.416
July	93	23	3	3	0	13	7	13	.247	.344	.343
August	103	32	7	0	1	10	14	11	.311	.408	.398
Sept./Oct.	101	29	4	2	5	14	6	14	.287	.515	.333
Leading Off Inn.	120	38	10	2	4	4	11	16	.317	.533	.379
Runners On	196	60	7	3	2	42	31	31	.306	.403	.403
Runners/Scor. Pos.	102	29	4	1	0	35	24	19	.284	.343	.414
Runners On/2 Out	75	21	1	2	0	18	11	13	.280	.347	.379
Scor. Pos./2 Out	47	11	1	1	0	17	9	10	.234	.298	.357
Late Inning Pressure	75	26	6	0	1	7	10	8	.347	.467	.419
Leading Off	21	8	2	0	1	1	1	4	.381	.619	.409
Runners On	30	10	3	0	0	6	5	1	.333	.433	.417
Runners/Scor. Pos.	14	3	2	0	0	5	4	0	.214	.357	.368

DRIVING IN RUNS	From 1B	From 2B	From 3B	Scoring Position
Totals	8/145	17/84	15/36	32/120
Percentage	6%	20%	42%	27%
Driving In Runners from 3B with Less than Two Out:			11/19	58%

Loves to face: Brad Havens (.500, 11-for-22, 1 HR)
Hates to face: Bobby Witt (0-for-9, 6 SO)

Led A.L. outfielders in fielding last season (.997), and became first player in A.L. history to lead league in fielding both in outfield and at an infield position; he had led league at shortstop in 1981. Pete Rose did it most recently in N.L.... Batted 84 points higher vs. right-handed pitchers than against left-handed pitchers, 4th-largest difference in A.L. (minimum: 100 AB vs. each).... Batting average vs. right-handed pitchers was his highest in 12 years of *The Player Analysis*.... Career batting average at the Metrodome (.366) is his highest at any A.L. ballpark.... From the Feast or Famine Dept.: yearly batting averages in Late-Inning Pressure Situations since 1982: .194, .351, .374, .191, .347.

Baltimore Orioles

	AB	H	2B	3B	HR	RRF	BB	SO	BA	SA	OBA
Season	5524	1425	223	13	169	696	563	862	.258	.395	.327
vs. Left-Handers	1527	413	68	3	57	190	145	223	.270	.431	.336
vs. Right-Handers	3997	1012	155	10	112	506	418	639	.253	.381	.324
Home	2625	667	98	2	91	344	271	407	.254	.397	.325
Road	2899	758	125	11	78	352	292	455	.261	.393	.329
Grass	4623	1169	177	8	140	578	478	716	.253	.385	.323
Artificial Turf	901	256	46	5	29	118	85	146	.284	.443	.348
April	673	176	35	1	15	81	73	106	.262	.383	.331
May	861	232	33	4	28	124	102	134	.269	.415	.347
June	960	246	34	1	30	116	91	156	.256	.388	.320
July	941	257	43	5	35	130	95	143	.273	.441	.344
August	987	244	33	1	32	128	101	149	.247	.380	.319
Sept./Oct.	1102	270	45	1	29	117	101	174	.245	.367	.309
Leading Off Inn.	1319	365	55	2	44	44	120	177	.277	.422	.341
Runners On	2485	630	100	5	76	602	251	392	.254	.390	.320
Runners/Scor. Pos.	1332	332	59	3	41	518	162	224	.249	.390	.325
Runners On/2 Out	993	221	38	3	30	218	102	173	.223	.358	.300
Scor. Pos./2 Out	596	129	25	1	21	192	79	103	.216	.367	.313
Late Inning Pressure	847	214	38	2	22	108	83	155	.253	.380	.319
Leading Off	213	52	10	0	5	5	13	31	.244	.362	.294
Runners On	370	99	15	1	9	95	33	68	.268	.386	.324
Runners/Scor. Pos.	205	53	13	1	3	82	24	40	.259	.376	.324

DRIVING IN RUNS	From 1B	From 2B	From 3B	Scoring Position
Totals	88/1922	183/1103	255/566	438/1669
Percentage	5%	17%	45%	26%
Driving In Runners from 3B with Less than Two Out:		186/304	61%	

Love to face: Mike Morgan (8–1 against him)
Hate to face: Kirk McCaskill (1–4 against him)
Grounded into 159 double plays, to lead A.L. for only second time during Weaver's tenure, despite his aversion to bunts and steals.... Speaking of which, ranked last in A.L. in stolen bases (41) for fourth consecutive season.... Also ranked last in majors in triples for third season in a row, with only *two* in home games. As we've said before, it's easier to hit a triple at Pimlico than at Memorial Stadium.... Batting average with two outs and runners on base was lowest in A.L. since 1982.... Won 13 games in which they trailed after six innings, highest total in A.L. last season.... Orioles' parting tribute to Earl: ranked 6th in A.L. in home runs, but tied for second with 26 home runs of three or more runs.

Boston Red Sox

	AB	H	2B	3B	HR	RRF	BB	SO	BA	SA	OBA
Season	5498	1488	320	21	144	782	595	707	.271	.415	.346
vs. Left-Handers	1553	418	86	9	39	222	170	180	.269	.411	.344
vs. Right-Handers	3945	1070	234	12	105	560	425	527	.271	.416	.347
Home	2671	721	179	10	55	383	311	330	.270	.406	.351
Road	2827	767	141	11	89	399	284	377	.271	.423	.341
Grass	4635	1245	267	17	123	674	519	591	.269	.413	.347
Artificial Turf	863	243	53	4	21	108	76	116	.282	.425	.343
April	639	165	40	4	16	82	75	62	.258	.408	.338
May	971	280	67	3	17	154	119	128	.288	.416	.371
June	911	243	47	5	21	117	86	132	.267	.398	.334
July	881	224	49	3	21	105	73	135	.254	.388	.315
August	1027	279	61	4	32	160	122	117	.272	.432	.353
Sept./Oct.	1069	297	56	2	37	164	120	133	.278	.438	.353
Leading Off Inn.	1298	347	73	6	32	32	108	167	.267	.407	.330
Runners On	2516	700	166	9	66	704	332	321	.278	.430	.364
Runners/Scor. Pos.	1459	392	89	6	34	614	235	200	.269	.408	.357
Runners On/2 Out	1057	291	64	5	26	302	169	144	.275	.419	.384
Scor. Pos./2 Out	698	191	44	5	16	273	131	103	.274	.420	.397
Late Inning Pressure	616	168	38	1	15	90	82	96	.273	.411	.367
Leading Off	153	44	11	0	4	4	10	20	.288	.438	.335
Runners On	286	77	22	1	8	83	52	50	.269	.437	.393
Runners/Scor. Pos.	170	42	13	1	4	74	41	33	.247	.406	.405

DRIVING IN RUNS	From 1B	From 2B	From 3B	Scoring Position
Totals	99/1887	233/1195	305/645	538/1840
Percentage	5%	19%	47%	29%
Driving In Runners from 3B with Less than Two Out:		201/341	59%	

Love to face: Neal Heaton (9–1)
Hate to face: Ron Guidry (6–14)
Led American League in doubles for third time in past four seasons.... Hit by 66 pitches last season, highest total in majors since 1978.... Average age of home run hitters last season was highest in majors (33.29).... Think you know Fenway? Red Sox hit 89 home runs on the road last season, 34 more than at home, the largest difference in the American League since 1982, when Milwaukee hit 38 more on the road than at home.... Second spot in batting order had composite .316 batting average, to rank third in A.L., behind third slot for New York (.331) and the *eighth* slot for Cleveland (.326).... Starting shortstops batted .221 last season, lowest mark by any position on any A.L. team excluding catchers.

California Angels

	AB	H	2B	3B	HR	RRF	BB	SO	BA	SA	OBA
Season	5433	1387	236	36	167	771	671	860	.255	.404	.338
vs. Left-Handers	1769	460	76	13	51	241	220	254	.260	.404	.341
vs. Right-Handers	3664	927	160	23	116	530	451	606	.253	.404	.337
Home	2607	661	104	13	88	367	343	416	.254	.405	.341
Road	2826	726	132	23	79	404	328	444	.257	.404	.336
Grass	4607	1181	193	29	137	650	580	735	.256	.400	.340
Artificial Turf	826	206	43	7	30	121	91	125	.249	.427	.326
April	713	194	36	4	33	114	77	101	.272	.473	.346
May	921	240	38	2	22	118	98	156	.261	.378	.332
June	889	223	40	10	23	130	115	144	.251	.396	.338
July	899	231	36	8	26	128	117	154	.257	.402	.343
August	940	240	42	3	31	131	119	138	.255	.405	.340
Sept./Oct.	1071	259	44	9	32	150	145	167	.242	.389	.332
Leading Off Inn.	1301	347	51	8	52	52	139	202	.267	.438	.343
Runners On	2391	633	101	16	68	671	354	384	.265	.406	.355
Runners/Scor. Pos.	1435	373	62	12	37	592	245	260	.260	.397	.359
Runners On/2 Out	1012	253	42	6	30	276	162	186	.250	.392	.357
Scor. Pos./2 Out	680	173	30	5	17	242	117	141	.254	.388	.368
Late Inning Pressure	790	189	23	5	20	98	96	138	.239	.357	.324
Leading Off	194	43	4	1	4	4	21	33	.222	.314	.304
Runners On	344	89	12	1	11	88	46	67	.259	.395	.345
Runners/Scor. Pos.	191	44	8	1	3	70	36	42	.230	.330	.348

DRIVING IN RUNS	From 1B	From 2B	From 3B	Scoring Position
Totals	87/1711	238/1157	277/620	515/1777
Percentage	5%	21%	45%	29%
Driving In Runners from 3B with Less than Two Out:		198/332	60%	

Love to face: Mike Flanagan (8–4)
Hate to face: Bert Blyleven (12–27)
Led A.L. in sacrifice bunts (91) for fifth time in past six seasons. Only exception: 1984, under John McNamara.... Led league in walks for second consecutive season.... Won seven games in which they trailed after eight innings, most in A.L. last season.... Third-place hitters in batting order drove in 126 runs last season, highest total for any slot on any team in A.L.... Run producers are growing old: average age weighted by RBIs was highest in majors last season (32.34 years).... Best record in A.L. against right-handed starters (67–43), but below .500 against southpaw starters (25–27).... 2d-highest batting average in A.L. during April, 3d lowest after the All-Star break (.247).

Chicago White Sox

	AB	H	2B	3B	HR	RRF	BB	SO	BA	SA	OBA
Season	5406	1335	197	34	121	631	487	940	.247	.363	.310
vs. Left-Handers	1901	446	70	10	37	196	167	396	.235	.340	.298
vs. Right-Handers	3505	889	127	24	84	435	320	544	.254	.375	.317
Home	2640	682	99	23	51	333	274	427	.258	.371	.329
Road	2766	653	98	11	70	298	213	513	.236	.355	.292
Grass	4476	1109	151	30	100	531	419	763	.248	.362	.313
Artificial Turf	930	226	46	4	21	100	68	177	.243	.369	.299
April	635	152	21	6	19	77	63	117	.239	.381	.308
May	925	223	29	6	13	93	86	156	.241	.328	.308
June	926	236	46	6	22	159	124	168	.255	.389	.346
July	865	225	29	6	20	100	67	149	.260	.377	.313
August	964	240	29	4	29	102	58	155	.249	.374	.291
Sept./Oct.	1091	259	43	6	19	100	89	195	.237	.340	.297
Leading Off Inn.	1323	331	53	12	29	29	119	232	.250	.374	.317
Runners On	2257	592	85	11	53	562	224	383	.262	.379	.325
Runners/Scor. Pos.	1269	330	49	8	29	502	145	226	.260	.380	.327
Runners On/2 Out	921	221	31	5	22	213	100	157	.240	.356	.316
Scor. Pos./2 Out	574	139	19	4	14	191	76	104	.242	.362	.333
Late Inning Pressure	842	190	23	7	13	93	77	178	.226	.316	.291
Leading Off	218	53	9	3	0	0	17	41	.243	.312	.298
Runners On	337	87	7	2	8	88	40	69	.258	.362	.332
Runners/Scor. Pos.	191	51	5	1	4	78	31	40	.267	.366	.356

DRIVING IN RUNS	From 1B	From 2B	From 3B	Scoring Position
Totals	73/1637	176/956	261/603	437/1559
Percentage	4%	18%	43%	28%
Driving In Runners from 3B with Less than Two Out:		174/323	54%	

Love to face: Bob Stanley (9–4)
Hate to face: Dave Stieb (3–14)
Ranked last in A.L. in batting average for second time in past three seasons, last in slugging for first time since 1968.... Also ranked last in runs scored (644), home runs, and extra-base hits.... Lowest road-game batting average in A.L. last season.... Hit only six first-inning home runs, fewest in A.L.... Batted higher with runners on base than with bases empty for sixth consecutive season.... Batting average in Late-Inning Pressure Situations was lowest in majors over past two seasons.... Starting second basemen had only 19 extra-base hits, 2d-lowest total by any position on any team in A.L. The big loser: Orioles second basemen (14).

Cleveland Indians

	AB	H	2B	3B	HR	RRF	BB	SO	BA	SA	OBA
Season	5702	1620	270	45	157	817	456	944	.284	.430	.337
vs. Left-Handers	1574	469	81	11	46	231	139	268	.298	.451	.356
vs. Right-Handers	4128	1151	189	34	111	586	317	676	.279	.422	.330
Home	2749	799	119	26	80	396	216	430	.291	.440	.341
Road	2953	821	151	19	77	421	240	514	.278	.420	.333
Grass	4790	1367	217	38	133	685	384	773	.285	.430	.338
Artificial Turf	912	253	53	7	24	132	72	171	.277	.430	.332
April	641	175	34	4	17	81	58	101	.273	.418	.333
May	938	239	40	7	19	120	88	151	.255	.373	.319
June	905	258	44	8	32	140	67	151	.285	.457	.334
July	929	261	39	5	25	145	83	150	.281	.414	.338
August	1139	326	45	7	32	140	80	195	.286	.422	.334
Sept./Oct.	1150	361	68	14	32	191	80	196	.314	.481	.359
Leading Off Inn.	1347	399	63	12	35	35	100	211	.296	.439	.346
Runners On	2580	743	129	19	70	730	214	424	.288	.434	.340
Runners/Scor. Pos.	1502	427	80	14	36	630	157	261	.284	.428	.345
Runners On/2 Out	1062	285	51	13	29	277	103	187	.268	.423	.334
Scor. Pos./2 Out	697	182	38	12	19	249	79	135	.261	.432	.337
Late Inning Pressure	727	209	38	4	15	103	68	141	.287	.413	.349
Leading Off	178	41	7	0	2	2	15	37	.230	.303	.294
Runners On	326	100	21	2	6	94	31	61	.307	.439	.366
Runners/Scor. Pos.	198	62	10	2	3	83	22	43	.313	.429	.374

DRIVING IN RUNS	From 1B	From 2B	From 3B	Scoring Position
Totals	114/1785	257/1152	285/618	542/1770
Percentage	6%	22%	46%	31%
Driving In Runners from 3B with Less than Two Out:			198/331	60%

Love to face: Floyd Bannister (9–3)
Hate to face: Charlie Hough (4–11)
Led American League in batting average and runs scored (831) for first time since 1959. . . . Only the second A.L. batting leader during divisional era to lead league in stolen bases as well (141). Ranked last in walks. . . . Finally! Cory Snyder was first Indians first-round draft selection (June or January draft, regular or secondary phase) to have a major impact on team since Chris Chambliss (chosen in 1970). Only two other first-round selections since 1976—and we're talking about 44 players here—have even worn Cleveland uniforms. And you were wondering how we'd get John Bohnet's name in the book, not to mention Dave Clark's. (Shouldn't he play third, so we can enter in our scorebooks, "Dave Clark 5"?)

Detroit Tigers

	AB	H	2B	3B	HR	RRF	BB	SO	BA	SA	OBA
Season	5512	1447	234	30	198	774	613	885	.263	.424	.338
vs. Left-Handers	1879	489	87	12	54	249	184	288	.260	.406	.328
vs. Right-Handers	3633	958	147	18	144	525	429	597	.264	.433	.344
Home	2684	683	99	16	96	393	317	431	.254	.411	.335
Road	2828	764	135	14	102	381	296	454	.270	.436	.341
Grass	4659	1204	191	27	164	656	527	740	.258	.417	.335
Artificial Turf	853	243	43	3	34	118	86	145	.285	.462	.354
April	647	164	30	7	20	90	63	106	.253	.414	.321
May	900	240	47	6	30	119	90	145	.267	.432	.336
June	978	246	42	3	33	133	110	154	.252	.402	.328
July	976	265	38	3	36	137	106	174	.272	.427	.349
August	1012	274	41	5	41	161	123	149	.271	.443	.350
Sept./Oct.	999	258	36	6	38	134	121	157	.258	.420	.338
Leading Off Inn.	1305	328	52	7	44	44	128	200	.251	.403	.321
Runners On	2404	635	100	9	88	664	287	392	.264	.423	.342
Runners/Scor. Pos.	1356	352	52	6	43	551	193	241	.260	.402	.347
Runners On/2 Out	1057	274	55	2	35	277	127	173	.259	.414	.343
Scor. Pos./2 Out	667	169	31	1	20	232	96	115	.253	.393	.352
Late Inning Pressure	758	198	24	0	22	102	94	138	.261	.380	.344
Leading Off	190	55	3	0	8	8	16	33	.289	.432	.345
Runners On	341	91	12	0	8	88	48	57	.267	.372	.358
Runners/Scor. Pos.	176	51	5	0	4	78	32	33	.290	.386	.392

DRIVING IN RUNS	From 1B	From 2B	From 3B	Scoring Position
Totals	104/1766	228/1086	244/587	472/1673
Percentage	6%	21%	42%	28%
Driving In Runners from 3B with Less than Two Out:			173/313	55%

Love to face: Jim Clancy (13–4)
Hate to face: Bret Saberhagen (2–8)
Led A.L. in home runs for second time in past three seasons. . . . Had nine first-inning sacrifice bunts last season, 2d most in majors to Angels' 11. . . . Faced 55 left-handed starters last season, most in A.L. (27–28 record in those games). . . . Won only five games in which they trailed after six innings, lowest total in A.L. last season. . . . Led majors in multirun innings (212) for second time in past three seasons. . . . Grounded into one double play for every 13.69 opportunities, lowest rate in A.L. . . . That stat was aided by the lowest ground outs-to-air outs ratio in the majors (0.95). . . . Ninth position in batting order contributed a .276 batting average, highest bottom slot in A.L. last season.

Kansas City Royals

	AB	H	2B	3B	HR	RRF	BB	SO	BA	SA	OBA
Season	5561	1403	264	45	137	649	474	919	.252	.390	.313
vs. Left-Handers	1505	376	58	13	39	173	128	260	.250	.383	.308
vs. Right-Handers	4056	1027	206	32	98	476	346	659	.253	.392	.315
Home	2744	718	140	29	60	340	239	412	.262	.399	.324
Road	2817	685	124	16	77	309	235	507	.243	.381	.303
Grass	2148	511	86	11	64	235	190	386	.238	.378	.302
Artificial Turf	3413	892	178	34	73	414	284	533	.261	.398	.321
April	630	141	32	5	14	73	53	90	.224	.357	.288
May	963	243	52	3	21	112	101	158	.252	.378	.325
June	988	266	50	11	20	125	92	157	.269	.403	.335
July	897	207	39	6	24	89	77	140	.231	.368	.293
August	977	259	40	5	30	126	79	182	.265	.408	.322
Sept./Oct.	1106	287	51	15	28	124	72	192	.259	.409	.308
Leading Off Inn.	1342	335	69	10	43	44	101	206	.250	.412	.306
Runners On	2400	633	104	18	56	567	215	399	.264	.392	.324
Runners/Scor. Pos.	1368	352	59	10	30	486	156	234	.257	.381	.330
Runners On/2 Out	1016	248	36	6	21	198	101	175	.244	.353	.315
Scor. Pos./2 Out	639	138	19	4	12	169	74	114	.216	.315	.299
Late Inning Pressure	867	215	33	7	18	91	68	143	.248	.364	.304
Leading Off	212	54	12	3	7	7	15	30	.255	.439	.310
Runners On	382	98	14	3	8	81	33	70	.257	.372	.314
Runners/Scor. Pos.	212	49	6	2	4	67	26	38	.231	.335	.307

DRIVING IN RUNS	From 1B	rrom 2B	From 3B	Scoring Position
Totals	d9/1745	195/1070	226/524	421/1594
Percentage	5%	18%	43%	26%
Driving In Runners from 3B with Less than Two Out:			172/275	63%

Love to face: Oil Can Boyd (5–1)
Hate to face: Floyd Bannister (6–14)
Tied with Toronto for last in A.L. with 24 sacrifice bunts. . . . Batted higher with runners on base than with bases empty for fifth consecutive season. . . . Ground outs-to-air outs ratio of 1.02, 3d lowest in A.L. . . . Advanced two bases on singles only 23.8 percent of the time last season, lowest A.L. average in the 12-year history of *The Player Analysis*. . . . Only A.L. team to use its opening-day combination of starters more than 10 times during the season. . . . Ranked 8th in A.L. in home-game batting average, 12th in road games. . . . Cleanup position hit only 15 home runs, fewest in A.L. last season. . . . Eighth slot (.201) and seventh slot (.202) had two lowest batting averages in league last season.

Milwaukee Brewers

	AB	H	2B	3B	HR	RRF	BB	SO	BA	SA	OBA
Season	5461	1393	255	38	127	655	530	986	.255	.385	.321
vs. Left-Handers	1396	353	55	11	36	179	146	264	.253	.385	.325
vs. Right-Handers	4065	1040	200	27	91	476	384	722	.256	.385	.320
Home	2660	673	119	23	63	331	273	443	.253	.386	.322
Road	2801	720	136	15	64	324	257	543	.257	.385	.320
Grass	4648	1188	214	34	109	567	464	835	.256	.387	.323
Artificial Turf	813	205	41	4	18	88	66	151	.252	.379	.310
April	605	157	29	7	10	79	74	119	.260	.380	.342
May	970	272	51	7	25	147	102	153	.280	.425	.351
June	938	235	40	6	15	96	75	144	.251	.354	.305
July	862	218	48	5	15	92	84	162	.253	.372	.322
August	1037	268	43	4	35	127	108	194	.258	.409	.325
Sept./Oct.	1049	243	44	9	27	114	87	214	.232	.368	.291
Leading Off Inn.	1335	351	67	12	32	32	106	220	.263	.403	.319
Runners On	2356	595	108	13	56	583	264	422	.253	.381	.325
Runners/Scor. Pos.	1336	326	55	8	28	500	187	240	.244	.360	.329
Runners On/2 Out	986	228	47	6	21	227	124	190	.231	.355	.322
Scor. Pos./2 Out	626	144	26	5	12	196	96	116	.230	.345	.338
Late Inning Pressure	834	214	33	5	14	88	81	157	.257	.359	.321
Leading Off	211	59	11	1	4	4	17	31	.280	.398	.333
Runners On	352	87	13	2	4	78	43	65	.247	.330	.326
Runners/Scor. Pos.	206	52	5	1	2	69	29	35	.252	.316	.336

DRIVING IN RUNS	From 1B	From 2B	From 3B	Scoring Position
Totals	89/1725	189/1055	248/564	437/1619
Percentage	5%	18%	44%	27%
Driving In Runners from 3B with Less than Two Out:			179/311	58%

Love to face: Charlie Hough (6–1)
Hate to face: Neal Heaton (3–6)
Faced only 38 left-handed starters last season, but damned if we can figure out why. Milwaukee was 15–23 in games started by southpaws, 62–61 vs. right-handers. . . . Scored 62 first-inning runs, fewest in A.L. last season. . . . Had fewest multirun innings in A.L. (157). . . . Advanced two bases on singles 41.3 percent of time when winning (2d-highest mark in A.L.), 29.0 percent at other times (12th in A.L.). . . . Used 129 combinations of starting players, one short of highest total in majors during five years we've kept track. California used 130 combinations in 1983. . . . No single combination started as many as five games. . . . Cleanup position drove in only 71 runs, lowest total in A.L. last season.

Minnesota Twins

	AB	H	2B	3B	HR	RRF	BB	SO	BA	SA	OBA
Season	5531	1446	257	39	196	729	501	977	.261	.428	.325
vs. Left-Handers	1433	400	76	6	55	212	128	271	.279	.456	.338
vs. Right-Handers	4098	1046	181	33	141	517	373	706	.255	.419	.320
Home	2780	756	142	29	116	420	257	487	.272	.469	.336
Road	2751	690	115	10	80	309	244	490	.251	.387	.313
Grass	2103	523	90	7	63	233	193	390	.249	.388	.313
Artificial Turf	3428	923	167	32	133	496	308	587	.269	.453	.332
April	722	193	32	5	29	97	61	115	.267	.446	.325
May	922	256	49	7	49	148	104	159	.278	.505	.350
June	969	264	45	10	34	134	86	160	.272	.445	.336
July	853	199	42	5	24	92	74	147	.233	.379	.298
August	994	254	46	7	26	130	89	177	.256	.394	.318
Sept./Oct.	1071	280	43	5	34	128	87	219	.261	.406	.321
Leading Off Inn.	1341	353	49	7	49	49	93	196	.263	.420	.317
Runners On	2325	613	101	16	80	612	241	421	.264	.424	.331
Runners/Scor. Pos.	1289	320	59	6	42	501	165	267	.248	.401	.327
Runners On/2 Out	984	253	42	4	33	263	115	190	.257	.409	.337
Scor. Pos./2 Out	629	148	26	2	17	215	87	138	.235	.364	.329
Late Inning Pressure	776	180	31	4	20	84	73	163	.232	.360	.301
Leading Off	194	38	2	0	5	5	10	31	.196	.284	.243
Runners On	316	75	11	3	8	72	34	66	.237	.367	.307
Runners/Scor. Pos.	170	38	5	2	4	59	22	39	.224	.347	.305

DRIVING IN RUNS	From 1B	From 2B	From 3B	Scoring Position
Totals	114/1699	207/1037	208/496	415/1533
Percentage	7%	20%	42%	27%
Driving In Runners from 3B with Less than Two Out:	141/259		54%	

Love to face: Richard Dotson (10–5)
Hate to face: Roger Clemens (0–7)
One of three A.L. teams with no first-inning sacrifices last season; the others: Kansas City and Toronto. . . . Combination of Salas, Hrbek-Lombardozzi-Gaetti-Gagne, Bush-Puckett-Brunansky, and Smalley started 27 games last season, highest total in majors by any group. . . . Average age of home run hitters was lowest in A.L. last season (27.33 years), slightly younger than Seattle's (27.45) and Toronto's (27.53). San Francisco led the majors (27.29). . . . Third-place hitters in batting order hit 35 home runs last season, highest total for any slot on any team in A.L. . . . Have lost 11 of 12 extra-inning road games over past three seasons.

New York Yankees

	AB	H	2B	3B	HR	RRF	BB	SO	BA	SA	OBA
Season	5570	1512	275	23	188	778	645	911	.271	.430	.347
vs. Left-Handers	1938	493	95	11	53	239	214	343	.254	.397	.330
vs. Right-Handers	3632	1019	180	12	135	539	431	568	.281	.448	.357
Home	2655	713	132	14	93	375	338	418	.269	.434	.351
Road	2915	799	143	9	95	403	307	493	.274	.427	.344
Grass	4642	1258	228	19	155	647	552	731	.271	.428	.349
Artificial Turf	928	254	47	4	33	131	93	180	.274	.440	.339
April	679	177	33	2	13	100	104	101	.261	.373	.359
May	956	256	52	5	39	146	137	159	.268	.455	.359
June	1008	299	61	1	39	147	105	154	.297	.475	.361
July	878	237	44	5	34	131	102	124	.270	.448	.347
August	970	234	34	6	31	107	93	183	.241	.385	.308
Sept./Oct.	1079	309	51	4	32	147	104	190	.286	.430	.353
Leading Off Inn.	1290	353	60	6	61	61	144	210	.274	.471	.350
Runners On	2514	670	122	10	70	660	318	397	.267	.407	.346
Runners/Scor. Pos.	1430	358	69	3	41	575	220	252	.250	.389	.343
Runners On/2 Out	1049	256	40	2	27	238	150	195	.244	.363	.340
Scor. Pos./2 Out	657	148	22	0	17	209	112	130	.225	.336	.340
Late Inning Pressure	694	193	30	4	21	97	85	132	.278	.424	.358
Leading Off	174	43	7	1	7	7	18	37	.247	.420	.321
Runners On	290	82	13	1	6	82	47	53	.283	.397	.381
Runners/Scor. Pos.	160	48	9	0	3	74	34	29	.300	.413	.415

DRIVING IN RUNS	From 1B	From 2B	From 3B	Scoring Position
Totals	90/1843	223/1103	274/627	497/1730
Percentage	5%	20%	44%	29%
Driving In Runners from 3B with Less than Two Out:	196/324		60%	

Love to face: Scott McGregor (14–7)
Hate to face: Vida Blue (9–16)
Scored 116 first-inning runs, highest total in A.L. last season. Hit 38 first-inning home runs, 10 more than closest rival in either league. . . . Led American League in slugging average for first time since 1962. . . . Highest batting average in A.L. during the month of June, lowest during August. . . . Third position in batting order had .331 composite average (thanks, Don), highest of any position on any A.L. team last season. Second spot batted .310 to rank fifth, making Yankees only team with two spots in top five. . . . One of four teams whose starting shortstops did not hit a home run last season. The others: Seattle, Pittsburgh, and St. Louis.

Oakland A's

	AB	H	2B	3B	HR	RRF	BB	SO	BA	SA	OBA
Season	5435	1370	213	25	163	715	553	983	.252	.390	.322
vs. Left-Handers	1743	454	71	9	53	228	155	314	.260	.403	.322
vs. Right-Handers	3692	916	142	16	110	487	398	669	.248	.385	.322
Home	2716	687	93	11	75	357	311	473	.253	.378	.330
Road	2719	683	120	14	88	358	242	510	.251	.403	.314
Grass	4542	1118	166	19	131	567	464	812	.246	.378	.317
Artificial Turf	893	252	47	6	32	148	89	171	.282	.456	.348
April	697	178	24	1	13	96	91	119	.255	.349	.343
May	955	233	36	3	39	129	79	175	.244	.410	.303
June	959	240	45	4	22	116	111	171	.250	.374	.329
July	877	230	26	4	22	111	86	158	.262	.376	.328
August	936	233	41	6	36	131	88	179	.249	.421	.314
Sept./Oct.	1011	256	41	7	31	132	98	181	.253	.400	.321
Leading Off Inn.	1304	339	56	5	41	41	132	225	.260	.405	.330
Runners On	2318	629	91	14	60	611	391	391	.271	.400	.339
Runners/Scor. Pos.	1337	360	51	10	35	532	182	229	.269	.401	.350
Runners On/2 Out	977	257	36	6	21	250	122	158	.263	.377	.349
Scor. Pos./2 Out	646	172	22	4	14	223	94	102	.266	.378	.365
Late Inning Pressure	800	188	27	8	23	99	86	155	.235	.375	.309
Leading Off	198	52	7	0	9	9	20	24	.263	.434	.330
Runners On	328	81	14	7	6	82	44	63	.247	.387	.332
Runners/Scor. Pos.	186	49	7	5	5	73	28	31	.263	.435	.353

DRIVING IN RUNS	From 1B	From 2B	From 3B	Scoring Position
Totals	92/1693	206/1022	253/595	459/1617
Percentage	5%	20%	43%	28%
Driving In Runners from 3B with Less than Two Out:	166/315		53%	

Love to face: New Dodgers (3–0 vs. Tim Leary, 8–2 vs. Matt Young)
Hate to face: Scott McGregor (3–11)
Made fewest DPs in A.L. (120) for 7th time in 12 seasons. . . . Lowest home batting average in A.L. last season. . . . Higher batting averages with runners on base than with the bases empty in each of last 12 seasons. . . . Advanced two bases on singles 37.7% of the time, highest mark in A.L. last season. . . . At least Jackie Moore preserved this cherished mark: No manager since Connie Mack has lasted longer than three consecutive seasons for this franchise. Ninth-place hitters drove in 62 runs, highest total in A.L. last season. . . . Starting catchers batted .214, 2d-lowest by any position in A.L.; Baltimore catchers batted .194.

Seattle Mariners

	AB	H	2B	3B	HR	RRF	BB	SO	BA	SA	OBA
Season	5498	1392	243	41	158	699	572	1148	.253	.399	.326
vs. Left-Handers	1378	362	63	9	29	164	145	287	.263	.385	.336
vs. Right-Handers	4120	1030	180	32	129	535	427	861	.250	.403	.322
Home	2779	741	147	30	97	396	293	552	.267	.446	.340
Road	2719	651	96	11	61	303	279	596	.239	.350	.312
Grass	2029	457	56	7	51	213	219	453	.225	.335	.302
Artificial Turf	3469	935	187	34	107	486	353	695	.270	.436	.340
April	667	134	24	2	21	73	77	202	.201	.337	.284
May	967	247	50	10	30	122	104	205	.255	.421	.329
June	989	267	49	6	34	149	105	177	.270	.435	.344
July	880	248	39	9	19	129	93	166	.282	.411	.352
August	956	242	41	5	28	109	96	181	.253	.394	.325
Sept./Oct.	1039	254	40	9	26	117	97	217	.244	.375	.312
Leading Off Inn.	1328	335	62	13	31	31	122	252	.252	.389	.320
Runners On	2368	614	105	20	69	609	269	509	.259	.408	.335
Runners/Scor. Pos.	1331	349	65	13	39	518	178	287	.262	.418	.345
Runners On/2 Out	979	233	30	8	28	253	129	221	.238	.371	.329
Scor. Pos./2 Out	616	147	18	5	16	216	92	149	.239	.362	.339
Late Inning Pressure	803	189	28	5	29	101	96	191	.235	.391	.322
Leading Off	203	43	6	0	3	3	20	42	.212	.286	.286
Runners On	314	79	13	4	14	86	47	82	.252	.452	.356
Runners/Scor. Pos.	177	50	6	4	11	76	36	41	.282	.548	.399

DRIVING IN RUNS	From 1B	From 2B	From 3B	Scoring Position
Totals	102/1682	205/1041	232/578	437/1619
Percentage	6%	20%	40%	27%
Driving In Runners from 3B with Less than Two Out:	152/300		51%	

Love to face: Bud Black (6–1)
Hate to face: Ken Schrom (1–6)
Set all-time A.L. record for strikeouts. Previous mark (1125) was set in 1965 by Washington Senators. . . . Led American League in double plays (191) for first time in team history. . . . First team to make two triple plays in a season since the 1982 New York Mets. . . . Have batted higher with runners on base than with bases empty in all 10 seasons in team history. . . . Scored 56 runs in sixth inning last season, tying Chicago's seventh inning for lowest total in A.L. last season (ninth inning and overtime excluded). . . . Have lost 121 consecutive road games in which they trailed after eight innings. Last win: June 2, 1984, at Texas. . . . Highest ground outs-to-air outs ratio in A.L. (1.17).

Texas Rangers

	AB	H	2B	3B	HR	RRF	BB	SO	BA	SA	OBA
Season	5529	1479	248	43	184	753	511	1088	.267	.428	.331
vs. Left-Handers	1592	437	80	12	55	227	164	325	.274	.443	.340
vs. Right-Handers	3937	1042	168	31	129	526	347	763	.265	.421	.327
Home	2666	717	113	22	87	363	225	532	.269	.426	.327
Road	2863	762	135	21	97	390	286	556	.266	.430	.334
Grass	4562	1208	189	35	149	612	426	904	.265	.420	.329
Artificial Turf	967	271	59	8	35	141	85	184	.280	.466	.340
April	645	174	35	3	28	102	63	123	.270	.464	.338
May	943	241	42	7	26	120	86	194	.256	.398	.321
June	994	262	41	12	26	114	74	199	.264	.407	.317
July	906	244	44	8	26	113	73	152	.269	.422	.326
August	1020	294	52	8	34	157	98	201	.288	.455	.352
Sept./Oct.	1021	264	34	5	44	147	117	219	.259	.431	.332
Leading Off Inn.	1351	353	63	8	49	49	96	266	.261	.429	.313
Runners On	2248	641	96	21	63	630	239	421	.285	.431	.353
Runners/Scor. Pos.	1271	373	65	13	34	545	154	258	.293	.445	.363
Runners On/2 Out	964	261	37	10	24	250	106	200	.271	.405	.347
Scor. Pos./2 Out	614	167	28	5	15	223	73	133	.272	.407	.354
Late Inning Pressure	733	204	32	7	27	105	78	160	.278	.452	.351
Leading Off	189	54	9	1	9	9	8	41	.286	.487	.322
Runners On	300	84	13	4	7	85	42	61	.280	.420	.370
Runners/Scor. Pos.	166	48	7	3	4	73	28	38	.289	.440	.387

DRIVING IN RUNS	From 1B	From 2B	From 3B	Scoring Position
Totals	99/1633	223/1003	241/507	464/1510
Percentage	6%	22%	48%	31%
Driving In Runners from 3B with Less than Two Out:	164/262		63%	

Love to face: Floyd Bannister (10–5)
Hate to face: Mike Boddicker (0–7)

Led A.L. in batting average with runners in scoring position for first time in *Player Analysis* history, with a team record .293 mark.... Grounded into one double play for every 9.37 opportunities, 2d-highest rate in majors. The leader: Baltimore (9.12).... Highest batting average in A.L. during the month of August.... Were not shut out at Arlington Stadium until final Saturday of last season, when John Candelaria and Vern Ruhle combined for two-hitter. Last complete-game shutout vs. Texas at home: May 21, 1985, a three-hitter by Bud Black.... Ranked second in A.L. with a .267 batting average after the All-Star break.

Toronto Blue Jays

	AB	H	2B	3B	HR	RRF	BB	SO	BA	SA	OBA
Season	5716	1540	285	35	181	797	496	848	.269	.427	.329
vs. Left-Handers	1675	453	85	6	55	241	136	273	.270	.427	.327
vs. Right-Handers	4041	1087	200	29	126	556	360	575	.269	.426	.330
Home	2738	743	148	19	87	407	264	417	.271	.435	.337
Road	2978	797	137	16	94	390	232	431	.268	.419	.321
Grass	2311	608	104	10	70	290	192	336	.263	.408	.321
Artificial Turf	3405	932	181	25	111	507	304	512	.274	.439	.334
April	690	181	29	3	16	90	62	126	.262	.383	.324
May	1018	280	46	8	32	147	111	127	.275	.430	.348
June	1003	295	58	7	42	169	83	137	.294	.492	.348
July	939	248	51	10	30	131	89	139	.264	.436	.329
August	1038	295	58	5	34	162	92	145	.284	.448	.344
Sept./Oct.	1028	241	43	2	27	98	59	174	.234	.359	.277
Leading Off Inn.	1367	358	58	5	44	45	97	205	.262	.408	.316
Runners On	2462	704	130	16	76	691	220	332	.286	.444	.341
Runners/Scor. Pos.	1424	386	73	8	37	573	161	211	.271	.412	.336
Runners On/2 Out	1028	271	47	7	32	270	99	149	.264	.416	.331
Scor. Pos./2 Out	661	168	29	5	17	227	79	93	.254	.390	.336
Late Inning Pressure	939	252	31	5	29	126	80	143	.268	.405	.325
Leading Off	235	62	9	1	9	9	20	38	.264	.426	.324
Runners On	392	115	16	3	9	106	35	53	.293	.418	.348
Runners/Scor. Pos.	220	59	7	1	6	91	26	29	.268	.391	.340

DRIVING IN RUNS	From 1B	From 2B	From 3B	Scoring Position
Totals	123/1751	219/1087	273/615	492/1702
Percentage	7%	20%	44%	29%
Driving In Runners from 3B with Less than Two Out:	189/335		56%	

Love to face: Frank Viola (9–1)
Hate to face: Mike Flanagan (7–17)

Led American League in fielding percentage (.984) for first time in team history. Committed only 35 errors after the All-Star break, nine fewer than any other A.L. team.... Hit six extra-inning home runs, tying Philadelphia for major-league lead.... Weren't shut out at Exhibition Stadium last season; last shutout vs. Jays at home was tossed by Phil Niekro, for his 300th career victory, on final day of 1985 season.... Balanced lineup contributed to fewest intentional walks in majors (23).... Least productive spot in batting order (ninth position) still hit nine home runs with 59 RBIs.

American League

	AB	H	2B	3B	HR	RRF	BB	SO	BA	SA	OBA
Season	77376	20237	3520	468	2290	10246	7667	13058	.262	.408	.330
vs. Left-Handers	22863	6023	1051	135	659	2992	2241	3946	.263	.408	.330
vs. Right-Handers	54513	14214	2469	333	1631	7254	5426	9112	.261	.408	.329
Home	37714	9961	1732	267	1139	5205	3932	6175	.264	.415	.335
Road	39662	10276	1788	201	1151	5041	3735	6883	.259	.401	.324
Grass	54775	14146	2329	291	1589	7138	5607	9165	.258	.398	.328
Artificial Turf	22601	6091	1191	177	701	3108	2060	3893	.270	.431	.333
April	9283	2361	434	54	264	1235	994	1588	.254	.398	.328
May	13210	3482	632	78	390	1799	1407	2200	.264	.412	.334
June	13417	3580	642	90	393	1845	1324	2204	.267	.416	.334
July	12583	3294	567	82	357	1633	1219	2093	.262	.405	.329
August	13997	3682	606	70	450	1871	1346	2345	.263	.413	.329
Sept./Oct.	14886	3838	639	94	436	1863	1377	2628	.258	.401	.322
Leading Off Inn.	18551	4894	831	113	586	588	1605	2969	.264	.416	.326
Runners On	33624	9032	1538	197	950	8896	3675	5588	.269	.411	.339
Runners/Scor. Pos.	19139	5030	887	120	506	7637	2540	3390	.263	.401	.343
Runners On/2 Out	14085	3552	596	83	379	3512	1709	2498	.252	.387	.344
Scor. Pos./2 Out	9000	2215	377	58	227	3057	1285	1676	.246	.377	.344
Late Inning Pressure	11026	2803	429	64	288	1385	1147	2090	.254	.383	.326
Leading Off	2762	693	107	11	76	76	220	469	.251	.380	.310
Runners On	4678	1244	196	34	112	1208	575	885	.266	.394	.345
Runners/Scor. Pos.	2628	696	106	24	60	1047	415	511	.265	.392	.359

DRIVING IN RUNS	From 1B	From 2B	From 3B	Scoring Position
Totals	1363/24479	2982/15067	3582/8145	6564/23212
Percentage	6%	20%	44%	28%
Driving In Runners from 3B with Less than Two Out:	2489/4325		58%	

Runs were scored in 28.6 percent of innings last season, broken down this way: 16.7 percent when leadoff batter was retired, 51.9 percent when leadoff batter reached base (43.8 when he reached first, 62.7 when he reached second, 85.5 when he reached third, 100.0 when he reached home).... Set all-time record for home runs in a season, but real story was increase in strikeouts. Home run record was broken by 5.1 percent, whiff mark by 10.9 percent.... Four grand slam home runs were hit on one day, August 10 (three in A.L.), for only ninth time in major-league history, and first time since 1974.... A.L. pitchers still 0-for-the-1980s in World Series play. Hitless streak now at 59 at bats with 0-for-10 by Red Sox. Last hit: Tim Stoddard, in Game Four of 1979 Series.

National League

Mike Aldrete
San Francisco Giants

Bats Left

	AB	H	2B	3B	HR	RRF	BB	SO	BA	SA	OBA
Season	216	54	18	3	2	27	33	34	.250	.389	.353
vs. Left-Handers	26	5	1	0	0	1	1	6	.192	.231	.222
vs. Right-Handers	190	49	17	3	2	26	32	28	.258	.411	.369
Home	117	35	9	2	1	16	20	16	.299	.436	.401
Road	99	19	9	1	1	11	13	18	.192	.333	.296
Grass	165	44	12	3	2	22	26	24	.267	.412	.370
Artificial Turf	51	10	6	0	0	5	7	10	.196	.314	.300
April	0	0	0	0	0	0	0	0	—	—	—
May	10	1	0	0	0	0	1	1	.100	.100	.250
June	74	16	6	0	1	9	12	12	.216	.338	.322
July	15	2	2	0	0	0	5	5	.133	.267	.350
August	48	17	4	2	1	9	3	8	.354	.583	.404
Sept./Oct.	69	18	6	1	0	9	12	8	.261	.377	.370
Leading Off Inn.	40	10	3	0	1	1	4	6	.250	.400	.333
Runners On	101	24	9	2	0	25	21	17	.238	.366	.371
Runners/Scor. Pos.	67	16	6	2	0	23	18	11	.239	.388	.402
Runners On/2 Out	46	13	5	1	0	11	13	7	.283	.435	.450
Scor. Pos./2 Out	35	8	3	1	0	10	13	6	.229	.371	.449
Late Inning Pressure	40	14	4	1	1	8	8	3	.350	.575	.449
Leading Off	5	1	1	0	0	0	0	0	.200	.400	.200
Runners On	22	6	1	1	0	7	6	3	.273	.409	.414
Runners/Scor. Pos.	16	4	0	1	0	7	4	2	.250	.375	.381

DRIVING IN RUNS	From 1B	From 2B	From 3B	Scoring Position
Totals	3/72	11/59	11/23	22/82
Percentage	4%	19%	48%	27%
Driving In Runners from 3B with Less than Two Out:		8/11		73%

Loves to face: Jeff Dedmon (.500, 3-for-6, 1 HR)
Hates to face: Bob Knepper (0-for-3, 2 SO)
Six of his 18 doubles were hit against the Expos. . . . Batted .350 in Late-Inning Pressure Situations, .227 in nonpressure situations. . . . Had 23 extra-base hits in only 216 at bats, 4th-best rate among N.L. rookies (minimum: 15 XBH). . . . Did he possess unusual patience for a rookie, or get some rare rookie respect from umpires? His rate of one walk every 7.8 plate appearances was 3d highest among N.L. rookies with 200+ plate appearances, behind John Kruk (one every 7.3) and Barry Bonds (one every 7.4); league average for rookies: one walk every 12.7 times up, 14 percent higher than veterans' rate. . . . Wielded a big stick at the 'Stick: .299 at home, compared to .192 on the road.

Dave Anderson
Los Angeles Dodgers

Bats Right

	AB	H	2B	3B	HR	RRF	BB	SO	BA	SA	OBA
Season	216	53	9	0	1	19	22	39	.245	.301	.314
vs. Left-Handers	75	18	2	0	0	9	8	17	.240	.267	.313
vs. Right-Handers	141	35	7	0	1	10	14	22	.248	.319	.314
Home	97	28	4	0	0	10	10	13	.289	.330	.355
Road	119	25	5	0	1	9	12	26	.210	.277	.280
Grass	156	43	7	0	0	14	17	23	.276	.321	.347
Artificial Turf	60	10	2	0	1	5	5	16	.167	.250	.227
April	46	11	0	0	0	4	4	9	.239	.239	.300
May	39	10	4	0	0	2	2	4	.256	.359	.292
June	29	8	1	0	0	1	0	4	.276	.310	.276
July	0	0	0	0	0	0	0	0	—	—	—
August	27	8	3	0	0	2	4	5	.296	.407	.387
Sept./Oct.	75	16	1	0	1	10	12	17	.213	.267	.318
Leading Off Inn.	52	11	1	0	0	0	4	14	.212	.231	.268
Runners On	89	22	4	0	1	19	7	12	.247	.326	.299
Runners/Scor. Pos.	56	12	2	0	0	16	3	8	.214	.250	.250
Runners On/2 Out	33	3	1	0	0	5	1	3	.091	.121	.118
Scor. Pos./2 Out	25	2	0	0	0	4	1	2	.080	.080	.115
Late Inning Pressure	42	13	4	0	0	5	4	7	.310	.405	.370
Leading Off	9	3	1	0	0	0	1	2	.333	.444	.400
Runners On	14	3	2	0	0	5	2	3	.214	.357	.313
Runners/Scor. Pos.	10	1	1	0	0	4	0	2	.100	.200	.100

DRIVING IN RUNS	From 1B	From 2B	From 3B	Scoring Position
Totals	2/60	7/46	9/20	16/66
Percentage	3%	15%	45%	24%
Driving In Runners from 3B with Less than Two Out:		8/14		57%

Loves to face: Bob Knepper (.500, 8-for-16)
Hates to face: Mark Davis (0-for-10, 5 SO)
Started 57 games last season, despite a two-month stay on the disabled list: 31 starts at shortstop, 24 at third base, two at second base. . . . Frequently inserted at third base late in games, he wound up with more innings at third (270) than at short (265.1). . . . Batted for a higher average against right-handers than he did against left-handers for the first time in his career. . . . Stole only five bases last season, three vs. the Expos. . . . Grounded into 11 double plays in only 44 opportunities (runner on first, less than two outs) last season, highest rate in N.L. among players with 40+ opportunities. . . . Only player to hit below .100 with two outs and runners in scoring position in each of the past two seasons (minimum: 15 AB in each).

Bill Almon
Pittsburgh Pirates

Bats Right

	AB	H	2B	3B	HR	RRF	BB	SO	BA	SA	OBA
Season	196	43	7	2	7	28	30	38	.219	.383	.319
vs. Left-Handers	121	24	2	2	3	10	22	26	.198	.322	.317
vs. Right-Handers	75	19	5	0	4	18	8	12	.253	.480	.321
Home	108	23	5	0	4	15	21	20	.213	.370	.336
Road	88	20	2	2	3	13	9	18	.227	.398	.296
Grass	52	7	1	1	2	8	6	11	.135	.308	.220
Artificial Turf	144	36	6	1	5	20	24	27	.250	.410	.353
April	30	9	4	0	3	9	5	4	.300	.733	.400
May	40	10	0	0	3	9	9	10	.250	.475	.380
June	61	13	1	1	1	7	8	12	.213	.311	.296
July	45	6	2	1	0	3	8	10	.133	.222	.264
August	13	2	0	0	0	0	0	1	.154	.154	.154
Sept./Oct.	7	3	0	0	0	0	0	1	.429	.429	.429
Leading Off Inn.	56	9	1	0	2	2	7	14	.161	.286	.254
Runners On	79	23	6	1	3	24	14	13	.291	.506	.385
Runners/Scor. Pos.	40	11	3	0	2	20	10	10	.275	.500	.396
Runners On/2 Out	30	8	1	0	2	7	6	4	.267	.500	.389
Scor. Pos./2 Out	16	5	1	0	2	7	6	3	.313	.750	.500
Late Inning Pressure	61	12	1	0	2	7	5	13	.197	.311	.250
Leading Off	16	0	0	0	0	0	4	6	.000	.000	.200
Runners On	27	7	1	0	1	6	0	3	.259	.407	.241
Runners/Scor. Pos.	14	2	0	0	1	6	0	2	.143	.357	.125

DRIVING IN RUNS	From 1B	From 2B	From 3B	Scoring Position
Totals	4/56	7/36	9/19	16/55
Percentage	7%	19%	47%	29%
Driving In Runners from 3B with Less than Two Out:		7/12		58%

Loves to face: Dan Schatzeder (.500, 5-for-10, 1 HR)
Hates to face: Bob Ojeda (.091, 2-for-22, 8 SO)
Batted .421 (8-for-19) with two home runs vs. Phillies last season. . . . Committed seven errors in 49 games on the road, only one error in 53 games at Three Rivers Stadium. . . . Started 30 of 58 games in which Pirates faced a left-hander in '86; only 11 of 104 vs. right-handed starters. . . . Hit only four home runs in first seven years in majors (1,471 at bats), but has demonstrated moderate power over last six years (32 homers in 1,759 at bats). . . . Career rate of 2.5 strikeouts for every walk, but with bases loaded since 1975, he has 21 strikeouts and only two walks. Has hit .243 with sacks full; had two grand-slams in '86.

Alan Ashby
Houston Astros

Bats Left and Right

	AB	H	2B	3B	HR	RRF	BB	SO	BA	SA	OBA
Season	315	81	15	0	7	38	39	56	.257	.371	.333
vs. Left-Handers	116	32	7	0	2	13	8	16	.276	.388	.315
vs. Right-Handers	199	49	8	0	5	25	31	40	.246	.362	.343
Home	155	39	7	0	1	18	18	25	.252	.316	.326
Road	160	42	8	0	6	20	21	31	.263	.425	.341
Grass	94	23	3	0	3	9	13	25	.245	.372	.330
Artificial Turf	221	58	12	0	4	29	26	31	.262	.371	.335
April	40	11	2	0	3	6	8	3	.275	.550	.396
May	23	2	0	0	0	1	4	7	.087	.087	.222
June	30	8	1	0	0	2	3	7	.267	.300	.333
July	57	17	2	0	1	11	9	10	.298	.386	.394
August	84	22	5	0	0	7	6	14	.262	.321	.301
Sept./Oct.	81	21	5	0	3	11	9	15	.259	.432	.323
Leading Off Inn.	62	16	2	0	5	5	3	18	.258	.532	.292
Runners On	154	41	9	0	2	33	23	24	.266	.364	.350
Runners/Scor. Pos.	90	22	4	0	1	29	15	11	.244	.322	.333
Runners On/2 Out	73	18	2	0	2	10	12	12	.247	.356	.353
Scor. Pos./2 Out	49	11	1	0	1	8	10	7	.224	.306	.356
Late Inning Pressure	49	12	2	0	1	7	4	14	.245	.347	.302
Leading Off	10	4	0	0	1	1	0	1	.400	.700	.400
Runners On	23	5	2	0	0	6	3	6	.217	.304	.308
Runners/Scor. Pos.	15	3	1	0	0	5	3	5	.200	.267	.333

DRIVING IN RUNS	From 1B	From 2B	From 3B	Scoring Position
Totals	3/106	7/64	21/47	28/111
Percentage	3%	11%	45%	25%
Driving In Runners from 3B with Less than Two Out:		16/26		62%

Loves to face: Chris Welsh (.417, 5-for-12, 2 HR)
Hates to face: Joe Price (.118, 2-for-17)
Caught 103 games last season, his highest total since 1980. . . . Caught 52 percent of team's innings; Mark Bailey, 28 percent; John Mizerock, 18 percent; Robbie Wine, two percent; Jim Pankovits, one inning. . . . Couldn't hit lefties early in his career, and that label stuck with him long after he turned things around. 1975–80: .251 vs. right-handers, .165 vs. left-handers; 1981–86: .257 vs. right-handers, .260 vs. left-handers. Had a career-high number of at bats vs. left-handers last season. . . . Ninth player in major-league history to catch as many as three no-hitters. Ray Schalk caught four; the others: Lou Criger, Bill Carrigan, Val Picinich, Luke Sewell, Jim Hegan, Roy Campanella, and Del Crandall.

Wally Backman

New York Mets — Bats Left and Right

	AB	H	2B	3B	HR	RRF	BB	SO	BA	SA	OBA
Season	387	124	18	2	1	28	36	32	.320	.385	.376
vs. Left-Handers	52	10	1	1	0	6	5	10	.192	.250	.259
vs. Right-Handers	335	114	17	1	1	22	31	22	.340	.406	.394
Home	180	56	6	1	1	10	19	12	.311	.372	.377
Road	207	68	12	1	0	18	17	20	.329	.396	.374
Grass	260	80	10	1	1	17	26	20	.308	.365	.367
Artificial Turf	127	44	8	1	0	11	10	12	.346	.425	.394
April	35	13	1	1	0	2	4	2	.371	.457	.425
May	48	16	6	0	0	4	2	3	.333	.458	.360
June	84	28	2	0	0	5	9	6	.333	.357	.398
July	76	24	3	0	0	8	3	7	.316	.355	.342
August	75	24	4	0	0	7	9	8	.320	.373	.384
Sept./Oct.	69	19	2	1	1	2	9	6	.275	.377	.359
Leading Off Inn.	68	24	4	0	1	1	5	6	.353	.456	.397
Runners On	149	45	6	0	0	27	16	15	.302	.342	.363
Runners/Scor. Pos.	84	19	4	0	0	26	9	13	.226	.274	.292
Runners On/2 Out	51	20	4	0	0	15	6	5	.392	.471	.456
Scor. Pos./2 Out	39	13	4	0	0	15	1	5	.333	.436	.350
Late Inning Pressure	55	20	1	0	0	2	7	6	.364	.382	.435
Leading Off	18	6	0	0	0	0	3	3	.333	.333	.429
Runners On	17	7	1	0	0	2	2	2	.412	.471	.474
Runners/Scor. Pos.	8	1	1	0	0	2	2	2	.125	.250	.300

DRIVING IN RUNS	From 1B	From 2B	From 3B	Scoring Position
Totals	4/92	12/74	11/23	23/97
Percentage	4%	16%	48%	24%
Driving In Runners from 3B with Less than Two Out:		8/13		62%

Loves to face: Rick Mahler (.536, 15-for-28)
Hates to face: Fernando Valenzuela (0-for-16)

Maintains his title as Mr. Ground Ball: Career rate of 2.49 ground outs for every air out is highest in majors over past 12 years.... Hit his only home run last season on his birthday (Sept. 22).... Batted second in the lineup in each of his 92 games started, after being Mets' leadoff hitter for most of two previous years.... Career average of .144 vs. left-handers, 11 points lower than the combined career-vs.-lefties average of the five pitchers in Mets' starting rotation last year.... Career average of .312 vs. right-handers.... Five hits in 11 career at bats with two outs and the bases loaded.... Lowest fielding average (.966) of any N.L. second baseman (minimum: 80 games).

Kevin Bass

Houston Astros — Bats Left and Right

	AB	H	2B	3B	HR	RRF	BB	SO	BA	SA	OBA
Season	591	184	33	5	20	85	38	72	.311	.486	.357
vs. Left-Handers	248	80	18	0	12	43	7	31	.323	.540	.345
vs. Right-Handers	343	104	15	5	8	42	31	41	.303	.446	.365
Home	296	93	14	2	5	42	18	37	.314	.426	.361
Road	295	91	19	3	15	43	20	35	.308	.546	.353
Grass	170	51	11	3	10	26	9	20	.300	.576	.333
Artificial Turf	421	133	22	2	10	59	29	52	.316	.449	.366
April	73	19	2	1	2	6	6	9	.260	.397	.308
May	101	29	8	0	2	10	3	12	.287	.426	.308
June	98	37	5	1	7	15	12	10	.378	.663	.460
July	104	31	4	0	3	15	5	17	.298	.423	.333
August	100	29	3	3	4	14	7	13	.290	.500	.349
Sept./Oct.	115	39	11	0	2	25	5	11	.339	.487	.358
Leading Off Inn.	143	45	12	3	6	7	3	16	.315	.566	.329
Runners On	256	75	15	2	5	69	26	33	.293	.426	.360
Runners/Scor. Pos.	148	46	9	1	3	60	19	22	.311	.446	.384
Runners On/2 Out	114	31	3	0	4	33	17	17	.272	.404	.375
Scor. Pos./2 Out	82	22	2	0	3	29	14	14	.268	.402	.375
Late Inning Pressure	89	27	1	1	3	11	6	13	.303	.438	.347
Leading Off	26	7	1	0	1	1	1	4	.269	.423	.296
Runners On	42	10	0	1	0	8	3	6	.238	.286	.347
Runners/Scor. Pos.	23	7	0	0	0	7	2	5	.304	.304	.360

DRIVING IN RUNS	From 1B	From 2B	From 3B	Scoring Position
Totals	10/184	29/120	25/65	54/185
Percentage	5%	24%	38%	29%
Driving In Runners from 3B with Less than Two Out:		15/25		60%

Loves to face: Kent Tekulve (.714, 5-for-7, 2 triples)
Hates to face: Jay Tibbs (.111, 2-for-18)

Led N.L. in hits (80) and extra-base hits (30) off left-handed pitchers.... Right side is his power side; career figures: batting .278, slugging .454, one homer every 30.2 at bats batting right-handed; .270, .385, and one every 62.2 batting lefty.... Has homered in every N.L. ballpark except Veterans Stadium (51 career AB).... Hit five of his 20 home runs vs. Padres.... Led N.L. in batting for the month of June (minimum: 75 AB).... Had hit only 20 home runs in 1,098 at bats in majors before start of 1986 season; matched that total in 591 at bats last year.... Only N.L. player with at least 10 more homers on the road than at his home park in 1986.

Buddy Bell

Cincinnati Reds — Bats Right

	AB	H	2B	3B	HR	RRF	BB	SO	BA	SA	OBA
Season	568	158	29	3	20	81	73	49	.278	.445	.362
vs. Left-Handers	174	47	9	1	8	27	22	16	.270	.471	.348
vs. Right-Handers	394	111	20	2	12	54	51	33	.282	.434	.368
Home	276	85	12	3	14	47	34	19	.308	.525	.387
Road	292	73	17	0	6	34	39	30	.250	.370	.339
Grass	176	44	11	0	4	22	23	20	.250	.381	.338
Artificial Turf	392	114	18	3	16	59	50	29	.291	.474	.373
April	51	8	4	0	0	2	3	4	.157	.235	.228
May	88	24	4	1	1	9	10	10	.273	.375	.354
June	96	23	4	0	3	15	14	7	.240	.375	.325
July	94	30	6	0	3	13	8	7	.319	.479	.379
August	106	32	4	0	10	22	24	9	.302	.623	.431
Sept./Oct.	133	41	7	2	3	20	14	12	.308	.459	.376
Leading Off Inn.	109	31	6	0	3	3	15	10	.284	.422	.376
Runners On	247	70	13	2	11	71	33	21	.283	.486	.369
Runners/Scor. Pos.	148	36	7	1	8	62	24	15	.243	.466	.348
Runners On/2 Out	100	26	6	0	3	23	14	11	.260	.410	.357
Scor. Pos./2 Out	72	15	2	0	3	21	12	10	.208	.361	.321
Late Inning Pressure	84	25	5	0	2	12	16	9	.298	.429	.406
Leading Off	20	6	2	0	0	0	3	4	.300	.400	.391
Runners On	39	12	2	0	2	12	7	4	.308	.513	.404
Runners/Scor. Pos.	29	6	2	0	1	10	6	3	.207	.379	.333

DRIVING IN RUNS	From 1B	From 2B	From 3B	Scoring Position
Totals	12/170	23/114	25/62	48/176
Percentage	7%	20%	40%	27%
Driving In Runners from 3B with Less than Two Out:		18/29		62%

Loves to face: Ed Whitson (.400, 6-for-15, 2 HR)
Hates to face: Rick Reuschel (.067, 1-for-15, 1 HR)

Has played in 2133 regular-season games, the 2d-highest total among players active in 1986 who had never played in *any* postseason games.... Raised his average against right-handers from .214 in 1985 to .284 in 1986 while his average vs. left-handers remained at .270.... Batting average of .157 in April was 4th lowest in N.L. (minimum: 50 AB); drove in only one run in 24 games through May 15.... On-base percentage after the All-Star break (.403) was 6th highest in N.L.; Schmidt (18) was only N.L. player with more 2d-half homers than Bell (15).... Had six home runs and 17 RBI vs. San Diego last season.... Committed only one error in 46 games on grass fields, nine in 105 on artificial turf.

Rafael Belliard

Pittsburgh Pirates — Bats Right

	AB	H	2B	3B	HR	RRF	BB	SO	BA	SA	OBA
Season	309	72	5	2	0	34	26	54	.233	.262	.298
vs. Left-Handers	122	30	0	0	0	12	9	17	.246	.246	.298
vs. Right-Handers	187	42	5	2	0	22	17	37	.225	.273	.298
Home	144	30	2	1	0	17	12	18	.208	.236	.278
Road	165	42	3	1	0	17	14	36	.255	.285	.315
Grass	95	29	2	1	0	11	6	23	.305	.347	.353
Artificial Turf	214	43	3	1	0	23	20	31	.201	.224	.274
April	30	7	1	0	0	4	1	9	.233	.267	.258
May	17	1	0	0	0	1	1	5	.059	.059	.111
June	82	22	0	1	0	13	7	14	.268	.293	.341
July	50	12	1	1	0	6	5	5	.240	.300	.321
August	54	13	1	0	0	6	3	8	.241	.259	.281
Sept./Oct.	76	17	2	0	0	4	9	13	.224	.250	.302
Leading Off Inn.	65	18	0	0	0	0	5	11	.277	.277	.329
Runners On	138	31	2	2	0	34	10	21	.225	.268	.285
Runners/Scor. Pos.	90	22	2	1	0	31	7	15	.244	.289	.310
Runners On/2 Out	56	11	0	1	0	15	7	11	.196	.232	.308
Scor. Pos./2 Out	40	10	0	1	0	15	6	7	.250	.300	.375
Late Inning Pressure	23	5	1	0	0	1	5	9	.217	.261	.357
Leading Off	7	2	0	0	0	1	2	2	.286	.286	.444
Runners On	10	2	1	0	0	1	1	3	.200	.300	.273
Runners/Scor. Pos.	7	2	1	0	0	1	0	1	.286	.429	.375

DRIVING IN RUNS	From 1B	From 2B	From 3B	Scoring Position
Totals	4/91	14/69	16/40	30/109
Percentage	4%	20%	40%	28%
Driving In Runners from 3B with Less than Two Out:		11/24		46%

Loves to face: Scott Sanderson (.444, 4-for-9)
Hates to face: John Tudor (0-for-6)

Had 122 at bats without an extra-base hit vs. left-handed pitchers, the most by anyone in the 12 years that we've been keeping track. Old "record" was 113 at bats by Rick Miller in 1979.... Drove in only 31 runs last season, 10 of them vs. Cubs.... Career breakdown: .307 on grass fields, .202 on artificial turf.... Four hits in nine career at bats with the bases loaded.... Ranked third among major-league shortstops with an average of 3.46 assists per nine innings (minimum: 500 innings).... Played 48 percent of shortstop innings for Pirates last year; Sammy Khalifa, 30 percent; U.L. Washington, 19 percent; Bill Almon, three percent; Jim Morrison, one inning.

Dann Bilardello
Montreal Expos — Bats Right

	AB	H	2B	3B	HR	RRF	BB	SO	BA	SA	OBA
Season	191	37	5	0	4	18	14	32	.194	.283	.249
vs. Left-Handers	40	7	0	0	0	1	3	6	.175	.175	.233
vs. Right-Handers	151	30	5	0	4	17	11	26	.199	.311	.253
Home	84	19	4	0	1	8	10	18	.226	.310	.309
Road	107	18	1	0	3	10	4	14	.168	.262	.198
Grass	59	9	0	0	2	4	1	11	.153	.254	.167
Artificial Turf	132	28	5	0	2	14	13	21	.212	.295	.283
April	25	4	1	0	2	5	3	3	.160	.440	.250
May	29	5	1	0	0	2	2	10	.172	.207	.226
June	15	3	0	0	0	0	1	1	.200	.200	.250
July	20	3	1	0	0	0	1	2	.150	.200	.190
August	68	13	0	0	0	5	4	11	.191	.191	.236
Sept./Oct.	34	9	2	0	2	6	3	5	.265	.500	.324
Leading Off Inn.	47	10	1	0	0	0	6	6	.213	.234	.302
Runners On	88	18	3	0	3	17	6	16	.205	.341	.255
Runners/Scor. Pos.	52	10	0	0	2	13	5	14	.192	.308	.263
Runners On/2 Out	42	6	1	0	0	4	5	9	.143	.167	.234
Scor. Pos./2 Out	26	3	0	0	0	3	4	8	.115	.115	.233
Late Inning Pressure	25	5	1	0	0	3	5	7	.200	.240	.333
Leading Off	6	2	0	0	0	0	1	2	.333	.333	.429
Runners On	14	2	0	0	0	3	3	4	.143	.143	.294
Runners/Scor. Pos.	10	2	0	0	0	3	2	3	.200	.200	.333

DRIVING IN RUNS	From 1B	From 2B	From 3B	Scoring Position
Totals	3/58	6/42	5/13	11/55
Percentage	5%	14%	38%	20%
Driving In Runners from 3B with Less than Two Out:		3/7		43%

Loves to face: Andy Hawkins (.313, 5-for-16, 2 HR)
Hates to face: Bill Gullickson (.050, 1-for-20)
Only major-league player with 100+ at bats in both 1985 and 1986 and sub-.200 batting average in each year (.167 and .194). . . . Hit 21 and 17 home runs in last two full years in minors (1981 and 1982, in Texas and California Leagues, respectively), but has hit only 16 homers in 773 at bats in majors. . . . Came to Expos with three pitchers in exchange for Bill Gullickson and Sal Butera in December 1985. Reds got the best of the backup catcher part of the trade; Butera hit .239 in 56 games, had just one fewer RBI than Bilardello in 78 fewer at bats, had an on-base percentage of .363, and even pitched a scoreless inning, striking out Chico Walker.

Bobby Bonilla
Pittsburgh Pirates — Bats Left and Right

	AB	H	2B	3B	HR	RRF	BB	SO	BA	SA	OBA
Season	192	46	6	2	1	17	29	39	.240	.307	.342
vs. Left-Handers	89	24	4	1	0	9	14	13	.270	.337	.375
vs. Right-Handers	103	22	2	1	1	8	15	26	.214	.282	.314
Home	92	23	3	1	0	9	13	18	.250	.304	.349
Road	100	23	3	1	1	8	16	21	.230	.310	.336
Grass	32	11	0	0	1	3	7	4	.344	.438	.462
Artificial Turf	160	35	6	2	0	14	22	35	.219	.281	.317
April	1	0	0	0	0	0	1	0	.000	.000	.500
May	0	0	0	0	0	0	0	0	—	—	—
June	0	0	0	0	0	0	0	0	—	—	—
July	11	3	0	0	0	2	2	2	.273	.273	.385
August	86	22	6	1	0	14	12	15	.256	.349	.354
Sept./Oct.	94	21	0	1	1	3	14	22	.223	.277	.324
Leading Off Inn.	39	6	0	0	0	0	4	8	.154	.154	.250
Runners On	74	24	5	2	0	16	12	13	.324	.446	.419
Runners/Scor. Pos.	42	11	4	0	0	15	10	7	.262	.405	.404
Runners On/2 Out	23	8	0	0	0	1	1	6	.348	.348	.375
Scor. Pos./2 Out	14	2	0	0	0	1	1	4	.143	.143	.200
Late Inning Pressure	37	6	1	0	1	4	5	9	.162	.270	.262
Leading Off	12	1	0	0	0	0	2	3	.083	.083	.214
Runners On	11	3	1	0	0	2	2	2	.273	.364	.385
Runners/Scor. Pos.	6	2	1	0	0	3	1	0	.333	.500	.429

DRIVING IN RUNS	From 1B	From 2B	From 3B	Scoring Position
Totals	3/51	7/31	6/20	13/51
Percentage	6%	23%	30%	25%
Driving In Runners from 3B with Less than Two Out:		6/12		50%

Loves to face: Dennis Eckersley (.667, 2-for-3)
Hates to face: Jim Deshaies (0-for-6)
Figures above are for N.L. only. See also the A.L. Batters section. . . . Full-time starter vs. southpaws for Pittsburgh (24 starts in 29 games after joining Pirates), part-timer against right-handers (23 in 43). . . . Two-league totals indicate better contact from the right side, more power from the left: .269 batting average, no home runs, one SO per 11.8 plate appearances vs. left-handers; .246, 3 HR, one SO per 4.5 PA vs. right-handers. . . . Drove in only four of 20 base-runners from scoring position, including one of nine from third base, in Late-Inning Pressure Situations.

Barry Bonds
Pittsburgh Pirates — Bats Left

	AB	H	2B	3B	HR	RRF	BB	SO	BA	SA	OBA
Season	413	92	26	3	16	51	65	102	.223	.416	.330
vs. Left-Handers	151	33	10	2	3	14	29	39	.219	.371	.348
vs. Right-Handers	262	59	16	1	13	37	36	63	.225	.443	.319
Home	211	51	17	2	9	28	36	56	.242	.469	.355
Road	202	41	9	1	7	23	29	46	.203	.361	.303
Grass	94	22	5	0	4	12	13	29	.234	.415	.327
Artificial Turf	319	70	21	3	12	39	52	73	.219	.417	.331
April	1	1	0	0	0	2	0	0	1.000	1.000	1.000
May	8	1	1	0	0	0	2	3	.125	.250	.300
June	111	27	9	1	6	15	20	33	.243	.505	.364
July	73	13	4	1	2	6	10	24	.178	.342	.274
August	108	27	8	1	6	19	18	20	.250	.509	.354
Sept./Oct.	112	23	4	0	2	9	15	22	.205	.295	.305
Leading Off Inn.	153	36	10	1	7	8	24	35	.235	.451	.343
Runners On	139	36	9	1	4	38	20	38	.259	.424	.352
Runners/Scor. Pos.	96	20	3	1	2	32	14	27	.208	.323	.304
Runners On/2 Out	62	11	3	0	2	13	6	17	.177	.323	.261
Scor. Pos./2 Out	28	5	1	0	2	12	4	15	.154	.288	.214
Late Inning Pressure	70	12	2	1	1	5	13	23	.171	.271	.301
Leading Off	19	3	1	0	0	0	2	3	.158	.211	.238
Runners On	33	5	0	0	1	5	5	15	.152	.242	.263
Runners/Scor. Pos.	20	1	0	0	0	3	4	10	.050	.050	.208

DRIVING IN RUNS	From 1B	From 2B	From 3B	Scoring Position
Totals	6/81	14/71	14/44	28/115
Percentage	7%	20%	32%	24%
Driving In Runners from 3B with Less than Two Out:		12/22		55%

Loves to face: Tim Conroy (.800, 4-for-5, 1 HR)
Hates to face: Mike Maddux (.091, 1-for-11)
Led N.L. rookies with 48 RBI and 36 stolen bases. . . . Made his *de facto* major-league debut on May 30 vs. Dodgers, but his game-winning pinch-hit on August 11 vs. Cubs occurred in completion of suspended game of April 20. Statistically speaking, accordingly, his debut was in the game of April 20. Rotisserie commissioners earned their pay on that one. . . . Teammate Barry Jones was the Pirates' winning pitcher in the April 20 game. Pretty neat trick considering he was credited with a save for Hawaii (PCL) on the same night. Joel Youngblood (hits for two teams in one day), eat your heart out. . . . Papa Bobby's 1968 rookie totals: 81 games, 307 at bats, batted .254, 9 homers, 35 RBI.

Sid Bream
Pittsburgh Pirates — Bats Left

	AB	H	2B	3B	HR	RRF	BB	SO	BA	SA	OBA
Season	522	140	37	5	16	80	60	73	.268	.450	.341
vs. Left-Handers	152	34	11	1	2	23	11	23	.224	.349	.268
vs. Right-Handers	370	106	26	4	14	57	49	50	.286	.492	.370
Home	262	74	23	3	5	35	27	34	.282	.450	.348
Road	260	66	14	2	11	45	33	39	.254	.450	.333
Grass	136	32	7	1	5	22	14	23	.235	.412	.303
Artificial Turf	386	108	30	4	11	58	46	50	.280	.464	.354
April	54	13	4	0	4	9	11	8	.241	.537	.364
May	95	28	8	2	3	15	14	10	.295	.516	.382
June	86	21	5	1	3	13	12	19	.244	.430	.340
July	71	22	4	1	1	12	6	7	.310	.437	.359
August	95	28	6	1	3	14	6	11	.295	.474	.333
Sept./Oct.	121	28	10	0	2	17	11	18	.231	.364	.291
Leading Off Inn.	134	33	9	2	6	6	15	12	.246	.478	.322
Runners On	241	72	18	2	8	72	34	34	.299	.490	.378
Runners/Scor. Pos.	119	35	8	2	3	57	26	18	.294	.471	.405
Runners On/2 Out	96	25	8	0	1	19	17	15	.260	.375	.372
Scor. Pos./2 Out	52	11	4	0	0	15	11	10	.212	.288	.349
Late Inning Pressure	96	21	5	0	2	13	12	19	.219	.333	.300
Leading Off	28	3	1	0	0	0	3	3	.107	.143	.194
Runners On	37	12	3	0	0	13	8	5	.324	.568	.426
Runners/Scor. Pos.	16	5	1	0	1	10	6	2	.313	.563	.458

DRIVING IN RUNS	From 1B	From 2B	From 3B	Scoring Position
Totals	15/178	22/91	27/54	49/145
Percentage	8%	24%	50%	34%
Driving In Runners from 3B with Less than Two Out:		22/26		85%

Loves to face: Mike Scott (.389, 7-for-18, 2 HR)
Hates to face: Dave Dravecky (0-for-8)
Set N.L. record for first basemen with 166 assists last season. Old record: 161, by the man whose name is synonymous with ground balls to first base, Bill Buckner. (Buckner still holds the A.L. record, 184). . . . Batted 118 points higher in night games (.303) than in day games (.184), largest difference in N.L. (minimum: 50 AB in each). . . . Drove in 22 of 26 (.846) runners from third base with less than two out, 2d-highest percentage in N.L. (minimum: 10 RRF). . . . Started 35 of 58 games in which Bucs faced a lefty starter. . . . Career breakdown: .220 on grass fields; .270 on artificial surfaces. . . . Batted over .300 in all five seasons in minors.

Bob Brenly
San Francisco Giants — Bats Right

	AB	H	2B	3B	HR	RRF	BB	SO	BA	SA	OBA
Season	472	116	26	0	16	67	74	97	.246	.403	.350
vs. Left-Handers	157	42	16	0	6	25	29	31	.268	.484	.378
vs. Right-Handers	315	74	10	0	10	42	45	66	.235	.362	.335
Home	235	55	10	0	8	34	34	53	.234	.379	.331
Road	237	61	16	0	8	33	40	44	.257	.426	.368
Grass	354	86	18	0	12	47	57	72	.243	.395	.348
Artificial Turf	118	30	8	0	4	20	17	25	.254	.424	.355
April	59	15	2	0	3	8	17	13	.254	.441	.421
May	73	16	4	0	0	7	17	19	.219	.274	.359
June	68	18	1	0	1	8	12	12	.265	.324	.383
July	73	17	6	0	3	12	6	10	.233	.438	.291
August	85	22	7	0	2	11	8	16	.259	.412	.330
Sept./Oct.	114	28	6	0	7	21	14	27	.246	.482	.331
Leading Off Inn.	98	27	6	0	4	4	13	23	.276	.459	.366
Runners On	201	47	11	0	7	58	31	32	.234	.393	.335
Runners/Scor. Pos.	127	33	9	0	7	56	25	22	.260	.496	.378
Runners On/2 Out	71	14	4	0	3	21	16	13	.197	.380	.345
Scor. Pos./2 Out	50	11	3	0	3	20	12	8	.220	.460	.371
Late Inning Pressure	90	20	5	0	1	9	9	25	.222	.311	.293
Leading Off	21	5	2	0	0	0	3	6	.238	.333	.333
Runners On	37	7	1	0	0	8	4	7	.189	.216	.268
Runners/Scor. Pos.	26	6	1	0	0	8	2	7	.231	.269	.286

DRIVING IN RUNS	From 1B	From 2B	From 3B	Scoring Position
Totals	9/142	22/103	20/51	42/154
Percentage	6%	21%	39%	27%
Driving In Runners from 3B with Less than Two Out:		14/29		48%

Loves to face: Steve Trout (.467, 7-for-15, 2 HR)
Hates to face: Danny Cox (0-for-12)

First N.L. third baseman since Lewis Whistler in 1891 to commit four errors in one inning (Sept. 14). Redeemed himself with two home runs in that game, the second one a game-winner in the ninth inning. ... Career batting average of .216 at Dodger Stadium, the only N.L. ballpark in which he has not homered (102 AB). ... A bases-loaded bust: 60 career plate appearances have resulted in only 35 runs (.58 every PA; 1986 major-league average: .74) and a .196 (10-for-51) average. Even worse (3-for-28) with bases loaded and two outs. ... Career average of .261 on road, .247 at home. Rule of thumb: Mentally add five points to a Giant player's overall batting average in consideration of the effect of Candlestick.

Greg Brock
Los Angeles Dodgers — Bats Left

	AB	H	2B	3B	HR	RRF	BB	SO	BA	SA	OBA
Season	325	76	13	0	16	52	37	60	.234	.422	.309
vs. Left-Handers	59	6	3	0	0	1	9	23	.102	.153	.221
vs. Right-Handers	266	70	10	0	16	51	28	37	.263	.481	.329
Home	140	33	0	0	5	20	15	25	.236	.343	.306
Road	185	43	13	0	11	32	22	35	.232	.481	.311
Grass	239	53	5	0	8	36	33	41	.222	.343	.313
Artificial Turf	86	23	8	0	8	16	4	19	.267	.640	.297
April	74	14	1	0	3	7	10	13	.189	.324	.286
May	56	12	0	0	1	8	9	10	.214	.268	.323
June	44	11	3	0	4	9	4	9	.250	.477	.306
July	17	5	1	0	1	6	4	2	.294	.529	.391
August	60	18	5	0	4	15	5	11	.300	.583	.348
Sept./Oct.	74	16	3	0	3	7	5	15	.216	.378	.266
Leading Off Inn.	75	18	3	0	4	4	10	17	.240	.440	.329
Runners On	148	38	3	0	8	44	19	30	.257	.439	.333
Runners/Scor. Pos.	93	22	3	0	4	36	14	18	.237	.398	.324
Runners On/2 Out	70	15	0	0	3	16	9	15	.214	.343	.304
Scor. Pos./2 Out	50	10	0	0	1	12	5	10	.200	.260	.273
Late Inning Pressure	52	3	1	0	0	0	8	11	.058	.077	.183
Leading Off	16	2	1	0	0	0	4	6	.125	.188	.300
Runners On	21	1	0	0	0	0	3	3	.048	.048	.167
Runners/Scor. Pos.	15	1	0	0	0		2	1	.067	.067	.176

DRIVING IN RUNS	From 1B	From 2B	From 3B	Scoring Position
Totals	7/102	13/71	16/41	29/112
Percentage	7%	18%	39%	26%
Driving In Runners from 3B with Less than Two Out:		11/22		50%

Loves to face: Joaquin Andujar (.455, 5-for-11, 1 HR)
Hates to face: Joe Niekro (.083, 2-for-24)
.058 batting average in Late-Inning Pressure Situations was lowest by any major leaguer over past 12 years (minimum: 50 AB). ... Career breakdown: .182, one home run every 31.3 at bats vs. left-handers; .246, one every 19.6 at bats vs. right-handers. ... Leaving one bad home-run stadium for another: Dodger Stadium has depressed homers by 16 percent over past five years; County Stadium by 13 percent. ... Has been hit by a pitch once (in 1983) in 1,737 major-league plate appearances. ... Annual batting averages vs. left-handers: .219 in 1983, .208 in '84, .176 in '85, .102 in '86. Reserve 1988 copy of Analyst now to see if he dips into double figures.

Hubie Brooks
Montreal Expos — Bats Right

	AB	H	2B	3B	HR	RRF	BB	SO	BA	SA	OBA
Season	306	104	18	5	14	59	25	60	.340	.569	.388
vs. Left-Handers	85	31	6	3	5	17	13	13	.365	.682	.450
vs. Right-Handers	221	73	12	2	9	42	12	47	.330	.525	.361
Home	137	48	8	2	3	26	14	24	.350	.504	.409
Road	169	56	10	3	11	33	11	36	.331	.621	.370
Grass	103	34	8	0	8	21	6	24	.330	.641	.366
Artificial Turf	203	70	10	5	6	38	19	36	.345	.532	.398
April	77	24	6	0	5	16	8	11	.312	.584	.384
May	85	29	4	3	7	24	6	27	.341	.706	.379
June	79	28	4	2	2	9	9	15	.354	.532	.420
July	63	22	3	0	0	10	1	6	.349	.397	.348
August	2	1	1	0	0	0	1	1	.500	1.000	.667
Sept./Oct.	0	0	0	0	0	0	0	0	—	—	—
Leading Off Inn.	76	25	4	3	1	1	5	12	.329	.500	.370
Runners On	148	47	9	1	5	50	15	36	.318	.493	.373
Runners/Scor. Pos.	92	26	6	0	4	45	11	30	.283	.478	.349
Runners On/2 Out	66	19	4	0	3	17	10	15	.288	.485	.382
Scor. Pos./2 Out	40	10	2	0	1	16	8	13	.250	.525	.375
Late Inning Pressure	56	21	3	1	2	10	3	12	.375	.571	.426
Leading Off	11	5	1	0	1	1	0	3	.455	.818	.455
Runners On	32	13	1	1	1	9	2	9	.406	.594	.457
Runners/Scor. Pos.	19	5	1	0	1	8	2	8	.263	.474	.364

DRIVING IN RUNS	From 1B	From 2B	From 3B	Scoring Position
Totals	7/99	16/76	22/44	38/120
Percentage	7%	21%	50%	32%
Driving In Runners from 3B with Less than Two Out:		17/29		59%

Loves to face: Bob Walk (.615, 8-for-13, 1 HR)
Hates to face: Bruce Sutter, (.100, 2-for-20)
Batting average vs. left-handed pitchers has improved in each season since 1982: .259, .272, .290, .310, .365. ... Hit 13 home runs in his first 43 games, one homer in 37 games thereafter. ... Has homered in every N.L. ballpark except the Astrodome (108 career AB). ... Only N.L. player to hit better in Late-Inning Pressure Situations than overall for each of the last six seasons. ... Has not had a sacrifice bunt since 1983. ... Has quit third base cold turkey; not one inning there since coming to the Expos. ... First Montreal shortstop ever selected for All-Star Game. ... Ah, Expos' history; remember when Gene Mauch had catcher Ron Brand playing shortstop for 41 games in 1970–71?

Chris Brown
San Francisco Giants — Bats Right

	AB	H	2B	3B	HR	RRF	BB	SO	BA	SA	OBA
Season	416	132	16	3	7	51	33	43	.317	.421	.376
vs. Left-Handers	137	40	8	1	3	12	6	14	.292	.431	.331
vs. Right-Handers	279	92	8	2	4	39	27	29	.330	.416	.396
Home	228	76	7	2	3	31	23	25	.333	.421	.400
Road	188	56	9	1	4	20	10	18	.298	.420	.345
Grass	311	101	9	3	4	40	27	30	.325	.412	.387
Artificial Turf	105	31	7	0	3	11	6	13	.295	.448	.339
April	63	22	2	1	1	12	5	5	.349	.460	.408
May	72	23	3	1	2	10	7	8	.319	.472	.375
June	92	31	4	0	3	10	12	8	.337	.478	.413
July	94	31	5	1	1	11	6	10	.330	.436	.381
August	90	25	2	0	0	8	3	10	.278	.300	.327
Sept./Oct.	5	0	0	0	0	0	0	2	.000	.000	.000
Leading Off Inn.	90	20	3	1	1	1	5	12	.222	.311	.278
Runners On	172	65	8	1	2	46	17	15	.378	.471	.440
Runners/Scor. Pos.	92	34	4	1	0	42	13	6	.370	.435	.447
Runners On/2 Out	66	23	2	0	0	16	6	9	.348	.379	.434
Scor. Pos./2 Out	44	16	1	0	0	16	5	4	.364	.386	.462
Late Inning Pressure	73	24	1	1	1	9	9	8	.329	.425	.395
Leading Off	19	5	1	0	0	0	2	4	.263	.316	.333
Runners On	30	11	1	0	1	9	5	1	.367	.500	.436
Runners/Scor. Pos.	13	3	0	0	0	7	4	1	.231	.231	.381

DRIVING IN RUNS	From 1B	From 2B	From 3B	Scoring Position
Totals	2/132	15/66	26/43	41/109
Percentage	2%	23%	60%	38%
Driving In Runners from 3B with Less than Two Out:		17/27		63%

Loves to face: Rick Reuschel (.667, 6-for-9, 2 HR)
Hates to face: Mario Soto (.053, 1-for-19)
Batted 103 points higher with runners on base than with bases empty, 7th-largest difference in majors (minimum: 100 AB each way); see Giants essay on page 163 for detailed analysis of fabulous clutch-hitting statistics. ... Just one teaser: .355 career batting average with runners in scoring position. ... Career batting average of .378 (17-for-45) at Wrigley Field, .170 (9-for-53) at Riverfront Stadium. ... Committed 18 errors in 111 games at third base last season (.933 fielding percentage) after leading N.L. third basemen with a .971 fielding percentage in 1985. ... First Giants' third baseman chosen for All-Star Game since Jim Ray Hart in 1966. ... No, Steve Ontiveros never made it.

Mike Brown
Pittsburgh Pirates — Bats Right

	AB	H	2B	3B	HR	RRF	BB	SO	BA	SA	OBA
Season	243	53	7	0	4	28	27	32	.218	.296	.293
vs. Left-Handers	117	23	2	0	1	9	17	13	.197	.239	.292
vs. Right-Handers	126	30	5	0	3	19	10	19	.238	.349	.294
Home	130	27	3	0	1	16	10	14	.208	.254	.261
Road	113	26	4	0	3	12	17	18	.230	.345	.328
Grass	74	18	3	0	2	8	15	9	.243	.365	.367
Artificial Turf	169	35	4	0	2	20	12	23	.207	.266	.257
April	61	16	4	0	2	8	8	6	.262	.410	.348
May	87	22	4	0	1	16	8	16	.253	.333	.313
June	39	7	0	0	0	2	2	2	.179	.179	.209
July	29	4	0	0	1	2	6	5	.138	.241	.286
August	5	0	0	0	0	0	0	0	.000	.000	.000
Sept./Oct.	22	4	0	0	0		3	3	.182	.182	.280
Leading Off Inn.	51	11	4	0	1	1	6	8	.216	.353	.298
Runners On	118	24	2	0	3	27	13	13	.203	.297	.276
Runners/Scor. Pos.	69	13	2	0	2	24	8	9	.188	.304	.263
Runners On/2 Out	50	10	2	0	1	11	6	6	.200	.300	.286
Scor. Pos./2 Out	29	6	2	0	1	10	4	5	.207	.379	.303
Late Inning Pressure	46	12	1	0	1	5	4	7	.261	.348	.314
Leading Off	11	3	1	0	0	0	2	1	.273	.364	.385
Runners On	23	6	0	0	1	5	0	3	.261	.391	.250
Runners/Scor. Pos.	10	3	0	0	1	5	0	2	.300	.600	.273

DRIVING IN RUNS	From 1B	From 2B	From 3B	Scoring Position
Totals	6/90	4/54	14/27	18/81
Percentage	7%	7%	52%	22%
Driving In Runners from 3B with Less than Two Out:		11/15		73%

Loves to face: John Denny (.467, 7-for-15)
Hates to face: Doyle Alexander (0-for-8, 3 SO)
Had batted .304 for Angels and Pirates in 1985, including .337 mark against left-handers. . . . When he played last season, it was always in right field (38 percent of team's innings there, to lead the team). . . . Career batting average of .212 in Late-Inning Pressure Situations, .278 in nonpressure situations. . . . Four hits in 25 career at bats with the bases loaded. . . . Career breakdown: .303 in day games, .250 in night games. . . . Career on-base average of .353 when leading off inning, 27 points higher than his overall average. League average OBA last year was .322, but for players leading off an inning, it was only .316.

Enos Cabell
Los Angeles Dodgers — Bats Right

	AB	H	2B	3B	HR	RRF	BB	SO	BA	SA	OBA
Season	277	71	11	0	2	30	14	26	.256	.318	.294
vs. Left-Handers	197	56	11	0	2	22	10	16	.284	.371	.321
vs. Right-Handers	80	15	0	0	0	8	4	10	.188	.188	.230
Home	144	39	7	0	2	23	7	13	.271	.361	.308
Road	133	32	4	0	0	7	7	13	.241	.271	.279
Grass	212	57	9	0	2	27	10	21	.269	.340	.304
Artificial Turf	65	14	2	0	0	3	4	5	.215	.246	.261
April	33	4	0	0	0	1	2	3	.121	.121	.194
May	48	17	2	0	0	5	5	5	.354	.396	.385
June	49	10	2	0	0	6	2	5	.204	.245	.235
July	39	11	3	0	0	7	1	3	.282	.359	.286
August	62	20	3	0	2	9	2	5	.323	.468	.344
Sept./Oct.	46	9	1	0	0	2	4	5	.196	.217	.275
Leading Off Inn.	68	16	4	0	1	0	3	6	.235	.294	.268
Runners On	111	29	4	0	1	29	7	10	.261	.324	.309
Runners/Scor. Pos.	73	17	3	0	1	28	7	8	.233	.315	.289
Runners On/2 Out	41	8	1	0	0	6	1	5	.195	.220	.233
Scor. Pos./2 Out	32	4	0	0	0	5	1	4	.125	.125	.152
Late Inning Pressure	46	15	1	0	1	12	4	9	.326	.413	.385
Leading Off	14	1	0	0	0	0	1	4	.071	.071	.133
Runners On	18	7	0	0	1	12	2	2	.389	.556	.455
Runners/Scor. Pos.	15	5	0	0	1	12	2	2	.333	.533	.389

DRIVING IN RUNS	From 1B	From 2B	From 3B	Scoring Position
Totals	2/72	13/63	13/29	26/92
Percentage	3%	21%	45%	28%
Driving In Runners from 3B with Less than Two Out:		11/16		69%

Loves to face: Bob Ojeda (.500, 8-for-16, 1 HR)
Hates to face: David Palmer (.056, 1-for-18)
Did not have an extra-base hit against right-handed pitching last season. Batting average against righties (.188) was his lowest in the last 12 seasons. . . . But his .326 average in Late-Inning Pressure Situations was his highest over that same span. . . . Batted .118 (4-for-34, one RBI) as a pinch-hitter last season, hitless in his last 10 at bats. . . . Has played parts of 15 seasons in major leagues; career-high walks in a season: 30 in 1985. . . . Should be set with cocktail party stories from now till the milennium; he's the only man to play in the major leagues for Earl Weaver, Sparky Anderson, and Tommy Lasorda.

Gary Carter
New York Mets — Bats Right

	AB	H	2B	3B	HR	RRF	BB	SO	BA	SA	OBA
Season	490	125	14	2	24	108	62	63	.255	.439	.337
vs. Left-Handers	171	47	5	0	10	33	37	16	.275	.480	.397
vs. Right-Handers	319	78	9	2	14	75	25	47	.245	.417	.301
Home	228	61	5	2	13	51	33	28	.268	.478	.352
Road	262	64	9	0	11	57	29	35	.244	.405	.323
Grass	312	82	7	2	19	75	41	41	.263	.481	.342
Artificial Turf	178	43	7	0	5	33	21	22	.242	.365	.327
April	64	18	3	0	3	19	10	6	.281	.469	.364
May	85	17	3	0	5	15	12	16	.200	.412	.300
June	86	24	1	0	5	22	13	9	.279	.465	.362
July	92	21	2	0	4	19	12	13	.228	.380	.324
August	56	13	2	1	2	15	6	10	.232	.411	.323
Sept./Oct.	107	32	3	1	5	18	9	9	.299	.486	.347
Leading Off Inn.	111	30	6	0	4	4	9	15	.270	.432	.331
Runners On	262	68	6	1	14	98	38	36	.260	.450	.347
Runners/Scor. Pos.	163	46	3	1	8	84	29	22	.282	.460	.374
Runners On/2 Out	121	30	3	1	5	34	21	17	.248	.413	.359
Scor. Pos./2 Out	75	18	1	1	2	27	16	10	.240	.360	.374
Late Inning Pressure	69	24	1	0	2	12	8	11	.348	.449	.438
Leading Off	15	7	0	0	0	0	1	1	.467	.467	.529
Runners On	37	14	1	0	2	10	5	8	.378	.405	.477
Runners/Scor. Pos.	20	9	0	0	0	9	3	5	.450	.450	.542

DRIVING IN RUNS	From 1B	From 2B	From 3B	Scoring Position
Totals	16/196	27/123	41/78	68/201
Percentage	8%	22%	53%	34%
Driving In Runners from 3B with Less than Two Out:		31/48		65%

Loves to face: Joe Price (.526, 10-for-19, 4 HR)
Hates to face: Don Robinson (.065, 3-for-46)
Has batted for a higher average with men on base than with bases empty in each of last nine seasons. . . . Has hit six opening-day home runs, one short of modern N.L. record shared by Willie Mays and Eddie Mathews. . . . Finished '86 regular season with a 13-game hitting streak, matching longest of career. . . . Longest stretch of games without an RBI last season were the six games he spent in anticipation of his 100th RBI. . . . Batted .304 in day games last season. . . . Career fielding percentage of .9914 as catcher is just shy of Johnny Edwards's N.L. record of .9916. . . . Did not have an error in 73 chances at first base, but suffered his thumb injury, which cost him 14 games, while trying to imitate Keith Hernandez.

Ron Cey
Chicago Cubs — Bats Right

	AB	H	2B	3B	HR	RRF	BB	SO	BA	SA	OBA
Season	256	70	21	0	13	37	44	66	.273	.508	.384
vs. Left-Handers	80	26	10	0	5	15	18	19	.325	.638	.460
vs. Right-Handers	176	44	11	0	8	22	26	47	.250	.449	.346
Home	137	33	10	0	4	19	23	43	.241	.401	.354
Road	119	37	11	0	9	18	21	23	.311	.630	.418
Grass	192	51	16	0	9	28	31	54	.266	.490	.370
Artificial Turf	64	19	5	0	4	9	13	12	.297	.563	.423
April	22	3	1	0	0	1	6	5	.136	.182	.345
May	61	17	5	0	3	9	6	16	.279	.508	.343
June	46	16	5	0	3	9	6	12	.348	.652	.423
July	47	14	7	0	2	9	9	16	.298	.574	.414
August	72	20	3	0	4	9	15	15	.278	.528	.404
Sept./Oct.	8	0	0	0	0	0	2	2	.000	.000	.200
Leading Off Inn.	52	18	7	0	3	3	9	9	.346	.654	.443
Runners On	109	25	9	0	1	25	25	34	.229	.339	.377
Runners/Scor. Pos.	58	18	6	0	1	24	15	17	.310	.455	.455
Runners On/2 Out	48	11	5	0	0	11	9	17	.229	.333	.373
Scor. Pos./2 Out	29	8	4	0	0	11	5	9	.276	.414	.417
Late Inning Pressure	45	11	4	0	1	6	9	14	.244	.400	.370
Leading Off	9	3	1	0	0	0	2	3	.333	.444	.455
Runners On	19	5	2	0	0	5	5	6	.263	.368	.417
Runners/Scor. Pos.	11	4	1	0	0	5	2	2	.364	.455	.533

DRIVING IN RUNS	From 1B	From 2B	From 3B	Scoring Position
Totals	3/83	12/49	9/23	21/72
Percentage	4%	24%	39%	29%
Driving In Runners from 3B with Less than Two Out:		5/10		50%

Loves to face: Bob Knepper (.333, 17-for-51, 7 HR)
Hates to face: John Tudor (.188, 2-for-17)
Had about as unproductive a 13-home run season as one can: 12 solo shots, one two-run homer. . . . Slugged above .500 for first time in his career. . . . Batted .325 vs. left-handed pitchers, highest since 1975. . . . Did not start a game last season after Sept. 1. . . . Batted 77 points lower with runners on base than with bases empty, 7th-largest difference in N.L. (minimum: 100 AB each way). . . . Batting average with runners on base (.229) was his lowest in 12 years we've been recording such things. . . . Batted .406 with four home runs and 11 RBI vs. Mets. . . . Needs 14 games at third base to become 6th major leaguer to play 2000 games there; N.L. record is 2154 by Eddie Mathews.

Jack Clark
St. Louis Cardinals   Bats Right

	AB	H	2B	3B	HR	RRF	BB	SO	BA	SA	OBA
Season	232	55	12	2	9	25	45	61	.237	.422	.362
vs. Left-Handers	89	27	6	1	6	13	16	20	.303	.596	.415
vs. Right-Handers	143	28	6	1	3	12	29	41	.196	.315	.329
Home	117	32	7	1	4	13	23	32	.274	.453	.393
Road	115	23	5	1	5	12	22	29	.200	.391	.331
Grass	55	9	1	0	0	2	9	13	.164	.182	.281
Artificial Turf	177	46	11	2	9	23	36	48	.260	.497	.386
April	65	15	3	1	3	6	11	18	.231	.446	.342
May	87	24	4	0	2	9	18	22	.276	.391	.400
June	80	16	5	1	4	10	16	21	.200	.438	.337
July	0	0	0	0	0	0	0	0	—	—	—
August	0	0	0	0	0	0	0	0	—	—	—
Sept./Oct.	0	0	0	0	0	0	0	0	—	—	—
Leading Off Inn.	67	17	3	2	3	3	9	23	.254	.493	.342
Runners On	102	21	6	0	2	18	28	28	.206	.324	.379
Runners/Scor. Pos.	59	10	5	0	0	12	21	18	.169	.254	.390
Runners On/2 Out	46	8	4	0	0	5	17	16	.174	.261	.406
Scor. Pos./2 Out	30	4	3	0	0	4	13	11	.133	.233	.409
Late Inning Pressure	55	14	3	1	2	5	8	17	.255	.455	.349
Leading Off	19	6	2	1	1	1	4	8	.316	.684	.435
Runners On	20	4	0	0	0	3	3	5	.200	.200	.304
Runners/Scor. Pos.	9	2	0	0	0	2	2	2	.222	.222	.364

DRIVING IN RUNS	From 1B	From 2B	From 3B	Scoring Position
Totals	5/62	5/38	6/28	11/66
Percentage	8%	13%	21%	17%
Driving In Runners from 3B with Less than Two Out:	4/10			40%

Loves to face: Craig Lefferts (.600, 3-for-5, 3 HR)
Hates to face: Bruce Berenyi (.088, 3-for-24)

Don't blame his 23 RBIs on lack of opportunities; his rate of 11-of-66 runners driven in from scoring position was 4th lowest in N.L. (minimum: 50 opportunities). ... Did not drive in a run in 14 straight games (May 9–27), his longest RBI drought since final 16 games of 1979 season. ... Batting averages with runners on base (.206) and in scoring position (.169) were his lowest of career. ... Averaged one walk every 6.2 plate appearances last season, 2d-highest rate in N.L. (minimum: 40 BB). ... Last game in 1984 was on June 22, last game in 1986 on June 24. We'd advise him to stay home on June 26, 1988. ... Maybe not if team is in Pittsburgh, where his career slugging percentage is .661.

Will Clark
San Francisco Giants   Bats Left

	AB	H	2B	3B	HR	RRF	BB	SO	BA	SA	OBA
Season	408	117	27	2	11	45	34	76	.287	.444	.343
vs. Left-Handers	130	40	8	0	2	14	8	27	.308	.415	.348
vs. Right-Handers	278	77	19	2	9	31	26	49	.277	.457	.341
Home	220	74	15	1	7	27	19	35	.336	.509	.388
Road	188	43	12	1	4	18	15	41	.229	.367	.290
Grass	311	98	21	2	9	36	31	61	.315	.482	.378
Artificial Turf	97	19	6	0	2	9	3	15	.196	.320	.225
April	82	26	6	0	3	7	8	25	.317	.500	.374
May	104	23	5	2	3	11	8	23	.221	.394	.283
June	6	1	0	0	0	4	1	0	.167	.167	.286
July	5	3	2	0	0	1	1	1	.600	1.000	.667
August	98	32	5	0	4	13	8	6	.327	.500	.370
Sept./Oct.	113	32	9	0	1	10	8	21	.283	.389	.339
Leading Off Inn.	83	26	4	1	1	1	7	10	.313	.422	.374
Runners On	158	38	11	0	4	38	23	32	.241	.386	.337
Runners/Scor. Pos.	92	18	5	0	1	29	19	20	.196	.283	.333
Runners On/2 Out	54	12	6	0	2	12	11	13	.222	.444	.373
Scor. Pos./2 Out	35	7	3	0	1	7	8	8	.200	.371	.378
Late Inning Pressure	78	31	7	0	5	12	7	9	.397	.679	.442
Leading Off	17	6	1	0	0	0	1	1	.353	.412	.389
Runners On	25	8	0	0	1	8	6	5	.320	.480	.438
Runners/Scor. Pos.	14	6	1	0	0	6	4	4	.429	.500	.571

DRIVING IN RUNS	From 1B	From 2B	From 3B	Scoring Position
Totals	6/111	16/74	12/41	28/115
Percentage	5%	22%	29%	24%
Driving In Runners from 3B with Less than Two Out:	12/27			44%

Loves to face: Bob Knepper (.700, 7-for-10)
Hates to face: Nolan Ryan (.091, 1-for-11, 4 SO)

Some very strange breakdowns. Exhibit A: Unimpressive clutch progression: .316 with bases empty, .241 with runners on, .196 with runners in scoring position, 0-for-12 with the bases loaded; but he did bat 137 points higher in Late-Inning Pressure Situations (.397) than in unpressured at bats (.261), 7th-highest difference in majors (minimum: 25 LIP AB). Exhibit B: Batted 107 points higher at home than on the road—even though Candlestick has deflated batting averages more than any other N.L. stadium over past five years. Exhibit C: Hit 31 points higher vs. left-handers than vs. right-handers. Only one N.L. left-handed batter had a larger pro-lefty difference: Dave Parker (45 points).

Vince Coleman
St. Louis Cardinals   Bats Left and Right

	AB	H	2B	3B	HR	RRF	BB	SO	BA	SA	OBA
Season	600	139	13	8	0	31	60	98	.232	.280	.301
vs. Left-Handers	227	54	5	2	0	12	31	31	.238	.278	.327
vs. Right-Handers	373	85	8	6	0	19	29	67	.228	.282	.285
Home	320	86	5	5	0	13	36	56	.269	.316	.345
Road	280	53	8	3	0	18	24	42	.189	.239	.250
Grass	139	22	2	1	0	9	14	21	.158	.187	.231
Artificial Turf	461	117	11	7	0	22	46	77	.254	.308	.323
April	78	18	3	2	0	5	8	14	.231	.321	.302
May	94	30	1	3	0	10	11	15	.319	.394	.380
June	97	21	1	2	0	3	11	16	.216	.268	.303
July	100	21	4	0	0	5	11	13	.210	.250	.292
August	116	31	2	0	0	6	9	17	.267	.284	.320
Sept./Oct.	115	18	2	1	0	2	10	23	.157	.191	.222
Leading Off Inn.	264	66	8	3	0	0	25	46	.250	.303	.317
Runners On	193	41	2	4	0	31	16	31	.212	.264	.270
Runners/Scor. Pos.	125	25	1	4	0	30	14	24	.200	.272	.276
Runners On/2 Out	86	17	1	2	0	9	6	18	.198	.256	.258
Scor. Pos./2 Out	63	10	0	2	0	8	6	16	.159	.222	.243
Late Inning Pressure	96	24	5	1	0	10	10	15	.250	.323	.315
Leading Off	23	7	3	0	0	0	4	2	.304	.435	.407
Runners On	43	12	2	1	0	10	2	6	.279	.372	.298
Runners/Scor. Pos.	25	6	1	1	0	1		3	.240	.360	.250

DRIVING IN RUNS	From 1B	From 2B	From 3B	Scoring Position
Totals	1/100	12/99	18/57	30/156
Percentage	1%	12%	32%	19%
Driving In Runners from 3B with Less than Two Out:	14/24			58%

Loves to face: Jerry Reuss (.375, 6-for-16)
Hates to face: Kevin Gross (.067, 1-for-15, 6 SO)

Batting average on Busch Stadium carpet fell from .305 in 1985 to .269 last year; it's not easy to hit with one eye on the tarp. ... Became the first player to score fewer than 100 runs in a 100-steal season; Coleman had 107 steals, 94 runs. ... Stole 20 bases vs. Phillies last season without being caught. ... Wonder what he would do against them if he could hit at Veterans Stadium; his average there (.138) is his lowest at any park. ... Batting average with two out and runners in scoring position dropped from .323 in 1985 to .159 last season. ... Batting average after Sept. 1 (.157) was 2d lowest in N.L. (minimum: 50 AB).

Dave Concepcion
Cincinnati Reds   Bats Right

	AB	H	2B	3B	HR	RRF	BB	SO	BA	SA	OBA
Season	311	81	13	2	3	33	26	43	.260	.344	.314
vs. Left-Handers	101	34	9	0	1	7	9	10	.337	.455	.384
vs. Right-Handers	210	47	4	2	2	26	17	33	.224	.290	.279
Home	135	37	6	2	0	15	12	16	.274	.348	.331
Road	176	44	7	0	3	18	14	27	.250	.341	.301
Grass	102	28	2	0	3	13	12	14	.275	.382	.309
Artificial Turf	209	53	11	2	0	20	20	29	.254	.325	.316
April	57	10	1	0	2	9	2	12	.175	.298	.200
May	90	24	5	0	0	8	15	10	.267	.322	.368
June	90	25	3	2	0	7	4	8	.278	.356	.309
July	33	10	2	0	0	4	1	7	.303	.364	.306
August	0	0	0	0	0	0	0	0	—	—	—
Sept./Oct.	41	12	2	0	1	5	4	6	.293	.415	.356
Leading Off Inn.	71	19	5	0	1	1	2	10	.268	.380	.288
Runners On	127	27	3	1	0	30	13	18	.213	.252	.278
Runners/Scor. Pos.	78	16	2	0	0	29	11	14	.205	.231	.290
Runners On/2 Out	55	14	1	1	0	12	7	8	.255	.309	.339
Scor. Pos./2 Out	39	9	1	0	0	11	7	6	.231	.256	.348
Late Inning Pressure	61	19	4	1	0	5	3	10	.311	.459	.344
Leading Off	18	7	2	0	1	1	1	2	.389	.667	.421
Runners On	25	5	0	0	0	4	2	3	.200	.280	.259
Runners/Scor. Pos.	15	2	0	0	0	3	2	3	.133	.133	.235

DRIVING IN RUNS	From 1B	From 2B	From 3B	Scoring Position
Totals	3/93	8/58	17/41	25/99
Percentage	3%	14%	41%	25%
Driving In Runners from 3B with Less than Two Out:	12/20			60%

Loves to face: Zane Smith (.409, 9-for-22, 1 HR)
Hates to face: Ed Lynch (.059, 1-for-17)

Started only eight games from Sept. 1 till end of season, none at shortstop. ... Two of his three homers were hit in the same game (at Atlanta, April 16). ... Batted 113 points higher vs. left-handed pitchers than against right-handers, 6th-largest difference in N.L. (minimum: 100 AB vs. both). ... Batting average with runners in scoring position (.205) was his lowest in past 12 years. ... Made nine errors in 48 games on the road, one in 42 games at Riverfront Stadium. ... Cooperstown-bound? Has played 2163 games at shortstop, 4th in history behind Aparicio, Bowa, and Appling; 314 stolen bases. A yea vote here, even if he was outhomered by Yankees shortstop Jim Mason in the '76 Series.

Jose Cruz

Houston Astros — Bats Left

	AB	H	2B	3B	HR	RRF	BB	SO	BA	SA	OBA
Season	479	133	22	4	10	74	55	86	.278	.403	.351
vs. Left-Handers	194	55	7	4	2	29	12	41	.284	.392	.325
vs. Right-Handers	285	78	15	0	8	45	43	45	.274	.411	.367
Home	245	73	10	2	5	44	32	46	.298	.416	.378
Road	234	60	12	2	5	30	23	40	.256	.389	.322
Grass	141	31	6	0	2	14	14	28	.220	.305	.288
Artificial Turf	338	102	16	4	8	60	41	58	.302	.444	.376
April	33	4	1	0	0	3	3	8	.121	.152	.194
May	82	24	3	1	0	10	7	11	.293	.354	.348
June	94	27	4	1	0	14	12	17	.287	.351	.364
July	84	21	2	1	2	9	8	22	.250	.369	.312
August	98	32	5	1	3	18	8	14	.327	.490	.377
Sept./Oct.	88	25	7	0	5	20	17	14	.284	.534	.400
Leading Off Inn.	105	20	4	1	1	1	10	19	.190	.276	.261
Runners On	207	73	11	3	6	70	27	34	.353	.522	.424
Runners/Scor. Pos.	126	49	7	2	4	63	20	23	.389	.571	.466
Runners On/2 Out	71	24	4	1	4	31	10	11	.338	.592	.420
Scor. Pos./2 Out	45	18	2	1	2	25	7	6	.400	.622	.481
Late Inning Pressure	70	17	0	1	3	10	13	14	.243	.400	.361
Leading Off	20	2	0	0	0	0	1	3	.100	.100	.143
Runners On	31	9	0	1	1	8	11	7	.290	.452	.476
Runners/Scor. Pos.	13	5	0	1	0	6	9	2	.385	.538	.636

DRIVING IN RUNS	From 1B	From 2B	From 3B	Scoring Position
Totals	10/132	26/99	27/46	53/145
Percentage	8%	26%	59%	37%
Driving In Runners from 3B with Less than Two Out:			19/29	66%

Loves to face: Mike Krukow (.386, 22-for-57, 2 HR)
Hates to face: Floyd Youmans (.077, 1-for-13, 5 SO)
Only N.L. player to bat .300 with runners in scoring position in each of last four years (minimum: 100 AB each year): .317, .331, .331, .389.... Career total of 2051 games in the outfield trails only Reggie (2082) among active players.... However, Reggie has played in 27 World Series games; Cruz is still waiting to play in his first.... Batted 132 points higher with runners on base than with bases empty, 3d-largest difference in majors (minimum: 100 AB each way); he's one of nine players with higher batting averages with runners on than with bases empty for the last eight seasons.... Five-for-eight with the bases loaded last season; batting .472 (17-for-36) with bags bulgin' since 1983.

Kal Daniels

Cincinnati Reds — Bats Left

	AB	H	2B	3B	HR	RRF	BB	SO	BA	SA	OBA
Season	181	58	10	4	6	23	22	30	.320	.519	.398
vs. Left-Handers	32	6	1	0	0	0	3	7	.188	.219	.278
vs. Right-Handers	149	52	9	4	6	23	19	23	.349	.584	.424
Home	110	34	4	3	3	15	10	22	.309	.482	.369
Road	71	24	6	1	3	8	12	8	.338	.577	.440
Grass	37	13	4	0	2	5	9	5	.351	.622	.489
Artificial Turf	144	45	6	4	4	18	13	25	.313	.493	.371
April	34	12	2	1	2	5	3	3	.353	.647	.405
May	12	1	0	0	0	0	3	3	.083	.083	.267
June	7	3	0	0	0	2	1	3	.429	.429	.500
July	35	13	3	1	0	5	5	4	.371	.514	.465
August	81	25	4	1	3	6	6	10	.309	.494	.356
Sept./Oct.	12	4	1	1	1	5	4	2	.333	.833	.500
Leading Off Inn.	64	24	7	3	3	5	5	13	.375	.656	.429
Runners On	66	20	2	2	2	19	9	9	.303	.485	.390
Runners/Scor. Pos.	34	8	1	0	0	12	8	6	.235	.265	.386
Runners On/2 Out	31	8	0	2	1	9	3	3	.258	.484	.324
Scor. Pos./2 Out	16	4	0	0	0	5	3	2	.250	.250	.368
Late Inning Pressure	28	9	4	0	2	6	6	4	.321	.679	.429
Leading Off	8	5	2	0	1	1	2	0	.625	1.250	.700
Runners On	12	2	1	0	1	5	3	3	.167	.500	.313
Runners/Scor. Pos.	7	1	1	0	0	3	3	3	.143	.286	.364

DRIVING IN RUNS	From 1B	From 2B	From 3B	Scoring Position
Totals	5/48	6/30	6/12	12/42
Percentage	10%	20%	50%	29%
Driving In Runners from 3B with Less than Two Out:			4/7	57%

Loves to face: Mike LaCoss (.800, 4-for-5)
Hates to face: Ron Darling (0-for-7)
Twenty extra-base hits in 181 at bats, best rate among N.L. rookies (minimum: 15 XBH).... Batted .478 (11-for-23) as pinch-hitter, tied with Terry Kennedy for N.L. lead (minimum: 20 AB). Also walked six times for a .552 pinch-hit OBA.... 15 steals in 17 attempts (88.2 percent) last season, 4th-best rate in N.L. (minimum: 15 SB).... Last at bat of the season was a 10th-inning game-winning home run vs. Charlie Puleo on Oct. 2.... Batted .420 (21-for-50) when leading off innings vs. right-handed pitchers.... Born Aug. 20, 1963; rookie Pete Rose went 0-for-3 that night, but scored the only run as Joe Nuxhall won his 100th in a Cincinnati uniform, a 1–0 decision over the Colt .45s.

Darren Daulton

Philadelphia Phillies — Bats Left

	AB	H	2B	3B	HR	RRF	BB	SO	BA	SA	OBA
Season	138	31	4	0	8	22	38	41	.225	.428	.391
vs. Left-Handers	17	4	1	0	0	0	5	9	.235	.294	.409
vs. Right-Handers	121	27	3	0	8	22	33	32	.223	.446	.389
Home	65	15	3	0	4	12	23	18	.231	.462	.438
Road	73	16	1	0	4	10	15	23	.219	.397	.344
Grass	44	8	1	0	2	5	6	15	.182	.341	.269
Artificial Turf	94	23	3	0	6	17	32	26	.245	.468	.441
April	36	11	1	0	4	7	10	8	.306	.667	.457
May	57	8	1	0	2	5	14	19	.140	.263	.315
June	45	12	2	0	2	10	14	14	.267	.444	.433
July	0	0	0	0	0	0	0	0	—	—	—
August	0	0	0	0	0	0	0	0	—	—	—
Sept./Oct.	0	0	0	0	0	0	0	0	—	—	—
Leading Off Inn.	40	9	2	0	1	1	1	6	.225	.350	.244
Runners On	55	14	1	0	4	18	22	20	.255	.491	.463
Runners/Scor. Pos.	36	7	0	0	2	14	16	16	.194	.361	.426
Runners On/2 Out	21	5	0	0	2	7	12	8	.238	.524	.529
Scor. Pos./2 Out	17	3	0	0	1	5	11	8	.176	.353	.500
Late Inning Pressure	26	3	1	0	0	0	4	8	.115	.154	.233
Leading Off	10	2	0	0	0	0	0	0	.200	.200	.200
Runners On	8	0	0	0	0	0	4	5	.000	.000	.333
Runners/Scor. Pos.	5	0	0	0	0	0	3	3	.000	.000	.375

DRIVING IN RUNS	From 1B	From 2B	From 3B	Scoring Position
Totals	4/38	3/25	7/15	10/40
Percentage	11%	12%	47%	25%
Driving In Runners from 3B with Less than Two Out:			5/8	63%

Loves to face: Andy McGaffigan (.400, 4-for-10, 1 HR)
Hates to face: Andy Hawkins (0-for-6, 4 SO)
On disabled list for 39 days in 1984 (in minors), 84 days in 1985, and 105 days last season. Had 19 home runs and 83 RBI in 113 games for Reading in 1983, his last full season.... Allowed 52 stolen bases in 384.2 innings, one every 7.39 innings (N.L. average: one steal every 9.48 innings).... Batted 135 points lower in Late-Inning Pressure Situations (.115) than in nonpressure situations (.250), 7th-largest difference in N.L. (minimum: 25 LIP AB).... Has 79 strikeouts in 244 major-league at bats. After his season-ending injury, John Russell and Ronn Reynolds picked up the slack: Russell fanned 103 times in 315 at bats; Reynolds, 30 times in 126 at bats. (Don't you just love the Phillies?)

Chili Davis

San Francisco Giants — Bats Left and Right

	AB	H	2B	3B	HR	RRF	BB	SO	BA	SA	OBA
Season	526	146	28	3	13	74	84	96	.278	.416	.375
vs. Left-Handers	168	38	3	1	5	26	10	24	.226	.345	.267
vs. Right-Handers	358	108	25	2	8	48	74	72	.302	.450	.420
Home	258	75	14	0	7	38	43	52	.291	.426	.389
Road	268	71	14	3	6	36	41	44	.265	.407	.361
Grass	395	116	21	1	10	57	66	77	.294	.428	.392
Artificial Turf	131	30	7	2	3	17	18	19	.229	.382	.322
April	72	19	3	0	3	15	7	12	.264	.431	.321
May	81	25	4	1	2	20	9	7	.309	.457	.374
June	96	29	9	2	2	17	20	14	.302	.500	.419
July	88	24	3	0	2	8	9	20	.273	.364	.337
August	84	20	3	0	4	15	22	23	.238	.274	.354
Sept./Oct.	105	29	7	0	4	10	24	21	.276	.457	.415
Leading Off Inn.	146	37	8	1	3	3	15	28	.253	.384	.323
Runners On	218	73	12	2	6	67	51	39	.335	.491	.453
Runners/Scor. Pos.	141	44	6	1	4	60	42	30	.312	.454	.457
Runners On/2 Out	101	32	4	0	3	24	28	24	.317	.446	.465
Scor. Pos./2 Out	71	20	2	0	2	21	26	20	.282	.394	.474
Late Inning Pressure	97	27	8	1	4	16	18	16	.278	.505	.393
Leading Off	26	5	1	0	1	1	2	6	.192	.346	.250
Runners On	34	13	2	1	1	13	12	5	.382	.588	.532
Runners/Scor. Pos.	20	7	1	1	1	13	11	4	.350	.650	.563

DRIVING IN RUNS	From 1B	From 2B	From 3B	Scoring Position
Totals	9/142	21/99	31/62	52/161
Percentage	6%	21%	50%	32%
Driving In Runners from 3B with Less than Two Out:			25/37	68%

Loves to face: Ted Power (.583, 7-for-12)
Hates to face: Jeff Dedmon (0-for-11)
Drove in his 50th run in the Giants' 66th game, but drove in only five runs in 44 games from Aug. 6 to Sept. 26, and finished the season with 70 RBI.... A switch-hitter who is far stronger from left side; 1984–86: batting .303, slugging .478 vs. right-handers; batting .242, slugging .348 vs. left-handers.... Has hit exactly seven home runs at Candlestick Park in each of last four years.... Has homered in every N.L. ballpark except Busch Stadium (108 AB). ... Hit four of his 13 home runs vs. Dodgers last season.... Higher batting average with runners on base than with bases empty in five of his six seasons in majors.... Caught stealing 13 times last season, one fewer than Vince Coleman in 92 fewer attempts.

Eric Davis
Cincinnati Reds — Bats Right

	AB	H	2B	3B	HR	RRF	BB	SO	BA	SA	OBA
Season	415	115	15	3	27	77	68	100	.277	.523	.378
vs. Left-Handers	144	46	4	1	11	28	27	25	.319	.590	.422
vs. Right-Handers	271	69	11	2	16	49	41	75	.255	.487	.354
Home	197	52	6	2	12	36	32	42	.264	.497	.368
Road	218	63	9	1	15	41	36	58	.289	.546	.387
Grass	130	36	4	1	5	14	16	29	.277	.438	.356
Artificial Turf	285	79	11	2	22	63	52	71	.277	.561	.387
April	54	10	1	0	3	7	8	10	.185	.370	.290
May	36	8	0	1	1	6	5	11	.222	.361	.310
June	61	22	1	1	5	13	11	12	.361	.656	.458
July	84	32	9	0	6	17	14	23	.381	.702	.465
August	82	21	2	0	7	19	17	16	.256	.537	.384
Sept./Oct.	98	22	2	1	5	15	13	28	.224	.418	.319
Leading Off Inn.	130	33	5	1	9	9	18	24	.254	.515	.345
Runners On	175	51	4	1	13	62	32	50	.291	.549	.398
Runners/Scor. Pos.	103	29	1	1	8	50	25	32	.282	.544	.417
Runners On/2 Out	81	23	1	1	5	28	20	23	.284	.506	.426
Scor. Pos./2 Out	47	15	0	1	4	25	16	12	.319	.617	.492
Late Inning Pressure	66	20	2	0	3	15	10	16	.303	.470	.390
Leading Off	19	5	1	0	1	1	3	4	.263	.474	.364
Runners On	31	8	0	0	2	14	4	7	.258	.452	.333
Runners/Scor. Pos.	20	4	0	0	1	12	2	7	.200	.350	.261

DRIVING IN RUNS	From 1B	From 2B	From 3B	Scoring Position
Totals	12/129	16/66	21/55	37/121
Percentage	9%	24%	38%	31%
Driving In Runners from 3B with Less than Two Out:	10/28			36%

Loves to face: Greg Mathews (2-for-2, 2 HR)
Hates to face: Fernando Valenzuela (0-for-8, 6 SO)
Also loves to face: anyone at Candlestick (.315, 17-for-54, 9 HR). . . . Had 80 stolen bases last season, one shy of Reds' single-season record (Bob Bescher, 1911). . . . Batted 4th in batting order in 89 games last season (82 starts); stole 58 bases in those 89 games, to account for 35 percent of N.L. total of 164 stolen bases from cleanup spot; 2d place: Darryl Strawberry, 18; 3d: Sid Bream, 11. . . . Career stolen-base percentage (.869) is 2d highest among active players with 100 steals. . . . Averaged one home run every 15.4 at bats last season, 2d-best rate in N.L. (minimum: 10 HR). . . . Drove in only 36 percent (10-of-28) of runners from third base with less than two out, 3d-lowest rate in N.L. (minimum: 15 opportunities).

Glenn Davis
Houston Astros — Bats Right

	AB	H	2B	3B	HR	RRF	BB	SO	BA	SA	OBA
Season	574	152	32	3	31	103	64	72	.265	.493	.344
vs. Left-Handers	211	57	13	1	12	43	28	23	.270	.512	.359
vs. Right-Handers	363	95	19	2	19	60	36	49	.262	.482	.335
Home	285	85	16	2	17	59	32	30	.298	.547	.372
Road	289	67	16	1	14	44	32	42	.232	.439	.316
Grass	169	39	9	0	6	19	15	26	.231	.391	.299
Artificial Turf	405	113	23	3	25	84	49	46	.279	.536	.362
April	75	17	4	1	4	15	5	10	.227	.467	.268
May	93	28	5	0	4	14	10	13	.301	.484	.377
June	108	30	6	1	8	21	8	10	.278	.574	.336
July	104	28	6	0	7	24	10	17	.269	.529	.339
August	94	18	4	0	3	8	15	12	.191	.330	.313
Sept./Oct.	100	31	7	1	5	21	16	10	.310	.550	.410
Leading Off Inn.	152	38	5	1	8	8	10	16	.250	.454	.317
Runners On	265	68	14	1	15	87	40	36	.257	.487	.352
Runners/Scor. Pos.	162	43	8	1	7	66	29	24	.265	.457	.367
Runners On/2 Out	128	33	5	0	9	37	24	18	.258	.508	.375
Scor. Pos./2 Out	78	20	3	0	5	27	17	14	.256	.487	.389
Late Inning Pressure	90	27	3	0	5	16	8	13	.300	.500	.370
Leading Off	23	7	1	0	1	1	1	2	.304	.478	.360
Runners On	36	8	0	0	2	13	7	4	.222	.389	.364
Runners/Scor. Pos.	24	6	0	0	1	11	5	2	.250	.375	.400

DRIVING IN RUNS	From 1B	From 2B	From 3B	Scoring Position
Totals	19/173	23/125	30/68	53/193
Percentage	11%	18%	44%	27%
Driving In Runners from 3B with Less than Two Out:	22/37			59%

Loves to face: Dennis Martinez (2-for-2, 2 HR)
Hates to face: Lance McCullers (0-for-11)
Hit 17 home homers, one short of the Astrodome record (Lee May, 1974). . . . Stood tied for N.L. lead in homers on August 12 before Mike Schmidt charged past. No Houston player has led the league in home runs, and only one has ever come close: Jim Wynn led as late as Sept. 13, 1967, but finished second to Hank Aaron. . . . Career batting averages: .299 at the Astrodome; .230 in road games; .340 at Dodger Stadium; .123 at San Diego Stadium. . . . Career average of 62.7 RBI every 100 games ranks in between Dave Winfield (62.8) and George Foster (62.7). Not bad company. . . . Homered vs. every N.L. team except the Mets last season, then got them on his first time up in Game One of the N.L.C.S.

Jody Davis
Chicago Cubs — Bats Right

	AB	H	2B	3B	HR	RRF	BB	SO	BA	SA	OBA
Season	528	132	27	2	21	75	41	110	.250	.428	.300
vs. Left-Handers	133	31	7	0	3	12	11	15	.233	.353	.286
vs. Right-Handers	395	101	20	2	18	63	30	95	.256	.453	.305
Home	262	70	12	1	14	49	20	57	.267	.481	.315
Road	266	62	15	1	7	26	21	53	.233	.376	.285
Grass	377	90	18	1	16	56	32	80	.239	.419	.295
Artificial Turf	151	42	9	1	5	19	9	30	.278	.450	.313
April	71	18	3	0	2	9	3	20	.254	.380	.280
May	96	23	5	1	7	17	10	25	.240	.531	.308
June	91	25	5	1	1	10	5	15	.275	.385	.313
July	92	19	4	0	3	9	4	18	.207	.348	.240
August	99	21	6	0	3	11	6	20	.212	.364	.248
Sept./Oct.	79	26	4	0	5	19	13	12	.329	.570	.415
Leading Off Inn.	113	31	10	0	4	4	13	22	.274	.469	.349
Runners On	250	66	12	1	11	65	13	45	.264	.452	.292
Runners/Scor. Pos.	137	34	6	0	7	54	9	24	.248	.445	.279
Runners On/2 Out	102	19	6	0	4	24	8	20	.186	.363	.245
Scor. Pos./2 Out	66	13	3	0	4	22	7	13	.197	.424	.274
Late Inning Pressure	100	22	4	0	5	12	8	29	.220	.410	.270
Leading Off	23	7	2	0	1	1	3	7	.304	.522	.385
Runners On	38	10	0	0	2	9	3	10	.263	.421	.295
Runners/Scor. Pos.	22	4	0	0	1	7	1	5	.182	.318	.192

DRIVING IN RUNS	From 1B	From 2B	From 3B	Scoring Position
Totals	11/182	21/114	22/53	43/167
Percentage	6%	18%	42%	26%
Driving In Runners from 3B with Less than Two Out:	16/31			52%

Loves to face: Bryn Smith (.395, 15-for-38, 3 HR)
Hates to face: Nolan Ryan (.056, 1-for-18)
Batting average vs. left-handed pitchers has decreased every year in the majors. Since 1981: .328, .311, .281, .271, .235, .233. 1986 home run rate vs. lefties (one every 44.3 AB) was his lowest since 1982. . . . Caught 145 games last season, most in majors; has caught 579 over last four years, one behind Tony Pena, who leads majors over that span. . . . Batted below .200 for 2d straight year with runners on base and two outs, and with runners in scoring position and two outs. . . . Has hit 10+ home runs at Wrigley Field in each of last four years, and has not reached 10 home runs on the road in *any* of those four years. Career: 62 homers in the friendly confines; 35, as Howard might say, when not so amicably confined.

Andre Dawson
Montreal Expos — Bats Right

	AB	H	2B	3B	HR	RRF	BB	SO	BA	SA	OBA
Season	496	141	32	2	20	83	37	79	.284	.478	.338
vs. Left-Handers	160	53	12	1	11	28	14	20	.331	.625	.384
vs. Right-Handers	336	88	20	1	9	55	23	59	.262	.408	.315
Home	243	72	11	0	11	35	19	39	.296	.477	.356
Road	253	69	21	2	9	48	18	40	.273	.478	.320
Grass	143	42	10	1	4	23	10	25	.294	.462	.340
Artificial Turf	353	99	22	1	16	60	27	54	.280	.484	.337
April	66	22	4	1	6	10	8	6	.333	.697	.395
May	95	25	5	1	3	13	7	21	.263	.432	.320
June	14	4	0	0	3	5	0	1	.286	.929	.286
July	90	20	5	0	2	15	8	20	.222	.344	.267
August	103	28	9	0	3	19	4	15	.272	.447	.313
Sept./Oct.	128	42	9	0	3	21	10	16	.328	.469	.381
Leading Off Inn.	94	24	7	0	4	4	2	9	.255	.457	.286
Runners On	242	67	16	0	6	69	28	45	.277	.417	.346
Runners/Scor. Pos.	161	42	10	0	5	63	24	33	.261	.416	.346
Runners On/2 Out	105	28	7	0	2	26	11	16	.267	.390	.342
Scor. Pos./2 Out	67	18	5	0	2	23	9	10	.269	.433	.355
Late Inning Pressure	97	32	4	1	2	11	8	15	.330	.454	.394
Leading Off	22	7	2	0	1	1	0	2	.318	.545	.348
Runners On	48	14	2	0	1	10	7	10	.292	.396	.386
Runners/Scor. Pos.	30	7	1	0	0	8	7	8	.233	.267	.368

DRIVING IN RUNS	From 1B	From 2B	From 3B	Scoring Position
Totals	8/158	22/120	33/68	55/188
Percentage	5%	18%	49%	29%
Driving In Runners from 3B with Less than Two Out:	22/43			51%

Loves to face: Bob Knepper (.385, 20-for-52, 7 HR)
Hates to face: Craig McMurtry (0-for-13)
Last year we told you that he had higher batting average in day games than in night games in each of his 10 major-league seasons. Make that 11: .293 in day games last season, .280 at night. Over past three seasons, he has averaged one home run every 16.8 at bats during the day, one homer every 37.1 at bats at night. . . . Not surprising that his career average of .346 at Wrigley Field is his highest anywhere; his home run production is best, however, at Cincinnati (one every 13.6 at bats). . . . Expos' career leader in games, home runs, RBI, hits, doubles, and triples. . . . Lefty/righty imbalance is growing. 1976–82: batted .288 vs. left-handers, .283 vs. right-handers; 1983–86: .303 vs. lefties, .260 vs. righties.

Bob Dernier
Chicago Cubs   Bats Right

	AB	H	2B	3B	HR	RRF	BB	SO	BA	SA	OBA
Season	324	73	14	1	4	21	22	41	.225	.312	.275
vs. Left-Handers	105	32	7	0	2	11	9	5	.305	.429	.360
vs. Right-Handers	219	41	7	1	2	10	13	36	.187	.256	.233
Home	157	40	7	1	2	10	10	14	.255	.350	.299
Road	167	33	7	0	2	11	12	27	.198	.275	.251
Grass	214	53	10	1	4	17	14	26	.248	.360	.294
Artificial Turf	110	20	4	0	0	4	8	15	.182	.218	.237
April	79	14	3	0	1	7	7	8	.177	.253	.244
May	62	13	3	0	0	3	6	11	.210	.258	.279
June	29	3	1	0	0	0	1	6	.103	.138	.133
July	20	7	2	0	0	2	2	3	.350	.450	.409
August	99	24	3	1	2	5	4	9	.242	.354	.272
Sept./Oct.	35	12	2	0	1	4	2	4	.343	.486	.378
Leading Off Inn.	116	27	3	0	1	1	10	12	.233	.284	.294
Runners On	106	20	3	0	2	19	6	17	.189	.274	.232
Runners/Scor. Pos.	64	13	2	0	1	17	5	9	.203	.281	.261
Runners On/2 Out	52	11	2	0	0	9	4	9	.212	.250.	.268
Scor. Pos./2 Out	34	7	2	0	0	9	3	9	.206	.265	.270
Late Inning Pressure	52	10	3	0	1	6	2	4	.192	.308	.222
Leading Off	14	5	1	0	1	1	2	2	.357	.643	.438
Runners On	21	4	2	0	0	5	0	2	.190	.286	.190
Runners/Scor. Pos.	13	3	1	0	0	5	0	2	.231	.308	.231

DRIVING IN RUNS	From 1B	From 2B	From 3B	Scoring Position
Totals	4/71	6/53	7/20	13/73
Percentage	6%	11%	35%	18%
Driving In Runners from 3B with Less than Two Out:			4/9	44%

Loves to face: Kevin Gross (.500, 7-for-14)
Hates to face: Tom Hume .071, 1-for-14
27 steals in 29 attempts (93.1 percent) last season, best rate in N.L. (minimum: 15 SB). Only batteries to catch him: Rhoden-Pena on April 12, Dedmon-Virgil on Aug. 31. . . . Career batting average of .254, but only .226 with runners on base and two outs, and .175 with runners on and two outs in Late-Inning Pressure Situations. . . . Drove in only 16.4 percent (12-of-73) of runners from scoring position last year, 3d-lowest rate in N.L. (minimum: 50 opportunities). . . . Batted 118 points higher vs. left-handers than vs. right-handers, 5th-largest difference in N.L. (minimum: 100 AB vs. both). . . . On the platoon threshold? Despite worst overall batting average of his career, he had his best season vs. lefties since 1982.

Bo Diaz
Cincinnati Reds   Bats Right

	AB	H	2B	3B	HR	RRF	BB	SO	BA	SA	OBA
Season	474	129	21	0	10	58	40	52	.272	.380	.327
vs. Left-Handers	133	36	8	0	3	18	13	11	.271	.398	.333
vs. Right-Handers	341	93	13	0	7	40	27	41	.273	.372	.324
Home	220	63	12	0	8	31	17	27	.286	.450	.338
Road	254	66	9	0	2	27	23	25	.260	.319	.318
Grass	168	52	6	0	2	21	12	13	.310	.381	.352
Artificial Turf	306	77	15	0	8	37	28	39	.252	.379	.313
April	56	14	2	0	2	5	5	5	.250	.393	.311
May	66	17	4	0	1	7	11	10	.258	.364	.354
June	92	23	4	0	0	11	5	13	.250	.293	.289
July	67	19	3	0	2	10	4	7	.284	.418	.324
August	105	28	5	0	3	12	10	9	.267	.400	.328
Sept./Oct.	88	28	3	0	2	13	5	8	.318	.420	.355
Leading Off Inn.	121	32	3	0	5	5	4	12	.264	.413	.288
Runners On	195	55	7	0	2	50	24	19	.282	.349	.356
Runners/Scor. Pos.	126	36	5	0	1	46	20	15	.286	.349	.376
Runners On/2 Out	83	18	1	0	0	19	13	10	.217	.229	.323
Scor. Pos./2 Out	60	16	1	0	0	19	13	9	.267	.283	.397
Late Inning Pressure	78	27	1	0	4	15	5	15	.346	.513	.381
Leading Off	18	8	0	0	3	3	0	3	.444	.944	.444
Runners On	32	11	1	0	1	11	4	6	.344	.375	.405
Runners/Scor. Pos.	23	7	1	0	0	11	3	6	.304	.348	.370

DRIVING IN RUNS	From 1B	From 2B	From 3B	Scoring Position
Totals	5/129	17/92	26/62	43/154
Percentage	4%	18%	42%	28%
Driving In Runners from 3B with Less than Two Out:			17/31	55%

Loves to face: Greg Maddux (4-for-4, 1 HR)
Hates to face: Ron Darling (1-for-17)
Has batted for a higher average with runners on base than with bases empty in each of last five seasons. . . . A .324 career hitter with the bases loaded; he also drew three bases-loaded walks last season. . . . Batting .306 with runners in scoring position over last two years. . . . Career batting average of .315 in Late-Inning Pressure Situations, .248 in nonpressure situations. . . . Bounced back from a somewhat brittle past to have 2d-highest at-bat total of his career. . . . Started 129 games behind the bat; in N.L., only Jody Davis (141) and Tony Pena (133) had more. . . . Has been on disabled list seven times since coming to majors. . . . Career batting average of .149 at the Astrodome.

Mike Diaz
Pittsburgh Pirates   Bats Right

	AB	H	2B	3B	HR	RRF	BB	SO	BA	SA	OBA
Season	209	56	9	0	12	37	19	43	.268	.483	.330
vs. Left-Handers	131	35	5	0	9	19	11	32	.267	.511	.326
vs. Right-Handers	78	21	4	0	3	18	8	11	.269	.436	.337
Home	95	24	3	0	6	19	6	21	.253	.474	.301
Road	114	32	6	0	6	18	13	22	.281	.491	.354
Grass	58	13	2	0	4	11	7	15	.224	.466	.313
Artificial Turf	151	43	7	0	8	26	12	28	.285	.490	.337
April	16	4	0	0	0	2	1	5	.250	.250	.333
May	13	2	1	0	0	1	2	4	.154	.231	.267
June	27	8	2	0	1	4	2	7	.296	.481	.367
July	26	7	2	0	3	5	1	8	.269	.692	.296
August	38	14	1	0	6	12	6	6	.368	.868	.444
Sept./Oct.	89	21	3	0	2	13	7	13	.236	.337	.286
Leading Off Inn.	39	8	1	0	2	2	2	6	.205	.385	.244
Runners On	106	29	4	0	4	29	13	25	.274	.425*	.355
Runners/Scor. Pos.	60	14	1	0	2	23	10	14	.233	.350	.338
Runners On/2 Out	46	8	1	0	1	9	9	13	.174	.261	.321
Scor. Pos./2 Out	27	5	0	0	0	6	7	7	.185	.185	.353
Late Inning Pressure	51	20	4	0	1	11	6	9	.392	.529	.475
Leading Off	9	2	0	0	0	0	2	2	.222	.222	.364
Runners On	29	14	3	0	1	11	4	4	.483	.690	.571
Runners/Scor. Pos.	18	8	1	0	1	9	3	2	.444	.667	.545

DRIVING IN RUNS	From 1B	From 2B	From 3B	Scoring Position
Totals	5/75	9/53	11/25	20/78
Percentage	7%	17%	44%	26%
Driving In Runners from 3B with Less than Two Out:			9/15	60%

Loves to face: John Tudor (.556, 5-for-9, 2 HR)
Hates to face: Bob Ojeda (.083, 1-for-12)
A well-kept secret: averaged one home run every 17.4 at bats last season, 4th-best rate in N.L. (minimum: 10 HR). . . . Batted 164 points higher in Late-Inning Pressure Situations (.392) than in non-pressure situations (.228), 3d-largest difference in N.L. (minimum: 25 LIP AB). . . . Batted 111 points higher in night games (.301) than in day games (.190), also 3d-largest difference in N.L (minimum; 50 AB each). . . . Had seven at bats with the Cubs in 1983, after they selected him in 30th round of 1978 amateur draft. . . . Led N.L. rookies in pinch-hit RBI (10); tied Kal Daniels for N.L. rookie lead with 11 pinch-hits. . . . Started 41 of 58 games in which Pittsburgh faced a left-handed starter, including 24 of the last 25.

Bill Doran
Houston Astros   Bats Left and Right

	AB	H	2B	3B	HR	RRF	BB	SO	BA	SA	OBA
Season	550	152	29	3	6	37	81	57	.276	.373	.368
vs. Left-Handers	214	65	13	0	3	19	25	18	.304	.407	.371
vs. Right-Handers	336	87	16	3	3	18	56	39	.259	.351	.366
Home	270	74	18	0	3	20	44	24	.274	.374	.379
Road	280	78	11	3	3	17	37	33	.279	.371	.358
Grass	171	42	8	2	3	10	21	23	.246	.368	.325
Artificial Turf	379	110	21	1	3	27	60	34	.290	.375	.387
April	72	22	4	0	0	3	15	8	.306	.361	.425
May	88	21	3	0	1	6	12	9	.239	.307	.327
June	110	31	3	2	4	9	16	8	.282	.455	.370
July	110	31	6	0	0	7	13	10	.282	.336	.360
August	69	18	5	0	0	3	12	10	.261	.333	.373
Sept./Oct.	101	29	8	1	1	9	13	12	.287	.416	.365
Leading Off Inn.	221	66	8	0	6	6	25	15	.299	.416	.370
Runners On	157	42	8	1	0	31	28	21	.268	.331	.375
Runners/Scor. Pos.	91	22	1	1	0	29	22	16	.242	.275	.383
Runners On/2 Out	66	18	2	0	0	13	19	7	.273	.303	.435
Scor. Pos./2 Out	49	13	0	0	0	13	16	6	.265	.265	.446
Late Inning Pressure	71	14	4	0	1	6	8	10	.197	.296	.280
Leading Off	17	4	0	0	1	1	1	1	.235	.412	.278
Runners On	30	4	1	0	0	5	5	7	.133	.167	.263
Runners/Scor. Pos.	16	1	0	0	0	5	4	5	.063	.063	.261

DRIVING IN RUNS	From 1B	From 2B	From 3B	Scoring Position
Totals	2/111	12/78	17/37	29/115
Percentage	2%	15%	46%	25%
Driving In Runners from 3B with Less than Two Out:			17/17	65%

Loves to face: Roger McDowell (.800, 4-for-5, 1 HR)
Hates to face: Jesse Orosco (.083, 1-for-12)
Batting average vs. left-handed pitchers has improved in each of his major-league seasons. Since 1982: .200, .220, .295, .300, .304. . . . Led off 115 games last season; only Vince Coleman (145) had more in N.L. . . . Just because he plays in Dome, don't think he doesn't appreciate the finer things in life: He owns a .420 career batting average, with three home runs, at Wrigley Field. . . . Became first Houston player since 1980 to steal at least one base in five consecutive games. . . . Averaged only 2.38 assists per nine innings last season, lowest among major-league second basemen (minimum: 500 innings). . . . Led N.L. regular second basemen in walks, and tied Juan Samuel for lead in stolen bases (42).

Mariano Duncan

Los Angeles Dodgers — Bats Left and Right

	AB	H	2B	3B	HR	RRF	BB	SO	BA	SA	OBA
Season	407	93	7	0	8	31	30	78	.229	.305	.284
vs. Left-Handers	173	45	3	0	4	16	8	28	.260	.347	.295
vs. Right-Handers	234	48	4	0	4	15	22	50	.205	.274	.276
Home	205	45	2	0	2	10	15	44	.220	.259	.275
Road	202	48	5	0	6	21	15	34	.238	.351	.294
Grass	334	74	6	0	6	24	25	68	.222	.293	.279
Artificial Turf	73	19	1	0	2	7	5	10	.260	.356	.308
April	91	17	2	0	1	4	9	14	.187	.242	.260
May	88	19	2	0	2	6	9	19	.216	.307	.296
June	77	21	0	0	3	10	2	13	.273	.390	.291
July	65	16	1	0	1	6	6	14	.246	.308	.306
August	46	15	2	0	1	2	2	8	.326	.435	.354
Sept./Oct.	40	5	0	0	0	3	2	10	.125	.125	.186
Leading Off Inn.	136	23	1	0	2	2	9	23	.169	.221	.221
Runners On	162	39	4	0	2	25	10	30	.241	.302	.287
Runners/Scor. Pos.	99	21	2	0	2	25	7	17	.212	.293	.269
Runners On/2 Out	79	17	2	0	1	13	4	15	.215	.278	.262
Scor. Pos./2 Out	52	11	1	0	1	13	3	7	.212	.288	.268
Late Inning Pressure	56	20	1	0	1	5	4	5	.357	.429	.400
Leading Off	14	6	0	0	1	1	1	2	.429	.643	.467
Runners On	23	7	1	0	0	4	1	1	.304	.348	.333
Runners/Scor. Pos.	13	3	0	0	0	3	1	1	.231	.231	.286

DRIVING IN RUNS

	From 1B	From 2B	From 3B	Scoring Position
Totals	2/105	5/72	16/41	21/113
Percentage	2%	7%	39%	19%
Driving In Runners from 3B with Less than Two Out:		9/19		47%

Loves to face: Tim Conroy (.417, 5-for-12)
Hates to face: Dwight Gooden (.067, 1-for-15, 8 SO)
Who Would Have Thought: that Duncan would hit 10 triples in spring training and wouldn't hit a single one during the regular season. In fact, the Dodgers *as a team* wouldn't exceed Duncan's spring-training total until Sept. 18.... Batted 149 points higher in Late-Inning Pressure Situations (.357) than in nonpressure situations (.208), 6th-highest difference in majors (minimum: 25 LIP AB).... Tough hops or tough scorers? He had 17 errors in 56 home games last season, eight errors in 53 road games.... Career breakdown: .273 vs. left-handers, .217 vs. right-handers.... Batted .212 in 56 games batting leadoff; Steve Sax replaced him and batted .340 from the leadoff spot.

Shawon Dunston

Chicago Cubs — Bats Right

	AB	H	2B	3B	HR	RRF	BB	SO	BA	SA	OBA
Season	581	145	37	3	17	69	21	114	.250	.411	.278
vs. Left-Handers	156	36	10	1	6	25	4	27	.231	.423	.247
vs. Right-Handers	425	109	27	2	11	44	17	87	.256	.407	.290
Home	305	80	23	1	10	39	9	61	.262	.443	.287
Road	276	65	14	2	7	30	12	53	.236	.377	.269
Grass	427	111	29	3	13	54	13	78	.260	.433	.284
Artificial Turf	154	34	8	0	4	15	8	36	.221	.351	.264
April	65	17	5	0	3	7	4	10	.262	.477	.304
May	115	36	8	1	3	11	4	16	.313	.478	.342
June	106	26	8	0	2	13	6	24	.245	.377	.292
July	96	23	6	2	3	14	3	19	.240	.438	.260
August	96	19	3	0	3	13	1	25	.198	.323	.212
Sept./Oct.	103	24	7	0	3	11	3	20	.233	.388	.255
Leading Off Inn.	169	40	9	0	6	6	4	29	.237	.396	.254
Runners On	230	64	21	1	6	58	13	41	.278	.457	.320
Runners/Scor. Pos.	137	37	12	1	3	51	9	23	.270	.438	.311
Runners On/2 Out	92	21	6	1	2	20	8	12	.228	.380	.297
Scor. Pos./2 Out	58	13	5	1	1	18	7	8	.224	.397	.308
Late Inning Pressure	107	23	3	2	4	12	2	22	.215	.393	.229
Leading Off	20	3	0	0	2	2	0	1	.150	.450	.150
Runners On	50	10	1	1	1	9	1	10	.200	.320	.216
Runners/Scor. Pos.	31	4	1	1	0	7	1	9	.129	.226	.156

DRIVING IN RUNS

	From 1B	From 2B	From 3B	Scoring Position
Totals	9/155	21/117	22/48	43/165
Percentage	6%	18%	46%	26%
Driving In Runners from 3B with Less than Two Out:		18/33		55%

Loves to face: Don Robinson (.625, 5-for-8, 1 HR)
Hates to face: Sid Fernandez (.083, 1-for-12, 5 SO)
Averaged one walk every 29.1 plate appearances, lowest rate in N.L. last season. Walked twice in a game only once (June 3 at Cincinnati).... Streak of 12 errorless games to end season matched longest of his career.... Career .275 hitter with runners on base, .238 with bases empty.... Better hitter for average vs. right-handers, but for power vs. left-handers: career batting: .260 vs. righties, .229 vs. lefties; career slugging: .403 vs. righties, .408 vs. lefties.... Hit .258 with a league-leading 11 home runs from the 8th spot in the batting order; batted .241 with six home runs, in roughly equal times at bat, from other spots. Only one N.L. *team* had more home runs from the 8th spot than Dunston (Montreal, 14).

Leon Durham

Chicago Cubs — Bats Left

	AB	H	2B	3B	HR	RRF	BB	SO	BA	SA	OBA
Season	484	127	18	7	20	66	67	98	.262	.452	.350
vs. Left-Handers	128	29	3	3	3	15	9	28	.227	.367	.275
vs. Right-Handers	356	98	15	4	17	51	58	70	.275	.483	.375
Home	279	79	13	5	13	43	35	48	.283	.505	.360
Road	205	48	5	2	7	23	32	50	.234	.380	.338
Grass	349	98	14	6	15	52	40	61	.281	.484	.351
Artificial Turf	135	29	4	1	5	14	27	37	.215	.370	.348
April	62	14	0	0	3	9	10	12	.226	.371	.324
May	83	23	3	1	2	9	8	14	.277	.410	.341
June	95	21	2	2	3	16	15	20	.221	.379	.324
July	69	19	2	1	3	12	9	10	.275	.464	.359
August	84	21	6	3	2	5	9	25	.250	.464	.319
Sept./Oct.	91	29	5	0	7	15	16	17	.319	.604	.422
Leading Off Inn.	120	32	4	3	6	6	8	23	.267	.500	.318
Runners On	202	57	5	2	10	56	38	37	.282	.475	.388
Runners/Scor. Pos.	98	24	3	0	3	39	30	20	.245	.367	.406
Runners On/2 Out	83	25	2	1	5	22	22	18	.301	.530	.448
Scor. Pos./2 Out	45	10	1	0	2	15	17	14	.222	.378	.435
Late Inning Pressure	86	21	3	0	5	12	22	16	.244	.453	.398
Leading Off	26	6	1	0	3	3	3	4	.231	.615	.310
Runners On	28	8	1	0	2	9	15	5	.286	.536	.535
Runners/Scor. Pos.	13	4	1	0	1	7	10	1	.308	.615	.609

DRIVING IN RUNS

	From 1B	From 2B	From 3B	Scoring Position
Totals	13/155	16/78	17/40	33/118
Percentage	8%	21%	43%	28%
Driving In Runners from 3B with Less than Two Out:		12/19		63%

Loves to face: Tom Hume (.563, 9-for-16, 1 HR)
Hates to face: Bruce Ruffin (0-for-8, 6 SO)
Batting average with runners in scoring position has been declining since 1982: .346, .321, .294, .286, .245.... Another lopsided home/road year; since coming to Cubs, has batted .305 with 73 home runs at home, .256 with 35 home runs on road.... Led majors with 22 walks last season in Late-Inning Pressure Situations. ... Has walked between 64 and 69 times in each of the last five seasons.... Drove in at least one run in eight consecutive games, June 15–23. ... Hit six of his 20 home runs vs. Pirates.... No sacrifice bunts in his six seasons with the Cubs.... As rookie in 1980, was struck out by Tommy Hutton, the Expos first baseman making his only major-league appearance as a pitcher.

Len Dykstra

New York Mets — Bats Left

	AB	H	2B	3B	HR	RRF	BB	SO	BA	SA	OBA
Season	431	127	27	7	8	45	58	55	.295	.445	.377
vs. Left-Handers	103	24	6	0	0	9	16	20	.233	.291	.336
vs. Right-Handers	328	103	21	7	8	36	42	35	.314	.494	.390
Home	211	68	16	4	4	24	27	25	.322	.493	.397
Road	220	59	11	3	4	21	31	30	.268	.400	.357
Grass	301	93	22	5	4	29	37	38	.309	.455	.383
Artificial Turf	130	34	5	2	4	16	21	17	.262	.423	.362
April	55	18	1	1	1	5	8	7	.327	.436	.413
May	68	15	2	1	0	1	7	6	.221	.279	.293
June	58	23	7	2	1	11	8	9	.397	.638	.470
July	84	30	9	2	3	15	9	10	.357	.619	.415
August	89	20	4	1	2	9	11	14	.225	.360	.307
Sept./Oct.	77	21	4	0	1	4	15	9	.273	.364	.391
Leading Off Inn.	183	56	13	2	5	5	26	26	.306	.481	.392
Runners On	124	37	5	3	2	39	19	13	.298	.435	.386
Runners/Scor. Pos.	80	28	5	2	2	38	12	10	.350	.538	.406
Runners On/2 Out	63	17	3	1	0	20	10	5	.270	.349	.370
Scor. Pos./2 Out	48	16	3	1	0	20	6	5	.333	.438	.407
Late Inning Pressure	61	20	4	0	0	5	10	10	.328	.393	.423
Leading Off	19	8	3	0	0	0	3	5	.421	.579	.500
Runners On	21	6	1	0	0	5	3	2	.286	.333	.375
Runners/Scor. Pos.	11	3	1	0	0	5	2	1	.273	.364	.385

DRIVING IN RUNS

	From 1B	From 2B	From 3B	Scoring Position
Totals	3/78	21/69	13/30	34/99
Percentage	4%	30%	43%	34%
Driving In Runners from 3B with Less than Two Out:		5/10		50%

Loves to face: Kevin Gross (.444, 8-for-18, 1 HR)
Hates to face: Bob Forsch (0-for-11)
No home runs in 89 career regular season at bats in Late-Inning Pressure Situations. Tell that to Dave Smith (9th inning, Game Three).... No triples in 159 career regular season at bats vs. left-handers. Tell that to Bob Knepper (9th inning, Game Six).... Knepper's response: Lenny has a .469 career on-base average when leading off innings in Late-Inning Pressure Situations.... Has started 151 games in major-league career: 103 wins, 48 losses, a .682 percentage. Tell that to Lou Gehrig (.618 career).... Batting average crested at .349 at All-Star break; in six games before the break he batted .640 (16-for-25) with seven extra-base hits.... Has never homered against a left-hander.

Nick Esasky
Cincinnati Reds — Bats Right

	AB	H	2B	3B	HR	RRF	BB	SO	BA	SA	OBA
Season	330	76	17	2	12	43	47	97	.230	.403	.325
vs. Left-Handers	118	28	9	1	5	11	17	30	.237	.458	.331
vs. Right-Handers	212	48	8	1	7	32	30	67	.226	.373	.321
Home	159	36	10	0	9	24	19	55	.226	.459	.306
Road	171	40	7	2	3	19	28	42	.234	.351	.342
Grass	97	24	5	1	1	13	19	26	.247	.351	.373
Artificial Turf	233	52	12	1	11	30	28	71	.223	.425	.303
April	51	10	2	1	3	6	8	16	.196	.451	.317
May	63	14	4	0	1	5	13	12	.222	.333	.355
June	29	8	2	0	2	6	3	9	.276	.552	.333
July	39	11	2	0	1	3	4	13	.282	.410	.349
August	83	19	5	1	2	13	8	23	.229	.386	.287
Sept./Oct.	65	14	2	0	3	10	11	24	.215	.385	.329
Leading Off Inn.	82	25	6	1	3	3	8	19	.305	.512	.367
Runners On	143	32	5	0	8	39	26	45	.224	.427	.339
Runners/Scor. Pos.	84	14	5	0	2	27	19	30	.167	.298	.315
Runners On/2 Out	67	13	2	0	2	13	16	23	.194	.313	.349
Scor. Pos./2 Out	41	6	2	0	1	11	12	15	.146	.268	.340
Late Inning Pressure	45	8	0	0	3	8	8	14	.178	.200	.296
Leading Off	5	1	0	0	1	1	2	0	.200	.800	.429
Runners On	23	6	0	0	2	7	5	8	.261	.522	.379
Runners/Scor. Pos.	15	3	0	0	1	5	3	5	.200	.400	.316

DRIVING IN RUNS	From 1B	From 2B	From 3B	Scoring Position
Totals	8/103	7/54	15/48	22/102
Percentage	8%	13%	31%	22%
Driving In Runners from 3B with Less than Two Out:			11/24	46%

Loves to face: Steve Bedrosian (.545, 6-for-11, 1 HR)
Hates to face: Jeff Robinson (0-for-12)

America's Villain: .421 career batting average at Atlanta Stadium (32-for-76), with eight home runs and .868 slugging average.... Yearly batting average in Late-Inning Pressure Situations since 1983: .346, .218, .211, .178.... Ended season with 26 consecutive errorless games at first base.... Had hit a grand slam home run in each of his first three seasons, but failed last year, when he was 1-for-7 with the bases loaded.... Strikeout rate rose to once every 25.3 plate appearances last season; his career rate is once every 25.6.

Mike Fitzgerald
Montreal Expos — Bats Right

	AB	H	2B	3B	HR	RRF	BB	SO	BA	SA	OBA
Season	209	59	13	1	6	37	27	34	.282	.440	.364
vs. Left-Handers	66	15	4	0	1	8	9	7	.227	.333	.320
vs. Right-Handers	143	44	9	1	5	29	18	27	.308	.490	.384
Home	97	27	2	1	1	13	12	21	.278	.351	.355
Road	112	32	11	0	5	24	15	13	.286	.518	.372
Grass	63	19	8	0	3	16	8	5	.302	.571	.384
Artificial Turf	146	40	5	1	3	21	19	29	.274	.384	.355
April	12	3	0	0	2	4	0	0	.250	.750	.250
May	63	14	2	0	3	10	7	10	.222	.397	.300
June	75	27	6	1	1	14	16	11	.360	.507	.467
July	57	14	5	0	0	9	4	12	.246	.333	.302
August	2	1	0	0	0	0	0	0	.500	.500	.500
Sept./Oct.	0	0	0	0	0	0	0	0	—	—	—
Leading Off Inn.	44	14	3	1	1	1	5	4	.318	.500	.388
Runners On	82	25	7	0	2	33	17	12	.305	.463	.422
Runners/Scor. Pos.	51	17	3	0	2	30	14	8	.333	.510	.471
Runners On/2 Out	30	9	5	0	1	11	6	7	.300	.567	.432
Scor. Pos./2 Out	20	5	2	0	1	9	5	5	.250	.500	.423
Late Inning Pressure	41	11	2	0	1	5	6	10	.268	.390	.354
Leading Off	7	3	1	0	1	1	1	1	.429	1.000	.500
Runners On	19	2	0	0	0	4	5	5	.105	.105	.280
Runners/Scor. Pos.	13	1	0	0	0	4	3	4	.077	.077	.235

DRIVING IN RUNS	From 1B	From 2B	From 3B	Scoring Position
Totals	5/60	9/38	17/27	26/65
Percentage	8%	24%	63%	40%
Driving In Runners from 3B with Less than Two Out:			14/18	78%

Loves to face: Joe Price (.625, 5-for-8)
Hates to face: Steve Bedrosian (0-for-12)

One of two N.L. players to drive in at least 40 percent of runners from scoring position last season (minimum: 25 RRF).... Mismatched with his home stadium: career batting average at The Big O (.208) is 2d lowest anywhere in N.L. (.161 at Dodger Stadium). ... Batted .524 (11-for-21) vs. Mets last season; Carter hit .224 against the Expos.... June batting average was 2d best in N.L. (minimum: 75 AB).... Batted .410 (25-for-61) with 10 walks and 20 RBI during a 19-game span from June 13 to July 6.... Caught 37 percent of Expos' innings last season; Dann Bilardello had 36 percent; Tom Nieto, 12 percent; Randy Hunt, 10 percent; Wilfredo Tejada, five percent.

Tim Flannery
San Diego Padres — Bats Left

	AB	H	2B	3B	HR	RRF	BB	SO	BA	SA	OBA
Season	368	103	11	2	3	30	54	61	.280	.345	.378
vs. Left-Handers	56	8	3	0	1	3	4	14	.143	.250	.200
vs. Right-Handers	312	95	8	2	2	27	50	47	.304	.362	.407
Home	183	54	4	1	1	19	27	33	.295	.344	.392
Road	185	49	7	1	2	11	27	28	.265	.346	.364
Grass	268	77	5	1	3	28	40	40	.287	.347	.387
Artificial Turf	100	26	6	1	0	2	14	21	.260	.340	.353
April	62	17	5	1	0	4	8	7	.274	.387	.357
May	61	17	2	1	2	10	10	9	.279	.443	.389
June	43	13	1	0	1	5	9	5	.302	.395	.426
July	56	16	1	0	0	3	10	9	.286	.304	.397
August	90	28	2	0	0	3	11	19	.311	.333	.398
Sept./Oct.	56	12	0	0	0	5	6	12	.214	.214	.290
Leading Off Inn.	124	34	4	1	1	1	22	21	.274	.347	.396
Runners On	133	37	5	1	1	28	15	21	.278	.353	.351
Runners/Scor. Pos.	80	21	1	0	0	23	10	15	.263	.275	.337
Runners On/2 Out	60	11	2	0	0	9	7	7	.183	.217	.269
Scor. Pos./2 Out	45	8	1	0	0	9	5	6	.178	.200	.260
Late Inning Pressure	62	12	0	0	0	2	11	13	.194	.242	.315
Leading Off	13	4	0	0	0	0	4	1	.308	.308	.471
Runners On	30	3	0	0	0	1	4	8	.100	.100	.290
Runners/Scor. Pos.	22	2	0	0	0	1	2	7	.091	.091	.167

DRIVING IN RUNS	From 1B	From 2B	From 3B	Scoring Position
Totals	4/95	9/61	13/37	22/98
Percentage	4%	15%	35%	22%
Driving In Runners from 3B with Less than Two Out:			12/20	60%

Loves to face: Bob Welch (.341, 14-for-40)
Hates to face: Dennis Eckersley (0-for-11)

Batted leadoff in 62 games last season; stole one base in those games. Padres had just 17 steals from leadoff position last year; other 11 N.L. teams averaged 51.8.... A .242 hitter in first five major-league seasons (through 1983); .280 since then.... Homered off Steve Carlton on May 22, his only home run in 251 career at bats vs. left-handers. Maybe that's what got Bill Giles thinking.... Batting average vs. right-handers (.304) was best of career. Highest he ever batted against left-handers was .172 in 1982.... Read aloud: "Flannery's career batting average against southpaws is .147"; now look around, quick: If you see someone not snickering, get his autograph. That's Wally Backman!

Tom Foley
Phillies/Expos — Bats Left

	AB	H	2B	3B	HR	RRF	BB	SO	BA	SA	OBA
Season	263	70	15	3	1	23	30	37	.266	.357	.337
vs. Left-Handers	31	9	1	0	0	4	3	8	.290	.323	.343
vs. Right-Handers	232	61	14	3	1	19	27	29	.263	.362	.336
Home	120	29	5	1	1	10	18	21	.242	.325	.333
Road	143	41	10	2	0	13	12	16	.287	.385	.340
Grass	66	21	4	2	0	6	5	5	.318	.439	.361
Artificial Turf	197	49	11	1	1	17	25	32	.249	.330	.329
April	0	0	0	0	0	0	0	0	—	—	—
May	15	7	2	0	0	1	4	0	.467	.600	.579
June	18	4	0	1	0	2	3	6	.222	.333	.318
July	56	16	1	0	0	4	5	8	.286	.304	.344
August	83	23	8	2	0	9	8	12	.277	.422	.333
Sept./Oct.	91	20	4	0	1	7	10	11	.220	.297	.294
Leading Off Inn.	71	19	3	0	0		5	11	.268	.310	.316
Runners On	108	26	6	1	0	22	14	18	.241	.315	.317
Runners/Scor. Pos.	64	13	5	1	0	21	10	10	.203	.313	.295
Runners On/2 Out	49	8	5	1	0	11	9	11	.163	.306	.293
Scor. Pos./2 Out	38	7	4	1	0	10	7	7	.184	.342	.311
Late Inning Pressure	55	16	2	0	0	4	10	10	.291	.364	.400
Leading Off	13	5	0	0	0	0	2	4	.385	.385	.467
Runners On	26	5	0	0	0	4	4	7	.192	.192	.300
Runners/Scor. Pos.	14	3	0	0	0	2	4	2	.214	.214	.389

DRIVING IN RUNS	From 1B	From 2B	From 3B	Scoring Position
Totals	3/81	7/49	12/28	19/77
Percentage	4%	14%	43%	25%
Driving In Runners from 3B with Less than Two Out:			8/12	67%

Loves to face: Mike LaCoss (.714, 5-for-7, 1 HR)
Hates to face: Dwight Gooden (.105, 2-for-19)

Ron Hunt, he ain't: has more at bats (888) without being hit by a pitch than any active N.L. player (though he did spend 23 days on the DL after being hit in spring training last year).... Had four hits in last five pinch-hit at bats with Phillies before being traded. He then went 0-for-6 pinch-hitting for Expos.... Hit safely in his first 14 of 15 games as Expos' leadoff batter, but drew only one walk in those games. Expos had 4–11 record with Foley leading off.... Similar career batting averages against right-handers (.249) and left-handers (.239), but has only two extra-base hits in 142 career at bats vs. left-handers.... Yearly batting averages with runners in scoring position since 1983: .333, .234, .232, .203.

Curt Ford
St. Louis Cardinals — Bats Left

	AB	H	2B	3B	HR	RRF	BB	SO	BA	SA	OBA
Season	214	53	15	2	2	31	23	29	.248	.364	.318
vs. Left-Handers	29	6	2	0	0	5	3	7	.207	.276	.281
vs. Right-Handers	185	47	13	2	2	26	20	22	.254	.378	.324
Home	94	26	11	1	0	19	12	13	.277	.415	.355
Road	120	27	4	1	2	12	11	16	.225	.325	.288
Grass	49	6	1	0	0	3	3	8	.122	.143	.170
Artificial Turf	165	47	14	2	2	28	20	21	.285	.430	.360
April	0	0	0	0	0	0	0	0	—	—	—
May	0	0	0	0	0	0	0	0	—	—	—
June	49	14	5	1	1	5	6	7	.286	.490	.364
July	64	18	5	0	0	11	5	8	.281	.359	.333
August	78	16	3	1	1	12	7	10	.205	.308	.264
Sept./Oct.	23	5	2	0	0	3	5	4	.217	.304	.357
Leading Off Inn.	50	12	3	0	1	1	4	9	.240	.360	.296
Runners On	111	30	8	1	1	30	11	11	.270	.387	.331
Runners/Scor. Pos.	75	20	7	0	0	27	10	10	.267	.360	.345
Runners On/2 Out	54	17	5	0	1	15	4	5	.315	.463	.362
Scor. Pos./2 Out	41	12	4	0	0	13	3	4	.293	.390	.341
Late Inning Pressure	39	13	4	1	0	3	7	5	.333	.487	.435
Leading Off	10	2	0	0	0	0	1	1	.200	.200	.273
Runners On	19	7	2	0	0	3	5	3	.368	.474	.500
Runners/Scor. Pos.	12	3	1	0	0	3	4	3	.250	.333	.438

DRIVING IN RUNS	From 1B	From 2B	From 3B	Scoring Position
Totals	3/74	14/59	12/29	26/88
Percentage	4%	24%	41%	30%
Driving In Runners from 3B with Less than Two Out:			7/12	58%

Loves to face: Kevin Gross (.500, 4-for-8)
Hates to face: Mike LaCoss (0-for-6)

How likely is it that both leadoff batters in a game will hit first-inning home runs? Let's put it this way: It has happened in three times in 111 N.L. seasons. . . . Ford and Jeff Stone of Phillies did it last June 20, joining tandems of Eric Davis and Dan Gladden (1985), and Abner Dalrymple and George Wood (1884) as the only double leadoff home run hitters in N.L. history. That latter game was Chicago's home opener for 1884 at Lake Front Park, with its sub-200 foot foul lines. . . . Had seven RBI as pinch-hitter, 2d most among N.L. rookies (Mike Diaz had 10). . . . Started only 50 games last season, but had at least one start in every batting order position except 9th.

George Foster
New York Mets — Bats Right

	AB	H	2B	3B	HR	RRF	BB	SO	BA	SA	OBA
Season	233	53	6	1	13	39	21	53	.227	.429	.289
vs. Left-Handers	104	23	2	0	7	17	6	24	.221	.442	.261
vs. Right-Handers	129	30	4	1	6	22	15	29	.233	.419	.310
Home	120	25	3	0	9	24	13	25	.208	.458	.284
Road	113	28	3	1	4	15	8	28	.248	.398	.295
Grass	164	34	3	0	12	31	17	37	.207	.445	.279
Artificial Turf	69	19	3	1	1	8	4	16	.275	.391	.315
April	47	14	3	0	6	16	5	6	.298	.362	.365
May	65	13	0	0	7	16	6	17	.200	.523	.264
June	69	19	2	0	6	12	8	15	.275	.565	.346
July	47	7	1	1	0	5	2	11	.149	.213	.184
August	5	0	0	0	0	0	0	4	.000	.000	.000
Sept./Oct.	0	0	0	0	0	0	0	0	—	—	—
Leading Off Inn.	55	16	2	0	3	4	4	11	.291	.491	.339
Runners On	109	24	3	1	5	31	9	30	.220	.404	.275
Runners/Scor. Pos.	64	16	2	1	3	27	4	19	.250	.453	.286
Runners On/2 Out	43	9	1	1	1	13	2	15	.209	.349	.244
Scor. Pos./2 Out	30	7	1	1	1	13	1	11	.233	.433	.258
Late Inning Pressure	35	6	1	0	0	1	6	7	.171	.200	.293
Leading Off	6	1	0	0	0	0	2	0	.167	.333	.375
Runners On	18	4	0	0	0	1	2	7	.222	.222	.300
Runners/Scor. Pos.	9	2	0	0	0	1	1	5	.222	.222	.300

DRIVING IN RUNS	From 1B	From 2B	From 3B	Scoring Position
Totals	6/88	10/52	10/26	20/78
Percentage	7%	19%	38%	26%
Driving In Runners from 3B with Less than Two Out:			6/13	46%

Loves to face: Donnie Moore (.636, 7-for-11)
Hates to face: Orel Hershiser (0-for-14, 5 SO)

Figures above are for N.L. only. . . . Averaged one home run every 17.9 at bats last season, 7th-best rate in N.L. (minimum: 10 HR). . . . Hit his only A.L. homer on his 2d at bat, off Bill Wegman on Aug. 15. . . His career home run total (348) is between Dick Allen (351) and Ron Santo (342) on all-time list. . . . Percentage of runners driven in from scoring position last year was his lowest in past twelve years; drove in only one of ten in Late-Inning Pressure Situations. . . . Koufax made Hall of Fame on the basis of five great years. Will Foster be considered on the basis of three (1976–78: 121 home runs, 390 RBI)? We think not; we know of no recent Hall of Famers whose careers ended so unhappily.

Andres Galarraga
Montreal Expos — Bats Right

	AB	H	2B	3B	HR	RRF	BB	SO	BA	SA	OBA
Season	321	87	13	0	10	43	30	79	.271	.405	.338
vs. Left-Handers	120	40	5	0	4	14	13	23	.333	.475	.398
vs. Right-Handers	201	47	8	0	6	29	17	56	.234	.363	.302
Home	161	46	8	0	4	22	15	39	.286	.410	.348
Road	160	41	5	0	6	21	15	40	.256	.400	.328
Grass	86	20	3	0	3	13	8	20	.233	.372	.305
Artificial Turf	235	67	10	0	7	30	22	59	.285	.417	.350
April	41	17	2	0	3	8	8	9	.415	.683	.500
May	75	14	1	0	2	7	6	18	.187	.280	.256
June	87	22	4	0	3	12	6	19	.253	.402	.309
July	17	2	0	0	0	0	0	8	.118	.118	.167
August	3	0	0	0	0	0	1	0	.000	.000	.250
Sept./Oct.	98	32	6	0	2	16	9	25	.327	.449	.383
Leading Off Inn.	76	23	5	0	4	4	9	24	.303	.526	.376
Runners On	145	41	4	0	4	37	14	33	.283	.393	.356
Runners/Scor. Pos.	92	24	3	0	2	33	13	23	.261	.359	.367
Runners On/2 Out	71	23	3	0	2	26	8	14	.324	.451	.400
Scor. Pos./2 Out	55	18	3	0	1	24	8	12	.327	.436	.422
Late Inning Pressure	65	18	5	0	2	8	8	14	.277	.446	.356
Leading Off	18	9	2	0	2	2	1	2	.500	.944	.526
Runners On	33	6	1	0	0	6	5	9	.182	.212	.289
Runners/Scor. Pos.	21	4	1	0	0	6	4	7	.190	.238	.320

DRIVING IN RUNS	From 1B	From 2B	From 3B	Scoring Position
Totals	4/102	13/66	16/38	29/104
Percentage	4%	20%	42%	28%
Driving In Runners from 3B with Less than Two Out:			4/15	27%

Loves to face: Steve Trout (.545, 6-for-11)
Hates to face: Shane Rawley (.133, 2-for-15)

Returned to Expos lineup on Sept. 4 following an injury and terrorized pitchers (.535, 38-for-71) over his next 19 games to raise average from a season-low .247 to .279. . . . Batted .289 with 10 homers and 40 RBIs in 79 starts last season; in 82 other games, Montreal's starting first basemen batted .260, with one home run and 22 RBI. . . . Season total of 42 RBIs was only six behind N.L. rookie leader, Barry Bonds. . . . Drove in only 27 percent (4-of-15) of runners from third base with less than 2 out, lowest rate in N.L. (minimum: 15 opportunities). . . . Born on June 18, 1961, the day that Eddie Gaedel died.

Phil Garner
Houston Astros — Bats Right

	AB	H	2B	3B	HR	RRF	BB	SO	BA	SA	OBA
Season	313	83	14	3	9	45	30	45	.265	.415	.329
vs. Left-Handers	192	56	10	3	6	32	20	22	.292	.469	.356
vs. Right-Handers	121	27	4	0	3	13	10	23	.223	.331	.282
Home	151	40	5	2	2	21	16	20	.265	.364	.335
Road	162	43	9	1	7	24	14	25	.265	.463	.322
Grass	92	25	4	1	4	16	11	14	.272	.467	.346
Artificial Turf	221	58	10	2	5	29	19	31	.262	.394	.321
April	51	17	4	1	4	12	3	7	.333	.686	.370
May	64	17	5	0	0	3	4	9	.266	.344	.309
June	70	18	1	1	2	14	11	7	.257	.386	.354
July	38	9	1	0	2	9	5	9	.237	.421	.333
August	43	10	1	0	0	4	3	7	.233	.256	.283
Sept./Oct.	47	12	2	1	1	3	4	6	.255	.404	.308
Leading Off Inn.	69	22	2	0	3	3	1	9	.319	.478	.329
Runners On	144	31	5	2	3	39	16	19	.215	.340	.293
Runners/Scor. Pos.	86	19	3	2	2	36	9	14	.221	.372	.293
Runners On/2 Out	59	15	2	2	1	21	7	9	.254	.458	.333
Scor. Pos./2 Out	35	11	1	2	1	19	5	5	.314	.543	.400
Late Inning Pressure	50	15	2	1	2	12	5	9	.300	.500	.357
Leading Off	16	5	0	0	1	1	1	1	.313	.500	.353
Runners On	25	7	1	1	1	11	2	7	.280	.520	.321
Runners/Scor. Pos.	18	4	1	1	0	9	1	6	.222	.389	.250

DRIVING IN RUNS	From 1B	From 2B	From 3B	Scoring Position
Totals	8/94	9/65	18/39	27/104
Percentage	9%	14%	46%	26%
Driving In Runners from 3B with Less than Two Out:			10/21	48%

Loves to face: Ted Power (.438, 7-for-16)
Hates to face: Alejandro Pena (.091, 2-for-22)

Batted 92 points lower with runners on base than with bases empty, 2d-largest difference in N.L. (minimum: 100 AB each way). . . . Batting averages with runners on base (.215) and runners in scoring position (.221) were lowest of his career. . . . Even with last season's decline, still has some strong clutch stats: .263 overall average over past 12 years, but .303 with runners in scoring position in Late-Inning Pressure Situations. . . . Batting .395 (15-for-38) with the bases loaded over the past four years. . . . Committed nine errors at third base in an 18-game span (April 14 to May 14). He topped that with five errors in four games, June 23–27.

Steve Garvey
San Diego Padres — Bats Right

	AB	H	2B	3B	HR	RBI	BB	SO	BA	SA	OBA
Season	557	142	22	0	21	85	23	72	.255	.408	.284
vs. Left-Handers	184	52	9	0	12	36	8	19	.283	.527	.311
vs. Right-Handers	373	90	13	0	9	49	15	53	.241	.349	.271
Home	279	68	10	0	11	43	15	37	.244	.398	.282
Road	278	74	12	0	10	42	8	35	.266	.417	.287
Grass	409	100	17	0	13	57	15	51	.244	.381	.271
Artificial Turf	148	42	5	0	8	28	8	21	.284	.480	.321
April	79	17	4	0	3	7	3	10	.215	.380	.241
May	101	30	3	0	8	19	5	7	.297	.564	.330
June	103	21	3	0	2	11	1	11	.204	.291	.212
July	86	21	2	0	1	12	6	10	.244	.302	.287
August	116	37	7	0	6	27	5	18	.319	.534	.352
Sept./Oct.	72	16	3	0	1	9	3	16	.222	.306	.253
Leading Off Inn.	130	40	4	0	5	5	3	14	.308	.469	.323
Runners On	279	68	14	0	9	73	17	34	.244	.391	.284
Runners/Scor. Pos.	166	41	6	0	7	64	11	23	.247	.410	.289
Runners On/2 Out	125	31	7	0	6	33	6	16	.248	.448	.282
Scor. Pos./2 Out	76	21	4	0	6	31	4	11	.276	.566	.313
Late Inning Pressure	97	25	4	0	1	14	6	19	.258	.330	.301
Leading Off	20	7	0	0	0	0	2	1	.350	.350	.409
Runners On	48	10	3	0	1	14	2	14	.208	.333	.240
Runners/Scor. Pos.	29	6	2	0	1	13	2	5	.207	.379	.258

DRIVING IN RUNS	From 1B	From 2B	From 3B	Scoring Position
Totals	11/194	25/127	28/63	53/190
Percentage	6%	20%	44%	28%
Driving In Runners from 3B with Less than Two Out:		19/36	53%	

Loves to face: Larry McWilliams (.353, 12-for-34, 4 HR)
Hates to face: Roger McDowell (0-for-10)

More career hits (2583) than any active player—at least until May 15, when Pete is eligible to return.... Batting average was his lowest since he hit .227 in 1971; we don't go that far back for his average with runners in scoring position, but we know that it was his lowest since we started keeping track in 1975.... Averaged one walk every 25.4 plate appearances last season, 2d-lowest rate in N.L.... Committed seven errors last season, most since joining Padres in 1983. ... On Aug. 11 he became 11th player in history to play 2000 games at first base. Current total of 2039 games is only 208 shy of Jake Beckley's N.L. record.... Maybe if he buys the team, he'll stay on to break Jake's record the way that Pete hung on to break Ty's.

Dan Gladden
San Francisco Giants — Bats Right

	AB	H	2B	3B	HR	RBI	BB	SO	BA	SA	OBA
Season	351	97	16	1	4	32	39	59	.276	.362	.357
vs. Left-Handers	123	34	6	0	0	9	17	24	.276	.325	.373
vs. Right-Handers	228	63	10	1	4	23	22	35	.276	.382	.348
Home	162	44	5	0	1	10	26	30	.272	.321	.376
Road	189	53	11	1	3	22	13	29	.280	.397	.340
Grass	249	64	8	0	3	19	31	42	.257	.325	.349
Artificial Turf	102	33	8	1	1	13	8	17	.324	.451	.378
April	87	25	3	0	0	6	7	13	.287	.322	.361
May	89	22	5	0	2	7	8	14	.247	.371	.316
June	9	5	1	0	0	2	0	0	.556	.667	.556
July	24	6	3	0	0	4	5	2	.250	.375	.379
August	89	28	4	1	0	7	16	15	.315	.382	.419
Sept./Oct.	53	11	0	0	2	6	3	15	.208	.321	.263
Leading Off Inn.	139	38	3	1	1	1	21	21	.273	.331	.377
Runners On	111	33	5	0	2	30	6	18	.297	.396	.339
Runners/Scor. Pos.	76	19	4	0	2	30	4	14	.250	.382	.296
Runners On/2 Out	48	10	2	0	1	14	4	11	.208	.313	.269
Scor. Pos./2 Out	37	6	1	0	1	14	2	10	.162	.270	.205
Late Inning Pressure	67	11	1	0	0	3	11	13	.164	.179	.291
Leading Off	15	3	1	0	0	0	4	3	.200	.267	.400
Runners On	29	5	0	0	0	3	5	3	.172	.172	.294
Runners/Scor. Pos.	19	2	0	0	0	3	4	1	.105	.105	.261

DRIVING IN RUNS	From 1B	From 2B	From 3B	Scoring Position
Totals	2/63	10/58	16/33	26/91
Percentage	3%	17%	48%	29%
Driving In Runners from 3B with Less than Two Out:		9/12	75%	

Loves to face: Doyle Alexander (.455, 5-for-11)
Hates to face: Don Carman (0-for-7, 5 SO)

Accounted for 50.6 percent of the 763 plate appearances by Giants' leadoff batters last season; he outhit the others, .281 to .254, and outwalked them, 36 to 26. But they outpowered him, 10 home runs to four.... Batted 139 points lower in Late-Inning Pressure Situations (.164) than in nonpressure situations (.303), 6th-largest difference in N.L. (minimum: 25 LIP AB).... That maintained a trend: career average of .220 in Late-Inning Pressure Situations, .294 in non-pressure situations.... Has hit 13 of 16 career home runs vs. right-handed pitchers.... Has never struck out in 29 career plate appearances with the bases loaded (8-for-26, one walk, one HBP).

Ken Griffey
Atlanta Braves — Bats Left

	AB	H	2B	3B	HR	RBI	BB	SO	BA	SA	OBA
Season	292	90	15	3	12	33	20	43	.308	.503	.351
vs. Left-Handers	85	22	7	0	3	12	5	13	.259	.447	.300
vs. Right-Handers	207	68	8	3	9	21	15	30	.329	.527	.372
Home	155	53	11	0	9	20	12	19	.342	.587	.387
Road	137	37	4	3	3	13	8	24	.270	.409	.310
Grass	227	73	13	0	10	27	15	33	.322	.511	.362
Artificial Turf	65	17	2	3	2	6	5	10	.262	.477	.314
April	0	0	0	0	0	0	0	0	—	—	—
May	0	0	0	0	0	0	0	0	—	—	—
June	5	1	0	0	0	0	0	1	.200	.200	.200
July	102	30	6	1	5	11	7	14	.294	.520	.339
August	99	33	5	2	5	17	4	18	.333	.576	.356
Sept./Oct.	86	26	4	0	2	5	9	10	.302	.419	.368
Leading Off Inn.	74	30	3	2	4	4	1	8	.405	.662	.413
Runners On	115	28	6	0	3	24	12	18	.243	.374	.313
Runners/Scor. Pos.	66	12	3	0	1	20	11	11	.182	.273	.295
Runners On/2 Out	58	13	2	0	2	16	7	7	.224	.359	.308
Scor. Pos./2 Out	39	9	2	0	1	14	7	4	.231	.359	.348
Late Inning Pressure	57	23	2	0	5	13	3	6	.404	.702	.433
Leading Off	17	10	2	0	3	3	0	2	.588	1.235	.588
Runners On	23	7	0	0	1	9	2	3	.304	.435	.360
Runners/Scor. Pos.	16	5	0	0	1	9	2	3	.313	.500	.389

DRIVING IN RUNS	From 1B	From 2B	From 3B	Scoring Position
Totals	3/90	11/56	7/19	18/75
Percentage	3%	20%	37%	24%
Driving In Runners from 3B with Less than Two Out:		2/6	33%	

Loves to face: Greg Minton (.667, 8-for-12)
Hates to face: Bob Ojeda (.143, 3-for-21)

Figures above are for N.L. only; see also the A.L. Batters section. ... Was 9-for-his-last-18, lifting career average to .30020; an 0-for-4 opening day would drop him to .30000.... Batted .313 after the All-Star break, 10th highest in N.L.... Batted .421 (8-for-19) as pinch-hitter, 4-for-4 in N.L.... Played 128 games at first base in A.L., mostly pre-Mattingly, but only action there last year was one-third of an inning on July 31 for Braves.... Taking his 1986 two-league totals, he hit 84 points lower with runners on base than with bases empty, 6th-largest difference in majors (minimum: 100 AB each way).... Combined batting average with runners in scoring position (.189) was his lowest in the last 12 years.

Tony Gwynn
San Diego Padres — Bats Left

	AB	H	2B	3B	HR	RBI	BB	SO	BA	SA	OBA
Season	642	211	33	7	14	59	52	35	.329	.467	.381
vs. Left-Handers	235	77	13	6	7	30	21	12	.328	.523	.384
vs. Right-Handers	407	134	20	1	7	29	31	23	.329	.435	.379
Home	317	108	14	4	8	26	27	20	.341	.486	.392
Road	325	103	19	3	6	33	25	15	.317	.449	.369
Grass	474	158	24	6	10	40	36	29	.333	.473	.381
Artificial Turf	168	53	9	1	4	19	16	6	.315	.452	.380
April	87	28	7	0	3	7	7	12	.322	.506	.372
May	97	35	1	1	2	6	12	5	.361	.454	.432
June	109	38	7	3	2	14	11	2	.349	.523	.410
July	101	31	5	1	4	17	6	5	.307	.495	.346
August	123	42	6	0	2	10	6	4	.341	.439	.372
Sept./Oct.	125	37	7	2	1	5	10	7	.296	.408	.353
Leading Off Inn.	142	53	11	1	1	7	7	3	.373	.486	.403
Runners On	237	75	7	2	6	51	29	13	.316	.439	.390
Runners/Scor. Pos.	110	36	4	2	3	43	20	6	.327	.482	.424
Runners On/2 Out	78	20	2	1	1	16	14	4	.256	.346	.389
Scor. Pos./2 Out	46	12	1	1	1	15	13	3	.261	.391	.443
Late Inning Pressure	103	37	7	0	3	11	12	8	.359	.515	.426
Leading Off	34	11	3	0	1	2	1	2	.324	.500	.361
Runners On	40	16	1	0	2	10	8	2	.400	.575	.500
Runners/Scor. Pos.	21	6	0	0	2	9	7	1	.286	.571	.464

DRIVING IN RUNS	From 1B	From 2B	From 3B	Scoring Position
Totals	10/181	20/91	15/35	35/126
Percentage	6%	22%	43%	28%
Driving In Runners from 3B with Less than Two Out:		10/18	56%	

Loves to face: Ron Darling (.542, 13-for-24)
Hates to face: Rick Reuschel (.118, 2-for-17)

N.L. has had same outfielders starting All-Star Game (Gwynn, Murphy, Strawberry) for three straight years. That's a first for them; A.L. All-Stars did it from 1955 to 1957, with Williams, Mantle, and Kaline.... Tied modern N.L. record with five stolen bases in game vs. Houston on Sept. 20.... Had three assists in first five innings of game vs. Mets on Aug. 27; no outfielder has had four in a nine-inning game since Elton Langford in 1928.... Last year's batting average leading off innings (.373) was only a slight improvement over his career average of .370.... Career average of .469 (15-for-32) with the bases loaded.... Yearly batting averages in Late-Inning Pressure Situations since 1983: .340, .361, .347, .359.

Batters: National League

Terry Harper

Atlanta Braves	AB	H	2B	3B	HR	RRF	BB	SO	BA	SA	OBA
Season	265	68	12	0	8	32	29	39	.257	.392	.330
vs. Left-Handers	133	36	6	0	2	13	11	13	.271	.361	.326
vs. Right-Handers	132	32	6	0	6	19	18	26	.242	.424	.333
Home	110	33	9	0	3	16	15	15	.300	.464	.386
Road	155	35	3	0	5	16	14	24	.226	.342	.288
Grass	175	49	10	0	3	19	20	27	.280	.389	.355
Artificial Turf	90	19	2	0	5	13	9	12	.211	.400	.280
April	57	11	2	0-	0	5	7	12	.193	.228	.288
May	63	12	0	0	5	13	10	9	.190	.429	.297
June	43	9	3	0	0	3	2	5	.209	.279	.244
July	40	13	1	0	1	3	5	6	.325	.425	.400
August	21	6	2	0	0	1	1	2	.286	.381	.318
Sept./Oct.	41	17	4	0	2	7	4	5	.415	.659	.467
Leading Off Inn.	63	14	3	0	3	3	9	11	.222	.413	.319
Runners On	118	30	4	0	3	27	17	19	.254	.364	.343
Runners/Scor. Pos.	69	18	2	0	2	24	10	11	.261	.377	.377
Runners On/2 Out	51	15	3	0	1	18	9	10	.294	.412·	.400
Scor. Pos./2 Out	37	13	2	0	1	17	7	6	.351	.486	.455
Late Inning Pressure	46	17	5	0	2	8	5	4	.370	.609	.431
Leading Off	10	1	1	0	0	0	2	1	.100	.200	.250
Runners On	21	7	2	0	1	7	3	2	.333	.571	.417
Runners/Scor. Pos.	12	4	1	0	1	7	1	1	.333	.667	.385

DRIVING IN RUNS	From 1B	From 2B	From 3B	Scoring Position
Totals	4/87	15/62	5/17	20/79
Percentage	5%	24%	29%	25%
Driving In Runners from 3B with Less than Two Out:			3/7	43%

Loves to face: John Candelaria (.462, 6-for-13, 1 HR)
Hates to face: New Yankees (0-for-7 against both Hudson and Guante)

Started season as Braves' regular left fielder against both types of pitching. Started 28 of team's first 30 games, but .202 average made him a platoon player thereafter. . . . Started just 37 of Atlanta's last 131 games. . . . Batted 137 points higher in Late-Inning Pressure Situations (.370) than in nonpressure situations (.233), 8th-largest difference in majors (minimum: 25 LIP AB). . . . Batted 98 points higher in night games (.284) than in day games (.187), 4th-largest difference in N.L (minimum: 50 AB each). Career breakdown: .265 at night, .228 under sun. . . . Career batting average of .305 with two out and runners in scoring position.

Billy Hatcher

Houston Astros	AB	H	2B	3B	HR	RRF	BB	SO	BA	SA	OBA
Season	419	108	15	4	6	38	22	52	.258	.356	.302
vs. Left-Handers	210	60	5	4	3	23	13	23	.286	.390	.346
vs. Right-Handers	209	48	10	0	3	15	9	29	.230	.321	.278
Home	218	56	8	2	2	18	10	23	.257	.339	.300
Road	201	52	7	2	4	20	12	29	.259	.373	.304
Grass	124	31	3	2	3	15	10	18	.250	.379	.311
Artificial Turf	295	77	12	2	3	23	12	34	.261	.346	.298
April	27	6	0	0	0	0	1	8	.222	.222	.250
May	42	13	3	0	0	3	2	4	.310	.381	.341
June	92	22	3	1	1	9	2	14	.239	.326	.255
July	52	12	4	0	1	3	1	6	.231	.308	.268
August	87	28	4	1	2	11	6	8	.322	.460	.366
Sept./Oct.	119	27	1	2	3	12	10	12	.227	.345	.303
Leading Off Inn.	109	30	1	0	0	7	13	.275	.321	.331
Runners On	159	38	5	1	2	34	6	19	.239	.321	.278
Runners/Scor. Pos.	90	20	3	1	1	32	5	10	.222	.311	.283
Runners On/2 Out	53	11	0	0	2	16	3	4	.208	.321	.288
Scor. Pos./2 Out	34	7	0	0	1	14	3	4	.206	.294	.325
Late Inning Pressure	52	16	2	0	1	10	2	8	.308	.404	.333
Leading Off	12	5	0	0	0	1	1	.417	.417	.462
Runners On	23	6	1	0	0	9	0	3	.261	.304	.261
Runners/Scor. Pos.	16	6	1	0	0	9	0	2	.375	.438	.375

DRIVING IN RUNS	From 1B	From 2B	From 3B	Scoring Position
Totals	3/106	14/73	15/36	29/109
Percentage	3%	19%	42%	27%
Driving In Runners from 3B with Less than Two Out:			10/17	59%

Loves to face: Tim Conroy (.667, 4-for-6, 1 HR)
Hates to face: Sid Fernandez (.091, 1-for-11)

Batted .277 in 57 games batting in 2d spot in order, Houston's most frequent hitter in that spot. Astros as a team batted .275 in two hole; only Padres, with Gwynn, and Mets, with Backman, hit higher. . . . Career batting average of .444 (16-for-36) at Dodger Stadium, .095 (2-for-21) at Atlanta Stadium. . . . Career breakdown: .270 with bases empty, .221 with runners on base, .216 with runners in scoring position, .195 with runners on base and two outs. . . . Batted .417 leading off innings in Late-Inning Pressure Situations. Up in that situation in 14th inning of Game Six of N.L.C.S., he hit a game-tying home run off Jesse Orosco.

Von Hayes

Philadelphia Phillies	AB	H	2B	3B	HR	RRF	BB	SO	BA	SA	OBA
Season	610	186	46	2	19	101	74	77	.305	.480	.379
vs. Left-Handers	195	45	10	0	3	34	19	27	.231	.328	.301
vs. Right-Handers	415	141	36	2	16	67	55	50	.340	.552	.414
Home	296	93	19	2	11	55	38	36	.314	.503	.393
Road	314	93	27	0	8	46	36	41	.296	.459	.365
Grass	170	59	15	0	6	27	14	23	.347	.541	.392
Artificial Turf	440	127	31	2	13	74	60	54	.289	.457	.374
April	60	11	4	0	1	9	8	5	.183	.300	.275
May	98	34	11	0	2	13	15	20	.347	.520	.434
June	108	35	9	0	1	18	15	17	.324	.435	.405
July	103	30	4	0	5	20	12	10	.291	.476	.365
August	115	36	6	2	2	18	10	14	.313	.452	.365
Sept./Oct.	126	40	12	0	8	23	14	11	.317	.603	.386
Leading Off Inn.	133	49	14	1	8	8	18	13	.368	.669	.444
Runners On	273	91	16	1	8	90	32	26	.333	.487	.400
Runners/Scor. Pos.	171	58	13	1	3	78	27	18	.339	.480	.424
Runners On/2 Out	115	37	8	0	3	39	18	14	.322	.470	.414
Scor. Pos./2 Out	81	28	6	0	2	36	15	10	.346	.494	.448
Late Inning Pressure	102	29	5	0	3	14	8	15	.284	.422	.333
Leading Off	25	14	3	0	1	1	2	2	.560	.800	.593
Runners On	45	10	1	0	1	12	4 - 6	.222	.311	.280
Runners/Scor. Pos.	27	7	1	0	1	12	4	3	.259	.407	.323

DRIVING IN RUNS	From 1B	From 2B	From 3B	Scoring Position
Totals	12/183	33/123	37/78	70/201
Percentage	7%	27%	47%	35%
Driving In Runners from 3B with Less than Two Out:			23/37	62%

Loves to face: Mike Krukow (.471, 16-for-34, 1 HR)
Hates to face: Floyd Youmans (.118, 2-for-17, 6 SO)

Led N.L. with 46 doubles, 15th time in last 16 years that N.L. leader in that category (or a player who shared lead) played on artificial-turf home field. The only exception: 1981, when Cubs' Bill Buckner led (Buckner also tied for lead in '83). . . . One of two N.L. players (other: Darryl Strawberry) to have 20+ stolen bases and 90+ RBI last season. . . . Had 58 multiple-hit games last season, 3d most in N.L. . . . Batted 109 points higher vs. right-handed pitchers than against left-handers, 2d-largest difference in majors (minimum: 100 AB vs. each). . . . Batting average with runners in scoring position has increased in every season since 1983: .239, .247, .291, .339. . . . Career batting average of .212 (14-for-66) with the bases loaded.

Mike Heath

St. Louis Cardinals	AB	H	2B	3B	HR	RRF	BB	SO	BA	SA	OBA
Season	190	39	8	1	4	25	23	36	.205	.321	.293
vs. Left-Handers	121	26	6	1	4	18	14	24	.215	.380	.294
vs. Right-Handers	69	13	2	0	0	7	9	12	.188	.217	.291
Home	104	22	4	1	1	9	13	15	.212	.298	.305
Road	86	17	4	0	3	16	10	21	.198	.349	.278
Grass	38	4	1	0	1	5	6	13	.105	.211	.222
Artificial Turf	152	35	7	1	3	20	17	23	.230	.349	.312
April	50	4	2	0	1	3	5	10	.080	.180	.179
May	57	16	3	1	1	12	10	8	.281	.421	.388
June	47	8	2	0	1	5	5	6	.170	.277	.262
July	31	9	1	0	1	5	1	11	.290	.419	.303
August	5	2	0	0	0	0	2	1	.400	.400	.571
Sept./Oct.	0	0	0	0	0	0	0	0	—	—	—
Leading Off Inn.	55	12	2	1	0	0	4	10	.218	.291	.271
Runners On	84	19	6	0	3	24	13	13	.226	.405	.333
Runners/Scor. Pos.	49	11	4	0	1	19	12	9	.224	.367	.381
Runners On/2 Out	38	9	2	0	1	11	6	6	.237	.368	.341
Scor. Pos./2 Out	25	6	1	0	0	9	6	4	.240	.280	.387
Late Inning Pressure	34	4	1	0	0	2	7	7	.118	.147	.268
Leading Off	11	3	0	0	0	0	1	2	.273	.273	.333
Runners On	14	1	0	0	0	2	3	3	.071	.143	.235
Runners/Scor. Pos.	8	1	1	0	0	2	2	3	.125	.250	.250

DRIVING IN RUNS	From 1B	From 2B	From 3B	Scoring Position
Totals	5/59	9/45	7/17	16/62
Percentage	8%	20%	41%	26%
Driving In Runners from 3B with Less than Two Out:			4/7	57%

Loves to face: Oil Can Boyd (.500, 6-for-12, 2 HR)
Hates to face: Mike Boddicker (.059, 1-for-17)

Figures above are for N.L. only. . . . April batting average was lowest in the majors (minimum: 50 AB). . . . Competition for Cabell on the cocktail circuit: he's played for Steinbrenner's Yankees, Finley's A's, Martin in New York and Oakland, Whitey, and Sparky. . . . Combined-league batting average with runners in scoring position (.216) was the lowest of his career. . . . Goodbye, St. Louis; hello, Detroit: Batting average on grass has been higher than on artificial turf in eight of his nine seasons in majors. . . . Made error in his only chance at third base last season. . . . Must not call for a lot of knockdown pitches: has been hit by pitch only nine times in nine big-league seasons.

Danny Heep

New York Mets — Bats Left

	AB	H	2B	3B	HR	RRF	BB	SO	BA	SA	OBA
Season	195	55	8	2	5	35	30	31	.282	.421	.379
vs. Left-Handers	12	1	0	0	0	0	4	3	.083	.083	.353
vs. Right-Handers	183	54	8	2	5	35	26	28	.295	.443	.381
Home	94	28	3	1	3	17	14	9	.298	.447	.391
Road	101	27	5	1	2	18	16	22	.267	.396	.368
Grass	137	36	5	1	4	21	17	21	.263	.401	.346
Artificial Turf	58	19	3	1	1	14	13	10	.328	.466	.451
April	19	7	1	1	1	8	1	3	.368	.684	.400
May	35	9	1	0	1	4	4	8	.257	.371	.333
June	37	10	2	0	1	6	14	3	.270	.405	.471
July	32	7	0	0	0	1	4	4	.219	.219	.306
August	35	11	1	0	2	6	2	7	.314	.514	.351
Sept./Oct.	37	11	3	1	0	10	5	6	.297	.432	.386
Leading Off Inn.	42	7	0	1	0	0	4	8	.167	.214	.239
Runners On	87	33	5	1	4	34	15	13	.379	.598	.466
Runners/Scor. Pos.	52	21	3	1	3	32	13	8	.404	.673	.515
Runners On/2 Out	44	15	3	1	1	16	5	6	.341	.523	.408
Scor. Pos./2 Out	27	10	3	1	1	16	5	4	.370	.667	.469
Late Inning Pressure	34	9	1	0	0	6	4	8	.265	.294	.342
Leading Off	10	0	0	0	0	0	0	0	.000	.000	.000
Runners On	14	7	1	0	0	6	1	3	.500	.571	.533
Runners/Scor. Pos.	8	4	0	0	0	6	1	1	.500	.500	.556

DRIVING IN RUNS	From 1B	From 2B	From 3B	Scoring Position
Totals	5/64	13/41	12/23	25/64
Percentage	8%	32%	52%	39%
Driving In Runners from 3B with Less than Two Out:		7/11		64%

Loves to face: Jeff Reardon (.600, 9-for-15)
Hates to face: Bill Gullickson (.095, 2-for-21)
Drove in 39.1 percent (25-of-64) of runners from scoring position, 3d-highest percentage in N.L. (minimum: 25 RRF) and best percentage of his career. . . . Had four hits in 10 at bats last season in Late-Inning Pressure Situations with runners in scoring position; had been 6-for-53 in those situations before last season. . . . Batted .278 in 50 games in the starting lineup, .303 in 36 games off the bench. . . . Career batting average of .346 at Olympic Stadium is his highest anywhere in N.L. . . . Batted only 17 times vs. left-handers last season, his lowest total since his major-league debut in 1979, but his average against right-handers (.295) was highest of his career.

Keith Hernandez

New York Mets — Bats Left

	AB	H	2B	3B	HR	RRF	BB	SO	BA	SA	OBA
Season	551	171	34	1	13	87	94	69	.310	.446	.413
vs. Left-Handers	218	68	12	0	4	29	32	31	.312	.422	.409
vs. Right-Handers	333	103	22	1	9	58	62	38	.309	.462	.415
Home	239	74	9	1	6	38	46	31	.310	.431	.422
Road	312	97	25	0	7	49	48	38	.311	.458	.405
Grass	372	119	19	1	11	64	66	49	.320	.465	.422
Artificial Turf	179	52	15	0	2	23	28	20	.291	.408	.392
April	66	20	6	0	0	7	9	4	.303	.394	.403
May	102	37	7	0	3	17	14	11	.363	.520	.436
June	97	22	2	0	2	9	15	15	.227	.318	.318
July	88	22	4	1	3	12	20	10	.250	.420	.394
August	114	42	11	0	3	26	22	16	.368	.544	.464
Sept./Oct.	84	28	4	0	2	16	16	13	.333	.452	.446
Leading Off Inn.	96	25	3	0	2	9	9	16	.260	.354	.330
Runners On	276	93	20	1	6	80	54	27	.337	.482	.445
Runners/Scor. Pos.	164	49	9	1	5	72	39	15	.299	.457	.430
Runners On/2 Out	81	22	5	0	2	22	20	9	.272	.407	.422
Scor. Pos./2 Out	55	12	2	0	2	19	17	5	.218	.364	.411
Late Inning Pressure	74	20	3	0	2	13	14	8	.270	.392	.389
Leading Off	15	5	0	0	0	0	2	4	.333	.333	.444
Runners On	39	7	1	0	1	12	8	3	.179	.282	.313
Runners/Scor. Pos.	25	5	1	0	1	12	7	2	.200	.360	.364

DRIVING IN RUNS	From 1B	From 2B	From 3B	Scoring Position
Totals	11/179	32/119	30/71	62/190
Percentage	6%	27%	42%	33%
Driving In Runners from 3B with Less than Two Out:		23/42		55%

Loves to face: Steve Trout (.577, 15-for-26)
Hates to face: Dan Schatzeder (.182, 8-for-44)
Has batted .311, .309, .310 in three full seasons with Mets. . . . Only player to have batted over .300 with runners on base in each of past eight years. . . . One of four players to hit better with runners on base than bases empty in each of last nine seasons. Others: Gary Carter, Graig Nettles, Jerry Royster. . . . Has batted 3d in every game he's started for the Mets. . . . Batted .343 after All-Star break, 3d highest in N.L. . . . Had RBI in eight straight games, Aug. 6–11, a team record. . . . Needs 100 RBI, 83 walks, 31 runs to reach 1,000 in each. Only five players active in 1986 had 1,000+ in all three: Darrell Evans, Reggie, Nettles, Rose, and Schmidt. Of those, only Rose, like Hernandez, has a .300 career average.

Tommy Herr

St. Louis Cardinals — Bats Left and Right

	AB	H	2B	3B	HR	RRF	BB	SO	BA	SA	OBA
Season	559	141	30	4	2	66	73	75	.252	.331	.342
vs. Left-Handers	219	69	14	1	1	23	31	24	.315	.402	.407
vs. Right-Handers	340	72	16	3	1	43	42	51	.212	.285	.299
Home	273	71	10	2	1	42	44	36	.260	.322	.367
Road	286	70	20	2	1	24	29	39	.245	.339	.315
Grass	146	30	9	1	1	8	10	21	.205	.301	.255
Artificial Turf	413	111	21	3	1	58	63	54	.269	.341	.370
April	68	10	3	0	0	6	9	7	.147	.191	.244
May	83	15	2	0	1	6	11	16	.181	.241	.277
June	101	31	4	1	1	12	13	16	.307	.396	.397
July	79	24	5	0	0	9	9	7	.304	.367	.396
August	110	24	8	2	0	20	17	15	.218	.327	.315
Sept./Oct.	118	37	8	1	0	13	14	14	.314	.398	.386
Leading Off Inn.	104	21	8	0	0	0	14	16	.202	.279	.297
Runners On	232	64	9	4	1	65	29	29	.276	.362	.358
Runners/Scor. Pos.	157	38	3	2	1	57	21	24	.242	.306	.335
Runners On/2 Out	83	23	1	1	0	14	14	14	.277	.313	.388
Scor. Pos./2 Out	61	12	0	0	0	12	11	12	.197	.197	.329
Late Inning Pressure	102	18	1	0	0	7	9	14	.176	.216	.250
Leading Off	27	3	0	0	0	0	0	2	.111	.111	.111
Runners On	45	10	1	0	1	7	7	7	.222	.311	.340
Runners/Scor. Pos.	32	6	0	0	1	6	5	6	.188	.281	.316

DRIVING IN RUNS	From 1B	From 2B	From 3B	Scoring Position
Totals	9/135	26/104	29/81	55/185
Percentage	7%	25%	36%	30%
Driving In Runners from 3B with Less than Two Out:		23/48		48%

Loves to face: John Denny (.400, 10-for-25)
Hates to face: Rick Sutcliffe (.111, 2-for-18)
All right, Tommy Herr fans, here's your question: What was the only measurable category in which your guy's batting average improved from 1985 to 1986? Anyone who said "against left-handed pitching" wins honorary membership in the Herr Fan(ny) Club, last seen during the '85 Series. Herr went from .283 in 1985 to .315, a career high, last season. . . . His average dropped in all other categories, including a plunge against right-handers from .313 to .212. . . . Batting averages of .147 in April and .181 in May were both 2d lowest in N.L. (minimum: 50 AB). In 1985 he hit .391 in April, .358 in May. . . . Ended season with 50 consecutive errorless games at second base, his best streak since a 57-gamer in 1984.

Bob Horner

Atlanta Braves — Bats Right

	AB	H	2B	3B	HR	RRF	BB	SO	BA	SA	OBA
Season	517	141	22	0	27	89	52	72	.273	.472	.336
vs. Left-Handers	166	52	10	0	7	27	20	19	.313	.500	.385
vs. Right-Handers	351	89	12	0	20	62	32	53	.254	.459	.312
Home	268	82	11	0	20	60	26	29	.306	.571	.360
Road	249	59	11	0	7	29	26	43	.237	.365	.309
Grass	405	113	17	0	23	73	37	57	.279	.491	.335
Artificial Turf	112	28	5	0	4	16	15	15	.250	.402	.338
April	62	12	1	0	2	9	7	12	.194	.306	.278
May	101	29	6	0	6	23	13	16	.287	.525	.361
June	99	32	5	0	5	16	9	9	.323	.525	.380
July	60	15	1	0	4	9	2	9	.250	.467	.270
August	79	23	3	0	2	12	7	9	.291	.405	.345
Sept./Oct.	116	30	6	0	8	20	14	17	.259	.517	.333
Leading Off Inn.	137	39	5	0	8	8	9	12	.285	.496	.333
Runners On	242	62	11	0	10	72	34	31	.256	.421	.334
Runners/Scor. Pos.	126	37	9	0	6	63	26	15	.294	.508	.393
Runners On/2 Out	119	23	4	0	5	25	20	19	.193	.353	.314
Scor. Pos./2 Out	59	10	2	0	3	20	16	8	.169	.356	.355
Late Inning Pressure	73	18	3	0	1	10	12	15	.247	.329	.348
Leading Off	19	4	1	0	0	0	1	2	.211	.263	.250
Runners On	27	7	2	0	1	10	9	5	.259	.444	.425
Runners/Scor. Pos.	15	5	2	0	1	10	6	2	.333	.667	.480

DRIVING IN RUNS	From 1B	From 2B	From 3B	Scoring Position
Totals	11/192	18/94	33/57	51/151
Percentage	6%	19%	58%	34%
Driving In Runners from 3B with Less than Two Out:		24/33		73%

Loves to face: Andy McGaffigan (.400, 6-for-15, 4 HR)
Hates to face: Tom Niedenfuer (.059, 1-for-17)
Hit four home runs in a game before he hit his first career grand slam, which finally happened on Sept. 6, in his 87th career plate appearance with the bases loaded. Until then, he held major-league record of 209 career home runs without a grand slam. The king is dead, long live the new king: Willie Kirkland, with 148 career home runs, no slams (Claudell Washington, the active leader, trails by 18 homers). . . . Went 2-for-23 with no RBIs at Shea Stadium last year. Career average of .174 (21-for-121) there. . . . Career average of one home run every 12.6 at bats at Atlanta-Fulton County Stadium, one HR every 24.4 at bats in road games. . . . Has batted over .300 in day games in five of the last six seasons.

Glenn Hubbard

Atlanta Braves   **Bats Right**

	AB	H	2B	3B	HR	RRF	BB	SO	BA	SA	OBA
Season	408	94	16	1	4	40	66	74	.230	.304	.340
vs. Left-Handers	127	28	6	0	1	13	29	23	.220	.291	.365
vs. Right-Handers	281	66	10	1	3	27	37	51	.235	.310	.328
Home	203	50	8	1	4	24	39	31	.246	.355	.370
Road	205	44	8	0	0	16	27	43	.215	.254	.309
Grass	304	74	11	1	4	30	53	52	.243	.326	.361
Artificial Turf	104	20	5	0	0	10	13	22	.192	.240	.277
April	54	12	2	0	1	5	10	11	.222	.315	.338
May	88	24	8	0	1	12	10	16	.273	.398	.350
June	53	11	1	0	1	7	16	9	.208	.283	.394
July	47	13	3	0	0	9	10	9	.277	.340	.407
August	88	15	1	0	0	3	10	14	.170	.182	.263
Sept./Oct.	78	19	1	1	1	4	10	15	.244	.321	.330
Leading Off Inn.	98	18	2	1	0	0	10	20	.184	.224	.273
Runners On	160	40	8	0	2	38	42	31	.250	.338	.401
Runners/Scor. Pos.	77	21	7	0	1	36	35	19	.273	.403	.487
Runners On/2 Out	64	18	3	0	0	10	28	11	.281	.328	.500
Scor. Pos./2 Out	34	9	2	0	0	10	26	8	.265	.324	.583
Late Inning Pressure	50	11	3	0	0	1	6	11	.220	.280	.316
Leading Off	12	4	1	0	0	0	3	5	.333	.417	.500
Runners On	14	0	0	0	0	1	2	3	.000	.000	.125
Runners/Scor. Pos.	5	0	0	0	0	1	2	1	.000	.000	.286

DRIVING IN RUNS	From 1B	From 2B	From 3B	Scoring Position
Totals	5/137	15/59	16/37	31/96
Percentage	4%	25%	43%	32%
Driving In Runners from 3B with Less than Two Out:			10/23	43%

Loves to face: Mike LaCoss (.412, 14-for-34)
Hates to face: Bryn Smith (.043, 1-for-23)
Has committed only three errors in 102 games on artificial surfaces since 1984, while making 34 errors in 303 games on grass fields (24 in 224 games at home, 10 in 79 games on other grass fields). . . . Before you call him a Home Grass Dog, consider that his career *batting* average on grass fields is .250, on artificial turf, .219. . . . Led major-league second basemen with an average of 3.72 assists per nine innings (minimum: 500 innings). . . . Batted in the 8th spot in the lineup in all but four of his 139 games started. . . . N.L. 8th-spot hitters batted a composite .237, slugged .326; Hubbard came up short (.231, .307 batting 8th). . . . Has homered in every N.L. park except Olympic Stadium (99 career AB).

Steve Jeltz

Philadelphia Phillies   **Bats Left and Right**

	AB	H	2B	3B	HR	RRF	BB	SO	BA	SA	OBA
Season	439	96	11	4	0	39	65	97	.219	.262	.320
vs. Left-Handers	140	31	3	1	0	8	19	36	.221	.257	.314
vs. Right-Handers	299	65	8	3	0	31	46	61	.217	.264	.324
Home	226	49	8	3	0	24	28	53	.217	.279	.301
Road	213	47	3	1	0	15	37	44	.221	.244	.339
Grass	119	27	2	0	0	9	14	22	.227	.244	.313
Artificial Turf	320	69	9	4	0	30	51	75	.216	.269	.322
April	56	14	0	2	0	7	12	12	.250	.321	.382
May	69	14	4	0	0	6	10	18	.203	.261	.304
June	85	21	2	0	0	10	20	8	.247	.271	.387
July	61	12	1	0	0	3	10	21	.197	.213	.319
August	88	18	2	2	0	5	7	19	.205	.273	.263
Sept./Oct.	80	17	2	0	0	8	6	19	.213	.238	.264
Leading Off Inn.	95	21	1	0	0	0	15	20	.221	.232	.327
Runners On	189	40	5	4	0	39	31	39	.212	.280	.320
Runners/Scor. Pos.	112	25	4	3	0	35	22	21	.223	.313	.346
Runners On/2 Out	87	17	3	0	0	19	18	16	.195	.230	.333
Scor. Pos./2 Out	63	13	2	0	0	17	15	13	.206	.238	.359
Late Inning Pressure	61	16	0	1	0	5	15	13	.262	.295	.408
Leading Off	14	4	0	0	0	0	5	4	.286	.286	.474
Runners On	27	8	0	1	0	5	3	4	.296	.370	.367
Runners/Scor. Pos.	13	5	0	1	0	5	3	0	.385	.538	.500

DRIVING IN RUNS	From 1B	From 2B	From 3B	Scoring Position
Totals	7/138	16/101	15/32	31/133
Percentage	5%	16%	47%	23%
Driving In Runners from 3B with Less than Two Out:			9/14	64%

Loves to face: Joe Hesketh (.500, 4-for-8)
Hates to face: Bob Forsch (0-for-15)
13 errors in last 45 games cost him the N.L. fielding title for shortstops. . . . Had made only nine errors in first 96 games, and led N.L. shortstops in fielding (.980) on Aug. 10, before his decline; fielded only .939 the rest of the way, finishing at .967, 4th among the six qualifying N.L. shortstops. . . . Hit his only major-league home run off John Tudor, Sept. 23, 1984, at Pittsburgh. . . . Has 635 at bats over past two years, most by anyone in majors without a home run over that span. . . . Had the fewest extra-base hits (15) of any player with 502+ plate appearances last season. . . . Career batting average of .385 (5-for-13) with the bases loaded.

Howard Johnson

New York Mets   **Bats Left and Right**

	AB	H	2B	3B	HR	RRF	BB	SO	BA	SA	OBA
Season	220	54	14	0	10	40	31	64	.245	.445	.341
vs. Left-Handers	47	10	3	0	2	8	8	14	.213	.404	.339
vs. Right-Handers	173	44	11	0	8	32	23	50	.254	.457	.342
Home	92	20	7	0	5	21	17	25	.217	.457	.345
Road	128	34	7	0	5	19	14	39	.266	.438	.338
Grass	157	38	11	0	7	29	24	44	.242	.446	.346
Artificial Turf	63	16	3	0	3	11	7	20	.254	.444	.329
April	28	10	2	0	1	4	3	7	.357	.536	.419
May	57	12	5	0	0	8	9	15	.211	.298	.328
June	6	2	0	0	2	2	2	3	.333	1.333	.500
July	44	11	3	0	4	13	3	14	.250	.591	.298
August	42	9	3	0	1	2	7	14	.214	.357	.327
Sept./Oct.	43	10	1	0	2	11	7	11	.233	.395	.340
Leading Off Inn.	52	7	1	0	2	2	3	13	.135	.269	.196
Runners On	95	27	8	0	5	35	18	35	.284	.526	.398
Runners/Scor. Pos.	47	17	7	0	4	32	14	15	.362	.766	.508
Runners On/2 Out	39	11	5	0	1	15	8	14	.282	.487	.404
Scor. Pos./2 Out	23	8	5	0	0	13	7	10	.348	.565	.500
Late Inning Pressure	53	13	2	0	3	9	5	18	.245	.453	.310
Leading Off	14	1	0	0	1	1	1	5	.071	.286	.133
Runners On	25	7	0	0	2	8	3	11	.280	.520	.357
Runners/Scor. Pos.	13	4	0	0	2	8	2	6	.308	.769	.400

DRIVING IN RUNS	From 1B	From 2B	From 3B	Scoring Position
Totals	7/77	12/35	11/23	23/58
Percentage	9%	34%	48%	40%
Driving In Runners from 3B with Less than Two Out:			7/11	64%

Loves to face: Nolan Ryan (.500, 4-for-8, 2 doubles)
Hates to face: Mario Soto (.063, 1-for-16, 5 SO)
Started 49 of 100 games in which Mets faced a starting right-hander, and three of 62 against left-handers. . . . Credited by Mets and Cardinals with striking the blow that crushed the Cards' pennant hopes: a two-run, ninth-inning homer off Todd Worrell on April 24 that ignited a Mets sweep of four-game series. . . . Career batting average of .071 at Dodger Stadium, the only N.L. ballpark in which he does not have an extra-base hit. Held hitless in 16 at bats vs. Dodgers last season. . . . Batted .200 with runners in scoring position in 1985, .362 in 1986. . . . Career batting average of .200 vs. left-handers, .266 vs. right-handers. . . . Tied Bill Russell for N.L. lead for most hits last season without having a 3-hit game.

Terry Kennedy

San Diego Padres   **Bats Left**

	AB	H	2B	3B	HR	RRF	BB	SO	BA	SA	OBA
Season	432	114	22	1	12	57	37	74	.264	.403	.324
vs. Left-Handers	96	22	7	0	3	10	7	23	.229	.396	.288
vs. Right-Handers	336	92	15	1	9	47	30	51	.274	.405	.334
Home	214	60	9	0	7	26	20	39	.280	.421	.346
Road	218	54	13	1	5	31	17	35	.248	.385	.302
Grass	320	87	12	0	10	38	29	55	.272	.403	.335
Artificial Turf	112	27	10	1	2	19	8	19	.241	.402	.292
April	67	15	2	1	2	10	8	11	.224	.373	.307
May	82	20	4	0	2	15	8	11	.244	.366	.308
June	76	24	4	0	2	7	7	12	.316	.447	.381
July	78	21	5	0	2	4	6	14	.269	.410	.329
August	80	18	2	0	2	6	5	16	.225	.325	.271
Sept./Oct.	49	16	5	0	2	15	3	10	.327	.551	.360
Leading Off Inn.	107	25	3	1	2	2	8	16	.234	.336	.287
Runners On	166	45	8	0	5	50	22	36	.271	.410	.358
Runners/Scor. Pos.	99	30	7	0	3	45	16	22	.303	.465	.378
Runners On/2 Out	78	22	4	0	2	29	12	15	.282	.410	.378
Scor. Pos./2 Out	54	19	4	0	1	27	11	10	.352	.481	.462
Late Inning Pressure	80	26	7	0	2	12	12	13	.325	.488	.413
Leading Off	22	3	1	0	0	0	3	5	.136	.182	.240
Runners On	33	11	2	0	2	12	8	7	.333	.576	.463
Runners/Scor. Pos.	17	5	2	0	1	10	7	3	.294	.588	.500

DRIVING IN RUNS	From 1B	From 2B	From 3B	Scoring Position
Totals	7/120	21/77	17/35	38/112
Percentage	6%	27%	49%	34%
Driving In Runners from 3B with Less than Two Out:			7/15	47%

Loves to face: Joaquin Andujar, (.341, 15-for-44)
Hates to face: Jose DeLeon (.133, 2-for-15, 1 HR)
Good news, Terry: Typical A.L. team averaged only .98 stolen-base attempts per game last season, 29 percent fewer than typical N.L. team (1.39). . . . Batted .478 (11-for-23) as pinch-hitter, tied with Kal Daniels for N.L. lead (minimum: 20 AB). . . . Failed to drive in a run from July 13 to Aug. 15; that's 26 consecutive games, 22 of which he started. . . . Hit left-handers much better earlier in his career than he has recently: .297 in 404 at bats, with 38 extra-base hits, 1981–83; .223 in 403 at bats, with 28 extra-base hits, 1984–86. . . . Should be the first left-handed batter to be Orioles' primary catcher since Johnny Oates in 1972. . . . Orioles starting catchers had only 40 RBI last year, fewest in majors.

Ray Knight
New York Mets — Bats Right

	AB	H	2B	3B	HR	RRF	BB	SO	BA	SA	OBA
Season	486	145	24	2	11	80	40	63	.298	.424	.351
vs. Left-Handers	198	75	15	1	9	37	11	17	.379	.601	.408
vs. Right-Handers	288	70	9	1	2	43	29	46	.243	.302	.315
Home	228	66	12	2	7	38	22	34	.289	.452	.353
Road	258	79	12	0	4	42	18	29	.306	.399	.350
Grass	326	98	18	2	7	54	32	47	.301	.433	.363
Artificial Turf	160	47	6	0	4	26	8	16	.294	.406	.326
April	49	15	2	0	6	12	5	4	.306	.714	.364
May	89	31	10	0	0	11	8	13	.348	.461	.396
June	98	28	1	1	2	15	6	16	.286	.378	.327
July	70	13	1	1	1	9	11	15	.186	.271	.306
August	97	32	5	0	0	18	5	6	.330	.381	.359
Sept./Oct.	83	26	5	0	2	15	5	9	.313	.446	.356
Leading Off Inn.	111	32	5	1	2	2	9	12	.288	.405	.342
Runners On	210	69	10	0	4	73	19	19	.329	.433	.377
Runners/Scor. Pos.	113	40	3	0	1	61	16	10	.354	.407	.413
Runners On/2 Out	90	36	5	0	3	38	10	7	.400	.556	.465
Scor. Pos./2 Out	53	21	1	0	0	27	8	4	.396	.415	.484
Late Inning Pressure	68	24	6	0	3	17	3	9	.353	.574	.375
Leading Off	18	6	3	0	0	2	1	3	.333	.500	.400
Runners On	27	9	3	0	1	15	0	2	.333	.556	.321
Runners/Scor. Pos.	16	5	2	0	0	13	0	1	.313	.438	.294

DRIVING IN RUNS	From 1B	From 2B	From 3B	Scoring Position
Totals	10/181	26/88	32/56	58/144
Percentage	6%	30%	57%	40%
Driving In Runners from 3B with Less than Two Out:			21/34	62%

Loves to face: Craig Lefferts (.583, 7-for-12)
Hates to face: Kent Tekulve (.069, 2-for-29)
Drove in 40.3 percent (58-of-144) of runners from scoring position last season, best rate in N.L. (minimum: 25 RRF). . . . Batted 136 points higher vs. left-handers than vs. right-handers, 3d-largest difference in N.L. (minimum: 100 AB vs. both). . . . Matched 1985 home run total in first nine games of '86, RBI total by June 30. . . . Batting average never dropped below .279; would have been his high-water mark in 1984 or '85. . . . Homered in Mets' season opener, season finale, and World Series clincher. . . . Batting average with runners in scoring position (.354) is career high. . . . Has homered in every N.L. ballpark except Olympic Stadium (147 career AB).

Wayne Krenchicki
Montreal Expos — Bats Left

	AB	H	2B	3B	HR	RRF	BB	SO	BA	SA	OBA
Season	221	53	6	2	2	24	22	32	.240	.312	.306
vs. Left-Handers	7	0	0	0	0	0	0	4	.000	.000	.000
vs. Right-Handers	214	53	6	2	2	24	22	28	.248	.322	.315
Home	91	21	1	2	1	11	17	17	.231	.319	.345
Road	130	32	5	0	1	13	5	15	.246	.308	.274
Grass	70	18	3	0	1	11	5	10	.257	.343	.307
Artificial Turf	151	35	3	2	1	13	17	22	.232	.298	.306
April	14	3	0	0	1	2	1	4	.214	.429	.267
May	26	4	2	0	1	4	1	3	.154	.346	.172
June	31	10	0	1	0	3	4	4	.323	.387	.400
July	60	16	3	0	0	4	8	8	.267	.317	.353
August	53	13	1	0	0	7	4	7	.245	.264	.298
Sept./Oct.	37	7	0	1	0	4	4	6	.189	.243	.268
Leading Off Inn.	41	10	0	0	1	1	2	4	.244	.317	.279
Runners On	101	23	3	0	0	21	13	18	.228	.257	.310
Runners/Scor. Pos.	69	16	1	0	0	20	10	10	.232	.246	.321
Runners On/2 Out	44	8	2	0	0	6	6	6	.182	.227	.280
Scor. Pos./2 Out	30	6	1	0	0	6	5	2	.200	.233	.314
Late Inning Pressure	51	9	0	0	1	5	3	7	.176	.235	.218
Leading Off	11	2	0	0	1	1	0	1	.182	.455	.182
Runners On	20	3	0	0	0	4	2	5	.150	.150	.217
Runners/Scor. Pos.	17	3	0	0	0	4	1	4	.176	.176	.211

DRIVING IN RUNS	From 1B	From 2B	From 3B	Scoring Position
Totals	1/60	8/56	12/26	20/82
Percentage	2%	14%	46%	24%
Driving In Runners from 3B with Less than Two Out:			10/16	63%

Loves to face: Dennis Eckersley (.474, 9-for-19)
Hates to face: Danny Cox (0-for-15)
Career batting average of .420 (21-for-50, 3 HR) at San Diego Stadium. . . . Started 54 of 107 games in which Montreal faced a right-handed starter; no starts against lefties. . . . One of those hitters whose .266 career batting average must be taken with a grain of salt, since he is always used in situations with favorable pitching matchups. . . . Career average of .188 vs. left-handers (13-for-69) with no extra-base hits, only three walks, and 21 strikeouts. . . . A .312 career hitter in day games, .246 at night. . . . In his wildest dreams, did he ever envision batting cleanup in eight games for a major-league team, which he did last season?

John Kruk
San Diego Padres — Bats Left

	AB	H	2B	3B	HR	RRF	BB	SO	BA	SA	OBA
Season	278	86	16	2	4	39	45	58	.309	.424	.403
vs. Left-Handers	79	24	3	0	0	13	13	20	.304	.342	.402
vs. Right-Handers	199	62	13	2	4	26	32	38	.312	.457	.403
Home	103	32	11	0	1	12	17	25	.311	.447	.408
Road	175	54	5	2	3	27	28	33	.309	.411	.400
Grass	187	55	12	0	3	24	26	44	.294	.406	.377
Artificial Turf	91	31	4	2	1	15	19	14	.341	.462	.455
April	27	6	2	0	0	1	1	8	.222	.296	.250
May	23	9	1	0	1	4	3	4	.391	.565	.462
June	21	6	1	0	0	5	6	3	.286	.333	.444
July	35	12	3	0	0	4	4	7	.343	.429	.410
August	91	28	8	1	2	10	19	19	.308	.484	.427
Sept./Oct.	81	25	1	1	1	15	12	17	.309	.383	.389
Leading Off Inn.	54	14	2	0	0	0	8	10	.259	.296	.355
Runners On	124	48	6	1	2	37	19	22	.387	.500	.462
Runners/Scor. Pos.	73	23	2	1	0	32	12	19	.315	.370	.402
Runners On/2 Out	43	20	1	1	1	22	8	6	.465	.605	.549
Scor. Pos./2 Out	31	15	1	1	0	20	7	6	.484	.581	.579
Late Inning Pressure	49	15	2	0	0	8	8	12	.306	.347	.404
Leading Off	13	4	0	0	0	0	3	2	.308	.308	.438
Runners On	21	9	1	0	0	8	3	4	.429	.476	.500
Runners/Scor. Pos.	15	7	0	0	0	8	3	3	.467	.467	.556

DRIVING IN RUNS	From 1B	From 2B	From 3B	Scoring Position
Totals	5/89	13/54	17/32	30/86
Percentage	6%	24%	53%	35%
Driving In Runners from 3B with Less than Two Out:			9/15	60%

Loves to face: Ted Power (.800, 4-for-5)
Hates to face: Mike LaCoss (0-for-7)
No, those clutch-hitting stats are not misprints. . . . Batted 140 points higher with runners on base than with bases empty, largest difference in majors (minimum: 100 AB each way). . . . Has now hit .300 in each of last five years, with Reno, Beaumont, Las Vegas twice, and San Diego. . . . Among N.L. rookies with 200 plate appearances, only Kruk and Kal Daniels (.320) batted over .300. . . . Had highest walk rate, one every 7.3 plate appearances, among N.L. rookies (minimum: 200 PA). . . . On-base percentage after the All-Star break (.405) was 5th highest in N.L. . . . Drove in 13 runs in 17 games vs. Atlanta. . . . Three hits in five at bats with the bases loaded.

Randy Kutcher
San Francisco Giants — Bats Right

	AB	H	2B	3B	HR	RRF	BB	SO	BA	SA	OBA
Season	186	44	9	1	7	16	11	41	.237	.409	.279
vs. Left-Handers	69	14	3	1	1	5	5	18	.203	.319	.257
vs. Right-Handers	117	30	6	0	6	11	6	23	.256	.462	.293
Home	92	24	6	0	5	9	7	21	.261	.489	.313
Road	94	20	3	1	2	7	4	20	.213	.330	.245
Grass	150	34	6	1	7	12	9	39	.227	.420	.270
Artificial Turf	36	10	3	0	0	4	2	2	.278	.361	.316
April	0	0	0	0	0	0	0	0	—	—	—
May	0	0	0	0	0	0	0	0	—	—	—
June	54	14	3	0	2	4	0	14	.259	.426	.259
July	76	17	3	1	5	9	6	13	.224	.487	.280
August	26	5	1	0	0	1	3	5	.192	.231	.276
Sept./Oct.	30	8	2	0	0	2	2	9	.267	.333	.313
Leading Off Inn.	74	21	4	0	5	5	5	13	.284	.541	.329
Runners On	62	12	1	1	0	9	2	18	.194	.242	.219
Runners/Scor. Pos.	42	7	1	0	0	8	2	11	.167	.190	.205
Runners On/2 Out	35	7	0	0	0	5	1	11	.200	.200	.222
Scor. Pos./2 Out	26	5	0	0	0	5	1	7	.192	.192	.222
Late Inning Pressure	39	8	2	0	0	0	3	8	.205	.256	.262
Leading Off	14	5	2	0	0	0	2	2	.357	.500	.438
Runners On	14	2	0	0	0	0	1	4	.143	.143	.200
Runners/Scor. Pos.	9	1	0	0	0	0	1	3	.111	.111	.200

DRIVING IN RUNS	From 1B	From 2B	From 3B	Scoring Position
Totals	1/39	4/36	4/15	8/51
Percentage	3%	11%	27%	16%
Driving In Runners from 3B with Less than Two Out:			2/6	33%

Loves to face: Rick Reuschel (2-for-2, 1 double, 1 HR)
Hates to face: Greg Mathews (0-for-6)
Seven home runs, 13 RBI through first 25 games; no home runs, three RBI after that. . . . Even so, those seven home runs were only three less than the total for all other Giants' starting center fielders last season; Kutcher started only 33 games there, compared to 129 for the others. . . . Drove in only 15.7 percent (8-of-51) of runners from scoring position, lowest rate in N.L. (minimum: 50 opportunities). . . . Played six positions, including four starts at shortstop and one at third after Sept. 1; did not pitch, catch, or play first base. . . . Born April 20, 1960, the day that Mike McCormick pitched the first Giants' shutout at Candlestick Park, a 1–0 win over Don Drysdale and Dodgers.

Ken Landreaux

Bats Left

Los Angeles Dodgers	AB	H	2B	3B	HR	RRF	BB	SO	BA	SA	OBA
Season	283	74	13	2	4	30	22	39	.261	.364	.313
vs. Left-Handers	45	12	3	0	0	8	2	5	.267	.333	.313
vs. Right-Handers	238	62	10	2	4	22	20	34	.261	.370	.313
Home	127	30	4	0	1	14	14	14	.236	.291	.308
Road	156	44	9	2	3	16	8	25	.282	.423	.317
Grass	205	50	10	1	3	19	18	28	.244	.346	.303
Artificial Turf	78	24	3	1	1	11	4	11	.308	.410	.341
April	73	18	5	0	2	10	5	5	.247	.397	.288
May	63	16	2	1	1	8	8	14	.254	.365	.333
June	53	14	2	1	0	3	3	9	.264	.340	.298
July	73	22	4	0	1	9	5	8	.301	.397	.354
August	0	0	0	0	0	0	0	0	—	—	—
Sept./Oct.	21	4	0	0	0	0	1	3	.190	.190	.227
Leading Off Inn.	51	17	4	0	1	1	2	8	.333	.471	.358
Runners On	111	29	6	1	1	27	14	11	.261	.360	.333
Runners/Scor. Pos.	65	15	4	1	0	23	12	9	.231	.323	.333
Runners On/2 Out	33	4	1	1	0	7	8	4	.121	.212	.293
Scor. Pos./2 Out	21	4	1	1	0	6	8	4	.190	.333	.414
Late Inning Pressure	55	11	2	0	0	4	3	4	.200	.236	.237
Leading Off	10	3	1	0	0	0	0	1	.300	.400	.300
Runners On	24	5	1	0	0	4	3	1	.208	.250	.286
Runners/Scor. Pos.	13	2	0	0	0	4	3	1	.154	.154	.294

DRIVING IN RUNS	From 1B	From 2B	From 3B	Scoring Position
Totals	4/75	7/56	15/29	22/85
Percentage	5%	13%	52%	26%
Driving In Runners from 3B with Less than Two Out:		11/16		69%

Loves to face: Eric Show (.359, 14-for-39, 1 HR)
Hates to face: Andy Hawkins (.095, 2-for-21)
Batted .344 in 27 games in 3d position in lineup; .231 in 38 games batting 2d. . . . Batted .326 in day games, .234 at night. . . . Career batting average of .434 at Veterans Stadium, .219 at Candlestick Park. . . . Has batted over .300 in five of last six seasons when leading off in Late-Inning Pressure Situations. . . . Batting average was higher vs. left-handers than vs. right-handers for third time in past six seasons. . . . Has batted .155 with runners in scoring position and two outs over past two years. . . . Did not walk twice in any game last season. . . . Does not show any indication of being the next Manny Mota. Pinch-hitting: 6-for-31 (.194) last year; 21-for-105 (.200) for career.

Tito Landrum

Bats Right

St. Louis Cardinals	AB	H	2B	3B	HR	RRF	BB	SO	BA	SA	OBA
Season	205	43	7	1	2	20	20	41	.210	.283	.279
vs. Left-Handers	171	31	6	1	2	18	19	31	.181	.263	.263
vs. Right-Handers	34	12	1	0	0	2	1	10	.353	.382	.371
Home	91	19	5	0	2	10	10	12	.209	.330	.286
Road	114	24	2	1	0	10	10	29	.211	.246	.274
Grass	58	9	1	1	0	8	5	18	.155	.207	.222
Artificial Turf	147	34	6	0	2	12	15	23	.231	.313	.301
April	31	5	0	0	1	4	1	4	.161	.258	.212
May	38	8	4	0	0	7	3	8	.211	.316	.273
June	26	3	0	0	0	2	6	7	.115	.115	.273
July	42	9	3	0	0	3	2	9	.214	.286	.250
August	45	13	0	0	0	1	4	8	.289	.289	.340
Sept./Oct.	23	5	0	1	1	3	4	5	.217	.435	.333
Leading Off Inn.	40	7	1	1	1	1	4	8	.175	.325	.267
Runners On	102	24	3	0	0	18	11	19	.235	.265	.302
Runners/Scor. Pos.	56	13	3	0	0	18	8	10	.232	.286	.313
Runners On/2 Out	49	8	0	0	0	4	4	12	.163	.163	.226
Scor. Pos./2 Out	30	4	0	0	0	4	4	8	.133	.133	.235
Late Inning Pressure	42	11	1	0	1	8	7	10	.262	.357	.365
Leading Off	8	1	0	0	1	1	2	2	.125	.500	.364
Runners On	20	7	1	0	0	7	4	5	.350	.400	.423
Runners/Scor. Pos.	12	4	1	0	0	7	4	4	.333	.417	.444

DRIVING IN RUNS	From 1B	From 2B	From 3B	Scoring Position
Totals	0/81	7/42	11/23	18/65
Percentage	0%	17%	48%	28%
Driving In Runners from 3B with Less than Two Out:		9/12		75%

Loves to face: Tom Browning (.444, 4-for-9)
Hates to face: Fernando Valenzuela (.111, 3-for-27, 10 SO)
.347 career postseason average (17-for-49), .256 in regular season. . . . Drove in only three runs over second half of '86 season, but each was a game-winner. . . . Started 45 of 61 games in which Cardinals faced a left-handed starter, only three of 100 against righties. . . . Has never played regularly against right-handed pitching, but this career breakdown suggests that he should: .241 vs. left-handers, .302 vs. right-handers. Only home run hit vs. a right-hander was off Bill Laskey in 1985. . . . Career batting average of .444 (8-for-18, 3 HR) at Atlanta Stadium. . . . This surprised us: 15 career stolen bases, 16 times caught stealing.

Mike LaValliere

Bats Left

St. Louis Cardinals	AB	H	2B	3B	HR	RRF	BB	SO	BA	SA	OBA
Season	303	71	10	2	3	31	36	37	.234	.310	.318
vs. Left-Handers	57	12	4	0	1	9	5	12	.211	.333	.274
vs. Right-Handers	246	59	6	2	2	22	31	25	.240	.305	.327
Home	150	33	4	1	1	14	18	17	.220	.280	.304
Road	153	38	6	1	2	17	18	20	.248	.340	.331
Grass	67	16	3	1	0	8	10	9	.239	.313	.338
Artificial Turf	236	55	7	1	3	23	26	28	.233	.309	.312
April	16	4	0	0	0	0	1	4	.250	.250	.294
May	20	5	0	0	0	2	3	2	.250	.250	.348
June	57	17	2	1	1	9	8	7	.298	.421	.385
July	61	11	2	0	0	7	9	6	.180	.213	.286
August	69	12	4	1	1	5	7	7	.174	.304	.260
Sept./Oct.	80	22	2	0	1	8	8	11	.275	.338	.341
Leading Off Inn.	62	17	2	2	1	1	8	5	.274	.419	.357
Runners On	133	32	5	0	2	30	21	15	.241	.323	.348
Runners/Scor. Pos.	82	22	5	0	2	28	14	11	.268	.366	.381
Runners On/2 Out	50	13	2	0	2	16	12	3	.260	.420	.403
Scor. Pos./2 Out	40	11	2	0	1	14	9	3	.275	.400	.408
Late Inning Pressure	52	13	2	1	2	7	4	7	.250	.442	.304
Leading Off	9	4	0	1	1	1	1	0	.444	1.000	.500
Runners On	26	6	1	0	1	6	1	4	.231	.385	.259
Runners/Scor. Pos.	13	3	1	0	0	4	1	3	.231	.308	.286

DRIVING IN RUNS	From 1B	From 2B	From 3B	Scoring Position
Totals	2/87	10/61	16/35	26/96
Percentage	2%	16%	46%	27%
Driving In Runners from 3B with Less than Two Out:		10/19		53%

Loves to face: Dennis Martinez (.750, 3-for-4)
Hates to face: Rick Reuschel (.188, 3-for-16)
Drove in runners from third base with less than two out in 10 of his first 12 attempts last season. "Mr. Squeeze Play" had four sacrifice bunts and a bunt single last season while a runner occupied third base. . . . Had 10 sacrifice bunts during the season, the most by any catcher in N.L. . . . Caught 56 percent of Cardinals innings last season; Heath had 33 percent; Steve Lake, nine percent; Clint Hurdle, two percent; Alan Knicely, three innings. . . . Even started 11 games against left-handers last season, and batted .257 in those games. . . . Charged with only one passed ball in 827.1 innings caught, lowest rate in majors; the average for a major-league catcher is one every 103 innings.

Vance Law

Bats Right

Montreal Expos	AB	H	2B	3B	HR	RRF	BB	SO	BA	SA	OBA
Season	360	81	17	2	5	47	37	66	.225	.325	.298
vs. Left-Handers	127	32	7	1	4	21	11	20	.252	.417	.307
vs. Right-Handers	233	49	10	1	1	26	26	46	.210	.275	.292
Home	177	46	11	1	3	28	20	25	.260	.384	.333
Road	183	35	6	1	2	19	17	41	.191	.268	.262
Grass	105	16	5	0	1	10	7	23	.152	.229	.204
Artificial Turf	255	65	12	2	4	37	30	43	.255	.365	.334
April	66	15	4	0	1	8	8	13	.227	.333	.311
May	80	19	2	0	2	9	5	17	.238	.338	.282
June	78	15	4	1	0	10	12	18	.192	.269	.254
July	56	9	0	1	0	8	7	6	.161	.196	.254
August	63	17	4	0	1	6	4	10	.270	.381	.319
Sept./Oct.	17	6	3	0	1	6	1	2	.353	.706	.368
Leading Off Inn.	78	15	2	1	0	0	8	15	.192	.244	.276
Runners On	160	44	8	1	2	44	17	26	.275	.375	.344
Runners/Scor. Pos.	97	26	4	1	1	39	13	17	.268	.361	.348
Runners On/2 Out	59	12	0	1	2	18	6	10	.203	.339	.277
Scor. Pos./2 Out	42	9	0	1	1	16	4	6	.214	.333	.283
Late Inning Pressure	68	17	3	1	1	8	9	10	.250	.368	.338
Leading Off	20	3	0	1	0	0	3	2	.150	.250	.261
Runners On	33	9	1	0	0	7	5	5	.273	.303	.368
Runners/Scor. Pos.	17	4	1	0	0	7	3	3	.235	.294	.350

DRIVING IN RUNS	From 1B	From 2B	From 3B	Scoring Position
Totals	5/121	17/77	20/40	37/117
Percentage	4%	22%	50%	32%
Driving In Runners from 3B with Less than Two Out:		13/22		59%

Loves to face: Rick Mahler (.471, 8-for-17)
Hates to face: Bob Ojeda (.100, 2-for-20)
A modern-day Gil McDougald, who has spent different seasons playing primarily at shortstop (1982), third base (1983–84) and second base (1985–86). . . . Has also played outfield, first base, and last year pitched in three games (four innings, 2.25 ERA, opponents were 0-for-4 with runners in scoring position). . . . Stole his last base on May 27; caught stealing five times after that. . . . Ranked second among N.L. second basemen with an average of 3.38 assists per nine innings (minimum: 500 innings). . . . Batted .400 over an eight-game stretch in late August and early September, before having to leave team to attend to family illness.

Jeffrey Leonard

San Francisco Giants   Bats Right

	AB	H	2B	3B	HR	RRF	BB	SO	BA	SA	OBA
Season	341	95	11	3	6	44	20	62	.279	.381	.322
vs. Left-Handers	119	39	4	0	3	20	4	9	.328	.437	.350
vs. Right-Handers	222	56	7	3	3	24	16	53	.252	.351	.307
Home	168	53	5	3	2	21	8	30	.315	.417	.350
Road	173	42	6	0	4	23	12	32	.243	.347	.294
Grass	256	78	10	3	5	36	16	48	.305	.426	.347
Artificial Turf	85	17	1	0	1	8	4	14	.200	.247	.244
April	85	28	4	2	4	18	6	9	.329	.565	.370
May	92	29	2	0	2	14	5	17	.315	.402	.360
June	97	22	3	1	0	8	4	25	.227	.278	.262
July	67	16	2	0	0	4	5	11	.239	.269	.292
August	0	0	0	0	0	0	0	0	—	—	—
Sept./Oct.	0	0	0	0	0	0	0	0	—	—	—
Leading Off Inn.	68	21	3	2	1	2	1	10	.309	.456	.319
Runners On	175	50	4	1	4	41	12	31	.286	.389	.330
Runners/Scor. Pos.	103	31	3	1	4	41	8	20	.301	.466	.348
Runners On/2 Out	81	20	1	1	1	16	6	13	.247	.321	.307
Scor. Pos./2 Out	44	13	1	1	1	16	5	8	.295	.432	.380
Late Inning Pressure	56	15	1	1	2	7	5	12	.268	.429	.333
Leading Off	15	6	1	1	1	2	1	2	.400	.800	.438
Runners On	27	8	0	0	1	5	3	5	.296	.407	.375
Runners/Scor. Pos.	12	4	0	0	1	5	1	3	.333	.583	.400

DRIVING IN RUNS	From 1B	From 2B	From 3B	Scoring Position
Totals	5/115	13/75	19/42	32/117
Percentage	4%	17%	45%	27%
Driving In Runners from 3B with Less than Two Out:			14/26	54%

Loves to face: Steve Trout (.524, 11-for-21, 2 HR)
Hates to face: Rich Gossage (0-for-13, 8 SO)
Batted 128 points higher in day games (.348) than in night games (.220), largest difference in N.L. (minimum: 50 AB each). . . . Has hit 40 of 81 career home runs in day games, despite having less than 40 percent of his at bats in day games. . . . Has homered in every N.L. ballpark except Olympic Stadium (76 AB). . . . Career batting average of .302 (one HR every 25.5 AB) vs. left-handers, .252 (one HR every 47.9 AB) vs. right-handers. . . . Hitless in last 29 at bats with two outs and runners in scoring position in Late-Inning Pressure Situations. . . . Career .970 fielding percentage ranks in bottom 10 among active outfielders with 500 games; the group includes Dave Kingman, Lonnie Smith, and Reggie Jackson.

Dave Lopes

Cubs/Astros   Bats Right

	AB	H	2B	3B	HR	RRF	BB	SO	BA	SA	OBA
Season	255	70	10	3	7	37	43	25	.275	.420	.381
vs. Left-Handers	94	24	4	0	3	15	21	12	.255	.394	.391
vs. Right-Handers	161	46	6	3	4	22	22	13	.285	.435	.374
Home	122	38	4	2	4	19	24	12	.311	.475	.422
Road	133	32	6	1	3	18	19	13	.241	.368	.342
Grass	150	45	6	2	6	21	31	13	.300	.487	.421
Artificial Turf	105	25	4	1	1	16	12	12	.238	.324	.319
April	31	7	3	1	0	4	5	4	.226	.387	.333
May	38	13	1	0	2	7	10	4	.342	.526	.469
June	58	18	2	1	3	11	11	5	.310	.534	.429
July	50	13	2	1	1	5	7	6	.260	.400	.362
August	51	12	1	0	1	4	4	4	.235	.314	.291
Sept./Oct.	27	7	1	0	0	6	6	2	.259	.296	.382
Leading Off Inn.	68	22	4	0	1	1	13	2	.324	.426	.439
Runners On	104	28	3	1	2	32	18	12	.269	.375	.376
Runners/Scor. Pos.	67	17	3	0	0	27	12	9	.254	.299	.366
Runners On/2 Out	40	12	2	0	1	14	9	8	.300	.425	.429
Scor. Pos./2 Out	33	11	2	0	0	12	8	7	.333	.394	.463
Late Inning Pressure	50	16	3	0	2	13	6	3	.320	.500	.382
Leading Off	11	3	1	0	0	0	2	0	.273	.364	.385
Runners On	26	8	1	0	1	12	2	3	.308	.462	.357
Runners/Scor. Pos.	20	6	1	0	0	10	1	3	.300	.350	.333

DRIVING IN RUNS	From 1B	From 2B	From 3B	Scoring Position
Totals	3/65	12/54	15/34	27/88
Percentage	5%	22%	44%	31%
Driving In Runners from 3B with Less than Two Out:			10/19	53%

Loves to face: Dave Dravecky (.700, 7-for-10, 2 HR)
Hates to face: Bob Welch (0-for-10)
Career stolen-base percentage of .831 is 5th best among active players with 100+ steals; over the past four years, his percentage is .872. . . . Averaged one walk every 7.1 plate appearances last season, 6th-highest rate in N.L. (minimum: 40 BB). . . . Has a streak going: 33 consecutive plate appearances with the bases loaded without striking out. . . . Batted 121 points higher in day games (.331) than in night games (.210), 4th-largest difference in majors (minimum: 50 AB each). Also, batting average on grass fields (.300) was his highest in the last 12 years. So what happens? Cubs trade him to Houston, the first of his four teams to have an artificial-turf home field.

Bill Madlock

Los Angeles Dodgers   Bats Right

	AB	H	2B	3B	HR	RRF	BB	SO	BA	SA	OBA
Season	379	106	17	0	10	63	30	43	.280	.404	.336
vs. Left-Handers	141	44	6	0	6	25	11	11	.312	.482	.364
vs. Right-Handers	238	62	11	0	4	38	19	32	.261	.357	.320
Home	186	49	6	0	4	32	19	22	.263	.360	.336
Road	193	57	11	0	6	31	11	21	.295	.446	.335
Grass	262	74	11	0	6	40	23	26	.282	.393	.345
Artificial Turf	117	32	6	0	4	23	7	17	.274	.427	.315
April	38	9	1	0	1	2	1	3	.237	.342	.275
May	71	17	1	0	0	11	3	12	.239	.254	.267
June	65	14	3	0	3	10	7	8	.215	.400	.292
July	41	14	2	0	1	6	4	2	.341	.463	.400
August	97	33	5	0	3	20	8	10	.340	.485	.405
Sept./Oct.	67	19	5	0	2	14	7	8	.284	.448	.338
Leading Off Inn.	76	19	4	0	1	1	6	8	.250	.342	.305
Runners On	158	46	4	0	7	60	18	15	.291	.449	.362
Runners/Scor. Pos.	94	30	3	0	2	49	14	8	.319	.415	.397
Runners On/2 Out	59	17	2	0	0	11	7	6	.288	.322	.373
Scor. Pos./2 Out	37	11	2	0	0	11	5	3	.297	.351	.395
Late Inning Pressure	62	15	3	0	1	11	4	8	.242	.339	.294
Leading Off	19	3	1	0	0	0	0	2	.158	.211	.158
Runners On	22	8	0	0	1	11	3	1	.364	.500	.423
Runners/Scor. Pos.	13	5	0	0	0	9	2	0	.385	.385	.438

DRIVING IN RUNS	From 1B	From 2B	From 3B	Scoring Position
Totals	8/100	20/80	25/37	45/117
Percentage	8%	25%	68%	38%
Driving In Runners from 3B with Less than Two Out:			22/25	88%

Loves to face: Mark Davis (.500, 9-for-18, 3 HR)
Hates to face: Jay Tibbs (.077, 1-for-13)
Drove in 88 percent (22-of-25) of runners from third base with less than two out last season, best rate in N.L. . . . Drove in at least one run in seven consecutive games (May 11–20), longest streak of career. . . . Has 11 hits in 21 at bats with bases loaded over past three years; batting .429 in that situation over past 12 years. . . . Played his first 87 games in majors for four different managers, his last 1,277 for three (Altobelli, Tanner, Lasorda). . . . Got off to a fast start in that regard: his major league debut, on Sept. 7, 1973, came for Del Wilber, in Del's only game as major-league "manager," filling in between the time when the Rangers fired Whitey Herzog and hired Billy Martin. Madlock's second game was Martin's first.

Candy Maldonado

San Francisco Giants   Bats Right

	AB	H	2B	3B	HR	RRF	BB	SO	BA	SA	OBA
Season	405	102	31	3	18	88	20	77	.252	.477	.289
vs. Left-Handers	132	31	10	2	6	32	3	20	.235	.477	.252
vs. Right-Handers	273	71	21	1	12	56	17	57	.260	.476	.307
Home	197	45	16	1	6	44	8	39	.228	.411	.258
Road	208	57	15	2	12	44	12	38	.274	.538	.318
Grass	282	73	23	2	13	66	11	55	.259	.493	.289
Artificial Turf	123	29	8	1	5	22	9	22	.236	.439	.291
April	25	8	1	1	2	6	0	6	.320	.680	.346
May	68	16	5	0	3	12	2	9	.235	.441	.257
June	63	15	8	1	0	7	4	14	.238	.397	.284
July	33	10	0	0	1	14	3	6	.303	.394	.342
August	83	21	4	0	6	24	8	12	.253	.518	.326
Sept./Oct.	133	32	13	1	6	25	3	30	.241	.489	.259
Leading Off Inn.	116	20	6	0	4	4	2	30	.172	.328	.193
Runners On	183	57	16	3	11	81	12	32	.311	.612	.353
Runners/Scor. Pos.	121	37	12	2	7	71	12	20	.306	.612	.362
Runners On/2 Out	80	25	6	1	4	38	4	16	.313	.638	.353
Scor. Pos./2 Out	55	17	6	1	3	31	4	9	.309	.582	.356
Late Inning Pressure	97	32	10	1	6	28	7	19	.330	.639	.371
Leading Off	23	6	1	0	2	2	0	7	.261	.565	.261
Runners On	42	16	7	1	1	23	5	7	.381	.667	.438
Runners/Scor. Pos.	31	12	5	1	1	23	5	5	.387	.710	.459

DRIVING IN RUNS	From 1B	From 2B	From 3B	Scoring Position
Totals	16/122	24/93	30/59	54/152
Percentage	13%	26%	51%	36%
Driving In Runners from 3B with Less than Two Out:			21/30	70%

Loves to face: Frank DiPino (.714, 5-for-7)
Hates to face: Shane Rawley (.095, 2-for-21)
One of four N.L. players to drive in 50+ runs after the All-Star break (Parker 57, Hayes 56, Schmidt 53, Maldonado 51). . . . His 17 extra-base hits in Late-Inning Pressure Situations fell one short of Dave Parker's 1979 *Player Analysis* record. Ten hits with bases loaded (in 19 AB) also fell one short of top mark. . . . Batted 109 points higher with runners on than with bases empty, 5th-largest difference in majors (minimum: 100 AB each way). . . . Career breakdown: .282 with runners on base, .212 with bases empty. . . . Batted .425 (17-for-40) with four HR and five game-winning RBI as pinch-hitter, .221 with 60 RBI in 88 games in the starting lineup. . . . Led N.L. with five 9th-inning homers.

Mike Marshall

Los Angeles Dodgers — Bats Right

	AB	H	2B	3B	HR	RRF	BB	SO	BA	SA	OBA
Season	330	77	11	0	19	55	27	90	.233	.439	.298
vs. Left-Handers	129	32	7	0	9	23	16	34	.248	.512	.329
vs. Right-Handers	201	45	4	0	10	32	11	56	.224	.393	.278
Home	179	43	7	0	13	35	16	40	.240	.497	.305
Road	151	34	4	0	6	20	11	50	.225	.371	.291
Grass	261	67	9	0	18	49	22	63	.257	.498	.323
Artificial Turf	69	10	2	0	1	6	5	27	.145	.217	.203
April	89	20	2	0	6	17	3	25	.225	.449	.266
May	91	27	6	0	7	21	10	22	.297	.593	.379
June	87	24	3	0	4	9	10	22	.276	.448	.347
July	25	3	0	0	1	2	0	7	.120	.240	.120
August	38	3	0	0	1	6	4	14	.079	.158	.167
Sept./Oct.	0	0	0	0	0	0	0	0	—	—	—
Leading Off Inn.	84	19	1	0	7	7	7	25	.226	.488	.286
Runners On	155	40	8	0	7	43	13	38	.258	.445	.322
Runners/Scor. Pos.	82	20	3	0	2	29	12	19	.244	.354	.337
Runners On/2 Out	66	14	3	0	4	18	6	16	.212	.439	.288
Scor. Pos./2 Out	35	8	1	0	2	12	5	7	.229	.429	.325
Late Inning Pressure	53	13	1	0	2	6	3	10	.245	.377	.305
Leading Off	11	3	0	0	1	1	1	2	.273	.545	.333
Runners On	27	7	1	0	1	5	1	6	.259	.407	.276
Runners/Scor. Pos.	12	3	1	0	0	3	1	3	.250	.333	.286

DRIVING IN RUNS	From 1B	From 2B	From 3B	Scoring Position
Totals	11/111	9/61	16/36	25/97
Percentage	10%	15%	44%	26%
Driving In Runners from 3B with Less than Two Out:		12/22	55%	

Loves to face: Scott Garrelts (.444, 8-for-18, 3 HR)
Hates to face: John Franco (0-for-7, 4 SO)

Played in 103 games last season, three short of the other Mike Marshall's total with Dodgers in 1974. . . . N.L.'s home run leader as late as July 1, but chronic back problems limited him to only 44 at bats in 27 games after All-Star break. . . . Started his last game on Aug. 25; his last 13 games were as a pinch-runner or defensive replacement. . . . Marshall and Pedro Guerrero appeared in the same starting lineup only once last season, a 7–3 victory over Houston on Aug. 4. They had combined for 61 home runs and 182 RBI in 1985, leading Dodgers to division title. . . . Very little career left/right imbalance: batting .270, slugging .455 vs. right-handers; .262 and .461 vs. lefties.

Carmelo Martinez

San Diego Padres — Bats Right

	AB	H	2B	3B	HR	RRF	BB	SO	BA	SA	OBA
Season	244	58	10	0	9	26	35	46	.238	.389	.333
vs. Left-Handers	110	31	5	0	7	16	24	18	.282	.518	.407
vs. Right-Handers	134	27	5	0	2	10	11	28	.201	.284	.265
Home	123	22	4	0	6	15	21	26	.179	.358	.297
Road	121	36	6	0	3	11	14	20	.298	.421	.372
Grass	191	41	7	0	8	22	30	39	.215	.377	.318
Artificial Turf	53	17	3	0	1	4	5	7	.321	.434	.390
April	40	11	3	0	1	2	5	13	.275	.425	.356
May	64	17	1	0	2	4	8	12	.266	.375	.347
June	63	15	4	0	2	6	14	7	.238	.397	.377
July	15	1	0	0	0	1	4	1	.067	.067	.250
August	11	3	0	0	1	2	0	3	.273	.545	.273
Sept./Oct.	51	11	2	0	3	11	4	10	.216	.431	.281
Leading Off Inn.	54	16	2	0	2	2	13	8	.296	.444	.433
Runners On	106	23	4	0	4	21	13	19	.217	.368	.303
Runners/Scor. Pos.	57	9	3	0	1	14	9	18	.158	.263	.275
Runners On/2 Out	44	8	0	0	1	6	8	6	.182	.318	.308
Scor. Pos./2 Out	27	1	0	0	0	2	4	6	.037	.037	.161
Late Inning Pressure	53	12	2	0	3	11	4	9	.226	.434	.288
Leading Off	6	3	0	0	1	1	2	2	.500	1.000	.571
Runners On	31	6	1	0	1	9	2	6	.194	.323	.257
Runners/Scor. Pos.	18	4	1	0	0	7	2	5	.222	.278	.318

DRIVING IN RUNS	From 1B	From 2B	From 3B	Scoring Position
Totals	6/79	5/42	6/24	11/66
Percentage	8%	12%	25%	17%
Driving In Runners from 3B with Less than Two Out:		6/14	43%	

Loves to face: Tom Hume (.500, 4-for-8, 2 HR)
Hates to face: Bill Gullickson (.063, 1-for-16)

Limited to 60 starts last season by addition of Marvell Wynne, emergence of John Kruk, and his own poor year. . . . Started 60 percent of games in which Padres faced a left-handed starter, only 24 percent vs. right-handers. . . . Started only two games from June 30 to August 30. . . . Drove in 16.7 percent (11-of-66) of runners from scoring position, 4th-lowest percentage in N.L. (minimum: 50 opportunities). . . . Batted 120 points higher in day games (.317) than in night games (.198), 5th-largest difference in majors (minimum: 50 AB each). . . . Batting average with runners on base was lower than average with bases empty for the first time in four-year career. Annual averages with runners on base: .289, .283, .288, .217.

Gary Matthews

Chicago Cubs — Bats Right

	AB	H	2B	3B	HR	RRF	BB	SO	BA	SA	OBA
Season	370	96	16	1	21	49	60	59	.259	.478	.361
vs. Left-Handers	105	37	6	1	6	15	23	9	.352	.600	.465
vs. Right-Handers	265	59	10	0	15	34	37	50	.223	.430	.317
Home	185	53	7	1	11	30	30	31	.286	.514	.382
Road	185	43	9	0	10	19	30	28	.232	.443	.340
Grass	274	75	11	1	18	42	43	43	.274	.518	.370
Artificial Turf	96	21	5	0	3	7	17	16	.219	.365	.336
April	31	5	1	0	0	2	7	3	.161	.194	.316
May	66	15	3	0	4	9	12	12	.227	.455	.346
June	54	13	3	1	1	4	15	8	.241	.389	.406
July	80	25	5	0	7	16	10	11	.313	.638	.389
August	93	24	3	0	5	12	9	14	.258	.452	.317
Sept./Oct.	46	14	1	0	4	6	7	11	.304	.587	.396
Leading Off Inn.	77	22	2	0	4	4	11	10	.286	.468	.375
Runners On	149	33	5	1	6	34	27	25	.221	.389	.337
Runners/Scor. Pos.	88	18	2	1	4	27	16	17	.205	.386	.321
Runners On/2 Out	46	12	2	1	0	7	8	6	.261	.348	.370
Scor. Pos./2 Out	33	8	1	1	0	7	6	5	.242	.333	.359
Late Inning Pressure	57	12	0	0	3	8	9	9	.211	.316	.308
Leading Off	18	4	0	0	1	1	4	2	.222	.389	.364
Runners On	21	4	0	0	0	1	3	4	.190	.190	.292
Runners/Scor. Pos.	12	2	0	0	0	1	2	3	.167	.167	.286

DRIVING IN RUNS	From 1B	From 2B	From 3B	Scoring Position
Totals	7/95	8/67	13/35	21/102
Percentage	7%	12%	37%	21%
Driving In Runners from 3B with Less than Two Out:		11/20	55%	

Loves to face: Sid Fernandez (.533, 8-for-15, 2 HR)
Hates to face: Bryn Smith (.040, 1-for-25)

0-for-the-season as a pinch-hitter last season, in 16 at bats; counting 1985, has gone 0-for-19 off the bench since hitting a pinch homer off Expos' John Dopson, Sept. 24, 1985. . . . When he wasn't pinch-hitting, his stroke wasn't bad: averaged one home run every 17.6 at bats last season, 6th-best rate in N.L. (minimum: 10 HR). . . . Batted 130 points higher vs. left-handed pitchers than against right-handers, 4th-largest difference in N.L. (minimum: 100 AB vs. both). . . . Had lowest fielding percentage (.940) of any N.L. outfielder last season (minimum: 100 games). . . . Batting average with runners in scoring position (.205) was his lowest in last 12 years.

Len Matuszek

Los Angeles Dodgers — Bats Left

	AB	H	2B	3B	HR	RRF	BB	SO	BA	SA	OBA
Season	199	52	7	0	9	29	21	47	.261	.432	.333
vs. Left-Handers	13	2	0	0	0	0	1	7	.154	.154	.214
vs. Right-Handers	186	50	7	0	9	29	20	40	.269	.452	.341
Home	89	28	1	0	7	20	13	16	.315	.562	.404
Road	110	24	6	0	2	9	8	31	.218	.327	.271
Grass	129	38	4	0	8	25	16	28	.295	.512	.374
Artificial Turf	70	14	3	0	1	4	5	19	.200	.286	.253
April	0	0	0	0	0	0	0	0	—	—	—
May	3	0	0	0	0	0	0	1	.000	.000	.000
June	24	7	0	0	2	5	4	8	.292	.542	.393
July	59	17	4	0	4	10	5	13	.288	.559	.344
August	61	15	1	0	2	8	7	15	.246	.361	.329
Sept./Oct.	52	13	2	0	1	6	5	10	.250	.346	.329
Leading Off Inn.	56	10	2	0	0	0	4	17	.179	.214	.233
Runners On	73	26	1	0	6	26	12	13	.356	.616	.448
Runners/Scor. Pos.	42	12	1	0	4	21	7	10	.286	.595	.392
Runners On/2 Out	37	10	0	0	4	14	6	8	.270	.595	.400
Scor. Pos./2 Out	27	6	0	0	3	11	5	6	.222	.556	.344
Late Inning Pressure	34	7	1	0	2	6	3	9	.206	.412	.270
Leading Off	9	1	0	0	0	0	0	2	.111	.111	.111
Runners On	14	3	0	0	2	6	2	5	.214	.643	.313
Runners/Scor. Pos.	8	3	0	0	2	6	2	3	.375	1.125	.500

DRIVING IN RUNS	From 1B	From 2B	From 3B	Scoring Position
Totals	5/57	6/24	9/27	15/51
Percentage	9%	25%	33%	29%
Driving In Runners from 3B with Less than Two Out:		5/9	56%	

Loves to face: Kevin Gross (.714, 5-for-7)
Hates to face: Mark Davis (0-for-7)

One of seven Dodgers to start at first base last season, tying Brewers for major-league lead. Dodgers win on a tie-breaker, though: They also had three guys who didn't start but played there as substitutes, while Milwaukee had none. . . . The Tooz was also one of 10 left fielders and one of nine right fielders used by Lasorda last season. . . . One hit in 18 career at bats at the Astrodome, the only N.L. ballpark in which he does not have an extra-base hit. . . . Started only one game vs. a left-handed pitcher last season (July 30 vs. Terry Mulholland). Only 21 plate appearances against lefties over the past two seasons. . . . Career breakdown: .277 on grass fields, .204 on artificial surfaces.

Lee Mazzilli

Pirates/Mets — Bats Left and Right

	AB	H	2B	3B	HR	RRF	BB	SO	BA	SA	OBA
Season	151	37	5	1	3	18	38	36	.245	.351	.401
vs. Left-Handers	52	9	2	0	1	4	6	17	.173	.269	.259
vs. Right-Handers	99	28	3	1	2	14	32	19	.283	.394	.463
Home	80	23	5	0	1	8	17	21	.288	.388	.408
Road	71	14	0	1	2	10	21	15	.197	.310	.394
Grass	81	20	3	1	2	13	17	20	.247	.383	.378
Artificial Turf	70	17	2	0	1	5	21	16	.243	.314	.426
April	17	4	0	0	0	5	8	6	.235	.235	.480
May	28	6	1	0	0	7	7	8	.214	.250	.371
June	33	6	1	1	0	3	8	8	.182	.273	.333
July	15	5	0	0	1	3	3	3	.333	.533	.444
August	24	5	0	0	2	4	3	5	.208	.458	.296
Sept./Oct.	34	11	3	0	0	3	9	6	.324	.412	.489
Leading Off Inn.	27	5	2	0	0	0	9	9	.185	.259	.389
Runners On	70	15	1	0	2	17	21	11	.214	.314	.404
Runners/Scor. Pos.	41	10	1	0	0	13	16	9	.244	.268	.467
Runners On/2 Out	22	4	0	0	1	6	7	2	.182	.318	.400
Scor. Pos./2 Out	12	3	0	0	0	4	6	2	.250	.250	.526
Late Inning Pressure	56	11	0	0	1	5	10	14	.196	.250	.324
Leading Off	15	1	0	0	0	0	6	6	.067	.067	.333
Runners On	22	3	0	0	0	4	2	4	.136	.136	.231
Runners/Scor. Pos.	13	2	0	0	0	4	1	2	.154	.154	.250

DRIVING IN RUNS	From 1B	From 2B	From 3B	Scoring Position
Totals	2/50	5/33	8/16	13/49
Percentage	4%	15%	50%	27%
Driving In Runners from 3B with Less than Two Out:		6/9		67%

Loves to face: Kent Tekulve (.391, 9-for-23, 2 HR)
Hates to face: Andy Hawkins (0-for-14)
Started season with majors' worst team, finished with the best; among others to have done that in recent history are Todd Cruz (Seattle to Baltimore, 1983), Rico Carty (Texas to Oakland, 1973), Ted Kubiak and Don Mincher (Texas to Oakland, 1972), and Donn Clendenon (Montreal to Mets, 1969). . . . Has batted for a higher average with runners on base than with the bases empty in nine of his 11 seasons (1980 being the other exception). . . . Became 3d player to get pinch-hits in both 6th and 7th games of a World Series; multiple choice quiz for the other two: (a) Ken Boswell and Dr. Bobby Brown; (b) Dr. Bobby Brown and Bart Giamatti; (c) Bart Giamatti and Ron Darling.

Willie McGee

St. Louis Cardinals — Bats Left and Right

	AB	H	2B	3B	HR	RRF	BB	SO	BA	SA	OBA
Season	497	127	22	7	7	55	37	82	.256	.370	.306
vs. Left-Handers	199	49	7	3	5	23	15	40	.246	.387	.301
vs. Right-Handers	298	78	15	4	2	32	22	42	.262	.359	.310
Home	264	74	15	6	7	34	17	47	.280	.462	.325
Road	233	53	7	1	0	21	20	35	.227	.266	.285
Grass	127	26	3	0	0	6	7	13	.205	.228	.244
Artificial Turf	370	101	19	7	7	49	30	69	.273	.419	.327
April	81	18	0	0	2	11	3	18	.222	.296	.247
May	109	29	2	4	0	11	6	19	.266	.358	.308
June	113	26	5	1	1	11	12	19	.230	.319	.299
July	67	20	2	2	3	10	5	8	.299	.522	.347
August	20	6	2	0	0	3	5	1	.300	.400	.440
Sept./Oct.	107	28	11	0	1	9	6	17	.262	.393	.301
Leading Off Inn.	110	32	4	2	2	6	15	.291	.418	.328	
Runners On	203	48	10	4	2	50	21	35	.236	.355	.303
Runners/Scor. Pos.	131	33	7	2	1	45	15	26	.252	.359	.320
Runners On/2 Out	79	16	3	2	0	17	10	11	.203	.291	.292
Scor. Pos./2 Out	55	13	3	1	0	16	8	7	.236	.327	.333
Late Inning Pressure	88	20	2	0	0	7	7	17	.227	.250	.278
Leading Off	19	8	1	0	0	2	3	.421	.474	.476	
Runners On	36	5	1	0	0	7	2	8	.139	.167	.175
Runners/Scor. Pos.	24	4	1	0	0	7	1	7	.167	.208	.185

DRIVING IN RUNS	From 1B	From 2B	From 3B	Scoring Position
Totals	5/115	23/98	19/52	42/150
Percentage	4%	23%	37%	28%
Driving In Runners from 3B with Less than Two Out:		14/30		47%

Loves to face: Scott Sanderson (.429, 15-for-35, 1 HR)
Hates to face: Jeff Reardon (.143, 3-for-21)
Career batting average of .379 with the bases loaded (22-for-58, with five "grand slam triples"). . . . Hit two home runs in game vs. Giants on July 21, first two-homer game by a St. Louis player since David Green (remember him?) in July 1984. . . . You've heard of a player taking his batting slump into the field? McGee evidently took his slump onto the basepaths. In 1985, he stole 56 of 72 bases (.778); last season he dropped to 19 of 35 (.543). N.L. average stolen base percentage in 1986 was .682. . . . Through games of Sept. 13, his 1986 slugging average (.3526) was lower than his 1985 final batting average (.3529). Rallied during last three weeks of season to avoid finishing with that distinction.

Kevin McReynolds

San Diego Padres — Bats Right

	AB	H	2B	3B	HR	RRF	BB	SO	BA	SA	OBA
Season	560	161	31	6	26	98	66	83	.288	.504	.358
vs. Left-Handers	192	65	12	3	10	34	22	21	.339	.589	.395
vs. Right-Handers	368	96	19	3	16	64	44	62	.261	.459	.339
Home	276	81	13	3	14	46	35	46	.293	.514	.368
Road	284	80	18	3	12	52	31	37	.282	.493	.349
Grass	410	111	19	4	18	65	49	63	.271	.468	.344
Artificial Turf	150	50	12	2	8	33	17	20	.333	.600	.399
April	76	19	2	0	3	8	8	11	.250	.395	.321
May	94	31	8	1	6	21	15	16	.330	.628	.414
June	99	24	6	2	3	13	8	16	.242	.434	.294
July	81	22	5	0	2	8	16	11	.272	.407	.384
August	88	27	4	0	6	22	9	9	.307	.557	.364
Sept./Oct.	122	38	6	3	6	26	10	20	.311	.557	.366
Leading Off Inn.	110	35	6	2	5	5	7	12	.318	.545	.359
Runners On	263	76	16	2	14	86	33	42	.289	.525	.359
Runners/Scor. Pos.	159	43	9	0	8	69	26	31	.270	.478	.359
Runners On/2 Out	90	27	7	1	5	32	13	14	.300	.567	.388
Scor. Pos./2 Out	63	18	4	0	3	26	10	12	.286	.492	.384
Late Inning Pressure	98	25	4	0	5	21	12	26	.255	.449	.330
Leading Off	19	7	1	0	0	0	0	3	.368	.421	.368
Runners On	50	13	3	0	4	20	10	16	.260	.560	.371
Runners/Scor. Pos.	35	8	3	0	2	16	9	14	.229	.486	.370

DRIVING IN RUNS	From 1B	From 2B	From 3B	Scoring Position
Totals	16/187	22/128	34/66	56/194
Percentage	9%	17%	52%	29%
Driving In Runners from 3B with Less than Two Out:		22/39		56%

Loves to face: Jay Tibbs (.591, 13-for-22, 3 HR)
Hates to face: Mark Davis (.063, 1-for-16)
Hit more home runs last season than any player ever acquired by defending World Series champs in a postseason trade. . . . Has homered in every N.L. ballpark except Three Rivers Stadium (54 career AB). . . . Played more than one outfield position in 64 games last season: played 54 percent of Padres' innings in center, 35 percent in left, one percent (18 innings) in right. . . . Batted .422 (19-for-45) with six home runs in 12 games vs. Expos last season. . . . Batted over .300 with runners in scoring position in both 1984 and 1985. . . . Career breakdown: .283, one HR every 24.4 at bats vs. left-handers, .253, one HR every 29.2 at bats vs. righties.

Bob Melvin

San Francisco Giants — Bats Right

	AB	H	2B	3B	HR	RRF	BB	SO	BA	SA	OBA
Season	268	60	14	2	5	31	15	69	.224	.347	.262
vs. Left-Handers	104	32	7	0	3	14	7	18	.308	.462	.348
vs. Right-Handers	164	28	7	2	2	17	8	51	.171	.274	.207
Home	109	24	8	0	2	9	4	27	.220	.349	.248
Road	159	36	6	2	3	22	11	42	.226	.346	.272
Grass	176	31	8	0	4	20	8	48	.176	.290	.209
Artificial Turf	92	29	6	2	1	11	7	21	.315	.457	.364
April	39	6	2	0	0	7	0	10	.154	.205	.150
May	37	8	3	1	0	4	0	11	.216	.351	.216
June	49	20	3	0	1	3	3	11	.408	.531	.442
July	55	11	2	0	3	3	11	.200	.236	.241	
August	27	4	0	1	1	5	3	7	.148	.333	.226
Sept./Oct.	61	11	4	0	3	9	6	19	.180	.393	.250
Leading Off Inn.	55	11	2	1	2	3	14	.200	.382	.241	
Runners On	124	31	9	1	2	28	9	33	.250	.387	.294
Runners/Scor. Pos.	81	14	6	1	0	24	8	22	.173	.272	.239
Runners On/2 Out	57	11	2	0	0	10	2	11	.193	.228	.220
Scor. Pos./2 Out	42	5	2	0	0	10	2	8	.119	.167	.159
Late Inning Pressure	40	6	2	0	0	6	3	12	.150	.200	.200
Leading Off	11	1	0	0	0	0	1	3	.091	.091	.167
Runners On	18	4	1	0	0	6	2	6	.222	.278	.273
Runners/Scor. Pos.	13	3	1	0	0	6	2	4	.231	.308	.294

DRIVING IN RUNS	From 1B	From 2B	From 3B	Scoring Position
Totals	5/85	9/55	12/40	21/95
Percentage	6%	16%	30%	22%
Driving In Runners from 3B with Less than Two Out:		9/21		43%

Loves to face: Bob Knepper (.636, 7-for-11)
Hates to face: Fernando Valenzuela (.083, 1-for-12, 5 SO)
Batted 137 points higher vs. left-handed pitchers than against right-handers, 2d-largest difference in N.L. (minimum: 100 AB vs. both). . . . In 82 at bats with Detroit in 1985, batted .263 vs. lefties, .182 vs. righties. . . . Had lowest on-base average of any N.L. player with 250+ plate appearances last season. . . . His only hit in 24 career at bats at Dodger Stadium was a home run in his final at bat of the '86 season. Melvin's only two hits against Los Angeles last season (.071, 2-for-28) were both home runs. . . . Giants' starting catchers had only 49 RBI last season, tied for fewest in N.L. More surprising is that the team they were tied with was the Dodgers.

Eddie Milner

Cincinnati Reds	AB	H	2B	3B	HR	RRF	BB	SO	BA	SA	OBA
Season	424	110	22	6	15	51	36	56	.259	.446	.317
vs. Left-Handers	58	13	3	0	0	4	3	10	.224	.276	.262
vs. Right-Handers	366	97	19	6	15	47	33	46	.265	.473	.325
Home	208	60	11	3	8	29	19	27	.288	.486	.346
Road	216	50	11	3	7	22	17	29	.231	.407	.288
Grass	133	36	6	2	5	11	10	19	.271	.459	.322
Artificial Turf	291	74	16	4	10	40	26	37	.254	.440	.314
April	22	5	1	0	0	1	1	3	.227	.273	.261
May	76	18	2	3	2	13	11	9	.237	.421	.333
June	98	24	4	1	2	7	6	8	.245	.367	.288
July	88	20	7	0	5	7	7	14	.227	.477	.284
August	48	9	2	0	2	3	3	7	.188	.354	.235
Sept./Oct.	92	34	6	2	4	20	8	15	.370	.609	.416
Leading Off Inn.	153	37	6	2	6	6	6	21	.242	.425	.270
Runners On	140	38	8	4	3	39	17	14	.271	.450	.348
Runners/Scor. Pos.	80	19	4	2	1	30	12	7	.238	.375	.333
Runners On/2 Out	59	19	4	3	1	18	9	6	.322	.542	.412
Scor. Pos./2 Out	37	10	1	1	1	14	7	3	.270	.432	.386
Late Inning Pressure	52	10	0	2	2	8	4	9	.192	.385	.250
Leading Off	15	2	0	1	1	0	5		.133	.467	.133
Runners On	21	4	0	1	0	6	1	4	.190	.286	.227
Runners/Scor. Pos.	12	2	0	1	0	6	1	2	.167	.333	.231

DRIVING IN RUNS	From 1B	From 2B	From 3B	Scoring Position
Totals	11/94	10/58	14/39	24/97
Percentage	12%	17%	36%	25%
Driving In Runners from 3B with Less than Two Out:			50%	

Loves to face: Frank Williams (.667, 6-for-9, 3 2B)
Hates to face: Tom Niedenfuer (.067, 1-for-15)
Out of frying pan, into the fire: joins an already crowded Giants outfield.... Reached base safely in 26 consecutive games from Sept. 3 to Oct. 4 (streak was snapped in season finale). Raised his batting average from .228 to .261 over that 26-game span. Batting average of .370 after Sept. 1 was 2d highest in N.L.... Batted .200 (3-for-15) as pinch-hitter.... Career batting average of .219 with the bases loaded.... Only two of his 38 career home runs have been hit against left-handed pitchers (none since 1984).... Drove in only four base runners with his 15 home runs last season.... What Launching Pad? He has a career total of 138 at bats at Atlanta Stadium, most among active players without a home run there.

Kevin Mitchell

New York Mets	AB	H	2B	3B	HR	RRF	BB	SO	BA	SA	OBA
Season	328	91	22	2	12	44	33	61	.277	.466	.344
vs. Left-Handers	199	61	16	1	7	28	16	29	.307	.503	.358
vs. Right-Handers	129	30	6	1	5	16	17	32	.233	.411	.330
Home	162	49	15	1	4	25	18	30	.302	.481	.370
Road	166	42	7	1	8	19	15	31	.253	.452	.319
Grass	234	66	17	1	7	31	25	48	.282	.453	.350
Artificial Turf	.94	25	5	1	5	13	8	13	.266	.500	.330
April	23	9	3	0	1	4	1	3	.391	.652	.417
May	41	11	2	0	1	4	2	9	.268	.390	.302
June	61	26	10	0	2	13	9	8	.426	.689	.500
July	66	16	2	0	5	7	7	12	.242	.500	.315
August	85	17	4	2	2	8	10	23	.200	.365	.292
Sept./Oct.	52	12	1	0	1	8	4	6	.231	.308	.281
Leading Off Inn.	69	16	2	1	3	3	5	11	.232	.420	.284
Runners On	136	40	11	0	5	37	18	33	.294	.485	.374
Runners/Scor. Pos.	91	25	10	0	3	32	12	24	.275	.484	.356
Runners On/2 Out	59	18	5	0	2	16	7	16	.305	.492	.379
Scor. Pos./2 Out	40	13	5	0	2	16	4	10	.325	.600	.386
Late Inning Pressure	49	14	2	0	3	7	1	10	.286	.510	.314
Leading Off	8	3	0	0	1	0	2		.375	.750	.375
Runners On	21	7	1	0	2	6	0	4	.333	.667	.333
Runners/Scor. Pos.	13	3	1	0	1	4	0	4	.231	.538	.231

DRIVING IN RUNS	From 1B	From 2B	From 3B	Scoring Position
Totals	4/88	15/71	13/39	28/110
Percentage	5%	21%	33%	25%
Driving In Runners from 3B with Less than Two Out:			8/24	33%

Loves to face: John Tudor (.667, 6-for-9, 2 HR)
Hates to face: Bob Knepper (.133, 2-for-15)
Batted .342 before All-Star break, as a jack-of-all-trades handyman; batted .225 after break, when he was basically a platooned left fielder.... Started at six fielding positions (1B-3B-SS-LF-CF-RF) last season. The last major leaguer to do that was Alan Bannister of 1984 Rangers, who started at 1B-2B-3B-LF-CF-RF (and also at DH).... Committed errors in four consecutive games (June 9–15) at three different positions (SS-1B-RF).... Drove in only 33 percent (8-of-24) of runners from third base with less than 2 outs, 2d-lowest rate in N.L. (minimum: 15 opportunities).... Batting average vs. Padres (.444) was his highest against any club; the irony, as Vin would say, is that he's from San Diego.

Keith Moreland

Chicago Cubs	AB	H	2B	3B	HR	RRF	BB	SO	BA	SA	OBA
Season	586	159	30	0	12	83	53	48	.271	.384	.326
vs. Left-Handers	147	45	6	0	5	17	23	7	.306	.449	.395
vs. Right-Handers	439	114	24	0	7	66	30	41	.260	.362	.301
Home	297	87	19	0	8	48	22	24	.293	.438	.339
Road	289	72	11	0	4	35	31	24	.249	.329	.314
Grass	417	120	24	0	10	61	38	38	.288	.417	.344
Artificial Turf	169	39	6	0	2	22	15	10	.231	.302	.283
April	75	24	3	0	1	10	8	6	.320	.400	.376
May	100	25	2	0	4	12	11	9	.250	.390	.324
June	103	28	7	0	2	18	9	9	.272	.398	.316
July	90	29	7	0	0	16	12	7	.322	.400	.398
August	109	23	5	0	1	10	6	10	.211	.284	.248
Sept./Oct.	109	30	6	0	4	17	7	7	.275	.440	.316
Leading Off Inn.	162	49	10	0	3	3	12	10	.302	.420	.351
Runners On	265	65	15	0	5	76	25	25	.245	.358	.299
Runners/Scor. Pos.	159	40	10	0	3	68	21	17	.252	.371	.319
Runners On/2 Out	141	29	7	0	1	29	12	14	.206	.277	.268
Scor. Pos./2 Out	90	22	6	0	1	27	11	10	.244	.344	.327
Late Inning Pressure	105	33	6	0	5	19	13	5	.314	.514	.383
Leading Off	28	6	1	0	1	1	2	1	.214	.357	.267
Runners On	46	15	3	0	4	18	4	4	.326	.652	.365
Runners/Scor. Pos.	27	6	0	0	2	12	3	3	.222	.444	.281

DRIVING IN RUNS	From 1B	From 2B	From 3B	Scoring Position
Totals	10/180	25/123	36/69	61/192
Percentage	6%	20%	52%	32%
Driving In Runners from 3B with Less than Two Out:			28/40	70%

Loves to face: Roger McDowell (.500, 7-for-14, 1 HR)
Hates to face: Scott Garrelts (0-for-14)
Last season was the first of his seven full years in majors in which he batted higher with bases empty than with runners on base.... Has homered in every N.L. ballpark except Dodger Stadium (121 career AB).... Yearly batting averages vs. left-handers since 1982: .298, .382, .298, .315, .306.... Hitless in eight at bats with the bases loaded last season.... Has hit 48 home runs at Wrigley Field, 25 on the road, during five seasons with Cubs.... Has hit exactly 30 doubles in three of last five seasons, exactly 17 in the other two.... Warning to fans sitting behind first base: career .886 fielding average (13 errors in 114 chances) in 56 games at third base.

Omar Moreno

Atlanta Braves	AB	H	2B	3B	HR	RRF	BB	SO	BA	SA	OBA
Season	359	84	18	6	4	29	21	77	.234	.351	.276
vs. Left-Handers	41	6	1	1	0	2	3	17	.146	.220	.205
vs. Right-Handers	318	78	17	5	4	27	18	60	.245	.368	.286
Home	181	51	10	3	3	15	11	41	.282	.420	.323
Road	178	33	8	3	1	14	10	36	.185	.281	.229
Grass	282	71	17	4	4	22	17	64	.252	.383	.294
Artificial Turf	77	13	1	2	0	7	4	13	.169	.234	.210
April	29	5	0	2	1	4	4	6	.172	.414	.273
May	61	19	8	3	0	5	3	8	.311	.541	.344
June	69	15	2	0	0	4	6	18	.217	.246	.280
July	63	14	1	1	1	8	1	12	.222	.317	.234
August	98	26	6	0	2	8	3	21	.265	.388	.287
Sept./Oct.	39	5	1	0	0	0	4	12	.128	.154	.287
Leading Off Inn.	143	36	9	0	1	1	5	24	.252	.336	.277
Runners On	118	23	2	2	3	28	11	32	.195	.322	.264
Runners/Scor. Pos.	81	18	1	1	2	24	8	25	.222	.333	.292
Runners On/2 Out	63	16	2	2	3	23	6	18	.254	.492	.319
Scor. Pos./2 Out	53	13	1	1	2	19	5	17	.245	.415	.319
Late Inning Pressure	51	10	1	1	1	7	3	10	.196	.314	.241
Leading Off	17	3	0	0	0	0	0	3	.176	.176	.176
Runners On	18	4	0	1	1	7	3	4	.222	.500	.333
Runners/Scor. Pos.	13	4	0	1	1	7	2	4	.308	.692	.400

DRIVING IN RUNS	From 1B	From 2B	From 3B	Scoring Position
Totals	4/72	11/62	9/30	20/92
Percentage	6%	18%	30%	22%
Driving In Runners from 3B with Less than Two Out:			3/8	38%

Loves to face: Lance McCullers (.800, 4-for-5, 1 HR)
Hates to face: Jesse Orosco (0-for-11, 6 SO)
Ended 1986 season with an 0-for-23 slump and did not drive in a run in his last 28 games.... Braves were his fifth team in the last five seasons.... Once stole 96 bases in a season, but has made good on only 18 of 36 attempts over past two seasons, and was caught seven times in last 11 tries in '86.... One hit in last 10 at bats as pinch-hitter.... Drove in a runner from first base in a Late-Inning Pressure Situation last year; he's now driven in three, in 204 chances, in his career.... OK, now the good news: his .196 batting average in Late-Inning Pressure Situations. Why is that good news? Because the year before, he batted .056 in those situations.

Jim Morrison

Pittsburgh Pirates — Bats Right

	AB	H	2B	3B	HR	RRF	BB	SO	BA	SA	OBA
Season	537	147	35	4	23	88	47	88	.274	.482	.334
vs. Left-Handers	192	51	13	1	6	26	20	24	.266	.438	.329
vs. Right-Handers	345	96	22	3	17	62	27	64	.278	.507	.337
Home	269	80	15	4	11	49	30	46	.297	.506	.374
Road	268	67	20	0	12	39	17	42	.250	.459	.292
Grass	142	42	9	0	8	21	9	25	.296	.528	.338
Artificial Turf	395	105	26	4	15	67	38	63	.266	.466	.333
April	48	10	0	0	2	4	3	11	.208	.333	.269
May	91	23	2	1	5	16	14	21	.253	.462	.352
June	94	21	7	1	2	16	8	18	.223	.383	.282
July	84	25	6	0	3	13	9	11	.298	.476	.362
August	111	30	8	1	4	18	5	10	.270	.468	.311
Sept./Oct.	109	38	12	1	7	21	8	17	.349	.670	.392
Leading Off Inn.	136	41	11	1	7	7	12	17	.301	.551	.358
Runners On	251	73	13	3	11	76	22	40	.291	.498	.351
Runners/Scor. Pos.	139	42	8	2	5	61	18	25	.302	.496	.378
Runners On/2 Out	103	26	3	1	5	28	8	20	.252	.447	.313
Scor. Pos./2 Out	61	17	2	1	2	22	8	14	.279	.443	.371
Late Inning Pressure	96	22	4	1	5	15	13	24	.229	.448	.327
Leading Off	18	4	0	0	1	1	5	3	.222	.389	.391
Runners On	46	13	3	1	2	12	6	11	.283	.522	.377
Runners/Scor. Pos.	22	5	2	0	0	6	6	6	.227	.318	.393

DRIVING IN RUNS	From 1B	From 2B	From 3B	Scoring Position
Totals	14/183	22/94	29/73	51/167
Percentage	8%	23%	40%	31%
Driving In Runners from 3B with Less than Two Out:			23/43	53%

Loves to face: Ron Robinson (.625, 5-for-8, 3 HR)
Hates to face: Dwight Gooden (.056, 1-for-18, 9 SO)
Only N.L. player to go 4-for-4 in three different games last season; only Gary Gaetti did it in A.L. . . . In all, had four four-hit games, one behind N.L. leader Tony Gwynn. . . . Impressive 2d-half numbers: batted .314 (9th best in N.L.); slugged .558 (2d best); had 37 extra-base hits (tied Von Hayes for N.L. lead). . . . Has homered in every current major-league outdoor stadium; indoors, he's missing the Astrodome (51 career AB) and Metrodome (never played there). . . . Finished season with 21 straight errorless games, matching his longest streak of season. . . . Hit his first grand slam homer and triple last year; .333 career batting average with bases loaded, 8-for-20 over last two years.

Jerry Mumphrey

Chicago Cubs — Bats Left and Right

	AB	H	2B	3B	HR	RRF	BB	SO	BA	SA	OBA
Season	309	94	11	2	5	32	26	45	.304	.401	.355
vs. Left-Handers	61	12	1	0	0	2	7	9	.197	.213	.279
vs. Right-Handers	248	82	10	2	5	30	19	36	.331	.448	.374
Home	147	53	7	2	4	22	15	19	.361	.517	.417
Road	162	41	4	0	1	10	11	26	.253	.296	.297
Grass	235	77	9	2	5	25	23	36	.328	.447	.386
Artificial Turf	74	17	2	0	0	7	3	9	.230	.257	.253
April	31	9	1	0	1	3	1	7	.290	.419	.303
May	53	16	3	0	0	2	9	9	.302	.358	.403
June	70	17	2	0	0	6	10	7	.243	.271	.338
July	74	28	3	1	1	4	5	9	.378	.486	.418
August	62	19	2	1	2	12	1	10	.306	.468	.313
Sept./Oct.	19	5	0	0	1	5	0	3	.263	.421	.250
Leading Off Inn.	75	28	4	0	1	1	7	8	.373	.467	.427
Runners On	136	38	1	1	3	30	14	24	.279	.368	.340
Runners/Scor. Pos.	74	21	1	1	1	26	8	17	.284	.365	.341
Runners On/2 Out	55	15	1	1	2	13	6	12	.273	.436	.344
Scor. Pos./2 Out	34	9	1	1	1	11	4	10	.265	.441	.342
Late Inning Pressure	71	15	0	0	2	12	8	14	.211	.296	.280
Leading Off	17	3	0	0	0	0	3	4	.176	.176	.300
Runners On	36	10	0	0	2	12	4	7	.278	.444	.326
Runners/Scor. Pos.	19	5	0	0	1	10	3	4	.263	.421	.320

DRIVING IN RUNS	From 1B	From 2B	From 3B	Scoring Position
Totals	3/101	9/56	15/33	24/89
Percentage	3%	16%	45%	27%
Driving In Runners from 3B with Less than Two Out:			9/16	56%

Loves to face: Danny Cox (.529, 9-for-17, 1 HR)
Hates to face: Andy McGaffigan (.056, 1-for-18, 7 SO)
Started in every batting order position except 9th spot last season. Batted cleanup just once, Aug. 9 vs. Philadelphia, after homering in two of his previous three games. . . . Has a higher average from the left side of the plate in each of the last 10 seasons. . . . Batted .345 (10-for-29) as a pinch-hitter last season. . . . Walked only once in his last 84 plate appearances. . . . Adapts well to changes in scenery: He's topped .300 in home games in each of the last six seasons for three different teams. . . . Won't get a Band Aid endorsement: He's been hit by a pitch once in 3762 plate appearances over past eight years, and only four times in 5126 career plate appearances.

Dale Murphy

Atlanta Braves — Bats Right

	AB	H	2B	3B	HR	RRF	BB	SO	BA	SA	OBA
Season	614	163	29	7	29	87	75	141	.265	.477	.347
vs. Left-Handers	193	54	7	5	9	24	32	37	.280	.508	.382
vs. Right-Handers	421	109	22	2	20	63	43	104	.259	.463	.330
Home	298	80	11	4	17	41	44	66	.268	.503	.366
Road	316	83	18	3	12	46	31	75	.263	.453	.328
Grass	453	124	18	6	24	64	61	98	.274	.499	.362
Artificial Turf	161	39	11	1	5	23	14	43	.242	.416	.301
April	64	22	5	1	5	10	11	16	.344	.688	.440
May	108	31	5	0	4	16	16	26	.287	.444	.379
June	107	26	3	1	4	8	16	27	.243	.402	.339
July	100	22	6	0	2	7	9	23	.220	.340	.284
August	104	35	9	2	10	32	16	23	.337	.750	.430
Sept./Oct.	131	27	1	3	4	14	7	26	.206	.351	.252
Leading Off Inn.	105	29	6	2	5	5	11	22	.276	.514	.345
Runners On	263	73	11	1	16	74	39	61	.278	.510	.372
Runners/Scor. Pos.	146	43	8	1	9	60	27	37	.295	.548	.406
Runners On/2 Out	92	28	4	0	6	33	14	21	.304	.543	.402
Scor. Pos./2 Out	58	18	4	0	3	27	11	14	.310	.534	.429
Late Inning Pressure	95	27	6	3	7	17	17	28	.284	.632	.398
Leading Off	19	6	3	0	2	2	3	3	.316	.789	.409
Runners On	41	10	1	1	3	13	12	13	.244	.537	.426
Runners/Scor. Pos.	24	7	1	1	2	11	10	8	.292	.667	.514

DRIVING IN RUNS	From 1B	From 2B	From 3B	Scoring Position
Totals	15/177	23/106	20/48	43/154
Percentage	8%	22%	42%	28%
Driving In Runners from 3B with Less than Two Out:			12/30	40%

Loves to face: Rick Ownbey (.875, 7-for-8, 2 HR)
Hates to face: Jeff Robinson (.095, 2-for-21)
Failed to hit a home run in his final 67 at bats, finishing the season with 29; he had hit 30+ in every season since the strike. . . . Also failed to drive in a run over his last 12 games. . . . Career batting average at Three Rivers Stadium (.201) is his lowest at any ballpark. . . . Held without an RBI in 11 games vs. Phillies last season; he homered against every other N.L. club. . . . Didn't start vs. Dwight Gooden on April 30 and seemed to be on verge of ending his streak of 675 consecutive games; then he pinch-hit and slammed a home run. . . . Stole 30 bases in 34 attempts in 1983, but has tapered off to 19, 10, and seven steals in last three years. . . . First N.L. outfielder since Hank Aaron to start five straight All-Star Games.

Graig Nettles

San Diego Padres — Bats Left

	AB	H	2B	3B	HR	RRF	BB	SO	BA	SA	OBA
Season	354	77	9	0	16	57	41	62	.218	.379	.300
vs. Left-Handers	53	9	1	0	3	9	2	13	.170	.358	.224
vs. Right-Handers	301	68	8	0	13	48	39	49	.226	.382	.313
Home	166	44	5	0	13	40	27	36	.265	.530	.374
Road	188	33	4	0	3	17	14	26	.176	.245	.229
Grass	253	59	7	0	15	52	35	49	.233	.439	.330
Artificial Turf	101	18	2	0	1	5	6	13	.178	.228	.220
April	49	8	0	0	2	9	7	7	.163	.286	.288
May	63	15	0	0	6	12	5	8	.238	.524	.304
June	57	16	0	0	4	12	5	15	.281	.491	.349
July	70	14	4	0	2	8	6	8	.200	.343	.260
August	66	10	0	0	2	8	8	15	.152	.242	.240
Sept./Oct.	49	14	5	0	0	8	8	9	.286	.388	.386
Leading Off Inn.	76	13	1	0	1	1	8	10	.171	.224	.250
Runners On	164	42	4	0	10	51	19	29	.256	.463	.335
Runners/Scor. Pos.	92	21	1	0	5	39	16	20	.228	.402	.339
Runners On/2 Out	80	15	2	0	4	21	8	19	.188	.363	.278
Scor. Pos./2 Out	55	10	0	0	4	19	8	14	.182	.400	.297
Late Inning Pressure	62	15	1	0	3	11	10	17	.242	.403	.347
Leading Off	20	4	0	0	1	1	2	6	.200	.350	.273
Runners On	29	7	0	0	1	9	5	7	.241	.345	.353
Runners/Scor. Pos.	19	5	0	0	0	5	5	6	.263	.263	.417

DRIVING IN RUNS	From 1B	From 2B	From 3B	Scoring Position
Totals	11/116	18/76	12/36	30/112
Percentage	9%	24%	33%	27%
Driving In Runners from 3B with Less than Two Out:			9/12	75%

Loves to face: Jeff Robinson (.571, 8-for-14, 3 HR)
Hates to face: Dan Schatzeder (0-for-13)
The only player to hit for a higher average with men on base than with bases empty in each of the past 12 seasons. . . . Among players active last season, only Rose, Perez, and Reggie have appeared in more games than Nettles (2508). . . Despite career batting average of .354 at Three Rivers Stadium (his highest at any current park) it remains the only current major league stadium in which he has not homered (48 AB). . . . Homered in four straight games (May 21–26). . . . Last home run was hit on Aug. 11; he finished the season with 88 consecutive homerless at bats. . . . An Elias Retrospective: His first major-league box score includes the names Leon Wagner, Al Worthington, and Carroll Hardy.

Al Newman

Montreal Expos — Bats Left and Right

	AB	H	2B	3B	HR	RRF	BB	SO	BA	SA	OBA
Season	185	37	3	0	1	9	21	20	.200	.232	.279
vs. Left-Handers	41	9	1	0	1	3	7	6	.220	.317	.327
vs. Right-Handers	144	28	2	0	0	6	14	14	.194	.208	.264
Home	84	16	1	0	0	5	11	11	.190	.202	.278
Road	101	21	2	0	1	4	10	9	.208	.257	.279
Grass	32	6	0	0	1	2	4	3	.188	.281	.278
Artificial Turf	153	31	3	0	0	7	17	17	.203	.222	.279
April	14	4	0	0	0	0	1	1	.286	.286	.333
May	39	10	0	0	0	4	4	5	.256	.256	.318
June	46	10	2	0	0	1	7	0	.217	.261	.321
July	38	7	0	0	1	3	6	3	.184	.263	.289
August	28	4	0	0	0	0	3	5	.143	.143	.226
Sept./Oct.	20	2	1	0	0	1	0	6	.100	.150	.100
Leading Off Inn.	66	8	0	0	0	0	6	9	.121	.121	.194
Runners On	63	17	2	0	1	9	7	4	.270	.349	.333
Runners/Scor. Pos.	35	7	1	0	1	9	5	1	.200	.314	.286
Runners On/2 Out	28	7	0	0	1	3	2	1	.250	.357	.300
Scor. Pos./2 Out	19	4	0	0	1	3	2	1	.211	.368	.286
Late Inning Pressure	39	8	1	0	0	3	2	6	.205	.256	.238
Leading Off	16	3	0	0	0	2	2	3	.188	.188	.278
Runners On	13	3	2	0	0	3	0	1	.231	.385	.214
Runners/Scor. Pos.	8	1	1	0	0	3	0	1	.125	.250	.111

DRIVING IN RUNS	From 1B	From 2B	From 3B	Scoring Position
Totals	0/45	3/30	5/13	8/43
Percentage	0%	10%	38%	19%
Driving In Runners from 3B with Less than Two Out:			5/8	63%

Loves to face: Charlie Kerfeld (2-for-2)
Hates to face: Nolan Ryan (0-for-6, 3 SO)
Made 33 starts at second base, 10 at shortstop. . . . N.L. second basemen average 9.4 RBI per 100 at bats; Newman had four RBI in 118 at bats in his starts there, with one extra-base hit, a home run off Zane Smith. . . . Expos have no lack of second-base candidates; they were only team in majors to have four players with 15+ starts there last season. But Vance Law (87 starts), Newman, Casey Candaele (22) and Tom Foley (19) batted a combined .207, the lowest composite average by the starters at *any* position by any N.L. team. . . . Starting second basemen for all N.L. teams batted a combined .2695, a shade behind .2697 by first basemen, winners of distinction as the best-hitting N.L. position.

Ken Oberkfell

Atlanta Braves — Bats Left

	AB	H	2B	3B	HR	RRF	BB	SO	BA	SA	OBA
Season	503	136	24	3	5	51	83	40	.270	.360	.373
vs. Left-Handers	129	30	4	0	2	21	19	17	.233	.310	.333
vs. Right-Handers	374	106	20	3	3	30	64	23	.283	.377	.387
Home	268	76	11	2	2	25	43	18	.284	.362	.382
Road	235	60	13	1	3	26	40	22	.255	.357	.363
Grass	384	107	19	2	3	31	64	28	.279	.362	.380
Artificial Turf	119	29	5	1	2	20	19	12	.244	.353	.350
April	62	20	4	0	0	8	8	6	.323	.387	.389
May	76	24	1	0	1	9	12	3	.316	.368	.416
June	89	25	5	0	4	13	13	7	.281	.472	.424
July	86	24	4	0	0	9	12	9	.279	.326	.374
August	83	20	6	2	0	7	22	6	.241	.361	.396
Sept./Oct.	107	23	4	1	0	5	16	9	.215	.271	.317
Leading Off Inn.	115	21	6	0	1	1	11	7	.183	.261	.254
Runners On	201	58	9	2	2	48	35	10	.289	.383	.388
Runners/Scor. Pos.	118	35	5	2	2	48	29	9	.297	.424	.424
Runners On/2 Out	84	24	4	1	0	21	22	4	.286	.357	.434
Scor. Pos./2 Out	55	14	1	1	0	21	18	3	.255	.309	.438
Late Inning Pressure	80	20	3	0	1	7	17	5	.250	.325	.381
Leading Off	26	5	1	0	0	0	2	3	.192	.231	.250
Runners On	32	8	1	0	1	7	9	1	.250	.375	.415
Runners/Scor. Pos.	22	6	0	0	1	7	8	1	.273	.409	.467

DRIVING IN RUNS	From 1B	From 2B	From 3B	Scoring Position
Totals	2/137	21/97	23/43	44/140
Percentage	1%	22%	53%	31%
Driving In Runners from 3B with Less than Two Out:			13/19	68%

Loves to face: Bob Walk (.478, 11-for-23)
Hates to face: Dave Dravecky (.063, 1-for-16)
One of two N.L. regulars last season with walk/strikeout ratio over 2.00 (minimum: 502 PA); other: Ozzie Smith. . . . Ranked second among major-league third basemen with an average of 2.28 assists per nine innings (minimum: 500 innings). . . . Two home runs off left-handers last season doubled his previous career total. Has batted for a higher average against right-handers than left-handers in each of 10 years in majors. . . . Despite his 6'1", 210-pound frame, has hit only 20 career home runs in 1,059 games. Only three active players (minimum: 1,000 games) have hit fewer: Greg Gross (5'11", 175 pounds), Ozzie Smith (5'10", 150), and Alfredo Griffin (5'11", 165).

Ron Oester

Cincinnati Reds — Bats Left and Right

	AB	H	2B	3B	HR	RRF	BB	SO	BA	SA	OBA
Season	523	135	23	2	8	48	52	84	.258	.356	.325
vs. Left-Handers	136	25	5	0	1	11	15	22	.184	.243	.263
vs. Right-Handers	387	110	18	2	7	37	37	62	.284	.395	.347
Home	261	73	14	1	6	24	27	43	.280	.410	.349
Road	262	62	9	1	2	24	25	41	.237	.302	.300
Grass	151	37	6	1	1	10	13	26	.245	.318	.301
Artificial Turf	372	98	17	1	7	38	39	58	.263	.371	.334
April	60	12	2	0	0	2	3	14	.200	.233	.238
May	78	21	3	0	5	15	12	16	.269	.500	.359
June	101	23	5	0	0	7	7	14	.228	.277	.278
July	97	30	5	1	0	11	9	13	.309	.381	.374
August	98	26	3	0	1	6	7	13	.265	.327	.314
Sept./Oct.	89	23	5	1	2	7	14	14	.258	.404	.356
Leading Off Inn.	115	30	7	1	2	2	9	22	.261	.391	.315
Runners On	246	64	8	1	3	43	34	35	.260	.337	.346
Runners/Scor. Pos.	124	33	4	1	1	37	28	20	.266	.339	.394
Runners On/2 Out	98	29	3	1	1	15	19	17	.296	.378	.410
Scor. Pos./2 Out	49	13	2	1	0	13	17	11	.265	.347	.455
Late Inning Pressure	93	27	4	0	2	10	7	17	.290	.398	.340
Leading Off	23	8	1	0	1	1	1	4	.348	.522	.375
Runners On	37	10	1	0	1	9	4	7	.270	.378	.341
Runners/Scor. Pos.	17	5	1	0	1	9	4	4	.294	.529	.429

DRIVING IN RUNS	From 1B	From 2B	From 3B	Scoring Position
Totals	5/188	15/103	20/42	35/145
Percentage	3%	15%	48%	24%
Driving In Runners from 3B with Less than Two Out:			15/26	58%

Loves to face: Kevin Gross (.625, 10-for-16)
Hates to face: Rick Honeycutt (.067, 1-for-15)
Batted 100 points higher vs. right-handed pitchers than against left-handers, 3d-largest difference in majors (minimum: 100 AB vs. each). . . . Committed 11 errors in 44 games on grass fields, eight errors in 109 games on artificial surfaces. . . . Career average of .295 in Late-Inning Pressure Situations, .260 in nonpressure situations. . . . Has played 601 games at second base over past four years, 3d in majors over that span behind Sandberg (619) and Ray (612). . . . Born May 5, 1956 in Cincinnati; Reds presented him with 7–6 win that day, with Gus Bell, father of Oester's current teammate Buddy, driving in Rocky Bridges with winning run in 10th inning.

Joe Orsulak

Pittsburgh Pirates — Bats Left

	AB	H	2B	3B	HR	RRF	BB	SO	BA	SA	OBA
Season	401	100	19	6	2	20	28	38	.249	.342	.299
vs. Left-Handers	50	13	1	1	0	1	2	5	.260	.320	.288
vs. Right-Handers	351	87	18	5	2	19	26	33	.248	.345	.301
Home	183	41	8	3	0	5	16	15	.224	.301	.285
Road	218	59	11	3	2	15	12	23	.271	.376	.312
Grass	110	37	7	2	2	10	6	11	.336	.491	.376
Artificial Turf	291	63	12	4	0	10	22	27	.216	.285	.271
April	57	14	6	1	1	7	5	5	.246	.439	.302
May	85	20	3	0	0	3	5	10	.235	.271	.278
June	66	18	3	0	0	7	7	3	.273	.318	.351
July	74	23	3	1	1	2	5	6	.311	.473	.354
August	63	17	4	1	0	1	0	4	.270	.365	.270
Sept./Oct.	56	8	0	1	0	0	6	10	.143	.179	.226
Leading Off Inn.	118	35	5	1	1	1	9	11	.297	.381	.352
Runners On	122	23	3	0	0	18	12	6	.189	.213	.259
Runners/Scor. Pos.	72	15	3	0	0	18	11	3	.208	.250	.310
Runners On/2 Out	55	10	2	0	0	8	7	3	.182	.218	.274
Scor. Pos./2 Out	39	7	2	0	0	8	7	2	.179	.231	.304
Late Inning Pressure	66	14	3	0	0	4	4	7	.212	.258	.254
Leading Off	24	7	1	0	0	0	2	4	.292	.333	.346
Runners On	25	2	0	0	0	4	2	0	.080	.080	.143
Runners/Scor. Pos.	16	1	0	0	0	4	2	0	.063	.063	.158

DRIVING IN RUNS	From 1B	From 2B	From 3B	Scoring Position
Totals	0/74	7/55	11/32	18/87
Percentage	0%	13%	34%	21%
Driving In Runners from 3B with Less than Two Out:			7/14	50%

Loves to face: David Palmer (.700, 7-for-10)
Hates to face: Mike Scott (.067, 1-for-15)
Drove in only one run in his last 63 games of the season, which included 37 starts. . . . Batting average after Sept. 1 (.143) was lowest in majors (minimum: 50 AB). . . . Batted 87 points lower with runners on base than with bases empty, 4th-largest difference in N.L. (minimum: 100 AB each way). . . . Bucs lost nine of last 10 games in which he was starting leadoff batter. . . . Pirate fans and Orsulak family members may skip this career breakdown, featuring the old ski-slope clutch effect: .299 with bases empty, .212 with runners on base, .199 with runners in scoring position, .187 with two out and runners in scoring position. . . . Has had 24 stolen bases and 11 times caught stealing in each of last two years.

Dave Parker

Bats Left

Cincinnati Reds

	AB	H	2B	3B	HR	RRF	BB	SO	BA	SA	OBA
Season	637	174	31	3	31	121	56	126	.273	.477	.330
vs. Left-Handers	232	70	13	3	10	52	9	48	.302	.513	.325
vs. Right-Handers	405	104	18	0	21	69	47	78	.257	.457	.333
Home	313	84	19	2	17	59	28	59	.268	.505	.325
Road	324	90	12	1	14	62	28	67	.278	.451	.335
Grass	190	54	5	1	9	36	19	40	.284	.463	.352
Artificial Turf	447	120	26	2	22	85	37	86	.268	.483	.320
April	70	20	4	0	5	15	3	16	.286	.557	.315
May	106	35	5	0	6	20	13	21	.330	.547	.400
June	113	28	6	0	4	17	13	22	.248	.407	.323
July	99	29	6	0	8	25	9	17	.293	.596	.352
August	121	26	4	2	3	22	9	23	.215	.355	.269
Sept./Oct.	128	36	6	1	5	22	9	27	.281	.461	.326
Leading Off Inn.	95	29	8	1	6	6	3	13	.305	.600	.327
Runners On	295	97	15	2	22	112	34	59	.329	.617	.393
Runners/Scor. Pos.	154	53	7	2	15	93	29	31	.344	.708	.437
Runners On/2 Out	97	40	7	1	10	47	17	13	.412	.814	.500
Scor. Pos./2 Out	62	26	3	1	7	41	14	10	.419	.839	.526
Late Inning Pressure	96	26	7	0	5	18	14	21	.271	.500	.360
Leading Off	22	6	3	0	1	1	0	4	.273	.545	.273
Runners On	48	15	4	0	4	17	11	9	.313	.646	.433
Runners/Scor. Pos.	24	8	1	0	3	15	11	5	.333	.750	.528

DRIVING IN RUNS	From 1B	From 2B	From 3B	Scoring Position
Totals	22/217	34/110	34/68	68/178
Percentage	10%	31%	50%	38%
Driving In Runners from 3B with Less than Two Out:			26/46	57%

Loves to face: Mike Bielecki (.583, 7-for-12, 3 HR)
Hates to face: Craig Lefferts (.056, 1-for-18)

What do the following southpaws have in common: Dravecky, Hensley, Horton, McClure, Niemann, Ojeda, and Rawley? Each allowed only one home run to a left-handed batter last season, and all were to No. 39.... Batted 104 points higher with runners on base than with bases empty, 6th-largest difference in majors (minimum: 100 AB each way). Has a higher average with runners on than with bases empty in eight of last nine seasons.... Has hit .353 with runners in scoring position since joining the Reds.... Only N.L. batter (minimum: 10 HR) to average more than two RBI on each home run in '86.... Only sacrifice bunt of career: Aug. 5, 1973, in his 18th major-league game.

Tony Pena

Bats Right

Pittsburgh Pirates

	AB	H	2B	3B	HR	RRF	BB	SO	BA	SA	OBA
Season	510	147	26	2	10	54	53	69	.288	.406	.356
vs. Left-Handers	174	58	8	2	4	17	20	18	.333	.471	.405
vs. Right-Handers	336	89	18	0	6	37	33	51	.265	.372	.330
Home	255	76	12	0	5	26	35	29	.298	.404	.384
Road	255	71	14	2	5	28	18	40	.278	.408	.326
Grass	137	35	5	0	2	14	12	21	.255	.336	.315
Artificial Turf	373	112	21	2	8	40	41	48	.300	.432	.370
April	61	15	4	0	1	5	8	11	.246	.361	.333
May	79	17	3	1	2	10	8	15	.215	.354	.295
June	98	25	8	0	2	13	10	14	.255	.398	.324
July	81	23	2	0	2	7	9	10	.284	.383	.352
August	90	32	4	1	2	12	10	10	.356	.489	.420
Sept./Oct.	101	35	5	0	1	7	8	9	.347	.426	.394
Leading Off Inn.	112	38	6	0	2	2	8	16	.339	.446	.383
Runners On	247	65	11	1	1	45	23	29	.263	.328	.327
Runners/Scor. Pos.	157	35	8	0	0	40	17	21	.223	.274	.297
Runners On/2 Out	98	23	2	1	0	16	7	15	.235	.276	.286
Scor. Pos./2 Out	68	13	1	0	0	15	5	11	.191	.206	.286
Late Inning Pressure	111	28	3	0	0	8	8	17	.252	.279	.303
Leading Off	24	10	1	0	0	0	1	3	.417	.458	.440
Runners On	61	15	1	0	0	8	4	6	.246	.262	.292
Runners/Scor. Pos.	33	8	1	0	0	8	3	3	.242	.273	.306

DRIVING IN RUNS	From 1B	From 2B	From 3B	Scoring Position
Totals	4/165	20/125	20/60	40/185
Percentage	2%	16%	33%	22%
Driving In Runners from 3B with Less than Two Out:			12/27	44%

Loves to face: Mike Krukow (.410, 16-for-39, 2 HR)
Hates to face: Kent Tekulve (0-for-10)

Led N.L. with a .348 batting average after the All-Star break.... Since 1981, Pirates are 341–399 (.461) with Pena in starting lineup, 69–102 (.404) without him.... One-for-15 at bats with the bases loaded last season. Has walked only once in 92 career plate appearances with bags full.... Career average of .321 leading off innings. ... Nine of 10 home runs were solo shots last season, the other was with one man on.... One of two players (other: Bob Boone) to have caught 135+ games in each of last five years.... Walked a career-high 53 times last season, just about doubling his previous career walk rate (1986: once every 10.7 plate appearances; before that: once every 20.9).

Terry Pendleton

Bats Left and Right

St. Louis Cardinals

	AB	H	2B	3B	HR	RRF	BB	SO	BA	SA	OBA
Season	578	138	26	5	1	59	34	59	.239	.306	.279
vs. Left-Handers	209	58	12	3	0	27	16	16	.278	.364	.325
vs. Right-Handers	369	80	14	2	1	32	18	43	.217	.274	.253
Home	286	73	15	4	0	28	17	26	.255	.336	.294
Road	292	65	11	1	1	31	17	33	.223	.277	.264
Grass	135	25	3	0	1	8	11	16	.185	.230	.245
Artificial Turf	443	113	23	5	0	51	23	43	.255	.330	.290
April	67	13	2	0	0	1	8	13	.194	.224	.280
May	87	20	7	0	0	9	8	9	.230	.310	.289
June	111	24	6	0	0	9	5	15	.216	.270	.256
July	84	21	4	0	0	13	5	9	.250	.298	.280
August	115	29	3	3	1	15	6	7	.252	.357	.289
Sept./Oct.	114	31	4	2	0	12	2	6	.272	.342	.282
Leading Off Inn.	126	33	5	2	0	0	5	15	.262	.333	.290
Runners On	257	61	12	2	0	58	22	24	.237	.300	.290
Runners/Scor. Pos.	168	39	8	2	0	56	19	19	.232	.304	.299
Runners On/2 Out	110	30	6	1	0	20	14	8	.273	.345	.355
Scor. Pos./2 Out	80	17	3	1	0	19	11	8	.213	.275	.308
Late Inning Pressure	105	22	7	0	0	7	8	12	.210	.276	.265
Leading Off	32	7	2	0	0	0	1	6	.219	.281	.242
Runners On	40	6	2	0	0	7	6	3	.150	.200	.261
Runners/Scor. Pos.	24	2	1	0	0	6	5	3	.083	.125	.241

DRIVING IN RUNS	From 1B	From 2B	From 3B	Scoring Position
Totals	5/166	25/133	28/63	53/196
Percentage	3%	19%	44%	27%
Driving In Runners from 3B with Less than Two Out:			23/30	77%

Loves to face: Zane Smith (.643, 9-for-14)
Hates to face: Jesse Orosco (0-for-14)

Advanced 63 runners with outs last season, most in N.L.; all right, so he did make out more than most batters.... Led major-league third basemen with an average of 2.42 assists per nine innings (minimum: 500 innings).... Finished season with 20 consecutive errorless games at third base, one game short of career-best 21-game streak in 1985.... Career batting average of .128 (5-for-39) at Dodger Stadium.... Career averages vs. right-handers (.255) and left-handers (.256) are virtually identical despite a lopsided 1986 season. Yearly averages vs. right-handers since 1984: .356, .245, .217.... Career batting average of .342 (13-for-38) with the bases loaded; two of his seven career homers have been grand slams.

Tony Perez

Bats Right

Cincinnati Reds

	AB	H	2B	3B	HR	RRF	BB	SO	BA	SA	OBA
Season	200	51	12	1	2	32	25	25	.255	.355	.333
vs. Left-Handers	115	31	6	0	1	12	16	16	.270	.348	.359
vs. Right-Handers	85	20	6	1	1	20	9	9	.235	.365	.299
Home	96	24	4	1	2	22	18	6	.250	.375	.362
Road	104	27	8	0	0	10	7	19	.260	.337	.304
Grass	78	19	7	0	0	7	4	15	.244	.333	.277
Artificial Turf	122	32	5	1	2	25	10	10	.262	.369	.366
April	10	2	0	0	0	1	2	2	.200	.200	.333
May	25	3	0	0	0	1	3	7	.120	.120	.214
June	29	9	2	0	0	3	5	4	.310	.379	.412
July	31	8	1	0	0	8	5	3	.258	.290	.361
August	43	8	2	1	1	3	5	5	.186	.349	.271
Sept./Oct.	62	21	7	0	1	16	5	4	.339	.500	.371
Leading Off Inn.	39	7	1	0	0	0	2	4	.179	.205	.220
Runners On	91	28	5	1	1	31	14	7	.308	.418	.389
Runners/Scor. Pos.	59	17	4	1	0	28	12	6	.288	.390	.392
Runners On/2 Out	43	10	1	0	1	9	4	6	.233	.326	.298
Scor. Pos./2 Out	31	6	1	0	0	7	3	5	.194	.226	.265
Late Inning Pressure	39	15	3	0	0	10	4	3	.385	.462	.432
Leading Off	7	2	0	0	0	0	0	0	.286	.286	.286
Runners On	21	9	1	0	0	10	4	2	.429	.476	.500
Runners/Scor. Pos.	15	6	1	0	0	10	3	2	.400	.467	.474

DRIVING IN RUNS	From 1B	From 2B	From 3B	Scoring Position
Totals	4/63	7/36	19/35	26/71
Percentage	6%	19%	54%	37%
Driving In Runners from 3B with Less than Two Out:			15/19	79%

Loved to face: Pete Vuckovich (.556, 10-for-18, 1 HR)
Hated to face: Rich Gossage (.133, 2-for-15, 6 SO)

Drove in 56 percent (20-of-36) of runners from scoring position with less than two out, highest rate in majors last season (minimum: 15 RRF) and 6th highest over last 12 years.... Batted 161 points higher in Late-Inning Pressure Situations (.385) than in nonpressure situations (.224), 5th-largest difference in majors (minimum: 25 LIP AB). Yearly LIP averages since 1983: .281, .318, .343, .385.... Had 106 career sacrifice flies, 15 shy of Hank Aaron's major-league record (121).... No wonder he felt he could dig in against left-handers—the last time a lefty hit him with a pitch, LBJ was in the White House. It was 1968, and the pitcher was Mets' Al Jackson.

Tim Raines

Montreal Expos — Bats Left and Right

	AB	H	2B	3B	HR	RRF	BB	SO	BA	SA	OBA
Season	580	194	35	10	9	63	78	60	.334	.476	.413
vs. Left-Handers	181	57	9	2	4	28	20	17	.315	.453	.382
vs. Right-Handers	399	137	26	8	5	35	58	43	.343	.486	.427
Home	282	92	17	3	4	37	39	28	.326	.450	.409
Road	298	102	18	7	5	26	39	32	.342	.500	.417
Grass	155	52	9	1	2	13	25	16	.335	.445	.425
Artificial Turf	425	142	26	9	7	50	53	44	.334	.487	.409
April	74	20	7	1	2	4	14	5	.270	.473	.382
May	98	34	5	3	2	9	17	13	.347	.520	.443
June	95	34	8	1	2	5	7	13	.358	.526	.402
July	100	36	3	4	2	13	7	10	.360	.530	.398
August	101	31	7	1	0	13	17	7	.307	.396	.412
Sept./Oct.	112	39	5	0	1	8	16	12	.348	.420	.431
Leading Off Inn.	190	66	13	3	4	8	17	21	.347	.511	.404
Runners On	209	70	7	4	3	57	29	22	.335	.450	.413
Runners/Scor. Pos.	127	42	3	1	2	50	25	17	.331	.417	.432
Runners On/2 Out	78	20	2	1	1	19	16	12	.256	.346	.389
Scor. Pos./2 Out	55	14	1	0	1	18	14	10	.255	.327	.406
Late Inning Pressure	99	37	5	1	2	9	16	13	.374	.505	.466
Leading Off	27	12	2	0	1	1	5	2	.444	.630	.531
Runners On	40	14	1	1	1	8	6	6	.350	.500	.447
Runners/Scor. Pos.	18	6	0	0	0	5	6	5	.333	.333	.500

DRIVING IN RUNS	From 1B	From 2B	From 3B	Scoring Position
Totals	8/140	17/95	28/53	45/148
Percentage	6%	18%	53%	30%
Driving In Runners from 3B with Less than Two Out:			19/29	66%

Loves to face: Orel Hershiser (.455, 10-for-22)
Hates to face: Doug Sisk (.083, 1-for-12)
Career batting average of .347 in Late-Inning Pressure Situations, 3d highest over past 12 years, behind Boggs (.369) and Gwynn (.348). . . . Career stolen base percentage of .870, highest in major-league history (minimum: 300 SB). . . . Caught stealing three times in nine attempts vs. Mets last season; no one else caught him *twice*. . . . 24 steals in his last 25 attempts. . . . One of three players to hit 30 or more doubles in each of last five seasons. . . . Led N.L. with 65 multiple-hit games last season. . . . Four of his six errors last season came in a 10-game span (July 23 to Aug. 3). . . . Led N.L. left fielders with 13 assists. . . . Has homered in every N.L. ballpark except Dodger Stadium (117 career AB).

Rafael Ramirez

Atlanta Braves — Bats Right

	AB	H	2B	3B	HR	RRF	BB	SO	BA	SA	OBA
Season	496	119	21	1	8	33	21	60	.240	.335	.273
vs. Left-Handers	179	37	4	0	2	5	9	20	.207	.263	.247
vs. Right-Handers	317	82	17	1	6	28	12	40	.259	.375	.288
Home	238	56	13	1	1	18	15	31	.235	.311	.287
Road	258	63	8	0	7	15	6	29	.244	.357	.260
Grass	369	86	17	1	6	28	18	48	.233	.333	.273
Artificial Turf	127	33	4	0	2	5	3	12	.260	.339	.275
April	75	22	4	0	2	9	2	9	.293	.427	.312
May	102	25	8	0	1	6	1	9	.245	.353	.250
June	101	21	5	0	1	3	3	12	.208	.287	.236
July	67	9	0	0	0	3	7	10	.134	.134	.224
August	82	28	2	1	2	6	1	8	.341	.463	.349
Sept./Oct.	69	14	2	0	2	6	7	12	.203	.319	.286
Leading Off Inn.	99	30	7	1	1	1	4	12	.303	.424	.330
Runners On	198	35	7	0	2	27	9	24	.177	.242	.213
Runners/Scor. Pos.	111	15	3	0	1	24	7	13	.135	.189	.182
Runners On/2 Out	84	14	2	0	1	9	6	10	.167	.226	.222
Scor. Pos./2 Out	58	6	1	0	0	6	5	6	.103	.121	.175
Late Inning Pressure	84	21	5	0	2	8	3	12	.250	.381	.289
Leading Off	21	6	3	0	1	0	0	3	.286	.571	.286
Runners On	36	7	2	0	0	6	2	7	.194	.250	.250
Runners/Scor. Pos.	23	4	1	0	0	6	2	5	.174	.217	.231

DRIVING IN RUNS	From 1B	From 2B	From 3B	Scoring Position
Totals	3/146	9/89	13/46	22/135
Percentage	2%	10%	28%	16%
Driving In Runners from 3B with Less than Two Out:			11/22	50%

Loves to face: Larry Andersen (.833, 5-for-6)
Hates to face: Sid Fernandez (0-for-12, 4 SO)
What's the difference between Ramirez's 33 RBI and Danny Heep's 33 RBI? Ramirez batted with 135 runners in scoring position and drove in 16 percent of them; Heep batted with 64, and drove in 39 percent of them. . . . Ramirez's rate of 16 percent was 2d lowest in N.L. (minimum: 50 opportunities). . . . Batted 105 points lower with runners on base than with bases empty, largest difference in the N.L. (minimum: 100 AB each way). . . . One walk every 25.2 plate appearances last season, 3d-lowest rate in N.L. . . . Ranked second among major-league shortstops with an average of 3.58 assists per nine innings (minimum: 500 innings). . . . July batting average (.134) was lowest in majors (minimum: 50 AB).

Johnny Ray

Pittsburgh Pirates — Bats Left and Right

	AB	H	2B	3B	HR	RRF	BB	SO	BA	SA	OBA
Season	579	174	33	0	7	82	58	47	.301	.394	.363
vs. Left-Handers	222	58	8	0	1	26	19	18	.261	.311	.318
vs. Right-Handers	357	116	25	0	6	56	39	29	.325	.445	.390
Home	298	85	18	0	2	39	33	28	.285	.366	.356
Road	281	89	15	0	5	43	25	19	.317	.423	.371
Grass	146	45	7	0	2	24	14	12	.308	.397	.372
Artificial Turf	433	129	26	0	5	58	44	35	.298	.393	.360
April	73	28	5	0	1	19	7	4	.384	.493	.432
May	96	33	9	0	1	11	12	9	.344	.469	.413
June	87	16	5	0	0	12	10	12	.184	.241	.265
July	91	25	4	0	1	10	10	9	.275	.352	.359
August	119	42	6	0	2	17	7	6	.353	.454	.386
Sept./Oct.	113	30	4	0	2	13	12	7	.265	.354	.333
Leading Off Inn.	100	34	7	0	2	2	8	3	.340	.470	.394
Runners On	259	78	17	0	2	77	24	26	.301	.390	.354
Runners/Scor. Pos.	154	44	10	0	1	69	19	16	.286	.370	.354
Runners On/2 Out	75	16	0	0	1	18	6	9	.213	.253	.280
Scor. Pos./2 Out	58	13	0	0	1	18	6	8	.224	.276	.308
Late Inning Pressure	106	34	7	0	2	10	13	12	.321	.443	.395
Leading Off	16	6	3	0	0	0	1	1	.375	.563	.412
Runners On	46	11	1	0	1	9	8	6	.239	.326	.352
Runners/Scor. Pos.	25	6	0	0	1	9	7	3	.240	.360	.406

DRIVING IN RUNS	From 1B	From 2B	From 3B	Scoring Position
Totals	12/169	26/111	36/71	62/182
Percentage	7%	23%	51%	34%
Driving In Runners from 3B with Less than Two Out:			29/42	69%

Loves to face: Bill Campbell (.563, 9-for-16)
Hates to face: Tom Niedenfuer (.077, 1-for-13, 4 SO)
Has played 777 games over past five years; in N.L., only Dale Murphy (808) has played more. . . . One of three players to top 30 doubles in each of last five seasons. . . . Set career highs in RBIs (78), walks (58), strikeouts (47), and fielding percentage (.993). . . . Only two pitchers fanned Ray twice in one game last season: Joe Johnson (May 26) and Mike Krukow (July 12). . . . Outhomered Reggie, 2–0, last October. . . . Ranked third among N.L. second basemen with rate of 3.35 assists per nine innings (minimum: 500 innings). . . . Batting average vs. right-handers (.325) was highest of his career; home run off Tim Conroy on Aug. 14 was second of his career against a lefty.

Gary Redus

Philadelphia Phillies — Bats Right

	AB	H	2B	3B	HR	RRF	BB	SO	BA	SA	OBA
Season	340	84	22	4	11	33	47	78	.247	.432	.343
vs. Left-Handers	109	27	7	1	2	10	27	26	.248	.385	.397
vs. Right-Handers	231	57	15	3	9	23	20	52	.247	.455	.314
Home	170	49	15	3	8	23	22	40	.288	.553	.374
Road	170	35	7	1	3	10	25	38	.206	.312	.311
Grass	71	15	3	0	1	6	12	18	.211	.296	.325
Artificial Turf	269	69	19	4	10	27	35	60	.257	.468	.347
April	54	15	6	0	1	3	6	12	.278	.444	.361
May	0	0	0	0	0	0	0	0	—	—	—
June	0	0	0	0	0	0	0	0	—	—	—
July	103	24	10	1	3	10	13	18	.233	.437	.319
August	91	21	3	2	6	10	15	21	.231	.505	.349
Sept./Oct.	92	24	3	1	1	10	13	27	.261	.348	.352
Leading Off Inn.	141	32	11	0	3	3	16	27	.227	.369	.306
Runners On	105	25	6	1	3	25	16	28	.238	.400	.341
Runners/Scor. Pos.	75	19	4	1	2	22	11	21	.253	.413	.352
Runners On/2 Out	51	15	3	0	3	17	8	13	.294	.529	.400
Scor. Pos./2 Out	45	12	2	0	2	14	6	13	.267	.444	.365
Late Inning Pressure	52	12	5	0	1	5	7	12	.231	.385	.322
Leading Off	19	3	0	0	0	0	1	3	.158	.158	.200
Runners On	18	3	2	0	0	4	5	5	.167	.278	.348
Runners/Scor. Pos.	8	2	1	0	0	3	3	3	.250	.375	.455

DRIVING IN RUNS	From 1B	From 2B	From 3B	Scoring Position
Totals	2/62	15/67	5/16	20/83
Percentage	3%	22%	31%	24%
Driving In Runners from 3B with Less than Two Out:			3/9	33%

Loves to face: Rick Mahler (.389, 7-for-18, 2 HR)
Hates to face: Andy Hawkins (.053, 1-for-19)
Has batted between .247 and .254 in each of last four seasons. . . . Hit six of his 11 home runs within a two-week stretch in August. . . . Hit eight of those 11 home runs with bases empty, bringing career totals to 31 homers with bases empty, 11 with runners on base. . . . Career batting average of .224 on grass fields, .257 on artificial surfaces. . . . Still ranks number one on career list of lowest ground out-to-air out ratio, among all players with 1,000 plate appearances over last 12 years. . . . It follows, then, that he doesn't ground into many double plays: only two in 75 double-play situations over the last two years.

Craig Reynolds
Houston Astros — Bats Left

	AB	H	2B	3B	HR	RRF	BB	SO	BA	SA	OBA
Season	313	78	7	3	6	43	12	31	.249	.348	.274
vs. Left-Handers	35	5	1	0	0	1	0	7	.143	.171	.143
vs. Right-Handers	278	73	6	3	6	42	12	24	.263	.371	.290
Home	144	46	3	1	4	22	5	14	.319	.438	.340
Road	169	32	4	2	2	21	7	17	.189	.272	.219
Grass	110	22	4	0	1	15	4	14	.200	.264	.226
Artificial Turf	203	56	3	3	5	28	8	17	.276	.394	.300
April	29	11	1	0	2	10	2	1	.379	.621	.419
May	44	9	0	2	0	4	3	6	.205	.295	.255
June	54	16	1	0	1	8	0	4	.296	.370	.286
July	63	13	1	0	2	4	3	9	.206	.317	.242
August	67	19	3	0	1	9	0	4	.284	.373	.284
Sept./Oct.	56	10	1	1	0	8	4	7	.179	.232	.230
Leading Off Inn.	69	11	0	0	1	0	0	13	.159	.203	.159
Runners On	138	45	4	3	2	39	8	8	.326	.442	.356
Runners/Scor. Pos.	76	27	2	2	1	36	7	5	.355	.474	.395
Runners On/2 Out	48	17	2	2	2	17	3	4	.354	.604	.392
Scor. Pos./2 Out	27	10	1	1	1	14	3	3	.370	.593	.433
Late Inning Pressure	52	15	1	1	1	8	3	4	.288	.404	.327
Leading Off	9	1	0	0	0	0	0	2	.111	.111	.111
Runners On	24	9	1	1	0	7	2	0	.375	.500	.423
Runners/Scor. Pos.	11	6	1	1	0	7	2	0	.545	.818	.615

DRIVING IN RUNS	From 1B	From 2B	From 3B	Scoring Position
Totals	4/96	16/61	17/30	33/91
Percentage	4%	26%	57%	36%
Driving In Runners from 3B with Less than Two Out:			11/20	55%

Loves to face: Scott Garrelts & Jeff Robinson (.583, 7-for-12)
Hates to face: Matt Keough (.083, 1-for-12)
Batted 138 points higher with runners on base than with bases empty, 2d-largest difference in majors (minimum: 100 AB each way). . . . Batting average with runners in scoring position (.355) was a career high. Previous high was .307 in 1981. . . . Batted .409 (9-for-22) as a pinch-hitter last season. . . . Drove in 18 runs in 15 games vs. Atlanta. . . . Five hits in six at bats with the bases loaded last season. . . . Has not been hit by a pitch since May 9, 1982. . . . Career total of 114 sacrifice bunts ranks him 2d among active non-pitchers behind Ozzie Smith (125); no, Craig, we don't regard you as a pitcher—despite, or maybe because of, your one-inning, 3 earned run performance vs. Mets last July.

R.J. Reynolds
Pittsburgh Pirates — Bats Left and Right

	AB	H	2B	3B	HR	RRF	BB	SO	BA	SA	OBA
Season	402	108	30	2	9	49	40	78	.269	.420	.335
vs. Left-Handers	105	23	5	1	0	12	9	21	.219	.286	.278
vs. Right-Handers	297	85	25	1	9	37	31	57	.286	.468	.355
Home	198	56	18	2	6	29	24	34	.283	.485	.357
Road	204	52	12	0	3	20	16	44	.255	.358	.312
Grass	114	35	5	0	3	12	11	26	.307	.430	.368
Artificial Turf	288	73	25	2	6	37	29	52	.253	.417	.322
April	71	21	8	0	2	9	6	16	.296	.493	.351
May	82	22	6	0	2	7	10	17	.268	.415	.348
June	84	25	8	1	2	11	10	18	.298	.488	.372
July	75	27	4	0	3	13	8	9	.360	.533	.422
August	79	13	4	1	0	9	5	17	.165	.241	.209
Sept./Oct.	11	0	0	0	0	0	1	1	.000	.000	.154
Leading Off Inn.	103	32	9	0	4	4	14	13	.311	.515	.398
Runners On	166	43	11	2	4	44	14	32	.259	.422	.313
Runners/Scor. Pos.	105	26	8	1	2	37	11	21	.248	.400	.314
Runners On/2 Out	62	15	5	1	2	18	8	13	.242	.452	.329
Scor. Pos./2 Out	42	11	5	0	1	15	6	9	.262	.452	.354
Late Inning Pressure	81	17	6	0	1	5	7	20	.210	.321	.273
Leading Off	15	7	3	0	0	0	3	2	.467	.667	.556
Runners On	34	3	2	0	0	4	2	10	.088	.147	.139
Runners/Scor. Pos.	19	1	1	0	0	3	1	5	.053	.105	.100

DRIVING IN RUNS	From 1B	From 2B	From 3B	Scoring Position
Totals	10/110	12/85	18/38	30/123
Percentage	9%	14%	47%	24%
Driving In Runners from 3B with Less than Two Out:			12/19	63%

Loves to face: Bill Gullickson (.400, 6-for-15, 1 HR)
Hates to face: Dave Dravecky (.083, 1-for-12)
Good early, bad late: homered off Gooden leading off bottom of first inning of season opener. Finished the season hitless in last 14 at bats. . . . Started 78 of 104 games vs. right-handed starters, but only 19 of 58 against lefties. . . . Played 41 percent of team's innings in left field, 15 percent in right, six percent in center. . . . Committed nine errors in 84 games in left field, no errors in 43 games in right. . . . Has hit only one of 16 career home runs against a left-handed pitcher: June 22, 1984 off Pete Falcone. . . . Career batting average of .346 (9-for-26) with the bases loaded. . . . July batting average of .360 was 2d highest in N.L. (minimum: 75 AB), August average (.165) was 4th lowest (minimum: 50 AB).

Bip Roberts
San Diego Padres — Bats Left and Right

	AB	H	2B	3B	HR	RRF	BB	SO	BA	SA	OBA
Season	241	61	5	2	1	12	14	29	.253	.303	.293
vs. Left-Handers	138	28	4	1	1	6	8	16	.203	.268	.247
vs. Right-Handers	103	33	1	1	0	6	6	13	.320	.350	.355
Home	118	28	2	1	0	8	8	16	.237	.271	.283
Road	123	33	3	1	1	4	6	13	.268	.333	.302
Grass	187	48	4	1	0	10	11	27	.257	.289	.296
Artificial Turf	54	13	1	1	1	2	3	2	.241	.352	.281
April	20	0	0	0	0	0	1	8	.000	.000	.048
May	46	16	1	1	0	2	3	5	.348	.413	.388
June	65	13	3	1	0	5	2	6	.200	.277	.224
July	25	6	1	0	0	2	3	2	.240	.280	.310
August	48	12	0	0	1	2	3	2	.250	.313	.294
Sept./Oct.	37	14	0	0	0	1	2	6	.378	.378	.410
Leading Off Inn.	90	17	1	0	0		2	17	.189	.200	.200
Runners On	81	22	3	1	0	11	5	6	.272	.333	.310
Runners/Scor. Pos.	44	11	1	0	0	10	3	3	.250	.273	.292
Runners On/2 Out	40	14	3	0	0	5	1	2	.350	.425	.366
Scor. Pos./2 Out	20	6	1	0	0	5	1	0	.300	.350	.333
Late Inning Pressure	29	6	0	0	0	1	4	3	.207	.207	.303
Leading Off	6	1	0	0	0	0	0	1	.167	.167	.167
Runners On	10	3	0	0	0	1	2	1	.300	.300	.417
Runners/Scor. Pos.	7	2	0	0	0	1	1	0	.286	.286	.375

DRIVING IN RUNS	From 1B	From 2B	From 3B	Scoring Position
Totals	2/57	3/35	6/18	9/53
Percentage	4%	9%	33%	17%
Driving In Runners from 3B with Less than Two Out:			5/9	56%

Loves to face: Dennis Eckersley (.750, 3-for-4)
Hates to face: Rick Honeycutt (0-for-11)
Batted 117 points higher vs. right-handed pitchers than against left-handers, largest difference in majors (minimum: 100 AB vs. each). . . . Hitless in first 20 at bats before an infield hit on May 3 got him rolling on a 14-for-29 tear. . . . Started 72 percent of Padres' games vs. left-handers, 22 percent against right-handers. . . . Like Rob Thompson, arrived in majors without having played a game at AAA level. . . . Hit his only major-league home run off Reds' Tom Browning, Aug. 15. . . . Walked only twice in 92 innings as leadoff batter; his .207 on-base average when leading off was 2d lowest in majors last year (minimum: 80 innings led off); only Candy Maldonado's (.193) was lower.

Ron Roenicke
Philadelphia Phillies — Bats Left and Right

	AB	H	2B	3B	HR	RRF	BB	SO	BA	SA	OBA
Season	275	68	13	1	5	43	61	52	.247	.356	.381
vs. Left-Handers	107	33	5	0	3	17	27	23	.308	.439	.441
vs. Right-Handers	168	35	8	1	2	26	34	29	.208	.304	.340
Home	142	38	8	1	4	24	40	33	.268	.423	.424
Road	133	30	5	0	1	19	21	19	.226	.286	.329
Grass	70	16	3	0	0	9	10	13	.229	.271	.325
Artificial Turf	205	52	10	1	5	34	51	39	.254	.385	.398
April	0	0	0	0	0	0	0	0	—	—	—
May	40	11	2	0	1	8	3	8	.275	.325	.326
June	103	33	7	1	3	14	24	18	.320	.495	.445
July	60	11	1	0	1	14	10	9	.183	.250	.296
August	32	7	1	0	1	4	10	5	.219	.344	.395
Sept./Oct.	40	6	2	0	0	3	14	12	.150	.200	.370
Leading Off Inn.	55	12	3	0	1	1	10	12	.218	.327	.338
Runners On	130	37	7	0	1	39	29	22	.285	.362	.407
Runners/Scor. Pos.	84	25	2	0	1	36	20	17	.298	.357	.421
Runners On/2 Out	49	15	2	0	0	15	13	13	.306	.347	.452
Scor. Pos./2 Out	35	11	0	0	0	13	10	10	.314	.314	.467
Late Inning Pressure	53	13	2	0	0	5	13	10	.245	.283	.388
Leading Off	10	2	1	0	0	0	1	1	.200	.300	.273
Runners On	25	8	1	0	0	9	7	4	.320	.360	.455
Runners/Scor. Pos.	14	6	1	0	0	9	5	3	.429	.500	.550

DRIVING IN RUNS	From 1B	From 2B	From 3B	Scoring Position
Totals	3/83	17/73	18/34	35/107
Percentage	4%	23%	53%	33%
Driving In Runners from 3B with Less than Two Out:			13/21	62%

Loves to face: Bob Ojeda (.625, 5-for-8, 1 HR)
Hates to face: Mario Soto (.091, 1-for-11, 7 SO)
Averaged one walk every 5.6 plate appearances, highest rate in N.L. (minimum: 40 BB). . . . Posted career-high totals in virtually every offensive category. . . . Drove in his 40th run on Aug. 15; had two RBI in 29 games thereafter. . . . Batted .190 (4-for-21) as a pinch-hitter. . . . Career batting average of .448 (13-for-29) with the bases loaded. . . . Career batting average of .284 in Late-Inning Pressure Situations, .313 in those situations with runners on base, and .375 (15-for-40) in such situations with runners on base and two outs. . . . Just a West Coast kind of guy: Phillies were his fifth team in four seasons, but the first one east of San Diego.

Pete Rose
Cincinnati Reds   Bats Left and Right

	AB	H	2B	3B	HR	RRF	BB	SO	BA	SA	OBA
Season	237	52	8	2	0	25	30	31	.219	.270	.316
vs. Left-Handers	22	6	0	1	0	2	1	4	.273	.364	.304
vs. Right-Handers	215	46	8	1	0	23	29	27	.214	.260	.317
Home	121	31	6	1	0	13	12	17	.256	.322	.341
Road	116	21	2	1	0	12	18	14	.181	.216	.291
Grass	65	15	1	1	0	9	8	7	.231	.277	.315
Artificial Turf	172	37	7	1	0	16	22	24	.215	.267	.317
April	10	0	0	0	0	0	3	2	.000	.000	.231
May	62	12	2	0	0	8	6	9	.194	.226	.271
June	81	21	4	1	0	10	12	8	.259	.333	.368
July	60	11	1	1	0	3	7	7	.183	.233	.279
August	24	8	1	0	0	4	2	5	.333	.375	.385
Sept./Oct.	0	0	0	0	0	0	0	0			
Leading Off Inn.	48	8	2	0	0	0	4	6	.167	.208	.245
Runners On	80	29	3	2	0	25	15	7	.363	.450	.464
Runners/Scor. Pos.	46	16	3	1	0	24	10	4	.348	.457	.466
Runners On/2 Out	39	16	2	2	0	17	10	2	.410	.564	.531
Scor. Pos./2 Out	27	12	2	1	0	16	7	2	.444	.593	.559
Late Inning Pressure	23	5	1	1	0	3	6	5	.217	.348	.400
Leading Off	8	0	0	0	0	0	1	2	.000	.000	.111
Runners On	8	3	0	1	0	3	3	1	.375	.625	.545
Runners/Scor. Pos.	4	1	0	0	0	2	2	1	.250	.250	.500

DRIVING IN RUNS	From 1B	From 2B	From 3B	Scoring Position
Totals	4/49	14/37	7/21	21/58
Percentage	8%	38%	33%	36%
Driving In Runners from 3B with Less than Two Out:		3/7		43%

Loves to face: Juan Berenguer (.833, 5-for-6)
Hates to face: Rick Aguilera (.071, 1-for-14)
Batted .363 with runners on base, .146 with bases empty, his first time over .300 with runners on base since 1982. . . . Five-hit game on Aug. 11 was 10th of career, breaking Max Carey's N.L. record. . . . There were 13 N.L. players who had five-hit games last season; none had a season average as low as Rose's .219. . . . Reds were 34–38 in games that Rose played last season, bringing his all-time record to 1972–1583-7. Pete has said that he would like to play in 2000 wins. . . . Needs two steals to reach 200; he'll have to hang around a while longer to become the oldest guy to steal a base in the majors: Arlie Latham (yes, "The Freshest Man on Earth" himself) stole a base for 1909 Giants at age 50.

Jerry Royster
San Diego Padres   Bats Right

	AB	H	2B	3B	HR	RRF	BB	SO	BA	SA	OBA
Season	257	66	12	0	5	27	32	45	.257	.362	.336
vs. Left-Handers	187	51	12	0	3	19	24	28	.273	.385	.352
vs. Right-Handers	70	15	0	0	2	8	8	17	.214	.300	.291
Home	118	29	8	0	2	13	13	18	.246	.364	.316
Road	139	37	4	0	3	14	19	27	.266	.360	.352
Grass	181	47	9	0	3	17	20	30	.260	.359	.330
Artificial Turf	76	19	3	0	2	10	12	15	.250	.368	.348
April	32	9	3	0	0	3	1	3	.281	.375	.294
May	46	11	5	0	1	7	4	4	.239	.413	.288
June	45	8	0	0	0	1	7	12	.178	.178	.288
July	35	13	1	0	1	4	6	7	.371	.486	.463
August	47	12	0	0	3	4	6	16	.255	.447	.340
Sept./Oct.	52	13	3	0	0	8	8	3	.250	.308	.350
Leading Off Inn.	89	19	3	0	3	4	9	16	.213	.348	.286
Runners On	100	27	3	0	2	23	16	19	.270	.360	.361
Runners/Scor. Pos.	53	13	1	0	0	18	12	12	.245	.264	.368
Runners On/2 Out	38	11	2	0	0	9	7	5	.289	.342	.400
Scor. Pos./2 Out	26	7	1	0	0	8	6	5	.269	.308	.406
Late Inning Pressure	49	11	2	0	0	4	7	8	.224	.265	.321
Leading Off	13	1	0	0	0	0	0	2	.077	.077	.077
Runners On	25	7	1	0	0	4	4	6	.280	.320	.379
Runners/Scor. Pos.	16	3	0	0	0	3	2	5	.188	.188	.278

DRIVING IN RUNS	From 1B	From 2B	From 3B	Scoring Position
Totals	3/76	8/42	10/24	18/66
Percentage	4%	19%	42%	27%
Driving In Runners from 3B with Less than Two Out:		6/10		60%

Loves to face: Doug Bair (.667, 6-for-9, 1 HR)
Hates to face: Joaquin Andujar (.195, 8-for-41)
Has batted for a higher average with runners on base than with bases empty in 11 consecutive seasons. The only player active last year with a longer streak was his platoon partner, Graig Nettles. . . . Started 51 of 58 games in which Padres faced left-handed starters, but only nine of 104 against right-handers. . . . Had his lowest fielding average (.931) at third base of any full season in majors. . . . There's been little impact on preventing runs over past two years according to who San Diego's third baseman is; with Nettles in game, team has allowed 4.01 runs per nine innings; with Royster, 4.05. . . . Nine hits in 18 at bats with the bases loaded since 1983.

Bill Russell
Los Angeles Dodgers   Bats Right

	AB	H	2B	3B	HR	RRF	BB	SO	BA	SA	OBA
Season	216	54	11	0	0	18	15	23	.250	.301	.302
vs. Left-Handers	114	37	5	0	0	11	11	5	.325	.368	.386
vs. Right-Handers	102	17	6	0	0	7	4	18	.167	.225	.204
Home	110	26	4	0	0	13	11	10	.236	.273	.309
Road	106	28	7	0	0	5	4	13	.264	.330	.295
Grass	158	39	8	0	0	15	13	16	.247	.297	.309
Artificial Turf	58	15	3	0	0	3	2	7	.259	.310	.283
April	26	5	2	0	0	3	2	2	.192	.269	.269
May	13	3	0	0	0	1	0	3	.231	.231	.231
June	42	11	2	0	0	3	3	5	.262	.310	.319
July	45	11	1	0	0	4	4	1	.244	.267	.306
August	66	16	4	0	0	6	5	9	.242	.303	.292
Sept./Oct.	24	8	2	0	0	1	1	3	.333	.417	.385
Leading Off Inn.	49	14	3	0	0	0	0	1	.286	.347	.286
Runners On	77	23	4	0	0	18	11	8	.299	.351	.391
Runners/Scor. Pos.	44	10	1	0	0	16	9	7	.227	.250	.357
Runners On/2 Out	34	8	2	0	0	5	3	5	.235	.294	.297
Scor. Pos./2 Out	21	3	0	0	0	4	2	4	.143	.143	.217
Late Inning Pressure	61	15	2	0	0	4	1	8	.246	.279	.266
Leading Off	11	3	0	0	0	0	0	1	.273	.273	.273
Runners On	23	6	0	0	0	4	1	3	.261	.261	.308
Runners/Scor. Pos.	15	2	0	0	0	4	1	3	.133	.133	.176

DRIVING IN RUNS	From 1B	From 2B	From 3B	Scoring Position
Totals	2/58	7/38	9/21	16/59
Percentage	3%	18%	43%	27%
Driving In Runners from 3B with Less than Two Out:		7/9		78%

Loved to face: Steve Trout (.500, 11-for-22)
Hated to face: Bruce Berenyi (.063, 1-for-16)
One of 22 players active in 1986 with 2000+ career games played, but one of only three of those guys who has played for only one major league team; others: Dave Concepcion and Mike Schmidt. . . . Has bled Dodger Blue for 2181 games in his career, passing Pee Wee Reese on Sept. 7. Only Zack Wheat (2318) played in more games for the Dodgers. . . . Batted 158 points higher vs. left-handed pitchers than against right-handers, largest difference in majors (minimum: 100 AB vs. both). . . . First major-league hit: double off Jim Merritt in 1969; last career hit: bunt single off Greg Minton. . . . Batted .323 (10 for 31) as a pinch-hitter last season.

John Russell
Philadelphia Phillies   Bats Right

	AB	H	2B	3B	HR	RRF	BB	SO	BA	SA	OBA
Season	315	76	21	2	13	60	25	103	.241	.444	.300
vs. Left-Handers	122	31	10	1	4	19	13	38	.254	.451	.338
vs. Right-Handers	193	45	11	1	9	41	12	65	.233	.440	.274
Home	159	45	12	2	8	35	11	49	.283	.535	.331
Road	156	31	9	0	5	25	14	54	.199	.353	.269
Grass	61	14	4	0	3	9	10	20	.230	.443	.347
Artificial Turf	254	62	17	2	10	51	15	83	.244	.445	.287
April	25	8	1	0	1	5	3	9	.320	.480	.414
May	31	5	1	0	2	4	4	16	.161	.387	.257
June	53	16	9	0	2	15	5	18	.302	.585	.373
July	74	16	2	0	3	11	2	24	.216	.365	.231
August	60	14	4	1	2	8	4	13	.233	.433	.277
Sept./Oct.	72	17	4	1	3	17	7	23	.236	.444	.309
Leading Off Inn.	75	12	4	0	2	8	25		.160	.293	.250
Runners On	150	44	11	2	7	54	9	46	.293	.533	.329
Runners/Scor. Pos.	88	25	9	2	2	43	8	23	.284	.500	.337
Runners On/2 Out	73	23	6	2	4	29	2	20	.315	.616	.333
Scor. Pos./2 Out	47	16	5	2	2	25	2	13	.340	.660	.367
Late Inning Pressure	60	13	2	0	3	7	4	21	.217	.400	.262
Leading Off	13	3	0	0	1	1	1	4	.231	.462	.286
Runners On	33	5	1	0	0	4	2	13	.152	.182	.194
Runners/Scor. Pos.	21	3	1	0	0	4	1		.143	.190	.174

DRIVING IN RUNS	From 1B	From 2B	From 3B	Scoring Position
Totals	11/122	21/74	15/38	36/112
Percentage	9%	28%	39%	32%
Driving In Runners from 3B with Less than Two Out:		10/17		59%

Loves to face: Ray Fontenot (.714, 5-for-7)
Hates to face: Sid Fernandez (0-for-10, 7 SO)
Has 696 career plate appearances, roughly the equivalent of what a number-five hitter would get in a full season if he never came out of a game; 208 of those appearances have resulted in strikeouts, far in excess of Bobby Bonds's major-league season record of 189. . . . Averaged one strikeout every 3.4 plate appearances last season, worst rate in N.L. . . . Some interesting career breakdowns submitted for your approval: .280 with runners on base, .206 with bases empty; .196 leading off innings; .412 with the bases loaded; .290 at home, .182 on road. . . . Returned to catcher last season and led major leagues in passed balls (17), without a knuckleball pitcher in sight.

Billy Sample

Atlanta Braves — Bats Right

	AB	H	2B	3B	HR	RRF	BB	SO	BA	SA	OBA
Season	200	57	11	0	6	17	14	26	.285	.430	.338
vs. Left-Handers	142	41	8	0	4	10	10	15	.289	.430	.346
vs. Right-Handers	58	16	3	0	2	7	4	11	.276	.431	.317
Home	93	26	6	0	1	5	7	17	.280	.376	.350
Road	107	31	5	0	5	12	7	9	.290	.477	.328
Grass	142	39	6	0	3	9	10	22	.275	.380	.335
Artificial Turf	58	18	5	0	3	8	4	4	.310	.552	.344
April	24	7	0	0	1	4	0	1	.292	.417	.292
May	47	13	0	0	3	5	3	8	.277	.468	.314
June	49	11	1	0	1	2	5	6	.224	.306	.321
July	35	8	3	0	0	0	0	5	.229	.314	.229
August	21	9	5	0	1	4	2	2	.429	.667	.500
Sept./Oct.	24	9	2	0	1	5	2	4	.375	.583	.444
Leading Off Inn.	81	20	2	0	3	3	4	7	.247	.383	.291
Runners On	55	14	3	0	2	13	7	8	.277	.418	.328
Runners/Scor. Pos.	40	7	1	0	2	12	6	5	.175	.350	.271
Runners On/2 Out	23	5	0	0	0	2	2	4	.217	.217	.280
Scor. Pos./2 Out	18	1	0	0	0	1	1	4	.056	.056	.105
Late Inning Pressure	30	10	5	0	0	2	5	5	.333	.500	.429
Leading Off	9	3	0	0	0	0	2	2	.333	.333	.455
Runners On	11	2	2	0	0	2	2	2	.182	.364	.308
Runners/Scor. Pos.	7	1	1	0	0	2	2	1	.143	.286	.308

DRIVING IN RUNS	From 1B	From 2B	From 3B	Scoring Position
Totals	2/34	4/34	5/16	9/50
Percentage	6%	12%	31%	18%
Driving In Runners from 3B with Less than Two Out:			5/11	45%

Loves to face: John Tudor (.407, 11-for-27, 1 HR)
Hates to face: Rick Sutcliffe (.071, 1-for-14)
One of 10 players to play right field for Atlanta last year; one of seven who started; one of five who started 10 or more games (the most by any team in majors). . . . Started 39 of 58 games against left-handed pitchers, three of 103 vs. right-handers. . . . Batting average with runners in scoring position (.175) was the lowest of his career; had hit .393 in such situations in limited action with Yankees in 1985. . . . Only one extra-base hit in 48 career at bats with the bases loaded. . . . Came up 25 times in double-play situations last season, didn't ground into any. . . . Has hit higher vs. lefties than vs. righties in each of last three years, after going the other way in each of the previous three.

Juan Samuel

Philadelphia Phillies — Bats Right

	AB	H	2B	3B	HR	RRF	BB	SO	BA	SA	OBA
Season	591	157	36	12	16	83	26	142	.266	.448	.302
vs. Left-Handers	180	46	13	4	5	31	5	46	.256	.456	.283
vs. Right-Handers	411	111	23	8	11	52	21	96	.270	.445	.310
Home	286	76	19	7	10	46	18	71	.266	.486	.313
Road	305	81	17	5	6	37	8	71	.266	.413	.292
Grass	157	46	7	0	4	16	5	39	.293	.414	.329
Artificial Turf	434	111	29	12	12	67	21	103	.256	.461	.292
April	14	4	1	0	0	1	2	2	.286	.357	.375
May	99	25	3	0	1	8	4	25	.253	.313	.290
June	124	31	10	3	5	28	4	35	.250	.500	.288
July	113	32	6	5	3	15	6	24	.283	.504	.322
August	118	30	8	2	5	21	4	27	.254	.483	.280
Sept./Oct.	123	35	8	2	2	10	6	29	.285	.431	.321
Leading Off Inn.	101	28	7	1	1	4	4	22	.277	.396	.305
Runners On	262	71	19	8	9	75	13	62	.271	.508	.315
Runners/Scor. Pos.	150	40	12	5	6	63	8	35	.267	.533	.312
Runners On/2 Out	98	26	7	3	5	31	8	17	.265	.551	.333
Scor. Pos./2 Out	68	19	4	2	5	29	6	12	.279	.618	.355
Late Inning Pressure	93	24	3	1	4	11	5	20	.258	.441	.310
Leading Off	25	7	1	0	0	0	2	6	.280	.320	.333
Runners On	40	11	1	1	2	9	3	10	.275	.500	.341
Runners/Scor. Pos.	19	5	0	0	1	5	3	5	.263	.421	.391

DRIVING IN RUNS	From 1B	From 2B	From 3B	Scoring Position
Totals	15/175	24/116	27/63	51/179
Percentage	9%	21%	43%	28%
Driving In Runners from 3B with Less than Two Out:			17/34	50%

Loves to face: Jamie Moyer (.625, 5-for-8, 1 HR)
Hates to face: Tom Browning (.087, 2-for-23)
Led N.L. in strikeouts (142) last season and had the 4th-lowest walk rate in the league (one BB every 24.3 PA). . . . Has struck out 451 times in the past three seasons, tying Steve Balboni for most in majors. . . . Also leads major-league second basemen in errors (73) during those three years; that's 14 more than the guy who gets all the pub, Steve Sax. . . . Has homered in every N.L. ballpark except the Astrodome (78 career AB). Didn't get one in Busch Stadium until last June 29, when he hit a 9th-inning grand slam off Todd Worrell to beat Cardinals. . . . 2-for-2 (1 2B, 1 HR) as a pinch-hitter last season. . . . Seven steals in seven attempts vs. Mets last season, one in five vs. Cubs.

Ryne Sandberg

Chicago Cubs — Bats Right

	AB	H	2B	3B	HR	RRF	BB	SO	BA	SA	OBA
Season	627	178	28	5	14	81	46	79	.284	.411	.330
vs. Left-Handers	159	42	4	1	4	23	12	15	.264	.377	.314
vs. Right-Handers	468	136	24	4	10	58	34	64	.291	.423	.335
Home	321	97	18	2	8	45	23	42	.302	.445	.344
Road	306	81	10	3	6	36	23	37	.265	.376	.315
Grass	445	125	22	2	11	56	35	59	.281	.413	.330
Artificial Turf	182	53	6	3	3	25	11	20	.291	.407	.330
April	81	20	4	1	2	9	6	12	.247	.395	.295
May	104	35	7	1	3	18	12	12	.337	.510	.395
June	116	30	4	1	3	20	4	10	.259	.388	.283
July	94	25	3	0	3	8	5	13	.266	.394	.300
August	110	32	4	0	2	8	8	15	.291	.382	.339
Sept./Oct.	122	36	6	2	1	18	11	17	.295	.402	.351
Leading Off Inn.	107	23	5	1	4	4	6	13	.215	.393	.257
Runners On	267	82	12	1	6	73	22	35	.307	.427	.353
Runners/Scor. Pos.	165	50	6	1	3	64	19	25	.303	.406	.363
Runners On/2 Out	97	24	4	0	3	30	11	14	.247	.381	.324
Scor. Pos./2 Out	74	21	4	0	2	28	9	11	.284	.419	.361
Late Inning Pressure	98	25	1	2	0	9	8	15	.255	.306	.308
Leading Off	20	2	0	0	0	0	3	4	.100	.100	.217
Runners On	39	9	1	1	0	9	5	9	.231	.308	.311
Runners/Scor. Pos.	24	6	1	1	0	9	5	6	.250	.375	.367

DRIVING IN RUNS	From 1B	From 2B	From 3B	Scoring Position
Totals	9/172	25/129	33/63	58/192
Percentage	5%	19%	52%	30%
Driving In Runners from 3B with Less than Two Out:			19/32	59%

Loves to face: Mark Davis (.455, 10-for-22)
Hates to face: Scott Garrelts (.125, 2-for-16)
Only major leaguer with 175+ hits who did not have a four-hit game last season. . . . Homered only once in last 48 games, but batted .301 during that span. . . . Batting .500 (12-for-24) with the bases loaded over the past three years; 18-for-50 in his career. . . . Has homered in every N.L. ballpark except the Astrodome (88 career AB). . . . Batting average with runners in scoring position (.303) was a career high. . . . Led major-league second basemen with a .994 fielding average last season. Committed five errors, but only one in his last 63 games. . . . Did not commit an error in 44 games on artificial fields last season, running his two-season streak to 65 games; last error on plastic: July 2, 1985.

Rafael Santana

New York Mets — Bats Right

	AB	H	2B	3B	HR	RRF	BB	SO	BA	SA	OBA
Season	394	86	11	0	1	33	36	43	.218	.254	.285
vs. Left-Handers	163	40	4	0	1	17	20	19	.245	.288	.328
vs. Right-Handers	231	46	7	0	0	16	16	24	.199	.229	.254
Home	191	36	6	0	0	16	21	25	.188	.220	.270
Road	203	50	5	0	1	17	15	18	.246	.286	.300
Grass	271	59	9	0	1	24	26	30	.218	.262	.289
Artificial Turf	123	27	2	0	0	9	10	13	.220	.236	.276
April	47	8	1	0	0	4	4	8	.170	.191	.226
May	38	6	2	0	0	4	2	7	.158	.211	.220
June	71	12	1	0	0	5	8	5	.169	.183	.253
July	60	12	0	0	0	7	7	7	.200	.200	.284
August	105	31	6	0	1	9	8	7	.295	.381	.351
Sept./Oct.	73	17	1	0	0	10	7	9	.233	.247	.296
Leading Off Inn.	86	15	2	0	0	0	5	11	.174	.198	.228
Runners On	170	38	4	0	1	33	24	12	.224	.265	.315
Runners/Scor. Pos.	90	17	2	0	0	31	19	10	.189	.211	.321
Runners On/2 Out	70	14	2	0	0	10	17	5	.200	.229	.356
Scor. Pos./2 Out	43	7	1	0	0	10	15	4	.163	.186	.379
Late Inning Pressure	55	7	3	0	0	2	3	8	.127	.182	.172
Leading Off	16	2	2	0	0	0	1		.125	.250	.176
Runners On	17	2	0	0	0	2	2	0	.118	.118	.211
Runners/Scor. Pos.	9	2	0	0	0	2	2	0	.222	.222	.364

DRIVING IN RUNS	From 1B	From 2B	From 3B	Scoring Position
Totals	3/135	10/67	19/43	29/110
Percentage	2%	15%	44%	26%
Driving In Runners from 3B with Less than Two Out:			15/23	65%

Loves to face: Bob Kipper (.500, 7-for-14)
Hates to face: Scott Sanderson (.063, 1-for-16)
Pound for pound, the best non–base stealer in baseball. Shares distinction of having fewest career stolen bases (one) of all nonpitchers active in 1986 with at least 1000 plate appearances. Fellow members: Steve Balboni, Chris Bando, Marc Hill, Clint Hurdle, Tim Laudner, five guys who average 213 pounds among them. Raffy, at 160, is in the lightweight division. . . . He's in one other select group: guys with at least 1000 plate appearances, and career slugging and on base averages below .300: Santana, Mike Fischlin, Jose Uribe and Curtis Wilkerson make up the entire active membership. . . . Batted .164 before All-Star break, .265 after the break; career averages: .218 before the break, .266 after.

Steve Sax
Los Angeles Dodgers — Bats Right

	AB	H	2B	3B	HR	RRF	BB	SO	BA	SA	OBA
Season	633	210	43	4	6	58	59	58	.332	.441	.390
vs. Left-Handers	225	74	20	1	3	21	18	17	.329	.467	.374
vs. Right-Handers	408	136	23	3	3	37	41	41	.333	.426	.398
Home	306	95	19	1	1	22	33	27	.310	.389	.377
Road	327	115	24	3	5	36	26	31	.352	.489	.402
Grass	447	138	27	4	4	37	51	43	.309	.414	.380
Artificial Turf	186	72	16	0	2	21	8	15	.387	.505	.413
April	66	22	2	0	1	4	7	8	.333	.409	.397
May	108	34	8	0	3	15	6	13	.315	.472	.345
June	113	36	8	2	0	9	16	11	.319	.425	.403
July	92	32	6	0	1	4	9	7	.348	.446	.412
August	121	33	8	0	0	9	7	10	.273	.339	.315
Sept./Oct.	133	53	11	2	1	17	14	9	.398	.534	.459
Leading Off Inn.	249	80	16	2	2	2	15	25	.321	.426	.365
Runners On	174	59	12	1	2	54	27	19	.339	.454	.422
Runners/Scor. Pos.	114	39	9	1	1	51	22	13	.342	.465	.439
Runners On/2 Out	71	22	5	0	0	21	17	9	.310	.380	.443
Scor. Pos./2 Out	55	17	4	0	0	20	15	6	.309	.382	.457
Late Inning Pressure	98	37	6	0	3	13	12	10	.378	.531	.445
Leading Off	35	14	3	0	0	0	3	4	.400	.486	.447
Runners On	35	11	1	0	2	12	8	5	.314	.514	.442
Runners/Scor. Pos.	23	7	1	0	1	10	7	5	.304	.478	.467

DRIVING IN RUNS	From 1B	From 2B	From 3B	Scoring Position
Totals	4/101	22/89	26/51	48/140
Percentage	4%	25%	51%	34%
Driving In Runners from 3B with Less than Two Out:	14/21		67%	

Loves to face: Zane Smith (.421, 8-for-19)
Hates to face: Eric Show (.083, 2-for-24)

Led N.L. with a .398 average after Sept. 1.... Reached base safely in each of his last 34 games last season, including a league-high 25-game hitting streak.... Set career-high marks in hits, batting average, home runs, and RBI to complement the best defensive season (.980 percentage) of his career...Raised his batting average against left-handed pitchers over 100 points from .215 in 1985.... Had 64 multiple-hit games last season, 2d most in N.L.... Career batting average at Shea Stadium (.189) is his lowest at any ballpark.... Career total of 161 at bats at Candlestick Park, most among active players without a home run there.... Career average of .311 in Late-Inning Pressure Situations.

Mike Schmidt
Philadelphia Phillies — Bats Right

	AB	H	2B	3B	HR	RRF	BB	SO	BA	SA	OBA
Season	552	160	29	1	37	125	89	84	.290	.547	.390
vs. Left-Handers	157	56	10	0	15	43	33	11	.357	.707	.474
vs. Right-Handers	395	104	19	1	22	82	56	73	.263	.484	.354
Home	258	77	17	0	20	67	46	43	.298	.597	.406
Road	294	83	12	1	17	58	43	41	.282	.503	.374
Grass	150	43	4	0	7	29	21	22	.287	.453	.378
Artificial Turf	402	117	25	1	30	96	68	62	.291	.582	.394
April	67	22	2	0	5	20	8	11	.328	.582	.385
May	87	24	7	0	3	18	13	17	.276	.460	.382
June	104	32	6	1	6	18	9	13	.308	.558	.386
July	90	22	1	0	8	24	16	13	.244	.522	.381
August	97	29	8	0	7	20	18	12	.299	.598	.410
Sept./Oct.	107	31	5	0	8	25	23	18	.290	.561	.396
Leading Off Inn.	142	39	8	1	10	10	12	16	.275	.556	.340
Runners On	265	81	12	0	21	108	56	47	.306	.589	.419
Runners/Scor. Pos.	162	51	6	0	12	86	48	37	.315	.574	.455
Runners On/2 Out	129	43	4	0	9	48	36	25	.333	.574	.482
Scor. Pos./2 Out	81	29	1	0	6	40	30	18	.358	.593	.532
Late Inning Pressure	91	26	4	0	5	13	15	14	.286	.495	.387
Leading Off	27	9	2	0	1	1	1	3	.333	.519	.357
Runners On	39	7	0	0	2	10	11	8	.179	.333	.360
Runners/Scor. Pos.	18	5	0	0	1	8	7	4	.278	.444	.480

DRIVING IN RUNS	From 1B	From 2B	From 3B	Scoring Position
Totals	22/166	34/121	31/69	65/190
Percentage	13%	28%	45%	34%
Driving In Runners from 3B with Less than Two Out:	19/31		61%	

Loves to face: Larry McWilliams (.356, 16-for-45, 7 HR)
Hates to face: Orel Hershiser (.111, 2-for-13)

Led league in home runs for the eighth time in his career, breaking the N.L. record he shared with Ralph Kiner. Led league in RBI for the 4th time, tying Hornsby and Aaron for N.L. record.... 30+ homers this season would tie Eddie Mathews's N.L. record of nine straight 30-homer seasons; amazing part is that Schmidt hit 31 in strike-shortened 1981.... Five home runs short of 500. Some 500th home run trivia: Jimmie Foxx had the longest wait between Nos. 499 and 500, 16 games. Ruth, Williams, Mays, Mathews, and Robinson each hit 499 and 500 in consecutive games. No one has hit them in the same game. Consider that a challenge, Mike, and best of luck.

Rick Schu
Philadelphia Phillies — Bats Right

	AB	H	2B	3B	HR	RRF	BB	SO	BA	SA	OBA
Season	208	57	10	1	8	25	18	44	.274	.447	.335
vs. Left-Handers	104	29	4	1	4	10	7	17	.279	.452	.330
vs. Right-Handers	104	28	6	0	4	15	11	27	.269	.442	.339
Home	100	27	7	1	1	10	9	25	.270	.390	.327
Road	108	30	3	0	7	15	9	19	.278	.500	.342
Grass	66	14	3	0	2	7	8	15	.212	.348	.303
Artificial Turf	142	43	7	1	6	18	10	29	.303	.493	.351
April	22	9	0	0	2	3	1	6	.409	.682	.435
May	77	16	4	0	1	3	8	20	.208	.299	.276
June	42	13	3	0	0	6	5	4	.310	.381	.396
July	21	8	1	0	1	3	0	2	.381	.571	.409
August	30	7	1	1	3	9	2	6	.233	.633	.281
Sept./Oct.	16	4	1	0	1	1	2	6	.250	.500	.333
Leading Off Inn.	36	10	1	0	1	1	3	5	.278	.389	.350
Runners On	106	25	6	1	4	21	9	25	.236	.425	.297
Runners/Scor. Pos.	53	10	3	0	2	16	7	15	.189	.358	.274
Runners On/2 Out	50	12	3	1	2	13	5	10	.240	.440	.321
Scor. Pos./2 Out	31	8	2	0	1	10	5	8	.258	.419	.361
Late Inning Pressure	34	5	0	0	1	2	2	7	.147	.235	.216
Leading Off	8	1	0	0	0	0	1	1	.125	.125	.222
Runners On	18	3	0	0	1	2	1	3	.167	.333	.250
Runners/Scor. Pos.	7	0	0	0	0	0	1	2	.000	.000	.125

DRIVING IN RUNS	From 1B	From 2B	From 3B	Scoring Position
Totals	3/82	6/42	8/23	14/65
Percentage	4%	14%	35%	22%
Driving In Runners from 3B with Less than Two Out:	4/7		57%	

Loves to face: Danny Cox (.500, 7-for-14)
Hates to face: Mike Krukow (.083, 1-for-12)

Grounded into only one double play in 47 opportunities (runner on first, less than two outs) last season, lowest rate in majors among players with 40+ opportunities.... Started 42 games last season (21 against each type of pitching), but only eight after the All-Star break.... Batted 152 points lower in Late-Inning Pressure Situations (.147) than in nonpressure situations (.299), 4th-largest difference in N.L. (minimum: 25 LIP AB).... Batted 78 points lower with runners on base than with bases empty, 6th-largest difference in N.L. (minimum: 100 AB each way).... Batted .241 (7 for 29) as a pinch-hitter. Last two pinch-hits were home runs.

Mike Scioscia
Los Angeles Dodgers — Bats Left

	AB	H	2B	3B	HR	RRF	BB	SO	BA	SA	OBA
Season	374	94	18	1	5	28	62	23	.251	.345	.359
vs. Left-Handers	107	25	2	0	2	7	18	7	.234	.308	.341
vs. Right-Handers	267	69	16	1	3	21	44	16	.258	.360	.366
Home	169	42	7	0	2	10	25	12	.249	.325	.350
Road	205	52	11	1	3	18	37	11	.254	.361	.366
Grass	277	70	14	0	5	19	47	21	.253	.357	.365
Artificial Turf	97	24	4	1	0	9	15	2	.247	.309	.342
April	64	18	4	0	2	6	13	10	.281	.438	.418
May	69	18	3	0	0	2	15	3	.261	.304	.400
June	25	7	2	0	0	2	5	0	.280	.360	.400
July	39	15	2	0	0	7	3	1	.385	.436	.409
August	81	18	4	1	1	6	16	5	.222	.333	.347
Sept./Oct.	96	18	3	0	2	5	10	4	.188	.281	.262
Leading Off Inn.	84	21	5	0	2	2	11	4	.250	.381	.337
Runners On	149	36	6	0	1	24	30	11	.242	.302	.361
Runners/Scor. Pos.	76	11	2	0	0	20	16	7	.145	.171	.281
Runners On/2 Out	56	11	2	0	1	8	12	5	.196	.286	.338
Scor. Pos./2 Out	33	3	0	0	0	6	6	3	.091	.091	.268
Late Inning Pressure	71	15	3	0	0	6	16	7	.211	.254	.352
Leading Off	18	3	1	0	0	0	4	1	.167	.222	.318
Runners On	29	7	1	0	0	6	9	3	.241	.276	.395
Runners/Scor. Pos.	12	5	1	0	0	6	6	3	.417	.500	.579

DRIVING IN RUNS	From 1B	From 2B	From 3B	Scoring Position
Totals	4/111	7/60	12/30	19/90
Percentage	4%	12%	40%	21%
Driving In Runners from 3B with Less than Two Out:	10/16		63%	

Loves to face: Lee Smith (.600, 6-for-10, 1 HR)
Hates to face: Jay Tibbs (.125, 2-for-16)

Dodgers jumped from last place to third in two weeks after Scioscia's return from the DL following the All-Star break.... One strikeout every 17.8 career plate appearances; among active N.L. players (minimum: 1000 PA), only Tony Gwynn, Greg Gross, and Ozzie Smith strike out less frequently.... One of three N.L. players with lower averages in Late-Inning Pressure situations than overall for last seven seasons. Others: Gary Matthews and Mario Soto.... Had batted higher with runners on base than with bases empty in six straight seasons until 1986.... Career breakdown: .281 on grass, .217 on artificial turf.... Six career homers at Dodger Stadium, 20 on the road.

Ozzie Smith
St. Louis Cardinals — Bats Left and Right

	AB	H	2B	3B	HR	RRF	BB	SO	BA	SA	OBA
Season	514	144	19	4	0	59	79	27	.280	.333	.376
vs. Left-Handers	203	56	8	0	0	16	31	9	.276	.315	.370
vs. Right-Handers	311	88	11	4	0	43	48	18	.283	.344	.380
Home	254	73	13	1	0	33	47	16	.287	.346	.400
Road	260	71	6	3	0	26	32	11	.273	.319	.352
Grass	126	28	3	2	0	12	14	6	.222	.278	.298
Artificial Turf	388	116	16	2	0	47	65	21	.299	.351	.400
April	58	18	3	0	0	6	8	5	.310	.362	.394
May	79	23	7	1	0	7	14	3	.291	.405	.404
June	100	30	1	1	0	13	16	4	.300	.330	.397
July	86	22	3	1	0	13	11	2	.256	.314	.337
August	93	18	3	0	0	8	14	8	.194	.226	.299
Sept./Oct.	98	33	2	1	0	12	16	5	.337	.378	.427
Leading Off Inn.	113	38	6	1	0	0	21	5	.336	.407	.440
Runners On	192	57	7	3	0	59	39	7	.297	.365	.415
Runners/Scor. Pos.	127	39	4	1	0	56	34	7	.307	.354	.452
Runners On/2 Out	69	16	1	2	0	21	19	3	.232	.304	.404
Scor. Pos./2 Out	57	14	1	1	0	20	18	3	.246	.298	.434
Late Inning Pressure	92	26	4	1	0	7	20	2	.283	.348	.411
Leading Off	30	10	3	1	0	0	8	0	.333	.500	.474
Runners On	31	7	0	0	0	7	10	1	.226	.226	.415
Runners/Scor. Pos.	22	6	0	0	0	7	8	1	.273	.273	.467

DRIVING IN RUNS	From 1B	From 2B	From 3B	Scoring Position
Totals	5/115	20/90	33/62	53/152
Percentage	4%	22%	53%	35%
Driving In Runners from 3B with Less than Two Out:			22/29	76%

Loves to face: Dan Schatzeder (.462, 12-for-26, 2 HR)
Hates to face: David Palmer (.040, 1-for-25)

Second shortstop to start All-Star Game in four consecutive years; other: Marty Marion (1943–47; no game in '45). ... Toughest to fan in N.L. last season: averaged one strikeout every 22.6 plate appearances. ... Six hits in eight at bats with bases loaded last season; has struck out only once in 105 bases-loaded plate appearances in his career; Steve Trout got him in 1985, in game in which Cards clinched division title. ... Leads active nonpitchers with 125 sacrifice bunts. ... Batted career-high .280 last season, but career average is only .247; lowest among Hall of Fame nonpitchers chosen for major-league playing ability is .253, by former catcher Ray Schalk.

Kurt Stillwell
Cincinnati Reds — Bats Left and Right

	AB	H	2B	3B	HR	RRF	BB	SO	BA	SA	OBA
Season	279	64	6	1	0	27	30	47	.229	.258	.309
vs. Left-Handers	86	21	3	0	0	8	16	14	.244	.279	.363
vs. Right-Handers	193	43	3	1	0	19	14	33	.223	.249	.282
Home	151	33	4	0	0	13	15	29	.219	.245	.298
Road	128	31	2	1	0	14	15	18	.242	.273	.322
Grass	99	21	1	0	0	9	11	12	.212	.222	.291
Artificial Turf	180	43	5	1	0	18	19	35	.239	.278	.318
April	21	6	0	0	0	1	2	6	.286	.286	.348
May	38	6	1	1	0	3	8	10	.158	.237	.304
June	43	6	0	0	0	1	5	11	.140	.140	.229
July	51	12	2	0	0	7	4	8	.235	.275	.291
August	69	18	2	0	0	7	8	6	.261	.290	.338
Sept./Oct.	57	16	1	0	0	8	3	6	.281	.298	.339
Leading Off Inn.	72	11	2	0	0	0	8	18	.153	.181	.256
Runners On	119	30	2	1	0	27	10	16	.252	.286	.310
Runners/Scor. Pos.	78	23	1	1	0	27	8	9	.295	.333	.360
Runners On/2 Out	49	12	1	0	0	14	7	9	.245	.265	.339
Scor. Pos./2 Out	39	11	1	0	0	14	5	5	.282	.308	.364
Late Inning Pressure	48	10	1	0	0	8	6	11	.208	.229	.296
Leading Off	12	0	0	0	0	0	3	4	.000	.000	.200
Runners On	24	8	1	0	0	8	0	2	.333	.375	.333
Runners/Scor. Pos.	20	8	1	0	0	8	0	2	.400	.450	.400

DRIVING IN RUNS	From 1B	From 2B	From 3B	Scoring Position
Totals	1/73	13/61	13/32	26/93
Percentage	1%	21%	41%	28%
Driving In Runners from 3B with Less than Two Out:			6/16	38%

Loves to face: Orel Hershiser (.500, 3-for-6)
Hates to face: Jay Tibbs (0-for-10)

Had eight game-winning RBI last season, tying Will Clark for the most among N.L. rookies. ... Committed 14 errors after the All-Star break, 2d most in N.L. ... Played regularly at shortstop after Concepcion was injured, but of Reds' last 46 games, fellow rookie Barry Larkin started 34, and Stillwell only 12. ... Lowest fielding percentage of any N.L. shortstop (minimum: 80 games). ... Four hits in 11 at bats with the bases loaded. ... Spent most of the summer as the youngest player in N.L.; Cubs' Greg Maddux, 10 months younger, succeeded to the title when he was called up in September. ... Born June 4, 1965; by then, Pete Rose had 368 career hits.

Jeff Stone
Philadelphia Phillies — Bats Left

	AB	H	2B	3B	HR	RRF	BB	SO	BA	SA	OBA
Season	249	69	6	4	6	20	20	52	.277	.406	.341
vs. Left-Handers	63	20	2	1	2	2	5	10	.317	.476	.377
vs. Right-Handers	186	49	4	3	4	18	15	42	.263	.382	.328
Home	113	36	2	2	4	12	7	21	.319	.478	.369
Road	136	33	4	2	2	8	13	31	.243	.346	.318
Grass	77	19	3	0	2	4	5	20	.247	.364	.301
Artificial Turf	172	50	3	4	4	16	15	32	.291	.424	.358
April	0	0	0	0	0	0	0	0	—	—	—
May	32	7	0	0	0	2	1	10	.219	.219	.242
June	87	23	1	1	2	6	9	16	.264	.368	.340
July	49	11	3	1	1	5	4	9	.224	.388	.296
August	63	22	2	2	3	5	4	11	.349	.587	.406
Sept./Oct.	18	6	0	0	0	2	2	6	.333	.333	.400
Leading Off Inn.	90	19	2	0	1	1	9	21	.211	.267	.283
Runners On	74	21	3	1	2	16	5	19	.284	.432	.338
Runners/Scor. Pos.	45	10	1	0	1	13	3	15	.222	.311	.286
Runners On/2 Out	28	7	1	1	2	6	2	10	.250	.571	.300
Scor. Pos./2 Out	18	2	0	0	1	3	1	8	.111	.278	.158
Late Inning Pressure	43	12	1	0	2	6	3	10	.279	.442	.326
Leading Off	14	2	0	0	0	0	1	3	.143	.143	.200
Runners On	11	3	0	0	1	5	1	4	.273	.545	.333
Runners/Scor. Pos.	7	1	0	0	0	3	1	3	.143	.143	.250

DRIVING IN RUNS	From 1B	From 2B	From 3B	Scoring Position
Totals	2/41	7/37	5/15	12/52
Percentage	5%	19%	33%	23%
Driving In Runners from 3B with Less than Two Out:			5/12	42%

Loves to face: Scott Garrelts (3-for-3, 1 HR)
Hates to face: Orel Hershiser (0-for-17, 5 SO)

Rodney Dangerfield Award Winner: only active major leaguer who has played in 150+ games with career batting average over .290, but who has never received an intentional walk. ... Reason for award? Maybe opponents are hip to his lack of clutch hits. Has career rate of driving in only 20.5 percent of runners in scoring position when he bats. ... Committed only two errors last season, and they came in successive games, June 2–3. ... Hitless in nine career at bats with the bases loaded. ... Career batting average of .331 at Veterans Stadium, .262 in road games. ...Batted .341 in 11 starts vs. left-handers last season; career average vs. lefties is .322; vs. righties, .293.

Darryl Strawberry
New York Mets — Bats Left

	AB	H	2B	3B	HR	RRF	BB	SO	BA	SA	OBA
Season	475	123	27	5	27	99	72	141	.259	.507	.358
vs. Left-Handers	187	39	8	2	5	30	21	65	.209	.353	.296
vs. Right-Handers	288	84	19	3	22	69	51	76	.292	.608	.396
Home	211	48	11	1	11	39	30	69	.227	.445	.324
Road	264	75	16	4	16	60	42	72	.284	.557	.385
Grass	309	82	18	1	18	66	46	94	.265	.505	.362
Artificial Turf	166	41	9	4	9	33	26	47	.247	.512	.350
April	64	20	6	0	3	14	10	15	.313	.547	.400
May	77	16	4	1	3	13	12	24	.208	.403	.319
June	71	25	7	1	4	13	16	16	.352	.648	.466
July	87	24	7	1	6	20	12	31	.276	.586	.363
August	91	16	1	1	3	17	11	29	.176	.308	.276
Sept./Oct.	85	22	2	1	8	22	11	26	.259	.588	.347
Leading Off Inn.	105	23	4	2	7	20	21	30	.219	.495	.344
Runners On	240	70	12	3	14	86	38	76	.292	.542	.383
Runners/Scor. Pos.	134	35	5	1	6	64	30	47	.261	.448	.386
Runners On/2 Out	120	33	6	3	5	34	25	36	.275	.500	.408
Scor. Pos./2 Out	73	15	2	1	3	25	19	24	.205	.384	.383
Late Inning Pressure	74	20	3	1	4	16	6	25	.270	.500	.325
Leading Off	15	3	0	0	1	1	0	2	.200	.400	.200
Runners On	43	13	1	1	3	15	4	13	.302	.581	.347
Runners/Scor. Pos.	18	8	1	1	2	13	3	7	.444	.944	.478

DRIVING IN RUNS	From 1B	From 2B	From 3B	Scoring Position
Totals	17/201	25/102	28/71	53/173
Percentage	8%	25%	39%	31%
Driving In Runners from 3B with Less than Two Out:			20/37	54%

Loves to face: Bob Forsch (.444, 8-for-18, 5 HR)
Hates to face: Mike Krukow (.048, 1-for-21, 9 SO)

Only player to total at least 100 home runs and 100 stolen bases over the last four seasons. Kirk Gibson missed by a single homer. ... Led N.L. with 60 RBI in road games. ... First N.L. player to start All-Star Game in each of first three full seasons. ... Grounded into only four double plays in 117 opportunities last season, 5th-lowest rate in N.L. (minimum: 40 opportunities). ... Had only one hit in his last 36 regular-season at bats vs. lefties at Shea Stadium, but took Knepper deep in playoffs. ... Struck out 65 times vs. left-handed pitchers last season, 4th-highest total by anyone over last 12 years, but highest by anyone not named Reggie Jackson (79, 75, and 69 in 1978, 1982, and 1980).

Franklin Stubbs
Los Angeles Dodgers — Bats Left

	AB	H	2B	3B	HR	RRF	BB	SO	BA	SA	OBA
Season	420	95	11	1	23	58	37	107	.226	.421	.291
vs. Left-Handers	97	22	3	0	4	10	3	16	.227	.381	.250
vs. Right-Handers	323	73	8	1	19	48	34	91	.226	.433	.302
Home	195	51	5	1	12	33	17	48	.262	.482	.318
Road	225	44	6	0	11	25	20	59	.196	.369	.267
Grass	296	64	7	1	15	41	27	81	.216	.399	.280
Artificial Turf	124	31	4	0	8	17	10	26	.250	.476	.316
April	52	9	0	0	4	10	4	25	.173	.404	.228
May	46	12	2	1	2	7	4	12	.261	.478	.327
June	100	31	2	0	9	17	12	17	.310	.600	.384
July	70	17	3	0	4	12	3	15	.243	.457	.284
August	81	13	0	0	2	2	6	22	.160	.235	.218
Sept./Oct.	71	13	4	0	2	10	8	16	.183	.324	.266
Leading Off Inn.	89	22	3	0	6	6	3	11	.247	.483	.272
Runners On	187	42	5	1	8	43	28	60	.225	.390	.326
Runners/Scor. Pos.	111	20	3	1	4	35	21	37	.180	.333	.311
Runners On/2 Out	85	14	1	1	3	17	10	31	.165	.306	.253
Scor. Pos./2 Out	59	9	1	1	2	15	7	23	.153	.305	.242
Late Inning Pressure	57	16	1	1	3	8	9	11	.281	.491	.388
Leading Off	20	6	1	0	2	2	0	2	.300	.650	.300
Runners On	22	7	0	1	1	6	8	8	.318	.545	.516
Runners/Scor. Pos.	13	4	0	1	1	6	4	5	.308	.692	.500

DRIVING IN RUNS

	From 1B	From 2B	From 3B	Scoring Position
Totals	7/130	14/84	14/46	28/130
Percentage	5%	17%	30%	22%

Driving In Runners from 3B with Less than Two Out: 11/21 — 52%

Loves to face: Bryn Smith (.500, 5-for-10, 3 HR)
Hates to face: Ron Darling (.071, 1-for-14, 9 SO)

.215 career batting average vs. right-handers; same vs. left-handers, but with significant power disparity: one home run every 19.3 at bats vs. righties, every 28.8 vs. lefties. . . . Will apparently have a good shot at first base with Brock traded to Milwaukee; good thing: He was 0-for-12 as a pinch-hitter last season, 6-for-41 in his career. . . . Started in every batting order position except the first and ninth spots last season. . . . Career batting average of .063 (2-for-32) at Candlestick Park. . . . Homered vs. every N.L. club except New York last season (26 AB). . . . Batting average of .160 in August was 3d lowest in N.L. (minimum: 50 AB); failed to drive in a run in 17 consecutive games, Aug. 5–24.

Garry Templeton
San Diego Padres — Bats Left and Right

	AB	H	2B	3B	HR	RRF	BB	SO	BA	SA	OBA
Season	510	126	21	2	2	44	35	86	.247	.308	.296
vs. Left-Handers	175	45	7	1	2	14	17	28	.257	.343	.323
vs. Right-Handers	335	81	14	1	0	30	18	58	.242	.290	.281
Home	269	62	10	2	1	24	20	54	.230	.294	.284
Road	241	64	11	0	1	20	15	32	.266	.324	.309
Grass	380	92	14	2	1	32	30	71	.242	.297	.298
Artificial Turf	130	34	7	0	1	12	5	15	.262	.338	.289
April	75	16	0	0	0	2	7	17	.213	.213	.280
May	93	17	2	0	0	3	3	12	.183	.204	.208
June	87	26	2	1	2	17	9	14	.299	.414	.365
July	91	18	5	0	0	8	4	21	.198	.253	.227
August	98	27	7	1	0	10	5	12	.276	.367	.317
Sept./Oct.	66	22	5	0	0	4	7	10	.333	.409	.397
Leading Off Inn.	127	32	5	0	0	2	0	18	.252	.291	.264
Runners On	211	51	9	2	1	43	27	41	.242	.318	.328
Runners/Scor. Pos.	120	31	8	1	1	42	25	22	.258	.367	.381
Runners On/2 Out	92	22	3	0	0	16	16	18	.239	.272	.358
Scor. Pos./2 Out	59	15	2	0	0	16	16	10	.254	.288	.413
Late Inning Pressure	108	35	6	0	0	13	8	21	.324	.380	.371
Leading Off	30	9	2	0	0	0	1	7	.300	.367	.323
Runners On	48	15	3	0	0	13	5	7	.313	.375	.397
Runners/Scor. Pos.	29	11	2	0	0	13	5	3	.379	.448	.471

DRIVING IN RUNS

	From 1B	From 2B	From 3B	Scoring Position
Totals	2/124	19/89	20/49	39/138
Percentage	2%	21%	41%	28%

Driving In Runners from 3B with Less than Two Out: 12/24 — 50%

Loves to face: Craig McMurtry (.591, 13-for-22, 1 HR)
Hates to face: Ken Dayley (.071, 1-for-14)

Which slugger has received the most intentional walks in majors over past three years? Parker has 50; Durham, 51; Brett, 55. Those guys pale compared to Tarzan Templeton, who leads the majors with 68; those other fellows are the only others over 50. Fifty-three of those walks have occurred while T.T. was in the eight spot in the lineup. . . . Career breakdown: .310 with runners on base, .267 with bases empty. . . . Career walk rate is one every 23 plate appearances; only one walk in 101 times up with bases loaded. . . . Four hits in last six at bats as pinch-hitter last season, after going 1-for-26 in career in that role before then. . . . Fielding average of .953 with 15 errors through June 30; .981 with five errors after July 1.

Tim Teufel
New York Mets — Bats Right

	AB	H	2B	3B	HR	RRF	BB	SO	BA	SA	OBA
Season	279	69	20	1	4	32	32	42	.247	.369	.324
vs. Left-Handers	196	48	14	1	3	22	22	22	.245	.372	.318
vs. Right-Handers	83	21	6	0	1	10	10	20	.253	.361	.337
Home	140	33	10	0	2	17	16	27	.236	.350	.308
Road	139	36	10	1	2	15	16	15	.259	.388	.340
Grass	194	47	11	0	3	23	24	34	.242	.345	.321
Artificial Turf	85	22	9	1	1	9	8	8	.259	.424	.330
April	39	9	4	0	1	7	4	9	.231	.410	.311
May	53	11	1	0	0	4	8	7	.208	.226	.311
June	39	12	4	1	1	9	0	4	.308	.538	.300
July	37	8	3	0	0	2	5	6	.216	.297	.310
August	57	18	3	0	2	7	8	6	.316	.474	.394
Sept./Oct.	54	11	5	0	0	3	7	10	.204	.296	.295
Leading Off Inn.	43	9	5	0	0	0	5	5	.209	.326	.292
Runners On	129	39	12	1	2	30	14	11	.302	.457	.363
Runners/Scor. Pos.	77	18	6	0	1	27	13	8	.234	.351	.333
Runners On/2 Out	51	16	4	1	1	12	6	5	.294	.471	.350
Scor. Pos./2 Out	34	8	2	0	0	9	6	4	.235	.294	.350
Late Inning Pressure	44	12	4	0	1	9	5	8	.273	.432	.347
Leading Off	5	0	0	0	0	0	1	0	.000	.000	.167
Runners On	26	11	4	0	1	9	3	3	.423	.692	.483
Runners/Scor. Pos.	17	5	2	0	1	9	3	3	.294	.588	.400

DRIVING IN RUNS

	From 1B	From 2B	From 3B	Scoring Position
Totals	4/89	12/65	12/30	24/95
Percentage	4%	18%	40%	25%

Driving In Runners from 3B with Less than Two Out: 9/16 — 56%

Loves to face: Storm Davis (.417, 5-for-12)
Hates to face: Jamie Moyer (.091, 1-for-11)

Game-winning home run off Tom Hume on June 10 was only the 8th pinch-hit, extra-inning grand slam homer in major-league history. Others: Rogers Hornsby, 1931; Harvey Hendrick, 1933; Frank Secory, 1946; Steve Souchock (only A.L. player), 1952; Rick Joseph, 1967; Roger Freed, 1979; and Mike Vail, 1979. . . . Started 60 of 62 games in which Mets faced a left-handed starter, but only 10 of 100 (eight in May while Backman was hurt, two in September) against right-handers. However, has higher career average vs. right-handed pitchers (.266) than against lefties (.254). . . . Fielding average at second base has declined in each of his seasons in majors: .990, .984, .980, .971.

Andres Thomas
Atlanta Braves — Bats Right

	AB	H	2B	3B	HR	RRF	BB	SO	BA	SA	OBA
Season	323	81	17	2	6	34	8	49	.251	.372	.267
vs. Left-Handers	139	37	9	1	2	10	1	17	.266	.388	.271
vs. Right-Handers	184	44	8	1	4	24	7	32	.239	.359	.264
Home	135	27	5	1	1	11	6	16	.200	.274	.231
Road	188	54	12	1	5	23	2	33	.287	.441	.295
Grass	220	46	6	1	1	17	7	33	.209	.259	.231
Artificial Turf	103	35	11	1	5	17	1	16	.340	.612	.346
April	14	4	2	0	0	2	1	0	.286	.429	.333
May	51	17	5	0	1	6	2	8	.333	.490	.358
June	56	15	1	1	3	6	0	5	.268	.482	.268
July	79	25	7	1	2	12	3	15	.316	.506	.337
August	47	7	1	0	0	3	1	10	.149	.170	.163
Sept./Oct.	76	13	1	0	0	5	1	11	.171	.184	.182
Leading Off Inn.	63	16	4	0	2	2	0	10	.254	.413	.254
Runners On	148	38	8	0	2	29	5	16	.257	.351	.277
Runners/Scor. Pos.	82	19	7	0	1	26	5	9	.232	.354	.270
Runners On/2 Out	57	18	7	0	1	16	3	11	.316	.491	.350
Scor. Pos./2 Out	41	13	6	0	1	15	3	7	.317	.537	.364
Late Inning Pressure	50	12	2	0	1	7	4	9	.240	.340	.296
Leading Off	14	4	0	0	0	0	0	3	.286	.286	.286
Runners On	24	7	1	0	0	7	2	3	.292	.458	.346
Runners/Scor. Pos.	14	4	1	0	0	5	2	3	.286	.357	.375

DRIVING IN RUNS

	From 1B	From 2B	From 3B	Scoring Position
Totals	4/112	12/68	10/32	22/100
Percentage	4%	18%	31%	22%

Driving In Runners from 3B with Less than Two Out: 7/17 — 41%

Loves to face: Bruce Ruffin (.500, 4-for-8)
Hates to face: Greg Mathews (0-for-6)

Led major-league shortstops with an average of 3.65 assists per nine innings (minimum: 500 innings). . . . All Braves infielders were helped by fact that worm-killing Atlanta staff had ground outs-to-air outs ratio of 1.78 last season, the highest by any pitching staff over last 12 years. . . . Eight walks in 335 plate appearances gave him the lowest rate in N.L. (minimum: 300 PA), one walk every 41.9 times up; did not walk twice in a game, and two of the eight were intentional. . . . Did not hit a home run in his final 48 games after homering in back-to-back games July 18 and 19. . . . Leading hitter among N.L. visitors at Veterans Stadium last season (.519, 14-for-27, seven doubles), but hitless in 19 at bats vs. Cardinals.

Milt Thompson
Philadelphia Phillies — Bats Left

	AB	H	2B	3B	HR	RRF	BB	SO	BA	SA	OBA
Season	299	75	7	1	6	24	26	62	.251	.341	.311
vs. Left-Handers	50	11	1	0	0	3	3	13	.220	.240	.264
vs. Right-Handers	249	64	6	1	6	21	23	49	.257	.361	.320
Home	154	42	4	1	4	13	14	33	.273	.390	.331
Road	145	33	3	0	2	11	12	29	.228	.290	.289
Grass	85	19	2	0	2	6	6	19	.224	.318	.280
Artificial Turf	214	56	5	1	4	18	20	43	.262	.350	.323
April	62	12	1	0	1	4	5	13	.194	.258	.250
May	81	16	2	0	1	4	4	17	.198	.259	.244
June	21	6	0	0	1	5	2	3	.286	.429	.348
July	0	0	0	0	0	0	0	0			
August	53	16	2	1	0	5	2	12	.302	.377	.321
Sept./Oct.	82	25	2	0	3	6	13	17	.305	.439	.400
Leading Off Inn.	88	21	1	0	1	1	8	15	.239	.284	.302
Runners On	101	28	3	1	1	19	9	23	.277	.356	.336
Runners/Scor. Pos.	59	17	2	0	1	18	5	17	.288	.373	.343
Runners On/2 Out	42	13	0	0	1	6	3	6	.310	.381	.370
Scor. Pos./2 Out	26	8	0	0	1	6	1	5	.308	.423	.357
Late Inning Pressure	46	12	1	0	0	4	5	16	.261	.283	.333
Leading Off	11	1	0	0	0	0	1	2	.091	.091	.167
Runners On	22	8	0	0	0	4	2	9	.364	.364	.417
Runners/Scor. Pos.	13	5	0	0	0	4	1	7	.385	.385	.429

DRIVING IN RUNS	From 1B	From 2B	From 3B	Scoring Position
Totals	1/64	8/52	9/20	17/72
Percentage	2%	15%	45%	24%
Driving In Runners from 3B with Less than Two Out:		8/10	80%	

Loves to face: Andy Hawkins (.438, 7-for-16)
Hates to face: Orel Hershiser (.077, 1-for-13, 5 SO)
Averaged 2.95 putouts per nine innings in center field, highest in N.L. among center fielders who led their teams in games there.... Starting center fielder in 34 of Phillies' first 43 games, but was removed from lineup on May 31, batting .196; started two games in June, and was sent to Portland July 1.... Recalled on Aug. 15, he did not fail to hit safely in more than two consecutive games the rest of the way, batting .304.... Batted .213 in day games, .272 in night games.... Career batting average of .320 in Late-Inning Pressure Situations, .266 in nonpressure situations.... Career breakdown: .173 vs. left-handers (with one extra-base hit, a double, in 81 at bats), .257 vs. right-handers.

Rob Thompson
San Francisco Giants — Bats Right

	AB	H	2B	3B	HR	RRF	BB	SO	BA	SA	OBA
Season	549	149	27	3	7	51	42	112	.271	.370	.328
vs. Left-Handers	168	48	10	1	3	15	14	33	.286	.411	.342
vs. Right-Handers	381	101	17	2	4	36	28	79	.265	.352	.321
Home	255	75	17	2	4	30	26	43	.294	.424	.363
Road	294	74	10	1	3	21	16	69	.252	.323	.296
Grass	395	116	22	3	7	42	38	75	.294	.418	.361
Artificial Turf	154	33	5	0	0	9	4	37	.214	.247	.238
April	78	19	5	0	0	9	10	17	.244	.308	.337
May	82	25	5	0	2	9	6	15	.305	.439	.348
June	98	24	3	0	1	9	7	15	.245	.306	.292
July	93	26	5	2	1	9	7	27	.280	.409	.350
August	115	31	5	0	2	8	5	20	.270	.365	.300
Sept./Oct.	83	24	4	1	1	7	7	18	.289	.398	.352
Leading Off Inn.	110	33	7	0	3	3	10	21	.300	.445	.364
Runners On	212	54	8	2	2	46	23	55	.255	.340	.328
Runners/Scor. Pos.	124	30	3	1	1	40	18	27	.242	.306	.338
Runners On/2 Out	74	17	3	0	1	15	12	15	.230	.311	.345
Scor. Pos./2 Out	51	11	2	0	0	12	6	13	.216	.255	.333
Late Inning Pressure	96	27	3	0	2	7	6	17	.281	.375	.324
Leading Off	25	11	2	0	1	1	1	3	.440	.640	.462
Runners On	31	9	0	0	0	5	4	2	.290	.290	.371
Runners/Scor. Pos.	20	6	0	0	0	5	2	2	.300	.300	.364

DRIVING IN RUNS	From 1B	From 2B	From 3B	Scoring Position
Totals	7/127	12/93	24/54	36/147
Percentage	5%	13%	44%	24%
Driving In Runners from 3B with Less than Two Out:		18/33	55%	

Loves to face: Doyle Alexander (.818, 9-for-11, 1 HR)
Hates to face: John Denny (0-for-14, 7 SO)
Led N.L. rookies in games (149), at bats (549), runs (73), hits (149), total bases (203), and sacrifice bunts (18).... Had his share of embarrassing moments, too: combined with Jose Uribe to let a 9th-inning popup fall in game vs. Mets, turning a win into a loss; had three errors in a game vs. St. Louis; and set a major league record by being caught stealing four times in an extra-inning game.... Only N.L. player with 10+ stolen bases who was caught more times (15) than he succeeded (12); Gary Gaetti was the only one in the A.L. (14 SB, 15 CS).... Will he be the man to end this schneid? No Giants' second baseman has been chosen for the All-Star Game since Davey Williams in 1953.

Dickie Thon
Houston Astros — Bats Right

	AB	H	2B	3B	HR	RRF	BB	SO	BA	SA	OBA
Season	278	69	13	1	3	23	29	49	.248	.335	.318
vs. Left-Handers	177	43	6	1	1	10	20	26	.243	.305	.318
vs. Right-Handers	101	26	7	0	2	13	9	23	.257	.386	.318
Home	148	37	9	1	0	10	16	26	.250	.324	.321
Road	130	32	4	0	3	13	13	23	.246	.346	.315
Grass	69	14	0	0	2	6	8	17	.203	.290	.286
Artificial Turf	209	55	13	1	1	17	21	32	.263	.349	.329
April	49	12	5	0	0	6	6	11	.245	.347	.327
May	56	12	3	1	1	5	6	9	.214	.357	.286
June	30	7	1	0	0	1	2	6	.233	.267	.281
July	46	13	2	0	0	2	3	3	.283	.326	.327
August	40	8	0	0	1	5	5	7	.200	.275	.289
Sept./Oct.	57	17	2	0	1	4	7	13	.298	.386	.375
Leading Off Inn.	66	23	3	0	1	1	5	9	.348	.439	.394
Runners On	117	23	5	1	1	21	17	22	.197	.282	.296
Runners/Scor. Pos.	66	14	4	1	1	20	12	11	.212	.348	.329
Runners On/2 Out	48	9	4	0	1	11	10	6	.188	.333	.328
Scor. Pos./2 Out	32	6	3	0	1	10	9	4	.188	.375	.366
Late Inning Pressure	33	14	0	0	2	4	6	7	.424	.606	.513
Leading Off	13	6	0	0	1	1	1	2	.462	.692	.500
Runners On	10	3	0	0	0	2	3	2	.300	.300	.462
Runners/Scor. Pos.	6	1	0	0	0	2	2	2	.167	.167	.375

DRIVING IN RUNS	From 1B	From 2B	From 3B	Scoring Position
Totals	2/84	8/53	10/24	18/77
Percentage	2%	15%	42%	23%
Driving In Runners from 3B with Less than Two Out:		6/11	55%	

Loves to face: Bob Forsch (.476, 10-for-21, 2 HR)
Hates to face: Mario Soto (.100, 2-for-20)
Strikeout frequency: pre-injury, once every 9.6 plate appearances; since injury, once every 5.9.... Averaged only 2.68 assists per nine innings, worst among N.L. shortstops (minimum: 500 innings).... Batted 200 points higher in Late-Inning Pressure Situations (.424) than in non-pressure situations (.224), largest difference in N.L. (minimum: 25 LIP AB).... Batted 89 points lower with runners on base than with bases empty, 3d-largest difference in N.L. (minimum: 100 AB each way).... Has not been hit by a pitch since he suffered his eye injury the opening week of the 1984 season; Houston's other shortstop, Craig Reynolds, hasn't been hit since 1982.

Alex Trevino
Los Angeles Dodgers — Bats Right

	AB	H	2B	3B	HR	RRF	BB	SO	BA	SA	OBA
Season	202	53	13	0	4	28	27	35	.262	.386	.351
vs. Left-Handers	125	29	6	0	2	13	14	25	.232	.328	.309
vs. Right-Handers	77	24	7	0	2	15	13	10	.312	.481	.413
Home	112	30	7	0	2	17	8	23	.268	.384	.314
Road	90	23	6	0	2	11	19	12	.256	.389	.391
Grass	148	40	7	0	4	24	19	26	.270	.399	.355
Artificial Turf	54	13	6	0	0	4	8	9	.241	.352	.339
April	13	3	1	0	0	0	1	1	.231	.308	.286
May	22	5	0	0	0	2	2	6	.227	.227	.292
June	62	19	5	0	3	7	13	12	.306	.532	.427
July	48	12	3	0	0	8	7	9	.250	.313	.339
August	27	5	3	0	0	3	3	4	.185	.407	.267
Sept./Oct.	30	9	1	0	1	8	1	3	.300	.333	.344
Leading Off Inn.	38	15	3	0	2	2	5	5	.395	.632	.465
Runners On	94	24	6	0	2	24	11	15	.255	.319	.336
Runners/Scor. Pos.	59	15	5	0	0	23	9	9	.254	.339	.357
Runners On/2 Out	31	11	5	0	0	12	7	4	.355	.516	.474
Scor. Pos./2 Out	23	8	4	0	0	11	6	2	.348	.522	.483
Late Inning Pressure	47	14	4	0	1	9	4	6	.298	.447	.358
Leading Off	9	4	1	0	0	0	1	1	.444	.556	.500
Runners On	23	6	2	0	0	8	2	3	.261	.348	.333
Runners/Scor. Pos.	17	5	2	0	0	8	2	2	.294	.412	.381

DRIVING IN RUNS	From 1B	From 2B	From 3B	Scoring Position
Totals	5/67	12/49	7/20	19/69
Percentage	7%	24%	35%	28%
Driving In Runners from 3B with Less than Two Out:		4/12	33%	

Loves to face: Ted Power (.600, 6-for-10)
Hates to face: Bob Welch (.100, 3-for-30)
Committed 11 errors in just 63 games as catcher last season; 10 of them came on wild throws to second base on stolen-base attempts.... Drove in 21 runs in the 50 games that he started behind the plate; in 108 starts, Mike Scioscia contributed only 26 RBI. As a team, Dodgers and Giants had the fewest RBI from their starting catchers, 49 apiece (Jack Fimple had the other two for L.A.).... Reached base safely in each of his last 17 games started.... Career batting average of .372 with the bases loaded.... Played one-third of inning at first base last season, the 7th position he has played in majors; he hasn't pitched or played center field.

Jose Uribe

San Francisco Giants

	AB	H	2B	3B	HR	RRF	BB	SO	BA	SA	OBA
Season	453	101	15	1	3	47	61	76	.223	.280	.315
vs. Left-Handers	145	31	7	0	3	19	15	33	.214	.324	.288
vs. Right-Handers	308	70	8	1	0	28	46	43	.227	.260	.328
Home	219	48	7	0	1	19	37	35	.219	.265	.332
Road	234	53	8	1	2	28	24	41	.226	.295	.298
Grass	337	79	10	0	2	36	50	53	.234	.282	.333
Artificial Turf	116	22	5	1	1	11	11	23	.190	.276	.260
April	62	16	2	0	0	6	6	11	.258	.290	.324
May	84	22	5	0	0	14	10	15	.262	.321	.340
June	94	19	0	0	1	5	9	7	.202	.234	.272
July	73	14	2	0	2	6	11	9	.192	.301	.298
August	68	13	4	1	0	7	7	20	.191	.279	.267
Sept./Oct.	72	17	2	0	0	9	18	14	.236	.264	.389
Leading Off Inn.	112	28	3	0	1	1	15	14	.250	.304	.339
Runners On	196	49	10	1	1	45	28	33	.250	.327	.344
Runners/Scor. Pos.	114	33	8	1	0	42	27	22	.289	.377	.426
Runners On/2 Out	87	19	1	1	0	18	21	17	.218	.253	.370
Scor. Pos./2 Out	47	15	1	1	0	18	21	11	.319	.383	.529
Late Inning Pressure	48	9	1	0	0	2	10	9	.188	.208	.328
Leading Off	15	4	1	0	0	0	7	5	.267	.333	.500
Runners On	16	3	0	0	0	2	1	4	.188	.188	.235
Runners/Scor. Pos.	9	2	0	0	0	2	1	3	.222	.222	.300

DRIVING IN RUNS	From 1B	From 2B	From 3B	Scoring Position
Totals	5/134	22/93	17/42	39/135
Percentage	4%	24%	40%	29%
Driving In Runners from 3B with Less than Two Out:			10/23	43%

Loves to face: Rick Mahler (.500, 8-for-16)

Hates to face: Fernando Valenzuela (.053, 1-for-19, 8 SO)

Most plate appearances (1050) of any active player without a sacrifice fly. That's part of his low career rate of driving in runners from third with less than two outs (41 percent, 17-of-41). . . . Career breakdown: .211 with bases empty, .256 with runners on base, .279 with runners in scoring position. . . . Grounded into two double plays in 77 opportunities last season, 3d-lowest rate in majors (minimum: 40 opps.). . . . Was walked intentionally 19 times last season, all while batting 8th. That's the most intentional walks in one season by a player with a slugging average below .300 since baseball started tracking intentional walks in 1955; old mark is 15 by Fred Patek in 1969.

Andy Van Slyke

St. Louis Cardinals   Bats Left

	AB	H	2B	3B	HR	RRF	BB	SO	BA	SA	OBA
Season	418	113	23	7	13	63	47	85	.270	.452	.343
vs. Left-Handers	116	24	6	4	1	13	14	26	.207	.353	.290
vs. Right-Handers	302	89	17	3	12	50	33	59	.295	.490	.364
Home	211	59	11	6	6	41	30	39	.280	.474	.365
Road	207	54	12	1	7	22	17	46	.261	.430	.320
Grass	112	29	5	1	3	8	10	25	.259	.402	.320
Artificial Turf	306	84	18	6	10	55	37	60	.275	.471	.352
April	40	9	1	0	0	6	6	11	.225	.250	.326
May	66	16	3	0	2	10	7	9	.242	.379	.315
June	75	16	1	3	2	9	9	15	.213	.387	.298
July	60	20	2	2	1	11	9	13	.333	.533	.414
August	65	23	10	1	2	11	7	10	.354	.631	.419
Sept./Oct.	112	29	6	1	5	16	9	27	.259	.464	.311
Leading Off Inn.	103	31	8	2	7	7	8	18	.301	.621	.351
Runners On	192	55	10	3	6	56	28	39	.286	.464	.375
Runners/Scor. Pos.	111	31	6	2	3	46	16	28	.279	.450	.366
Runners On/2 Out	72	24	3	2	2	21	17	15	.333	.514	.461
Scor. Pos./2 Out	44	13	2	1	1	17	12	10	.295	.455	.446
Late Inning Pressure	80	23	5	0	4	8	14	23	.288	.500	.394
Leading Off	24	10	2	0	4	4	1	5	.417	1.000	.440
Runners On	31	8	2	0	0	4	8	10	.258	.323	.410
Runners/Scor. Pos.	13	1	0	0	0	3	6	6	.077	.077	.368

DRIVING IN RUNS	From 1B	From 2B	From 3B	Scoring Position
Totals	9/123	23/80	18/48	41/128
Percentage	7%	29%	38%	32%
Driving In Runners from 3B with Less than Two Out:			13/28	46%

Loves to face: Rick Mahler (.478, 11-for-23, 2 HR)

Hates to face: Steve Trout (0-for-15)

104 stolen bases in 130 career attempts, exactly 80 percent; he's one of seven active players with 100+ career steals and a better stolen-base percentage than Rickey Henderson. . . . Stole seven-for-seven vs. Expos last season. . . . Totals of hits and RBI have increased each year in majors. . . . Slugged .551 after All-Star break, 4th highest in N.L. . . . Batted 88 points higher vs. right-handed pitchers than against left-handers, 4th-largest difference in N.L. (minimum: 100 AB vs. each). Career figures: .272 vs. right-handers, .201 vs. lefties. . . . Grounded into two DPs in 91 opportunities last season, 2d-lowest rate in majors (minimum: 40 opportunities). . . . Ten-for-29 career with the bases loaded.

Ozzie Virgil

Atlanta Braves   Bats Right

	AB	H	2B	3B	HR	RRF	BB	SO	BA	SA	OBA
Season	359	80	9	0	15	51	63	73	.223	.373	.343
vs. Left-Handers	107	28	4	0	2	13	25	10	.262	.355	.396
vs. Right-Handers	252	52	5	0	13	38	38	63	.206	.381	.319
Home	170	45	6	0	6	26	20	37	.265	.406	.344
Road	189	35	3	0	9	25	43	36	.185	.344	.342
Grass	265	62	6	0	11	35	49	59	.234	.381	.358
Artificial Turf	94	18	3	0	4	16	14	14	.191	.351	.297
April	35	3	0	0	1	5	6	8	.086	.171	.220
May	83	18	2	0	6	15	12	15	.217	.458	.320
June	61	19	2	0	4	12	18	7	.311	.541	.476
July	58	8	2	0	0	3	9	14	.138	.172	.250
August	70	18	2	0	3	9	10	16	.257	.414	.350
Sept./Oct.	52	14	1	0	1	7	8	13	.269	.346	.377
Leading Off Inn.	76	14	0	0	4	4	11	9	.184	.395	.303
Runners On	155	38	2	0	6	42	36	33	.245	.374	.381
Runners/Scor. Pos.	91	21	1	0	2	34	24	23	.231	.308	.381
Runners On/2 Out	61	15	2	0	2	18	19	13	.246	.377	.425
Scor. Pos./2 Out	41	12	1	0	1	16	12	9	.293	.390	.453
Late Inning Pressure	64	16	1	0	1	9	9	14	.250	.313	.347
Leading Off	10	2	0	0	0	0	1	0	.200	.200	.333
Runners On	34	8	0	0	0	8	6	8	.235	.235	.341
Runners/Scor. Pos.	20	4	0	0	0	8	4	4	.200	.200	.320

DRIVING IN RUNS	From 1B	From 2B	From 3B	Scoring Position
Totals	5/114	15/69	16/37	31/106
Percentage	4%	22%	43%	29%
Driving In Runners from 3B with Less than Two Out:			13/25	52%

Loves to face: Tom Browning (.474, 9-for-19, 2 HR)

Hates to face: Sid Fernandez (0-for-19)

.223 batting average, when blended with Benedict's and Simmons's, left Braves with composite .217 mark from their starting catchers, lowest by any N.L. team. League average was .248; only starting shortstops (.245) hit lower. . . . Played on a grass home field for first time last year, and even though he hit higher on such fields in '86, his career average is .256 on artificial turf, only .216 on grass. . . . Averaged one walk every 6.8 plate appearances last season, 3d-highest rate in N.L. (minimum: 40 BB). . . . Has been a late-inning horse throughout his career: has driven in 36.5 percent of runners in scoring position in Late-Inning Pressure Situations, compared to 23.5 percent at all other times.

Tim Wallach

Montreal Expos   Bats Right

	AB	H	2B	3B	HR	RRF	BB	SO	BA	SA	OBA
Season	480	112	22	1	18	72	44	72	.233	.396	.308
vs. Left-Handers	135	29	10	0	3	16	17	19	.215	.356	.305
vs. Right-Handers	345	83	12	1	15	56	27	53	.241	.412	.309
Home	230	52	8	1	6	34	21	34	.226	.348	.309
Road	250	60	14	0	12	38	23	38	.240	.440	.307
Grass	137	28	8	0	6	19	15	27	.204	.394	.284
Artificial Turf	343	84	14	1	12	53	29	45	.245	.397	.318
April	64	19	4	0	4	13	8	10	.297	.547	.384
May	102	27	8	1	4	17	4	13	.265	.480	.313
June	88	24	4	0	4	17	13	12	.273	.455	.374
July	97	21	3	0	4	12	10	17	.216	.371	.290
August	97	17	2	0	2	11	6	15	.175	.258	.238
Sept./Oct.	32	4	1	0	0	2	3	5	.125	.156	.200
Leading Off Inn.	106	27	3	0	6	6	11	17	.255	.453	.347
Runners On	222	56	15	0	7	61	21	30	.252	.414	.324
Runners/Scor. Pos.	143	32	9	0	4	52	17	20	.224	.371	.318
Runners On/2 Out	96	25	6	0	3	24	11	17	.260	.417	.349
Scor. Pos./2 Out	65	17	5	0	2	22	9	11	.262	.431	.368
Late Inning Pressure	81	20	3	0	2	10	12	12	.247	.358	.367
Leading Off	20	6	0	0	1	1	4	5	.300	.450	.481
Runners On	39	10	3	0	1	9	6	4	.256	.410	.348
Runners/Scor. Pos.	24	7	3	0	1	9	5	1	.292	.542	.400

DRIVING IN RUNS	From 1B	From 2B	From 3B	Scoring Position
Totals	10/153	18/106	26/61	44/167
Percentage	7%	17%	43%	26%
Driving In Runners from 3B with Less than Two Out:			18/31	58%

Loves to face: Steve Trout (.452, 14-for-31, 3 HR)

Hates to face: Alejandro Pena (.056, 1-for-18)

One of three N.L. players with 18+ home runs and 70+ RBI in each of past five years; others: Dale Murphy and Mike Schmidt. . . . Has hit more home runs on road than at home in all seven seasons in majors (even including 11 at bats in Sept. 1980); career totals: 40 homers at home (one every 36.7 at bats), 70 on road (one every 22.3 at bats). . . . Olympic Stadium has depressed home runs by 16.2 percent over past five years. . . . Batting average at season's end (.233) was at lowest point since opening week of season. . . . Homered against every N.L. club except Padres last season; hasn't connected in 31 games vs. San Diego since May 17, 1984. . . . Career average of .180 (11-for-61) with bases loaded.

Denny Walling

Houston Astros — Bats Left

	AB	H	2B	3B	HR	RRF	BB	SO	BA	SA	OBA
Season	382	119	23	1	13	60	36	31	.312	.479	.367
vs. Left-Handers	58	11	1	0	0	8	6	6	.190	.207	.266
vs. Right-Handers	324	108	22	1	13	52	30	25	.333	.528	.385
Home	190	56	10	0	5	29	17	13	.295	.426	.349
Road	192	63	13	1	8	31	19	18	.328	.531	.385
Grass	110	38	7	1	5	19	10	14	.345	.564	.397
Artificial Turf	272	81	16	0	8	41	26	17	.298	.445	.355
April	38	11	1	0	1	2	4	5	.289	.395	.349
May	64	20	5	0	0	8	4	3	.313	.391	.353
June	45	12	2	0	1	4	8	3	.267	.378	.370
July	76	23	6	0	4	18	12	6	.303	.539	.393
August	74	26	2	1	5	19	3	7	.351	.608	.372
Sept./Oct.	85	27	7	0	2	9	5	7	.318	.471	.356
Leading Off Inn.	75	24	3	0	3	3	3	10	.320	.480	.346
Runners On	170	48	7	1	7	54	27	13	.282	.459	.373
Runners/Scor. Pos.	100	25	4	1	4	46	23	9	.250	.430	.378
Runners On/2 Out	56	18	4	0	3	20	10	2	.321	.554	.424
Scor. Pos./2 Out	38	11	2	0	2	17	8	1	.289	.500	.413
Late Inning Pressure	71	21	2	0	2	9	10	6	.296	.408	.378
Leading Off	18	4	0	0	1	1	0	2	.222	.389	.222
Runners On	31	11	2	0	1	8	9	1	.355	.516	.488
Runners/Scor. Pos.	21	5	1	0	1	8	8	1	.238	.429	.433

DRIVING IN RUNS	From 1B	From 2B	From 3B	Scoring Position
Totals	9/121	18/84	20/39	38/123
Percentage	7%	21%	51%	31%
Driving In Runners from 3B with Less than Two Out:			15/23	65%

Loves to face: Danny Cox (.520, 13-for-25)
Hates to face: Floyd Youmans (0-for-12)
Career games played: 252 in outfield, 218 at first base, 218 at third base; if you believe that Rose is retired, then Walling is the only active player with 200+ games at each of those positions; then again, if you believe that, there's some land in Florida we'd like to talk with you about. . . . Despite last year's poor average vs. left-handers, he has .248 career mark vs. lefties, with three home runs, in 302 at bats; batting average vs. right-handers last season was a career high. . . . Has never hit a grand slam home run, but who cares: 5-for-11 with bases loaded last season, .422 (19-for-45) in his career. . . . Career batting average of .400 (26-for-65, two HR) at Busch Stadium.

Mitch Webster

Montreal Expos — Bats Left and Right

	AB	H	2B	3B	HR	RRF	BB	SO	BA	SA	OBA
Season	576	167	31	13	8	49	57	78	.290	.431	.355
vs. Left-Handers	199	67	16	2	5	20	11	23	.337	.513	.376
vs. Right-Handers	377	100	15	11	3	29	46	55	.265	.387	.345
Home	283	75	15	8	2	24	28	34	.265	.396	.329
Road	293	92	16	5	6	25	29	44	.314	.464	.380
Grass	148	52	10	0	3	12	13	21	.351	.480	.411
Artificial Turf	428	115	21	13	5	37	44	57	.269	.414	.336
April	69	17	6	0	1	7	5	13	.246	.377	.297
May	80	24	5	0	2	9	13	6	.300	.438	.396
June	104	25	5	2	1	6	17	12	.240	.356	.347
July	85	30	5	2	1	9	7	15	.353	.494	.402
August	115	38	6	5	0	9	5	9	.330	.470	.364
Sept./Oct.	123	33	4	4	3	9	10	23	.268	.439	.326
Leading Off Inn.	118	39	11	1	3	3	7	14	.331	.517	.368
Runners On	237	69	10	4	2	43	29	28	.291	.392	.371
Runners/Scor. Pos.	132	33	4	2	2	39	22	15	.250	.356	.358
Runners On/2 Out	90	25	3	1	1	17	13	11	.278	.367	.375
Scor. Pos./2 Out	63	14	1	1	1	16	10	7	.222	.317	.338
Late Inning Pressure	102	25	3	0	1	13	11	11	.245	.304	.325
Leading Off	21	2	0	0	1	1	0	0	.095	.238	.095
Runners On	49	13	3	0	0	10	8	6	.265	.327	.379
Runners/Scor. Pos.	32	8	1	0	0	10	7	4	.250	.281	.400

DRIVING IN RUNS	From 1B	From 2B	From 3B	Scoring Position
Totals	5/154	17/113	19/41	36/154
Percentage	3%	15%	46%	23%
Driving In Runners from 3B with Less than Two Out:			13/22	59%

Loves to face: Zane Smith (.727, 8-for-11)
Hates to face: Nolan Ryan (0-for-6, 5 SO)
Made 114 starts in center field, 3d most in N.L., behind Dale Murphy (154) and Willie McGee (121); led N.L. center fielders with 10 assists. . . . Led N.L. with 13 triples last season; all 13 came on fields with artificial turf. Half (484 of 969) of the N.L.'s games last year were played on artificial turf, but 63 percent of triples were hit in those games. . . . Despite the triples, for 2d consecutive season Webster had a much better average on grass fields than on artificial surfaces. Career breakdown: .339 grass, .262 artificial. . . . Batted .500 (18-for-36) vs. Braves. . . . Six hits in 12 career at bats with bases loaded. . . . Batting average of .353 in July was 4th highest in N.L.

Reggie Williams

Los Angeles Dodgers — Bats Right

	AB	H	2B	3B	HR	RRF	BB	SO	BA	SA	OBA
Season	303	84	14	2	4	37	23	57	.277	.376	.331
vs. Left-Handers	170	50	9	2	1	18	15	28	.294	.388	.355
vs. Right-Handers	133	34	5	0	3	19	8	29	.256	.361	.301
Home	151	41	7	1	1	16	12	27	.272	.351	.327
Road	152	43	7	1	3	21	11	30	.283	.401	.335
Grass	214	62	10	2	2	25	15	38	.290	.383	.338
Artificial Turf	89	22	4	0	2	12	8	19	.247	.360	.316
April	6	1	0	0	0	0	0	0	.167	.167	.167
May	51	14	4	0	0	3	4	10	.275	.353	.339
June	65	24	6	1	0	12	4	12	.369	.492	.406
July	76	19	3	0	2	10	1	17	.250	.368	.256
August	54	13	1	0	1	5	8	8	.241	.315	.349
Sept./Oct.	51	13	0	1	1	7	6	10	.255	.353	.333
Leading Off Inn.	68	23	4	0	0	0	1	11	.338	.397	.348
Runners On	123	36	6	0	3	35	14	21	.293	.415	.371
Runners/Scor. Pos.	70	19	1	0	1	30	11	14	.271	.329	.381
Runners On/2 Out	48	14	2	0	1	16	8	7	.292	.396	.393
Scor. Pos./2 Out	31	10	0	0	1	15	8	4	.323	.419	.462
Late Inning Pressure	52	14	5	0	1	4	3	12	.269	.423	.309
Leading Off	14	3	1	0	0	0	0	4	.214	.286	.214
Runners On	17	8	3	0	1	4	1	3	.471	.824	.500
Runners/Scor. Pos.	4	2	1	0	0	2	1	0	.500	.750	.600

DRIVING IN RUNS	From 1B	From 2B	From 3B	Scoring Position
Totals	5/88	13/49	14/34	27/83
Percentage	6%	27%	41%	33%
Driving In Runners from 3B with Less than Two Out:			8/17	47%

Loves to face: Tim Conroy (.556, 5-for-9)
Hates to face: Sid Fernandez (.125, 1-for-8, 5 SO)
Started 63 games in center field, most on team; Dodgers and Phillies were only teams in majors that did not have one player start the majority of their games in center. . . . Batted .285 in his 63 starts there; in 99 other games, L.A.'s starting center fielders batted .247. . . . Also started 16 games in right and eight games in left. . . . Total of 128 games played was 2d highest among N.L. rookies, behind Rob Thompson's 149. . . . Batted in six different lineup positions. . . . It's just a one-year sample, but something to watch: Dodgers allowed 4.04 runs per nine innings with Williams in center; with others in center, that average was 4.30—a difference of 42 runs over a 162-game season.

Glenn Wilson

Philadelphia Phillies — Bats Right

	AB	H	2B	3B	HR	RRF	BB	SO	BA	SA	OBA
Season	584	158	30	4	15	87	42	91	.271	.413	.319
vs. Left-Handers	185	41	9	0	4	22	12	25	.222	.335	.271
vs. Right-Handers	399	117	21	4	11	65	30	66	.293	.449	.341
Home	285	86	22	2	7	41	24	41	.302	.467	.357
Road	299	72	8	2	8	46	18	50	.241	.361	.283
Grass	163	36	5	2	2	21	5	25	.221	.313	.251
Artificial Turf	421	122	25	2	13	66	37	66	.290	.451	.344
April	62	10	1	0	0	4	8	9	.161	.177	.260
May	93	18	3	0	3	15	8	15	.194	.323	.260
June	117	36	10	0	3	19	6	21	.308	.470	.341
July	85	21	3	0	4	13	10	10	.247	.424	.316
August	117	37	7	2	4	20	4	14	.316	.513	.344
Sept./Oct.	110	36	6	2	1	16	6	22	.327	.445	.362
Leading Off Inn.	122	30	8	1	3	3	11	19	.246	.402	.308
Runners On	272	77	10	2	8	80	17	45	.283	.423	.325
Runners/Scor. Pos.	158	47	6	1	6	73	13	28	.297	.462	.344
Runners On/2 Out	108	26	4	1	3	29	7	16	.241	.380	.299
Scor. Pos./2 Out	77	19	3	0	2	25	4	14	.247	.364	.301
Late Inning Pressure	96	25	4	0	0	9	9	17	.260	.302	.327
Leading Off	29	5	2	0	0	2	5	7	.172	.241	.226
Runners On	45	15	1	0	0	8	4	9	.333	.356	.392
Runners/Scor. Pos.	25	9	1	0	0	8	3	4	.360	.400	.414

DRIVING IN RUNS	From 1B	From 2B	From 3B	Scoring Position
Totals	12/213	28/131	32/61	60/192
Percentage	6%	21%	52%	31%
Driving In Runners from 3B with Less than Two Out:			22/32	69%

Loves to face: Frank DiPino (.857, 6-for-7, 2 HR)
Hates to face: Ted Power (0-for-10)
Led N.L. outfielders in assists (20) and double plays (five) for second straight season. . . . His edge over Tony Gwynn (19 assists) and over Kevins Bass and McReynolds (four DPs) was an up-the-middle double play grounder with Wilson used as a fifth infielder. . . . Batting average hit its highest point at season's end. Drove in at least one run in seven consecutive games twice last season. . . . Has batted 68 times in his career without a walk with bases loaded (.203, 12-for-59). . . . Career average is higher vs. left-handers (.274) than vs. right-handers (.268) despite 1986 breakdown. But home run frequency is higher against righties (one every 37.1 at bats, compared with one every 50.7).

Mookie Wilson
New York Mets   Bats Left and Right

	AB	H	2B	3B	HR	RRF	BB	SO	BA	SA	OBA
Season	381	110	17	5	9	47	32	72	.289	.430	.345
vs. Left-Handers	196	57	6	5	3	25	15	37	.291	.418	.341
vs. Right-Handers	185	53	11	0	6	22	17	35	.286	.443	.348
Home	173	50	9	1	4	18	17	32	.289	.422	.351
Road	208	60	8	4	5	29	15	40	.288	.438	.339
Grass	262	82	11	4	6	36	23	43	.313	.454	.367
Artificial Turf	119	28	6	1	3	11	9	29	.235	.378	.295
April	0	0	0	0	0	0	0	0	—	—	—
May	55	15	2	2	1	5	8	8	.273	.436	.365
June	84	25	6	0	3	8	3	19	.298	.476	.322
July	57	17	1	0	2	7	5	11	.298	.421	.355
August	94	31	5	2	2	17	10	14	.330	.489	.400
Sept./Oct.	91	22	3	1	1	10	6	20	.242	.330	.286
Leading Off Inn.	141	37	6	2	5	5	10	31	.262	.440	.316
Runners On	129	42	7	3	4	42	16	14	.326	.519	.397
Runners/Scor. Pos.	76	28	4	2	1	34	14	7	.368	.513	.462
Runners On/2 Out	55	17	2	2	2	16	7	10	.309	.527	.387
Scor. Pos./2 Out	34	11	1	1	0	11	7	5	.324	.412	.439
Late Inning Pressure	62	17	3	1	1	11	5	16	.274	.403	.328
Leading Off	19	4	0	0	0	0	1	7	.211	.211	.250
Runners On	24	8	2	1	1	11	4	3	.333	.625	.429
Runners/Scor. Pos.	13	8	2	1	1	11	4	2	.615	1.154	.706

DRIVING IN RUNS	From 1B	From 2B	From 3B	Scoring Position
Totals	6/85	17/61	15/31	32/92
Percentage	7%	28%	48%	35%
Driving In Runners from 3B with Less than Two Out:			12/18	67%

Loves to face: Joe Hesketh (.583, 7-for-12)
Hates to face: Andy Hawkins (0-for-16)
1986 was first full season in major-league career in which he did not hit in .270s. He's one of only three N.L. players to hit .270 or better in each of past six seasons. Others: Keith Hernandez and Tim Raines. . . . Has hit for a higher average at Shea Stadium than in road games in six of seven seasons. . . . Averaged 3.09 putouts per nine innings in center field, highest in N.L. (minimum: 25 CF starts); Dykstra averaged 2.66 putouts per nine innings. . . . Outstanding performance (8-for-15) in Late-Inning Pressure Situations with runners in scoring position raised his career mark in that category to .330. Can also do damage in those situations without even getting a hit: Check World Series, Game Six.

Herm Winningham
Montreal Expos   Bats Left

	AB	H	2B	3B	HR	RRF	BB	SO	BA	SA	OBA
Season	185	40	6	3	4	11	18	51	.216	.346	.286
vs. Left-Handers	26	8	0	0	1	2	1	9	.308	.423	.333
vs. Right-Handers	159	32	6	3	3	9	17	42	.201	.333	.278
Home	85	13	1	2	1	4	13	26	.153	.247	.265
Road	100	27	5	1	3	7	5	25	.270	.430	.305
Grass	37	6	0	1	0	0	3	12	.162	.216	.225
Artificial Turf	148	34	6	2	4	11	15	39	.230	.378	.301
April	21	5	0	0	1	2	6	6	.238	.381	.407
May	50	11	2	1	2	5	6	11	.220	.420	.304
June	66	15	3	1	1	3	2	20	.227	.348	.250
July	0	0	0	0	0	0	0	0	—	—	—
August	13	2	0	1	0	0	2	4	.154	.308	.267
Sept./Oct.	35	7	1	0	0	1	2	10	.200	.229	.243
Leading Off Inn.	54	14	3	1	1	1	5	14	.259	.407	.322
Runners On	71	13	2	1	1	8	8	22	.183	.282	.266
Runners/Scor. Pos.	42	7	1	1	0	6	6	19	.167	.238	.271
Runners On/2 Out	32	5	0	0	1	4	3	11	.156	.250	.229
Scor. Pos./2 Out	23	3	0	0	0	2	3	11	.130	.130	.231
Late Inning Pressure	41	11	2	1	0	3	7	11	.268	.366	.375
Leading Off	15	5	1	0	0	0	3	4	.333	.400	.444
Runners On	14	4	0	1	0	3	3	5	.286	.429	.412
Runners/Scor. Pos.	10	3	0	1	0	2	3	2	.300	.500	.417

DRIVING IN RUNS	From 1B	From 2B	From 3B	Scoring Position
Totals	1/46	5/38	1/11	6/49
Percentage	2%	13%	9%	12%
Driving In Runners from 3B with Less than Two Out:			1/5	20%

Loves to face: Kevin Gross (.467, 7-for-15)
Hates to face: Dwight Gooden (0-for-11, 4 SO)
Went 5-for-10 in a series at Olympic Stadium while with Mets in Sept. 1984, and Expos took the bait; over past two seasons, has hit .191 and .153 in Canada, .287 and .270 in United States. . . . Ten career extra-base hits at the Big O: two doubles, seven triples, one homer. . . . On the whole, would rather be in Philadelphia, where he is 20-for-40 with two home runs. . . . Hitless in seven career at bats with bases loaded. . . . Has hit under .200 with runners in scoring position in both seasons with Montreal. . . . Comme frappeur supplant: en 1985, 6-en-13, bon; en 1986, 3-en-23, mal. . . . Can never tell when a French publisher might be out there. European rights to the *Analyst*, anyone?

Marvell Wynne
San Diego Padres   Bats Left

	AB	H	2B	3B	HR	RRF	BB	SO	BA	SA	OBA
Season	288	76	19	2	7	38	15	45	.264	.417	.300
vs. Left-Handers	70	13	4	0	2	6	4	19	.186	.329	.230
vs. Right-Handers	218	63	15	2	5	32	11	26	.289	.445	.322
Home	177	55	13	2	5	25	5	30	.311	.492	.328
Road	111	21	6	0	2	13	10	15	.189	.297	.258
Grass	222	65	15	2	6	29	15	37	.293	.459	.335
Artificial Turf	66	11	4	0	1	9	0	8	.167	.273	.176
April	29	9	1	0	2	4	1	5	.310	.552	.323
May	23	6	1	0	0	2	2	2	.261	.304	.320
June	63	19	3	0	1	7	2	7	.302	.397	.318
July	92	25	10	1	3	14	2	13	.272	.500	.287
August	54	8	1	0	1	3	4	12	.148	.222	.207
Sept./Oct.	27	9	3	1	0	8	4	6	.333	.519	.424
Leading Off Inn.	85	25	4	1	5	5	1	11	.294	.541	.302
Runners On	125	31	12	1	1	31	8	22	.248	.360	.292
Runners/Scor. Pos.	81	19	7	1	0	28	5	17	.235	.346	.278
Runners On/2 Out	51	11	4	0	0	5	4	10	.216	.294	.286
Scor. Pos./2 Out	32	4	1	0	0	3	3	8	.125	.156	.222
Late Inning Pressure	69	20	4	0	3	10	5	12	.290	.478	.338
Leading Off	18	8	1	0	3	3	0	0	.444	1.000	.444
Runners On	38	10	3	0	0	7	3	11	.263	.342	.317
Runners/Scor. Pos.	25	6	2	0	0	6	1	9	.240	.320	.269

DRIVING IN RUNS	From 1B	From 2B	From 3B	Scoring Position
Totals	7/90	12/65	12/30	24/95
Percentage	8%	18%	40%	25%
Driving In Runners from 3B with Less than Two Out:			12/20	60%

Loves to face: Rick Reuschel (.500, 8-for-16)
Hates to face: Jeff Russell (0-for-16)
Started 59 games in center field last season: 48-of-104 vs. right-handers, 11-of-58 vs. left-handers; he started in center in all the games in which McReynolds didn't. McReynolds isn't there this year; sounds like a genuine opportunity for Wynne. . . . John Havlicek Award Winner: Batted .234 in his 59 starts, but hit .386 in 78 games off the bench. . . . August batting average of .148 was lowest in majors (minimum: 50 AB). . . . Pinch-runner in 19 games last season, 3d most in N.L. . . . Catch me before I steal again: 57 career steals, 45 times caught stealing, a percentage of .559. Over past four years, only one active player with 50+ steals (a compulsive thief?) has a lower stolen-base percentage: Rafael Ramirez, .542 (51-of-94).

Joel Youngblood
San Francisco Giants   Bats Right

	AB	H	2B	3B	HR	RRF	BB	SO	BA	SA	OBA
Season	184	47	12	0	5	29	18	34	.255	.402	.320
vs. Left-Handers	76	16	5	0	0	8	6	13	.211	.276	.265
vs. Right-Handers	108	31	7	0	5	21	12	21	.287	.491	.358
Home	77	18	8	0	0	10	8	15	.234	.338	.295
Road	107	29	4	0	5	19	10	19	.271	.449	.339
Grass	130	32	8	0	3	20	13	28	.246	.377	.308
Artificial Turf	54	15	4	0	2	9	5	6	.278	.463	.350
April	19	4	1	0	0		4	3	.211	.263	.348
May	11	4	0	0	1	3	0	4	.364	.636	.364
June	31	9	2	0	2	7	5	5	.290	.548	.395
July	57	16	2	0	2	12	3	8	.281	.421	.311
August	42	5	3	0	0	4	2	9	.119	.190	.156
Sept./Oct.	24	9	4	0	0	3	4	5	.375	.542	.464
Leading Off Inn.	44	11	3	0	2	2	2	6	.250	.455	.283
Runners On	81	28	7	0	2	26	10	16	.346	.506	.404
Runners/Scor. Pos.	54	21	5	0	0	21	7	11	.389	.481	.438
Runners On/2 Out	37	10	3	0	0	8	4	9	.270	.351	.341
Scor. Pos./2 Out	29	9	2	0	0	8	2	7	.310	.414	.355
Late Inning Pressure	61	14	2	0	1	9	7	13	.230	.311	.304
Leading Off	19	4	1	0	0		1	3	.211	.263	.250
Runners On	24	10	1	0	1	9	5	5	.417	.583	.500
Runners/Scor. Pos.	16	7	1	0	0	7	4	3	.438	.500	.524

DRIVING IN RUNS	From 1B	From 2B	From 3B	Scoring Position
Totals	3/46	13/43	8/20	21/63
Percentage	7%	30%	40%	33%
Driving In Runners from 3B with Less than Two Out:			7/12	58%

Loves to face: Ed Whitson (.536, 15-for-28)
Hates to face: Alejandro Pena (.067, 1-for-15)
Has batted for a higher average with runners on base than with the bases empty in each of last seven seasons. . . . Batting average with runners in scoring position (.389) was a career high. . . . Looks for his licks with the bases loaded: his overall career walk rate is one for every 12.2 plate appearances; but with the bases loaded, he has walked only once in 86 plate appearances. . . . Six hits in his last 10 at bats as a pinch-hitter. . . . Started only 28 games last season, never more than six in succession; played six positions in '86, including seven games at first base, and has now played every position in majors except pitcher.

Atlanta Braves

	AB	H	2B	3B	HR	RRF	BB	SO	BA	SA	OBA
Season	5384	1348	241	24	138	605	538	904	.250	.381	.319
vs. Left-Handers	1754	433	83	8	37	180	181	264	.247	.367	.318
vs. Right-Handers	3630	915	158	16	101	425	357	640	.252	.388	.319
Home	2667	694	122	12	77	325	290	421	.260	.402	.333
Road	2717	654	119	12	61	280	248	483	.241	.361	.305
Grass	3989	1006	172	15	106	448	422	671	.252	.383	.325
Artificial Turf	1395	342	69	9	32	157	116	233	.245	.376	.302
April	629	155	27	3	16	72	72	108	.246	.375	.323
May	963	252	57	3	31	134	96	160	.262	.424	.328
June	927	234	36	2	26	99	105	137	.252	.380	.330
July	878	212	39	3	17	87	78	155	.241	.351	.305
August	932	250	49	8	26	117	90	164	.268	.422	.331
Sept./Oct.	1055	245	33	5	22	96	97	180	.232	.336	.298
Leading Off Inn.	1343	336	64	7	39	39	92	195	.250	.395	.301
Runners On	2198	537	92	5	57	523	297	371	.244	.369	.331
Runners/Scor. Pos.	1254	301	57	4	34	466	231	224	.240	.373	.350
Runners On/2 Out	980	240	48	3	25	243	157	174	.245	.377	.351
Scor. Pos./2 Out	637	152	30	2	16	215	129	117	.239	.367	.368
Late Inning Pressure	869	227	40	4	24	116	100	158	.261	.399	.338
Leading Off	213	58	12	0	7	7	18	35	.272	.427	.335
Runners On	382	88	15	2	11	103	63	72	.230	.366	.336
Runners/Scor. Pos.	228	54	8	2	9	98	50	42	.237	.408	.366

DRIVING IN RUNS	From 1B	From 2B	From 3B	Scoring Position
Totals	68/1633	184/989	212/506	396/1495
Percentage	4%	19%	42%	26%
Driving In Runners from 3B with Less than Two Out:			135/250	54%

Love to face: Mike Scott (8–2 against him)
Hate to face: Bob Welch (5–15 against him)

Scored fewest first-inning runs in majors (51) last season and had lowest first-inning batting average (.224). ... Also had the fewest innings of three or more runs (52) in the majors. ... Had fewest strikeouts in N.L. with 904. ... Led N.L. in turning DPs (181) for fourth time in past five seasons. ... Lowest batting average in N.L. during September/October. ... Starting catchers batted .217 last season, lowest mark for that position in N.L. ... Chuck Tanner is the first manager to finish last in different divisions in consecutive seasons. ... Dave Bristol avoided that distinction when he was fired by Milwaukee during the 1972 season after he led Brewers to a last-place finish in 1971, their last season in A.L. West.

Chicago Cubs

	AB	H	2B	3B	HR	RRF	BB	SO	BA	SA	OBA
Season	5499	1409	258	27	155	666	508	966	.256	.398	.318
vs. Left-Handers	1399	365	72	6	40	180	148	217	.261	.407	.330
vs. Right-Handers	4100	1044	186	21	115	486	360	749	.255	.394	.314
Home	2768	754	141	17	89	385	261	495	.272	.432	.334
Road	2731	655	117	10	66	281	247	471	.240	.363	.302
Grass	3877	1007	184	21	119	487	361	695	.260	.410	.322
Artificial Turf	1622	402	74	6	36	179	147	271	.248	.367	.309
April	679	156	30	3	15	76	71	118	.230	.349	.301
May	913	242	41	4	30	112	96	159	.265	.417	.335
June	940	239	43	6	20	120	95	150	.254	.377	.323
July	866	229	49	4	25	112	72	166	.264	.417	.320
August	1045	256	45	5	30	108	81	205	.245	.384	.297
Sept./Oct.	1056	287	50	5	35	138	93	168	.272	.428	.329
Leading Off Inn.	1342	355	68	5	39	39	113	207	.265	.410	.323
Runners On	2293	589	109	9	60	571	239	400	.257	.391	.323
Runners/Scor. Pos.	1334	341	68	4	31	489	171	247	.256	.382	.331
Runners On/2 Out	955	213	48	4	21	213	120	179	.223	.348	.312
Scor. Pos./2 Out	624	142	37	3	12	188	93	128	.228	.354	.331
Late Inning Pressure	992	243	36	6	31	120	113	175	.245	.387	.319
Leading Off	242	60	8	1	12	12	30	40	.248	.438	.331
Runners On	413	101	13	2	12	101	60	74	.245	.373	.333
Runners/Scor. Pos.	250	53	7	2	5	84	40	49	.212	.316	.308

DRIVING IN RUNS	From 1B	From 2B	From 3B	Scoring Position
Totals	91/1603	189/1066	231/525	420/1591
Percentage	6%	18%	44%	26%
Driving In Runners from 3B with Less than Two Out:			170/292	58%

Love to face: Mark Davis (7–0)
Hate to face: Bob Walk (1–6)

One of two N.L. teams not to have any first-inning sacrifice bunts last season; the other: Cincinnati. ... Had seven players with 10 or more home runs, tying New York for N.L. lead. ... Led N.L. in home runs for 2d consecutive season (only seventh time in team history), but cleanup hitters hit only 13, lowest total in either league. ... Lowest ground outs-to-air outs ratio in N.L. last season (1.12). Unusual stat for a home run–hitting team. ... Recalled only two announced pinch-hitters before they batted, lowest total in N.L. last season. ... Who was 1986 Chicago Interim Manager of the Year? John Vukovich was 1–1 for Cubs, Doug Rader 1–1 for White Sox. Close vote expected; big turnout should favor the incumbent.

Cincinnati Reds

	AB	H	2B	3B	HR	RRF	BB	SO	BA	SA	OBA
Season	5536	1404	237	35	144	713	586	920	.254	.387	.325
vs. Left-Handers	1668	441	81	8	45	211	175	257	.264	.403	.332
vs. Right-Handers	3868	963	156	27	99	502	411	663	.249	.380	.322
Home	2719	705	119	21	84	371	284	449	.259	.411	.330
Road	2817	699	118	14	60	342	302	471	.248	.364	.320
Grass	1697	437	69	8	35	204	169	280	.258	.369	.324
Artificial Turf	3839	967	168	27	109	509	417	640	.252	.395	.325
April	572	124	22	2	18	56	48	112	.217	.357	.280
May	903	213	35	6	18	110	122	156	.236	.348	.325
June	989	249	40	6	17	118	101	143	.252	.356	.321
July	938	259	55	4	27	128	93	151	.276	.430	.343
August	1031	255	36	6	33	127	113	167	.247	.390	.321
Sept./Oct.	1103	304	49	11	31	174	109	191	.276	.424	.340
Leading Off Inn.	1360	345	62	7	43	43	100	219	.254	.404	.307
Runners On	2332	629	89	21	68	635	300	379	.270	.413	.350
Runners/Scor. Pos.	1385	355	54	12	39	547	235	244	.256	.397	.358
Runners On/2 Out	1004	266	38	13	25	265	160	177	.265	.403	.367
Scor. Pos./2 Out	673	171	22	7	17	236	132	125	.254	.383	.376
Late Inning Pressure	841	230	36	4	24	127	108	152	.273	.411	.354
Leading Off	211	60	11	1	10	10	18	38	.284	.488	.341
Runners On	376	104	13	3	12	115	58	60	.277	.423	.367
Runners/Scor. Pos.	235	58	10	1	7	103	46	49	.247	.387	.364

DRIVING IN RUNS	From 1B	From 2B	From 3B	Scoring Position
Totals	101/1648	199/1020	263/647	462/1667
Percentage	6%	20%	41%	28%
Driving In Runners from 3B with Less than Two Out:			178/335	53%

Love to face: 300-game-winners-to-be (see below)
Hate to face: Rick Mahler (2–9)

Led N.L. with 23 three-run homers; also had three grand slams. ... Scored in 17.6 percent of innings in which leadoff batter was retired, highest rate in N.L. ... Reds have all-time winning record against each of 300-game winners active in 1986 (20–12 vs. Seaver, 34–29 vs. Niekro, 25–22 vs. Sutton, and 21–14 vs. Carlton). ... Hit by only 15 pitches, fewest in majors. Mario Soto missed half the season. Hmmmm. ... Highest night-game batting average in N.L. last season (.262), lowest average in day games (.238). ... Used 59 pinch-runners, 2d-highest total in N.L. last season. The leader: San Diego (72). ... Starting first basemen batted .233 last season, lowest mark for that position in N.L.

Houston Astros

	AB	H	2B	3B	HR	RRF	BB	SO	BA	SA	OBA
Season	5441	1388	244	32	125	643	536	916	.255	.381	.322
vs. Left-Handers	2117	550	92	15	44	255	201	355	.260	.380	.324
vs. Right-Handers	3324	838	152	17	81	388	335	561	.252	.381	.322
Home	2643	692	110	16	49	321	266	428	.262	.371	.331
Road	2798	696	134	16	76	322	270	488	.249	.390	.314
Grass	1666	399	77	9	44	183	157	309	.239	.376	.305
Artificial Turf	3775	989	167	23	81	460	379	607	.262	.383	.330
April	643	150	28	3	16	68	64	123	.233	.361	.301
May	884	216	42	4	13	89	80	136	.244	.345	.307
June	957	248	33	8	27	116	99	162	.259	.395	.330
July	921	232	38	2	22	116	99	182	.252	.374	.327
August	939	251	40	6	21	108	81	139	.267	.390	.327
Sept./Oct.	1097	291	63	7	26	146	113	174	.265	.407	.333
Leading Off Inn.	1349	347	48	8	40	41	93	216	.257	.394	.308
Runners On	2295	576	98	15	48	565	280	383	.251	.369	.330
Runners/Scor. Pos.	1352	344	54	12	25	496	209	241	.254	.348	.348
Runners On/2 Out	965	232	35	5	32	249	143	180	.240	.387	.341
Scor. Pos./2 Out	626	157	18	4	18	212	115	117	.251	.379	.370
Late Inning Pressure	783	213	21	4	23	106	92	135	.272	.397	.349
Leading Off	199	53	4	0	9	9	12	27	.266	.422	.311
Runners On	341	91	10	4	5	88	58	60	.267	.364	.373
Runners/Scor. Pos.	205	55	6	3	2	79	43	43	.268	.356	.394

DRIVING IN RUNS	From 1B	From 2B	From 3B	Scoring Position
Totals	77/1576	197/1075	241/573	438/1648
Percentage	5%	18%	42%	27%
Driving In Runners from 3B with Less than Two Out:			158/287	55%

Love to face: Tom Browning (6–3, 5–0 last season)
Hate to face: Orel Hershiser (1–6)

Faced 66 left-handed starters last season, most by any team in majors. ... Won five consecutive games in their last at bat from July 19 through July 23. ... Further evidence of team's new image: tied Montreal for last in N.L. with 53 sacrifice bunts. ... Made fewest double plays in N.L. (108). ... Had 69–21 record in games in which they scored the first run, 27–45 in games in which their opponents struck first. ... Eighth position in batting order batted .211, lowest mark by any position for any team in majors, with exception of ninth spots for N.L. teams. ... Won last five extra-inning games of *regular* season, two short of team record set in 1980–81.

Los Angeles Dodgers

	AB	H	2B	3B	HR	RRF	BB	SO	BA	SA	OBA
Season	5471	1373	232	14	130	629	478	966	.251	.370	.313
vs. Left-Handers	2044	540	98	4	39	224	166	323	.264	.373	.320
vs. Right-Handers	3427	833	134	10	91	405	312	643	.243	.368	.309
Home	2635	667	91	5	57	321	242	441	.253	.356	.317
Road	2836	706	141	9	73	308	236	525	.249	.382	.309
Grass	4002	1000	157	11	95	470	376	696	.250	.366	.316
Artificial Turf	1469	373	75	3	35	159	102	270	.254	.381	.303
April	759	164	22	1	20	75	70	137	.216	.327	.286
May	884	229	35	2	17	101	79	158	.259	.361	.322
June	940	254	42	4	28	112	93	163	.270	.413	.335
July	831	221	40	1	18	106	60	141	.266	.381	.315
August	950	234	42	2	18	104	84	162	.246	.352	.311
Sept./Oct.	1107	271	51	4	29	131	92	205	.245	.377	.305
Leading Off Inn.	1375	346	61	4	33	33	87	248	.252	.374	.297
Runners On	2191	564	84	5	52	550	384	291	.257	.372	.333
Runners/Scor. Pos.	1308	309	46	3	25	472	187	241	.236	.333	.328
Runners On/2 Out	932	202	34	2	17	197	119	180	.217	.312	.309
Scor. Pos./2 Out	616	128	16	2	10	167	92	113	.208	.289	.314
Late Inning Pressure	900	228	36	1	18	101	88	153	.253	.360	.322
Leading Off	235	59	11	2	4	4	18	43	.251	.366	.304
Runners On	357	93	12	1	9	92	50	62	.261	.375	.352
Runners/Scor. Pos.	211	53	7	1	5	83	39	37	.251	.365	.363

DRIVING IN RUNS	From 1B	From 2B	From 3B	Scoring Position
Totals	79/1496	178/1027	241/560	419/1587
Percentage	5%	17%	43%	26%
Driving In Runners from 3B with Less than Two Out:		171/293		58%

Love to face: Bob Knepper (15–7)
Hate to face: Craig Lefferts (0–5)
Equalled their worst record of past 40 years with 73–89 mark last season. Have posted consecutive losing seasons only once during that period (1967–68). . . . Ranked last in N.L. with 478 walks. . . . Led N.L. in errors (181) for first time since 1972. . . . Batting average with two outs and runners on base was lowest in majors since New York Mets hit .211 in 1981. . . . Only team in majors that failed to put at least 30 percent of its leadoff batters on base last season. . . . Advanced two bases on singles 39.0 percent of the time, highest average in majors last season. . . . Record of 4–11 vs. left-handed pitchers on artificial surfaces. As Vin would say, "No big deal. But it's a fact."

Montreal Expos

	AB	H	2B	3B	HR	RRF	BB	SO	BA	SA	OBA
Season	5508	1401	255	50	110	624	537	1016	.254	.379	.322
vs. Left-Handers	1642	442	89	14	40	191	157	293	.269	.414	.333
vs. Right-Handers	3866	959	166	36	70	433	380	723	.248	.364	.318
Home	2648	663	110	24	42	292	289	502	.250	.358	.326
Road	2860	738	145	26	68	332	248	514	.258	.398	.319
Grass	1470	381	77	8	37	173	133	273	.259	.398	.322
Artificial Turf	4038	1020	178	42	73	451	404	743	.253	.372	.322
April	654	171	41	3	28	83	87	123	.261	.462	.348
May	905	226	39	9	28	115	85	191	.250	.406	.316
June	904	238	43	11	19	110	111	167	.263	.398	.344
July	859	221	34	7	12	100	74	156	.257	.355	.317
August	1008	243	46	12	8	102	81	153	.241	.334	.302
Sept./Oct.	1178	302	52	8	15	114	99	226	.256	.352	.315
Leading Off Inn.	1350	362	66	14	28	28	113	225	.268	.400	.329
Runners On	2319	602	108	14	40	553	259	440	.260	.370	.333
Runners/Scor. Pos.	1422	345	63	7	27	493	204	295	.243	.354	.335
Runners On/2 Out	985	233	46	6	20	227	137	206	.237	.356	.334
Scor. Pos./2 Out	673	152	30	4	14	202	108	143	.226	.345	.337
Late Inning Pressure	1012	275	41	8	16	111	114	182	.272	.375	.350
Leading Off	253	76	11	1	10	10	26	36	.300	.470	.375
Runners On	456	115	14	4	4	99	63	96	.252	.327	.343
Runners/Scor. Pos.	280	65	9	2	2	91	51	67	.232	.300	.347

DRIVING IN RUNS	From 1B	From 2B	From 3B	Scoring Position
Totals	72/1575	187/1106	253/581	440/1687
Percentage	5%	17%	44%	26%
Driving In Runners from 3B with Less than Two Out:		171/309		55%

Love to face: Mario Soto (11–4)
Hate to face: Fernando Valenzuela (2–9)
Led N.L. in triples for first time in team history. . . . Won only two games in which they trailed after seven innings, lowest total in majors last season. . . . Used 110 different combinations of eight starting players last season, highest total in N.L. . . . Starting second basemen batted .207 last season, lowest mark by any position on any N.L. team excluding pitchers. . . . Starting third basemen batted .240, lowest mark for that position in N.L. . . . Hit only 28 home runs after the All-Star break. Even St. Louis hit more than that (30). . . . Five games above .500 against right-handed pitchers (56–51), 10 games below vs. left-handers (22–32).

New York Mets

	AB	H	2B	3B	HR	RRF	BB	SO	BA	SA	OBA
Season	5558	1462	261	31	148	766	631	968	.263	.401	.339
vs. Left-Handers	2115	550	99	12	54	282	229	388	.260	.395	.334
vs. Right-Handers	3443	912	162	19	94	484	402	580	.265	.405	.342
Home	2634	691	124	15	77	370	326	457	.262	.409	.343
Road	2924	771	137	16	71	396	305	511	.264	.394	.335
Grass	3812	1019	176	19	108	539	448	669	.267	.408	.344
Artificial Turf	1746	443	85	12	40	227	183	299	.254	.385	.328
April	585	169	33	3	17	94	68	90	.289	.443	.361
May	894	216	46	5	21	112	99	168	.242	.375	.318
June	967	272	47	5	32	139	116	159	.281	.440	.356
July	931	229	39	6	30	125	106	175	.246	.397	.325
August	1118	302	54	7	23	155	118	200	.270	.393	.341
Sept./Oct.	1063	274	42	5	25	141	124	176	.258	.377	.337
Leading Off Inn.	1333	334	62	9	35	35	123	222	.251	.389	.316
Runners On	2421	677	114	15	70	688	329	409	.280	.426	.362
Runners/Scor. Pos.	1425	388	65	10	39	598	249	258	.272	.414	.373
Runners On/2 Out	1052	282	50	10	25	279	155	192	.268	.406	.365
Scor. Pos./2 Out	677	172	31	6	12	237	120	129	.254	.371	.370
Late Inning Pressure	787	218	35	2	20	114	86	155	.277	.403	.353
Leading Off	191	47	10	0	3	3	20	39	.246	.346	.324
Runners On	348	107	16	2	11	105	40	64	.307	.460	.380
Runners/Scor. Pos.	190	62	11	2	8	98	32	41	.326	.532	.421

DRIVING IN RUNS	From 1B	From 2B	From 3B	Scoring Position
Totals	102/1781	248/1116	264/621	512/1737
Percentage	6%	22%	43%	29%
Driving In Runners from 3B with Less than Two Out:		184/334		55%

Love to face: Rick Reuschel (21–10)
Hate to face: Mike Krukow (6–17, 0–4 last season)
20th team to win 100 games in the divisional era. The honor roll: Balt., 5; Yanks, Reds, 3; Phils, Mets, 2; Det., K.C., Oak., L.A., and St.L. 1. . . . Third team in history to place its hitters three-four-five in the All-Star lineup. Others: Maris-Mantle-Skowron for 1960 Yankees; Goodman-McCormick-Lombardi for 1939 Reds. . . . Went 85 games into season before being shut out (by Bob Knepper); only one N.L. team since 1900 advanced farther (1970 Reds, 96 games). . . . Led N.L. in batting for first time in their 25-year history. Ditto slugging and runs. . . . Lost all 40 home games over past two seasons in which they trailed after eight, then rallied for win in Game Three of N.L.C.S.

Phila. Phillies

	AB	H	2B	3B	HR	RRF	BB	SO	BA	SA	OBA
Season	5483	1386	266	39	154	724	589	1154	.253	.400	.327
vs. Left-Handers	1712	430	80	10	49	221	193	350	.251	.395	.331
vs. Right-Handers	3771	956	186	29	105	503	396	804	.254	.402	.325
Home	2660	720	155	26	86	403	308	578	.271	.445	.347
Road	2823	666	111	13	68	321	281	576	.236	.357	.307
Grass	1473	358	60	2	32	155	133	316	.243	.352	.309
Artificial Turf	4010	1028	206	37	122	569	456	838	.256	.417	.333
April	582	135	19	3	17	73	74	111	.232	.363	.321
May	884	204	44	0	15	92	96	211	.231	.331	.310
June	1015	289	66	7	28	165	125	195	.285	.446	.364
July	908	213	35	7	29	125	93	184	.235	.384	.308
August	1025	260	48	15	34	129	85	203	.254	.429	.314
Sept./Oct.	1069	285	54	7	31	140	116	250	.267	.417	.338
Leading Off Inn.	1323	328	72	5	34	34	125	246	.248	.387	.315
Runners On	2352	617	111	22	72	640	281	504	.262	.420	.340
Runners/Scor. Pos.	1403	371	71	14	40	549	207	329	.264	.421	.354
Runners On/2 Out	1034	264	46	9	34	277	148	221	.255	.416	.353
Scor. Pos./2 Out	698	185	28	5	23	241	114	161	.265	.418	.373
Late Inning Pressure	892	224	33	2	20	92	109	183	.251	.360	.334
Leading Off	234	65	11	0	3	3	22	34	.278	.363	.340
Runners On	393	93	8	2	8	80	56	86	.237	.328	.333
Runners/Scor. Pos.	210	53	5	1	4	69	41	51	.252	.343	.375

DRIVING IN RUNS	From 1B	From 2B	From 3B	Scoring Position
Totals	100/1654	234/1135	233/537	467/1672
Percentage	6%	21%	43%	28%
Driving In Runners from 3B with Less than Two Out:		156/264		59%

Love to face: Bob Welch (10–5)
Hate to face: Andy McGaffigan (2–6, 1–4 last season)
Led N.L. in extra-base hits (459) for third consecutive season. First team to do that since Big Red Machine had four from 1967–70. Also led league in strikeouts for third consecutive season. . . . Hit by 40 pitches last season, highest total in N.L. since 1978, when Phillies and Pirates were hit by 42 each. . . . Won 33 of 39 home games in which they scored the first run. . . . Lowest batting average in N.L. in May, highest in June, lowest in July. . . . Ninth position in batting order drove in nearly as many runs (42) as eighth spot (47). . . . Outscored opponents by 78 runs over first four innings, were outscored by 52 runs from there on.

Pittsburgh Pirates

	AB	H	2B	3B	HR	RRF	BB	SO	BA	SA	OBA
Season	5456	1366	273	33	111	644	569	929	.250	.374	.321
vs. Left-Handers	1917	470	80	12	29	198	207	315	.245	.345	.317
vs. Right-Handers	3539	896	193	21	82	446	362	614	.253	.389	.323
Home	2688	679	145	19	49	321	308	445	.253	.375	.330
Road	2768	687	128	14	62	323	261	484	.248	.372	.312
Grass	1468	376	59	6	37	174	144	282	.256	.380	.323
Artificial Turf	3988	990	214	27	74	470	425	647	.248	.371	.320
April	614	152	37	1	17	86	70	112	.248	.394	.325
May	891	215	46	4	17	97	108	179	.241	.359	.323
June	999	242	56	7	17	127	114	185	.242	.363	.321
July	845	221	33	10	18	96	93	140	.262	.388	.334
August	1021	270	56	7	23	136	82	142	.264	.401	.318
Sept./Oct.	1086	266	45	4	19	102	102	171	.245	.346	.309
Leading Off Inn.	1335	353	72	7	35	36	130	213	.264	.407	.332
Runners On	2346	603	112	15	41	573	262	386	.257	.370	.329
Runners/Scor. Pos.	1397	340	66	9	19	492	199	255	.243	.344	.332
Runners On/2 Out	947	210	35	4	16	190	114	174	.222	.318	.309
Scor. Pos./2 Out	620	132	22	2	9	165	93	128	.213	.298	.319
Late Inning Pressure	1012	232	39	3	16	98	113	202	.229	.321	.307
Leading Off	244	57	11	1	1	1	33	43	.234	.299	.325
Runners On	459	104	16	1	9	91	50	81	.227	.325	.301
Runners/Scor. Pos.	255	50	8	0	5	77	38	46	.196	.286	.294

DRIVING IN RUNS	From 1B	From 2B	From 3B	Scoring Position
Totals	92/1615	190/1071	248/611	438/1682
Percentage	6%	18%	41%	26%
Driving In Runners from 3B with Less than Two Out:	191/330	58%		

Love to face: Dan Schatzeder (8–2)
Hate to face: Danny Cox (3–10)

What did last season's Pirates have in common with the Mets and Astros? They were the only N.L. teams that never used their opening-day combination of starters again during the season. ... Led N.L. with 273 doubles, 11th time they've led league; 16 more years and they can catch St. Louis. ... Leadoff batters had a composite .216 batting average. With exception of ninth slots, only two other N.L. batting-order positions had lower marks: the eighth spots for Houston (.211) and Philadelphia (.214). ... Eighth position in Pirates order was only slot on any team in majors not to produce a home run last season; chief culprits were Rafael Belliard (46.8% of their PA), Sammy Khalifa (23.8%), and U.L. Washington (13.5%).

St. Louis Cardinals

	AB	H	2B	3B	HR	RRF	BB	SO	BA	SA	OBA
Season	5378	1270	216	48	58	588	568	905	.236	.327	.309
vs. Left-Handers	2042	502	87	17	26	226	228	335	.246	.343	.321
vs. Right-Handers	3336	768	129	31	32	362	340	570	.230	.316	.302
Home	2659	667	119	30	27	312	310	440	.251	.349	.330
Road	2719	603	97	18	31	276	258	465	.222	.305	.288
Grass	1344	260	37	9	9	104	119	236	.193	.254	.257
Artificial Turf	4034	1010	179	39	49	484	449	669	.250	.351	.326
April	627	129	18	4	7	56	64	122	.206	.281	.280
May	841	208	42	10	7	98	101	145	.247	.346	.327
June	1002	230	38	12	12	104	117	176	.230	.327	.311
July	836	206	32	6	8	101	85	139	.246	.328	.316
August	1005	239	43	9	6	115	100	144	.238	.316	.311
Sept./Oct.	1067	258	43	7	18	114	93	179	.242	.346	.302
Leading Off Inn.	1335	338	62	17	18	18	128	222	.253	.366	.320
Runners On	2299	550	92	23	23	553	286	390	.239	.329	.332
Runners/Scor. Pos.	1457	346	63	15	12	505	219	284	.237	.326	.332
Runners On/2 Out	979	216	35	11	8	191	150	195	.221	.303	.327
Scor. Pos./2 Out	691	138	23	7	4	173	122	154	.200	.271	.323
Late Inning Pressure	959	222	36	7	14	91	118	177	.231	.327	.315
Leading Off	246	67	14	3	7	7	30	39	.272	.439	.356
Runners On	410	89	13	3	2	79	58	80	.217	.278	.310
Runners/Scor. Pos.	248	49	7	3	1	72	44	59	.198	.262	.311

DRIVING IN RUNS	From 1B	From 2B	From 3B	Scoring Position
Totals	64/1454	214/1089	250/632	464/1721
Percentage	4%	20%	40%	27%
Driving In Runners from 3B with Less than Two Out:	184/315	58%		

Love to face: Larry McWilliams (7–3)
Hate to face: Fernando Valenzuela (4–10, 0–4 last season)

First team in major league history to fall from first to last in its league in both runs scored and batting average in one year. ... It gets worse: also ranked last in slugging average, on-base percentage, home runs, and doubles. ... Led N.L. in stolen bases for fifth straight season, longest streak in either league since Los Angeles tied N.L. mark of 8, 1958–65. Brooklyn coholds N.L. record; White Sox hold major-league mark (11). ... Led N.L. in fielding percentage (.981) for fifth time in past six seasons. ... Won only four games in which they trailed after six innings, lowest total in majors last season. ... Leadoff position contributed only 33 RBIs; 10 teams, including Cards, got more from ninth position.

San Diego Padres

	AB	H	2B	3B	HR	RRF	BB	SO	BA	SA	OBA
Season	5515	1442	239	25	136	649	484	917	.261	.388	.321
vs. Left-Handers	1888	492	93	12	62	236	170	314	.261	.421	.321
vs. Right-Handers	3627	950	146	13	74	413	314	603	.262	.371	.321
Home	2722	709	118	13	80	337	251	502	.260	.402	.323
Road	2793	733	121	12	56	312	233	415	.262	.375	.319
Grass	4058	1052	166	16	103	472	356	692	.259	.384	.319
Artificial Turf	1457	390	73	9	33	177	128	225	.268	.398	.327
April	724	176	31	3	19	69	61	134	.243	.373	.300
May	892	241	31	4	33	113	83	122	.270	.425	.332
June	952	240	37	7	21	119	87	140	.252	.372	.316
July	843	216	47	2	17	92	75	135	.256	.388	.315
August	1026	274	43	2	27	118	89	177	.267	.392	.327
Sept./Oct.	1078	295	50	7	19	138	89	209	.274	.386	.330
Leading Off Inn.	1358	368	57	6	31	32	102	203	.271	.390	.323
Runners On	2333	615	106	11	57	569	237	404	.264	.394	.330
Runners/Scor. Pos.	1338	337	61	6	30	488	176	275	.252	.374	.333
Runners On/2 Out	973	238	39	4	22	231	112	166	.245	.361	.326
Scor. Pos./2 Out	640	151	22	3	16	208	95	122	.236	.355	.336
Late Inning Pressure	965	259	44	0	25	129	105	195	.268	.392	.340
Leading Off	239	68	9	0	7	7	19	41	.285	.410	.337
Runners On	449	118	22	0	11	115	60	95	.263	.385	.350
Runners/Scor. Pos.	277	69	13	0	6	101	50	67	.249	.361	.363

DRIVING IN RUNS	From 1B	From 2B	From 3B	Scoring Position
Totals	95/1697	196/1044	220/536	416/1580
Percentage	6%	19%	41%	26%
Driving In Runners from 3B with Less than Two Out:	148/278	53%		

Love to face: Bill Laskey (9–4)
Hate to face: John Franco (0–5)

Padres' average game lasted 2:38, *shortest* in majors. ... Hit 19 ninth-inning homers last season, tying San Francisco for major-league lead. ... Led majors with 62 homers off left-handed pitchers. ... Consolation prize: Padres led N.L. with 1,042 singles. ... Ground outs-to-air outs ratio of 1.31, 2d-highest in majors. The leader: St. Louis (1.36). ... Used 60 different combinations of starting players last season, lowest total in N.L. ... Combination of Kennedy, Garvey-Flannery-Templeton-Nettles, McReynolds-Wynne-Gwynn started 24 games together, highest total in league by any single group. ... Used 72 pinch-runners, highest total in N.L. last season. ... Also used the most pinch-hitters (351).

San Francisco Giants

	AB	H	2B	3B	HR	RRF	BB	SO	BA	SA	OBA
Season	5501	1394	269	29	114	682	536	1087	.253	.375	.322
vs. Left-Handers	1728	444	95	6	37	220	131	329	.257	.383	.310
vs. Right-Handers	3773	950	174	23	77	462	405	758	.252	.371	.327
Home	2705	716	139	12	50	335	289	520	.265	.380	.336
Road	2796	678	130	17	64	347	247	567	.242	.370	.308
Grass	4082	1063	194	19	87	515	419	807	.260	.381	.331
Artificial Turf	1419	331	75	10	27	167	117	280	.233	.357	.296
April	753	197	33	4	16	98	78	167	.262	.380	.335
May	908	236	45	5	17	121	79	167	.260	.377	.320
June	942	250	47	7	17	109	96	162	.265	.384	.334
July	867	212	39	4	21	114	74	171	.245	.371	.306
August	943	238	43	5	16	107	88	180	.252	.359	.319
Sept./Oct.	1088	261	62	4	27	133	121	252	.240	.379	.319
Leading Off Inn.	1336	330	59	9	30		119	255	.247	.370	.313
Runners On	2310	631	122	15	50	617	269	437	.273	.404	.349
Runners/Scor. Pos.	1448	387	82	11	31	558	222	295	.267	.403	.362
Runners On/2 Out	995	243	44	5	20	240	138	215	.244	.359	.343
Scor. Pos./2 Out	687	167	33	4	13	217	118	155	.243	.360	.360
Late Inning Pressure	1019	264	55	6	24	132	115	198	.259	.395	.333
Leading Off	257	66	16	2	5	6	27	54	.257	.393	.330
Runners On	415	118	18	3	7	114	66	71	.284	.393	.377
Runners/Scor. Pos.	261	73	12	3	4	107	54	49	.280	.395	.393

DRIVING IN RUNS	From 1B	From 2B	From 3B	Scoring Position
Totals	83/1541	220/1123	262/620	482/1743
Percentage	5%	20%	42%	28%
Driving In Runners from 3B with Less than Two Out:	189/337	56%		

Love to face: Ray Burris (10–3)
Hate to face: Bob Welch (3–17)

Led major leagues with nine wins in games in which they trailed going to 9th inning. ... Grounded into one double play for every 14.98 opportunities, 2d-lowest rate in majors. The leader: St. Louis (15.37). ... Second-place hitters in lineup struck out 145 times, more than any other position in the lineup except the ninth spot. ... Youngest team in majors last season. Excluding pitchers, team had average age of 26.98 years, weighted by plate appearances. ... Lowest batting average in N.L. after the All-Star break (.241), after posting 2d-highest mark during first half of season (.264).

National League

	AB	H	2B	3B	HR	RRF	BB	SO	BA	SA	OBA
Season	65730	16643	2991	387	1523	7933	6560	11648	.253	.380	.322
vs. Left-Handers	22026	5659	1049	124	502	2624	2186	3740	.257	.384	.324
vs. Right-Handers	43704	10984	1942	263	1021	5309	4374	7908	.251	.378	.320
Home	32148	8357	1493	210	767	4093	3424	5678	.260	.391	.332
Road	33582	8286	1498	177	756	3840	3136	5970	.247	.369	.312
Grass	32938	8358	1428	143	812	3924	3237	5926	.254	.380	.321
Artificial Turf	32792	8285	1563	244	711	4009	3323	5722	.253	.380	.322
April	7821	1878	341	33	206	906	827	1445	.240	.371	.313
May	10762	2698	503	56	247	1294	1124	1952	.251	.377	.322
June	11534	2985	528	82	264	1438	1259	1939	.259	.387	.332
July	10523	2671	480	58	244	1302	1002	1895	.254	.380	.319
August	12043	3072	545	84	265	1426	1100	2036	.255	.380	.318
Sept./Oct.	13047	3339	594	74	297	1567	1248	2381	.256	.381	.321
Leading Off Inn.	16139	4142	753	98	404	408	1325	2671	.257	.391	.316
Runners On	27689	7190	1237	170	638	7037	3290	4887	.260	.386	.336
Runners/Scor. Pos.	16523	4164	750	107	352	6153	2509	3188	.252	.374	.345
Runners On/2 Out	11801	2839	498	76	265	2802	1653	2259	.241	.363	.337
Scor. Pos./2 Out	7862	1847	312	49	164	2461	1331	1592	.235	.350	.349
Late Inning Pressure	11031	2835	452	49	255	1337	1261	2065	.257	.376	.334
Leading Off	2764	736	128	11	78	79	273	469	.266	.405	.335
Runners On	4799	1221	170	27	101	1182	682	907	.254	.364	.345
Runners/Scor. Pos.	2850	694	103	20	58	1062	532	600	.244	.355	.356

DRIVING IN RUNS	From 1B	From 2B	From 3B	Scoring Position
Totals	1024/19273	2436/12861	2918/6949	5354/19810
Percentage	5%	19%	42%	27%
Driving In Runners from 3B with Less than Two Out:		2035/3624	56%	

Runs were scored in 26.6 percent of innings last season, broken down this way: 15.5 percent when leadoff batter was retired, 49.4 percent when leadoff batter reached base (42.1 when he reached first, 59.3 when he reached second, 80.5 when he reached third, 100 when he reached home). . . . No N.L. team used its opening-day combination of starters after June 25 last season. . . . Both playoff teams reached championship series with five-game winning streaks, longest by a postseason contender since 1980 when Philadelphia and Yankees won the last six. Those with good memories will recall that in 1969 both Atlanta and the Mets prepped for the first ever N.L.C.S. by winning nine in a row to conclude the regular season. . . . More than twice as many pinch-hitters batted in N.L. last season (3.48 per game) as in A.L. (1.72).

IV
Pitcher Section

Pitcher Section

The Pitcher Section is an alphabetical listing of every pitcher who faced at least 250 batters in either the American or the National League last season. Also included are several key pitchers who did not face the required 250 batters. Pitchers are listed alphabetically within each league, followed by the totals for each team and the league as a whole.

Column Headings Information

Don Aase

Baltimore Orioles	W-L	ERA	AB	H	HR	BB	SO	BA	SA	OBA

W-L	Won-Lost Record
ERA	Earned-Run Average
AB	At Bats
H	Hits
HR	Home Runs
BB	Bases on Balls
SO	Strikeouts
BA	Batting Average
SA	Slugging Average
OBA	On-Base Average

In addition to the expected categories for pitchers (won-lost record, ERA, walks, and strikeouts), this book includes a unique perspective on each pitcher's season: the batting performance of the league against him. While this method may be unfamiliar at first, it enables us to look at the pitcher and his abilities in fascinating detail.

By compiling pitching statistics in this way, we can examine a pitcher's performance in the same "within the game" contexts we've used to look at batters. To take one example, we're all familiar with platoon differentials for batters; we know that some right-handed batters are far more effective against left-handed pitchers than they are against righties. The same must be true of pitchers, but because the specific information was never available before, who knew how big those differences were? Well,

we know now, and the differences can be huge: to take one example, Mark Eichhorn of Toronto last season allowed a .259 average to left-handed batters, while limiting right-handed hitters to a .135 average—a whopping 124-point difference. Given that large a variance, a manager should think twice about letting him face a lefty hitter in a clutch situation.

Moreover, by looking at the opponents' batting figures with runners on base or in scoring position, we can show conclusively for the first time who are those underrated pitchers who may give up a lot of hits or home runs, but rarely give them up with men on or in clutch situations. And we can also see those pitchers who (whisper the word, please) fold under the same pressure. (Bear in mind that overall batting averages increase with men on base. This makes any pitcher who holds opponents to a lower average with runners on all the more impressive.)

Season Summary Information

	W-L	ERA	AB	H	HR	BB	SO	BA	SA	OBA
Season	19-7	2.87	910	204	19	74	170	.224	.330	.285
vs. Left-Handed Batters			475	95	7	42	93	.200	.282	.269
vs. Right-Handed Batters			435	109	12	32	77	.251	.382	.302
Home	10-2	3.23	468	118	10	30	86	.252	.357	.297
Road	9-5	2.50	442	86	9	44	84	.195	.301	.272
Grass	14-6	3.06	702	163	16	59	128	.232	.343	.291
Artificial Turf	5-1	2.22	208	41	3	15	42	.197	.284	.264
April	3-1	3.00	132	32	2	11	31	.242	.364	.301
May	1-1	4.26	103	29	1	13	20	.282	.379	.356
June	2-1	3.26	114	25	4	10	15	.219	.342	.291
July	4-1	2.93	163	32	7	16	30	.196	.337	.269
August	5-1	2.51	173	38	2	14	27	.220	.277	.282
Sept./Oct.	4-2	2.23	225	48	3	10	47	.213	.316	.249

Each pitcher's seasonal performance is broken down into a variety of special categories. The first line for each pitcher gives his totals for the whole season. This is followed by breakdowns of his performance against left- and right-handed hitters, in home and road games, on grass fields and on artificial turf, and by month. (For pitchers who pitched for more than one team within a league, all totals are combined. The "home" totals for Tom Seaver, for example, include all games he pitched in Chicago while with the White Sox, and all games he pitched in Boston while with the Red Sox.)

Leading Off Inn.	240	59	6	14	37	.246	.367	.287
Runners On	350	79	8	32	63	.226	.343	.290
Runners/Scor. Pos.	178	40	4	21	41	.225	.343	.301
Runners On/2 Out	152	30	3	14	31	.197	.309	.278
Scor. Pos./2 Out	89	20	2	9	20	.225	.371	.310

Following these breakdowns, each pitcher's performance is divided into specific game situations. Totals are given for each pitcher against batters who led off an inning, and against players batting with runners on base. These are followed by his performance with runners in scoring position (on second or third base, or both), with runners on base and two out, and with runners in scoring position and two out.

Late Inning Pressure	79	19	2	11	19	.241	.342	.333
Leading Off	24	7	1	3	5	.292	.458	.370
Runners On	26	7	1	3	4	.269	.385	.345
Runners/Scor. Pos.	10	1	0	3	2	.100	.100	.308

The next group shows the pitcher's performance in late-inning pressure situations, which are defined a little differently for pitchers than they are for batters. For pitchers, late-inning pressure is defined as any situation occurring in the seventh inning or later with the score tied, or with his team leading or trailing by one or two runs.

Each pitcher's totals are listed for all late-inning pressure situations, then broken out for his performance when facing a leadoff batter, with runners on base, and with runners in scoring position.

First 9 Batters	240	50	2	27	44	.208	.288	.288
Second 9 Batters	362	81	8	23	75	.224	.340	.272
All Batters Thereafter	308	73	9	24	51	.237	.351	.297

The last set of breakdowns tracks a pitcher's performance throughout each appearance by listing the opponents' batting record according to the number of batters he has faced, regardless of when he entered the game. This allows us to spotlight those pitchers who get stronger as the game progresses, and to pick out those who can breeze through the order once, but falter the second or third time around.

Following the statistics for each pitcher are a series of comments, beginning with the batter each pitcher loves to face and hates to face. The statistics listed for each individual match-up are from regular season games in the last ten years. Contained within the comments for each pitcher is his "Ground outs-to-air outs" ratio, which consists of his total of ground outs divided by outs on balls hit in the air. (Also included are plays in which the batter reaches base on an error.) An average figure, appropriately enough, is roughly 1.000, although a slight majority of pitchers exceeds that figure. (The median is 1.040.) Pitchers with ratios below 0.750 have their games charted by NASA; those above 1.500 receive hate mail from burrowing animals.

American League

Don Aase
Baltimore Orioles — Throws Right

	W-L	ERA	AB	H	HR	BB	SO	BA	SA	OBA
Season	6-7	2.98	304	71	6	28	67	.234	.352	.296
vs. Left-Handers			156	36	3	13	33	.231	.359	.290
vs. Right-Handers			148	35	3	15	34	.236	.345	.303
Home	5-3	2.91	170	37	3	12	36	.218	.324	.269
Road	1-4	3.06	134	34	3	16	31	.254	.388	.329
Grass	6-7	2.92	264	61	5	25	59	.231	.341	.297
Artificial Turf	0-0	3.38	40	10	1	3	8	.250	.425	.295
April	1-2	1.64	39	6	0	6	7	.154	.231	.267
May	1-0	0.69	48	10	1	5	12	.208	.292	.283
June	1-1	2.87	57	13	2	4	18	.228	.351	.279
July	1-0	2.76	60	16	0	5	14	.267	.333	.318
August	1-3	4.26	49	14	1	4	7	.286	.429	.333
Sept./Oct.	1-1	5.54	51	12	2	4	9	.235	.451	.291
Leading Off Inn.			57	10	0	2	11	.175	.246	.203
Runners On			151	40	6	20	36	.265	.457	.347
Runners/Scor. Pos.			89	27	2	14	18	.303	.472	.390
Runners On/2 Out			81	25	4	12	21	.309	.556	.398
Scor. Pos./2 Out			50	18	2	10	11	.360	.600	.467
Late Inning Pressure			218	52	5	22	50	.239	.385	.306
Leading Off			40	7	0	1	8	.175	.275	.195
Runners On			112	28	5	16	27	.250	.473	.338
Runners/Scor. Pos.			68	18	1	12	15	.265	.426	.366
First 9 Batters			297	68	5	27	66	.229	.337	.291
Second 9 Batters			7	3	1	1	1	.429	1.000	.500
All Batters Thereafter			0	0	0	0	0	—	—	—

Loves to face: Doug DeCinces (.050, 1-for-20, 1 HR)
Hates to face: Tom Paciorek (.538, 7-for-13)
Ground outs-to-air outs ratio: 0.66, 8th lowest in A.L. last season (minimum: 250 BFP), 0.96 for career. . . . Additional statistics: 7 double-play ground outs in 62 opportunities, 12 doubles, 3 triples in 81.2 innings last season. . . . Faced only one batter once, pitched two or more innings 18 times, finished 58 games in 66 relief appearances. . . . More saves last season (34) than previous three seasons combined (26). . . . Led A.L. with 9 saves in May, and with 7 in July. . . . Career record of 7–0 vs. Kansas City. . . . Opponents' batting average of over .300 with runners in scoring position in each of the last three seasons. . . . Twelve of the last 13 home runs he's allowed have been hit with runners on base.

Jim Acker
Toronto Blue Jays — Throws Right

	W-L	ERA	AB	H	HR	BB	SO	BA	SA	OBA
Season	2-4	4.35	224	63	6	22	32	.281	.424	.344
vs. Left-Handers			106	36	6	14	8	.340	.575	.407
vs. Right-Handers			118	27	0	8	24	.229	.288	.285
Home	1-1	5.76	115	36	4	10	17	.313	.504	.357
Road	1-3	2.97	109	27	2	12	15	.248	.339	.331
Grass	1-2	3.66	72	19	2	11	8	.264	.389	.376
Artificial Turf	1-2	4.69	152	44	4	11	24	.289	.441	.327
April	0-1	2.08	45	9	0	4	8	.200	.244	.260
May	1-2	4.74	93	26	2	6	12	.280	.419	.317
June	1-1	4.91	70	24	4	11	9	.343	.543	.440
July	0-0	6.75	16	4	0	1	3	.250	.438	.278
August			0	0	0	0	0	—	—	—
Sept./Oct.			0	0	0	0	0	—	—	—
Leading Off Inn.			51	15	0	2	8	.294	.353	.333
Runners On			102	27	4	13	13	.265	.461	.339
Runners/Scor. Pos.			67	16	3	10	8	.239	.478	.325
Runners On/2 Out			42	14	3	8	5	.333	.595	.451
Scor. Pos./2 Out			31	9	2	6	3	.290	.548	.421
Late Inning Pressure			67	22	1	7	6	.328	.403	.403
Leading Off			15	8	0	1	0	.533	.600	.588
Runners On			39	9	1	4	5	.231	.308	.311
Runners/Scor. Pos.			26	3	1	4	3	.115	.231	.250
First 9 Batters			142	41	4	10	18	.289	.430	.333
Second 9 Batters			59	17	1	8	12	.288	.441	.362
All Batters Thereafter			23	5	1	4	2	.217	.348	.357

Loves to face: Willie Wilson (.077, 1-for-13)
Hates to face: Gary Pettis (.800, 4-for-5)
Figures above are for A.L. only. . . . Ground outs-to-air outs ratio: 1.91 last season, 2.11 for career. . . . Additional statistics: 15 double-play ground outs in 125 opportunities, 26 doubles, 5 triples in 155.0 innings last season. . . . Allowed 4 first-inning runs in 19 starts last season. . . . Batting support: 2.74 runs per start. . . . Faced only one batter twice, pitched two or more innings 12 times, finished 9 games in 25 relief appearances. . . . Opponents' career batting average of .422 (19-for-45, 5 BB) with the bases loaded. . . . Struck out 21 times in 28 at bats last season. . . . Additional comments in N.L. Pitchers section.

Doyle Alexander
Toronto Blue Jays — Throws Right

	W-L	ERA	AB	H	HR	BB	SO	BA	SA	OBA
Season	5-4	4.46	440	120	18	20	65	.273	.468	.308
vs. Left-Handers			228	61	7	11	25	.268	.417	.303
vs. Right-Handers			212	59	11	9	40	.278	.524	.314
Home	2-2	3.65	234	54	9	10	42	.231	.419	.267
Road	3-2	5.47	206	66	9	10	23	.320	.524	.355
Grass	3-1	4.50	160	51	4	6	15	.319	.469	.349
Artificial Turf	2-3	4.44	280	69	14	14	50	.246	.468	.285
April	3-1	2.21	153	35	3	4	24	.229	.353	.256
May	0-1	7.01	142	44	11	7	19	.310	.599	.344
June	2-1	3.00	129	33	4	7	21	.256	.419	.292
July	0-1	23.63	16	8	0	2	1	.500	.813	.579
August			0	0	0	0	0	—	—	—
Sept./Oct.			0	0	0	0	0	—	—	—
Leading Off Inn.			115	30	5	1	18	.261	.452	.274
Runners On			170	50	8	4	29	.294	.524	.313
Runners/Scor. Pos.			88	22	3	3	16	.250	.398	.281
Runners On/2 Out			73	17	0	2	16	.233	.342	.273
Scor. Pos./2 Out			49	10	0	2	11	.204	.306	.264
Late Inning Pressure			60	8	0	0	7	.133	.250	.133
Leading Off			16	0	0	0	2	.000	.000	.000
Runners On			9	0	0	0	3	.000	.000	.000
Runners/Scor. Pos.			1	0	0	0	0	.000	.000	.000
First 9 Batters			139	42	3	9	21	.302	.432	.351
Second 9 Batters			145	39	7	5	17	.269	.497	.296
All Batters Thereafter			156	39	8	6	27	.250	.474	.280

Loves to face: Jose Cruz (.167, 4-for-24)
Hates to face: Rob Thompson (.818, 9-for-11, 1 HR)
Figures above are for A.L. only. . . . Ground outs-to-air outs ratio: 0.87 last season, 0.94 for career. . . . Additional statistics: 17 double-play ground outs in 161 opportunities, 54 doubles (2d most in majors), 4 triples in 228.1 innings last season. Allowed 85 extra-base hits, 6th most in majors. . . . Allowed 19 first-inning runs in 34 starts last season. . . . Batting support: 4.97 runs per start (5.71 with Blue Jays was 5th best in A.L. among pitchers with 15 starts). . . . Has not walked in a run since June 8, 1979, when he walked Dave Skaggs with the bases loaded. Since then he has faced 53 batters with the bases full. . . . Additional comments in N.L. Pitchers section.

Neil Allen
Chicago White Sox — Throws Right

	W-L	ERA	AB	H	HR	BB	SO	BA	SA	OBA
Season	7-2	3.82	414	101	8	38	57	.244	.365	.306
vs. Left-Handers			211	49	4	18	27	.232	.360	.290
vs. Right-Handers			203	52	4	20	30	.256	.369	.322
Home	5-0	4.70	208	55	3	18	34	.264	.380	.323
Road	2-2	3.03	206	46	5	20	23	.223	.350	.289
Grass	7-2	3.67	358	82	5	27	52	.229	.335	.283
Artificial Turf	0-0	4.80	56	19	3	11	5	.339	.554	.435
April	0-0	13.50	24	11	0	1	5	.458	.500	.444
May	1-0	3.63	128	34	5	19	16	.266	.430	.356
June	3-0	5.28	109	30	2	12	17	.275	.431	.350
July	3-2	1.85	137	24	1	4	15	.175	.255	.201
August			0	0	0	0	0	—	—	—
Sept./Oct.	0-0	1.80	16	2	0	2	4	.125	.125	.222
Leading Off Inn.			109	25	1	9	16	.229	.349	.294
Runners On			147	39	3	22	22	.265	.388	.311
Runners/Scor. Pos.			71	20	1	6	6	.282	.408	.318
Runners On/2 Out			66	14	0	5	8	.212	.258	.268
Scor. Pos./2 Out			34	7	0	2	2	.206	.265	.250
Late Inning Pressure			17	6	1	1	1	.353	.529	.389
Leading Off			6	3	0	0	0	.500	.500	.500
Runners On			3	0	0	1	0	.000	.000	.250
Runners/Scor. Pos.			2	0	0	1	0	.000	.000	.333
First 9 Batters			152	36	3	20	26	.237	.362	.326
Second 9 Batters			138	29	2	10	23	.210	.304	.260
All Batters Thereafter			124	36	3	8	8	.290	.435	.331

Loves to face: Andre Thornton (.083, 1-for-12)
Hates to face: Larry Parrish (.583, 7-for-12)
Ground outs-to-air outs ratio: 1.17 last season, 1.22 for career. . . . Additional statistics: 5 double-play ground outs in 69 opportunities, 22 doubles, 2 triples in 113.0 innings last season. . . . Allowed 10 first-inning runs in 17 starts last season. . . . Batting support: 5.47 runs per start, 9th best in A.L. . . . Averaged 6.26 innings per start, highest on the White Sox' staff. . . . Warning to White Sox: Keep this guy! Allen had a record of 3–0 vs. the Mets in the season they traded him. Last season he came back to haunt the Yankees, beating them twice after being traded away in February 1986. . . . Has never hit a left-handed batter with a pitch. Has faced 1636 lefties in his career.

Allan Anderson

Throws Left

Minnesota Twins	W–L	ERA	AB	H	HR	BB	SO	BA	SA	OBA
Season	3-6	5.55	335	106	11	30	51	.316	.501	.371
vs. Left-Handers			89	30	3	8	12	.337	.551	.392
vs. Right-Handers			246	76	8	22	39	.309	.484	.364
Home	1-4	6.52	197	66	9	18	27	.335	.563	.385
Road	2-2	4.25	138	40	2	12	24	.290	.413	.351
Grass	2-1	4.41	126	37	2	10	21	.294	.413	.350
Artificial Turf	1-5	6.27	209	69	9	20	30	.330	.555	.384
April			0	0	0	0	0	—	—	—
May			0	0	0	0	0	—	—	—
June	2-1	3.69	113	28	3	10	20	.248	.425	.306
July	1-2	8.46	96	37	5	6	12	.385	.646	.423
August	0-2	4.97	52	16	1	8	8	.308	.462	.400
Sept./Oct.	0-1	5.60	74	25	2	6	11	.338	.459	.383
Leading Off Inn.			81	27	3	6	12	.333	.543	.379
Runners On			147	49	3	14	16	.333	.490	.388
Runners/Scor. Pos.			81	28	1	10	12	.346	.469	.404
Runners On/2 Out			58	21	0	2	12	.362	.500	.393
Scor. Pos./2 Out			35	12	0	2	9	.343	.429	.378
Late Inning Pressure			27	6	0	4	6	.222	.259	.323
Leading Off			9	1	0	0	2	.111	.111	.111
Runners On			9	2	0	1	2	.222	.222	.300
Runners/Scor. Pos.			2	1	0	0	0	.500	.500	.500
First 9 Batters			151	46	4	15	24	.305	.457	.365
Second 9 Batters			114	41	7	9	15	.360	.640	.403
All Batters Thereafter			70	19	0	6	12	.271	.371	.333

Loves to face: Steve Buechele (0-for-6, 4 SO)
Hates to face: Don Mattingly (.750, 3-for-4)
Ground outs-to-air outs ratio: 0.91 last season, his first in majors. . . . Additional statistics: 10 double-play ground outs in 76 opportunities, 27 doubles, 1 triple in 84.1 innings last season. . . . Allowed 4 first-inning runs in 10 starts last season. . . . Batting support: 3.70 runs per start. . . . 2–5, 5.93 ERA as a starter; 1–1, 4.85 ERA in 11 relief appearances. . . . Eleven of his last 15 appearances were as a reliever, after starting his first six games. His only complete game was his first victory, a 3-hit, nine-strikeout effort at Chicago on June 24. . . . Average of 2.21 strikeouts per walk in day games, 1.25 in night games. . . . Has never faced Andy Allanson.

Joaquin Andujar

Throws Right

Oakland As	W–L	ERA	AB	H	HR	BB	SO	BA	SA	OBA
Season	12-7	3.82	582	139	23	56	72	.239	.399	.308
vs. Left-Handers			307	78	15	29	28	.254	.453	.318
vs. Right-Handers			275	61	8	27	44	.222	.338	.297
Home	8-4	3.87	328	76	15	33	47	.232	.402	.301
Road	4-3	3.76	254	63	8	23	25	.248	.394	.318
Grass	11-6	3.46	508	117	20	48	64	.230	.386	.298
Artificial Turf	1-1	6.62	74	22	3	8	8	.297	.486	.373
April	2-1	4.43	82	16	3	9	12	.195	.341	.277
May	2-1	3.27	81	17	3	6	9	.210	.383	.264
June	0-0	0.00	0	0	0	1	0	—	—	1.000
July	2-1	3.72	77	19	3	7	9	.247	.390	.310
August	2-3	4.26	166	47	6	21	17	.283	.440	.368
Sept./Oct.	4-1	3.45	176	40	8	12	25	.227	.398	.279
Leading Off Inn.			144	36	10	15	19	.250	.493	.333
Runners On			206	49	7	31	25	.238	.388	.335
Runners/Scor. Pos.			121	24	3	16	11	.198	.314	.289
Runners On/2 Out			85	17	3	13	11	.200	.341	.313
Scor. Pos./2 Out			53	8	1	9	7	.151	.226	.286
Late Inning Pressure			66	14	1	11	10	.212	.258	.325
Leading Off			18	5	1	1	2	.278	.444	.316
Runners On			28	3	0	9	5	.107	.107	.324
Runners/Scor. Pos.			15	3	0	6	1	.200	.200	.429
First 9 Batters			202	45	9	20	22	.223	.406	.298
Second 9 Batters			180	47	8	17	25	.261	.433	.330
All Batters Thereafter			200	47	6	19	25	.235	.360	.299

Loves to face: Wade Boggs (0-for-6)
Hates to face: Brian Downing (.600, 6-for-10)
Ground outs-to-air outs ratio: 1.11 last season, 1.34 for career. . . . Additional statistics: 12 double-play ground outs in 106 opportunities, 16 doubles, 4 triples in 155.1 innings last season. . . . Allowed 18 first-inning runs in 26 starts last season. . . . Batting support: 4.27 runs per start. . . . Leads active pitchers in innings (2,014) without allowing a grand slam homer. All-time leaders: Old Hoss Radbourn (4543); Jim McCormick (4264); Eddie Plank (4234); Jim Palmer (3947.1). . . . Andujar and Gary Peters are the only pitchers in postwar era to have hit a grand slam but not allowed one. . . . How can this be true: Andujar has batted 667 times in his career and was never hit by a pitch!

Keith Atherton

Throws Right

As/Twins	W–L	ERA	AB	H	HR	BB	SO	BA	SA	OBA
Season	6-10	4.08	372	100	11	46	67	.269	.419	.347
vs. Left-Handers			182	55	8	28	29	.302	.478	.393
vs. Right-Handers			190	45	3	18	38	.237	.363	.300
Home	4-3	3.68	191	46	5	25	38	.241	.382	.324
Road	2-7	4.53	181	54	6	21	29	.298	.459	.371
Grass	1-3	3.89	128	33	2	22	22	.258	.359	.366
Artificial Turf	5-7	4.19	244	67	9	24	45	.275	.451	.336
April	1-1	5.00	34	10	1	6	5	.294	.559	.381
May	1-1	4.86	67	18	1	8	11	.269	.343	.347
June	2-1	1.26	98	17	0	10	16	.173	.214	.248
July	1-0	6.19	68	24	3	9	17	.353	.559	.429
August	0-7	5.59	75	23	5	11	13	.307	.560	.393
Sept./Oct.	1-0	3.68	30	8	1	2	5	.267	.433	.313
Leading Off Inn.			70	15	4	9	13	.214	.429	.313
Runners On			206	57	5	26	41	.277	.403	.350
Runners/Scor. Pos.			135	37	4	14	25	.274	.415	.331
Runners On/2 Out			88	20	2	7	19	.227	.352	.284
Scor. Pos./2 Out			64	11	1	3	15	.172	.250	.209
Late Inning Pressure			152	41	6	21	28	.270	.428	.356
Leading Off			34	10	2	5	6	.294	.529	.385
Runners On			79	20	2	9	14	.253	.354	.326
Runners/Scor. Pos.			46	9	1	5	11	.196	.261	.269
First 9 Batters			307	88	10	34	58	.287	.456	.354
Second 9 Batters			57	9	1	11	8	.158	.228	.294
All Batters Thereafter			8	3	0	1	1	.375	.375	.444

Loves to face: Brook Jacoby (0-for-9)
Hates to face: Eddie Murray (.571, 4-for-7, 2 HR)
Ground outs-to-air outs ratio: 0.63, 5th lowest in A.L. last season (minimum: 250 BFP), 0.52 for career. . . . Additional statistics: 6 double-play ground outs in 117 opportunities, 19 doubles, 2 triples in 97.0 innings last season. . . . Faced only one batter 5 times, pitched two or more innings 22 times, finished 36 games in 60 relief appearances. . . . Only A.L. pitcher to lose 10 games in relief last season. . . . June ERA was best in A.L. . . . Led A.L. in losses in August. . . . Career record of 0–6 vs. Toronto. . . . Opponents' career batting average of .167 (9-for-54) with the bases loaded. . . . In his four seasons in the majors, opponents have never hit above .200 with two outs and runners in scoring position. . . . Has not committed a balk in his last 186 games.

Scott Bailes

Throws Left

Cleveland Indians	W–L	ERA	AB	H	HR	BB	SO	BA	SA	OBA
Season	10-10	4.95	445	123	12	43	60	.276	.411	.339
vs. Left-Handers			117	35	3	11	17	.299	.427	.354
vs. Right-Handers			328	88	9	32	43	.268	.405	.333
Home	5-5	4.29	237	58	5	22	27	.245	.354	.309
Road	5-5	5.80	208	65	7	21	33	.313	.476	.371
Grass	10-9	4.88	406	111	10	38	51	.273	.404	.336
Artificial Turf	0-1	5.79	39	12	2	5	9	.308	.487	.370
April	3-1	5.06	60	17	2	8	14	.283	.467	.368
May	2-3	4.73	54	17	0	5	7	.315	.333	.367
June	2-0	4.60	62	17	1	7	8	.274	.403	.367
July	1-2	2.45	42	10	0	4	5	.238	.262	.292
August	1-2	4.46	133	33	5	13	15	.248	.398	.320
Sept./Oct.	1-2	7.25	94	29	4	6	11	.309	.511	.350
Leading Off Inn.			96	28	3	5	14	.292	.406	.327
Runners On			226	61	7	24	27	.270	.420	.335
Runners/Scor. Pos.			120	41	5	15	11	.342	.550	.403
Runners On/2 Out			94	28	4	7	5	.298	.500	.347
Scor. Pos./2 Out			56	20	3	6	1	.357	.625	.419
Late Inning Pressure			130	39	1	16	21	.300	.385	.376
Leading Off			25	7	0	0	7	.280	.320	.280
Runners On			78	25	1	12	7	.321	.423	.402
Runners/Scor. Pos.			55	21	1	8	6	.382	.509	.446
First 9 Batters			282	79	5	31	42	.280	.397	.349
Second 9 Batters			103	29	6	6	11	.282	.476	.321
All Batters Thereafter			60	15	1	6	7	.250	.367	.318

Loves to face: Dick Schofield (0-for-7)
Hates to face: Tom Brunansky (4-for-4)
Ground outs-to-air outs ratio: 1.13 last season, his first in majors. . . . Additional statistics: 10 double-play ground outs in 133 opportunities, 22 doubles, 1 triple in 112.2 innings last season. . . . Allowed 2 first-inning runs in 10 starts last season. . . . Batting support: 5.30 runs per start. . . . Faced only one batter 5 times, pitched two or more innings 10 times, finished 22 games in 52 relief appearances. . . . Opponents batted .462 (6-for-13) with the bases loaded. . . . Used in relief for his first 51 appearances, started 10 of his last 11 games. . . . 2–3, 5.26 ERA as a starter; 8–7 (7 saves), 4.68 ERA in relief. . . . Did not reach the ninth inning in any of his starts. . . . ERA after Sept. 1 was 2d worst in majors (minimum: 20 IP).

Scott Bankhead

Kansas City Royals — Throws Right

	W–L	ERA	AB	H	HR	BB	SO	BA	SA	OBA
Season	8-9	4.61	467	121	14	37	94	.259	.418	.314
vs. Left-Handers			273	66	11	21	54	.242	.414	.296
vs. Right-Handers			194	55	3	16	40	.284	.423	.340
Home	4-6	5.80	245	67	7	19	47	.273	.424	.328
Road	4-3	3.30	222	54	7	18	47	.243	.410	.299
Grass	3-1	2.45	142	34	2	11	26	.239	.345	.294
Artificial Turf	5-8	5.55	325	87	12	26	68	.268	.449	.323
April			0	0	0	0	0	—	—	—
May	1-0	0.00	19	2	0	1	7	.105	.158	.150
June	2-1	3.74	127	30	3	10	29	.236	.354	.300
July	1-4	5.03	131	35	6	11	21	.267	.466	.319
August	4-2	4.34	148	41	4	8	28	.277	.466	.310
Sept./Oct.	0-2	9.90	42	13	1	7	9	.310	.405	.420
Leading Off Inn.			121	35	5	4	23	.289	.463	.317
Runners On			184	47	3	21	33	.255	.359	.327
Runners/Scor. Pos.			113	26	2	18	25	.230	.345	.328
Runners On/2 Out			74	14	2	11	16	.189	.297	.302
Scor. Pos./2 Out			50	7	2	11	14	.140	.300	.306
Late Inning Pressure			56	9	2	8	12	.161	.286	.277
Leading Off			16	4	1	2	2	.250	.438	.333
Runners On			13	1	0	5	3	.077	.077	.368
Runners/Scor. Pos.			8	0	0	5	3	.000	.000	.429
First 9 Batters			193	51	6	12	39	.264	.415	.313
Second 9 Batters			148	38	4	14	34	.257	.405	.319
All Batters Thereafter			126	32	4	11	21	.254	.437	.312

Loves to face: Jose Canseco (0-for-5)
Hates to face: George Bell (.833, 5-for-6, 1 HR)
Ground outs-to-air outs ratio: 0.83 last season, his first in majors. . . . Additional statistics: 7 double-play ground outs in 89 opportunities, 24 doubles, 4 triples in 121.0 innings last season. . . . Allowed 10 first-inning runs in 17 starts last season. . . . Batting support: 4.53 runs per start. . . . Didn't complete a start last season, but did last nine innings in two of his starts, a 12-inning Royals victory at Oakland on June 16, and a 13-inning loss to Baltimore on July 8. . . . Four losses in July were tied for most in A.L. . . . Opponents batted .161 in Late-Inning Pressure Situations, .273 in unpressured situations.

Floyd Bannister

Chicago White Sox — Throws Left

	W–L	ERA	AB	H	HR	BB	SO	BA	SA	OBA
Season	10-14	3.54	626	162	17	48	92	.259	.398	.311
vs. Left-Handers			98	20	2	6	16	.204	.316	.255
vs. Right-Handers			528	142	15	42	76	.269	.413	.322
Home	5-6	2.84	356	78	9	27	61	.219	.354	.275
Road	5-8	4.57	270	84	8	21	31	.311	.456	.360
Grass	7-13	3.59	550	142	14	42	80	.258	.389	.311
Artificial Turf	3-1	3.15	76	20	3	6	12	.263	.461	.317
April	1-2	3.00	90	21	1	9	6	.233	.344	.303
May	1-2	2.70	89	22	2	11	19	.247	.337	.337
June	1-0	6.75	5	1	0	0	0	.200	.200	.200
July	2-4	5.61	131	38	7	7	17	.290	.496	.324
August	3-2	3.68	140	39	2	9	26	.279	.393	.318
Sept./Oct.	2-4	2.53	171	41	5	12	24	.240	.392	.290
Leading Off Inn.			168	46	3	6	26	.274	.381	.299
Runners On			235	59	6	28	33	.251	.362	.327
Runners/Scor. Pos.			131	28	3	15	21	.214	.321	.289
Runners On/2 Out			91	20	3	14	12	.220	.363	.330
Scor. Pos./2 Out			56	8	1	10	8	.143	.250	.284
Late Inning Pressure			50	12	1	5	11	.240	.340	.309
Leading Off			16	4	0	2	4	.250	.313	.333
Runners On			14	4	0	3	3	.286	.357	.412
Runners/Scor. Pos.			5	2	0	1	1	.400	.600	.500
First 9 Batters			225	61	7	16	32	.271	.436	.320
Second 9 Batters			207	60	7	18	31	.290	.459	.348
All Batters Thereafter			194	41	3	14	29	.211	.289	.262

Loves to face: Darrell Porter (0-for-17)
Hates to face: Gary Gaetti (.464, 13-for-28, 5 HR)
Ground outs-to-air outs ratio: 1.00 last season, 0.91 for career. . . . Additional statistics: 16 double-play ground outs in 122 opportunities, 26 doubles, 5 triples in 165.1 innings last season. . . . Allowed 15 first-inning runs in 27 starts last season. . . . White Sox scored an average of 3.30 runs in his 27 starts, 2d-poorest run support in A.L. (minimum: 15 GS). . . . Four losses in July were tied for most in A.L. . . . Has lost 11 straight decisions to the Red Sox since shuting them out at Fenway Park on May 18, 1982. Last season he had a record of 0–4 against the A.L. champs. . . . Since 1984, opponents have batted .395 (15-for-38, 3 HR) with the bases loaded.

Bud Black

Kansas City Royals — Throws Left

	W–L	ERA	AB	H	HR	BB	SO	BA	SA	OBA
Season	5-10	3.20	445	100	14	43	68	.225	.373	.301
vs. Left-Handers			137	30	3	11	27	.219	.336	.285
vs. Right-Handers			308	70	11	32	41	.227	.390	.307
Home	3-2	2.63	223	45	4	18	35	.202	.323	.271
Road	2-8	3.79	222	55	10	25	33	.248	.423	.329
Grass	2-6	3.97	165	37	7	16	22	.224	.400	.297
Artificial Turf	3-4	2.74	280	63	7	27	46	.225	.357	.303
April	1-2	6.14	63	21	3	4	7	.333	.540	.368
May	2-1	4.34	66	15	3	7	17	.227	.409	.311
June	1-1	2.79	71	15	1	9	9	.211	.352	.300
July	0-1	2.82	84	20	3	4	14	.238	.357	.293
August	0-2	2.55	87	15	2	11	12	.172	.322	.275
Sept./Oct.	1-3	1.69	74	14	2	8	9	.189	.297	.277
Leading Off Inn.			103	27	2	8	11	.262	.369	.321
Runners On			199	41	9	24	31	.206	.367	.302
Runners/Scor. Pos.			113	25	5	20	19	.221	.372	.343
Runners On/2 Out			90	25	7	12	16	.278	.544	.375
Scor. Pos./2 Out			57	17	5	12	11	.298	.579	.429
Late Inning Pressure			150	28	5	19	23	.187	.300	.295
Leading Off			38	12	2	2	4	.316	.474	.350
Runners On			68	9	2	9	13	.132	.221	.263
Runners/Scor. Pos.			28	5	0	8	7	.179	.179	.395
First 9 Batters			331	70	9	33	54	.211	.338	.290
Second 9 Batters			90	22	3	9	12	.244	.433	.320
All Batters Thereafter			24	8	2	1	2	.333	.625	.385

Loves to face: Bob Boone (.091, 3-for-33)
Hates to face: Alfredo Griffin (.571, 12-for-21)
Ground outs-to-air outs ratio: 1.00 last season, 1.05 for career. . . . Additional statistics: 9 double-play ground outs in 101 opportunities, 18 doubles, 3 triples in 121.0 innings last season. . . . Faced only one batter 3 times, pitched two or more innings 26 times (4th most in A.L.), finished 26 games in 52 relief appearances. . . . Averaged 4.25 innings per game in his four starts. . . . Opponents batted .077 (1-for-13) with the bases loaded last season. . . . Has lost his last five decisions to the Yankees. . . . Has allowed only 26 career home runs at Royals Stadium, 56 in road games. Opponents' career batting, slugging: .251, .351 at home; .249, .414 on the road.

Bert Blyleven

Minnesota Twins — Throws Right

	W–L	ERA	AB	H	HR	BB	SO	BA	SA	OBA
Season	17-14	4.01	1049	262	50	58	215	.250	.448	.294
vs. Left-Handers			638	152	26	35	138	.238	.415	.279
vs. Right-Handers			411	110	24	23	77	.268	.498	.318
Home	12-5	4.12	604	159	31	29	133	.263	.469	.301
Road	5-9	3.86	445	103	19	29	82	.231	.420	.285
Grass	4-7	4.34	320	71	16	23	58	.222	.413	.284
Artificial Turf	13-7	3.86	729	191	34	35	157	.262	.464	.299
April	2-1	3.57	152	38	5	14	28	.250	.408	.321
May	2-3	6.39	183	51	14	5	35	.279	.568	.300
June	2-3	6.37	150	45	8	9	21	.300	.560	.352
July	3-3	2.85	171	38	6	11	33	.222	.351	.283
August	5-0	1.45	177	32	5	7	46	.181	.299	.211
Sept./Oct.	3-4	4.23	216	58	12	12	52	.269	.495	.306
Leading Off Inn.			266	69	9	12	60	.259	.425	.296
Runners On			386	95	23	23	81	.246	.469	.298
Runners/Scor. Pos.			206	47	10	15	55	.228	.427	.294
Runners On/2 Out			154	42	14	11	32	.273	.604	.333
Scor. Pos./2 Out			96	23	8	8	25	.240	.542	.318
Late Inning Pressure			87	28	5	6	15	.322	.563	.366
Leading Off			25	8	2	0	4	.320	.600	.320
Runners On			26	10	1	3	4	.385	.615	.448
Runners/Scor. Pos.			18	7	0	1	3	.389	.556	.421
First 9 Batters			296	60	8	19	74	.203	.334	.262
Second 9 Batters			299	82	21	15	56	.274	.535	.314
All Batters Thereafter			454	120	21	24	85	.264	.465	.303

Loves to face: Don Slaught (.038, 1-for-26)
Hates to face: Brett Butler (.462, 6-for-13, 1 HR)
Ground outs-to-air outs ratio: 1.02 last season, 1.20 for career. . . . Additional statistics: 18 double-play ground outs in 191 opportunities, 42 doubles, 8 triples in 271.2 innings last season. . . . Allowed 16 first-inning runs in 36 starts last season. . . . Batting support: 4.56 runs per start. . . . Allowed exactly 100 extra-base hits, most by any pitcher in last 12 years. . . . Gave up a home run to the first batter he faced in his first major-league start (Lee Maye in 1970), but went on to pitch seven innings of a 2–1 win. . . . In 12-year *Player Analysis* history, only Nolan Ryan has fanned more left-handed batters in a season than Blyleven did in '86. Ryan did it four times.

Mike Boddicker

Baltimore Orioles — Throws Right

	W–L	ERA	AB	H	HR	BB	SO	BA	SA	OBA
Season	14-12	4.70	840	214	30	74	175	.255	.410	.321
vs. Left-Handers			428	114	12	37	72	.266	.404	.329
vs. Right-Handers			412	100	18	37	103	.243	.415	.313
Home	7-4	4.66	390	96	15	44	87	.246	.395	.333
Road	7-8	4.73	450	118	15	30	88	.262	.422	.311
Grass	10-10	5.15	657	171	26	67	138	.260	.425	.335
Artificial Turf	4-2	3.14	183	43	4	7	37	.235	.355	.267
April	2-0	3.38	78	19	1	8	21	.244	.346	.314
May	3-1	3.34	121	27	2	15	29	.223	.298	.324
June	5-2	5.07	188	44	10	16	32	.234	.457	.300
July	3-2	3.74	167	40	5	6	31	.240	.359	.278
August	1-4	5.31	170	47	8	16	33	.276	.447	.335
Sept./Oct.	0-3	7.06	116	37	4	13	29	.319	.509	.393
Leading Off Inn.			207	64	7	20	33	.309	.469	.378
Runners On			357	98	16	21	88	.275	.457	.317
Runners/Scor. Pos.			187	56	13	12	46	.299	.556	.338
Runners On/2 Out			144	38	6	12	37	.264	.417	.321
Scor. Pos./2 Out			91	28	6	8	19	.308	.538	.364
Late Inning Pressure			76	20	2	6	13	.263	.382	.333
Leading Off			24	8	0	1	3	.333	.417	.360
Runners On			27	7	0	2	6	.259	.259	.333
Runners/Scor. Pos.			11	4	0	0	2	.364	.364	.417
First 9 Batters			263	72	8	26	49	.274	.433	.339
Second 9 Batters			252	61	10	22	55	.242	.405	.306
All Batters Thereafter			325	81	12	26	71	.249	.394	.318

Loves to face: Brook Jacoby (.056, 1-for-18, 8 SO)
Hates to face: Kirk Gibson (.474, 9-for-19, 3 HR)
Ground outs-to-air outs ratio: 1.21 last season, 1.51 for career. . . . Additional statistics: 12 double-play ground outs in 162 opportunities, 32 doubles, 4 triples in 218.1 innings last season. . . . Allowed 28 first-inning runs (5th most in A.L.) in 33 starts last season. . . . Batting support: 5.06 runs per start. . . . Had a 10–1 record after June 20, and a 14–5 record after Aug. 4, before losing his last seven decisions. . . . Allowed seven 3-run homers last season, tied with Mike Witt for most in A.L. . . . Has faced 41 batters with the bases loaded in his career and has walked in eight runs. . . . Opponents' annual batting averages with runners in scoring position since 1984: .178, .237, .299. . . . Career record of 7–0 vs. Texas.

Rich Bordi

Baltimore Orioles — Throws Right

	W–L	ERA	AB	H	HR	BB	SO	BA	SA	OBA
Season	6-4	4.46	413	105	13	41	83	.254	.392	.325
vs. Left-Handers			172	53	6	22	28	.308	.477	.383
vs. Right-Handers			241	52	7	19	55	.216	.332	.283
Home	4-3	2.82	254	61	6	22	50	.240	.339	.302
Road	2-1	7.20	159	44	7	19	33	.277	.478	.361
Grass	6-3	4.41	373	97	11	36	72	.260	.397	.328
Artificial Turf	0-1	4.91	40	8	2	5	11	.200	.350	.304
April	0-0	2.65	61	14	1	10	11	.230	.361	.342
May	3-0	2.12	60	13	2	6	15	.217	.350	.288
June	0-0	7.62	56	19	2	8	8	.339	.536	.415
July	1-1	2.17	105	20	2	5	30	.190	.286	.232
August	1-1	7.80	61	18	3	3	10	.295	.443	.328
Sept./Oct.	1-2	7.31	70	21	3	9	9	.300	.457	.395
Leading Off Inn.			85	29	5	8	18	.341	.541	.404
Runners On			215	54	4	19	50	.251	.358	.308
Runners/Scor. Pos.			131	33	2	12	31	.252	.366	.308
Runners On/2 Out			89	20	1	3	24	.225	.303	.250
Scor. Pos./2 Out			61	14	0	3	15	.230	.295	.266
Late Inning Pressure			138	40	5	17	22	.290	.428	.369
Leading Off			32	11	2	5	3	.344	.531	.432
Runners On			65	20	0	7	13	.308	.369	.370
Runners/Scor. Pos.			40	10	0	6	8	.250	.350	.340
First 9 Batters			289	77	11	35	60	.266	.426	.348
Second 9 Batters			107	24	2	5	22	.224	.327	.265
All Batters Thereafter			17	4	0	1	1	.235	.235	.278

Loves to face: Brett Butler (0-for-9)
Hates to face: Marty Barrett (.800, 4-for-5)
Ground outs-to-air outs ratio: 0.82 last season, 0.98 for career. . . . Additional statistics: 7 double-play ground outs in 113 opportunities, 12 doubles, 3 triples in 107.0 innings. . . . Faced only one batter 2 times, pitched two or more innings 20 times, finished 22 games in 51 relief appearances. . . . Held top 15 A.L. batters to combined .146 average last season (6-for-41), 3d lowest in A.L. (minimum: 20 at bats). . . . One of four pitchers whose opponents have hit better in Late-Inning Pressure Situations than overall for the last five seasons. Others: Jim Clancy, Ken Dayley, Ricky Wright. . . . Opponents' career batting average of .315 in LIP Situations, .242 in unpressured situations. . . . Nearly identical opposing batting averages in 1985: .309 by left-handers, .209 by right-handers.

Oil Can Boyd

Boston Red Sox — Throws Right

	W–L	ERA	AB	H	HR	BB	SO	BA	SA	OBA
Season	16-10	3.78	837	222	32	45	129	.265	.430	.302
vs. Left-Handers			442	123	18	19	59	.278	.452	.306
vs. Right-Handers			395	99	14	26	70	.251	.405	.298
Home	9-6	3.66	479	139	13	24	75	.290	.432	.326
Road	7-4	3.93	358	83	19	21	54	.232	.427	.271
Grass	16-9	3.67	814	216	30	43	126	.265	.426	.302
Artificial Turf	0-1	7.50	23	6	2	2	3	.261	.565	.308
April	1-2	4.66	108	26	4	8	15	.241	.435	.288
May	5-1	2.66	177	37	8	5	24	.209	.379	.234
June	4-2	3.46	165	50	5	14	21	.303	.455	.358
July	1-1	6.75	46	14	3	3	10	.304	.543	.347
August	2-3	3.98	175	51	7	6	28	.291	.440	.315
Sept./Oct.	3-1	3.80	166	44	5	9	31	.265	.416	.302
Leading Off Inn.			212	59	6	10	30	.278	.406	.314
Runners On			308	78	13	19	44	.253	.425	.293
Runners/Scor. Pos.			144	35	8	10	21	.243	.444	.286
Runners On/2 Out			131	31	4	7	18	.237	.344	.281
Scor. Pos./2 Out			72	18	3	6	10	.250	.375	.316
Late Inning Pressure			75	23	2	3	8	.307	.413	.333
Leading Off			23	6	0	1	2	.261	.261	.292
Runners On			21	8	0	2	0	.381	.476	.435
Runners/Scor. Pos.			8	3	0	1	0	.375	.500	.444
First 9 Batters			248	59	5	17	40	.238	.339	.287
Second 9 Batters			252	75	15	13	47	.298	.536	.331
All Batters Thereafter			337	88	12	15	42	.261	.418	.292

Loves to face: Pete Incaviglia (0-for-11, 8 SO)
Hates to face: Larry Parrish (.500, 7-for-14, 3 HR)
Ground outs-to-air outs ratio: 1.12 last season, 1.07 for career. . . . Additional statistics: 15 double-play ground outs in 152 opportunities, 30 doubles, 6 triples in 214.1 innings last season. . . . Allowed 9 first-inning runs in 30 starts last season. . . . Batting support: 5.50 runs per start. . . . Allowed 32 home runs last season, but before you say, "Aha, Fenway," check the home/road distribution: one every nine innings at home, one every five innings on road. Allowed as many *road* homers (19) as did Bert Blyleven; at home: Bert 31, Boyd 13. . . . You want consistency? Opponents' annual batting since 1983: .269, .269, .261, .265. . . . Career ratio of 2.87 strikeouts per walk in day games, 4th highest in *Player Analysis* history (minimum: 100 SO).

Mike Brown

Red Sox/Mariners — Throws Right

	W–L	ERA	AB	H	HR	BB	SO	BA	SA	OBA
Season	4-6	5.79	291	91	14	36	41	.313	.540	.387
vs. Left-Handers			140	47	6	18	15	.336	.571	.409
vs. Right-Handers			151	44	8	18	26	.291	.510	.366
Home	2-3	5.63	195	63	10	23	27	.323	.569	.394
Road	2-3	6.12	96	28	4	13	14	.292	.479	.373
Grass	3-5	6.58	212	72	10	25	26	.340	.552	.407
Artificial Turf	1-1	3.86	79	19	4	11	15	.241	.506	.333
April	1-0	2.35	27	6	2	1	3	.222	.481	.250
May	2-1	5.27	108	33	5	12	13	.306	.537	.377
June	1-3	4.00	71	22	1	7	11	.310	.394	.363
July	0-0	16.62	22	11	2	5	5	.500	.955	.593
August	0-2	8.31	31	8	2	8	4	.258	.484	.410
Sept./Oct.	0-0	6.43	32	11	2	3	5	.344	.688	.468
Leading Off Inn.			68	27	4	9	4	.397	.721	.468
Runners On			130	35	5	16	24	.269	.454	.347
Runners/Scor. Pos.			80	20	1	9	19	.250	.375	.323
Runners On/2 Out			60	21	1	9	14	.350	.517	.435
Scor. Pos./2 Out			44	15	0	5	13	.341	.477	.408
Late Inning Pressure			21	8	1	7	3	.381	.667	.536
Leading Off			5	1	1	2	0	.200	.800	.429
Runners On			8	3	0	3	1	.375	.500	.545
Runners/Scor. Pos.			4	3	0	1	0	.750	1.000	.800
First 9 Batters			140	48	4	19	13	.343	.557	.420
Second 9 Batters			87	25	7	9	16	.287	.575	.354
All Batters Thereafter			64	18	3	8	12	.281	.453	.356

Loves to face: Cal Ripken (0-for-6)
Hates to face: Willie Wilson (.800, 8-for-10)
Ground outs-to-air outs ratio: 1.21 last season, 1.20 for career. . . . Additional statistics: 7 double-play ground outs in 53 opportunities, 16 doubles, 4 triples in 73.0 innings last season. . . . Allowed 8 first-inning runs in 12 starts last season. . . . Batting support: 3.25 runs per start. . . . 4-6, 5.02 ERA as a starter; 0-0, 9.75 ERA in nine relief appearances. . . . Opposing left-handed batters have a career batting average of .346 (177-for-511), and slugging percentage of .544. Both of those figures are the highest for any pitcher in the last 12 years (minimum: 500 AB). . . . Has faced 24 batters in his career with the bases loaded, has not walked in a run.

John Butcher

Twins/Indians — Throws Right

	W-L	ERA	AB	H	HR	BB	SO	BA	SA	OBA
Season	1-8	6.56	503	168	17	37	45	.334	.503	.380
vs. Left-Handers			300	102	11	23	21	.340	.517	.388
vs. Right-Handers			203	66	6	14	24	.325	.483	.369
Home	0-2	8.35	149	59	1	8	7	.396	.497	.422
Road	1-6	5.91	354	109	16	29	38	.308	.506	.362
Grass	1-7	7.48	323	113	13	25	30	.350	.526	.396
Artificial Turf	0-1	4.95	180	55	4	12	15	.306	.461	.351
April	0-2	4.79	138	34	6	11	18	.246	.428	.302
May	0-1	6.75	89	28	4	12	8	.315	.517	.394
June	0-2	8.64	75	28	3	3	5	.373	.627	.400
July	1-2	5.13	142	50	1	6	8	.352	.430	.377
August	0-1	16.88	46	24	3	5	5	.522	.761	.566
Sept./Oct.	0-0	3.00	13	4	0	0	1	.308	.385	.308
Leading Off Inn.			120	47	5	5	12	.392	.633	.425
Runners On			236	82	6	19	16	.347	.483	.389
Runners/Scor. Pos.			148	49	5	15	11	.331	.514	.382
Runners On/2 Out			86	26	1	7	8	.302	.384	.355
Scor. Pos./2 Out			58	16	1	6	5	.276	.397	.344
Late Inning Pressure			27	6	2	3	2	.222	.556	.300
Leading Off			9	3	0	1	1	.333	.556	.400
Runners On			8	2	1	1	0	.250	.750	.333
Runners/Scor. Pos.			6	2	1	1	0	.333	1.000	.429
First 9 Batters			208	68	5	17	18	.327	.462	.379
Second 9 Batters			158	58	5	11	20	.367	.538	.406
All Batters Thereafter			137	42	7	9	7	.307	.526	.351

Loves to face: Ron Hassey (0-for-12)
Hates to face: Harold Baines (.500, 13-for-26, 3 HR)
Ground outs-to-air outs ratio: 1.37 last season, 1.41 for career. . . . Additional statistics: 19 double-play ground outs in 116 opportunities, 5th-highest average in A.L. (minimum: 10 GDP), 30 doubles, 2 triples in 120.2 innings last season. . . . Allowed 11 first-inning runs in 18 starts last season. . . . Batting support: 4.89 runs per start. . . . 1–7, 5.97 ERA as a starter; 0–1, 9.13 ERA in 11 relief appearances. . . . Allowed only one home run in home games in 1986, 16 in road games; but his "home games" were split between two ballparks. All 11 allowed while with the Twins were hit in road games. . . . Has walked the leadoff batter in only 13 of 348 innings over the past two seasons. . . . Career record of 0–5 vs. the Yankees.

Ernie Camacho

Cleveland Indians — Throws Right

	W-L	ERA	AB	H	HR	BB	SO	BA	SA	OBA
Season	2-4	4.08	223	60	1	31	36	.269	.332	.355
vs. Left-Handers			109	31	1	19	16	.284	.367	.376
vs. Right-Handers			114	29	0	12	20	.254	.298	.333
Home	1-0	5.65	119	36	0	14	16	.303	.370	.374
Road	1-4	2.51	104	24	1	17	20	.231	.288	.333
Grass	2-1	3.78	183	47	0	24	30	.257	.306	.340
Artificial Turf	0-3	5.59	40	13	1	7	6	.325	.450	.426
April	0-0	3.09	45	10	0	7	14	.222	.289	.327
May	1-0	6.35	22	7	0	7	1	.318	.364	.467
June	0-1	4.50	29	7	0	4	5	.241	.276	.324
July	0-1	2.16	31	8	0	7	4	.258	.290	.385
August	1-0	4.09	44	12	0	4	6	.273	.318	.327
Sept./Oct.	0-2	4.97	52	16	1	2	6	.308	.423	.345
Leading Off Inn.			33	13	0	7	5	.394	.485	.500
Runners On			150	37	0	22	22	.247	.300	.331
Runners/Scor. Pos.			92	23	0	18	15	.250	.293	.353
Runners On/2 Out			69	13	0	14	8	.188	.203	.325
Scor. Pos./2 Out			45	8	0	12	7	.178	.178	.351
Late Inning Pressure			171	45	1	27	25	.263	.333	.358
Leading Off			26	11	0	6	2	.423	.538	.531
Runners On			112	25	0	19	15	.223	.277	.324
Runners/Scor. Pos.			68	17	0	15	9	.250	.279	.364
First 9 Batters			213	57	1	30	35	.268	.329	.355
Second 9 Batters			10	3	0	1	1	.300	.400	.364
All Batters Thereafter			0	0	0	0	0	—	—	—

Loves to face: Jim Rice (0-for-12)
Hates to face: Dwight Evans (.714, 5-for-7, 2 HR)
Ground outs-to-air outs ratio: 1.59 last season, 1.60 for career. . . . Additional statistics: 2 double-play ground outs in 77 opportunities, 4th-lowest average in A.L. (minimum: 40 opp.), 9 doubles, 1 triple in 57.1 innings last season. . . . Faced only one batter 2 times, pitched two or more innings 5 times, finished 37 games in 51 relief appearances. . . . Led A.L. with six saves in April. . . . Opponents have hit for a higher average with the bases empty than with runners on base in each of his six seasons in the majors. . . . Opponents' career batting in Late-Inning Pressure Situations: .212 with runners on base, .283 with bases empty. . . . Last home run by a right-handed batter: Aug. 31, 1984, by Dwight Evans.

John Candelaria

California Angels — Throws Left

	W-L	ERA	AB	H	HR	BB	SO	BA	SA	OBA
Season	10-2	2.55	330	68	4	26	81	.206	.306	.268
vs. Left-Handers			59	11	0	5	17	.186	.271	.254
vs. Right-Handers			271	57	4	21	64	.210	.314	.271
Home	5-1	2.66	166	30	2	14	44	.181	.295	.250
Road	5-1	2.44	164	38	2	12	37	.232	.317	.287
Grass	10-2	1.95	296	56	2	22	74	.189	.270	.250
Artificial Turf	0-0	8.31	34	12	2	4	7	.353	.618	.421
April	0-0	18.00	10	6	0	1	0	.600	.800	.636
May			0	0	0	0	0	—	—	—
June			0	0	0	0	0	—	—	—
July	4-1	2.67	98	21	1	9	20	.214	.316	.291
August	3-1	2.15	134	26	3	11	34	.194	.299	.257
Sept./Oct.	3-0	1.80	88	15	0	5	27	.170	.250	.215
Leading Off Inn.			88	18	0	8	24	.205	.261	.271
Runners On			130	28	2	11	28	.215	.338	.271
Runners/Scor. Pos.			63	14	2	7	12	.222	.413	.288
Runners On/2 Out			53	9	2	7	12	.170	.340	.267
Scor. Pos./2 Out			28	5	2	6	5	.179	.429	.324
Late Inning Pressure			14	2	0	3	3	.143	.143	.278
Leading Off			3	0	0	2	0	.000	.000	.400
Runners On			5	2	0	1	2	.400	.400	.429
Runners/Scor. Pos.			1	1	0	1	0	1.000	1.000	.667
First 9 Batters			127	31	2	12	32	.244	.370	.314
Second 9 Batters			128	23	2	7	26	.180	.273	.232
All Batters Thereafter			75	14	0	7	23	.187	.253	.250

Loves to face: Brett Butler (0-for-9, 4 SO)
Hates to face: Larry Herndon (.439, 18-for-41, 3 HR)
Ground outs-to-air outs ratio: 0.65, 6th lowest in A.L. last season (minimum: 250 BFP), 0.87 for career. . . . Additional statistics: 5 double-play ground outs in 60 opportunities, 13 doubles, 4 triples in 91.2 innings last season. . . . Allowed 4 first-inning runs in 16 starts last season. . . . Batting support: 6.00 runs per start, 3d best in A.L. (minimum: 15 GS). . . . Did not walk more than three batters in a game last season. Has not walked more than four batters in any game since April 28, 1978. . . . Finished regular season holding opponents hitless in their last 29 at bats with two outs and runners on base. . . . Has allowed 120 of 181 career home runs with the bases empty, 163 to right-handed batters.

Tom Candiotti

Cleveland Indians — Throws Right

	W-L	ERA	AB	H	HR	BB	SO	BA	SA	OBA
Season	16-12	3.57	952	234	18	106	167	.246	.357	.324
vs. Left-Handers			497	118	7	56	74	.237	.334	.311
vs. Right-Handers			455	116	11	50	93	.255	.382	.337
Home	10-6	3.35	517	129	10	56	96	.250	.356	.330
Road	6-6	3.82	435	105	8	50	71	.241	.359	.316
Grass	15-9	3.15	772	185	15	91	130	.240	.339	.324
Artificial Turf	1-3	5.52	180	49	3	15	37	.272	.433	.322
April	1-2	2.28	99	16	1	21	24	.162	.202	.308
May	2-3	4.68	126	33	2	17	24	.262	.349	.363
June	3-1	4.60	176	55	3	18	39	.313	.432	.379
July	4-1	2.90	155	38	2	11	21	.245	.381	.292
August	3-2	3.42	182	41	8	21	21	.225	.379	.309
Sept./Oct.	3-3	3.34	214	51	2	18	38	.238	.336	.297
Leading Off Inn.			239	68	5	20	45	.285	.418	.345
Runners On			415	92	4	58	64	.222	.301	.318
Runners/Scor. Pos.			228	52	3	44	36	.228	.325	.346
Runners On/2 Out			162	36	2	26	23	.222	.302	.337
Scor. Pos./2 Out			105	21	2	22	19	.200	.314	.344
Late Inning Pressure			88	21	2	13	15	.239	.352	.343
Leading Off			25	4	0	2	3	.160	.160	.250
Runners On			31	11	1	6	3	.355	.581	.459
Runners/Scor. Pos.			13	6	1	4	0	.462	.923	.588
First 9 Batters			264	65	2	36	51	.246	.326	.342
Second 9 Batters			257	67	6	28	42	.261	.385	.333
All Batters Thereafter			431	102	10	42	74	.237	.360	.306

Loves to face: Jim Presley (0-for-11, 7 SO)
Hates to face: Don Baylor (.545, 6-for-11, 3 HR)
Ground outs-to-air outs ratio: 1.14 last season, 1.20 for career (2.30 in Late-Inning Pressure Situations). . . . Additional statistics: 26 double-play ground outs (4th in A.L.) in 222 opportunities, 44 doubles (6th most in A.L.), 4 triples in 252.1 innings last season. . . . Allowed 15 first-inning runs in 34 starts last season. . . . Batting support: 5.21 runs per start. . . . Led A.L. in complete games (17). . . . Averaged 7.36 innings per start, best on Cleveland's staff. . . . Opponents' batting average has decreased in each of his seasons in the majors: .291, .277, .246. . . . Appeared for Brewers in 1983 and 1984, but spent the entire 1985 season in the minors, compiling a 10–13 record.

Steve Carlton
Chicago White Sox   *Throws Left*

	W–L	ERA	AB	H	HR	BB	SO	BA	SA	OBA
Season	4–3	3.69	230	58	6	25	40	.252	.400	.323
vs. Left-Handers			16	3	0	1	4	.188	.188	.235
vs. Right-Handers			214	55	6	24	36	.257	.416	.329
Home	2–0	3.51	115	25	1	15	18	.217	.322	.303
Road	2–3	3.90	115	33	5	10	22	.287	.478	.344
Grass	2–3	4.28	177	46	4	22	28	.260	.407	.338
Artificial Turf	2–0	1.80	53	12	2	3	12	.226	.377	.268
April			0	0	0	0	0	—	—	—
May			0	0	0	0	0	—	—	—
June			0	0	0	0	0	—	—	—
July			0	0	0	0	0	—	—	—
August	2–2	5.87	85	22	3	12	15	.259	.447	.347
Sept./Oct.	2–1	2.45	145	36	3	13	25	.248	.372	.308
Leading Off Inn.			58	16	2	9	8	.276	.448	.373
Runners On			87	24	3	9	11	.276	.425	.337
Runners/Scor. Pos.			45	13	2	5	6	.289	.467	.346
Runners On/2 Out			33	9	1	3	3	.273	.394	.333
Scor. Pos./2 Out			15	5	1	3	1	.333	.533	.444
Late Inning Pressure			29	10	0	3	2	.345	.483	.406
Leading Off			8	2	0	2	1	.250	.375	.400
Runners On			12	5	0	0	0	.417	.667	.417
Runners/Scor. Pos.			4	3	0	0	0	.750	1.250	.750
First 9 Batters			80	19	2	9	19	.238	.413	.315
Second 9 Batters			79	17	2	8	10	.215	.304	.281
All Batters Thereafter			71	22	2	8	11	.310	.493	.380

Loves to face: Omar Moreno (.171, 12-for-70, 27 SO)
Hates to face: Lee Lacy (.372, 29-for-78, 2 HR)
Figures above are for A.L. only; see also N.L. Pitchers section. . . .
Ground outs-to-air outs ratio: 1.23 last season, 1.09 for career. . . .
Additional statistics: 22 double-play ground outs in 149 opportunities, 30 doubles, 5 triples in 176.1 innings. . . . Allowed 21 first-inning runs in 32 starts last season. . . . Batting support: 4.72 runs per start. . . . Led majors in balks in 8 of the past 12 seasons. . . . Future as a reliever? 18 career relief appearances, with no saves. . . . Leads active pitchers with 13 homers, followed by Seaver, 12; Bob Forsch, 10; Rhoden, 9; Lollar, 8; and Phil Niekro 7.

John Cerutti
Toronto Blue Jays   *Throws Left*

	W–L	ERA	AB	H	HR	BB	SO	BA	SA	OBA
Season	9–4	4.15	559	150	25	47	89	.268	.449	.324
vs. Left-Handers			129	31	5	7	24	.240	.380	.281
vs. Right-Handers			430	119	20	40	65	.277	.470	.336
Home	2–1	5.12	231	66	14	15	41	.286	.524	.329
Road	7–3	3.50	328	84	11	32	48	.256	.396	.320
Grass	5–3	3.42	258	66	8	27	39	.256	.376	.324
Artificial Turf	4–1	4.79	301	84	17	20	50	.279	.512	.323
April			0	0	0	0	0	—	—	—
May	1–1	2.65	59	11	2	7	12	.186	.322	.273
June	2–0	4.40	125	40	6	10	16	.320	.512	.368
July	2–2	4.11	113	31	3	12	14	.274	.398	.344
August	3–0	5.24	138	39	8	8	26	.283	.514	.322
Sept./Oct.	1–1	3.58	124	29	6	10	21	.234	.419	.287
Leading Off Inn.			136	38	7	14	15	.279	.493	.347
Runners On			230	59	5	17	42	.257	.365	.304
Runners/Scor. Pos.			116	29	2	11	24	.250	.336	.308
Runners On/2 Out			91	23	0	7	18	.253	.308	.313
Scor. Pos./2 Out			52	13	0	6	11	.250	.288	.339
Late Inning Pressure			44	12	4	1	9	.273	.568	.289
Leading Off			11	2	1	1	3	.182	.545	.250
Runners On			10	2	0	0	3	.200	.200	.200
Runners/Scor. Pos.			4	0	0	0	2	.000	.000	.000
First 9 Batters			242	69	10	17	41	.285	.463	.330
Second 9 Batters			169	39	6	16	28	.231	.385	.296
All Batters Thereafter			148	42	9	14	20	.284	.500	.346

Loves to face: Dwight Evans (0-for-6, 2 SO)
Hates to face: Jim Rice (.667, 4-for-6, 2 2B, 2 HR)
Ground outs-to-air outs ratio: 0.92 last season, 0.89 for career. . . .
Additional statistics: 16 double-play ground outs in 115 opportunities, 24 doubles, 1 triple in 145.1 innings last season. . . . Allowed 13 first-inning runs in 20 starts last season. . . . Batting support: 5.70 runs per start, 6th best in A.L. (minimum: 15 GS). . . . 7–4, 4.49 ERA as a starter; 2–0 (1 save), 2.90 ERA in 14 relief appearances. . . . Compiled a 6.70 ERA in nine no-decision starts. . . . Opponents' career batting: .193 in day games (3–2 record, 3.65 ERA); .304 in night games (6–4, 4.47). . . . Has allowed 26 career home runs, only one with more than one runner on base.

Jim Clancy
Toronto Blue Jays   *Throws Right*

	W–L	ERA	AB	H	HR	BB	SO	BA	SA	OBA
Season	14–14	3.94	832	202	24	63	126	.243	.373	.296
vs. Left-Handers			441	101	9	36	66	.229	.333	.287
vs. Right-Handers			391	101	15	27	60	.258	.417	.307
Home	5–6	5.26	347	94	12	26	57	.271	.418	.320
Road	9–8	3.07	485	108	12	37	69	.223	.340	.279
Grass	5–7	2.93	346	76	6	29	53	.220	.312	.280
Artificial Turf	9–7	4.72	486	126	18	34	73	.259	.416	.308
April	2–1	3.00	103	26	2	8	11	.252	.379	.310
May	3–2	4.17	163	45	8	13	29	.276	.460	.326
June	2–2	5.86	110	30	3	12	19	.273	.382	.350
July	5–0	1.54	138	20	3	12	23	.145	.232	.211
August	2–2	4.42	141	37	6	7	17	.262	.418	.300
Sept./Oct.	0–7	4.89	177	44	2	11	27	.249	.356	.292
Leading Off Inn.			220	55	7	15	28	.250	.386	.298
Runners On			315	89	9	20	40	.283	.410	.321
Runners/Scor. Pos.			172	51	5	9	28	.297	.436	.319
Runners On/2 Out			136	36	5	11	14	.265	.441	.324
Scor. Pos./2 Out			88	26	1	6	12	.295	.398	.340
Late Inning Pressure			66	25	2	8	9	.379	.515	.440
Leading Off			19	9	1	2	1	.474	.737	.524
Runners On			29	12	1	3	3	.414	.552	.455
Runners/Scor. Pos.			12	6	0	2	2	.500	.583	.533
First 9 Batters			274	55	4	26	48	.201	.296	.267
Second 9 Batters			267	72	11	14	36	.270	.438	.309
All Batters Thereafter			291	75	9	23	42	.258	.385	.313

Loves to face: Larry Herndon (0-for-18)
Hates to face: Dave Winfield (.429, 9-for-21, 4 HR)
Ground outs-to-air outs ratio: 1.03 last season, 1.01 for career. . . .
Additional statistics: 13 double-play ground outs in 156 opportunities, 28 doubles, 4 triples in 219.1 innings last season. . . . Allowed 19 first-inning runs in 34 starts last season. . . . Batting support: 4.68 runs per start. . . . Tied for A.L. lead in wins in July. . . . Seven losses after Sept. 1 were the most in the A.L. . . . Enters 1987 season tied with Dave Stieb as Blue Jays' all-time leader in wins (102). . . . Career total of 277 games started, has pitched only two games in relief. . . . Only active pitcher with more than 1000 innings (actually 1768.1) and no balks. . . . Opponents' career batting: .246 with bases empty, .276 with runners on base, .279 with runners in scoring position.

Mark Clear
Milwaukee Brewers   *Throws Right*

	W–L	ERA	AB	H	HR	BB	SO	BA	SA	OBA
Season	5–5	2.20	264	53	4	36	85	.201	.280	.295
vs. Left-Handers			106	20	1	25	35	.189	.226	.346
vs. Right-Handers			158	33	3	11	50	.209	.316	.256
Home	5–2	0.86	143	25	2	17	48	.175	.231	.261
Road	0–3	3.98	121	28	2	19	37	.231	.339	.333
Grass	5–4	1.53	227	41	3	31	74	.181	.260	.279
Artificial Turf	0–1	7.00	37	12	1	5	11	.324	.405	.395
April	0–1	1.42	24	6	0	4	9	.250	.333	.345
May	2–1	0.73	44	8	0	6	20	.182	.182	.280
June	0–1	4.15	30	7	2	12	9	.233	.433	.392
July	0–1	2.03	44	6	1	5	14	.136	.250	.224
August	3–0	0.00	69	11	0	5	19	.159	.188	.211
Sept./Oct.	0–1	6.23	53	15	1	4	14	.283	.396	.345
Leading Off Inn.			54	10	0	7	20	.185	.222	.279
Runners On			131	24	2	23	42	.183	.267	.302
Runners/Scor. Pos.			83	13	1	13	29	.157	.229	.267
Runners On/2 Out			57	8	1	12	16	.140	.263	.290
Scor. Pos./2 Out			39	6	1	9	10	.154	.282	.313
Late Inning Pressure			150	28	0	23	44	.187	.227	.295
Leading Off			31	7	0	5	7	.226	.290	.333
Runners On			76	13	0	13	23	.171	.224	.293
Runners/Scor. Pos.			42	7	0	7	15	.167	.214	.288
First 9 Batters			256	53	4	36	82	.207	.289	.303
Second 9 Batters			8	0	0	0	3	.000	.000	.000
All Batters Thereafter			—	—	—	—	—	—	—	—

Loves to face: Tony Armas (0-for-14, 9 SO)
Hates to face: Pat Tabler (.583, 7-for-12)
Also loves to face: Reggie Jackson (.071, 1-for-14, 10 SO) Ground outs-to-air outs ratio: 1.03 last season, 0.86 for career. . . . Additional statistics: 5 double-play ground outs in 67 opportunities, 5 doubles, 2 triples in 73.2 innings last season. . . . Faced only one batter 2 times, pitched two or more innings 12 times, finished 52 games in 59 relief appearances. . . . Opponents' batting average with runners in scoring position was the lowest of his career. . . . Recorded career highs in games (59), saves (16), and ERA (2.20) last season. . . . Home run by Rich Gedman on June 5 was first by a left-handed batter since the 1983 season. . . . Next start will be first of career, tying Cesar Tovar on all-time list.

Roger Clemens

Throws Right

Boston Red Sox

	W–L	ERA	AB	H	HR	BB	SO	BA	SA	OBA
Season	24-4	2.48	916	179	21	67	238	.195	.306	.252
vs. Left-Handers			523	110	8	45	115	.210	.317	.274
vs. Right-Handers			393	69	13	22	123	.176	.290	.221
Home	11-3	2.56	438	89	11	24	121	.203	.313	.245
Road	13-1	2.41	478	90	10	43	117	.188	.299	.258
Grass	19-4	2.54	775	153	19	56	204	.197	.307	.253
Artificial Turf	5-0	2.20	141	26	2	11	34	.184	.298	.245
April	4-0	1.62	121	22	4	10	39	.182	.314	.244
May	4-0	3.57	148	28	6	11	42	.189	.338	.250
June	6-0	1.44	182	32	3	9	44	.176	.269	.215
July	3-3	3.56	153	31	4	10	37	.203	.346	.253
August	3-1	2.70	165	31	4	17	45	.188	.297	.265
Sept./Oct.	4-0	1.99	147	35	0	10	31	.238	.279	.288
Leading Off Inn.			241	49	5	19	63	.203	.315	.262
Runners On			317	64	8	25	78	.202	.312	.258
Runners/Scor. Pos.			154	29	1	12	36	.188	.253	.238
Runners On/2 Out			138	27	4	15	37	.196	.333	.279
Scor. Pos./2 Out			81	15	0	8	22	.185	.247	.258
Late Inning Pressure			110	23	3	9	26	.209	.318	.267
Leading Off			28	6	1	3	7	.214	.321	.290
Runners On			42	7	1	4	12	.167	.310	.234
Runners/Scor. Pos.			21	3	0	0	6	.143	.286	.136
First 9 Batters			274	44	2	20	91	.161	.223	.223
Second 9 Batters			263	58	5	19	68	.221	.308	.273
All Batters Thereafter			379	77	14	28	79	.203	.364	.258

Loves to face: Joe Carter (0-for-12)
Hates to face: Eddie Murray (.462, 6-for-13, 2 HR)
Ground outs-to-air outs ratio: 0.83 last season, 0.90 for career. . . . Additional statistics: 14 double-play ground outs in 150 opportunities, 34 doubles, 2 triples in 254.0 innings last season. . . . Allowed 4 first-inning runs in 33 starts last season. . . . . . The new math: best ERA in A.L. (2.48) plus best run support in majors (6.09 runs per game) equals 24–4 record, Cy Young, and MVP. . . . Won his 20th game in his 27th appearance, equalling the pace of Steve Stone in 1980. The last pitchers to win 20 games in fewer appearances were Denny McLain and Juan Marichal, who reached the 20 mark in 26 games in 1968. Bobby Shantz won 20 in his first 23 games in 1952. . . . 1986 ERA breakdown: 1st–3d innings, 1.75; 4th–6th innings, 2.59; 7th–9th innings, 3.45.

Bryan Clutterbuck

Throws Right

Milwaukee Brewers

	W–L	ERA	AB	H	HR	BB	SO	BA	SA	OBA
Season	0-1	4.29	230	68	8	16	38	.296	.448	.345
vs. Left-Handers			103	39	6	11	14	.379	.592	.444
vs. Right-Handers			127	29	2	5	24	.228	.331	.258
Home	0-0	4.18	115	32	4	7	19	.278	.426	.325
Road	0-1	4.40	115	36	4	9	19	.313	.470	.365
Grass	0-1	3.88	196	57	6	14	28	.291	.429	.340
Artificial Turf	0-0	6.75	34	11	2	2	10	.324	.559	.378
April			0	0	0	0	0	—	—	—
May			0	0	0	0	0	—	—	—
June			0	0	0	0	0	—	—	—
July	0-0	0.00	22	6	0	3	3	.273	.273	.346
August	0-1	5.00	118	40	6	5	17	.339	.568	.371
Sept./Oct.	0-0	4.76	90	22	2	8	18	.244	.333	.313
Leading Off Inn.			46	18	2	3	6	.391	.609	.429
Runners On			122	34	4	9	20	.279	.410	.326
Runners/Scor. Pos.			77	20	3	7	16	.260	.403	.318
Runners On/2 Out			50	13	2	6	7	.260	.400	.339
Scor. Pos./2 Out			35	7	1	4	6	.200	.286	.282
Late Inning Pressure			13	5	0	1	4	.385	.462	.429
Leading Off			3	3	0	0	0	1.000	1.333	1.000
Runners On			10	2	0	1	4	.200	.200	.273
Runners/Scor. Pos.			6	1	0	1	3	.167	.167	.286
First 9 Batters			148	51	4	12	20	.345	.473	.395
Second 9 Batters			63	13	2	4	12	.206	.349	.265
All Batters Thereafter			19	4	2	0	6	.211	.579	.211

Loves to face: Jim Sundberg (0-for-3, 3 SO)
Hates to face: Ruben Sierra (.750, 3-for-4)
Ground outs-to-air outs ratio: 0.66, 7th lowest in A.L. last season (minimum: 250 BFP), his first in majors. . . . Additional statistics: 2 double-play ground outs in 51 opportunities, 6th-lowest average in A.L. (minimum: 40 opp.), 11 doubles, 0 triples in 56.2 innings last season. . . . Brewers lost all seven games in which he allowed a home run. . . . Faced 250 batters last season, but only 23 while the Brewers held a lead. . . . Joined Milwaukee after five consecutive winning seasons in minors. Career minor-league record: 54–35 (.607). . . . Before any diminutive columnists poke fun at Mr. Clutterbuck's name, they should be aware that he's listed at 6'4", 225 pounds.

Chris Codiroli

Throws Right

Oakland As

	W–L	ERA	AB	H	HR	BB	SO	BA	SA	OBA
Season	5-8	4.03	364	91	15	38	43	.250	.431	.323
vs. Left-Handers			193	50	7	22	20	.259	.430	.338
vs. Right-Handers			171	41	8	16	23	.240	.433	.307
Home	4-2	3.17	186	42	6	19	18	.226	.344	.296
Road	1-6	4.98	178	49	9	19	25	.275	.522	.352
Grass	4-8	4.29	337	87	14	36	39	.258	.442	.332
Artificial Turf	1-0	1.17	27	4	1	2	4	.148	.296	.207
April	2-2	2.20	114	26	2	14	15	.228	.368	.318
May	1-4	4.89	153	43	9	16	14	.281	.490	.351
June	2-2	4.81	97	22	4	8	14	.227	.412	.286
July			0	0	0	0	0	—	—	—
August			0	0	0	0	0	—	—	—
Sept./Oct.			0	0	0	0	0	—	—	—
Leading Off Inn.			89	21	4	9	10	.236	.427	.306
Runners On			147	36	7	20	14	.245	.429	.341
Runners/Scor. Pos.			91	19	2	13	12	.209	.319	.311
Runners On/2 Out			67	18	3	8	8	.269	.433	.355
Scor. Pos./2 Out			43	9	1	7	7	.209	.326	.320
Late Inning Pressure			17	6	0	1	2	.353	.412	.389
Leading Off			5	1	0	0	1	.200	.200	.200
Runners On			5	2	0	1	1	.400	.400	.500
Runners/Scor. Pos.			3	0	0	0	1	.000	.000	.000
First 9 Batters			123	24	1	18	17	.195	.285	.303
Second 9 Batters			131	32	7	8	16	.244	.458	.286
All Batters Thereafter			110	35	7	12	10	.318	.564	.390

Loves to face: Dick Schofield (0-for-10)
Hates to face: Andre Thornton (6-for-6, 1 HR)
Ground outs-to-air outs ratio: 1.02 last season, 1.28 for career. . . . Additional statistics: 4 double-play ground outs in 61 opportunities, 17 doubles, 2 triples in 91.2 innings last season. . . . Allowed 9 first-inning runs in 16 starts last season. . . . Batting support: 4.81 runs per start. . . . In five seasons with the A's he has allowed 29 home runs at the Oakland Coliseum, 43 home runs in road games. . . . Career record of 21–12 in day games, 17–28 in night games. . . . Opponents' batting average with runners in scoring position was the lowest of his career. . . . Opponents' career batting average of .464 (13-for-28, 3 HR) with the bases loaded.

Doug Corbett

Throws Right

California Angels

	W–L	ERA	AB	H	HR	BB	SO	BA	SA	OBA
Season	4-2	3.66	286	66	11	22	36	.231	.378	.286
vs. Left-Handers			118	32	5	6	8	.271	.441	.304
vs. Right-Handers			168	34	6	16	28	.202	.333	.274
Home	4-1	2.45	141	28	4	8	19	.199	.319	.240
Road	0-1	4.93	145	38	7	14	17	.262	.434	.329
Grass	4-2	4.13	254	58	11	20	33	.228	.394	.286
Artificial Turf	0-0	0.00	32	8	0	2	3	.250	.250	.286
April	0-0	1.93	31	5	1	5	6	.161	.258	.278
May	0-1	4.60	58	13	2	1	8	.224	.397	.233
June	2-0	3.07	51	11	2	5	4	.216	.373	.293
July	0-1	4.97	49	12	1	3	9	.245	.327	.288
August	1-0	3.68	55	14	4	3	7	.255	.491	.293
Sept./Oct.	1-0	3.09	42	11	1	5	2	.262	.357	.340
Leading Off Inn.			60	13	3	4	6	.217	.417	.277
Runners On			124	35	4	11	16	.282	.419	.336
Runners/Scor. Pos.			67	20	3	8	6	.299	.448	.364
Runners On/2 Out			44	9	1	5	11	.205	.318	.286
Scor. Pos./2 Out			26	5	0	3	5	.192	.231	.276
Late Inning Pressure			98	22	2	6	12	.224	.337	.274
Leading Off			21	6	1	0	3	.286	.524	.318
Runners On			43	13	1	5	5	.302	.419	.367
Runners/Scor. Pos.			26	8	0	3	2	.308	.346	.367
First 9 Batters			253	58	8	17	34	.229	.356	.278
Second 9 Batters			32	7	3	5	2	.219	.531	.324
All Batters Thereafter			1	1	0	0	0	1.000	1.000	1.000

Loves to face: Rick Dempsey (0-for-11)
Hates to face: Gary Ward (4-for-4, 1 HR)
Ground outs-to-air outs ratio: 2.76, 2d highest in A.L. last season (minimum: 250 BFP), 3.01 for career. . . . One of two active pitchers with a career G/A ratio above 3.00. The other: Roger McDowell (3.31). . . . Additional statistics: 14 double-play ground outs in 68 opportunities, highest average in A.L. (minimum: 10 GDP), 7 doubles, 1 triple in 78.2 innings last season. . . . Faced only one batter twice, pitched two or more innings 22 times, finished 32 games in 46 relief appearances. . . . Allowed home runs in five straight appearances, Aug. 15 to Sept. 1. . . . Has never allowed a grand slam home run. . . . Opponents' career batting average of .211 (15-for-71) with the bases loaded. . . . Career record of 0–4 vs. Texas.

Ed Correa
Throws Right

Texas Rangers	W–L	ERA	AB	H	HR	BB	SO	BA	SA	OBA
Season	12-14	4.23	750	167	15	126	189	.223	.324	.336
vs. Left-Handers			397	89	3	61	88	.224	.290	.327
vs. Right-Handers			353	78	12	65	101	.221	.363	.345
Home	6-6	3.98	309	64	5	41	89	.207	.291	.305
Road	6-8	4.40	441	103	10	85	100	.234	.347	.356
Grass	11-10	4.06	604	129	10	103	153	.214	.308	.330
Artificial Turf	1-4	4.93	146	38	5	23	36	.260	.390	.361
April	1-2	4.62	96	22	0	13	21	.229	.271	.327
May	2-1	1.67	131	23	3	26	37	.176	.282	.321
June	2-3	5.59	144	35	2	20	35	.243	.340	.333
July	1-3	6.66	102	27	3	18	29	.265	.402	.372
August	2-2	6.67	107	30	5	23	18	.280	.439	.405
Sept./Oct.	4-3	2.25	170	30	2	26	49	.176	.253	.286
Leading Off Inn.			178	41	2	34	39	.230	.303	.354
Runners On			341	84	8	51	86	.246	.364	.347
Runners/Scor. Pos.			218	45	3	36	60	.206	.294	.318
Runners On/2 Out			140	34	3	22	37	.243	.371	.350
Scor. Pos./2 Out			100	21	1	17	30	.210	.300	.325
Late Inning Pressure			51	5	1	6	11	.098	.176	.220
Leading Off			14	2	0	3	1	.143	.143	.294
Runners On			13	0	0	2	4	.000	.000	.235
Runners/Scor. Pos.			6	0	0	2	3	.000	.000	.250
First 9 Batters			233	49	5	50	62	.210	.296	.350
Second 9 Batters			243	54	5	40	57	.222	.337	.332
All Batters Thereafter			209	64	5	36	70	.234	.336	.326

Loves to face: Bruce Bochte (0-for-8, 5 SO)
Hates to face: Don Baylor (.333, 3-for-9, 2 HR)
Ground outs-to-air outs ratio: 1.09 last season, 1.08 for career. . . .
Additional statistics: 9 double-play ground outs in 166 opportunities, 29 doubles, 1 triple in 202.1 innings last season. . . . Allowed 11 first-inning runs in 32 starts last season. . . . Batting support: 3.91 runs per start, 8th lowest in A.L. (minimum: 15 GS). . . . Led major-league rookies in innings pitched (202.1) and strikeouts (189). . . . Had a 24.2-inning scoreless streak snapped by the Angels in his final appearance last season. . . . May ERA was 2d best in A.L., August ERA was 3d worst (minimum: 20 IP). . . . Has faced 174 batters in day games in his career, allowed only one home run. . . . Opposing hitters were 0-for-13 with runners on base in Late-Inning Pressure Situations.

Joe Cowley
Throws Right

Chicago White Sox	W–L	ERA	AB	H	HR	BB	SO	BA	SA	OBA
Season	11-11	3.88	596	133	20	83	132	.223	.369	.319
vs. Left-Handers			323	80	10	48	58	.248	.390	.345
vs. Right-Handers			273	53	10	35	74	.194	.344	.288
Home	6-5	2.37	280	56	6	36	67	.200	.311	.291
Road	5-6	5.33	316	77	14	47	65	.244	.421	.344
Grass	9-9	3.97	447	99	18	65	105	.221	.391	.320
Artificial Turf	2-2	3.60	149	34	2	18	27	.228	.302	.315
April	0-1	19.29	10	3	1	3	2	.300	.600	.462
May	1-1	4.50	45	9	1	5	11	.200	.311	.280
June	3-1	3.07	144	28	1	17	36	.194	.285	.278
July	2-3	5.40	107	27	6	10	17	.252	.467	.316
August	2-3	5.81	110	36	8	21	21	.327	.600	.440
Sept./Oct.	3-2	2.00	180	30	3	27	45	.167	.239	.276
Leading Off Inn.			152	29	4	20	38	.191	.309	.285
Runners On			235	55	5	39	50	.234	.349	.341
Runners/Scor. Pos.			137	33	3	28	37	.241	.365	.361
Runners On/2 Out			97	24	3	16	24	.247	.392	.354
Scor. Pos./2 Out			66	18	2	12	16	.273	.424	.385
Late Inning Pressure			51	11	1	3	11	.216	.294	.259
Leading Off			15	5	0	2	3	.333	.400	.412
Runners On			17	4	1	1	4	.235	.412	.278
Runners/Scor. Pos.			10	3	1	1	3	.300	.600	.364
First 9 Batters			196	42	8	40	53	.214	.372	.351
Second 9 Batters			191	47	9	18	40	.246	.429	.310
All Batters Thereafter			209	44	3	25	39	.211	.311	.295

Loves to face: Bill Buckner (.043, 1-for-23)
Hates to face: Jim Traber (2-for-2, 1 HR)
Ground outs-to-air outs ratio: 0.93 last season, 0.80 for career. . . .
Additional statistics: 9 double-play ground outs in 120 opportunities, 25 doubles, 1 triple in 162.1 innings last season. . . . Allowed 17 first-inning runs in 27 starts last season. . . . Batting support: 4.63 runs per start. . . . Lowest opponents' batting average in A.L. with runners in scoring position in both 1984 (.149) and 1985 (.148). Lost that distinction to Jose DeLeon last season. . . . Opponents' career batting: .245 by left-handed batters, .213 by right-handed batters; .211 in Late-Inning Pressure Situations, .233 in unpressured situations. . . . Career record of 5–0 vs. the Angels.

Steve Crawford
Throws Right

Boston Red Sox	W–L	ERA	AB	H	HR	BB	SO	BA	SA	OBA
Season	0-2	3.92	224	69	5	19	32	.308	.429	.359
vs. Left-Handers			99	39	4	15	7	.394	.576	.466
vs. Right-Handers			125	30	1	4	25	.240	.312	.264
Home	0-1	4.26	121	38	3	11	22	.314	.421	.366
Road	0-1	3.51	103	31	2	8	10	.301	.437	.351
Grass	0-2	4.12	175	57	5	16	26	.326	.457	.378
Artificial Turf	0-0	3.29	49	12	0	3	6	.245	.327	.288
April	0-0	0.00	24	8	0	3	2	.333	.375	.407
May	0-0	8.18	46	15	2	4	8	.326	.674	.380
June	0-0	2.40	58	16	0	4	10	.276	.293	.317
July	0-0	3.68	26	7	0	2	4	.269	.308	.310
August			0	0	0	0	0	—	—	—
Sept./Oct.	0-2	4.00	70	23	3	6	8	.329	.586	.382
Leading Off Inn.			48	16	1	1	6	.333	.479	.347
Runners On			118	33	1	16	17	.280	.356	.360
Runners/Scor. Pos.			85	23	1	13	13	.271	.365	.360
Runners On/2 Out			39	9	1	7	6	.231	.308	.348
Scor. Pos./2 Out			30	6	1	6	5	.200	.300	.333
Late Inning Pressure			96	27	0	10	17	.281	.323	.346
Leading Off			20	5	0	1	4	.250	.350	.286
Runners On			50	14	0	8	7	.280	.320	.373
Runners/Scor. Pos.			32	11	0	7	4	.344	.406	.450
First 9 Batters			206	61	5	17	31	.296	.413	.347
Second 9 Batters			18	8	0	2	1	.444	.611	.500
All Batters Thereafter			0	0	0	0	0			

Loves to face: Cliff Johnson (0-for-13, 6 SO)
Hates to face: Harold Baines (.636, 7-for-11, 1 HR)
Ground outs-to-air outs ratio: 0.93 last season, 1.59 for career. . . .
Additional statistics: 9 double-play ground outs in 62 opportunities, 12 doubles, 0 triples in 57.1 innings last season. . . . Never faced only one batter, pitched two or more innings 11 times, finished 15 games in 40 relief appearances. . . . Only home run allowed to a right-handed batter last season was by Joe Carter. . . . Opposing left-handed batters have hit over .300 in four of the last five seasons. . . . Opponents' career batting average of .422 (19-for-45) with two out and runners in scoring position in Late-Inning Pressure Situations. . . . Percentage of batters faced in LIP situations, year by year starting with 1980: 6%, 6%, 24%, 29%, 38%, 44%.

Danny Darwin
Throws Right

Milwaukee Brewers	W–L	ERA	AB	H	HR	BB	SO	BA	SA	OBA
Season	6-8	3.52	488	120	13	35	80	.246	.375	.297
vs. Left-Handers			243	63	8	27	30	.259	.412	.332
vs. Right-Handers			245	57	5	8	50	.233	.339	.260
Home	2-6	3.75	286	72	8	22	48	.252	.374	.306
Road	4-2	3.21	202	48	5	13	32	.238	.376	.284
Grass	4-8	3.74	417	103	12	31	70	.247	.374	.298
Artificial Turf	2-0	2.29	71	17	1	4	10	.239	.380	.289
April	1-1	4.35	40	8	3	6	8	.200	.450	.304
May	2-0	1.40	88	18	1	5	17	.205	.330	.253
June	1-3	3.68	143	36	2	7	22	.252	.364	.292
July	2-2	2.93	155	37	3	12	22	.239	.316	.292
August	0-2	7.98	62	21	4	5	11	.339	.565	.386
Sept./Oct.			0	0	0	0	0	—	—	—
Leading Off Inn.			120	30	4	10	21	.250	.400	.308
Runners On			196	57	6	16	20	.291	.439	.338
Runners/Scor. Pos.			118	35	2	8	14	.297	.441	.326
Runners On/2 Out			88	30	4	8	10	.341	.591	.402
Scor. Pos./2 Out			61	18	2	4	8	.295	.557	.338
Late Inning Pressure			117	31	5	11	18	.265	.444	.328
Leading Off			30	8	2	2	5	.267	.533	.313
Runners On			49	15	1	4	3	.306	.429	.358
Runners/Scor. Pos.			28	11	1	3	1	.393	.607	.452
First 9 Batters			199	49	7	17	37	.246	.417	.305
Second 9 Batters			126	28	2	8	23	.222	.302	.270
All Batters Thereafter			163	43	4	10	20	.264	.380	.284

Loves to face: Tim Teufel (.136, 3-for-22, 7 SO)
Hates to face: Vance Law (.400, 6-for-15, 1 HR)
Figures above are for A.L. only. . . . Ground outs-to-air outs ratio: 0.76 last season, 0.85 for career. . . . Additional statistics: 15 double-play ground outs in 132 opportunities, 27 doubles, 4 triples in 184.2 innings last season. . . . Allowed 11 first-inning runs in 22 starts last season. . . . Batting support: 3.82 runs per start. . . . 8–9, 3.26 ERA as a starter; 3–1, 2.78 ERA in 17 relief appearances. . . . Ranked 3d in N.L. in wins (5) and ERA (1.94) after September 1. . . . Career averages: one extra-base hit per 11.2 at bats vs. left-handers, one per 17.6 at bats vs. right-handers. . . . Opponents have batted for a higher average with runners on base than with the bases empty in each of his nine seasons in the majors.

Joel Davis

Chicago White Sox — Throws Right

	W–L	ERA	AB	H	HR	BB	SO	BA	SA	OBA
Season	4-5	4.70	411	115	9	51	54	.280	.426	.359
vs. Left-Handers			215	63	7	32	27	.293	.470	.384
vs. Right-Handers			196	52	2	19	27	.265	.378	.330
Home	2-2	4.13	201	56	1	23	27	.279	.373	.350
Road	2-3	5.26	210	59	8	28	27	.281	.476	.368
Grass	4-4	4.20	332	93	4	40	44	.280	.395	.356
Artificial Turf	0-1	6.86	79	22	5	11	10	.278	.557	.374
April	1-1	3.29	100	22	1	11	15	.220	.320	.297
May	1-1	3.76	152	41	4	22	27	.270	.414	.362
June	2-2	7.09	113	37	4	16	9	.327	.531	.409
July	0-1	5.91	46	15	0	2	3	.326	.435	.354
August			0	0	0	0	0	—	—	—
Sept./Oct.			0	0	0	0	0	—	—	—
Leading Off Inn.			105	22	4	8	14	.210	.390	.272
Runners On			168	57	4	22	20	.339	.470	.411
Runners/Scor. Pos.			100	31	2	15	11	.310	.440	.393
Runners On/2 Out			77	29	2	7	8	.377	.506	.429
Scor. Pos./2 Out			51	18	2	6	4	.353	.490	.421
Late Inning Pressure			51	17	1	5	10	.333	.490	.393
Leading Off			16	5	1	1	2	.313	.563	.353
Runners On			17	9	0	1	3	.529	.706	.556
Runners/Scor. Pos.			9	6	0	0	0	.667	.778	.667
First 9 Batters			148	39	3	20	19	.264	.351	.351
Second 9 Batters			134	39	3	15	18	.291	.500	.362
All Batters Thereafter			129	37	3	16	17	.287	.434	.366

Loves to face: Greg Gagne (0-for-8)
Hates to face: Lloyd Moseby (.500, 4-for-8, 2 2B, 2 3B)
Ground outs-to-air outs ratio: 1.19 last season, 1.15 for career. . . . Additional statistics: 7 double-play ground outs in 83 opportunities, 19 doubles, 7 triples in 105.1 innings last season. . . . Allowed 7 first-inning runs in 19 starts last season. . . . Batting support: 4.16 runs per start. . . . Averaged 5.54 innings pitched per start, lowest on the White Sox staff (minimum: 10 GS). . . . June ERA was 2d worst in A.L. (minimum: 20 IP). . . . Opponents' career batting: .243 with bases empty; .311 with runners on base; .303 with runners in scoring position; .325 in Late-Inning Pressure Situations, .263 in unpressured situations. . . . Career ERA: 3.07 in first two innings, 4.04 in 3d through 5th innings, 6.69 thereafter.

Storm Davis

Baltimore Orioles — Throws Right

	W–L	ERA	AB	H	HR	BB	SO	BA	SA	OBA
Season	9-12	3.62	603	166	16	49	96	.275	.400	.329
vs. Left-Handers			300	88	11	31	42	.293	.453	.358
vs. Right-Handers			303	78	5	18	54	.257	.347	.298
Home	5-7	3.35	334	99	8	23	58	.296	.413	.340
Road	4-5	3.95	269	67	8	26	38	.249	.383	.315
Grass	8-11	3.31	551	150	14	46	88	.272	.387	.327
Artificial Turf	1-1	7.11	52	16	2	3	8	.308	.538	.345
April	1-1	2.73	93	17	3	11	17	.183	.333	.269
May	3-3	4.33	146	45	3	11	26	.308	.445	.357
June	2-4	2.82	150	41	2	9	20	.273	.347	.314
July	1-0	5.56	44	13	2	4	9	.295	.455	.354
August	2-4	3.63	160	48	5	12	22	.300	.425	.345
Sept./Oct.	0-0	6.00	10	2	1	2	2	.200	.500	.333
Leading Off Inn.			153	48	8	12	21	.314	.516	.364
Runners On			248	75	4	16	38	.302	.399	.342
Runners/Scor. Pos.			139	40	2	8	19	.288	.388	.322
Runners On/2 Out			91	23	2	3	18	.253	.341	.277
Scor. Pos./2 Out			58	14	1	0	11	.241	.328	.241
Late Inning Pressure			67	19	4	5	6	.284	.478	.329
Leading Off			19	4	2	3	1	.211	.526	.318
Runners On			19	6	0	1	1	.316	.368	.333
Runners/Scor. Pos.			6	0	0	1	0	.000	.000	.125
First 9 Batters			205	53	4	17	33	.259	.361	.315
Second 9 Batters			183	54	5	15	30	.295	.443	.348
All Batters Thereafter			215	59	7	17	33	.274	.400	.325

Loves to face: Dave Collins (.133, 2-for-15)
Hates to face: Mike Easler (.556, 10-for-18, 5 2B)
Ground outs-to-air outs ratio: 1.41 last season, 1.18 for career. . . . Additional statistics: 15 double-play ground outs in 130 opportunities, 21 doubles, 3 triples in 154.0 innings last season. . . . Allowed 9 first-inning runs in 25 starts last season. . . . Batting support: 3.96 runs per start, 9th lowest in A.L. (minimum: 15 GS). . . . Opponents' annual batting averages since 1983: .238, .247, .256, .275. Opponents have batted over .300 with runners on base in each of the last two seasons. . . . Has faced 1820 left-handed batters in his career and has never hit one with a pitch. . . . Lost his last five decisions to the Yankees, now hopes for better luck against the Mets.

Bill Dawley

Chicago White Sox — Throws Right

	W–L	ERA	AB	H	HR	BB	SO	BA	SA	OBA
Season	0-7	3.32	368	91	10	28	66	.247	.370	.300
vs. Left-Handers			148	43	6	15	14	.291	.480	.354
vs. Right-Handers			220	48	4	13	52	.218	.295	.263
Home	0-4	2.96	176	38	4	13	40	.216	.307	.268
Road	0-3	3.67	192	53	6	15	26	.276	.427	.329
Grass	0-4	3.16	329	78	9	25	59	.237	.359	.289
Artificial Turf	0-3	4.82	39	13	1	3	7	.333	.462	.386
April	0-0	1.93	35	8	1	4	6	.229	.371	.308
May	0-3	3.00	68	17	0	5	6	.250	.279	.293
June	0-1	2.76	59	13	2	3	16	.220	.339	.270
July	0-0	5.71	70	23	5	8	10	.329	.586	.392
August	0-1	2.70	72	14	0	5	10	.194	.264	.247
Sept./Oct.	0-2	3.24	64	16	2	3	18	.250	.375	.284
Leading Off Inn.			84	21	0	4	12	.250	.333	.284
Runners On			167	40	6	17	25	.240	.371	.305
Runners/Scor. Pos.			103	27	6	13	11	.262	.466	.336
Runners On/2 Out			71	11	1	7	9	.155	.225	.231
Scor. Pos./2 Out			46	7	1	4	4	.152	.261	.220
Late Inning Pressure			135	36	1	12	23	.267	.326	.327
Leading Off			36	10	0	1	5	.278	.333	.297
Runners On			59	15	0	7	10	.254	.271	.324
Runners/Scor. Pos.			35	10	0	5	3	.286	.286	.357
First 9 Batters			287	74	9	22	61	.258	.394	.311
Second 9 Batters			76	16	1	6	5	.211	.289	.265
All Batters Thereafter			5	1	0	0	0	.200	.200	.200

Loves to face: Dave Kingman (0-for-6, 3 SO)
Hates to face: Bill Buckner (.800, 4-for-5, 3 2B, 1 HR)
Ground outs-to-air outs ratio: 0.62, 4th lowest in A.L. last season (minimum: 250 BFP), 0.74 for career. . . . Additional statistics: 4 double-play ground outs in 81 opportunities, 13 doubles, 1 triple in 97.2 innings last season. . . . Faced only one batter twice, pitched two or more innings 25 times, finished 23 games in 46 relief appearances. . . . Career averages: one extra-base hit per 21.7 at bats in day games, one per 55.9 at bats in night games. . . . Opponents' year-by-year batting averages in Late-Inning Pressure Situations, starting with 1983: .169, .200, .241, .267. . . . Opponents have batted .391 (18-for-46, 1 HR) with the bases loaded.

Jose DeLeon

Chicago White Sox — Throws Right

	W–L	ERA	AB	H	HR	BB	SO	BA	SA	OBA
Season	4-5	2.96	274	49	7	42	68	.179	.285	.296
vs. Left-Handers			136	25	4	24	25	.184	.309	.306
vs. Right-Handers			138	24	3	18	43	.174	.261	.286
Home	2-3	3.94	108	20	6	16	27	.185	.389	.296
Road	2-2	2.30	166	29	1	26	41	.175	.217	.296
Grass	4-4	3.05	206	37	6	34	52	.180	.301	.303
Artificial Turf	0-1	2.70	68	12	1	8	16	.176	.235	.273
April			0	0	0	0	0	—	—	—
May			0	0	0	0	0	—	—	—
June			0	0	0	0	0	—	—	—
July	1-0	2.70	36	7	1	8	8	.194	.333	.341
August	2-4	3.22	129	25	5	22	32	.194	.341	.325
Sept./Oct.	1-1	2.76	109	17	1	12	28	.156	.202	.244
Leading Off Inn.			68	17	1	14	13	.250	.353	.393
Runners On			124	20	5	13	34	.161	.298	.250
Runners/Scor. Pos.			63	9	2	7	18	.143	.270	.247
Runners On/2 Out			43	9	4	5	13	.209	.488	.306
Scor. Pos./2 Out			26	5	2	4	5	.192	.423	.323
Late Inning Pressure			20	6	1	3	2	.300	.600	.391
Leading Off			6	3	0	1	0	.500	1.000	.571
Runners On			10	3	1	0	1	.300	.600	.300
Runners/Scor. Pos.			6	2	0	0	1	.333	.333	.333
First 9 Batters			96	14	2	18	27	.146	.229	.291
Second 9 Batters			100	23	2	10	21	.230	.310	.306
All Batters Thereafter			78	12	3	14	20	.154	.321	.290

Loves to face: Jim Rice (0-for-6)
Hates to face: Pete O'Brien (2-for-2, 1 2B, 1 HR)
Figures above are for A.L. only. . . . Ground outs-to-air outs ratio: 0.71 last season, 0.81 for career. . . . Additional statistics: 3 double-play ground outs in 85 opportunities, 7th-lowest average in majors (minimum: 40 opp.), 9 doubles, 3 triples in 95.1 innings last season. . . . Allowed 6 first-inning runs in 14 starts. . . . Batting support: 3.50 runs per start. . . . Defeated Roger Clemens in consecutive starts (July 30 and Aug. 4) after losing 27 of his last 31 decisions. No one else has beaten Clemens twice. . . . Held opposing right-handed batters below .200 in each of the past three seasons. The other: Eric Show.

Ken Dixon

Baltimore Orioles   Throws Right

	W–L	ERA	AB	H	HR	BB	SO	BA	SA	OBA
Season	11-13	4.58	779	194	33	83	170	.249	.438	.320
vs. Left-Handers			385	93	15	46	70	.242	.418	.320
vs. Right-Handers			394	101	18	37	100	.256	.457	.320
Home	4-10	5.24	390	104	23	54	87	.267	.479	.353
Road	7-3	3.92	389	90	10	29	83	.231	.396	.284
Grass	7-12	5.13	624	167	29	71	140	.268	.465	.340
Artificial Turf	4-1	2.53	155	27	4	12	30	.174	.329	.238
April	2-1	2.63	91	20	4	7	20	.220	.385	.283
May	3-1	5.23	120	27	11	11	25	.225	.583	.290
June	1-4	6.89	126	34	7	23	23	.270	.484	.380
July	3-2	1.57	155	25	2	15	41	.161	.258	.233
August	1-2	6.44	123	37	4	10	25	.301	.480	.351
Sept./Oct.	1-3	5.49	164	51	5	17	36	.311	.463	.372
Leading Off Inn.			202	47	11	15	40	.233	.450	.286
Runners On			309	80	9	36	78	.259	.408	.332
Runners/Scor. Pos.			174	41	6	28	44	.236	.397	.332
Runners On/2 Out			134	36	3	18	35	.269	.381	.355
Scor. Pos./2 Out			86	24	3	16	22	.279	.442	.392
Late Inning Pressure			81	18	4	10	11	.222	.444	.308
Leading Off			25	3	1	1	4	.120	.240	.154
Runners On			21	5	1	4	4	.238	.524	.360
Runners/Scor. Pos.			6	3	1	4	1	.500	1.333	.700
First 9 Batters			272	66	14	27	72	.243	.445	.313
Second 9 Batters			232	52	6	31	51	.224	.371	.310
All Batters Thereafter			275	76	13	25	47	.276	.487	.336

Loves to face: Chris Bando (0-for-10)
Hates to face: Ron Hassey (.714, 5-for-7, 1 HR)
Ground outs-to-air outs ratio: 0.72 last season, 0.73 for career. . . .
Additional statistics: 14 double-play ground outs in 142 opportunities, 30 doubles, 9 triples (most in A.L.) in 202.1 innings last season.
. . . Allowed 18 first-inning runs in 33 starts last season. . . . Batting support: 4.30 runs per start. . . . Averaged 6.08 innings per start, 4th best in Baltimore's five-man rotation. . . . 3d-highest ERA in A.L. during June (minimum: 20 IP), 3d lowest during July. . . . Has allowed 54 home runs in his career, 39 of them at Memorial Stadium. . . . Opponents' career batting: .257 at Memorial Stadium (9–14, 4.75 ERA), .229 in road games (10–4, 3.45); .259 on grass fields (13–17, 4.56), .179 on artificial surfaces (6–1, 2.47 ERA).

Richard Dotson

Chicago White Sox   Throws Right

	W–L	ERA	AB	H	HR	BB	SO	BA	SA	OBA
Season	10-17	5.48	782	226	24	69	110	.289	.435	.347
vs. Left-Handers			408	108	14	37	56	.265	.407	.324
vs. Right-Handers			374	118	10	32	54	.316	.465	.371
Home	7-9	4.84	416	115	13	36	63	.276	.423	.333
Road	3-8	6.23	366	111	11	33	47	.303	.448	.362
Grass	9-14	5.26	661	186	20	58	97	.281	.424	.340
Artificial Turf	1-3	6.75	121	40	4	11	13	.331	.496	.383
April	1-2	7.62	111	31	5	18	14	.279	.486	.380
May	1-3	4.28	112	35	4	13	12	.313	.464	.386
June	4-2	4.57	161	45	3	12	15	.280	.379	.330
July	1-4	9.82	94	36	2	6	7	.383	.489	.420
August	2-2	4.30	149	45	4	8	30	.302	.430	.335
Sept./Oct.	1-4	4.46	155	34	6	12	32	.219	.406	.275
Leading Off Inn.			202	63	5	11	24	.312	.446	.347
Runners On			320	95	11	34	41	.297	.463	.362
Runners/Scor. Pos.			169	50	7	25	22	.296	.491	.382
Runners On/2 Out			123	29	1	14	16	.236	.325	.324
Scor. Pos./2 Out			79	19	1	12	11	.241	.329	.341
Late Inning Pressure			65	17	1	5	8	.262	.338	.314
Leading Off			20	5	0	0	2	.250	.300	.250
Runners On			16	3	0	3	3	.188	.188	.316
Runners/Scor. Pos.			5	1	0	3	1	.200	.200	.500
First 9 Batters			279	84	6	20	45	.301	.416	.347
Second 9 Batters			256	76	10	29	37	.297	.480	.367
All Batters Thereafter			247	66	8	20	28	.267	.409	.325

Loves to face: Jerry Willard (0-for-11)
Hates to face: Julio Franco (.500, 11-for-22)
Ground outs-to-air outs ratio: 1.49 last season, 1.36 for career. . . .
Additional statistics: 21 double-play ground outs in 171 opportunities, 34 doubles, 4 triples in 197.0 innings last season. . . . Allowed 22 first-inning runs in 34 starts last season. . . . Batting support: 3.85 runs per start, 7th lowest in A.L. (minimum: 15 GS). . . . Highest ERA of any A.L. starting pitcher (minimum: 25 GS). Highest in N.L. belonged to former teammate LaMarr Hoyt. . . . Averaged 5.79 innings per start last season. . . . April ERA was worst in the major leagues, and July ERA was 2d worst in A.L. (minimum: 20 IP). . . . Four losses in July were tied for most in A.L.

Doug Drabek

New York Yankees   Throws Right

	W–L	ERA	AB	H	HR	BB	SO	BA	SA	OBA
Season	7-8	4.10	501	126	13	50	76	.251	.397	.322
vs. Left-Handers			259	72	9	32	31	.278	.456	.356
vs. Right-Handers			242	54	4	18	45	.223	.335	.284
Home	2-3	3.75	243	63	8	18	39	.259	.403	.314
Road	5-5	4.41	258	63	5	32	37	.244	.391	.329
Grass	4-7	4.45	371	94	11	38	57	.253	.399	.327
Artificial Turf	3-1	3.12	130	32	2	12	19	.246	.392	.308
April			0	0	0	0	0	—	—	—
May	0-0	2.08	13	1	0	3	4	.077	.154	.250
June	0-1	7.85	73	18	3	10	9	.247	.425	.337
July	2-3	4.76	131	35	5	10	14	.267	.473	.331
August	1-3	3.66	154	42	3	15	30	.273	.403	.335
Sept./Oct.	4-1	2.27	130	30	2	12	19	.231	.323	.296
Leading Off Inn.			128	32	4	13	20	.250	.398	.329
Runners On			198	50	2	21	26	.253	.364	.324
Runners/Scor. Pos.			104	30	0	13	15	.288	.365	.361
Runners On/2 Out			79	18	0	11	10	.228	.266	.330
Scor. Pos./2 Out			48	13	0	6	7	.271	.313	.352
Late Inning Pressure			34	8	2	8	5	.235	.500	.381
Leading Off			7	2	1	5	2	.286	.714	.583
Runners On			13	4	0	2	1	.308	.385	.400
Runners/Scor. Pos.			9	2	0	2	1	.222	.333	.364
First 9 Batters			201	45	2	24	35	.224	.318	.313
Second 9 Batters			165	44	6	6	23	.267	.424	.295
All Batters Thereafter			135	37	5	20	18	.274	.481	.365

Loves to face: Jesse Barfield & George Bell (each 0-for-8)
Hates to face: Reggie Jackson (.600, 3-for-5, 2 HR)
Ground outs-to-air outs ratio: 0.72 last season, his first in majors.
. . . Additional statistics: 5 double-play ground outs in 97 opportunities, 26 doubles, 4 triples in 131.2 innings last season. . . . Allowed 6 first-inning runs in 21 starts last season. . . . Batting support: 4.33 runs per start. . . . Started his last 16 games after being used in relief in six of his first 11 games. . . . Allowed 13 homers: 11 with the bases empty, two with one man on. . . . Opponents collected four hits in six at bats with the bases loaded. . . . Walked only 13 of 143 leadoff batters last season, but five of 12 in Late-Inning Pressure Situations.

Mark Eichhorn

Toronto Blue Jays   Throws Right

	W–L	ERA	AB	H	HR	BB	SO	BA	SA	OBA
Season	14-6	1.72	548	105	8	45	166	.192	.288	.261
vs. Left-Handers			251	65	7	29	54	.259	.434	.345
vs. Right-Handers			297	40	1	16	112	.135	.165	.186
Home	7-5	1.94	274	56	5	23	90	.204	.314	.275
Road	7-1	1.50	274	49	3	22	76	.179	.263	.247
Grass	7-1	1.49	210	37	3	18	55	.176	.252	.247
Artificial Turf	7-5	1.86	338	68	5	27	111	.201	.311	.270
April	2-1	0.48	60	5	1	3	20	.083	.150	.152
May	2-1	1.37	93	15	1	9	26	.161	.226	.243
June	2-1	1.32	45	7	1	6	18	.156	.289	.250
July	1-0	3.69	123	36	3	9	34	.293	.439	.351
August	5-1	1.13	131	21	1	7	36	.160	.267	.203
Sept./Oct.	2-2	1.67	96	21	1	11	32	.219	.271	.312
Leading Off Inn.			126	27	2	4	30	.214	.317	.250
Runners On			224	41	2	34	67	.183	.246	.299
Runners/Scor. Pos.			155	30	1	28	41	.194	.258	.328
Runners On/2 Out			101	17	1	22	34	.168	.218	.323
Scor. Pos./2 Out			76	13	0	19	23	.171	.197	.344
Late Inning Pressure			305	60	2	30	92	.197	.249	.272
Leading Off			80	20	1	2	20	.250	.325	.277
Runners On			113	20	0	22	35	.177	.204	.314
Runners/Scor. Pos.			74	14	0	18	22	.189	.230	.351
First 9 Batters			426	80	7	34	130	.188	.286	.253
Second 9 Batters			118	22	1	11	36	.186	.280	.273
All Batters Thereafter			4	3	0	0	0	.750	.750	.750

Loves to face: Bruce Bochte (0-for-8, 3 SO)
Hates to face: Mike Davis (.583, 7-for-12, 3 HR)
Ground outs-to-air outs ratio: 2.05, 9th highest in A.L. last season (minimum: 250 BFP), 1.85 for career. . . . Additional statistics: 11 double-play ground outs in 103 opportunities, 23 doubles, 3 triples in 157.0 innings last season. . . . Never faced only one batter, pitched two or more innings 41 times (most in majors), finished 38 games in 69 relief appearances. . . . Opposing right-handed batters hit only .135, 2d lowest against any pitcher over last 12 years (minimum: 175 BFP). The lowest: .124 vs. J.R. Richard in 1980. . . . Allowed only one home run to a right-handed batter: Larry Parrish. . . . Tied Roger McDowell for most wins by a reliever. His 14 wins also led major-league rookies. . . . Only A.L. pitcher with a winning record in every month (except October).

Steve Farr
Kansas City Royals — Throws Right

	W–L	ERA	AB	H	HR	BB	SO	BA	SA	OBA
Season	8-4	3.13	395	90	10	39	83	.228	.359	.302
vs. Left-Handers			203	45	2	21	35	.222	.310	.300
vs. Right-Handers			192	45	8	18	48	.234	.411	.305
Home	7-0	2.23	218	47	3	20	51	.216	.303	.285
Road	1-4	4.25	177	43	7	19	32	.243	.429	.323
Grass	1-3	4.20	161	36	7	15	29	.224	.398	.298
Artificial Turf	7-1	2.38	234	54	3	24	54	.231	.333	.305
April	1-0	2.19	41	7	1	5	7	.171	.244	.277
May	2-1	1.38	86	15	1	7	20	.174	.279	.234
June	2-0	2.01	74	11	2	8	17	.149	.284	.232
July	2-1	2.95	79	20	1	10	19	.253	.367	.341
August	0-1	4.82	76	25	3	5	11	.329	.474	.378
Sept./Oct.	1-1	9.35	39	12	2	4	9	.308	.564	.386
Leading Off Inn.			92	25	3	7	12	.272	.402	.323
Runners On			173	36	3	24	41	.208	.324	.308
Runners/Scor. Pos.			94	18	1	22	25	.191	.245	.345
Runners On/2 Out			82	21	1	13	15	.256	.354	.365
Scor. Pos./2 Out			53	13	1	13	10	.245	.340	.403
Late Inning Pressure			126	29	3	13	30	.230	.389	.302
Leading Off			33	9	1	1	4	.273	.424	.294
Runners On			49	12	2	8	12	.245	.510	.351
Runners/Scor. Pos.			29	5	1	8	8	.172	.345	.351
First 9 Batters			330	72	8	36	76	.218	.348	.299
Second 9 Batters			65	18	2	3	7	.277	.415	.319
All Batters Thereafter			0	0	0	0	0	—	—	—

Loves to face: Darnell Coles (0-for-7, 3 SO)
Hates to face: Bill Schroeder (.600, 3-for-5, 1 2B, 2 HR)
Ground outs-to-air outs ratio: 1.10 last season, 1.21 for career. . . . Additional statistics: 10 double-play ground outs in 80 opportunities, 14 doubles, 4 triples in 109.1 innings last season. . . . Faced only one batter once, pitched two or more innings 31 times (2d-most in A.L.), finished 33 games in 56 relief appearances. . . . Won seven of his first eight decisions, including a career-high five-game winning streak. . . . Opponents' annual averages with runners in scoring position: .295, .220, .191. . . . Opposing right-handed batters have outhit left-handed ones in all three seasons in majors. Three-year averages: .228 by left-handers, .248 by right-handers.

Brian Fisher
New York Yankees — Throws Right

	W–L	ERA	AB	H	HR	BB	SO	BA	SA	OBA
Season	9-5	4.93	379	105	14	37	67	.277	.438	.341
vs. Left-Handers			152	48	6	22	28	.316	.493	.400
vs. Right-Handers			227	57	8	15	39	.251	.401	.299
Home	2-3	5.91	174	54	7	16	27	.310	.494	.366
Road	7-2	4.17	205	51	7	21	40	.249	.390	.320
Grass	7-5	4.59	320	87	11	35	56	.272	.422	.344
Artificial Turf	2-0	6.91	59	18	3	2	11	.305	.525	.328
April	0-1	3.78	61	16	1	8	11	.262	.328	.348
May	1-1	7.50	50	17	2	5	9	.340	.560	.386
June	3-3	4.41	62	13	2	9	10	.210	.371	.310
July	0-0	3.20	77	22	3	6	10	.286	.416	.337
August	3-0	6.43	86	25	3	3	21	.291	.477	.315
Sept./Oct.	2-0	4.91	43	12	3	6	6	.279	.512	.380
Leading Off Inn.			80	22	4	3	16	.275	.438	.301
Runners On			181	52	6	25	23	.287	.453	.370
Runners/Scor. Pos.			117	32	5	20	18	.274	.470	.374
Runners On/2 Out			79	23	3	11	9	.291	.456	.378
Scor. Pos./2 Out			59	16	3	10	7	.271	.475	.377
Late Inning Pressure			189	51	6	17	30	.270	.439	.333
Leading Off			43	9	1	2	9	.209	.279	.244
Runners On			80	23	2	10	7	.288	.475	.367
Runners/Scor. Pos.			57	16	2	8	7	.281	.491	.369
First 9 Batters			341	96	13	36	61	.282	.449	.350
Second 9 Batters			38	9	1	1	6	.237	.342	.256
All Batters Thereafter								—	—	—

Loves to face: Ted Simmons (0-for-7)
Hates to face: Darrell Evans (3-for-3, 1 2B, 1 HR)
Ground outs-to-air outs ratio: 0.96 last season, 1.00 for career. . . . Additional statistics: 13 double-play ground outs in 96 opportunities, 13 doubles, 3 triples in 96.2 innings last season. . . . Faced only one batter once, pitched two or more innings 22 times, finished 26 games in 62 relief appearances. . . . Allowed 14 home runs, 2d most among major-league relievers. . . . Strikeout-to-walk ratio dropped from 2.93 in 1985 to 1.81 last season. . . . Opposing left-handed batters hit .225 in 1985. . . . Opponents' career batting average of .435 (10-for-23, 1 HR) with the bases loaded. . . . Only 66 of his 424 batters faced last season came while protecting a lead of three runs or less in the 8th inning or later.

Mike Flanagan
Baltimore Orioles — Throws Left

	W–L	ERA	AB	H	HR	BB	SO	BA	SA	OBA
Season	7-11	4.24	664	179	15	66	96	.270	.410	.334
vs. Left-Handers			129	32	1	11	19	.248	.349	.312
vs. Right-Handers			535	147	14	55	77	.275	.424	.339
Home	5-2	3.73	283	77	6	28	39	.272	.424	.338
Road	2-9	4.61	381	102	9	38	57	.268	.399	.331
Grass	6-7	4.14	524	147	10	50	76	.281	.412	.343
Artificial Turf	1-4	4.58	140	32	5	16	20	.229	.400	.302
April	1-2	4.33	107	31	1	12	13	.290	.383	.361
May	0-2	3.86	109	30	1	14	15	.275	.394	.352
June	0-1	5.56	46	14	3	3	3	.304	.587	.360
July	4-1	3.32	157	38	4	14	27	.242	.369	.302
August	2-2	3.00	150	36	2	10	24	.240	.333	.284
Sept./Oct.	0-3	7.61	95	30	4	13	14	.316	.558	.394
Leading Off Inn.			172	49	6	14	21	.285	.465	.339
Runners On			303	84	9	24	43	.277	.436	.324
Runners/Scor. Pos.			154	38	2	18	22	.247	.364	.315
Runners On/2 Out			106	23	3	11	15	.217	.358	.291
Scor. Pos./2 Out			66	14	1	8	10	.212	.333	.297
Late Inning Pressure			58	18	1	14	7	.310	.517	.432
Leading Off			19	8	0	3	1	.421	.632	.500
Runners On			26	8	1	7	3	.308	.538	.429
Runners/Scor. Pos.			14	4	0	7	1	.286	.429	.478
First 9 Batters			235	64	4	19	31	.272	.383	.324
Second 9 Batters			215	51	5	17	34	.237	.349	.291
All Batters Thereafter			214	64	6	30	31	.299	.500	.385

Loves to face: Wally Joyner (0-for-8)
Hates to face: Don Baylor (.392, 20-for-51, 6 HR)
Ground outs-to-air outs ratio: 1.43 last season, 1.31 for career. . . . Additional statistics: 21 double-play ground outs in 162 opportunities, 38 doubles, 5 triples in 172.0 innings last season. . . . Allowed 13 first-inning runs in 28 starts last season. . . . Batting support: 4.07 runs per start. . . . ERA after Sept. 1 was worst in major leagues (minimum: 20 IP). . . . Only home run allowed to a left-handed batter last season was hit by Greg Walker. . . . Career averages: one extra-base hit per 17.8 at bats vs. left-handers, one per 12.6 at bats vs. right-handers. . . . Opponents' averages for the last three seasons with two out and runners in scoring position: .197, .211, .212.

Mark Gubicza
Kansas City Royals — Throws Right

	W–L	ERA	AB	H	HR	BB	SO	BA	SA	OBA
Season	12-6	3.64	664	155	8	84	118	.233	.325	.321
vs. Left-Handers			352	87	4	52	59	.247	.332	.345
vs. Right-Handers			312	68	4	32	59	.218	.317	.292
Home	8-4	2.91	430	98	5	50	79	.228	.309	.309
Road	4-2	5.00	234	57	3	34	39	.244	.355	.341
Grass	4-2	5.87	143	35	2	24	28	.245	.357	.355
Artificial Turf	8-4	3.04	521	120	6	60	90	.230	.317	.311
April	0-3	6.75	69	17	1	12	6	.246	.420	.361
May	3-1	3.72	143	29	2	15	32	.203	.273	.278
June	0-0	4.35	38	10	0	8	6	.263	.368	.380
July	1-1	3.76	98	22	2	14	21	.224	.327	.322
August	4-1	3.57	148	37	1	13	27	.250	.324	.307
Sept./Oct.	4-0	2.14	168	40	2	22	26	.238	.321	.333
Leading Off Inn.			168	41	1	17	22	.244	.310	.321
Runners On			295	74	2	34	55	.251	.325	.324
Runners/Scor. Pos.			170	43	1	23	35	.253	.312	.332
Runners On/2 Out			121	29	1	12	23	.240	.339	.313
Scor. Pos./2 Out			77	17	1	10	16	.221	.312	.310
Late Inning Pressure			47	11	1	12	12	.234	.362	.390
Leading Off			13	2	0	5	4	.154	.154	.389
Runners On			17	6	0	4	4	.353	.471	.476
Runners/Scor. Pos.			9	3	0	3	2	.333	.444	.500
First 9 Batters			265	63	0	33	49	.238	.283	.320
Second 9 Batters			214	45	5	31	40	.210	.350	.316
All Batters Thereafter			185	47	3	20	29	.254	.357	.327

Loves to face: Joe Carter (0-for-10)
Hates to face: Greg Walker (.462, 6-for-13, 2 HR)
Ground outs-to-air outs ratio: 1.28 last season, 1.43 for career (0.80 in Late-Inning Pressure Situations). . . . Additional statistics: 12 double-play ground outs in 143 opportunities, 31 doubles, 3 triples in 180.2 innings last season. . . . Allowed 9 first-inning runs in 24 starts last season. . . . Batting support: 5.33 runs per start. . . . 11–5, 3.74 ERA as a starter; 1–1, 3.18 ERA in 11 relief appearances. . . . 7–4 vs. teams with winning records last season. . . . Opponents have batted for a higher average with runners on base than with the bases empty in each of his three seasons in the majors. . . . Yearly batting averages by right-handed batters: .248, .219, .218.

Lee Guetterman

Seattle Mariners — Throws Left

	W–L	ERA	AB	H	HR	BB	SO	BA	SA	OBA
Season	0–4	7.34	311	108	7	30	38	.347	.489	.406
vs. Left-Handers			102	34	2	10	10	.333	.471	.404
vs. Right-Handers			209	74	5	20	28	.354	.498	.407
Home	0–3	8.26	170	60	4	15	20	.353	.488	.414
Road	0–1	6.31	141	48	3	15	18	.340	.489	.396
Grass	0–1	6.59	113	37	3	12	16	.327	.478	.386
Artificial Turf	0–3	7.80	198	71	4	18	22	.359	.495	.417
April	0–0	3.38	38	12	0	4	3	.316	.447	.395
May	0–0	8.27	68	23	3	9	7	.338	.529	.418
June	0–3	7.23	78	24	2	7	14	.308	.423	.368
July	0–0	4.40	53	17	0	4	6	.321	.434	.356
August	0–0	10.61	41	15	2	3	5	.366	.585	.409
Sept./Oct.	0–1	13.50	33	17	0	3	3	.515	.576	.553
Leading Off Inn.			70	27	0	6	10	.386	.486	.442
Runners On			164	61	7	18	17	.372	.585	.429
Runners/Scor. Pos.			99	37	4	15	13	.374	.556	.437
Runners On/2 Out			51	16	2	9	6	.314	.471	.417
Scor. Pos./2 Out			33	10	2	8	3	.303	.515	.439
Late Inning Pressure			45	19	1	5	5	.422	.533	.509
Leading Off			13	5	0	1	1	.385	.385	.467
Runners On			22	10	1	4	4	.455	.636	.556
Runners/Scor. Pos.			12	6	1	3	3	.500	.833	.600
First 9 Batters			223	78	4	24	28	.350	.489	.415
Second 9 Batters			71	24	3	4	8	.338	.493	.382
All Batters Thereafter			17	6	0	2	2	.353	.471	.381

Loves to face: Curtis Wilkerson (0-for-5)
Hates to face: Lou Whitaker (3-for-3, 1 HR)
Ground outs-to-air outs ratio: 1.47 last season, 1.55 for career. . . .
Additional statistics: 15 double-play ground outs in 94 opportunities, 7th-highest average in A.L. (minimum: 10 GDP), 17 doubles, 3 triples in 76.0 innings last season. . . . Faced only one batter twice, pitched two or more innings 13 times, finished 8 games in 37 relief appearances. . . . Allowed seven home runs, all with runners on base. . . . 0–2, 8.10 ERA in 4 games started; 0–2, 7.13 ERA in relief. . . . Opponents' career on-base percentage of .463 leading off inning, worst of any pitcher (minimum: 75 PA) over the last 12 years. . . . Has made 44 career appearances, most of any winless pitcher active in 1986.

Ron Guidry

New York Yankees — Throws Left

	W–L	ERA	AB	H	HR	BB	SO	BA	SA	OBA
Season	9–12	3.98	761	202	28	38	140	.265	.424	.300
vs. Left-Handers			137	34	4	8	32	.248	.394	.290
vs. Right-Handers			624	168	24	30	108	.269	.431	.302
Home	6–8	4.39	483	137	19	22	84	.284	.449	.313
Road	3–4	3.28	278	65	9	16	56	.234	.381	.277
Grass	8–11	3.93	673	179	24	34	127	.266	.426	.301
Artificial Turf	1–1	4.37	88	23	4	4	13	.261	.409	.293
April	3–0	2.45	130	35	3	5	21	.269	.385	.296
May	1–4	4.25	167	40	6	9	40	.240	.377	.277
June	0–3	5.92	106	36	3	9	12	.340	.472	.385
July	1–1	3.00	46	13	1	1	12	.283	.435	.298
August	1–2	5.06	149	40	10	7	32	.268	.523	.301
Sept./Oct.	3–2	3.12	163	38	5	7	23	.233	.380	.267
Leading Off Inn.			196	54	7	5	33	.276	.423	.294
Runners On			290	80	9	17	47	.276	.428	.312
Runners/Scor. Pos.			159	40	5	12	21	.252	.390	.297
Runners On/2 Out			134	37	3	9	17	.276	.418	.322
Scor. Pos./2 Out			86	23	2	8	10	.267	.395	.330
Late Inning Pressure			99	24	5	6	14	.242	.434	.286
Leading Off			29	4	1	0	7	.138	.241	.138
Runners On			25	6	0	1	1	.240	.240	.296
Runners/Scor. Pos.			13	5	0	1	1	.385	.385	.429
First 9 Batters			257	76	14	9	51	.296	.521	.321
Second 9 Batters			237	54	5	13	46	.228	.329	.265
All Batters Thereafter			267	72	9	16	43	.270	.416	.311

Loves to face: Oddibe McDowell (0-for-14, 5 SO)
Hates to face: Jim Rice (.365, 27-for-74, 6 HR)
Ground outs-to-air outs ratio: 0.99 last season, 0.91 for career. . . .
Additional statistics: 10 double-play ground outs in 124 opportunities, 27 doubles, 5 triples in 192.1 innings last season. . . . Allowed 16 first-inning runs in 30 starts last season. . . . Batting support: 4.07 runs per start. . . . Has played 12 consecutive years for the Yankees. Only three pitchers in the history of the team had longer tours of duty: Whitey Ford (16 years), Red Ruffing (14), and Lefty Gomez (13). . . . Has walked progressively fewer batters in every season since strike-shortened 1981: 69, 60, 44, 42, 38. . . . Lost five starts decided by one run, tying Richard Dotson for most in A.L. last season. . . . Has won his last eight decisions vs. Seattle.

Jose Guzman

Texas Rangers — Throws Right

	W–L	ERA	AB	H	HR	BB	SO	BA	SA	OBA
Season	9–15	4.54	680	199	23	60	87	.293	.446	.353
vs. Left-Handers			375	116	13	34	46	.309	.480	.367
vs. Right-Handers			305	83	10	26	41	.272	.403	.336
Home	6–7	3.92	410	118	8	37	59	.288	.398	.349
Road	3–8	5.48	270	81	15	23	28	.300	.519	.360
Grass	8–13	4.40	589	173	17	55	75	.294	.431	.357
Artificial Turf	1–2	5.48	91	26	6	5	12	.286	.538	.330
April	1–4	5.53	115	37	3	7	13	.322	.478	.363
May	3–1	2.20	128	33	3	12	19	.258	.391	.321
June	3–3	4.46	163	44	6	15	24	.270	.429	.331
July	1–2	3.45	114	32	2	13	18	.281	.342	.369
August	1–2	7.32	78	27	3	8	7	.346	.538	.398
Sept./Oct.	0–3	5.91	82	26	6	5	6	.317	.573	.367
Leading Off Inn.			171	47	7	16	25	.275	.456	.337
Runners On			272	79	9	36	30	.290	.445	.377
Runners/Scor. Pos.			157	38	4	21	21	.242	.357	.332
Runners On/2 Out			107	26	6	13	17	.243	.439	.336
Scor. Pos./2 Out			65	13	2	10	11	.200	.292	.316
Late Inning Pressure			45	14	1	7	4	.311	.444	.404
Leading Off			14	4	0	2	2	.286	.357	.375
Runners On			15	5	1	3	2	.333	.533	.444
Runners/Scor. Pos.			8	1	0	1	2	.125	.125	.222
First 9 Batters			243	65	5	15	35	.267	.379	.313
Second 9 Batters			225	65	8	22	21	.289	.453	.354
All Batters Thereafter			212	69	10	23	31	.325	.514	.397

Loves to face: Dave Henderson (0-for-8)
Hates to face: Kent Hrbek (.833, 5-for-6, 1 HR)
Ground outs-to-air outs ratio: 1.41 last season, 1.38 for career. . . .
Additional statistics: 19 double-play ground outs in 143 opportunities, 35 doubles, 0 triples in 172.1 innings last season. . . . Allowed 10 first-inning runs in 29 starts last season. . . . Batting support: 3.79 runs per start, 6th lowest in A.L. (minimum: 15 GS). . . . Lost 15 games, most among major-league rookies. . . . Tied for A.L. lead with four losses in April. . . . Started Rangers' opener in 1986, becoming first major-league rookie to start an opening-day game since Mike Smithson opened for Texas in 1983. The last rookie to win an opener was Fernando Valenzuela in 1981. . . . Opponents' career batting: .286 with bases empty, .272 with runners on base, .227 with runners in scoring position.

Moose Haas

Oakland As — Throws Right

	W–L	ERA	AB	H	HR	BB	SO	BA	SA	OBA
Season	7–2	2.74	266	58	4	19	40	.218	.316	.271
vs. Left-Handers			120	34	3	13	12	.283	.392	.351
vs. Right-Handers			146	24	1	6	28	.164	.253	.201
Home	2–1	2.49	99	24	1	10	19	.242	.333	.312
Road	5–1	2.87	167	34	3	9	21	.204	.305	.246
Grass	4–2	3.10	190	48	3	15	25	.253	.358	.304
Artificial Turf	3–0	1.96	76	10	1	4	15	.132	.211	.185
April	4–0	1.26	98	17	1	6	21	.173	.255	.229
May	3–1	3.69	123	29	2	10	12	.236	.341	.293
June	0–1	12.00	13	6	1	2	1	.462	.692	.471
July	0–0	2.25	16	4	0	1	4	.250	.375	.294
August			0	0	0	0	0	—	—	—
Sept./Oct.	0–0	0.00	16	2	0	0	2	.125	.125	.125
Leading Off Inn.			69	15	1	4	11	.217	.304	.270
Runners On			95	17	1	13	14	.179	.284	.273
Runners/Scor. Pos.			46	9	0	7	9	.196	.196	.291
Runners On/2 Out			40	7	1	7	7	.175	.325	.298
Scor. Pos./2 Out			21	3	0	5	6	.143	.190	.308
Late Inning Pressure			14	3	0	1	3	.214	.286	.267
Leading Off			4	0	0	0	0	.000	.000	.000
Runners On			4	1	0	1	0	.250	.250	.400
Runners/Scor. Pos.			2	1	0	1	0	.500	.500	.667
First 9 Batters			99	24	1	7	16	.242	.323	.290
Second 9 Batters			88	20	3	6	14	.227	.375	.274
All Batters Thereafter			79	14	0	6	10	.177	.241	.244

Loves to face: Tim Laudner (.125, 2-for-16, 10 SO)
Hates to face: Bob Kearney (.615, 8-for-13, 5 2B)
Ground outs-to-air outs ratio: 0.91 last season, 1.00 for career. . . .
Additional statistics: 4 double-play ground outs in 46 opportunities, 14 doubles, 0 triples in 72.1 innings last season. . . . Allowed 2 first-inning runs in 12 starts last season. . . . Batting support: 7.42 runs per start. . . . Only homer allowed to a right-handed batter was hit by Jesse Barfield on May 6. . . . April ERA was 2d best in A.L. . . . Opponents' batting average was lowest since his rookie year (.207 in 1976). . . . Opponents' average with runners in scoring position was over .300 in each of the previous two seasons. . . . Annual batting average by right-handers since 1984: .295, .260, .164.

Greg Harris

Texas Rangers — Throws Right

	W–L	ERA	AB	H	HR	BB	SO	BA	SA	OBA
Season	10-8	2.83	410	103	12	42	95	.251	.402	.318
vs. Left-Handers			179	45	5	24	30	.251	.397	.335
vs. Right-Handers			231	58	7	18	65	.251	.407	.304
Home	9-4	2.64	239	60	5	12	50	.251	.368	.286
Road	1-4	3.09	171	43	7	30	45	.251	.450	.358
Grass	10-7	2.86	358	90	11	37	82	.251	.405	.318
Artificial Turf	0-1	2.63	52	13	1	5	13	.250	.385	.316
April	2-3	6.06	64	23	4	7	12	.359	.641	.411
May	1-3	1.61	85	19	1	9	17	.224	.318	.298
June	0-1	2.35	59	14	0	5	14	.237	.322	.308
July	2-1	2.41	67	20	1	10	19	.299	.448	.375
August	3-0	2.05	76	15	3	7	13	.197	.342	.262
Sept./Oct.	2-0	3.24	59	12	3	4	20	.203	.373	.254
Leading Off Inn.			82	21	3	8	15	.256	.427	.322
Runners On			215	51	7	23	51	.237	.391	.306
Runners/Scor. Pos.			132	30	4	19	32	.227	.379	.312
Runners On/2 Out			99	25	4	13	20	.253	.424	.345
Scor. Pos./2 Out			72	17	2	11	15	.236	.375	.337
Late Inning Pressure			236	52	4	27	57	.220	.331	.297
Leading Off			44	9	0	5	7	.205	.273	.286
Runners On			122	28	2	18	30	.230	.344	.322
Runners/Scor. Pos.			77	20	1	14	17	.260	.377	.354
First 9 Batters			366	88	8	38	83	.240	.366	.307
Second 9 Batters			44	15	4	4	12	.341	.705	.408
All Batters Thereafter			0	0	0	0	0	—	—	—

Loves to face: Jim Presley (0-for-6, 4 SO)
Hates to face: Willie Upshaw (.556, 5-for-9, 2 2B, 2 HR)
Ground outs-to-air outs ratio: 1.12 last season, 1.30 for career.... Additional statistics: 13 double-play ground outs in 105 opportunities, 22 doubles, 2 triples in 111.1 innings last season.... Faced only one batter 3 times, pitched two or more innings 25 times, finished 63 games in 73 relief appearances.... Opposing batters had hit below .200 in each of the two previous seasons.... Opposing leadoff batters had hit .115 over two seasons prior to 1986, .143 with two outs and runners on base.... Opponents have a .189 career batting average with the bases loaded (no HR in 53 AB).... Other career batting averages: .234 by left-handers, .234 by right-handers. So why bother trying to pitch left-handed?

Brad Havens

Baltimore Orioles — Throws Left

	W–L	ERA	AB	H	HR	BB	SO	BA	SA	OBA
Season	3-3	4.56	258	64	7	29	57	.248	.403	.323
vs. Left-Handers			99	17	2	10	26	.172	.273	.245
vs. Right-Handers			159	47	5	19	31	.296	.484	.371
Home	1-2	5.27	154	42	5	20	36	.273	.442	.356
Road	2-1	3.60	104	22	2	9	21	.212	.346	.272
Grass	2-3	4.10	230	55	7	26	51	.239	.391	.315
Artificial Turf	1-0	8.59	28	9	0	3	6	.321	.500	.387
April	1-1	7.36	43	13	2	6	8	.302	.488	.388
May	1-0	4.73	48	12	0	3	12	.250	.375	.294
June	0-0	3.52	56	14	0	9	9	.250	.375	.348
July	1-0	3.52	28	7	2	2	6	.250	.500	.300
August	0-1	4.80	52	11	2	4	11	.212	.385	.268
Sept./Oct.	0-1	3.12	31	7	1	5	11	.226	.323	.333
Leading Off Inn.			56	9	2	7	14	.161	.321	.254
Runners On			118	33	3	15	26	.280	.432	.358
Runners/Scor. Pos.			78	23	2	12	18	.295	.462	.385
Runners On/2 Out			56	14	1	6	13	.250	.357	.323
Scor. Pos./2 Out			39	10	0	5	10	.256	.333	.341
Late Inning Pressure			67	19	2	7	15	.284	.403	.351
Leading Off			17	3	1	3	6	.176	.412	.300
Runners On			26	10	0	2	5	.385	.385	.429
Runners/Scor. Pos.			17	5	0	2	4	.294	.294	.368
First 9 Batters			201	52	6	19	44	.259	.428	.321
Second 9 Batters			43	9	1	10	9	.209	.302	.358
All Batters Thereafter			14	3	0	0	4	.214	.357	.214

Loves to face: Al Cowens (.067, 1-for-15, 5 SO)
Hates to face: Dave Henderson (.636, 7-for-11, 2 HR)
Ground outs-to-air outs ratio: 1.07 last season, 0.80 for career.... Additional statistics: 8 double-play ground outs in 53 opportunities, 13 doubles, 3 triples in 71.0 innings last season.... Faced only one batter 5 times, pitched two or more innings 11 times, finished 19 games in 46 relief appearances.... Opposing left-handed batters had outhit right-handers .295 to .267 prior to last season.... Opponents' on-base average of .259 leading off innings is 4th lowest over past 12 seasons (minimum: 250 BFP).... Opponents' career batting: .241 with bases empty, .314 with runners on base, .326 with runners in scoring position.... Opponents were hitless in 8 at bats with the bases loaded last season, although Havens did force in two runs with walks.

Neal Heaton

Indians/Twins — Throws Left

	W–L	ERA	AB	H	HR	BB	SO	BA	SA	OBA
Season	7-15	4.08	756	201	26	81	90	.266	.427	.336
vs. Left-Handers			144	36	6	10	19	.250	.431	.297
vs. Right-Handers			612	165	20	71	71	.270	.426	.345
Home	4-8	3.26	383	99	13	38	54	.258	.413	.324
Road	3-7	4.93	373	102	13	43	36	.273	.442	.349
Grass	5-9	4.43	466	127	17	49	40	.273	.433	.342
Artificial Turf	2-6	3.55	290	74	9	32	50	.255	.417	.327
April	0-1	3.63	66	16	1	9	7	.242	.333	.333
May	2-3	5.14	136	36	3	15	13	.265	.353	.338
June	1-2	2.48	128	29	4	10	11	.227	.367	.288
July	1-4	3.68	131	32	5	18	20	.244	.412	.336
August	1-2	4.31	124	38	4	10	17	.306	.516	.350
Sept./Oct.	2-3	4.73	171	50	9	19	22	.292	.515	.363
Leading Off Inn.			189	60	8	20	28	.317	.529	.386
Runners On			316	72	12	45	36	.228	.399	.322
Runners/Scor. Pos.			159	38	9	30	19	.239	.453	.351
Runners On/2 Out			121	27	6	22	10	.223	.438	.343
Scor. Pos./2 Out			69	18	4	19	5	.261	.507	.420
Late Inning Pressure			60	14	2	9	8	.233	.417	.329
Leading Off			20	6	1	0	5	.300	.550	.300
Runners On			17	5	1	8	2	.294	.647	.500
Runners/Scor. Pos.			12	2	1	6	1	.167	.500	.421
First 9 Batters			262	76	8	27	35	.290	.435	.356
Second 9 Batters			250	61	5	23	27	.244	.360	.307
All Batters Thereafter			244	64	13	31	28	.262	.488	.345

Loves to face: John Shelby (.121, 4-for-33)
Hates to face: George Bell (.409, 9-for-22, 3 HR)
Ground outs-to-air outs ratio: 1.05 last season, 0.93 for career.... Additional statistics: 21 double-play ground outs in 166 opportunities, 34 doubles, 5 triples in 198.2 innings last season.... Allowed 18 first-inning runs in 29 starts last season.... Batting support: 3.66 runs per start, 4th lowest in A.L. (minimum: 15 GS).... Tied for A.L. lead with 4 losses during the month of July.... Opponents' career batting average of .408 (20-for-49, 3 HR) with the bases loaded.... Has faced 94 batters leading off innings in Late-Inning Pressure Situations, and walked only one.... Opposing left-handers had batted over .300 in each of the two previous seasons.

Tom Henke

Toronto Blue Jays — Throws Right

	W–L	ERA	AB	H	HR	BB	SO	BA	SA	OBA
Season	9-5	3.35	329	63	6	32	118	.191	.286	.261
vs. Left-Handers			177	39	4	20	62	.220	.322	.299
vs. Right-Handers			152	24	2	12	56	.158	.243	.216
Home	5-2	3.16	154	28	3	12	46	.182	.273	.234
Road	4-3	3.51	175	35	3	20	72	.200	.297	.284
Grass	3-1	3.16	134	27	2	11	54	.201	.269	.260
Artificial Turf	6-4	3.48	195	36	4	21	64	.185	.297	.261
April	2-1	11.57	29	8	2	4	13	.276	.586	.364
May	2-2	4.15	66	12	1	9	27	.182	.303	.276
June	2-0	1.15	55	12	2	5	14	.218	.327	.274
July	1-0	2.45	47	6	0	8	19	.128	.128	.263
August	1-0	2.08	63	13	1	2	20	.206	.317	.231
Sept./Oct.	1-2	3.26	69	12	0	4	25	.174	.188	.213
Leading Off Inn.			65	8	1	6	24	.123	.185	.208
Runners On			158	35	3	18	51	.222	.323	.291
Runners/Scor. Pos.			96	21	1	13	36	.219	.271	.296
Runners On/2 Out			77	15	1	9	26	.195	.273	.279
Scor. Pos./2 Out			51	13	1	7	17	.255	.333	.345
Late Inning Pressure			217	37	6	24	87	.171	.290	.255
Leading Off			41	5	1	4	16	.122	.220	.217
Runners On			105	21	3	13	40	.200	.314	.286
Runners/Scor. Pos.			67	13	1	11	30	.194	.239	.304
First 9 Batters			308	59	6	25	112	.192	.286	.250
Second 9 Batters			21	4	0	7	6	.190	.286	.393
All Batters Thereafter			0	0	0	0	0	—	—	—

Loves to face: Dwayne Murphy (0-for-6, 6 SO)
Hates to face: Reggie Jackson (.667, 4-for-6)
Ground outs-to-air outs ratio: 0.51, lowest in A.L. last season (minimum: 250 BFP), 0.68 for career.... Additional statistics: 4 double-play ground outs in 73 opportunities, 13 doubles, 0 triples in 91.1 innings last season.... Faced only one batter twice, pitched two or more innings 18 times, finished 51 games in 63 relief appearances.... Prior to 1986, had faced 46 leadoff batters in Late-Inning Pressure Situations without walking one. Last season, he faced 46 and walked four.... Opponents' career batting: .213 with bases empty, .237 with runners on, .245 with runners in scoring position.... No home runs by right-handed batters until '86. Career batting averages: .248 by left-handers, .200 by right-handers.

Willie Hernandez

Detroit Tigers   Throws Left

	W–L	ERA	AB	H	HR	BB	SO	BA	SA	OBA
Season	8-7	3.55	346	87	13	21	77	.251	.413	.301
vs. Left-Handers			97	20	1	3	20	.206	.268	.238
vs. Right-Handers			249	67	12	18	57	.269	.470	.325
Home	6-3	3.77	168	42	4	12	39	.250	.369	.316
Road	2-4	3.35	178	45	9	9	38	.253	.455	.287
Grass	7-5	3.35	303	76	8	19	65	.251	.380	.303
Artificial Turf	1-2	5.06	43	11	5	2	12	.256	.651	.289
April	1-1	5.56	49	16	2	1	12	.327	.510	.340
May	1-1	2.30	64	15	2	5	18	.234	.359	.290
June	1-1	2.82	84	24	4	4	17	.286	.476	.326
July	4-2	2.08	65	13	2	3	10	.200	.323	.235
August	0-1	6.75	51	12	3	5	12	.235	.471	.333
Sept./Oct.	1-1	3.12	33	7	0	3	8	.212	.303	.278
Leading Off Inn.			70	14	2	2	13	.200	.329	.233
Runners On			160	41	6	9	34	.256	.413	.303
Runners/Scor. Pos.			89	23	3	6	22	.258	.393	.310
Runners On/2 Out			86	23	3	5	20	.267	.407	.315
Scor. Pos./2 Out			58	15	3	2	14	.259	.448	.295
Late Inning Pressure			206	52	8	13	45	.252	.417	.300
Leading Off			45	9	0	0	10	.200	.267	.200
Runners On			89	23	4	6	16	.258	.427	.313
Runners/Scor. Pos.			50	12	1	4	9	.240	.360	.309
First 9 Batters			325	82	12	19	75	.252	.415	.301
Second 9 Batters			21	5	1	2	2	.238	.381	.304
All Batters Thereafter			0	0	0	0	0	—	—	—

Loves to face: Pete O'Brien (0-for-16)
Hates to face: Dick Schofield (.625, 5-for-8, 1 HR)
Ground outs-to-air outs ratio: 0.76 last season, 1.10 for career. . . .
Additional statistics: 4 double-play ground outs in 67 opportunities, 17 doubles, 0 triples in 88.2 innings last season. . . . Faced only one batter 5 times, pitched two or more innings 22 times, finished 53 games in 64 relief appearances. . . . Led A.L. with eight saves in June. . . . Allowed three extra-inning home runs last season, tied for most in the majors. . . . Only left-handed batter to take him deep last season was Rich Gedman. He did it with the bases full. . . . Hernandez allowed grand slams to the last two batters he faced with the bases loaded last season (Gedman and Dick Schofield). . . . Career averages: 1.94 strikeouts per walk in day games, 3.07 in night games.

Charlie Hough

Texas Rangers   Throws Right

	W–L	ERA	AB	H	HR	BB	SO	BA	SA	OBA
Season	17-10	3.79	850	188	32	89	146	.221	.379	.301
vs. Left-Handers			436	89	13	43	78	.204	.335	.282
vs. Right-Handers			414	99	19	46	68	.239	.425	.322
Home	8-5	3.99	394	93	15	39	69	.236	.388	.308
Road	9-5	3.62	456	95	17	50	77	.208	.371	.296
Grass	14-8	3.67	682	148	25	72	121	.217	.365	.298
Artificial Turf	3-2	4.30	168	40	7	17	25	.238	.435	.316
April			0	0	0	0	0	—	—	—
May	3-2	5.23	119	29	4	7	16	.244	.420	.297
June	4-1	1.51	181	25	4	15	34	.138	.238	.208
July	2-3	4.40	156	39	8	24	28	.250	.455	.352
August	3-2	5.40	161	42	5	22	24	.261	.398	.357
Sept./Oct.	5-2	3.59	233	53	11	21	44	.227	.403	.300
Leading Off Inn.			226	41	9	15	47	.181	.341	.239
Runners On			296	74	10	35	45	.250	.402	.334
Runners/Scor. Pos.			175	48	6	27	30	.274	.434	.376
Runners On/2 Out			121	23	4	19	21	.190	.331	.300
Scor. Pos./2 Out			74	17	4	14	14	.230	.446	.352
Late Inning Pressure			117	23	2	8	25	.197	.291	.254
Leading Off			37	3	0	1	14	.081	.135	.105
Runners On			22	5	0	3	5	.227	.227	.346
Runners/Scor. Pos.			11	3	0	1	3	.273	.273	.333
First 9 Batters			260	50	9	28	49	.192	.331	.280
Second 9 Batters			246	59	9	31	34	.240	.402	.330
All Batters Thereafter			344	79	14	30	63	.230	.398	.297

Loves to face: Marc Hill (0-for-19)
Hates to face: Mark Salas (.524, 11-for-21, 2 HR)
Ground outs-to-air outs ratio: 0.98 last season, 1.04 for career. . . .
Additional statistics: 19 double-play ground outs in 123 opportunities, 32 doubles, 3 triples in 230.1 innings last season. . . . Allowed 12 first-inning runs in 33 starts last season. . . . Batting support: 5.00 runs per start. . . . June ERA was 3d best in A.L. . . . Has won his last eight decisions vs. Cleveland, lost his last six vs. Milwaukee. . . . One of three major leaguers to pitch 225 or more innings in each of the last five seasons (Valenzuela and Morris). . . . Has allowed three grand slam home runs in his career: to Carmen Fanzone, Pat Sheridan, and George Vukovich.

Ted Higuera

Milwaukee Brewers   Throws Left

	W–L	ERA	AB	H	HR	BB	SO	BA	SA	OBA
Season	20-11	2.79	936	226	26	74	207	.241	.379	.296
vs. Left-Handers			152	37	4	7	37	.243	.382	.275
vs. Right-Handers			784	189	22	67	170	.241	.379	.300
Home	10-3	1.79	484	106	10	36	108	.219	.335	.270
Road	10-8	3.91	452	120	16	38	99	.265	.427	.323
Grass	17-8	2.40	794	185	20	68	171	.233	.361	.291
Artificial Turf	3-3	5.14	142	41	6	6	36	.289	.479	.327
April	3-1	2.23	145	30	5	12	34	.207	.324	.266
May	3-3	2.60	171	39	5	14	40	.228	.374	.294
June	4-2	2.25	162	39	4	13	36	.241	.383	.298
July	3-1	3.52	119	30	3	11	26	.252	.378	.308
August	4-1	3.02	174	47	2	9	37	.270	.374	.308
Sept./Oct.	3-3	3.30	165	41	7	15	34	.248	.436	.308
Leading Off Inn.			237	55	10	18	46	.232	.392	.289
Runners On			367	88	7	25	90	.240	.354	.282
Runners/Scor. Pos.			175	36	7	18	53	.206	.389	.265
Runners On/2 Out			170	35	3	14	41	.206	.306	.266
Scor. Pos./2 Out			92	15	3	10	27	.163	.326	.245
Late Inning Pressure			120	28	1	11	27	.233	.292	.293
Leading Off			31	8	1	3	6	.258	.419	.324
Runners On			46	11	0	6	13	.239	.261	.315
Runners/Scor. Pos.			21	3	0	4	8	.143	.143	.259
First 9 Batters			282	69	6	20	75	.245	.369	.292
Second 9 Batters			260	62	12	21	58	.238	.423	.298
All Batters Thereafter			394	95	8	33	74	.241	.358	.297

Loves to face: Brian Downing (0-for-12)
Hates to face: Eddie Murray (.500, 7-for-14, 3 HR)
Ground outs-to-air outs ratio: 0.76 last season, 0.79 for career. . . .
Additional statistics: 13 double-play ground outs in 167 opportunities, 43 doubles (8th most in A.L.), 4 triples in 248.1 innings last season. . . . Allowed 8 first-inning runs in 34 starts last season. . . . . .Batting support: 3.97 runs per 34 start. Eleven A.L. starting pitchers (minimum: 25 GS) were supported with less than 4 runs per start; only Higuera posted a winning record. . . . Career average of one extra-base hit allowed per 26.7 at bats in Late-Inning Pressure Situations, one per 13.0 AB overall. . . . Has allowed 48 career home runs, 41 of them to right-handed batters.

Jay Howell

Oakland As   Throws Right

	W–L	ERA	AB	H	HR	BB	SO	BA	SA	OBA
Season	3-6	3.38	202	53	3	23	42	.262	.351	.339
vs. Left-Handers			97	32	2	15	16	.330	.464	.420
vs. Right-Handers			105	21	1	8	26	.200	.248	.261
Home	1-3	3.72	112	32	1	8	25	.286	.357	.339
Road	2-3	2.96	90	21	2	15	17	.233	.344	.340
Grass	2-6	4.04	166	50	2	20	33	.301	.392	.378
Artificial Turf	1-0	0.82	36	3	1	3	9	.083	.167	.154
April	0-2	4.91	60	17	3	2	15	.283	.467	.306
May	0-2	9.82	18	7	0	5	3	.389	.556	.522
June			0	0	0	0	0	—	—	—
July	0-0	0.00	13	2	0	0	1	.154	.154	.154
August	2-0	0.51	60	11	0	7	11	.183	.200	.279
Sept./Oct.	1-2	4.73	51	16	0	9	12	.314	.373	.410
Leading Off Inn.			42	11	0	2	6	.262	.310	.295
Runners On			101	29	2	12	18	.287	.396	.365
Runners/Scor. Pos.			54	18	1	8	9	.333	.444	.413
Runners On/2 Out			45	9	1	2	11	.200	.289	.250
Scor. Pos./2 Out			25	4	0	0	6	.160	.200	.160
Late Inning Pressure			140	40	2	16	30	.286	.386	.361
Leading Off			28	9	0	1	4	.321	.393	.345
Runners On			71	21	1	9	14	.296	.394	.378
Runners/Scor. Pos.			37	14	1	7	6	.378	.514	.467
First 9 Batters			186	45	3	20	39	.242	.339	.320
Second 9 Batters			18	8	0	3	3	.444	.444	.524
All Batters Thereafter			0	0	0	0	0	—	—	—

Loves to face: Andre Thornton (0-for-10, 2 SO)
Hates to face: Jim Gantner (.700, 7-for-10)
Ground outs-to-air outs ratio: 1.27 last season, 1.10 for career. . . .
Additional statistics: 7 double-play ground outs in 54 opportunities, 9 doubles, 0 triples in 53.1 innings last season. . . . Faced only one batter once, pitched two or more innings 11 times, finished 33 games in 38 relief appearances. . . . Has faced 158 leadoff batters in Late-Inning Pressure Situations, and walked only three, lowest average in *Player Analysis* history (minimum: 100 BFP). . . . Opponents' career batting: .243 with bases empty, .287 with runners on base, .304 with runners in scoring position. . . . Yearly batting averages by opposing left-handers since 1984: .220, .254, .330.

Mark Huismann
Throws Right

Royals/Mariners	W–L	ERA	AB	H	HR	BB	SO	BA	SA	OBA
Season	3-4	3.79	379	98	19	25	72	.259	.462	.304
vs. Left-Handers			198	61	8	10	21	.308	.485	.341
vs. Right-Handers			181	37	11	15	51	.204	.436	.265
Home	2-2	3.45	221	57	13	15	42	.258	.471	.305
Road	1-2	4.28	158	41	6	10	30	.259	.449	.302
Grass	0-1	5.54	103	27	6	7	18	.262	.520	.306
Artificial Turf	3-3	3.15	276	71	13	18	54	.257	.460	.303
April	0-0	2.38	40	7	0	4	10	.175	.175	.250
May	1-2	4.32	67	21	4	5	13	.313	.507	.356
June	0-0	5.09	68	20	5	6	9	.294	.574	.342
July	1-1	6.50	75	24	4	6	12	.320	.627	.378
August	1-0	1.69	79	14	3	2	14	.177	.316	.198
Sept./Oct.	0-1	2.19	50	12	3	2	14	.240	.440	.269
Leading Off Inn.			83	23	6	5	12	.277	.518	.318
Runners On			170	40	4	12	31	.235	.365	.281
Runners/Scor. Pos.			108	22	2	7	21	.204	.333	.246
Runners On/2 Out			68	13	1	8	10	.191	.309	.276
Scor. Pos./2 Out			53	8	1	5	7	.151	.283	.224
Late Inning Pressure			92	23	5	12	20	.250	.446	.333
Leading Off			23	6	3	2	2	.261	.696	.320
Runners On			38	9	1	6	8	.237	.368	.333
Runners/Scor. Pos.			24	6	0	3	5	.250	.333	.321
First 9 Batters			290	72	13	19	57	.248	.445	.293
Second 9 Batters			84	24	5	6	14	.286	.476	.337
All Batters Thereafter			5	2	1	0	1	.400	1.200	.400

Loves to face: Rudy Law (0-for-7)
Hates to face: Don Mattingly (.750, 3-for-4, 2 HR)
Ground outs-to-air outs ratio: 1.64 last season, 1.55 for career.... Additional statistics: 12 double-play ground outs in 82 opportunities, 14 doubles, 3 triples in 97.1 innings last season.... Faced only one batter once, pitched two or more innings 24 times, finished 19 games in 45 relief appearances.... Allowed 16 home runs in relief, highest total in majors last season.... Opponents' career batting: .284 with bases empty, .241 with runners on base, .225 with runners in scoring position, .175 with two outs and runners in scoring position.... Career breakdown: left-handers .298, right-handers .232.

Bruce Hurst
Throws Left

Boston Red Sox	W–L	ERA	AB	H	HR	BB	SO	BA	SA	OBA
Season	13-8	2.99	660	169	18	50	167	.256	.392	.310
vs. Left-Handers			86	22	4	7	20	.256	.442	.312
vs. Right-Handers			574	147	14	43	147	.256	.385	.310
Home	8-3	2.37	378	89	11	26	106	.235	.368	.287
Road	5-5	3.88	282	80	7	24	61	.284	.426	.340
Grass	12-7	2.96	613	160	18	44	159	.261	.400	.312
Artificial Turf	1-1	3.46	47	9	0	6	8	.191	.298	.283
April	1-2	3.78	122	29	1	13	41	.238	.344	.311
May	4-1	2.05	165	42	3	7	48	.255	.364	.286
June	0	0	0	0	0	0	0	—	—	—
July	0-2	8.00	40	12	4	5	5	.300	.700	.378
August	3-2	3.73	155	40	8	16	26	.258	.452	.327
Sept./Oct.	5-1	1.72	178	46	2	9	47	.258	.331	.300
Leading Off Inn.			165	51	8	16	30	.309	.497	.374
Runners On			277	64	2	17	75	.231	.314	.275
Runners/Scor. Pos.			133	29	1	11	35	.218	.293	.277
Runners On/2 Out			110	21	1	7	38	.191	.264	.246
Scor. Pos./2 Out			62	12	1	5	20	.194	.306	.265
Late Inning Pressure			61	15	0	4	16	.246	.311	.292
Leading Off			19	6	0	1	6	.316	.421	.350
Runners On			25	6	0	1	6	.240	.320	.269
Runners/Scor. Pos.			9	2	0	1	2	.222	.222	.300
First 9 Batters			202	46	4	19	73	.228	.327	.291
Second 9 Batters			206	60	8	17	38	.291	.485	.345
All Batters Thereafter			252	63	6	14	56	.250	.369	.296

Loves to face: Bob Kearney (0-for-15)
Hates to face: Lance Parrish (.478, 11-for-23, 6 HR)
Ground outs-to-air outs ratio: 0.89 last season, 1.09 for career.... Additional statistics: 14 double-play ground outs in 137 opportunities, 28 doubles, 4 triples in 174.1 innings.... Allowed 5 first-inning runs in 25 starts last season.... Batting support: 4.20 runs per start.... First left-hander since Lefty Grove (1936) to pitch four shutouts at Fenway in one season.... Had 3d-lowest ERA in A.L. at home (2.37); only Higuera (1.79) and Curt Young (2.37), in pitchers parks, were lower.... Allowed 18 home runs, 16 with the bases empty. The other two were hit with only one man on.... Nearly untouchable in the 8th and 9th innings last season, allowing one run in 20 innings pitched after the 7th inning.

Danny Jackson
Throws Left

Kansas City Royals	W–L	ERA	AB	H	HR	BB	SO	BA	SA	OBA
Season	11-12	3.20	692	177	13	79	115	.256	.364	.334
vs. Left-Handers			137	40	2	15	25	.292	.409	.362
vs. Right-Handers			555	137	11	64	90	.247	.353	.327
Home	6-4	2.15	297	73	6	36	45	.246	.367	.324
Road	5-8	3.99	395	104	7	43	70	.263	.362	.336
Grass	5-5	3.93	322	86	6	34	59	.267	.357	.337
Artificial Turf	6-7	2.55	370	91	7	45	56	.246	.370	.331
April	0-0	4.05	23	6	0	7	3	.261	.304	.433
May	2-1	3.28	96	25	1	10	20	.260	.333	.330
June	2-4	4.21	144	44	4	14	23	.306	.465	.366
July	2-1	3.33	87	19	2	11	14	.218	.356	.320
August	3-3	3.96	135	37	2	13	23	.274	.370	.336
Sept./Oct.	2-3	1.88	207	46	4	24	32	.222	.314	.305
Leading Off Inn.			166	39	3	25	29	.235	.325	.335
Runners On			305	80	5	32	46	.262	.364	.334
Runners/Scor. Pos.			171	45	3	20	28	.263	.374	.343
Runners On/2 Out			126	31	4	14	22	.246	.397	.336
Scor. Pos./2 Out			81	17	3	10	15	.210	.370	.319
Late Inning Pressure			98	22	1	13	14	.224	.276	.321
Leading Off			28	7	0	1	5	.250	.250	.276
Runners On			41	7	0	6	5	.171	.195	.292
Runners/Scor. Pos.			19	3	0	4	3	.158	.158	.333
First 9 Batters			236	56	4	30	40	.237	.339	.323
Second 9 Batters			221	61	6	23	33	.276	.425	.344
All Batters Thereafter			235	60	3	26	42	.255	.332	.335

Loves to face: Greg Gagne (.059, 1-for-17)
Hates to face: Kent Hrbek (.478, 11-for-23, 1 HR)
Ground outs-to-air outs ratio: 1.70 last season, 1.55 for career.... Additional statistics: 23 double-play ground outs (7th in A.L.) in 155 opportunities, 24 doubles, 6 triples in 185.2 innings last season.... Allowed 22 first-inning runs in 27 starts last season.... Poorest run support (2.93 runs per start) in majors last season (minimum: 15 GS).... ERA after Sept. 1 was 2d best in A.L.... Opponents batted .538 (7-for-13) with the bases loaded last season.... Over the last three seasons his effectiveness against left-handers has diminished (.217, .272, .292) while batting average of opposing right-handers has decreased in every year since 1983: .324, .302, .258, .247.

Bob James
Throws Right

Chicago White Sox	W–L	ERA	AB	H	HR	BB	SO	BA	SA	OBA
Season	5-4	5.25	228	61	8	23	32	.268	.478	.340
vs. Left-Handers			113	27	5	16	18	.239	.469	.344
vs. Right-Handers			115	34	3	7	14	.296	.487	.336
Home	3-2	6.30	124	38	4	13	18	.306	.540	.371
Road	2-2	4.13	104	23	4	10	14	.221	.404	.302
Grass	5-3	4.91	198	50	7	18	30	.253	.465	.321
Artificial Turf	0-1	7.71	30	11	1	5	2	.367	.567	.457
April	1-1	5.06	43	12	1	1	9	.279	.442	.311
May	1-3	7.13	71	21	3	8	6	.296	.577	.366
June	1-0	4.02	62	17	3	9	9	.274	.484	.361
July	1-0	6.30	38	10	1	3	6	.263	.474	.341
August	0-0	0.00	10	0	0	1	1	.000	.000	.091
Sept./Oct.	1-0	0.00	4	1	0	1	1	.250	.250	.400
Leading Off Inn.			41	9	2	5	3	.220	.439	.319
Runners On			133	36	3	11	21	.271	.466	.327
Runners/Scor. Pos.			85	21	2	9	14	.247	.435	.320
Runners On/2 Out			63	17	2	4	8	.270	.460	.313
Scor. Pos./2 Out			39	7	1	3	7	.179	.282	.238
Late Inning Pressure			154	40	5	17	24	.260	.468	.335
Leading Off			28	4	1	3	3	.143	.321	.250
Runners On			93	27	2	8	16	.290	.516	.343
Runners/Scor. Pos.			57	17	2	7	9	.298	.561	.368
First 9 Batters			216	57	8	21	31	.264	.481	.331
Second 9 Batters			12	4	0	2	1	.333	.417	.471
All Batters Thereafter			0	0	0	0	0			

Loves to face: Lloyd Moseby (0-for-8, 2 SO)
Hates to face: Randy Bush (2-for-2, 1 HR)
Ground outs-to-air outs ratio: 1.06 last season, 1.03 for career.... Additional statistics: 3 double-play ground outs in 59 opportunities, 18 doubles, 3 triples in 58.1 innings last season.... Faced only one batter 6 times, pitched two or more innings 12 times, finished 40 games in 49 relief appearances.... Percent of batters faced in Late-Inning Pressure Situations has increased in each season in the majors: Since 1982: 7.6, 36.1, 44.2, 65.8, 70.0.... Opposing batters have hit better with runners on base than with the bases empty in each of the past five seasons.... Opponents' carrer batting average of .244 with runners in scoring position drops to .197 with two men out.

Tommy John
New York Yankees   Throws Left

	W–L	ERA	AB	H	HR	BB	SO	BA	SA	OBA
Season	5-3	2.93	265	73	8	15	28	.275	.392	.316
vs. Left-Handers			42	12	2	4	4	.286	.500	.354
vs. Right-Handers			223	61	6	11	24	.274	.372	.308
Home	2-2	3.76	160	46	6	10	14	.288	.431	.326
Road	3-1	1.80	105	27	2	5	14	.257	.333	.301
Grass	4-2	3.07	213	60	6	13	23	.282	.399	.319
Artificial Turf	1-1	2.40	52	13	2	2	5	.250	.365	.304
April			0	0	0	0	0	—	—	—
May	2-0	2.82	80	19	3	7	5	.238	.388	.300
June	1-1	4.80	63	20	3	2	7	.317	.492	.338
July			0	0	0	0	0	—	—	—
August	2-2	2.16	122	34	2	6	16	.279	.344	.315
Sept./Oct.			0	0	0	0	0	—	—	—
Leading Off Inn.			68	25	0	1	4	.368	.397	.394
Runners On			110	22	4	9	15	.200	.336	.254
Runners/Scor. Pos.			54	8	2	6	9	.148	.296	.222
Runners On/2 Out			39	9	1	6	7	.231	.359	.333
Scor. Pos./2 Out			22	4	1	4	4	.182	.364	.308
Late Inning Pressure			18	4	0	0	2	.222	.222	.222
Leading Off			5	2	0	0	0	.400	.400	.400
Runners On			5	1	0	0	1	.200	.200	.200
Runners/Scor. Pos.			4	1	0	0	0	.250	.250	.250
First 9 Batters			102	28	1	5	10	.275	.324	.312
Second 9 Batters			91	23	5	5	11	.253	.451	.296
All Batters Thereafter			72	22	2	5	7	.306	.417	.346

Loves to face: Lloyd Moseby (.143, 5-for-35, 7 SO, 1 HR)
Hates to face: John Shelby (.643, 9-for-14, 2 HR)
Ground outs-to-air outs ratio: 3.14, highest in A.L. last season (minimum: 250 BFP), 2.49 for career. . . . Additional statistics: 10 double-play ground outs in 61 opportunities, 4th-highest average in A.L. (minimum: 10 GDP), 7 doubles, 0 triples in 70.2 innings last season. . . . Allowed 3 first-inning runs in 10 starts last season. . . . Batting support: 4.30 runs per start. . . . August ERA was 6th best in A.L. . . . Held top 15 A.L. batters to combined .115 average last year (3-for-26), lowest in A.L. (minimum: 20 AB). . . . First major-league win was a 3-hit shutout vs. Baltimore on May 3, 1963. He threw only 74 pitches. The time of game was 1:34.

Joe Johnson
Toronto Blue Jays   Throws Right

	W–L	ERA	AB	H	HR	BB	SO	BA	SA	OBA
Season	7-2	3.89	335	94	3	22	39	.281	.349	.327
vs. Left-Handers			184	53	3	14	25	.288	.391	.332
vs. Right-Handers			151	41	0	8	14	.272	.298	.321
Home	4-1	2.83	157	42	2	5	18	.268	.350	.297
Road	3-1	4.82	178	52	1	17	21	.292	.348	.352
Grass	2-1	5.40	153	46	1	13	18	.301	.359	.353
Artificial Turf	5-1	2.63	182	48	2	9	21	.264	.341	.304
April			0	0	0	0	0	—	—	—
May			0	0	0	0	0	—	—	—
June			0	0	0	0	0	—	—	—
July	1-0	3.22	84	24	0	10	12	.286	.321	.358
August	3-1	4.67	134	39	3	5	15	.291	.410	.326
Sept./Oct.	3-1	3.48	117	31	0	7	12	.265	.299	.305
Leading Off Inn.			91	21	0	4	13	.231	.297	.271
Runners On			124	44	3	7	15	.355	.460	.382
Runners/Scor. Pos.			58	20	2	4	10	.345	.466	.373
Runners On/2 Out			47	11	1	0	10	.234	.234	.234
Scor. Pos./2 Out			20	5	1	0	6	.250	.450	.250
Late Inning Pressure			18	6	0	1	2	.333	.444	.350
Leading Off			6	2	0	0	2	.333	.500	.333
Runners On			5	3	0	0	0	.600	.800	.500
Runners/Scor. Pos.			1	1	0	0	0	1.000	1.000	.500
First 9 Batters			137	44	1	5	17	.321	.394	.343
Second 9 Batters			110	25	1	10	13	.227	.264	.295
All Batters Thereafter			88	25	1	7	9	.284	.386	.343

Loves to face: Paul Molitor (0-for-5)
Hates to face: Jim Dwyer (2-for-2, 1 2B, 1 HR)
Figures above are for A.L. only; see also N.L. Pitchers section. . . . Ground outs-to-air outs ratio: 1.34 last season, 1.32 for career. . . . Additional statistics: 16 double-play ground outs in 158 opportunities, 30 doubles, 3 triples in 175.0 innings last season. . . . Allowed 14 first-inning runs in 30 starts last season. . . . Batting support: 4.60 runs per start. . . . Allowed only three home runs in his last 18 starts. . . . Opponents' career batting averages: .314 with runners on base, .264 with the bases empty. . . . Atlanta's winningest pitcher through end of May, Toronto's after the All-Star break (tied with Eichhorn).

Jimmy Key
Toronto Blue Jays   Throws Left

	W–L	ERA	AB	H	HR	BB	SO	BA	SA	OBA
Season	14-11	3.57	866	222	24	74	141	.256	.403	.315
vs. Left-Handers			190	51	1	12	45	.268	.321	.319
vs. Right-Handers			676	171	23	62	96	.253	.426	.314
Home	7-9	4.50	438	121	16	40	69	.276	.454	.335
Road	7-2	2.67	428	101	8	34	72	.236	.350	.294
Grass	6-2	2.04	362	78	6	30	65	.215	.320	.278
Artificial Turf	8-9	4.76	504	144	18	44	76	.286	.462	.341
April	0-1	11.85	59	20	1	7	7	.339	.593	.403
May	3-2	5.19	132	34	6	17	19	.258	.447	.342
June	3-2	2.09	174	40	5	11	38	.230	.356	.274
July	3-1	3.24	153	46	3	14	25	.301	.425	.359
August	2-3	3.51	155	40	3	9	22	.258	.387	.303
Sept./Oct.	3-2	2.01	193	42	6	16	30	.218	.352	.278
Leading Off Inn.			231	69	6	15	40	.299	.455	.341
Runners On			340	78	14	25	49	.229	.406	.282
Runners/Scor. Pos.			164	35	4	17	26	.213	.354	.286
Runners On/2 Out			138	29	5	5	25	.210	.362	.238
Scor. Pos./2 Out			69	13	1	5	17	.188	.275	.243
Late Inning Pressure			106	32	3	7	12	.302	.425	.345
Leading Off			31	7	0	2	2	.226	.290	.273
Runners On			38	12	2	1	7	.316	.500	.333
Runners/Scor. Pos.			14	4	1	1	3	.286	.500	.333
First 9 Batters			287	62	11	22	60	.216	.397	.273
Second 9 Batters			263	69	4	27	40	.262	.373	.327
All Batters Thereafter			316	91	9	25	41	.288	.434	.343

Loves to face: Mike Davis (0-for-10, 6 SO)
Hates to face: Floyd Rayford (.556, 5-for-9, 2 2B, 2 HR)
Ground outs-to-air outs ratio: 1.13 last season, 1.31 for career. . . . Additional statistics: 21 double-play ground outs in 169 opportunities, 47 doubles (4th most in A.L.), 4 triples in 232.0 innings last season. Allowed 75 extra-base hits, 10th most in A.L. . . . Allowed 12 first-inning runs in 35 starts last season. . . . Batting support: 5.11 runs per start. . . . Averaged 6.62 innings per start, highest on Blue Jays staff. . . . June ERA was 4th best in A.L. . . . Season totals of 14-8, 2.70 ERA if you throw out his first seven games (0–3, 13.05 ERA). . . . 9–4 vs. teams above the .500 mark, 5–7 vs. teams with losing records. . . . Allowed only one home run to a left-handed batter: Rich Gedman. . . . Career averages: one extra-base hit per 24.2 at bats in day games, one per 47.2 at bats in night games.

Eric King
Detroit Tigers   Throws Right

	W–L	ERA	AB	H	HR	BB	SO	BA	SA	OBA
Season	11-4	3.51	501	108	11	63	79	.216	.329	.312
vs. Left-Handers			247	59	8	28	35	.239	.389	.326
vs. Right-Handers			254	49	3	35	44	.193	.272	.299
Home	6-0	2.00	231	36	3	25	33	.156	.221	.250
Road	5-4	4.97	270	72	8	38	46	.267	.422	.364
Grass	9-3	3.05	397	80	8	46	66	.202	.302	.293
Artificial Turf	2-1	5.47	104	28	3	17	13	.269	.433	.382
April			0	0	0	0	0	—	—	—
May	1-0	1.20	49	6	0	4	9	.122	.122	.189
June	3-0	2.64	159	30	1	20	28	.189	.233	.283
July	4-2	3.96	134	33	5	18	22	.246	.433	.344
August	1-2	6.38	89	24	2	14	8	.270	.416	.394
Sept./Oct.	2-0	2.89	70	15	3	7	12	.214	.386	.286
Leading Off Inn.			126	28	4	15	20	.222	.341	.310
Runners On			219	50	2	24	25	.228	.315	.309
Runners/Scor. Pos.			120	27	0	16	12	.225	.283	.319
Runners On/2 Out			87	14	0	13	12	.161	.207	.277
Scor. Pos./2 Out			56	8	0	9	7	.143	.196	.262
Late Inning Pressure			65	15	2	6	12	.231	.338	.296
Leading Off			19	6	1	1	2	.316	.474	.350
Runners On			22	5	0	2	4	.227	.273	.292
Runners/Scor. Pos.			11	3	0	1	2	.273	.364	.333
First 9 Batters			217	46	4	19	35	.212	.309	.285
Second 9 Batters			138	25	2	23	25	.181	.254	.311
All Batters Thereafter			146	37	5	21	19	.253	.432	.353

Loves to face: Eddie Murray (0-for-12)
Hates to face: Tony Bernazard (4-for-7, 2 HR)
Ground outs-to-air outs ratio: 1.14 last season, his first in majors. . . . Additional statistics: 10 double-play ground outs in 112 opportunities, 24 doubles, 0 triples in 138.1 innings last season. . . . Allowed 12 first-inning runs in 16 starts last season. . . . Batting support: 5.63 runs per start, 7th best in A.L. (minimum: 15 GS). . . . 8–4, 4.31 ERA in 16 games started; 3–0 (3 saves), 1.25 ERA in 17 relief appearances. . . . Allowed 11 home runs—nine with the bases empty, two with one man on. . . . Tied major-league record for pitchers with six putouts in a nine-inning game (July 8). . . . Best winning percentage (.733) of any A.L. rookie (minimum: 10 decisions). . . . Opponents are 3-for-25 with the bases loaded.

Pete Ladd
Seattle Mariners — Throws Right

	W–L	ERA	AB	H	HR	BB	SO	BA	SA	OBA
Season	8-6	3.82	267	69	10	18	53	.258	.476	.306
vs. Left-Handers			107	31	7	11	22	.290	.598	.358
vs. Right-Handers			160	38	3	7	31	.238	.394	.270
Home	6-1	3.57	150	36	6	10	35	.240	.473	.282
Road	2-5	4.15	117	33	4	8	18	.282	.479	.336
Grass	1-5	5.00	70	17	3	5	10	.243	.471	.304
Artificial Turf	7-1	3.42	197	52	7	13	43	.264	.477	.307
April	1-1	3.48	40	8	3	2	10	.200	.450	.244
May	2-0	2.95	64	12	2	3	11	.188	.375	.217
June	0-1	7.00	38	14	1	4	4	.368	.605	.432
July	2-0	1.93	54	16	1	2	12	.296	.444	.316
August	3-2	2.13	43	7	2	5	8	.163	.349	.250
Sept./Oct.	0-2	9.95	28	12	1	2	8	.429	.821	.484
Leading Off Inn.			55	17	3	3	10	.309	.600	.356
Runners On			126	30	3	10	25	.238	.405	.292
Runners/Scor. Pos.			91	21	3	9	21	.231	.451	.296
Runners On/2 Out			46	3	0	5	11	.065	.087	.173
Scor. Pos./2 Out			38	3	0	4	10	.079	.105	.186
Late Inning Pressure			151	35	4	11	31	.232	.397	.285
Leading Off			33	9	2	3	7	.273	.545	.351
Runners On			66	15	0	6	14	.227	.303	.284
Runners/Scor. Pos.			48	9	0	5	11	.188	.271	.255
First 9 Batters			249	65	10	18	50	.261	.494	.312
Second 9 Batters			18	4	0	0	3	.222	.222	.222
All Batters Thereafter			0	0	0	0	0	—	—	—

Loves to face: Bruce Bochte (0-for-9)
Hates to face: Eddie Murray (.667, 4-for-6, 2 HR)
Ground outs-to-air outs ratio: 0.58, 3d lowest in A.L. last season (minimum: 250 BFP), 0.60 for career. . . . Additional statistics: 7 double-play ground outs in 56 opportunities, 22 doubles, 3 triples in 70.2 innings last season. . . . Faced only one batter 5 times, pitched two or more innings 16 times, finished 33 games in 52 relief appearances. . . . Had a winning record for the first time in his career. . . . At his best with two out. Opponents' career batting with runners on: .299 with less than two out, .190 with two out; with runners in scoring position: .299 with less than two out, .181 with two out. . . . Has walked leadoff batters in 9 of 99 innings in Late-Inning Pressure Situations, but only 4 in 136 unpressured innings.

Dennis Lamp
Toronto Blue Jays — Throws Right

	W–L	ERA	AB	H	HR	BB	SO	BA	SA	OBA
Season	2-6	5.05	301	93	5	23	30	.309	.405	.357
vs. Left-Handers			126	44	1	13	7	.349	.405	.410
vs. Right-Handers			175	49	4	10	23	.280	.406	.317
Home	1-5	5.44	169	47	3	13	20	.278	.373	.328
Road	1-1	4.50	132	46	2	10	10	.348	.447	.394
Grass	1-1	4.91	114	40	2	9	8	.351	.465	.398
Artificial Turf	1-5	5.13	187	53	3	14	22	.283	.369	.332
April	0-2	7.53	60	19	3	2	7	.317	.500	.339
May	1-1	9.31	46	17	1	5	6	.370	.500	.431
June	1-1	4.50	79	23	1	8	9	.291	.380	.356
July	0-1	3.38	45	17	0	5	4	.378	.422	.440
August	0-1	3.00	49	13	0	1	3	.265	.286	.280
Sept./Oct.	0-0	1.42	22	4	0	2	1	.182	.273	.240
Leading Off Inn.			69	16	0	5	9	.232	.275	.284
Runners On			136	52	4	11	13	.382	.544	.426
Runners/Scor. Pos.			83	36	4	9	7	.434	.675	.484
Runners On/2 Out			57	20	3	7	8	.351	.561	.422
Scor. Pos./2 Out			36	17	3	6	5	.472	.806	.548
Late Inning Pressure			50	26	3	8	6	.520	.760	.586
Leading Off			12	6	0	3	1	.500	.500	.600
Runners On			29	18	3	3	4	.621	1.034	.656
Runners/Scor. Pos.			18	15	3	2	1	.833	1.500	.850
First 9 Batters			231	70	2	15	25	.303	.377	.344
Second 9 Batters			69	22	3	8	5	.319	.478	.390
All Batters Thereafter			1	1	0	0	0	1.000	2.000	1.000

Loves to face: Lance Parrish (.152, 5-for-33, 14 SO, 1 HR)
Hates to face: Brett Butler (.700, 7-for-10)
Ground outs-to-air outs ratio: 2.03, 10th highest in A.L. last season (minimum: 250 BFP), 2.35 for career. . . . Additional statistics: 9 double-play ground outs in 60 opportunities, 12 doubles, 1 triple in 73.0 innings last season. . . . Faced only one batter once, pitched two or more innings 15 times, finished 11 games in 38 relief appearances. . . . Only home run allowed to a left-handed batter was hit by Pete O'Brien in Lamp's first outing of the season (April 10). . . . Fewest innings pitched (73) since his rookie season in 1977, and his first losing season since 1980. . .Career record of 8–0 vs. Detroit, 6–0 vs. Minnesota. . . . Opponents' batting average with runners in scoring position has been above .300 in three of the last four seasons.

Rick Langford
Oakland As — Throws Right

	W–L	ERA	AB	H	HR	BB	SO	BA	SA	OBA
Season	1-10	7.36	230	69	13	18	30	.300	.526	.351
vs. Left-Handers			104	35	6	7	12	.337	.567	.381
vs. Right-Handers			126	34	7	11	18	.270	.492	.326
Home	1-2	5.13	98	20	5	8	16	.204	.378	.269
Road	0-8	9.42	132	49	8	10	14	.371	.636	.413
Grass	1-9	6.15	212	58	12	16	28	.274	.491	.325
Artificial Turf	0-1	34.71	18	11	1	2	2	.611	.944	.650
April	1-2	4.32	59	11	5	6	12	.186	.441	.262
May	0-2	12.00	43	18	0	8	2	.419	.535	.510
June	0-4	6.31	109	32	6	2	15	.294	.514	.307
July	0-2	17.18	19	8	2	2	1	.421	.842	.476
August			0	0	0	0	0	—	—	—
Sept./Oct.			0	0	0	0	0	—	—	—
Leading Off Inn.			56	12	0	4	6	.214	.268	.267
Runners On			85	33	6	10	8	.388	.682	.443
Runners/Scor. Pos.			41	19	2	7	2	.463	.732	.520
Runners On/2 Out			32	11	3	6	2	.344	.688	.447
Scor. Pos./2 Out			16	6	1	5	1	.375	.688	.524
Late Inning Pressure			9	2	0	0	2	.222	.222	.222
Leading Off			3	0	0	0	0	.000	.000	.000
Runners On			1	0	0	0	0	.000	.000	.000
Runners/Scor. Pos.			0	0	0	0	0	—	—	—
First 9 Batters			113	37	8	12	15	.327	.619	.394
Second 9 Batters			78	22	3	4	10	.282	.410	.313
All Batters Thereafter			39	10	2	2	5	.256	.487	.293

Loves to face: Don Baylor (.059, 3-for-51, 10 SO)
Hates to face: Cecil Cooper (.463, 19-for-41, 4 HR)
Also hates to face: Brook Jacoby (.714, 5-for-7, 2 HR). . . . Ground outs-to-air outs ratio: 0.89 last season, 1.09 for career. . . . Additional statistics: 3 double-play ground outs in 48 opportunities, 9 doubles, 2 triples in 55.0 innings. . . . Allowed 10 first-inning runs in 11 starts. . . . Batting support: 2.18 runs per start, lowest in majors (minimum: 10 GS). . . . 1–8, 7.91 ERA as a starter; 0–2, 4.32 in five relief appearances. . . . Mark of .463 with runners in scoring position was the highest in majors since 1978, when Dave Hamilton was drummed to a .476 beat (minimum: 40 AB). . . . Opponents are 9-for-13 with the bases loaded since 1983.

Mark Langston
Seattle Mariners — Throws Left

	W–L	ERA	AB	H	HR	BB	SO	BA	SA	OBA
Season	12-14	4.85	917	234	30	123	245	.255	.425	.343
vs. Left-Handers			163	30	4	16	50	.184	.294	.260
vs. Right-Handers			754	204	26	107	195	.271	.454	.361
Home	5-7	5.39	457	115	20	65	142	.252	.457	.342
Road	7-7	4.31	460	119	10	58	103	.259	.393	.344
Grass	5-7	4.72	396	107	9	54	88	.270	.407	.359
Artificial Turf	7-7	4.94	521	127	21	69	157	.244	.440	.331
April	1-2	6.20	99	30	5	18	19	.303	.535	.408
May	3-2	4.60	174	49	4	23	35	.282	.431	.365
June	5-1	3.35	152	31	1	19	45	.204	.296	.297
July	0-2	5.74	117	27	5	17	34	.231	.419	.328
August	2-3	6.14	170	43	7	25	47	.253	.429	.347
Sept./Oct.	1-4	4.00	205	54	8	21	65	.263	.463	.330
Leading Off Inn.			220	57	8	30	64	.259	.441	.351
Runners On			403	111	14	51	89	.275	.449	.353
Runners/Scor. Pos.			258	70	10	28	55	.271	.457	.333
Runners On/2 Out			160	35	5	22	41	.219	.356	.313
Scor. Pos./2 Out			108	22	4	13	24	.204	.352	.289
Late Inning Pressure			125	41	4	10	23	.328	.488	.375
Leading Off			33	13	3	3	3	.394	.697	.444
Runners On			57	17	1	5	10	.298	.439	.349
Runners/Scor. Pos.			35	7	1	4	5	.200	.343	.275
First 9 Batters			286	62	7	41	87	.217	.346	.316
Second 9 Batters			271	66	8	40	89	.244	.413	.340
All Batters Thereafter			360	106	15	42	69	.294	.497	.368

Loves to face: Don Slaught (0-for-11, 5 SO)
Hates to face: Rick Dempsey (3-for-6, 2 HR)
Ground outs-to-air outs ratio: 1.00 last season, 1.02 for career. . . . Additional statistics: 22 double-play ground outs (9th in A.L.) in 193 opportunities, 52 doubles (2d most in A.L.), 7 triples in 239.1 innings last season. Allowed 89 XBH, 2d most in majors, including 79 vs. right-handed batters, a *Player Analysis* record. . . . Allowed 25 first-inning runs in 36 starts last season. . . . Batting support: 4.17 runs per start. . . . April ERA was 4th worst in A.L. (minimum: 20 IP). . . . Also set a *Player Analysis* record for walks to right-handers. . . . Compiled a 5.49 ERA in 10 no-decision starts. . . . Career breakdown: .194 (one home run per 42.4 at bats) vs. left-handers; .256 (one HR per 31.1 AB) vs. right-handers.

Dave LaPoint
Detroit Tigers — Throws Left

	W–L	ERA	AB	H	HR	BB	SO	BA	SA	OBA
Season	3-6	5.72	277	85	11	32	36	.307	.473	.377
vs. Left-Handers			61	17	0	6	6	.279	.328	.343
vs. Right-Handers			216	68	11	26	30	.315	.514	.387
Home	1-1	4.06	126	37	4	12	16	.294	.421	.355
Road	2-5	7.12	151	48	7	20	20	.318	.517	.395
Grass	3-4	5.34	226	70	8	28	31	.310	.465	.384
Artificial Turf	0-2	7.50	51	15	3	4	5	.294	.510	.345
April	0-0	4.00	37	11	2	2	5	.297	.486	.333
May	2-3	4.79	136	36	4	18	17	.265	.382	.351
June	0-3	9.60	73	28	5	5	10	.384	.658	.423
July	1-0	4.50	31	10	0	7	4	.323	.419	.436
August			0	0	0	0	0	—	—	—
Sept./Oct.			0	0	0	0	0	—	—	—
Leading Off Inn.			65	18	1	4	5	.277	.323	.319
Runners On			122	43	7	19	19	.352	.598	.437
Runners/Scor. Pos.			68	24	4	11	12	.353	.588	.438
Runners On/2 Out			55	19	1	11	10	.345	.509	.455
Scor. Pos./2 Out			34	9	0	7	7	.265	.324	.390
Late Inning Pressure			17	4	0	2	1	.235	.235	.316
Leading Off			4	1	0	1	0	.250	.250	.400
Runners On			7	2	0	1	0	.286	.286	.375
Runners/Scor. Pos.			3	1	0	0	0	.333	.333	.333
First 9 Batters			120	41	7	13	16	.342	.558	.403
Second 9 Batters			93	20	0	12	15	.215	.258	.305
All Batters Thereafter			64	24	4	7	5	.375	.625	.437

Loves to face: Tim Wallach (.118, 4-for-34, 7 SO)
Hates to face: Tim Raines (.459, 17-for-37, 2 2B, 3 3B, 2 HR)
Figures above are for A.L. only; see also N.L. Pitchers section.... Ground outs-to-air outs ratio: 1.14 last season, 1.30 for career.... Additional statistics: 9 double-play ground outs in 124 opportunities, 25 doubles, 2 triples in 129.0 innings last season.... Allowed 12 first-inning runs in 12 starts.... Batting support: 4.33 runs per start.... Faced only one batter once, pitched two or more innings 17 times, finished 6 games in 28 relief appearances.... Pitched fewer innings than in any of the previous four seasons, but still allowed a career high home runs total.... Allowed grand slams in consecutive appearances: May 29 to Dick Schofield, June 3 to Dave Kingman.

Tim Leary
Milwaukee Brewers — Throws Right

	W–L	ERA	AB	H	HR	BB	SO	BA	SA	OBA
Season	12-12	4.21	747	216	20	53	110	.289	.422	.339
vs. Left-Handers			369	104	11	42	47	.282	.423	.354
vs. Right-Handers			378	112	9	11	63	.296	.421	.324
Home	5-8	4.30	374	103	11	24	57	.275	.406	.320
Road	7-4	4.11	373	113	9	29	53	.303	.437	.359
Grass	10-10	4.14	592	175	13	47	87	.296	.407	.351
Artificial Turf	2-2	4.46	155	41	7	6	23	.265	.477	.292
April	2-1	4.50	94	30	4	9	19	.319	.521	.387
May	1-3	6.39	158	50	8	12	25	.316	.532	.368
June	3-3	3.02	167	43	3	9	26	.257	.359	.299
July	1-3	5.23	84	24	1	6	9	.286	.345	.337
August	2-1	3.62	111	36	2	10	16	.324	.423	.380
Sept./Oct.	3-1	2.94	133	33	2	7	15	.248	.346	.287
Leading Off Inn.			185	59	8	13	16	.319	.530	.370
Runners On			324	96	8	24	54	.296	.417	.343
Runners/Scor. Pos.			179	43	3	16	34	.240	.335	.294
Runners On/2 Out			118	30	5	10	20	.254	.424	.318
Scor. Pos./2 Out			74	15	2	9	14	.203	.311	.289
Late Inning Pressure			64	20	2	5	7	.313	.438	.362
Leading Off			18	7	1	1	0	.389	.611	.421
Runners On			28	9	1	1	7	.321	.464	.345
Runners/Scor. Pos.			10	2	0	1	2	.200	.200	.273
First 9 Batters			273	72	6	17	44	.264	.374	.313
Second 9 Batters			258	82	7	15	36	.318	.461	.359
All Batters Thereafter			216	62	7	21	30	.287	.435	.349

Loves to face: Spike Owen (0-for-14)
Hates to face: Tom Foley (2-for-2, 1 HR)
Ground outs-to-air outs ratio: 1.08 last season, 1.22 for career.... Additional statistics: 17 double-play ground outs in 170 opportunities, 31 doubles, 4 triples in 188.1 innings last season.... Allowed 15 first-inning runs in 30 starts last season.... Batting support: 4.43 runs per start.... Bring on the Mets! 9–4 record last season vs. teams with winning records, 3–8 vs. teams below the .500 mark.... Opposing batters have hit .233 with runners in scoring position over past two seasons, compared to .313 over two previous seasons.... Made only appearance of career at Dodger Stadium on May 13, 1984. Entered game with the bases loaded, walking Bob Bailor; ball four was a wild pitch that allowed two runs to score. He then retired Steve Yeager to end the inning, but then, who hasn't?

Charlie Leibrandt
Kansas City Royals — Throws Left

	W–L	ERA	AB	H	HR	BB	SO	BA	SA	OBA
Season	14-11	4.09	889	238	18	63	108	.268	.399	.317
vs. Left-Handers			178	50	3	13	27	.281	.388	.342
vs. Right-Handers			711	188	15	50	81	.264	.402	.311
Home	7-7	4.25	427	125	7	21	45	.293	.440	.326
Road	7-4	3.94	462	113	11	42	63	.245	.361	.310
Grass	5-4	4.04	373	89	9	36	44	.239	.354	.307
Artificial Turf	9-7	4.12	516	149	9	27	64	.289	.432	.325
April	4-0	3.38	126	26	4	16	12	.206	.349	.296
May	0-3	4.31	119	32	2	12	14	.269	.387	.336
June	4-2	3.86	169	48	1	7	20	.284	.367	.313
July	1-2	5.11	143	42	5	12	11	.294	.476	.354
August	2-3	3.55	147	36	3	6	22	.245	.381	.277
Sept./Oct.	3-1	4.28	185	54	3	10	29	.292	.427	.327
Leading Off Inn.			230	60	4	9	14	.261	.387	.292
Runners On			354	98	7	36	47	.277	.410	.343
Runners/Scor. Pos.			203	52	3	26	28	.256	.384	.336
Runners On/2 Out			139	31	3	22	18	.223	.331	.333
Scor. Pos./2 Out			87	16	0	18	14	.184	.230	.330
Late Inning Pressure			84	24	1	9	9	.286	.393	.355
Leading Off			23	11	1	1	2	.478	.783	.500
Runners On			37	5	0	7	4	.135	.135	.273
Runners/Scor. Pos.			18	2	0	7	2	.111	.111	.360
First 9 Batters			285	85	5	18	33	.298	.446	.344
Second 9 Batters			274	75	11	18	29	.274	.464	.316
All Batters Thereafter			330	78	2	27	46	.236	.306	.295

Loves to face: Andre Thornton (0-for-14)
Hates to face: Alan Trammell (.500, 8-for-16, 2 2B, 2 HR)
Ground outs-to-air outs ratio: 1.05 last season, 1.17 for career.... Additional statistics: 23 double-play ground outs (7th in A.L.) in 163 opportunities, 53 doubles (most in A.L.), 5 triples in 231.1 innings last season. Allowed 76 extra-base hits, 8th most in A.L. Allowed 23 first-inning runs in 34 starts last season.... Batting support: 4.41 runs per start.... Averaged 6.69 innings per start, highest on Royals staff.... Tied for A.L. lead with four wins in April.... 42–27 in three A.L. seasons after compiling a 16–17 record in four seasons with Cincinnati.... Opponents collected only three hits in 13 at bats with the bases loaded last season, but all three were extra-base hits (two doubles, one HR).

Dennis Leonard
Kansas City Royals — Throws Right

	W–L	ERA	AB	H	HR	BB	SO	BA	SA	OBA
Season	8-13	4.44	753	207	22	51	114	.275	.425	.321
vs. Left-Handers			391	120	15	34	46	.307	.496	.356
vs. Right-Handers			362	87	7	17	68	.240	.348	.280
Home	6-5	3.63	435	115	9	23	57	.264	.400	.299
Road	2-8	5.61	318	92	13	28	57	.289	.459	.350
Grass	1-6	5.83	234	68	11	22	45	.291	.474	.355
Artificial Turf	7-7	3.83	519	139	11	29	69	.268	.403	.305
April	2-2	0.90	113	23	1	4	14	.204	.239	.237
May	3-2	2.54	164	36	4	9	29	.220	.348	.263
June	1-3	6.61	139	44	5	9	24	.317	.576	.359
July	0-3	7.16	117	39	6	9	14	.333	.547	.359
August	0-1	4.39	109	33	3	6	18	.303	.450	.331
Sept./Oct.	2-2	6.07	111	32	3	14	15	.288	.387	.365
Leading Off Inn.			190	50	5	10	20	.263	.384	.307
Runners On			308	84	9	24	57	.273	.422	.319
Runners/Scor. Pos.			161	45	4	16	30	.280	.422	.332
Runners On/2 Out			122	28	4	10	29	.230	.410	.293
Scor. Pos./2 Out			71	14	2	8	16	.197	.352	.288
Late Inning Pressure			89	23	2	5	10	.258	.393	.306
Leading Off			26	7	0	1	2	.269	.308	.321
Runners On			30	7	0	1	4	.233	.267	.242
Runners/Scor. Pos.			11	3	0	1	1	.273	.273	.286
First 9 Batters			271	76	9	19	47	.280	.446	.325
Second 9 Batters			238	67	7	21	31	.282	.437	.328
All Batters Thereafter			244	64	6	11	36	.262	.389	.297

Loves to face: Harold Baines (0-for-15, 4 SO)
Hates to face: Andre Thornton (.405, 15-for-37, 6 HR)
Ground outs-to-air outs ratio: 0.92 last season, 0.97 for career.... Additional statistics: 12 double-play ground outs in 153 opportunities, 31 doubles, 8 triples (tied for 2d most in A.L.) in 192.2 innings last season.... Allowed 20 first-inning runs in 30 starts last season.... Batting support: 3.77 runs per start, 5th lowest in A.L. (minimum: 15 GS).... The Baseball Writers of America should have sealed their votes for the A.L. Comeback Award on the afternoon of April 12 when Leonard hurled a three-hit, 1–0 shutout against the Blue Jays at Royals Stadium. Before taking the mound that day he had pitched only two innings for the Royals (September 1985) since a torn tendon below his left knee nearly ended his career on May 28, 1983.... Led A.L. in ERA for the month of April.

Mickey Mahler — Throws Left

Rangers/Blue Jays	W–L	ERA	AB	H	HR	BB	SO	BA	SA	OBA
Season	0-2	4.08	246	72	3	29	28	.293	.407	.371
vs. Left-Handers			68	26	1	7	5	.382	.485	.450
vs. Right-Handers			178	46	2	22	23	.258	.376	.340
Home	0-0	4.33	102	32	2	15	11	.314	.471	.410
Road	0-2	3.89	144	40	1	14	17	.278	.361	.342
Grass	0-2	3.63	214	62	2	28	26	.290	.393	.373
Artificial Turf	0-0	7.71	32	10	1	1	2	.313	.500	.353
April	0-1	2.70	61	18	0	7	7	.295	.344	.377
May	0-0	4.15	52	15	1	7	5	.288	.442	.367
June	0-1	5.40	75	23	2	10	12	.307	.453	.379
July	0-0	4.05	53	15	0	5	4	.283	.396	.361
August			0	0	0	0	0	—	—	—
Sept./Oct.	0-0	0.00	5	1	0	0	0	.200	.200	.333
Leading Off Inn.			58	14	2	6	8	.241	.397	.323
Runners On			116	36	0	18	10	.310	.388	.396
Runners/Scor. Pos.			68	22	0	14	5	.324	.426	.425
Runners On/2 Out			46	11	0	6	5	.239	.348	.327
Scor. Pos./2 Out			30	8	0	4	2	.267	.367	.353
Late Inning Pressure			24	4	0	1	6	.167	.167	.231
Leading Off			8	1	0	0	3	.125	.125	.125
Runners On			6	2	0	1	0	.333	.333	.429
Runners/Scor. Pos.			2	1	0	1	0	.500	.500	.667
First 9 Batters			176	45	2	20	21	.256	.358	.340
Second 9 Batters			56	22	1	7	6	.393	.554	.453
All Batters Thereafter			14	5	0	2	1	.357	.429	.438

Loves to face: Mike Pagliarulo (.167, 1-for-6, 4 SO)
Hates to face: Mike Young (.833, 5-for-6)
One of Pagliarulo's strikeouts was in his only major league righty at bat, ordered by Billy Martin. . . . Ground outs-to-air outs ratio: 0.82 last season, 0.87 for career. . . . Additional statistics: 9 double-play ground outs in 64 opportunities, 15 doubles, 2 triples in 64.0 innings last season. . . . Faced only one batter once, pitched two or more innings 10 times, finished 8 games in 26 relief appearances. Opponents' career batting: .264 with bases empty, .287 with runners on base, .297 with runners in scoring position. . . . Home run by Mike Davis on June 22 was first one off Mahler by a lefty since Sept. 22, 1978 (Joe Morgan). . . . Only player to play for four different clubs (Expos, Tigers, Rangers, and Blue Jays) in last two seasons.

Mike Mason — Throws Left

Texas Rangers	W–L	ERA	AB	H	HR	BB	SO	BA	SA	OBA
Season	7-3	4.33	525	135	11	56	85	.257	.371	.327
vs. Left-Handers			94	25	2	6	11	.266	.372	.307
vs. Right-Handers			431	110	9	50	74	.255	.371	.331
Home	4-1	4.02	268	62	6	30	57	.231	.343	.308
Road	3-2	4.66	257	73	5	26	28	.284	.401	.347
Grass	6-2	3.62	418	98	10	42	70	.234	.354	.303
Artificial Turf	1-1	7.36	107	37	1	14	15	.346	.439	.418
April	1-0	4.44	95	29	2	9	16	.305	.411	.358
May	3-2	3.89	157	40	2	20	23	.255	.350	.337
June	0-0	9.82	29	7	1	5	7	.241	.345	.353
July	2-1	2.45	81	16	1	5	12	.198	.296	.244
August	0-0	5.89	73	21	3	9	14	.288	.438	.366
Sept./Oct.	1-0	3.80	90	22	2	8	13	.244	.389	.306
Leading Off Inn.			129	37	1	17	19	.287	.395	.370
Runners On			239	63	6	19	41	.264	.377	.314
Runners/Scor. Pos.			123	30	3	10	20	.244	.341	.294
Runners On/2 Out			91	15	2	6	16	.165	.264	.216
Scor. Pos./2 Out			49	7	2	3	8	.143	.265	.192
Late Inning Pressure			9	5	1	4	0	.556	.889	.692
Leading Off			6	2	0	0	0	.333	.333	.333
Runners On			2	2	1	1	0	1.000	2.500	1.000
Runners/Scor. Pos.			0	0	0	0	0	—	—	—
First 9 Batters			202	49	3	24	46	.243	.337	.322
Second 9 Batters			172	48	4	21	26	.279	.413	.356
All Batters Thereafter			151	38	4	11	13	.252	.371	.301

Loves to face: Larry Herndon (0-for-12)
Hates to face: Alejandro Sanchez (4-for-4, 3 HR)
Ground outs-to-air outs ratio: 1.12 last season, 1.16 for career. . . . Additional statistics: 9 double-play ground outs in 123 opportunities, 23 doubles, 2 triples in 135.0 innings last season. . . . Allowed 9 first-inning runs in 22 starts last season. . . . Batting support: 6.09 runs per start, tied for best in majors (minimum: 15 GS). . . . Narrow escapes: Had an ERA of 5.58 on 12 no-decision starts. . . . Career record of 0–5 vs. Cleveland. . . . Opponents' career batting average of .429 (12-for-28, 2 HR) with the bases loaded. . . . Career home run rate of one per 51.8 at bats by opposing left-handed batters, one per 34.5 by right-handers.

Kirk McCaskill — Throws Right

California Angels	W–L	ERA	AB	H	HR	BB	SO	BA	SA	OBA
Season	17-10	3.36	905	207	19	92	202	.229	.341	.302
vs. Left-Handers			504	118	11	55	98	.234	.355	.311
vs. Right-Handers			401	89	8	37	104	.222	.324	.291
Home	6-5	2.93	407	88	8	40	86	.216	.324	.289
Road	11-5	3.73	498	119	11	52	116	.239	.355	.312
Grass	15-9	3.17	793	174	16	84	183	.219	.325	.296
Artificial Turf	2-1	4.88	112	33	3	8	19	.295	.455	.347
April	2-1	3.13	113	26	0	13	24	.230	.274	.315
May	2-2	4.54	147	36	5	17	39	.245	.408	.323
June	4-2	3.38	165	37	2	15	40	.224	.297	.291
July	4-1	1.64	158	33	1	15	37	.209	.278	.286
August	2-1	5.08	154	41	8	18	22	.266	.487	.341
Sept./Oct.	3-3	2.77	168	34	3	14	40	.202	.298	.263
Leading Off Inn.			231	54	2	26	46	.234	.329	.311
Runners On			359	94	11	30	82	.262	.401	.316
Runners/Scor. Pos.			180	51	7	15	44	.283	.444	.330
Runners On/2 Out			159	41	4	18	33	.258	.377	.333
Scor. Pos./2 Out			86	23	2	9	18	.267	.384	.337
Late Inning Pressure			125	20	4	14	34	.160	.296	.255
Leading Off			36	5	0	4	10	.139	.222	.225
Runners On			41	6	1	2	10	.146	.220	.186
Runners/Scor. Pos.			17	2	0	0	1	.118	.118	.118
First 9 Batters			269	65	8	31	70	.242	.379	.325
Second 9 Batters			262	67	4	25	50	.256	.347	.316
All Batters Thereafter			374	75	7	36	82	.201	.310	.275

Loves to face: Rick Dempsey (0-for-8, 3 SO)
Hates to face: Kirk Gibson (.571, 8-for-14, 4 HR)
Ground outs-to-air outs ratio: 1.11 last season, 1.10 for career. . . . Additional statistics: 18 double-play ground outs in 167 opportunities, 33 doubles, 6 triples in 246.1 innings last season. . . . Allowed 14 first-inning runs in 33 starts last season. . . . Batting support: 4.58 runs per start. . . . Averaged 7.40 innings per start, 5th highest among A.L. pitchers (minimum: 15 GS). . . . July ERA was 4th best in A.L. . . . Had 4.59 ERA in first three innings of his 33 starts last season; 2.72 in middle three innings; 2.37 in last three innings. . . . Ended regular season by fanning last five Texas batters in his last start. . . . Opponents' career batting: .279 with runners on base, .218 with the bases empty.

Scott McGregor — Throws Left

Baltimore Orioles	W–L	ERA	AB	H	HR	BB	SO	BA	SA	OBA
Season	11-15	4.52	799	216	35	57	95	.270	.457	.319
vs. Left-Handers			166	37	10	8	26	.223	.452	.260
vs. Right-Handers			633	179	25	49	69	.283	.458	.334
Home	5-8	4.53	344	96	18	25	43	.279	.465	.329
Road	6-7	4.51	455	120	17	32	52	.264	.451	.312
Grass	10-14	4.42	718	193	32	49	85	.269	.451	.316
Artificial Turf	1-1	5.40	81	23	3	8	10	.284	.506	.344
April	2-2	4.32	99	24	5	1	12	.242	.434	.257
May	2-1	4.73	130	40	3	9	16	.308	.438	.348
June	2-4	3.83	181	43	8	18	22	.238	.414	.303
July	1-3	7.66	95	31	7	8	8	.326	.589	.375
August	1-1	4.32	99	26	5	12	13	.263	.455	.348
Sept./Oct.	3-4	3.86	195	52	7	9	24	.267	.456	.301
Leading Off Inn.			205	61	11	12	20	.298	.512	.336
Runners On			310	82	13	20	38	.265	.442	.310
Runners/Scor. Pos.			163	42	6	14	19	.258	.429	.306
Runners On/2 Out			125	30	4	13	14	.240	.392	.312
Scor. Pos./2 Out			75	18	4	11	8	.240	.467	.337
Late Inning Pressure			71	25	4	4	8	.352	.606	.387
Leading Off			22	9	1	0	3	.409	.591	.409
Runners On			27	7	1	1	4	.259	.407	.286
Runners/Scor. Pos.			19	3	0	0	4	.158	.211	.158
First 9 Batters			270	79	16	24	35	.293	.537	.348
Second 9 Batters			250	52	4	17	32	.208	.296	.257
All Batters Thereafter			279	85	15	16	28	.305	.523	.347

Loves to face: Mike Davis (0-for-12, 3 SO)
Hates to face: Don Mattingly (.500, 16-for-32, 3 HR)
Ground outs-to-air outs ratio: 0.73 last season, 0.79 for career. . . . Additional statistics: 14 double-play ground outs in 148 opportunities, 34 doubles, 5 triples in 203.0 innings last season. . . . Allowed 27 first-inning runs in 33 starts last season. . . . Batting support: 4.70 runs per start. . . . July ERA was 4th worst in A.L. . . . Averaged 6.09 innings per start, just a bit better than teammates Ken Dixon (6.08) and Mike Flanagan (6.07). . . . First losing season since he went 3–5 in 1977; career winning percentage dropped below .600 (136–98, .581). He was the only pitcher to have a record of .500 or better in every year from 1978 to 1985. . . . Has won his last eight decisions vs. Oakland, lost his last seven vs. Cleveland.

Dale Mohorcic
Texas Rangers   Throws Right

	W–L	ERA	AB	H	HR	BB	SO	BA	SA	OBA
Season	2-4	2.51	308	86	5	15	29	.279	.373	.315
vs. Left-Handers			123	35	1	11	11	.285	.358	.343
vs. Right-Handers			185	51	4	4	18	.276	.384	.295
Home	2-0	1.56	154	39	0	7	15	.253	.299	.290
Road	0-4	3.49	154	47	5	8	14	.305	.448	.340
Grass	2-2	2.19	248	67	4	11	26	.270	.359	.304
Artificial Turf	0-2	4.05	60	19	1	4	3	.317	.433	.359
April			0	0	0	0	0	—	—	—
May	0-0	0.00	4	1	0	1	0	.250	.250	.400
June	1-0	1.59	67	20	0	5	3	.299	.358	.347
July	0-0	2.20	58	15	1	1	4	.259	.345	.271
August	1-1	2.42	89	23	1	2	11	.258	.337	.275
Sept./Oct.	0-3	3.57	90	27	3	6	11	.300	.444	.351
Leading Off Inn.			63	22	2	2	8	.349	.476	.369
Runners On			153	41	1	10	13	.268	.353	.313
Runners/Scor. Pos.			89	21	0	9	6	.236	.270	.306
Runners On/2 Out			66	17	0	4	4	.258	.288	.300
Scor. Pos./2 Out			45	11	0	4	3	.244	.244	.306
Late Inning Pressure			147	43	2	8	16	.293	.381	.333
Leading Off			36	13	1	2	4	.361	.500	.395
Runners On			64	17	0	5	7	.266	.328	.319
Runners/Scor. Pos.			29	8	0	5	3	.276	.276	.382
First 9 Batters			289	77	4	14	28	.266	.353	.303
Second 9 Batters			19	9	1	1	1	.474	.684	.500
All Batters Thereafter			0	0	0	0	0	—	—	—

Loves to face: Rob Deer (.200, 1-for-5, 4 SO)
Hates to face: Dick Schofield (3-for-3)
Ground outs-to-air outs ratio: 2.09, 6th highest in A.L. last season (minimum: 250 BFP), his first in majors. . .Additional statistics: 10 double-play ground outs in 74 opportunities, 14 doubles, 0 triples in 79.0 innings. . . Faced only one batter 6 times, pitched two or more innings 16 times, finished 20 games in 58 relief appearances. . . . Appeared in 13 consecutive games to tie Mike Marshall's major-league mark. Record breaker was literally "one for the book": He relieved Charlie Hough after 8.2 innings of 3-hit ball, with the bases empty and Texas leading 7–2. It's enough to make a record-keeper sick. . . . Made major-league debut in '86 at age 30. Joins Mets' Rick Anderson in the "It's Never Too Late" Club.

Bill Mooneyham
Oakland As   Throws Right

	W–L	ERA	AB	H	HR	BB	SO	BA	SA	OBA
Season	4-5	4.52	381	103	4	67	75	.270	.352	.382
vs. Left-Handers			189	51	1	38	28	.270	.323	.394
vs. Right-Handers			192	52	3	29	47	.271	.380	.369
Home	4-2	4.27	193	47	3	39	40	.244	.321	.372
Road	0-3	4.79	188	56	1	28	35	.298	.383	.393
Grass	4-3	4.27	337	88	3	62	70	.261	.332	.377
Artificial Turf	0-2	7.00	44	15	1	5	5	.341	.500	.420
April	0-0	0.00	15	3	0	3	4	.200	.200	.333
May	1-0	3.20	72	18	0	15	14	.250	.347	.375
June	1-2	3.99	109	31	1	20	17	.284	.339	.400
July	1-1	5.81	112	34	2	12	20	.304	.420	.378
August	1-1	6.48	34	9	1	5	5	.265	.412	.359
Sept./Oct.	0-1	5.40	39	8	0	12	15	.205	.205	.392
Leading Off Inn.			78	21	1	21	14	.269	.359	.424
Runners On			214	52	1	33	47	.243	.313	.347
Runners/Scor. Pos.			135	29	1	20	27	.215	.289	.316
Runners On/2 Out			87	23	0	7	22	.264	.310	.326
Scor. Pos./2 Out			63	14	0	7	16	.222	.254	.310
Late Inning Pressure			92	29	2	22	16	.315	.446	.443
Leading Off			17	2	0	9	3	.118	.176	.423
Runners On			54	15	0	10	11	.278	.370	.385
Runners/Scor. Pos.			37	10	0	6	8	.270	.378	.364
First 9 Batters			252	62	2	50	53	.246	.313	.372
Second 9 Batters			90	29	2	15	14	.322	.456	.415
All Batters Thereafter			39	12	0	2	8	.308	.359	.372

Loves to face: Brook Jacoby (0-for-6, 3 SO)
Hates to face: Phil Bradley (2-for-2)
Ground outs-to-air outs ratio: 2.07, 8th highest in A.L. last season (minimum: 250 BFP), his first in majors. . . . Additional statistics: 14 double-play ground outs in 125 opportunities, 17 doubles, 1 triple in 99.2 innings last season. . . . Faced only one batter 5 times, pitched two or more innings 20 times, finished 18 games in 39 relief appearances. . . . 0–2, 6.39 ERA in six games started; 4–3 (2 saves), 3.67 ERA in 39 relief appearances. . . . One walk per 4.7 leadoff batters was the highest rate in the majors last season (minimum: 50 PA), and things got worse in Late-Inning Pressure Situations: 9 walks to 26 leadoff batters. . . . Astrologers, note the lunar factor: Mooneyham was born August 16, 1960; on that day, Wally Moon hit a game-tying inside-the-park home run at Wrigley Field.

Donnie Moore
California Angels   Throws Right

	W–L	ERA	AB	H	HR	BB	SO	BA	SA	OBA
Season	4-5	2.97	263	60	10	22	53	.228	.373	.285
vs. Left-Handers			146	31	2	13	25	.212	.295	.275
vs. Right-Handers			117	29	8	9	28	.248	.470	.297
Home	4-0	2.30	111	22	6	5	21	.198	.378	.231
Road	0-5	3.48	152	38	4	17	32	.250	.368	.322
Grass	4-3	2.83	216	49	8	17	45	.227	.370	.280
Artificial Turf	0-2	3.65	47	11	2	5	8	.234	.383	.308
April	1-1	4.63	40	7	3	3	12	.175	.425	.227
May	0-2	6.14	27	9	2	6	3	.333	.556	.441
June	0-0	0.00	2	0	0	1	1	.000	.000	.333
July	0-0	1.29	50	11	2	5	9	.220	.380	.291
August	2-2	2.29	73	15	1	5	17	.205	.288	.256
Sept./Oct.	1-0	2.84	71	18	2	2	11	.254	.366	.270
Leading Off Inn.			53	14	1	4	13	.264	.340	.316
Runners On			119	32	6	11	20	.269	.462	.323
Runners/Scor. Pos.			69	17	3	10	14	.246	.449	.329
Runners On/2 Out			49	12	2	2	9	.245	.429	.275
Scor. Pos./2 Out			30	6	0	2	7	.200	.300	.250
Late Inning Pressure			172	38	7	18	35	.221	.360	.290
Leading Off			35	9	0	3	10	.257	.286	.316
Runners On			73	20	5	8	11	.274	.507	.333
Runners/Scor. Pos.			44	12	3	7	7	.273	.523	.352
First 9 Batters			254	56	10	19	52	.220	.370	.273
Second 9 Batters			9	4	0	3	1	.444	.444	.538
All Batters Thereafter			0	0	0	0	0	—	—	—

Loves to face: Roy Smalley (0-for-7)
Hates to face: George Bell (.571, 4-for-7, 2 HR)
Ground outs-to-air outs ratio: 0.75 last season, 1.09 for career. . . . Additional statistics: 6 double-play ground outs in 68 opportunities, 6 doubles, 1 triple in 72.2 innings last season. . . . Never faced only one batter, pitched two or more innings 14 times, finished 42 games in 49 relief appearances. . . . Ranks third in A.L. with 52 saves over the last two seasons, behind Dave Righetti (75) and Willie Hernandez (55). . . . Opponents' career average of .193 (34-for-176, 2 HR) with two out and runners on base in Late-Inning Pressure Situations. . . . Opponents' career batting average of .415 (27-for-65, 1 HR) with the bases loaded.

Mike Moore
Seattle Mariners   Throws Right

	W–L	ERA	AB	H	HR	BB	SO	BA	SA	OBA
Season	11-13	4.30	1023	279	28	94	146	.273	.408	.339
vs. Left-Handers			529	149	11	66	58	.282	.405	.363
vs. Right-Handers			494	130	17	28	88	.263	.411	.313
Home	7-4	4.18	495	135	16	47	75	.273	.420	.344
Road	4-9	4.40	528	144	12	47	71	.273	.396	.335
Grass	3-6	4.31	394	110	8	37	57	.279	.386	.340
Artificial Turf	8-7	4.29	629	169	20	57	89	.269	.421	.339
April	1-2	2.36	155	38	5	15	23	.245	.387	.320
May	1-4	6.87	151	45	8	19	16	.298	.503	.382
June	2-1	5.04	175	49	5	10	27	.280	.451	.321
July	2-3	4.98	175	50	4	12	22	.286	.417	.339
August	3-1	2.98	179	45	3	18	28	.251	.330	.318
Sept./Oct.	2-2	3.99	188	52	3	20	30	.277	.372	.357
Leading Off Inn.			256	76	7	23	24	.297	.434	.362
Runners On			426	117	15	41	53	.275	.427	.344
Runners/Scor. Pos.			236	54	5	26	34	.229	.326	.309
Runners On/2 Out			167	45	5	17	20	.269	.407	.344
Scor. Pos./2 Out			105	25	2	13	15	.238	.343	.328
Late Inning Pressure			132	41	5	20	20	.311	.485	.409
Leading Off			35	12	1	6	5	.343	.486	.439
Runners On			54	17	4	8	7	.315	.611	.422
Runners/Scor. Pos.			25	7	2	7	3	.280	.520	.455
First 9 Batters			299	87	13	28	35	.291	.492	.354
Second 9 Batters			292	65	3	29	43	.223	.298	.297
All Batters Thereafter			432	127	12	37	68	.294	.424	.358

Loves to face: Mike Young (.115, 3-for-26, 8 SO)
Hates to face: Doug DeCinces (.472, 17-for-36, 6 HR)
Ground outs-to-air outs ratio: 1.44 last season, 1.28 for career. . . . Additional statistics: 28 double-play ground outs (2d in A.L.) in 230 opportunities, 42 doubles (10th most in A.L.), 6 triples in 266.0 innings last season. . . . Allowed 76 extra-base hits, 8th most in A.L. . . . Allowed 25 first-inning runs in 37 starts last season. . . . Batting support: 4.84 runs per start. . . . Averaged 7.16 innings per start, highest on Mariners staff. . . . Opposing batters have hit better with runners on base than with the bases empty in all five major-league seasons. . . . Opponents batted .091 (2-for-22) with the bases loaded last season, .077 (1-for-13) in 1985. Has faced 81 batters with the bags full in his career, and allowed only one extra-base hit.

Mike Morgan

Seattle Mariners　　　　　　　　Throws Right

	W–L	ERA	AB	H	HR	BB	SO	BA	SA	OBA
Season	11-17	4.53	851	243	24	86	116	.286	.427	.353
vs. Left-Handers			441	121	10	48	56	.274	.390	.347
vs. Right-Handers			410	122	14	38	60	.298	.466	.359
Home	4-10	5.11	397	116	14	42	64	.292	.461	.360
Road	7-7	4.03	454	127	10	44	52	.280	.396	.347
Grass	3-6	3.96	296	79	8	27	40	.267	.385	.331
Artificial Turf	8-11	4.86	555	164	16	59	76	.295	.449	.364
April	1-2	2.00	96	21	2	13	10	.219	.292	.312
May	2-4	6.67	124	42	3	20	20	.339	.468	.431
June	2-1	3.50	142	42	3	10	19	.296	.387	.344
July	3-3	5.65	154	50	3	14	10	.325	.506	.386
August	1-4	4.32	155	40	7	15	32	.258	.439	.326
Sept./Oct.	2-3	4.76	180	48	6	14	25	.267	.422	.320
Leading Off Inn.			202	54	9	26	28	.267	.441	.354
Runners On			387	104	7	39	54	.269	.370	.333
Runners/Scor. Pos.			218	56	3	24	37	.257	.344	.327
Runners On/2 Out			151	38	2	23	24	.252	.325	.351
Scor. Pos./2 Out			102	23	1	17	18	.225	.284	.336
Late Inning Pressure			71	26	1	7	13	.366	.437	.423
Leading Off			18	4	1	3	4	.222	.444	.333
Runners On			30	13	0	3	6	.433	.433	.485
Runners/Scor. Pos.			14	7	0	2	2	.500	.500	.563
First 9 Batters			281	76	6	35	39	.270	.416	.352
Second 9 Batters			265	68	6	25	42	.257	.374	.323
All Batters Thereafter			305	99	12	26	35	.325	.482	.379

Loves to face: Eddie Murray (.083, 2-for-24, 6 SO)
Hates to face: Bo Jackson (5-for-6)
Ground outs-to-air outs ratio: 1.48 last season, 1.48 for career. . . .
Additional statistics: 27 double-play ground outs (3d in A.L.) in 190 opportunities, 44 doubles (6th most in A.L.), 2 triples in 216.1 innings last season. . . . Allowed 15 first-inning runs in 33 starts last season. . . . Batting support: 4.76 runs per start. . . . April ERA was 4th best in A.L. . . . Has had a losing record in five of six seasons in the majors. Only exception was 1985 when he had a 1–1 record with Seattle. . . . Wins last season exceeded his previous career total (10). . . . One of 16 pitchers to record both a save and a shutout last season. . . . Complete game victories in consecutive starts (June 11–17) for the first time in his career.

Jack Morris

Detroit Tigers　　　　　　　　Throws Right

	W–L	ERA	AB	H	HR	BB	SO	BA	SA	OBA
Season	21-8	3.27	1000	229	40	82	223	.229	.403	.287
vs. Left-Handers			529	118	13	43	114	.223	.344	.281
vs. Right-Handers			471	111	27	39	109	.236	.469	.293
Home	10-3	2.76	411	91	16	32	88	.221	.392	.278
Road	11-5	3.63	589	138	24	50	135	.234	.411	.293
Grass	17-8	3.40	784	185	30	66	165	.236	.409	.294
Artificial Turf	4-0	2.81	216	44	10	16	58	.204	.380	.259
April	3-2	5.60	145	40	10	10	31	.276	.545	.323
May	1-2	3.06	114	23	5	14	37	.202	.395	.289
June	3-1	4.34	188	52	9	15	36	.277	.457	.330
July	5-1	0.54	176	33	1	8	47	.188	.261	.222
August	3-2	5.21	147	38	6	17	24	.259	.490	.333
Sept./Oct.	6-0	2.26	230	43	9	18	48	.187	.326	.245
Leading Off Inn.			261	63	15	13	47	.241	.456	.277
Runners On			370	78	9	30	81	.211	.332	.268
Runners/Scor. Pos.			187	36	3	23	52	.193	.299	.277
Runners On/2 Out			169	38	4	16	38	.225	.349	.292
Scor. Pos./2 Out			98	17	1	13	28	.173	.265	.270
Late Inning Pressure			137	36	8	14	27	.263	.474	.331
Leading Off			37	12	2	2	4	.324	.568	.359
Runners On			52	10	2	7	13	.192	.308	.288
Runners/Scor. Pos.			22	6	1	6	6	.273	.409	.429
First 9 Batters			282	64	15	31	75	.227	.450	.304
Second 9 Batters			285	63	8	20	59	.221	.361	.272
All Batters Thereafter			433	102	17	31	89	.236	.400	.290

Loves to face: Ken Phelps (0-for-20, 12 SO)
Hates to face: George Brett (.422, 19-for-45, 3 HR)
Ground outs-to-air outs ratio: 0.93 last season, 1.17 for career. . . .
Additional statistics: 20 double-play ground outs in 159 opportunities, 38 doubles, 8 triples in 267.0 innings last season. Allowed 86 extra-base hits, 4th most in A.L. . . . Allowed 15 first-inning runs in 35 starts last season. . . . Batting support: 5.43 runs per start, 10th best in A.L. (minimum: 15 GS). . . . Averaged 7.63 innings per start, 4th highest in the major leagues (minimum: 15 GS). . . . Became 4th pitcher in Tigers history to pitch three consecutive shutouts. The others: Harry Coveleski (1914), Ed Wells (1926), and Mickey Lolich (1964 and 1967). . . . Winning record in every season since 1979, the longest current streak of its type. Second longest belongs to John Tudor (every season since 1980).

Gene Nelson

Chicago White Sox　　　　　　　　Throws Right

	W–L	ERA	AB	H	HR	BB	SO	BA	SA	OBA
Season	6-6	3.85	436	118	7	41	70	.271	.406	.337
vs. Left-Handers			193	55	3	22	27	.285	.430	.359
vs. Right-Handers			243	63	4	19	43	.259	.387	.318
Home	3-2	3.47	225	63	3	24	42	.280	.400	.355
Road	3-4	4.25	211	55	4	17	28	.261	.412	.317
Grass	6-3	3.65	354	93	6	32	58	.263	.390	.328
Artificial Turf	0-3	4.71	82	25	1	9	12	.305	.476	.374
April	1-1	4.08	66	18	0	8	12	.273	.348	.351
May	3-1	0.95	97	18	0	7	18	.186	.216	.240
June	0-2	8.79	65	23	2	10	8	.354	.615	.440
July	1-0	2.70	76	21	1	4	11	.276	.434	.325
August	0-1	6.55	87	26	4	3	9	.299	.506	.322
Sept./Oct.	1-1	1.46	45	12	0	9	12	.267	.356	.400
Leading Off Inn.			94	27	2	9	17	.287	.479	.350
Runners On			223	58	3	23	36	.260	.377	.331
Runners/Scor. Pos.			145	32	2	17	30	.221	.324	.305
Runners On/2 Out			92	23	0	7	19	.250	.326	.310
Scor. Pos./2 Out			62	14	0	5	16	.226	.306	.294
Late Inning Pressure			145	36	0	19	21	.248	.338	.335
Leading Off			34	8	0	3	5	.235	.294	.297
Runners On			66	21	0	12	10	.318	.470	.423
Runners/Scor. Pos.			41	12	0	9	7	.293	.439	.420
First 9 Batters			341	93	5	31	60	.273	.405	.339
Second 9 Batters			87	22	2	8	9	.253	.402	.313
All Batters Thereafter			8	3	0	2	1	.375	.500	.500

Loves to face: Kent Hrbek (.059, 1-for-17, 8 SO, 1 HR)
Hates to face: Cal Ripken (.529, 9-for-17, 2 2B, 2 3B, 2 HR)
Ground outs-to-air outs ratio: 1.09 last season, 1.27 for career. . . .
Additional statistics: 9 double-play ground outs in 99 opportunities, 26 doubles, 6 triples in 114.2 innings last season. . . . Faced only one batter 4 times, pitched two or more innings 28 times (3d most in A.L.), finished 26 games in 53 relief appearances. . . . May ERA was best in A.L., August ERA was 5th worst (minimum: 20 IP). . . . Allowed one home run per 62.3 at bats last season, considerably better than career rate of one per 27.1 at bats through the 1985 season. . . . Opponents' career batting average of .253 on grass fields, .304 on artificial surfaces. . . . Opponents' batting average with runners in scoring position, year by year since 1982: .304, .353, .250, .207, .221.

Joe Niekro

New York Yankees　　　　　　　　Throws Right

	W–L	ERA	AB	H	HR	BB	SO	BA	SA	OBA
Season	9-10	4.87	505	139	15	63	59	.275	.432	.357
vs. Left-Handers			238	65	5	39	25	.273	.395	.378
vs. Right-Handers			267	74	10	24	34	.277	.464	.337
Home	4-5	5.97	255	78	9	34	28	.306	.475	.388
Road	5-5	3.86	250	61	6	29	31	.244	.388	.325
Grass	8-9	4.90	468	128	15	54	56	.274	.432	.350
Artificial Turf	1-1	4.50	37	11	0	9	3	.297	.432	.435
April	3-0	3.16	122	29	2	11	16	.238	.328	.301
May	2-3	3.96	144	37	4	11	17	.257	.403	.314
June	2-3	6.46	95	24	5	19	9	.253	.484	.377
July	1-1	6.75	54	20	1	2	8	.370	.556	.393
August	1-2	5.40	80	26	2	16	9	.325	.475	.438
Sept./Oct.	0-1	11.57	10	3	1	4	0	.300	.600	.500
Leading Off Inn.			126	30	4	10	18	.238	.373	.294
Runners On			217	70	7	36	25	.323	.498	.419
Runners/Scor. Pos.			140	37	1	28	18	.264	.343	.387
Runners On/2 Out			90	28	2	18	9	.311	.456	.426
Scor. Pos./2 Out			69	19	0	14	8	.275	.362	.398
Late Inning Pressure			6	1	0	0	1	.167	.167	.167
Leading Off			2	0	0	0	0	.000	.000	.000
Runners On			0	0	0	0	0	—	—	—
Runners/Scor. Pos.			0	0	0	0	0	—	—	—
First 9 Batters			205	53	9	17	30	.259	.434	.318
Second 9 Batters			180	45	5	23	20	.250	.411	.335
All Batters Thereafter			120	41	1	23	9	.342	.458	.448

Loves to face: Wally Joyner (.091, 1-for-11)
Hates to face: Doug DeCinces (.667, 4-for-6, 3 HR)
Ground outs-to-air outs ratio: 0.99 last season, 1.11 for career. . . .
Additional statistics: 9 double-play ground outs in 93 opportunities, 26 doubles, 4 triples in 125.2 innings last season. . . . Allowed 14 first-inning runs in 25 starts last season. . . . Batting support: 4.96 runs per start. . . . Yes, there is still an active player who allowed home runs to Roger Maris, Rocky Colavito, Roberto Clemente, Orlando Cepeda, and Tony Oliva. He is one of two active pitchers who shut out the Washington Senators at RFK Stadium. The other: Tommy John. Bert Blyleven and Vida Blue also won there. . . . Failed to complete six innings in any of his last 12 starts. Opponents batted .354 during that span.

Phil Niekro

Cleveland Indians — Throws Right

	W–L	ERA	AB	H	HR	BB	SO	BA	SA	OBA
Season	11-11	4.32	841	241	24	95	81	.287	.429	.362
vs. Left-Handers			455	129	9	52	37	.284	.404	.360
vs. Right-Handers			386	112	15	43	44	.290	.459	.365
Home	6-5	4.05	379	105	12	44	41	.277	.422	.353
Road	5-6	4.55	462	136	12	51	40	.294	.435	.370
Grass	8-10	4.59	698	200	22	86	69	.287	.438	.367
Artificial Turf	3-1	3.03	143	41	2	9	12	.287	.385	.338
April	1-2	2.57	111	26	3	16	12	.234	.360	.328
May	2-2	5.40	150	51	3	17	12	.340	.453	.407
June	1-2	5.52	122	35	5	13	15	.287	.508	.365
July	3-1	3.50	169	45	4	14	16	.266	.391	.326
August	3-3	4.81	154	44	5	23	16	.286	.435	.380
Sept./Oct.	1-1	4.05	135	40	4	12	10	.296	.430	.362
Leading Off Inn.			201	53	4	21	21	.264	.383	.339
Runners On			389	107	10	46	37	.275	.406	.353
Runners/Scor. Pos.			197	60	4	37	22	.305	.431	.416
Runners On/2 Out			168	52	5	27	17	.310	.458	.405
Scor. Pos./2 Out			102	34	2	23	12	.333	.471	.456
Late Inning Pressure			78	25	7	11	9	.321	.615	.400
Leading Off			24	5	1	3	5	.208	.375	.296
Runners On			25	8	1	4	3	.320	.440	.400
Runners/Scor. Pos.			6	2	0	3	1	.333	.333	.500
First 9 Batters			268	76	3	27	19	.284	.388	.355
Second 9 Batters			256	78	5	24	25	.305	.426	.364
All Batters Thereafter			317	87	16	44	37	.274	.467	.367

Loves to face: Rich Gedman (.053, 1-for-19)
Hates to face: Kirk Gibson (.478, 11-for-23, 4 HR)
Ground outs-to-air outs ratio: 0.96 last season, 1.08 for career. . . .
Additional statistics: 22 double-play ground outs (9th in A.L.) in 198 opportunities, 40 doubles, 4 triples in 210.1 innings last season. . . . Allowed 16 first-inning runs in 32 starts last season. . . . Batting support: 4.97 runs per start. . . . Has compiled a .543 career winning percentage with teams that have a composite winning percentage of .486 without him. . . . One of two pitchers to win 10 or more games in each full season since 1977 (that excludes 1981). The other: Nolan Ryan. . . . Has given up homers to, among others, Roger Maris, Ron Swoboda, Bill Mazeroski, Clay Dalrymple, Joe Pepitone, Curt Flood, and the broadcasting tandem of Bill White and Tim McCarver.

Scott Nielsen

New York Yankees — Throws Right

	W–L	ERA	AB	H	HR	BB	SO	BA	SA	OBA
Season	4-4	4.02	221	66	12	12	20	.299	.507	.340
vs. Left-Handers			111	36	6	9	6	.324	.505	.375
vs. Right-Handers			110	30	6	3	14	.273	.509	.304
Home	1-3	6.53	90	32	8	1	7	.356	.656	.370
Road	3-1	2.55	131	34	4	11	13	.260	.405	.322
Grass	3-4	4.79	191	60	12	8	16	.314	.545	.348
Artificial Turf	1-0	0.00	30	6	0	4	4	.200	.267	.294
April			0	0	0	0	0	—	—	—
May			0	0	0	0	0	—	—	—
June			0	0	0	0	0	—	—	—
July	2-3	6.94	104	39	7	6	11	.375	.635	.409
August			0	0	0	0	0	—	—	—
Sept./Oct.	2-1	1.93	117	27	5	6	9	.231	.393	.280
Leading Off Inn.			56	15	2	1	6	.268	.446	.293
Runners On			82	23	5	7	8	.280	.476	.337
Runners/Scor. Pos.			42	13	2	6	6	.310	.452	.396
Runners On/2 Out			34	10	1	4	3	.294	.412	.368
Scor. Pos./2 Out			17	5	0	4	3	.294	.294	.429
Late Inning Pressure			13	2	0	1	2	.154	.154	.267
Leading Off			3	0	0	0	2	.000	.000	.000
Runners On			4	0	0	0	0	.000	.000	.000
Runners/Scor. Pos.			0	0	0	0	0	—	—	—
First 9 Batters			81	23	2	6	9	.284	.407	.341
Second 9 Batters			61	21	6	4	3	.344	.705	.385
All Batters Thereafter			79	22	4	2	8	.278	.456	.305

Loves to face: Marty Barrett (0-for-6)
Hates to face: Joel Skinner (3-for-3, 1 2B, 1 HR)
Ground outs-to-air outs ratio: 1.53 last season, his first in majors. . . . Additional statistics: 9 double-play ground outs in 33 opportunities, 10 doubles, 0 triples in 56.0 innings. . . . ERA after Sept. 1 was 3d best in A.L. . . . Completed two of nine starts, but both were shutouts (vs. Minnesota and Boston), accounting for half his team's total. . . . Five-hit shutout in season finale at Fenway completed a 4-game sweep. Boston lost eight games to New York teams in October. . . . Issued one leadoff walk in 58 innings. . . . Allowed two or more homers in five of his starts.

Juan Nieves

Milwaukee Brewers — Throws Left

	W–L	ERA	AB	H	HR	BB	SO	BA	SA	OBA
Season	11-12	4.92	748	224	17	77	116	.299	.418	.363
vs. Left-Handers			132	42	1	14	30	.318	.409	.384
vs. Right-Handers			616	182	16	63	86	.295	.420	.359
Home	4-6	6.35	333	105	6	38	49	.315	.423	.385
Road	7-6	3.88	415	119	11	39	67	.287	.414	.346
Grass	9-11	4.92	659	197	14	72	99	.299	.413	.367
Artificial Turf	2-1	4.91	89	27	3	5	17	.303	.461	.337
April	0-1	4.63	90	23	2	13	19	.256	.344	.346
May	5-0	4.71	168	49	1	20	20	.292	.363	.363
June	1-1	3.41	126	34	2	8	15	.270	.397	.319
July	4-2	3.16	135	35	2	21	30	.259	.319	.357
August	0-3	10.42	91	39	4	5	11	.429	.626	.454
Sept./Oct.	1-5	5.68	138	44	6	10	21	.319	.514	.365
Leading Off Inn.			177	52	4	24	29	.294	.441	.378
Runners On			344	111	8	34	47	.323	.439	.380
Runners/Scor. Pos.			187	61	4	19	27	.326	.460	.382
Runners On/2 Out			143	51	5	18	19	.357	.517	.432
Scor. Pos./2 Out			90	33	3	12	11	.367	.556	.447
Late Inning Pressure			64	15	1	6	10	.234	.297	.300
Leading Off			20	7	1	1	4	.350	.550	.381
Runners On			17	5	0	3	1	.294	.294	.400
Runners/Scor. Pos.			6	2	0	3	1	.333	.333	.556
First 9 Batters			287	94	3	20	42	.328	.425	.373
Second 9 Batters			235	62	6	31	43	.264	.374	.347
All Batters Thereafter			226	68	8	26	31	.301	.456	.369

Loves to face: Chet Lemon (0-for-11)
Hates to face: Kirby Puckett (.800, 8-for-10)
Ground outs-to-air outs ratio: 0.92 last season, his first in majors. . . . Additional statistics: 20 double-play ground outs in 166 opportunities, 36 doubles, 1 triple in 184.2 innings last season. . . . Allowed 34 first-inning runs (most in majors) in 33 starts last season. . . . Batting support: 4.88 runs per start. . . . Averaged 5.43 innings per start, 4th fewest among A.L. pitchers (minimum: 15 GS). . . . Led rookie pitchers in games started, 33; complete games, 4 (tied with Ed Correa); and shutouts, 3. . . . Record could have been a lot worse: Compiled a 5.52 ERA in 11 no-decision starts. . . . Allowed only one home run to a left-handed batter last season: Harold Baines.

Al Nipper

Boston Red Sox — Throws Right

	W–L	ERA	AB	H	HR	BB	SO	BA	SA	OBA
Season	10-12	5.38	642	186	24	47	79	.290	.480	.340
vs. Left-Handers			348	106	8	30	41	.305	.463	.358
vs. Right-Handers			294	80	16	17	38	.272	.500	.317
Home	3-5	5.17	315	93	11	20	43	.295	.483	.339
Road	7-7	5.58	327	93	13	27	36	.284	.477	.340
Grass	7-9	5.49	503	145	18	40	67	.288	.467	.341
Artificial Turf	3-3	4.98	139	41	6	7	12	.295	.525	.333
April	2-2	2.14	120	22	2	10	15	.183	.275	.250
May	1-2	5.87	93	28	8	9	18	.301	.634	.369
June	1-0	8.76	53	19	2	2	5	.358	.585	.390
July	1-3	5.12	138	44	3	5	14	.319	.478	.343
August	3-2	5.87	122	36	6	8	12	.295	.516	.338
Sept./Oct.	2-3	7.16	116	37	3	13	15	.319	.483	.382
Leading Off Inn.			160	52	3	8	22	.325	.469	.357
Runners On			269	79	12	23	32	.294	.520	.348
Runners/Scor. Pos.			152	46	8	12	23	.303	.546	.343
Runners On/2 Out			110	30	7	11	16	.273	.545	.339
Scor. Pos./2 Out			67	22	5	5	10	.328	.627	.375
Late Inning Pressure			53	12	1	3	6	.226	.321	.268
Leading Off			17	2	0	0	3	.118	.118	.118
Runners On			12	3	0	1	0	.250	.333	.308
Runners/Scor. Pos.			2	1	0	0	0	.500	.500	.500
First 9 Batters			210	60	8	22	24	.286	.457	.353
Second 9 Batters			210	69	10	10	27	.329	.590	.363
All Batters Thereafter			222	57	6	15	28	.257	.396	.305

Loves to face: Rance Mulliniks (.059, 1-for-17)
Hates to face: Wally Joyner (.833, 5-for-6, 2 HR)
Ground outs-to-air outs ratio: 1.06 last season, 1.12 for career. . . . Additional statistics: 11 double-play ground outs in 124 opportunities, 40 doubles, 5 triples in 159.0 innings last season. . . . Allowed 17 first-inning runs in 26 starts last season. . . . Batting support: 4.85 runs per start. . . . ERA was 3d highest among A.L. starting pitchers (minimum: 25 GS). . . . April ERA was 5th best in A.L., ERA after Sept. 1 was 3d worst in major leagues (minimum: 20 IP). . . . A.L.'s top 15 batters hit .484 (30-for-62) against him, and Boggs didn't even get a crack! . . .Career total of 77 games started, most among active pitchers without a shutout. . . . Opponents' career batting average of .381 (8-for-21, 1 HR) with the bases loaded.

Dickie Nolcs

Cleveland Indians — Throws Right

	W–L	ERA	AB	H	HR	BB	SO	BA	SA	OBA
Season	3-2	5.10	208	56	9	30	32	.269	.418	.367
vs. Left-Handers			98	29	6	19	13	.296	.500	.418
vs. Right-Handers			110	27	3	11	19	.245	.345	.317
Home	1-0	6.23	84	28	3	18	6	.333	.452	.450
Road	2-2	4.36	124	28	6	12	26	.226	.395	.302
Grass	3-0	4.35	184	47	5	29	28	.255	.359	.360
Artificial Turf	0-2	12.60	24	9	4	1	4	.375	.875	.423
April	0-0	3.00	9	0	0	2	3	.000	.000	.182
May			0	0	0	0	0	—	—	—
June	1-1	9.53	26	9	3	1	4	.346	.692	.393
July	1-1	5.50	75	23	3	9	10	.307	.467	.398
August	1-0	4.64	78	21	3	15	11	.269	.397	.385
Sept./Oct.	0-0	2.70	20	3	0	3	4	.150	.150	.240
Leading Off Inn.			38	7	2	9	5	.184	.395	.354
Runners On			101	32	4	18	12	.317	.455	.417
Runners/Scor. Pos.			69	17	2	16	9	.246	.348	.367
Runners On/2 Out			48	14	1	8	6	.292	.354	.414
Scor. Pos./2 Out			37	8	1	7	4	.216	.297	.341
Late Inning Pressure			55	11	2	8	14	.200	.309	.302
Leading Off			11	2	1	3	3	.182	.455	.357
Runners On			18	5	0	4	5	.278	.278	.409
Runners/Scor. Pos.			13	3	0	4	4	.231	.231	.412
First 9 Batters			170	43	9	22	30	.253	.435	.343
Second 9 Batters			35	12	0	7	2	.343	.343	.457
All Batters Thereafter			3	1	0	1	0	.333	.333	.500

Loves to face: Tony Armas (0-for-8, 6 SO)
Hates to face: Terry Kennedy (.500, 8-for-16, 2 HR)
Ground outs-to-air outs ratio: 1.18 last season, 1.19 for career....
Additional statistics: 5 double-play ground outs in 50 opportunities, 4 doubles, 0 triples in 54.2 innings last season.... Faced only one batter twice, pitched two or more innings 13 times, finished 9 games in 32 relief appearances.... Enjoyed the first winning season in his 8-year major-league career.... Only major leaguer with an ERA above 5.00 in the last three seasons (minimum: 50 IP in each season).... Opponents' career batting: .263 with bases empty, .285 with runners on base, .294 with runners in scoring position.

Bryan Oelkers

Cleveland Indians — Throws Left

	W–L	ERA	AB	H	HR	BB	SO	BA	SA	OBA
Season	3-3	4.70	267	70	13	40	33	.262	.449	.368
vs. Left-Handers			95	22	4	12	13	.232	.432	.339
vs. Right-Handers			172	48	9	28	20	.279	.459	.384
Home	2-2	4.36	162	41	7	28	18	.253	.426	.372
Road	1-1	5.26	105	29	6	12	15	.276	.486	.361
Grass	2-3	4.75	233	61	10	37	27	.262	.438	.374
Artificial Turf	1-0	4.32	34	9	3	3	6	.265	.529	.324
April			0	0	0	0	0	—	—	—
May			0	0	0	0	0	—	—	—
June	0-0	2.91	80	20	5	15	10	.250	.463	.388
July	1-2	3.78	58	11	2	11	12	.190	.328	.319
August	1-1	6.75	108	34	5	9	8	.315	.500	.372
Sept./Oct.	1-0	5.06	21	5	1	5	3	.238	.476	.407
Leading Off Inn.			61	19	5	7	7	.311	.607	.391
Runners On			127	30	4	20	15	.236	.362	.349
Runners/Scor. Pos.			69	17	0	13	7	.246	.304	.379
Runners On/2 Out			58	16	2	12	7	.276	.397	.425
Scor. Pos./2 Out			36	11	0	8	3	.306	.333	.468
Late Inning Pressure			40	9	3	11	4	.225	.500	.404
Leading Off			12	3	2	2	2	.250	.750	.357
Runners On			12	4	1	4	1	.333	.750	.529
Runners/Scor. Pos.			4	2	0	4	0	.500	1.000	.778
First 9 Batters			175	40	3	30	23	.229	.320	.344
Second 9 Batters			73	24	8	8	8	.329	.712	.417
All Batters Thereafter			19	6	2	2	2	.316	.632	.409

Loves to face: Reggie Jackson (0-for-5, 3 SO)
Hates to face: Rickey Henderson (5-for-5)
Ground outs-to-air outs ratio: 0.92 last season, 0.99 for career....
Additional statistics: 8 double-play ground outs in 63 opportunities, 7 doubles, 2 triples in 69.0 innings last season.... Faced only one batter 5 times, pitched two or more innings 13 times, finished 8 games in 31 relief appearances.... August ERA was 2d worst in A.L. (minimum: 20 IP). ..Cleveland had a record of 1–8 in games in which he allowed a home run.... One of three active pitchers with a career opponents' batting average above .300 (minimum: 100 IP). The others: Don Schulze and Mike Brown.... One of two pitchers selected before Dwight Gooden in June 1982 free-agent draft. The other: San Diego rookie Jimmy Jones.

Randy O'Neal

Detroit Tigers — Throws Right

	W–L	ERA	AB	H	HR	BB	SO	BA	SA	OBA
Season	3-7	4.33	466	121	13	44	68	.260	.412	.324
vs. Left-Handers			222	50	9	30	21	.225	.396	.318
vs. Right-Handers			244	71	4	14	47	.291	.426	.330
Home	2-4	3.47	213	53	5	25	33	.249	.385	.326
Road	1-3	5.07	253	68	8	19	35	.269	.435	.321
Grass	3-5	3.99	399	102	12	36	56	.256	.396	.317
Artificial Turf	0-2	6.48	67	19	1	8	12	.284	.507	.364
April	0-1	2.57	56	16	2	2	7	.286	.411	.317
May	0-1	10.38	33	10	0	11	6	.303	.485	.467
June	1-1	3.93	69	19	1	5	7	.275	.362	.333
July	0-2	3.52	115	26	4	10	17	.226	.435	.291
August	2-2	6.59	107	31	4	13	13	.290	.458	.358
Sept./Oct.	0-0	1.90	86	19	2	3	18	.221	.337	.247
Leading Off Inn.			113	28	4	6	19	.248	.398	.298
Runners On			185	50	5	25	25	.270	.416	.347
Runners/Scor. Pos.			108	24	1	18	18	.222	.296	.318
Runners On/2 Out			86	22	2	10	16	.256	.372	.333
Scor. Pos./2 Out			54	12	1	9	12	.222	.315	.333
Late Inning Pressure			73	23	2	6	7	.315	.425	.363
Leading Off			16	4	0	1	2	.250	.250	.294
Runners On			37	12	1	3	2	.324	.459	.366
Runners/Scor. Pos.			18	5	0	1	2	.278	.333	.300
First 9 Batters			234	65	6	24	35	.278	.436	.342
Second 9 Batters			144	37	3	14	26	.257	.396	.327
All Batters Thereafter			88	19	4	6	7	.216	.375	.266

Loves to face: Tony Fernandez (0-for-8)
Hates to face: John Shelby (.500, 3-for-6, 2 HR)
Ground outs-to-air outs ratio: 1.34 last season, 1.37 for career....
Additional statistics: 13 double-play ground outs in 79 opportunities, 3d-highest average in A.L. (minimum: 10 GDP), 26 doubles, 3 triples in 122.2 innings last season.... Allowed 5 first-inning runs in 11 starts last season.... Batting support: 4.73 runs per start.... Faced only one batter once, pitched two or more innings 12 times, finished 9 games in 26 relief appearances.... 3–4, 4.19 ERA as a starter; 0–3 (2 saves), 4.48 ERA in relief.... August ERA was 4th worst in A.L. (minimum: 20 IP).... Opponents' career average of .143 (2-for-14) with the bases loaded.... Right-handers hit him for a higher average (.271, one HR per 54.0 at bats), left-handers for more power (.228, one HR per 34.5 AB).

Steve Ontiveros

Oakland As — Throws Right

	W–L	ERA	AB	H	HR	BB	SO	BA	SA	OBA
Season	2-2	4.71	272	72	10	25	54	.265	.430	.322
vs. Left-Handers			132	40	3	17	24	.303	.424	.373
vs. Right-Handers			140	32	7	8	30	.229	.436	.272
Home	2-2	3.20	139	28	4	14	29	.201	.317	.277
Road	0-0	6.48	133	44	6	11	25	.331	.549	.369
Grass	2-2	4.26	235	61	8	21	49	.260	.409	.316
Artificial Turf	0-0	7.71	37	11	2	4	5	.297	.568	.366
April	0-0	2.76	62	14	1	5	10	.226	.323	.284
May	1-2	7.29	83	27	6	9	14	.325	.578	.375
June	0-0	2.37	64	13	1	4	16	.203	.328	.257
July	0-0	5.40	42	12	1	4	11	.286	.429	.340
August			0	0	0	0	0	—	—	—
Sept./Oct.	1-0	7.71	21	6	1	3	3	.286	.476	.375
Leading Off Inn.			54	18	5	6	8	.333	.685	.400
Runners On			131	33	2	15	26	.252	.351	.316
Runners/Scor. Pos.			83	22	1	10	15	.265	.337	.323
Runners On/2 Out			62	18	0	8	10	.290	.323	.371
Scor. Pos./2 Out			47	14	0	6	7	.298	.319	.377
Late Inning Pressure			141	36	5	11	27	.255	.426	.308
Leading Off			30	9	2	2	4	.300	.600	.344
Runners On			59	17	2	7	13	.288	.458	.348
Runners/Scor. Pos.			38	11	1	5	8	.289	.395	.348
First 9 Batters			242	63	9	19	49	.260	.426	.311
Second 9 Batters			30	9	1	6	5	.300	.467	.405
All Batters Thereafter			0	0	0	0	0	—	—	—

Loves to face: Lance Parrish (0-for-8)
Hates to face: Kirk Gibson (.800, 4-for-5, 2 HR)
Ground outs-to-air outs ratio: 1.15 last season, 1.34 for career....
Additional statistics: 8 double-play ground outs in 59 opportunities, 13 doubles, 1 triple in 72.2 innings last season.... Faced only one batter 3 times, pitched two or more innings 18 times, finished 27 games in 46 relief appearances.... Only 15 of his 56 appearances were in 8th inning or later to protect leads of three runs or less.... Lowest opponents' batting average (.174) in the A.L. in 1985.... Opponents' career batting averages: .178 at Oakland Coliseum, .181 by right-handed batters. Combine the two for a stunning .118 mark (17-for-144) by right-handed opponents at the Oakland Coliseum.... Opponents are 2-for-19 with the bases loaded.

Dan Petry
Detroit Tigers   Throws Right

	W–L	ERA	AB	H	HR	BB	SO	BA	SA	OBA
Season	5-10	4.66	456	122	15	53	56	.268	.439	.348
vs. Left-Handers			242	56	12	28	36	.231	.442	.311
vs. Right-Handers			214	66	3	25	20	.308	.435	.389
Home	1-7	4.65	258	76	10	24	31	.295	.481	.360
Road	4-3	4.67	198	46	5	29	25	.232	.384	.333
Grass	4-10	4.96	427	118	14	48	49	.276	.450	.353
Artificial Turf	1-0	1.00	29	4	1	5	7	.138	.276	.286
April	1-2	6.10	130	41	5	13	15	.315	.515	.375
May	3-2	3.15	127	29	4	14	17	.228	.346	.319
June	0-1	∞	0	0	0	0	3	—	—	1.000
July			0	0	0	0	0	—	—	—
August	0-2	2.33	71	17	1	7	8	.239	.366	.316
Sept./Oct.	1-3	5.46	128	35	5	16	16	.273	.492	.354
Leading Off Inn.			108	31	4	14	11	.287	.454	.379
Runners On			212	53	4	27	26	.250	.387	.333
Runners/Scor. Pos.			120	30	3	16	18	.250	.425	.331
Runners On/2 Out			84	21	2	11	15	.250	.417	.337
Scor. Pos./2 Out			53	11	1	7	10	.208	.377	.300
Late Inning Pressure			26	6	0	6	3	.231	.231	.375
Leading Off			5	0	0	3	1	.000	.000	.375
Runners On			13	5	0	2	1	.385	.385	.467
Runners/Scor. Pos.			7	2	0	2	1	.286	.286	.444
First 9 Batters			149	43	5	19	20	.289	.477	.376
Second 9 Batters			143	35	7	10	13	.245	.469	.303
All Batters Thereafter			164	44	3	24	23	.268	.378	.360

Loves to face: Mike Pagliarulo (0-for-15)
Hates to face: George Brett (.438, 14-for-32, 5 HR)
Ground outs-to-air outs ratio: 1.60 last season, 1.48 for career. . . . Additional statistics: 12 double-play ground outs in 106 opportunities, 27 doubles, 3 triples in 116.0 innings last season. . . . Allowed 16 first-inning runs in 20 starts last season. . . . Batting support: 4.15 runs per start. . . . April ERA was 5th worst in A.L. (minimum: 20 IP). . . . Has lost his last six decisions to Seattle. . . . Had a winning record in every season from 1979 to 1985. . . . Strikeout-walk ratio (1.06) and opponents' batting average were the worst of his career. . . . Opponents' career batting average of .195 (15-for-77, 4 HR) with the bases loaded.

Dan Plesac
Milwaukee Brewers   Throws Left

	W–L	ERA	AB	H	HR	BB	SO	BA	SA	OBA
Season	10-7	2.97	337	81	5	29	75	.240	.341	.296
vs. Left-Handers			79	21	1	9	17	.266	.367	.333
vs. Right-Handers			258	60	4	20	58	.233	.333	.285
Home	6-3	3.58	192	50	3	17	43	.260	.391	.315
Road	4-4	2.21	145	31	2	12	32	.214	.276	.272
Grass	9-6	3.26	294	71	5	26	66	.241	.354	.298
Artificial Turf	1-1	0.82	43	10	0	3	9	.233	.256	.283
April	1-1	4.66	34	6	1	3	8	.176	.353	.243
May	2-2	3.12	66	17	1	5	13	.258	.394	.310
June	1-2	2.25	41	10	1	5	9	.244	.341	.313
July	1-1	3.55	48	13	0	5	9	.271	.354	.327
August	4-0	1.77	75	16	1	6	20	.213	.280	.268
Sept./Oct.	1-1	3.32	73	19	1	5	17	.260	.342	.308
Leading Off Inn.			76	21	1	3	12	.276	.382	.304
Runners On			167	38	3	16	35	.228	.329	.287
Runners/Scor. Pos.			100	22	2	11	26	.220	.320	.284
Runners On/2 Out			83	14	0	8	17	.169	.181	.242
Scor. Pos./2 Out			55	8	0	6	15	.145	.164	.230
Late Inning Pressure			199	51	3	19	44	.256	.362	.317
Leading Off			45	14	1	2	7	.311	.444	.340
Runners On			103	24	2	10	23	.233	.340	.293
Runners/Scor. Pos.			58	14	1	8	18	.241	.345	.319
First 9 Batters			285	66	4	27	70	.232	.330	.293
Second 9 Batters			52	15	1	2	5	.288	.404	.315
All Batters Thereafter			0	0	0	0	0	—	—	—

Loves to face: Brook Jacoby (0-for-6, 3 SO)
Hates to face: Cory Snyder (.667, 2-for-3, 1 2B, 1 HR)
Ground outs-to-air outs ratio: 0.73 last season, his first in majors. . . . Additional statistics: 4 double-play ground outs in 73 opportunities, 11 doubles, 4 triples in 91.0 innings last season. . . . Faced only one batter 4 times, pitched two or more innings 24 times, finished 33 games in 51 relief appearances. . . . Compiled his lowest ERA at any level of his professional career last season, his first in the majors. . . . Led A.L. rookies with 14 saves. . . . Allowed 10.88 base runners per nine innings, 2d fewest among A.L. rookies (minimum: 81 innings). . . . Opponents batted .100 (1-for-10) with the bases loaded.

Eric Plunk
Oakland As   Throws Right

	W–L	ERA	AB	H	HR	BB	SO	BA	SA	OBA
Season	4-7	5.31	425	91	14	102	98	.214	.341	.370
vs. Left-Handers			239	54	7	58	45	.226	.339	.377
vs. Right-Handers			186	37	7	44	53	.199	.344	.362
Home	3-3	5.68	224	50	10	59	54	.223	.384	.389
Road	1-4	4.89	201	41	4	43	44	.204	.294	.348
Grass	3-6	5.33	358	76	14	84	84	.212	.360	.367
Artificial Turf	1-1	5.21	67	15	0	18	14	.224	.239	.384
April			0	0	0	0	0			
May	0-1	4.76	77	15	4	17	17	.195	.377	.337
June	2-2	5.45	122	25	5	31	32	.205	.344	.365
July	1-4	5.34	111	26	4	26	18	.234	.378	.384
August	1-0	4.91	63	12	1	12	15	.190	.270	.329
Sept./Oct.	0-0	6.28	52	13	0	16	16	.250	.288	.443
Leading Off Inn.			112	28	3	16	25	.250	.357	.344
Runners On			194	47	8	39	40	.242	.397	.375
Runners/Scor. Pos.			106	27	3	25	31	.255	.387	.388
Runners On/2 Out			78	16	3	18	19	.205	.333	.354
Scor. Pos./2 Out			52	11	1	11	16	.212	.288	.349
Late Inning Pressure			29	10	3	6	2	.345	.655	.457
Leading Off			11	5	1	0	0	.455	.727	.455
Runners On			9	4	1	3	1	.444	.778	.583
Runners/Scor. Pos.			4	3	0	1	0	.750	.750	.800
First 9 Batters			184	37	2	37	53	.201	.266	.344
Second 9 Batters			131	27	7	40	22	.206	.397	.394
All Batters Thereafter			110	27	5	25	23	.245	.400	.382

Loves to face: Ruben Sierra (0-for-7, 6 SO)
Hates to face: Harold Baines (.750, 3-for-4)
Ground outs-to-air outs ratio: 0.84 last season, his first in majors. . .Additional statistics: 13 double-play ground outs in 111 opportunities, 12 doubles, 0 triples in 120.1 innings last season. . . . Allowed 2 first-inning runs in 15 starts last season. . . . Batting support: 4.07 runs per start. . . . Third pitcher in A.L. history to allow two grand slams in one game (July 31). Others: Tex Shirley (1946) and Jack Morris (1984). . . . Held top 15 A.L. batters to combined .146 average last season (7-for-48), 2d lowest in A.L. (minimum: 20 AB). . . . Allowed 6.81 hits per nine innings, 3d best among major-league rookies (minimum: 81 IP). . . . Led American League with six balks, but despite his name, 21 pitchers hit more batters.

Mark Portugal
Minnesota Twins   Throws Right

	W–L	ERA	AB	H	HR	BB	SO	BA	SA	OBA
Season	6-10	4.31	422	112	10	50	67	.265	.391	.342
vs. Left-Handers			206	45	3	30	39	.218	.325	.314
vs. Right-Handers			216	67	7	20	28	.310	.454	.371
Home	3-3	4.09	161	43	4	23	25	.267	.416	.357
Road	3-7	4.46	261	69	6	27	42	.264	.375	.333
Grass	1-6	4.28	187	51	4	14	29	.273	.396	.325
Artificial Turf	5-4	4.34	235	61	6	36	38	.260	.387	.355
April	0-2	23.14	11	6	1	3	0	.545	.818	.643
May	1-3	4.71	82	23	3	9	8	.280	.476	.344
June	1-2	5.19	97	28	2	14	22	.289	.443	.378
July	0-1	4.35	36	9	1	5	5	.250	.333	.341
August	2-0	3.42	90	25	3	14	10	.278	.411	.371
Sept./Oct.	2-2	2.45	106	21	0	5	22	.198	.236	.241
Leading Off Inn.			105	37	4	15	16	.352	.533	.433
Runners On			195	46	5	22	34	.236	.354	.312
Runners/Scor. Pos.			101	20	4	13	15	.198	.366	.282
Runners On/2 Out			64	12	0	10	17	.188	.219	.297
Scor. Pos./2 Out			41	7	0	6	9	.171	.220	.277
Late Inning Pressure			33	15	1	3	3	.455	.636	.514
Leading Off			11	6	0	1	2	.545	.545	.583
Runners On			15	7	1	1	0	.467	.800	.529
Runners/Scor. Pos.			10	3	1	0	0	.300	.600	.300
First 9 Batters			171	44	2	25	27	.257	.363	.352
Second 9 Batters			120	33	4	13	19	.275	.408	.341
All Batters Thereafter			131	35	4	12	21	.267	.412	.331

Loves to face: Mel Hall (0-for-8, 4 SO)
Hates to face: Mike Davis (2-for-2, 1 2B, 1 HR)
Ground outs-to-air outs ratio: 1.24 last season, 1.30 for career. . . . Additional statistics: 16 double-play ground outs in 119 opportunities, 21 doubles, 1 triple in 112.2 innings last season. . . . Allowed 3 first-inning runs in 15 starts last season. . . . Batting support: 5.27 runs per start. . . . 4–6, 3.73 ERA as a starter; 2–4 (1 save), 6.86 ERA in 12 relief appearances. . . . Lost his first five decisions last season. . . . Opponents' career batting: .459 in Late-Inning Pressure Situations, .251 in unpressured situations, .195 with runners in scoring position. . . . Battle for the Iberian peninsula: Franco has a career 3-for-10 mark with two doubles vs. Portugal.

Dan Quisenberry
Kansas City Royals — Throws Right

	W–L	ERA	AB	H	HR	BB	SO	BA	SA	OBA
Season	3-7	2.77	316	92	2	24	36	.291	.348	.342
vs. Left-Handers			145	45	1	18	14	.310	.379	.380
vs. Right-Handers			171	47	1	6	22	.275	.322	.308
Home	2-3	2.45	142	36	1	11	15	.254	.310	.310
Road	1-4	3.02	174	56	1	13	21	.322	.379	.368
Grass	0-3	3.03	134	45	1	10	17	.336	.410	.376
Artificial Turf	3-4	2.59	182	47	1	14	19	.258	.302	.317
April	0-0	0.00	35	9	0	0	6	.257	.257	.257
May	0-1	4.97	52	20	1	5	5	.385	.500	.450
June	0-0	0.61	56	13	0	4	7	.232	.250	.274
July	0-3	5.27	59	20	0	7	4	.339	.373	.403
August	.1-1	1.20	53	10	0	5	8	.189	.245	.254
Sept./Oct.	2-2	4.02	61	20	1	3	6	.328	.426	.369
Leading Off Inn.			68	21	0	3	4	.309	.353	.338
Runners On			164	49	1	18	23	.299	.354	.365
Runners/Scor. Pos.			103	34	1	16	15	.330	.388	.408
Runners On/2 Out			74	20	0	8	12	.270	.311	.349
Scor. Pos./2 Out			52	15	0	8	9	.288	.327	.383
Late Inning Pressure			136	42	0	16	18	.309	.346	.382
Leading Off			29	11	0	1	3	.379	.448	.400
Runners On			80	24	0	12	10	.300	.313	.392
Runners/Scor. Pos.			53	17	0	11	6	.321	.340	.426
First 9 Batters			303	87	2	24	33	.287	.340	.340
Second 9 Batters			13	5	0	0	3	.385	.538	.385
All Batters Thereafter			0	0	0	0	0	—	—	—

Loves to face: Julio Franco (0-for-14)
Hates to face: Brett Butler (.778, 7-for-9)
Ground outs-to-air outs ratio: 2.07, 7th highest in A.L. last season (minimum: 250 BFP), 2.31 for career. . . . Additional statistics: 10 double-play ground outs in 92 opportunities, 8 doubles, 2 triples in 81.1 innings last season. . . . Faced only one batter 5 times, pitched two or more innings 18 times, finished 54 games in 62 relief appearances. . . . Has walked the leadoff batter in three of the last 41 innings he has started (since June 22). Prior to that, he had walked only two of the previous 426 leadoff batters he faced, dating back to July 1982. . . . For the first time in his career less than half the batters he faced were in Late-Inning Pressure Situations (45.7 percent). Previous low was 59.0 percent in 1983.

Dennis Rasmussen
New York Yankees — Throws Left

	W–L	ERA	AB	H	HR	BB	SO	BA	SA	OBA
Season	18-6	3.88	737	160	28	74	131	.217	.366	.289
vs. Left-Handers			136	25	2	12	23	.184	.250	.247
vs. Right-Handers			601	135	26	62	108	.225	.393	.298
Home	8-2	4.32	269	55	10	33	54	.204	.353	.291
Road	10-4	3.61	468	105	18	41	77	.224	.374	.287
Grass	13-5	3.92	559	121	20	63	96	.216	.354	.296
Artificial Turf	5-1	3.72	178	39	8	11	35	.219	.404	.265
April	2-0	2.41	63	12	2	6	13	.190	.333	.257
May	3-1	4.70	136	27	3	17	33	.199	.294	.286
June	3-1	3.56	154	33	5	17	21	.214	.325	.289
July	4-0	1.74	106	16	3	14	26	.151	.274	.256
August	2-2	4.71	109	26	6	8	20	.239	.459	.291
Sept./Oct.	4-2	5.10	169	46	9	12	18	.272	.473	.322
Leading Off Inn.			197	38	5	20	34	.193	.294	.267
Runners On			247	65	12	38	48	.263	.445	.322
Runners/Scor. Pos.			101	31	8	13	17	.307	.604	.375
Runners On/2 Out			100	24	3	9	14	.240	.360	.309
Scor. Pos./2 Out			47	12	3	5	8	.255	.468	.340
Late Inning Pressure			58	12	2	6	7	.207	.328	.277
Leading Off			20	3	1	1	1	.150	.300	.190
Runners On			11	5	1	1	2	.455	.727	.462
Runners/Scor. Pos.			2	1	1	1	0	.500	2.000	.500
First 9 Batters			254	50	7	21	46	.197	.327	.256
Second 9 Batters			246	55	12	22	50	.224	.402	.288
All Batters Thereafter			237	55	9	31	35	.232	.371	.322

Loves to face: Harold Baines (.053, 1-for-19, 1 HR)
Hates to face: Tom Brookens (.467, 7-for-15, 1 HR)
Ground outs-to-air outs ratio: 0.55, 2d lowest in A.L. last season (minimum: 250 BFP), 0.68 for career. . . . Additional statistics: 15 double-play ground outs in 135 opportunities, 24 doubles, 1 triple in 202.0 innings last season. . . . Allowed 10 first-inning runs in 31 starts last season. . . . Batting support: 5.84 runs per start, 4th best in A.L. (minimum: 15 GS). . . . Averaged 6.52 innings per start, highest on Yankees staff. . . . Had a 5–0 record in starts decided by one run, tied with Oil Can Boyd and Bob Ojeda for best in the majors. . . . July ERA was 5th best in A.L. . . . Opponents' career batting: .207 with bases empty, .270 with runners on base, .282 with runners in scoring position. . . . Opponents' 9-for-18 career with bases loaded is bad enough, but *five of the nine hits are grand slams.*

Dave Righetti
New York Yankees — Throws Left

	W–L	ERA	AB	H	HR	BB	SO	BA	SA	OBA
Season	8-8	2.45	389	88	4	35	83	.226	.296	.291
vs. Left-Handers			69	21	1	8	16	.304	.391	.388
vs. Right-Handers			320	67	3	27	67	.209	.275	.269
Home	5-5	1.99	180	37	1	12	48	.206	.256	.255
Road	3-3	2.84	209	51	3	23	35	.244	.330	.319
Grass	7-7	2.35	319	71	3	29	72	.223	.288	.287
Artificial Turf	1-1	2.89	70	17	1	6	11	.243	.329	.308
April	2-1	4.61	51	15	1	9	11	.294	.373	.400
May	2-1	1.69	59	10	1	3	16	.169	.254	.210
June	1-2	6.08	55	17	1	9	7	.309	.436	.403
July	2-0	1.00	63	12	0	3	16	.190	.254	.227
August	0-3	1.23	78	15	0	6	17	.192	.218	.259
Sept./Oct.	1-1	1.90	83	19	1	5	16	.229	.289	.267
Leading Off Inn.			83	21	1	5	18	.253	.325	.295
Runners On			199	45	3	21	37	.226	.302	.301
Runners/Scor. Pos.			120	26	1	15	25	.217	.283	.300
Runners On/2 Out			91	18	3	8	17	.198	.308	.270
Scor. Pos./2 Out			60	11	1	4	11	.183	.250	.246
Late Inning Pressure			253	62	3	26	52	.245	.328	.316
Leading Off			53	16	1	3	10	.302	.415	.339
Runners On			128	32	2	18	21	.250	.336	.342
Runners/Scor. Pos.			81	18	0	12	14	.222	.284	.323
First 9 Batters			371	82	4	28	81	.221	.288	.277
Second 9 Batters			18	6	0	7	2	.333	.444	.500
All Batters Thereafter			0	0	0	0	0	—	—	—

Loves to face: Dwight Evans (.133, 4-for-30, 9 SO, 1 HR)
Hates to face: Ben Oglivie (.455, 5-for-11, 1 HR)
Ground outs-to-air outs ratio: 1.18 last season, 1.04 for career. . . . Additional statistics: 13 double-play ground outs in 106 opportunities, 15 doubles, 0 triples in 106.2 innings last season. . . . Faced only one batter 5 times, pitched two or more innings 25 times, finished 68 games in 74 relief appearances. . . . Recorded a save in 10 consecutive appearances from Aug. 28 to Sept. 15, one shy of major-league record set by Yanks' Sparky Lyle in 1973. . . . In three seasons in the bullpen Righetti has 106 saves, most in the majors. Others over 90: Reardon, 99; L. Smith, 97; Quisenberry, 93. . . . Opponents' career batting average of .240 in Late-Inning Pressure Situations, .220 in unpressured situations.

Jose Rijo
Oakland As — Throws Right

	W–L	ERA	AB	H	HR	BB	SO	BA	SA	OBA
Season	9-11	4.65	725	172	24	108	176	.237	.406	.336
vs. Left-Handers			395	95	11	71	82	.241	.403	.354
vs. Right-Handers			330	77	13	37	94	.233	.409	.312
Home	3-4	3.90	322	66	10	59	85	.205	.348	.326
Road	6-7	5.30	403	106	14	49	91	.263	.452	.343
Grass	7-10	4.07	565	123	14	88	137	.218	.359	.322
Artificial Turf	2-1	6.92	160	49	10	20	39	.306	.569	.384
April	1-2	4.89	122	23	6	14	47	.189	.418	.275
May	1-0	3.77	103	21	3	23	27	.204	.330	.344
June	0-5	6.55	92	28	2	18	26	.304	.457	.420
July	2-1	2.65	141	32	3	14	32	.227	.369	.295
August	2-2	6.19	136	37	6	22	21	.272	.463	.373
Sept./Oct.	3-1	4.46	131	31	4	17	23	.237	.397	.325
Leading Off Inn.			178	35	4	26	48	.197	.331	.302
Runners On			300	82	12	50	75	.273	.467	.373
Runners/Scor. Pos.			180	49	4	37	45	.272	.411	.389
Runners On/2 Out			125	31	6	29	28	.248	.432	.394
Scor. Pos./2 Out			83	19	1	21	18	.229	.277	.390
Late Inning Pressure			92	24	3	13	21	.261	.446	.352
Leading Off			26	2	0	3	10	.077	.115	.172
Runners On			34	14	0	6	10	.412	.618	.500
Runners/Scor. Pos.			19	10	0	6	3	.526	.789	.640
First 9 Batters			254	64	12	41	78	.252	.472	.354
Second 9 Batters			196	53	7	29	43	.270	.469	.367
All Batters Thereafter			275	55	5	38	55	.200	.298	.297

Loves to face: Kirk Gibson (0-for-11, 5 SO)
Hates to face: George Bell (.714, 5-for-7, 2 2B)
Ground outs-to-air outs ratio: 1.04 last season, 0.99 for career. . . . Additional statistics: 3 double-play ground outs in 138 opportunities, lowest average in majors (minimum: 40 opp.), 34 doubles, 8 triples (tied for 2d most in A.L.) in 193.2 innings last season. . . . Allowed 11 first-inning runs in 26 starts last season. . . . Batting support: 4.77 runs per start. . . . 9-7, 4.38 ERA as a starter; 0-4 (1 save), 8.53 ERA in 13 relief appearances. . . . Led A.L. with five losses in June. . . . Batting average by opposing left-handers has decreased in every season: .353, .280, .241. . . . Opponents' career batting average of .222 (6-for-27, 1 HR) with the bases loaded; .390 with runners in scoring position in Late-Inning Pressure Situations.

Ron Romanick

California Angels   Throws Right

	W–L	ERA	AB	H	HR	BB	SO	BA	SA	OBA
Season	5-8	5.50	418	124	13	44	38	.297	.450	.360
vs. Left-Handers			214	64	3	23	16	.299	.411	.361
vs. Right-Handers			204	60	10	21	22	.294	.490	.358
Home	2-6	5.43	213	65	9	19	17	.305	.484	.356
Road	3-2	5.57	205	59	4	25	21	.288	.415	.364
Grass	4-7	5.01	355	104	10	37	32	.293	.439	.355
Artificial Turf	1-1	8.59	63	20	3	7	6	.317	.508	.386
April	2-1	4.88	87	23	4	10	15	.264	.414	.337
May	1-1	3.89	128	34	1	17	10	.266	.359	.342
June	2-4	5.85	140	45	6	7	7	.321	.507	.354
July	0-2	9.39	63	22	2	10	6	.349	.556	.438
August			0	0	0	0	0	—	—	—
Sept./Oct.			0	0	0	0	0	—	—	—
Leading Off Inn.			105	27	1	9	13	.257	.343	.316
Runners On			190	58	9	18	14	.305	.505	.357
Runners/Scor. Pos.			88	31	4	10	7	.352	.580	.398
Runners On/2 Out			85	31	5	9	7	.365	.600	.426
Scor. Pos./2 Out			48	18	3	6	6	.375	.646	.444
Late Inning Pressure			28	11	2	1	3	.393	.679	.400
Leading Off			10	4	1	0	2	.400	.800	.400
Runners On			12	5	1	0	1	.417	.667	.385
Runners/Scor. Pos.			8	3	1	0	1	.375	.750	.333
First 9 Batters			144	39	2	17	16	.271	.375	.346
Second 9 Batters			135	38	6	15	12	.281	.467	.353
All Batters Thereafter			139	47	5	12	10	.338	.511	.381

Loves to face: Alvin Davis (.056, 1-for-18, 1 HR)
Hates to face: Kirby Puckett (.857, 6-for-7, 1 HR)
Ground outs-to-air outs ratio: 1.28 last season, 0.94 for career. . . .
Additional statistics: 9 double-play ground outs in 95 opportunities, 19 doubles, 3 triples in 106.1 innings last season. . . . Allowed 5 first-inning runs in 18 starts last season. . . . Batting support: 4.83 runs per start. . . . Good news for Yankees: Career record of 3–0 vs. Bosox. . . . Opponents' yearly batting averages since 1984: .270, .280, .297. ERA has also escalated: 3.76, 4.11, 5.50. . . . Has started all 64 of his major-league games. . . . Career at Yankee Stadium: 1–2, 3.87 ERA. . . . Opponents' career batting average of .357 (10-for-28) with the bases loaded.

Jeff Russell

Texas Rangers   Throws Right

	W–L	ERA	AB	H	HR	BB	SO	BA	SA	OBA
Season	5-2	3.40	303	74	11	31	54	.244	.396	.315
vs. Left-Handers			124	36	5	17	20	.290	.452	.376
vs. Right-Handers			179	38	6	14	34	.212	.358	.270
Home	2-0	3.30	107	27	2	9	16	.252	.336	.308
Road	3-2	3.46	196	47	9	22	38	.240	.429	.318
Grass	4-0	3.23	235	57	8	24	37	.243	.370	.312
Artificial Turf	1-2	4.00	68	17	3	7	17	.250	.485	.325
April			0	0	0	0	0	—	—	—
May			0	0	0	0	0	—	—	—
June	1-1	5.17	61	15	2	9	12	.246	.377	.338
July	1-0	5.40	73	19	4	10	12	.260	.466	.349
August	3-1	2.15	106	25	4	11	18	.236	.396	.311
Sept./Oct.	0-0	1.59	63	15	1	1	12	.238	.333	.250
Leading Off Inn.			64	14	3	6	12	.219	.406	.286
Runners On			138	38	3	15	24	.275	.391	.346
Runners/Scor. Pos.			101	24	3	11	19	.238	.376	.307
Runners On/2 Out			61	20	2	8	12	.328	.459	.414
Scor. Pos./2 Out			47	14	2	8	10	.298	.468	.400
Late Inning Pressure			55	7	2	6	13	.127	.291	.226
Leading Off			18	3	1	1	4	.167	.333	.211
Runners On			13	2	0	1	4	.154	.308	.267
Runners/Scor. Pos.			7	2	0	1	1	.286	.571	.375
First 9 Batters			232	57	6	23	38	.246	.375	.313
Second 9 Batters			66	17	5	8	15	.258	.500	.342
All Batters Thereafter			5	0	0	0	1	.000	.000	.000

Loves to face: Tom Brunansky (0-for-6)
Hates to face: Jim Presley (3-for-3, 1 2B, 2 HR)
Ground outs-to-air outs ratio: 1.72 last season, 1.06 for career (1.26 on grass surfaces, 0.86 on artificial turf). . . . Additional statistics: 9 double-play ground outs in 64 opportunities, 9 doubles, 2 triples in 82.0 innings last season. . . . Faced only one batter once, pitched two or more innings 21 times, finished 9 games in 37 relief appearances. . . . August ERA was 4th best in A.L. . . . Opponents' career batting average of .170 in Late-Inning Pressure Situations is the lowest in the majors over the past 12 seasons. Yearly averages in LIP: .125, .209, .167, .127. . . . Walked only one batter in his last 17 innings in 1986. . . . Has never walked a batter with the bases loaded (39 career PA).

Bret Saberhagen

Kansas City Royals   Throws Right

	W–L	ERA	AB	H	HR	BB	SO	BA	SA	OBA
Season	7-12	4.15	615	165	15	29	112	.268	.402	.302
vs. Left-Handers			368	93	8	18	76	.253	.394	.288
vs. Right-Handers			247	72	7	11	36	.291	.413	.323
Home	2-5	3.67	306	88	4	12	55	.288	.399	.313
Road	5-7	4.61	309	77	11	17	57	.249	.405	.292
Grass	4-5	3.86	262	59	10	14	50	.225	.382	.264
Artificial Turf	3-7	4.40	353	106	5	15	62	.300	.416	.331
April	1-2	4.56	91	23	2	5	12	.253	.407	.292
May	1-3	3.21	170	47	1	10	31	.276	.359	.317
June	2-4	4.91	144	39	4	6	23	.271	.382	.305
July	2-1	4.71	110	25	7	3	23	.227	.464	.246
August	0-0	6.00	10	3	1	2	3	.300	.600	.417
Sept./Oct.	1-2	3.27	90	28	0	3	20	.311	.411	.333
Leading Off Inn.			150	43	2	9	36	.287	.360	.335
Runners On			244	67	4	14	40	.275	.422	.310
Runners/Scor. Pos.			112	35	2	11	17	.313	.482	.365
Runners On/2 Out			103	28	2	8	20	.272	.388	.324
Scor. Pos./2 Out			54	16	2	6	13	.296	.444	.367
Late Inning Pressure			70	16	2	3	11	.229	.343	.260
Leading Off			20	5	0	0	6	.250	.250	.250
Runners On			20	5	0	1	4	.250	.250	.286
Runners/Scor. Pos.			6	1	0	1	2	.167	.167	.286
First 9 Batters			238	54	5	14	53	.227	.332	.272
Second 9 Batters			204	68	7	7	39	.333	.529	.355
All Batters Thereafter			173	43	3	8	20	.249	.347	.283

Loves to face: Reggie Jackson (0-for-22, 8 SO)
Hates to face: Jim Traber (2-for-2, 2 HR)
Ground outs-to-air outs ratio: 1.29 last season, 1.21 for career. . . .
Additional statistics: 9 double-play ground outs in 115 opportunities, 21 doubles, 8 triples (tied for 2d most in A.L.) in 156.0 innings last season. . . . Allowed 14 first-inning runs in 25 starts last season. . . . Royals scored an average of 3.32 runs in his 25 starts, 3d poorest run support in A.L. (minimum: 15 GS). . . . Royals had a 2–10 record in games in which he allowed a home run. . . . Highest ratio of strikeouts to walks in majors (4.22) for second consecutive season (minimum: 50 SO). . . . Fanned only four of 67 batters with runners in scoring position and less than two outs. . . . Opponents' batting average with runners on base was .217 in his Cy Young season, .275 in 1986.

Calvin Schiraldi

Boston Red Sox   Throws Right

	W–L	ERA	AB	H	HR	BB	SO	BA	SA	OBA
Season	4-2	1.41	179	36	5	15	55	.201	.318	.265
vs. Left-Handers			94	16	2	9	27	.170	.277	.248
vs. Right-Handers			85	20	3	6	28	.235	.365	.286
Home	3-1	1.99	81	18	4	6	26	.222	.432	.281
Road	1-1	0.95	98	18	1	9	29	.184	.224	.252
Grass	4-2	1.43	154	31	5	13	47	.201	.338	.266
Artificial Turf	0-0	1.29	25	5	0	2	8	.200	.200	.259
April			0	0	0	0	0	—	—	—
May			0	0	0	0	0	—	—	—
June			0	0	0	0	0	—	—	—
July	0-0	0.71	42	10	0	6	12	.238	.238	.333
August	2-1	1.33	70	11	1	3	24	.157	.229	.189
Sept./Oct.	2-1	2.00	67	15	4	6	19	.224	.463	.297
Leading Off Inn.			43	9	4	2	10	.209	.488	.244
Runners On			73	12	1	7	26	.164	.219	.235
Runners/Scor. Pos.			44	5	0	6	16	.114	.114	.216
Runners On/2 Out			34	4	1	2	12	.118	.235	.167
Scor. Pos./2 Out			22	2	0	2	7	.091	.091	.167
Late Inning Pressure			84	18	4	6	26	.214	.405	.275
Leading Off			18	3	3	0	4	.167	.667	.167
Runners On			30	6	1	4	10	.200	.300	.294
Runners/Scor. Pos.			23	2	0	4	9	.087	.087	.222
First 9 Batters			158	35	5	12	50	.222	.348	.281
Second 9 Batters			21	1	0	3	5	.048	.048	.160
All Batters Thereafter			0	0	0	0	0			

Loves to face: Jim Dwyer (0-for-4, 2 SO)
Hates to face: Gary Carter with 2 strikes and 2 outs
Carter was also 2-for-2 against him in N.L. . . . Ground outs-to-air outs ratio: 0.67 last season, 0.86 for career. . . . Additional statistics: 4 double-play ground outs in 35 opportunities, 6 doubles, 0 triples in 51.0 innings. . . . Faced only one batter once, pitched two or more innings 15 times, finished 21 games in 25 relief appearances. . . . No XBH by the first 65 right-handed batters he faced last season, but five by his last 27 righties in the regular season and Ray Knight's HR in postseason. . . . Opponents' batting average dropped from .368 (43-for-117) in 1985 to .201 last season.

Dave Schmidt
Chicago White Sox   Throws Right

	W-L	ERA	AB	H	HR	BB	SO	BA	SA	OBA
Season	3-6	3.31	356	94	10	27	67	.264	.427	.322
vs. Left-Handers			162	43	3	17	28	.265	.426	.341
vs. Right-Handers			194	51	7	10	39	.263	.428	.306
Home	2-1	3.00	164	39	3	9	30	.238	.372	.291
Road	1-5	3.61	192	55	7	18	37	.286	.474	.349
Grass	2-6	3.33	300	78	7	23	59	.260	.403	.321
Artificial Turf	1-0	3.21	56	16	3	4	8	.286	.554	.328
April	0-0	6.97	44	16	3	2	7	.364	.705	.391
May	0-2	4.82	77	24	1	7	9	.312	.416	.372
June	0-0	2.66	73	15	2	5	20	.205	.425	.272
July	0-1	1.93	70	17	1	6	14	.243	.329	.312
August	1-2	1.98	53	14	2	4	10	.264	.434	.328
Sept./Oct.	2-1	2.53	39	8	1	3	7	.205	.308	.256
Leading Off Inn.			84	21	2	3	13	.250	.381	.276
Runners On			161	37	2	16	36	.230	.311	.310
Runners/Scor. Pos.			109	25	2	14	23	.229	.330	.320
Runners On/2 Out			79	19	2	6	19	.241	.354	.302
Scor. Pos./2 Out			58	16	2	6	14	.276	.431	.354
Late Inning Pressure			105	34	4	8	17	.324	.486	.383
Leading Off			25	9	0	1	1	.360	.360	.385
Runners On			48	12	0	6	11	.250	.292	.357
Runners/Scor. Pos.			29	7	0	6	3	.241	.241	.389
First 9 Batters			286	78	7	22	57	.273	.430	.333
Second 9 Batters			63	13	3	3	8	.206	.381	.239
All Batters Thereafter			7	3	0	2	2	.429	.714	.556

Loves to face: Ben Oglivie (0-for-14)
Hates to face: Kent Hrbek (.571, 4-for-7, 1 HR)
Ground outs-to-air outs ratio: 1.22 last season, 1.44 for career. . . . Additional statistics: 12 double-play ground outs in 71 opportunities, 16 doubles, 6 triples in 92.1 innings last season. . . . Faced only one batter 4 times, pitched two or more innings 23 times, finished 21 games in 48 relief appearances. . . . Career record of 0–5 vs. Baltimore. . . . Career average of one extra-base hit per 23.1 at bats in Late-Inning Pressure Situations, to one per 15.0 at bats overall. . . . Has faced 50 batters with the bases loaded in his career without allowing an extra-base hit, a *Player Analysis* record. . . . Opponents' career batting average of .180 (9-for-50) with the bases loaded. . . . Has walked the leadoff batters in only eight of the 398 innings he has started.

Ken Schrom
Cleveland Indians   Throws Right

	W-L	ERA	AB	H	HR	BB	SO	BA	SA	OBA
Season	14-7	4.54	802	217	34	49	87	.271	.455	.318
vs. Left-Handers			447	131	17	27	44	.293	.472	.335
vs. Right-Handers			355	86	17	22	43	.242	.434	.297
Home	9-4	3.88	451	115	16	29	51	.255	.412	.306
Road	5-3	5.44	351	102	18	20	36	.291	.510	.332
Grass	11-7	4.73	673	186	29	44	75	.276	.462	.323
Artificial Turf	3-0	3.58	129	31	5	5	12	.240	.419	.288
April	3-1	3.52	113	30	4	10	9	.265	.416	.317
May	0-1	4.84	139	39	7	6	18	.281	.511	.327
June	5-0	3.25	132	28	7	10	18	.212	.402	.266
July	3-1	4.17	143	35	7	8	17	.245	.441	.290
August	0-3	7.06	127	45	4	7	10	.354	.520	.394
Sept./Oct.	3-1	4.74	148	40	5	8	15	.270	.439	.317
Leading Off Inn.			202	59	11	16	17	.292	.530	.362
Runners On			318	77	10	22	40	.242	.390	.289
Runners/Scor. Pos.			163	35	3	15	23	.215	.319	.275
Runners On/2 Out			123	29	2	9	23	.236	.350	.299
Scor. Pos./2 Out			74	17	1	7	15	.230	.324	.305
Late Inning Pressure			65	16	2	4	8	.246	.369	.310
Leading Off			21	7	1	2	2	.333	.667	.364
Runners On			20	4	0	1	4	.200	.200	.304
Runners/Scor. Pos.			7	0	0	1	2	.000	.000	.300
First 9 Batters			272	72	16	15	34	.265	.485	.307
Second 9 Batters			261	72	10	13	32	.276	.456	.323
All Batters Thereafter			269	73	8	21	21	.271	.424	.323

Loves to face: Alvin Davis (.045, 1-for-22, 1 HR)
Hates to face: Rickey Henderson (.500, 5-for-10, 3 HR)
Ground outs-to-air outs ratio: 0.69, 9th lowest in A.L. last season (minimum: 250 BFP), 0.80 for career. . . . Additional statistics: 17 double-play ground outs in 160 opportunities, 40 doubles, 3 triples in 206.0 innings last season. Allowed 77 extra-base hits, 7th most in A.L. . . . Allowed 26 first-inning runs in 33 starts last season. . . . Batting support: 5.21 runs per start. . . . Made seven consecutive starts without a win from July 28 to Aug. 28. . . . August ERA was worst in A.L. (minimum: 20 IP). . . . Allowed nine first-inning home runs last season, most in the major leagues. . . . Opponents' career batting average of .087 (4-for-46, 1 HR) with the bases loaded.

Don Schulze
Cleveland Indians   Throws Right

	W-L	ERA	AB	H	HR	BB	SO	BA	SA	OBA
Season	4-4	5.00	331	88	9	34	33	.266	.417	.342
vs. Left-Handers			152	45	5	17	14	.296	.467	.368
vs. Right-Handers			179	43	4	17	19	.240	.374	.320
Home	1-2	4.30	173	41	5	13	15	.237	.382	.302
Road	3-2	5.82	158	47	4	21	18	.297	.456	.385
Grass	3-3	4.66	283	75	8	29	30	.265	.406	.341
Artificial Turf	1-1	7.15	48	13	1	5	3	.271	.479	.352
April	2-0	2.77	52	16	0	5	10	.308	.346	.368
May	1-2	4.40	112	22	3	11	9	.196	.321	.274
June	1-2	6.33	114	38	5	12	8	.333	.553	.412
July	0-0	4.66	36	8	0	3	3	.222	.361	.282
August			0	0	0	0	0	—	—	—
Sept./Oct.	0-0	8.31	17	4	1	3	3	.235	.471	.350
Leading Off Inn.			81	22	2	9	7	.272	.395	.344
Runners On			148	42	5	14	16	.284	.493	.352
Runners/Scor. Pos.			86	26	4	8	8	.302	.581	.365
Runners On/2 Out			60	18	1	4	6	.300	.517	.354
Scor. Pos./2 Out			38	13	1	2	4	.342	.605	.390
Late Inning Pressure			19	3	2	7	2	.158	.474	.385
Leading Off			6	1	0	2	1	.167	.167	.375
Runners On			8	2	2	2	1	.250	1.000	.400
Runners/Scor. Pos.			3	2	2	2	0	.667	2.667	.800
First 9 Batters			140	35	4	18	15	.250	.400	.344
Second 9 Batters			112	28	2	9	11	.250	.366	.317
All Batters Thereafter			79	25	3	7	7	.316	.519	.375

Loves to face: Jim Sundberg (0-for-9, 3 SO)
Hates to face: Jim Gantner (.833, 5-for-6, 2 HR)
Ground outs-to-air outs ratio: 0.98 last season, 1.33 for career. . . . Additional statistics: 3 double-play ground outs in 72 opportunities, 8th-lowest average in A.L. (minimum: 40 opp.), 19 doubles, 2 triples in 84.2 innings last season. . . . Allowed 2 first-inning runs in 13 starts last season. . . . Batting support: 4.69 runs per start. . . . Has pitched in exactly 19 games in each of the last three seasons. What's he got, an incentive clause at 20? . . . Career batting average by opposing left-handed batters (.336) is 3d worst (minimum: 500 AB) in the 12 years we've been keeping track (see Mike Brown, Bill Swift). . . . Opponents' career batting: .287 with bases empty, .323 with runners on base, .331 with runners in scoring position.

Tom Seaver
White Sox/Red Sox   Throws Right

	W-L	ERA	AB	H	HR	BB	SO	BA	SA	OBA
Season	7-13	4.03	683	180	17	56	103	.264	.401	.323
vs. Left-Handers			348	97	8	32	52	.279	.437	.339
vs. Right-Handers			335	83	9	24	51	.248	.364	.306
Home	3-7	4.65	318	87	11	21	40	.274	.447	.323
Road	4-6	3.51	365	93	6	35	63	.255	.362	.323
Grass	5-11	4.15	551	147	15	43	81	.267	.416	.325
Artificial Turf	2-2	3.51	132	33	2	13	22	.250	.341	.315
April	2-2	2.79	107	22	2	7	14	.206	.318	.267
May	0-0	5.68	50	15	1	10	4	.300	.460	.419
June	0-4	5.34	116	29	6	10	13	.250	.474	.318
July	2-3	3.43	157	46	3	13	21	.293	.420	.347
August	3-2	3.51	159	41	4	9	38	.258	.371	.298
Sept./Oct.	0-2	4.88	94	27	1	7	13	.287	.394	.337
Leading Off Inn.			178	42	6	7	24	.236	.382	.269
Runners On			271	71	7	30	41	.262	.399	.335
Runners/Scor. Pos.			160	41	5	21	26	.256	.400	.335
Runners On/2 Out			120	29	2	13	21	.242	.325	.321
Scor. Pos./2 Out			75	20	2	10	14	.267	.400	.353
Late Inning Pressure			56	19	0	5	5	.339	.482	.397
Leading Off			18	6	0	0	0	.333	.500	.333
Runners On			21	7	0	2	3	.333	.381	.375
Runners/Scor. Pos.			12	3	0	1	1	.250	.333	.286
First 9 Batters			224	54	5	24	34	.241	.379	.316
Second 9 Batters			226	64	10	15	33	.283	.438	.331
All Batters Thereafter			233	62	2	17	36	.266	.386	.323

Loves to face: Eddie Murray (.120, 3-for-25, 11 SO)
Hates to face: Chris Bando (.714, 5-for-7, 1 HR)
Ground outs-to-air outs ratio: 1.20 last season, 1.09 for career. . . . Additional statistics: 14 double-play ground outs in 120 opportunities, 31 doubles, 6 triples in 176.1 innings last season. . . . Allowed 12 first-inning runs in 28 starts last season. . . . Batting support: 3.64 runs per start, 4th lowest in A.L. (minimum: 25 GS). . . . Has compiled a .603 winning percentage over his 20-year career. Discounting his own decisions, teams he has played for during that span have a .481 composite winning percentage. Approaches numbers of Cy Young, who won at a .620 clip for teams that played .484 ball without him. . . . Seaver's first game, April 13, 1967, was won for him in relief by Chuck Estrada; the loser was Vern Law.

Jeff Sellers
Boston Red Sox — Throws Right

	W–L	ERA	AB	H	HR	BB	SO	BA	SA	OBA
Season	3-7	4.94	319	90	13	40	51	.282	.448	.365
vs. Left-Handers			185	55	4	22	22	.297	.411	.373
vs. Right-Handers			134	35	9	18	29	.261	.500	.355
Home	2-4	4.81	186	52	9	20	28	.280	.478	.351
Road	1-3	5.13	133	38	4	20	23	.286	.406	.385
Grass	3-6	4.33	273	75	12	31	43	.275	.454	.351
Artificial Turf	0-1	8.74	46	15	1	9	8	.326	.413	.446
April			0	0	0	0	0	—	—	—
May			0	0	0	0	0	—	—	—
June	1-3	3.50	138	37	4	15	22	.268	.391	.346
July	2-3	6.00	120	35	6	19	18	.292	.467	.386
August			0	0	0	0	0	—	—	—
Sept./Oct.	0-1	6.19	61	18	3	6	11	.295	.541	.368
Leading Off Inn.			76	22	3	12	15	.289	.500	.393
Runners On			144	44	7	16	20	.306	.486	.370
Runners/Scor. Pos.			79	25	5	11	11	.316	.544	.391
Runners On/2 Out			50	15	3	9	6	.300	.500	.407
Scor. Pos./2 Out			30	9	2	7	3	.300	.533	.432
Late Inning Pressure			22	8	1	3	2	.364	.591	.440
Leading Off			8	4	1	1	1	.500	1.000	.556
Runners On			5	2	0	1	1	.400	.600	.500
Runners/Scor. Pos.			3	2	0	1	0	.667	1.000	.750
First 9 Batters			103	25	2	20	22	.243	.350	.373
Second 9 Batters			109	35	7	11	14	.321	.560	.385
All Batters Thereafter			107	30	4	9	15	.280	.430	.336

Loves to face: Jose Canseco (0-for-4, 2 SO)
Hates to face: Don Mattingly (.667, 2-for-3, 1 2B, 1 HR)
Ground outs-to-air outs ratio: 1.16 last season, 1.30 for career (1.97 vs. left-handers, 0.59 vs. right-handers).... Additional statistics: 12 double-play ground outs in 75 opportunities, 6th-highest average in A.L. (minimum: 10 GDP), 12 doubles, 1 triple in 82.0 innings last season.... Allowed 4 first-inning runs in 13 starts last season.... Batting support: 4.15 runs per start.... His three victories last season came in consecutive starts.... Opposing right-handed batters hit only .232 at Fenway last season, but belted six home runs in 82 at bats.... Opponents' career batting: .254 with bases empty, .313 with runners on base, .320 with runners in scoring position.

Bob Shirley
New York Yankees — Throws Left

	W–L	ERA	AB	H	HR	BB	SO	BA	SA	OBA
Season	0-4	5.04	398	108	13	40	64	.271	.427	.336
vs. Left-Handers			113	23	2	7	29	.204	.274	.252
vs. Right-Handers			285	85	11	33	35	.298	.488	.355
Home	0-4	5.46	240	71	8	26	39	.296	.446	.366
Road	0-0	4.47	158	37	5	14	25	.234	.399	.290
Grass	0-4	4.29	374	96	11	38	62	.257	.393	.325
Artificial Turf	0-0	21.21	24	12	2	2	2	.500	.958	.500
April	0-1	7.71	30	12	2	4	3	.400	.667	.486
May	0-1	4.34	107	25	2	13	18	.234	.336	.323
June	0-1	7.66	86	28	4	9	15	.326	.570	.378
July	0-1	5.40	67	21	4	4	13	.313	.433	.342
August	0-0	7.59	47	16	3	4	7	.340	.596	.392
Sept./Oct.	0-0	0.46	61	6	0	6	8	.098	.131	.176
Leading Off Inn.			92	23	5	6	14	.250	.457	.303
Runners On			175	57	8	18	30	.326	.537	.376
Runners/Scor. Pos.			110	31	3	8	24	.282	.427	.310
Runners On/2 Out			82	21	2	10	13	.256	.378	.337
Scor. Pos./2 Out			55	14	1	4	11	.255	.382	.305
Late Inning Pressure			75	20	2	2	8	.267	.427	.282
Leading Off			21	6	2	0	2	.286	.571	.286
Runners On			29	9	0	0	4	.310	.483	.300
Runners/Scor. Pos.			18	3	0	0	4	.167	.222	.158
First 9 Batters			220	63	6	26	46	.286	.436	.357
Second 9 Batters			121	33	5	10	11	.273	.455	.331
All Batters Thereafter			57	12	2	4	7	.211	.333	.262

Loves to face: Lou Whitaker (0-for-10, 3 SO)
Hates to face: Joe Carter (.636, 7-for-11)
Ground outs-to-air outs ratio: 0.89 last season, 1.01 for career.... Additional statistics: 4 double-play ground outs in 88 opportunities, 21 doubles, 1 triple in 105.1 innings last season.... Faced only one batter 3 times, pitched two or more innings 17 times, finished 9 games in 33 relief appearances.... June ERA was worst in A.L. (minimum: 20 IP).... Career averages: .217 (one extra-base hit per 20.7 at bats) vs. left-handers, .278 (one XBH per 11.4 AB) vs. right-handers.... Allowed two home runs to left-handed batters last season, equalling his career high.... Claims not to have walked Tony Armas intentionally to set up Dave Righetti's A.L. record-tying save situation on October 2, but nothing came near the plate. Who knows?

Jim Slaton
Angels/Tigers — Throws Right

	W–L	ERA	AB	H	HR	BB	SO	BA	SA	OBA
Season	4-6	5.08	445	130	14	40	43	.292	.467	.349
vs. Left-Handers			202	58	8	23	17	.287	.485	.357
vs. Right-Handers			243	72	6	17	26	.296	.453	.342
Home	2-2	4.06	256	74	7	21	27	.289	.441	.340
Road	2-4	6.43	189	56	7	19	16	.296	.503	.360
Grass	2-5	5.42	377	113	12	34	34	.300	.485	.354
Artificial Turf	2-1	3.38	68	17	2	6	9	.250	.368	.320
April	2-1	3.96	94	25	3	6	14	.266	.394	.311
May	2-3	5.09	140	41	3	16	11	.293	.436	.367
June	0-2	10.38	51	18	3	7	6	.353	.667	.410
July	0-0	2.89	37	9	0	3	3	.243	.324	.300
August	0-0	3.33	96	27	4	5	8	.281	.510	.320
Sept./Oct.	0-0	8.53	27	10	1	3	1	.370	.556	.419
Leading Off Inn.			108	34	3	7	11	.315	.509	.362
Runners On			199	57	9	22	20	.286	.492	.351
Runners/Scor. Pos.			111	30	6	18	8	.270	.486	.360
Runners On/2 Out			79	23	3	12	4	.291	.443	.398
Scor. Pos./2 Out			52	15	3	11	1	.288	.500	.431
Late Inning Pressure			33	12	0	5	3	.364	.515	.436
Leading Off			11	6	0	0	0	.545	.818	.545
Runners On			14	4	0	4	2	.286	.429	.421
Runners/Scor. Pos.			11	3	0	2	2	.273	.455	.357
First 9 Batters			223	67	7	23	21	.300	.502	.365
Second 9 Batters			127	32	3	8	11	.252	.346	.294
All Batters Thereafter			95	31	4	9	11	.326	.547	.380

Loves to face: Rickey Henderson (.125, 3-for-24)
Hates to face: Fred Lynn (.464, 26-for-56, 3 HR)
Ground outs-to-air outs ratio: 0.78 last season, 0.94 for career.... Additional statistics: 8 double-play ground outs in 95 opportunities, 28 doubles, 4 triples in 113.1 innings last season.... Allowed 16 first-inning runs in 12 starts, highest average in A.L. last season. Batting support: 4.67 runs per start.... 3–6, 6.33 ERA as a starter; 1–0 (2 saves), 3.47 ERA in 24 relief appearances.... Only active pitcher with at least 125 wins and a career winning percentage below .500 (151–158, .488).... Has won his last six decisions vs. the White Sox.... Don't tell Slaton that "you can't go home again." He has been reacquired by two of his former teams: Milwaukee (1971–77, 1979–83) and Detroit (1978, 1986). California, here he comes?

Mike Smithson
Minnesota Twins — Throws Right

	W–L	ERA	AB	H	HR	BB	SO	BA	SA	OBA
Season	13-14	4.77	796	234	26	57	114	.294	.462	.349
vs. Left-Handers			485	153	18	41	48	.315	.501	.368
vs. Right-Handers			311	81	8	16	66	.260	.402	.318
Home	9-6	4.34	449	135	13	26	73	.301	.457	.346
Road	4-8	5.32	347	99	13	31	41	.285	.470	.352
Grass	3-5	4.77	235	68	7	24	23	.289	.447	.357
Artificial Turf	10-9	4.77	561	166	19	33	91	.296	.469	.345
April	2-2	4.01	128	33	5	7	22	.258	.438	.292
May	3-2	3.40	190	56	4	12	23	.295	.447	.347
June	2-2	6.10	93	34	2	4	11	.366	.505	.404
July	1-3	9.86	91	32	6	9	12	.352	.648	.412
August	1-3	4.71	137	36	6	18	17	.263	.438	.361
Sept./Oct.	4-2	3.72	157	43	3	7	29	.274	.389	.313
Leading Off Inn.			196	58	8	12	32	.296	.505	.352
Runners On			354	107	9	22	44	.302	.435	.351
Runners/Scor. Pos.			202	59	4	19	31	.292	.401	.346
Runners On/2 Out			141	40	2	12	19	.284	.390	.344
Scor. Pos./2 Out			92	29	2	10	15	.315	.424	.382
Late Inning Pressure			52	14	2	6	10	.269	.423	.350
Leading Off			13	4	0	2	3	.308	.308	.438
Runners On			21	5	2	3	2	.238	.524	.320
Runners/Scor. Pos.			11	2	2	3	1	.182	.727	.333
First 9 Batters			276	90	16	18	37	.326	.580	.376
Second 9 Batters			238	70	7	13	35	.294	.458	.336
All Batters Thereafter			282	74	3	26	42	.262	.351	.332

Loves to face: Dick Schofield (0-for-15)
Hates to face: George Brett (.607, 17-for-28, 2 HR)
Ground outs-to-air outs ratio: 1.25 last season, 1.22 for career (0.97 vs. left-handers, 1.66 vs. right-handers).... Additional statistics: 24 double-play ground outs (6th in A.L.) in 162 opportunities, 50 doubles (3d most in A.L.), 3 triples in 198.0 innings last season. Allowed 79 extra-base hits, 5th most in A.L. after leading majors in two previous seasons.... Allowed 30 first-inning runs (3d most in A.L.) in 33 starts last season.... Batting support: 4.91 runs per start.... Only A.L. pitcher to complete three games in April.... July ERA was worst in A.L. (minimum: 20 IP).... Tied Twins' club record of 15 wild pitches set by Dave Goltz in 1976.... Opponents' career batting average of .164 (9-for-55) with the bases loaded.

Nate Snell
Baltimore Orioles — Throws Right

	W–L	ERA	AB	H	HR	BB	SO	BA	SA	OBA
Season	2-1	3.86	268	69	9	22	29	.257	.410	.313
vs. Left-Handers			104	28	4	9	9	.269	.452	.327
vs. Right-Handers			164	41	5	13	20	.250	.384	.304
Home	0-0	3.48	153	39	4	10	16	.255	.399	.295
Road	2-1	4.35	115	30	5	12	13	.261	.426	.336
Grass	1-1	3.88	212	57	6	15	23	.269	.406	.316
Artificial Turf	1-0	3.78	56	12	3	7	6	.214	.429	.302
April	0-0	2.70	10	0	0	1	1	.000	.000	.091
May	2-0	1.93	78	16	2	4	15	.205	.333	.244
June	0-0	4.38	47	13	1	6	7	.277	.383	.364
July	0-1	6.23	68	21	3	8	0	.309	.500	.377
August	0-0	2.45	13	3	0	0	1	.231	.385	.231
Sept./Oct.	0-0	4.38	52	16	3	3	5	.308	.519	.339
Leading Off Inn.			59	14	3	5	7	.237	.424	.297
Runners On			125	34	5	9	9	.272	.456	.319
Runners/Scor. Pos.			69	17	1	7	6	.246	.362	.313
Runners On/2 Out			54	13	1	6	3	.241	.352	.317
Scor. Pos./2 Out			33	7	0	4	3	.212	.303	.297
Late Inning Pressure			50	13	3	6	2	.260	.480	.339
Leading Off			12	4	1	2	0	.333	.583	.429
Runners On			25	6	2	1	0	.240	.520	.269
Runners/Scor. Pos.			14	3	1	1	0	.214	.286	.267
First 9 Batters			180	51	7	16	17	.283	.461	.340
Second 9 Batters			68	13	0	5	11	.191	.235	.247
All Batters Thereafter			20	5	2	1	1	.250	.550	.286

Loves to face: Jim Presley (0-for-6, 3 SO)
Hates to face: Bill Buckner (.600, 6-for-10, 2 HR)
Ground outs-to-air outs ratio: 2.12, 4th highest in A.L. last season (minimum: 250 BFP), 2.05 for career (1.40 vs. left-handers, 2.88 vs. right-handers). . . . Additional statistics: 11 double-play ground outs in 58 opportunities, 2d-highest average in A.L. (minimum: 10 GDP), 14 doubles, 0 triples in 72.1 innings last season. . . . Faced only one batter 2 times, pitched two or more innings 13 times, finished 18 games in 54 relief appearances. . . . Finished 18 games last season, most of any A.L. pitcher without a save. . . . Faced 81 consecutive batters without a strikeout from June 28 to Aug. 4. . . . Opponents have a career batting average of .215 with two outs and runners in scoring position.

Bob Stanley
Boston Red Sox — Throws Right

	W–L	ERA	AB	H	HR	BB	SO	BA	SA	OBA
Season	6-6	4.37	338	109	9	22	54	.322	.462	.360
vs. Left-Handers			154	52	3	15	16	.338	.442	.392
vs. Right-Handers			184	57	6	7	38	.310	.478	.332
Home	3-1	6.00	163	59	5	11	26	.362	.528	.395
Road	3-5	2.91	175	50	4	11	28	.286	.400	.326
Grass	5-4	4.83	266	93	7	20	41	.350	.481	.390
Artificial Turf	1-2	2.84	72	16	2	2	13	.222	.389	.243
April	0-1	4.70	34	11	1	1	4	.324	.412	.343
May	2-1	3.95	52	14	3	5	8	.269	.519	.328
June	3-0	3.32	78	21	0	3	11	.269	.321	.293
July	0-1	4.50	65	20	3	8	15	.308	.508	.378
August	0-2	7.07	61	25	2	3	6	.410	.623	.438
Sept./Oct.	1-1	3.00	48	18	0	2	10	.375	.396	.392
Leading Off Inn.			66	19	3	3	8	.288	.500	.319
Runners On			179	58	4	17	29	.324	.441	.375
Runners/Scor. Pos.			121	35	2	14	23	.289	.372	.353
Runners On/2 Out			70	14	1	11	16	.200	.286	.309
Scor. Pos./2 Out			49	9	1	9	12	.184	.245	.310
Late Inning Pressure			147	48	3	18	23	.327	.429	.395
Leading Off			24	6	2	3	1	.250	.500	.333
Runners On			85	29	1	13	15	.341	.435	.420
Runners/Scor. Pos.			60	19	1	11	12	.317	.433	.411
First 9 Batters			315	101	7	18	53	.321	.448	.353
Second 9 Batters			17	4	1	4	1	.235	.471	.381
All Batters Thereafter			6	4	1	0	0	.667	1.167	.667

Loves to face: Ernie Whitt (.143, 3-for-21, 5 SO)
Hates to face: Greg Walker (.833, 5-for-6, 2 HR)
Ground outs-to-air outs ratio: 2.11, 5th highest in A.L. last season (minimum: 250 BFP), 2.33 for career. . . . Additional statistics: 12 double-play ground outs in 96 opportunities, 16 doubles, 2 triples in 82.1 innings last season. . . . Faced only one batter 3 times, pitched two or more innings 12 times, finished 50 games in 65 relief appearances. . . . Does booing have an effect? Check home/road figures. What comes first, the booing or the egg? . . . Career average of one wild pitch per 105.2 innings. . . . Mickey Owen's name will forever live in infamy, but Hugh Casey's is only a footnote because tough-to-handle pitch in dirt was ruled an error on catcher. Similarly, official scorers' borderline wild pitch call guaranteed Stanley of a spot in baseball history, while Rich Gedman will escape blameless.

Dave Stewart
Oakland As — Throws Right

	W–L	ERA	AB	H	HR	BB	SO	BA	SA	OBA
Season	9-5	3.74	567	137	15	65	102	.242	.374	.321
vs. Left-Handers			284	67	7	35	45	.236	.366	.318
vs. Right-Handers			283	70	8	30	57	.247	.382	.324
Home	5-3	2.86	318	72	6	41	63	.226	.318	.313
Road	4-2	4.90	249	65	9	24	39	.261	.446	.331
Grass	8-4	3.64	474	116	10	53	84	.245	.361	.320
Artificial Turf	1-1	4.21	93	21	5	12	18	.226	.441	.324
April			0	0	0	0	0	—	—	—
May	0-0	3.00	12	4	0	1	1	.333	.333	.385
June	0-0	5.16	89	25	2	9	15	.281	.427	.350
July	4-0	3.52	140	27	5	15	23	.193	.343	.269
August	4-1	2.53	172	38	5	21	31	.221	.343	.308
Sept./Oct.	1-4	4.62	154	43	3	19	32	.279	.409	.360
Leading Off Inn.			140	36	6	14	23	.257	.464	.329
Runners On			238	51	4	33	44	.214	.303	.305
Runners/Scor. Pos.			144	31	2	19	30	.215	.306	.299
Runners On/2 Out			100	18	2	20	27	.180	.290	.317
Scor. Pos./2 Out			70	14	2	10	20	.200	.343	.300
Late Inning Pressure			62	15	0	8	9	.242	.274	.329
Leading Off			17	1	0	2	2	.059	.059	.158
Runners On			19	3	0	5	5	.158	.158	.333
Runners/Scor. Pos.			11	2	0	1	4	.182	.182	.250
First 9 Batters			217	51	8	21	45	.235	.387	.307
Second 9 Batters			169	39	6	23	27	.231	.391	.326
All Batters Thereafter			181	47	1	21	30	.260	.343	.332

Loves to face: Pat Corrales (1-for-1, KO)
Hates to face: Lou Whitaker (.875, 7-for-8, 4 BB)
Figures above are for A.L. only. . . . Ground outs-to-air outs ratio: 1.02 last season, 0.90 for career. . . . Additional statistics: 9 double-play ground outs in 116 opportunities, 25 doubles, 6 triples in 149.1 innings last season. . . . Allowed 8 first-inning runs in 17 starts last season. . . . 9–5, 3.35 ERA as a starter; 0–0, 5.61 ERA in 20 relief appearances (combined league totals). . . . Batting support: 4.12 runs per start. . . . 6–1 record vs. teams with winning records, 3–4 vs. teams below the .500 mark. . . . 5–0 vs. California, 0–5 vs. Minnesota. . . . One of four players to play for two different clubs in each of the last two seasons. One more trade wins him a free trip to Japan on Dick Littlefield Frequent Flier program.

Sammy Stewart
Boston Red Sox — Throws Right

	W–L	ERA	AB	H	HR	BB	SO	BA	SA	OBA
Season	4-1	4.38	241	64	7	48	47	.266	.415	.381
vs. Left-Handers			115	34	2	26	18	.296	.374	.423
vs. Right-Handers			126	30	5	22	29	.238	.452	.342
Home	4-0	3.13	115	27	1	22	25	.235	.313	.350
Road	0-1	5.63	126	37	6	26	22	.294	.508	.409
Grass	4-1	3.96	192	49	6	36	38	.255	.417	.365
Artificial Turf	0-0	6.35	49	15	1	12	9	.306	.408	.443
April	1-1	2.25	31	7	1	6	2	.226	.323	.351
May	2-0	0.56	59	11	0	8	10	.186	.203	.284
June	0-0	7.71	9	3	0	2	3	.333	.667	.417
July	0-0	8.10	12	3	1	2	2	.250	.667	.333
August	0-0	5.71	67	20	2	14	11	.299	.448	.410
Sept./Oct.	1-0	6.48	63	20	3	16	11	.317	.540	.450
Leading Off Inn.			53	12	2	8	8	.226	.396	.328
Runners On			121	29	4	26	28	.240	.388	.362
Runners/Scor. Pos.			71	16	1	20	17	.225	.310	.375
Runners On/2 Out			53	10	0	9	14	.189	.226	.306
Scor. Pos./2 Out			39	9	0	6	9	.231	.282	.333
Late Inning Pressure			77	16	1	8	17	.208	.299	.279
Leading Off			23	3	0	4	4	.130	.217	.130
Runners On			26	4	1	4	7	.154	.269	.258
Runners/Scor. Pos.			16	2	0	3	4	.125	.125	.250
First 9 Batters			188	50	6	36	38	.266	.431	.376
Second 9 Batters			53	14	1	11	9	.264	.358	.391
All Batters Thereafter			0	0	0	1	0	—	—	1.000

Loves to face: Tony Phillips (0-for-7, 5 SO)
Hates to face: Kirby Puckett (.833, 5-for-6)
Ground outs-to-air outs ratio: 0.75 last season, 1.01 for career. . . . Additional statistics: 6 double-play ground outs in 67 opportunities, 9 doubles, 3 triples in 63.2 innings last season. . . . Never faced only one batter, pitched two or more innings 21 times, finished 5 games in 27 relief appearances. . . . Has never allowed an earned run in 12 postseason innings; kept that streak intact by sitting out all 14 postseason games for Sox in '86. . . . Streak of 21 consecutive scoreless innings that began on opening day was snapped by an unearned run on May 31. . . . Fewest appearances (27) in any season since 1978, when he played two games in September as a rookie for the Orioles.

Dave Stieb

Toronto Blue Jays — Throws Right

	W–L	ERA	AB	H	HR	BB	SO	BA	SA	OBA
Season	7-12	4.74	805	239	29	87	127	.297	.476	.373
vs. Left-Handers			416	137	17	52	48	.329	.546	.410
vs. Right-Handers			389	102	12	35	79	.262	.401	.333
Home	5-5	3.93	504	147	13	53	77	.292	.448	.366
Road	2-7	6.17	301	92	16	34	50	.306	.522	.387
Grass	1-5	6.57	210	68	10	25	35	.324	.519	.407
Artificial Turf	6-7	4.14	595	171	19	62	92	.287	.461	.361
April	0-3	6.75	113	36	7	11	12	.319	.593	.388
May	1-3	5.36	151	43	6	20	28	.285	.470	.383
June	1-2	4.97	151	47	5	15	25	.311	.457	.371
July	1-2	5.01	93	28	5	13	12	.301	.570	.405
August	1-0	4.96	129	38	3	13	20	.295	.450	.364
Sept./Oct.	3-2	2.45	168	47	3	15	30	.280	.387	.346
Leading Off Inn.			198	53	8	18	29	.268	.455	.335
Runners On			356	113	13	35	52	.317	.494	.385
Runners/Scor. Pos.			183	56	4	19	29	.306	.437	.379
Runners On/2 Out			149	48	4	12	22	.322	.463	.380
Scor. Pos./2 Out			85	25	0	9	14	.294	.365	.375
Late Inning Pressure			42	19	4	6	6	.452	.857	.540
Leading Off			13	8	0	1	1	.615	.692	.643
Runners On			25	9	4	3	4	.360	.960	.467
Runners/Scor. Pos.			8	3	2	1	3	.375	1.250	.500
First 9 Batters			274	88	6	33	45	.321	.482	.404
Second 9 Batters			270	68	10	21	43	.252	.422	.322
All Batters Thereafter			261	83	13	33	39	.318	.525	.393

Loves to face: Tim Hulett (0-for-12, 5 SO)
Hates to face: Larry Parrish (.500, 15-for-30, 3 HR)
Ground outs-to-air outs ratio: 1.22 last season, 1.15 for career. . . . Additional statistics: 21 double-play ground outs in 184 opportunities, 43 doubles (8th most in A.L.), 7 triples in 205.0 innings last season. Allowed 79 extra-base hits, 5th-most in A.L. . . . Allowed 29 first-inning runs (4th most in A.L.) in 34 starts last season. . . . Batting support: 4.71 runs per start. . . . April ERA was 2d worst in A.L. (minimum: 20 IP). . . . Led A.L. in hit batters (15) for fourth time in past six seasons. Only three other pitchers have led A.L. four times: Howard Ehmke (6), Tommy Byrne (5), and Frank Lary (4). . . . Tied for A.L. lead with 15 no-decision starts last season. . . . Opponents' yearly batting averages since 1983: .219, .221, .213, .297.

Don Sutton

California Angels — Throws Right

	W–L	ERA	AB	H	HR	BB	SO	BA	SA	OBA
Season	15-11	3.74	795	192	31	49	116	.242	.411	.287
vs. Left-Handers			407	91	11	34	53	.224	.346	.282
vs. Right-Handers			388	101	20	15	63	.260	.479	.293
Home	10-6	3.23	482	111	19	30	69	.230	.400	.279
Road	5-5	4.58	313	81	12	19	47	.259	.428	.299
Grass	13-9	3.56	665	156	25	39	91	.235	.394	.279
Artificial Turf	2-2	4.68	130	36	6	10	25	.277	.500	.326
April	0-2	10.31	79	27	8	7	12	.342	.709	.391
May	2-3	4.78	107	34	4	2	14	.318	.542	.333
June	4-0	2.84	161	31	7	7	30	.193	.348	.231
July	3-2	2.94	127	29	3	8	21	.228	.378	.279
August	3-2	3.38	144	34	5	10	21	.236	.382	.286
Sept./Oct.	3-2	2.30	177	37	4	15	18	.209	.305	.269
Leading Off Inn.			209	42	9	8	31	.201	.354	.234
Runners On			267	72	9	19	37	.270	.434	.317
Runners/Scor. Pos.			133	35	7	15	20	.263	.489	.331
Runners On/2 Out			137	39	4	13	22	.285	.438	.347
Scor. Pos./2 Out			79	21	3	11	11	.266	.443	.356
Late Inning Pressure			41	9	3	3	7	.220	.463	.289
Leading Off			15	5	2	0	1	.333	.733	.333
Runners On			10	1	0	1	1	.100	.100	.250
Runners/Scor. Pos.			5	0	0	1	0	.000	.000	.167
First 9 Batters			285	65	10	19	34	.228	.382	.276
Second 9 Batters			265	69	10	14	46	.260	.426	.295
All Batters Thereafter			245	58	11	16	36	.237	.429	.291

Loves to face: Curtis Wilkerson (0-for-15, 4 SO)
Hates to face: Gary Gaetti (.429, 12-for-28, 3 HR)
Ground outs-to-air outs ratio: 0.86 last season, 0.89 for career. . . . Additional statistics: 11 double-play ground outs in 107 opportunities, 36 doubles, 3 triples in 207.0 innings last season. . . . Allowed 22 first-inning runs in 34 starts last season. . . . Batting support: 4.65 runs per start. . . . 10–5 vs. winning teams last season, 5–6 vs. teams below the .500 mark. . . . Has started 30 or more games in every season since 1969 (excluding 1981). . . . 21 major-league seasons, never been on the disabled list. . . . First home run he allowed in majors was hit by Ferguson Jenkins in 1966. . . . Total of 31 home runs allowed was 2d highest of his career. He surrendered 38 round-trippers in 1970.

Bill Swift

Seattle Mariners — Throws Right

	W–L	ERA	AB	H	HR	BB	SO	BA	SA	OBA
Season	2-9	5.46	464	148	5	55	55	.319	.416	.397
vs. Left-Handers			255	98	2	36	22	.384	.486	.463
vs. Right-Handers			209	50	3	19	33	.239	.330	.313
Home	2-3	4.23	247	76	2	31	36	.308	.372	.390
Road	0-6	6.88	217	72	3	24	19	.332	.465	.405
Grass	0-5	6.60	172	55	3	20	14	.320	.471	.399
Artificial Turf	2-4	4.77	292	93	2	35	41	.318	.384	.396
April	0-0	3.86	69	17	0	17	14	.246	.275	.395
May	0-3	6.58	114	40	0	8	13	.351	.412	.408
June	1-1	6.17	90	32	1	9	6	.356	.500	.417
July			0	0	0	0	0	—	—	—
August	1-1	4.57	82	21	2	9	10	.256	.354	.337
Sept./Oct.	0-4	5.61	109	38	2	12	12	.349	.486	.415
Leading Off Inn.			105	25	2	16	14	.238	.333	.350
Runners On			228	76	3	26	33	.333	.439	.399
Runners/Scor. Pos.			136	48	2	20	20	.353	.456	.431
Runners On/2 Out			95	28	1	11	16	.295	.379	.368
Scor. Pos./2 Out			60	17	0	8	10	.283	.333	.368
Late Inning Pressure			49	16	2	3	8	.327	.490	.377
Leading Off			14	3	2	0	3	.214	.643	.214
Runners On			16	6	0	1	4	.375	.375	.412
Runners/Scor. Pos.			8	2	0	1	2	.250	.250	.333
First 9 Batters			210	58	1	28	27	.276	.362	.366
Second 9 Batters			168	59	2	16	18	.351	.458	.414
All Batters Thereafter			86	31	2	11	10	.360	.465	.440

Loves to face: Willie Wilson (.077, 1-for-13, 3 SO)
Hates to face: Darrell Evans & Alan Trammell (.800, 4-for-5, 1 HR)
Ground outs-to-air outs ratio: 2.21, 3d highest in A.L. last season (minimum: 250 BFP), 2.23 for career. . . . Additional statistics: 17 double-play ground outs in 111 opportunities, 24 doubles, 3 triples in 115.1 innings last season. . . . Allowed 14 first-inning runs in 17 starts last season. . . . Batting support: 4.53 runs per start. . . . 2–9, 6.51 ERA as a starter; 0–0, 2.78 ERA in 12 relief appearances. Averaged 4.88 innings per start, fewest among A.L. pitchers (minimum: 15 GS). . . . Career averages: .346 (one extra-base hit per 10.3 at bats) vs. left-handers, .241 (one XBH per 22.1 AB) vs. right-handers. Career batting average by left-handers is the 2d worst in *Player Analysis* history (minimum: 500 AB).

Greg Swindell

Cleveland Indians — Throws Left

	W–L	ERA	AB	H	HR	BB	SO	BA	SA	OBA
Season	5-2	4.23	235	57	9	15	46	.243	.391	.290
vs. Left-Handers			26	4	0	1	3	.154	.192	.185
vs. Right-Handers			209	53	9	14	43	.254	.416	.302
Home	3-1	4.09	129	32	6	8	21	.248	.403	.297
Road	2-1	4.40	106	25	3	7	25	.236	.377	.281
Grass	5-1	4.21	176	42	7	12	31	.239	.381	.291
Artificial Turf	0-1	4.30	59	15	2	3	15	.254	.424	.286
April			0	0	0	0	0	—	—	—
May			0	0	0	0	0	—	—	—
June			0	0	0	0	0	—	—	—
July			0	0	0	0	0	—	—	—
August	0-1	4.91	45	12	1	4	7	.267	.333	.327
Sept./Oct.	5-1	4.09	190	45	8	11	39	.237	.405	.281
Leading Off Inn.			63	16	2	3	9	.254	.397	.288
Runners On			84	22	3	6	17	.262	.393	.315
Runners/Scor. Pos.			51	15	2	5	15	.294	.451	.351
Runners On/2 Out			35	10	0	2	6	.286	.314	.324
Scor. Pos./2 Out			22	8	0	2	6	.364	.409	.417
Late Inning Pressure			23	6	0	1	2	.261	.261	.292
Leading Off			8	2	0	0	1	.250	.250	.250
Runners On			5	2	0	0	0	.400	.400	.400
Runners/Scor. Pos.			3	0	0	0	0	.000	.000	.000
First 9 Batters			73	14	3	5	23	.192	.342	.244
Second 9 Batters			74	21	2	6	11	.284	.419	.333
All Batters Thereafter			88	22	4	4	12	.250	.409	.290

Loves to face: Tim Laudner (0-for-6, 2 SO)
Hates to face: Gary Gaetti (.714, 5-for-7, 1 HR)
Ground outs-to-air outs ratio: 0.83 last season, his first in majors. . . . Additional statistics: 1 double-play ground out in 40 opportunities, 3d-lowest average in A.L. (minimum: 40 opp.), 8 doubles, 0 triples in 61.2 innings last season. . . . Nine games last season were all starts. . . . Won five of his last six starts. . . . Only extra-base hit allowed to a left-handed batter was a double by Ernest Riles on Sept. 6. . . . If Scott Bailes remains in the starting rotation in 1987, the Tribe may have two southpaws starting as many as 20 games apiece for the first time since 1978 (Rick Waits and David Clyde).

Frank Tanana

Detroit Tigers — Throws Left

	W-L	ERA	AB	H	HR	BB	SO	BA	SA	OBA
Season	12-9	4.16	731	196	23	65	119	.268	.431	.328
vs. Left-Handers			123	39	2	7	12	.317	.447	.354
vs. Right-Handers			608	157	21	58	107	.258	.428	.323
Home	8-6	3.87	433	112	12	28	84	.259	.411	.303
Road	4-3	4.58	298	84	11	37	35	.282	.460	.364
Grass	12-7	3.71	649	168	17	58	108	.259	.408	.319
Artificial Turf	0-2	8.20	82	28	6	7	11	.341	.610	.400
April	3-1	3.13	117	28	2	12	16	.239	.385	.308
May	1-2	8.14	104	34	6	10	15	.327	.587	.386
June	3-1	2.41	148	34	4	16	23	.230	.372	.307
July	1-0	5.96	95	30	3	11	10	.316	.474	.387
August	2-2	4.31	126	39	3	7	19	.310	.437	.346
Sept./Oct.	2-3	3.13	141	31	5	9	36	.220	.383	.270
Leading Off Inn.			186	49	6	9	34	.263	.419	.301
Runners On			290	72	10	38	49	.248	.403	.330
Runners/Scor. Pos.			156	37	5	31	26	.237	.372	.354
Runners On/2 Out			125	31	5	14	30	.248	.408	.324
Scor. Pos./2 Out			75	22	4	10	17	.293	.507	.376
Late Inning Pressure			73	19	0	5	5	.260	.342	.308
Leading Off			17	4	0	3	0	.235	.235	.350
Runners On			28	7	0	2	4	.250	.321	.300
Runners/Scor. Pos.			12	5	0	1	0	.417	.583	.462
First 9 Batters			263	71	6	17	55	.270	.418	.318
Second 9 Batters			215	64	12	27	36	.298	.530	.372
All Batters Thereafter			253	61	5	21	28	.241	.360	.299

Loves to face: Ernie Whitt (0-for-7, 6 SO)
Hates to face: Paul Molitor (.438, 21-for-48, 1 HR)
Ground outs-to-air outs ratio: 0.91 last season, 0.99 for career. . . . Additional statistics: 18 double-play ground outs in 145 opportunities, 34 doubles, 8 triples (tied for 2d most in A.L.) in 188.1 innings last season. . . . Allowed 31 first-inning runs (2d most in majors) in 31 starts last season. . . . Batting support: 4.77 runs per start. . . . May ERA was worst in the majors (minimum: 20 IP), June ERA was 6th best in A.L. . . . Allowed only two home runs to left-handed batters last season. Both were hit by Red Sox: Boggs and Gedman. . . . Career winning percentage was .580 (91–66) after the 1979 season. It slipped to only three games over .500 (147–144) at the start of the 1986 season. Last season was his first winning season (12–9) since 1979.

Walt Terrell

Detroit Tigers — Throws Right

	W-L	ERA	AB	H	HR	BB	SO	BA	SA	OBA
Season	15-12	4.56	812	199	30	98	93	.245	.415	.328
vs. Left-Handers			422	102	11	52	38	.242	.389	.324
vs. Right-Handers			390	97	19	46	55	.249	.444	.331
Home	10-3	3.35	425	89	14	42	53	.209	.362	.281
Road	5-9	5.93	387	110	16	56	40	.284	.473	.376
Grass	15-9	4.20	699	163	26	78	80	.233	.392	.311
Artificial Turf	0-3	6.91	113	36	4	20	13	.319	.558	.422
April	2-1	6.08	94	29	5	10	7	.309	.511	.368
May	4-1	3.47	169	41	4	19	18	.243	.385	.317
June	1-4	4.75	130	32	4	20	12	.246	.408	.347
July	2-2	3.22	133	26	5	15	29	.195	.331	.287
August	2-3	5.85	149	33	6	23	14	.221	.409	.326
Sept./Oct.	4-1	4.67	137	38	6	11	13	.277	.482	.326
Leading Off Inn.			201	47	6	29	28	.234	.358	.330
Runners On			337	93	10	36	30	.276	.445	.347
Runners/Scor. Pos.			159	42	5	19	18	.264	.415	.337
Runners On/2 Out			121	31	5	21	11	.256	.471	.371
Scor. Pos./2 Out			71	18	2	15	9	.254	.408	.384
Late Inning Pressure			78	14	3	7	7	.179	.333	.256
Leading Off			24	7	1	2	1	.292	.458	.346
Runners On			22	4	1	2	2	.182	.409	.280
Runners/Scor. Pos.			12	3	1	2	2	.250	.667	.357
First 9 Batters			262	67	6	37	41	.256	.366	.350
Second 9 Batters			241	52	10	28	18	.216	.407	.297
All Batters Thereafter			309	80	14	33	34	.259	.463	.331

Loves to face: Bill Schroeder (0-for-6, 6 SO)
Hates to face: Jim Rice (.471, 8-for-17, 2 HR)
Ground outs-to-air outs ratio: 1.13 last season, 1.33 for career. . . . Additional statistics: 25 double-play ground outs (5th in A.L.) in 190 opportunities, 38 doubles, 5 triples in 217.1 innings last season. . . . Allowed 18 first-inning runs in 33 starts last season. . . . Batting support: 4.79 runs per start. . . . Only A.L. pitcher to complete four games during the month of May. . . . Allowed one home run per 27.1 at bats last season, compared to one per 96.1 at bats in 1985. . . . Has allowed more homers in road games (22) than in Tiger Stadium (17) over the last two seasons. . . . Career record of 7–2 in April, has won six of his first seven decisions in both seasons with Detroit.

Bob Tewksbury

New York Yankees — Throws Right

	W-L	ERA	AB	H	HR	BB	SO	BA	SA	OBA
Season	9-5	3.31	511	144	8	31	49	.282	.397	.325
vs. Left-Handers			266	67	6	13	21	.252	.380	.286
vs. Right-Handers			245	77	2	18	28	.314	.416	.365
Home	4-1	2.56	229	64	5	13	22	.279	.397	.319
Road	5-4	3.95	282	80	3	18	27	.284	.397	.330
Grass	8-4	3.24	434	123	6	28	36	.283	.389	.328
Artificial Turf	1-1	3.72	77	21	2	3	13	.273	.442	.305
April	2-1	3.33	104	27	2	4	10	.260	.462	.294
May	2-1	5.30	82	29	1	3	9	.354	.463	.376
June	1-0	2.45	117	35	1	6	9	.299	.368	.331
July	1-2	4.08	70	20	1	5	7	.286	.414	.333
August		—	0	0	0	0	0	—	—	—
Sept./Oct.	3-1	2.63	138	33	3	13	15	.239	.326	.310
Leading Off Inn.			133	41	2	5	13	.308	.429	.333
Runners On			218	61	2	14	18	.280	.349	.322
Runners/Scor. Pos.			122	33	0	11	7	.270	.320	.319
Runners On/2 Out			94	27	2	6	8	.287	.404	.337
Scor. Pos./2 Out			58	18	0	6	3	.310	.397	.375
Late Inning Pressure			35	9	0	3	0	.257	.343	.308
Leading Off			14	6	0	0	0	.429	.643	.429
Runners On			10	2	0	1	0	.200	.200	.250
Runners/Scor. Pos.			8	1	0	0	0	.125	.125	.111
First 9 Batters			186	53	3	14	20	.285	.366	.338
Second 9 Batters			163	46	3	10	18	.282	.405	.326
All Batters Thereafter			162	45	2	7	11	.278	.426	.308

Loves to face: Willie Upshaw (0-for-6)
Hates to face: Roy Smalley (2-for-2, 1 HR)
Ground outs-to-air outs ratio: 1.92 last season, his first in majors. . . . Additional statistics: 13 double-play ground outs in 101 opportunities, 21 doubles, 7 triples in 130.1 innings last season. . . . Allowed 10 first-inning runs in 20 starts. . . . Batting support: 5.00 runs per start. . . . Faced 40 batters in Late-Inning Pressure Situations without a strikeout, highest total in majors since 1980, when Jerry Augustine set the *Player Analysis* record that won't be broken (80). . . . 2.14 walks per nine innings, 2d best among major-league rookies (minimum: 81 innings). . . . Drabek, Nielsen, Tewksbury. After a year of talk by Yankee brass about the need to develop pitchers from within, only "Tewks" remains in pinstripes.

Frank Viola

Minnesota Twins — Throws Left

	W-L	ERA	AB	H	HR	BB	SO	BA	SA	OBA
Season	16-13	4.51	958	257	37	83	191	.268	.442	.327
vs. Left-Handers			154	42	5	8	21	.273	.409	.311
vs. Right-Handers			804	215	32	75	170	.267	.448	.330
Home	6-6	4.58	499	142	21	38	100	.285	.473	.338
Road	10-7	4.43	459	115	16	45	91	.251	.407	.316
Grass	8-6	4.16	382	92	14	35	74	.241	.403	.302
Artificial Turf	8-7	4.75	576	165	23	48	117	.286	.467	.343
April	3-1	2.97	139	32	3	15	29	.230	.309	.303
May	1-4	7.93	161	56	8	13	24	.348	.584	.398
June	4-1	3.48	166	42	5	17	40	.253	.416	.322
July	3-2	4.76	152	35	8	10	28	.230	.408	.278
August	2-2	4.46	155	41	5	15	25	.265	.445	.333
Sept./Oct.	3-3	3.91	185	51	8	13	45	.276	.465	.322
Leading Off Inn.			240	68	12	17	51	.283	.488	.333
Runners On			393	97	15	34	83	.247	.420	.306
Runners/Scor. Pos.			185	53	7	17	48	.286	.470	.338
Runners On/2 Out			159	37	2	14	35	.233	.352	.303
Scor. Pos./2 Out			86	22	0	9	24	.256	.372	.326
Late Inning Pressure			95	29	4	4	16	.305	.526	.337
Leading Off			27	7	2	0	8	.259	.519	.259
Runners On			33	12	2	2	8	.364	.667	.405
Runners/Scor. Pos.			20	8	1	0	6	.400	.750	.381
First 9 Batters			302	68	7	23	84	.225	.358	.281
Second 9 Batters			291	74	14	27	53	.254	.450	.318
All Batters Thereafter			365	115	16	33	54	.315	.504	.371

Loves to face: Rick Cerone (.056, 1-for-18)
Hates to face: Lee Lacy (.429, 9-for-21, 2 HR)
Ground outs-to-air outs ratio: 0.72 last season, 0.78 for career. . . . Additional statistics: 16 double-play ground outs in 200 opportunities, 45 doubles (5th most in A.L.), 5 triples in 245.2 innings last season. Allowed 87 extra-base hits, 3d most in majors. . . . Allowed 15 first-inning runs in 37 starts last season. . . . Batting support: 4.89 runs per start. . . . May ERA was 2d worst in the major leagues (minimum: 20 IP). . . . 10–6 vs. teams with winning records, 6–7 vs. teams below the .500 mark. . . . Allowed 32 homers to right-handed batters, most in the 12-year history of the *Player Analysis*. . . . Has won more games over the past three seasons (52) than any other left-hander in baseball. . . . Opponents' annual batting averages in Late-Inning Pressure Situations since 1984: .185, .204, .305.

Bill Wegman

Milwaukee Brewers · Throws Right

	W–L	ERA	AB	H	HR	BB	SO	BA	SA	OBA
Season	5-12	5.13	777	217	32	43	82	.279	.463	.321
vs. Left-Handers			437	117	19	29	42	.268	.446	.313
vs. Right-Handers			340	100	13	14	40	.294	.485	.331
Home	2-5	5.06	429	123	15	17	49	.287	.459	.319
Road	3-7	5.22	348	94	17	26	33	.270	.468	.323
Grass	4-9	5.16	684	190	29	40	71	.278	.463	.321
Artificial Turf	1-3	4.84	93	27	3	3	11	.290	.462	.320
April	0-1	4.07	95	26	3	8	6	.274	.442	.330
May	0-4	4.96	182	53	7	10	18	.291	.500	.333
June	2-1	5.61	128	34	5	4	18	.266	.438	.299
July	1-3	5.53	107	28	2	6	8	.262	.346	.304
August	1-1	4.40	165	45	8	7	21	.273	.461	.306
Sept./Oct.	1-2	6.66	100	31	7	8	11	.310	.580	.358
Leading Off Inn.			197	54	11	11	19	.274	.487	.313
Runners On			296	91	10	15	31	.307	.480	.340
Runners/Scor. Pos.			159	52	5	9	16	.327	.503	.353
Runners On/2 Out			126	44	6	9	12	.349	.603	.393
Scor. Pos./2 Out			80	29	4	4	9	.363	.638	.393
Late Inning Pressure			74	18	1	3	8	.243	.378	.273
Leading Off			20	4	0	1	2	.200	.350	.238
Runners On			25	6	1	1	3	.240	.400	.269
Runners/Scor. Pos.			10	2	0	1	2	.200	.200	.273
First 9 Batters			282	69	13	15	34	.245	.418	.291
Second 9 Batters			262	80	10	15	23	.305	.492	.343
All Batters Thereafter			233	68	9	13	25	.292	.485	.332

Loves to face: Brett Butler & Mel Hall (.083, 1-for-12)
Hates to face: Bill Bathe (2-for-2, 2 HR)
Ground outs-to-air outs ratio: 0.94 last season, 0.99 for career. . . . Additional statistics: 20 double-play ground outs in 135 opportunities, 37 doubles, 5 triples in 198.1 innings last season. . . . Allowed 15 first-inning runs in 32 starts last season. . . . Batting support: 4.03 runs per start. . . . Tied for A.L. lead with 15 no-decision starts last season. Led league with 15 starts in games decided by one run. . . . Allowed 32 home runs, most among major-league rookies. . . . Allowed an average of 1.95 walks per nine innings, best among major-league rookies (minimum: 81 innings). . . . Pitched more innings than any rookie except Ed Correa. . . . ERA was 4th highest among A.L. starting pitchers.

Milt Wilcox

Seattle Mariners · Throws Right

	W–L	ERA	AB	H	HR	BB	SO	BA	SA	OBA
Season	0-8	5.50	226	74	11	28	26	.327	.553	.399
vs. Left-Handers			123	46	8	19	12	.374	.650	.455
vs. Right-Handers			103	28	3	9	14	.272	.437	.330
Home	0-3	5.48	86	23	4	13	13	.267	.488	.370
Road	0-5	5.51	140	51	7	15	13	.364	.593	.418
Grass	0-3	4.34	79	27	4	12	9	.342	.506	.424
Artificial Turf	0-5	6.08	147	47	7	16	17	.320	.578	.386
April	0-4	5.59	75	25	4	15	11	.333	.560	.435
May	0-2	3.49	109	29	4	11	12	.266	.450	.339
June	0-2	12.38	42	20	3	2	3	.476	.810	.489
July			0	0	0	0	0	—	—	—
August			0	0	0	0	0	—	—	—
Sept./Oct.			0	0	0	0	0	—	—	—
Leading Off Inn.			53	16	5	4	12	.302	.604	.362
Runners On			102	31	2	12	10	.304	.431	.368
Runners/Scor. Pos.			54	17	2	7	5	.315	.481	.375
Runners On/2 Out			49	17	1	7	5	.347	.490	.429
Scor. Pos./2 Out			31	11	1	6	2	.355	.516	.459
Late Inning Pressure			20	7	2	0	1	.350	.800	.350
Leading Off			4	2	1	0	1	.500	1.250	.500
Runners On			9	3	1	0	0	.333	.778	.333
Runners/Scor. Pos.			8	3	1	0	0	.375	.875	.375
First 9 Batters			94	26	4	13	13	.277	.479	.361
Second 9 Batters			85	31	4	5	11	.365	.576	.398
All Batters Thereafter			47	17	3	10	2	.362	.660	.474

Loves to face: Tony Phillips (0-for-16)
Hates to face: Carney Lansford (.429, 24-for-56, 5 HR)
Ground outs-to-air outs ratio: 0.89 last season, 1.17 for career. . . . Additional statistics: 6 double-play ground outs in 53 opportunities, 14 doubles, 2 triples in 55.2 innings last season. . . . Allowed 6 first-inning runs in 10 starts last season. . . . Batting support: 2.70 runs per start, 2d lowest in A.L. (minimum: 10 GS). . . . Lasted an average of 4.87 innings in his 10 starts. . . . Opponents' yearly batting averages since 1983: .237, .252, .315, .327. . . . Has lost 11 of 12 decisions since his victory over the Padres in Game 3 on the 1984 World Series, snapping streak of seven consecutive winning seasons. . . . Was once traded for Ted Uhlaender.

Mitch Williams

Texas Rangers · Throws Left

	W–L	ERA	AB	H	HR	BB	SO	BA	SA	OBA
Season	8-6	3.58	341	69	8	79	90	.202	.331	.366
vs. Left-Handers			118	24	3	19	29	.203	.322	.331
vs. Right-Handers			223	45	5	60	61	.202	.336	.384
Home	3-3	3.46	180	38	5	37	44	.211	.350	.350
Road	5-3	3.72	161	31	3	42	46	.193	.311	.372
Grass	6-5	3.20	280	56	5	69	68	.200	.304	.373
Artificial Turf	2-1	5.51	61	13	3	10	22	.213	.459	.333
April	1-0	5.14	25	7	1	5	5	.280	.400	.419
May	2-0	0.00	41	4	0	4	15	.098	.195	.178
June	3-1	3.32	72	18	3	13	26	.250	.486	.379
July	1-1	4.05	68	17	1	18	15	.250	.338	.424
August	1-2	2.96	89	13	1	22	18	.146	.202	.327
Sept./Oct.	0-2	7.30	46	10	2	17	11	.217	.413	.439
Leading Off Inn.			69	14	3	15	18	.203	.362	.368
Runners On			183	40	4	39	47	.219	.344	.371
Runners/Scor. Pos.			112	20	2	30	31	.179	.286	.358
Runners On/2 Out			81	19	2	20	20	.235	.383	.392
Scor. Pos./2 Out			58	10	1	16	15	.172	.293	.351
Late Inning Pressure			186	42	4	46	49	.226	.355	.392
Leading Off			38	7	1	7	11	.184	.289	.326
Runners On			100	25	2	24	23	.250	.390	.412
Runners/Scor. Pos.			61	12	1	18	14	.197	.311	.386
First 9 Batters			321	64	7	74	86	.199	.327	.363
Second 9 Batters			20	5	1	5	4	.250	.400	.423
All Batters Thereafter			0	0	0	0	0	—	—	—

Loves to face: Lloyd Moseby (0-for-6, 3 SO)
Hates to face: Billy Jo Robidoux (2-for-2, 1 HR)
Ground outs-to-air outs ratio: 0.89 last season, his first in majors. . . . Additional statistics: 16 double-play ground outs in 100 opportunities, 14 doubles, 3 triples in 98.0 innings last season. . . . Faced only one batter 6 times, pitched two or more innings 16 times, finished 38 games in 80 relief appearances. . . . Texas lost all seven games in which he allowed a home run. . . . First rookie to lead A.L. in appearances (80) since Ed Vande Berg in 1982. . . . Allowed 6.34 hits per nine innings, struck out 8.27 batters per nine innings; both figures were 4th best among A.L. relievers (minimum: 40 games). . . . On the negative side, he allowed 7.26 walks per nine innings. No other A.L. reliever (minimum: 40 games) averaged more than 5.00.

Bobby Witt

Texas Rangers · Throws Right

	W–L	ERA	AB	H	HR	BB	SO	BA	SA	OBA
Season	11-9	5.48	583	130	18	143	174	.223	.369	.374
vs. Left-Handers			314	78	7	86	81	.248	.382	.409
vs. Right-Handers			269	52	11	57	93	.193	.353	.330
Home	6-3	4.00	333	69	9	69	94	.207	.333	.345
Road	5-6	7.45	250	61	9	74	80	.244	.416	.410
Grass	10-8	5.58	520	118	17	131	155	.227	.375	.380
Artificial Turf	1-1	4.67	63	12	1	12	19	.190	.317	.320
April	2-0	3.80	71	11	1	24	27	.155	.225	.361
May	0-4	7.53	105	25	6	29	14	.238	.467	.401
June	2-2	6.39	118	31	2	27	37	.263	.390	.412
July	1-3	8.47	64	15	2	18	21	.234	.391	.412
August	2-0	3.86	100	23	2	22	34	.230	.330	.363
Sept./Oct.	4-0	3.71	125	25	5	23	41	.200	.368	.322
Leading Off Inn.			133	33	6	36	40	.248	.414	.412
Runners On			281	65	8	72	90	.231	.374	.380
Runners/Scor. Pos.			176	39	5	53	58	.222	.341	.389
Runners On/2 Out			119	28	2	34	37	.235	.370	.405
Scor. Pos./2 Out			91	20	1	30	30	.220	.341	.413
Late Inning Pressure			22	7	0	1	5	.318	.409	.348
Leading Off			6	1	0	1	1	.167	.167	.286
Runners On			6	4	0	0	0	.667	.833	.667
Runners/Scor. Pos.			2	1	0	0	0	.500	.500	.500
First 9 Batters			220	48	8	53	74	.218	.391	.367
Second 9 Batters			198	44	6	60	58	.222	.348	.405
All Batters Thereafter			165	38	4	30	42	.230	.364	.343

Loves to face: Tom Brunansky (0-for-8, 7 SO)
Hates to face: Chet Lemon (2-for-2, 1 HR)
Also loves to face: Robin Yount (0-for-9, 6 SO). . . . Ground outs-to-air outs ratio: 0.89 last season, his first in majors. . . . Additional statistics: 6 double-play ground outs in 149 opportunities, 7th-lowest average in A.L. (minimum: 40 opp.), 31 doubles, 0 triples in 157.2 innings last season. . . . Allowed 22 first-inning runs in 31 starts last season. . . . Batting support: 5.03 runs per start. . . . Set A.L. single-season record with 22 wild pitches. He pitched only 157.2 innings, more than 50 fewer than any of the three men who previously shared the record. Old record of 21 was set by Walter Johnson (374 IP in 1910) and equalled by Earl Wilson (211 IP in 1963) and Nolan Ryan (299 IP in 1977). . . . Averaged a walk an inning through the end of July.

Mike Witt
California Angels — Throws Right

	W-L	ERA	AB	H	HR	BB	SO	BA	SA	OBA
Season	18-10	2.84	987	218	22	73	208	.221	.335	.275
vs. Left-Handers			578	124	15	43	104	.215	.339	.270
vs. Right-Handers			409	94	7	30	104	.230	.330	.282
Home	11-5	2.62	510	106	12	37	114	.208	.331	.261
Road	7-5	3.09	477	112	10	36	94	.235	.340	.290
Grass	17-9	2.83	876	196	20	69	177	.224	.337	.280
Artificial Turf	1-1	2.97	111	22	2	4	31	.198	.324	.239
April	2-1	2.91	130	31	2	9	31	.238	.323	.291
May	2-3	3.43	154	37	3	18	30	.240	.338	.322
June	4-2	3.42	191	47	7	13	40	.246	.382	.298
July	3-1	2.59	177	39	4	11	39	.220	.339	.265
August	5-0	0.21	147	17	1	8	28	.116	.170	.161
Sept./Oct.	2-3	4.21	188	47	5	14	40	.250	.420	.299
Leading Off Inn.			257	47	4	20	59	.183	.265	.242
Runners On			363	86	12	31	67	.237	.386	.295
Runners/Scor. Pos.			174	46	8	18	31	.264	.448	.325
Runners On/2 Out			153	38	6	14	31	.248	.412	.331
Scor. Pos./2 Out			84	26	4	9	15	.310	.476	.376
Late Inning Pressure			158	38	4	11	30	.241	.354	.295
Leading Off			44	8	1	2	8	.182	.250	.217
Runners On			56	17	3	5	10	.304	.500	.359
Runners/Scor. Pos.			23	8	1	5	5	.348	.522	.433
First 9 Batters			287	57	7	19	80	.199	.321	.250
Second 9 Batters			280	63	5	20	52	.225	.311	.275
All Batters Thereafter			420	98	10	34	76	.233	.362	.293

Loves to face: Jerry Hairston (0-for-14)
Hates to face: John Shelby (.417, 10-for-24, 2 HR)
Ground outs-to-air outs ratio: 1.41 last season, 1.52 for career.... Additional statistics: 29 double-play ground outs (most in A.L.) in 183 opportunities, 39 doubles, 4 triples in 269.0 innings last season. ... Allowed 11 first-inning runs in 34 starts last season.... Batting support: 5.24 runs per start.... Pitched at least seven innings 29 times, tying for A.L. lead.... Won seven consecutive starts from July 28 to Aug. 28.... Opponents stole only five bases in 15 attempts last season, including only one success in last 10 tries.... One of two pitchers to hold opponents below .250 in Late-Inning Pressure Situations each of last six years; other: Nolan Ryan.... Opposing left-handers' yearly batting averages since 1983: .307, .258, .263, .215.

Rich Yett
Cleveland Indians — Throws Right

	W-L	ERA	AB	H	HR	BB	SO	BA	SA	OBA
Season	5-3	5.15	306	84	10	37	50	.275	.428	.351
vs. Left-Handers			170	46	3	18	23	.271	.382	.337
vs. Right-Handers			136	38	7	19	27	.279	.485	.367
Home	3-1	5.49	154	48	5	18	32	.312	.474	.381
Road	2-2	4.81	152	36	5	19	18	.237	.382	.320
Grass	5-3	4.98	281	78	8	34	47	.278	.423	.353
Artificial Turf	0-0	7.11	25	6	2	3	3	.240	.480	.321
April	0-0	5.79	19	6	0	0	3	.316	.421	.316
May	2-0	4.11	58	16	1	7	12	.276	.379	.353
June	1-0	4.22	40	12	1	6	9	.300	.400	.383
July	1-1	6.38	72	20	4	7	10	.278	.514	.338
August	0-1	9.00	56	18	2	8	5	.321	.518	.406
Sept./Oct.	1-1	2.16	61	12	2	9	11	.197	.311	.300
Leading Off Inn.			66	12	2	8	9	.182	.318	.270
Runners On			128	42	4	21	18	.328	.492	.416
Runners/Scor. Pos.			76	26	2	17	10	.342	.513	.449
Runners On/2 Out			68	24	3	13	10	.353	.574	.457
Scor. Pos./2 Out			45	15	1	10	4	.333	.511	.455
Late Inning Pressure			50	15	3	8	9	.300	.520	.400
Leading Off			11	2	1	2	2	.182	.455	.308
Runners On			23	8	1	4	3	.348	.565	.448
Runners/Scor. Pos.			14	5	1	4	3	.357	.571	.500
First 9 Batters			212	53	6	26	35	.250	.382	.329
Second 9 Batters			68	22	1	8	14	.324	.441	.395
All Batters Thereafter			26	9	3	3	1	.346	.769	.414

Loves to face: Larry Parrish (0-for-5, 2 SO)
Hates to face: Scott Fletcher (.750, 3-for-4, 2 2B, 1 HR)
Ground outs-to-air outs ratio: 0.74 last season, 0.74 for career.... Additional statistics: 3 double-play ground outs in 54 opportunities, 15 doubles, 1 triple in 78.2 innings last season. ... Faced only one batter once, pitched two or more innings 15 times, finished 17 games in 36 relief appearances. ... A.L.'s top 15 batters hit .550 against him (11-for-20), highest vs. any A.L. pitcher (minimum: 20 at bats). ... Opponents batted .429 (6-for-14, 1 HR) with the bases loaded. ... Yett another member of the Cleveland-Minnesota Pitchers Exchange Program that includes Bert Blyleven, John Butcher, George Frazier (via the Cubs), Neal Heaton, Bryan Oelkers, Ramon Romero, Ken Schrom, Roy Smith, and Curt Wardle.

Curt Young
Oakland As — Throws Left

	W-L	ERA	AB	H	HR	BB	SO	BA	SA	OBA
Season	13-9	3.45	745	176	19	57	116	.236	.365	.293
vs. Left-Handers			146	32	1	10	30	.219	.260	.286
vs. Right-Handers			599	144	18	47	86	.240	.391	.295
Home	9-2	2.37	442	88	9	31	69	.199	.299	.260
Road	4-7	5.19	303	88	10	26	47	.290	.462	.341
Grass	11-7	3.11	668	153	17	46	103	.229	.353	.282
Artificial Turf	2-2	6.75	77	23	2	11	13	.299	.468	.385
April			0	0	0	0	0	—	—	—
May	3-1	2.60	131	31	2	6	18	.237	.366	.282
June	2-4	4.35	156	37	3	16	24	.237	.359	.309
July	2-1	3.41	117	30	1	12	16	.256	.333	.321
August	3-2	3.32	159	41	5	12	30	.258	.403	.310
Sept./Oct.	3-1	3.44	182	37	8	11	28	.203	.357	.255
Leading Off Inn.			192	48	6	11	25	.250	.422	.304
Runners On			293	75	10	24	48	.256	.403	.310
Runners/Scor. Pos.			163	40	6	15	33	.245	.393	.305
Runners On/2 Out			122	26	3	15	17	.213	.320	.309
Scor. Pos./2 Out			75	16	2	10	11	.213	.320	.322
Late Inning Pressure			63	12	1	4	9	.190	.302	.246
Leading Off			21	7	0	1	2	.333	.429	.391
Runners On			16	2	1	1	1	.125	.313	.167
Runners/Scor. Pos.			9	1	1	0	1	.111	.444	.100
First 9 Batters			227	52	6	23	34	.229	.366	.302
Second 9 Batters			229	53	7	18	36	.231	.362	.288
All Batters Thereafter			289	71	6	16	46	.246	.367	.290

Loves to face: Bill Buckner (0-for-11)
Hates to face: Gorman Thomas (.750, 3-for-4, 2 HR)
Ground outs-to-air outs ratio: 0.74 last season, 0.74 for career.... Additional statistics: 7 double-play ground outs in 135 opportunities, 33 doubles, 3 triples in 198.0 innings last season.... Allowed 18 first-inning runs in 27 starts last season.... Batting support: 4.22 runs per start.... Averaged 7.05 innings per start, highest on A's staff.... Career averages: .236 (one extra-base hit per 24.3 at bats) vs. left-handers, .267 (one XBH per 9.8 AB) vs. right-handers. ... Led A's with 27 starts last season, lowest total to lead any major-league team.... Visibly upset to the point of removing himself from the game when his inside pitch broke Mike Pagliarulo's nose (May 30).

Matt Young
Seattle Mariners — Throws Left

	W-L	ERA	AB	H	HR	BB	SO	BA	SA	OBA
Season	8-6	3.82	397	108	9	46	82	.272	.401	.357
vs. Left-Handers			129	27	2	13	35	.209	.310	.306
vs. Right-Handers			268	81	7	33	47	.302	.444	.381
Home	6-2	3.52	233	57	4	23	50	.245	.343	.331
Road	2-4	4.31	164	51	5	23	32	.311	.482	.394
Grass	2-4	4.94	130	42	5	18	22	.323	.531	.403
Artificial Turf	6-2	3.34	267	66	4	28	60	.247	.337	.334
April	2-2	6.30	83	26	2	12	10	.313	.458	.402
May	2-1	3.13	88	25	3	14	17	.284	.455	.394
June	3-1	1.84	50	7	2	3	15	.140	.300	.204
July	0-0	1.83	76	21	1	5	18	.276	.342	.321
August	0-1	5.25	40	9	1	5	10	.225	.375	.327
Sept./Oct.	1-1	5.02	60	20	0	7	12	.333	.417	.420
Leading Off Inn.			74	19	0	10	12	.257	.324	.345
Runners On			236	60	3	23	55	.254	.360	.332
Runners/Scor. Pos.			150	37	3	16	37	.247	.387	.333
Runners On/2 Out			107	31	2	13	26	.290	.449	.377
Scor. Pos./2 Out			77	22	2	10	19	.286	.468	.375
Late Inning Pressure			180	52	4	15	43	.289	.417	.355
Leading Off			33	10	0	1	5	.303	.394	.324
Runners On			113	30	2	9	30	.265	.381	.333
Runners/Scor. Pos.			74	20	2	5	21	.270	.419	.337
First 9 Batters			297	78	5	38	64	.263	.377	.355
Second 9 Batters			69	20	3	6	12	.290	.464	.355
All Batters Thereafter			31	10	1	2	6	.323	.484	.382

Loved to face: Wade Boggs (.053, 1-for-19)
Hated to face: Dave Kingman (.667, 6-for-9, 4 HR)
Ground outs-to-air outs ratio: 1.90 last season, 1.67 for career (1.27 on grass surfaces, 1.91 on artificial turf).... Additional statistics: 15 double-play ground outs in 110 opportunities, 20 doubles, 2 triples in 103.2 innings last season.... Faced only one batter 7 times (5th most in A.L.), pitched two or more innings 17 times, finished 32 games in 60 relief appearances.... 2–3, 6.30 ERA in 5 starts; 6–3 (13 saves), 3.23 ERA in relief.... Lasted an average of four innings in his starts; that includes one complete game.... April ERA was 3d worst in A.L.... Opponents' career batting average of .381 (24-for-63, 4 HR) with the bases loaded.

Baltimore Orioles

	W–L	ERA	AB	H	HR	BB	SO	BA	SA	OBA
Season	73-89	4.30	5518	1451	177	535	954	.263	.418	.328
vs. Left-Handers			2165	566	67	227	356	.261	.417	.331
vs. Right-Handers			3353	885	110	308	598	.264	.419	.326
Home	37-42	4.11	2769	739	98	279	493	.267	.420	.335
Road	36-47	4.50	2749	712	79	256	461	.259	.417	.322
Grass	59-78	4.35	4703	1260	153	464	810	.268	.422	.334
Artificial Turf	14-11	4.07	815	191	24	71	144	.234	.396	.297
April	10-10	3.79	662	158	18	67	113	.239	.382	.311
May	18-8	3.76	871	226	25	81	167	.259	.410	.323
June	11-17	4.58	945	247	35	100	150	.261	.432	.332
July	16-11	3.66	928	225	28	74	177	.242	.381	.299
August	10-19	4.30	1001	271	30	82	169	.271	.410	.324
Sept./Oct.	8-24	5.39	1111	324	41	131	178	.292	.473	.365
Leading Off Inn.			1328	378	56	107	201	.285	.474	.340
Runners On			2428	664	75	230	443	.273	.427	.333
Runners/Scor. Pos.			1365	372	40	168	244	.273	.431	.344
Runners On/2 Out			1007	263	29	105	199	.261	.401	.331
Scor. Pos./2 Out			645	174	21	84	120	.270	.434	.354
Late Inning Pressure			946	264	34	109	152	.279	.449	.353
Leading Off			241	70	10	20	32	.290	.473	.345
Runners On			400	114	11	54	66	.285	.438	.366
Runners/Scor. Pos.			231	63	3	45	37	.273	.403	.384
First 9 Batters			2590	697	82	271	455	.269	.426	.337
Second 9 Batters			1499	362	36	141	268	.241	.368	.306
All Batters Thereafter			1429	392	59	123	231	.274	.456	.335

Starting pitchers: 54–69, 4.42 ERA
Relief pitchers: 19–20, 4.07 ERA
Ground outs-to-air outs ratio: 1.07. . . . First A.L. team to post progressively lower winning percentages in three consecutive seasons since Minnesota Twins of 1980–82. . . . Only team in either league with five pitchers who started at least 25 games each last season. . . . Opposing batters hit .279 in Late-Inning Pressure Situations, highest mark against Orioles in 12-year history of *The Player Analysis*. . . . Highest ERA in A.L. after September 1. . . . Record of 8–20 was team's worst ever during the month of September, and third losing September in a row following an 11-year winning streak. . . . Also was worst full-month record of Weaver's career. Sad to see Earl go out that way.

Boston Red Sox

	W–L	ERA	AB	H	HR	BB	SO	BA	SA	OBA
Season	95-66	3.93	5516	1469	167	474	1033	.266	.414	.325
vs. Left-Handers			2615	730	65	246	412	.279	.417	.341
vs. Right-Handers			2901	739	102	228	621	.255	.410	.310
Home	51-30	3.98	2859	788	85	223	563	.276	.423	.329
Road	44-36	3.89	2657	681	82	251	470	.256	.403	.320
Grass	82-55	3.91	4720	1270	146	399	897	.269	.415	.326
Artificial Turf	13-11	4.05	796	199	21	75	136	.250	.403	.316
April	11-8	2.93	621	136	15	59	134	.219	.348	.286
May	21-7	3.52	947	229	38	71	188	.242	.418	.296
June	17-10	3.88	934	258	20	82	151	.276	.395	.335
July	10-16	4.86	921	269	32	88	159	.292	.461	.353
August	17-13	4.28	1018	275	37	81	193	.270	.424	.324
Sept./Oct.	19-12	3.87	1075	302	25	93	208	.281	.412	.339
Leading Off Inn.			1328	365	46	100	222	.275	.438	.328
Runners On			2359	617	67	230	443	.262	.399	.324
Runners/Scor. Pos.			1329	335	34	150	256	.252	.380	.320
Runners On/2 Out			983	227	27	98	215	.231	.357	.305
Scor. Pos./2 Out			622	148	15	66	139	.238	.355	.315
Late Inning Pressure			878	233	18	82	162	.265	.376	.329
Leading Off			216	50	8	14	34	.231	.384	.281
Runners On			365	100	6	45	70	.274	.378	.352
Runners/Scor. Pos.			212	57	2	32	40	.269	.363	.357
First 9 Batters			2537	668	60	258	524	.263	.390	.331
Second 9 Batters			1436	410	58	113	251	.286	.467	.338
All Batters Thereafter			1543	391	49	103	258	.253	.402	.301

Starting pitchers: 77–56 (most wins in A.L.), 3.74 ERA (lowest in A.L.)
Relief pitchers: 18–10 (fewest losses in majors), 4.53 ERA
Ground outs-to-air outs ratio: 1.04. . . . Haven't led A.L. in ERA since 1914, but led the league as late as August 9 last season. . . . Won 10 consecutive one-run decisions from June 10 through July 2, longest A.L. streak since Toronto won 19 in a row in 1984. . . . Have won 89 consecutive home games in which they led after eight innings. Last loss: Sept. 7, 1984, vs. New York. . . . Allowed 58 first-inning runs, fewest in A.L. . . . Opposing batters had a lower batting average with runners in scoring position than overall for fifth consecutive season, longest current streak in majors.

California Angels

	W–L	ERA	AB	H	HR	BB	SO	BA	SA	OBA
Season	92-70	3.84	5476	1356	153	478	955	.248	.385	.309
vs. Left-Handers			2720	664	66	264	412	.244	.371	.311
vs. Right-Handers			2756	692	87	214	543	.251	.399	.306
Home	50-32	3.60	2776	664	84	226	479	.239	.383	.297
Road	42-38	4.09	2700	692	69	252	476	.256	.387	.321
Grass	80-58	3.76	4677	1145	130	418	811	.245	.380	.307
Artificial Turf	12-12	4.33	799	211	23	60	144	.264	.413	.318
April	13-8	4.65	693	178	23	71	139	.257	.400	.326
May	10-17	4.82	911	252	25	97	142	.277	.430	.347
June	17-10	4.29	914	238	36	74	147	.260	.419	.317
July	15-11	3.04	900	208	18	83	172	.231	.349	.299
August	19-10	3.34	963	214	31	76	167	.222	.359	.279
Sept./Oct.	18-14	3.26	1095	266	20	77	188	.243	.361	.293
Leading Off Inn.			1341	314	31	113	242	.234	.357	.296
Runners On			2263	614	71	193	380	.271	.422	.324
Runners/Scor. Pos.			1177	333	43	129	202	.283	.450	.344
Runners On/2 Out			970	262	32	99	173	.270	.420	.338
Scor. Pos./2 Out			561	154	18	70	98	.275	.421	.356
Late Inning Pressure			969	234	30	92	187	.241	.376	.311
Leading Off			248	56	8	20	52	.226	.371	.289
Runners On			386	103	13	37	69	.267	.409	.327
Runners/Scor. Pos.			203	59	7	28	33	.291	.443	.362
First 9 Batters			2600	645	72	244	385	.248	.385	.314
Second 9 Batters			1480	369	40	115	234	.249	.378	.302
All Batters Thereafter			1396	342	41	119	243	.245	.393	.306

Starting pitchers: 70–56, 3.85 ERA
Relief pitchers: 22–14, 3.82 ERA
Ground outs-to-air outs ratio: 1.11. . . . Only A.L. team to retire more than 70 percent of opposing leadoff batters. . . . Led A.L. in night-game ERA (3.59). . . . Used fewest left-handed starters of any team in majors last season (16). . . . Still another irony to Game Five loss in A.L.C.S.: Angels have won every regular-season home game in which they led after eight innings for two consecutive seasons. Current streak: 92 in a row. Last loss: Aug. 11, 1984, vs. Oakland. . . . Opposing batters hit 40 points better with runners on base than with the bases empty, largest difference in majors last season. . . . Allowed 33 home runs with two or more runners on base, most in majors.

Chicago White Sox

	W–L	ERA	AB	H	HR	BB	SO	BA	SA	OBA
Season	72-90	3.93	5424	1361	143	561	895	.251	.392	.323
vs. Left-Handers			2338	581	64	275	354	.249	.395	.328
vs. Right-Handers			3086	780	79	286	541	.253	.390	.318
Home	41-40	3.64	2731	655	63	271	477	.240	.373	.309
Road	31-50	4.24	2693	706	80	290	418	.262	.411	.336
Grass	62-73	3.81	4492	1104	112	461	756	.246	.382	.317
Artificial Turf	10-17	4.51	932	257	31	100	139	.276	.441	.347
April	7-12	4.85	650	170	15	68	93	.262	.405	.333
May	11-16	3.70	949	249	21	116	137	.262	.387	.343
June	15-13	4.79	946	246	27	102	149	.260	.427	.334
July	11-15	4.29	859	225	25	64	120	.262	.412	.334
August	12-17	3.73	951	242	28	104	177	.254	.394	.330
Sept./Oct.	16-17	2.79	1069	229	27	107	219	.214	.340	.293
Leading Off Inn.			1333	326	30	109	206	.245	.377	.305
Runners On			2279	589	59	274	375	.258	.392	.337
Runners/Scor. Pos.			1332	331	37	188	232	.248	.391	.337
Runners On/2 Out			954	228	21	113	158	.239	.352	.322
Scor. Pos./2 Out			612	143	15	87	100	.234	.353	.333
Late Inning Pressure			1021	266	17	104	162	.261	.379	.331
Leading Off			260	71	3	19	31	.273	.373	.325
Runners On			445	121	4	56	77	.272	.393	.354
Runners/Scor. Pos.			262	73	3	44	40	.279	.405	.381
First 9 Batters			2783	693	69	301	508	.249	.387	.324
Second 9 Batters			1482	382	49	142	221	.258	.416	.338
All Batters Thereafter			1159	286	25	118	166	.247	.373	.318

Starting pitchers: 51–66, 4.19 ERA
Relief pitchers: 21–24, 3.46 ERA
Ground outs-to-air outs ratio: 1.07. . . . Led A.L. in ERA after September 1. . . . Lost 14 games in which they led after seven innings, most in majors. . . . One of two teams in majors without a pitcher who worked at least 200 innings. The other: Oakland. . . . Lost seven consecutive one-run decisions (May 24–June 18), for third consecutive season. In fact, in 1984 they had two streaks at least that long. . . . Used relief pitchers to face just one batter 36 times, highest total in majors. . . . Eight different pitchers started at least 10 games last season, tying Oakland for highest total in majors.

Cleveland Indians

	W–L	ERA	AB	H	HR	BB	SO	BA	SA	OBA
Season	84-78	4.58	5662	1548	167	605	744	.273	.415	.346
vs. Left-Handers			2616	730	63	286	303	.279	.408	.350
vs. Right-Handers			3046	818	104	319	441	.269	.422	.343
Home	45-35	4.44	2876	788	80	298	374	.274	.407	.346
Road	39-43	4.72	2786	760	87	307	370	.273	.424	.346
Grass	73-64	4.49	4772	1306	135	531	614	.274	.409	.349
Artificial Turf	11-14	5.03	890	242	32	74	130	.272	.449	.331
April	11-8	3.29	634	156	13	91	104	.246	.358	.340
May	12-16	5.47	966	277	22	111	114	.287	.406	.364
June	15-11	4.39	891	250	36	98	122	.281	.458	.358
July	15-12	4.11	940	251	24	84	110	.267	.403	.328
August	12-19	5.44	1132	331	41	136	126	.292	.451	.369
Sept./Oct.	19-12	4.22	1099	283	31	85	168	.258	.396	.314
Leading Off Inn.			1316	379	43	122	164	.288	.448	.355
Runners On			2619	701	68	326	330	.268	.400	.347
Runners/Scor. Pos.			1482	405	36	243	192	.273	.408	.368
Runners On/2 Out			1102	293	26	158	135	.266	.396	.363
Scor. Pos./2 Out			704	187	16	129	88	.266	.403	.384
Late Inning Pressure			909	246	26	131	130	.271	.404	.365
Leading Off			216	59	8	24	34	.273	.426	.349
Runners On			418	118	9	76	50	.282	.411	.391
Runners/Scor. Pos.			246	72	6	63	30	.293	.427	.433
First 9 Batters			2680	725	69	320	387	.271	.400	.350
Second 9 Batters			1506	432	45	136	181	.287	.432	.350
All Batters Thereafter			1476	391	53	149	176	.265	.426	.335

Starting pitchers: 55–53, 4.33 ERA
Relief pitchers: 29–25, 5.33 ERA
Ground outs-to-air outs ratio: 1.00 (3d lowest in A.L.).... Opponents grounded into one double play for every 11.96 opportunities, 2d-lowest rate in A.L. ... Fewest strikeouts in A.L. for second consecutive season.... Led majors for second consecutive season by hitting 57 opposing batters with pitches, highest total in either league since Seattle hit 61 in 1977.... Highest night-game ERA in A.L. (4.78), ranked 7th in day games (4.18); highest during months of May and August as well.... Young pitching staff with exception of Niekro: Average age of other winning pitchers was 27.5 years. Only three teams had lower averages.

Detroit Tigers

	W–L	ERA	AB	H	HR	BB	SO	BA	SA	OBA
Season	87-75	4.02	5475	1374	183	571	880	.251	.410	.323
vs. Left-Handers			2278	545	66	236	334	.239	.382	.311
vs. Right-Handers			3197	829	117	335	546	.259	.429	.332
Home	49-32	3.25	2792	657	83	255	454	.235	.377	.302
Road	38-43	4.84	2683	717	100	316	426	.267	.444	.345
Grass	78-60	3.78	4657	1151	145	467	732	.247	.396	.317
Artificial Turf	9-15	5.45	818	223	38	104	148	.273	.488	.358
April	10-9	4.61	679	194	28	56	97	.286	.473	.338
May	13-13	4.26	871	214	29	114	154	.246	.403	.334
June	14-15	4.18	967	247	32	105	156	.255	.407	.331
July	17-11	3.15	940	218	22	101	167	.232	.357	.308
August	14-16	4.79	1004	263	36	107	127	.262	.438	.337
Sept./Oct.	19-11	3.37	1014	238	36	88	179	.235	.395	.296
Leading Off Inn.			1329	331	49	113	201	.249	.405	.311
Runners On			2288	582	65	277	345	.254	.399	.333
Runners/Scor. Pos.			1252	298	32	191	213	.238	.371	.333
Runners On/2 Out			981	237	28	136	181	.242	.382	.337
Scor. Pos./2 Out			607	135	18	99	122	.222	.366	.333
Late Inning Pressure			863	213	27	84	134	.247	.386	.314
Leading Off			213	52	4	18	25	.244	.352	.303
Runners On			347	90	10	38	53	.259	.386	.334
Runners/Scor. Pos.			187	51	4	27	30	.273	.406	.364
First 9 Batters			2509	646	80	261	450	.257	.414	.330
Second 9 Batters			1445	345	49	160	217	.239	.397	.316
All Batters Thereafter			1521	383	54	150	213	.252	.415	.319

Starting pitchers: 70–54, 4.15 ERA
Relief pitchers: 17–21, 3.69 ERA
Ground outs-to-air outs ratio: 1.08.... Opponents grounded into one double play for every 9.35 opportunities, 2d-highest rate in A.L. ... Lowest home-game ERA in A.L., but ranked 12th in road games.... Ranked last in league in ERA on artificial surfaces.... Allowed 117 first-inning runs, highest total in majors last season. ... One of two A.L. teams not to lose more than three consecutive home games last season. The other: Kansas City.... Best record in Eastern Division after the All-Star break (44–31).... Issued 60 intentional walks, highest total in A.L. last season.

Kansas City Royals

	W–L	ERA	AB	H	HR	BB	SO	BA	SA	OBA
Season	76-86	3.82	5477	1413	121	479	888	.258	.384	.319
vs. Left-Handers			2301	617	52	217	377	.268	.399	.332
vs. Right-Handers			3176	796	69	262	511	.251	.373	.310
Home	45-36	3.40	2848	727	46	229	444	.255	.370	.312
Road	31-50	4.28	2629	686	75	250	444	.261	.399	.327
Grass	25-37	4.24	2004	511	59	189	332	.255	.390	.320
Artificial Turf	51-49	3.58	3473	902	62	290	556	.260	.380	.319
April	9-10	3.50	628	150	13	60	80	.239	.352	.307
May	14-14	3.32	942	232	16	78	178	.246	.350	.306
June	14-15	4.09	993	264	20	77	164	.266	.398	.320
July	9-17	4.55	908	242	32	81	141	.267	.427	.329
August	14-14	3.78	939	244	19	73	153	.260	.389	.313
Sept./Oct.	16-16	3.65	1067	281	21	110	172	.263	.379	.335
Leading Off Inn.			1343	360	25	94	179	.268	.373	.321
Runners On			2345	612	47	249	393	.261	.380	.331
Runners/Scor. Pos.			1325	347	25	187	235	.262	.376	.348
Runners On/2 Out			974	237	26	121	180	.243	.377	.334
Scor. Pos./2 Out			620	142	18	102	125	.229	.360	.345
Late Inning Pressure			886	216	18	107	143	.244	.352	.330
Leading Off			233	71	5	15	32	.305	.416	.349
Runners On			373	83	5	59	63	.223	.295	.336
Runners/Scor. Pos.			194	44	2	52	37	.227	.278	.395
First 9 Batters			2626	663	52	243	454	.252	.368	.318
Second 9 Batters			1530	418	46	132	238	.273	.436	.331
All Batters Thereafter			1321	332	23	104	196	.251	.356	.308

Starting pitchers: 57–64, 4.14 ERA
Relief pitchers: 19–22, 3.10 ERA (lowest in A.L.)
Ground outs-to-air outs ratio: 1.17 (2d highest in A.L.).... Allowed fewest home runs in A.L. for second consecutive season.... Lost only five games in which they led after six innings (tied for fewest in majors), including all 34 home games.... One of three A.L. teams not to win more than four consecutive games last season. The others: Minnesota and Seattle.... Relief pitchers faced an average of 8.00 batters, 2d-highest total in majors last season; 56 relief appearances lasted at least three innings, highest total in either league.... Led A.L. with a 3.82 ERA after the All-Star break.

Milwaukee Brewers

	W–L	ERA	AB	H	HR	BB	SO	BA	SA	OBA
Season	77-84	4.01	5536	1478	158	494	952	.267	.405	.328
vs. Left-Handers			2049	553	61	231	306	.270	.410	.343
vs. Right-Handers			3487	925	97	263	646	.265	.402	.318
Home	41-39	4.02	2845	752	79	236	491	.264	.399	.321
Road	36-45	4.00	2691	726	79	258	461	.270	.412	.334
Grass	66-71	3.94	4724	1251	134	437	805	.265	.401	.327
Artificial Turf	11-13	4.46	812	227	24	57	147	.280	.433	.330
April	9-9	3.58	602	149	20	73	116	.248	.394	.329
May	15-13	3.89	938	251	25	86	163	.268	.413	.331
June	13-15	3.57	945	241	22	77	154	.255	.383	.314
July	12-13	3.69	847	213	17	95	138	.251	.348	.325
August	15-15	4.72	1091	318	34	75	202	.291	.438	.336
Sept./Oct.	13-19	4.32	1113	306	40	88	179	.275	.436	.329
Leading Off Inn.			1317	373	47	114	192	.283	.446	.342
Runners On			2442	671	63	229	414	.275	.406	.334
Runners/Scor. Pos.			1371	358	35	148	260	.261	.397	.324
Runners On/2 Out			1026	272	31	111	170	.265	.416	.339
Scor. Pos./2 Out			654	160	18	77	120	.245	.396	.325
Late Inning Pressure			941	234	15	107	184	.249	.348	.325
Leading Off			237	71	6	22	33	.300	.447	.359
Runners On			417	103	6	50	88	.247	.341	.326
Runners/Scor. Pos.			217	54	3	37	57	.249	.350	.354
First 9 Batters			2665	692	66	244	508	.260	.387	.323
Second 9 Batters			1538	424	47	136	248	.276	.418	.336
All Batters Thereafter			1333	362	45	114	196	.272	.428	.328

Starting pitchers: 54–65, 4.29 ERA
Relief pitchers: 23–19, 3.48 ERA
Ground outs-to-air outs ratio: 0.91 (lowest in majors).... Led A.L. in ERA through games of August 29, but compiled an 8.61 mark over next 11 games and couldn't challenge thereafter despite strong rebound (2.63 through end of season).... Lost only five games in which they led after six innings, tied for fewest in majors.... Only team in majors to win every home game in which it led after seven innings (29 games).... Left-handers pitched 606.1 innings last season, 2d-highest total in A.L. behind New York.... Used relief pitchers to face an average of 8.13 batters, highest average in majors last season; relievers faced just one batter only nine times, the major-league low.

Minnesota Twins

	W–L	ERA	AB	H	HR	BB	SO	BA	SA	OBA
Season	71-91	4.77	5619	1579	200	503	937	.281	.454	.342
vs. Left-Handers			2398	666	87	230	365	.278	.453	.341
vs. Right-Handers			3221	913	113	273	572	.283	.455	.343
Home	43-38	4.67	2966	857	107	239	521	.289	.467	.343
Road	28-53	4.88	2653	722	93	264	416	.272	.441	.341
Grass	22-40	4.92	2026	550	73	197	307	.271	.439	.339
Artificial Turf	49-51	4.68	3593	1029	127	306	630	.286	.463	.344
April	8-13	4.92	714	192	26	66	122	.269	.429	.334
May	11-16	5.38	954	292	35	85	135	.306	.491	.365
June	14-13	4.52	957	266	23	82	160	.278	.442	.337
July	10-16	5.21	887	251	38	84	139	.283	.469	.348
August	12-17	4.10	1000	265	36	104	165	.265	.436	.337
Sept./Oct.	16-16	4.62	1107	313	42	82	216	.283	.455	.333
Leading Off Inn.			1329	387	52	98	249	.291	.485	.345
Runners On			2487	701	85	251	395	.282	.447	.347
Runners/Scor. Pos.			1415	399	50	173	252	.282	.447	.355
Runners On/2 Out			998	258	30	100	182	.259	.416	.333
Scor. Pos./2 Out			637	161	20	72	133	.253	.405	.336
Late Inning Pressure			837	253	30	94	141	.302	.480	.374
Leading Off			211	57	9	13	47	.270	.445	.319
Runners On			345	119	13	55	55	.345	.542	.430
Runners/Scor. Pos.			219	70	10	41	37	.320	.534	.415
First 9 Batters			2547	707	76	255	460	.278	.438	.346
Second 9 Batters			1534	442	66	120	239	.288	.480	.341
All Batters Thereafter			1538	430	58	128	238	.280	.455	.336

Starting pitchers: 56–65, 4.52 ERA
Relief pitchers: 15–26 (tied for fewest wins in majors), 5.51 ERA (highest in majors)
Ground outs-to-air outs ratio: 1.02. . . . Highest ERA in American League for third time in team's history, all since moving to Metrodome in 1982. . . . Also led league with 39 complete games, to become first A.L. team to finish last in ERA and first in CG since the 1916 Philadelphia A's. . . . Lost 17 games in which they led after six innings, most in A.L. . . . Opposing batters hit .302 in Late-Inning Pressure Situations, highest mark in majors since 1980, when Seattle set *Player Analysis* record of .304. . . . Made the record books for average of .345 with runners on base in LIP situations, 18 points higher than previous worst, set in 1975 by Chicago Cubs.

New York Yankees

	W–L	ERA	AB	H	HR	BB	SO	BA	SA	OBA
Season	90-72	4.11	5564	1461	175	492	878	.263	.410	.323
vs. Left-Handers			1821	487	56	201	265	.267	.414	.340
vs. Right-Handers			3743	974	119	291	613	.260	.408	.314
Home	41-39	4.31	2846	779	96	234	455	.274	.423	.329
Road	49-33	3.91	2718	682	79	258	423	.251	.396	.317
Grass	71-65	4.12	4691	1235	147	423	741	.263	.408	.324
Artificial Turf	19-7	4.03	873	226	28	69	137	.259	.422	.314
April	14-6	3.52	695	182	15	66	104	.262	.393	.327
May	16-12	4.13	953	233	26	88	177	.244	.376	.308
June	12-16	5.14	993	277	34	106	124	.279	.438	.345
July	14-12	3.89	891	245	29	61	151	.275	.432	.324
August	14-15	4.30	997	265	35	82	185	.266	.422	.322
Sept./Oct.	20-11	3.53	1035	259	36	89	137	.250	.395	.311
Leading Off Inn.			1351	352	38	90	215	.261	.388	.310
Runners On			2354	645	73	245	357	.274	.423	.339
Runners/Scor. Pos.			1334	351	37	167	217	.263	.400	.337
Runners On/2 Out			1003	256	24	117	143	.255	.371	.336
Scor. Pos./2 Out			640	165	14	81	100	.258	.370	.344
Late Inning Pressure			969	244	24	93	162	.252	.380	.318
Leading Off			245	60	7	16	42	.245	.363	.291
Runners On			386	103	6	47	60	.267	.376	.342
Runners/Scor. Pos.			240	60	4	33	41	.250	.358	.333
First 9 Batters			2846	741	81	256	518	.260	.397	.322
Second 9 Batters			1530	388	55	122	220	.254	.412	.309
All Batters Thereafter			1188	332	39	114	140	.279	.437	.343

Starting pitchers: 63–55, 4.16 ERA
Relief pitchers: 27–17, 4.02 ERA
Ground outs-to-air outs ratio: 1.01. . . . Ranked last in majors with 13 complete games for first time since 1918. . . . Highest ERA in A.L. during the month of June. . . . Used four consecutive rookie starting pitchers (Drabek, Nielsen, Pulido, Tewksbury), July 6–7–8 –9. They hadn't used as many as *three* in a row since 1947 (Vic Raschi, Dick Starr, Karl Drews). . . . Lost 10 consecutive home games from May 26 through June 29, longest streak in A.L. last season. . . . Won all 44 road games in which they led after eight innings. . . . Only American League team to start left-handed pitchers in half its games last season.

Oakland A's

	W–L	ERA	AB	H	HR	BB	SO	BA	SA	OBA
Season	76-86	4.31	5407	1334	166	667	937	.247	.394	.330
vs. Left-Handers			2469	635	68	353	375	.257	.396	.350
vs. Right-Handers			2938	699	98	314	562	.238	.392	.314
Home	47-36	3.80	2817	638	81	377	511	.226	.352	.319
Road	29-50	4.89	2590	696	85	290	426	.269	.439	.343
Grass	62-75	4.16	4558	1110	132	567	784	.244	.382	.328
Artificial Turf	14-11	5.16	849	224	34	100	153	.264	.456	.345
April	11-10	3.59	678	142	23	72	145	.209	.375	.287
May	12-16	4.63	954	249	32	126	136	.261	.418	.346
June	7-22	4.76	960	246	28	123	179	.256	.399	.341
July	14-12	3.94	888	215	22	108	151	.242	.372	.325
August	17-11	4.19	928	232	30	118	155	.250	.398	.337
Sept./Oct.	15-15	4.52	999	250	31	120	171	.250	.394	.332
Leading Off Inn.			1284	309	46	143	208	.241	.407	.322
Runners On			2331	595	71	332	405	.255	.403	.345
Runners/Scor. Pos.			1383	350	30	216	256	.253	.376	.346
Runners On/2 Out			990	229	28	155	179	.231	.363	.340
Scor. Pos./2 Out			654	145	10	109	127	.222	.312	.338
Late Inning Pressure			895	226	21	130	162	.253	.372	.347
Leading Off			222	47	4	26	26	.212	.311	.300
Runners On			378	101	9	72	73	.267	.399	.379
Runners/Scor. Pos.			225	65	4	47	44	.289	.396	.400
First 9 Batters			2600	634	76	342	501	.244	.390	.332
Second 9 Batters			1440	363	55	180	223	.252	.418	.336
All Batters Thereafter			1367	337	35	145	213	.247	.375	.320

Starting pitchers: 61–57, 4.29 ERA
Relief pitchers: 15–29 (most losses in A.L.), 4.38 ERA
Ground outs-to-air outs ratio: 1.00 (2d lowest in A.L.). . . . Opponents grounded into one double play for every 14.33 opportunities, lowest rate in A.L. . . . Lost 10 consecutive one-run games from June 19 through July 11, the franchise's longest streak since losing the last 11 one-run games it played in Kansas City. . . . Lost 15 consecutive road games from May 24 through June 29, longest streak in majors last season. . . . First team since 1980 without a pitcher who made at least 30 starts. Padres and Mets had none in 1980, Oakland none in 1979. A's leader last season: Curt Young (27). . . . Set an A.L. record with 19 balks. Previous mark was set in 1985 by Seattle. . . . Highest road-game ERA in A.L.

Seattle Mariners

	W–L	ERA	AB	H	HR	BB	SO	BA	SA	OBA
Season	67-95	4.65	5626	1590	171	585	944	.283	.441	.353
vs. Left-Handers			2428	699	68	279	343	.288	.434	.365
vs. Right-Handers			3198	891	103	306	601	.279	.446	.344
Home	41-41	4.53	2924	799	99	308	544	.273	.437	.346
Road	26-54	4.79	2702	791	72	277	400	.293	.445	.361
Grass	17-44	4.95	2031	592	58	224	314	.291	.441	.364
Artificial Turf	50-51	4.48	3595	998	113	361	630	.278	.441	.347
April	7-14	4.08	704	196	22	103	109	.278	.429	.372
May	11-17	5.34	1007	299	34	116	156	.297	.461	.373
June	14-15	4.84	998	288	27	80	164	.289	.448	.344
July	13-12	4.63	895	263	24	76	131	.294	.464	.352
August	13-16	4.38	953	238	32	109	179	.250	.396	.327
Sept./Oct.	9-21	4.48	1069	306	32	101	205	.286	.444	.332
Leading Off Inn.			1299	355	45	136	212	.273	.438	.348
Runners On			2589	745	70	272	417	.288	.433	.355
Runners/Scor. Pos.			1569	430	41	179	280	.274	.416	.344
Runners On/2 Out			1063	283	23	139	189	.266	.394	.354
Scor. Pos./2 Out			726	176	15	102	131	.242	.364	.338
Late Inning Pressure			988	296	33	95	187	.300	.467	.366
Leading Off			234	69	14	22	39	.295	.526	.363
Runners On			457	140	12	46	91	.306	.457	.374
Runners/Scor. Pos.			285	83	8	33	56	.291	.453	.367
First 9 Batters			2706	737	78	300	470	.272	.433	.347
Second 9 Batters			1530	427	43	147	265	.279	.423	.345
All Batters Thereafter			1390	426	50	138	209	.306	.476	.372

Starting pitchers: 44–75 (fewest wins, most losses in A.L.), 4.87 ERA (highest in majors)
Relief pitchers: 23–20, 4.24 ERA
Ground outs-to-air outs ratio: 1.31 (highest in A.L.). . . . Opponents grounded into one double play for every 8.57 opportunities, highest rate in A.L. . . . Retired only 65.2 percent of opposing leadoff batters, lowest average in majors Twins sat down only 64.7 percent in 1983. . . . One of two A.L. teams without a road-game shutout last season. The other: Oakland. . . . Lost 19 of 20 one-run decisions in road games, including their last 17. . . . Allowed 23 innings of five runs or more, most in majors last season. . . . Relief pitchers faced an average of 6.42 batters per appearance, 2d-lowest mark in A.L.

Texas Rangers

	W-L	ERA	AB	H	HR	BB	SO	BA	SA	OBA
Season	87-75	4.11	5455	1356	145	736	1059	.249	.380	.340
vs. Left-Handers			2412	617	54	332	431	.256	.377	.347
vs. Right-Handers			3043	739	91	404	628	.243	.383	.334
Home	51-30	3.72	2791	683	61	329	561	.245	.359	.327
Road	36-45	4.52	2664	673	84	407	498	.253	.403	.353
Grass	77-59	3.92	4549	1109	116	628	884	.244	.369	.338
Artificial Turf	10-16	5.11	906	247	29	108	175	.273	.437	.352
April	9-10	4.82	641	183	12	90	117	.285	.398	.372
May	15-13	3.54	936	214	21	135	167	.229	.357	.328
June	16-13	4.17	988	241	22	129	206	.244	.366	.332
July	12-14	4.41	883	227	25	124	172	.257	.393	.353
August	17-12	4.52	1000	260	30	142	176	.260	.395	.353
Sept./Oct.	18-13	3.47	1007	231	35	116	221	.229	.379	.313
Leading Off Inn.			1278	310	39	169	253	.243	.384	.335
Runners On			2469	640	62	357	478	.259	.390	.352
Runners/Scor. Pos.			1487	359	31	259	305	.241	.357	.349
Runners On/2 Out			1028	245	27	163	201	.238	.372	.346
Scor. Pos./2 Out			696	159	17	131	145	.228	.352	.351
Late Inning Pressure			939	216	17	121	196	.230	.338	.324
Leading Off			234	48	3	24	49	.205	.286	.282
Runners On			387	98	6	61	78	.253	.364	.363
Runners/Scor. Pos.			216	51	2	45	46	.236	.329	.363
First 9 Batters			2846	682	60	388	575	.240	.354	.333
Second 9 Batters			1404	368	45	142	258	.262	.414	.361
All Batters Thereafter			1205	306	40	136	226	.254	.403	.332

Starting pitchers: 59–55, 4.48 ERA
Relief pitchers: 28–20, 3.40 ERA
Ground outs-to-air outs ratio: 1.15 (3d highest in A.L.). . . . Led A.L. with 1,059 strikeouts, highest total in A.L. since Cleveland had 1,076 in 1970. . . . Walked 736 batters to lead majors with highest in either league since Cleveland walked 770 in 1971. . . . Also set a major-league record with 94 wild pitches. Had as many by August 2 as runner-up Cleveland had all season. Bobby Witt (22), Ed Correa (19), and Charlie Hough (16) ranked one-two-three in majors. . . . Won all 42 home games in which they led after eight innings. . . . Swept all three doubleheaders last season.

Toronto Blue Jays

	W-L	ERA	AB	H	HR	BB	SO	BA	SA	OBA
Season	86-76	4.08	5621	1467	164	487	1002	.261	.406	.322
vs. Left-Handers			2410	670	68	235	394	.278	.425	.344
vs. Right-Handers			3211	797	96	252	608	.248	.392	.306
Home	42-39	4.30	2822	750	89	231	516	.266	.423	.323
Road	44-37	3.86	2799	717	75	256	486	.256	.389	.322
Grass	34-29	3.66	2171	552	49	202	378	.254	.368	.321
Artificial Turf	52-47	4.35	3450	915	115	285	624	.265	.428	.323
April	9-11	4.73	682	175	21	52	115	.257	.425	.315
May	14-15	4.99	1011	265	41	103	186	.262	.440	.332
June	17-11	3.80	986	271	31	89	178	.275	.414	.334
July	15-11	3.89	896	242	21	96	165	.270	.400	.344
August	18-10	3.92	1020	264	31	57	171	.259	.416	.301
Sept./Oct.	13-18	3.36	1026	250	19	90	187	.244	.384	.307
Leading Off Inn.			1375	355	21	97	225	.258	.401	.311
Runners On			2371	656	74	210	413	.277	.428	.335
Runners/Scor. Pos.			1318	362	35	142	246	.275	.417	.342
Runners On/2 Out			1006	262	27	94	193	.260	.399	.329
Scor. Pos./2 Out			622	166	12	76	128	.267	.386	.354
Late Inning Pressure			1067	284	32	104	254	.266	.404	.334
Leading Off			263	73	6	19	52	.278	.392	.333
Runners On			458	130	16	55	115	.284	.443	.362
Runners/Scor. Pos.			259	75	10	43	71	.290	.459	.390
First 9 Batters			2807	719	69	245	580	.256	.390	.318
Second 9 Batters			1526	384	45	130	242	.252	.397	.314
All Batters Thereafter			1288	364	50	112	180	.283	.451	.342

Starting pitchers: 54–52 (fewest losses in A.L.), 4.16 ERA
Relief pitchers: 32–24 (most wins in A.L.), 3.91 ERA
Ground outs-to-air outs ratio: 1.12. . . . Lowest road-game ERA in A.L., but ranked 10th in home games. . . . Only team in A.L. not to allow more than five runs in an inning last season. . . . One of three major-league teams not to lose more than four consecutive road games last season. The others: the league champions, Boston and the Mets. . . . Left-handers pitched only 54.0 innings in relief, lowest total in either league last season. Seven southpaws compiled a 6.00 relief ERA; John Cerutti had both wins and the only save. . . . Ranked 12th in A.L. with a 4.59 ERA before the All-Star break, second with a 3.46 mark during second half.

American League

	W-L	ERA	AB	H	HR	BB	SO	BA	SA	OBA
Season	1134-1134	4.18	77376	20237	2290	7667	13058	.262	.408	.330
vs. Left-Handers			33020	8760	905	3612	5027	.265	.407	.338
vs. Right-Handers			44356	11477	1385	4055	8031	.259	.409	.323
Home	624-509	3.98	39662	10276	1151	3735	6883	.259	.401	.324
Road	509-624	4.38	37714	9961	1139	3932	6175	.264	.415	.335
Grass	809-809	4.08	54775	14146	1589	5607	9165	.258	.398	.328
Artificial Turf	325-325	4.40	22601	6091	701	2060	3893	.270	.431	.333
April	138-138	4.07	9283	2361	264	994	1588	.254	.398	.328
May	193-193	4.34	13210	3482	390	1407	2200	.264	.412	.336
June	196-196	4.36	13417	3580	393	1324	2204	.267	.416	.334
July	183-183	4.08	12583	3294	357	1219	2093	.262	.405	.329
August	205-205	4.28	13997	3682	450	1346	2345	.263	.413	.329
Sept./Oct.	219-219	3.91	14886	3838	436	1377	2628	.258	.401	.322
Leading Off Inn.			18551	4894	586	1605	2969	.264	.416	.326
Runners On			33624	9032	950	3675	5588	.269	.411	.339
Runners/Scor. Pos.			19139	5030	506	2540	3390	.263	.401	.343
Runners On/2 Out			14085	3552	379	1709	2498	.252	.387	.337
Scor. Pos./2 Out			9000	2215	227	1285	1676	.246	.377	.344
Late Inning Pressure			13108	3425	342	1453	2356	.261	.393	.337
Leading Off			3273	854	95	272	528	.261	.397	.321
Runners On			5562	1523	126	751	1008	.274	.403	.360
Runners/Scor. Pos.			3196	877	68	570	599	.274	.403	.379
First 9 Batters			37342	9649	990	3928	6868	.258	.397	.330
Second 9 Batters			20880	5514	679	1986	3305	.264	.418	.329
All Batters Thereafter			19154	5074	621	1753	2885	.265	.418	.328

No gripes last season: For only the third time since the leagues split into divisions in 1969, the teams with the four best records in the majors advanced to the playoffs. The other occasions: 1969 (Baltimore, Minnesota, New York Mets, and Atlanta); 1975 (Boston, Oakland, Philadelphia, and Los Angeles). . . . Starting pitchers completed 355 of 2268 starts last season (15.6 percent), the lowest rate since the dawn of the DH in 1972. Starters pitched an average of 6.20 innings, only marginally higher than N.L. average (6.18). . . . Used 3.32 relief pitchers per game, 15 percent fewer than N.L. (3.91). . . . League ERA was highest since 1979. . . . Last season was first time four 300-game winners were active at same time since 1891, when Old Hoss Radbourn won his 300th to join Pud Galvin, Tim Keefe, and Mickey Welch.

National League

Jim Acker
Atlanta Braves — Throws Right

	W–L	ERA	AB	H	HR	BB	SO	BA	SA	OBA
Season	3-8	3.79	365	100	7	26	37	.274	.392	.321
vs. Left-Handers			222	67	2	17	22	.302	.396	.347
vs. Right-Handers			143	33	5	9	15	.231	.385	.279
Home	1-4	3.14	190	46	3	11	18	.242	.358	.284
Road	2-4	4.57	175	54	4	15	19	.309	.429	.359
Grass	3-5	3.39	274	69	5	19	28	.252	.369	.299
Artificial Turf	0-3	5.23	91	31	2	7	9	.341	.462	.388
April			0	0	0	0	0	—	—	—
May			0	0	0	0	0	—	—	—
June			0	0	0	0	0	—	—	—
July	1-1	3.72	84	26	2	7	6	.310	.405	.363
August	2-2	2.70	122	33	2	6	12	.270	.369	.300
Sept./Oct.	0-5	4.68	159	41	3	13	19	.258	.403	.314
Leading Off Inn.			92	32	4	5	5	.348	.543	.381
Runners On			153	41	3	15	18	.268	.386	.329
Runners/Scor. Pos.			96	24	2	12	15	.250	.354	.321
Runners On/2 Out			54	10	1	7	11	.185	.241	.279
Scor. Pos./2 Out			39	8	0	6	10	.205	.205	.311
Late Inning Pressure			33	11	0	1	1	.333	.455	.361
Leading Off			9	2	0	0	0	.222	.222	.222
Runners On			15	5	0	0	0	.333	.600	.353
Runners/Scor. Pos.			4	3	0	0	0	.750	1.000	.600
First 9 Batters			147	43	2	12	21	.293	.395	.344
Second 9 Batters			106	26	1	7	11	.245	.321	.287
All Batters Thereafter			112	31	4	7	5	.277	.455	.322

Loves to face: Kevin Bass (.083, 1-for-12)
Hates to face: Howard Johnson (.667, 4-for-6, 2 HR)
Figures above are for N.L. only; see also A.L. Pitchers section. . . . Ground outs-to-air outs ratio: 1.91 last season, 2.11 for career. . . . Additional statistics: 15 double-play ground outs in 125 opportunities, 26 doubles, 5 triples in 155.0 innings last season. . . . Allowed 4 first-inning runs in 19 starts last season. . . . Batting support: 2.74 runs per start. . . . Faced only one batter twice, pitched two or more innings 12 times, finished 9 games in 25 relief appearances. . . . 3–10, 3.77 ERA as a starter; 2–2, 4.69 ERA in relief. . . . Lost his last six decisions in 1986. . . . Opponents have batted over .300 in Late-Inning Pressure Situations in each of his four seasons in the majors.

Rick Aguilera
New York Mets — Throws Right

	W–L	ERA	AB	H	HR	BB	SO	BA	SA	OBA
Season	10-7	3.88	551	145	15	36	104	.263	.425	.314
vs. Left-Handers			269	78	4	19	34	.290	.442	.341
vs. Right-Handers			282	67	11	17	70	.238	.408	.288
Home	5-2	3.72	266	69	8	17	52	.259	.429	.313
Road	5-5	4.01	285	76	7	19	52	.267	.421	.315
Grass	7-5	3.89	407	109	13	20	75	.268	.430	.306
Artificial Turf	3-2	3.82	144	36	2	16	29	.250	.410	.335
April	0-1	6.00	48	13	4	2	12	.271	.625	.300
May	0-2	7.24	51	14	6	7	14	.275	.667	.373
June	1-0	4.76	69	17	1	13	12	.246	.362	.366
July	3-0	2.62	137	40	0	5	21	.292	.387	.319
August	3-3	3.32	141	31	1	5	28	.220	.333	.261
Sept./Oct.	3-1	3.04	105	30	3	4	17	.286	.429	.315
Leading Off Inn.			134	34	2	9	31	.254	.381	.315
Runners On			227	60	8	14	40	.264	.441	.309
Runners/Scor. Pos.			132	33	3	9	21	.250	.394	.297
Runners On/2 Out			105	32	3	8	19	.305	.467	.371
Scor. Pos./2 Out			66	17	2	7	11	.258	.394	.347
Late Inning Pressure			28	10	2	3	7	.357	.643	.419
Leading Off			6	2	0	2	3	.333	.500	.500
Runners On			13	5	2	0	2	.385	.846	.385
Runners/Scor. Pos.			6	3	2	0	1	.500	1.500	.500
First 9 Batters			215	45	5	20	49	.209	.363	.286
Second 9 Batters			175	48	9	13	29	.274	.514	.325
All Batters Thereafter			161	52	1	3	26	.323	.410	.341

Loves to face: Pete Rose (.071, 1-for-14)
Hates to face: Bill Madlock (.833, 5-for-6, 2 HR)
Ground outs-to-air outs ratio: 1.38 last season, 1.15 for career. . . . Additional statistics: 8 double-play ground outs in 85 opportunities, 32 doubles, 6 triples in 141.2 innings last season. . . . Allowed 9 first-inning runs in 20 starts last season. . . . Batting support: 5.00 runs per start, 7th best in N.L. (minimum: 15 GS). . . . Allowed 10 home runs in 25.2 innings pitched through the end of May, but surrendered only five homers in 116 innings after June 1. . . . Almost half of the home runs he allowed were hit in the fourth inning (7 of 15). . . . Walked only 1.10 batters per nine innings after the All-Star break, best rate in N.L. . . . Has never walked an opposing pitcher in N.L. career (has faced 74).

Doyle Alexander
Atlanta Braves — Throws Right

	W–L	ERA	AB	H	HR	BB	SO	BA	SA	OBA
Season	6-6	3.84	470	135	9	17	74	.287	.409	.311
vs. Left-Handers			217	64	4	15	39	.295	.424	.339
vs. Right-Handers			253	71	5	2	35	.281	.395	.286
Home	4-2	4.09	249	73	6	12	46	.293	.410	.324
Road	2-4	3.56	221	62	3	5	28	.281	.407	.296
Grass	5-4	4.04	364	104	8	15	61	.286	.415	.313
Artificial Turf	1-2	3.12	106	31	1	2	13	.292	.387	.306
April			0	0	0	0	0	—	—	—
May			0	0	0	0	0	—	—	—
June			0	0	0	0	0	—	—	—
July	1-3	3.03	138	32	4	5	23	.232	.370	.259
August	3-2	5.05	170	53	3	5	27	.312	.435	.330
Sept./Oct.	2-1	3.32	162	50	2	7	24	.309	.414	.337
Leading Off Inn.			119	27	1	3	17	.227	.328	.246
Runners On			193	54	3	10	32	.280	.383	.314
Runners/Scor. Pos.			111	30	1	7	20	.270	.333	.311
Runners On/2 Out			80	21	1	3	15	.263	.313	.289
Scor. Pos./2 Out			52	16	1	3	10	.308	.365	.345
Late Inning Pressure			44	19	3	2	4	.432	.773	.457
Leading Off			14	4	0	0	1	.286	.357	.286
Runners On			14	7	2	2	1	.500	1.071	.563
Runners/Scor. Pos.			10	5	1	2	1	.500	.900	.583
First 9 Batters			145	40	1	4	30	.276	.359	.293
Second 9 Batters			149	34	3	3	26	.228	.342	.243
All Batters Thereafter			176	61	5	10	18	.347	.506	.382

Loves to face: Mike Scioscia (.091, 1-for-11)
Hates to face: Mike Easler (.484, 15-for-31, 3 HR)
Figures above are for N.L. only; see also A.L. Pitchers section. . . . Ground outs-to-air outs ratio: 0.87 last season, 0.94 for career. . . . Additional statistics: 17 double-play ground outs in 161 opportunities, 54 doubles (2d most in majors), 4 triples in 228.1 innings last season. Allowed 85 extra-base hits, 6th most in majors. . . . Allowed 19 first-inning runs in 34 starts last season. . . . Batting support: 4.97 runs per start. . . . Walked 1.50 batters per nine innings with the Braves, 3d-best rate in N.L. after the All-Star break. . . . Winning percentage of .634 over past three seasons ranks 9th in majors (minimum: 25 wins).

Larry Andersen
Phillies/Astros — Throws Right

	W–L	ERA	AB	H	HR	BB	SO	BA	SA	OBA
Season	2-1	3.03	281	83	2	26	42	.295	.384	.351
vs. Left-Handers			128	39	1	14	22	.305	.383	.373
vs. Right-Handers			153	44	1	12	20	.288	.386	.333
Home	2-0	2.68	127	31	1	16	17	.244	.299	.322
Road	0-1	3.35	154	52	1	10	25	.338	.455	.377
Grass	0-1	2.96	97	37	0	6	15	.381	.485	.419
Artificial Turf	2-0	3.06	184	46	2	20	27	.250	.332	.317
April	0-0	7.36	32	14	0	2	6	.438	.656	.457
May	0-0	0.66	43	12	0	7	7	.279	.326	.380
June	1-0	4.41	63	20	0	8	5	.317	.444	.389
July	0-0	2.63	49	15	2	2	6	.306	.429	.327
August	1-1	4.91	38	10	0	3	7	.263	.289	.302
Sept./Oct.	0-0	0.59	56	12	0	4	11	.214	.232	.279
Leading Off Inn.			61	23	1	4	8	.377	.492	.415
Runners On			154	43	1	17	22	.279	.377	.345
Runners/Scor. Pos.			107	33	0	17	16	.308	.402	.388
Runners On/2 Out			65	18	0	9	11	.277	.385	.373
Scor. Pos./2 Out			50	16	0	9	9	.320	.460	.424
Late Inning Pressure			92	24	1	14	9	.261	.315	.355
Leading Off			24	10	0	3	1	.417	.458	.481
Runners On			46	10	1	9	4	.217	.283	.339
Runners/Scor. Pos.			28	7	0	9	3	.250	.250	.421
First 9 Batters			255	78	2	21	41	.306	.400	.356
Second 9 Batters			26	5	0	5	1	.192	.231	.313
All Batters Thereafter			0	0	0	0	0	—	—	—

Loves to face: Ryne Sandberg (.118, 2-for-17)
Hates to face: Wally Backman (.636, 7-for-11)
Ground outs-to-air outs ratio: 1.48 last season, 1.17 for career. . . . Additional statistics: 9 double-play ground outs in 65 opportunities, 13 doubles, 3 triples in 77.1 innings. . . . Faced Faced one batter once, pitched two or more innings 20 times, finished 8 games in 48 relief appearances. . . . Career averages: one HR allowed per 119 at bats in day games, one per 39 at bats at night. . . . Opponents' career breakdown: .255 with bases empty, .284 with runners on, .298 with runners in scoring position. . . . Opposing left-handed batters have hit above .300 in four of the last five seasons. . . . Among pitchers active in 1986 with nine or more seasons in the majors, only Paul Mirabella has fewer wins (11) than Andersen (12).

Paul Assenmacher

Atlanta Braves — Throws Left

	W–L	ERA	AB	H	HR	BB	SO	BA	SA	OBA
Season	7-3	2.50	253	61	5	26	56	.241	.332	.311
vs. Left-Handers			82	22	1	10	19	.268	.354	.348
vs. Right-Handers			171	39	4	16	37	.228	.322	.293
Home	4-1	1.15	135	24	4	11	35	.178	.281	.238
Road	3-2	4.30	118	37	1	15	21	.314	.390	.391
Grass	5-3	2.77	192	45	5	21	47	.234	.328	.308
Artificial Turf	2-0	1.65	61	16	0	5	9	.262	.344	.318
April	0-0	2.45	28	7	0	4	7	.250	.393	.333
May	2-1	1.15	50	6	0	5	10	.120	.140	.200
June	1-1	3.14	56	17	2	5	11	.304	.411	.361
July	1-0	6.23	32	10	1	5	5	.313	.438	.405
August	1-0	2.00	31	7	1	5	8	.226	.323	.333
Sept./Oct.	2-1	1.35	56	14	1	2	15	.250	.339	.276
Leading Off Inn.			58	14	2	6	13	.241	.431	.313
Runners On			115	29	0	14	25	.252	.278	.331
Runners/Scor. Pos.			73	18	0	12	16	.247	.274	.349
Runners On/2 Out			49	10	0	6	11	.204	.265	.291
Scor. Pos./2 Out			31	6	0	6	9	.194	.258	.324
Late Inning Pressure			163	36	4	14	40	.221	.307	.281
Leading Off			40	9	2	4	9	.225	.425	.295
Runners On			68	13	0	7	19	.191	.191	.263
Runners/Scor. Pos.			43	6	0	7	12	.140	.140	.255
First 9 Batters			246	60	5	24	54	.244	.337	.310
Second 9 Batters			7	1	0	2	2	.143	.143	.333
All Batters Thereafter			0	0	0	0	0	—	—	—

Loves to face: Johnny Ray (0-for-6)
Hates to face: Jerry Royster (.667, 2-for-3, 1 HR)
Ground outs-to-air outs ratio: 2.23 last season, his first in majors.
. . . Additional statistics: 8 double-play ground outs in 56 opportunities, 4 doubles, 2 triples in 68.1 innings last season. . . . Faced only one batter 8 times (4th most in N.L.), pitched two or more innings 14 times, finished 27 games in 61 relief appearances. . . . Held top 15 N.L. batters to combined .129 average (4-for-31), 2d lowest in N.L. (minimum: 20 at bats); only Worrell did better against the cream of the crop. . . . Allowed four hits in 13 at bats with the bases loaded. . . . Allowed one home run per 40.8 at bats in Late-Inning Pressure Situations, only one home run in 90 at bats in nonpressure situations. . . . Tied for 2d among N.L. rookies with 61 appearances.

Steve Bedrosian

Philadelphia Phillies — Throws Right

	W–L	ERA	AB	H	HR	BB	SO	BA	SA	OBA
Season	8-6	3.39	341	79	12	34	82	.232	.364	.299
vs. Left-Handers			178	38	10	23	43	.213	.410	.300
vs. Right-Handers			163	41	2	11	39	.252	.313	.297
Home	2-3	3.00	144	28	6	7	31	.194	.354	.232
Road	6-3	3.68	197	51	6	27	51	.259	.371	.344
Grass	2-2	4.44	93	25	4	12	25	.269	.409	.346
Artificial Turf	6-4	3.00	248	54	8	22	57	.218	.347	.280
April	1-1	7.27	37	13	1	5	5	.351	.514	.429
May	1-1	2.13	42	7	2	3	11	.167	.310	.213
June	3-1	3.18	64	14	2	10	15	.219	.359	.324
July	2-0	1.13	59	11	0	8	14	.186	.186	.279
August	1-0	2.53	78	17	4	4	23	.218	.372	.256
Sept./Oct.	0-3	6.14	61	17	3	4	14	.279	.475	.323
Leading Off Inn.			70	20	5	5	17	.286	.514	.333
Runners On			167	39	4	20	39	.234	.347	.311
Runners/Scor. Pos.			104	17	1	17	29	.163	.212	.274
Runners On/2 Out			73	14	0	11	12	.192	.233	.298
Scor. Pos./2 Out			49	9	0	9	10	.184	.224	.310
Late Inning Pressure			240	50	10	23	54	.208	.358	.275
Leading Off			52	13	4	3	11	.250	.500	.291
Runners On			105	20	3	14	22	.190	.314	.281
Runners/Scor. Pos.			60	10	1	13	15	.167	.250	.307
First 9 Batters			331	78	12	31	79	.236	.372	.299
Second 9 Batters			10	1	0	3	3	.100	.100	.308
All Batters Thereafter			0	0	0	0	0	—	—	—

Loves to face: Mike Fitzgerald (0-for-12)
Hates to face: Ray Knight (.478, 11-for-23, 2 HR)
Ground outs-to-air outs ratio: 0.67, 9th lowest in N.L. last season (minimum: 250 BFP), 0.85 for career. . . . Additional statistics: 4 double-play ground outs in 83 opportunities, 9 doubles, 0 triples in 90.1 innings last season. . . . Faced only one batter 4 times, pitched two or more innings 26 times, finished 56 games in 68 relief appearances. . . . Allowed 10 home runs in Late-Inning Pressure Situations, most in majors. . . . Opponents' batting average with runners in scoring position was the lowest of his career. Has held opponents below .200 in four of six major-league seasons. . . . Opponents' batting average was lower at home than on the road for the first time in his career. Do you think he misses Atlanta?

Juan Berenguer

San Francisco Giants — Throws Right

	W–L	ERA	AB	H	HR	BB	SO	BA	SA	OBA
Season	2-3	2.70	265	64	4	44	72	.242	.343	.353
vs. Left-Handers			134	34	2	22	41	.254	.366	.359
vs. Right-Handers			131	30	2	22	31	.229	.321	.346
Home	1-2	2.94	124	32	1	23	31	.258	.347	.378
Road	1-1	2.50	141	32	3	21	41	.227	.340	.329
Grass	2-2	2.80	162	38	2	28	45	.235	.321	.349
Artificial Turf	0-1	2.54	103	26	2	16	27	.252	.379	.358
April	0-0	6.75	12	4	1	3	2	.333	.667	.467
May	0-0	2.70	75	20	0	6	19	.267	.347	.325
June	1-0	0.47	65	9	0	8	24	.138	.154	.233
July	0-2	6.30	33	7	1	8	10	.212	.364	.366
August	1-0	2.25	44	13	1	11	10	.295	.477	.436
Sept./Oct.	0-1	2.89	36	11	1	8	7	.306	.389	.444
Leading Off Inn.			66	12	1	5	21	.182	.303	.250
Runners On			112	32	2	20	24	.286	.393	.396
Runners/Scor. Pos.			68	17	1	17	14	.250	.353	.402
Runners On/2 Out			51	14	0	13	13	.275	.333	.422
Scor. Pos./2 Out			35	7	0	12	8	.200	.257	.404
Late Inning Pressure			87	19	1	18	25	.218	.276	.349
Leading Off			23	2	0	2	10	.087	.174	.160
Runners On			34	10	1	7	7	.294	.382	.405
Runners/Scor. Pos.			19	4	0	6	3	.211	.211	.385
First 9 Batters			217	48	3	36	66	.221	.309	.336
Second 9 Batters			38	11	0	5	6	.289	.395	.372
All Batters Thereafter			10	5	1	3	0	.500	.900	.615

Loves to face: Dane Iorg (.091, 1-for-11)
Hates to face: Pete Rose (.833, 5-for-6)
Ground outs-to-air outs ratio: 0.54, 3d lowest in N.L. last season (minimum: 250 BFP), 0.62 for career. . . . Additional statistics: 5 double-play ground outs in 47 opportunities, 13 doubles, 1 triple in 73.1 innings last season. . . . Faced only one batter twice, pitched two or more innings 14 times, finished 17 games in 42 relief appearances. . . . Has faced 61 batters with the bases loaded in his career and has walked in 12 runs. . . . Lowest ERA of his 9-year career. . . . Opponents' career breakdown: .222 with bases empty, .249 with runners on base, .266 with runners in scoring position. . . . Opponents' career on-base percentage of .281 leading off innings is considerably lower than his overall mark of .330.

Mike Bielecki

Pittsburgh Pirates — Throws Right

	W–L	ERA	AB	H	HR	BB	SO	BA	SA	OBA
Season	6-11	4.66	569	149	10	83	83	.262	.394	.355
vs. Left-Handers			306	80	7	36	31	.261	.412	.333
vs. Right-Handers			263	69	3	47	52	.262	.373	.378
Home	2-6	4.64	291	72	6	44	46	.247	.388	.349
Road	4-5	4.69	278	77	4	39	37	.277	.399	.360
Grass	4-1	3.89	155	36	2	20	20	.232	.329	.316
Artificial Turf	2-10	4.96	414	113	8	63	63	.273	.418	.369
April	1-0	6.75	60	22	0	7	8	.367	.467	.429
May	2-3	5.14	106	24	4	18	13	.226	.368	.339
June	1-2	3.75	135	36	2	17	22	.267	.393	.349
July	2-1	4.70	86	19	1	15	16	.221	.337	.333
August	0-3	3.94	123	30	3	16	18	.244	.407	.333
Sept./Oct.	0-2	5.51	59	18	0	10	6	.305	.424	.394
Leading Off Inn.			138	36	3	18	13	.261	.406	.350
Runners On			258	70	5	38	48	.271	.411	.358
Runners/Scor. Pos.			154	38	4	29	28	.247	.370	.354
Runners On/2 Out			114	25	1	19	31	.219	.272	.331
Scor. Pos./2 Out			74	17	0	17	18	.230	.243	.374
Late Inning Pressure			18	4	0	3	3	.222	.333	.333
Leading Off			5	1	0	3	0	.200	.200	.500
Runners On			5	3	0	0	1	.600	1.000	.600
Runners/Scor. Pos.			2	1	0	0	0	.500	.500	.500
First 9 Batters			225	52	3	26	38	.231	.338	.315
Second 9 Batters			203	57	4	25	32	.281	.404	.355
All Batters Thereafter			141	40	3	32	13	.284	.468	.411

Loves to face: Von Hayes (.077, 1-for-13)
Hates to face: Dave Parker (.583, 7-for-12, 3 HR)
Ground outs-to-air outs ratio: 1.17 last season, 1.18 for career. . . . Additional statistics: 7 double-play ground outs in 111 opportunities, 27 doubles, 9 triples (tied for 2d most in majors) in 148.2 innings (most among N.L. rookies) last season. . . . Allowed 10 first-inning runs in 27 starts last season. . . . Batting support: 4.44 runs per start. . . . Led N.L. rookie pitchers with 27 starts. . . . Allowed only one hit in 11 at bats with the bases loaded last season: a grand-slam by Bob Forsch. . . . Career record of 0–4 against the Reds. . . . One of five pitchers active in 1986 with more career walks than strikeouts but at least 25 career starts. . . . Hitless in 23 career at bats vs. left-handed pitchers.

Vida Blue

San Francisco Giants — Throws Left

	W-L	ERA	AB	H	HR	BB	SO	BA	SA	OBA
Season	10-10	3.27	573	137	19	77	100	.239	.394	.326
vs. Left-Handers			88	19	3	9	19	.216	.386	.289
vs. Right-Handers			485	118	16	68	81	.243	.396	.333
Home	6-6	3.01	344	79	14	47	57	.230	.398	.320
Road	4-4	3.69	229	58	5	30	43	.253	.389	.336
Grass	7-6	3.03	396	90	15	53	62	.227	.391	.315
Artificial Turf	3-4	3.86	177	47	4	24	38	.266	.401	.351
April	1-2	4.73	51	15	3	5	9	.294	.529	.357
May	0-1	7.11	25	8	2	1	5	.320	.600	.333
June	4-1	1.69	108	17	2	14	22	.157	.241	.252
July	2-2	4.60	104	27	2	19	18	.260	.385	.365
August	2-3	2.08	177	40	5	21	32	.226	.373	.308
Sept./Oct.	1-1	4.18	108	30	5	17	14	.278	.481	.373
Leading Off Inn.			144	37	7	19	24	.257	.486	.344
Runners On			243	49	3	27	40	.202	.263	.275
Runners/Scor. Pos.			127	27	3	16	19	.213	.299	.289
Runners On/2 Out			108	26	1	13	19	.241	.324	.322
Scor. Pos./2 Out			65	14	1	9	11	.215	.292	.311
Late Inning Pressure			40	10	3	2	3	.250	.600	.286
Leading Off			12	1	0	0	0	.083	.167	.083
Runners On			9	3	0	0	0	.333	.444	.333
Runners/Scor. Pos.			5	2	0	0	0	.400	.400	.400
First 9 Batters			214	46	5	30	43	.215	.332	.305
Second 9 Batters			216	50	7	26	44	.231	.380	.313
All Batters Thereafter			143	41	7	21	13	.287	.510	.378

Loves to face: Cal Ripken (0-for-8, 3 SO)
Hates to face: Eddie Murray (.615, 8-for-13)
Ground outs-to-air outs ratio: 0.64, 6th lowest in N.L. last season (minimum: 250 BFP), 0.90 for career.... Additional statistics: 10 double-play ground outs in 122 opportunities, 24 doubles, 4 triples in 156.2 innings last season.... Allowed 13 first-inning runs in 28 starts last season.... Batting support: 3.96 runs per start.... Youngest active pitcher to have played in the 1960s. Is it too early to think about the next group of potential "four-decade" players? ... Opponents' batting average with runners on base was his lowest in the last 12 years.... In six seasons with the Giants (1978–81, 1985–86) he has allowed 60 homers at Candlestick Park, 32 in road games.... Ranked 3d in N.L. in ERA during month of June, 4th during August.

Tom Browning

Cincinnati Reds — Throws Left

	W-L	ERA	AB	H	HR	BB	SO	BA	SA	OBA
Season	14-13	3.81	918	225	26	70	147	.245	.375	.296
vs. Left-Handers			133	32	4	17	23	.241	.353	.325
vs. Right-Handers			785	193	22	53	124	.246	.378	.291
Home	7-6	3.80	393	93	10	38	59	.237	.346	.300
Road	7-7	3.82	525	132	16	32	88	.251	.396	.292
Grass	5-3	3.50	344	82	13	14	57	.238	.404	.268
Artificial Turf	9-10	3.99	574	143	13	56	90	.249	.357	.311
April	0-3	6.08	92	25	4	9	11	.272	.478	.333
May	2-2	4.54	155	45	4	14	22	.290	.426	.345
June	3-2	3.35	150	34	8	12	23	.227	.420	.287
July	4-1	3.00	146	34	3	7	31	.233	.342	.266
August	2-3	4.31	182	45	6	17	26	.247	.379	.305
Sept./Oct.	3-2	2.73	193	42	1	11	29	.218	.269	.256
Leading Off Inn.			234	51	6	18	50	.218	.338	.277
Runners On			329	89	7	30	42	.271	.392	.321
Runners/Scor. Pos.			162	44	1	22	24	.272	.358	.337
Runners On/2 Out			155	39	4	18	23	.252	.368	.329
Scor. Pos./2 Out			87	22	1	15	12	.253	.322	.363
Late Inning Pressure			63	9	1	5	14	.143	.190	.206
Leading Off			19	2	1	1	3	.105	.263	.150
Runners On			15	4	0	0	3	.267	.267	.267
Runners/Scor. Pos.			7	1	0	0	3	.143	.143	.143
First 9 Batters			308	75	7	28	58	.244	.338	.303
Second 9 Batters			309	72	12	23	51	.233	.401	.284
All Batters Thereafter			301	78	7	19	38	.259	.385	.299

Loves to face: Vince Coleman (0-for-11)
Hates to face: Kevin Bass (.464, 13-for-28, 2 HR)
Ground outs-to-air outs ratio: 0.71 last season, 0.67 for career.... Additional statistics: 16 double-play ground outs in 157 opportunities, 37 doubles, 2 triples in 243.1 innings last season.... Allowed 24 first-inning runs (4th most in N.L.) in 39 starts last season.... Batting support: 4.72 runs per start.... One of five N.L. pitchers to allow four home runs in a game last season. The others: Rick Aguilera, Don Carman, David Palmer, and Mario Soto.... Won his first game in his ninth start last season; made 12 no-decision starts in all, with a 2.88 ERA in those games.... Reds finished 10 games out of first place last season, but could have tied Houston for N.L. West title had Browning reversed his 0–5 record vs. the Astros.

Tim Burke

Montreal Expos — Throws Right

	W-L	ERA	AB	H	HR	BB	SO	BA	SA	OBA
Season	9-7	2.93	393	103	7	46	82	.262	.369	.344
vs. Left-Handers			205	62	5	31	37	.302	.415	.391
vs. Right-Handers			188	41	2	15	45	.218	.319	.290
Home	4-2	1.74	174	41	3	24	36	.236	.345	.330
Road	5-5	3.95	219	62	4	22	46	.283	.388	.355
Grass	4-2	1.74	117	26	2	8	26	.222	.291	.278
Artificial Turf	5-5	3.45	276	77	5	38	56	.279	.402	.370
April	1-0	0.96	67	10	1	6	19	.149	.209	.230
May	1-1	2.08	80	19	3	8	10	.238	.375	.307
June	3-1	2.70	71	17	0	10	18	.239	.324	.337
July	2-2	5.79	61	20	0	16	10	.328	.377	.468
August	1-2	2.45	72	21	1	5	17	.292	.389	.350
Sept./Oct.	1-1	6.23	42	16	2	1	8	.381	.643	.395
Leading Off Inn.			91	26	2	7	22	.286	.429	.337
Runners On			183	50	2	31	35	.273	.355	.381
Runners/Scor. Pos.			127	29	1	28	29	.228	.283	.367
Runners On/2 Out			71	16	0	11	13	.225	.254	.329
Scor. Pos./2 Out			53	10	0	11	11	.189	.189	.328
Late Inning Pressure			246	64	5	32	55	.260	.370	.348
Leading Off			57	14	1	5	14	.246	.386	.306
Runners On			115	33	1	21	25	.287	.400	.400
Runners/Scor. Pos.			80	19	1	19	20	.238	.300	.382
First 9 Batters			344	90	7	41	73	.262	.381	.345
Second 9 Batters			38	10	0	5	6	.263	.289	.349
All Batters Thereafter			11	3	0	0	3	.273	.273	.273

Loves to face: Howard Johnson (0-for-8, 4 SO)
Hates to face: Glenn Davis (.857, 6-for-7, 2 HR)
Ground outs-to-air outs ratio: 1.48 last season, 1.68 for career.... Additional statistics: 7 double-play ground outs in 95 opportunities, 19 doubles, 1 triple in 101.1 innings last season.... Faced only one batter once, pitched two or more innings 24 times, finished 25 games in 66 relief appearances.... Opposing batters were even worse with two outs and runners in scoring position in 1985 (.134).... Opponents' career batting average of .201 on grass fields, .247 on artificial surfaces.... Opponents career batting, slugging: left-handers .279, .389; right-handers .189, .291.... Another Yankee pitching prospect that got away, acquired by the Expos in 1983 for outfielder Pat Rooney.... Immediately preceded Jeff Reardon in 13 of Reardon's 35 saves last season.

Ray Burris

St. Louis Cardinals — Throws Right

	W-L	ERA	AB	H	HR	BB	SO	BA	SA	OBA
Season	4-5	5.60	321	92	13	32	34	.287	.483	.359
vs. Left-Handers			143	42	5	15	10	.294	.476	.350
vs. Right-Handers			178	50	8	17	24	.281	.489	.350
Home	3-1	3.95	156	42	5	9	15	.269	.442	.317
Road	1-4	7.24	165	50	8	23	19	.303	.521	.395
Grass	1-1	8.59	64	22	2	6	10	.344	.547	.408
Artificial Turf	3-4	4.95	257	70	11	26	24	.272	.467	.346
April			0	0	0	0	0	—	—	—
May	2-1	3.92	77	19	2	4	4	.247	.390	.310
June	2-2	3.86	139	35	6	16	15	.252	.446	.329
July	0-1	18.69	47	22	3	4	11	.468	.766	.519
August	0-1	4.70	58	16	2	8	4	.276	.466	.364
Sept./Oct.			0	0	0	0	0	—	—	—
Leading Off Inn.			73	17	5	7	8	.233	.479	.325
Runners On			141	48	8	17	16	.340	.553	.415
Runners/Scor. Pos.			88	26	4	13	12	.295	.511	.392
Runners On/2 Out			58	21	1	10	5	.362	.466	.456
Scor. Pos./2 Out			44	16	1	8	3	.364	.477	.462
Late Inning Pressure			24	5	1	0	3	.208	.417	.208
Leading Off			7	1	1	0	1	.143	.571	.143
Runners On			6	0	0	0	0	.000	.000	.000
Runners/Scor. Pos.			2	0	0	0	0	.000	.000	.000
First 9 Batters			143	44	10	16	18	.308	.580	.381
Second 9 Batters			101	22	2	11	10	.218	.347	.301
All Batters Thereafter			77	26	1	5	6	.338	.481	.393

Loves to face: Ray Knight (0-for-19)
Hates to face: Darryl Strawberry (.500, 5-for-10, 2 HR)
Ground outs-to-air outs ratio: 1.10 last season, 0.96 for career.... Additional statistics: 9 double-play ground outs in 69 opportunities, 24 doubles, 0 triples in 82.0 innings last season.... Allowed 4 first-inning runs in 10 starts last season.... Batting support: 4.20 runs per start.... Has defeated every major-league team except the Angels, A's, and Rangers.... Has lost his last eight decisions to the Padres; his last victory against them was in 1978.... Cardinals were his seventh team in the last eight years after he spent his first six seasons with the Cubs.... Has made 43 relief appearances without a save over the past four seasons.

Steve Carlton
Phillies/Giants — Throws Left

	W–L	ERA	AB	H	HR	BB	SO	BA	SA	OBA
Season	5-11	5.89	462	138	19	61	80	.299	.474	.380
vs. Left-Handers			65	19	2	8	12	.292	.462	.370
vs. Right-Handers			397	119	17	53	68	.300	.476	.381
Home	2-4	6.31	214	70	7	24	35	.327	.486	.396
Road	3-7	5.55	248	68	12	37	45	.274	.464	.366
Grass	1-6	5.33	198	60	6	28	40	.303	.455	.390
Artificial Turf	4-5	6.33	264	78	13	33	40	.295	.489	.371
April	1-3	6.91	115	34	5	20	23	.296	.452	.397
May	2-3	2.80	133	31	6	8	23	.233	.421	.277
June	1-2	11.07	95	37	4	17	16	.389	.589	.474
July	1-2	3.42	101	29	4	13	15	.287	.436	.374
August	0-1	17.18	18	7	0	3	3	.389	.611	.476
Sept./Oct.			0	0	0	0	0			
Leading Off Inn.			106	27	5	13	19	.255	.406	.342
Runners On			197	60	7	39	34	.305	.472	.414
Runners/Scor. Pos.			122	31	4	32	20	.254	.418	.401
Runners On/2 Out			83	28	4	20	13	.337	.566	.466
Scor. Pos./2 Out			59	21	3	16	8	.356	.610	.493
Late Inning Pressure			14	6	0	1	2	.429	.429	.467
Leading Off			4	1	0	0	1	.250	.250	.250
Runners On			5	3	0	1	0	.600	.600	.667
Runners/Scor. Pos.			4	2	0	1	0	.500	.500	.600
First 9 Batters			175	40	3	20	35	.229	.309	.311
Second 9 Batters			166	55	10	27	29	.331	.572	.418
All Batters Thereafter			121	43	6	14	16	.355	.579	.422

Loves to face: Candy Maldonado (.080, 2-for-25)
Hates to face: Steve Sax (.423, 11-for-26)
Figures above are for N.L. only.... Ground outs-to-air outs ratio: 1.23 last season, 1.09 for career.... Additional statistics: 22 double-play ground outs in 149 opportunities, 30 doubles, 5 triples in 176.1 innings last season.... Allowed 21 first-inning runs in 32 starts last season.... Batting support: 4.72 runs per start.... Failed to complete five innings in 10 starts last season, tied for 2d most in majors. The leader: Juan Nieves (12).... Has completed only one of his last 88 starts, and that was in August 1984.... Additional comments in the A.L. Pitchers section.

Don Carman
Philadelphia Phillies — Throws Left

	W–L	ERA	AB	H	HR	BB	SO	BA	SA	OBA
Season	10-5	3.22	482	113	11	52	98	.234	.359	.311
vs. Left-Handers			90	21	3	5	18	.233	.389	.289
vs. Right-Handers			392	92	8	47	80	.235	.352	.316
Home	6-2	3.90	245	60	5	29	57	.245	.388	.325
Road	4-3	2.54	237	53	6	23	41	.224	.329	.297
Grass	2-1	2.52	123	26	6	11	23	.211	.390	.276
Artificial Turf	8-4	3.47	359	87	5	41	75	.242	.348	.323
April	0-0	5.00	34	9	0	3	10	.265	.324	.342
May	2-0	5.54	47	13	2	7	8	.277	.426	.370
June	1-1	4.30	56	17	0	9	16	.304	.393	.394
July	2-1	2.05	79	19	1	6	13	.241	.278	.307
August	2-3	3.26	173	35	4	20	36	.202	.358	.284
Sept./Oct.	3-0	1.73	93	20	4	7	15	.215	.387	.270
Leading Off Inn.			122	34	2	12	14	.279	.385	.343
Runners On			183	39	1	27	43	.213	.295	.316
Runners/Scor. Pos.			95	22	0	23	23	.232	.337	.382
Runners On/2 Out			81	18	1	12	21	.222	.333	.330
Scor. Pos./2 Out			47	11	0	12	12	.234	.319	.400
Late Inning Pressure			148	43	0	18	30	.291	.372	.365
Leading Off			39	13	0	2	5	.333	.410	.354
Runners On			67	15	0	14	14	.224	.299	.354
Runners/Scor. Pos.			41	10	0	12	9	.244	.366	.407
First 9 Batters			266	72	6	34	61	.271	.395	.351
Second 9 Batters			116	23	5	9	25	.198	.353	.273
All Batters Thereafter			100	18	0	9	12	.180	.270	.245

Loves to face: Jim Morrison (.091, 1-for-11)
Hates to face: Gary Carter (.750, 6-for-8, 1 HR)
Ground outs-to-air outs ratio: 0.54, 4th lowest in N.L. last season (minimum: 250 BFP), 0.57 for career.... Additional statistics: 9 double-play ground outs in 92 opportunities, 23 doubles, 2 triples in 134.1 innings last season.... Allowed 9 first-inning runs in 14 starts last season.... Batting support: 3.43 runs per start.... Faced only one batter 3 times, pitched two or more innings 8 times, finished 13 games in 36 relief appearances.... Career home run breakdown: five with men on base, 14 with the bases empty.... Hitless in 31 at bats last season, most hitless at bats for any N.L. pitcher last season. Now 0-for-34 in his career. Did someone mention Bob Buhl?

Pat Clements
Pittsburgh Pirates — Throws Left

	W–L	ERA	AB	H	HR	BB	SO	BA	SA	OBA
Season	0-4	2.80	211	53	1	32	31	.251	.303	.349
vs. Left-Handers			67	19	1	14	10	.284	.373	.412
vs. Right-Handers			144	34	0	18	21	.236	.271	.317
Home	0-0	2.90	98	22	0	20	15	.224	.276	.344
Road	0-4	2.70	113	31	1	12	16	.274	.327	.354
Grass	0-2	2.60	62	15	1	6	8	.242	.323	.329
Artificial Turf	0-2	2.89	149	38	0	26	23	.255	.295	.358
April	0-1	2.79	30	7	0	4	4	.233	.267	.324
May	0-0	3.27	40	10	0	8	6	.250	.325	.375
June	0-3	2.92	47	14	0	10	7	.298	.319	.421
July	0-0	4.91	35	9	1	6	6	.257	.343	.364
August	0-0	1.59	41	11	0	3	6	.268	.341	.304
Sept./Oct.	0-0	0.00	18	2	0	1	2	.111	.111	.200
Leading Off Inn.			53	15	0	6	11	.283	.321	.356
Runners On			103	25	0	21	16	.243	.282	.364
Runners/Scor. Pos.			61	17	0	16	7	.279	.295	.415
Runners On/2 Out			40	10	0	5	7	.250	.250	.348
Scor. Pos./2 Out			26	6	0	5	4	.231	.231	.375
Late Inning Pressure			94	29	0	19	13	.309	.362	.410
Leading Off			24	11	0	4	5	.458	.542	.536
Runners On			53	13	0	14	7	.245	.283	.380
Runners/Scor. Pos.			32	11	0	10	3	.344	.375	.457
First 9 Batters			206	51	1	31	30	.248	.296	.346
Second 9 Batters			5	2	0	1	1	.400	.600	.500
All Batters Thereafter			0	0	0	0	0			

Loves to face: Bill Buckner (0-for-6)
Hates to face: Cecil Cooper (.833, 5-for-6, 1 HR)
Ground outs-to-air outs ratio: 1.56 last season, 1.36 for career.... Additional statistics: 8 double-play ground outs in 67 opportunities, 8 doubles, 0 triples in 61.0 innings last season.... Faced only one batter 11 times (most in N.L.; A.L. leader: Joe "One-Third" Sambito, with 14), pitched two or more innings 12 times, finished 19 games in 65 relief appearances.... Career record of 5-0 in A.L., 0-6 in N.L.... Opponents' career batting: .236 with bases empty, .260 with runners on base, .306 with runners in scoring position.... Opposing left-handers outhit right-handers in 1985 also.... Has faced leadoff hitters in 146 innings, and never allowed a homer.

Tim Conroy
St. Louis Cardinals — Throws Left

	W–L	ERA	AB	H	HR	BB	SO	BA	SA	OBA
Season	5-11	5.23	444	122	15	56	79	.275	.446	.353
vs. Left-Handers			89	19	3	14	13	.213	.393	.321
vs. Right-Handers			355	103	12	42	66	.290	.459	.361
Home	2-7	5.37	246	70	9	31	32	.285	.463	.358
Road	3-4	5.05	198	52	6	25	47	.263	.424	.346
Grass	1-2	4.24	89	20	1	9	21	.225	.326	.303
Artificial Turf	4-9	5.48	355	102	14	47	58	.287	.476	.365
April	1-0	0.96	29	1	0	2	6	.034	.069	.097
May	1-3	4.97	99	31	2	9	9	.313	.444	.357
June	0-0		0	0	0	0	0	—	—	—
July	1-3	7.85	80	24	4	6	19	.300	.500	.364
August	1-2	3.93	130	34	3	15	23	.262	.431	.338
Sept./Oct.	1-3	6.75	106	32	6	24	22	.302	.528	.418
Leading Off Inn.			108	26	5	12	29	.241	.472	.322
Runners On			185	53	10	22	20	.286	.514	.349
Runners/Scor. Pos.			92	24	3	16	10	.261	.424	.339
Runners On/2 Out			78	20	5	13	8	.256	.487	.363
Scor. Pos./2 Out			40	9	2	9	4	.225	.400	.367
Late Inning Pressure			32	5	1	0	5	.156	.313	.156
Leading Off			10	1	0	0	2	.100	.200	.100
Runners On			4	1	1	0	0	.250	1.000	.250
Runners/Scor. Pos.			1	1	1	0	0	1.000	4.000	1.000
First 9 Batters			185	45	6	21	38	.243	.411	.316
Second 9 Batters			147	42	3	22	24	.286	.415	.385
All Batters Thereafter			112	35	6	13	17	.313	.545	.362

Loves to face: Buddy Bell (.105, 2-for-19)
Hates to face: Barry Bonds (.800, 4-for-5, 1 HR)
Ground outs-to-air outs ratio: 0.71 last season, 0.67 for career.... Additional statistics: 11 double-play ground outs in 86 opportunities, 25 doubles, 3 triples in 115.1 innings last season.... Allowed 14 first-inning runs in 21 starts last season.... Batting support: 3.71 runs per start.... Career average of one home run allowed for every 66.8 at bats by left-handed batters (.234 career average); one HR per 30.1 AB by right-handers (.247).... Opponents' career average of .207 in Late-Inning Pressure Situations, .247 in nonpressure situations.... One of three N.L. pitchers who failed to complete five innings in nine starts last season. The others: Rick Mahler and Mark Thurmond.

Danny Cox
St. Louis Cardinals   Throws Right

	W–L	ERA	AB	H	HR	BB	SO	BA	SA	OBA
Season	12-13	2.90	808	189	14	60	108	.234	.347	.288
vs. Left-Handers			433	101	9	33	48	.233	.351	.286
vs. Right-Handers			375	88	5	27	60	.235	.341	.290
Home	6-6	2.90	452	97	11	31	52	.215	.341	.266
Road	6-7	2.92	356	92	3	29	56	.258	.354	.314
Grass	2-5	2.51	177	43	2	16	30	.243	.350	.308
Artificial Turf	10-8	3.01	631	146	12	44	78	.231	.345	.282
April	0-1	12.00	13	7	1	0	0	.538	.846	.538
May	0-3	3.51	148	35	2	17	20	.236	.338	.313
June	2-1	4.22	121	34	3	9	16	.281	.405	.336
July	3-3	2.53	171	33	4	3	21	.193	.310	.206
August	3-3	2.09	157	32	2	15	24	.204	.306	.272
Sept./Oct.	4-2	2.14	198	48	2	16	27	.242	.348	.302
Leading Off Inn.			214	53	5	14	33	.248	.364	.294
Runners On			302	77	3	20	38	.255	.354	.301
Runners/Scor. Pos.			177	44	1	14	21	.249	.345	.303
Runners On/2 Out			116	26	1	11	12	.224	.319*	.291
Scor. Pos./2 Out			77	16	1	9	8	.208	.325	.291
Late Inning Pressure			99	22	0	8	6	.222	.293	.280
Leading Off			28	7	0	3	1	.250	.357	.323
Runners On			29	9	0	5	4	.310	.379	.412
Runners/Scor. Pos.			18	4	0	5	3	.222	.333	.391
First 9 Batters			264	70	5	18	45	.265	.379	.311
Second 9 Batters			258	52	7	16	35	.202	.341	.249
All Batters Thereafter			286	67	2	26	28	.234	.322	.300

Loves to face: Wayne Krenchicki (0-for-15)
Hates to face: Bob Horner (.500, 7-for-14, 3 HR)
Ground outs-to-air outs ratio: 1.35 last season, 1.40 for career....
Additional statistics: 19 double-play ground outs (8th in N.L.), in 129 opportunities, 43 doubles (7th most in N.L.), 3 triples in 220.0 innings last season.... Allowed 22 first-inning runs in 32 starts last season.... Batting support: 3.44 runs per start, 5th lowest in N.L. (minimum: 15 GS).... Record of 9–6 with 2.20 ERA after the All-Star break.... Ranked 5th in N.L. in ERA in road games last season.... Has allowed 28 home runs in his career at Busch Stadium, 20 in road games.... Only Cardinals pitcher to start at least 25 games in each of the last three seasons.... Career total of 33 batters faced with the bases loaded, has allowed two grand slams.

Ron Darling
New York Mets   Throws Right

	W–L	ERA	AB	H	HR	BB	SO	BA	SA	OBA
Season	15-6	2.81	867	203	21	81	184	.234	.354	.300
vs. Left-Handers			503	114	12	44	105	.227	.344	.288
vs. Right-Handers			364	89	9	37	79	.245	.368	.316
Home	10-2	2.36	434	95	10	30	95	.219	.327	.272
Road	5-4	3.26	433	108	11	51	89	.249	.381	.326
Grass	12-3	2.77	600	138	15	51	127	.230	.348	.291
Artificial Turf	3-3	2.91	267	65	6	30	57	.243	.367	.319
April	1-0	6.75	82	23	5	9	14	.280	.500	.359
May	5-0	1.63	134	23	2	17	28	.172	.254	.263
June	2-2	2.93	142	34	4	13	31	.239	.373	.304
July	3-1	1.47	169	36	3	11	41	.213	.320	.260
August	1-2	4.81	153	45	4	13	28	.294	.425	.345
Sept./Oct.	3-1	1.80	187	42	3	18	42	.225	.321	.296
Leading Off Inn.			228	66	8	15	45	.289	.439	.333
Runners On			328	68	4	34	70	.207	.287	.281
Runners/Scor. Pos.			186	37	1	20	46	.199	.253	.272
Runners On/2 Out			133	19	1	17	32	.143	.211	.240
Scor. Pos./2 Out			85	11	1	10	23	.129	.212	.221
Late Inning Pressure			97	20	1	10	16	.206	.289	.287
Leading Off			27	10	1	2	4	.370	.556	.414
Runners On			39	3	0	6	8	.077	.103	.217
Runners/Scor. Pos.			22	2	0	3	5	.091	.091	.200
First 9 Batters			271	65	5	30	60	.240	.343	.317
Second 9 Batters			278	58	12	22	67	.209	.374	.267
All Batters Thereafter			318	80	4	29	57	.252	.346	.313

Loves to face: Tommy Herr (.067, 2-for-30, 1 HR)
Hates to face: Tony Gwynn (.542, 13-for-24)
Ground outs-to-air outs ratio: 1.15 last season, 1.16 for career....
Additional statistics: 18 double-play ground outs in 164 opportunities, 35 doubles, 3 triples in 237.0 innings last season.... Allowed 13 first-inning runs in 34 starts last season.... Batting support: 4.91 runs per start, 8th best in N.L. (minimum: 15 GS).... Allowed 38 home runs over the past two seasons, but only nine with runners on base.... Highest ERA in N.L. during April (minimum: 20 IP), lowest during May and July.... Mets won 26 of his 34 starts last season, best such record in the N.L.... Career record of 6–0 vs. Atlanta.... Opponents' career batting: .250 with bases empty, .216 with runners on base, .202 with runners in scoring position, .181 with two out and runners in scoring position.

Mark Davis
San Francisco Giants   Throws Left

	W–L	ERA	AB	H	HR	BB	SO	BA	SA	OBA
Season	5-7	2.99	297	63	6	34	90	.212	.310	.291
vs. Left-Handers			84	11	1	9	36	.131	.190	.213
vs. Right-Handers			213	52	5	25	54	.244	.357	.321
Home	3-2	2.50	141	34	3	14	42	.241	.362	.304
Road	2-5	3.43	156	29	3	20	48	.186	.263	.279
Grass	3-6	2.71	224	49	5	24	66	.219	.321	.292
Artificial Turf	2-1	3.80	73	14	1	10	24	.192	.274	.286
April	1-1	1.89	65	14	1	4	20	.215	.308	.264
May	0-2	3.12	30	6	0	6	12	.200	.233	.324
June	1-1	2.77	45	10	1	11	10	.222	.311	.375
July	0-0	4.73	48	12	2	1	13	.250	.438	.260
August	2-0	1.65	54	8	0	8	18	.148	.167	.254
Sept./Oct.	1-3	4.50	55	13	2	4	17	.236	.382	.288
Leading Off Inn.			71	13	1	5	20	.183	.239	.237
Runners On			124	31	2	22	35	.250	.347	.355
Runners/Scor. Pos.			76	19	1	14	27	.250	.342	.347
Runners On/2 Out			52	16	1	15	13	.308	.442	.463
Scor. Pos./2 Out			39	13	0	8	9	.333	.410	.447
Late Inning Pressure			131	28	3	16	40	.214	.328	.293
Leading Off			33	4	0	4	10	.121	.121	.216
Runners On			52	16	1	10	10	.308	.442	.400
Runners/Scor. Pos.			30	11	1	5	9	.367	.567	.421
First 9 Batters			275	61	5	31	84	.222	.316	.298
Second 9 Batters			20	2	1	3	6	.100	.250	.217
All Batters Thereafter			2	0	0	0	0	.000	.000	.000

Loves to face: Kevin McReynolds (.063, 1-for-16)
Hates to face: Bill Madlock (.500, 9-for-18, 3 HR)
Ground outs-to-air outs ratio: 0.80 last season, 0.86 for career....
Additional statistics: 4 double-play ground outs in 70 opportunities, 11 doubles, 0 triples in 84.1 innings last season.... Faced only one batter 10 times (2d most in N.L.), pitched two or more innings 17 times, finished 20 games in 65 relief appearances.... Career record of 0–7 vs. the Cubs.... Opponents' career batting average of .198 in Late-Inning Pressure Situations (19 percent of total at bats), .267 in unpressured situations.... Only home run allowed to a left-handed batter last season was hit by Andy Van Slyke.... Opponents' career batting averages: .195 by left-handers, .267 by right-handers.

Ron Davis
Twins/Cubs   Throws Right

	W–L	ERA	AB	H	HR	BB	SO	BA	SA	OBA
Season	2-8	8.59	249	86	10	32	40	.345	.550	.425
vs. Left-Handers			115	40	6	19	14	.348	.600	.445
vs. Right-Handers			134	46	4	13	26	.343	.507	.407
Home	2-3	7.58	120	40	5	18	22	.333	.533	.426
Road	0-5	9.62	129	46	5	14	18	.357	.566	.425
Grass	0-5	10.67	125	47	4	14	19	.376	.576	.447
Artificial Turf	2-3	6.61	124	39	6	18	21	.315	.524	.404
April	1-2	15.43	30	10	3	4	11	.333	.667	.429
May	0-2	5.91	42	13	0	11	9	.310	.452	.455
June	1-1	4.50	35	10	1	5	4	.286	.457	.375
July	0-0	12.96	44	19	3	3	3	.432	.795	.479
August	0-3	7.11	52	15	1	7	9	.288	.423	.383
Sept./Oct.	0-0	9.00	46	19	2	2	4	.413	.587	.429
Leading Off Inn.			47	18	2	2	3	.383	.596	.408
Runners On			143	51	6	25	26	.357	.559	.453
Runners/Scor. Pos.			107	33	4	21	22	.308	.477	.424
Runners On/2 Out			62	20	2	9	12	.323	.484	.425
Scor. Pos./2 Out			48	14	1	9	10	.292	.396	.424
Late Inning Pressure			80	27	5	15	18	.338	.613	.454
Leading Off			17	6	2	2	3	.353	.824	.421
Runners On			42	15	2	10	9	.357	.595	.491
Runners/Scor. Pos.			24	7	1	9	6	.292	.458	.500
First 9 Batters			240	81	9	31	40	.338	.529	.420
Second 9 Batters			9	5	1	1	0	.556	1.111	.545
All Batters Thereafter			0	0	0	0	0	.000	.000	.000

Loves to face: Dave Lopes (.111, 1-for-9)
Hates to face: Graig Nettles (.500, 2-for-4, 2 HR)
Ground outs-to-air outs ratio: 1.34 last season, 0.96 for career....
Additional statistics: 4 double-play ground outs in 76 opportunities, 17 doubles, 2 triples in 58.2 innings last season.... Faced only one batter 3 times, pitched two or more innings 10 times, finished 33 games in 53 relief appearances.... Led A.L. in winning percentage (14–2, .875) in 1979 and was 9–3 in '80. Only pitcher in majors with a losing record in all six years since, dropping his career mark to 46–52, .469.... Opponents' batting average with runners in scoring position was the highest of his career.... Saved first two appearances in '86, didn't allow a run in first five outings, then had a 10.33 ERA in next 31 games, prompting trade to Cubs.

Jeff Dedmon

Atlanta Braves   Throws Right

	W–L	ERA	AB	H	HR	BB	SO	BA	SA	OBA
Season	6-6	2.98	372	90	8	39	58	.242	.344	.319
vs. Left-Handers			165	41	5	18	24	.248	.370	.321
vs. Right-Handers			207	49	3	21	34	.237	.324	.318
Home	4-3	3.67	214	57	8	15	34	.266	.425	.325
Road	2-3	2.08	158	33	0	24	24	.209	.234	.311
Grass	6-4	3.02	310	74	8	32	49	.239	.348	.316
Artificial Turf	0-2	2.76	62	16	0	7	9	.258	.323	.333
April	0-1	7.00	31	5	2	6	8	.161	.452	.289
May	2-0	2.38	49	15	1	7	11	.306	.429	.393
June	1-2	1.40	69	14	0	6	11	.203	.246	.267
July	0-2	2.78	88	24	0	10	13	.273	.295	.366
August	2-1	2.37	68	17	4	6	9	.250	.456	.307
Sept./Oct.	1-0	3.93	67	15	1	4	6	.224	.284	.278
Leading Off Inn.			79	22	4	8	11	.278	.456	.345
Runners On			181	41	2	23	27	.227	.298	.324
Runners/Scor. Pos.			121	25	1	19	17	.207	.273	.329
Runners On/2 Out			74	15	1	13	10	.203	.257	.337
Scor. Pos./2 Out			54	9	0	11	7	.167	.167	.328
Late Inning Pressure			201	49	6	17	36	.244	.363	.308
Leading Off			46	10	3	3	7	.217	.457	.265
Runners On			83	19	1	11	12	.229	.277	.330
Runners/Scor. Pos.			54	12	1	10	6	.222	.296	.358
First 9 Batters			323	78	7	31	51	.241	.341	.312
Second 9 Batters			49	12	1	8	7	.245	.367	.362
All Batters Thereafter			0	0	0	0	0	—	—	—

Loves to face: Chili Davis (0-for-11)
Hates to face: Tim Raines (.625, 5-for-8, 1 HR)
Ground outs-to-air outs ratio: 2.56, 4th highest in N.L. last season (minimum: 250 BFP), 2.72 for career. . . . Additional statistics: 9 double-play ground outs in 80 opportunities, 12 doubles, 1 triple in 99.2 innings last season. . . . Faced only one batter 3 times, pitched two or more innings 30 times (3d most in N.L.), finished 22 games in 57 relief appearances. . . . Has not allowed a home run in a road game since Alex Trevino connected on the final day of the 1985 season at Candlestick Park. Has allowed 14 of 19 career home runs at Atlanta Stadium. . . . Opponents batted .133 (2-for-15) with the bases loaded last season. . . . One of nine N.L. pitchers with 50 or more relief appearances in each of the past three seasons.

John Denny

Cincinnati Reds   Throws Right

	W–L	ERA	AB	H	HR	BB	SO	BA	SA	OBA
Season	11-10	4.20	658	179	15	56	115	.272	.410	.331
vs. Left-Handers			327	104	8	32	38	.318	.486	.381
vs. Right-Handers			331	75	7	24	77	.227	.335	.281
Home	6-5	4.43	342	95	6	27	53	.278	.424	.331
Road	5-5	3.95	316	84	9	29	62	.266	.396	.331
Grass	3-2	3.28	174	45	5	15	38	.259	.374	.319
Artificial Turf	8-8	4.55	484	134	10	41	77	.277	.424	.335
April	1-2	4.50	92	27	2	5	14	.293	.446	.327
May	2-3	6.21	158	51	5	15	28	.323	.532	.392
June	2-2	2.72	152	42	4	16	28	.276	.395	.347
July	2-3	5.21	146	36	3	18	28	.247	.370	.325
August	4-0	2.35	110	23	1	2	17	.209	.282	.223
Sept./Oct.			0	0	0	0	0	—	—	—
Leading Off Inn.			163	50	3	16	36	.307	.429	.372
Runners On			272	72	8	27	43	.265	.430	.331
Runners/Scor. Pos.			152	35	4	21	28	.230	.388	.324
Runners On/2 Out			108	23	3	12	29	.213	.343	.298
Scor. Pos./2 Out			68	11	2	11	21	.162	.279	.288
Late Inning Pressure			54	12	1	5	7	.222	.352	.300
Leading Off			16	3	0	1	3	.188	.188	.278
Runners On			15	2	1	4	0	.133	.400	.316
Runners/Scor. Pos.			8	1	1	3	0	.125	.500	.364
First 9 Batters			220	57	6	16	44	.259	.409	.312
Second 9 Batters			214	58	4	22	42	.271	.393	.335
All Batters Thereafter			224	64	5	18	29	.286	.429	.346

Loves to face: Rob Thompson (0-for-14) & Jose Uribe (0-for-15)
Hates to face: Shawon Dunston (.500, 6-for-12)
Ground outs-to-air outs ratio: 2.38, 7th highest in N.L. last season (minimum: 250 BFP), 2.21 for career. . . . Additional statistics: 18 double-play ground outs in 134 opportunities, 36 doubles, 5 triples in 171.1 innings last season. . . . Allowed 15 first-inning runs in 27 starts last season. . . . Batting support: 4.04 runs per start. . . . Has defeated every major league club in his career except Cleveland and Texas. . . . Left-handed batters have hit for a higher average off him than right-handers in each of the past 10 seasons, but never to the degree exhibited in 1986. . . . Has had a winning record only once in the last five seasons, but won the Cy Young Award in that season (19–6 in 1983).

Jim Deshaies

Houston Astros   Throws Left

	W–L	ERA	AB	H	HR	BB	SO	BA	SA	OBA
Season	12-5	3.25	531	124	16	59	128	.234	.379	.311
vs. Left-Handers			87	21	3	12	20	.241	.402	.333
vs. Right-Handers			444	103	13	47	108	.232	.374	.306
Home	6-3	3.39	315	72	11	30	71	.229	.378	.295
Road	6-2	3.05	216	52	5	29	57	.241	.380	.333
Grass	2-1	3.67	100	27	3	8	29	.270	.450	.330
Artificial Turf	10-4	3.15	431	97	13	51	99	.225	.362	.307
April	0-0	4.15	32	8	2	2	6	.250	.469	.294
May	1-1	5.40	49	12	2	5	17	.245	.408	.309
June	4-1	3.08	144	32	3	15	27	.222	.368	.294
July	1-1	3.63	80	18	3	12	28	.225	.413	.326
August	3-1	3.18	126	30	3	18	25	.238	.349	.340
Sept./Oct.	3-1	1.95	100	24	3	7	25	.240	.360	.290
Leading Off Inn.			137	37	4	15	32	.270	.423	.342
Runners On			206	37	6	24	48	.180	.311	.265
Runners/Scor. Pos.			114	16	0	15	27	.140	.184	.241
Runners On/2 Out			86	13	1	11	24	.151	.244	.247
Scor. Pos./2 Out			48	6	0	10	13	.125	.167	.276
Late Inning Pressure			18	5	0	0	3	.278	.278	.278
Leading Off			6	1	0	0	0	.167	.167	.167
Runners On			3	1	0	0	1	.333	.333	.333
Runners/Scor. Pos.			0	0	0	0	0	—	—	—
First 9 Batters			202	48	5	25	65	.238	.356	.320
Second 9 Batters			190	41	6	20	40	.216	.384	.294
All Batters Thereafter			139	35	5	14	23	.252	.403	.320

Loves to face: Willie McGee (0-for-8, 4 SO)
Hates to face: Steve Sax (.467, 7-for-15)
Ground outs-to-air outs ratio: 0.56, 5th lowest in N.L. last season (minimum: 250 BFP), 0.58 for career. . . . Additional statistics: 4 double-play ground outs in 91 opportunities, 27 doubles, 1 triple in 144.0 innings last season. . . . Allowed 7 first-inning runs in 26 starts last season. . . . Batting support: 4.23 runs per start. . . . Opponents' batting average with runners in scoring position (.140) is lowest in majors in last 12 years (minimum: 125 BFP in such situations). . . . Set modern major-league record by striking out the first eight batters (vs. Dodgers, Sept. 23). . . . Has never allowed a home run with more than one runner on. . . . Led majors with seven balks last season. . . . 2.51 ERA in the first three innings, 4.06 thereafter.

Frank DiPino

Astros/Cubs   Throws Left

	W–L	ERA	AB	H	HR	BB	SO	BA	SA	OBA
Season	3-7	4.37	301	74	11	30	70	.246	.409	.315
vs. Left-Handers			93	16	3	7	23	.172	.290	.235
vs. Right-Handers			208	58	8	23	47	.279	.462	.350
Home	2-2	3.51	150	35	4	14	26	.233	.360	.299
Road	1-5	5.26	151	39	7	16	44	.258	.457	.331
Grass	1-4	5.77	133	38	5	16	30	.286	.466	.362
Artificial Turf	2-3	3.33	168	36	6	14	40	.214	.363	.277
April	0-1	1.74	37	5	0	3	7	.135	.162	.195
May	1-1	1.46	43	8	0	7	8	.186	.186	.314
June	0-1	6.10	35	7	2	5	5	.200	.429	.300
July	0-2	6.60	61	19	3	4	15	.311	.492	.358
August	1-2	4.02	59	16	3	7	20	.271	.475	.343
Sept./Oct.	1-0	5.40	66	19	3	4	15	.288	.500	.329
Leading Off Inn.			66	13	0	9	19	.197	.273	.312
Runners On			142	39	3	12	26	.275	.408	.325
Runners/Scor. Pos.			87	21	1	9	18	.241	.299	.303
Runners On/2 Out			61	18	1	4	10	.295	.393	.338
Scor. Pos./2 Out			38	12	0	4	6	.316	.342	.381
Late Inning Pressure			150	43	5	18	32	.287	.447	.368
Leading Off			33	6	0	6	12	.182	.212	.341
Runners On			72	23	3	9	9	.319	.542	.390
Runners/Scor. Pos.			41	10	1	7	9	.244	.341	.347
First 9 Batters			281	67	10	28	65	.238	.399	.310
Second 9 Batters			20	7	1	2	5	.350	.550	.391
All Batters Thereafter			0	0	0	0	0	—	—	—

Loves to face: Von Hayes (.071, 1-for-14)
Hates to face: Glenn Wilson (.857, 6-for-7, 2 HR)
Ground outs-to-air outs ratio: 1.34 last season, 1.20 for career. . . . Additional statistics: 4 double-play ground outs in 69 opportunities, 12 doubles, 2 triples in 80.1 innings last season. . . . Faced only one batter 5 times, pitched two or more innings 23 times, finished 26 games in 61 relief appearances. . . . Career record of 0–5 vs. Los Angeles. . . . Has allowed more home runs in road games than in home games in each of the last five years. Of course, he now pitches in Wrigley Field after calling the Astrodome home for several seasons. . . . Annual total of saves since 1983: 20, 14, 6, 3. . . . Has never had a winning record in the majors (six seasons); one of three pitchers with losing records in each of past four seasons.

Kelly Downs

San Francisco Giants — Throws Right

	W–L	ERA	AB	H	HR	BB	SO	BA	SA	OBA
Season	4-4	2.75	331	78	5	30	64	.236	.323	.302
vs. Left-Handers			171	40	2	18	31	.234	.327	.313
vs. Right-Handers			160	38	3	12	33	.238	.319	.290
Home	2-2	3.79	140	32	3	14	26	.229	.343	.304
Road	2-2	1.97	191	46	2	16	38	.241	.309	.300
Grass	4-3	2.97	257	60	5	24	50	.233	.335	.300
Artificial Turf	0-1	1.93	74	18	0	6	14	.243	.284	.309
April			0	0	0	0	0	—	—	—
May			0	0	0	0	0	—	—	—
June			0	0	0	0	0	—	—	—
July	0-1	3.60	17	5	0	3	4	.294	.294	.364
August	1-3	3.93	144	40	3	11	28	.278	.396	.327
Sept./Oct.	3-0	1.74	170	33	2	16	32	.194	.265	.274
Leading Off Inn.			85	22	2	5	18	.259	.365	.308
Runners On			141	27	1	17	26	.191	.248	.276
Runners/Scor. Pos.			87	17	1	12	19	.195	.253	.282
Runners On/2 Out			67	17	1	9	9	.254	.313	.342
Scor. Pos./2 Out			48	14	1	8	7	.292	.354	.393
Late Inning Pressure			18	3	0	4	2	.167	.222	.318
Leading Off			4	1	0	2	0	.250	.500	.500
Runners On			9	1	0	2	0	.111	.111	.273
Runners/Scor. Pos.			6	1	0	1	0	.167	.167	.286
First 9 Batters			117	24	0	6	29	.205	.231	.240
Second 9 Batters			110	28	3	11	14	.255	.391	.320
All Batters Thereafter			104	26	2	13	21	.250	.356	.347

Loves to face: Bo Diaz (0-for-6)
Hates to face: Len Matuszek (.667, 4-for-6)
Ground outs-to-air outs ratio: 1.46 last season, his first in majors. . . . Additional statistics: 5 double-play ground outs in 61 opportunities, 12 doubles, 1 triple in 88.1 innings last season. . . . Allowed 1 first-inning run in 14 starts last season. . . . Batting support: 3.21 runs per start, 2d lowest in N.L. (minimum: 15 GS). . . . Attention rotisserie-league scouts: Ranked 7th in N.L. with an ERA of 2.75 after the All-Star break. Two other rookies also ranked among the top 10: Bruce Ruffin (2.38, 4th) and Jim Deshaies (2.81, 10th). . . . Led the league in ERA after September 1. . . . Allowed one home run per 17.7 innings, 7th-best ratio in N.L. (minimum: 10 GS).

Dave Dravecky

San Diego Padres — Throws Left

	W–L	ERA	AB	H	HR	BB	SO	BA	SA	OBA
Season	9-11	3.07	605	149	17	54	87	.246	.387	.307
vs. Left-Handers			84	19	1	5	20	.226	.333	.261
vs. Right-Handers			521	130	16	49	67	.250	.395	.314
Home	3-6	3.45	319	77	9	27	55	.241	.382	.300
Road	6-5	2.63	286	72	8	27	32	.252	.392	.314
Grass	5-7	2.82	412	98	11	35	64	.238	.364	.296
Artificial Turf	4-4	3.62	193	51	6	19	23	.264	.435	.329
April	2-1	0.75	122	21	2	8	20	.172	.279	.221
May	3-3	3.14	164	39	3	10	30	.238	.341	.284
June	2-3	3.82	140	40	3	16	12	.286	.436	.359
July	0-1	3.52	82	21	2	10	12	.256	.366	.330
August	2-3	4.88	97	28	7	10	13	.289	.546	.352
Sept./Oct.			0	0	0	0	0	—	—	—
Leading Off Inn.			159	39	5	11	25	.245	.403	.294
Runners On			220	50	7	26	25	.227	.377	.306
Runners/Scor. Pos.			134	26	4	16	20	.194	.328	.276
Runners On/2 Out			109	27	4	12	11	.248	.431	.328
Scor. Pos./2 Out			71	15	3	7	9	.211	.408	.291
Late Inning Pressure			48	16	2	3	3	.333	.542	.358
Leading Off			13	3	0	2	1	.231	.308	.333
Runners On			17	7	1	1	1	.412	.588	.400
Runners/Scor. Pos.			11	4	0	1	1	.364	.364	.357
First 9 Batters			204	55	6	24	35	.270	.417	.345
Second 9 Batters			200	42	6	18	30	.210	.345	.276
All Batters Thereafter			201	52	5	12	22	.259	.398	.298

Loves to face: Ken Oberkfell (.063, 1-for-16)
Hates to face: Dave Lopes (.700, 7-for-10, 2 HR)
Ground outs-to-air outs ratio: 1.11 last season, 1.07 for career. . . . Additional statistics: 9 double-play ground outs in 97 opportunities, 28 doubles, 3 triples in 161.1 innings last season. . . . Allowed 10 first-inning runs in 26 starts last season. . . . Batting support: 3.46 runs per start, 7th lowest in N.L. (minimum: 15 GS). . . . Led N.L. in ERA in April. . . . Career ERA of 2.63 before the All-Star break, 3.62 thereafter. . . . Opponents' career batting average of .211 (8-for-38, no XBH) with the bases loaded. . . . Opponents' career batting: .252 with bases empty, .230 with runners on, .219 with runners in scoring position. . . . Has allowed 68 career homers, but only five to left-handed batters—one each in the last five seasons.

Dennis Eckersley

Chicago Cubs — Throws Right

	W–L	ERA	AB	H	HR	BB	SO	BA	SA	OBA
Season	6-11	4.57	793	226	21	43	137	.285	.455	.320
vs. Left-Handers			425	128	9	32	54	.301	.471	.347
vs. Right-Handers			368	98	12	11	83	.266	.438	.289
Home	4-5	5.18	336	100	13	20	59	.298	.500	.334
Road	2-6	4.13	457	126	8	23	78	.276	.422	.310
Grass	6-8	4.74	574	166	17	28	107	.289	.469	.320
Artificial Turf	0-3	4.13	219	60	4	15	30	.274	.420	.321
April	0-2	4.37	127	31	5	8	30	.244	.441	.295
May	2-1	7.53	154	55	6	5	16	.357	.610	.377
June	0-1	4.91	95	21	1	8	15	.221	.316	.274
July	3-2	2.57	154	33	5	6	31	.214	.370	.247
August	1-2	3.89	154	49	1	9	25	.318	.442	.352
Sept./Oct.	0-3	4.73	109	37	3	7	20	.339	.514	.373
Leading Off Inn.			200	52	3	8	29	.260	.385	.288
Runners On			313	92	12	25	52	.294	.505	.340
Runners/Scor. Pos.			194	55	5	15	39	.284	.448	.326
Runners On/2 Out			136	34	2	14	27	.250	.412	.325
Scor. Pos./2 Out			96	23	1	8	20	.240	.365	.305
Late Inning Pressure			41	10	1	2	6	.244	.390	.279
Leading Off			13	3	0	0	3	.231	.231	.231
Runners On			12	3	0	1	3	.250	.250	.308
Runners/Scor. Pos.			7	1	0	1	3	.143	.143	.250
First 9 Batters			268	77	4	14	59	.287	.440	.317
Second 9 Batters			263	69	9	15	41	.262	.411	.305
All Batters Thereafter			262	80	8	14	37	.305	.515	.339

Loves to face: Jose Cruz (.077, 1-for-13)
Hates to face: Ken Griffey (.500, 7-for-14, 1 HR)
Ground outs-to-air outs ratio: 0.87 last season, 0.70 for career. . . . Additional statistics: 6 double-play ground outs in 127 opportunities, 6th-lowest average in N.L. (minimum: 40 opp.), 58 doubles (most in majors), 7 triples in 201.0 innings last season. Allowed 86 extra-base hits, most in N.L. . . . Allowed 18 first-inning runs in 32 starts last season. . . . Batting support: 4.03 runs per start. . . . Highest ERA in N.L. during May (minimum: 20 IP). . . . Career record of 0–5 vs. Pittsburgh. . . . Committed four balks in nine and a half years in the A.L., 10 balks in two and a half years with the Cubs. . . . Opposing batters have a career batting average of .221 with two outs and runners in scoring position.

Sid Fernandez

New York Mets — Throws Left

	W–L	ERA	AB	H	HR	BB	SO	BA	SA	OBA
Season	16-6	3.52	746	161	13	91	200	.216	.324	.300
vs. Left-Handers			98	22	1	18	33	.224	.286	.347
vs. Right-Handers			648	139	12	73	167	.215	.330	.293
Home	8-3	2.17	376	67	4	45	109	.178	.258	.265
Road	8-3	5.03	370	94	9	46	91	.254	.392	.337
Grass	10-5	3.39	521	110	10	61	139	.211	.313	.294
Artificial Turf	6-1	3.84	225	51	3	30	61	.227	.351	.315
April	2-0	2.66	66	6	0	12	20	.091	.091	.231
May	3-1	3.10	147	30	3	18	35	.204	.306	.293
June	4-1	3.41	118	21	3	18	29	.178	.314	.283
July	3-2	3.35	145	35	2	14	41	.241	.352	.311
August	3-0	5.46	124	34	5	12	30	.274	.460	.336
Sept./Oct.	1-2	3.15	146	35	0	17	45	.240	.315	.315
Leading Off Inn.			187	39	3	24	48	.209	.294	.299
Runners On			310	66	7	38	84	.213	.348	.297
Runners/Scor. Pos.			162	33	5	25	49	.204	.352	.299
Runners On/2 Out			135	25	2	13	40	.185	.289	.267
Scor. Pos./2 Out			80	15	2	8	27	.188	.325	.261
Late Inning Pressure			38	11	0	7	5	.289	.368	.391
Leading Off			8	3	0	4	1	.375	.375	.583
Runners On			21	5	0	2	3	.238	.333	.292
Runners/Scor. Pos.			10	1	0	1	3	.100	.100	.167
First 9 Batters			249	46	3	30	80	.185	.273	.270
Second 9 Batters			256	56	4	25	70	.219	.316	.286
All Batters Thereafter			241	59	6	36	50	.245	.386	.345

Loves to face: John Russell (0-for-10, 7 SO)
Hates to face: Mitch Webster (.417, 5-for-12)
Ground outs-to-air outs ratio: 0.48, lowest in majors last season (minimum: 250 BFP), 0.49 for career. . . . Additional statistics: 10 double-play ground outs in 158 opportunities, 34 doubles, 4 triples in 204.1 innings last season. . . . Allowed 12 first-inning runs in 31 starts last season. . . . Batting support: 5.16 runs per start, 3d best in N.L. (minimum: 15 GS). . . . Only home run allowed to a left-handed batter was a mammoth shot by Graig Nettles. . . . ERA in home games (2.17) was 2d best in the N.L. . . . The only starting pitcher in the majors to average more than a strikeout per inning over the past two seasons (minimum: 10 GS in each). . . . Opponents batted .500 (6-for-12) with the bases loaded last season.

Bob Forsch
St. Louis Cardinals — Throws Right

	W–L	ERA	AB	H	HR	BB	SO	BA	SA	OBA
Season	14-10	3.25	855	211	19	68	104	.247	.374	.301
vs. Left-Handers			421	111	10	44	48	.264	.394	.332
vs. Right-Handers			434	100	9	24	56	.230	.355	.270
Home	8-4	2.66	461	107	5	28	49	.232	.321	.277
Road	6-6	3.94	394	104	14	40	55	.264	.437	.328
Grass	2-5	3.57	218	61	6	25	34	.280	.436	.350
Artificial Turf	12-5	3.14	637	150	13	43	70	.235	.353	.283
April	1-1	2.60	105	25	3	9	19	.238	.390	.298
May	3-2	2.95	146	36	1	19	18	.247	.315	.331
June	2-1	1.79	142	27	3	14	22	.190	.303	.264
July	4-2	2.82	147	45	2	7	10	.306	.408	.340
August	3-2	3.23	170	38	4	9	20	.224	.341	.260
Sept./Oct.	1-2	6.14	145	40	6	10	15	.276	.497	.316
Leading Off Inn.			231	56	9	9	24	.242	.429	.271
Runners On			294	75	3	39	33	.255	.330	.337
Runners/Scor. Pos.			158	45	3	28	19	.285	.411	.381
Runners On/2 Out			122	28	0	15	17	.230	.287	.319
Scor. Pos./2 Out			70	18	0	11	11	.257	.343	.366
Late Inning Pressure			80	18	4	7	6	.225	.413	.287
Leading Off			24	6	2	2	1	.250	.542	.308
Runners On			15	2	0	3	1	.133	.133	.278
Runners/Scor. Pos.			6	1	0	1	0	.167	.167	.286
First 9 Batters			274	69	7	19	36	.252	.398	.297
Second 9 Batters			274	71	4	12	35	.259	.372	.292
All Batters Thereafter			307	71	8	37	33	.231	.355	.311

Loves to face: Marvell Wynne (0-for-17)
Hates to face: Darryl Strawberry (.444, 8-for-18, 5 HR)
Ground outs-to-air outs ratio: 1.15 last season, 1.47 for career. . . .
Additional statistics: 27 double-play ground outs in 150 opportunities, 6th-highest average in N.L. (minimum: 10 GDP), 38 doubles, 7 triples in 230.0 innings last season. . . . Allowed 17 first-inning runs in 33 starts last season. . . . Batting support: 4.30 runs per start. . . . 9–4 vs. teams with winning records, 5–6 vs. teams below the .500 mark. . . . Leads major-league pitchers with 13 consecutive seasons of service with a single team. . . . Opponents batted .176 (3-for-17) with the bases loaded last season, following .464 mark (13-for-28) over four previous seasons. . . . One of four pitchers to hit two home runs last season. He led all pitchers with 12 RBI.

John Franco
Cincinnati Reds — Throws Left

	W–L	ERA	AB	H	HR	BB	SO	BA	SA	OBA
Season	6-6	2.94	371	90	7	44	84	.243	.332	.324
vs. Left-Handers			76	16	0	3	13	.211	.250	.250
vs. Right-Handers			295	74	7	41	71	.251	.353	.341
Home	2-2	3.02	204	51	5	20	37	.250	.377	.319
Road	4-4	2.85	167	39	2	24	47	.234	.275	.330
Grass	2-3	2.70	107	23	2	14	30	.215	.271	.309
Artificial Turf	4-3	3.04	264	67	5	30	54	.254	.356	.330
April	0-0	3.46	46	12	1	6	10	.261	.413	.346
May	0-1	1.64	76	15	0	11	22	.197	.224	.303
June	1-3	2.66	70	16	1	8	10	.229	.271	.304
July	2-0	1.15	57	12	1	7	16	.211	.263	.308
August	2-0	4.38	49	12	2	5	8	.245	.388	.315
Sept./Oct.	1-2	5.09	73	23	2	7	18	.315	.466	.370
Leading Off Inn.			77	16	1	4	14	.208	.247	.250
Runners On			189	45	4	28	48	.238	.349	.332
Runners/Scor. Pos.			113	26	1	22	31	.230	.327	.348
Runners On/2 Out			88	18	0	18	27	.205	.284	.340
Scor. Pos./2 Out			60	16	0	14	17	.267	.383	.405
Late Inning Pressure			274	62	5	36	65	.226	.307	.318
Leading Off			57	11	1	4	11	.193	.246	.258
Runners On			136	29	3	22	37	.213	.309	.319
Runners/Scor. Pos.			83	16	1	18	26	.193	.277	.330
First 9 Batters			354	88	7	41	79	.249	.339	.328
Second 9 Batters			17	2	0	3	5	.118	.176	.250
All Batters Thereafter			0	0	0	0	0	—	—	—

Loves to face: Von Hayes (0-for-12)
Hates to face: Bill Doran (.667, 6-for-9)
Ground outs-to-air outs ratio: 2.00 last season, 1.85 for career. . . .
Additional statistics: 7 double-play ground outs in 96 opportunities, 10 doubles, 1 triple in 101.0 innings last season. . . . Faced only one batter 5 times, pitched two or more innings 23 times, finished 52 games in 74 relief appearances. . . . Has allowed 15 career home runs, only two to left-handed batters. Hasn't allowed a home run to a lefty since his first appearance of the 1985 season when Darryl Strawberry connected. . . . Career average of one extra-base hit for every 39.5 at bats by left-handed batters is lowest in 12-year *Player Analysis* history (minimum: 200 AB). . . . Opponents have a career mark of .194 (7-for-36) with the bases loaded.

Gene Garber
Atlanta Braves — Throws Right

	W–L	ERA	AB	H	HR	BB	SO	BA	SA	OBA
Season	5-5	2.54	292	76	3	20	56	.260	.332	.309
vs. Left-Handers			138	34	0	14	26	.246	.297	.316
vs. Right-Handers			154	42	3	6	30	.273	.364	.302
Home	3-3	2.55	134	35	2	7	24	.261	.343	.301
Road	2-2	2.53	158	41	1	13	32	.259	.323	.316
Grass	4-5	2.83	216	58	2	17	40	.269	.347	.323
Artificial Turf	1-0	1.74	76	18	1	3	16	.237	.289	.266
April	0-1	3.38	32	10	0	4	4	.313	.406	.389
May	1-0	0.48	67	15	1	2	14	.224	.299	.257
June	3-0	1.26	49	10	0	4	10	.204	.224	.264
July	0-1	1.42	46	8	1	3	7	.174	.239	.224
August	1-1	2.76	62	18	0	5	13	.290	.323	.343
Sept./Oct.	0-2	10.13	36	15	1	2	8	.417	.611	.436
Leading Off Inn.			58	15	1	4	12	.259	.345	.306
Runners On			146	37	0	15	29	.253	.295	.321
Runners/Scor. Pos.			98	27	0	12	16	.276	.327	.351
Runners On/2 Out			67	17	0	7	13	.254	.299	.324
Scor. Pos./2 Out			47	15	0	5	9	.319	.383	.385
Late Inning Pressure			183	49	3	16	32	.268	.355	.330
Leading Off			35	11	1	4	4	.314	.457	.385
Runners On			96	24	0	12	20	.250	.281	.333
Runners/Scor. Pos.			64	20	0	10	10	.313	.359	.405
First 9 Batters			288	75	3	20	54	.260	.333	.310
Second 9 Batters			4	1	0	0	2	.250	.250	.250
All Batters Thereafter			0	0	0	0	0	—	—	—

Loves to face: Dane Iorg (.091, 1-for-11)
Hates to face: Jerry Mumphrey (.500, 10-for-20)
Ground outs-to-air outs ratio: 2.40 last season, 6th highest in N.L. last season (minimum: 250 BFP), 2.17 for career. . . . Additional statistics: 11 double-play ground outs in 67 opportunities, 9th-highest average in N.L. (minimum: 10 GDP), 12 doubles, 0 triples in 78.0 innings last season. . . . Faced only one batter 5 times, pitched two or more innings 17 times, finished 48 games in 61 relief appearances. . . . The only major-league pitcher with at least one decision in every season since 1979, but without a winning season during that time. . . . More saves last season (24) than in previous three seasons combined (21). . . . Unusual streak: hasn't allowed a triple to a right-handed batter since July 11, 1979. He has faced 1375 righties since then.

Scott Garrelts
San Francisco Giants — Throws Right

	W–L	ERA	AB	H	HR	BB	SO	BA	SA	OBA
Season	13-9	3.11	624	144	17	74	125	.231	.351	.311
vs. Left-Handers			337	80	6	43	56	.237	.320	.322
vs. Right-Handers			287	64	11	31	69	.223	.387	.298
Home	8-4	2.23	345	66	10	33	66	.191	.307	.261
Road	5-5	4.23	279	78	7	41	59	.280	.405	.370
Grass	11-6	2.81	517	114	16	55	99	.221	.340	.296
Artificial Turf	2-3	4.60	107	30	1	19	26	.280	.402	.380
April	3-2	2.65	138	33	5	13	20	.239	.370	.303
May	2-3	4.32	153	38	6	19	24	.248	.418	.328
June	1-1	1.91	114	26	2	8	19	.228	.316	.282
July	3-1	7.16	65	17	3	8	16	.262	.477	.338
August	2-2	2.21	71	15	1	15	21	.211	.296	.352
Sept./Oct.	2-0	1.44	83	15	0	11	25	.181	.193	.274
Leading Off Inn.			158	40	4	14	24	.253	.380	.314
Runners On			254	56	8	38	61	.220	.343	.317
Runners/Scor. Pos.			160	34	5	28	43	.213	.338	.321
Runners On/2 Out			104	17	5	19	30	.163	.317	.298
Scor. Pos./2 Out			73	12	3	16	20	.164	.301	.322
Late Inning Pressure			207	46	4	28	53	.222	.309	.316
Leading Off			49	14	1	6	8	.286	.367	.364
Runners On			94	21	2	15	29	.223	.319	.333
Runners/Scor. Pos.			58	10	1	14	19	.172	.259	.338
First 9 Batters			315	70	7	49	78	.222	.327	.323
Second 9 Batters			161	40	4	12	27	.248	.354	.303
All Batters Thereafter			148	34	6	13	20	.230	.399	.292

Loves to face: Keith Moreland (0-for-14)
Hates to face: Craig Reynolds (.583, 7-for-12)
Ground outs-to-air outs ratio: 1.34 last season, 1.25 for career. . . . Additional statistics: 20 double-play ground outs (6th in N.L.) in 126 opportunities, 20 doubles, 2 triples in 173.2 innings last season. . . . Allowed 12 first-inning runs in 18 starts last season. . . . Batting support: 3.56 runs per start, 8th lowest in N.L. (minimum: 15 GS). . . . Never faced only one batter, pitched two or more innings 17 times, finished 27 games in 35 relief appearances. . . . ERA in home games (2.23) was 5th best in N.L. . . . Career batting averages: .247 by left-handers, .212 by right-handers. . . . And forget Incaviglia, Canseco, and Deer—Garrelts struck out 25 times in 45 at bats last season.

Dwight Gooden

Throws Right

New York Mets	W–L	ERA	AB	H	HR	BB	SO	BA	SA	OBA
Season	17-6	2.84	917	197	17	80	200	.215	.321	.278
vs. Left-Handers			527	111	7	50	111	.211	.306	.283
vs. Right-Handers			390	86	10	30	89	.221	.341	.273
Home	9-3	2.20	431	79	8	42	103	.183	.288	.257
Road	8-3	3.47	486	118	9	38	97	.243	.350	.298
Grass	12-4	2.60	666	139	11	60	152	.209	.303	.274
Artificial Turf	5-2	3.53	251	58	6	20	48	.231	.367	.290
April	4-0	1.26	151	28	2	6	32	.185	.285	.215
May	2-2	2.83	134	31	2	8	30	.231	.299	.275
June	3-1	3.97	162	35	4	23	32	.216	.352	.312
July	1-1	4.32	97	25	2	10	13	.258	.371	.327
August	3-0	2.89	170	41	3	14	42	.241	.353	.302
Sept./Oct.	4-2	2.45	203	37	4	19	51	.182	.286	.254
Leading Off Inn.			225	56	5	25	40	.249	.378	.332
Runners On			384	78	8	35	89	.203	.297	.265
Runners/Scor. Pos.			221	37	5	25	58	.167	.262	.244
Runners On/2 Out			154	26	3	12	40	.169	.253	.229
Scor. Pos./2 Out			101	15	2	8	28	.149	.228	.211
Late Inning Pressure			101	18	2	12	27	.178	.277	.270
Leading Off			23	3	0	4	4	.130	.130	.286
Runners On			46	9	1	3	12	.196	.304	.240
Runners/Scor. Pos.			21	1	0	3	7	.048	.095	.160
First 9 Batters			267	55	1	20	71	.206	.262	.261
Second 9 Batters			263	63	6	26	48	.240	.365	.308
All Batters Thereafter			387	79	10	34	81	.204	.331	.270

Loves to face: Jim Morrison (.056, 1-for-18, 9 SO)
Hates to face: Chili Davis (.522, 12-for-23)
Ground outs-to-air outs ratio: 1.26 last season, 1.06 for career. . . .
Additional statistics: 13 double-play ground outs in 174 opportunities, 36 doubles, 5 triples in 250.0 innings last season. . . . Allowed 13 first-inning runs in 33 starts last season. . . . Batting support: 4.64 runs per start. . . . Has not lost consecutive regular-season starts since May 20–25, 1985. . . . Compiled a 2.80 ERA in 10 no-decision starts last season. . . . Opponents' annual batting averages leading off innings: .178, .196, .249. . . . Yearly averages with two outs and runners on base: .174, .158, .169. . . . With two out and runners in scoring position in Late-Inning Pressure Situations, Gooden has allowed opponents only two hits in 39 at bats, and both of those hits came in his rookie year.

Kevin Gross

Throws Right

Philadelphia Phillies	W–L	ERA	AB	H	HR	BB	SO	BA	SA	OBA
Season	12-12	4.02	923	240	28	94	154	.260	.417	.332
vs. Left-Handers			530	144	16	70	84	.272	.445	.360
vs. Right-Handers			393	96	12	24	70	.244	.379	.291
Home	7-7	3.56	510	128	14	47	99	.251	.402	.317
Road	5-5	4.60	413	112	14	47	55	.271	.436	.350
Grass	3-3	5.11	263	73	11	30	36	.278	.452	.350
Artificial Turf	9-9	3.59	660	167	17	64	118	.253	.403	.325
April	1-3	4.30	114	33	4	14	12	.289	.456	.364
May	3-2	4.32	163	42	6	14	19	.258	.417	.316
June	2-0	4.39	154	40	3	19	29	.260	.422	.345
July	0-3	3.44	136	34	6	9	17	.250	.456	.301
August	3-2	3.27	201	50	3	21	45	.249	.333	.330
Sept./Oct.	3-2	4.65	155	41	6	17	32	.265	.458	.339
Leading Off Inn.			228	59	13	24	34	.259	.478	.335
Runners On			390	103	7	42	69	.264	.379	.338
Runners/Scor. Pos.			230	62	4	23	46	.270	.374	.335
Runners On/2 Out			178	53	2	19	27	.298	.388	.375
Scor. Pos./2 Out			124	34	1	12	21	.274	.331	.343
Late Inning Pressure			99	26	3	10	14	.263	.434	.336
Leading Off			25	3	1	2	4	.120	.240	.214
Runners On			38	10	1	5	6	.263	.447	.349
Runners/Scor. Pos.			21	4	0	1	4	.190	.238	.227
First 9 Batters			295	65	10	30	55	.220	.366	.294
Second 9 Batters			275	74	9	32	39	.269	.440	.353
All Batters Thereafter			353	101	9	32	60	.286	.442	.348

Loves to face: Vince Coleman (.067, 1-for-15, 6 SO)
Hates to face: Len Dykstra (.444, 8-for-18, 1 HR)
Ground outs-to-air outs ratio: 0.76 last season, 1.05 for career. . . .
Additional statistics: 12 double-play ground outs in 178 opportunities, 41 doubles, 10 triples (most in majors) in 241.2 innings last season. Allowed 79 extra-base hits, 2d most in N.L., including league-leading 28 home runs. . . . Allowed 18 first-inning runs in 36 starts last season. . . . Batting support: 4.50 runs per start. . . . One of three N.L. pitchers to hit for the cycle last year (in the season, not a game); others: Bob Forsch and Dan Schatzeder. . . . One of three N.L. pitchers to defeat the Mets three times last season. The others: Mike Krukow (4) and Bob Knepper. . . . Hit 8 batters with pitches, most in N.L. last season.

Rich Gossage

Throws Right

San Diego Padres	W–L	ERA	AB	H	HR	BB	SO	BA	SA	OBA
Season	5-7	4.45	253	69	8	20	63	.273	.419	.326
vs. Left-Handers			128	36	4	14	26	.281	.445	.347
vs. Right-Handers			125	33	4	6	37	.264	.392	.304
Home	5-5	3.79	151	44	4	11	39	.291	.417	.337
Road	0-2	5.40	102	25	4	9	24	.245	.422	.310
Grass	5-6	4.37	215	58	6	19	56	.270	.400	.329
Artificial Turf	0-1	5.00	38	11	2	1	7	.289	.526	.308
April	2-1	3.00	48	14	1	3	14	.292	.396	.340
May	1-2	4.15	51	13	2	6	11	.255	.431	.328
June	0-0	5.25	41	8	1	7	10	.195	.317	.320
July	2-1	3.27	43	12	2	2	14	.279	.465	.311
August	0-3	5.52	61	19	1	2	13	.311	.410	.328
Sept./Oct.	0-0	9.00	9	3	1	0	1	.333	.778	.333
Leading Off Inn.			48	12	2	5	12	.250	.417	.321
Runners On			136	37	5	10	32	.272	.419	.318
Runners/Scor. Pos.			84	21	4	7	24	.250	.452	.295
Runners On/2 Out			58	15	4	4	16	.259	.517	.306
Scor. Pos./2 Out			39	9	3	4	11	.231	.538	.302
Late Inning Pressure			196	54	6	16	47	.276	.413	.330
Leading Off			37	11	2	5	9	.297	.514	.381
Runners On			109	27	4	7	27	.248	.376	.289
Runners/Scor. Pos.			68	15	4	4	20	.221	.426	.250
First 9 Batters			241	67	8	20	60	.278	.432	.336
Second 9 Batters			12	2	0	0	3	.167	.167	.143
All Batters Thereafter			0	0	0	0	0	—	—	—

Loves to face: Jeffrey Leonard (0-for-13, 8 SO)
Hates to face: Sid Bream (2-for-2, 2 HR)
Ground outs-to-air outs ratio: 0.97 last season, 0.83 for career. . . .
Additional statistics: 5 double-play ground outs in 64 opportunities, 9 doubles, 2 triples in 64.2 innings last season. . . . Faced only one batter once, pitched two or more innings 18 times, finished 38 games in 45 relief appearances. . . . Fanned Pete Rose as a pinch-hitter in what may have been his final at bat (Aug. 17). . . . Yeah, sure. . . . Only pitcher in majors with 20 or more saves in each of the past seven seasons. . . . The heat is on. Again. Strikeouts per nine innings over past four seasons, starting with 1983: 9.31, 7.39, 5.92, 8.77. . . . Led N.L. relief pitchers with a ratio of 3.15 strikeouts per walk (minimum: 40 appearances).

Cecilio Guante

Throws Right

Pittsburgh Pirates	W–L	ERA	AB	H	HR	BB	SO	BA	SA	OBA
Season	5-2	3.35	289	65	11	29	63	.225	.398	.300
vs. Left-Handers			119	22	2	17	24	.185	.286	.292
vs. Right-Handers			170	43	9	12	39	.253	.476	.306
Home	1-1	3.35	156	31	6	14	37	.199	.372	.272
Road	4-1	3.34	133	34	5	15	26	.256	.429	.333
Grass	2-1	4.87	83	24	4	9	16	.289	.494	.355
Artificial Turf	3-1	2.81	206	41	7	20	47	.199	.359	.278
April	1-0	1.80	53	8	1	7	12	.151	.245	.262
May	1-0	2.70	62	11	3	7	12	.177	.323	.261
June	0-1	2.28	88	23	2	9	15	.261	.386	.333
July	2-1	7.11	49	14	3	4	13	.286	.571	.333
August	1-0	4.50	37	9	2	2	11	.243	.541	.300
Sept./Oct.			0	0	0	0	0	—	—	—
Leading Off Inn.			61	12	1	6	5	.197	.328	.279
Runners On			138	37	7	12	34	.268	.471	.322
Runners/Scor. Pos.			89	21	4	7	21	.236	.427	.286
Runners On/2 Out			62	15	4	9	16	.242	.468	.338
Scor. Pos./2 Out			45	10	3	6	10	.222	.467	.314
Late Inning Pressure			133	24	4	17	38	.180	.316	.278
Leading Off			32	9	1	3	2	.281	.469	.361
Runners On			59	9	3	8	24	.153	.322	.254
Runners/Scor. Pos.			30	4	1	6	12	.133	.267	.278
First 9 Batters			270	59	11	29	61	.219	.396	.299
Second 9 Batters			19	6	0	0	2	.316	.421	.316
All Batters Thereafter			0	0	0	0	0	—	—	—

Loves to face: Danny Heep (0-for-5)
Hates to face: George Hendrick (.778, 7-for-9)
Ground outs-to-air outs ratio: 0.65, 7th lowest in N.L. last season (minimum: 250 BFP), 0.69 for career. . . . Additional statistics: 4 double-play ground outs in 64 opportunities, 17 doubles, 0 triples in 78.0 innings last season. . . . Faced only one batter twice, pitched two or more innings 22 times, finished 24 games in 52 relief appearances. . . . Opponents have career average of .153 with two outs and runners in scoring position, lowest in 12-year history of *The Player Analysis* (minimum: 100 AB). . . . Sharp form reversal last season: Opposing left-handers had hit .288 over two previous seasons, right-handers .168.

Bill Gullickson

Cincinnati Reds — Throws Right

	W–L	ERA	AB	H	HR	BB	SO	BA	SA	OBA
Season	15-12	3.38	927	245	24	60	121	.264	.392	.306
vs. Left-Handers			483	133	10	39	56	.275	.400	.328
vs. Right-Handers			444	112	14	21	65	.252	.383	.282
Home	9-6	3.70	473	131	10	31	74	.277	.397	.318
Road	6-6	3.06	454	114	14	29	47	.251	.385	.294
Grass	2-5	3.98	278	74	13	19	29	.266	.450	.312
Artificial Turf	13-7	3.13	649	171	11	41	92	.263	.367	.304
April	0-2	3.10	73	16	3	9	3	.219	.370	.301
May	4-2	4.03	169	48	3	16	15	.284	.385	.337
June	1-2	4.86	147	41	7	7	17	.279	.449	.308
July	2-0	2.45	159	37	5	10	26	.233	.365	.275
August	5-2	0.79	208	46	2	9	36	.221	.298	.253
Sept./Oct.	3-4	6.05	171	57	5	9	24	.333	.497	.368
Leading Off Inn.			233	55	4	19	30	.236	.335	.296
Runners On			365	98	7	18	46	.268	.364	.295
Runners/Scor. Pos.			188	46	2	16	23	.245	.309	.289
Runners On/2 Out			155	36	3	12	26	.232	.329	.287
Scor. Pos./2 Out			90	20	0	12	14	.222	.256	.314
Late Inning Pressure			92	18	0	6	9	.196	.239	.242
Leading Off			27	7	0	1	3	.259	.296	.286
Runners On			29	2	0	5	3	.069	.069	.200
Runners/Scor. Pos.			16	2	0	5	1	.125	.125	.318
First 9 Batters			304	73	1	19	49	.240	.293	.281
Second 9 Batters			301	84	15	17	36	.279	.472	.314
All Batters Thereafter			322	88	8	24	36	.273	.410	.323

Loves to face: Candy Maldonado (0-for-11)
Hates to face: Keith Hernandez (.373, 22-for-59)
Ground outs-to-air outs ratio: 1.02 last season, 0.93 for career. . . . Additional statistics: 16 double-play ground outs in 176 opportunities, 42 doubles (8th most in N.L.), 2 triples in 244.2 innings last season. Allowed 68 extra-base hits, 7th most in N.L. . . . Allowed 14 first-inning runs in 37 starts last season. . . . Batting support: 4.24 runs per start. . . . Only N.L. pitcher with a winning record and at least 10 wins in each of the past four seasons. . . . Led N.L. in ERA during month of August. . . . Has allowed only four career home runs in Late-Inning Pressure Situations (532 AB). . . . Has walked only two of the 78 batters he has faced with bases loaded; opposing batters are 3 for 32 with two outs and bags full. . . . Lost six starts decided by one run, tied for 2d most in majors.

Dave Gumpert

Chicago Cubs — Throws Right

	W–L	ERA	AB	H	HR	BB	SO	BA	SA	OBA
Season	2-0	4.37	225	60	4	28	45	.267	.369	.349
vs. Left-Handers			96	34	2	6	9	.354	.510	.392
vs. Right-Handers			129	26	2	22	36	.202	.264	.320
Home	1-0	3.96	148	39	2	18	31	.264	.351	.343
Road	1-0	5.14	77	21	2	10	14	.273	.403	.360
Grass	2-0	3.47	186	46	3	21	36	.247	.344	.322
Artificial Turf	0-0	8.71	39	14	1	7	9	.359	.487	.468
April	0-0	0.00	3	1	0	0	0	.333	.333	.333
May	0-0	—	0	0	0	0	0	—	—	—
June	0-0	1.93	17	5	0	2	1	.294	.353	.368
July	2-0	2.75	74	18	1	11	16	.243	.351	.337
August	0-0	4.37	84	21	3	8	17	.250	.405	.315
Sept./Oct.	0-0	8.25	47	15	0	7	11	.319	.340	.418
Leading Off Inn.			47	13	2	3	6	.277	.447	.320
Runners On			116	34	1	15	26	.293	.379	.376
Runners/Scor. Pos.			75	28	1	12	15	.373	.493	.461
Runners On/2 Out			53	13	1	10	19	.245	.340	.365
Scor. Pos./2 Out			36	12	1	9	12	.333	.472	.467
Late Inning Pressure			96	32	2	10	13	.333	.469	.393
Leading Off			22	9	1	1	1	.409	.636	.435
Runners On			50	16	0	6	9	.320	.380	.386
Runners/Scor. Pos.			33	12	0	6	6	.364	.455	.450
First 9 Batters			203	54	4	26	38	.266	.379	.351
Second 9 Batters			22	6	0	2	7	.273	.273	.333
All Batters Thereafter			0	0	0	0	0	—	—	—

Loves to face: Mariano Duncan (0-for-3, 3 SO)
Hates to face: Howard Johnson (2-for-2, 1 HR)
Ground outs-to-air outs ratio: 2.10 last season, 1.92 for career. . . . Additional statistics: 5 double-play ground outs in 56 opportunities, 7 doubles, 2 triples in 59.2 innings last season. . . . Never faced only one batter, pitched two or more innings 12 times, finished 12 games in 38 relief appearances. . . . Made 34 career appearances before winning his first game in majors on July 1. Won another four days later, and finished the season with an 0-for-32 streak. . . . Outstanding career winning percentage in minors (36–19, .655). . . . Career opponents' batting averages: .309 by left-handers (one extra-base hit per 10.1 at bats), .248 by right-handers (one XBH per 23 AB); .500 (8-for-16, no extra-base hits) with the bases loaded.

Andy Hawkins

San Diego Padres — Throws Right

	W–L	ERA	AB	H	HR	BB	SO	BA	SA	OBA
Season	10-8	4.30	812	218	24	75	117	.268	.411	.332
vs. Left-Handers			405	131	11	42	58	.323	.462	.384
vs. Right-Handers			407	87	13	33	59	.214	.361	.279
Home	6-2	3.07	417	109	11	32	54	.261	.388	.319
Road	4-6	5.61	395	109	13	43	63	.276	.435	.345
Grass	8-4	3.44	636	165	19	46	91	.259	.403	.313
Artificial Turf	2-4	7.51	176	53	5	29	26	.301	.443	.395
April	1-2	4.55	106	24	2	10	19	.226	.321	.299
May	2-1	3.55	130	34	5	5	16	.262	.400	.294
June	2-1	4.72	130	36	4	15	19	.277	.454	.358
July	2-3	4.91	148	46	4	15	19	.311	.432	.371
August	2-1	4.03	145	39	5	12	24	.269	.421	.323
Sept./Oct.	1-0	4.08	153	39	4	18	21	.255	.418	.331
Leading Off Inn.			200	56	5	21	31	.280	.395	.348
Runners On			336	92	13	38	46	.274	.446	.349
Runners/Scor. Pos.			173	49	9	29	26	.283	.491	.384
Runners On/2 Out			133	34	5	22	23	.256	.421	.365
Scor. Pos./2 Out			83	20	5	15	17	.241	.458	.357
Late Inning Pressure			42	15	2	4	8	.357	.595	.426
Leading Off			13	6	2	2	2	.462	1.000	.533
Runners On			11	3	0	2	2	.273	.273	.385
Runners/Scor. Pos.			5	0	0	2	2	.000	.000	.286
First 9 Batters			292	71	3	31	48	.243	.325	.320
Second 9 Batters			274	70	9	22	39	.255	.398	.310
All Batters Thereafter			246	77	12	22	30	.313	.528	.370

Loves to face: Lee Mazzilli (0-for-14)
Hates to face: Milt Thompson (.438, 7-for-16)
Ground outs-to-air outs ratio: 0.98 last season, 0.99 for career. . . . Additional statistics: 12 double-play ground outs in 169 opportunities, 38 doubles, 3 triples in 209.1 innings last season. Allowed 65 extra-base hits, 10th most in N.L. . . . Allowed 20 first-inning runs in 35 starts last season. . . . Batting support: 4.66 runs per start. . . . Snapped streak of eight consecutive no-decision starts with victory on final day of season. . . . Made 18 no-decision starts, three more than any other pitcher in the majors. . . . Career averages: one home run per 30 at bats in day games, one per 58 at bats in night games. . . . Opposing left-handed batters have outhit right-handers in each of the past four seasons.

Orel Hershiser

Los Angeles Dodgers — Throws Right

	W–L	ERA	AB	H	HR	BB	SO	BA	SA	OBA
Season	14-14	3.85	877	213	13	86	153	.243	.339	.312
vs. Left-Handers			469	118	7	49	72	.252	.354	.320
vs. Right-Handers			408	95	6	37	81	.233	.321	.303
Home	10-5	3.07	484	112	8	41	85	.231	.329	.294
Road	4-9	4.84	393	101	5	45	68	.257	.351	.334
Grass	12-9	3.38	655	157	10	53	102	.240	.339	.298
Artificial Turf	2-5	5.25	222	56	3	33	51	.252	.338	.350
April	3-2	2.06	136	34	0	14	24	.250	.301	.318
May	2-1	2.55	154	30	2	19	36	.195	.266	.287
June	2-2	5.27	160	42	3	18	25	.263	.369	.344
July	3-2	5.46	109	30	2	11	24	.275	.394	.339
August	2-3	4.62	147	36	3	12	23	.245	.367	.339
Sept./Oct.	2-4	3.52	171	41	3	12	21	.240	.345	.290
Leading Off Inn.			225	57	5	13	37	.253	.364	.294
Runners On			352	87	4	51	63	.247	.313	.342
Runners/Scor. Pos.			217	49	3	41	46	.226	.290	.343
Runners On/2 Out			168	48	3	25	29	.286	.381	.378
Scor. Pos./2 Out			113	30	3	21	23	.265	.381	.381
Late Inning Pressure			100	26	2	14	16	.260	.400	.353
Leading Off			26	8	1	3	4	.308	.462	.379
Runners On			41	10	1	10	4	.244	.341	.396
Runners/Scor. Pos.			27	7	1	7	2	.259	.407	.400
First 9 Batters			281	61	3	27	49	.217	.278	.286
Second 9 Batters			266	76	4	25	48	.286	.387	.347
All Batters Thereafter			330	76	6	34	56	.230	.352	.306

Loves to face: Jeff Stone (0-for-17)
Hates to face: Keith Hernandez (.455, 10-for-22, 1 HR)
Ground outs-to-air outs ratio: 1.79 last season, 2.19 for career. . . . Additional statistics: 16 double-play ground outs in 166 opportunities, 33 doubles, 6 triples in 231.1 innings last season. . . . Allowed 14 first-inning runs in 35 starts last season. . . . Batting support: 3.74 runs per start. . . . Has allowed two or more home runs in a game only once in his career (Aug. 18, 1986 vs. Mets); has surrendered a first-inning shot only once (Bob Brenly, Sept. 22, 1985). . . . Prior to May 30, 1986, had made 27 consecutive regular-season starts without allowing more than three earned runs; then, over next 10 starts, it happened eight times. . . . Opposing right-handers have a career batting average of .206 at Dodger Stadium, with nine home runs in 664 at bats.

Joe Hesketh
Montreal Expos — Throws Left

	W-L	ERA	AB	H	HR	BB	SO	BA	SA	OBA
Season	6-5	5.01	325	92	11	31	67	.283	.471	.347
vs. Left-Handers			44	11	0	6	12	.250	.318	.353
vs. Right-Handers			281	81	11	25	55	.288	.495	.346
Home	3-2	5.61	180	59	5	11	43	.328	.528	.368
Road	3-3	4.35	145	33	6	20	24	.228	.400	.323
Grass	2-1	2.61	70	12	2	14	13	.171	.286	.318
Artificial Turf	4-4	5.81	255	80	9	17	54	.314	.522	.356
April	0-3	7.63	64	22	4	7	13	.344	.719	.417
May	3-0	4.61	104	26	4	12	22	.250	.423	.328
June	3-1	4.45	131	40	3	6	26	.305	.450	.321
July	0-1	3.52	26	4	0	6	6	.154	.154	.333
August			0	0	0	0	0	—	—	—
Sept./Oct.			0	0	0	0	0	—	—	—
Leading Off Inn.			81	19	3	5	17	.235	.444	.279
Runners On			129	40	6	15	25	.310	.535	.381
Runners/Scor. Pos.			83	28	3	13	15	.337	.566	.424
Runners On/2 Out			58	15	1	10	14	.259	.345	.368
Scor. Pos./2 Out			41	13	1	8	7	.317	.439	.429
Late Inning Pressure			40	10	0	3	11	.250	.275	.302
Leading Off			11	2	0	0	2	.182	.182	.182
Runners On			12	3	0	2	3	.250	.250	.357
Runners/Scor. Pos.			6	2	0	1	1	.333	.333	.429
First 9 Batters			119	40	4	13	29	.336	.555	.396
Second 9 Batters			102	33	6	11	17	.324	.598	.400
All Batters Thereafter			104	19	1	7	21	.183	.250	.234

Loves to face: Tony Pena (0-for-9)
Hates to face: Mookie Wilson (.583, 7-for-12)
Ground outs-to-air outs ratio: 0.83 last season, 1.01 for career. . . . Additional statistics: 4 double-play ground outs in 41 opportunities, 20 doubles, 4 triples in 82.2 innings last season. . . . Allowed 15 first-inning runs in 15 starts last season. . . . Batting support: 3.93 runs per start. . . . Has allowed 23 career home runs, 22 to right-handed batters. Only home run by a lefty: Jose Cruz, May 13, 1985. . . . Has never allowed a home run in Late-Inning Pressure Situations (115 AB). . . . Has retired the leadoff batter in 213 of 292 innings (72.9 percent). . . . Hitless in 23 at bats last season, stretching streak to 43 in a row without a hit (with 30 strikeouts), to lower his lifetime batting average to .065 (5-for-77).

Guy Hoffman
Chicago Cubs — Throws Left

	W-L	ERA	AB	H	HR	BB	SO	BA	SA	OBA
Season	6-2	3.86	319	92	6	29	47	.288	.411	.348
vs. Left-Handers			65	16	0	12	11	.246	.308	.367
vs. Right-Handers			254	76	6	17	36	.299	.437	.343
Home	4-0	3.33	185	50	6	11	32	.270	.427	.310
Road	2-2	4.58	134	42	0	18	15	.313	.388	.397
Grass	4-1	3.82	232	67	6	20	36	.289	.431	.343
Artificial Turf	2-1	3.97	87	25	0	9	11	.287	.356	.364
April	0-0	2.57	25	6	1	1	5	.240	.400	.269
May	1-1	6.04	88	29	3	8	11	.330	.534	.388
June	2-1	3.20	101	29	1	8	15	.287	.337	.345
July	1-0	5.79	34	11	0	5	4	.324	.441	.400
August			0	0	0	0	0	—	—	—
Sept./Oct.	2-0	1.80	71	17	1	7	12	.239	.352	.304
Leading Off Inn.			75	25	0	6	12	.333	.427	.390
Runners On			143	41	3	17	17	.287	.413	.360
Runners/Scor. Pos.			82	25	2	15	13	.305	.451	.400
Runners On/2 Out			62	18	1	11	8	.290	.387	.405
Scor. Pos./2 Out			39	12	1	10	5	.308	.436	.449
Late Inning Pressure			50	18	0	3	6	.360	.380	.389
Leading Off			13	5	0	1	3	.385	.385	.429
Runners On			19	8	0	2	1	.421	.421	.455
Runners/Scor. Pos.			8	5	0	2	0	.625	.625	.636
First 9 Batters			181	52	3	17	28	.287	.387	.348
Second 9 Batters			85	25	1	7	13	.294	.447	.348
All Batters Thereafter			53	15	2	5	6	.283	.434	.350

Loves to face: Lance Parrish (0-for-6)
Hates to face: Darrell Porter (5-for-5)
Ground outs-to-air outs ratio: 1.24 last season, 1.33 for career (1.58 vs. left-handers, 0.75 vs. right-handers). . . . Additional statistics: 10 double-play ground outs in 64 opportunities, 21 doubles, 0 triples in 84.0 innings last season. . . . Made eight starts, 24 relief appearances last season; only one start among 58 appearances in three previous seasons. . . . Split four decisions as a starter, won all four in relief. . . . See ya in 1989: Made first major-league appearance in 1979, then pitched in majors in 1980, 1983, and 1986. . . . Could reach Cooperstown if he remains at Wrigley Field. Won all five decisions in day games last season to improve career day-game mark to 7–0, but has lost seven of eight decisions in night games.

Rick Honeycutt
Los Angeles Dodgers — Throws Left

	W-L	ERA	AB	H	HR	BB	SO	BA	SA	OBA
Season	11-9	3.32	658	164	9	45	100	.249	.368	.300
vs. Left-Handers			105	25	0	3	23	.238	.343	.266
vs. Right-Handers			553	139	9	42	77	.251	.373	.306
Home	6-4	2.69	376	93	4	21	50	.247	.340	.290
Road	5-5	4.14	282	71	5	24	50	.252	.404	.314
Grass	8-7	3.19	550	137	7	35	81	.249	.362	.296
Artificial Turf	3-2	3.90	108	27	2	10	19	.250	.398	.317
April	0-2	4.05	84	24	3	8	14	.286	.488	.348
May	2-1	2.31	83	19	0	10	13	.229	.289	.312
June	2-1	0.50	126	25	0	4	19	.198	.262	.229
July	2-2	5.75	86	26	1	4	14	.302	.465	.341
August	3-3	3.79	141	33	2	8	23	.234	.362	.280
Sept./Oct.	2-0	4.54	138	37	3	11	17	.268	.384	.320
Leading Off Inn.			169	31	4	8	22	.183	.296	.225
Runners On			238	67	4	24	34	.282	.424	.348
Runners/Scor. Pos.			119	38	4	21	15	.319	.487	.423
Runners On/2 Out			117	26	0	15	19	.222	.274	.316
Scor. Pos./2 Out			58	17	0	13	9	.293	.328	.431
Late Inning Pressure			43	12	0	4	5	.279	.326	.340
Leading Off			11	3	0	1	1	.273	.273	.333
Runners On			17	5	0	2	2	.294	.353	.368
Runners/Scor. Pos.			7	2	0	2	1	.286	.286	.444
First 9 Batters			249	54	4	18	48	.217	.337	.275
Second 9 Batters			232	59	2	13	33	.254	.358	.297
All Batters Thereafter			177	51	3	14	19	.288	.424	.339

Loves to face: Ron Oester (.067, 1-for-15)
Hates to face: Jack Clark (.583, 7-for-12, 2 HR)
Ground outs-to-air outs ratio: 1.74 last season, 1.90 for career. . . . Additional statistics: 7 double-play ground outs in 89 opportunities, 39 doubles, 6 triples in 171.0 innings last season. . . . Allowed 8 first-inning runs in 28 starts last season. . . . Batting support: 4.04 runs per start. . . . Last home run allowed to a left-handed batter was hit by Terry Kennedy on June 25, 1984. . . . Won five of six decisions in day games last season. . . . Led N.L. in ERA during month of June. . . . Has not allowed a home run in Late-Inning Pressure Situations since June 5, 1982 (to Harold Baines). Faced 254 batters in LIP since then. . . . Walked eight times last season, most among pitchers, including a pair in his only two plate appearances with bases loaded.

Ricky Horton
St. Louis Cardinals — Throws Left

	W-L	ERA	AB	H	HR	BB	SO	BA	SA	OBA
Season	4-3	2.24	354	77	7	26	49	.218	.331	.271
vs. Left-Handers			81	18	1	4	13	.222	.296	.267
vs. Right-Handers			273	59	6	22	36	.216	.341	.272
Home	1-1	2.66	156	36	4	10	19	.231	.359	.280
Road	3-2	1.92	198	41	3	16	30	.207	.308	.264
Grass	1-1	2.51	98	17	3	7	14	.173	.306	.226
Artificial Turf	3-2	2.13	256	60	4	19	35	.234	.340	.288
April	0-3	4.39	97	25	3	11	14	.258	.443	.330
May	0-0	2.57	25	5	1	1	6	.200	.360	.259
June	1-0	0.00	13	2	0	1	2	.154	.154	.214
July	0-0	0.00	47	7	0	1	7	.149	.170	.163
August	1-0	1.42	43	8	1	3	7	.186	.302	.239
Sept./Oct.	2-0	1.98	129	30	2	9	13	.233	.326	.281
Leading Off Inn.			94	18	2	3	9	.191	.298	.216
Runners On			118	29	1	16	13	.246	.339	.328
Runners/Scor. Pos.			67	17	1	10	7	.254	.388	.338
Runners On/2 Out			52	12	0	8	7	.231	.288	.333
Scor. Pos./2 Out			34	8	0	6	4	.235	.324	.350
Late Inning Pressure			107	21	1	10	16	.196	.262	.263
Leading Off			29	5	0	0	2	.172	.172	.172
Runners On			37	9	1	6	5	.243	.405	.341
Runners/Scor. Pos.			16	6	1	4	2	.375	.750	.476
First 9 Batters			194	35	3	15	27	.180	.258	.242
Second 9 Batters			89	21	3	5	12	.236	.393	.271
All Batters Thereafter			71	21	1	6	10	.296	.451	.351

Loves to face: Mookie Wilson (0-for-16)
Hates to face: Johnny Ray (.455, 10-for-22)
Ground outs-to-air outs ratio: 1.51 last season, 1.38 for career. . . . Additional statistics: 12 double-play ground outs in 59 opportunities, 3d-highest average in N.L. (minimum: 10 GDP), 17 doubles, 1 triple in 100.1 innings last season. . . . Faced only one batter 9 times (3d most in N.L.), pitched two or more innings 8 times, finished 12 games in 33 relief appearances. . . . Opponents' career batting averages: .226 (one extra-base hit per 33.9 at bats) by left-handers, .265 (one XBH per 11.2 AB) by right-handers. . . . Made 18 consecutive scoreless relief appearances from June 27 through August 11. Streak of 26.1 shutout innings was longest in N.L. last season. . . . Dave Parker's home run on May 20 was the only one ever off him in Late-Inning Pressure Situations.

Ken Howell
Los Angeles Dodgers Throws Right

	W–L	ERA	AB	H	HR	BB	SO	BA	SA	OBA
Season	6-12	3.87	360	86	7	63	104	.239	.339	.354
vs. Left-Handers			193	46	3	39	51	.238	.332	.366
vs. Right-Handers			167	40	4	24	53	.240	.347	.340
Home	5-5	2.65	197	43	3	25	57	.218	.305	.311
Road	1-7	5.40	163	43	4	38	47	.264	.380	.402
Grass	6-8	3.79	269	63	6	44	79	.234	.346	.343
Artificial Turf	0-4	4.13	91	23	1	19	25	.253	.319	.387
April	0-1	1.15	53	9	0	10	18	.170	.189	.318
May	1-1	1.04	63	13	0	8	21	.206	.206	.296
June	1-4	3.48	72	18	0	17	15	.250	.306	.389
July	2-0	5.25	43	9	2	5	13	.209	.349	.286
August	1-2	5.27	53	13	1	8	15	.245	.377	.344
Sept./Oct.	1-4	7.36	76	24	4	15	22	.316	.553	.435
Leading Off Inn.			87	22	1	7	21	.253	.299	.309
Runners On			176	40	5	40	51	.227	.375	.371
Runners/Scor. Pos.			103	26	3	22	27	.252	.417	.380
Runners On/2 Out			73	16	4	14	21	.219	.397	.345
Scor. Pos./2 Out			51	10	2	7	15	.196	.333	.293
Late Inning Pressure			285	71	7	50	81	.249	.372	.362
Leading Off			72	17	1	6	16	.236	.292	.295
Runners On			131	33	5	32	36	.252	.443	.399
Runners/Scor. Pos.			79	22	3	19	21	.278	.481	.412
First 9 Batters			327	77	7	54	95	.235	.343	.347
Second 9 Batters			33	9	0	9	9	.273	.303	.419
All Batters Thereafter			0	0	0	0	0			

Loves to face: Rafael Ramirez (0-for-9)
Hates to face: Tony Gwynn (.455, 5-for-11)
Ground outs-to-air outs ratio: 1.09 last season, 1.12 for career. . . .
Additional statistics: 5 double-play ground outs in 111 opportunities, 4th-lowest average in N.L. (minimum: 40 opp.), 9 doubles, 3 triples in 97.2 innings last season. . . . Faced only one batter once, pitched two or more innings 26 times, finished 36 games in 62 relief appearances. . . . First pitcher to walk 50 batters in Late-Inning Pressure Situations since 1977, when Charlie Hough set *Player Analysis* record of 59. . . . Faced 348 batters in Late-Inning Pressure Situations last season, tying Todd Worrell for tops in majors. . . . Career records: 7–6 in day games, 8–18 in night games. . . . Did not allow an HR in first 31 games; allowed 4 in his last 7.

LaMarr Hoyt
San Diego Padres Throws Right

	W–L	ERA	AB	H	HR	BB	SO	BA	SA	OBA
Season	8-11	5.15	615	170	27	68	85	.276	.467	.350
vs. Left-Handers			308	84	10	44	34	.273	.422	.365
vs. Right-Handers			307	86	17	24	51	.280	.511	.333
Home	5-3	3.95	323	82	13	36	44	.254	.427	.330
Road	3-8	6.59	292	88	14	32	41	.301	.510	.372
Grass	6-9	5.05	477	132	21	50	62	.277	.459	.346
Artificial Turf	2-2	5.50	138	38	6	18	23	.275	.493	.363
April	0-0	1.17	24	2	0	1	3	.083	.125	.115
May	2-1	4.80	121	35	8	8	15	.289	.570	.333
June	0-3	8.54	111	43	4	17	11	.387	.550	.465
July	3-2	3.00	135	34	3	11	24	.252	.348	.306
August	2-3	5.35	144	39	6	13	19	.271	.472	.335
Sept./Oct.	1-2	6.14	80	17	6	18	13	.213	.488	.370
Leading Off Inn.			149	45	3	14	15	.302	.456	.366
Runners On			262	69	13	36	37	.263	.454	.353
Runners/Scor. Pos.			170	41	10	30	28	.241	.459	.356
Runners On/2 Out			101	21	3	15	20	.208	.347	.316
Scor. Pos./2 Out			74	14	2	14	17	.189	.311	.326
Late Inning Pressure			41	9	2	7	7	.220	.439	.333
Leading Off			11	5	1	3	0	.455	.818	.571
Runners On			16	1	0	4	3	.063	.063	.250
Runners/Scor. Pos.			12	0	0	3	3	.000	.000	.200
First 9 Batters			236	63	9	38	31	.267	.436	.368
Second 9 Batters			203	50	8	19	30	.246	.433	.317
All Batters Thereafter			176	57	10	11	24	.324	.545	.362

Loves to face: Keith Hernandez (.083, 1-for-12)
Hates to face: Wayne Gross (.600, 14-for-32, 4 HR)
Ground outs-to-air outs ratio: 1.04 last season, 1.19 for career. . . .
Additional statistics: 10 double-play ground outs in 125 opportunities, 30 doubles, 3 triples in 159.0 innings last season. . . . Allowed 29 first-inning runs (2d most in N.L.) in 25 starts last season, only six runs in 2d inning. . . . Batting support: 4.32 runs per start. . . . Only N.L. pitcher to allow three or more homers in a game four times last season. . . . Walks per nine innings ballooned from a career-best 0.86 in '85 to a career-worst 3.85. . . . Allowed five XBH to opposing pitchers, most in N.L. . . . From last season's *Analyst*: "Hawkins and Hoyt are not likely to combine for more than 70 wins over the next three seasons; a total of 60 would be more like it." Well, Andy, you're on your own.

Charles Hudson
Philadelphia Phillies Throws Right

	W–L	ERA	AB	H	HR	BB	SO	BA	SA	OBA
Season	7-10	4.94	567	165	20	58	82	.291	.450	.355
vs. Left-Handers			319	90	11	38	43	.282	.436	.358
vs. Right-Handers			248	75	9	20	39	.302	.468	.352
Home	3-5	4.52	276	80	7	22	36	.290	.424	.342
Road	4-5	5.33	291	85	13	36	46	.292	.474	.367
Grass	1-2	6.67	120	41	6	13	25	.342	.525	.403
Artificial Turf	6-8	4.51	447	124	14	45	57	.277	.430	.342
April	2-1	3.60	61	18	2	4	4	.295	.459	.338
May	1-2	3.62	107	29	1	11	9	.271	.355	.336
June	1-4	5.60	134	37	7	16	18	.276	.500	.353
July	2-3	5.40	105	30	4	12	16	.286	.457	.353
August	1-0	6.94	96	31	6	12	17	.323	.542	.398
Sept./Oct.	0-0	3.31	64	20	0	3	18	.313	.344	.343
Leading Off Inn.			143	38	9	12	22	.266	.510	.323
Runners On			244	78	6	16	39	.320	.451	.357
Runners/Scor. Pos.			131	44	2	10	27	.336	.450	.375
Runners On/2 Out			112	39	3	7	21	.348	.482	.387
Scor. Pos./2 Out			70	24	1	3	15	.343	.457	.370
Late Inning Pressure			20	7	0	0	4	.350	.400	.350
Leading Off			5	1	0	0	2	.200	.400	.200
Runners On			8	3	0	0	1	.375	.375	.375
Runners/Scor. Pos.			6	2	0	0	1	.333	.333	.333
First 9 Batters			251	70	7	20	45	.279	.394	.330
Second 9 Batters			182	50	9	24	23	.275	.500	.357
All Batters Thereafter			134	45	4	14	14	.336	.485	.399

Loves to face: Lonnie Smith (.125, 2-for-16)
Hates to face: Darrell Porter (.450, 9-for-20, 1 HR)
Ground outs-to-air outs ratio: 1.02 last season, 0.91 for career. . . .
Additional statistics: 12 double-play ground outs in 111 opportunities, 24 doubles, 3 triples in 144.0 innings last season. . . . Allowed 12 first-inning runs in 23 starts last season. . . . Batting support: 3.96 runs per start. . . . Pitched an average of only 5.38 innings per start. . . . One of three N.L. pitchers to strike out Ozzie Smith twice in one game last season. . . . Career records: 15–7 in day games, 17–35 in night games. . . . Batting averages prior to last season: .273 by left-handers, .235 by right-handers. . . . He'll be happy to put his bat in moth balls (at least until the World Series). Batted .047 (2-for-43) last season. One hit in 40 at bats vs. left-handed pitchers since 1984.

Tom Hume
Philadelphia Phillies Throws Right

	W–L	ERA	AB	H	HR	BB	SO	BA	SA	OBA
Season	4-1	2.77	353	89	5	34	51	.252	.354	.317
vs. Left-Handers			192	48	4	22	25	.250	.370	.329
vs. Right-Handers			161	41	1	12	26	.255	.335	.303
Home	3-0	2.21	196	45	1	17	33	.230	.301	.297
Road	1-1	3.48	157	44	4	17	18	.280	.420	.343
Grass	0-1	4.95	80	27	3	6	6	.338	.525	.375
Artificial Turf	4-0	2.18	273	62	2	28	45	.227	.304	.301
April			0	0	0	0	0	—	—	—
May	0-0	6.75	23	8	0	3	2	.348	.391	.393
June	0-0	4.34	72	17	3	10	11	.236	.431	.337
July	3-0	2.22	106	27	1	8	15	.255	.368	.310
August	1-0	0.00	45	9	0	4	5	.200	.200	.260
Sept./Oct.	0-1	2.60	107	28	1	9	18	.262	.346	.317
Leading Off Inn.			81	20	1	6	6	.247	.346	.299
Runners On			172	40	3	21	34	.233	.349	.315
Runners/Scor. Pos.			105	25	2	19	17	.238	.362	.351
Runners On/2 Out			80	21	1	12	14	.263	.375	.372
Scor. Pos./2 Out			59	16	1	10	8	.271	.390	.394
Late Inning Pressure			84	21	1	7	12	.250	.357	.312
Leading Off			21	7	0	0	0	.333	.476	.391
Runners On			40	7	1	2	10	.175	.275	.227
Runners/Scor. Pos.			23	4	1	2	4	.174	.304	.259
First 9 Batters			304	77	5	30	47	.253	.355	.322
Second 9 Batters			48	12	0	4	4	.250	.354	.296
All Batters Thereafter			1	0	0	0	0	.000	.000	.000

Loves to face: Bill Almon (0-for-11)
Hates to face: Leon Durham (.563, 9-for-16, 1 HR)
Ground outs-to-air outs ratio: 1.33 last season, 1.34 for career. . . .
Additional statistics: 8 double-play ground outs in 80 opportunities, 17 doubles, 2 triples in 94.1 innings last season. . . . Faced only one batter once, pitched two or more innings 29 times (4th most in N.L.), finished 9 games in 47 relief appearances. . . . Pitched a six-inning one-hitter for a victory in his only start last season, his first since 1984. . . . Faced only 94 batters in Late-Inning Pressure Situations, his lowest total since 1978. . . . Snapped streak of four consecutive losing seasons. . . . Has walked 200 left-handed batters in his career, struck out only 170. Totals vs. right-handers: 141 **walks, 333 strikeouts.**

Joe Johnson
Atlanta Braves — Throws Right

	W–L	ERA	AB	H	HR	BB	SO	BA	SA	OBA
Season	6-7	4.97	349	101	8	35	49	.289	.421	.357
vs. Left-Handers			193	59	4	23	36	.306	.425	.382
vs. Right-Handers			156	42	4	12	13	.269	.417	.324
Home	3-4	4.25	170	49	3	13	21	.288	.406	.342
Road	3-3	5.64	179	52	5	22	28	.291	.436	.369
Grass	5-5	4.14	269	79	5	26	38	.294	.420	.360
Artificial Turf	1-2	7.78	80	22	3	9	11	.275	.425	.344
April	3-1	2.86	108	26	3	9	16	.241	.370	.299
May	3-2	4.70	145	39	4	15	19	.269	.414	.344
June	0-3	7.64	83	30	1	8	13	.361	.470	.418
July	0-1	13.50	13	6	0	3	1	.462	.615	.563
August			0	0	0	0	0	—	—	—
Sept./Oct.			0	0	0	0	0	—	—	—
Leading Off Inn.			85	22	1	6	11	.259	.376	.308
Runners On			160	48	3	17	23	.300	.413	.372
Runners/Scor. Pos.			98	26	2	12	13	.265	.378	.348
Runners On/2 Out			62	18	0	7	5	.290	.371	.380
Scor. Pos./2 Out			43	10	0	7	3	.233	.326	.353
Late Inning Pressure			25	6	0	6	3	.240	.280	.387
Leading Off			7	2	0	1	2	.286	.429	.375
Runners On			14	2	0	3	1	.143	.143	.294
Runners/Scor. Pos.			8	1	0	2	1	.125	.125	.300
First 9 Batters			132	35	2	15	20	.265	.364	.345
Second 9 Batters			117	36	4	10	19	.308	.470	.364
All Batters Thereafter			100	30	2	10	10	.300	.440	.364

Loves to face: Larry Parrish (.143, 1-for-7)
Hates to face: Greg Brock (.500, 4-for-8, 1 HR)
Figures above are for N.L. only.... Ground outs-to-air outs ratio: 1.34 last season, 1.32 for career.... Additional statistics: 16 double-play ground outs in 158 opportunities, 30 doubles, 3 triples in 175.0 innings last season.... Allowed 14 first-inning runs in 30 starts last season.... Batting support: 4.60 runs per start.... Completed two of his first three starts last season, and none thereafter.... Has made 44 career starts without a complete game.... No home runs allowed to 71 batters faced in Late-Inning Pressure Situations.... Additional comments in the A.L. Pitchers section.

Matt Keough
Cubs/Astros — Throws Right

	W–L	ERA	AB	H	HR	BB	SO	BA	SA	OBA
Season	5-4	3.94	236	58	9	30	44	.246	.403	.335
vs. Left-Handers			114	28	2	12	16	.246	.351	.326
vs. Right-Handers			122	30	7	18	28	.246	.451	.343
Home	0-1	6.88	68	21	5	9	13	.309	.574	.385
Road	5-3	2.87	168	37	4	21	31	.220	.333	.314
Grass	4-3	4.74	140	35	7	22	32	.250	.429	.360
Artificial Turf	1-1	2.77	96	23	2	8	12	.240	.365	.295
April	1-1	3.09	39	9	3	4	8	.231	.462	.302
May	1-0	6.23	57	21	1	6	9	.368	.509	.438
June	0-1	6.23	18	6	0	2	2	.333	.444	.400
July			0	0	0	0	0	—	—	—
August	1-1	4.50	49	11	3	10	10	.224	.408	.350
Sept./Oct.	2-1	2.14	73	11	2	8	15	.151	.274	.244
Leading Off Inn.			55	16	2	9	10	.291	.473	.391
Runners On			99	25	6	17	17	.253	.465	.364
Runners/Scor. Pos.			56	11	2	11	11	.196	.357	.324
Runners On/2 Out			39	10	2	8	8	.256	.436	.383
Scor. Pos./2 Out			25	6	1	7	6	.240	.440	.406
Late Inning Pressure			38	11	2	7	9	.289	.474	.413
Leading Off			9	3	1	3	1	.333	.667	.500
Runners On			15	3	0	4	3	.200	.200	.400
Runners/Scor. Pos.			6	0	0	4	2	.000	.000	.400
First 9 Batters			149	42	6	19	30	.282	.450	.371
Second 9 Batters			63	9	0	9	10	.143	.190	.247
All Batters Thereafter			24	7	3	2	4	.292	.667	.346

Loves to face: Jim Morrison (.077, 1-for-13)
Hates to face: Dale Murphy (.500, 3-for-6, 1 HR)
Ground outs-to-air outs ratio: 1.13 last season, 0.90 for career.... Additional statistics: 6 double-play ground outs in 50 opportunities, 10 doubles, 0 triples in 64.0 innings last season.... Faced only one batter once, pitched two or more innings 4 times, finished 5 games in 22 relief appearances.... Definition of desperate: Keough started fourth game of season for Cubs last year.... Completed 40 starts during last three full seasons with Oakland, none of 24 in four seasons since then.... Astros purchased him on July 30, but sent him to Tucson on August 17. Wasn't recalled until September 1, making him ineligible for N.L.C.S.... Batted .375 (6-for-16) last season.

Charlie Kerfeld
Houston Astros — Throws Right

	W–L	ERA	AB	H	HR	BB	SO	BA	SA	OBA
Season	11-2	2.59	333	71	5	42	77	.213	.291	.299
vs. Left-Handers			154	38	4	20	28	.247	.383	.328
vs. Right-Handers			179	33	1	22	49	.184	.212	.275
Home	5-0	1.64	149	28	0	17	34	.188	.228	.266
Road	6-2	3.44	184	43	5	25	43	.234	.342	.326
Grass	4-1	4.45	117	30	3	16	28	.256	.368	.338
Artificial Turf	7-1	1.71	216	41	2	26	49	.190	.250	.278
April	2-0	0.52	61	7	1	7	15	.115	.180	.206
May	3-1	2.14	66	12	1	8	16	.182	.242	.282
June	0-0	5.79	20	6	1	1	2	.300	.500	.333
July	2-0	3.45	55	16	0	8	7	.291	.345	.364
August	1-1	3.86	71	17	1	7	18	.239	.310	.304
Sept./Oct.	3-0	2.20	60	13	1	11	19	.217	.317	.333
Leading Off Inn.			79	17	1	8	22	.215	.278	.295
Runners On			144	32	2	24	34	.222	.306	.320
Runners/Scor. Pos.			95	15	1	18	24	.158	.221	.275
Runners On/2 Out			65	10	0	11	14	.154	.185	.276
Scor. Pos./2 Out			48	6	0	7	12	.125	.146	.236
Late Inning Pressure			171	35	2	22	32	.205	.281	.296
Leading Off			45	10	0	3	12	.222	.267	.286
Runners On			67	14	1	13	12	.209	.299	.321
Runners/Scor. Pos.			42	7	1	10	5	.167	.286	.304
First 9 Batters			302	65	4	35	68	.215	.288	.295
Second 9 Batters			31	6	1	7	9	.194	.323	.342
All Batters Thereafter			0	0	0	0	0	—	—	—

Loves to face: Glenn Hubbard (0-for-7, 5 SO)
Hates to face: Leon Durham (.600, 3-for-5, 1 2B, 1 HR)
Ground outs-to-air outs ratio: 2.17 last season, 2.09 for career.... Additional statistics: 8 double-play ground outs in 76 opportunities, 7 doubles, 2 triples in 93.2 innings last season.... Faced only one batter 3 times, pitched two or more innings 26 times, finished 29 games in 61 relief appearances.... Allowed first major-league home run on Aug. 5, 1985, at the Astrodome. Since then he has allowed six home runs, all in road games.... Opponents' career batting averages: .273 (one extra-base hit per 14.2 at bats) by left-handers, .196 (one XBH per 67.5 AB) by right-handers.... Highest winning percentage (.846) among major-league rookies last season (minimum: 10 decisions).

Bob Kipper
Pittsburgh Pirates — Throws Left

	W–L	ERA	AB	H	HR	BB	SO	BA	SA	OBA
Season	6-8	4.03	453	123	17	34	81	.272	.455	.323
vs. Left-Handers			71	19	0	1	15	.268	.338	.278
vs. Right-Handers			382	104	17	33	66	.272	.476	.331
Home	2-4	4.75	221	65	9	19	41	.294	.480	.351
Road	4-4	3.36	232	58	8	15	40	.250	.431	.296
Grass	1-3	4.73	108	29	6	8	16	.269	.519	.325
Artificial Turf	5-5	3.81	345	94	11	26	65	.272	.435	.323
April	0-2	5.40	42	12	1	6	6	.286	.476	.375
May	1-2	4.31	156	46	8	14	27	.295	.519	.349
June	2-2	4.50	90	25	4	5	19	.278	.467	.316
July			0	0	0	0	0	—	—	—
August			0	0	0	0	0	—	—	—
Sept./Oct.	3-2	3.19	165	40	4	9	29	.242	.382	.288
Leading Off Inn.			110	31	5	8	23	.282	.473	.331
Runners On			180	49	7	14	26	.272	.467	.320
Runners/Scor. Pos.			102	24	4	11	17	.235	.422	.302
Runners On/2 Out			85	24	2	8	12	.282	.471	.344
Scor. Pos./2 Out			54	15	2	7	8	.278	.463	.361
Late Inning Pressure			44	13	1	1	7	.295	.409	.326
Leading Off			12	3	1	1	3	.250	.500	.308
Runners On			15	3	0	0	1	.200	.200	.200
Runners/Scor. Pos.			4	0	0	0	0	.000	.000	.000
First 9 Batters			164	33	5	8	36	.201	.348	.238
Second 9 Batters			146	49	10	16	24	.336	.603	.400
All Batters Thereafter			143	41	2	10	21	.287	.427	.335

Loves to face: Ryne Sandberg (0-for-10)
Hates to face: Bruce Bochy (3-for-3, 1 2B, 2 HR)
Ground outs-to-air outs ratio: 0.66, 8th lowest in N.L. last season (minimum: 250 BFP), 0.69 for career.... Additional statistics: 3 double-play ground outs in 72 opportunities, 3d-lowest average in N.L. (minimum: 40 opp.), 26 doubles, 3 triples in 114.0 innings last season.... Allowed 5 first-inning runs in 19 starts last season.... Batting support: 3.63 runs per start.... 0–7, 6.03 ERA in 11 starts vs. teams with winning records.... Has allowed 22 career home runs, all to right-handed batters.... Has faced 94 left-handers, walked only two.... Has made 24 career starts without a complete game. Leader among active players: Steve Bedrosian (46).

Bob Knepper
Houston Astros — Throws Left

	W–L	ERA	AB	H	HR	BB	SO	BA	SA	OBA
Season	17-12	3.14	960	232	19	62	143	.242	.367	.289
vs. Left-Handers			154	35	4	6	36	.227	.383	.255
vs. Right-Handers			806	197	15	56	107	.244	.364	.295
Home	9-6	3.62	496	123	11	24	77	.248	.375	.285
Road	8-6	2.64	464	109	8	38	66	.235	.358	.293
Grass	4-4	2.72	309	70	6	21	44	.227	.350	.276
Artificial Turf	13-8	3.34	651	162	13	41	99	.249	.375	.295
April	4-0	1.27	127	28	2	9	19	.220	.299	.275
May	4-2	2.74	174	41	3	15	29	.236	.397	.297
June	2-4	3.78	188	48	5	8	26	.255	.410	.286
July	3-1	2.33	162	30	3	5	27	.185	.278	.214
August	2-3	3.40	176	45	4	10	24	.256	.398	.296
Sept./Oct.	2-2	5.63	133	40	2	15	18	.301	.398	.372
Leading Off Inn.			251	63	4	13	38	.251	.355	.288
Runners On			348	85	7	34	46	.244	.374	.315
Runners/Scor. Pos.			205	47	5	26	31	.229	.380	.315
Runners On/2 Out			143	28	2	15	24	.196	.294	.281
Scor. Pos./2 Out			100	17	1	12	18	.170	.260	.259
Late Inning Pressure			77	17	1	8	11	.221	.338	.291
Leading Off			22	8	0	2	4	.364	.500	.417
Runners On			27	5	1	5	2	.185	.407	.303
Runners/Scor. Pos.			18	5	1	4	1	.278	.611	.391
First 9 Batters			320	70	4	22	50	.219	.294	.270
Second 9 Batters			315	69	3	17	50	.219	.305	.263
All Batters Thereafter			325	93	12	23	43	.286	.498	.333

Loves to face: Darryl Strawberry (.100, 2-for-20, 1 HR, 9 SO)
Hates to face: Will Clark (.700, 7-for-10, 1 HR)
Ground outs-to-air outs ratio: 1.27 last season, 1.27 for career.…
Additional statistics: 24 double-play ground outs (4th in N.L.) in 180 opportunities, 47 doubles (2d most in N.L.), 8 triples in 258.0 innings last season (74 XBH was 3d most in N.L.).… Allowed 16 first-inning runs in 38 starts last season.… Batting support: 4.16 runs per start.… One of two N.L. pitchers with 15 wins each of last three seasons; other: Dwight Gooden.… Allowed four homers to left-handers last season, *highest* total of his career. Tony Gwynn became 2d lefty batter to homer off him in the Dome.… Pitched a scoreless 9th all eight times he reached it in the regular season. Then came Game Six.… Batted 16 times with a runner on 3d without driving one in, a *Player Analysis* record of sorts.

Mike Krukow
San Francisco Giants — Throws Right

	W–L	ERA	AB	H	HR	BB	SO	BA	SA	OBA
Season	20-9	3.05	913	204	24	55	178	.223	.355	.269
vs. Left-Handers			520	118	11	41	95	.227	.352	.284
vs. Right-Handers			393	86	13	14	83	.219	.359	.249
Home	12-4	2.47	461	95	15	17	92	.206	.354	.235
Road	8-5	3.67	452	109	9	38	86	.241	.356	.302
Grass	17-6	3.15	715	161	21	32	138	.225	.364	.258
Artificial Turf	3-3	2.70	198	43	3	23	40	.217	.323	.307
April	3-1	3.77	112	22	3	9	23	.196	.357	.254
May	3-2	3.50	162	36	3	9	31	.222	.333	.266
June	3-1	3.07	168	40	6	9	27	.238	.381	.278
July	2-2	3.77	114	27	6	5	18	.237	.439	.275
August	2-2	2.68	140	34	2	7	30	.243	.336	.275
Sept./Oct.	7-1	2.16	217	45	4	16	49	.207	.318	.261
Leading Off Inn.			239	56	5	11	40	.234	.368	.271
Runners On			325	74	11	28	61	.228	.369	.289
Runners/Scor. Pos.			184	36	5	21	39	.196	.299	.278
Runners On/2 Out			129	22	5	15	27	.171	.333	.278
Scor. Pos./2 Out			81	10	2	12	20	.123	.222	.237
Late Inning Pressure			92	23	2	3	14	.250	.337	.274
Leading Off			22	7	0	2	1	.318	.318	.375
Runners On			39	8	0	1	8	.205	.256	.256
Runners/Scor. Pos.			19	2	0	1	5	.105	.105	.150
First 9 Batters			278	60	4	21	58	.216	.324	.269
Second 9 Batters			280	59	8	15	52	.211	.354	.257
All Batters Thereafter			355	85	12	19	68	.239	.380	.279

Loves to face: Keith Moreland (.088, 3-for-34)
Hates to face: Gerald Perry (.600, 6-for-10, 2 HR)
Ground outs-to-air outs ratio: 1.10 last season, 1.23 for career.…
Additional statistics: 13 double-play ground outs in 153 opportunities, 36 doubles, 6 triples in 245.0 innings last season.… Allowed 16 first-inning runs in 34 starts last season.… Batting support: 5.09 runs per start, 5th best in N.L. (minimum: 15 GS); it was 2.89 in 1985.… 4–0 vs. Mets in '86. Seven others since 1969 won four vs. a 100-game winner: Dierker (1969, vs. N.Y.), Hands (1970, vs. Cin.), John (1971, vs. Oak.), Lolich (1971, vs. Balt.), Barr (1976, vs. Cin.), Eckersley (1978, vs. N.Y.), and Flanagan (1978, vs. N.Y.).… More home wins (12) than any N.L. pitcher.… Opposing batters hit below .200 with two outs and runners in scoring position five times in last eight seasons.

Mike LaCoss
San Francisco Giants — Throws Right

	W–L	ERA	AB	H	HR	BB	SO	BA	SA	OBA
Season	10-13	3.57	747	179	14	70	86	.240	.343	.309
vs. Left-Handers			425	97	5	42	48	.228	.322	.297
vs. Right-Handers			322	82	9	28	38	.255	.370	.324
Home	7-4	2.83	387	78	5	33	45	.202	.289	.267
Road	3-9	4.39	360	101	9	37	41	.281	.400	.352
Grass	9-8	3.50	547	125	12	53	65	.229	.335	.299
Artificial Turf	1-5	3.74	200	54	2	17	21	.270	.365	.335
April	1-0	2.20	54	11	1	3	6	.204	.259	.250
May	4-1	2.82	157	32	4	13	18	.204	.318	.265
June	2-2	2.86	152	35	3	16	15	.230	.322	.308
July	2-3	3.05	145	30	1	12	21	.207	.290	.266
August	0-4	10.71	95	36	3	13	9	.379	.558	.468
Sept./Oct.	1-3	2.43	144	35	2	13	17	.243	.333	.310
Leading Off Inn.			197	48	2	16	23	.244	.305	.300
Runners On			277	78	9	31	26	.282	.433	.357
Runners/Scor. Pos.			157	49	3	21	15	.312	.433	.390
Runners On/2 Out			122	34	7	8	9	.279	.484	.333
Scor. Pos./2 Out			76	23	3	5	6	.303	.474	.346
Late Inning Pressure			71	14	1	7	5	.197	.310	.269
Leading Off			21	4	0	4	2	.190	.238	.320
Runners On			17	4	1	1	0	.235	.471	.278
Runners/Scor. Pos.			5	1	0	1	0	.200	.200	.333
First 9 Batters			276	68	6	22	34	.246	.330	.302
Second 9 Batters			238	62	4	25	27	.261	.374	.337
All Batters Thereafter			233	49	4	23	25	.210	.326	.287

Loves to face: Terry Pendleton (0-for-12)
Hates to face: Tom Foley (.714, 5-for-7, 2 3B, 1 HR)
Ground outs-to-air outs ratio: 1.93 last season, 1.89 for career.…
Additional statistics: 17 double-play ground outs in 142 opportunities, 21 doubles, 7 triples in 204.1 innings last season.… Allowed 22 first-inning runs in 31 starts last season.… Batting support: 5.16 runs per start, 4th best in N.L. (minimum: 15 GS).… Nine of his 13 losses were in games decided by a single run, three more than any other pitcher in majors.… Struck out 16 more batters than he walked, to even his career totals at 487.… Opposing batters have had a higher batting average with runners on base than with the bases empty in each of the past six seasons.… Ranked 10th in N.L. in ERA (2.76) and wins (9) at the All-Star break; 1–10, 4.89 ERA thereafter.

Dave LaPoint
San Diego Padres — Throws Left

	W–L	ERA	AB	H	HR	BB	SO	BA	SA	OBA
Season	1-4	4.26	243	67	8	24	41	.276	.440	.342
vs. Left-Handers			57	11	2	5	8	.193	.333	.258
vs. Right-Handers			186	56	6	19	33	.301	.473	.367
Home	0-0	3.00	110	28	5	13	19	.255	.436	.333
Road	1-4	5.46	133	39	3	11	22	.293	.444	.349
Grass	0-1	3.69	153	43	6	19	27	.281	.464	.362
Artificial Turf	1-3	5.24	90	24	2	5	14	.267	.400	.305
April			0	0	0	0	0	—	—	—
May			0	0	0	0	0	—	—	—
June			0	0	0	0	0	—	—	—
July	0-0	10.29	30	11	0	1	5	.367	.467	.387
August	0-1	2.86	86	22	2	11	10	.256	.384	.340
Sept./Oct.	1-3	3.90	127	34	6	12	26	.268	.472	.333
Leading Off Inn.			60	16	1	3	11	.267	.367	.302
Runners On			103	31	2	14	18	.301	.456	.387
Runners/Scor. Pos.			59	20	2	11	10	.339	.576	.444
Runners On/2 Out			37	6	0	7	7	.162	.216	.295
Scor. Pos./2 Out			23	5	0	5	2	.217	.304	.357
Late Inning Pressure			20	4	0	3	4	.200	.200	.304
Leading Off			6	1	0	2	2	.167	.167	.167
Runners On			6	2	0	2	0	.333	.333	.500
Runners/Scor. Pos.			2	1	0	2	0	.500	.500	.750
First 9 Batters			148	39	3	14	26	.264	.372	.325
Second 9 Batters			66	18	4	4	10	.273	.561	.324
All Batters Thereafter			29	10	1	6	5	.345	.517	.457

Loves to face: Keith Hernandez (.148, 4-for-27)
Hates to face: Dave Parker (.457, 16-for-35, 2 HR)
Figures above are for N.L. only; see also A.L. Pitchers section.…
Ground outs-to-air outs ratio: 1.14 last season, 1.30 for career.…
Additional statistics: 9 double-play ground outs in 124 opportunities, 25 doubles, 2 triples in 129.0 innings last season.… Allowed 12 first-inning runs in 12 starts.… Batting support: 4.33 runs per start.… Faced only one batter once, pitched two or more innings 17 times, finished 6 games in 28 relief appearances.… Record of 11–27 over past two seasons, for 2d-lowest winning percentage (.289) in majors during that time (minimum: 20 losses). The big loser: Jose DeLeon (7–27, .206).

Craig Lefferts
San Diego Padres — Throws Left

	W–L	ERA	AB	H	HR	BB	SO	BA	SA	OBA
Season	9-8	3.09	387	98	7	44	72	.253	.370	.327
vs. Left-Handers			90	20	1	6	24	.222	.289	.271
vs. Right-Handers			297	78	6	38	48	.263	.394	.343
Home	7-5	2.48	207	48	5	18	45	.232	.357	.291
Road	2-3	3.81	180	50	2	26	27	.278	.383	.367
Grass	9-6	2.74	302	73	6	29	61	.242	.361	.305
Artificial Turf	0-2	4.43	85	25	1	15	11	.294	.400	.398
April	3-0	2.92	45	9	2	3	10	.200	.378	.250
May	0-2	1.89	64	12	1	8	13	.188	.313	.274
June	2-0	1.99	76	19	1	12	16	.250	.342	.344
July	2-2	1.74	68	10	1	7	17	.147	.221	.234
August	0-1	3.79	77	25	2	7	9	.325	.455	.376
Sept./Oct.	2-3	7.71	57	23	0	7	7	.404	.526	.469
Leading Off Inn.			89	20	3	8	13	.225	.348	.289
Runners On			173	46	1	25	32	.266	.353	.353
Runners/Scor. Pos.			102	26	1	22	19	.255	.353	.377
Runners On/2 Out			73	18	1	9	17	.247	.384	.329
Scor. Pos./2 Out			46	10	1	7	13	.217	.348	.321
Late Inning Pressure			262	65	5	26	53	.248	.359	.316
Leading Off			61	13	1	6	9	.213	.279	.284
Runners On			111	29	1	14	20	.261	.351	.344
Runners/Scor. Pos.			61	18	1	13	11	.295	.410	.416
First 9 Batters			376	96	7	44	67	.255	.367	.331
Second 9 Batters			11	2	0	0	5	.182	.455	.182
All Batters Thereafter			0	0	0	0	0			

Loves to face: Ozzie Smith (0-for-11)
Hates to face: Jack Clark (.600, 3-for-5, 3 HR)
Ground outs-to-air outs ratio: 0.75 last season, 0.78 for career. . . .
Additional statistics: 11 double-play ground outs in 97 opportunities, 16 doubles, 4 triples in 107.2 innings last season. . . . Faced only one batter 5 times, pitched two or more innings 25 times, finished 36 games in 83 relief appearances. . . . First left-hander to lead majors in appearances since Gary Lucas in 1981. . . . Career records: 21–13 on grass fields, 1–9 on artificial turf. . . . Has faced 46 career batters with the bases loaded without walking in a run. . . . Career batting averages: .210 (one extra-base hit per 21.8 at bats) by left-handers, .254 (one XBH per 11.7 AB) by right-handers.

Aurelio Lopez
Houston Astros — Throws Right

	W–L	ERA	AB	H	HR	BB	SO	BA	SA	OBA
Season	3-3	3.46	289	64	6	25	44	.221	.325	.280
vs. Left-Handers			153	28	4	16	27	.183	.288	.260
vs. Right-Handers			136	36	2	9	17	.265	.368	.302
Home	1-2	5.45	139	36	4	14	18	.259	.396	.323
Road	2-1	1.73	150	28	2	11	26	.187	.260	.239
Grass	2-1	3.27	85	22	2	7	14	.259	.376	.309
Artificial Turf	1-2	3.54	204	42	4	18	30	.206	.304	.268
April			0	0	0	0	0			
May			0	0	0	0	0			
June	1-1	2.95	72	17	0	4	13	.236	.278	.276
July	1-0	1.53	58	7	2	4	5	.121	.259	.175
August	1-0	3.86	78	18	3	8	14	.231	.410	.299
Sept./Oct.	0-2	5.14	81	22	1	9	12	.272	.333	.337
Leading Off Inn.			75	15	1	2	9	.200	.280	.221
Runners On			117	27	0	12	22	.231	.265	.293
Runners/Scor. Pos.			74	18	0	7	11	.243	.270	.294
Runners On/2 Out			58	14	0	1	14	.241	.259	.290
Scor. Pos./2 Out			41	12	0	1	6	.293	.317	.310
Late Inning Pressure			135	33	4	10	19	.244	.370	.293
Leading Off			38	10	1	1	3	.263	.421	.282
Runners On			50	12	0	6	10	.240	.240	.310
Runners/Scor. Pos.			29	10	0	4	4	.345	.345	.400
First 9 Batters			263	56	6	21	38	.213	.323	.267
Second 9 Batters			26	8	0	4	6	.308	.346	.400
All Batters Thereafter			0	0	0	0	0			

Loves to face: Jim Morrison (0-for-7)
Hates to face: Tony Gwynn (2-for-2, 1 2B)
Ground outs-to-air outs ratio: 0.82 last season, 0.67 for career. . . .
Additional statistics: 2 double-play ground outs in 49 opportunities, 10 doubles, 1 triple in 78.0 innings last season. . . . Faced only one batter once, pitched two or more innings 24 times, finished 22 games in 45 relief appearances. . . . Allowed seven home runs last season, all with runners on base. Minority of his gopher balls have been solo shots in each of the past four seasons. . . . Has retired more than 70 percent of leadoff batters in four of the past six seasons. . . . Losing pitcher in longest game in postseason history.

Ed Lynch
Mets/Cubs — Throws Right

	W–L	ERA	AB	H	HR	BB	SO	BA	SA	OBA
Season	7-5	3.73	384	107	10	23	58	.279	.396	.319
vs. Left-Handers			215	65	5	14	26	.302	.414	.343
vs. Right-Handers			169	42	5	9	32	.249	.373	.287
Home	4-4	4.76	227	73	7	12	28	.322	.445	.351
Road	3-1	2.42	157	34	3	11	30	.217	.325	.272
Grass	5-4	3.79	280	81	7	16	37	.289	.389	.327
Artificial Turf	2-1	3.58	104	26	3	7	21	.250	.413	.297
April	0-0	0.00	7	2	0	0	1	.286	.286	.286
May			0	0	0	0	0	——	——	——
June			0	0	0	0	0	——	——	——
July	2-1	3.38	120	32	2	8	13	.267	.333	.318
August	2-2	3.86	158	45	5	6	27	.285	.430	.309
Sept./Oct.	3-2	4.21	99	28	3	9	17	.283	.424	.336
Leading Off Inn.			100	25	2	5	18	.250	.330	.292
Runners On			144	43	3	12	20	.299	.389	.346
Runners/Scor. Pos.			78	28	2	9	9	.359	.474	.411
Runners On/2 Out			58	17	2	5	11	.293	.431	.349
Scor. Pos./2 Out			36	14	1	5	3	.389	.500	.463
Late Inning Pressure			51	12	1	7	7	.235	.333	.328
Leading Off			14	3	0	2	3	.214	.214	.313
Runners On			20	6	1	4	1	.300	.550	.417
Runners/Scor. Pos.			12	3	1	4	1	.250	.583	.438
First 9 Batters			182	42	2	9	33	.231	.297	.266
Second 9 Batters			107	35	4	10	13	.327	.486	.390
All Batters Thereafter			95	30	4	4	12	.316	.484	.337

Loves to face: Vince Coleman (0-for-9)
Hates to face: Dave Parker (.440, 11-for-25, 3 HR)
Ground outs-to-air outs ratio: 1.07 last season, 0.96 for career. . . .
Additional statistics: 9 double-play ground outs in 76 opportunities, 15 doubles, 0 triples in 101.1 innings last season. . . . Allowed 7 first-inning runs in 13 starts last season. . . . Batting support: 4.46 runs per start. . . . 4-4, 4.22 ERA in 13 starts, 3–1, 1.77 ERA in 11 relief appearances. . . . Has pitched only two complete-game shutouts in 98 career starts. . . . Opposing batters had hit .300 or better on artificial turf in each of the four previous seasons. . . . Has faced 56 batters with the bases loaded during career, walked in only one run. . . . Tied Jamie Moyer for most wins on Cubs after the All-Star break (6).

Mike Maddux
Philadelphia Phillies — Throws Right

	W–L	ERA	AB	H	HR	BB	SO	BA	SA	OBA
Season	3-7	5.42	308	88	6	34	44	.286	.396	.359
vs. Left-Handers			189	48	3	25	27	.254	.344	.347
vs. Right-Handers			119	40	3	9	17	.336	.479	.380
Home	3-3	5.02	156	49	2	11	24	.314	.397	.365
Road	0-4	5.80	152	39	4	23	20	.257	.395	.354
Grass	0-2	6.63	71	18	2	12	10	.254	.394	.365
Artificial Turf	3-5	5.03	237	70	4	22	34	.295	.397	.357
April			0	0	0	0	0	——	——	——
May			0	0	0	0	0	——	——	——
June	0-3	9.98	63	19	3	7	9	.302	.508	.380
July	0-0	1.69	19	6	0	5	4	.316	.421	.458
August	2-2	4.71	108	28	1	14	12	.259	.352	.339
Sept./Oct.	1-2	4.40	118	35	2	8	19	.297	.373	.349
Leading Off Inn.			74	24	1	8	10	.324	.446	.412
Runners On			141	43	5	16	22	.305	.468	.369
Runners/Scor. Pos.			81	28	4	12	13	.346	.580	.417
Runners On/2 Out			52	17	4	6	10	.327	.577	.397
Scor. Pos./2 Out			34	10	3	5	8	.294	.588	.385
Late Inning Pressure			14	4	0	0	0	.286	.357	.286
Leading Off			4	2	0	0	0	.500	.750	.500
Runners On			5	0	0	0	0	.000	.000	.000
Runners/Scor. Pos.			2	0	0	0	0	.000	.000	.000
First 9 Batters			123	33	6	11	16	.268	.455	.336
Second 9 Batters			102	29	0	15	17	.284	.343	.378
All Batters Thereafter			83	26	0	8	11	.313	.373	.370

Loves to face: Tony Gwynn (0-for-7)
Hates to face: Keith Moreland and Ryne Sandberg (each .500, 4-for-8, 2 2B)
Ground outs-to-air outs ratio: 1.97 last season, his first in majors. . . . Additional statistics: 5 double-play ground outs in 68 opportunities, 16 doubles, 0 triples in 78.0 innings. . . . Allowed 22 first-inning runs in 16 starts, highest average in either league; allowed only four runs in 2d inning. . . . Batting support: 4.19 runs per start. . . . Lost first five decisions with 8.10 ERA; was 3–2, 3.75 thereafter. . . . Retired 59 percent of opposing leadoff batters, 2d-worst average in N.L. (minimum: 75 BFP). . . . Averaged 4.88 innings per start, 2d lowest in N.L. . . . Lost three games to Cubs, including one to brother Greg on Sept. 29.

Rick Mahler

Atlanta Braves — Throws Right

	W–L	ERA	AB	H	HR	BB	SO	BA	SA	OBA
Season	14-18	4.88	940	283	25	95	137	.301	.439	.364
vs. Left-Handers			520	174	14	57	70	.335	.498	.398
vs. Right-Handers			420	109	11	38	67	.260	.367	.321
Home	8-6	4.56	458	130	16	44	56	.284	.445	.346
Road	6-12	5.20	482	153	9	51	81	.317	.434	.381
Grass	11-11	4.23	692	198	21	69	92	.286	.428	.352
Artificial Turf	3-7	6.86	248	85	4	26	45	.343	.472	.399
April	1-4	5.34	127	41	6	12	12	.323	.512	.383
May	3-1	4.33	170	49	5	24	32	.288	.441	.371
June	6-0	3.31	199	52	3	20	25	.261	.362	.327
July	0-5	10.44	113	44	5	12	16	.389	.593	.452
August	1-4	5.54	149	49	2	16	21	.329	.423	.398
Sept./Oct.	3-4	3.38	182	48	4	11	31	.264	.390	.301
Leading Off Inn.			239	65	5	13	38	.272	.381	.310
Runners On			381	122	10	58	49	.320	.475	.403
Runners/Scor. Pos.			211	64	8	41	36	.303	.507	.404
Runners On/2 Out			156	48	5	32	23	.308	.468	.426
Scor. Pos./2 Out			101	28	3	25	19	.277	.436	.421
Late Inning Pressure			51	18	1	11	3	.353	.431	.468
Leading Off			14	4	1	2	1	.286	.500	.375
Runners On			21	7	0	7	2	.333	.333	.500
Runners/Scor. Pos.			8	2	0	6	1	.250	.250	.571
First 9 Batters			317	78	7	28	53	.246	.350	.306
Second 9 Batters			304	100	11	26	47	.329	.520	.385
All Batters Thereafter			319	105	7	41	37	.329	.451	.400

Loves to face: Chris Speier (.091, 2-for-22, 1 HR, 6 SO)
Hates to face: Wally Backman (.536, 15-for-28)
Ground outs-to-air outs ratio: 1.54 last season, 1.58 for career. . . .
Additional statistics: 27 double-play ground outs (tied for 2d in N.L.) in 203 opportunities, 41 doubles (9th most in N.L.), 7 triples in 237.2 innings last season. Allowed 73 extra-base hits, 4th most in N.L. . . . Allowed 23 first-inning runs (5th most in N.L.) in 39 starts last season. . . . Batting support: 4.05 runs per start. . . . Pitched two opening-day shutouts (1982 and '86) and left a scoreless tie after seven innings in 1985. Modern N.L. record is three by Chris Short (1965, '68, and '70). . . . Has lost his last six decisions vs. the Mets. . . . Allowed most hits in N.L. for second consecutive season. Set *Player Analysis* record with 174 hits allowed to left-handed batters. . . . Led majors with 18 losses.

Roger Mason

San Francisco Giants — Throws Right

	W–L	ERA	AB	H	HR	BB	SO	BA	SA	OBA
Season	3-4	4.80	224	56	5	30	43	.250	.379	.342
vs. Left-Handers			128	34	4	21	25	.266	.398	.367
vs. Right-Handers			96	22	1	9	18	.229	.354	.309
Home	2-3	3.58	117	26	1	15	23	.222	.316	.311
Road	1-1	6.26	107	30	4	15	20	.280	.449	.376
Grass	2-3	3.64	173	40	2	21	38	.231	.329	.317
Artificial Turf	1-1	9.00	51	16	3	9	5	.314	.549	.426
April	1-1	2.25	97	16	2	9	24	.165	.247	.243
May	1-3	7.13	95	29	1	16	13	.305	.432	.409
June			0	0	0	0	0	—	—	—
July	1-0	6.75	32	11	2	5	6	.344	.625	.421
August			0	0	0	0	0	—	—	—
Sept./Oct.			0	0	0	0	0	—	—	—
Leading Off Inn.			55	17	1	7	11	.309	.455	.397
Runners On			94	25	3	17	21	.266	.426	.379
Runners/Scor. Pos.			54	15	2	13	14	.278	.481	.400
Runners On/2 Out			35	9	2	7	7	.257	.486	.381
Scor. Pos./2 Out			23	6	1	6	6	.261	.478	.414
Late Inning Pressure			7	1	0	2	3	.143	.143	.333
Leading Off			2	1	0	0	1	.500	.500	.500
Runners On			3	0	0	2	1	.000	.000	.400
Runners/Scor. Pos.			1	0	0	2	0	.000	.000	.667
First 9 Batters			80	20	0	16	16	.250	.350	.367
Second 9 Batters			81	24	4	8	15	.296	.481	.374
All Batters Thereafter			63	12	1	6	12	.190	.286	.268

Loves to face: Franklin Stubbs (0-for-6, 2 SO)
Hates to face: R.J. Reynolds (.667, 2-for-3, 1 HR)
Ground outs-to-air outs ratio: 0.86 last season, 0.89 for career. . . .
Additional statistics: 4 double-play ground outs in 55 opportunities, 14 doubles, 0 triples in 60.0 innings last season. . . . Allowed 5 first-inning runs in 11 starts last season. . . . Batting support: 3.91 runs per start. . . . This Mason handles Stone quite well: Philadelphia's Jeff is 0-for-3 against him. . . . 2d-highest ERA in N.L. during May (minimum: 20 IP). . . . One of two pitchers from 1984 Tigers on Roger Craig's Giants. The other: Juan Berenguer. . . . Opponents' career batting averages: .277 by left-handers, .229 by right-handers. . . . Hitless in 15 career at bats at Candlestick Park.

Dennis Martinez

Montreal Expos — Throws Right

	W–L	ERA	AB	H	HR	BB	SO	BA	SA	OBA
Season	3-6	4.59	376	103	11	28	63	.274	.415	.328
vs. Left-Handers			209	51	5	17	35	.244	.359	.300
vs. Right-Handers			167	52	6	11	28	.311	.485	.365
Home	1-4	5.29	197	58	5	21	36	.294	.442	.367
Road	2-2	3.83	179	45	6	7	27	.251	.385	.283
Grass	0-1	5.48	88	25	4	3	15	.284	.466	.315
Artificial Turf	3-5	4.32	288	78	7	25	48	.271	.399	.332
April			0	0	0	0	0	—	—	—
May			0	0	0	0	0	—	—	—
June	0-0	9.39	31	11	1	4	2	.355	.484	.417
July	0-3	6.85	86	27	5	7	18	.314	.593	.372
August	2-2	3.31	124	30	3	5	14	.242	.363	.277
Sept./Oct.	1-1	3.31	135	35	2	12	29	.259	.333	.324
Leading Off Inn.			97	26	2	1	21	.268	.412	.283
Runners On			145	37	7	21	25	.255	.448	.355
Runners/Scor. Pos.			93	27	5	15	21	.290	.516	.391
Runners On/2 Out			67	20	5	10	8	.299	.522	.397
Scor. Pos./2 Out			45	16	4	6	8	.356	.667	.431
Late Inning Pressure			29	10	0	2	0	.345	.448	.406
Leading Off			7	1	0	0	0	.143	.286	.143
Runners On			11	5	0	2	0	.455	.636	.571
Runners/Scor. Pos.			7	5	0	2	0	.714	1.000	.800
First 9 Batters			143	29	5	9	33	.203	.350	.253
Second 9 Batters			126	39	4	12	18	.310	.452	.374
All Batters Thereafter			107	35	2	7	12	.327	.458	.374

Loves to face: Will Clark (0-for-6)
Hates to face: Glenn Davis (2-for-2, 2 HR)
Figures above are for N.L. only. . . . Ground outs-to-air outs ratio: 1.29 last season, 1.16 for career. . . . Additional statistics: 3 double-play ground outs in 58 opportunities, 22 doubles, 2 triples in 104.2 innings last season. . . . Allowed 5 first-inning runs in 15 starts last season. . . . Batting support: 3.00 runs per start, lowest in N.L. (minimum: 15 GS). . . . Lost all 6 starts vs. N.L. teams with winning records (7.44 ERA). . . . Weirdest breakdown of the year: Martinez held the top 15 batters in the N.L. to a .191 average (9-for-47), but opposing pitchers hit .292 (7-for-24) against him. . . . Opposing right-handed hitters outhit lefties for sixth consecutive season. During that time: left-handers, .254; right-handers, .305.

Greg Mathews

St. Louis Cardinals — Throws Left

	W–L	ERA	AB	H	HR	BB	SO	BA	SA	OBA
Season	11-8	3.65	537	139	15	44	67	.259	.406	.317
vs. Left-Handers			91	23	2	7	12	.253	.396	.306
vs. Right-Handers			446	116	13	37	55	.260	.408	.319
Home	5-2	3.19	194	45	3	13	24	.232	.356	.284
Road	6-6	3.93	343	94	12	31	43	.274	.434	.335
Grass	2-2	3.10	150	37	5	12	17	.247	.393	.302
Artificial Turf	9-6	3.87	387	102	10	32	50	.264	.411	.322
April			0	0	0	0	0	—	—	—
May			0	0	0	0	0	—	—	—
June	4-1	2.89	163	37	3	15	23	.227	.344	.291
July	2-1	4.13	95	27	1	6	9	.284	.421	.333
August	4-2	3.00	151	37	5	10	16	.245	.384	.292
Sept./Oct.	1-4	5.23	128	38	6	13	19	.297	.500	.366
Leading Off Inn.			134	35	5	14	17	.261	.440	.340
Runners On			212	57	4	16	23	.269	.396	.319
Runners/Scor. Pos.			125	33	3	13	19	.264	.376	.331
Runners On/2 Out			85	22	2	8	8	.259	.400	.323
Scor. Pos./2 Out			55	12	2	6	7	.218	.345	.295
Late Inning Pressure			39	6	1	2	3	.154	.256	.195
Leading Off			11	1	0	1	1	.091	.182	.167
Runners On			8	2	0	0	1	.250	.250	.250
Runners/Scor. Pos.			1	1	0	0	0	1.000	1.000	1.000
First 9 Batters			189	49	3	15	23	.259	.365	.312
Second 9 Batters			180	42	6	12	30	.233	.394	.289
All Batters Thereafter			168	48	6	17	14	.286	.464	.351

Loves to face: Jose Cruz & Glenn Davis (0-for-6)
Hates to face: Eric Davis (2-for-2, 2 HR)
Also hates to face: Mookie Wilson (.833, 5-for-6). . . . Ground outs-to-air outs ratio: 1.13 last season, his first in majors. . . . Additional statistics: 15 double-play ground outs in 89 opportunities, 7th-highest average in N.L. (minimum: 10 GDP), 32 doubles, 1 triple in 145.1 innings last season. . . . Allowed 8 first-inning runs in 22 starts last season. . . . Batting support: 3.45 runs per start, 6th lowest in N.L. (minimum: 15 GS). . . . Tied Charlie Kerfeld for 2d among N.L. rookies with 11 wins, one fewer than league leader Jim Deshaies. . . . The only major-league pitcher to be hit by a pitch twice last season. . . . Was 0-for-22 with runners on base, 0-for-26 vs. right-handed pitchers, and 0-for-27 in road games.

Bob McClure

Montreal Expos — Throws Left

Montreal Expos	W–L	ERA	AB	H	HR	BB	SO	BA	SA	OBA
Season	2-5	3.02	228	53	2	23	42	.232	.316	.303
vs. Left-Handers			76	14	1	6	18	.184	.329	.238
vs. Right-Handers			152	39	1	17	24	.257	.309	.335
Home	2-2	4.25	114	28	1	13	20	.246	.360	.326
Road	0-3	1.91	114	25	1	10	22	.219	.272	.280
Grass	0-2	1.08	54	9	1	4	12	.167	.241	.220
Artificial Turf	2-3	3.72	174	44	1	19	30	.253	.339	.328
April			0	0	0	0	0	—	—	—
May			0	0	0	0	0	—	—	—
June	0-0	1.46	43	9	0	4	11	.209	.279	.277
July	0-1	6.28	54	16	2	6	10	.296	.500	.361
August	0-2	2.75	69	15	0	7	10	.217	.261	.299
Sept./Oct.	2-2	1.65	62	13	0	6	11	.210	.242	.275
Leading Off Inn.			57	12	0	6	13	.211	.246	.286
Runners On			101	26	1	8	19	.257	.347	.306
Runners/Scor. Pos.			56	16	1	7	14	.286	.393	.354
Runners On/2 Out			47	11	1	4	10	.234	.362	.294
Scor. Pos./2 Out			29	7	1	4	8	.241	.414	.333
Late Inning Pressure			165	40	2	16	32	.242	.339	.309
Leading Off			43	9	0	5	10	.209	.209	.292
Runners On			70	17	1	5	15	.243	.357	.293
Runners/Scor. Pos.			36	9	1	5	11	.250	.389	.341
First 9 Batters			208	48	1	21	39	.231	.308	.302
Second 9 Batters			20	5	1	2	3	.250	.400	.318
All Batters Thereafter			0	0	0	0	0			

Loves to face: Ken Griffey (.133, 2-for-15)
Hates to face: Jose Cruz (2-for-3, 1 3B)
Figures above are for N.L. only. . . . Ground outs-to-air outs ratio: 1.18 last season, 0.82 for career. . . . Additional statistics: 9 double-play ground outs in 75 opportunities, 7 doubles, 4 triples in 79.0 innings last season. . . . Faced only one batter 7 times, pitched two or more innings 14 times, finished 22 games in 65 relief appearances. . . . Opponents' slugging average was lowest since his rookie season of 1977. . . . Has retired more than 70 percent of leadoff batters in six of the past eight seasons. . . . Clean slate: starts 1987 season with a career record of 48–48.

Lance McCullers

San Diego Padres — Throws Right

San Diego Padres	W–L	ERA	AB	H	HR	BB	SO	BA	SA	OBA
Season	10-10	2.78	477	103	12	58	92	.216	.331	.304
vs. Left-Handers			237	66	5	35	30	.278	.388	.371
vs. Right-Handers			240	37	7	23	62	.154	.275	.236
Home	5-3	2.66	211	46	6	21	46	.218	.341	.289
Road	5-7	2.88	266	57	6	37	46	.214	.323	.316
Grass	8-8	2.84	345	79	11	48	74	.229	.365	.325
Artificial Turf	2-2	2.63	132	24	1	10	18	.182	.242	.248
April	1-1	2.25	27	7	1	2	7	.259	.481	.310
May	0-0	0.55	53	6	1	9	10	.113	.189	.238
June	3-1	2.39	93	21	1	9	19	.226	.269	.298
July	1-3	3.48	116	26	2	15	20	.224	.336	.318
August	2-1	2.78	111	24	3	8	19	.216	.324	.279
Sept./Oct.	3-4	4.09	77	19	4	15	17	.247	.455	.370
Leading Off Inn.			118	27	1	10	19	.229	.297	.300
Runners On			186	35	6	32	37	.188	.317	.306
Runners/Scor. Pos.			117	22	4	27	24	.188	.316	.338
Runners On/2 Out			88	13	2	17	19	.148	.239	.286
Scor. Pos./2 Out			59	9	1	14	15	.153	.220	.315
Late Inning Pressure			188	45	5	32	37	.239	.346	.353
Leading Off			46	11	0	6	9	.239	.261	.340
Runners On			82	16	2	19	17	.195	.268	.340
Runners/Scor. Pos.			53	11	1	17	10	.208	.264	.389
First 9 Batters			351	73	10	39	74	.208	.330	.291
Second 9 Batters			70	14	0	10	9	.200	.243	.300
All Batters Thereafter			56	16	2	9	9	.286	.446	.388

Loves to face: Glenn Davis (0-for-11, 3 SO)
Hates to face: Omar Moreno (.800, 4-for-5, 1 HR)
Ground outs-to-air outs ratio: 0.77 last season, 0.80 for career. . . . Additional statistics: 7 double-play ground outs in 75 opportunities, 17 doubles, 1 triple in 136.0 innings last season. . . . Faced only one batter 6 times, pitched two or more innings 19 times, finished 29 games in 63 relief appearances. . . . 1–4, 4.19 ERA in 7 starts; 9–6, 2.13 ERA in relief. . . . Opposing right-handed batters fared only slightly better in 1985 (.169). . . . Opposing batters also hit below .200 with runners on base in 1985. . . . ERA of 2.68 in two seasons in majors ranks 6th among N.L. pitchers with as many relief appearances (84) during that time.. . . . Has faced 692 batters in career, allowed only one triple.

Roger McDowell

New York Mets — Throws Right

New York Mets	W–L	ERA	AB	H	HR	BB	SO	BA	SA	OBA
Season	14-9	3.02	469	107	4	42	65	.228	.296	.294
vs. Left-Handers			227	56	4	32	24	.247	.366	.341
vs. Right-Handers			242	51	0	10	41	.211	.231	.246
Home	7-3	1.73	218	40	0	22	38	.183	.211	.261
Road	7-6	4.25	251	67	4	20	27	.267	.371	.322
Grass	10-5	2.58	331	73	2	26	50	.221	.269	.278
Artificial Turf	4-4	4.10	138	34	2	16	15	.246	.362	.331
April	2-0	2.63	52	10	0	5	14	.192	.269	.263
May	1-0	3.28	100	27	0	8	14	.270	.310	.330
June	4-0	0.69	85	13	0	10	11	.153	.165	.242
July	1-5	2.79	68	15	1	5	10	.221	.294	.289
August	4-2	3.38	88	18	1	3	8	.205	.295	.231
Sept./Oct.	2-2	5.75	76	24	2	11	8	.316	.447	.393
Leading Off Inn.			112	21	0	13	18	.188	.223	.272
Runners On			204	54	3	17	22	.265	.373	.326
Runners/Scor. Pos.			110	29	2	12	13	.264	.418	.344
Runners On/2 Out			80	15	3	8	8	.188	.375	.278
Scor. Pos./2 Out			54	8	2	5	5	.148	.352	.246
Late Inning Pressure			286	70	3	26	37	.245	.311	.308
Leading Off			68	14	0	9	10	.206	.235	.299
Runners On			127	34	2	9	13	.268	.354	.317
Runners/Scor. Pos.			74	19	2	8	7	.257	.405	.329
First 9 Batters			428	94	3	37	61	.220	.283	.283
Second 9 Batters			41	13	1	5	4	.317	.439	.404
All Batters Thereafter			0	0	0	0	0			

Loves to face: Steve Garvey (0-for-10)
Hates to face: Jerry Mumphrey (.600, 3-for-5, 2 HR)
Ground outs-to-air outs ratio: 3.47, highest in majors last season (minimum: 250 BFP), 3.31 for career. . . . Additional statistics: 15 double-play ground outs (most among N.L. relievers) in 108 opportunities, 14 doubles, 3 triples in 128.0 innings last season. . . . Faced only one batter twice, pitched two or more innings 37 times (most in N.L.), finished 52 games in 75 relief appearances. . . . Did not allow a home run at Shea Stadium last season, nor one to a right-handed batter. Allowed seven in both categories a year earlier. . . . Opposing right-handers managed only two extra-base hits (both doubles) in 106 at bats at Shea. By Schmidt and Dawson? Nope, Mike Fitzgerald and Chris James.

Andy McGaffigan

Montreal Expos — Throws Right

Montreal Expos	W–L	ERA	AB	H	HR	BB	SO	BA	SA	OBA
Season	10-5	2.65	511	114	9	55	104	.223	.325	.298
vs. Left-Handers			265	54	2	36	51	.204	.268	.296
vs. Right-Handers			246	60	7	19	53	.244	.386	.301
Home	3-2	1.99	217	43	2	25	43	.198	.249	.279
Road	7-3	3.18	294	71	7	30	61	.241	.381	.313
Grass	2-3	4.50	171	41	6	15	29	.240	.415	.304
Artificial Turf	8-2	1.77	340	73	3	40	75	.215	.279	.296
April	1-0	6.00	60	18	2	8	15	.300	.483	.391
May	2-1	2.73	106	22	1	15	15	.208	.264	.309
June	2-2	3.00	85	20	1	9	19	.235	.341	.309
July	0-1	3.52	91	22	4	7	16	.242	.429	.296
August	3-1	0.87	65	9	0	9	14	.138	.169	.237
Sept./Oct.	2-0	1.19	104	23	1	7	25	.221	.288	.265
Leading Off Inn.			130	31	5	14	23	.238	.400	.313
Runners On			207	42	3	27	41	.203	.275	.292
Runners/Scor. Pos.			130	28	2	22	27	.215	.292	.323
Runners On/2 Out			91	18	2	19	21	.198	.319	.342
Scor. Pos./2 Out			61	14	2	15	15	.230	.377	.390
Late Inning Pressure			90	23	0	15	18	.256	.333	.355
Leading Off			24	7	0	2	4	.292	.375	.346
Runners On			38	8	0	8	8	.211	.237	.333
Runners/Scor. Pos.			26	6	0	7	7	.231	.269	.371
First 9 Batters			302	55	3	28	66	.182	.252	.248
Second 9 Batters			134	36	4	10	26	.269	.440	.324
All Batters Thereafter			75	23	2	17	12	.307	.413	.441

Loves to face: Denny Walling (0-for-9, 3 SO)
Hates to face: Bob Horner (.400, 6-for-15, 4 HR)
Also hates to face: Kevin McReynolds (.529, 9-for-17, 2 HR). . . .
Ground outs-to-air outs ratio: 1.36 last season, 1.15 for career. . . . Additional statistics: 11 double-play ground outs in 84 opportunities, 25 doubles, 0 triples in 142.2 innings last season. . . . Allowed 2 first-inning runs in 14 starts last season. . . . Batting support: 5.00 runs per start. . . . Faced only one batter twice, pitched two or more innings 21 times, finished 8 games in 34 relief appearances. . . . Career records: 11–19, 4.18 ERA as a starter; 9–4, 2.16 ERA in relief. . . . Faced 583 batters last season, highest total among N.L. pitchers who did not allow a triple. . . . Opposing batting and slugging averages were lowest marks in his four full seasons in majors.

Craig McMurtry

Atlanta Braves — Throws Right

	W–L	ERA	AB	H	HR	BB	SO	BA	SA	OBA
Season	1-6	4.74	309	82	7	43	50	.265	.405	.357
vs. Left-Handers			147	46	3	27	19	.313	.476	.421
vs. Right-Handers			162	36	4	16	31	.222	.340	.292
Home	0-5	5.48	171	53	5	21	18	.310	.474	.388
Road	1-1	3.89	138	29	2	22	32	.210	.319	.319
Grass	0-5	5.95	226	69	6	27	33	.305	.478	.381
Artificial Turf	1-1	1.90	83	13	1	16	17	.157	.205	.293
April	0-1	5.40	35	6	1	5	8	.171	.257	.293
May	1-1	2.51	49	6	0	12	15	.122	.163	.295
June	0-2	3.15	111	35	2	10	17	.315	.441	.374
July	0-2	6.16	76	21	3	11	7	.276	.513	.364
August			0	0	0	0	0	—	—	—
Sept./Oct.	0-0	7.00	38	14	1	5	3	.368	.526	.442
Leading Off Inn.			68	24	0	10	10	.353	.471	.436
Runners On			155	38	5	26	25	.245	.387	.353
Runners/Scor. Pos.			107	26	3	20	19	.243	.355	.362
Runners On/2 Out			67	19	4	14	9	.284	.507	.407
Scor. Pos./2 Out			52	15	3	11	9	.288	.481	.413
Late Inning Pressure			46	12	1	7	6	.261	.413	.358
Leading Off			10	4	0	1	0	.400	.700	.455
Runners On			25	5	1	5	5	.200	.360	.333
Runners/Scor. Pos.			19	3	0	4	5	.158	.158	.304
First 9 Batters			195	48	4	26	37	.246	.385	.338
Second 9 Batters			65	20	2	12	8	.308	.462	.416
All Batters Thereafter			49	14	1	5	5	.286	.408	.352

Loves to face: Ron Cey (0-for-8)
Refuses to face: Rob Deer (0-for-0, 3 BB)
Ground outs-to-air outs ratio: 1.16 last season, 1.35 for career. . . .
Additional statistics: 9 double-play ground outs in 64 opportunities, 18 doubles, 2 triples in 79.2 innings last season. . . . Faced only one batter 3 times, pitched two or more innings 12 times, finished 5 games in 32 relief appearances. . . . Well-liked by other N.L. pitchers, who hit .320 (8-for-25) against him last season, highest collective average by the fraternity against any fellow member (minimum: 20 at bats). . . Opposing leadoff batters compiled .325 on-base average in first two seasons, .456 over last two. . . . Opponents batted .198 with runners on base in first two seasons, .274 in last two. . . . Has lost 10 consecutive decisions on grass fields.

Larry McWilliams

Pittsburgh Pirates — Throws Left

	W–L	ERA	AB	H	HR	BB	SO	BA	SA	OBA
Season	3-11	5.15	480	129	16	49	80	.269	.444	.345
vs. Left-Handers			80	17	3	7	24	.213	.400	.292
vs. Right-Handers			400	112	13	42	56	.280	.453	.356
Home	2-9	6.19	258	72	9	28	37	.279	.484	.354
Road	1-2	4.01	222	57	7	21	43	.257	.396	.335
Grass	0-1	5.13	134	38	5	12	23	.284	.455	.356
Artificial Turf	3-10	5.16	346	91	11	37	57	.263	.439	.341
April	0-2	4.66	73	17	3	10	11	.233	.384	.341
May	1-1	6.49	108	33	4	10	21	.306	.519	.364
June	0-1	3.32	82	20	3	7	14	.244	.402	.319
July	1-2	5.17	62	16	3	6	9	.258	.468	.324
August	0-4	5.79	111	30	3	12	20	.270	.441	.352
Sept./Oct.	1-1	4.76	44	13	0	4	5	.295	.409	.367
Leading Off Inn.			116	30	5	9	13	.259	.466	.312
Runners On			205	65	9	25	35	.317	.537	.397
Runners/Scor. Pos.			121	38	5	20	20	.314	.529	.420
Runners On/2 Out			96	32	4	16	17	.333	.573	.434
Scor. Pos./2 Out			63	19	2	14	11	.302	.476	.436
Late Inning Pressure			87	22	3	11	15	.253	.414	.337
Leading Off			19	3	1	4	3	.158	.316	.304
Runners On			37	12	2	3	4	.324	.541	.375
Runners/Scor. Pos.			18	6	2	3	2	.333	.722	.429
First 9 Batters			270	70	4	25	53	.259	.367	.327
Second 9 Batters			123	31	7	10	15	.252	.504	.319
All Batters Thereafter			87	28	5	14	12	.322	.598	.433

Loves to face: Glenn Hubbard (.045, 1-for-22, 7 SO)
Hates to face: Mike Schmidt (.356, 16-for-45, 7 HR)
Ground outs-to-air outs ratio: 1.30 last season, 1.17 for career. . . .
Additional statistics: 8 double-play ground outs in 90 opportunities, 32 doubles, 2 triples in 122.1 innings last season. . . . Allowed 12 first-inning runs in 15 starts last season. . . . Batting support: 4.67 runs per start. . . . Faced only one batter twice, pitched two or more innings 9 times, finished 11 games in 34 relief appearances. . . . Pitched an average of only 5.52 innings per start. . . . Has won all six career decisions against his former team, the Braves; 37–44 vs. other teams since leaving Atlanta. . . . Opposing batters have 14 hits in 25 at bats with the bases loaded over past two seasons.

Greg Minton

San Francisco Giants — Throws Right

	W–L	ERA	AB	H	HR	BB	SO	BA	SA	OBA
Season	4-4	3.93	251	63	4	34	34	.251	.371	.339
vs. Left-Handers			126	38	3	21	10	.302	.468	.396
vs. Right-Handers			125	25	1	13	24	.200	.272	.279
Home	1-2	3.16	113	24	1	10	15	.212	.283	.280
Road	3-2	4.58	138	39	3	24	19	.283	.442	.384
Grass	3-3	3.42	178	43	3	18	26	.242	.343	.312
Artificial Turf	1-1	5.30	73	20	1	16	8	.274	.438	.400
April	1-1	2.87	48	10	2	6	7	.208	.354	.291
May	1-2	5.06	60	15	0	8	10	.250	.317	.333
June	1-1	6.28	58	18	1	12	7	.310	.500	.423
July	0-0	1.23	27	7	0	3	5	.259	.333	.333
August	0-0	1.08	29	5	1	4	4	.172	.345	.294
Sept./Oct.	1-0	5.14	29	8	0	1	1	.276	.310	.300
Leading Off Inn.			55	14	1	3	8	.255	.345	.305
Runners On			127	33	0	23	16	.260	.354	.366
Runners/Scor. Pos.			100	25	0	21	14	.250	.370	.371
Runners On/2 Out			55	12	0	14	8	.218	.291	.377
Scor. Pos./2 Out			49	10	0	13	8	.204	.286	.371
Late Inning Pressure			139	36	3	17	20	.259	.396	.335
Leading Off			35	10	1	1	5	.286	.400	.306
Runners On			57	17	0	12	8	.298	.404	.408
Runners/Scor. Pos.			45	14	0	11	6	.311	.444	.431
First 9 Batters			228	58	3	33	32	.254	.360	.347
Second 9 Batters			22	5	1	1	2	.227	.500	.261
All Batters Thereafter			1	0	0	0	0	.000	.000	.000

Loves to face: Terry Puhl (0-for-14)
Hates to face: Ken Griffey (.667, 8-for-12)
Ground outs-to-air outs ratio: 2.37, 8th highest in N.L. last season (minimum: 250 BFP), 2.41 for career. . . . Additional statistics: 8 double-play ground outs in 63 opportunities, 10 doubles, 4 triples in 68.2 innings last season. . . . Faced only one batter twice, pitched two or more innings 14 times, finished 28 games in 48 relief appearances. . . . Only pitcher to appear in 50 or more games in six consecutive seasons through 1985. Streak was snapped with 48 appearances last season. . . . One of five pitchers with more walks than strikeouts in each season from 1983 through 1985. Snapped that streak last season, also, by the narrowest of margins. . . . Has faced 1668 left-handed batters in his career and never hit one with a pitch. . . . Career record of 0–5 vs. Philadelphia.

Jamie Moyer

Chicago Cubs — Throws Left

	W–L	ERA	AB	H	HR	BB	SO	BA	SA	OBA
Season	7-4	5.05	344	107	10	42	45	.311	.451	.388
vs. Left-Handers			40	12	2	8	5	.300	.575	.417
vs. Right-Handers			304	95	8	34	40	.313	.434	.384
Home	4-1	4.88	233	74	7	33	28	.318	.459	.405
Road	3-3	5.40	111	33	3	9	17	.297	.432	.350
Grass	5-2	4.81	265	84	7	37	33	.317	.449	.402
Artificial Turf	2-2	5.85	79	23	3	5	12	.291	.456	.337
April			0	0	0	0	0	—	—	—
May			0	0	0	0	0	—	—	—
June	1-1	10.00	39	15	2	4	5	.385	.641	.467
July	2-1	3.13	85	22	0	9	16	.259	.294	.326
August	2-2	5.81	102	29	3	13	13	.284	.412	.364
Sept./Oct.	2-0	4.34	118	41	5	16	11	.347	.534	.425
Leading Off Inn.			86	30	4	5	13	.349	.523	.391
Runners On			170	53	5	19	19	.312	.447	.381
Runners/Scor. Pos.			102	25	4	10	12	.245	.382	.310
Runners On/2 Out			60	18	1	8	8	.300	.400	.382
Scor. Pos./2 Out			39	9	1	5	7	.231	.333	.318
Late Inning Pressure			13	2	0	1	2	.154	.154	.214
Leading Off			4	0	0	0	0	.000	.000	.000
Runners On			3	2	0	0	0	.667	.667	.667
Runners/Scor. Pos.			2	1	0	0	0	.500	.500	.500
First 9 Batters			121	36	3	17	19	.298	.413	.386
Second 9 Batters			110	31	2	14	15	.282	.391	.365
All Batters Thereafter			113	40	5	11	11	.354	.549	.413

Loves to face: Tim Teufel (1-for-11)
Hates to face: Mike Schmidt (.625, 5-for-8, 2 HR)
Ground outs-to-air outs ratio: 1.54 last season, his first in majors. . . . Additional statistics: 13 double-play ground outs in 94 opportunities, 18 doubles, 0 triples in 87.1 innings last season. . . . Allowed 12 first-inning runs in 16 starts last season. . . . Batting support: 4.81 runs per start. . . . Top 15 batters in N.L. hit combined .414 against him, 3rd highest in N.L. (minimum: 20 at bats); the leader: Bob Patterson (.433, 13-for-30). . . . Retired all seven batters he faced with the bases loaded. . . . Tied Ed Lynch for most wins on Cubs after the All-Star break (6). . . . Allowed 15.66 base runners per nine innings, 3d-highest average in N.L. last season (minimum: 10 GS).

Tom Niedenfuer

Los Angeles Dodgers — Throws Right

	W–L	ERA	AB	H	HR	BB	SO	BA	SA	OBA
Season	6-6	3.71	307	86	11	29	55	.280	.453	.341
vs. Left-Handers			155	44	6	22	29	.284	.477	.371
vs. Right-Handers			152	42	5	7	26	.276	.428	.309
Home	4-4	3.33	170	43	6	7	31	.253	.412	.278
Road	2-2	4.24	137	43	5	22	24	.314	.504	.413
Grass	5-6	3.47	236	65	8	17	43	.275	.428	.323
Artificial Turf	1-0	4.58	71	21	3	12	12	.296	.507	.398
April	0-1	4.26	51	17	2	4	12	.333	.490	.382
May	3-1	2.37	69	15	4	9	17	.217	.449	.313
June	2-1	4.05	53	15	3	3	10	.283	.528	.321
July	0-1	2.95	66	16	1	8	10	.242	.333	.324
August	1-0	1.80	39	11	1	1	3	.282	.385	.293
Sept./Oct.	0-2	10.80	29	12	0	4	3	.414	.621	.471
Leading Off Inn.			67	19	2	3	14	.284	.433	.314
Runners On			152	40	5	21	30	.263	.428	.347
Runners/Scor. Pos.			92	26	3	20	18	.283	.467	.400
Runners On/2 Out			70	21	2	12	15	.300	.486	.402
Scor. Pos./2 Out			50	15	1	12	12	.300	.460	.435
Late Inning Pressure			200	63	7	23	34	.315	.495	.382
Leading Off			46	13	2	2	8	.283	.435	.313
Runners On			96	29	2	17	20	.302	.458	.400
Runners/Scor. Pos.			57	19	1	16	13	.333	.509	.467
First 9 Batters			291	78	10	28	54	.268	.430	.331
Second 9 Batters			16	8	1	1	1	.500	.875	.529
All Batters Thereafter			0	0	0	0	0	—	—	—

Loves to face: Vince Coleman (0-for-10)
Hates to face: Ray Knight (.462, 6-for-13)
Ground outs-to-air outs ratio: 0.54, 3d-lowest in majors last season (minimum: 250 BFP), 0.54 for career.... Additional statistics: 3 double-play ground outs in 74 opportunities, 2d-lowest average in N.L. (minimum: 40 opp.), 16 doubles, 2 triples in 80.0 innings last season.... Faced only one batter 4 times, pitched two or more innings 18 times, finished 27 games in 60 relief appearances.... Had never hit a right-handed batter with a pitch until he hit Ray Knight on May 27. Knight hit back.... Opposing right-handed hitters had never topped .235 prior to last season. They had 13 extra-base hits last season, compared to 19 in five previous years in majors.... Has made 295 career relief appearances without a start.

Bob Ojeda

New York Mets — Throws Left

	W–L	ERA	AB	H	HR	BB	SO	BA	SA	OBA
Season	18-5	2.57	804	185	15	52	148	.230	.330	.277
vs. Left-Handers			107	16	1	8	24	.150	.206	.207
vs. Right-Handers			697	169	14	44	124	.242	.349	.288
Home	9-2	2.86	397	89	7	23	81	.224	.325	.267
Road	9-3	2.28	407	96	8	29	67	.236	.334	.288
Grass	12-2	2.78	499	113	7	32	101	.226	.315	.272
Artificial Turf	6-3	2.21	305	72	8	20	47	.236	.354	.285
April	3-0	2.11	77	17	2	2	8	.221	.312	.241
May	3-2	2.90	152	40	0	12	32	.263	.329	.317
June	3-0	2.39	142	35	2	13	20	.246	.352	.308
July	3-0	1.54	128	28	5	7	26	.219	.352	.259
August	3-2	3.92	156	39	3	13	34	.250	.327	.312
Sept./Oct.	3-1	2.16	149	26	3	5	28	.174	.302	.200
Leading Off Inn.			206	51	4	13	33	.248	.354	.295
Runners On			323	66	4	21	63	.204	.291	.252
Runners/Scor. Pos.			180	37	3	12	36	.206	.311	.254
Runners On/2 Out			132	26	3	10	23	.197	.318	.254
Scor. Pos./2 Out			89	18	3	6	14	.202	.326	.253
Late Inning Pressure			96	28	2	7	16	.292	.375	.337
Leading Off			22	6	1	3	5	.273	.409	.360
Runners On			40	10	0	3	5	.250	.275	.295
Runners/Scor. Pos.			21	5	0	1	2	.238	.286	.261
First 9 Batters			270	64	2	14	65	.237	.304	.275
Second 9 Batters			243	49	5	20	35	.202	.309	.263
All Batters Thereafter			291	72	8	18	48	.247	.371	.292

Loves to face: Vance Law (.100, 2-for-20)
Hates to face: Ryne Sandberg (.500, 3-for-6, 2 HR)
Ground outs-to-air outs ratio: 1.10 last season (2.11 in DP situations, 0.92 at other times; league averages 1.74 and 1.11), 0.99 for career.... Additional statistics: 19 double-play ground outs (9th in N.L.) in 154 opportunities, 27 doubles, 4 triples in 217.1 innings last season.... Allowed 18 first-inning runs in 30 starts last season. First-inning ERA: 4.80; after that: 2.21.... Batting support: 4.83 runs per start, 9th best in N.L. (minimum: 15 GS).... Only pitcher in majors with a winning record in every month last season. Even if you eliminate October, only Mark Eichhorn joins Ojeda.... Career averages: 1.04 strikeouts per walk in Late-Inning Pressure Situations, 1.70 overall.... 13–0 in 18 starts in which he went at least seven innings.

Jesse Orosco

New York Mets — Throws Left

	W–L	ERA	AB	H	HR	BB	SO	BA	SA	OBA
Season	8-6	2.33	295	64	6	35	62	.217	.305	.304
vs. Left-Handers			75	14	1	5	24	.187	.253	.235
vs. Right-Handers			220	50	5	30	38	.227	.323	.325
Home	4-4	4.15	138	38	5	15	25	.275	.428	.346
Road	4-2	0.97	157	26	1	20	37	.166	.197	.267
Grass	6-6	3.55	197	49	6	22	36	.249	.376	.324
Artificial Turf	2-0	0.30	98	15	0	13	26	.153	.163	.263
April	0-0	0.00	30	4	0	6	9	.133	.167	.278
May	2-2	3.00	52	9	2	8	15	.173	.327	.283
June	1-2	5.40	34	9	1	9	8	.265	.382	.413
July	1-0	3.09	45	12	2	2	7	.267	.400	.306
August	1-1	1.04	68	15	0	6	11	.221	.235	.293
Sept./Oct.	3-1	2.08	66	15	1	4	12	.227	.318	.271
Leading Off Inn.			57	13	2	8	13	.228	.351	.323
Runners On			153	28	4	18	35	.183	.261	.277
Runners/Scor. Pos.			93	16	1	11	28	.172	.204	.266
Runners On/2 Out			75	12	2	10	16	.160	.240	.276
Scor. Pos./2 Out			52	10	1	7	14	.192	.250	.300
Late Inning Pressure			226	55	6	30	45	.243	.358	.335
Leading Off			41	11	2	7	8	.268	.439	.375
Runners On			124	26	4	18	28	.210	.306	.315
Runners/Scor. Pos.			78	16	1	11	22	.205	.244	.304
First 9 Batters			281	60	6	34	61	.214	.306	.302
Second 9 Batters			14	4	0	1	1	.286	.286	.333
All Batters Thereafter			0	0	0	0	0	—	—	—

Loves to face: Terry Pendleton (0-for-14, 3 SO)
Hates to face: Chili Davis (.571, 8-for-14, 1 HR)
Ground outs-to-air outs ratio: 0.71 last season, 0.88 for career.... Additional statistics: 7 double-play ground outs in 80 opportunities, 8 doubles, 0 triples in 81.0 innings last season.... Faced only one batter 8 times (4th most in N.L.), pitched two or more innings 22 times, finished 40 games in 58 relief appearances.... First pitcher in major-league history to win three games in relief in a postseason series.... Never allowed a run in Astrodome before Hatcher's homer in 14th inning of N.L.C.S. Game Six.... Hasn't allowed a HR to a left-hander at Shea Stadium since Aug. 15, 1982 (Leon Durham).... Career average of one XBH per 36.8 AB by left-handers is 2d lowest in *Player Analysis* history (minimum: 200 AB).

David Palmer

Atlanta Braves — Throws Right

	W–L	ERA	AB	H	HR	BB	SO	BA	SA	OBA
Season	11-10	3.65	773	181	17	102	170	.234	.343	.325
vs. Left-Handers			397	93	5	64	93	.234	.322	.343
vs. Right-Handers			376	88	12	38	77	.234	.364	.306
Home	5-2	2.90	380	93	5	42	72	.245	.313	.322
Road	6-8	4.36	393	88	12	60	98	.224	.372	.329
Grass	7-5	3.70	540	132	10	69	107	.244	.335	.332
Artificial Turf	4-5	3.55	233	49	7	33	63	.210	.361	.310
April	1-1	3.38	89	18	2	8	21	.202	.303	.268
May	2-3	2.51	153	29	3	20	39	.190	.301	.286
June	1-2	3.05	162	38	3	27	27	.235	.321	.344
July	3-2	5.40	103	28	6	16	26	.272	.456	.374
August	3-0	3.18	139	25	2	19	33	.180	.281	.284
Sept./Oct.	1-2	5.34	127	43	1	12	24	.339	.425	.396
Leading Off Inn.			194	46	2	26	41	.237	.325	.327
Runners On			322	76	7	42	72	.236	.342	.323
Runners/Scor. Pos.			180	42	4	32	41	.233	.344	.347
Runners On/2 Out			134	33	4	25	34	.246	.366	.369
Scor. Pos./2 Out			79	18	2	19	24	.228	.329	.384
Late Inning Pressure			62	26	1	5	8	.419	.532	.463
Leading Off			16	6	0	2	3	.375	.375	.444
Runners On			28	9	0	2	4	.321	.393	.367
Runners/Scor. Pos.			12	6	0	1	2	.500	.667	.538
First 9 Batters			266	56	8	44	59	.211	.338	.326
Second 9 Batters			257	57	8	33	64	.222	.358	.313
All Batters Thereafter			250	68	1	25	47	.272	.332	.338

Loves to face: Ozzie Smith (.040, 1-for-25)
Hates to face: Joe Orsulak (.700, 7-for-10)
Ground outs-to-air outs ratio: 2.10 last season, 2.11 for career.... Additional statistics: 15 double-play ground outs in 136 opportunities, 25 doubles, 4 triples in 209.2 innings last season.... Allowed 21 first-inning runs in 35 starts last season.... Batting support: 3.71 runs per start.... First time in pro career that he made more than 30 starts (35) or pitched more than 140 innings (209.2). Also set a personal record for wins.... Compiled a 3.19 ERA in 14 no-decision starts.... Walked the leadoff batter in 26 innings last season, 2d-highest total in N.L. Floyd Youmans set a 12-year *Player Analysis* record with 37.... Opposing batters hit .168 in day games last season, .256 in night games. Career averages: .221 and .252.

Alejandro Pena

Los Angeles Dodgers — Throws Right

	W–L	ERA	AB	H	HR	BB	SO	BA	SA	OBA
Season	1-2	4.89	274	74	6	30	46	.270	.394	.343
vs. Left-Handers			145	45	6	18	24	.310	.497	.390
vs. Right-Handers			129	29	0	12	22	.225	.279	.289
Home	1-1	2.25	127	23	1	13	25	.181	.236	.257
Road	0-1	7.68	147	51	5	17	21	.347	.531	.416
Grass	1-1	4.83	158	40	2	17	27	.253	.361	.324
Artificial Turf	0-1	4.97	116	34	4	13	19	.293	.440	.369
April			0	0	0	0	0	—	—	—
May	0-0	3.38	10	2	1	3	2	.200	.600	.385
June	0-1	8.10	45	16	0	7	11	.356	.422	.442
July	1-0	5.25	91	25	1	10	12	.275	.385	.343
August	0-1	1.69	77	14	3	5	13	.182	.312	.232
Sept./Oct.	0-0	7.50	51	17	1	5	8	.333	.471	.404
Leading Off Inn.			63	18	4	10	8	.286	.492	.384
Runners On			132	36	1	14	29	.273	.371	.345
Runners/Scor. Pos.			78	22	0	12	19	.282	.346	.374
Runners On/2 Out			50	14	0	6	9	.280	.380	.357
Scor. Pos./2 Out			35	11	0	5	7	.314	.400	.400
Late Inning Pressure			35	9	0	10	7	.257	.314	.422
Leading Off			6	2	0	4	0	.333	.333	.600
Runners On			23	5	0	6	7	.217	.261	.379
Runners/Scor. Pos.			14	3	0	5	5	.214	.286	.421
First 9 Batters			156	40	1	19	27	.256	.321	.339
Second 9 Batters			88	25	3	10	16	.284	.466	.357
All Batters Thereafter			30	9	2	1	3	.300	.567	.323

Loves to face: Dale Murphy (.167, 5-for-30, 12 SO)
Hates to face: Kal Daniels (.667, 2-for-3, 2 HR)

Ground outs-to-air outs ratio: 0.77 last season, 1.21 for career.... Additional statistics: 3 double-play ground outs in 66 opportunities, 5th-lowest average in N.L. (minimum: 40 opp.), 12 doubles, 2 triples in 70.0 innings last season.... Allowed 6 first-inning runs in 10 starts last season.... Batting support: 4.80 runs per start.... Failed to complete three innings three times in 10 starts, reached the seventh inning only once.... Strikeout percentage (one per 6.7 batters faced) was 21 percent below his mark in 1984 (one per 5.3) when he led N.L. in ERA.... Found his niche, even in lost year: Opposing right-handed batters hit .141 at Dodger Stadium (9-for-64, only three walks, no home runs).

Pat Perry

St. Louis Cardinals — Throws Left

	W–L	ERA	AB	H	HR	BB	SO	BA	SA	OBA
Season	2-3	3.80	247	59	5	34	29	.239	.364	.323
vs. Left-Handers			71	19	1	4	7	.268	.366	.307
vs. Right-Handers			176	40	4	30	22	.227	.364	.329
Home	0-1	5.90	111	34	3	13	15	.306	.468	.364
Road	2-2	2.27	136	25	2	21	14	.184	.279	.289
Grass	2-1	2.93	52	9	1	9	9	.173	.327	.290
Artificial Turf	0-2	4.05	195	50	4	25	20	.256	.374	.332
April	1-1	6.23	31	6	1	7	4	.194	.323	.333
May	0-0	1.69	18	4	1	2	4	.222	.444	.300
June	0-1	4.26	68	18	1	10	8	.265	.324	.350
July	0-0	6.23	33	10	0	2	4	.303	.455	.333
August	1-0	1.72	53	9	2	4	4	.170	.340	.220
Sept./Oct.	0-1	3.18	44	12	0	9	5	.273	.386	.389
Leading Off Inn.			58	9	1	7	8	.155	.259	.246
Runners On			102	34	2	15	7	.333	.441	.395
Runners/Scor. Pos.			58	20	1	13	4	.345	.466	.423
Runners On/2 Out			40	9	1	7	1	.225	.300	.340
Scor. Pos./2 Out			24	4	0	6	1	.167	.167	.333
Late Inning Pressure			81	21	2	17	11	.259	.383	.380
Leading Off			20	2	0	3	4	.100	.100	.217
Runners On			37	13	0	7	3	.351	.378	.435
Runners/Scor. Pos.			21	8	0	5	2	.381	.429	.464
First 9 Batters			226	57	4	34	25	.252	.376	.341
Second 9 Batters			21	2	1	0	4	.095	.238	.095
All Batters Thereafter			0	0	0	0	0			

Loves to face: Johnny Ray (0-for-6, 2 SO)
Hates to face: Keith Moreland (3-for-3, 1 2B, 1 HR)

Ground outs-to-air outs ratio: 0.85 last season, 0.81 for career.... Additional statistics: 8 double-play ground outs in 57 opportunities, 10 doubles, 3 triples in 68.2 innings last season.... Faced only one batter twice, pitched two or more innings 18 times, finished 20 games in 46 relief appearances.... Opponents' career batting averages: .167 on grass fields, .232 on artificial turf; .307 at Busch Stadium, .157 in road games.... Before you continue, look at his record against leadoff batters.... Also retired all 12 leadoff batters he faced in 1985. Career totals: has retired 61 of 77 leadoff batters (79.2 percent), highest average in *Player Analysis* history for pitchers with at least 50 leadoff batters faced.

Dennis Powell

Los Angeles Dodgers — Throws Left

	W–L	ERA	AB	H	HR	BB	SO	BA	SA	OBA
Season	2-7	4.27	239	65	5	25	31	.272	.381	.340
vs. Left-Handers			66	13	1	3	11	.197	.258	.232
vs. Right-Handers			173	52	4	22	20	.301	.428	.377
Home	0-2	6.08	54	19	3	6	6	.352	.519	.410
Road	2-5	3.81	185	46	2	19	25	.249	.341	.319
Grass	0-5	4.33	164	46	5	17	23	.280	.409	.350
Artificial Turf	2-2	4.15	75	19	0	8	8	.253	.320	.318
April	0-3	5.84	45	9	2	6	8	.200	.378	.294
May			0	0	0	0	0	—	—	—
June			0	0	0	0	0	—	—	—
July	1-0	4.26	42	12	0	4	3	.286	.381	.354
August	1-2	4.22	80	24	2	7	14	.300	.400	.356
Sept./Oct.	0-2	3.32	72	20	1	8	6	.278	.361	.341
Leading Off Inn.			61	20	2	6	9	.328	.475	.388
Runners On			102	26	2	10	9	.255	.373	.319
Runners/Scor. Pos.			58	15	1	10	4	.259	.379	.361
Runners On/2 Out			37	7	1	5	5	.189	.270	.302
Scor. Pos./2 Out			22	5	1	5	1	.227	.364	.393
Late Inning Pressure			49	15	1	10	3	.306	.408	.417
Leading Off			14	5	1	1	0	.357	.643	.400
Runners On			25	6	0	4	2	.240	.280	.333
Runners/Scor. Pos.			12	3	0	4	0	.250	.333	.412
First 9 Batters			153	39	4	19	21	.255	.359	.337
Second 9 Batters			56	16	0	2	7	.286	.357	.305
All Batters Thereafter			30	10	1	4	3	.333	.533	.412

Loves to face: Terry Kennedy (0-for-6)
Hates to face: Paul Zuvella (.667, 2-for-3)

Ground outs-to-air outs ratio: 1.41 last season, 1.56 for career.... Additional statistics: 9 double-play ground outs in 50 opportunities, 11 doubles, 0 triples in 65.1 innings last season.... Career records: 1–6, 6.31 ERA in 8 starts, 2–2, 3.51 ERA in 35 relief appearances.... Other two-year totals: 0–3, 6.41 ERA at Dodger Stadium; 3–5, 3.84 ERA in road games.... Has allowed nine home runs in 26.2 innings at home, three in 68 innings on the road.... Has failed to complete five innings in five of eight career starts.... Opponents' career batting averages: .169 (two extra-base hits in 89 at bats) by left-handers; .303 (one XBH per 11.0 AB) by right-handers.

Ted Power

Cincinnati Reds — Throws Right

	W–L	ERA	AB	H	HR	BB	SO	BA	SA	OBA
Season	10-6	3.70	469	115	13	52	95	.245	.371	.318
vs. Left-Handers			229	60	6	29	41	.262	.402	.342
vs. Right-Handers			240	55	7	23	54	.229	.342	.294
Home	6-2	3.38	259	67	8	25	52	.259	.386	.325
Road	4-4	4.07	210	48	5	27	43	.229	.352	.310
Grass	2-3	4.85	139	34	3	22	27	.245	.374	.341
Artificial Turf	8-3	3.20	330	81	10	30	68	.245	.370	.308
April	0-2	6.00	28	13	1	5	6	.464	.679	.529
May	2-1	3.94	55	13	2	7	14	.236	.400	.333
June	1-2	7.71	49	19	1	9	6	.388	.531	.483
July	1-0	3.44	65	12	3	5	9	.185	.354	.239
August	0-1	4.22	78	19	1	10	17	.244	.333	.330
Sept./Oct.	6-0	2.43	194	39	5	16	43	.201	.299	.261
Leading Off Inn.			118	34	2	8	19	.288	.398	.333
Runners On			200	48	8	28	49	.240	.410	.328
Runners/Scor. Pos.			121	29	3	22	31	.240	.388	.342
Runners On/2 Out			80	17	3	14	23	.213	.400	.330
Scor. Pos./2 Out			56	13	1	11	16	.232	.393	.358
Late Inning Pressure			97	33	5	15	12	.340	.526	.421
Leading Off			25	15	1	0	2	.600	.800	.600
Runners On			50	15	4	10	7	.300	.560	.403
Runners/Scor. Pos.			34	10	2	8	5	.294	.500	.409
First 9 Batters			300	80	10	40	57	.267	.417	.350
Second 9 Batters			97	20	1	9	26	.206	.268	.274
All Batters Thereafter			72	15	2	3	12	.208	.319	.237

Loves to face: Glenn Wilson (0-for-10, 3 SO)
Hates to face: Chris Chambliss (.429, 6-for-14, 3 HR)

Ground outs-to-air outs ratio: 1.07 last season, 0.86 for career.... Additional statistics: 13 double-play ground outs in 113 opportunities, 16 doubles, 2 triples in 129.0 innings last season.... Allowed 3 first-inning runs in 10 starts last season.... Batting support: 5.90 runs per start, most in N.L. (with minimum lowered to 10 GS).... Faced only one batter twice, pitched two or more innings 16 times, finished 30 games in 46 relief appearances.... 6–1, 2.59 as a starter last season.... Made 10 consecutive starts after August 22, his first since May 30, 1983.... Career batting averages: .287 (one extra-base hit per 22.2 at bats) by left-handers, .226 (one XBH per 11.1 AB) by right-handers.

Shane Rawley

Philadelphia Phillies — Throws Left

	W–L	ERA	AB	H	HR	BB	SO	BA	SA	OBA
Season	11-7	3.54	615	166	13	50	73	.270	.405	.325
vs. Left-Handers			80	23	1	3	15	.288	.425	.313
vs. Right-Handers			535	143	12	47	58	.267	.402	.326
Home	7-3	3.91	274	76	3	29	31	.277	.391	.348
Road	4-4	3.25	341	90	10	21	42	.264	.416	.306
Grass	1-2	5.20	114	36	3	3	15	.316	.456	.331
Artificial Turf	10-5	3.18	501	130	10	47	58	.259	.393	.324
April	3-1	2.41	159	37	3	12	14	.233	.340	.287
May	3-3	4.25	145	43	3	5	21	.297	.434	.316
June	4-0	1.76	183	40	2	16	23	.219	.301	.281
July	1-3	7.28	128	46	5	17	15	.359	.602	.438
August			0	0	0	0	0			
Sept./Oct.			0	0	0	0	0			
Leading Off Inn.			156	45	9	9	17	.288	.526	.327
Runners On			252	68	2	24	32	.270	.369	.333
Runners/Scor. Pos.			142	35	0	18	21	.246	.324	.327
Runners On/2 Out			112	30	1	10	14	.268	.366	.333
Scor. Pos./2 Out			71	13	0	8	11	.183	.225	.266
Late Inning Pressure			64	10	2	4	9	.156	.281	.206
Leading Off			19	4	2	0	2	.211	.579	.211
Runners On			15	1	0	3	2	.067	.067	.222
Runners/Scor. Pos.			7	0	0	2	1	.000	.000	.222
First 9 Batters			185	48	5	21	19	.259	.395	.335
Second 9 Batters			177	47	2	15	30	.266	.395	.320
All Batters Thereafter			253	71	6	14	24	.281	.419	.321

Loves to face: Billy Sample (.063, 1-for-16)
Hates to face: Andre Dawson (.440, 11-for-25, 4 HR)
Ground outs-to-air outs ratio: 1.10 last season, 1.29 for career.... Additional statistics: 12 double-play ground outs in 116 opportunities, 38 doubles, 3 triples in 157.2 innings last season.... Allowed 5 first-inning runs in 23 starts last season.... Batting support: 5.65 runs per start, best in N.L. (minimum: 15 GS).... Shared N.L. lead in wins as late as July 11.... Has never allowed more than two home runs to left-handed batters in one season. Only Dave Parker tagged him last season.... Career record of 5–0 vs. the Dodgers. ... Since joining the Phillies in 1984: 4–4, 4.06 ERA in day games; 30–17, 3.37 ERA in night games.... Even better: 5–13, 5.48 ERA on grass fields; 29–8, 2.67 on artificial turf.

Jeff Reardon

Montreal Expos — Throws Right

	W–L	ERA	AB	H	HR	BB	SO	BA	SA	OBA
Season	7-9	3.94	331	83	12	26	67	.251	.417	.306
vs. Left-Handers			172	43	5	20	31	.250	.390	.330
vs. Right-Handers			159	40	7	6	36	.252	.447	.279
Home	5-6	4.73	177	50	6	17	42	.282	.458	.347
Road	2-3	3.12	154	33	6	9	25	.214	.370	.258
Grass	1-1	3.26	67	13	3	4	10	.194	.373	.239
Artificial Turf	6-8	4.13	264	70	9	22	57	.265	.428	.323
April	2-2	3.86	52	13	2	4	10	.250	.423	.304
May	3-0	1.25	78	16	1	5	17	.205	.244	.253
June	1-2	4.12	71	15	1	7	17	.211	.352	.282
July	0-2	6.75	44	18	4	4	6	.409	.705	.458
August	0-2	4.76	36	6	3	4	5	.167	.472	.244
Sept./Oct.	1-1	5.40	50	15	1	2	12	.300	.480	.340
Leading Off Inn.			73	20	4	7	16	.274	.507	.338
Runners On			151	33	2	15	35	.219	.311	.287
Runners/Scor. Pos.			106	22	1	11	27	.208	.292	.280
Runners On/2 Out			59	10	1	4	17	.169	.254	.222
Scor. Pos./2 Out			46	7	1	3	12	.152	.217	.204
Late Inning Pressure			287	75	9	24	62	.261	.415	.319
Leading Off			66	19	4	5	16	.288	.545	.338
Runners On			128	30	1	15	30	.234	.313	.313
Runners/Scor. Pos.			91	20	1	11	23	.220	.308	.301
First 9 Batters			319	81	11	26	62	.254	.417	.311
Second 9 Batters			12	2	1	0	5	.167	.417	.167
All Batters Thereafter			0	0	0	0	0	—	—	—

Loves to face: Bob Dernier (0-for-11)
Hates to face: Nick Esasky (.750, 3-for-4, 2 HR)
Ground outs-to-air outs ratio: 0.69, 10th lowest in N.L. last season (minimum: 250 BFP), 0.59 for career.... Additional statistics: 8 double-play ground outs in 76 opportunities, 13 doubles, 3 triples in 89.0 innings last season.... Faced only one batter once, pitched two or more innings 25 times, finished 48 games in 62 relief appearances.... Allowed 12 home runs: 10 solo shots, the other two with one man on.... Allowed 23 extra-base hits in Late-Inning Pressure Situations, most in majors last season.... Opposing leadoff batters hit .161 over two previous seasons.... Career total of 665.2 innings without a balk, highest total among active N.L. pitchers.... Career record of 5–0 vs. Atlanta.

Rick Reuschel

Pittsburgh Pirates — Throws Right

	W–L	ERA	AB	H	HR	BB	SO	BA	SA	OBA
Season	9-16	3.96	845	232	20	57	125	.275	.408	.323
vs. Left-Handers			463	142	9	38	47	.307	.443	.360
vs. Right-Handers			382	90	11	19	78	.236	.366	.277
Home	5-8	3.28	394	105	7	32	60	.266	.391	.324
Road	4-8	4.61	451	127	13	25	65	.282	.424	.322
Grass	2-3	5.96	216	63	10	17	29	.292	.481	.345
Artificial Turf	7-13	3.34	629	169	10	40	96	.269	.383	.315
April	2-2	4.23	113	34	2	11	12	.301	.407	.357
May	1-2	2.43	135	34	2	9	19	.252	.370	.303
June	1-4	4.21	138	37	4	17	16	.268	.428	.344
July	2-4	6.88	143	45	3	10	24	.315	.462	.376
August	2-3	3.54	165	47	5	3	30	.285	.430	.300
Sept./Oct.	1-1	2.93	151	35	4	7	24	.232	.351	.264
Leading Off Inn.			205	67	7	13	23	.327	.512	.370
Runners On			368	97	7	28	51	.264	.380	.318
Runners/Scor. Pos.			217	51	3	21	33	.235	.332	.307
Runners On/2 Out			153	31	2	10	20	.203	.288	.269
Scor. Pos./2 Out			95	18	1	8	14	.189	.253	.280
Late Inning Pressure			68	25	2	4	8	.368	.559	.405
Leading Off			17	9	0	1	0	.529	.647	.556
Runners On			27	10	1	3	5	.370	.593	.438
Runners/Scor. Pos.			16	7	1	3	4	.438	.688	.524
First 9 Batters			277	75	7	22	42	.271	.426	.330
Second 9 Batters			275	75	7	21	47	.273	.393	.321
All Batters Thereafter			293	82	6	14	36	.280	.406	.317

Loves to face: Bill Doran (.059, 1-for-17)
Hates to face: Chris Brown (.667, 6-for-9, 2 HR)
Ground outs-to-air outs ratio: 2.20 last season, 2.15 for career.... Additional statistics: 15 double-play ground outs in 168 opportunities, 45 doubles (6th most in N.L.), 4 triples in 215.2 innings last season. Allowed 69 extra-base hits, 5th most in N.L.... Allowed 30 first-inning runs (most in N.L.) in 34 starts last season.... Batting support: 4.18 runs per start.... Has allowed two grand slam homers in his career, both to the same batter. Who is he? Hint: He was born the day that Babe Ruth died. Answer below.... Has faced 140 batters with bases loaded since last slam.... Walked 1.35 batters per nine innings after the All-Star break, 2d-best rate in N.L. ... Has won his last eight decisions vs. Atlanta; last loss against them was in 1979.... The mystery man is Mike Jorgensen.

Jerry Reuss

Los Angeles Dodgers — Throws Left

	W–L	ERA	AB	H	HR	BB	SO	BA	SA	OBA
Season	2-6	5.84	307	96	13	17	29	.313	.498	.353
vs. Left-Handers			50	11	1	2	7	.220	.320	.278
vs. Right-Handers			257	85	12	15	22	.331	.533	.368
Home	2-2	4.96	183	55	6	11	17	.301	.432	.344
Road	0-4	7.22	124	41	7	6	12	.331	.597	.366
Grass	2-4	4.98	241	69	8	14	24	.286	.440	.328
Artificial Turf	0-2	9.42	66	27	5	3	5	.409	.712	.443
April	1-0	2.93	59	18	0	6	6	.305	.339	.369
May	1-4	6.14	123	36	5	4	11	.293	.496	.315
June	0-2	7.59	93	31	6	3	9	.333	.581	.367
July	0-0	6.00	12	3	1	2	1	.250	.583	.357
August			0	0	0	0	0			
Sept./Oct.	0-0	5.40	20	8	1	2	2	.400	.550	.455
Leading Off Inn.			78	25	3	0	6	.321	.551	.321
Runners On			121	41	6	13	6	.339	.521	.407
Runners/Scor. Pos.			72	27	3	11	4	.375	.542	.464
Runners On/2 Out			57	21	2	8	3	.368	.526	.446
Scor. Pos./2 Out			35	15	1	7	2	.429	.600	.524
Late Inning Pressure			8	1	0	0	2	.125	.250	.125
Leading Off			2	0	0	0	0	.000	.000	.000
Runners On			3	0	0	0	0	.000	.000	.000
Runners/Scor. Pos.			3	0	0	0	0	.000	.000	.000
First 9 Batters			143	40	6	9	19	.280	.448	.327
Second 9 Batters			108	30	5	4	9	.278	.472	.310
All Batters Thereafter			56	26	2	4	1	.464	.679	.500

Loves to face: Terry Puhl (.154, 10-for-65)
Hates to face: Ronn Reynolds (.833, 5-for-6)
Ground outs-to-air outs ratio: 2.05 last season, 1.91 for career.... Additional statistics: 5 double-play ground outs in 49 opportunities, 12 doubles, 3 triples in 74.0 innings last season.... Allowed 11 first-inning runs in 13 starts last season.... Batting support: 4.38 runs per start.... Allowed 13 home runs in 74 innings, highest rate in N.L. last season (minimum: 10 GS).... Total of 194 career wins is 3d among pitchers without a 20-win season. The leaders: Milt Pappas (209) and Larry French (197).... Made major-league debut in 1969, winning his only game; could become 2d pitcher to win a game in four decades (other: Jack Quinn).... No walks to leadoff batters in 78 innings in '86, most in majors.

Rick Rhoden

Pittsburgh Pirates — Throws Right

	W–L	ERA	AB	H	HR	BB	SO	BA	SA	OBA
Season	15-12	2.84	926	211	17	76	159	.228	.347	.286
vs. Left-Handers			509	117	4	46	68	.230	.303	.294
vs. Right-Handers			417	94	13	30	91	.225	.400	.277
Home	9-6	2.76	509	111	13	42	93	.218	.352	.276
Road	6-6	2.93	417	100	4	34	66	.240	.341	.299
Grass	2-3	2.86	211	53	1	19	31	.251	.355	.315
Artificial Turf	13-9	2.83	715	158	16	57	128	.221	.344	.278
April	2-1	2.28	96	22	3	9	19	.229	.344	.292
May	1-2	3.19	137	32	1	13	21	.234	.299	.300
June	5-1	1.99	162	33	4	13	35	.204	.333	.261
July	2-2	1.87	156	37	1	17	27	.237	.353	.311
August	5-1	2.73	206	45	3	11	30	.218	.330	.261
Sept./Oct.	0-5	4.84	169	42	5	13	27	.249	.414	.302
Leading Off Inn.			245	54	8	12	35	.220	.359	.260
Runners On			332	75	4	35	68	.226	.328	.296
Runners/Scor. Pos.			185	44	3	28	34	.238	.378	.330
Runners On/2 Out			144	33	2	23	27	.229	.347	.335
Scor. Pos./2 Out			97	23	2	21	17	.237	.402	.373
Late Inning Pressure			107	23	2	12	20	.215	.318	.300
Leading Off			30	9	1	0	6	.300	.433	.323
Runners On			36	7	0	9	7	.194	.250	.356
Runners/Scor. Pos.			21	3	0	7	4	.143	.190	.357
First 9 Batters			273	57	5	27	59	.209	.319	.280
Second 9 Batters			286	80	4	16	50	.280	.420	.316
All Batters Thereafter			367	74	8	33	50	.202	.311	.269

Loves to face: Cliff Johnson (.063, 1-for-16, 3 SO)
Hates to face: Darrell Evans (.462, 12-for-26, 4 HR)
Ground outs-to-air outs ratio: 1.30 last season, 1.35 for career.... Additional statistics: 15 double-play ground outs in 149 opportunities, 45 doubles (6th most in N.L.), 7 triples in 253.2 innings last season. Allowed 69 extra-base hits, 5th most in N.L.... Allowed 12 first-inning runs in 34 starts last season.... Batting support: 4.44 runs per start.... Allowed fewer than two runs in 14 starts last season. Only one N.L. pitcher held his opponent to one run or less as often: Bob Ojeda.... Led N.L. with 5 losses after September 1 in aborted drive for 20 wins.... Batted .278 (25-for-90) last season, raising his career average to .239; led pitchers with 10 extra-base hits, ranked 2d with 10 RBIs. Are Yankees still in the market for a right-handed DH?

Don Robinson

Pittsburgh Pirates — Throws Right

	W–L	ERA	AB	H	HR	BB	SO	BA	SA	OBA
Season	3-4	3.38	257	61	5	27	53	.237	.342	.310
vs. Left-Handers			113	21	0	15	27	.186	.212	.282
vs. Right-Handers			144	40	5	12	26	.278	.444	.333
Home	3-3	3.19	140	33	2	13	36	.236	.307	.301
Road	0-1	3.58	117	28	3	14	17	.239	.385	.321
Grass	0-1	4.34	69	19	3	9	9	.275	.464	.350
Artificial Turf	3-3	3.02	188	42	2	18	44	.223	.298	.295
April	0-0	16.20	17	7	1	2	5	.412	.706	.474
May			0	0	0	0	0	—	—	—
June	2-0	2.40	55	14	0	6	12	.255	.291	.317
July	0-0	0.52	64	14	1	3	13	.219	.297	.254
August	0-3	6.60	58	15	3	8	8	.259	.431	.353
Sept./Oct.	1-1	1.93	63	11	0	8	15	.175	.254	.274
Leading Off Inn.			55	15	0	9	12	.273	.309	.375
Runners On			125	30	3	11	26	.240	.360	.303
Runners/Scor. Pos.			73	14	1	8	18	.192	.274	.276
Runners On/2 Out			55	10	2	3	12	.182	.327	.250
Scor. Pos./2 Out			36	4	1	3	9	.111	.250	.220
Late Inning Pressure			174	41	3	18	39	.236	.316	.310
Leading Off			38	8	0	6	9	.211	.211	.318
Runners On			85	20	2	6	20	.235	.329	.292
Runners/Scor. Pos.			51	8	1	4	14	.157	.235	.233
First 9 Batters			251	59	5	27	53	.235	.339	.310
Second 9 Batters			6	2	0	0	0	.333	.500	.333
All Batters Thereafter			0	0	0	0	0	—	—	—

Loves to face: Gary Carter (.065, 3-for-46)
Hates to face: Shawon Dunston (.625, 5-for-8, 2 2B, 1 HR)
Ground outs-to-air outs ratio: 1.07 last season, 0.90 for career.... Additional statistics: 4 double-play ground outs in 61 opportunities, 10 doubles, 1 triple in 69.1 innings last season.... Faced only one batter once, pitched two or more innings 17 times, finished 41 games in 50 relief appearances.... Made only 37 relief appearances over first six seasons in majors; has made more than that in each of three seasons since then.... Ranked 3d in relief appearances among N.L. pitchers named Robinson.... Opponents batted .296 in Late-Inning Pressure Situations over first four seasons, .211 over last five.... Added four hits in six at bats last season, raising his career batting average to .267, best among active pitchers (minimum: 100 AB).

Jeff Robinson

San Francisco Giants — Throws Right

	W–L	ERA	AB	H	HR	BB	SO	BA	SA	OBA
Season	6-3	3.36	394	92	8	32	90	.234	.332	.291
vs. Left-Handers			180	50	4	16	35	.278	.394	.337
vs. Right-Handers			214	42	4	16	55	.196	.280	.251
Home	2-1	3.19	202	47	4	13	49	.233	.342	.278
Road	4-2	3.55	192	45	4	19	41	.234	.323	.304
Grass	5-2	2.91	304	69	6	20	71	.227	.326	.274
Artificial Turf	1-1	4.88	90	23	2	12	19	.256	.356	.343
April	2-0	2.87	58	10	0	12	20	.172	.207	.314
May	0-1	4.86	66	20	2	3	15	.303	.439	.333
June	2-1	4.42	73	21	2	2	19	.288	.384	.303
July	1-0	3.24	64	14	1	7	15	.219	.359	.306
August	1-0	2.86	79	19	1	5	9	.241	.304	.279
Sept./Oct.	0-1	1.80	54	8	2	3	12	.148	.278	.193
Leading Off Inn.			103	21	2	1	17	.204	.272	.212
Runners On			145	42	4	19	38	.290	.428	.369
Runners/Scor. Pos.			82	23	2	18	22	.280	.427	.404
Runners On/2 Out			62	13	1	8	17	.210	.323	.300
Scor. Pos./2 Out			40	9	1	7	10	.225	.400	.340
Late Inning Pressure			161	44	4	13	46	.273	.385	.331
Leading Off			45	14	1	0	10	.311	.400	.311
Runners On			59	18	3	8	19	.305	.508	.397
Runners/Scor. Pos.			32	9	1	8	11	.281	.469	.439
First 9 Batters			339	80	8	29	80	.236	.342	.296
Second 9 Batters			53	10	0	3	10	.189	.245	.232
All Batters Thereafter			2	2	0	0	0	1.000	1.000	1.000

Loves to face: Nick Esasky (0-for-12)
Hates to face: Denny Walling (.667, 6-for-9, 2 2B)
Also loves to face: Dale Murphy (.095, 2-for-21).... Ground outs-to-air outs ratio: 1.55 last season, 1.67 for career.... Additional statistics: 8 double-play ground outs in 71 opportunities, 11 doubles, 2 triples in 104.1 innings last season.... Faced only one batter twice, pitched two or more innings 25 times, finished 22 games in 63 relief appearances.... Ranked 4th among N.L. relief pitchers with 89 strikeouts.... Opponents' career batting averages: .304 (one extra-base hit per 11.9 at bats) by left-handers; .236 (one XBH per 21.2 AB) by right-handers.... Walked only one of 104 leadoff batters last season, compared to 12 of 186 (6.5 percent) as a rookie in 1984.

Ron Robinson

Cincinnati Reds — Throws Right

	W–L	ERA	AB	H	HR	BB	SO	BA	SA	OBA
Season	10-3	3.24	435	110	10	43	117	.253	.384	.321
vs. Left-Handers			194	57	3	32	33	.294	.407	.394
vs. Right-Handers			241	53	7	11	84	.220	.365	.257
Home	3-1	3.55	247	61	7	17	61	.247	.405	.293
Road	7-2	2.84	188	49	3	26	56	.261	.356	.355
Grass	5-2	3.31	130	36	3	18	42	.277	.392	.371
Artificial Turf	5-1	3.21	305	74	7	25	75	.243	.380	.298
April	2-0	1.37	67	12	1	4	14	.179	.299	.225
May	1-0	2.08	62	13	2	10	18	.210	.339	.319
June	3-0	1.66	82	20	1	11	15	.244	.341	.347
July	2-2	4.58	72	24	2	4	16	.333	.458	.359
August	1-1	2.93	52	11	1	3	14	.212	.327	.255
Sept./Oct.	1-0	6.12	100	30	3	11	40	.300	.480	.366
Leading Off Inn.			107	28	3	7	28	.262	.421	.313
Runners On			177	43	5	26	42	.243	.379	.338
Runners/Scor. Pos.			112	24	2	21	27	.214	.304	.336
Runners On/2 Out			78	15	2	15	24	.192	.321	.330
Scor. Pos./2 Out			55	10	1	13	16	.182	.291	.348
Late Inning Pressure			293	82	5	29	72	.280	.382	.348
Leading Off			73	18	1	2	18	.247	.329	.276
Runners On			122	30	4	18	27	.246	.385	.345
Runners/Scor. Pos.			70	14	1	16	14	.200	.271	.337
First 9 Batters			401	106	9	38	107	.264	.399	.327
Second 9 Batters			34	4	1	5	10	.118	.206	.250
All Batters Thereafter			0	0	0	0	0	—	—	—

Loves to face: Jody Davis (0-for-8, 3 SO)
Hates to face: Jim Morrison (.625, 5-for-8, 3 HR)
Ground outs-to-air outs ratio: 1.22 last season, 1.15 for career.... Additional statistics: 7 double-play ground outs in 72 opportunities, 21 doubles, 3 triples in 116.2 innings last season.... Faced only one batter 3 times, pitched two or more innings 35 times (2d most in N.L.), finished 32 games in 70 relief appearances.... Faced 68 percent of his opposing batters in Late-Inning Pressure Situations last season, 11 percent in first two seasons.... Allowed 82 hits in LIP Situations, most in majors.... Led N.L. relief pitchers with 117 strikeouts last season. Also allowed the most hits (110).... Ranked 2d in majors with 7.64 strikeouts per walk vs. right-handed batters (minimum: 25 SO).

Bruce Ruffin — Philadelphia Phillies — Throws Left

	W–L	ERA	AB	H	HR	BB	SO	BA	SA	OBA
Season	9-4	2.46	549	138	6	44	70	.251	.346	.306
vs. Left-Handers			80	11	2	8	24	.138	.250	.216
vs. Right-Handers			469	127	4	36	46	.271	.362	.322
Home	6-2	2.16	330	82	2	25	36	.248	.333	.300
Road	3-2	2.91	219	56	4	19	34	.256	.365	.315
Grass	3-1	1.22	134	30	0	8	18	.224	.261	.264
Artificial Turf	6-3	2.88	415	108	6	36	52	.260	.373	.319
April			0	0	0	0	0	—	—	—
May			0	0	0	0	0	—	—	—
June	0-0	4.26	26	7	1	1	5	.269	.423	.321
July	3-2	3.00	168	42	3	14	18	.250	.363	.304
August	4-1	1.45	158	35	0	10	24	.222	.259	.265
Sept./Oct.	2-1	2.61	197	54	2	19	23	.274	.391	.338
Leading Off Inn.			141	30	1	10	14	.213	.277	.265
Runners On			224	56	3	19	25	.250	.353	.304
Runners/Scor. Pos.			119	27	2	12	12	.227	.328	.289
Runners On/2 Out			91	21	2	9	9	.231	.374	.300
Scor. Pos./2 Out			55	10	1	6	5	.182	.273	.262
Late Inning Pressure			50	12	1	3	4	.240	.340	.283
Leading Off			12	0	0	1	1	.000	.000	.077
Runners On			15	5	0	2	0	.333	.467	.412
Runners/Scor. Pos.			7	2	0	1	0	.286	.429	.375
First 9 Batters			171	33	1	14	29	.193	.257	.257
Second 9 Batters			170	46	2	15	19	.271	.376	.330
All Batters Thereafter			208	59	3	15	22	.284	.394	.327

Loves to face: Leon Durham (0-for-8, 6 SO)
Hates to face: Bob Dernier (.455, 5-for-11)
Ground outs-to-air outs ratio: 2.26, 10th highest in N.L. last season (minimum: 250 BFP), his first in majors.... Additional statistics: 17 double-play ground outs in 102 opportunities, 8th-highest average in N.L. (minimum: 10 GDP), 30 doubles, 2 triples in 146.1 innings last season.... Allowed 8 first-inning runs in 21 starts last season.... Batting support: 4.81 runs per start.... ERA in home games (2.16) was best in N.L.... Led major-league rookies with 6 complete games.... Allowed one home run per 29.3 innings after the All-Star break, best in majors during second half of season.... Opposing left-handers hit .123, 5th-lowest mark in majors over past 12 seasons (minimum: 75 at bats).

Nolan Ryan — Houston Astros — Throws Right

	W–L	ERA	AB	H	HR	BB	SO	BA	SA	OBA
Season	12-8	3.34	634	119	14	82	194	.188	.314	.283
vs. Left-Handers			309	57	4	50	89	.184	.278	.297
vs. Right-Handers			325	62	10	32	105	.191	.348	.269
Home	9-4	2.56	370	56	5	49	122	.151	.230	.251
Road	3-4	4.57	264	63	9	33	72	.239	.432	.329
Grass	1-2	3.86	151	34	5	15	38	.225	.411	.299
Artificial Turf	11-6	3.19	483	85	9	67	156	.176	.284	.278
April	3-3	5.56	129	32	6	15	31	.248	.473	.333
May	0-3	4.83	119	31	4	15	28	.261	.454	.350
June	1-0	1.64	36	5	0	8	12	.139	.194	.289
July	3-1	2.31	136	19	1	18	55	.140	.213	.239
August	2-1	2.82	80	14	0	12	22	.175	.238	.283
Sept./Oct.	3-0	2.03	134	18	3	14	46	.134	.216	.216
Leading Off Inn.			165	32	3	18	46	.194	.321	.273
Runners On			229	49	9	37	69	.214	.384	.324
Runners/Scor. Pos.			142	34	7	30	45	.239	.451	.371
Runners On/2 Out			105	21	0	17	37	.200	.286	.317
Scor. Pos./2 Out			70	15	0	15	28	.214	.300	.360
Late Inning Pressure			52	12	2	10	10	.231	.404	.355
Leading Off			15	3	0	2	4	.200	.267	.294
Runners On			14	5	2	6	1	.357	.786	.550
Runners/Scor. Pos.			9	4	2	3	1	.444	1.111	.583
First 9 Batters			225	33	5	33	78	.147	.249	.266
Second 9 Batters			225	47	5	22	71	.209	.356	.277
All Batters Thereafter			184	39	4	27	45	.212	.342	.311

Loves to face: Bo Diaz (0-for-23, 6 SO)
Hates to face: Rafael Ramirez (.353, 18-for-51, 2 HR)
Ground outs-to-air outs ratio: 1.04 last season, 1.09 for career.... Additional statistics: 9 double-play ground outs in 96 opportunities, 30 doubles, 4 triples in 178.0 innings last season.... Allowed 12 first-inning runs in 30 starts last season.... Batting support: 3.77 runs per start.... Opposing batters hit .140 after the All-Star break. Ranked 3d in N.L. with a 2.27 ERA during that time.... Made eight of his first 10 starts last season with three days' rest.... Hasn't won more than 16 games in a season since 1977.... Made first start of career at Astrodome on Sept. 18, 1966 in first game of twin bill. Crowd of 14,890 at the Dome on a football Sunday got to tell their friends they'd glimpsed the future; the Mets' starter in the nightcap was another youngster, Tug McGraw.

Scott Sanderson — Chicago Cubs — Throws Right

	W–L	ERA	AB	H	HR	BB	SO	BA	SA	OBA
Season	9-11	4.19	647	165	21	37	124	.255	.420	.295
vs. Left-Handers			358	93	13	19	58	.260	.439	.296
vs. Right-Handers			289	72	8	18	66	.249	.398	.295
Home	7-5	3.54	353	82	10	22	70	.232	.368	.278
Road	2-6	5.00	294	83	11	15	54	.282	.483	.316
Grass	9-9	3.99	524	132	17	30	104	.252	.406	.293
Artificial Turf	0-2	5.06	123	33	4	7	20	.268	.480	.305
April	1-1	4.58	68	18	2	4	13	.265	.382	.306
May	2-1	4.00	139	33	5	13	27	.237	.424	.307
June	0-3	4.94	104	28	6	5	19	.269	.529	.297
July	2-2	2.88	123	26	2	6	28	.211	.293	.252
August	2-3	5.45	139	42	4	7	26	.302	.496	.333
Sept./Oct.	2-1	3.20	74	18	2	2	11	.243	.365	.260
Leading Off Inn.			165	42	3	9	26	.255	.382	.293
Runners On			243	62	9	14	44	.255	.432	.295
Runners/Scor. Pos.			125	34	5	11	30	.272	.464	.324
Runners On/2 Out			101	19	2	10	19	.188	.287	.261
Scor. Pos./2 Out			57	10	1	8	11	.175	.263	.277
Late Inning Pressure			49	13	2	5	8	.265	.408	.333
Leading Off			11	1	0	3	0	.091	.091	.286
Runners On			18	4	1	1	2	.222	.389	.263
Runners/Scor. Pos.			4	2	1	0	0	.500	1.250	.500
First 9 Batters			270	59	8	16	58	.219	.347	.267
Second 9 Batters			227	66	5	9	43	.291	.436	.313
All Batters Thereafter			150	40	8	12	23	.267	.493	.319

Loves to face: Carmelo Martinez (0-for-9)
Hates to face: Willie McGee (.429, 15-for-35, 1 HR)
Ground outs-to-air outs ratio: 0.96 last season, 0.82 for career.... Additional statistics: 10 double-play ground outs in 108 opportunities, 34 doubles, 5 triples in 169.2 innings last season.... Allowed 20 first-inning runs in 28 starts last season.... Batting support: 3.82 runs per start.... 0–8, 6.19 ERA in 13 starts vs. teams with winning records.... 2–0, 1.23 ERA in nine relief appearances.... Allowed 1.96 walks per nine innings last season, 2d-best rate in N.L.... Opposing batters have hit below .200 with two outs and runners in scoring position in five of nine major-league seasons. Career average: .204.... Only N.L. batter with a higher average with runners in scoring position than in other at bats for six consecutive seasons. (Six-year composites: .206 and .072)

Dan Schatzeder — Expos/Phillies — Throws Left

	W–L	ERA	AB	H	HR	BB	SO	BA	SA	OBA
Season	6-5	3.26	332	81	9	35	47	.244	.392	.314
vs. Left-Handers			90	27	1	8	13	.300	.378	.354
vs. Right-Handers			242	54	8	27	34	.223	.397	.299
Home	4-2	1.75	194	42	3	20	34	.216	.325	.288
Road	2-3	5.35	138	39	6	15	13	.283	.486	.348
Grass	1-1	5.03	73	23	4	7	5	.315	.534	.370
Artificial Turf	5-4	2.75	259	58	5	28	42	.224	.351	.298
April	0-0	3.38	62	15	2	6	9	.242	.403	.309
May	2-1	3.18	61	13	1	7	6	.213	.311	.294
June	1-0	0.61	53	11	1	3	11	.208	.340	.250
July	0-1	5.02	55	16	2	5	9	.291	.436	.339
August	0-2	5.84	48	13	1	9	2	.271	.417	.379
Sept./Oct.	3-1	1.93	53	13	2	5	10	.245	.453	.310
Leading Off Inn.			80	17	3	5	12	.213	.388	.259
Runners On			136	35	5	19	14	.257	.441	.342
Runners/Scor. Pos.			85	21	3	12	10	.247	.412	.330
Runners On/2 Out			64	17	2	9	6	.266	.453	.356
Scor. Pos./2 Out			43	10	2	4	5	.233	.419	.298
Late Inning Pressure			149	34	4	21	22	.228	.362	.322
Leading Off			42	12	2	1	4	.286	.500	.302
Runners On			56	10	1	13	6	.179	.286	.329
Runners/Scor. Pos.			26	4	1	9	2	.154	.269	.361
First 9 Batters			281	67	6	29	43	.238	.367	.307
Second 9 Batters			50	14	3	5	3	.280	.540	.345
All Batters Thereafter			1	0	0	1	1	.000	.000	.500

Loves to face: Phil Garner (.107, 3-for-28, 1 HR)
Hates to face: Ozzie Smith (.462, 12-for-26, 9 BB, 2 HR)
Ground outs-to-air outs ratio: 1.27 last season, 0.77 for career.... Additional statistics: 8 double-play ground outs in 62 opportunities, 14 doubles, 4 triples in 88.1 innings last season.... Faced only one batter 3 times, pitched two or more innings 23 times, finished 19 games in 54 relief appearances.... Opposing batters have a career mark of .208 with two outs and runners in scoring position.... Opposing left-handers have batted .300 or better in three of past five seasons.... Five pinch-hits last season were the most by a pitcher since Don Larsen and Joe Nuxhall each collected six in 1961, and most by an N.L. pitcher since Don Newcombe in 1959.... Career batting average of .306 with runners in scoring position.

Mike Scott

Houston Astros — Throws Right

	W–L	ERA	AB	H	HR	BB	SO	BA	SA	OBA
Season	18-10	2.22	976	182	17	72	306	.186	.291	.242
vs. Left-Handers			508	109	6	49	111	.215	.307	.282
vs. Right-Handers			468	73	11	23	195	.156	.274	.198
Home	10-8	2.20	537	96	10	28	155	.179	.276	.222
Road	8-2	2.25	439	86	7	44	151	.196	.310	.266
Grass	3-1	1.98	209	40	3	18	77	.191	.301	.253
Artificial Turf	15-9	2.29	767	142	14	54	229	.185	.288	.239
April	3-2	3.18	149	35	2	11	34	.235	.329	.284
May	1-2	2.57	177	40	5	16	64	.226	.345	.289
June	3-1	1.46	171	26	2	9	50	.152	.211	.193
July	3-2	2.14	160	26	3	12	49	.163	.269	.218
August	4-2	2.01	160	32	0	17	44	.200	.294	.281
Sept./Oct.	4-1	2.14	159	23	5	7	65	.145	.302	.186
Leading Off Inn.			264	55	8	18	78	.208	.356	.261
Runners On			331	60	6	28	126	.181	.287	.243
Runners/Scor. Pos.			207	33	3	22	94	.159	.251	.237
Runners On/2 Out			138	15	1	16	55	.109	.181	.201
Scor. Pos./2 Out			101	12	1	13	45	.119	.208	.219
Late Inning Pressure			106	21	3	13	30	.198	.340	.286
Leading Off			31	6	1	1	10	.194	.323	.219
Runners On			36	6	1	7	9	.167	.333	.302
Runners/Scor. Pos.			15	2	0	6	7	.133	.333	.381
First 9 Batters			300	52	4	23	101	.173	.270	.234
Second 9 Batters			309	55	6	18	93	.178	.288	.222
All Batters Thereafter			367	75	7	31	112	.204	.311	.266

Loves to face: John Russell (0-for-8, all strikeouts)
Hates to face: Keith Hernandez (.377, 20-for-53, 5 HR)
Ground outs-to-air outs ratio: 1.02 last season, 1.21 for career. . . .
Additional statistics: 11 double-play ground outs in 133 opportunities, 41 doubles, 5 triples in 275.1 innings last season. . . . Allowed 8 first-inning runs in 37 starts last season. . . . Batting support: 3.92 runs per start. . . . Held opponents scoreless in first inning of 33 of his 37 starts. . . . Made 18 starts decided by a single run, tied for most in majors (5–5 record in those games). . . . Pitched at least seven innings in 30 starts, highest total in majors. . . . Set an N.L. *Player Analysis* record for strikeouts with runners on base. . . . Opposing batters have hit .164 in Late-Inning Pressure Situations over past two seasons, including .122 with runners on base.

Bob Sebra

Montreal Expos — Throws Right

	W–L	ERA	AB	H	HR	BB	SO	BA	SA	OBA
Season	5-5	3.55	343	82	9	25	66	.239	.373	.294
vs. Left-Handers			195	45	6	20	33	.231	.369	.311
vs. Right-Handers			148	37	3	5	33	.250	.378	.271
Home	2-2	3.23	173	40	4	13	29	.231	.347	.289
Road	3-3	3.89	170	42	5	12	37	.247	.400	.299
Grass	2-1	3.00	79	18	2	4	17	.228	.380	.265
Artificial Turf	3-4	3.71	264	64	7	21	49	.242	.371	.302
April			0	0	0	0	0	—	—	—
May			0	0	0	0	0	—	—	—
June			0	0	0	0	0	—	—	—
July	1-1	5.87	30	7	2	5	8	.233	.500	.361
August	2-1	3.73	157	41	3	7	26	.261	.376	.295
Sept./Oct.	2-3	2.95	156	34	4	13	32	.218	.346	.279
Leading Off Inn.			86	20	1	6	13	.233	.372	.283
Runners On			132	31	6	13	22	.235	.402	.307
Runners/Scor. Pos.			88	19	3	10	16	.216	.352	.301
Runners On/2 Out			59	14	2	7	9	.237	.407	.318
Scor. Pos./2 Out			43	10	1	5	6	.233	.372	.313
Late Inning Pressure			37	5	1	5	7	.135	.243	.250
Leading Off			10	2	1	1	2	.200	.500	.273
Runners On			10	2	0	3	0	.200	.300	.357
Runners/Scor. Pos.			2	0	0	3	0	.000	.000	.500
First 9 Batters			130	30	4	14	32	.231	.377	.315
Second 9 Batters			105	24	1	4	19	.229	.295	.252
All Batters Thereafter			108	28	4	7	15	.259	.444	.308

Loves to face: Wally Backman (0-for-9)
Hates to face: Johnny Ray (.833, 5-for-6)
Ground outs-to-air outs ratio: 1.08 last season, 0.99 for career (0.62 vs. left-handers, 1.23 vs. right-handers). . . . Additional statistics: 5 double-play ground outs in 49 opportunities, 15 doubles, 2 triples in 91.1 innings last season. . . . Allowed 11 first-inning runs in 13 starts last season. . . . Batting support: 3.54 runs per start. . . . One of three pitchers with two complete games vs. Mets last season. The others: Kevin Gross and Bob Knepper. Had N.L.'s best ERA vs. Mets (1.57). . . . One of three N.L. rookies with shutouts; others: Jim Deshaies and Jimmy Jones. . . . 7th in majors with 6.60 SO per walk vs. right-handed batters last season (minimum: 25 SO).

Eric Show

San Diego Padres — Throws Right

	W–L	ERA	AB	H	HR	BB	SO	BA	SA	OBA
Season	9-5	2.97	484	109	11	69	94	.225	.329	.326
vs. Left-Handers			272	68	4	45	44	.250	.342	.357
vs. Right-Handers			212	41	7	24	50	.193	.311	.285
Home	5-3	2.78	270	60	8	36	59	.222	.341	.319
Road	4-2	3.22	214	49	3	33	35	.229	.313	.335
Grass	6-4	3.14	367	85	10	48	70	.232	.349	.325
Artificial Turf	3-1	2.45	117	24	1	21	24	.205	.265	.331
April	0-2	2.89	136	28	4	10	25	.206	.324	.270
May	3-1	2.75	140	32	1	25	39	.229	.286	.347
June	3-1	2.45	99	25	4	20	15	.253	.404	.378
July	1-0	1.86	33	6	0	7	5	.182	.212	.325
August	2-1	4.79	76	18	2	7	10	.237	.368	.310
Sept./Oct.			0	0	0	0	0	—	—	—
Leading Off Inn.			127	29	4	16	28	.228	.339	.319
Runners On			188	36	4	26	35	.191	.277	.292
Runners/Scor. Pos.			110	16	1	12	26	.145	.191	.228
Runners On/2 Out			87	12	1	12	20	.138	.184	.250
Scor. Pos./2 Out			55	3	0	9	17	.055	.055	.188
Late Inning Pressure			39	10	2	3	9	.256	.436	.310
Leading Off			14	4	1	0	2	.286	.571	.286
Runners On			8	0	0	1	1	.000	.000	.111
Runners/Scor. Pos.			3	0	0	1	0	.000	.000	.250
First 9 Batters			177	39	3	26	33	.220	.328	.320
Second 9 Batters			148	32	4	25	28	.216	.311	.341
All Batters Thereafter			159	38	4	18	33	.239	.346	.318

Loves to face: Jody Davis (.077, 2-for-26, 1 HR)
Hates to face: Darryl Strawberry (.500, 10-for-20, 3 HR)
Ground outs-to-air outs ratio: 0.75 last season, 0.97 for career. . . .
Additional statistics: 6 double-play ground outs in 92 opportunities, 17 doubles, 0 triples in 136.1 innings last season. . . . Allowed 5 first-inning runs in 22 starts last season. . . . Batting support: 3.77 runs per start. . . . Held opposing pitchers to .028 average (1-for-36) in '86, lowest in N.L. (minimum: 20 AB). . . . Opponents' career BA is .116 with two outs and runners in scoring position in Late-Inning Pressure Situations. . . . One of two pitchers to hold opposing right-handers below .200 each of past three seasons. The other: Jose DeLeon. . . . Show's career batting: .261 (23-for-88) in day games, .135 in night games. Do Cubs need a righty pinch-hitter?

Doug Sisk

New York Mets — Throws Right

	W–L	ERA	AB	H	HR	BB	SO	BA	SA	OBA
Season	4-2	3.06	273	77	0	31	31	.282	.322	.366
vs. Left-Handers			117	31	0	17	13	.265	.316	.363
vs. Right-Handers			156	46	0	14	18	.295	.327	.368
Home	1-2	1.57	129	27	0	14	14	.209	.240	.292
Road	3-0	4.46	144	50	0	17	17	.347	.396	.430
Grass	2-2	3.38	198	56	0	23	20	.283	.318	.369
Artificial Turf	2-0	2.25	75	21	0	8	11	.280	.333	.357
April			0	0	0	0	0	—	—	—
May	0-0	3.86	22	8	0	1	3	.364	.364	.391
June	1-1	0.69	48	8	0	4	6	.167	.167	.259
July	1-1	5.30	78	24	0	5	8	.308	.372	.349
August	1-0	1.21	78	21	0	12	8	.269	.321	.380
Sept./Oct.	1-0	5.25	47	16	0	9	6	.340	.383	.456
Leading Off Inn.			60	17	0	9	4	.283	.317	.377
Runners On			144	43	0	16	17	.299	.326	.380
Runners/Scor. Pos.			92	28	0	12	10	.304	.326	.385
Runners On/2 Out			59	15	0	9	6	.254	.288	.362
Scor. Pos./2 Out			42	11	0	8	5	.262	.286	.380
Late Inning Pressure			118	33	0	14	13	.280	.314	.370
Leading Off			28	10	0	6	2	.357	.393	.471
Runners On			62	16	0	7	8	.258	.274	.352
Runners/Scor. Pos.			36	12	0	5	6	.333	.361	.415
First 9 Batters			242	65	0	30	29	.269	.310	.361
Second 9 Batters			31	12	0	1	2	.387	.419	.406
All Batters Thereafter			0	0	0	0	0	—	—	—

Loves to face: Andy Van Slyke (0-for-9, 7 ground outs)
Hates to face: Jeffrey Leonard (.667, 6-for-9)
Ground outs-to-air outs ratio: 2.70, 3d highest in N.L. last season (minimum: 250 BFP), 2.75 for career. . . . Additional statistics: 7 double-play ground outs in 77 opportunities, 11 doubles, 0 triples in 70.2 innings last season. . . . Never faced only one batter, pitched two or more innings 22 times, finished 15 games in 41 relief appearances. . . . Walk-strikeout ratio of 1.00 last season was his career *best*. . . . Career: has allowed six HR in 334.1 innings, lowest rate among active pitchers with at least 300 innings. Has faced 364 right-handed batters at Shea Stadium, without allowing a home run. . . . Career ratio of 2.61 walks per strikeout vs. left-handed batters is highest in 12-year *Player Analysis* history (minimum: 50 BB).

Bryn Smith — Throws Right
Montreal Expos

	W–L	ERA	AB	H	HR	BB	SO	BA	SA	OBA
Season	10-8	3.94	723	182	15	63	105	.252	.380	.316
vs. Left-Handers			409	117	8	40	56	.286	.421	.354
vs. Right-Handers			314	65	7	23	49	.207	.328	.265
Home	5-3	3.75	329	81	7	28	52	.246	.389	.311
Road	5-5	4.10	394	101	8	35	53	.256	.373	.319
Grass	2-5	4.76	256	69	7	27	26	.270	.402	.342
Artificial Turf	8-3	3.51	467	113	8	36	79	.242	.368	.301
April	2-2	3.58	123	28	4	13	19	.228	.390	.301
May	2-2	4.15	134	39	2	14	19	.291	.381	.362
June	1-1	3.97	128	31	3	11	21	.242	.391	.305
July	2-1	3.98	133	36	2	9	19	.271	.391	.319
August	2-2	3.80	158	36	2	14	19	.228	.329	.297
Sept./Oct.	1-0	4.63	47	12	2	2	8	.255	.468	.300
Leading Off Inn.			179	48	4	13	19	.268	.413	.325
Runners On			313	81	8	29	50	.259	.390	.325
Runners/Scor. Pos.			190	49	4	23	34	.258	.368	.342
Runners On/2 Out			130	37	1	17	19	.285	.385	.372
Scor. Pos./2 Out			89	26	1	15	15	.292	.393	.400
Late Inning Pressure			34	12	0	2	3	.353	.529	.389
Leading Off			10	4	0	1	0	.400	.700	.455
Runners On			16	5	0	0	3	.313	.500	.313
Runners/Scor. Pos.			10	3	0	0	1	.300	.600	.300
First 9 Batters			243	56	2	22	28	.230	.288	.295
Second 9 Batters			230	58	5	24	43	.252	.400	.331
All Batters Thereafter			250	68	8	17	34	.272	.452	.322

Loves to face: Gary Matthews (.040, 1-for-25)
Hates to face: Kevin McReynolds (.429, 6-for-14, 4 HR)
Ground outs-to-air outs ratio: 2.52, 5th highest in N.L. last season (minimum: 250 BFP), 1.82 for career.... Additional statistics: 12 double-play ground outs in 144 opportunities, 32 doubles, 8 triples (tied for 3d most in N.L.) in 187.1 innings last season.... Allowed 6 first-inning runs (2d most in N.L.) in 30 starts last season.... Batting support: 4.53 runs per start.... 6–1 vs. teams with winning records, 4–7 vs. teams below the .500 mark.... Career average of one extra-base hit allowed per 9.6 at bats in Late-Inning Pressure Situations, compared to one per 14.1 AB overall.... Opponents' batting average with two outs and runners in scoring position last season was highest of his career.... Hitless in 19 at bats vs. left-handed pitchers last season after 8-for-24 a year earlier.

Dave Smith — Throws Right
Houston Astros

	W–L	ERA	AB	H	HR	BB	SO	BA	SA	OBA
Season	4-7	2.73	195	39	5	22	46	.200	.292	.283
vs. Left-Handers			102	17	2	9	18	.167	.235	.234
vs. Right-Handers			93	22	3	13	28	.237	.355	.333
Home	3-1	2.92	89	18	3	7	24	.202	.315	.268
Road	1-6	2.59	106	21	2	15	22	.198	.274	.295
Grass	0-4	2.38	76	14	0	11	16	.184	.197	.284
Artificial Turf	4-3	2.97	119	25	5	11	30	.210	.353	.282
April	0-0	2.25	29	8	1	1	5	.276	.379	.300
May	1-2	1.80	35	7	0	5	8	.200	.229	.300
June	0-2	3.52	27	7	2	4	7	.259	.481	.355
July	2-2	4.91	39	7	2	5	9	.179	.385	.289
August	1-0	0.00	33	2	0	2	12	.061	.061	.114
Sept./Oct.	0-1	4.00	32	8	0	5	5	.250	.250	.342
Leading Off Inn.			36	5	1	9	6	.139	.250	.311
Runners On			97	19	3	8	23	.196	.299	.262
Runners/Scor. Pos.			64	11	2	5	16	.172	.281	.229
Runners On/2 Out			41	3	0	4	13	.073	.073	.156
Scor. Pos./2 Out			28	3	0	3	9	.107	.107	.194
Late Inning Pressure			151	34	5	17	32	.225	.344	.306
Leading Off			26	5	1	7	5	.192	.346	.364
Runners On			77	16	3	8	18	.208	.338	.287
Runners/Scor. Pos.			53	9	2	5	13	.170	.302	.237
First 9 Batters			194	39	5	22	46	.201	.294	.284
Second 9 Batters			1	0	0	0	0	.000	.000	.000
All Batters Thereafter			0	0	0	0	0	—	—	—

Loves to face: Dave Parker (0-for-11)
Hates to face: Tony Gwynn (.700, 7-for-10)
Ground outs-to-air outs ratio: 1.40 last season, 1.40 for career.... Additional statistics: 5 double-play ground outs in 50 opportunities, 3 doubles, 0 triples in 56.0 innings last season.... Faced one batter 5 times, pitched two or more innings 8 times, finished 51 games in 54 relief appearances.... Was over .500 in each of his six major-league seasons until last year.... Tied N.L. record with saves in eight straight appearances (April 11 to May 2); A.L. high is 11 by Sparky Lyle.... One of four major leaguers with 25+ saves in each of last two seasons.... Don't tell Len Dykstra, but opposing right-handers outhit lefties for 3d consecutive season. Career averages: .249 by right-handers, .214 by left-handers.

Lee Smith — Throws Right
Chicago Cubs

	W–L	ERA	AB	H	HR	BB	SO	BA	SA	OBA
Season	9-9	3.09	321	69	7	42	93	.215	.318	.303
vs. Left-Handers			172	38	5	33	53	.221	.349	.343
vs. Right-Handers			149	31	2	9	40	.208	.282	.252
Home	6-3	2.75	196	43	3	25	52	.219	.296	.305
Road	3-6	3.63	125	26	4	17	41	.208	.352	.301
Grass	7-5	2.70	244	50	5	30	72	.205	.299	.290
Artificial Turf	2-4	4.43	77	19	2	12	21	.247	.377	.344
April	1-2	7.11	25	6	1	6	7	.240	.400	.375
May	1-2	2.60	55	10	1	7	15	.182	.291	.274
June	2-2	1.96	59	9	1	9	19	.153	.237	.265
July	2-1	3.38	72	13	2	10	26	.181	.292	.274
August	2-2	1.80	56	14	1	2	14	.250	.339	.276
Sept./Oct.	1-0	4.50	54	17	1	8	12	.315	.463	.403
Leading Off Inn.			71	18	4	8	18	.254	.465	.329
Runners On			152	29	3	27	48	.191	.296	.308
Runners/Scor. Pos.			106	24	3	19	33	.226	.358	.336
Runners On/2 Out			70	15	3	12	22	.214	.386	.329
Scor. Pos./2 Out			51	13	3	10	17	.255	.490	.377
Late Inning Pressure			257	55	6	31	74	.214	.323	.297
Leading Off			58	15	4	6	14	.259	.500	.328
Runners On			116	23	2	19	36	.198	.302	.307
Runners/Scor. Pos.			83	19	2	15	27	.229	.361	.340
First 9 Batters			315	68	7	42	92	.216	.321	.306
Second 9 Batters			6	1	0	0	1	.167	.167	.167
All Batters Thereafter			0	0	0	0	0			

Loves to face: Andy Van Slyke (.053, 1-for-19, 1 HR, 5 SO)
Hates to face: Jack Clark (.524, 11-for-21, 2 3B, 2 HR)
Ground outs-to-air outs ratio: 1.00 last season, 1.21 for career.... Additional statistics: 8 double-play ground outs in 77 opportunities, 12 doubles, 0 triples in 90.1 innings last season.... Faced only one batter 3 times, pitched two or more innings 22 times, finished 59 games in 66 relief appearances.... Struck out in all five at bats last season, five of six at bats in 1985, and eight of 13 at bats in 1984. Career totals: 39 for 58.... Only pitcher in majors to have 25 or more saves in each of the past four seasons.... Has defeated every opposing N.L. club except the Reds.... Opponents' batting average with two outs and runners in scoring position was highest of career. Seven-year average: .185.

Zane Smith — Throws Left
Atlanta Braves

	W–L	ERA	AB	H	HR	BB	SO	BA	SA	OBA
Season	8-16	4.05	760	209	8	105	139	.275	.380	.364
vs. Left-Handers			115	26	0	7	33	.226	.304	.274
vs. Right-Handers			645	183	8	98	106	.284	.394	.379
Home	7-7	3.41	470	124	5	61	91	.264	.362	.350
Road	1-9	5.08	290	85	3	44	48	.293	.410	.387
Grass	8-12	4.20	631	177	7	84	115	.281	.384	.366
Artificial Turf	0-4	3.35	129	32	1	21	24	.248	.364	.358
April	1-2	2.67	120	24	0	13	26	.200	.242	.276
May	3-2	1.98	171	37	0	26	41	.216	.287	.323
June	2-4	4.20	163	52	1	22	22	.319	.429	.398
July	1-2	5.09	132	35	4	17	28	.265	.439	.358
August	0-3	6.56	85	30	3	16	8	.353	.541	.442
Sept./Oct.	1-3	6.23	89	31	0	11	14	.348	.416	.427
Leading Off Inn.			192	51	2	19	28	.266	.365	.335
Runners On			352	97	5	47	73	.276	.389	.360
Runners/Scor. Pos.			219	63	3	35	56	.288	.406	.382
Runners On/2 Out			143	37	3	22	34	.259	.399	.361
Scor. Pos./2 Out			93	25	1	17	28	.269	.387	.387
Late Inning Pressure			67	22	0	11	15	.328	.448	.423
Leading Off			19	6	0	2	3	.316	.474	.381
Runners On			29	9	0	8	8	.310	.414	.459
Runners/Scor. Pos.			24	8	0	6	7	.333	.458	.467
First 9 Batters			269	86	2	42	50	.320	.420	.413
Second 9 Batters			257	59	3	26	46	.230	.311	.302
All Batters Thereafter			234	64	3	37	43	.274	.410	.373

Loves to face: Darryl Strawberry (0-for-11, 5 SO)
Hates to face: Reggie Williams (.833, 5-for-6, 2 2B)
Ground outs-to-air outs ratio: 2.29, 9th highest in N.L. last season (minimum: 250 BFP), 2.25 for career.... Additional statistics: 36 double-play ground outs in 162 opportunities, highest average in majors (minimum: 10 GDP), 46 doubles (3d most in N.L.), 5 triples in 204.2 innings last season.... Allowed 29 first-inning runs in 32 starts.... Batting support: 3.72 runs per start.... Set an N.L. *Player Analysis* record for walks to right-handed batters.... 5–5 vs. teams with winning records, 3–11 vs. teams below .500.... Career records: 12–15, 3.38 ERA before All-Star break; 6–11, 4.62 thereafter.... Ranked 2d in N.L. in ERA during month of May.... Has allowed only one career HR to a left-handed hitter: on Sept. 18, **1984, to that noted** southpaw-basher, Greg Brock. (Just kidding.)

Mario Soto
Cincinnati Reds — Throws Right

	W–L	ERA	AB	H	HR	BB	SO	BA	SA	OBA
Season	5-10	4.71	404	113	15	46	67	.280	.480	.352
vs. Left-Handers			227	68	7	34	32	.300	.507	.390
vs. Right-Handers			177	45	8	12	35	.254	.446	.298
Home	2-7	6.02	196	64	12	23	28	.327	.622	.392
Road	3-3	3.56	208	49	3	23	39	.236	.346	.313
Grass	1-2	4.05	125	31	3	14	24	.248	.384	.326
Artificial Turf	4-8	5.02	279	82	12	32	43	.294	.523	.363
April	2-2	3.86	112	30	8	13	19	.268	.518	.339
May	1-4	4.41	127	34	2	14	17	.268	.417	.338
June	0-1	3.21	52	14	1	4	11	.269	.442	.321
July	0-1	7.00	38	12	1	4	6	.316	.526	.381
August	2-2	6.63	75	23	3	11	14	.307	.533	.398
Sept./Oct.			0	0	0	0	0	—	—	—
Leading Off Inn.			103	31	3	6	14	.301	.485	.339
Runners On			167	46	7	26	34	.275	.491	.369
Runners/Scor. Pos.			108	30	5	19	20	.278	.509	.379
Runners On/2 Out			69	20	3	14	15	.290	.493	.410
Scor. Pos./2 Out			50	14	3	10	7	.280	.500	.400
Late Inning Pressure			27	7	1	4	2	.259	.407	.355
Leading Off			8	2	0	1	0	.250	.250	.333
Runners On			8	4	1	2	1	.500	1.000	.600
Runners/Scor. Pos.			6	3	0	2	0	.500	.667	.625
First 9 Batters			146	42	5	17	23	.288	.486	.364
Second 9 Batters			141	41	7	12	24	.291	.546	.344
All Batters Thereafter			117	30	3	17	20	.256	.393	.346

Loves to face: Jeffrey Leonard (.143, 6-for-42, 23 SO)
Hates to face: Darryl Strawberry (.375, 12-for-32, 5 HR)
Ground outs-to-air outs ratio: 0.80 last season, 0.83 for career. . . .
Additional statistics: 6 double-play ground outs in 66 opportunities, 26 doubles, 5 triples in 105.0 innings last season. . . . Allowed 18 first-inning runs in 19 starts last season. . . . Batting support: 3.63 runs per start. . . . Only N.L. player to make three trips onto the disabled list last season. (Three A.L. players had three visits: Tippy Martinez, Paul Molitor, and Luis Salazar). . . . Became the first N.L. pitcher since the Dodgers' Ben Wade in 1954 to allow four home runs in one inning (Apr. 29). . . . Has lost his last six decisions vs. Los Angeles. . . . Opposing left-handed batters had hit .203 over three previous seasons.

Rick Sutcliffe
Chicago Cubs — Throws Right

	W–L	ERA	AB	H	HR	BB	SO	BA	SA	OBA
Season	5-14	4.64	659	166	18	96	122	.252	.393	.347
vs. Left-Handers			372	91	8	52	76	.245	.368	.339
vs. Right-Handers			287	75	10	44	46	.261	.425	.357
Home	3-6	4.35	376	98	11	58	73	.261	.410	.359
Road	2-8	5.00	283	68	7	38	49	.240	.371	.331
Grass	3-9	4.21	487	122	13	71	93	.251	.384	.345
Artificial Turf	2-5	5.83	172	44	5	25	29	.256	.419	.354
April	1-3	4.41	128	30	2	25	28	.234	.320	.359
May	2-3	3.40	140	30	4	16	29	.214	.343	.293
June	1-4	4.71	154	39	7	21	25	.253	.461	.347
July			0	0	0	0	0	—	—	—
August	0-2	4.78	123	33	2	19	17	.268	.364	.364
Sept./Oct.	1-2	6.35	114	34	3	15	23	.298	.421	.380
Leading Off Inn.			168	46	3	16	29	.274	.411	.337
Runners On			267	71	10	51	48	.266	.431	.381
Runners/Scor. Pos.			155	42	6	42	33	.271	.445	.422
Runners On/2 Out			114	27	3	36	23	.237	.412	.420
Scor. Pos./2 Out			77	19	2	29	19	.247	.416	.453
Late Inning Pressure			51	15	1	11	12	.294	.451	.413
Leading Off			15	8	0	2	2	.533	.867	.588
Runners On			25	6	1	6	7	.240	.360	.375
Runners/Scor. Pos.			16	3	1	5	6	.188	.375	.364
First 9 Batters			217	49	3	28	48	.226	.318	.316
Second 9 Batters			217	57	4	19	41	.263	.373	.322
All Batters Thereafter			225	60	11	49	33	.267	.484	.396

Loves to face: Darryl Strawberry (.059, 1-for-17, 1 HR, 8 SO)
Hates to face: Von Hayes (.435, 10-for-23, 4 2B, 2 HR)
Ground outs-to-air outs ratio: 0.93 last season, 0.86 for career. . . .
Additional statistics: 9 double-play ground outs in 120 opportunities, 25 doubles, 7 triples in 176.2 innings last season. . . . Allowed 9 first-inning runs in 27 starts last season. . . . Batting support: 3.26 runs per start, lowest in N.L. (minimum: 25 GS). . . . First losing season since 1980. . . . ERA might be misleading: allowed only one unearned run last season. . . . Two-year record of 13–22 since Leon Durham did his inverted goalpost imitation in final game of 1984 N.L.C.S. . . . Batting average by opposing right-handers was highest in any full season. . . . Threw more wild pitches last season (13) than in three previous years combined.

Bruce Sutter
Atlanta Braves — Throws Right

	W–L	ERA	AB	H	HR	BB	SO	BA	SA	OBA
Season	2-0	4.34	70	17	3	9	16	.243	.429	.329
vs. Left-Handers			40	7	0	5	9	.175	.225	.267
vs. Right-Handers			30	10	3	4	7	.333	.700	.412
Home	0-0	4.50	36	8	3	4	10	.222	.500	.300
Road	2-0	4.15	34	9	0	5	6	.265	.353	.359
Grass	1-0	3.29	49	11	3	5	13	.224	.449	.296
Artificial Turf	1-0	7.20	21	6	0	4	3	.286	.381	.400
April	1-0	5.14	27	7	2	4	9	.259	.519	.355
May	1-0	3.86	43	10	1	5	7	.233	.372	.313
June			0	0	0	0	0	—	—	—
July			0	0	0	0	0	—	—	—
August			0	0	0	0	0	—	—	—
Sept./Oct.			0	0	0	0	0	—	—	—
Leading Off Inn.			17	4	0	0	6	.235	.235	.235
Runners On			34	11	2	3	3	.324	.588	.378
Runners/Scor. Pos.			23	6	2	3	2	.261	.565	.346
Runners On/2 Out			15	5	1	2	1	.333	.600	.412
Scor. Pos./2 Out			13	4	1	2	1	.308	.615	.400
Late Inning Pressure			49	13	2	5	13	.265	.449	.333
Leading Off			11	4	0	0	3	.364	.364	.364
Runners On			26	7	1	3	3	.269	.462	.345
Runners/Scor. Pos.			20	4	1	3	2	.200	.400	.304
First 9 Batters			67	16	3	8	16	.239	.418	.320
Second 9 Batters			3	1	0	1	0	.333	.667	.500
All Batters Thereafter			0	0	0	0	0	—	—	—

Loves to face: Dickie Thon (0-for-9)
Hates to face: Leon Durham (.438, 7-for-16, 3 HR)
Ground outs-to-air outs ratio: 1.67 last season, 1.95 for career. . . .
Additional statistics: 2 double-play ground outs in 15 opportunities, 4 doubles, 0 triples in 18.2 innings last season. . . . Faced only one batter once, pitched two or more innings 3 times, finished 11 games in 16 relief appearances. . . . Has faced 2992 batters in Late-Inning Pressure Situations. Only two pitchers have reached 3000 in the 12 seasons we've kept the stat: Rich Gossage (3247) and Kent Tekulve (3150). . . . Career ratio of 2.76 strikeouts per walk leads all active relief pitchers (minimum: 200 relief games).

Kent Tekulve
Philadelphia Phillies — Throws Right

	W–L	ERA	AB	H	HR	BB	SO	BA	SA	OBA
Season	11-5	2.54	413	99	2	25	57	.240	.300	.281
vs. Left-Handers			197	50	1	14	12	.254	.305	.302
vs. Right-Handers			216	49	1	11	45	.227	.296	.261
Home	6-2	2.35	201	50	0	9	30	.249	.308	.278
Road	5-3	2.72	212	49	2	16	27	.231	.292	.283
Grass	4-3	3.21	130	32	1	11	17	.246	.292	.301
Artificial Turf	7-2	2.24	283	67	1	14	40	.237	.304	.271
April	0-0	1.93	20	6	0	1	4	.300	.350	.333
May	0-1	2.81	63	14	1	4	13	.222	.302	.265
June	2-0	2.96	101	26	0	4	11	.257	.307	.280
July	1-0	3.26	78	23	1	4	11	.295	.397	.329
August	5-2	1.74	74	14	0	7	6	.189	.216	.259
Sept./Oct.	3-2	2.05	77	16	0	5	12	.208	.260	.253
Leading Off Inn.			98	22	1	4	14	.224	.306	.255
Runners On			183	42	0	19	26	.230	.262	.296
Runners/Scor. Pos.			119	22	0	18	18	.185	.227	.284
Runners On/2 Out			81	14	0	11	15	.173	.222	.272
Scor. Pos./2 Out			63	11	0	11	13	.175	.238	.297
Late Inning Pressure			231	63	2	18	25	.273	.359	.324
Leading Off			59	17	1	1	7	.288	.390	.300
Runners On			98	23	0	16	11	.235	.296	.339
Runners/Scor. Pos.			68	11	0	16	9	.162	.235	.318
First 9 Batters			390	94	2	24	57	.241	.305	.283
Second 9 Batters			23	5	0	1	0	.217	.217	.240
All Batters Thereafter			0	0	0	0	0	—	—	—

Loves to face: Tony Pena (0-for-10)
Hates to face: Wayne Krenchicki (.625, 5-for-8, 1 HR)
Ground outs-to-air outs ratio: 1.68 last season, 2.27 for career. . . .
Additional statistics: 8 double-play ground outs in 85 opportunities, 13 doubles, 3 triples in 110.0 innings last season. . . . Faced only one batter twice, pitched two or more innings 29 times (4th most in N.L.), finished 34 games in 73 relief appearances. . . . Has now appeared in more N.L. games (853) than any pitcher in history. Broke Roy Face's old record (846). . . . Tied for N.L. lead with 5 wins during month of August, more than he'd won in either of the two previous *seasons*. . . . May be the one person in America who can imagine Wayne Krenchicki as a cleanup hitter.

Scott Terry
Cincinnati Reds — Throws Right

	W-L	ERA	AB	H	HR	BB	SO	BA	SA	OBA
Season	1-2	6.14	220	66	8	32	32	.300	.455	.387
vs. Left-Handers			108	37	3	13	15	.343	.500	.410
vs. Right-Handers			112	29	5	19	17	.259	.411	.366
Home	1-1	4.88	125	40	3	13	16	.320	.464	.381
Road	0-1	7.77	95	26	5	19	16	.274	.442	.395
Grass	0-1	8.04	65	19	4	8	10	.292	.492	.370
Artificial Turf	1-1	5.40	155	47	4	24	22	.303	.439	.394
April	0-0	1.08	29	7	1	5	4	.241	.345	.353
May	0-1	8.82	67	20	3	8	11	.299	.478	.373
June	0-1	4.32	33	12	1	5	4	.364	.455	.436
July	0-0	7.88	66	21	2	11	9	.318	.500	.416
August	0-0	0.00	6	1	0	0	1	.167	.167	.167
Sept./Oct.	1-0	5.79	19	5	1	3	3	.263	.474	.364
Leading Off Inn.			47	15	1	8	5	.319	.383	.418
Runners On			111	37	7	15	14	.333	.577	.409
Runners/Scor. Pos.			57	16	4	12	9	.281	.526	.400
Runners On/2 Out			48	15	3	5	8	.313	.563	.377
Scor. Pos./2 Out			31	9	3	4	6	.290	.613	.371
Late Inning Pressure			28	8	1	5	3	.286	.429	.382
Leading Off			7	2	0	2	0	.286	.286	.444
Runners On			15	4	1	1	2	.267	.467	.294
Runners/Scor. Pos.			7	1	0	0	1	.143	.143	.125
First 9 Batters			167	48	6	26	24	.287	.401	.381
Second 9 Batters			41	12	2	6	8	.293	.537	.383
All Batters Thereafter			12	6	0	0	0	.500	.917	.500

Loves to face: Dale Murphy (0-for-4)
Hates to face: Denny Walling (2-for-2, 1 HR)
Ground outs-to-air outs ratio: 1.25 last season, his first in majors. . . . Additional statistics: 4 double-play ground outs in 66 opportunities, 4 doubles, 3 triples in 55.2 innings last season. . . . Faced only one batter twice, pitched two or more innings 16 times, finished 7 games in 25 relief appearances. . . . Seven of eight home runs allowed were hit with men on base, including a grand slam by Dan Gladden, of all people. . . . Tough way to make a living: 21 pitchers last season walked at least as many batters as they struck out (minimum: 50 IP). They had a combined record of 87–127, and a 4.65 ERA. . . . Opponents' .577 slugging average with runners on base was highest against an N.L. pitcher since Nino Espinosa's .589 mark in 1981.

Mark Thurmond
San Diego Padres — Throws Left

	W-L	ERA	AB	H	HR	BB	SO	BA	SA	OBA
Season	3-7	6.50	295	96	7	27	32	.325	.454	.380
vs. Left-Handers			42	13	0	6	11	.310	.333	.396
vs. Right-Handers			253	83	7	21	21	.328	.474	.377
Home	2-4	6.05	154	41	5	9	19	.266	.396	.305
Road	1-3	7.03	141	55	2	18	13	.390	.518	.456
Grass	3-7	6.57	266	86	6	23	28	.323	.440	.375
Artificial Turf	0-0	5.87	29	10	1	4	4	.345	.586	.424
April	2-1	4.18	108	26	1	9	17	.241	.296	.299
May	0-3	12.27	52	24	2	5	5	.462	.692	.500
June	1-3	6.07	128	44	4	10	7	.344	.500	.388
July	0-0	13.50	7	2	0	3	3	.286	.286	.500
August			0	0	0	0	0	—	—	—
Sept./Oct.			0	0	0	0	0	—	—	—
Leading Off Inn.			74	24	1	2	8	.324	.378	.342
Runners On			126	49	4	18	12	.389	.563	.459
Runners/Scor. Pos.			71	29	3	15	5	.408	.648	.500
Runners On/2 Out			51	21	0	7	6	.412	.549	.483
Scor. Pos./2 Out			35	16	0	7	3	.457	.600	.548
Late Inning Pressure			6	2	0	0	2	.333	.333	.333
Leading Off			2	1	0	0	0	.500	.500	.500
Runners On			2	0	0	0	1	.000	.000	.000
Runners/Scor. Pos.			0	0	0	0	0	—	—	—
First 9 Batters			130	43	4	15	21	.331	.477	.397
Second 9 Batters			97	32	1	10	6	.330	.433	.389
All Batters Thereafter			68	21	2	2	5	.309	.441	.329

Loves to face: Mike Heath (0-for-4, 2 SO)
Hates to face: Lee Lacy (.667, 8-for-12)
Figures above are for N.L. only. . . . Ground outs-to-air outs ratio: 1.35 last season, 1.37 for career. . . . Additional statistics: 13 double-play ground outs in 117 opportunities, 16 doubles, 2 triples in 122.1 innings last season. . . . Allowed 11 first-inning runs in 19 starts last season. . . . Batting support: 3.89 runs per start. . . . 5–8, 5.18 ERA as a starter; 2–0, 2.81 ERA in 23 relief appearances. . . . Overall 1986 figures: .227, 2 HR vs. left-handed batters; .306, 12 HR vs. right-handed batters. . . . Failed to complete five innings in nine of 15 N.L. starts last season. . . . Opponents' .190 OBA in Late-Inning Pressure Situations was lowest in majors last season.

Jay Tibbs
Montreal Expos — Throws Right

	W-L	ERA	AB	H	HR	BB	SO	BA	SA	OBA
Season	7-9	3.97	706	181	12	70	117	.256	.375	.324
vs. Left-Handers			383	105	4	38	55	.274	.379	.338
vs. Right-Handers			323	76	8	32	62	.235	.372	.308
Home	3-6	3.93	391	92	6	38	63	.235	.366	.304
Road	4-3	4.03	315	89	6	32	54	.283	.387	.349
Grass	1-2	4.55	109	33	4	16	12	.303	.450	.391
Artificial Turf	6-7	3.87	597	148	8	54	105	.248	.362	.311
April	3-0	1.25	121	22	0	17	22	.182	.215	.281
May	0-1	4.36	127	33	3	11	16	.260	.370	.314
June	1-3	6.67	110	31	2	13	25	.282	.445	.358
July	1-2	3.53	127	33	1	15	23	.260	.354	.336
August	1-2	5.00	135	41	5	9	16	.304	.496	.361
Sept./Oct.	1-1	3.57	86	21	1	5	15	.244	.360	.286
Leading Off Inn.			185	46	1	12	31	.249	.319	.294
Runners On			272	79	6	33	47	.290	.430	.365
Runners/Scor. Pos.			160	44	3	28	31	.275	.369	.375
Runners On/2 Out			112	27	4	17	27	.241	.420	.341
Scor. Pos./2 Out			73	17	3	15	19	.233	.384	.364
Late Inning Pressure			53	12	0	6	8	.226	.226	.317
Leading Off			14	3	0	2	0	.214	.214	.313
Runners On			26	6	0	2	5	.231	.231	.286
Runners/Scor. Pos.			14	0	0	2	4	.000	.000	.125
First 9 Batters			265	68	4	26	42	.257	.385	.321
Second 9 Batters			238	60	2	23	45	.252	.349	.318
All Batters Thereafter			203	53	6	21	30	.261	.394	.336

Loves to face: Rafael Santana (0-for-11)
Hates to face: Kevin McReynolds (.591, 13-for-22, 3 HR)
Ground outs-to-air outs ratio: 1.59 last season, 1.55 for career. . . . Additional statistics: 18 double-play ground outs in 132 opportunities, 36 doubles, 6 triples in 190.1 innings last season. . . . Allowed 22 first-inning runs in 31 starts last season. . . . Batting support: 3.61 runs per start, 10th lowest in N.L. (minimum: 15 GS). . . . Faced 61 batters in Late-Inning Pressure Situations without allowing an extra-base hit, most in majors last season. . . . Tied for 2d in N.L. with 15 no-decision starts. . . . Opposing batters have hit better with runners on base than with the bases empty in all three major-league seasons. Career marks: .278 with runners on, .240 with runners off.

Steve Trout
Chicago Cubs — Throws Left

	W-L	ERA	AB	H	HR	BB	SO	BA	SA	OBA
Season	5-7	4.75	617	184	6	78	69	.298	.394	.375
vs. Left-Handers			104	37	0	4	8	.356	.433	.380
vs. Right-Handers			513	147	6	74	61	.287	.386	.374
Home	3-2	5.05	315	96	3	39	36	.305	.413	.381
Road	2-5	4.44	302	88	3	39	33	.291	.374	.368
Grass	3-4	4.78	414	121	3	61	54	.292	.382	.381
Artificial Turf	2-3	4.68	203	63	3	17	15	.310	.419	.360
April	1-0	4.61	98	23	4	11	8	.235	.408	.309
May	1-3	5.46	114	31	0	12	10	.272	.316	.336
June	1-0	3.96	145	42	0	15	17	.290	.366	.358
July	1-1	5.18	90	30	0	18	16	.333	.389	.436
August	1-2	6.56	101	39	2	13	11	.386	.554	.456
Sept./Oct.	0-1	2.45	69	19	0	9	7	.275	.333	.359
Leading Off Inn.			152	49	1	13	18	.322	.434	.376
Runners On			284	88	3	44	33	.310	.405	.395
Runners/Scor. Pos.			171	52	0	31	20	.304	.363	.399
Runners On/2 Out			120	35	1	26	17	.292	.375	.418
Scor. Pos./2 Out			83	23	0	21	12	.277	.325	.423
Late Inning Pressure			38	7	0	8	4	.184	.263	.326
Leading Off			10	2	0	2	0	.200	.300	.333
Runners On			15	3	0	4	3	.200	.267	.368
Runners/Scor. Pos.			6	2	0	4	2	.333	.500	.600
First 9 Batters			280	77	1	27	37	.275	.339	.335
Second 9 Batters			193	56	1	30	20	.290	.363	.386
All Batters Thereafter			144	51	4	21	12	.354	.542	.432

Loves to face: Andy Van Slyke (0-for-15)
Hates to face: Tim Wallach (.452, 14-for-31, 5 2B, 3 HR)
Ground outs-to-air outs ratio: 2.17 last season, 2.05 for career. . . . Additional statistics: 18 double-play ground outs in 139 opportunities, 31 doubles, 5 triples in 161.0 innings last season. . . . Allowed 9 first-inning runs in 25 starts last season. . . . Batting support: 5.24 runs per start, 2d best in N.L. (minimum: 15 GS). . . . 2d-highest ERA in N.L. (minimum: 25 GS). . . . Thanks, guys: Compiled a 5.76 ERA in 14 no-decision starts. . . . One home run allowed to a left-handed batter in the last four seasons (Terry Kennedy, July 22, 1985). . . . Walked Billy Hatcher with bases loaded on May 17, breaking a string of 72 bases-loaded batters faced without a walk. . . . Career averages: 0.66 strikeouts per walk in Late-Inning Pressure Situations, 1.21 overall.

John Tudor

St. Louis Cardinals — Throws Left

	W–L	ERA	AB	H	HR	BB	SO	BA	SA	OBA
Season	13-7	2.92	807	197	22	53	107	.244	.388	.289
vs. Left-Handers			143	27	1	6	39	.189	.273	.220
vs. Right-Handers			664	170	21	47	68	.256	.413	.303
Home	9-2	2.48	462	110	11	27	60	.238	.381	.279
Road	4-5	3.52	345	87	11	26	47	.252	.397	.302
Grass	1-4	3.70	209	56	6	20	27	.268	.407	.328
Artificial Turf	12-3	2.65	598	141	16	33	80	.236	.381	.275
April	3-1	2.08	141	30	3	8	18	.213	.312	.252
May	1-2	3.40	162	36	4	13	17	.222	.364	.282
June	2-1	1.79	178	30	4	10	27	.169	.292	.212
July	3-1	3.47	135	40	5	8	19	.296	.481	.329
August	4-1	3.96	152	47	5	13	24	.309	.487	.361
Sept./Oct.	0-1	3.72	39	14	1	1	2	.359	.487	.375
Leading Off Inn.			214	54	5	14	22	.252	.393	.301
Runners On			269	76	9	22	46	.283	.439	.328
Runners/Scor. Pos.			146	40	4	20	31	.274	.411	.345
Runners On/2 Out			115	34	7	11	23	.296	.539	.357
Scor. Pos./2 Out			65	17	3	11	16	.262	.446	.368
Late Inning Pressure			148	35	3	10	13	.236	.345	.288
Leading Off			43	13	1	3	4	.302	.419	.362
Runners On			49	10	1	4	5	.204	.265	.259
Runners/Scor. Pos.			23	8	1	2	4	.348	.478	.385
First 9 Batters			251	53	4	15	40	.211	.303	.255
Second 9 Batters			241	61	9	10	35	.253	.440	.280
All Batters Thereafter			315	83	9	28	32	.263	.416	.322

Loves to face: Jody Davis (.056, 1-for-18)
Hates to face: Kevin Mitchell (.667, 6-for-9, 2 HR)
Ground outs-to-air outs ratio: 1.05 last season, 0.89 for career.... Additional statistics: 18 double-play ground outs in 128 opportunities, 40 doubles, 5 triples in 219.0 innings last season. Allowed 67 extra-base hits, 8th most in N.L.... Allowed 11 first-inning runs in 30 starts last season.... Batting support: 3.90 runs per start.... Only pitcher in majors with at least five no-decision starts and a ERA below 2.00 in those games (1.93).... Won seven starts decided by one run, most in majors.... 29–7 on artificial turf over past two seasons, 5–8 on grass fields.... Highest career ratio of strikeouts to walks vs. left-handed batters (4.29) in 12-year history of *The Player Analysis* (minimum: 100 SO).

Fernando Valenzuela

Los Angeles Dodgers — Throws Left

	W–L	ERA	AB	H	HR	BB	SO	BA	SA	OBA
Season	21-11	3.14	998	226	18	85	242	.226	.325	.287
vs. Left-Handers			187	46	0	11	42	.246	.321	.286
vs. Right-Handers			811	180	18	74	200	.222	.326	.287
Home	11-3	2.20	481	104	4	30	121	.216	.279	.262
Road	10-8	4.02	517	122	14	55	121	.236	.368	.309
Grass	15-7	3.03	710	165	13	57	168	.232	.328	.289
Artificial Turf	6-4	3.42	288	61	5	28	74	.212	.316	.283
April	3-1	2.41	152	39	2	12	32	.257	.322	.309
May	4-2	2.88	174	31	4	17	44	.178	.287	.255
June	3-2	3.45	170	43	4	15	42	.253	.365	.312
July	4-1	2.48	143	26	1	11	40	.182	.245	.240
August	3-3	3.83	181	46	3	15	40	.254	.354	.311
Sept./Oct.	4-2	3.64	178	41	4	15	44	.230	.360	.289
Leading Off Inn.			254	49	2	18	70	.193	.272	.246
Runners On			400	102	8	34	79	.255	.355	.311
Runners/Scor. Pos.			236	60	3	27	53	.254	.331	.327
Runners On/2 Out			165	37	6	20	39	.224	.358	.308
Scor. Pos./2 Out			108	28	3	16	25	.259	.370	.355
Late Inning Pressure			149	43	2	9	38	.289	.362	.329
Leading Off			34	10	0	3	14	.294	.382	.351
Runners On			74	22	1	5	10	.297	.365	.342
Runners/Scor. Pos.			46	13	1	5	8	.283	.391	.353
First 9 Batters			274	59	6	22	72	.215	.325	.273
Second 9 Batters			268	51	5	31	78	.190	.291	.274
All Batters Thereafter			456	116	7	32	92	.254	.344	.303

Loves to face: Steve Jeltz (0-for-13)
Hates to face: Bob Horner (.423, 22-for-52, 6 HR)
Ground outs-to-air outs ratio: 1.30 last season, 1.38 for career.... Additional statistics: 16 double-play ground outs in 193 opportunities, 40 doubles, 2 triples in 269.1 innings last season.... Allowed 19 first-inning runs in 34 starts.... Batting support: 4.71 runs per start.... Most complete games (20) by an N.L. pitcher since Phil Niekro in 1979 (23).... Pitched to a decision in 32 of 34 starts, highest average in majors last season. The A.L. leader: Teodoro Valenzuela Higuera (31 of 34).... Career home run totals: 12 by opposing left-handers, 74 by right-handers.... Struck out more right-handed batters than any other pitcher in majors for 3d consecutive season.... Opposing batters have hit better with runners on than with bases empty in each of last four seasons.

Ed Vande Berg

Los Angeles Dodgers — Throws Left

	W–L	ERA	AB	H	HR	BB	SO	BA	SA	OBA
Season	1-5	3.41	286	83	8	33	42	.290	.427	.364
vs. Left-Handers			80	22	0	9	13	.275	.375	.348
vs. Right-Handers			206	61	8	24	29	.296	.447	.371
Home	1-2	3.00	132	40	4	14	18	.303	.371	.372
Road	0-3	3.76	154	43	6	19	24	.279	.474	.358
Grass	1-3	3.49	194	56	6	27	25	.289	.428	.377
Artificial Turf	0-2	3.22	92	27	2	6	17	.293	.424	.337
April	0-2	4.09	43	11	2	7	5	.256	.419	.373
May	0-0	3.14	54	14	2	4	8	.259	.370	.310
June	1-1	3.45	70	27	2	7	9	.386	.529	.442
July	0-1	5.40	21	6	1	2	4	.286	.571	.348
August	0-1	3.00	52	10	1	6	8	.192	.269	.271
Sept./Oct.	0-0	2.61	46	15	0	7	8	.326	.457	.415
Leading Off Inn.			59	18	1	5	6	.305	.441	.369
Runners On			153	40	4	20	23	.261	.392	.345
Runners/Scor. Pos.			99	26	2	17	15	.263	.374	.368
Runners On/2 Out			64	16	1	12	10	.250	.344	.368
Scor. Pos./2 Out			45	10	1	12	7	.222	.333	.386
Late Inning Pressure			106	35	4	13	13	.330	.509	.400
Leading Off			30	12	1	1	2	.400	.633	.419
Runners On			47	14	1	8	7	.298	.426	.393
Runners/Scor. Pos.			25	8	0	8	4	.320	.360	.471
First 9 Batters			273	82	8	31	41	.300	.443	.373
Second 9 Batters			13	1	0	2	1	.077	.077	.200
All Batters Thereafter			0	0	0	0	0	—	—	—

Loves to face: George Brett (0-for-14, 4 SO)
Hates to face: Alan Trammell (.500, 6-for-12, 3 HR)
Ground outs-to-air outs ratio: 1.30 last season, 1.44 for career.... Additional statistics: 2 double-play ground outs in 73 opportunities, lowest average in N.L. (minimum: 40 opp.), 11 doubles, 2 triples in 71.1 innings last season.... Faced only one batter 6 times, pitched two or more innings 18 times, finished 29 games (most of any major leaguer without a save) in 60 relief appearances.... Last allowed a home run to a left-handed batter on Aug. 26, 1985 (Darrell Evans).... Has made 254 appearances in four full seasons in majors, to rank 8th during that time.... Opposing right-handed batters have outhit left-handers in all five major-league seasons. Career averages: .292 by right-handers, .236 by left-handers.

Bob Walk

Pittsburgh Pirates — Throws Right

	W–L	ERA	AB	H	HR	BB	SO	BA	SA	OBA
Season	7-8	3.75	514	129	14	64	78	.251	.387	.334
vs. Left-Handers			260	66	6	39	34	.254	.381	.349
vs. Right-Handers			254	63	8	25	44	.248	.394	.319
Home	2-5	3.68	243	58	9	20	34	.239	.387	.300
Road	5-3	3.81	271	71	5	44	44	.262	.387	.364
Grass	2-2	3.44	131	30	2	17	25	.229	.344	.318
Artificial Turf	5-6	3.86	383	99	12	47	53	.258	.402	.340
April	0-0	1.53	58	9	0	6	13	.155	.224	.227
May	2-2	3.92	74	17	3	10	12	.230	.351	.322
June	1-2	4.39	99	28	2	15	16	.283	.414	.377
July	1-2	3.41	106	26	5	9	17	.245	.425	.304
August	3-1	3.92	143	37	3	16	14	.259	.385	.335
Sept./Oct.	0-1	6.23	34	12	1	8	6	.353	.559	.488
Leading Off Inn.			135	42	4	11	11	.311	.474	.367
Runners On			206	51	7	33	34	.248	.403	.347
Runners/Scor. Pos.			114	26	5	26	17	.228	.412	.359
Runners On/2 Out			84	23	6	12	15	.274	.536	.365
Scor. Pos./2 Out			52	11	4	10	8	.212	.481	.339
Late Inning Pressure			86	22	6	16	15	.256	.477	.371
Leading Off			26	6	2	3	4	.231	.500	.310
Runners On			30	11	4	8	4	.367	.767	.475
Runners/Scor. Pos.			18	5	3	6	3	.278	.778	.423
First 9 Batters			276	60	7	37	55	.217	.326	.309
Second 9 Batters			141	44	2	13	16	.312	.447	.374
All Batters Thereafter			97	25	5	14	7	.258	.474	.351

Loves to face: Ken Griffey (0-for-9)
Hates to face: Hubie Brooks (.615, 8-for-13, 3 2B, 1 HR)
Ground outs-to-air outs ratio: 2.07 last season, 1.18 for career.... Additional statistics: 20 double-play ground outs in 100 opportunities, 4th-highest average in N.L. (minimum: 10 GDP), 18 doubles, 5 triples in 141.2 innings last season.... Allowed 8 first-inning runs in 15 starts last season.... Batting support: 3.60 runs per start, 9th lowest in N.L. (minimum: 15 GS).... Never faced only one batter, pitched two or more innings 13 times, finished 7 games in 29 relief appearances.... 5–5, 3.97 ERA as a starter; 2–3, 3.38 ERA in relief.... Opponents have a career batting average of .317 in Late-Inning Pressure Situations.

Gene Walter — San Diego Padres (Throws Left)

	W–L	ERA	AB	H	HR	BB	SO	BA	SA	OBA
Season	2-2	3.86	361	89	7	49	84	.247	.352	.341
vs. Left-Handers			86	13	0	16	32	.151	.174	.292
vs. Right-Handers			275	76	7	33	52	.276	.407	.357
Home	1-0	3.21	172	41	2	24	38	.238	.326	.342
Road	1-2	4.47	189	48	5	25	46	.254	.376	.340
Grass	1-2	3.61	244	58	4	34	55	.238	.340	.338
Artificial Turf	1-0	4.40	117	31	3	15	29	.265	.376	.346
April	0-0	2.35	50	10	1	6	20	.200	.300	.298
May	1-0	3.97	42	11	0	5	11	.262	.357	.340
June	1-1	5.17	68	19	2	9	20	.279	.456	.364
July	0-0	2.63	46	8	1	7	9	.174	.261	.291
August	0-1	5.55	96	31	3	11	13	.323	.458	.394
Sept./Oct.	0-0	2.55	59	10	0	11	11	.169	.169	.306
Leading Off Inn.			80	20	1	12	20	.250	.313	.355
Runners On			165	46	4	22	39	.279	.424	.368
Runners/Scor. Pos.			100	25	2	15	26	.250	.430	.355
Runners On/2 Out			72	18	1	8	20	.250	.319	.333
Scor. Pos./2 Out			52	9	0	5	17	.173	.212	.259
Late Inning Pressure			103	24	2	19	29	.233	.369	.350
Leading Off			26	2	0	6	10	.077	.077	.250
Runners On			39	13	1	8	11	.333	.564	.438
Runners/Scor. Pos.			24	7	0	6	8	.292	.542	.419
First 9 Batters			309	75	7	41	74	.243	.356	.335
Second 9 Batters			52	14	0	8	10	.269	.327	.371
All Batters Thereafter			0	0	0	0	0	—	—	—

Loves to face: Kevin Bass (0-for-9)
Hates to face: Vance Law & Tony Pena (each 3-for-3)
Ground outs-to-air outs ratio: 1.59 last season, 1.58 for career (4.40 vs. left-handers, 1.26 vs. right-handers). . . . Additional statistics: 9 double-play ground outs in 91 opportunities, 13 doubles, 2 triples in 98.0 innings last season. . . . Faced only one batter 4 times, pitched two or more innings 27 times, finished 19 games in 57 relief appearances. . . . Ranked 6th among N.L. relievers with 84 strikeouts. . . . Interesting bullpen mate for Doug Sisk, who rarely allows home runs to *right*-handed batters. . . . Would you trust this man? San Diego didn't: He made 57 relief appearances, but only five in the 8th inning or later with the Padres leading; and only one when the lead was less than four runs.

Bob Welch — Los Angeles Dodgers (Throws Right)

	W–L	ERA	AB	H	HR	BB	SO	BA	SA	OBA
Season	7-13	3.28	904	227	14	55	183	.251	.357	.297
vs. Left-Handers			483	128	7	30	80	.265	.371	.308
vs. Right-Handers			421	99	7	25	103	.235	.342	.284
Home	5-6	2.66	502	124	5	30	93	.247	.327	.290
Road	2-7	4.08	402	103	9	25	90	.256	.396	.305
Grass	7-8	2.94	755	186	11	46	151	.246	.343	.291
Artificial Turf	0-5	5.11	149	41	3	9	32	.275	.430	.327
April	3-1	1.44	159	33	2	12	37	.208	.302	.262
May	0-3	6.44	125	42	3	7	32	.336	.488	.387
June	0-2	5.17	154	44	2	10	24	.286	.403	.327
July	2-3	2.45	163	39	3	6	34	.239	.356	.271
August	1-1	2.72	140	35	2	10	29	.250	.343	.299
Sept./Oct.	1-3	2.66	163	34	2	10	27	.209	.282	.254
Leading Off Inn.			231	64	5	12	34	.277	.416	.313
Runners On			361	88	3	32	82	.244	.321	.310
Runners/Scor. Pos.			221	53	0	24	51	.240	.290	.315
Runners On/2 Out			147	29	0	10	36	.197	.245	.253
Scor. Pos./2 Out			101	22	0	8	23	.218	.277	.282
Late Inning Pressure			116	28	6	7	22	.241	.431	.285
Leading Off			29	6	4	1	2	.207	.690	.233
Runners On			41	8	1	5	12	.195	.293	.283
Runners/Scor. Pos.			25	5	0	5	9	.200	.200	.333
First 9 Batters			271	70	2	20	62	.258	.358	.313
Second 9 Batters			273	60	1	14	61	.220	.289	.259
All Batters Thereafter			360	97	11	21	60	.269	.408	.313

Loves to face: Chris Speier (0-for-11)
Hates to face: Keith Hernandez (.406, 13-for-32, 1 HR)
Ground outs-to-air outs ratio: 1.04 last season, 0.89 for career. . . . Additional statistics: 15 double-play ground outs in 170 opportunities, 46 doubles (3d most in N.L.), 4 triples in 235.2 innings last season. . . . Allowed 16 first-inning runs in 33 starts last season. . . . Batting support: 3.27 runs per start, 4th lowest in N.L. (minimum: 15 GS). . . . Completed seven innings in 21 of his 33 starts, but won only seven of those games. . . . Compiled a 2.95 ERA in 13 no-decision starts. . . . Has faced 95 batters with the bases loaded, never allowed a grand slam home run. Hasn't allowed a three-run homer since Aug. 30, 1984. . . . Opposing batters have hit .200 or lower with two outs and runners on base in six of nine seasons in majors.

Chris Welsh — Cincinnati Reds (Throws Left)

	W–L	ERA	AB	H	HR	BB	SO	BA	SA	OBA
Season	6-9	4.78	541	163	9	40	40	.301	.418	.350
vs. Left-Handers			84	19	3	7	11	.226	.429	.280
vs. Right-Handers			457	144	6	33	29	.315	.416	.364
Home	3-6	4.73	298	86	7	24	25	.289	.413	.343
Road	3-3	4.84	243	77	2	16	15	.317	.424	.360
Grass	2-0	4.30	94	31	1	3	5	.330	.436	.351
Artificial Turf	4-9	4.87	447	132	8	37	35	.295	.414	.350
April			0	0	0	0	0	—	—	—
May			0	0	0	0	0	—	—	—
June	2-2	3.06	177	51	3	10	14	.288	.384	.333
July	1-1	5.74	63	17	0	6	4	.270	.365	.333
August	2-2	6.34	129	40	2	10	12	.310	.442	.359
Sept./Oct.	1-4	5.11	172	55	4	14	10	.320	.453	.367
Leading Off Inn.			131	37	4	12	3	.282	.427	.352
Runners On			242	75	3	13	23	.310	.426	.342
Runners/Scor. Pos.			136	42	3	11	17	.309	.463	.355
Runners On/2 Out			106	34	3	5	13	.321	.481	.348
Scor. Pos./2 Out			73	23	3	4	8	.315	.521	.359
Late Inning Pressure			31	10	1	6	2	.323	.452	.432
Leading Off			8	1	0	2	0	.125	.125	.300
Runners On			15	7	1	1	2	.467	.733	.500
Runners/Scor. Pos.			8	3	1	1	2	.375	.875	.444
First 9 Batters			185	51	3	17	20	.276	.395	.335
Second 9 Batters			186	51	3	8	12	.274	.360	.306
All Batters Thereafter			170	61	3	15	8	.359	.506	.414

Loves to face: Tim Wallach (.077, 1-for-13)
Hates to face: Keith Moreland (.625, 5-for-8, 4 BB)
Ground outs-to-air outs ratio: 2.03 last season, 1.67 for career. . . . Additional statistics: 24 double-play ground outs in 113 opportunities, 2d-highest average in N.L. (minimum: 10 GDP), 30 doubles, 3 triples in 139.1 innings last season. . . . Allowed 15 first-inning runs in 24 starts last season. . . . Batting support: 4.83 runs per start, 10th highest in N.L. (minimum: 15 GS). . . . Entering the 1986 season he had walked only three of the previous 105 leadoff batters he had faced. He walked 12 of 145 last season. . . . Over past two seasons, opposing right-handers have batted .329, left-handers, .228. . . . Opponents have a career batting average of .441 with the bases loaded, with three home runs in 34 at bats.

Ed Whitson — San Diego Padres (Throws Right)

	W–L	ERA	AB	H	HR	BB	SO	BA	SA	OBA
Season	1-7	5.59	296	85	8	37	46	.287	.439	.364
vs. Left-Handers			176	43	4	22	23	.244	.347	.327
vs. Right-Handers			120	42	4	15	23	.350	.575	.419
Home	1-3	4.30	145	38	2	14	20	.262	.352	.327
Road	0-4	6.87	151	47	6	23	26	.311	.523	.398
Grass	1-5	5.72	179	51	2	26	25	.285	.385	.374
Artificial Turf	0-2	5.40	117	34	6	11	21	.291	.521	.349
April			0	0	0	0	0	—	—	—
May			0	0	0	0	0	—	—	—
June			0	0	0	0	0	—	—	—
July	1-2	3.71	97	23	0	10	15	.237	.268	.306
August	0-4	7.36	102	31	2	14	14	.304	.451	.385
Sept./Oct.	0-1	5.79	97	31	6	13	17	.320	.598	.400
Leading Off Inn.			72	18	3	5	8	.250	.472	.299
Runners On			129	40	3	20	20	.310	.450	.397
Runners/Scor. Pos.			80	24	1	15	12	.300	.413	.402
Runners On/2 Out			52	15	0	9	8	.288	.365	.393
Scor. Pos./2 Out			37	11	0	6	4	.297	.405	.395
Late Inning Pressure			16	4	1	1	2	.250	.438	.294
Leading Off			5	2	0	0	1	.400	.400	.400
Runners On			6	1	1	0	1	.167	.667	.167
Runners/Scor. Pos.			0	0	0	0	0	—	—	—
First 9 Batters			127	37	1	19	21	.291	.386	.378
Second 9 Batters			93	25	5	8	15	.269	.495	.327
All Batters Thereafter			76	23	2	10	10	.303	.461	.384

Loves to face: Franklin Stubbs (0-for-8)
Hates to face: Terry Francona (4-for-4, 2 2B)
Figures above are for N.L. only. . . . Ground outs-to-air outs ratio: 1.10 last season, 0.95 career. . . . Additional statistics: 8 double-play ground outs in 106 opportunities, 25 doubles, 7 triples in 112.2 innings. . . . Allowed 18 first-inning runs in 16 starts. . . . Batting support: 4.56 runs per start. . . . 4–0 in relief with New York despite a 7.36 ERA. . . . 15–10, 5.38 ERA during year and a half with Yankees. During that time, nine others with 100+ innings had ERAs within 0.25 of Whitson's. Their combined record: 56–101. . . . Has defeated every major-league team except the Yankees.

Frank Williams

San Francisco Giants   Throws Right

	W–L	ERA	AB	H	HR	BB	SO	BA	SA	OBA
Season	3-1	1.20	165	35	0	21	33	.212	.218	.314
vs. Left-Handers			69	16	0	9	7	.232	.246	.338
vs. Right-Handers			96	19	0	12	26	.198	.198	.297
Home	1-0	1.16	68	8	0	11	17	.118	.118	.268
Road	2-1	1.24	97	27	0	10	16	.278	.289	.349
Grass	1-0	1.18	116	21	0	15	27	.181	.190	.291
Artificial Turf	2-1	1.26	49	14	0	6	6	.286	.286	.368
April			0	0	0	0	0	—	—	—
May			0	0	0	0	0	—	—	—
June	1-0	0.00	13	3	0	1	4	.231	.231	.286
July	0-0	1.35	46	12	0	7	6	.261	.283	.370
August	1-0	1.89	62	12	0	5	11	.194	.194	.275
Sept./Oct.	1-1	0.57	44	8	0	8	12	.182	.182	.315
Leading Off Inn.			39	11	0	3	6	.282	.308	.349
Runners On			71	14	0	10	13	.197	.197	.318
Runners/Scor. Pos.			41	9	0	8	10	.220	.220	.365
Runners On/2 Out			27	6	0	2	4	.222	.222	.300
Scor. Pos./2 Out			16	3	0	2	3	.188	.188	.316
Late Inning Pressure			43	11	0	8	10	.256	.256	.385
Leading Off			7	0	0	2	1	.000	.000	.300
Runners On			21	7	0	4	4	.333	.333	.440
Runners/Scor. Pos.			16	5	0	4	4	.313	.313	.450
First 9 Batters			158	34	0	20	33	.215	.222	.317
Second 9 Batters			7	1	0	1	0	.143	.143	.250
All Batters Thereafter			0	0	0	0	0			

Loves to face: Juan Samuel (0-for-6)
Hates to face: Glenn Wilson (.625, 5-for-8, 1 2B, 1 HR)
Ground outs-to-air outs ratio: 1.56 last season, 1.85 for career. . . . Additional statistics: 9 double-play ground outs in 46 opportunities, 1 double, 0 triples in 52.1 innings last season. . . . Faced one batter 4 times, pitched two or more innings 16 times, finished 12 games in 36 relief appearances. . . . Allowed one extra-base hit in 165 at bats in '86, lowest average in the majors over past 12 seasons. . . . Faced 113 right-handed batters without an XBH, another *Player Analysis* record. . . . In three seasons with Giants, opposing right-handed batters hit .137 (32-for-233, 3 XBH) at Candlestick. . . . Year-by-year vs. right-handed batters: .166, .164, .198.

Jim Winn

Pittsburgh Pirates   Throws Right

	W–L	ERA	AB	H	HR	BB	SO	BA	SA	OBA
Season	3-5	3.58	330	85	9	38	70	.258	.382	.335
vs. Left-Handers			129	38	6	17	29	.295	.473	.376
vs. Right-Handers			201	47	3	21	41	.234	.323	.308
Home	1-1	4.14	154	39	6	15	36	.253	.435	.320
Road	2-4	3.09	176	46	3	23	34	.261	.335	.348
Grass	2-1	2.25	99	22	1	17	19	.222	.293	.333
Artificial Turf	1-4	4.20	231	63	8	21	51	.273	.420	.336
April	0-0	2.08	30	6	2	1	8	.200	.400	.219
May	1-1	4.76	43	12	3	8	15	.279	.535	.392
June	0-1	3.42	100	28	1	9	19	.280	.370	.339
July	1-2	4.11	56	14	2	10	6	.250	.357	.373
August	1-1	3.60	75	18	1	7	18	.240	.360	.305
Sept./Oct.	0-0	2.84	26	7	0	3	4	.269	.269	.345
Leading Off Inn.			75	11	3	3	17	.147	.267	.190
Runners On			142	43	3	24	29	.303	.408	.400
Runners/Scor. Pos.			95	27	2	22	23	.284	.389	.413
Runners On/2 Out			60	17	3	12	13	.283	.483	.411
Scor. Pos./2 Out			44	12	2	11	11	.273	.455	.429
Late Inning Pressure			55	16	6	9	11	.291	.673	.385
Leading Off			11	2	2	0	2	.182	.727	.182
Runners On			19	8	2	8	4	.421	.789	.571
Runners/Scor. Pos.			14	4	1	8	4	.286	.571	.522
First 9 Batters			263	67	8	32	60	.255	.384	.337
Second 9 Batters			56	14	1	5	7	.250	.357	.311
All Batters Thereafter			11	4	0	1	3	.364	.455	.417

Loves to face: Jack Clark (0-for-6, 2 SO)
Hates to face: Ken Landreaux (.667, 4-for-6, 3 BB)
Ground outs-to-air outs ratio: 2.75, 2d highest in N.L. last season (minimum: 250 BFP), 1.90 for career. . . . Additional statistics: 13 double-play ground outs in 72 opportunities, 5th-highest average in N.L. (minimum: 10 GDP), 12 doubles, 1 triple in 88.0 innings last season. . . . Faced only one batter 4 times, pitched two or more innings 16 times, finished 18 games in 47 relief appearances. . . . Allowed five home runs in 55 at bats in Late-Inning Pressure Situations, 2d-highest average in N.L. over past 12 seasons. . . . Opponents' career batting average of .208 (5-for-24) with the bases loaded is pretty low, but Winn has walked seven of the 34 batters he's faced with the bases full.

Todd Worrell

St. Louis Cardinals   Throws Right

	W–L	ERA	AB	H	HR	BB	SO	BA	SA	OBA
Season	9-10	2.08	375	86	9	41	73	.229	.352	.303
vs. Left-Handers			181	48	7	26	36	.265	.425	.352
vs. Right-Handers			194	38	2	15	37	.196	.284	.254
Home	6-5	1.65	197	43	5	17	32	.218	.340	.282
Road	3-5	2.57	178	43	4	24	41	.242	.365	.324
Grass	2-3	3.08	98	25	2	9	19	.255	.388	.312
Artificial Turf	7-7	1.75	277	61	7	32	54	.220	.339	.299
April	1-1	1.08	55	11	1	15	7	.200	.309	.370
May	2-2	1.59	63	15	1	3	9	.238	.365	.273
June	2-5	2.05	80	19	1	13	24	.238	.313	.337
July	1-0	1.17	49	7	0	4	10	.143	.184	.204
August	2-1	3.68	59	18	2	3	7	.305	.508	.339
Sept./Oct.	1-1	3.00	69	16	4	3	16	.232	.406	.260
Leading Off Inn.			73	24	3	7	8	.329	.534	.388
Runners On			200	37	5	27	39	.185	.280	.275
Runners/Scor. Pos.			133	24	3	24	30	.180	.278	.294
Runners On/2 Out			96	16	4	11	17	.167	.323	.252
Scor. Pos./2 Out			68	10	2	10	15	.147	.279	.256
Late Inning Pressure			302	67	5	34	56	.222	.318	.296
Leading Off			58	20	1	6	5	.345	.466	.406
Runners On			163	26	3	23	30	.160	.233	.257
Runners/Scor. Pos.			104	16	1	21	21	.154	.212	.285
First 9 Batters			356	83	9	37	70	.233	.354	.303
Second 9 Batters			19	3	0	4	3	.158	.316	.304
All Batters Thereafter			0	0	0	0	0			

Loves to face: Gary Matthews (0-for-6, 3 SO)
Hates to face: Jose Cruz (2-for-2, 1 2B, 1 HR)
Ground outs-to-air outs ratio: 0.77 last season, 0.79 for career. . . . Additional statistics: 7 double-play ground outs in 94 opportunities, 17 doubles, 1 triple in 103.2 innings last season. . . . Faced only one batter 6 times, pitched two or more innings 23 times, finished 60 games in 74 relief appearances. . . . Held top 15 batters in league to combined .111 average (6-for-54), lowest by any pitcher in majors (minimum: 20 at bats). . . . More saves last season (36) than the next three major-league rookies combined (Dan Plesac, 14; Mark Eichhorn, 10; Mitch Williams, 8). . . . Opponents' career batting averages: .186 with runners on base, .272 with the bases empty; .131 with two outs and runners in scoring position.

Floyd Youmans

Montreal Expos   Throws Right

	W–L	ERA	AB	H	HR	BB	SO	BA	SA	OBA
Season	13-12	3.53	769	145	14	118	202	.189	.295	.297
vs. Left-Handers			420	79	8	77	106	.188	.298	.313
vs. Right-Handers			349	66	6	41	96	.189	.292	.278
Home	6-9	4.15	393	72	10	66	109	.183	.303	.300
Road	7-3	2.88	376	73	4	52	93	.194	.287	.294
Grass	4-1	2.96	189	38	2	31	39	.201	.286	.314
Artificial Turf	9-11	3.72	580	107	12	87	163	.184	.298	.292
April	0-2	6.89	60	15	2	15	15	.250	.383	.395
May	4-2	5.19	125	28	1	19	25	.224	.304	.324
June	3-1	2.97	143	29	3	23	35	.203	.322	.321
July	3-1	2.08	132	18	1	19	40	.136	.197	.242
August	1-3	3.50	128	30	2	18	26	.234	.375	.327
Sept./Oct.	2-3	2.98	181	25	5	24	61	.138	.254	.243
Leading Off Inn.			190	30	3	37	51	.158	.263	.298
Runners On			316	70	9	36	82	.222	.370	.297
Runners/Scor. Pos.			200	40	5	25	57	.200	.330	.283
Runners On/2 Out			141	32	4	18	38	.227	.376	.319
Scor. Pos./2 Out			94	19	2	15	26	.202	.319	.318
Late Inning Pressure			93	21	2	17	22	.226	.366	.342
Leading Off			25	5	1	5	7	.200	.400	.333
Runners On			35	12	1	5	6	.343	.571	.415
Runners/Scor. Pos.			24	7	0	5	4	.292	.417	.400
First 9 Batters			249	43	4	41	88	.173	.269	.292
Second 9 Batters			247	49	6	32	54	.198	.296	.291
All Batters Thereafter			273	53	4	45	60	.194	.319	.308

Loves to face: Denny Walling (0-for-12)
Hates to face: Mike Diaz (2-for-2, 1 HR)
Ground outs-to-air outs ratio: 0.86 last season, 0.88 for career. . . . Additional statistics: 9 double-play ground outs in 114 opportunities, 30 doubles, 5 triples in 219.0 innings last season. . . . Allowed 15 first-inning runs in 32 starts last season. . . . Batting support: 4.03 runs per start. . . . Only starting pitcher in majors to hold opposing batters below the .200 mark over past two seasons (minimum: 20 GS). . . . Allowed opposing pitchers only two hits in 54 at bats, but walked them a league-leading seven times. . . . Most batters walked in N.L. since J.R. Richard in 1978 (141). Walked more left-handed batters than any N.L. pitcher since Phil Niekro in 1977 (92). . . . Led majors with 37 leadoff walks, most by an N.L. pitcher since J.R. Richard in 1976 (44).

Atlanta Braves

	W–L	ERA	AB	H	HR	BB	SO	BA	SA	OBA
Season	72-89	3.97	5419	1443	117	576	932	.266	.388	.338
vs. Left-Handers			2440	681	46	279	432	.279	.400	.353
vs. Right-Handers			2979	762	71	297	500	.256	.377	.325
Home	41-40	3.64	2818	738	71	265	474	.262	.390	.327
Road	31-49	4.34	2601	705	46	311	458	.271	.385	.349
Grass	58-62	3.86	4107	1093	95	424	693	.266	.390	.336
Artificial Turf	14-27	4.34	1312	350	22	152	239	.267	.380	.343
April	7-12	3.96	629	153	18	65	117	.243	.383	.314
May	18-10	3.02	913	213	15	120	189	.233	.341	.324
June	14-14	3.57	966	268	16	111	144	.277	.384	.352
July	7-19	5.05	888	250	28	95	149	.282	.431	.355
August	15-13	4.13	927	254	20	92	152	.274	.392	.339
Sept./Oct.	11-21	4.17	1096	305	20	93	180	.278	.393	.336
Leading Off Inn.			1314	352	28	111	218	.268	.395	.326
Runners On			2389	637	45	304	413	.267	.379	.348
Runners/Scor. Pos.			1464	380	28	233	280	.260	.373	.358
Runners On/2 Out			983	250	24	154	183	.254	.374	.359
Scor. Pos./2 Out			663	167	13	125	144	.252	.359	.375
Late Inning Pressure			1009	277	26	107	183	.275	.402	.346
Leading Off			243	66	9	22	39	.272	.440	.332
Runners On			444	112	6	66	82	.252	.336	.351
Runners/Scor. Pos.			282	72	3	57	52	.255	.333	.381
First 9 Batters			2749	696	55	300	519	.253	.365	.328
Second 9 Batters			1408	369	38	140	245	.262	.398	.330
All Batters Thereafter			1262	378	24	136	168	.300	.426	.367

Starting pitchers: 49–68 (tied for most losses in N.L.), 4.19 ERA
Relief pitchers: 23–21, 3.52 ERA
Ground outs-to-air outs ratio: 1.78, highest in 12-year history of *The Player Analysis.* Previous record: 1.74, set in 1977 by Chicago Cubs. . . . Opponents grounded into one double play for every 8.46 opportunities, 2d-highest rate in N.L. . . . Lowest ERA in N.L. during the month of May, highest during the month of July. . . . Won every road game in which they led after eight innings for a second consecutive season. Current streak: 55. Last loss: Sept. 23, 1984 vs. San Diego. . . . Relief pitchers faced a single batter 27 times last season, highest total in N.L. . . . Two complete-game shutouts in first nine games of season, none thereafter.

Chicago Cubs

	W–L	ERA	AB	H	HR	BB	SO	BA	SA	OBA
Season	70-90	4.49	5551	1546	143	557	962	.279	.423	.344
vs. Left-Handers			2345	649	55	240	388	.277	.419	.343
vs. Right-Handers			3206	897	88	317	574	.280	.426	.344
Home	42-38	4.43	2905	813	79	300	509	.280	.419	.347
Road	28-52	4.55	2646	733	64	257	453	.277	.427	.341
Grass	54-59	4.28	3959	1092	103	396	707	.276	.413	.341
Artificial Turf	16-31	5.02	1592	454	40	161	255	.285	.448	.352
April	7-12	4.34	670	166	26	83	124	.248	.419	.331
May	12-15	4.63	930	260	24	86	149	.280	.431	.342
June	10-17	4.81	929	256	24	107	150	.276	.435	.351
July	15-11	3.49	843	208	14	81	166	.247	.343	.311
August	11-20	4.76	1091	324	26	93	189	.297	.450	.350
Sept./Oct.	15-15	4.75	1088	332	29	107	184	.305	.443	.366
Leading Off Inn.			1352	392	30	97	216	.290	.434	.339
Runners On			2405	692	67	297	391	.288	.437	.362
Runners/Scor. Pos.			1457	421	41	224	266	.289	.437	.376
Runners On/2 Out			1030	273	24	165	194	.265	.404	.368
Scor. Pos./2 Out			691	187	17	137	137	.271	.408	.393
Late Inning Pressure			1067	291	28	127	212	.273	.413	.349
Leading Off			269	80	8	24	45	.297	.480	.355
Runners On			446	124	10	73	85	.278	.399	.376
Runners/Scor. Pos.			276	73	9	65	59	.264	.420	.372
First 9 Batters			3030	806	67	307	598	.266	.395	.333
Second 9 Batters			1403	399	32	128	221	.284	.418	.344
All Batters Thereafter			1118	341	44	122	143	.305	.504	.372

Starting pitchers: 38–59 (fewest wins in majors), 4.67 ERA (highest in N.L.)
Relief pitchers: 32–31 (most wins in N.L.), 4.21 ERA (highest in N.L.)
Ground outs-to-air outs ratio: 1.26. . . . Highest ERA in N.L. for third time in past five years, but only seventh time in team history. . . . Ranked last in league with 11 complete games for 15th time in team history, breaking tie with Phillies for all-time N.L. lead. . . . Allowed five or more runs in 15 innings, most in N.L. last season. . . . Only team in majors without a 10-game winner last season. Team leaders: Scott Sanderson and Lee Smith with nine. . . . Entered 1986 season with streak of 70 consecutive wins in road games in which they led after seven innings. Lost five such games during season, tied for N.L. high.

Cincinnati Reds

	W–L	ERA	AB	H	HR	BB	SO	BA	SA	OBA
Season	86-76	3.91	5550	1465	136	524	924	.264	.394	.326
vs. Left-Handers			2062	579	46	227	297	.281	.418	.351
vs. Right-Handers			3488	886	90	297	627	.254	.380	.311
Home	43-38	4.08	2857	773	73	260	458	.271	.410	.330
Road	43-38	3.73	2693	692	63	264	466	.257	.377	.323
Grass	25-23	3.63	1612	409	50	146	291	.254	.391	.316
Artificial Turf	61-53	4.03	3938	1056	86	378	633	.268	.395	.330
April	5-12	3.65	575	149	22	59	91	.259	.431	.325
May	13-14	4.48	921	253	21	104	159	.275	.412	.346
June	14-15	3.60	989	273	28	91	138	.276	.406	.339
July	15-11	3.93	918	232	21	88	162	.253	.381	.316
August	19-12	3.60	1039	260	20	89	174	.250	.364	.309
Sept./Oct.	20-12	4.14	1108	298	24	93	200	.269	.387	.323
Leading Off Inn.			1347	362	30	118	215	.269	.389	.331
Runners On			2363	632	60	258	392	.267	.405	.334
Runners/Scor. Pos.			1335	341	28	203	245	.255	.386	.343
Runners On/2 Out			1007	243	25	131	204	.241	.369	.330
Scor. Pos./2 Out			651	156	15	108	126	.240	.361	.350
Late Inning Pressure			1077	277	22	124	204	.257	.362	.335
Leading Off			275	76	5	16	42	.276	.367	.323
Runners On			452	110	16	72	90	.243	.387	.343
Runners/Scor. Pos.			260	57	6	59	59	.219	.327	.356
First 9 Batters			2911	758	61	311	551	.260	.373	.330
Second 9 Batters			1418	363	47	115	229	.256	.413	.311
All Batters Thereafter			1221	344	28	98	144	.282	.420	.335

Starting pitchers: 57–57, 4.11 ERA
Relief pitchers: 29–19, 3.54 ERA
Ground outs-to-air outs ratio: 1.18. . . . Walked 81 batters intentionally, to lead N.L. for first time in 32 seasons that those figures have been compiled. . . . Highest day-game ERA in N.L. (4.40); ranked 6th in night games (3.65). . . . Lost 11 consecutive home games from April 9 to May 5, longest streak in N.L. last season, and longest by Cincinnati since it equalled team record of 12 from Sept. 26, 1945 through April 24, 1946. Mark was originally set in 1937–38. . . . Young bullpen: Average age of Reds pitchers with saves last season was 27.12 years, youngest in either league.

Houston Astros

	W–L	ERA	AB	H	HR	BB	SO	BA	SA	OBA
Season	96-66	3.15	5339	1203	116	523	1160	.225	.345	.295
vs. Left-Handers			2038	458	38	224	414	.225	.338	.301
vs. Right-Handers			3301	745	78	299	746	.226	.350	.291
Home	52-29	3.15	2717	593	56	239	581	.218	.326	.282
Road	44-37	3.14	2622	610	60	284	579	.233	.365	.309
Grass	23-25	3.39	1572	383	38	155	352	.244	.381	.313
Artificial Turf	73-41	3.04	3767	820	78	368	808	.218	.331	.288
April	14-6	2.93	660	152	16	61	125	.230	.355	.297
May	13-13	3.07	841	192	18	99	206	.228	.360	.312
June	14-15	3.38	956	233	18	88	169	.244	.367	.306
July	16-11	3.38	895	182	23	81	209	.203	.324	.270
August	16-12	3.38	912	211	17	98	186	.231	.345	.307
Sept./Oct.	23-9	2.92	1075	233	24	96	265	.217	.327	.282
Leading Off Inn.			1341	313	33	116	278	.233	.365	.297
Runners On			2111	478	46	252	472	.226	.343	.308
Runners/Scor. Pos.			1292	279	21	189	311	.216	.319	.310
Runners On/2 Out			927	186	7	125	226	.201	.278	.300
Scor. Pos./2 Out			632	127	3	100	162	.201	.272	.311
Late Inning Pressure			949	216	21	116	170	.228	.340	.313
Leading Off			237	58	3	29	44	.245	.346	.337
Runners On			388	88	11	65	68	.227	.353	.333
Runners/Scor. Pos.			236	54	6	50	44	.229	.356	.351
First 9 Batters			2733	595	57	296	602	.218	.325	.296
Second 9 Batters			1430	310	27	119	318	.217	.334	.307
All Batters Thereafter			1176	298	32	108	240	.253	.406	.315

Starting pitchers: 66–50, 3.06 ERA (lowest in majors)
Relief pitchers: 30–16 (fewest losses in N.L.), 3.38
Ground outs-to-air outs ratio: 1.05 (2d lowest in N.L.). . . . Opponents grounded into one double play for every 13.76 opportunities, 2d-lowest rate in N.L. . . . Led N.L. in shutouts for fifth time in past nine seasons. . . . Allowed fewest hits in N.L. for fifth time in past eight seasons, with lowest total in league since 1942, with the usual eliminations of 1972 and 1981. . . . Led N.L. in road-game ERA, but ranked only fourth in home games. . . . Allowed 53 first-inning runs, fewest in majors, with awesome record over final month: held opponents scoreless in first frame of final 20 games, including all six games of N.L.C.S.

Los Angeles Dodgers

	W–L	ERA	AB	H	HR	BB	SO	BA	SA	OBA
Season	73-89	3.76	5569	1428	115	499	1051	.256	.375	.319
vs. Left-Handers			2069	545	37	200	374	.263	.382	.329
vs. Right-Handers			3500	883	78	299	677	.252	.371	.313
Home	46-35	3.02	2832	699	46	210	526	.247	.340	.300
Road	27-54	4.54	2737	729	69	289	525	.266	.411	.338
Grass	58-62	3.56	4173	1059	82	351	762	.254	.368	.313
Artificial Turf	15-27	4.37	1396	369	33	148	289	.264	.396	.337
April	10-13	2.88	806	204	14	82	158	.253	.356	.323
May	13-13	3.45	880	208	21	86	184	.236	.357	.309
June	11-16	4.15	964	269	20	86	167	.279	.400	.340
July	15-10	3.86	831	207	14	65	168	.249	.367	.304
August	13-16	3.68	971	242	22	76	179	.249	.367	.304
Sept./Oct.	11-21	4.34	1117	298	24	104	195	.267	.395	.329
Leading Off Inn.			1378	347	33	83	243	.252	.380	.295
Runners On			2357	619	47	278	436	.263	.378	.340
Runners/Scor. Pos.			1410	375	24	221	275	.266	.368	.362
Runners On/2 Out			1013	249	20	140	202	.246	.348	.339
Scor. Pos./2 Out			668	175	13	117	136	.262	.364	.374
Late Inning Pressure			1167	324	31	150	234	.278	.414	.359
Leading Off			292	81	11	22	52	.277	.435	.328
Runners On			530	140	12	97	105	.264	.394	.376
Runners/Scor. Pos.			316	87	6	78	67	.275	.405	.412
First 9 Batters			2708	687	62	270	542	.254	.374	.323
Second 9 Batters			1419	355	21	117	274	.250	.359	.308
All Batters Thereafter			1442	386	32	112	235	.268	.393	.322

Starting pitchers: 56–61, 3.69 ERA
Relief pitchers: 17–28 (tied for fewest wins in N.L.), 3.94 ERA
Ground outs-to-air outs ratio: 1.29 (3d highest in N.L.). . . . Opponents grounded into one double play for every 14.57 opportunities, lowest rate in majors. . . . Led N.L. in complete games for fourth time in past six seasons. . . . Lost nine consecutive extra-inning games from Sept. 6, 1985 through May 10, 1986, tying the franchise record set in 1908. League record of 13 was set by St. Louis (1906–07), equalled by Montreal (1969–70). . . . Lost nine consecutive one-run games from June 17 through July 2, their longest streak since 1937–38. . . . Lost 18 games in which they led after six innings, most in majors.

Montreal Expos

	W–L	ERA	AB	H	HR	BB	SO	BA	SA	OBA
Season	78-83	3.78	5487	1350	119	566	1051	.246	.370	.318
vs. Left-Handers			2711	676	51	331	490	.249	.364	.331
vs. Right-Handers			2776	674	68	235	561	.243	.376	.305
Home	36-44	3.83	2773	674	58	298	547	.243	.372	.318
Road	42-39	3.73	2714	676	61	268	504	.249	.369	.318
Grass	20-22	3.86	1367	335	39	147	225	.245	.380	.319
Artificial Turf	58-61	3.76	4120	1015	80	419	826	.246	.367	.318
April	9-9	3.75	648	153	17	85	129	.236	.377	.327
May	17-10	3.83	901	218	19	100	147	.242	.344	.318
June	15-12	3.90	919	228	16	95	194	.248	.381	.320
July	9-16	4.47	864	229	25	105	166	.265	.412	.345
August	12-18	3.49	985	241	19	81	152	.245	.365	.307
Sept./Oct.	16-18	3.42	1170	281	23	100	263	.240	.352	.301
Leading Off Inn.			1347	321	29	122	257	.238	.367	.304
Runners On			2318	602	62	265	441	.260	.399	.335
Runners/Scor. Pos.			1462	367	35	208	311	.251	.377	.341
Runners On/2 Out			997	244	27	138	203	.245	.382	.339
Scor. Pos./2 Out			681	165	20	113	148	.242	.374	.353
Late Inning Pressure			1229	306	24	149	246	.249	.363	.332
Leading Off			311	75	8	26	62	.241	.379	.302
Runners On			518	136	7	80	103	.263	.365	.360
Runners/Scor. Pos.			328	80	5	67	74	.244	.348	.369
First 9 Batters			2915	698	59	308	600	.239	.357	.313
Second 9 Batters			1405	356	33	132	258	.253	.383	.320
All Batters Thereafter			1167	296	27	126	193	.254	.387	.330

Starting pitchers: 50–51, 3.92 ERA
Relief pitchers: 28–32 (most losses in majors), 3.50 ERA
Ground outs-to-air outs ratio: 1.28. . . . Only team in majors to allow more home runs with runners on base than with the bases empty last season. . . . Left-handers started fewer games (19) and pitched fewer innings (238.1) than for any other N.L. team last season. . . . Retired opposing leadoff batter in 69.6 percent of innings last season, a whisker short of the Expos' highest mark in 12-year history of *The Player Analysis* (69.7 percent in strike-shortened 1981 season). . . . Ranked 4th in N.L. in ERA in home games, 10th in road games. . . . Led majors in innings pitched by players named Floyd.

New York Mets

	W–L	ERA	AB	H	HR	BB	SO	BA	SA	OBA
Season	108-54	3.11	5519	1304	103	509	1083	.236	.342	.302
vs. Left-Handers			2174	504	35	229	405	.232	.336	.306
vs. Right-Handers			3345	800	68	280	678	.239	.345	.299
Home	55-26	2.72	2731	596	47	238	566	.218	.317	.282
Road	53-28	3.50	2788	708	56	271	517	.254	.366	.321
Grass	77-37	3.15	3880	911	74	339	767	.235	.337	.297
Artificial Turf	31-17	3.02	1639	393	29	170	316	.240	.353	.314
April	13-3	2.90	558	116	13	49	117	.208	.321	.273
May	18-9	3.26	915	216	18	91	193	.236	.334	.306
June	19-9	3.12	911	200	16	117	172	.220	.326	.309
July	16-11	2.85	957	243	17	69	174	.254	.357	.306
August	21-11	3.43	1089	271	20	86	205	.249	.358	.307
Sept./Oct.	21-11	3.00	1089	258	19	97	222	.237	.341	.300
Leading Off Inn.			1350	339	25	130	249	.251	.356	.321
Runners On			2335	538	45	230	458	.230	.334	.299
Runners/Scor. Pos.			1320	290	22	151	286	.220	.318	.295
Runners On/2 Out			978	195	18	112	202	.199	.302	.289
Scor. Pos./2 Out			638	120	13	74	142	.188	.288	.278
Late Inning Pressure			1097	279	18	125	180	.254	.341	.333
Leading Off			256	70	4	38	43	.273	.348	.369
Runners On			515	121	10	60	84	.235	.320	.319
Runners/Scor. Pos.			292	67	5	40	57	.229	.315	.319
First 9 Batters			2645	604	33	262	545	.228	.311	.300
Second 9 Batters			1430	348	40	124	270	.243	.380	.303
All Batters Thereafter			1444	352	30	123	268	.244	.359	.305

Starting pitchers: 78–33 (most wins, fewest losses in majors), 3.16 ERA
Relief pitchers: 30–21, 2.98 ERA
Ground outs-to-air outs ratio: 1.21. . . . Led N.L. in ERA for fourth time in team history. . . . Allowed fewest home runs for first time. . . . First team with four 15-game winners since 1980 Orioles; first in N.L. since 1978 Dodgers. . . . Ranked 3d in home-game ERA, but 10th in road games. . . . Only team in N.L. not to allow more than five runs in an inning last season. . . . Allowed only 10 home runs with two or more runners on base, fewest in majors. Only one other team in either league didn't allow a grand slam: Houston. . . . Only N.L. team not to lose more than four consecutive road games last season.

Phila. Phillies

	W–L	ERA	AB	H	HR	BB	SO	BA	SA	OBA
Season	86-75	3.85	5562	1473	130	553	874	.265	.395	.331
vs. Left-Handers			2184	577	57	255	336	.264	.402	.343
vs. Right-Handers			3378	896	73	298	538	.265	.390	.323
Home	49-31	3.60	2810	739	49	251	449	.263	.381	.324
Road	37-44	4.11	2752	734	81	302	425	.267	.410	.338
Grass	18-24	4.13	1399	381	43	135	231	.272	.409	.334
Artificial Turf	68-51	3.76	4163	1092	87	418	643	.262	.391	.330
April	8-9	4.30	619	175	16	69	86	.283	.422	.354
May	12-15	3.77	904	244	22	68	141	.270	.397	.316
June	15-13	5.01	1011	276	28	121	162	.273	.425	.351
July	14-13	3.90	956	265	21	95	134	.277	.412	.343
August	19-12	3.23	1010	239	19	103	173	.237	.340	.308
Sept./Oct.	18-13	3.25	1062	274	24	97	178	.258	.387	.322
Leading Off Inn.			1339	359	49	113	187	.268	.435	.328
Runners On			2453	648	42	279	409	.264	.377	.336
Runners/Scor. Pos.			1453	370	22	209	262	.255	.366	.342
Runners On/2 Out			1076	294	20	133	178	.273	.399	.352
Scor. Pos./2 Out			729	187	11	102	127	.257	.366	.352
Late Inning Pressure			1079	276	22	109	166	.256	.375	.324
Leading Off			271	72	10	14	36	.266	.432	.304
Runners On			450	99	5	73	70	.220	.316	.326
Runners/Scor. Pos.			267	50	2	60	45	.187	.270	.332
First 9 Batters			2955	752	66	287	509	.254	.374	.320
Second 9 Batters			1332	349	36	156	202	.262	.411	.340
All Batters Thereafter			1275	372	28	110	163	.292	.429	.348

Starting pitchers: 56–54, 3.98 ERA
Relief pitchers: 30–21, 3.64 ERA
Ground outs-to-air outs ratio: 1.12. . . . Highest ERA in N.L. during the month of June. . . . Only team in either league with fewer than three pitchers who started at least 25 games each last season. The Phillies had only one: Kevin Gross. . . . Opposing batters hit .220 with runners on base in Late-Inning Pressure Situations, a team record and the lowest mark in either league over past two seasons. . . . Relief pitchers worked three innings or more only 24 times, 2d-lowest total in N.L. (one more than Pittsburgh). . . . We're for turning the other cheek and all that, but there are limits. Pirates pitchers hit Phillies batters 11 times last season; Phillies didn't plunk a single Bucco.

Pittsburgh Pirates

	W–L	ERA	AB	H	HR	BB	SO	BA	SA	OBA
Season	64-98	3.90	5479	1397	138	570	924	.255	.393	.327
vs. Left-Handers			2327	595	44	265	347	.256	.374	.332
vs. Right-Handers			3152	802	94	305	577	.254	.408	.323
Home	31-50	3.81	2815	696	75	293	489	.247	.390	.320
Road	33-48	4.00	2664	701	63	277	435	.263	.397	.334
Grass	16-26	4.47	1410	374	42	159	227	.265	.417	.341
Artificial Turf	48-72	3.71	4069	1023	96	411	697	.251	.385	.322
April	7-10	3.75	608	154	13	68	109	.253	.375	.329
May	11-15	4.09	917	232	28	110	156	.253	.402	.334
June	12-18	3.55	1014	266	24	112	177	.262	.393	.336
July	11-14	4.22	834	215	24	90	144	.258	.406	.334
August	12-19	3.74	1020	259	25	88	164	.254	.396	.316
Sept./Oct.	11-22	4.07	1086	271	24	102	174	.250	.383	.316
Leading Off Inn.			1343	350	40	103	186	.261	.412	.317
Runners On			2325	624	61	283	407	.268	.412	.345
Runners/Scor. Pos.			1397	353	37	225	246	.253	.394	.352
Runners On/2 Out			1000	247	30	139	186	.247	.396	.344
Scor. Pos./2 Out			663	154	19	121	121	.232	.373	.358
Late Inning Pressure			1055	266	31	143	205	.252	.392	.343
Leading Off			263	73	10	28	42	.278	.441	.352
Runners On			449	117	14	81	91	.261	.401	.370
Runners/Scor. Pos.			265	62	6	66	56	.234	.385	.380
First 9 Batters			2915	691	70	325	568	.237	.363	.316
Second 9 Batters			1372	393	39	123	208	.286	.442	.344
All Batters Thereafter			1192	313	29	122	148	.263	.412	.334

Starting pitchers: 43–68 (tied for most losses in N.L.), 4.14 ERA
Relief pitchers: 21–30, 3.41 ERA
Ground outs-to-air outs ratio: 1.39 (2d highest in N.L.).... Highest ERA in N.L. on grass fields.... Lost 20 of 24 one-run decisions in road games.... Only N.L. team not to win more than four consecutive home games last season.... Lost nine consecutive one-run games from July 22 through Aug. 14, their longest streak since 1961. Team record: 14, set in 1923–24.... Made 356 relief appearances last season, highest total in majors, for an average of 5.69 batters faced, 2d-lowest mark in either league; only 23 relief appearances lasted three innings, fewest in N.L.

St. Louis Cardinals

	W–L	ERA	AB	H	HR	BB	SO	BA	SA	OBA
Season	79-82	3.37	5446	1364	135	485	761	.250	.387	.311
vs. Left-Handers			1892	478	44	181	264	.253	.380	.317
vs. Right-Handers			3554	886	91	304	497	.249	.390	.308
Home	42-39	3.16	2803	684	63	217	356	.244	.373	.298
Road	37-43	3.59	2643	680	72	268	405	.257	.401	.325
Grass	15-26	3.54	1353	346	34	131	208	.256	.397	.321
Artificial Turf	64-56	3.31	4093	1018	101	354	553	.249	.383	.308
April	8-10	3.21	630	149	15	71	101	.237	.365	.315
May	9-17	3.42	869	219	17	78	103	.252	.373	.315
June	15-14	3.01	1015	241	24	102	158	.237	.359	.307
July	14-12	3.69	866	226	20	47	123	.261	.396	.300
August	19-12	3.21	1019	254	27	84	136	.249	.397	.305
Sept./Oct.	14-17	3.68	1047	275	32	103	140	.263	.419	.327
Leading Off Inn.			1358	333	44	105	180	.245	.407	.303
Runners On			2143	575	47	225	286	.268	.392	.333
Runners/Scor. Pos.			1231	327	25	175	189	.266	.391	.347
Runners On/2 Out			899	221	22	115	119	.246	.372	.333
Scor. Pos./2 Out			569	133	11	92	87	.234	.344	.343
Late Inning Pressure			1169	276	23	108	171	.236	.352	.300
Leading Off			300	75	7	24	36	.250	.387	.308
Runners On			448	104	7	56	67	.232	.319	.314
Runners/Scor. Pos.			247	62	4	43	45	.251	.364	.354
First 9 Batters			2667	669	64	251	416	.251	.380	.314
Second 9 Batters			1412	334	35	100	197	.237	.377	.290
All Batters Thereafter			1367	361	36	134	148	.264	.410	.329

Starting pitchers: 62–58, 3.51 ERA
Relief pitchers: 17–24 (tied for fewest wins in N.L.), 3.06 ERA
Ground outs-to-air outs ratio: 1.09 (3d lowest in N.L.).... Opponents grounded into one double play for every 8.23 opportunities, highest rate in majors.... Fewest strikeouts in N.L. for sixth time in past seven seasons.... Led N.L. in ERA during the months of June and August.... Won 11 consecutive home games from July 21 through Aug. 8, longest streak in N.L. last season.... Left-handers started more games (82) and pitched more innings (690.1) than for any other N.L. team last season.... Only team in either league without a complete-game shutout last season.

San Diego Padres

	W–L	ERA	AB	H	HR	BB	SO	BA	SA	OBA
Season	74-88	3.99	5459	1406	150	607	934	.258	.395	.333
vs. Left-Handers			2143	566	47	281	357	.264	.381	.349
vs. Right-Handers			3316	840	103	326	577	.253	.403	.322
Home	43-38	3.39	2792	684	78	288	510	.245	.376	.317
Road	31-50	4.64	2667	722	72	319	424	.271	.414	.349
Grass	56-64	3.76	4084	1047	115	443	716	.256	.391	.330
Artificial Turf	18-24	4.68	1375	359	35	164	218	.261	.405	.341
April	12-9	2.74	699	146	16	58	145	.209	.318	.273
May	12-14	3.76	882	223	24	91	170	.253	.395	.323
June	14-14	4.46	959	270	29	133	147	.282	.428	.369
July	12-14	3.65	843	209	15	93	146	.248	.345	.323
August	11-19	4.52	1026	281	33	99	147	.274	.423	.339
Sept./Oct.	13-18	4.40	1050	277	33	133	179	.264	.428	.348
Leading Off Inn.			1325	342	33	116	215	.258	.383	.320
Runners On			2316	609	66	316	384	.263	.406	.351
Runners/Scor. Pos.			1393	352	44	242	252	.253	.412	.361
Runners On/2 Out			984	228	23	153	192	.232	.361	.339
Scor. Pos./2 Out			660	140	16	122	142	.212	.344	.338
Late Inning Pressure			1034	264	31	128	217	.255	.395	.338
Leading Off			254	64	9	31	49	.252	.398	.336
Runners On			428	105	11	69	88	.245	.360	.346
Runners/Scor. Pos.			254	59	7	59	56	.232	.366	.367
First 9 Batters			3011	756	71	365	573	.251	.377	.333
Second 9 Batters			1355	335	40	141	208	.247	.387	.321
All Batters Thereafter			1093	315	39	101	153	.288	.452	.348

Starting pitchers: 44–59, 4.27 ERA
Relief pitchers: 30–29, 3.52 ERA
Ground outs-to-air outs ratio: 1.01 (lowest in N.L.).... Allowed most home runs in N.L. for third time in five seasons since fences were cut in half.... Highest road-game ERA in N.L., but ranked 6th in home games.... Led N.L. in ERA during the month of April.... Allowed 103 first-inning runs, most in N.L.... Only N.L. team not to lose more than four consecutive games last season.... Left-handers pitched 249.1 innings in relief, highest total in N.L. last season. New York Yankees led the majors (285.0).... Margin of one run decided first 10 games last season of Padres as well as Dodgers (seven were played head to head), one short of modern National League record for any time during the season, set by Cincinnati in 1967.

San Francisco Giants

	W–L	ERA	AB	H	HR	BB	SO	BA	SA	OBA
Season	83-79	3.33	5350	1264	121	591	992	.236	.352	.313
vs. Left-Handers			2460	591	47	279	430	.240	.351	.318
vs. Right-Handers			2890	673	74	312	562	.233	.352	.309
Home	46-35	2.87	2729	597	61	277	505	.219	.333	.292
Road	37-44	3.83	2621	667	60	314	487	.254	.370	.335
Grass	65-55	3.19	4022	928	97	411	747	.231	.345	.303
Artificial Turf	18-24	3.76	1328	336	24	180	245	.253	.370	.344
April	13-8	3.28	719	161	20	77	143	.224	.345	.299
May	12-15	3.93	889	220	20	91	155	.247	.371	.317
June	16-12	3.04	901	205	21	96	160	.228	.339	.302
July	12-14	3.77	828	205	22	93	154	.248	.383	.324
August	12-16	3.45	954	236	17	111	179	.247	.357	.329
Sept./Oct.	18-14	2.69	1059	237	21	123	201	.224	.321	.307
Leading Off Inn.			1345	332	30	111	227	.247	.364	.308
Runners On			2174	536	50	303	398	.247	.360	.337
Runners/Scor. Pos.			1309	309	25	229	265	.236	.341	.343
Runners On/2 Out			907	209	25	148	170	.230	.341	.341
Scor. Pos./2 Out			617	136	13	120	120	.220	.329	.349
Late Inning Pressure			1058	254	21	125	226	.240	.345	.320
Leading Off			272	67	3	23	48	.246	.320	.307
Runners On			424	112	8	66	90	.264	.370	.361
Runners/Scor. Pos.			261	63	3	55	61	.241	.333	.369
First 9 Batters			2833	652	49	348	605	.230	.324	.314
Second 9 Batters			1376	338	37	131	219	.246	.381	.314
All Batters Thereafter			1141	274	35	112	168	.240	.386	.311

Starting pitchers: 54–60, 3.57 ERA
Relief pitchers: 29–19, 2.93 ERA (lowest in majors)
Ground outs-to-air outs ratio: 1.23.... Led N.L. in ERA after September 1.... Lost only five games in which they led after six innings, tied for fewest in majors.... Won all 27 road games in which they led after eight innings.... Left-handers pitched only 85.1 innings in relief, lowest total in N.L. last season.... Relief pitchers faced an average of 5.68 batters per appearance, the lowest mark in the majors.... Tough to get started against these guys: Opposing batters posted .296 on-base average with bases empty. Only one N.L. team had lower mark: Houston (.286).

National League

	W–L	ERA	AB	H	HR	BB	SO	BA	SA	OBA
Season	969-969	3.72	65730	16643	1523	6560	11648	.253	.380	.322
vs. Left-Handers			26845	6899	547	2991	4534	.257	.379	.332
vs. Right-Handers			38885	9744	976	3569	7114	.251	.381	.315
Home	526-443	3.48	33582	8286	756	3136	5970	.247	.369	.312
Road	443-526	3.97	32148	8357	767	3424	5678	.260	.391	.332
Grass	485-485	3.68	32938	8358	812	3237	5926	.254	.380	.321
Artificial Turf	484-484	3.75	32792	8285	711	3323	5722	.253	.380	.322
April	113-113	3.45	7821	1878	206	827	1445	.240	.371	.313
May	160-160	3.73	10762	2698	247	1124	1952	.251	.377	.322
June	169-169	3.79	11534	2985	264	1259	1939	.259	.387	.332
July	156-156	3.81	10523	2671	244	1002	1895	.254	.380	.319
August	180-180	3.72	12043	3072	265	1100	2036	.255	.380	.318
Sept./Oct.	191-191	3.73	13047	3339	297	1248	2381	.256	.381	.321
Leading Off Inn.			16139	4142	404	1325	2671	.257	.391	.316
Runners On			27689	7190	638	3290	4887	.260	.386	.336
Runners/Scor. Pos.			16523	4164	352	2509	3188	.252	.374	.345
Runners On/2 Out			11801	2839	265	1653	2259	.241	.363	.337
Scor. Pos./2 Out			7862	1847	164	1331	1592	.235	.350	.349
Late Inning Pressure			12990	3306	298	1511	2414	.255	.375	.333
Leading Off			3243	857	87	297	538	.264	.398	.329
Runners On			5492	1368	117	858	1023	.249	.360	.348
Runners/Scor. Pos.			3284	786	65	699	675	.239	.352	.367
First 9 Batters			34072	8364	714	3630	6628	.245	.360	.319
Second 9 Batters			16760	4249	425	1526	2849	.254	.390	.317
All Batters Thereafter			14898	4030	384	1404	2171	.271	.414	.334

Teams with best and 2d-best ERAs in league reached championship series for third time in past four seasons. . . . On momentum: Both playoff series were split after two games and won by teams that won the second game. In the 32 World Series under best-of-seven format in which first two games were split, second-game winner won 20 times, first-game winner won 12. . . . No balks have been called in N.L.C.S. since third game of 1982 series. . . . Last season was first in N.L. history in which more than 200 different pitchers were used (205). . . . League ERA was highest since 1979; has topped 4.00 only once during divisional era (4.05 in 1970). . . . Left-handers were combined 322–323, right-handers were 647–646. Maybe you never heard of Greg Booker (RHP, 1–0) or Ed Vosberg (LHP, 0–1), but without them, both sets would have been right at .500.

V
Rankings Section

Rankings Section

The Rankings Section consists of a series of lists ranking players in a wide variety of batting and pitching categories. Players are ranked in 24 batting categories and 24 pitching categories ranging from the simple (batting average, for example) to the more esoteric (like percentage of runners driven in from third base with less than two out). Listed are the players ranking in the top 20 and bottom 20 in each league.

The exact number of plate appearances required to qualify for ranking in each category varies. The number of eligible players for each ranking is determined by the number of players in each league who had 200 or more plate appearances, or who faced 250 or more batters. In the American League, the 169 players and 128 pitchers with the most plate appearances or batters faced in a given category are eligible for ranking; in the National League, the top 142 batters and 116 pitchers are eligible. (If there is a tie for the final position, all tied players are included.) In some categories, a large number of players tied for last place (as, for example, in Home Run

Percentage vs. Left-Handed Pitchers). In such cases, a line indicating "42 players tied with 0.00" is used in place of the Bottom 20 list.

The intent here is to rank all players who qualify as at least semiregulars for the season. To do this properly, it is necessary to look at the number of plate appearances in each specific situation. Craig Reynolds and Dickie Thon platooned at shortstop for Houston last year, and both can be considered as at least "semiregulars." But the vast majority of Reynolds's plate appearances were against right-handers, and Thon's were mostly against left-handers. Reynolds was one of the 142 batters who faced righties most often, so he is ranked there, but he failed to meet this qualification against lefties, so he is not ranked in that category. Thon, of course, is ranked against lefties but not against righties.

The material in this section is generally based on the categories used in the Batter and Pitcher Sections. If any of the breakdowns are unfamiliar, detailed descriptions can be found in the introductions to the Batter and Pitcher Sections.

Batting Average vs. Left-Handed Pitchers

American League

Top 20				Bottom 20		
1. Mike Felder	MIL	.409		173. Marc Sullivan	BOS	.137
2. Ernie Whitt	TOR	.370		172. Roy Smalley	MIN	.138
3. Mickey Hatcher	MIN	.364		171. Rudy Law	KC	.143
4. Cal Ripken	BAL	.360		170. Cecil Fielder	TOR	.150
5. Don Mattingly	NY	.358		169. Mark Davidson	MIN	.154
6. Wade Boggs	BOS	.352		168. Bobby Meacham	NY	.156
7. Jim Rice	BOS	.351		167. Stan Javier	OAK	.160
8. Gary Gaetti	MIN	.344		166. Ron Kittle	NY	.173
9. Julio Franco	CLE	.341		165. Gorman Thomas	MIL	.175
10. Tony Bernazard	CLE	.338		164. Ruppert Jones	CAL	.178
11. Juan Beniquez	BAL	.336		163. Rich Gedman	BOS	.186
12. Pat Tabler	CLE	.333		162. Buck Martinez	TOR	.191
13. George Bell	TOR	.330		161. Jim Sundberg	KC	.191
14. Phil Bradley	SEA	.325		160. Henry Cotto	NY	.193
15. Kirby Puckett	MIN	.325		159. Floyd Rayford	BAL	.194
16. Damaso Garcia	TOR	.324		158. Mike Pagliarulo	NY	.196
17. Jim Presley	SEA	.323		156. Darrell Miller	CAL	.200
18. Cory Snyder	CLE	.322		156. Jim Traber	BAL	.200
19. Marty Barrett	BOS	.322		155. Bill Bathe	OAK	.204
20. Tony Phillips	OAK	.321		153. Ron Shepherd	TOR	.205
				153. Harold Reynolds	SEA	.205

National League

Top 20				Bottom 20		
1. Ray Knight	NY	.379		143. Greg Brock	LA	.102
2. Hubie Brooks	MTL	.365		142. Tim Flannery	SD	.143
3. Mike Schmidt	PHI	.357		141. Luis Aguayo	PHI	.169
4. Gary Matthews	CHI	.352		140. Graig Nettles	SD	.170
5. Kevin McReynolds	SD	.339		139. Mark Bailey	HOU	.172
6. Mitch Webster	MTL	.337		138. Lee Mazzilli	NY	.173
7. Dave Concepcion	CIN	.337		137. Tito Landrum	STL	.181
8. Tony Pena	PIT	.333		136. Ron Oester	CIN	.184
8. Andres Galarraga	MTL	.333		135. Marvell Wynne	SD	.186
10. Andre Dawson	MTL	.331		134. Denny Walling	HOU	.190
11. Steve Sax	LA	.329		133. Wally Backman	NY	.192
12. Jeff Leonard	SF	.328		132. Mike Brown	PIT	.197
13. Tony Gwynn	SD	.328		131. Jerry Mumphrey	CHI	.197
14. Manny Trillo	CHI	.328		130. Bill Almon	PIT	.198
15. Ron Cey	CHI	.325		128. Bip Roberts	SD	.203
16. Bill Russell	LA	.325		128. Randy Kutcher	SF	.203
17. Kevin Bass	HOU	.323		127. Rafael Ramirez	ATL	.207
18. Eric Davis	CIN	.319		126. Andy Van Slyke	STL	.207
19. Tracy Jones	CIN	.317		125. Darryl Strawberry	NY	.209
19. Jeff Stone	PHI	.317		123. Mike Lavalliere	STL	.211
				123. Joel Youngblood	SF	.211

Batting Average vs. Right-Handed Pitchers

American League

Top 20				Bottom 20		
1. Wade Boggs	BOS	.359		171. Mickey Tettleton	OAK	.165
2. Don Mattingly	NY	.348		170. Rick Dempsey	BAL	.175
3. Johnny Grubb	DET	.342		169. Darryl Motley	KC	.177
4. Robin Yount	MIL	.332		168. Ed Romero	BOS	.191
5. Rick Burleson	CAL	.331		167. Gorman Thomas	MIL	.193
6. Kirby Puckett	MIN	.329		166. Billy Robidoux	MIL	.205
7. Ron Hassey	CHI	.329		165. Andy Allanson	CLE	.206
8. Rick Leach	TOR	.327		164. Bill Schroeder	MIL	.207
9. Mike Easler	NY	.323		163. Dave Kingman	OAK	.207
10. Pat Tabler	CLE	.322		162. Mickey Hatcher	MIN	.209
11. Ken Griffey	NY	.317		161. Toby Harrah	TEX	.210
12. Wally Joyner	CAL	.317		160. Rob Wilfong	CAL	.211
13. Harold Baines	CHI	.316		159. Steve Balboni	KC	.212
14. Gary Ward	TEX	.315		158. Julio Cruz	CHI	.213
15. George Brett	KC	.314		157. Rob Deer	MIL	.214
16. Jim Rice	BOS	.313		156. Argenis Salazar	KC	.214
17. Dan Pasqua	NY	.310		155. Glenn Braggs	MIL	.217
18. Tony Fernandez	TOR	.307		154. Tim Hulett	CHI	.218
19. Eddie Murray	BAL	.306		153. Spike Owen	BOS	.219
20. Scott Bradley	SEA	.306		152. Carlton Fisk	CHI	.220

National League

Top 20				Bottom 20		
1. Kal Daniels	CIN	.349		142. Bill Russell	LA	.167
2. Tim Raines	MTL	.343		141. Bob Melvin	SF	.171
3. Wally Backman	NY	.340		140. Bob Dernier	CHI	.187
4. Von Hayes	PHI	.340		139. U.L. Washington	PIT	.194
5. Denny Walling	HOU	.333		138. Al Newman	MTL	.194
6. Steve Sax	LA	.333		137. Jack Clark	STL	.196
7. Jerry Mumphrey	CHI	.331		136. Dann Bilardello	MTL	.199
8. Hubie Brooks	MTL	.330		135. Rafael Santana	NY	.199
9. Chris Brown	SF	.330		134. Clint Hurdle	STL	.200
10. Tony Gwynn	SD	.329		133. Herm Winningham	MTL	.201
11. Ken Griffey	ATL	.329		132. Carmelo Martinez	SD	.201
12. Johnny Ray	PIT	.325		131. Mariano Duncan	LA	.205
13. Chris Chambliss	ATL	.318		130. Ozzie Virgil	ATL	.206
14. Len Dykstra	NY	.314		129. Ron Roenicke	PHI	.208
15. John Kruk	SD	.312		128. Vance Law	MTL	.210
16. Keith Hernandez	NY	.309		127. Tom Herr	STL	.212
17. Mike Fitzgerald	MTL	.308		126. Bobby Bonilla	PIT	.214
18. Tim Flannery	SD	.304		125. Pete Rose	CIN	.214
19. Kevin Bass	HOU	.303		124. Terry Pendleton	STL	.217
20. Chili Davis	SF	.302		123. Steve Jeltz	PHI	.217

Slugging Average vs. Left-Handed Pitchers

American League

Top 20				Bottom 20		
1. Cal Ripken	BAL	.683		173. Rudy Law	KC	.167
2. Rob Deer	MIL	.605		172. Cecil Fielder	TOR	.175
3. Gary Gaetti	MIN	.603		171. Marc Sullivan	BOS	.196
4. Pete Incaviglia	TEX	.600		170. Bobby Meacham	NY	.200
5. Steve Balboni	KC	.590		169. Bruce Bochte	OAK	.216
6. Cory Snyder	CLE	.585		168. Henry Cotto	NY	.228
7. Cliff Johnson	TOR	.579		167. Mark Davidson	MIN	.231
8. Tom Brunansky	MIN	.575		166. Julio Cruz	CHI	.233
9. Larry Parrish	TEX	.569		165. Stan Javier	OAK	.240
10. Ernie Whitt	TOR	.565		163. Joel Skinner	NY	.250
11. Jim Rice	BOS	.560		163. Jim Gantner	MIL	.250
12. George Bell	TOR	.553		162. Reid Nichols	CHI	.267
13. Julio Franco	CLE	.537		161. Alvin Davis	SEA	.270
14. Joe Carter	CLE	.530		160. Rey Quinones	SEA	.272
15. Jesse Barfield	TOR	.527		159. Harold Reynolds	SEA	.274
16. Kirby Puckett	MIN	.524		158. Bob Boone	CAL	.276
17. Mickey Tettleton	OAK	.524		157. Reggie Jackson	CAL	.282
18. Dave Winfield	NY	.523		156. Dwayne Murphy	OAK	.287
19. Don Mattingly	NY	.523		155. Mike Pagliarulo	NY	.288
20. Fred Lynn	BAL	.521		154. Alfredo Griffin	OAK	.295

National League

Top 20				Bottom 20		
1. Mike Schmidt	PHI	.707		143. Greg Brock	LA	.153
2. Hubie Brooks	MTL	.682		142. Denny Walling	HOU	.207
3. Ron Cey	CHI	.638		141. Jerry Mumphrey	CHI	.213
4. Andre Dawson	MTL	.625		140. Mark Bailey	HOU	.234
5. Ray Knight	NY	.601		139. Mike Brown	PIT	.239
6. Gary Matthews	CHI	.600		138. Ron Oester	CIN	.243
7. Jack Clark	STL	.596		137. Rafael Belliard	PIT	.246
8. Eric Davis	CIN	.590		135. Wally Backman	NY	.250
9. Kevin McReynolds	SD	.589		135. Tim Flannery	SD	.250
10. Bruce Bochy	SD	.579		134. Steve Jeltz	PHI	.257
11. Kevin Bass	HOU	.540		133. Rafael Ramirez	ATL	.263
12. Steve Garvey	SD	.527		132. Tito Landrum	STL	.263
13. Tony Gwynn	SD	.523		131. Dave Anderson	LA	.267
14. Carmelo Martinez	SD	.518		130. Bip Roberts	SD	.268
15. Dave Parker	CIN	.513		129. Lee Mazzilli	NY	.269
16. Mitch Webster	MTL	.513		128. Eddie Milner	CIN	.276
17. Glenn Davis	HOU	.512		127. Joel Youngblood	SF	.276
18. Mike Marshall	LA	.512		126. Vince Coleman	STL	.278
19. Mike Diaz	PIT	.511		125. Kurt Stillwell	CIN	.279
20. Dale Murphy	ATL	.508		124. Luis Aguayo	PHI	.282

Slugging Average vs. Right-Handed Pitchers

American League

Top 20			Bottom 20		
1. Johnny Grubb	DET	.612	171. Julio Cruz	CHI	.221
2. Don Mattingly	NY	.601	170. Billy Robidoux	MIL	.253
3. Jesse Barfield	TOR	.569	169. Alan Wiggins	BAL	.256
4. Darrell Porter	TEX	.561	168. Andy Allanson	CLE	.258
5. Greg Walker	CHI	.554	167. Ed Romero	BOS	.259
6. Ken Phelps	SEA	.554	166. Mickey Hatcher	MIN	.266
7. Mike Pagliarulo	NY	.548	165. Argenis Salazar	KC	.278
8. Dan Pasqua	NY	.541	164. John Cangelosi	CHI	.280
9. Kirby Puckett	MIN	.541	163. Glenn Braggs	MIL	.287
10. Kirk Gibson	DET	.534	162. Steve Lyons	CHI	.290
11. George Brett	KC	.529	161. Garth Iorg	TOR	.292
12. Harold Baines	CHI	.527	160. Spike Owen	BOS	.292
13. Lance Parrish	DET	.527	159. Juan Bonilla	BAL	.293
14. George Bell	TOR	.524	158. Dave Bergman	DET	.295
15. Kent Hrbek	MIN	.515	157. Harold Reynolds	SEA	.296
16. Ken Griffey	NY	.512	156. Tony Phillips	OAK	.296
17. Mel Hall	CLE	.510	155. Rob Wilfong	CAL	.297
18. Ron Hassey	CHI	.509	154. Willie Randolph	NY	.298
19. Joe Carter	CLE	.508	153. Mickey Tettleton	OAK	.299
20. Wally Joyner	CAL	.506	152. John Moses	SEA	.301

National League

Top 20			Bottom 20		
1. Darryl Strawberry	NY	.608	142. Al Newman	MTL	.208
2. Kal Daniels	CIN	.584	141. Bill Russell	LA	.225
3. Von Hayes	PHI	.552	140. Rafael Santana	NY	.229
4. Denny Walling	HOU	.528	139. Kurt Stillwell	CIN	.249
5. Ken Griffey	ATL	.527	138. U.L. Washington	PIT	.255
6. Hubie Brooks	MTL	.525	137. Bob Dernier	CHI	.256
7. Jim Morrison	PIT	.507	136. Jose Uribe	SF	.260
8. Claudell Washington	ATL	.495	135. Pete Rose	CIN	.260
9. Len Dykstra	NY	.494	134. Steve Jeltz	PHI	.264
10. Sid Bream	PIT	.492	133. Rafael Belliard	PIT	.273
11. Joel Youngblood	SF	.491	132. Mariano Duncan	LA	.274
12. Andy Van Slyke	STL	.490	131. Terry Pendleton	STL	.274
13. Mike Fitzgerald	MTL	.490	130. Bob Melvin	SF	.274
14. Eric Davis	CIN	.487	129. Vance Law	MTL	.275
15. Tim Raines	MTL	.486	128. Vince Coleman	STL	.282
16. Mike Schmidt	PHI	.484	127. Bobby Bonilla	PIT	.282
17. Leon Durham	CHI	.483	126. Carmelo Martinez	SD	.284
18. Glenn Davis	HOU	.482	125. Tom Herr	STL	.285
19. Greg Brock	LA	.481	124. Garry Templeton	SD	.290
20. Candy Maldonado	SF	.476	123. Dave Concepcion	CIN	.290

Home Run Percentage vs. Left-Handed Pitchers

American League

Top 20			Bottom 20
1. Steve Balboni	KC	8.96	26 players tied with 0.00
2. Rob Deer	MIL	8.53	
3. Larry Parrish	TEX	8.46	
4. Dave Kingman	OAK	8.00	
5. Pete Incaviglia	TEX	7.50	
6. Cliff Johnson	TOR	7.48	
7. Cal Ripken	BAL	7.32	
8. Fred Lynn	BAL	7.29	
9. Gary Gaetti	MIN	7.28	
10. Mickey Tettleton	OAK	7.14	
11. Cory Snyder	CLE	6.78	
12. Butch Wynegar	NY	6.74	
13. Tom Brunansky	MIN	6.59	
14. Ernie Whitt	TOR	6.52	
15. Tim Laudner	MIN	6.31	
16. Bill Bathe	OAK	6.12	
16. Darrell Evans	DET	6.12	
18. Dave Winfield	NY	6.09	
19. Jesse Barfield	TOR	6.08	
20. Dave Henderson	BOS	5.94	

National League

Top 20			Bottom 20
1. Mike Schmidt	PHI	9.55	25 players tied with 0.00
2. Bruce Bochy	SD	8.42	
3. Eric Davis	CIN	7.64	
4. Mike Marshall	LA	6.98	
5. Andre Dawson	MTL	6.88	
6. Mike Diaz	PIT	6.87	
7. Jack Clark	STL	6.74	
8. George Foster	NY	6.73	
9. Steve Garvey	SD	6.52	
10. Carmelo Martinez	SD	6.36	
11. Ron Cey	CHI	6.25	
12. Hubie Brooks	MTL	5.88	
13. Gary Carter	NY	5.85	
14. Gary Matthews	CHI	5.71	
15. Glenn Davis	HOU	5.69	
16. Graig Nettles	SD	5.66	
17. Kevin McReynolds	SD	5.21	
18. Kevin Bass	HOU	4.84	
19. Dale Murphy	ATL	4.66	
20. Buddy Bell	CIN	4.60	

Home Run Percentage vs. Right-Handed Pitchers

American League

Top 20			Bottom 20		
1. Lance Parrish	DET	8.29	158. Dave Collins	DET	0.00
2. Darrell Porter	TEX	8.11	158. John Cangelosi	CHI	0.00
3. Ken Phelps	SEA	8.07	158. Juan Bonilla	BAL	0.00
4. Mike Pagliarulo	NY	7.62	158. Marty Barrett	BOS	0.00
5. Kirk Gibson	DET	7.58	158. Spike Owen	BOS	0.00
6. Ron Kittle	NY	7.11	158. Bobby Meacham	NY	0.00
7. Jesse Barfield	TOR	7.03	158. Garth Iorg	TOR	0.00
8. Johnny Grubb	DET	6.63	158. Julio Cruz	CHI	0.00
9. Rob Deer	MIL	6.53	158. Wayne Tolleson	NY	0.00
10. Kent Hrbek	MIN	6.28	158. Argenis Salazar	KC	0.00
11. Jim Traber	BAL	6.21	158. Billy Robidoux	MIL	0.00
12. Jose Canseco	OAK	6.05	158. Harold Reynolds	SEA	0.00
13. Don Baylor	BOS	6.00	158. Curtis Wilkerson	TEX	0.00
14. Don Mattingly	NY	5.99	158. Alan Wiggins	BAL	0.00
15. Danny Tartabull	SEA	5.70	157. Ozzie Guillen	CHI	0.26
15. Greg Walker	CHI	5.70	156. Scott Fletcher	TEX	0.28
17. Dan Pasqua	NY	5.68	155. Willie Randolph	NY	0.32
18. Darrell Evans	DET	5.56	154. John Moses	SEA	0.35
19. Ken Griffey	NY	5.49	153. Rudy Law	KC	0.38
20. Larry Sheets	BAL	5.45	152. Steve Lyons	CHI	0.47

National League

Top 20			Bottom 20		
1. Darryl Strawberry	NY	7.64	131. Al Newman	MTL	0.00
2. Darren Daulton	PHI	6.61	131. Steve Jeltz	PHI	0.00
3. Greg Brock	LA	6.02	131. Vince Coleman	STL	0.00
4. Eric Davis	CIN	5.90	131. Rafael Belliard	PIT	0.00
5. Franklin Stubbs	LA	5.88	131. Ozzie Smith	STL	0.00
6. Bob Horner	ATL	5.70	131. Rafael Santana	NY	0.00
7. Gary Matthews	CHI	5.66	131. Bill Russell	LA	0.00
8. Mike Schmidt	PHI	5.57	131. Pete Rose	CIN	0.00
9. Glenn Davis	HOU	5.23	131. U.L. Washington	PIT	0.00
10. Dave Parker	CIN	5.19	131. Jose Uribe	SF	0.00
11. Ozzie Virgil	ATL	5.16	131. Garry Templeton	SD	0.00
12. Randy Kutcher	SF	5.13	131. Kurt Stillwell	CIN	0.00
13. Mike Marshall	LA	4.98	130. Terry Pendleton	STL	0.27
14. Barry Bonds	PIT	4.96	129. Tom Herr	STL	0.29
15. Jim Morrison	PIT	4.93	128. Wally Backman	NY	0.30
16. Claudell Washington	ATL	4.85	127. Vance Law	MTL	0.43
17. Len Matuszek	LA	4.84	126. Tom Foley	MTL	0.43
18. Leon Durham	CHI	4.78	125. Joe Orsulak	PIT	0.57
19. Dale Murphy	ATL	4.75	124. Tim Flannery	SD	0.64
20. John Russell	PHI	4.66	123. Willie McGee	STL	0.67

Batting Average, Day Games

American League

Top 20				Bottom 20		
1. Johnny Grubb	DET	.377		171. Floyd Rayford	BAL	.117
2. Dwight Lowry	DET	.353		170. Kelly Gruber	TOR	.131
3. Charlie Moore	MIL	.352		169. Mark Salas	MIN	.154
4. Greg Walker	CHI	.345		168. Butch Wynegar	NY	.160
5. Ron Hassey	CHI	.344		167. Steve Lombardozzi	MIN	.165
6. Donnie Hill	OAK	.338		166. Curtis Wilkerson	TEX	.174
7. Don Mattingly	NY	.338		165. Buck Martinez	TOR	.186
8. Dave Henderson	BOS	.337		164. Jim Sundberg	KC	.187
9. Juan Beniquez	BAL	.333		161. Steve Lyons	CHI	.188
9. Pete O'Brien	TEX	.333		161. Lance Parrish	DET	.188
9. Bobby Grich	CAL	.333		161. Darryl Motley	KC	.188
12. Pat Tabler	CLE	.331		160. Steve Buechele	TEX	.190
13. George Brett	KC	.331		159. Chet Lemon	DET	.200
14. Mel Hall	CLE	.326		158. Argenis Salazar	KC	.202
15. Ben Oglivie	MIL	.326		157. Paul Molitor	MIL	.203
16. Wally Joyner	CAL	.324		156. Dusty Baker	OAK	.205
17. Larry Parrish	TEX	.324		155. Darnell Coles	DET	.205
18. Eddie Murray	BAL	.323		154. Don Baylor	BOS	.209
19. Kirby Puckett	MIN	.322		153. Rick Manning	MIL	.211
20. Wade Boggs	BOS	.321		152. Jose Canseco	OAK	.211

National League

Top 20				Bottom 20		
1. Denny Walling	HOU	.353		142. Dave Martinez	CHI	.128
2. Keith Hernandez	NY	.350		141. Pete Rose	CIN	.173
3. Jeff Leonard	SF	.348		140. Graig Nettles	SD	.182
4. Tim Raines	MTL	.339		139. Sid Bream	PIT	.184
5. Thad Bosley	CHI	.338		138. Terry Harper	ATL	.187
6. Tony Gwynn	SD	.337		137. Kurt Stillwell	CIN	.198
7. Wally Backman	NY	.336		135. Gary Redus	PHI	.200
8. Chris Brown	SF	.333		135. Tito Landrum	STL	.200
8. Johnny Ray	PIT	.333		134. Rafael Santana	NY	.201
8. Ken Oberkfell	ATL	.333		133. Glenn Hubbard	ATL	.203
11. Dave Lopes	HOU	.331		132. Herm Winningham	MTL	.203
12. John Kruk	SD	.327		131. Bob Melvin	SF	.204
13. Hubie Brooks	MTL	.326		130. Franklin Stubbs	LA	.208
14. Ken Landreaux	LA	.326		129. Jack Clark	STL	.208
15. Jerry Mumphrey	CHI	.321		128. Bob Brenly	SF	.212
16. Ozzie Smith	STL	.319		127. Milt Thompson	PHI	.213
17. Bill Doran	HOU	.319		126. Mike Heath	STL	.213
18. Tom Foley	MTL	.319		125. Vance Law	MTL	.214
19. Kal Daniels	CIN	.318		124. Mike Scioscia	LA	.215
20. Lee Mazzilli	NY	.317		123. Candy Maldonado	SF	.216

Batting Average, Night Games

American League

Top 20				Bottom 20		
1. Wade Boggs	BOS	.375		169. Gorman Thomas	MIL	.178
2. Don Mattingly	NY	.359		168. Charlie Moore	MIL	.185
3. Jim Rice	BOS	.341		167. Mickey Tettleton	OAK	.194
4. Kirby Puckett	MIN	.330		166. Ed Romero	BOS	.196
5. Gary Ward	TEX	.329		165. Tim Hulett	CHI	.198
6. Mike Easler	NY	.326		164. Floyd Rayford	BAL	.200
7. Ken Griffey	NY	.323		163. Steve Balboni	KC	.202
8. Rick Leach	TOR	.323		162. Rick Dempsey	BAL	.203
9. Pat Tabler	CLE	.322		161. Julio Cruz	CHI	.204
10. Paul Molitor	MIL	.322		160. Ron Kittle	NY	.204
11. Johnny Grubb	DET	.318		159. Harold Reynolds	SEA	.207
12. Tony Fernandez	TOR	.318		158. Dave Kingman	OAK	.209
13. George Bell	TOR	.315		157. Andy Allanson	CLE	.209
14. Ron Hassey	CHI	.314		156. Rob Wilfong	CAL	.211
15. Scott Bradley	SEA	.313		155. Rey Quinones	SEA	.211
16. Phil Bradley	SEA	.310		154. Jamie Quirk	KC	.212
17. Robin Yount	MIL	.309		153. Darryl Motley	KC	.212
18. Tony Bernazard	CLE	.308		152. Carlton Fisk	CHI	.213
19. Julio Franco	CLE	.306		151. Juan Bonilla	BAL	.213
20. Carmen Castillo	CLE	.303		150. Joel Skinner	NY	.213

National League

Top 20				Bottom 20		
1. Hubie Brooks	MTL	.351		142. Sammy Khalifa	PIT	.168
2. Steve Sax	LA	.339		141. Al Newman	MTL	.170
3. Tim Raines	MTL	.332		140. Clint Hurdle	STL	.173
4. Tony Gwynn	SD	.325		139. Mike Brown	PIT	.189
5. Kal Daniels	CIN	.322		138. Bruce Benedict	ATL	.194
6. Von Hayes	PHI	.319		137. Carmelo Martinez	SD	.198
7. Kevin Bass	HOU	.318		136. Mike Heath	STL	.200
8. Wally Backman	NY	.311		135. Bill Almon	PIT	.203
9. Ken Griffey	ATL	.309		134. Leon Durham	CHI	.206
9. Ray Knight	NY	.309		133. Steve Jeltz	PHI	.207
11. Buddy Bell	CIN	.306		132. Dave Lopes	HOU	.210
12. Sid Bream	PIT	.303		130. Dann Bilardello	MTL	.212
13. Chris Brown	SF	.302		130. Mariano Duncan	LA	.212
14. Mitch Webster	MTL	.302		129. Luis Rivera	MTL	.213
15. Will Clark	SF	.301		128. Tito Landrum	STL	.215
16. Mike Diaz	PIT	.301		127. Bip Roberts	SD	.216
17. John Kruk	SD	.297		126. Greg Brock	LA	.218
18. Claudell Washington	ATL	.295		125. Ozzie Virgil	ATL	.220
19. Mike Schmidt	PHI	.292		124. Jeff Leonard	SF	.220
20. Andy Van Slyke	STL	.290		123. Bobby Bonilla	PIT	.222

Batting Average, Grass Surfaces

American League

Top 20				Bottom 20		
1. Gary Gaetti	MIN	.364		169. Ken Phelps	SEA	.178
2. Wade Boggs	BOS	.352		168. Jackie Gutierrez	BAL	.179
3. Pat Tabler	CLE	.346		167. Harold Reynolds	SEA	.184
4. Ron Hassey	CHI	.343		166. Mickey Tettleton	OAK	.191
5. Don Mattingly	NY	.335		165. Steve Lombardozzi	MIN	.196
6. Johnny Grubb	DET	.328		164. Dave Kingman	OAK	.199
7. Garth Iorg	TOR	.326		163. Rick Dempsey	BAL	.199
8. Jim Rice	BOS	.317		161. Ron Kittle	NY	.200
9. Scott Fletcher	TEX	.312		161. Cliff Johnson	TOR	.200
10. Gary Ward	TEX	.311		160. Gorman Thomas	MIL	.202
11. Julio Franco	CLE	.309		159. Floyd Rayford	BAL	.202
12. Eddie Murray	BAL	.308		158. Bill Schroeder	MIL	.203
13. Robin Yount	MIL	.308		157. Jim Sundberg	KC	.205
14. Damaso Garcia	TOR	.306		156. Jim Dwyer	BAL	.206
15. Tony Bernazard	CLE	.305		155. Julio Cruz	CHI	.207
16. Harold Baines	CHI	.302		154. Ed Romero	BOS	.212
17. Dwight Lowry	DET	.300		153. Pat Sheridan	DET	.212
18. Juan Beniquez	BAL	.298		152. Rob Wilfong	CAL	.213
19. Jesse Barfield	TOR	.298		151. Jim Presley	SEA	.214
20. Mike Easler	NY	.297		150. Carlton Fisk	CHI	.214

National League

Top 20				Bottom 20		
1. Mitch Webster	MTL	.351		145. Dave Martinez	CHI	.113
2. Von Hayes	PHI	.347		144. Vance Law	MTL	.152
3. Denny Walling	HOU	.345		143. Vince Coleman	STL	.158
4. Joe Orsulak	PIT	.336		142. Luis Quinones	SF	.167
5. Tim Raines	MTL	.335		141. Mike Krukow	SF	.169
6. Tony Gwynn	SD	.333		140. Ted Simmons	ATL	.173
7. Hubie Brooks	MTL	.330		139. Bob Melvin	SF	.176
8. Jerry Mumphrey	CHI	.328		138. Terry Pendleton	STL	.185
9. Chris Brown	SF	.325		137. Dane Iorg	SD	.192
10. Harry Spilman	SF	.324		136. Craig Reynolds	HOU	.200
11. Ken Griffey	ATL	.322		135. Tim Wallach	MTL	.204
12. Keith Hernandez	NY	.320		134. Terry Francona	CHI	.205
13. Will Clark	SF	.315		133. Willie McGee	STL	.205
14. Mookie Wilson	NY	.313		132. Tom Herr	STL	.205
15. Bo Diaz	CIN	.310		131. George Foster	NY	.207
16. Len Dykstra	NY	.309		130. Andres Thomas	ATL	.209
17. Steve Sax	LA	.309		129. Gary Redus	PHI	.211
18. Johnny Ray	PIT	.308		127. Kurt Stillwell	CIN	.212
19. Wally Backman	NY	.308		127. Rick Schu	PHI	.212
20. R.J. Reynolds	PIT	.307		126. Jose Gonzalez	LA	.214

Batting Average, Artificial Surfaces

American League

Top 20			Bottom 20		
1. Don Mattingly	NY	.438	169. Floyd Rayford	BAL	.071
2. Kevin Seitzer	KC	.403	168. Mark Davidson	MIN	.128
3. Tom Brookens	DET	.400	167. Cecil Fielder	TOR	.136
4. Wade Boggs	BOS	.380	166. Mickey Brantley	SEA	.149
5. Dan Pasqua	NY	.379	165. Rey Quinones	SEA	.157
6. Cal Ripken	BAL	.369	164. Greg Pryor	KC	.160
7. Mike Davis	OAK	.366	163. Gorman Thomas	MIL	.165
8. Ron Washington	MIN	.362	162. Andre Thornton	CLE	.167
9. Jim Rice	BOS	.358	161. Paul Molitor	MIL	.170
10. Fred Lynn	BAL	.355	160. Charlie Moore	MIL	.178
11. Kirby Puckett	MIN	.352	159. Kelly Gruber	TOR	.181
12. Mel Hall	CLE	.349	158. Darryl Motley	KC	.190
13. Gary Ward	TEX	.347	157. Steve Lyons	CHI	.191
14. Rick Burleson	CAL	.344	156. Al Cowens	SEA	.192
15. Robin Yount	MIL	.343	155. Bobby Grich	CAL	.196
16. Alan Trammell	DET	.337	154. Toby Harrah	TEX	.200
17. Phil Bradley	SEA	.333	153. Pete Incaviglia	TEX	.203
18. Joe Carter	CLE	.327	152. Willie Randolph	NY	.203
19. Mike Easler	NY	.326	151. Bob Boone	CAL	.203
20. Rick Leach	TOR	.325	150. Reggie Jackson	CAL	.203

National League

Top 20			Bottom 20		
1. Tracy Jones	CIN	.395	143. Mike Scott	HOU	.149
2. Steve Sax	LA	.387	142. Omar Moreno	ATL	.169
3. Wally Backman	NY	.346	141. George Wright	MTL	.171
4. Hubie Brooks	MTL	.345	140. Graig Nettles	SD	.178
5. Junior Ortiz	PIT	.342	139. Bob Dernier	CHI	.182
6. John Kruk	SD	.341	138. Max Venable	CIN	.184
7. Andres Thomas	ATL	.340	137. Jose Uribe	SF	.190
8. Tim Raines	MTL	.334	136. Ozzie Virgil	ATL	.191
9. Kevin McReynolds	SD	.333	135. Glenn Hubbard	ATL	.192
10. Dan Gladden	SF	.324	134. Clint Hurdle	STL	.193
11. Kevin Bass	HOU	.316	133. Sal Butera	CIN	.194
12. Tony Gwynn	SD	.315	131. Will Clark	SF	.196
13. Bob Melvin	SF	.315	131. U.L. Washington	PIT	.196
14. Kal Daniels	CIN	.313	130. Sammy Khalifa	PIT	.196
15. Ken Landreaux	LA	.308	129. Jeff Leonard	SF	.200
16. Jose Oquendo	STL	.306	128. Rafael Belliard	PIT	.201
17. Rick Schu	PHI	.303	127. Al Newman	MTL	.203
18. Jose Cruz	HOU	.302	126. Mark Bailey	HOU	.206
19. Tony Pena	PIT	.300	125. Mike Brown	PIT	.207
20. Ozzie Smith	STL	.299	124. Luis Rivera	MTL	.210

Batting Average, Home Games

American League

Top 20			Bottom 20		
1. Kirby Puckett	MIN	.367	169. Gorman Thomas	MIL	.138
2. Johnny Grubb	DET	.366	168. Ed Romero	BOS	.176
3. Wade Boggs	BOS	.357	167. Bob Boone	CAL	.189
4. Pat Tabler	CLE	.348	166. Ron Kittle	NY	.191
5. Scott Bradley	SEA	.347	165. Bill Schroeder	MIL	.194
6. Jim Rice	BOS	.337	164. Darryl Motley	KC	.194
7. Don Mattingly	NY	.334	163. Jim Sundberg	KC	.196
8. Harold Baines	CHI	.331	162. Juan Bonilla	BAL	.197
9. Ron Hassey	CHI	.329	161. Mickey Tettleton	OAK	.198
10. Tony Bernazard	CLE	.329	160. John Shelby	BAL	.199
11. George Bell	TOR	.327	159. Steve Balboni	KC	.203
12. Phil Bradley	SEA	.324	158. Carlton Fisk	CHI	.207
13. George Brett	KC	.322	157. Toby Harrah	TEX	.207
14. Gary Ward	TEX	.321	156. Mark Salas	MIN	.211
15. Tony Fernandez	TOR	.320	155. Dave Kingman	OAK	.212
16. Carney Lansford	OAK	.319	154. Jose Canseco	OAK	.213
17. Lonnie Smith	KC	.317	153. Rich Gedman	BOS	.214
18. Carmen Castillo	CLE	.317	152. Rick Dempsey	BAL	.215
19. Mickey Hatcher	MIN	.314	151. Garth Iorg	TOR	.216
20. Joe Carter	CLE	.312	150. Rick Manning	MIL	.216

National League

Top 20			Bottom 20		
1. Jerry Mumphrey	CHI	.361	143. Herm Winningham	MTL	.153
2. Hubie Brooks	MTL	.350	142. Carmelo Martinez	SD	.179
3. Ken Griffey	ATL	.342	141. Rafael Santana	NY	.188
4. Tony Gwynn	SD	.341	140. Al Newman	MTL	.190
5. Will Clark	SF	.336	139. Andres Thomas	ATL	.200
6. Chris Brown	SF	.333	138. Luis Rivera	MTL	.207
7. Tim Raines	MTL	.326	137. Mike Brown	PIT	.208
8. Len Dykstra	NY	.322	135. Rafael Belliard	PIT	.208
9. Craig Reynolds	HOU	.319	135. George Foster	NY	.208
10. Jeff Stone	PHI	.319	134. Tito Landrum	STL	.209
11. Jeff Leonard	SF	.315	133. Mike Heath	STL	.212
12. Len Matuszek	LA	.315	132. Bill Almon	PIT	.213
13. Kevin Bass	HOU	.314	131. Steve Jeltz	PHI	.217
14. Von Hayes	PHI	.314	130. Howard Johnson	NY	.217
15. Dave Lopes	HOU	.311	129. Kurt Stillwell	CIN	.219
16. Wally Backman	NY	.311	128. Jose Uribe	SF	.219
17. Marvell Wynne	SD	.311	127. Mariano Duncan	LA	.220
18. John Kruk	SD	.311	126. Mike Lavalliere	STL	.220
19. Steve Sax	LA	.310	125. Bob Melvin	SF	.220
20. Keith Hernandez	NY	.310	124. Joe Orsulak	PIT	.224

Batting Average, Road Games

American League

Top 20			Bottom 20		
1. Don Mattingly	NY	.367	169. Floyd Rayford	BAL	.164
2. Wade Boggs	BOS	.356	168. Andre Thornton	CLE	.168
3. Ken Griffey	NY	.352	167. Julio Cruz	CHI	.171
4. Rick Leach	TOR	.328	166. Buck Martinez	TOR	.176
5. Robin Yount	MIL	.327	165. Butch Wynegar	NY	.178
6. Tom Paciorek	TEX	.325	164. Glenn Braggs	MIL	.186
7. Gary Gaetti	MIN	.323	163. Bob Kearney	SEA	.193
8. Juan Beniquez	BAL	.323	162. Rick Dempsey	BAL	.201
9. Julio Franco	CLE	.320	161. Rey Quinones	SEA	.201
10. Ron Hassey	CHI	.316	160. Steve Lombardozzi	MIN	.202
11. Mike Easler	NY	.315	159. Steve Lyons	CHI	.203
12. Dan Pasqua	NY	.314	158. Jamie Quirk	KC	.204
13. Mel Hall	CLE	.314	157. Ken Phelps	SEA	.206
14. Pete O'Brien	TEX	.311	156. Dave Kingman	OAK	.208
15. Jim Rice	BOS	.310	155. Mickey Tettleton	OAK	.210
16. Gary Ward	TEX	.310	154. Reggie Jackson	CAL	.210
17. Brook Jacoby	CLE	.307	153. Darryl Motley	KC	.211
18. Garth Iorg	TOR	.306	152. Pete Incaviglia	TEX	.211
19. Pat Tabler	CLE	.305	151. Andy Allanson	CLE	.212
20. Rick Burleson	CAL	.305	150. Rob Wilfong	CAL	.213

National League

Top 20			Bottom 20		
1. Steve Sax	LA	.352	142. Dann Bilardello	MTL	.168
2. Tim Raines	MTL	.342	141. Graig Nettles	SD	.176
3. Hubie Brooks	MTL	.331	140. Pete Rose	CIN	.181
4. Wally Backman	NY	.329	139. Ozzie Virgil	ATL	.185
5. Denny Walling	HOU	.328	138. Omar Moreno	ATL	.185
6. Tony Gwynn	SD	.317	137. Marvell Wynne	SD	.189
7. Johnny Ray	PIT	.317	136. Vince Coleman	STL	.189
8. Mitch Webster	MTL	.314	135. Craig Reynolds	HOU	.189
9. Ron Cey	CHI	.311	134. Vance Law	MTL	.191
10. Keith Hernandez	NY	.311	133. Mike Aldrete	SF	.192
11. John Kruk	SD	.309	132. Franklin Stubbs	LA	.196
12. Kevin Bass	HOU	.308	131. Bob Dernier	CHI	.198
13. Ray Knight	NY	.306	130. John Russell	PHI	.199
14. Chris Brown	SF	.298	129. Jack Clark	STL	.200
15. Carmelo Martinez	SD	.298	128. Barry Bonds	PIT	.203
16. Von Hayes	PHI	.296	127. Gary Redus	PHI	.206
17. Bill Madlock	LA	.295	126. Al Newman	MTL	.208
18. Billy Sample	ATL	.290	125. Dave Anderson	LA	.210
19. Eric Davis	CIN	.289	124. Tito Landrum	STL	.211
20. Mookie Wilson	NY	.288	123. Randy Kutcher	SF	.213

Slugging Average, Home Games

American League

	Top 20				Bottom 20		
1.	Johnny Grubb	DET	.652	169.	Juan Bonilla	BAL	.230
2.	Ken Phelps	SEA	.626	168.	Bob Boone	CAL	.250
3.	Kirby Puckett	MIN	.584	167.	Julio Cruz	CHI	.265
4.	George Bell	TOR	.567	166.	Dusty Baker	OAK	.268
5.	Don Mattingly	NY	.566	165.	Gary Pettis	CAL	.283
6.	Jim Traber	BAL	.559	164.	Bill Schroeder	MIL	.284
7.	Tim Laudner	MIN	.558	163.	Joel Skinner	NY	.284
8.	George Brett	KC	.556	162.	Andy Allanson	CLE	.286
9.	Jim Presley	SEA	.549	161.	Ed Romero	BOS	.287
10.	Scott Bradley	SEA	.542	160.	Jim Sundberg	KC	.287
11.	Dan Pasqua	NY	.536	159.	Carlton Fisk	CHI	.289
12.	Larry Parrish	TEX	.533	158.	Tom O'Malley	BAL	.290
13.	Cory Snyder	CLE	.532	157.	Rich Gedman	BOS	.299
14.	Kent Hrbek	MIN	.529	156.	Argenis Salazar	KC	.299
15.	Pete Incaviglia	TEX	.527	155.	Ozzie Guillen	CHI	.305
16.	Jesse Barfield	TOR	.526	154.	Garth Iorg	TOR	.305
17.	Jim Rice	BOS	.526	153.	Alan Wiggins	BAL	.306
18.	Randy Bush	MIN	.525	152.	Dave Collins	DET	.311
19.	Joe Carter	CLE	.522	151.	Gorman Thomas	MIL	.312
20.	Greg Walker	CHI	.517	150.	John Shelby	BAL	.312

National League

	Top 20				Bottom 20		
1.	Mike Schmidt	PHI	.597	143.	Al Newman	MTL	.202
2.	Ken Griffey	ATL	.587	142.	Rafael Santana	NY	.220
3.	Bob Horner	ATL	.571	141.	Rafael Belliard	PIT	.236
4.	Len Matuszek	LA	.562	140.	Kurt Stillwell	CIN	.245
5.	Gary Redus	PHI	.553	139.	Herm Winningham	MTL	.247
6.	Glenn Davis	HOU	.547	138.	Mike Brown	PIT	.254
7.	John Russell	PHI	.535	137.	Mariano Duncan	LA	.259
8.	Graig Nettles	SD	.530	136.	Jose Uribe	SF	.265
9.	Buddy Bell	CIN	.525	135.	Bip Roberts	SD	.271
10.	Jerry Mumphrey	CHI	.517	134.	Bill Russell	LA	.273
11.	Kevin McReynolds	SD	.514	133.	Andres Thomas	ATL	.274
12.	Gary Matthews	CHI	.514	132.	Steve Jeltz	PHI	.279
13.	Will Clark	SF	.509	131.	Mike Lavalliere	STL	.280
14.	Jim Morrison	PIT	.506	130.	Ken Landreaux	LA	.291
15.	Leon Durham	CHI	.505	129.	Luis Rivera	MTL	.293
16.	Dave Parker	CIN	.505	128.	Garry Templeton	SD	.294
17.	Hubie Brooks	MTL	.504	127.	Mike Heath	STL	.298
18.	Von Hayes	PHI	.503	126.	Joe Orsulak	PIT	.301
19.	Dale Murphy	ATL	.503	125.	Bruce Benedict	ATL	.301
20.	Eric Davis	CIN	.497	124.	Bobby Bonilla	PIT	.304

Slugging Average, Road Games

American League

	Top 20				Bottom 20		
1.	Jesse Barfield	TOR	.591	169.	Julio Cruz	CHI	.189
2.	Don Mattingly	NY	.580	168.	Alan Wiggins	BAL	.235
3.	Gary Gaetti	MIN	.563	167.	Rey Quinones	SEA	.240
4.	Lance Parrish	DET	.550	166.	Floyd Rayford	BAL	.242
5.	Rich Gedman	BOS	.542	165.	Harold Reynolds	SEA	.249
6.	Jose Canseco	OAK	.528	164.	Steve Lyons	CHI	.252
7.	Alan Trammell	DET	.521	163.	Buck Martinez	TOR	.253
8.	Johnny Grubb	DET	.520	162.	Spike Owen	BOS	.262
9.	Mel Hall	CLE	.517	161.	Andy Allanson	CLE	.274
10.	Dan Pasqua	NY	.514	159.	Bob Kearney	SEA	.275
11.	Steve Balboni	KC	.513	159.	Steve Lombardozzi	MIN	.275
12.	Dwight Evans	BOS	.510	158.	Glenn Braggs	MIL	.279
13.	Joe Carter	CLE	.507	157.	Ed Romero	BOS	.280
14.	George Bell	TOR	.501	156.	John Cangelosi	CHI	.284
15.	Ken Griffey	NY	.500	155.	Andre Thornton	CLE	.285
16.	Ron Kittle	NY	.498	154.	Curtis Wilkerson	TEX	.292
17.	Rickey Henderson	NY	.497	153.	Rob Wilfong	CAL	.294
18.	Don Baylor	BOS	.497	152.	Chris Bando	CLE	.301
19.	Pete O'Brien	TEX	.493	151.	Bobby Bonilla	CHI	.302
20.	Ruben Sierra	TEX	.490	150.	Willie Randolph	NY	.303

National League

	Top 20				Bottom 20		
1.	Ron Cey	CHI	.630	142.	Pete Rose	CIN	.216
2.	Hubie Brooks	MTL	.621	141.	Vince Coleman	STL	.239
3.	Darryl Strawberry	NY	.557	140.	Steve Jeltz	PHI	.244
4.	Eric Davis	CIN	.546	139.	Graig Nettles	SD	.245
5.	Kevin Bass	HOU	.546	138.	Tito Landrum	STL	.246
6.	Candy Maldonado	SF	.538	137.	Glenn Hubbard	ATL	.254
7.	Denny Walling	HOU	.531	136.	Al Newman	MTL	.257
8.	Mike Fitzgerald	MTL	.518	135.	Dann Bilardello	MTL	.262
9.	Mike Schmidt	PHI	.503	134.	Willie McGee	STL	.266
10.	Tim Raines	MTL	.500	133.	Vance Law	MTL	.268
10.	Rick Schu	PHI	.500	132.	Enos Cabell	LA	.271
12.	Kevin McReynolds	SD	.493	131.	Craig Reynolds	HOU	.272
13.	Mike Diaz	PIT	.491	130.	Kurt Stillwell	CIN	.273
14.	Steve Sax	LA	.489	129.	Bob Dernier	CHI	.275
15.	Greg Brock	LA	.481	128.	Dave Anderson	LA	.277
16.	Andre Dawson	MTL	.478	127.	Terry Pendleton	STL	.277
17.	Billy Sample	ATL	.477	126.	Omar Moreno	ATL	.281
18.	Mitch Webster	MTL	.464	125.	Rafael Belliard	PIT	.285
19.	Phil Garner	HOU	.463	123.	Rafael Santana	NY	.286
20.	Jim Morrison	PIT	.459	123.	Ron Roenicke	PHI	.286

Batting Average with Runners On Base

American League

	Top 20				Bottom 20		
1.	Johnny Grubb	DET	.387	170.	Rick Dempsey	BAL	.122
2.	Wade Boggs	BOS	.379	169.	Gorman Thomas	MIL	.151
3.	Rick Leach	TOR	.352	168.	Floyd Rayford	BAL	.161
4.	Gary Ward	TEX	.340	167.	Bill Schroeder	MIL	.176
5.	Jim Rice	BOS	.339	166.	Bobby Meacham	NY	.189
6.	Kirby Puckett	MIN	.333	165.	Butch Wynegar	NY	.193
7.	Don Mattingly	NY	.328	164.	Glenn Braggs	MIL	.198
8.	Tony Fernandez	TOR	.328	163.	Ed Romero	BOS	.198
9.	Pat Tabler	CLE	.325	162.	Jim Dwyer	BAL	.200
10.	Eddie Murray	BAL	.322	161.	Rick Cerone	MIL	.202
11.	Harold Baines	CHI	.322	160.	Harold Reynolds	SEA	.203
12.	Brook Jacoby	CLE	.322	159.	Darryl Motley	KC	.204
13.	Jorge Orta	KC	.320	158.	Tim Hulett	CHI	.207
14.	Wally Joyner	CAL	.320	157.	Steve Lombardozzi	MIN	.211
15.	Tony Phillips	OAK	.318	156.	Tim Laudner	MIN	.220
16.	George Bell	TOR	.317	155.	Don Baylor	BOS	.221
17.	Ron Hassey	CHI	.314	154.	Joel Skinner	NY	.222
18.	Don Slaught	TEX	.313	153.	Dave Kingman	OAK	.223
19.	Jerry Hairston	CHI	.313	152.	Dick Schofield	CAL	.224
19.	Rick Burleson	CAL	.313	151.	Mickey Tettleton	OAK	.225

National League

	Top 20				Bottom 20		
1.	John Kruk	SD	.387	144.	Mark Bailey	HOU	.141
2.	Danny Heep	NY	.379	143.	Clint Hurdle	STL	.169
3.	Chris Brown	SF	.378	142.	Rafael Ramirez	ATL	.177
4.	Pete Rose	CIN	.363	141.	Joe Orsulak	PIT	.189
5.	Len Matuszek	LA	.356	140.	Bob Dernier	CHI	.189
6.	Jose Cruz	HOU	.353	139.	Omar Moreno	ATL	.195
7.	Joel Youngblood	SF	.346	138.	Dickie Thon	HOU	.197
8.	Steve Sax	LA	.339	137.	Mike Brown	PIT	.203
9.	Keith Hernandez	NY	.337	136.	Dann Bilardello	MTL	.205
10.	Tim Raines	MTL	.335	135.	Jack Clark	STL	.206
11.	Chili Davis	SF	.335	134.	Steve Jeitz	PHI	.212
12.	Von Hayes	PHI	.333	133.	Terry Puhl	HOU	.212
13.	Dave Parker	CIN	.329	132.	Vince Coleman	STL	.212
14.	Ray Knight	NY	.329	131.	Dave Concepcion	CIN	.213
15.	Craig Reynolds	HOU	.326	130.	Lee Mazzilli	NY	.214
16.	Mookie Wilson	NY	.326	129.	Phil Garner	HOU	.215
17.	Bobby Bonilla	PIT	.324	128.	Carmelo Martinez	SD	.217
18.	Manny Trillo	CHI	.319	127.	George Foster	NY	.220
19.	Hubie Brooks	MTL	.318	126.	Gary Matthews	CHI	.221
20.	Tony Gwynn	SD	.316	125.	Rafael Santana	NY	.224

Batting Average in Pressure Situations

American League

Top 20				Bottom 20			
1. Wade Boggs	BOS	.433		171. Rey Quinones	SEA	.083	
2. Billy Robidoux	MIL	.423		170. Gorman Thomas	MIL	.100	
3. Ken Griffey	NY	.400		169. Rick Dempsey	BAL	.103	
4. Juan Beniquez	BAL	.393		168. Spike Owen	BOS	.125	
5. Ron Hassey	CHI	.378		167. Russ Morman	CHI	.130	
6. Tony Fernandez	TOR	.363		166. Darrell Porter	TEX	.138	
7. Marty Barrett	BOS	.359		165. Darryl Motley	KC	.143	
7. Kirk Gibson	DET	.359		163. Roy Smalley	MIN	.152	
9. Ernie Whitt	TOR	.353		163. Bill Schroeder	MIL	.152	
10. Don Mattingly	NY	.351		162. Harold Reynolds	SEA	.154	
10. Scott Bradley	SEA	.351		161. Joel Skinner	NY	.161	
12. Buck Martinez	TOR	.350		160. Gary Pettis	CAL	.164	
13. Darrell Evans	DET	.347		159. Mike Davis	OAK	.164	
14. Robin Yount	MIL	.347		158. Jack Howell	CAL	.167	
14. Brook Jacoby	CLE	.347		157. Dave Kingman	OAK	.169	
14. Rickey Henderson	NY	.347		156. Mickey Hatcher	MIN	.170	
14. Brett Butler	CLE	.347		155. Ron Kittle	NY	.175	
18. Ivan Calderon	CHI	.345		153. Mark Salas	MIN	.179	
19. Andy Allanson	CLE	.344		153. Mickey Tettleton	OAK	.179	
19. Tom Paciorek	TEX	.344		148. Reggie Jackson	CAL	.182	
				148. Tim Hulett	CHI	.182	
				148. Alan Wiggins	BAL	.182	

National League

Top 20				Bottom 20			
1. Ken Griffey	ATL	.404		142. Greg Brock	LA	.058	
2. Will Clark	SF	.397		141. Mike Heath	STL	.118	
3. Mike Diaz	PIT	.392		140. Rafael Santana	NY	.127	
4. Tony Perez	CIN	.385		139. Greg Gross	PHI	.143	
5. Steve Sax	LA	.378		138. Bob Melvin	SF	.150	
6. Hubie Brooks	MTL	.375		137. Bobby Bonilla	PIT	.162	
7. Tim Raines	MTL	.374		136. Dan Gladden	SF	.164	
8. Terry Harper	ATL	.370		135. Ted Simmons	ATL	.170	
9. Wally Backman	NY	.364		133. Terry Puhl	HOU	.171	
10. Tony Gwynn	SD	.359		133. Barry Bonds	PIT	.171	
11. Mariano Duncan	LA	.357		131. Wayne Krenchicki	MTL	.176	
12. Ray Knight	NY	.353		131. Tom Herr	STL	.176	
13. Mike Aldrete	SF	.350		130. Nick Esasky	CIN	.178	
14. Gary Carter	NY	.348		129. Jose Uribe	SF	.188	
15. Bo Diaz	CIN	.346		128. U.L. Washington	PIT	.191	
16. Curt Ford	STL	.333		126. Bob Dernier	CHI	.192	
17. Candy Maldonado	SF	.330		126. Eddie Milner	CIN	.192	
17. Andre Dawson	MTL	.330		125. Tim Flannery	SD	.194	
19. Chris Brown	SF	.329		124. Omar Moreno	ATL	.196	
20. Len Dykstra	NY	.328		123. Lee Mazzilli	NY	.196	

Home Run Percentage in Pressure Situations

American League

Top 20			Bottom 20
1. Darrell Evans	DET	11.11	63 players tied with 0.00
2. Don Slaught	TEX	9.30	
3. Jim Presley	SEA	9.20	
4. Dwight Evans	BOS	8.47	
5. Gorman Thomas	MIL	8.00	
6. Ken Phelps	SEA	7.84	
7. Kirk Gibson	DET	7.81	
8. Harold Baines	CHI	7.23	
9. Mickey Tettleton	OAK	7.14	
10. Dan Pasqua	NY	6.82	
10. Jim Dwyer	BAL	6.82	
12. Rickey Henderson	NY	6.67	
12. Jesse Barfield	TOR	6.67	
14. Don Baylor	BOS	6.56	
15. Frank White	KC	6.52	
16. Doug DeCinces	CAL	6.49	
17. Cal Ripken	BAL	6.32	
18. Dave Henderson	BOS	6.25	
19. Kirby Puckett	MIN	6.10	
20. Cliff Johnson	TOR	6.06	

National League

Top 20			Bottom 20
1. Ken Griffey	ATL	8.77	41 players tied with 0.00
2. Dale Murphy	ATL	7.37	
3. Nick Esasky	CIN	6.67	
4. Will Clark	SF	6.41	
5. Candy Maldonado	SF	6.19	
6. Kevin Mitchell	NY	6.12	
7. Leon Durham	CHI	5.81	
8. Howard Johnson	NY	5.66	
8. Carmelo Martinez	SD	5.66	
10. Glenn Davis	HOU	5.56	
11. Mike Schmidt	PHI	5.49	
12. Darryl Strawberry	NY	5.41	
13. Franklin Stubbs	LA	5.26	
14. Jim Morrison	PIT	5.21	
14. Dave Parker	CIN	5.21	
16. Bo Diaz	CIN	5.13	
17. Kevin McReynolds	SD	5.10	
18. Jody Davis	CHI	5.00	
18. Andy Van Slyke	STL	5.00	
18. John Russell	PHI	5.00	

% of Runners Driven in from Scoring Position, Pressure Situations

American League

Top 20				Bottom 20			
1. Greg Walker	CHI	.750		166. Mike Kingery	KC	.000	
2. Cliff Johnson	TOR	.619		166. Ivan Calderon	CHI	.000	
3. Mike Easler	NY	.615		166. Billy Beane	MIN	.000	
4. Darrell Evans	DET	.609		166. Gorman Thomas	MIL	.000	
5. Scott Bradley	SEA	.571		166. Domingo Ramos	SEA	.000	
6. Wade Boggs	BOS	.556		166. Rey Quinones	SEA	.000	
7. Rick Leach	TOR	.533		166. Darryl Motley	KC	.000	
8. Greg Gagne	MIN	.500		165. Rick Dempsey	BAL	.071	
9. Cal Ripken	BAL	.481		164. Bill Schroeder	MIL	.077	
10. Don Mattingly	NY	.464		160. Rick Cerone	MIL	.091	
11. Ozzie Guillen	CHI	.450		160. Rance Mulliniks	TOR	.091	
12. Carmen Castillo	CLE	.444		160. Mike Davis	OAK	.091	
12. Butch Wynegar	NY	.444		160. Alvin Davis	SEA	.091	
12. Kent Hrbek	MIN	.444		157. Wayne Tolleson	NY	.100	
15. Marty Barrett	BOS	.440		157. Jack Howell	CAL	.100	
16. Brook Jacoby	CLE	.438		157. Gary Gaetti	MIN	.100	
16. Gary Ward	TEX	.438		156. Lee Lacy	BAL	.107	
18. Kirk Gibson	DET	.435		154. Harold Reynolds	SEA	.111	
19. Jim Presley	SEA	.429		154. Damaso Garcia	TOR	.111	
19. Al Cowens	SEA	.429		152. Rob Deer	MIL	.118	
19. Jim Traber	BAL	.429		152. Lance Parrish	DET	.118	

National League

Top 20				Bottom 20			
1. Danny Heep	NY	.600		147. Greg Brock	LA	.000	
2. Mookie Wilson	NY	.563		147. Randy Kutcher	SF	.000	
3. Tony Perez	CIN	.556		146. Tim Flannery	SD	.036	
4. Ray Knight	NY	.550		145. Gary Matthews	CHI	.063	
5. Craig Reynolds	HOU	.538		144. Terry Puhl	HOU	.077	
6. Bill Madlock	LA	.500		142. Jerry White	STL	.083	
7. Ron Roenicke	PHI	.474		142. Mark Bailey	HOU	.083	
8. Tito Landrum	STL	.467		141. Barry Bonds	PIT	.087	
9. Candy Maldonado	SF	.463		140. R.J. Reynolds	PIT	.095	
10. Enos Cabell	LA	.455		139. Max Venable	CIN	.100	
11. Darryl Strawberry	NY	.435		138. Tom Herr	STL	.132	
12. John Kruk	SD	.421		137. Manny Trillo	CHI	.133	
13. Billy Hatcher	HOU	.409		136. Dan Gladden	SF	.136	
13. Chili Davis	SF	.409		135. John Russell	PHI	.143	
15. John Morris	STL	.400		134. Juan Samuel	PHI	.150	
15. Bob Horner	ATL	.400		132. Shawon Dunston	CHI	.154	
17. Ron Cey	CHI	.385		132. Luis Aguayo	PHI	.154	
18. Gary Carter	NY	.375		130. Jerry Royster	SD	.158	
18. Jerry Mumphrey	CHI	.375		130. Dave Concepcion	CIN	.158	
20. Garry Templeton	SD	.361		129. Chris Chambliss	ATL	.167	

On Base Average Leading Off the Inning

American League

Top 20				Bottom 20		
1. Ron Hassey	CHI	.500		170. Charlie Moore	MIL	.143
2. Bill Schroeder	MIL	.458		169. Ivan Calderon	CHI	.152
3. Juan Beniquez	BAL	.455		168. Rick Leach	TOR	.203
4. Bobby Bonilla	CHI	.450		167. Billy Beane	MIN	.204
5. Willie Randolph	NY	.438		166. Floyd Rayford	BAL	.215
6. Jerry Willard	OAK	.435		165. Mark Salas	MIN	.218
7. Wade Boggs	BOS	.433		164. Dave Kingman	OAK	.219
8. Phil Bradley	SEA	.426		163. Bob Kearney	SEA	.229
9. Don Mattingly	NY	.421		162. Rob Wilfong	CAL	.235
10. Cal Ripken	BAL	.402		161. Argenis Salazar	KC	.241
11. Dan Pasqua	NY	.400		160. Pat Sheridan	DET	.241
11. Rick Dempsey	BAL	.400		159. Carlton Fisk	CHI	.245
11. Kent Hrbek	MIN	.400		158. Ozzie Guillen	CHI	.246
14. Brian Downing	CAL	.395		157. Tim Hulett	CHI	.248
15. Gary Ward	TEX	.394		155. Damaso Garcia	TOR	.250
16. Pat Tabler	CLE	.391		155. Ruben Sierra	TEX	.250
17. Ben Oglivie	MIL	.391		154. Joel Skinner	NY	.253
18. Julio Franco	CLE	.389		152. Darryl Motley	KC	.255
19. Lee Lacy	BAL	.388		152. Buddy Biancalana	KC	.255
20. Doug DeCinces	CAL	.388		151. Tom O'Malley	BAL	.255

National League

Top 20				Bottom 20		
1. Wallace Johnson	MTL	.457		144. Craig Reynolds	HOU	.159
2. Von Hayes	PHI	.444		143. Candy Maldonado	SF	.193
3. Ron Cey	CHI	.443		142. Al Newman	MTL	.194
4. Ozzie Smith	STL	.440		141. Howard Johnson	NY	.196
5. Dave Lopes	HOU	.439		140. Bip Roberts	SD	.207
6. Carmelo Martinez	SD	.433		139. Mariano Duncan	LA	.221
7. Kal Daniels	CIN	.429		138. Rafael Santana	NY	.228
8. Jerry Mumphrey	CHI	.427		137. Len Matuszek	LA	.233
9. Ken Griffey	ATL	.413		136. Danny Heep	NY	.239
10. Tim Raines	MTL	.404		135. Bob Melvin	SF	.241
11. Tony Gwynn	SD	.403		134. Pete Rose	CIN	.245
12. R.J. Reynolds	PIT	.398		132. John Russell	PHI	.250
13. Wally Backman	NY	.397		132. Graig Nettles	SD	.250
14. Tim Flannery	SD	.396		129. Andres Thomas	ATL	.254
15. Johnny Ray	PIT	.394		129. Bill Almon	PIT	.254
16. Dickie Thon	HOU	.394		129. Ken Oberkfell	ATL	.254
17. Len Dykstra	NY	.392		128. Shawon Dunston	CHI	.254
18. Mike Fitzgerald	MTL	.388		127. U.L. Washington	PIT	.255
19. Tony Pena	PIT	.383		126. Kurt Stillwell	CIN	.256
20. Clint Hurdle	STL	.378		125. Ryne Sandberg	CHI	.257

Batting Average with Runners in Scoring Position

American League

Top 20				Bottom 20		
1. Johnny Grubb	DET	.393		169. Rick Cerone	MIL	.114
2. Larry Parrish	TEX	.393		168. Bill Schroeder	MIL	.123
3. Gary Ward	TEX	.378		167. Glenn Braggs	MIL	.125
4. Rudy Law	KC	.375		166. Rick Dempsey	BAL	.132
5. Eddie Murray	BAL	.366		165. Floyd Rayford	BAL	.137
6. Wade Boggs	BOS	.353		164. Mike Kingery	KC	.146
7. Paul Molitor	MIL	.351		163. Rick Manning	MIL	.151
8. Tony Phillips	OAK	.350		162. Bobby Meacham	NY	.160
9. Jose Canseco	OAK	.345		161. Tim Hulett	CHI	.175
10. Pete O'Brien	TEX	.344		160. Gorman Thomas	MIL	.178
11. Rick Leach	TOR	.343		159. Darryl Motley	KC	.180
12. Tony Fernandez	TOR	.342		158. Jamie Quirk	KC	.184
13. Jim Rice	BOS	.340		157. Ernest Riles	MIL	.190
14. Toby Harrah	TEX	.333		156. Steve Lombardozzi	MIN	.194
14. Charlie Moore	MIL	.333		155. Ruppert Jones	CAL	.194
16. Cecil Cooper	MIL	.329		154. Ken Griffey	NY	.196
17. Argenis Salazar	KC	.328		153. Spike Owen	BOS	.198
18. Gary Pettis	CAL	.328		149. Jim Gantner	MIL	.200
19. Julio Cruz	CHI	.320		149. Ron Kittle	NY	.200
20. Garth Iorg	TOR	.319		149. Lee Lacy	BAL	.200
				149. Ed Romero	BOS	.200

National League

Top 20				Bottom 20		
1. Danny Heep	NY	.404		144. Mark Bailey	HOU	.122
2. Jose Cruz	HOU	.389		143. Rafael Ramirez	ATL	.135
3. Joel Youngblood	SF	.389		142. Max Venable	CIN	.143
4. Chris Brown	SF	.370		141. Mike Scioscia	LA	.145
5. Mookie Wilson	NY	.368		140. Clint Hurdle	STL	.152
6. Howard Johnson	NY	.362		139. Carmelo Martinez	SD	.158
7. Craig Reynolds	HOU	.355		138. Nick Esasky	CIN	.167
8. Ray Knight	NY	.354		137. Jack Clark	STL	.169
9. Len Dykstra	NY	.350		136. Bob Melvin	SF	.173
10. Pete Rose	CIN	.348		135. Franklin Stubbs	LA	.180
11. Dave Parker	CIN	.344		134. Ken Griffey	ATL	.182
12. Steve Sax	LA	.342		133. Mike Brown	PIT	.188
13. Von Hayes	PHI	.339		132. Rick Schu	PHI	.189
14. Mike Fitzgerald	MTL	.333		131. Rafael Santana	NY	.189
14. Manny Trillo	CHI	.333		130. Terry Puhl	HOU	.190
16. Tim Raines	MTL	.331		129. Dann Bilardello	MTL	.192
17. Tony Gwynn	SD	.327		128. Darren Daulton	PHI	.194
18. Bill Madlock	LA	.319		127. Will Clark	SF	.196
19. John Kruk	SD	.315		126. Vince Coleman	STL	.200
20. Mike Schmidt	PHI	.315		124. Bob Dernier	CHI	.203
				124. Tom Foley	MTL	.203

Batting Average with Runners in Scoring Position and Two Outs

American League

Top 20				Bottom 20		
1. Tony Fernandez	TOR	.404		173. Rick Cerone	MIL	.045
2. Rudy Law	KC	.400		172. Rick Dempsey	BAL	.071
2. Paul Molitor	MIL	.400		171. Jamie Quirk	KC	.077
4. Larry Parrish	TEX	.392		170. Gorman Thomas	MIL	.093
5. Ozzie Guillen	CHI	.381		169. Bill Schroeder	MIL	.107
6. Tony Phillips	OAK	.366		168. Buddy Biancalana	KC	.120
7. Marc Sullivan	BOS	.364		167. Cal Ripken	BAL	.121
7. Jose Canseco	OAK	.364		166. Floyd Rayford	BAL	.130
7. Johnny Grubb	DET	.364		165. Tim Hulett	CHI	.136
10. Garth Iorg	TOR	.362		164. Mike Kingery	KC	.143
11. George Brett	KC	.361		163. Rickey Henderson	NY	.145
12. Wade Boggs	BOS	.361		162. Lloyd Moseby	TOR	.145
13. Rob Wilfong	CAL	.357		160. Reggie Jackson	CAL	.151
14. Dale Sveum	MIL	.351		160. Rob Deer	MIL	.151
15. Pete O'Brien	TEX	.349		159. Glenn Braggs	MIL	.154
16. Cliff Johnson	TOR	.348		158. Harold Reynolds	SEA	.155
17. Kirby Puckett	MIN	.345		157. Rey Quinones	SEA	.156
18. Marty Barrett	BOS	.343		156. Jim Sundberg	KC	.160
19. Don Slaught	TEX	.343		155. Ed Romero	BOS	.163
20. George Bell	TOR	.337		154. Mike Pagliarulo	NY	.163

National League

Top 20				Bottom 20		
1. John Kruk	SD	.484		145. Carmelo Martinez	SD	.037
2. Pete Rose	CIN	.444		144. Dave Anderson	LA	.080
3. Dave Parker	CIN	.419		143. Mike Scioscia	LA	.091
4. Jose Cruz	HOU	.400		142. Max Venable	CIN	.095
5. Ray Knight	NY	.396		141. Sammy Khalifa	PIT	.100
6. Danny Heep	NY	.370		140. Rafael Ramirez	ATL	.103
6. Craig Reynolds	HOU	.370		139. Dann Bilardello	MTL	.115
8. Chris Brown	SF	.364		138. Bob Melvin	SF	.119
9. Mike Schmidt	PHI	.358		136. Enos Cabell	LA	.125
10. Terry Kennedy	SD	.352		136. Marvell Wynne	SD	.125
11. Terry Harper	ATL	.351		134. Clint Hurdle	STL	.130
12. Howard Johnson	NY	.348		134. Herm Winningham	MTL	.130
12. Alex Trevino	LA	.348		132. Jack Clark	STL	.133
14. Von Hayes	PHI	.346		132. Tito Landrum	STL	.133
14. John Russell	PHI	.340		131. Terry Puhl	HOU	.136
16. Wally Backman	NY	.333		130. Bill Russell	LA	.143
16. Len Dykstra	NY	.333		129. Nick Esasky	CIN	.146
16. Dave Lopes	HOU	.333		128. Franklin Stubbs	LA	.153
19. Andres Galarraga	MTL	.327		127. Barry Bonds	PIT	.154
20. Kevin Mitchell	NY	.325		126. Vince Coleman	STL	.159

Batting Average with Runners On Base and Two Outs

American League

Top 20				Bottom 20		
1. Johnny Grubb	DET	.389	169.	Rick Dempsey	BAL	.079
2. Ozzie Guillen	CHI	.375	168.	Gorman Thomas	MIL	.089
3. Wade Boggs	BOS	.370	167.	Glenn Braggs	MIL	.114
4. Paul Molitor	MIL	.364	166.	Harold Reynolds	SEA	.133
5. Don Mattingly	NY	.358	165.	Bill Schroeder	MIL	.149
6. Phil Bradley	SEA	.356	164.	Ed Romero	BOS	.151
6. Jose Canseco	OAK	.350	163.	Rob Deer	MIL	.158
7. Wally Joyner	CAL	.350	162.	Dick Schofield	CAL	.159
9. Carmen Castillo	CLE	.349	161.	Tim Hulett	CHI	.160
10. Brook Jacoby	CLE	.346	160.	Buddy Biancalana	KC	.162
11. Kirby Puckett	MIN	.344	159.	Don Baylor	BOS	.165
12. Tony Fernandez	TOR	.343	158.	Rick Manning	MIL	.171
13. Tony Armas	BOS	.342	157.	Rick Cerone	MIL	.176
14. Lou Whitaker	DET	.341	156.	Jamie Quirk	KC	.178
15. George Bell	TOR	.326	155.	Jerry Hairston	CHI	.179
16. Larry Parrish	TEX	.325	154.	Lee Lacy	BAL	.183
17. Garth Iorg	TOR	.324	153.	Ken Phelps	SEA	.184
18. Jim Rice	BOS	.321	152.	Carlton Fisk	CHI	.186
19. Gary Ward	TEX	.319	149.	Mike Pagliarulo	NY	.188
20. Eddie Murray	BAL	.319	149.	Reggie Jackson	CAL	.188
			149.	Russ Morman	CHI	.188

National League

Top 20				Bottom 20		
1. John Kruk	SD	.465	142.	Sammy Khalifa	PIT	.103
2. Dave Parker	CIN	.412	141.	Clint Hurdle	STL	.111
3. Pete Rose	CIN	.410	140.	Ken Landreaux	LA	.121
4. Ray Knight	NY	.400	139.	Dann Bilardello	MTL	.143
5. Wally Backman	NY	.392	138.	Herm Winningham	MTL	.156
6. Alex Trevino	LA	.355	137.	Max Venable	CIN	.161
7. Craig Reynolds	HOU	.354	135.	Tito Landrum	STL	.163
8. Bip Roberts	SD	.350	135.	Tom Foley	MTL	.163
9. Chris Brown	SF	.348	134.	Franklin Stubbs	LA	.165
10. Danny Heep	NY	.341	133.	Rafael Ramirez	ATL	.167
11. Jose Cruz	HOU	.338	131.	Mike Diaz	PIT	.174
12. Mike Schmidt	PHI	.333	131.	Jack Clark	STL	.174
12. Andy Van Slyke	STL	.333	130.	Barry Bonds	PIT	.177
14. Andres Galarraga	MTL	.324	127.	Carmelo Martinez	SD	.182
15. Eddie Milner	CIN	.322	127.	Joe Orsulak	PIT	.182
16. Von Hayes	PHI	.322	127.	Wayne Krenchicki	MTL	.182
17. Denny Walling	HOU	.321	126.	Tim Flannery	SD	.183
18. Chili Davis	SF	.317	125.	Jody Davis	CHI	.186
19. Andres Thomas	ATL	.316	122.	Dickie Thon	HOU	.188
20. John Russell	PHI	.315	122.	Graig Nettles	SD	.188
			122.	Luis Rivera	MTL	.188

% of Runners Driven in from Scoring Position

American League

Top 20				Bottom 20		
1. Johnny Grubb	DET	.419	169.	Rick Dempsey	BAL	.118
2. Larry Parrish	TEX	.415	167.	Floyd Rayford	BAL	.143
3. Gary Ward	TEX	.402	167.	Bill Schroeder	MIL	.143
4. Greg Walker	CHI	.387	166.	Tim Hulett	CHI	.148
5. Rick Leach	TOR	.384	165.	Bobby Meacham	NY	.167
6. Eddie Murray	BAL	.381	164.	Gorman Thomas	MIL	.168
7. Don Mattingly	NY	.380	163.	Darryl Motley	KC	.172
8. Charlie Moore	MIL	.379	162.	Rey Quinones	SEA	.173
9. Tony Phillips	OAK	.377	161.	Steve Lombardozzi	MIN	.183
10. Pete O'Brien	TEX	.375	160.	Pat Sheridan	DET	.191
11. Mike Easler	NY	.371	159.	Ernest Riles	MIL	.194
12. Ben Oglivie	MIL	.369	158.	Donnie Hill	OAK	.206
13. Toby Harrah	TEX	.369	157.	Buck Martinez	TOR	.208
14. Wade Boggs	BOS	.368	156.	Reggie Jackson	CAL	.209
15. Rudy Law	KC	.366	155.	Glenn Braggs	MIL	.210
16. Joel Skinner	NY	.365	154.	Dave Collins	DET	.212
17. George Brett	KC	.364	153.	Mike Davis	OAK	.218
18. Paul Molitor	MIL	.363	152.	Tim Laudner	MIN	.219
19. Larry Sheets	BAL	.358	151.	Harold Reynolds	SEA	.220
20. Gary Pettis	CAL	.356	150.	Willie Wilson	KC	.221

National League

Top 20				Bottom 20		
1. Ray Knight	NY	.403	143.	Randy Kutcher	SF	.157
2. Mike Fitzgerald	MTL	.400	142.	Rafael Ramirez	ATL	.163
3. Howard Johnson	NY	.397	140.	Jack Clark	STL	.167
4. Danny Heep	NY	.391	140.	Carmelo Martinez	SD	.167
5. Bill Madlock	LA	.385	139.	Bip Roberts	SD	.170
6. Dave Parker	CIN	.382	138.	Terry Puhl	HOU	.173
7. Chris Brown	SF	.376	137.	Clint Hurdle	STL	.176
8. Tony Perez	CIN	.366	136.	Bob Dernier	CHI	.178
9. Jose Cruz	HOU	.366	135.	Mariano Duncan	LA	.186
10. Craig Reynolds	HOU	.363	134.	Vince Coleman	STL	.192
11. Pete Rose	CIN	.362	133.	Dann Bilardello	MTL	.200
12. Candy Maldonado	SF	.355	132.	Gary Matthews	CHI	.206
13. Ted Simmons	ATL	.352	131.	Joe Orsulak	PIT	.207
14. John Kruk	SD	.349	130.	Mike Scioscia	LA	.211
15. Ozzie Smith	STL	.349	128.	Rick Schu	PHI	.215
16. Von Hayes	PHI	.348	128.	Franklin Stubbs	LA	.215
17. Mookie Wilson	NY	.348	126.	Nick Esasky	CIN	.216
18. Len Dykstra	NY	.343	126.	Max Venable	CIN	.216
19. Steve Sax	LA	.343	125.	Tony Pena	PIT	.216
20. Mike Schmidt	PHI	.342	124.	Omar Moreno	ATL	.217

% of Runners Driven in from Third with Less than Two Out

American League

Top 20				Bottom 20		
1. Ben Oglivie	MIL	.913	169.	Steve Lombardozzi	MIN	.133
2. Argenis Salazar	KC	.900	168.	Bill Schroeder	MIL	.200
3. Johnny Grubb	DET	.857	167.	Bob Kearney	SEA	.231
4. Ron Hassey	CHI	.846	166.	Bobby Meacham	NY	.300
4. Toby Harrah	TEX	.846	165.	Dusty Baker	OAK	.308
6. Larry Sheets	BAL	.833	164.	Rick Dempsey	BAL	.313
7. Steve Buechele	TEX	.824	162.	Tim Hulett	CHI	.333
8. Billy Robidoux	MIL	.818	162.	Rick Burleson	CAL	.333
8. Tom Brookens	DET	.818	161.	Pat Sheridan	DET	.364
10. Jim Sundberg	KC	.800	160.	Dave Kingman	OAK	.395
11. Wayne Tolleson	NY	.786	156.	Buck Martinez	TOR	.400
12. Rick Cerone	MIL	.769	156.	Ivan Calderon	CHI	.400
13. Rick Leach	TOR	.765	156.	Tim Laudner	MIN	.400
14. Tony Bernazard	CLE	.760	156.	Billy Beane	MIN	.400
15. Gary Pettis	CAL	.758	155.	Joel Skinner	NY	.412
16. Fred Lynn	BAL	.750	153.	Ron Kittle	NY	.414
17. Scott Fletcher	TEX	.741	153.	Ernest Riles	MIL	.414
18. Wade Boggs	BOS	.739	151.	Glenn Braggs	MIL	.417
18. Don Mattingly	NY	.739	151.	Mark Salas	MIN	.417
20. Eddie Murray	BAL	.733	150.	Gorman Thomas	MIL	.421

National League

Top 20				Bottom 20		
1. Bill Madlock	LA	.880	143.	Andres Galarraga	MTL	.267
2. Sid Bream	PIT	.846	140.	Alex Trevino	LA	.333
3. Milt Thompson	PHI	.800	140.	Kevin Mitchell	NY	.333
4. Tony Perez	CIN	.789	140.	Gary Redus	PHI	.333
5. Mike Fitzgerald	MTL	.778	139.	Eric Davis	CIN	.357
5. Jeff Hamilton	LA	.778	138.	Kurt Stillwell	CIN	.375
5. Bill Russell	LA	.778	135.	Dale Murphy	ATL	.400
8. Terry Pendleton	STL	.767	135.	Fernando Valenzuela	LA	.400
9. Ozzie Smith	STL	.759	135.	Jack Clark	STL	.400
10. Graig Nettles	SD	.750	134.	Andres Thomas	ATL	.412
10. Dan Gladden	SF	.750	132.	Bruce Bochy	SD	.417
10. Tito Landrum	STL	.750	132.	Jeff Stone	PHI	.417
13. Mike Brown	PIT	.733	130.	Carmelo Martinez	SD	.429
14. Jose Oquendo	STL	.727	130.	Bob Melvin	SF	.429
14. Mike Aldrete	SF	.727	128.	Glenn Hubbard	ATL	.435
16. Bob Horner	ATL	.727	128.	Jose Uribe	SF	.435
17. Candy Maldonado	SF	.700	124.	Will Clark	SF	.444
17. Keith Moreland	CHI	.700	124.	Bob Dernier	CHI	.444
19. Johnny Ray	PIT	.690	124.	Bob Forsch	STL	.444
20. Enos Cabell	LA	.688	124.	Tony Pena	PIT	.444
20. Ken Landreaux	LA	.688				
20. Glenn Wilson	PHI	.688				

Opponents' Batting Average

American League

Top 20				Bottom 20		
1. Jose DeLeon	CHI	.179		128. Lee Guetterman	SEA	.347
2. Tom Henke	TOR	.191		127. John Butcher	CLE	.334
3. Mark Eichhorn	TOR	.192		126. Milt Wilcox	SEA	.327
4. Roger Clemens	BOS	.195		125. Bob Stanley	BOS	.322
5. Mark Clear	MIL	.201		124. Bill Swift	SEA	.319
6. Mitch Williams	TEX	.202		123. Allan Anderson	MIN	.316
7. John Candelaria	CAL	.206		122. Mike Brown	SEA	.313
8. Eric Plunk	OAK	.214		121. Dennis Lamp	TOR	.309
9. Eric King	DET	.216		120. Dave LaPoint	DET	.307
10. Dennis Rasmussen	NY	.217		119. Rick Langford	OAK	.300
11. Moose Haas	OAK	.218		118. Juan Nieves	MIL	.299
12. Mike Witt	CAL	.221		117. Dave Stieb	TOR	.297
13. Charlie Hough	TEX	.221		116. Ron Romanick	CAL	.297
14. Ed Correa	TEX	.223		115. Bryan Clutterbuck	MIL	.296
15. Bobby Witt	TEX	.223		114. Mike Smithson	MIN	.294
16. Joe Cowley	CHI	.223		113. Mickey Mahler	TOR	.293
17. Bud Black	KC	.225		112. Jose Guzman	TEX	.293
18. Dave Righetti	NY	.226		111. Jim Slaton	DET	.292
19. Steve Farr	KC	.228		110. Dan Quisenberry	KC	.291
20. Donnie Moore	CAL	.228		109. Al Nipper	BOS	.290

National League

Top 20				Bottom 20		
1. Mike Scott	HOU	.186		116. Mark Thurmond	SD	.325
2. Nolan Ryan	HOU	.188		115. Jerry Reuss	LA	.313
3. Floyd Youmans	MTL	.189		114. Jamie Moyer	CHI	.311
4. Mark Davis	SF	.212		113. Chris Welsh	CIN	.301
5. Charlie Kerfeld	HOU	.213		112. Rick Mahler	ATL	.301
6. Dwight Gooden	NY	.215		111. Scott Terry	CIN	.300
7. Lee Smith	CHI	.215		110. Steve Carlton	SF	.299
8. Sid Fernandez	NY	.216		109. Steve Trout	CHI	.298
9. Lance McCullers	SD	.216		108. Larry Andersen	HOU	.295
10. Jesse Orosco	NY	.217		107. Charles Hudson	PHI	.291
11. Ricky Horton	STL	.218		106. Ed Vande Berg	LA	.290
12. Aurelio Lopez	HOU	.221		105. Joe Johnson	ATL	.289
13. Andy McGaffigan	MTL	.223		104. Guy Hoffman	CHI	.288
14. Mike Krukow	SF	.223		103. Doyle Alexander	ATL	.287
15. Cecilio Guante	PIT	.225		102. Ed Whitson	SD	.287
16. Eric Show	SD	.225		101. Ray Burris	STL	.287
17. Fernando Valenzuela	LA	.226		100. Mike Maddux	PHI	.286
18. Rick Rhoden	PIT	.228		99. Dennis Eckersley	CHI	.285
19. Roger McDowell	NY	.228		98. Joe Hesketh	MTL	.283
20. Todd Worrell	STL	.229		97. Doug Sisk	NY	.282

Opponents' Slugging Average

American League

Top 20				Bottom 20		
1. Mark Clear	MIL	.280		128. Milt Wilcox	SEA	.553
2. Jose DeLeon	CHI	.285		127. Mike Brown	SEA	.540
3. Tom Henke	TOR	.286		126. Rick Langford	OAK	.526
4. Mark Eichhorn	TOR	.288		125. John Butcher	CLE	.503
5. Dave Righetti	NY	.296		124. Allan Anderson	MIN	.501
6. Roger Clemens	BOS	.306		123. Lee Guetterman	SEA	.489
7. John Candelaria	CAL	.306		122. Al Nipper	BOS	.480
8. Moose Haas	OAK	.316		121. Bob James	CHI	.478
9. Ed Correa	TEX	.324		120. Dave Stieb	TOR	.476
10. Mark Gubicza	KC	.325		119. Pete Ladd	SEA	.476
11. Eric King	DET	.329		118. Dave LaPoint	DET	.473
12. Mitch Williams	TEX	.331		117. Doyle Alexander	TOR	.468
13. Ernie Camacho	CLE	.332		116. Jim Slaton	DET	.467
14. Mike Witt	CAL	.335		115. Bill Wegman	MIL	.463
15. Eric Plunk	OAK	.341		114. Mike Smithson	MIN	.462
16. Dan Plesac	MIL	.341		113. Mark Huismann	SEA	.462
17. Kirk McCaskill	CAL	.341		112. Bob Stanley	BOS	.462
18. Dan Quisenberry	KC	.348		111. Scott McGregor	BAL	.457
19. Joe Johnson	TOR	.349		110. Ken Schrom	CLE	.455
20. Bill Mooneyham	OAK	.352		109. Ron Romanick	CAL	.450

National League

Top 20				Bottom 20		
1. Mike Scott	HOU	.291		116. Jerry Reuss	LA	.498
2. Charlie Kerfeld	HOU	.291		115. Ray Burris	STL	.483
3. Floyd Youmans	MTL	.295		114. Mario Soto	CIN	.480
4. Roger McDowell	NY	.296		113. Steve Carlton	SF	.474
5. Kent Tekulve	PHI	.300		112. Joe Hesketh	MTL	.471
6. Pat Clements	PIT	.303		111. LaMarr Hoyt	SD	.467
7. Jesse Orosco	NY	.305		110. Dennis Eckersley	CHI	.455
8. Mark Davis	SF	.310		109. Bob Kipper	PIT	.455
9. Nolan Ryan	HOU	.314		108. Scott Terry	CIN	.455
10. Bob McClure	MTL	.316		107. Mark Thurmond	SD	.454
11. Lee Smith	CHI	.318		106. Tom Niedenfuer	LA	.453
12. Dwight Gooden	NY	.321		105. Jamie Moyer	CHI	.451
13. Doug Sisk	NY	.322		104. Charles Hudson	PHI	.450
14. Kelly Downs	SF	.323		103. Tim Conroy	STL	.446
15. Sid Fernandez	NY	.324		102. Larry McWilliams	PIT	.444
16. Fernando Valenzuela	LA	.325		101. Dave LaPoint	SD	.440
17. Andy McGaffigan	MTL	.325		100. Rick Mahler	ATL	.439
18. Aurelio Lopez	HOU	.325		99. Ed Whitson	SD	.439
19. Eric Show	SD	.329		98. Ed Vande Berg	LA	.427
20. Bob Ojeda	NY	.330		97. Rick Aguilera	NY	.425

Opponents' Home Run Percentage

American League

Top 20				Bottom 20		
1. Ernie Camacho	CLE	0.45		128. Rick Langford	OAK	5.65
2. Dan Quisenberry	KC	0.63		127. Mark Huismann	SEA	5.01
3. Joe Johnson	TOR	0.90		126. Bryan Oelkers	CLE	4.87
4. Dave Righetti	NY	1.03		125. Milt Wilcox	SEA	4.87
5. Bill Mooneyham	OAK	1.05		124. Mike Brown	SEA	4.81
6. Bill Swift	SEA	1.08		123. Bert Blyleven	MIN	4.77
7. Mark Gubicza	KC	1.20		122. John Cerutti	TOR	4.47
8. John Candelaria	CAL	1.21		121. Scott McGregor	BAL	4.38
9. Mickey Mahler	TOR	1.22		120. Dickie Noles	CLE	4.33
10. Mark Eichhorn	TOR	1.46		119. Ken Schrom	CLE	4.24
11. Dan Plesac	MIL	1.48		118. Ken Dixon	BAL	4.24
12. Moose Haas	OAK	1.50		117. Chris Codiroli	OAK	4.12
13. Mark Clear	MIL	1.52		116. Bill Wegman	MIL	4.12
14. Bob Tewksbury	NY	1.57		115. Doyle Alexander	TOR	4.09
15. Gene Nelson	CHI	1.61		114. Jeff Sellers	BOS	4.08
16. Dale Mohorcic	TEX	1.62		113. Jack Morris	DET	4.00
17. Dennis Lamp	TOR	1.66		112. Dave LaPoint	DET	3.97
18. Tom Henke	TOR	1.82		111. Joaquin Andujar	OAK	3.95
19. Danny Jackson	KC	1.88		110. Don Sutton	CAL	3.90
20. Tom Candiotti	CLE	1.89		109. Frank Viola	MIN	3.86

National League

Top 20				Bottom 20		
1. Doug Sisk	NY	0.00		116. LaMarr Hoyt	SD	4.39
2. Pat Clements	PIT	0.47		115. Jerry Reuss	LA	4.23
3. Kent Tekulve	PHI	0.48		114. Steve Carlton	SF	4.11
4. Larry Andersen	HOU	0.71		113. Ray Burris	STL	4.05
5. Roger McDowell	NY	0.85		112. Matt Keough	HOU	3.81
6. Bob McClure	MTL	0.88		111. Cecilio Guante	PIT	3.81
7. Steve Trout	CHI	0.97		110. Bob Kipper	PIT	3.75
8. Gene Garber	ATL	1.03		109. Mario Soto	CIN	3.71
9. Zane Smith	ATL	1.05		108. Frank DiPino	CHI	3.65
10. Bruce Ruffin	PHI	1.09		107. Scott Terry	CIN	3.64
11. Rick Honeycutt	LA	1.37		106. Jeff Reardon	MTL	3.63
12. Tom Hume	PHI	1.42		105. Tom Niedenfuer	LA	3.58
13. Orel Hershiser	LA	1.48		104. Charles Hudson	PHI	3.53
14. Charlie Kerfeld	HOU	1.50		103. Steve Bedrosian	PHI	3.52
15. Juan Berenguer	SF	1.51		102. Joe Hesketh	MTL	3.38
16. Kelly Downs	SF	1.51		101. Tim Conroy	STL	3.38
17. Bob Welch	LA	1.55		100. Larry McWilliams	PIT	3.33
18. Greg Minton	SF	1.59		99. Vida Blue	SF	3.32
19. Chris Welsh	CIN	1.66		98. Dave LaPoint	SD	3.29
20. Jay Tibbs	MTL	1.70		97. Scott Sanderson	CHI	3.25

Opponents' Extra Base Hits per 100 At Bats

American League

Top 20				Bottom 20		
1. Dan Quisenberry	KC	3.80		128. Pete Ladd	SEA	13.11
2. Mark Clear	MIL	4.17		127. Bob James	CHI	12.72
3. Joe Johnson	TOR	4.48		126. Milt Wilcox	SEA	11.95
4. Dave Righetti	NY	4.88		125. Mike Brown	SEA	11.68
5. Ernie Camacho	CLE	4.93		124. Allan Anderson	MIN	11.64
6. Jose DeLeon	CHI	5.11		123. Doyle Alexander	TOR	11.14
7. Tommy John	NY	5.66		122. Al Nipper	BOS	10.75
8. Bill Mooneyham	OAK	5.77		121. Rick Langford	OAK	10.43
9. Tom Henke	TOR	5.78		120. Jim Slaton	DET	10.34
10. Dan Plesac	MIL	5.93		119. Mike Smithson	MIN	9.92
11. Dennis Lamp	TOR	5.98		118. Dan Petry	DET	9.87
12. Ed Correa	TEX	6.00		117. Dave Stieb	TOR	9.81
13. Eric Plunk	OAK	6.12		116. John Butcher	CLE	9.74
14. Dale Mohorcic	TEX	6.17		115. Mark Langston	SEA	9.71
15. Mark Eichhorn	TOR	6.20		114. Ken Schrom	CLE	9.60
16. Danny Jackson	KC	6.21		113. Bert Blyleven	MIN	9.53
17. Roger Clemens	BOS	6.22		112. Bill Wegman	MIL	9.52
18. Dickie Noles	CLE	6.25		111. Mark Huismann	SEA	9.50
19. Mark Gubicza	KC	6.33		110. Chris Codiroli	OAK	9.34
20. John Candelaria	CAL	6.36		109. Scott McGregor	BAL	9.26

National League

Top 20				Bottom 20		
1. Doug Sisk	NY	4.03		116. Ray Burris	STL	11.53
2. Charlie Kerfeld	HOU	4.20		115. Mario Soto	CIN	11.39
3. Pat Clements	PIT	4.27		114. Dennis Eckersley	CHI	10.84
4. Paul Assenmacher	ATL	4.35		113. Joe Hesketh	MTL	10.77
5. Kent Tekulve	PHI	4.36		112. Larry McWilliams	PIT	10.42
6. Roger McDowell	NY	4.48		111. Bob Kipper	PIT	10.15
7. Jesse Orosco	NY	4.75		110. LaMarr Hoyt	SD	9.76
8. John Franco	CIN	4.85		109. Cecilio Guante	PIT	9.69
9. Gene Garber	ATL	5.14		108. Tim Conroy	STL	9.68
10. Bob McClure	MTL	5.26		107. Rick Aguilera	NY	9.62
11. Ken Howell	LA	5.28		106. Dave LaPoint	SD	9.47
12. Jeff Robinson	SF	5.33		105. Tom Niedenfuer	LA	9.45
13. Kelly Downs	SF	5.44		104. Scott Sanderson	CHI	9.27
14. Mike LaCoss	SF	5.62		103. Jerry Reuss	LA	9.12
15. Jeff Dedmon	ATL	5.65		102. Steve Carlton	SF	9.09
16. Bob Ojeda	NY	5.72		101. Greg Mathews	STL	8.94
17. Mark Davis	SF	5.72		100. Ed Whitson	SD	8.78
18. Dave Gumpert	CHI	5.78		99. Shane Rawley	PHI	8.78
19. Eric Show	SD	5.79		98. Craig McMurtry	ATL	8.74
20. Aurelio Lopez	HOU	5.88		97. Kevin Gross	PHI	8.56

Opponents' Batting Average, Left-Handed Batters

American League

Top 20				Bottom 20		
1. Calvin Schiraldi	BOS	.170		129. Steve Crawford	BOS	.394
2. Brad Havens	BAL	.172		128. Ron Davis	MIN	.390
3. Jose DeLeon	CHI	.184		127. Bill Swift	SEA	.384
4. Dennis Rasmussen	NY	.184		126. Bryan Clutterbuck	MIL	.379
5. Mark Langston	SEA	.184		125. Milt Wilcox	SEA	.374
6. Mark Clear	MIL	.189		124. Dennis Lamp	TOR	.349
7. Mitch Williams	TEX	.203		123. John Butcher	CLE	.340
8. Bob Shirley	NY	.204		122. Jim Acker	TOR	.340
9. Floyd Bannister	CHI	.204		121. Bob Stanley	BOS	.338
10. Charlie Hough	TEX	.204		120. Allan Anderson	MIN	.337
11. Willie Hernandez	DET	.206		119. Rick Langford	OAK	.337
12. Matt Young	SEA	.209		118. Mike Brown	SEA	.336
13. Roger Clemens	BOS	.210		117. Lee Guetterman	SEA	.333
14. Donnie Moore	CAL	.212		116. Jay Howell	OAK	.330
15. Mike Witt	CAL	.215		115. Dave Stieb	TOR	.329
16. Mark Portugal	MIN	.218		114. Scott Nielsen	NY	.324
17. Bud Black	KC	.219		113. Juan Nieves	MIL	.318
18. Curt Young	OAK	.219		112. Frank Tanana	DET	.317
19. Tom Henke	TOR	.220		111. Brian Fisher	NY	.316
20. Steve Farr	KC	.222		110. Mike Smithson	MIN	.315

National League

Top 20				Bottom 20		
1. Mark Davis	SF	.131		117. Steve Trout	CHI	.356
2. Bruce Ruffin	PHI	.138		116. Dave Gumpert	CHI	.354
3. Bob Ojeda	NY	.150		115. Scott Terry	CIN	.343
4. Gene Walter	SD	.151		114. Rick Mahler	ATL	.335
5. Dave Smith	HOU	.167		112. Carl Willis	CIN	.333
6. Frank DiPino	CHI	.172		112. Ed Wojna	SD	.333
7. Aurelio Lopez	HOU	.183		111. Andy Hawkins	SD	.323
8. Bob McClure	MTL	.184		110. Bruce Berenyi	NY	.319
9. Nolan Ryan	HOU	.184		109. John Denny	CIN	.318
10. Cecilio Guante	PIT	.185		108. Craig McMurtry	ATL	.313
11. Don Robinson	PIT	.186		107. Alejandro Pena	LA	.310
12. Jesse Orosco	NY	.187		106. Rick Reuschel	PIT	.307
13. Floyd Youmans	MTL	.188		105. Joe Johnson	ATL	.306
14. John Tudor	STL	.189		104. Larry Andersen	HOU	.305
15. Andy McGaffigan	MTL	.204		103. Danny Darwin	HOU	.304
16. John Franco	CIN	.211		102. Tim Burke	MTL	.302
17. Dwight Gooden	NY	.211		101. Ed Lynch	CHI	.302
18. Larry McWilliams	PIT	.213		100. Jim Acker	ATL	.302
19. Tim Conroy	STL	.213		99. Greg Minton	SF	.302
19. Steve Bedrosian	PHI	.213		98. Dennis Eckersley	CHI	.301

Opponents' Batting Average, Right-Handed Batters

American League

Top 20				Bottom 20		
1. Mark Eichhorn	TOR	.135		130. Lee Guetterman	SEA	.354
2. Tom Henke	TOR	.158		129. John Butcher	CLE	.325
3. Moose Haas	OAK	.164		128. Richard Dotson	CHI	.316
4. Jose DeLeon	CHI	.174		127. Dave LaPoint	DET	.315
5. Roger Clemens	BOS	.176		126. Bob Tewksbury	NY	.314
6. Tim Stoddard	NY	.188		125. Mark Portugal	MIN	.310
7. Eric King	DET	.193		124. Bob Stanley	BOS	.310
8. Bobby Witt	TEX	.193		123. Allan Anderson	MIN	.309
9. Joe Cowley	CHI	.194		122. Dan Petry	DET	.308
10. Eric Plunk	OAK	.199		121. Matt Young	SEA	.302
11. Mitch Williams	TEX	.202		120. Bob Shirley	NY	.298
12. Doug Corbett	CAL	.202		119. Mike Morgan	SEA	.298
13. Mark Huismann	SEA	.204		117. Tim Leary	MIL	.296
14. Mark Clear	MIL	.209		117. Jim Slaton	DET	.296
15. Dave Righetti	NY	.209		116. Brad Havens	BAL	.296
16. John Candelaria	CAL	.210		115. Juan Nieves	MIL	.295
17. Jeff Russell	TEX	.212		113. Ron Romanick	CAL	.294
18. Rich Bordi	BAL	.216		113. Bill Wegman	MIL	.294
19. Mark Gubicza	KC	.218		112. Bret Saberhagen	KC	.291
20. Bill Dawley	CHI	.218		111. Mike Brown	SEA	.291

National League

Top 20				Bottom 20		
1. Lance McCullers	SD	.154		116. Jerry Reuss	LA	.331
2. Mike Scott	HOU	.156		115. Mark Thurmond	SD	.328
3. Rob Murphy	CIN	.163		114. Joe Price	CIN	.317
4. Charlie Kerfeld	HOU	.184		113. Chris Welsh	CIN	.315
5. Floyd Youmans	MTL	.189		112. Jamie Moyer	CHI	.313
6. Nolan Ryan	HOU	.191		111. Dennis Martinez	MTL	.311
7. Eric Show	SD	.193		110. Mike Madden	HOU	.305
8. Todd Worrell	STL	.196		109. Charles Hudson	PHI	.302
9. Jeff Robinson	SF	.196		108. Dave LaPoint	SD	.301
10. Greg Minton	SF	.200		107. Dennis Powell	LA	.301
11. Dave Gumpert	CHI	.202		106. Steve Carlton	SF	.300
12. Bryn Smith	MTL	.207		105. Guy Hoffman	CHI	.299
13. Lee Smith	CHI	.208		104. Ed Vande Berg	LA	.296
14. Roger McDowell	NY	.211		103. Doug Sisk	NY	.295
15. Andy Hawkins	SD	.214		102. Tim Conroy	STL	.290
16. Sid Fernandez	NY	.215		101. Joe Hesketh	MTL	.288
17. Ricky Horton	STL	.216		100. Larry Andersen	HOU	.288
18. Tim Burke	MTL	.218		99. Steve Trout	CHI	.287
19. Mike Krukow	SF	.219		98. Zane Smith	ATL	.284
20. Ron Robinson	CIN	.220		97. Ray Burris	STL	.281

Opponents' Slugging Average, Left-Handed Batters

American League

Top 20
1. Mark Clear	MIL	.226
2. Dennis Rasmussen	NY	.250
3. Curt Young	OAK	.260
4. Willie Hernandez	DET	.268
5. Brad Havens	BAL	.273
6. Bob Shirley	NY	.274
7. Calvin Schiraldi	BOS	.277
8. Ed Correa	TEX	.290
9. Mark Langston	SEA	.294
10. Donnie Moore	CAL	.295
11. Jose DeLeon	CHI	.309
12. Matt Young	SEA	.310
13. Steve Farr	KC	.310
14. Floyd Bannister	CHI	.316
15. Roger Clemens	BOS	.317
16. Jimmy Key	TOR	.321
17. Tom Henke	TOR	.322
17. Mitch Williams	TEX	.322
19. Bill Mooneyham	OAK	.323
20. Mike Trujillo	SEA	.323

Bottom 20
129. Ron Davis	MIN	.707
128. Milt Wilcox	SEA	.650
127. Pete Ladd	SEA	.598
126. Bryan Clutterbuck	MIL	.592
125. Steve Crawford	BOS	.576
124. Jim Acker	TOR	.575
123. Mike Brown	SEA	.571
122. Rick Langford	OAK	.567
121. Allan Anderson	MIN	.551
120. Dave Stieb	TOR	.546
119. John Butcher	CLE	.517
118. Scott Nielsen	NY	.505
117. Mike Smithson	MIN	.501
116. Dickie Noles	CLE	.500
115. Dennis Leonard	KC	.496
114. Brian Fisher	NY	.493
113. Bill Swift	SEA	.486
112. Jim Slaton	DET	.485
111. Mark Huismann	SEA	.485
110. Jose Guzman	TEX	.480

National League

Top 20
1. Gene Walter	SD	.174
2. Mark Davis	SF	.190
3. Bob Ojeda	NY	.206
4. Don Robinson	PIT	.212
5. Dave Smith	HOU	.235
6. Frank Williams	SF	.246
7. Bruce Ruffin	PHI	.250
7. John Franco	CIN	.250
9. Jesse Orosco	NY	.253
10. Andy McGaffigan	MTL	.268
11. John Tudor	STL	.273
12. Nolan Ryan	HOU	.278
13. Sid Fernandez	NY	.286
13. Cecilio Guante	PIT	.286
15. Aurelio Lopez	HOU	.288
16. Craig Lefferts	SD	.289
17. Frank DiPino	CHI	.290
18. Ricky Horton	STL	.296
19. Gene Garber	ATL	.297
20. Floyd Youmans	MTL	.298

Bottom 20
117. Dave Gumpert	CHI	.510
116. Mario Soto	CIN	.507
115. Scott Terry	CIN	.500
114. Rick Mahler	ATL	.498
113. Alejandro Pena	LA	.497
112. John Denny	CIN	.486
111. Tom Niedenfuer	LA	.477
110. Craig McMurtry	ATL	.476
109. Ray Burris	STL	.476
108. Jim Winn	PIT	.473
106. Danny Darwin	HOU	.471
106. Dennis Eckersley	CHI	.471
105. Greg Minton	SF	.468
104. Andy Hawkins	SD	.462
103. Bruce Berenyi	NY	.458
102. Rich Gossage	SD	.445
101. Kevin Gross	PHI	.445
100. Rick Reuschel	PIT	.443
99. Rick Aguilera	NY	.442
98. Ed Wojna	SD	.440

Opponents' Slugging Average, Right-Handed Batters

American League

Top 20
1. Mark Eichhorn	TOR	.165
2. Tom Henke	TOR	.243
3. Moose Haas	OAK	.253
4. Jose DeLeon	CHI	.261
5. Eric King	DET	.272
6. Dave Righetti	NY	.275
7. Roger Clemens	BOS	.290
8. Bill Dawley	CHI	.295
9. Joe Johnson	TOR	.298
10. John Candelaria	CAL	.314
11. Mark Clear	MIL	.316
12. Mark Gubicza	KC	.317
13. Dan Quisenberry	KC	.322
14. Kirk McCaskill	CAL	.324
15. Mike Witt	CAL	.330
16. Bill Swift	SEA	.330
17. Bryan Clutterbuck	MIL	.331
18. Rich Bordi	BAL	.332
19. Doug Corbett	CAL	.333
19. Dan Plesac	MIL	.333

Bottom 20
130. Doyle Alexander	TOR	.524
129. Dave LaPoint	DET	.514
128. Mike Brown	SEA	.510
126. Jeff Sellers	BOS	.500
126. Al Nipper	BOS	.500
125. Bert Blyleven	MIN	.499
124. Lee Guetterman	SEA	.498
123. Rick Langford	OAK	.492
122. Ron Romanick	CAL	.490
121. Bob Shirley	NY	.488
119. Bill Wegman	MIL	.485
119. Rich Yett	CLE	.485
118. Brad Havens	BAL	.484
117. Allan Anderson	MIN	.484
116. John Butcher	CLE	.483
115. Don Sutton	CAL	.479
114. Bob Stanley	BOS	.478
113. Donnie Moore	CAL	.470
112. Willie Hernandez	DET	.470
111. John Cerutti	TOR	.470

National League

Top 20
1. Rob Murphy	CIN	.187
2. Charlie Kerfeld	HOU	.212
3. Roger McDowell	NY	.231
4. Dave Gumpert	CHI	.264
5. Pat Clements	PIT	.271
6. Greg Minton	SF	.272
7. Mike Scott	HOU	.274
8. Lance McCullers	SD	.275
9. Alejandro Pena	LA	.279
10. Jeff Robinson	SF	.280
11. Lee Smith	CHI	.282
12. Todd Worrell	STL	.284
13. Floyd Youmans	MTL	.292
14. Kent Tekulve	PHI	.296
15. Bob McClure	MTL	.309
16. Eric Show	SD	.311
17. Steve Bedrosian	PHI	.313
18. Kelly Downs	SF	.319
19. Tim Burke	MTL	.319
20. Juan Berenguer	SF	.321

Bottom 20
116. Jerry Reuss	LA	.533
115. LaMarr Hoyt	SD	.511
114. Joe Hesketh	MTL	.495
113. Ray Burris	STL	.489
112. Joe Price	CIN	.488
111. Dennis Martinez	MTL	.485
110. Cecilio Guante	PIT	.476
109. Bob Kipper	PIT	.476
108. Steve Carlton	SF	.476
107. Mark Thurmond	SD	.474
106. Dave LaPoint	SD	.473
105. Charles Hudson	PHI	.468
104. Frank DiPino	CHI	.462
103. Tim Conroy	STL	.459
102. Larry McWilliams	PIT	.453
101. Ed Vande Berg	LA	.447
100. Jeff Reardon	MTL	.447
99. Mario Soto	CIN	.446
98. Don Robinson	PIT	.444
97. Carl Willis	CIN	.441

Opponents' Home Run Percentage, Left-Handed Batters

American League

Top 20
1. Jimmy Key	TOR	0.53
2. Bill Mooneyham	OAK	0.53
3. Curt Young	OAK	0.68
4. Dan Quisenberry	KC	0.69
5. Ed Correa	TEX	0.76
6. Juan Nieves	MIL	0.76
7. Mike Flanagan	BAL	0.78
8. Bill Swift	SEA	0.78
9. Dennis Lamp	TOR	0.79
10. Dale Mohorcic	TEX	0.81
11. Ernie Camacho	CLE	0.92
12. Mark Clear	MIL	0.94
13. Steve Farr	KC	0.99
14. Willie Hernandez	DET	1.03
15. Mark Gubicza	KC	1.14
16. Donnie Moore	CAL	1.37
17. Ron Romanick	CAL	1.40
18. Tom Candiotti	CLE	1.41
18. Jaime Cocanower	MIL	1.41
20. Mark Portugal	MIN	1.46

Bottom 20
129. Pete Ladd	SEA	6.54
128. Milt Wilcox	SEA	6.50
127. Dickie Noles	CLE	6.12
126. Ron Davis	MIN	6.10
125. Scott McGregor	BAL	6.02
124. Bryan Clutterbuck	MIL	5.83
123. Rick Langford	OAK	5.77
122. Jim Acker	TOR	5.66
121. Scott Nielsen	NY	5.41
120. Dan Petry	DET	4.96
119. Joaquin Andujar	OAK	4.89
118. Bruce Hurst	BOS	4.65
117. Bob James	CHI	4.42
116. Keith Atherton	MIN	4.40
115. Bill Wegman	MIL	4.35
114. Mike Brown	SEA	4.29
113. Doug Corbett	CAL	4.24
112. Bryan Oelkers	CLE	4.21
111. Neal Heaton	MIN	4.17
110. Dave Stieb	TOR	4.09

National League

Top 20
1. Frank Williams	SF	0.00
1. Carl Willis	CIN	0.00
1. Steve Trout	CHI	0.00
1. Fernando Valenzuela	LA	0.00
1. Ed Vande Berg	LA	0.00
1. Gene Walter	SD	0.00
1. Rick Honeycutt	LA	0.00
1. Don Robinson	PIT	0.00
1. Doug Sisk	NY	0.00
1. Zane Smith	ATL	0.00
1. John Franco	CIN	0.00
1. George Frazier	CHI	0.00
1. Gene Garber	ATL	0.00
14. Kent Tekulve	PHI	0.51
15. John Tudor	STL	0.70
16. Andy McGaffigan	MTL	0.75
17. Larry Andersen	HOU	0.78
18. Rick Rhoden	PIT	0.79
19. Jim Acker	ATL	0.90
20. Bob Ojeda	NY	0.93

Bottom 20
117. Steve Bedrosian	PHI	5.62
116. Jim Winn	PIT	4.65
115. Alejandro Pena	LA	4.14
114. Tom Niedenfuer	LA	3.87
113. Todd Worrell	STL	3.87
112. Larry McWilliams	PIT	3.75
111. Scott Sanderson	CHI	3.63
110. Chris Welsh	CIN	3.57
109. Ray Burris	STL	3.50
107. Charles Hudson	PHI	3.45
107. Jim Deshaies	HOU	3.45
106. Vida Blue	SF	3.41
105. Tim Conroy	STL	3.37
104. Don Carman	PHI	3.33
103. LaMarr Hoyt	SD	3.25
102. Frank DiPino	CHI	3.23
100. Rich Gossage	SD	3.13
100. Roger Mason	SF	3.13
99. Mario Soto	CIN	3.08
98. Bob Sebra	MTL	3.08

Opponents' Home Run Percentage, Right-Handed Batters

American League

Top 20			Bottom 20		
1. Joe Johnson	TOR	0.00	130. Donnie Moore	CAL	6.84
2. Mark Eichhorn	TOR	0.34	129. Jeff Sellers	BOS	6.72
3. Dan Quisenberry	KC	0.58	128. Mark Huismann	SEA	6.08
4. Moose Haas	OAK	0.68	127. Bert Blyleven	MIN	5.84
5. Bob Tewksbury	NY	0.82	126. Jack Morris	DET	5.73
6. Dave Righetti	NY	0.94	125. Rick Langford	OAK	5.56
7. Joel Davis	CHI	1.02	124. Al Nipper	BOS	5.44
8. Mickey Mahler	TOR	1.12	123. Mike Brown	SEA	5.30
9. Eric King	DET	1.18	122. Bryan Oelkers	CLE	5.23
10. Mark Gubicza	KC	1.28	121. Doyle Alexander	TOR	5.19
11. Tom Henke	TOR	1.32	120. Don Sutton	CAL	5.15
12. Dan Petry	DET	1.40	119. Rich Yett	CLE	5.15
13. Bill Swift	SEA	1.44	118. Dave LaPoint	DET	5.09
14. John Candelaria	CAL	1.48	117. Ray Searage	CHI	5.08
15. Scott Bankhead	KC	1.55	116. Steve Ontiveros	OAK	5.00
16. Dan Plesac	MIL	1.55	115. Ron Romanick	CAL	4.90
17. Bill Mooneyham	OAK	1.56	114. Walt Terrell	DET	4.87
18. Bryan Clutterbuck	MIL	1.57	113. Willie Hernandez	DET	4.82
18. John Johnson	MIL	1.57	112. Ken Schrom	CLE	4.79
20. Keith Atherton	MIN	1.58	111. Chris Codiroli	OAK	4.68

National League

Top 20			Bottom 20		
1. Rob Murphy	CIN	0.00	116. LaMarr Hoyt	SD	5.54
1. Alejandro Pena	LA	0.00	115. Cecilio Guante	PIT	5.29
1. Doug Sisk	NY	0.00	114. Jerry Reuss	LA	4.67
1. Pat Clements	PIT	0.00	113. Mario Soto	CIN	4.52
1. Roger McDowell	NY	0.00	112. Ray Burris	STL	4.49
6. Kent Tekulve	PHI	0.46	111. Bob Kipper	PIT	4.45
7. Charlie Kerfeld	HOU	0.56	110. Jeff Reardon	MTL	4.40
8. Tom Hume	PHI	0.62	109. Steve Carlton	SF	4.28
9. Larry Andersen	HOU	0.65	108. Joe Hesketh	MTL	3.91
10. Bob McClure	MTL	0.66	107. Rick Aguilera	NY	3.90
11. Greg Minton	SF	0.80	106. Ed Vande Berg	LA	3.88
12. Bruce Ruffin	PHI	0.85	105. Frank DiPino	CHI	3.85
13. Todd Worrell	STL	1.03	104. Scott Garrelts	SF	3.83
14. Tim Burke	MTL	1.06	103. Charles Hudson	PHI	3.63
15. Mike Bielecki	PIT	1.14	102. Dennis Martinez	MTL	3.59
16. Steve Trout	CHI	1.17	101. Jim Acker	ATL	3.50
17. Steve Bedrosian	PHI	1.23	100. Rick Sutcliffe	CHI	3.48
18. Zane Smith	ATL	1.24	99. Don Robinson	PIT	3.47
19. Terry Mulholland	SF	1.26	98. Carl Willis	CIN	3.39
20. Chris Welsh	CIN	1.31	97. Tim Conroy	STL	3.38

Opponents' Batting Average, Day Games

American League

Top 20			Bottom 20		
1. John Candelaria	CAL	.149	128. Bill Swift	SEA	.362
2. Don Aase	BAL	.170	127. Allan Anderson	MIN	.352
3. Mark Eichhorn	TOR	.179	126. Steve Crawford	BOS	.349
4. Roger Clemens	BOS	.180	125. Bob Stanley	BOS	.347
5. Mark Clear	MIL	.182	124. Lee Guetterman	SEA	.343
6. Jose DeLeon	CHI	.183	123. Keith Atherton	MIN	.333
7. Eric Plunk	OAK	.188	122. Dave Stieb	TOR	.331
8. Bobby Witt	TEX	.197	121. Jeff Sellers	BOS	.323
9. John Cerutti	TOR	.200	120. Jim Slaton	DET	.312
10. Moose Haas	OAK	.201	119. Storm Davis	BAL	.308
11. Ed Correa	TEX	.207	118. Mike Brown	SEA	.306
12. Joe Cowley	CHI	.208	117. Jose Guzman	TEX	.303
13. Ted Higuera	MIL	.212	116. Tommy John	NY	.301
14. Mark Gubicza	KC	.215	115. Tom Seaver	BOS	.301
15. Bert Blyleven	MIN	.215	114. Frank Tanana	DET	.300
16. Roy Jackson	MIN	.215	113. Joe Niekro	NY	.299
17. Walt Terrell	DET	.216	112. Al Nipper	BOS	.297
18. Jim Clancy	TOR	.218	110. Randy O'Neal	DET	.297
19. Floyd Bannister	CHI	.218	110. Pete Ladd	SEA	.297
20. Scott Bankhead	KC	.218	109. Dennis Lamp	TOR	.296

National League

Top 20			Bottom 20		
1. Aurelio Lopez	HOU	.165	116. Mark Thurmond	SD	.361
2. David Palmer	ATL	.168	115. Rick Mahler	ATL	.355
3. Jesse Orosco	NY	.169	114. Doug Sisk	NY	.346
4. Floyd Youmans	MTL	.178	113. Shane Rawley	PHI	.343
5. Frank Williams	SF	.179	112. Joe Hesketh	MTL	.341
6. Dave Smith	HOU	.194	111. Jerry Reuss	LA	.337
7. Mike Scott	HOU	.195	110. Scott Terry	CIN	.336
8. Nolan Ryan	HOU	.196	108. Dennis Martinez	MTL	.333
9. Ricky Horton	STL	.196	108. Larry Andersen	HOU	.333
10. Jeff Dedmon	ATL	.197	107. Ray Burris	STL	.322
11. Craig McMurtry	ATL	.197	106. Steve Carlton	SF	.319
12. Sid Fernandez	NY	.197	105. Jamie Moyer	CHI	.318
13. Gene Walter	SD	.200	104. Ed Lynch	CHI	.313
14. Charlie Kerfeld	HOU	.202	103. Bill Gullickson	CIN	.311
15. Roger McDowell	NY	.207	102. George Frazier	CHI	.310
16. John Franco	CIN	.208	101. Randy Niemann	NY	.309
17. Kelly Downs	SF	.211	100. LaMarr Hoyt	SD	.305
18. Ron Robinson	CIN	.211	99. Joe Johnson	ATL	.305
19. Bob Forsch	STL	.214	98. Steve Trout	CHI	.304
20. Bob Ojeda	NY	.217	97. Tim Conroy	STL	.303

Opponents' Batting Average, Night Games

American League

Top 20			Bottom 20		
1. Tom Henke	TOR	.171	129. John Butcher	CLE	.376
2. Jose DeLeon	CHI	.177	128. Lee Guetterman	SEA	.349
3. Mitch Williams	TEX	.193	127. Milt Wilcox	SEA	.342
4. Mark Eichhorn	TOR	.197	126. Jim Beattie	SEA	.341
5. Dennis Rasmussen	NY	.200	125. Rick Langford	OAK	.329
6. Roger Clemens	BOS	.202	124. Dave LaPoint	DET	.321
7. Eric King	DET	.208	123. Odell Jones	BAL	.320
8. Mike Witt	CAL	.209	122. Dennis Lamp	TOR	.319
9. Doug Corbett	CAL	.210	121. Mike Brown	SEA	.317
10. Mark Clear	MIL	.210	120. Bob Stanley	BOS	.308
11. Dave Righetti	NY	.211	119. Ed Whitson	NY	.307
12. Bud Black	KC	.214	118. Juan Nieves	MIL	.306
13. Mike Trujillo	SEA	.215	117. Mickey Mahler	TOR	.306
14. Charlie Hough	TEX	.216	116. Phil Niekro	CLE	.304
15. Donnie Moore	CAL	.220	115. Bill Swift	SEA	.298
16. Kirk McCaskill	CAL	.221	113. Joel Davis	CHI	.298
17. Ed Correa	TEX	.226	113. Mike Smithson	MIN	.298
18. Jack Morris	DET	.226	112. Ron Romanick	CAL	.298
19. Steve Farr	KC	.227	111. Doyle Alexander	TOR	.298
20. Bill Dawley	CHI	.229	110. Dennis Leonard	KC	.297

National League

Top 20			Bottom 20		
1. Rob Murphy	CIN	.134	116. Craig McMurtry	ATL	.313
2. Mike Scott	HOU	.183	115. Mark Thurmond	SD	.308
3. Nolan Ryan	HOU	.184	114. Ed Vande Berg	LA	.307
4. Floyd Youmans	MTL	.193	113. Charles Hudson	PHI	.303
5. Frank DiPino	CHI	.195	112. Mike Maddux	PHI	.302
6. Mark Davis	SF	.199	111. Jerry Reuss	LA	.301
7. Ed Lynch	CHI	.205	110. Chris Welsh	CIN	.301
8. Dwight Gooden	NY	.206	109. Tom Niedenfuer	LA	.296
9. Jeff Robinson	SF	.206	108. Ed Whitson	SD	.292
10. Lance McCullers	SD	.208	107. Scott Sanderson	CHI	.291
11. Fernando Valenzuela	LA	.212	106. Dennis Powell	LA	.290
12. Ed Olwine	ATL	.213	105. Dennis Eckersley	CHI	.290
13. Cecilio Guante	PIT	.218	104. Rick Aguilera	NY	.289
14. Charlie Kerfeld	HOU	.220	103. Rick Mahler	ATL	.288
15. Eric Show	SD	.220	102. Steve Trout	CHI	.286
16. Andy McGaffigan	MTL	.220	101. Andy Hawkins	SD	.285
17. Rick Sutcliffe	CHI	.221	100. Steve Carlton	SF	.284
18. Bob Knepper	HOU	.221	99. Joe Johnson	ATL	.281
19. Don Robinson	PIT	.222	98. Mario Soto	CIN	.281
20. Mike Krukow	SF	.223	97. Bob Kipper	PIT	.281

Opponents' Batting Average, Grass Surfaces

American League

Top 20				Bottom 20			
1. Mark Eichhorn	TOR	.176		128. John Butcher	CLE	.350
2. Jose DeLeon	CHI	.180		127. Bob Stanley	BOS	.350
3. Mark Clear	MIL	.181		126. Mike Brown	SEA	.340
4. John Candelaria	CAL	.189		125. Odell Jones	BAL	.327
5. Roger Clemens	BOS	.197		124. Steve Crawford	BOS	.326
6. Mitch Williams	TEX	.200		123. Dave Stieb	TOR	.324
7. Eric King	DET	.202		122. Bill Swift	SEA	.320
8. Eric Plunk	OAK	.212		121. Scott Nielsen	NY	.314
9. Ed Correa	TEX	.214		120. Tim Lollar	BOS	.312
10. Jimmy Key	TOR	.215		119. Dave LaPoint	DET	.310
11. Dennis Rasmussen	NY	.216		118. Jay Howell	OAK	.301
12. Charlie Hough	TEX	.217		117. Joe Johnson	TOR	.301
13. Jose Rijo	OAK	.218		116. Jim Slaton	DET	.300
14. Kirk McCaskill	CAL	.219		115. Juan Nieves	MIL	.299
15. Jim Clancy	TOR	.220		114. Tim Leary	MIL	.296
16. Joe Cowley	CHI	.221		113. Jose Guzman	TEX	.294
17. Bert Blyleven	MIN	.222		112. Ron Romanick	CAL	.293
18. Dave Righetti	NY	.223		111. Bryan Clutterbuck	MIL	.291
19. Bill Campbell	DET	.223		110. Dennis Leonard	KC	.291
20. Steve Farr	KC	.224		109. Joe Sambito	BOS	.290

National League

Top 20				Bottom 20			
1. Ricky Horton	STL	.173		117. Larry Andersen	HOU	.381
2. Frank Williams	SF	.181		116. Charles Hudson	PHI	.342
3. Tim Stoddard	SD	.186		115. Chris Welsh	CIN	.330
4. Mike Scott	HOU	.191		114. Mark Thurmond	SD	.323
5. Ed Olwine	ATL	.197		113. Jamie Moyer	CHI	.317
6. Floyd Youmans	MTL	.201		112. Shane Rawley	PHI	.316
7. Lee Smith	CHI	.205		111. Craig McMurtry	ATL	.305
8. Dwight Gooden	NY	.209		110. Steve Carlton	SF	.303
9. Sid Fernandez	NY	.211		109. Jay Tibbs	MTL	.303
10. Don Carman	PHI	.211		108. Bruce Berenyi	NY	.300
11. Cliff Speck	ATL	.213		107. Joe Johnson	ATL	.294
12. Danny Darwin	HOU	.214		106. Steve Trout	CHI	.292
13. John Franco	CIN	.215		105. Rick Reuschel	PIT	.292
14. Mark Davis	SF	.219		104. Ed Lynch	CHI	.289
15. Scott Garrelts	SF	.221		103. Dennis Eckersley	CHI	.289
16. Roger McDowell	NY	.221		102. Cecilio Guante	PIT	.289
17. Tim Burke	MTL	.222		101. Guy Hoffman	CHI	.289
18. Jim Winn	PIT	.222		100. Ed Vande Berg	LA	.289
19. Bruce Ruffin	PHI	.224		98. Ed Wojna	SD	.288
20. Tim Conroy	STL	.225		98. Jay Baller	CHI	.288

Opponents' Batting Average, Artificial Surfaces

American League

Top 20				Bottom 20			
1. Moose Haas	OAK	.132		130. Juan Agosto	MIN	.455
2. Ken Dixon	BAL	.174		129. Chuck Cary	DET	.425
3. Jose DeLeon	CHI	.176		128. Ray Fontenot	MIN	.407
4. Roger Clemens	BOS	.184		127. Lee Guetterman	SEA	.359
5. Tom Henke	TOR	.185		126. Mike Mason	TEX	.346
6. Bobby Witt	TEX	.190		125. Frank Tanana	DET	.341
7. Bruce Hurst	BOS	.191		124. Bill Mooneyham	OAK	.341
8. Mike Witt	CAL	.198		123. Neil Allen	CHI	.339
9. Rich Bordi	BAL	.200		122. Mike Birkbeck	MIL	.333
10. Mark Eichhorn	TOR	.201		121. Richard Dotson	CHI	.331
11. Jack Morris	DET	.204		120. Allan Anderson	MIN	.330
12. Mitch Williams	TEX	.213		119. Jeff Sellers	BOS	.326
13. Nate Snell	BAL	.214		118. Ernie Camacho	CLE	.325
14. Mike Trujillo	SEA	.216		117. Don Gordon	TOR	.323
15. Dennis Rasmussen	NY	.219		116. Jim Beattie	SEA	.321
16. Bob Stanley	BOS	.222		115. Alan Hargesheimer	KC	.320
17. Karl Best	SEA	.222		114. Milt Wilcox	SEA	.320
18. Eric Plunk	OAK	.224		113. Frank Pastore	MIN	.319
19. Bud Black	KC	.225		112. Walt Terrell	DET	.319
20. Dave Stewart	OAK	.226		111. Bill Swift	SEA	.318

National League

Top 20				Bottom 20			
1. Jesse Orosco	NY	.153		116. Rick Mahler	ATL	.343
2. Craig McMurtry	ATL	.157		115. Jim Acker	ATL	.341
3. Rob Murphy	CIN	.161		114. Joe Hesketh	MTL	.314
4. Nolan Ryan	HOU	.176		113. Carl Willis	CIN	.313
5. Lance McCullers	SD	.182		112. Steve Trout	CHI	.310
6. Floyd Youmans	MTL	.184		111. Greg Maddux	CHI	.309
7. Mike Scott	HOU	.185		110. Scott Terry	CIN	.303
8. Charlie Kerfeld	HOU	.190		109. Andy Hawkins	SD	.301
9. Cecilio Guante	PIT	.199		108. Rick Ownbey	STL	.296
10. Eric Show	SD	.205		107. Steve Carlton	SF	.295
11. Aurelio Lopez	HOU	.206		106. Mike Maddux	PHI	.295
12. Dave Smith	HOU	.210		105. Chris Welsh	CIN	.295
13. David Palmer	ATL	.210		104. Craig Lefferts	SD	.294
14. Fernando Valenzuela	LA	.212		103. Mario Soto	CIN	.294
15. Frank DiPino	CHI	.214		102. Ed Vande Berg	LA	.293
16. Andy McGaffigan	MTL	.215		101. Alejandro Pena	LA	.293
17. Mike Krukow	SF	.217		100. Doyle Alexander	ATL	.292
18. Steve Bedrosian	PHI	.218		99. Julio Solano	HOU	.292
19. Todd Worrell	STL	.220		98. Ed Whitson	SD	.291
20. Rick Rhoden	PIT	.221		97. Joe Price	CIN	.290

Opponents' Batting Average, Home Games

American League

Top 20				Bottom 20			
1. Eric King	DET	.156		128. John Butcher	CLE	.396
2. Mark Clear	MIL	.175		127. Bob Stanley	BOS	.362
3. John Candelaria	CAL	.181		126. Lee Guetterman	SEA	.353
4. Tom Henke	TOR	.182		125. Allan Anderson	MIN	.335
5. Jose DeLeon	CHI	.185		124. Mike Brown	SEA	.323
6. Bill Campbell	DET	.193		123. Juan Nieves	MIL	.315
7. Doug Corbett	CAL	.199		122. Steve Crawford	BOS	.314
8. Curt Young	OAK	.199		121. Jim Acker	TOR	.313
9. Joe Cowley	CHI	.200		120. Rich Yett	CLE	.312
10. Steve Ontiveros	OAK	.201		119. Brian Fisher	NY	.310
11. Bud Black	KC	.202		118. Bill Swift	SEA	.308
12. Roger Clemens	BOS	.203		117. Bob James	CHI	.306
13. Mark Eichhorn	TOR	.204		116. Joe Niekro	NY	.306
14. Dennis Rasmussen	NY	.204		115. Ron Romanick	CAL	.305
15. Jose Rijo	OAK	.205		114. Ernie Camacho	CLE	.303
16. Dave Righetti	NY	.206		113. Mike Smithson	MIN	.301
17. Ed Correa	TEX	.207		112. Storm Davis	BAL	.296
18. Bobby Witt	TEX	.207		111. Bob Shirley	NY	.296
19. Mike Witt	CAL	.208		110. Al Nipper	BOS	.295
20. Walt Terrell	DET	.209		109. Dan Petry	DET	.295

National League

Top 20				Bottom 20			
1. Nolan Ryan	HOU	.151		116. Joe Hesketh	MTL	.328
2. Paul Assenmacher	ATL	.178		115. Steve Carlton	SF	.327
3. Sid Fernandez	NY	.178		114. Mario Soto	CIN	.327
4. Mike Scott	HOU	.179		113. Ed Lynch	CHI	.322
5. Alejandro Pena	LA	.181		112. Scott Terry	CIN	.320
6. Floyd Youmans	MTL	.183		111. Jamie Moyer	CHI	.318
7. Dwight Gooden	NY	.183		110. Mike Maddux	PHI	.314
8. Roger McDowell	NY	.183		109. Craig McMurtry	ATL	.310
9. Charlie Kerfeld	HOU	.188		108. Pat Perry	STL	.306
10. Scott Garrelts	SF	.191		107. Steve Trout	CHI	.305
11. Steve Bedrosian	PHI	.194		106. Ed Vande Berg	LA	.303
12. Andy McGaffigan	MTL	.198		105. Jerry Reuss	LA	.301
13. Cecilio Guante	PIT	.199		104. Dennis Eckersley	CHI	.298
14. Terry Mulholland	SF	.200		103. Dennis Martinez	MTL	.294
15. Mike LaCoss	SF	.202		102. Bob Kipper	PIT	.294
16. Mike Krukow	SF	.206		101. Doyle Alexander	ATL	.293
17. Doug Sisk	NY	.209		100. Rich Gossage	SD	.291
18. Greg Minton	SF	.212		99. Charles Hudson	PHI	.290
19. Danny Cox	STL	.215		98. Chris Welsh	CIN	.289
20. Fernando Valenzuela	LA	.216		97. Joe Johnson	ATL	.288

Opponents' Batting Average, Road Games

American League							National League						
Top 20			**Bottom 20**				**Top 20**			**Bottom 20**			
1. Jose DeLeon	CHI	.175	128. Rick Langford	OAK	.371		1. Jesse Orosco	NY	.166	116. Mark Thurmond	SD	.390	
2. Mark Eichhorn	TOR	.179	127. Milt Wilcox	SEA	.364		2. Pat Perry	STL	.184	115. Doug Sisk	NY	.347	
3. Roger Clemens	BOS	.188	126. Dennis Lamp	TOR	.348		3. Mark Davis	SF	.186	114. Alejandro Pena	LA	.347	
4. Mitch Williams	TEX	.193	125. Lee Guetterman	SEA	.340		4. Aurelio Lopez	HOU	.187	113. Larry Andersen	HOU	.338	
5. Tom Henke	TOR	.200	124. Bill Swift	SEA	.332		5. Floyd Youmans	MTL	.194	112. Jerry Reuss	LA	.331	
6. Moose Haas	OAK	.204	123. Steve Ontiveros	OAK	.331		6. Mike Scott	HOU	.196	111. George Frazier	CHI	.328	
7. Eric Plunk	OAK	.204	122. Dan Quisenberry	KC	.322		7. Dave Smith	HOU	.198	110. Rick Mahler	ATL	.317	
8. Charlie Hough	TEX	.208	121. Doyle Alexander	TOR	.320		8. Danny Darwin	HOU	.199	109. Chris Welsh	CIN	.317	
9. Dan Plesac	MIL	.214	120. Dave LaPoint	DET	.318		9. Ricky Horton	STL	.207	108. Tom Niedenfuer	LA	.314	
10. Bob James	CHI	.221	119. Bryan Clutterbuck	MIL	.313		10. Lee Smith	CHI	.208	107. Paul Assenmacher	ATL	.314	
11. Jim Clancy	TOR	.223	118. Scott Bailes	CLE	.313		11. Jeff Dedmon	ATL	.209	106. Guy Hoffman	CHI	.313	
12. Neil Allen	CHI	.223	117. Floyd Bannister	CHI	.311		12. Craig McMurtry	ATL	.210	105. Ed Whitson	SD	.311	
13. Dennis Rasmussen	NY	.224	116. Matt Young	SEA	.311		13. Lance McCullers	SD	.214	104. Jim Acker	ATL	.309	
14. Dickie Noles	CLE	.226	115. John Butcher	CLE	.308		13. Jeff Reardon	MTL	.214	103. Ray Burris	STL	.303	
15. Ernie Camacho	CLE	.231	114. Dave Stieb	TOR	.306		15. Ed Lynch	CHI	.217	102. LaMarr Hoyt	SD	.301	
16. Ken Dixon	BAL	.231	113. Dale Mohorcic	TEX	.305		16. Bob McClure	MTL	.219	101. Dave LaPoint	SD	.293	
17. Mark Clear	MIL	.231	112. Richard Dotson	CHI	.303		17. Matt Keough	HOU	.220	100. Zane Smith	ATL	.293	
18. Bert Blyleven	MIN	.231	111. Tim Leary	MIL	.303		18. Don Carman	PHI	.224	99. Chris Hudson	PHI	.292	
19. John Candelaria	CAL	.232	110. Jose Guzman	TEX	.300		19. David Palmer	ATL	.224	98. Steve Trout	CHI	.291	
20. Oil Can Boyd	BOS	.232	109. Keith Atherton	MIN	.298		20. Juan Berenguer	SF	.227	97. Joe Johnson	ATL	.291	

Opponents' Batting Average with Runners On Base

American League							National League						
Top 20			**Bottom 20**				**Top 20**			**Bottom 20**			
1. Jose DeLeon	CHI	.161	131. Dennis Lamp	TOR	.382		1. Jim Deshaies	HOU	.180	116. Mark Thurmond	SD	.389	
2. Mark Eichhorn	TOR	.183	130. Lee Guetterman	SEA	.372		2. Mike Scott	HOU	.181	115. Ray Burris	STL	.340	
3. Mark Clear	MIL	.183	129. Joe Johnson	TOR	.355		3. Jesse Orosco	NY	.183	114. Jerry Reuss	LA	.339	
4. Tommy John	NY	.200	128. Dave LaPoint	DET	.352		4. Todd Worrell	STL	.185	112. Pat Perry	STL	.333	
5. Roger Clemens	BOS	.202	127. John Butcher	CLE	.347		5. Lance McCullers	SD	.188	112. Scott Terry	CIN	.333	
6. Bud Black	KC	.206	126. Joel Davis	CHI	.339		6. Lee Smith	CHI	.191	111. Rick Mahler	ATL	.320	
7. Steve Farr	KC	.208	124. Bill Swift	SEA	.333		7. Kelly Downs	SF	.191	110. Charles Hudson	PHI	.320	
8. Jack Morris	DET	.211	124. Allan Anderson	MIN	.333		8. Eric Show	SD	.191	109. Larry McWilliams	PIT	.317	
9. Dave Stewart	OAK	.214	123. Rich Yett	CLE	.328		9. Vida Blue	SF	.202	108. Jamie Moyer	CHI	.312	
10. John Candelaria	CAL	.215	122. Bob Shirley	NY	.326		10. Andy McGaffigan	MTL	.203	107. George Frazier	CHI	.311	
11. Mitch Williams	TEX	.219	121. Bob Stanley	BOS	.324		11. Dwight Gooden	NY	.203	105. Ed Whitson	SD	.310	
12. Tom Henke	TOR	.222	120. Juan Nieves	MIL	.323		12. Bob Ojeda	NY	.204	105. Joe Hesketh	MTL	.310	
13. Tom Candiotti	CLE	.222	119. Joe Niekro	NY	.323		13. Ron Darling	NY	.207	104. Chris Welsh	CIN	.310	
14. Dave Righetti	NY	.226	118. Dave Stieb	TOR	.317		14. Sid Fernandez	NY	.213	103. Steve Trout	CHI	.310	
15. Roy Jackson	MIN	.226	117. Ron Davis	MIN	.317		15. Don Carman	PHI	.213	102. Mike Maddux	PHI	.305	
16. Dan Plesac	MIL	.228	116. Dickie Noles	CLE	.317		16. Nolan Ryan	HOU	.214	101. Steve Carlton	SF	.305	
17. Neal Heaton	MIN	.228	115. Mickey Mahler	TOR	.310		17. Jeff Reardon	MTL	.219	100. Jim Winn	PIT	.303	
18. Eric King	DET	.228	114. Bill Wegman	MIL	.307		18. Scott Garrelts	SF	.220	99. Dave LaPoint	SD	.301	
19. Jimmy Key	TOR	.229	113. Jeff Sellers	BOS	.306		19. Floyd Youmans	MTL	.222	98. Joe Johnson	ATL	.300	
20. Dave Schmidt	CHI	.230	112. Ron Romanick	CAL	.305		20. Charlie Kerfeld	HOU	.222	96. Ed Lynch	CHI	.299	
										96. Doug Sisk	NY	.299	

Opponents' Batting Average with Bases Empty

American League							National League						
Top 20			**Bottom 20**				**Top 20**			**Bottom 20**			
1. Tom Henke	TOR	.164	128. Mike Brown	SEA	.348		1. Floyd Youmans	MTL	.166	116. Ed Vande Berg	LA	.323	
2. Mitch Williams	TEX	.184	127. Milt Wilcox	SEA	.347		2. Pat Perry	STL	.172	115. Larry Andersen	HOU	.315	
3. Eric Plunk	OAK	.190	126. Tommy John	NY	.329		3. Nolan Ryan	HOU	.173	114. Jamie Moyer	CHI	.310	
4. Doug Corbett	CAL	.191	125. John Butcher	CLE	.322		4. Mark Davis	SF	.185	113. Tom Niedenfuer	LA	.297	
5. Roger Clemens	BOS	.192	124. Bob Stanley	BOS	.321		5. Cecilio Guante	PIT	.185	112. Jerry Reuss	LA	.296	
6. Jose DeLeon	CHI	.193	123. Lee Guetterman	SEA	.320		6. Mike Scott	HOU	.189	111. Steve Carlton	SF	.294	
7. Dennis Rasmussen	NY	.194	122. Scott Nielsen	NY	.309		7. Roger McDowell	NY	.200	110. Chris Welsh	CIN	.294	
8. Donnie Moore	CAL	.194	121. Bill Mooneyham	OAK	.305		8. Jeff Robinson	SF	.201	109. Doyle Alexander	ATL	.292	
9. Mark Eichhorn	TOR	.198	120. Bill Swift	SEA	.305		9. Ricky Horton	STL	.203	108. Guy Hoffman	CHI	.290	
10. John Candelaria	CAL	.200	119. Allan Anderson	MIN	.303		10. Charlie Kerfeld	HOU	.206	107. Steve Trout	CHI	.288	
11. Don Aase	BAL	.203	118. Mike Morgan	SEA	.300		11. Fernando Valenzuela	LA	.207	106. Rick Mahler	ATL	.288	
12. Ed Correa	TEX	.203	117. Matt Young	SEA	.298		12. Juan Berenguer	SF	.209	105. LaMarr Hoyt	SD	.286	
13. Eric King	DET	.206	116. Jim Slaton	DET	.297		13. Bob McClure	MTL	.213	103. Dennis Martinez	MTL	.286	
14. Charlie Hough	TEX	.206	115. Phil Niekro	CLE	.296		14. Mike LaCoss	SF	.215	103. Craig McMurtry	ATL	.286	
15. Kirk McCaskill	CAL	.207	114. Jim Acker	TOR	.295		15. Aurelio Lopez	HOU	.215	102. Dennis Powell	LA	.285	
16. Mike Witt	CAL	.212	113. Jose Guzman	TEX	.294		16. Sid Fernandez	NY	.218	101. Rick Reuschel	PIT	.283	
17. Jose Rijo	OAK	.212	112. Neal Heaton	MIN	.293		17. Gene Walter	SD	.219	100. Mario Soto	CIN	.283	
18. Bill Campbell	DET	.214	111. Dave Schmidt	CHI	.292		18. Frank DiPino	CHI	.220	99. Joe Johnson	ATL	.280	
19. Bobby Witt	TEX	.215	110. Sammy Stewart	BOS	.292		19. Mike Krukow	SF	.221	98. Todd Worrell	STL	.280	
20. Danny Darwin	MIL	.216	109. Mark Portugal	MIN	.291		20. Danny Cox	STL	.221	97. Dennis Eckersley	CHI	.279	

Opponents' Home Run Percentage with Runners On Base

American League				National League			
Top 20		**Bottom 20**		**Top 20**		**Bottom 20**	
1. Ernie Camacho	CLE 0.00	131. Bert Blyleven	MIN 5.96	1. Doug Sisk	NY 0.00	116. Scott Terry	CIN 6.31
1. Mickey Mahler	TOR 0.00	130. Dave LaPoint	DET 5.74	1. Kent Tekulve	PHI 0.00	115. Matt Keough	HOU 6.06
3. Bill Mooneyham	OAK 0.47	129. Donnie Moore	CAL 5.04	1. Pat Clements	PIT 0.00	114. Tim Conroy	STL 5.41
4. Dan Quisenberry	KC 0.61	128. Jeff Sellers	BOS 4.86	1. Gene Garber	ATL 0.00	113. Cecilio Guante	PIT 5.07
5. Dale Mohorcic	TEX 0.65	127. Dennis Rasmussen	NY 4.86	1. Aurelio Lopez	HOU 0.00	112. LaMarr Hoyt	SD 4.96
6. Mark Gubicza	KC 0.68	126. Ron Davis	MIN 4.81	1. Greg Minton	SF 0.00	111. Jerry Reuss	LA 4.96
7. Bruce Hurst	BOS 0.72	125. Chris Codiroli	OAK 4.76	1. Paul Assenmacher	ATL 0.00	110. Dennis Martinez	MTL 4.83
8. Steve Crawford	BOS 0.85	124. Ron Romanick	CAL 4.74	8. Don Carman	PHI 0.55	109. Joe Hesketh	MTL 4.65
9. Mark Eichhorn	TOR 0.89	123. Doyle Alexander	TOR 4.71	9. Craig Lefferts	SD 0.58	108. Bob Sebra	MTL 4.55
10. Eric King	DET 0.91	122. Bob Shirley	NY 4.57	10. Larry Andersen	HOU 0.65	107. Larry McWilliams	PIT 4.39
11. Bob Tewksbury	NY 0.92	120. Jim Slaton	DET 4.52	11. Kelly Downs	SF 0.71	106. Ray Burris	STL 4.26
12. Tom Candiotti	CLE 0.96	120. Bud Black	KC 4.52	12. Alejandro Pena	LA 0.76	105. Mario Soto	CIN 4.19
13. Doug Drabek	NY 1.01	119. Mike Boddicker	BAL 4.48	13. Shane Rawley	PHI 0.79	104. Ted Power	CIN 4.00
13. Odell Jones	BAL 1.01	118. Al Nipper	BOS 4.46	14. Bob Welch	LA 0.83	103. Nolan Ryan	HOU 3.93
15. Dave Schmidt	CHI 1.24	117. Lee Guetterman	SEA 4.27	15. Ricky Horton	STL 0.85	102. Bob Kipper	PIT 3.89
16. Matt Young	SEA 1.27	116. Oil Can Boyd	BOS 4.22	16. Dave Gumpert	CHI 0.86	101. Andy Hawkins	SD 3.87
17. Bill Swift	SEA 1.32	115. Scott McGregor	BAL 4.19	17. Rick Rhoden	PIT 0.90	100. Dennis Eckersley	CHI 3.83
18. Gene Nelson	CHI 1.35	114. Eric Plunk	OAK 4.12	18. Danny Cox	STL 0.99	99. Rick Sutcliffe	CHI 3.75
19. Dave Righetti	NY 1.51	113. Jimmy Key	TOR 4.12	19. Carl Willis	CIN 1.01	98. Scott Sanderson	CHI 3.70
20. Steve Ontiveros	OAK 1.53	112. Jose DeLeon	CHI 4.03	20. Bob Forsch	STL 1.02	96. Rich Gossage	SD 3.68
20. Mark Clear	MIL 1.53					96. Dan Schatzeder	PHI 3.68

Opponents' Home Run Percentage Bases Empty

American League				National League			
Top 20		**Bottom 20**		**Top 20**		**Bottom 20**	
1. Don Aase	BAL 0.00	128. Milt Wilcox	SEA 7.26	1. Doug Sisk	NY 0.00	116. Jeff Reardon	MTL 5.56
1. Lee Guetterman	SEA 0.00	127. Mark Huismann	SEA 7.18	2. Roger McDowell	NY 0.38	115. Frank DiPino	CHI 5.03
1. Joe Johnson	TOR 0.00	126. Bryan Oelkers	CLE 6.43	3. Mike Maddux	PHI 0.60	114. Vida Blue	SF 4.85
4. Dave Righetti	NY 0.53	125. John Cerutti	TOR 6.08	4. Zane Smith	ATL 0.74	113. Steve Bedrosian	PHI 4.60
5. Dennis Lamp	TOR 0.61	124. Steve Ontiveros	OAK 5.67	5. Larry Andersen	HOU 0.79	112. Steve Carlton	SF 4.53
6. Dan Quisenberry	KC 0.66	123. Mike Brown	SEA 5.59	6. Bob McClure	MTL 0.79	111. Charles Hudson	PHI 4.33
7. Bill Swift	SEA 0.85	122. Ken Dixon	BAL 5.11	7. Terry Mulholland	SF 0.87	110. Dave LaPoint	SD 4.29
8. John Candelaria	CAL 1.00	121. Scott Nielsen	NY 5.04	7. Kent Tekulve	PHI 0.87	109. LaMarr Hoyt	SD 3.97
9. Dan Plesac	MIL 1.18	120. Pete Ladd	SEA 4.96	9. Steve Trout	CHI 0.90	108. Kevin Gross	PHI 3.94
10. Jose DeLeon	CHI 1.33	119. Ken Schrom	CLE 4.96	10. Bruce Ruffin	PHI 0.92	107. Ray Burris	STL 3.89
11. Kirk McCaskill	CAL 1.47	118. Jack Morris	DET 4.92	11. Mike LaCoss	SF 1.06	106. Tom Niedenfuer	LA 3.87
12. Mark Clear	MIL 1.50	117. Jeff Russell	TEX 4.85	11. Ken Howell	LA 1.09	105. Jerry Reuss	LA 3.76
13. Mike Witt	CAL 1.60	116. Rick Langford	OAK 4.83	13. Floyd Youmans	MTL 1.10	104. Bob Kipper	PIT 3.66
14. Mark Gubicza	KC 1.63	115. Bill Wegman	MIL 4.57	14. Tom Hume	PHI 1.10	103. Paul Assenmacher	ATL 3.62
15. Jim Acker	TOR 1.64	114. Rich Bordi	BAL 4.55	15. Rick Honeycutt	LA 1.19	102. Alejandro Pena	LA 3.52
16. Mike Flanagan	BAL 1.71	113. Dan Petry	DET 4.51	16. Nolan Ryan	HOU 1.23	101. Aurelio Lopez	HOU 3.49
17. Ed Correa	TEX 1.71	112. Scott McGregor	BAL 4.50	17. Craig McMurtry	ATL 1.30	100. Greg Mathews	STL 3.38
18. Mike Mason	TEX 1.75	111. Doug Corbett	CAL 4.32	18. Juan Berenguer	SF 1.31	99. Mario Soto	CIN 3.38
19. Ron Romanick	CAL 1.75	110. Mark Thurmond	DET 4.31	19. Sid Fernandez	NY 1.38	98. Don Carman	PHI 3.34
19. Moose Haas	OAK 1.75	109. Roy Jackson	MIN 4.27	20. Jay Tibbs	MTL 1.38	97. Jay Baller	CHI 3.33
19. Tom Henke	TOR 1.75						

Opponents' On Base Average Leading Off the Inning

American League				National League			
Top 20		**Bottom 20**		**Top 20**		**Bottom 20**	
1. Don Aase	BAL .203	129. Mike Brown	SEA .468	1. Jim Winn	PIT .190	117. Craig McMurtry	ATL .436
2. Tom Henke	TOR .208	128. Lee Guetterman	SEA .442	2. Jeff Robinson	SF .212	116. Scott Terry	CIN .418
3. Willie Hernandez	DET .233	127. Mark Portugal	MIN .433	3. Ricky Horton	STL .216	115. Larry Andersen	HOU .415
4. Don Sutton	CAL .234	126. Bryan Clutterbuck	MIL .429	4. Aurelio Lopez	HOU .221	114. Mike Maddux	PHI .412
5. Charlie Hough	TEX .239	125. John Butcher	CLE .425	5. Rick Honeycutt	LA .225	113. Roger Mason	SF .397
6. Mike Witt	CAL .242	124. Bill Mooneyham	OAK .424	6. Mark Davis	SF .237	112. Jamie Moyer	CHI .391
7. Mark Eichhorn	TOR .250	123. Bobby Witt	TEX .412	7. Danny Darwin	HOU .241	111. Matt Keough	HOU .391
8. Brad Havens	BAL .254	122. Rich Bordi	BAL .404	8. Doyle Alexander	ATL .246	110. Guy Hoffman	CHI .390
9. Roger Clemens	BOS .262	121. Steve Ontiveros	OAK .400	9. Pat Perry	STL .246	109. Dennis Powell	LA .388
10. Rick Langford	OAK .267	120. Tommy John	NY .394	10. Fernando Valenzuela	LA .246	108. Todd Worrell	STL .388
11. Dennis Rasmussen	NY .267	119. Jeff Sellers	BOS .393	11. Juan Berenguer	SF .250	107. Terry Mulholland	SF .387
12. Tom Seaver	BOS .269	118. Jose DeLeon	CHI .393	12. Kent Tekulve	PHI .255	106. Alejandro Pena	LA .384
13. Bill Campbell	DET .269	117. Bryan Oelkers	CLE .391	13. John Franco	CIN .256	105. Jim Acker	ATL .381
14. Moose Haas	OAK .270	116. Neal Heaton	MIN .386	14. Dan Schatzeder	PHI .259	104. Doug Sisk	NY .377
14. Rich Yett	CLE .270	115. Allan Anderson	MIN .379	15. Rick Rhoden	PIT .260	103. Steve Trout	CHI .376
16. Joe Johnson	TOR .271	114. Dan Petry	DET .379	16. Mike Scott	HOU .261	102. Don Robinson	PIT .375
16. John Candelaria	CAL .271	113. Mike Boddicker	BAL .378	17. Bruce Ruffin	PHI .265	101. John Denny	CIN .372
18. Joel Davis	CHI .272	112. Juan Nieves	MIL .378	18. Bob Forsch	STL .271	100. Rick Reuschel	PIT .370
19. Doyle Alexander	TOR .274	111. Bruce Hurst	BOS .374	19. Mike Krukow	SF .271	99. Ed Vande Berg	LA .369
20. Dave Schmidt	CHI .276	110. Steve Carlton	CHI .373	20. Roger McDowell	NY .272	98. Bob Walk	PIT .367

Opponents' Batting Average with Runners in Scoring Position

American League

Top 20				Bottom 20			
1.	Jose DeLeon	CHI	.143	130.	Dennis Lamp	TOR	.434
2.	Mark Clear	MIL	.157	129.	Lee Guetterman	SEA	.374
3.	Ray Searage	CHI	.161	127.	Dave LaPoint	DET	.353
4.	Mitch Williams	TEX	.179	127.	Bill Swift	SEA	.353
5.	Roy Jackson	MIN	.182	126.	Ron Romanick	CAL	.352
6.	Roger Clemens	BOS	.188	125.	Allan Anderson	MIN	.346
7.	Steve Farr	KC	.191	124.	Rich Yett	CLE	.342
8.	Jack Morris	DET	.193	123.	Scott Bailes	CLE	.342
9.	Mark Eichhorn	TOR	.194	122.	John Butcher	CLE	.331
10.	Mark Portugal	MIN	.198	121.	Dan Quisenberry	KC	.330
11.	Joaquin Andujar	OAK	.198	120.	Bill Wegman	MIL	.327
12.	Mark Huismann	SEA	.204	119.	Juan Nieves	MIL	.326
13.	Ted Higuera	MIL	.206	118.	Mickey Mahler	TOR	.324
14.	Ed Correa	TEX	.206	117.	Jeff Sellers	BOS	.316
15.	Chris Codiroli	OAK	.209	116.	Bret Saberhagen	KC	.313
16.	Jimmy Key	TOR	.213	115.	Odell Jones	BAL	.311
17.	Floyd Bannister	CHI	.214	114.	Joel Davis	CHI	.310
18.	Ken Schrom	CLE	.215	113.	Dennis Rasmussen	NY	.307
19.	Bill Mooneyham	OAK	.215	112.	Dave Stieb	TOR	.306
20.	Dave Stewart	OAK	.215	111.	Phil Niekro	CLE	.305

National League

Top 20				Bottom 20			
1.	Jim Deshaies	HOU	.140	119.	Mark Thurmond	SD	.408
2.	Eric Show	SD	.145	118.	Jerry Reuss	LA	.375
3.	Charlie Kerfeld	HOU	.158	117.	Dave Gumpert	CHI	.373
4.	Mike Scott	HOU	.159	116.	Ed Lynch	CHI	.359
5.	Steve Bedrosian	PHI	.163	115.	Mike Maddux	PHI	.346
6.	Dwight Gooden	NY	.167	114.	Pat Perry	STL	.345
7.	Jesse Orosco	NY	.172	113.	Dave LaPoint	SD	.339
8.	Todd Worrell	STL	.180	112.	Joe Hesketh	MTL	.337
9.	Kent Tekulve	PHI	.185	111.	Charles Hudson	PHI	.336
10.	Lance McCullers	SD	.188	110.	Rick Honeycutt	LA	.319
11.	Don Robinson	PIT	.192	109.	Jay Baller	CHI	.317
12.	Dave Dravecky	SD	.194	108.	Larry McWilliams	PIT	.314
13.	Kelly Downs	SF	.195	107.	Mike LaCoss	SF	.312
14.	Mike Krukow	SF	.196	106.	Chris Welsh	CIN	.309
15.	Ron Darling	NY	.199	105.	Larry Andersen	HOU	.308
16.	Floyd Youmans	MTL	.200	104.	Guy Hoffman	CHI	.305
17.	Sid Fernandez	NY	.204	103.	Doug Sisk	NY	.304
18.	Bob Ojeda	NY	.206	102.	Steve Trout	CHI	.304
19.	Jeff Dedmon	ATL	.207	101.	Rick Mahler	ATL	.303
20.	Jeff Reardon	MTL	.208	100.	Ed Whitson	SD	.300

Opponents' Batting Average in Pressure Situations

American League

Top 20				Bottom 20			
1.	Ed Correa	TEX	.098	128.	Dennis Lamp	TOR	.520
2.	Doug Bair	OAK	.108	127.	Juan Agosto	MIN	.487
3.	Jeff Russell	TEX	.127	126.	Dave Stieb	TOR	.452
4.	Doyle Alexander	TOR	.133	125.	Lee Guetterman	SEA	.422
5.	Kirk McCaskill	CAL	.160	124.	Jim Clancy	TOR	.379
6.	Scott Bankhead	KC	.161	123.	Mike Morgan	SEA	.366
7.	Joel McKeon	CHI	.170	122.	Jim Slaton	DET	.364
8.	Tom Henke	TOR	.171	121.	Ron Davis	MIN	.360
9.	Ray Searage	CHI	.176	120.	Scott McGregor	BAL	.352
10.	Walt Terrell	DET	.179	119.	Bill Caudill	TOR	.342
11.	Bill Campbell	DET	.185	118.	Tom Seaver	BOS	.339
12.	Mark Clear	MIL	.187	117.	Joel Davis	CHI	.333
12.	Bud Black	KC	.187	116.	Jim Acker	TOR	.328
14.	Joe Sambito	BOS	.188	115.	Mark Langston	SEA	.328
15.	Curt Young	OAK	.190	113.	Bob Stanley	BOS	.327
16.	Charlie Hough	TEX	.197	113.	Bill Swift	SEA	.327
17.	Mark Eichhorn	TOR	.197	112.	Dave Schmidt	CHI	.324
18.	Bobby Thigpen	CHI	.198	111.	Bert Blyleven	MIN	.322
19.	Dickie Noles	CLE	.200	110.	Phil Niekro	CLE	.321
20.	Dennis Rasmussen	NY	.207	109.	Frank Wills	CLE	.316

National League

Top 20				Bottom 20			
1.	Ed Olwine	ATL	.129	118.	Doyle Alexander	ATL	.432
2.	Bob Sebra	MTL	.135	117.	David Palmer	ATL	.419
3.	Jose DeLeon	PIT	.138	116.	Randy Niemann	NY	.405
4.	Tom Browning	CIN	.143	115.	Rick Ownbey	STL	.400
5.	Greg Mathews	STL	.154	114.	George Frazier	CHI	.390
6.	Shane Rawley	PHI	.156	113.	Rick Reuschel	PIT	.368
7.	Dwight Gooden	NY	.178	112.	Carl Willis	CIN	.364
8.	Cecilio Guante	PIT	.180	111.	Guy Hoffman	CHI	.360
9.	Steve Trout	CHI	.184	109.	Rick Aguilera	NY	.357
10.	Tim Stoddard	SD	.195	109.	Andy Hawkins	SD	.357
11.	Bill Gullickson	CIN	.196	107.	Rick Mahler	ATL	.353
12.	Ricky Horton	STL	.196	107.	Bryn Smith	MTL	.353
13.	Mike LaCoss	SF	.197	106.	Ted Power	CIN	.340
14.	Mike Scott	HOU	.198	102.	Bert Roberge	MTL	.333
15.	Charlie Kerfeld	HOU	.205	102.	Jim Acker	ATL	.333
16.	Ron Darling	NY	.206	102.	Dave Dravecky	SD	.333
17.	Steve Bedrosian	PHI	.208	102.	Dave Gumpert	CHI	.333
18.	Rob Murphy	CIN	.211	101.	Ed Vande Berg	LA	.330
19.	Mark Davis	SF	.214	100.	Zane Smith	ATL	.328
20.	Lee Smith	CHI	.214	99.	Chris Welsh	CIN	.323

Strikeout Percentage in Pressure Situations

American League

Top 20				Bottom 20			
1.	Tom Henke	TOR	35.51	128.	Bob Tewksbury	NY	0.00
2.	Calvin Schiraldi	BOS	28.57	127.	Dave Von Ohlen	OAK	2.50
3.	Mark Eichhorn	TOR	26.59	126.	Nate Snell	BAL	3.51
4.	Mark Clear	MIL	24.86	125.	Juan Agosto	MIN	4.44
5.	Bruce Hurst	BOS	24.62	124.	Frank Pastore	MIN	5.26
6.	Rod Scurry	NY	24.05	123.	Frank Tanana	DET	6.25
7.	Bill Caudill	TOR	23.81	122.	Doug Jones	CLE	6.67
8.	Doug Bair	OAK	23.60	121.	Jim Acker	TOR	7.23
9.	Kirk McCaskill	CAL	23.45	120.	Bryan Oelkers	CLE	7.41
10.	Chuck Finley	CAL	22.22	119.	Jim Slaton	DET	7.50
11.	Bill Campbell	DET	21.98	118.	Jose Guzman	TEX	7.55
12.	Dickie Noles	CLE	21.54	117.	Tom Seaver	BOS	7.81
13.	Roger Clemens	BOS	21.31	116.	Walt Terrell	DET	8.05
14.	Steve Farr	KC	21.28	115.	Storm Davis	BAL	8.22
15.	George Frazier	MIN	21.11	114.	Randy O'Neal	DET	8.64
16.	Matt Young	SEA	21.08	113.	Mike Flanagan	BAL	8.86
17.	Jeff Russell	TEX	20.97	112.	Lee Guetterman	SEA	9.26
18.	Greg Harris	TEX	20.96	111.	Charlie Leibrandt	KC	9.28
19.	Don Aase	BAL	20.41	110.	Phil Niekro	CLE	10.00
20.	Willie Hernandez	DET	20.36	109.	Dennis Leonard	KC	10.10

National League

Top 20				Bottom 20			
1.	Jeff Robinson	SF	26.14	118.	Jim Acker	ATL	2.78
2.	Mark Davis	SF	25.97	117.	Rick Mahler	ATL	4.76
3.	Joe Hesketh	MTL	25.58	116.	Dennis Powell	LA	4.84
4.	Lee Smith	CHI	25.00	115.	Chris Welsh	CIN	5.13
5.	Cecilio Guante	PIT	24.84	114.	Dave Dravecky	SD	5.45
6.	Mike Scott	HOU	24.59	113.	Danny Cox	STL	5.56
7.	Fernando Valenzuela	LA	23.75	112.	Mike LaCoss	SF	6.17
8.	Bruce Sutter	ATL	23.64	111.	Bob Forsch	STL	6.90
9.	Ken Howell	LA	23.28	110.	Vida Blue	SF	7.14
10.	Gene Walter	SD	23.20	109.	Greg Mathews	STL	7.32
11.	Juan Berenguer	SF	23.15	108.	Bruce Ruffin	PHI	7.55
12.	Dwight Gooden	NY	22.88	107.	John Tudor	STL	7.88
13.	Scott Garrelts	SF	22.18	105.	Larry Andersen	HOU	7.89
14.	Ron Robinson	CIN	21.88	105.	Bryn Smith	MTL	7.89
15.	Paul Assenmacher	ATL	21.74	104.	Rick Anderson	NY	8.11
16.	Rich Gossage	SD	21.36	102.	Bert Roberge	MTL	8.33
17.	Rick Aguilera	NY	21.21	102.	Doyle Alexander	ATL	8.33
17.	Rick Ownbey	STL	21.21	101.	Scott Terry	CIN	8.57
19.	Eric Show	SD	20.93	100.	Steve Trout	CHI	8.70
20.	Steve Bedrosian	PHI	20.15	99.	Bill Gullickson	CIN	9.00

VI
Single Season and Career Leaders

Single Season and Career Leaders

The Single Season and Career Leaders section lists, for a variety of batting and pitching categories, the top 25 performers since we began *The Player Analysis* in 1975.

When we began our analysis of play-by-play data from every game, we had a dual purpose: we recognized the value of the information for immediate use, and we knew we were accumulating and building a valuable resource for future study as well. This section gives us a chance to take stock of the results from our unparalleled files—files representing more than a million and a half plate appearances.

The leader categories for this section were chosen both for significance and for general interest (however quirky). The single season bests listed here provide an important context for evaluating the performances throughout this book. The career lists do considerably more; they combine twelve years' worth of statistics, and provide the definitive look at situational statistics since 1975.

Minimum qualifiers for most batting categories are expressed in hits rather than in the equivalent number of plate appearances. As a general rule, the number of hits is one third the number of at bats of the qualifying range, if you're more comfortable thinking about it in those terms.

In dealing with last season's statistics in the Ranking Section of this book, we used a more inclusive level for rankings qualification: the equivalent of 200 plate appearances. The levels used here are more stringent, corresponding more to everyday play than part-time or "semiregular" status.

In the pitching categories, it should not be too surprising that relievers dominate. They allow consistently lower batting averages than starters for a variety of reasons, not only in traditional statistics but in these situational statistics as well. We have tried to set qualifying levels that are meaningful for both starters and relievers; the levels are the equivalent of about one and a half seasons as a full-time starter, or three as a primary reliever.

Bear in mind that *The Player Analysis* began in 1975. For the vast majority of active players, this poses no obstacle to calling these "career" statistics. In some cases, the missing information is very minor (67 at bats out of Jim Rice's career; a little under 500 from George Brett's); in the case of a Pete Rose or Tony Perez, obviously, a larger chunk is missing. We'd love to be able to fill in the gaps; we'd also love to know how Lou Gehrig hit with runners in scoring position in late-inning pressure. Maybe someday . . .

CAREER BATTING AVERAGE VS. LEFT-HANDED PITCHERS

Min. 150 Hits

Kirby Puckett	.333
Jim Rice	.319
Bob Watson	.318
Keith Moreland	.317
Julio Franco	.317
Don Mattingly	.315
Paul Molitor	.312
Wade Boggs	.311
Buddy Bell	.310
Rod Carew	.310
Tony Pena	.309
Bill Madlock	.309
Ron LeFlore	.309
Gary Matthews	.308
Don Slaught	.308
Lee Lacy	.308
Ellis Valentine	.307
John Castino	.307
Carney Lansford	.306
Hubie Brooks	.306
Rickey Henderson	.306
Willie Wilson	.305
Gary Ward	.305
Hal McRae	.304
Jack Clark	.304

CAREER SLUGGING AVERAGE VS. LEFT-HANDED PITCHERS

Min. 200 Total Bases

Mike Schmidt	.585
Ellis Valentine	.562
Jack Clark	.543
Jim Rice	.541
Cal Ripken	.533
Johnny Bench	.531
George Foster	.530
Ron Cey	.528
Dave Winfield	.528
Tom Brunansky	.524
Dwight Evans	.522
Glenn Davis	.521
Dale Murphy	.519
Cliff Johnson	.518
Dave Kingman	.518
Lance Parrish	.518
Pedro Guerrero	.516
Don Mattingly	.515
Gary Carter	.514
Bill Robinson	.513
Andre Dawson	.512
Hal McRae	.509
Eric Soderholm	.509
Bob Horner	.509
Mike Ivie	.505

CAREER HOME RUN PCT. VS. LEFT-HANDED PITCHERS

Min. 20 Home Runs

Dave Kingman	7.58
Eric Davis	7.55
Mike Schmidt	7.21
Ron Cey	6.71
Tom Brunansky	6.20
Glenn Davis	6.19
Gorman Thomas	6.12
Ron Kittle	6.11
Ellis Valentine	6.07
Johnny Bench	6.03
Steve Balboni	5.95
George Foster	5.93
Gene Tenace	5.90
John Wockenfuss	5.85
Lance Parrish	5.81
Bob Horner	5.69
Cliff Johnson	5.57
Dale Murphy	5.54
Dave Winfield	5.43
Pedro Guerrero	5.39
Jack Clark	5.31
Gary Carter	5.29
Greg Luzinski	5.25
Eric Soderholm	5.25
Jim Rice	5.22

CAREER STRIKEOUT PCT. VS. LEFT-HANDED PITCHERS

Min. 500 PA

Ted Sizemore	2.90
Dave Cash	3.05
Tim Foli	3.08
Bob Bailor	3.41
Marty Barrett	3.46
Manny Sanguillen	3.48
Felix Millan	3.49
Doug Flynn	4.69
Rennie Stennett	4.72
Rich Dauer	4.96
Bruce Benedict	5.01
Bob Boone	5.08
Bucky Dent	5.09
Mickey Hatcher	5.20
Pete Rose	5.21
Don Kessinger	5.30
Bill Russell	5.34
Mario Guerrero	5.46
Rob Andrews	5.48
Jerry Terrell	5.54
Bill Buckner	5.69
Steve Nicosia	5.71
Willie Randolph	5.79
Eric Soderholm	6.03
Jim Essian	6.13

CAREER BATTING AVERAGE VS. RIGHT-HANDED PITCHERS

Min. 250 Hits

Wade Boggs	.370
Rod Carew	.341
Don Mattingly	.340
Tony Gwynn	.336
George Brett	.332
Al Oliver	.326
Lyman Bostock	.325
Phil Bradley	.317
Wally Backman	.312
Tim Raines	.309
Jose Cruz	.308
Cecil Cooper	.308
Mike Easler	.308
Fred Lynn	.307
Ken Griffey	.307
Pedro Guerrero	.306
Thurman Munson	.306
Dave Parker	.306
Bake McBride	.306
Mickey Rivers	.305
Bill Madlock	.305
Keith Hernandez	.304
Willie McGee	.304
Jerry Mumphrey	.304
Mike Hargrove	.301

CAREER SLUGGING AVERAGE VS. RIGHT-HANDED PITCHERS

Min. 300 Total Bases

Darryl Strawberry	.560
George Brett	.553
Don Mattingly	.552
Reggie Smith	.539
Mike Schmidt	.533
Willie Stargell	.532
Fred Lynn	.530
Greg Walker	.527
Ken Phelps	.520
Pedro Guerrero	.513
Reggie Jackson	.513
Jim Rice	.513
Kirk Gibson	.509
Jesse Barfield	.509
Eddie Murray	.508
Bob Horner	.507
Dave Parker	.502
Kent Hrbek	.501
Cecil Cooper	.500
Mike Pagliarulo	.499
Alvin Davis	.499
Oscar Gamble	.498
Leon Durham	.497
Mel Hall	.496
Willie Aikens	.494

CAREER HOME RUN PCT. VS. RIGHT-HANDED PITCHERS

Min. 40 Home Runs

Ken Phelps	7.87
Mike Schmidt	6.88
Darryl Strawberry	6.83
Ron Kittle	6.75
Dave Kingman	6.35
Reggie Jackson	6.22
Willie Stargell	6.19
Bob Horner	6.14
Reggie Smith	5.99
Mike Pagliarulo	5.95
Jesse Barfield	5.82
Gorman Thomas	5.80
Oscar Gamble	5.67
Steve Balboni	5.60
Tony Armas	5.52
Graig Nettles	5.49
Jason Thompson	5.29
Dale Murphy	5.22
Greg Walker	5.20
Andre Thornton	5.13
Greg Brock	5.11
John Mayberry	5.09
Greg Luzinski	5.03
Eddie Murray	5.00
George Foster	4.97

CAREER STRIKEOUT PCT. VS. RIGHT-HANDED PITCHERS

Min. 750 PA

Felix Millan	3.29
Bill Buckner	3.76
Dave Cash	4.30
Tony Gwynn	4.37
Johnny Ray	4.37
Larry Bowa	5.04
Ken Oberkfell	5.16
Jack Brohamer	5.17
Mike Squires	5.17
Ozzie Smith	5.19
Greg Gross	5.25
Rich Dauer	5.31
Terry Francona	5.32
Wade Boggs	5.33
Al Oliver	5.37
Rusty Staub	5.40
Don Mattingly	5.42
Mike Scioscia	5.45
George Brett	5.48
Tom Poquette	5.72
Pete Rose	5.83
Dan Meyer	5.95
Bob Bailor	5.98
Duane Kuiper	5.99
Mario Guerrero	6.01

SINGLE-SEASON BATTING AVERAGE VS. LEFT-HANDED PITCHERS		SINGLE-SEASON BATTING AVERAGE VS. RIGHT-HANDED PITCHERS		SINGLE-SEASON BATTING AVERAGE IN HOME GAMES		SINGLE-SEASON BATTING AVERAGE IN ROAD GAMES	
Min. 40 Hits		*Min. 75 Hits*		*Min. 75 Hits*		*Min. 75 Hits*	
Rennie Stennett, 1977	.435	George Brett, 1980	.437	Wade Boggs, 1985	.418	George Brett, 1980	.388
Sixto Lezcano, 1979	.411	Wade Boggs, 1983	.398	Rod Carew, 1977	.401	Cecil Cooper, 1980	.386
Steve Henderson, 1979	.395	Rod Carew, 1977	.398	Juan Beniquez, 1984	.399	Rod Carew, 1977	.374
Mike Vail, 1979	.395	Rod Carew, 1975	.379	Wade Boggs, 1983	.397	Johnny Ray, 1984	.370
Ken Griffey, 1976	.393	Wade Boggs, 1985	.377	George Brett, 1980	.391	Rod Carew, 1983	.369
Bill Buckner, 1978	.389	Tony Gwynn, 1984	.371	Rod Carew, 1975	.387	Don Mattingly, 1986	.367
Paul Molitor, 1979	.387	Oscar Gamble, 1979	.370	Fred Lynn, 1979	.386	Don Mattingly, 1984	.364
Brian Downing, 1979	.386	Cecil Cooper, 1980	.365	Al Oliver, 1980	.385	Brian Downing, 1979	.360
Chet Lemon, 1984	.384	Fred Lynn, 1979	.364	Hal McRae, 1976	.382	Bob Watson, 1975	.358
Keith Moreland, 1983	.382	Willie Wilson, 1982	.360	Miguel Dilone, 1980	.378	Mickey Rivers, 1977	.358
Buddy Bell, 1977	.382	Wade Boggs, 1986	.359	Tony Gwynn, 1984	.376	Bill Madlock, 1975	.357
Rico Carty, 1975	.381	Rod Carew, 1983	.358	Mike Easler, 1984	.375	Wade Boggs, 1986	.356
Don Baylor, 1975	.380	Bill Madlock, 1975	.357	George Brett, 1979	.373	Ken Singleton, 1977	.354
Jack Clark, 1980	.380	Mike Easler, 1980	.357	Bill Buckner, 1977	.372	Ben Oglivie, 1980	.353
Jeff Leonard, 1984	.380	Wade Boggs, 1982	.356	Jim Rice, 1979	.369	Willie McGee, 1985	.353
Jose Cardenal, 1975	.379	Wade Boggs, 1984	.356	Fred Lynn, 1975	.368	Steve Sax, 1986	.352
Ray Knight, 1986	.379	Willie McGee, 1985	.356	George Brett, 1985	.368	Keith Hernandez, 1979	.350
Lee Lacy, 1980	.379	Rod Carew, 1982	.355	Dave Parker, 1977	.368	Dave Winfield, 1984	.349
Gary Carter, 1977	.378	Al Oliver, 1979	.353	George Brett, 1976	.367	Enos Cabell, 1984	.348
Ken Singleton, 1977	.373	Miguel Dilone, 1980	.353	Kirby Puckett, 1986	.367	Al Oliver, 1978	.348
Joe Charboneau, 1980	.373	Keith Hernandez, 1979	.353	Dave Parker, 1978	.367	Robin Yount, 1982	.347
Dwight Evans, 1975	.372	George Brett, 1979	.352	Keith Hernandez, 1984	.366	Rod Carew, 1980	.347
Jeff Burroughs, 1978	.372	Al Oliver, 1980	.351	George Brett, 1975	.362	Bob Bailor, 1977	.347
Rod Carew, 1977	.371	Don Mattingly, 1984	.351	Gary Matthews, 1977	.362	Rod Carew, 1976	.346
Bill Madlock, 1983	.371	Fred Lynn, 1975	.350	Jim Rice, 1978	.361	Jose Cruz, 1984	.344

CAREER HOME RUN PCT. IN HOME GAMES		CAREER HOME RUN PCT. IN ROAD GAMES		CAREER BATTING AVERAGE IN HOME GAMES		CAREER BATTING AVERAGE IN ROAD GAMES	
Min. 25 Home Runs		*Min. 25 Home Runs*		*Min. 200 Hits*		*Min. 200 Hits*	
Ken Phelps	8.13	Eric Davis	7.47	Wade Boggs	.378	Don Mattingly	.337
Bob Horner	7.92	Ron Kittle	7.01	George Brett	.345	Rod Carew	.328
Rob Deer	7.78	Dave Kingman	6.90	Kirby Puckett	.340	Wade Boggs	.326
Mike Schmidt	7.02	Mike Schmidt	6.90	Rod Carew	.334	Tony Gwynn	.317
Jesse Barfield	6.59	Darryl Strawberry	6.86	Tony Gwynn	.334	Mickey Rivers	.308
Dave Kingman	6.52	Steve Balboni	6.83	Jim Rice	.326	Pedro Guerrero	.306
Oscar Gamble	6.31	Gorman Thomas	5.93	Al Oliver	.326	Lyman Bostock	.305
Willie Stargell	6.26	Pedro Guerrero	5.83	Don Mattingly	.326	Cecil Cooper	.305
Greg Luzinski	6.25	Ken Phelps	5.80	Lyman Bostock	.318	Bob Watson	.305
Dale Murphy	6.04	Reggie Jackson	5.55	Pat Tabler	.317	Tim Raines	.303
Ron Kittle	5.98	Glenn Davis	5.44	Dave Parker	.316	Bill Madlock	.303
Reggie Jackson	5.89	Willie Stargell	5.35	Kent Hrbek	.314	Manny Sanguillen	.303
Gorman Thomas	5.87	Willie Aikens	5.29	Phil Bradley	.314	Keith Hernandez	.300
George Foster	5.71	Tom Brunansky	5.23	Fred Lynn	.313	Ken Griffey	.299
Graig Nettles	5.49	Lance Parrish	5.18	Thurman Munson	.311	Dave Winfield	.299
Rick Monday	5.48	Tony Armas	5.11	Carney Lansford	.311	Cal Ripken	.297
Andre Thornton	5.47	Gene Tenace	5.08	Ryne Sandberg	.309	Thurman Munson	.297
Gary Alexander	5.46	Jack Clark	5.07	Bill Madlock	.309	Gene Richards	.297
Jim Rice	5.40	Reggie Smith	5.06	Mike Easler	.307	Willie McGee	.296
Reggie Smith	5.34	Johnny Bench	5.05	Hal McRae	.307	Rickey Henderson	.296
Glenn Davis	5.32	Mike Pagliarulo	5.01	Tim Raines	.306	Ken Singleton	.296
Champ Summers	5.31	Willie McCovey	5.00	Lou Brock	.306	Eddie Murray	.295
Fred Lynn	5.22	Eddie Murray	4.98	Keith Hernandez	.304	Willie Wilson	.294
Cliff Johnson	5.20	Bobby Bonds	4.93	Lonnie Smith	.304	Ray Knight	.294
Dwight Evans	5.09	John Mayberry	4.90	Bake McBride	.304	Glenn Adams	.293

CAREER BATTING AVERAGE WITH RUNNERS ON BASE

Min. 200 Hits

Wade Boggs	.362
Rod Carew	.348
Tony Gwynn	.339
George Brett	.327
Kirby Puckett	.326
Dave Parker	.326
Lyman Bostock	.326
Don Mattingly	.324
Thurman Munson	.321
Pete Rose	.319
Keith Hernandez	.319
Cecil Cooper	.317
Al Oliver	.316
Bill Madlock	.315
Jim Rice	.311
Eddie Murray	.311
Garry Templeton	.310
Tim Raines	.310
Mike Easler	.309
Bill Buckner	.308
Steve Garvey	.307
Manny Sanguillen	.307
Fred Lynn	.307
Pedro Guerrero	.306
Bruce Bochte	.305

SINGLE-SEASON BATTING AVERAGE WITH RUNNERS ON BASE

Min. 75 Hits

Rod Carew, 1977	.422
Tony Gwynn, 1984	.406
George Brett, 1980	.400
Garry Templeton, 1979	.388
Wade Boggs, 1985	.387
Fred Lynn, 1979	.387
Keith Hernandez, 1979	.383
Dave Parker, 1978	.383
Wade Boggs, 1986	.379
Garry Templeton, 1977	.378
Rod Carew, 1975	.377
Mickey Rivers, 1977	.373
Bill Madlock, 1975	.370
Manny Sanguillen, 1975	.370
Bill Madlock, 1976	.368
Hal McRae, 1976	.368
George Brett, 1985	.367
Hal McRae, 1982	.366
Pete Rose, 1975	.366
Fred Lynn, 1975	.365
Ken Griffey, 1976	.362
Cecil Cooper, 1980	.362
Eddie Murray, 1985	.361
Dave Parker, 1976	.360
Willie McGee, 1985	.360

CAREER BATTING AVERAGE WITH RUNNERS IN SCORING POSITION

Min. 100 Hits

Wade Boggs	.367
Rod Carew	.345
Tony Gwynn	.336
Thurman Munson	.329
Don Mattingly	.327
Pat Tabler	.324
Lyman Bostock	.324
Pete Rose	.323
Al Oliver	.323
George Brett	.322
Broderick Perkins	.318
Bill Madlock	.318
Jim Rice	.317
Rennie Stennett	.315
Cecil Cooper	.315
Lou Piniella	.314
Kirby Puckett	.313
Dane Iorg	.313
Lamar Johnson	.312
Dave Parker	.312
Willie McGee	.310
Keith Hernandez	.309
Bake McBride	.309
Julio Franco	.308
Kent Hrbek	.308

SINGLE-SEASON BATTING AVERAGE WITH RUNNERS IN SCORING POSITION

Min. 50 Hits

George Brett, 1980	.466
Cecil Cooper, 1980	.421
Tony Gwynn, 1984	.418
Bill Madlock, 1976	.414
Ken Griffey, 1976	.412
Pete Rose, 1975	.412
Don Mattingly, 1984	.405
Fred Lynn, 1975	.400
Mickey Rivers, 1977	.400
Kent Hrbek, 1982	.398
Wade Boggs, 1985	.392
Robin Yount, 1982	.392
Joe Morgan, 1976	.391
Willie McGee, 1985	.391
Hal McRae, 1982	.383
Rod Carew, 1977	.382
Bake McBride, 1980	.380
Bill Robinson, 1977	.380
Garry Templeton, 1977	.379
Thurman Munson, 1975	.376
Rod Carew, 1978	.375
Ted Simmons, 1983	.375
Dave Winfield, 1979	.371
Eddie Murray, 1985	.370
Joe Rudi, 1976	.369

CAREER BATTING AVERAGE WITH 2 OUTS AND RUNNERS ON BASE

Min. 75 Hits

Wade Boggs	.357
Kirby Puckett	.341
Larry Hisle	.321
Dave Parker	.321
Don Mattingly	.320
Thurman Munson	.320
Tony Gwynn	.316
Tony Fernandez	.311
Al Oliver	.311
Larry Biittner	.307
Cecil Cooper	.305
Keith Hernandez	.304
Jose Cardenal	.304
Bill Madlock	.303
Rico Carty	.303
George Brett	.302
Garry Templeton	.302
Rod Carew	.301
Gene Richards	.301
Lyman Bostock	.301
Garth Iorg	.299
Harold Baines	.298
Jose Cruz	.298
Pete Rose	.298
Oscar Gamble	.297

SINGLE-SEASON BATTING AVERAGE WITH 2 OUTS AND RUNNERS ON BASE

Min. 30 Hits

Barry Bonnell, 1977	.437
Lee Lacy, 1984	.432
Al Oliver, 1980	.424
Bruce Bochte, 1982	.418
Dave Parker, 1986	.412
Ted Simmons, 1983	.404
Sixto Lezcano, 1979	.402
Garry Templeton, 1979	.400
Ray Knight, 1986	.400
Rod Carew, 1977	.398
Harold Baines, 1985	.391
Greg Gross, 1975	.390
Lee Mazzilli, 1979	.390
Larry Parrish, 1979	.388
Rod Carew, 1975	.388
Joe Rudi, 1976	.386
Frank Taveras, 1978	.386
Rennie Stennett, 1975	.383
Larry Hisle, 1978	.379
Steve Garvey, 1979	.377
Rod Carew, 1978	.376
Garry Templeton, 1977	.376
Steve Kemp, 1980	.375
Ozzie Guillen, 1986	.375
Pete Rose, 1979	.373

CAREER BATTING AVERAGE WITH 2 OUTS & RUNNERS IN SCORING POSITION

Min. 50 Hits

Wade Boggs	.354
Kirby Puckett	.333
Larry Hisle	.332
Thurman Munson	.325
Al Oliver	.320
Marty Barrett	.312
Don Mattingly	.309
Lamar Johnson	.307
Kent Hrbek	.307
Gary Ward	.306
George Brett	.305
Terry Harper	.305
Dave Parker	.304
Lyman Bostock	.304
Tony Gwynn	.304
Gene Richards	.303
Pete Rose	.303
Lou Piniella	.303
John Castino	.302
Dane Iorg	.302
Bill Madlock	.302
Jose Morales	.301
Rod Carew	.299
Cecil Cooper	.297
Steve Garvey	.297

SINGLE-SEASON BATTING AVERAGE WITH 2 OUTS & RUNNERS IN SCORING POSITION

Min. 20 Hits

Kent Hrbek, 1982	.466
Bruce Bochte, 1982	.457
Al Oliver, 1980	.446
Rod Carew, 1975	.440
Ted Simmons, 1983	.437
George Foster, 1981	.426
Chris Speier, 1978	.426
Dave Parker, 1986	.419
Rod Carew, 1978	.414
Cecil Cooper, 1980	.414
Rod Carew, 1977	.412
Lee Mazzilli, 1978	.412
Joe Rudi, 1976	.410
Lyman Bostock, 1978	.407
Dave Winfield, 1979	.407
Mike Ivie, 1979	.404
Tony Fernandez, 1986	.404
Larry Hisle, 1978	.403
Lee Lacy, 1984	.400
Paul Molitor, 1986	.400
Rusty Staub, 1976	.397
Ray Knight, 1986	.396
Pete Rose, 1975	.395
Barry Bonnell, 1977	.393
Larry Parrish, 1986	.392

CAREER BATTING AVERAGE IN LATE-INNING PRESSURE SITUATIONS

Min. 50 Hits

Wade Boggs	.369
Tony Gwynn	.348
Tim Raines	.347
Chris Brown	.337
Ken Griffey	.328
Don Mattingly	.327
George Brett	.326
Joe Lefebvre	.320
Tony Fernandez	.318
Garth Iorg	.315
Bo Diaz	.315
Eddie Murray	.314
Cecil Cooper	.313
Cal Ripken	.312
Ron LeFlore	.312
Steve Sax	.311
Ed Romero	.311
Hubie Brooks	.310
Pedro Guerrero	.310
Tom Paciorek	.310
Thurman Munson	.309
Mickey Rivers	.309
Jose Cardenal	.309
Wally Backman	.308
Rickey Henderson	.308

SINGLE-SEASON BATTING AVERAGE IN LATE-INNING PRESSURE SITUATIONS

Min. 25 Hits

Manny Trillo, 1981	.466
Bill Madlock, 1975	.464
Mickey Rivers, 1977	.439
Wade Boggs, 1986	.433
George Brett, 1976	.433
Steve Kemp, 1979	.429
Ken Griffey, 1975	.423
Tom Paciorek, 1976	.419
Mike Easler, 1984	.416
Scot Thompson, 1979	.413
Cecil Cooper, 1982	.412
Lloyd Moseby, 1983	.410
Luis Salazar, 1981	.408
Bill Buckner, 1984	.403
Chris Chambliss, 1981	.403
Rick Manning, 1983	.402
Ken Griffey, 1986	.402
Cal Ripken, 1984	.398
Bill Buckner, 1978	.397
Will Clark, 1986	.397
Wade Boggs, 1985	.395
Rickey Henderson, 1983	.391
Dale Murphy, 1984	.391
Rico Carty, 1976	.389
Ken Singleton, 1977	.388

CAREER HOME RUN PCT. IN LATE-INNING PRESSURE SITUATIONS

Min. 10 Home Runs

Ken Phelps	7.95
Gary Alexander	7.80
Dave Kingman	6.90
Eddie Murray	6.80
Craig Kusick	6.78
Steve Balboni	6.54
Pedro Guerrero	6.38
Darryl Strawberry	6.34
Tony Armas	6.23
Andre Thornton	6.13
Mike Schmidt	5.96
Jim Presley	5.94
Graig Nettles	5.77
Mel Hall	5.64
Kirk Gibson	5.58
Oscar Gamble	5.57
Reggie Smith	5.56
Candy Maldonado	5.45
Bernie Carbo	5.41
Richie Zisk	5.32
Dwight Evans	5.29
Willie Stargell	5.25
Reggie Jackson	5.24
Cliff Johnson	5.24
Pat Putnam	5.14

CAREER BATTING AVG. IN LATE-INNING PRESSURE SITUATIONS WITH RUNNERS IN SCORING POSITION

Min. 25 Hits

Eric Soderholm	.429
Wade Boggs	.405
Cal Ripken	.396
Eddie Murray	.383
Don Mattingly	.372
Chili Davis	.359
Willie Montanez	.355
Lee May	.352
George Bell	.347
Pete Rose	.346
Ron Hassey	.346
Tony Gwynn	.346
Ken Griffey	.344
Oscar Gamble	.343
Thurman Munson	.341
Bruce Bochte	.337
Mike Ivie	.333
Reggie Smith	.333
Dave Chalk	.333
Rickey Henderson	.331
Mookie Wilson	.330
Cesar Geronimo	.330
Kent Hrbek	.330
Rod Carew	.328
Dave Cash	.325

CAREER BATTING AVERAGE IN LATE-INNING PRESSURE SITUATIONS WITH RUNNERS ON BASE

Min. 25 Hits

Wade Boggs	.393
Mike Ivie	.370
Dickie Thon	.368
Eddie Murray	.364
Chris Brown	.351
George Bell	.351
Eric Soderholm	.348
Garth Iorg	.346
Thad Bosley	.345
Tony Gwynn	.342
Manny Mota	.342
Phil Bradley	.341
Bill Buckner	.340
Greg Walker	.340
Don Mattingly	.340
Bo Diaz	.340
Don Slaught	.338
Jose Cardenal	.335
Reggie Smith	.333
Cal Ripken	.333
Dave Rader	.333
Pete Rose	.332
Thurman Munson	.331
Tim Raines	.330
U.L. Washington	.329

SINGLE-SEASON BATTING AVERAGE IN LATE-INNING PRESSURE SITUATIONS WITH RUNNERS ON BASE

Min. 10 Hits

Rance Mulliniks, 1984	.684
Eddie Murray, 1985	.567
Bill Buckner, 1984	.563
Rowland Office, 1975	.536
Rusty Staub, 1981	.536
Jack Clark, 1984	.526
Ron Oester, 1981	.524
Pedro Guerrero, 1980	.520
Manny Trillo, 1981	.520
Carl Yastrzemski, 1975	.500
Ken Griffey, 1975	.500
Bernie Carbo, 1976	.500
Mickey Rivers, 1977	.500
Ken Singleton, 1977	.500
Pete Rose, 1977	.500
Barry Foote, 1979	.500
Glenn Adams, 1979	.500
Dan Ford, 1983	.500
Rick Manning, 1983	.486
Cesar Geronimo, 1976	.485
Mike Diaz, 1986	.483
Toby Harrah, 1985	.481
Larry Biittner, 1975	.480
Greg Gross, 1982	.480
Johnnie LeMaster, 1982	.480

CAREER BATTING AVERAGE IN LATE-INNING PRESSURE SITUATIONS WITH 2 OUTS AND RUNNERS ON BASE

Min. 15 Hits

Eric Soderholm	.429
Garth Iorg	.417
Wade Boggs	.411
Marty Perez	.405
Mike Ivie	.387
Dave Rader	.383
Ron Roenicke	.375
Eddie Murray	.370
Thurman Munson	.365
Tony Gwynn	.364
Tim Raines	.362
Steve Henderson	.360
Oscar Gamble	.355
Vance Law	.349
Glenn Adams	.345
H. Pat Kelly	.344
Ed Ott	.343
George Brett	.342
Alan Trammell	.342
Manny Sanguillen	.341
Dickie Thon	.340
George Bell	.340
U.L. Washington	.338
Ken Griffey	.335
Chili Davis	.333

CAREER BATTING AVG. IN LATE-INNING PRESSURE SITUATIONS WITH 2 OUTS AND RUNNERS IN SCORING POSITION

Min. 10 Hits

Gary Pettis	.500
Eric Soderholm	.444
Chili Davis	.436
Marty Perez	.435
Jim Norris	.417
Rusty Staub	.405
Bo Diaz	.400
Kent Hrbek	.400
Don Mattingly	.400
Ron Roenicke	.400
Wade Boggs	.395
Garth Iorg	.393
Cesar Geronimo	.391
Eddie Murray	.391
Thurman Munson	.387
Dickie Thon	.387
Oscar Gamble	.381
Willie Horton	.373
Pete Rose	.372
Jose Cruz	.370
Steve Henderson	.356
Ernie Whitt	.353
Lee May	.352
Ken Griffey	.350
Mike Ivie	.349

HIGHEST CAREER RATIO OF GROUND OUTS TO AIR OUTS

Min. 1,000 PA

Wally Backman	2.49
Gary Pettis	2.31
Willie McGee	2.12
Juan Bonilla	2.10
Steve Henderson	2.02
Duane Kuiper	2.02
Billy North	2.02
Steve Carlton	1.99
Alan Wiggins	1.94
Tony Gwynn	1.93
Steve Sax	1.91
Gene Richards	1.91
Rod Carew	1.89
Ron LeFlore	1.82
Miguel Dilone	1.82
Pete Rose	1.79
Garry Templeton	1.79
Curtis Wilkerson	1.77
Jerry Mumphrey	1.74
Lyman Bostock	1.73
Wayne Tolleson	1.71
R.J. Reynolds	1.71
Claudell Washington	1.71
Mookie Wilson	1.70
Julio Cruz	1.70

LOWEST CAREER RATIO OF GROUND OUTS TO AIR OUTS

Min. 1,000 PA

Gary Redus	0.60
Jim Dwyer	0.62
Ken Phelps	0.62
Gene Tenace	0.63
Joe Morgan	0.65
Steve Balboni	0.65
Andre Thornton	0.65
Darrell Evans	0.66
Don Baylor	0.66
Tim Hulett	0.68
Richie Hebner	0.70
Mike Schmidt	0.70
Howard Johnson	0.71
Tom Brunansky	0.71
Buck Martinez	0.71
Dave Revering	0.72
Joe Carter	0.73
Ron Kittle	0.73
Bobby Murcer	0.73
Jerry White	0.74
Dave Kingman	0.75
Tony Solaita	0.75
Dave Henderson	0.76
Jim Wynn	0.76
Greg Luzinski	0.76

CAREER BATTING AVERAGE IN DAY GAMES

Min. 100 Hits

Rod Carew	.347
Wade Boggs	.347
Don Mattingly	.331
Willie McGee	.328
Tony Gwynn	.326
Tim Raines	.321
Thad Bosley	.317
Bake McBride	.316
George Brett	.315
Al Oliver	.315
Phil Bradley	.313
Lyman Bostock	.313
Ken Griffey	.313
Jerry Grote	.312
Wayne Krenchicki	.312
Thurman Munson	.311
Jose Morales	.311
Reggie Smith	.310
Gene Richards	.309
Don Slaught	.309
Dave Parker	.308
Tony Pena	.308
Mel Hall	.308
Carney Lansford	.307
Bill Madlock	.307

CAREER BATTING AVERAGE IN NIGHT GAMES

Min. 100 Hits

Wade Boggs	.354
Don Mattingly	.332
Tony Gwynn	.326
Rod Carew	.324
George Brett	.318
Pedro Guerrero	.313
Lyman Bostock	.310
Kirby Puckett	.310
Mickey Rivers	.309
Jim Rice	.307
Cecil Cooper	.307
Al Oliver	.306
Bill Madlock	.305
Mike Easler	.305
Manny Sanguillen	.303
Keith Hernandez	.302
Willie Wilson	.301
Rick Peters	.301
Thurman Munson	.300
Dave Parker	.298
Phil Bradley	.298
Chris Brown	.298
Steve Garvey	.298
Pete Rose	.298
Eddie Murray	.296

CAREER BATTING AVERAGE ON GRASS SURFACES

Min. 150 Hits

Wade Boggs	.354
Rod Carew	.331
Tony Gwynn	.330
Don Mattingly	.329
Al Oliver	.318
Keith Hernandez	.314
Lyman Bostock	.313
Bill Madlock	.307
Jim Rice	.307
Thurman Munson	.306
Bob Watson	.305
Tim Raines	.304
Steve Garvey	.303
Pedro Guerrero	.302
Chris Brown	.302
Willie Wilson	.302
Cecil Cooper	.302
Pat Tabler	.301
Jose Cardenal	.300
Reggie Smith	.300
Ryne Sandberg	.300
Andre Dawson	.300
Eddie Murray	.300
Jerry Mumphrey	.298
Fred Lynn	.297

CAREER BATTING AVERAGE ON ARTIFICIAL TURF

Min. 150 Hits

George Brett	.343
Rod Carew	.333
Kirby Puckett	.318
Alan Trammell	.316
Al Bumbry	.314
Cal Ripken	.314
Tony Gwynn	.313
Jeff Stone	.313
Mickey Rivers	.312
Von Joshua	.311
Pedro Guerrero	.310
Steve Sax	.310
Jim Gantner	.310
Mike Easler	.309
Phil Bradley	.308
Kent Hrbek	.308
Lee Lacy	.307
Dave Parker	.307
Ken Griffey	.306
Cecil Cooper	.306
Bill Madlock	.305
Tim Raines	.305
Chris Chambliss	.303
Mickey Hatcher	.303
Hal McRae	.303

SINGLE-SEASON BATTING AVERAGE ON GRASS SURFACES

Min. 60 Hits

George Brett, 1980	.396
Rod Carew, 1977	.393
Pete Rose, 1979	.373
Ray Knight, 1983	.370
Ken Griffey, 1976	.368
Rod Carew, 1975	.367
Keith Hernandez, 1979	.366
Gary Gaetti, 1986	.364
Wade Boggs, 1983	.364
Wade Boggs, 1985	.363
Cecil Cooper, 1980	.363
Oscar Gamble, 1979	.362
Pat Sheridan, 1984	.358
Dan Gladden, 1984	.357
Wade Boggs, 1982	.354
Wade Boggs, 1986	.352
Juan Beniquez, 1984	.352
Bill Buckner, 1978	.351
Fred Lynn, 1979	.350
Tony Gwynn, 1984	.349
Don Mattingly, 1984	.348
Glenn Adams, 1977	.346
Pat Tabler, 1986	.346
Al Oliver, 1975	.346
Miguel Dilone, 1980	.345

SINGLE-SEASON BATTING AVERAGE ON ARTIFICIAL TURF

Min. 60 Hits

Bill Madlock, 1975	.398
Steve Sax, 1986	.387
George Brett, 1980	.386
Hal McRae, 1976	.382
George Brett, 1979	.369
George Brett, 1976	.367
Keith Hernandez, 1985	.364
George Brett, 1978	.357
Lee Lacy, 1980	.356
Willie McGee, 1985	.356
George Brett, 1981	.356
Greg Gross, 1983	.356
Pete Rose, 1976	.354
Bake McBride, 1976	.354
George Brett, 1975	.352
Bill Madlock, 1981	.352
Kirby Puckett, 1986	.352
George Brett, 1985	.352
Mike Easler, 1980	.349
Kent Hrbek, 1984	.349
Willie Wilson, 1982	.349
Pete Rose, 1981	.348
Joe Morgan, 1975	.347
Pete LaCock, 1978	.347
Garry Maddox, 1976	.347

CAREER ON-BASE AVERAGE LEADING OFF INNINGS		SINGLE-SEASON ON-BASE AVERAGE LEADING OFF INNINGS		CAREER WALK PCT. LEADING OFF INNINGS		SINGLE-SEASON WALK PCT. LEADING OFF INNINGS	
Min. 200 PA		*Min. 100 PA*		*Min. 25 Walks*		*Min. 15 Walks*	
Wade Boggs	.440	Rod Carew, 1982	.523	Jim Wynn	19.71	Jim Wynn, 1975	23.85
Tony Gwynn	.404	Andre Thornton, 1975	.519	Gene Tenace	15.78	Lee Mazzilli, 1982	22.97
Rickey Henderson	.394	Carlton Fisk, 1977	.504	Rob Deer	15.76	Lee Mazzilli, 1983	22.50
Rod Carew	.392	Wade Boggs, 1983	.494	Joe Morgan	15.34	Joe Morgan, 1975	22.00
Willie Randolph	.392	Toby Harrah, 1981	.491	Bernie Carbo	15.05	Gene Tenace, 1977	21.43
Pepe Mangual	.384	Joe Morgan, 1975	.470	Pepe Mangual	14.76	Dwayne Murphy, 1981	21.43
Mike Schmidt	.384	Wade Boggs, 1985	.468	Otto Velez	14.55	Andre Thornton, 1975	21.30
Mike Hargrove	.382	Ken Griffey, 1977	.466	Jerry Hairston	14.43	Carlton Fisk, 1977	21.17
Tony Solaita	.382	Willie Randolph, 1980	.457	Glenn Borgmann	14.35	Bernie Carbo, 1975	21.05
Greg Gross	.381	Hal McRae, 1977	.456	Rickey Henderson	14.28	Jerry Hairston, 1984	20.55
Tim Raines	.380	Mike Hargrove, 1977	.453	Willie Randolph	14.26	Mike Scioscia, 1985	20.54
Pedro Guerrero	.379	Mitchell Page, 1977	.452	Tommy Hutton	14.00	Gary Matthews, 1984	19.82
Bob Stinson	.377	Cal Ripken, 1984	.452	Joe Ferguson	13.84	Toby Harrah, 1981	19.81
Bobby Grich	.377	Willie Randolph, 1985	.448	Lee Mazzilli	13.80	Steve Kemp, 1981	19.74
Don Mattingly	.376	Jose Cruz, 1979	.448	Carmelo Martinez	13.70	Toby Harrah, 1985	19.71
Gene Tenace	.375	Richie Zisk, 1981	.447	Mike Hargrove	13.67	Johnny Briggs, 1975	19.15
Otto Velez	.375	Von Hayes, 1986	.444	Billy North	13.62	Gene Tenace, 1979	19.05
Johnny Grubb	.375	Johnny Grubb, 1976	.443	Dwayne Murphy	13.60	Mike Hargrove, 1977	18.95
Cal Ripken	.374	John Stearns, 1977	.442	Bud Harrelson	13.56	Willie Randolph, 1980	18.78
Bernie Carbo	.374	Mike Schmidt, 1979	.441	Ken Phelps	13.39	Darrell Porter, 1975	18.75
Bobby Bonds	.374	Bobby Grich, 1976	.441	Merv Rettenmund	13.27	Willie Randolph, 1981	18.75
Jack Clark	.373	Ozzie Smith, 1986	.440	Toby Harrah	13.17	Tommy Herr, 1985	18.69
Len Dykstra	.373	Jose Cruz, 1976	.440	Tony Solaita	13.16	Reggie Jackson, 1986	18.42
Keith Hernandez	.372	Tommy Herr, 1983	.439	Rick Peters	13.13	Greg Luzinski, 1981	18.35
Joe Morgan	.372	Willie Randolph, 1986	.438	Steve Braun	12.96	Jim Wynn, 1976	18.18

CAREER BATTING AVERAGE WITH BASES LOADED		CAREER RRF RATIO (PER PA) WITH BASES LOADED		CAREER WALK PCT. WITH BASES LOADED		CAREER STRIKEOUT PCT. BASES LOADED	
Min. 15 Hits		*Min. 30 RRF*		*Min. 10 Walks*		*Min. 50 PA*	
Pat Tabler	.522	Eddie Murray	1.15	Oscar Gamble	17.65	Ozzie Smith	0.95
Rudy Law	.469	Darryl Motley	1.13	Mike Hargrove	17.48	Rico Carty	1.43
Tony Gwynn	.469	Pat Tabler	1.11	Sixto Lezcano	17.12	Jim Spencer	1.89
Eddie Murray	.447	John Milner	1.10	Gene Tenace	16.09	Biff Pocoroba	1.92
Miguel Dilone	.436	Biff Pocoroba	1.06	Pete Rose	15.57	Jerry Morales	2.02
Biff Pocoroba	.435	Terry Crowley	1.05	Gary Roenicke	14.81	Craig Reynolds	2.41
Bill Madlock	.429	Mike Cubbage	1.04	Ken Oberkfell	14.71	Ken Oberkfell	2.94
Rick Bosetti	.429	Dane Iorg	1.03	Joe Morgan	14.55	Dave Cash	3.03
Lou Brock	.423	Rico Carty	1.00	Darrell Porter	14.41	Brett Butler	3.17
Denny Walling	.422	Dale Berra	1.00	Terry Puhl	13.70	Bill Madlock	3.85
Ken Singleton	.417	Lee Stanton	1.00	Dwight Evans	13.04	Bruce Benedict	3.90
Ellis Valentine	.417	Candy Maldonado	1.00	Jeff Burroughs	12.90	Lyman Bostock	3.92
Rico Carty	.404	Roy Howell	0.99	Carl Yastrzemski	12.15	Jose Cardenal	4.00
Lee May	.402	Oscar Gamble	0.99	Dan Driessen	11.76	Ellis Valentine	4.00
Wade Boggs	.400	H. Pat Kelly	0.98	Bobby Murcer	11.58	Bill Buckner	4.05
Jay Johnstone	.400	Jose Cruz	0.98	Ken Singleton	11.48	Doug Flynn	4.08
Oscar Gamble	.392	Bill Madlock	0.98	Dave Winfield	11.32	Jose Cruz	4.24
Leon Durham	.391	Joe Rudi	0.98	Ruppert Jones	11.11	Rich Dauer	4.35
Dale Berra	.391	Greg Walker	0.97	Brian Downing	11.03	Lenny Randle	4.62
Larry Hisle	.389	Steve Garvey	0.97	Butch Wynegar	10.92	Frank Taveras	4.62
Rod Carew	.388	Joe Carter	0.97	Darrell Evans	10.74	Larry Bowa	4.81
Lloyd Moseby	.386	John Wockenfuss	0.96	Carney Lansford	10.68	Toby Harrah	5.19
Richie Zisk	.382	Rod Carew	0.96	Gorman Thomas	10.48	Lou Brock	5.36
Willie McGee	.379	Howard Johnson	0.96	Dusty Baker	10.37	Ted Sizemore	5.45
Lee Stanton	.375	Lee May	0.95	Dave Lopes	10.09	Terry Puhl	5.48

CAREER PCT. OF RUNNERS DRIVEN IN FROM SCORING POSITION

Min. 100 RRF

Don Mattingly	.375
Wade Boggs	.358
Thurman Munson	.352
Dane Iorg	.352
Kent Hrbek	.351
Broderick Perkins	.349
George Brett	.349
Al Oliver	.349
Rusty Staub	.349
Cecil Cooper	.347
Rod Carew	.346
Dave Parker	.346
Ted Simmons	.345
Keith Hernandez	.345
Eddie Murray	.342
Lou Piniella	.341
Rico Carty	.340
Mike Hargrove	.340
Larry Hisle	.338
Bill Madlock	.338
Dave Winfield	.336
Lyman Bostock	.334
Hal McRae	.333
Jose Cruz	.333
Greg Walker	.333

SINGLE-SEASON PCT. OF RUNNERS DRIVEN IN FROM SCORING POSITION

Min. 50 RRF

George Brett, 1980	.507
Bill Buckner, 1981	.476
Cecil Cooper, 1980	.470
Bill Madlock, 1976	.448
Dave Parker, 1976	.430
Eddie Murray, 1985	.428
Bill Buckner, 1978	.427
Richie Hebner, 1980	.422
Cecil Cooper, 1976	.420
Bake McBride, 1980	.419
Buddy Bell, 1984	.418
Larry Parrish, 1986	.415
John Milner, 1976	.412
Rod Carew, 1977	.411
Ted Simmons, 1983	.410
Tommy Herr, 1985	.409
Rod Carew, 1975	.408
Joe Morgan, 1978	.408
Joe Morgan, 1976	.408
Pat Tabler, 1985	.407
Kent Hrbek, 1984	.405
Ray Knight, 1986	.403
Hal McRae, 1982	.402
Bill Madlock, 1979	.401
Eddie Murray, 1982	.401

CAREER PCT. OF RUNNERS DRIVEN IN FROM SCORING POSITION IN LATE-INNING PRESSURE SITUATIONS

Min. 20 RRF

Eric Soderholm	.427
Eddie Murray	.420
Eddie Milner	.412
Jim Essian	.403
Wade Boggs	.402
Don Mattingly	.398
Jim Norris	.392
Pete LaCock	.379
Pedro Guerrero	.372
Mike Hargrove	.369
Tony Gwynn	.368
Ozzie Virgil	.365
Chili Davis	.364
Rico Carty	.364
Bill Melton	.361
Carmelo Martinez	.359
Rusty Staub	.357
Bo Diaz	.355
Reggie Smith	.354
Ellis Valentine	.352
Jose Cruz	.349
Oscar Gamble	.349
Ted Simmons	.348
Ken Singleton	.345
George Bell	.344

SINGLE-SEASON OPPORTUNITIES FROM SCORING POSITION

Tony Perez, 1975	268
Don Baylor, 1979	257
Jim Rice, 1986	250
Johnny Bench, 1975	246
George Foster, 1976	245
Julio Franco, 1985	244
George Foster, 1977	243
Bill Buckner, 1986	242
Keith Moreland, 1985	238
Jerry Morales, 1975	236
Bob Watson, 1976	236
Lance Parrish, 1983	235
Tommy Herr, 1985	232
Greg Luzinski, 1975	230
Thurman Munson, 1976	229
Cecil Cooper, 1983	229
Jim Rice, 1975	228
Jim Rice, 1984	228
Willie Montanez, 1975	227
Steve Garvey, 1978	227
Rusty Staub, 1978	227
Willie Horton, 1979	226
Thurman Munson, 1975	224
Joe Carter, 1986	224
Al Oliver, 1980	223

CAREER PCT. OF RUNNERS DRIVEN IN FROM 3D BASE WITH LESS THAN 2 OUTS

Min. 40 RRF

Broderick Perkins	.753
Don Mattingly	.739
Rico Carty	.722
Ed Kranepool	.720
Tony Solaita	.719
Rod Carew	.719
Wade Boggs	.702
Dave Winfield	.697
Manny Sanguillen	.695
Jerry Hairston	.694
Al Oliver	.692
Bill Madlock	.692
Pat Tabler	.692
Mike Hargrove	.689
Rusty Staub	.686
Wayne Krenchicki	.682
Cal Ripken	.681
Fred Lynn	.680
Pete Rose	.677
Toby Harrah	.674
George Brett	.671
Mel Hall	.671
Hal McRae	.671
Keith Hernandez	.670
Steve Kemp	.668

SINGLE-SEASON PCT. OF RUNNERS DRIVEN IN FROM 3D BASE WITH LESS THAN 2 OUTS

Min. 15 RRF

Ben Oglivie, 1986	.913
Rod Carew, 1983	.900
Toby Harrah, 1981	.889
Bill Madlock, 1986	.880
Elliott Maddox, 1978	.875
Bill Madlock, 1976	.868
Dave Revering, 1979	.857
Kevin McReynolds, 1984	.852
Al Oliver, 1983	.846
Jerry Mumphrey, 1985	.846
Sid Bream, 1986	.846
Paul Molitor, 1978	.842
Dave Bergman, 1984	.842
Pat Tabler, 1985	.840
George Brett, 1980	.838
Richie Hebner, 1976	.833
Denny Walling, 1978	.833
Rich Dauer, 1978	.833
Brian Downing, 1982	.833
Alan Wiggins, 1984	.833
Buddy Bell, 1984	.829
Jerry Remy, 1982	.826
Gene Richards, 1981	.818
Toby Harrah, 1982	.818
Don Kessinger, 1975	.815

CAREER PCT. OF RUNNERS DRIVEN IN FROM 1ST BASE

Min. 30 RRF

Willie Stargell	.110
Mike Schmidt	.098
Darryl Strawberry	.095
Alvin Davis	.093
Greg Luzinski	.092
Larry Hisle	.091
Dave Kingman	.091
Dale Murphy	.090
George Brett	.089
Hal McRae	.088
Dave Parker	.087
Reggie Jackson	.087
Oscar Gamble	.086
Fred Lynn	.086
Bill Robinson	.086
Steve Balboni	.085
Greg Walker	.085
Bob Horner	.084
Ron Kittle	.083
Lance Parrish	.083
Cliff Johnson	.083
Leon Durham	.082
Don Mattingly	.082
Clint Hurdle	.082
George Foster	.082

SINGLE-SEASON RUNNERS DRIVEN IN FROM 1ST BASE

Hal McRae, 1982	36
George Foster, 1977	31
Jim Rice, 1978	29
Don Mattingly, 1985	29
Greg Luzinski, 1977	28
Alvin Davis, 1984	28
Keith Hernandez, 1979	27
Joe Carter, 1986	26
Jim Rice, 1983	25
Fred Lynn, 1979	24
Steve Garvey, 1979	24
Dave Kingman, 1984	24
Jose Canseco, 1986	24
Jeff Burroughs, 1977	23
Ron Cey, 1977	23
Jim Rice, 1979	23
Tony Armas, 1980	23
Tony Perez, 1980	23
Mike Schmidt, 1983	23
Eddie Murray, 1985	23
Fred Lynn, 1975	22
Johnny Bench, 1975	22
Bob Watson, 1977	22
Dave Parker, 1978	22
Gorman Thomas, 1978	22

CAREER OPP. BATTING AVERAGE VS. LEFT-HANDED PITCHERS

Min. 400 PA

Jesse Orosco	.180
Mark Langston	.194
Mark Davis	.195
Floyd Youmans	.197
Rod Scurry	.199
Pat Underwood	.201
Bob Lacey	.201
John Candelaria	.207
Willie Hernandez	.207
Nolan Ryan	.208
Craig Lefferts	.210
Dwight Gooden	.213
Dave Righetti	.214
Dave Smith	.214
Joe Sambito	.215
Mike Norris	.216
John Fulgham	.216
Al Holland	.217
Bruce Sutter	.217
Bob Shirley	.217
Larry Gura	.218
John Henry Johnson	.219
John Tudor	.219
Bob McClure	.220
Dave Dravecky	.221

CAREER OPP. HOME RUN PCT. VS. LEFT-HANDED PITCHERS

Min. 400 PA

Mickey Lolich	0.46
Joe Sambito	0.47
Bert Roberge	0.51
Doug Sisk	0.54
Jim Crawford	0.64
Dave Smith	0.69
Bruce Berenyi	0.69
Paul Mirabella	0.75
Gary Lavelle	0.77
Greg Minton	0.77
Bob Shirley	0.79
Jeff Lahti	0.80
Frank Williams	0.82
Donnie Moore	0.89
Jerry Reuss	0.89
Shane Rawley	0.91
Dwight Gooden	0.92
Ken Howell	0.92
Bob Knepper	0.93
Pedro Borbon	0.94
Andy Hassler	0.95
Ed Correa	0.97
Steve Trout	0.99
Orel Hershiser	1.00
Dave Dravecky	1.01

CAREER OPP. WALK PCT. VS. LEFT-HANDED PITCHERS

Min. 400 PA

Steve Howe	2.86
Gary Nolan	3.23
Scott McGregor	3.97
Dick Bosman	4.75
Tom Burgmeier	4.80
Dan Quisenberry	5.13
Jim Kaat	5.13
Jon Matlack	5.14
Bret Saberhagen	5.22
Dennis Boyd	5.31
Dave Tomlin	5.37
John Tudor	5.38
Frank Tanana	5.42
Will McEnaney	5.42
John Candelaria	5.55
Ed Lynch	5.56
Randy Jones	5.63
Rick Honeycutt	5.64
Ron Guidry	5.68
Pedro Borbon	5.69
Bob Knepper	5.74
Larry Gura	5.82
Frank Viola	5.82
Glenn Abbott	5.86
Gary Ross	5.89

CAREER OPP. STRIKEOUT PCT. VS. LEFT-HANDED PITCHERS

Min. 100 Strikeouts

Tom Henke	28.19
Mark Davis	27.62
Mark Langston	25.17
Dave Righetti	24.89
Nolan Ryan	24.51
Jesse Orosco	24.16
John Candelaria	23.58
Al Holland	23.18
John Tudor	23.05
Joe Sambito	22.77
Matt Young	22.68
Rod Scurry	22.59
Steve Carlton	21.81
Tippy Martinez	21.61
Dwight Gooden	21.44
Gary Lavelle	20.88
Willie Hernandez	20.84
Bill Caudill	20.63
Bob Knepper	20.57
John Hiller	20.42
Mike Flanagan	20.34
Bob James	20.34
Mark Clear	20.18
Frank Tanana	20.03
Bob Shirley	19.99

CAREER OPP. BATTING AVERAGE VS. RIGHT-HANDED PITCHERS

Min. 600 PA

Jose DeLeon	.179
J.R. Richard	.190
Dwight Gooden	.197
Rich Gossage	.198
Luis DeLeon	.198
Mark Littell	.202
Eric Show	.204
Mario Soto	.204
Victor Cruz	.206
Sid Fernandez	.208
Andy Messersmith	.209
Orel Hershiser	.209
Nolan Ryan	.211
Scott Garrelts	.212
Skip Lockwood	.213
Joe Cowley	.213
Tom Niedenfuer	.213
Dan Warthen	.213
Don Carman	.213
Jeff Reardon	.213
Roger Clemens	.214
Mike Armstrong	.215
Jim Kern	.217
Bob Stoddard	.219
Mark Clear	.219

CAREER OPP. HOME RUN PCT. VS. RIGHT-HANDED PITCHERS

Min. 600 PA

Doug Sisk	0.44
Mark Fidrych	0.63
Steve Howe	0.65
Rick Lysander	0.70
Alejandro Pena	0.71
J.R. Richard	0.98
Kent Tekulve	0.98
Dave Heaverlo	1.00
Zane Smith	1.04
Dave Frost	1.09
Mike Barlow	1.14
Greg Minton	1.15
Pablo Torrealba	1.24
Ed Farmer	1.24
Mark Littell	1.26
Terry Forster	1.27
Jim Kern	1.28
Dave Righetti	1.30
Dale Murray	1.31
Gary Lucas	1.33
Dave Tomlin	1.34
Steve Hargan	1.34
Carl Morton	1.35
John Urrea	1.36
Steve Rogers	1.37

CAREER OPP. WALK PCT. VS. RIGHT-HANDED PITCHERS

Min. 600 PA

Dan Quisenberry	2.14
LaMarr Hoyt	3.49
Gary Nolan	3.51
Bret Saberhagen	3.91
Tim Leary	3.92
Bob Stanley	4.22
Ferguson Jenkins	4.52
Lary Sorensen	4.53
Larry Andersen	4.60
Luis DeLeon	4.64
Dick Bosman	4.65
Jim Barr	4.73
Ed Lynch	4.75
Fernando Arroyo	4.84
Dennis Leonard	4.95
Tom Hausman	4.96
Bill Gullickson	5.05
Roger Erickson	5.08
Moose Haas	5.09
Rick Wise	5.12
Rick Reuschel	5.18
Mike Caldwell	5.19
Scott Sanderson	5.19
Doug Bird	5.20
Vern Ruhle	5.21

CAREER OPP. STRIKEOUT PCT. VS. RIGHT-HANDED PITCHERS

Min. 150 Strikeouts

Dwight Gooden	29.88
Jose DeLeon	28.44
J.R. Richard	26.06
Roger Clemens	25.52
Lee Smith	25.36
Skip Lockwood	24.68
Victor Cruz	24.38
Mark Clear	24.37
Jeff Reardon	24.10
Cecilio Guante	23.88
Nolan Ryan	23.81
Rich Gossage	23.74
Mario Soto	23.65
Luis DeLeon	23.60
Mark Littell	22.95
Jose Rijo	22.78
Bill Caudill	22.71
Greg Harris	22.53
Steve Bedrosian	22.45
Tom Niedenfuer	22.30
Scott Garrelts	22.16
Ron Davis	22.12
Sid Fernandez	21.98
Joe Cowley	21.91
Don Carman	21.24

SINGLE-SEASON OPP. BATTING AVERAGE VS. LEFT-HANDED PITCHERS

Min. 125 PA

Bill Dawley, 1983	.142
Bob Lacey, 1977	.146
Mark Clear, 1984	.147
Dave Smith, 1984	.152
Nolan Ryan, 1981	.153
Ron Guidry, 1978	.156
Bob Shirley, 1978	.156
Larry McWilliams, 1983	.156
Matt Young, 1983	.158
Gary Lavelle, 1984	.158
Bill Scherrer, 1983	.158
Rich Wortham, 1979	.159
Larry Gura, 1983	.159
Tom Burgmeier, 1980	.159
Mike Caldwell, 1978	.160
Sid Monge, 1979	.161
Andy Hassler, 1980	.162
Larry Gura, 1978	.164
Bob Knepper, 1981	.164
Gene Garber, 1978	.165
Mike Flanagan, 1982	.167
Tim Lollar, 1982	.170
Bruce Sutter, 1979	.170
Willie Hernandez, 1984	.173
John Candelaria, 1975	.173

SINGLE-SEASON OPP. BATTING AVERAGE VS. RIGHT-HANDED PITCHERS

Min. 175 PA

J.R. Richard, 1980	.124
Mark Eichhorn, 1986	.135
Dave LaRoche, 1976	.139
Rich Gossage, 1977	.140
Mario Soto, 1980	.147
Lance McCullers, 1986	.154
Hank Webb, 1975	.156
Mike Scott, 1986	.156
Mark Clear, 1979	.157
Don Carman, 1985	.161
Jim Kern, 1979	.161
Jeff Reardon, 1984	.161
Aurelio Lopez, 1983	.162
Tom Niedenfuer, 1983	.162
Luis DeLeon, 1982	.163
Sid Monge, 1978	.164
Frank Williams, 1985	.164
Frank Williams, 1984	.166
Tim Burke, 1985	.166
Cecilio Guante, 1985	.166
Jose DeLeon, 1984	.168
Dwight Gooden, 1984	.170
Jose DeLeon, 1986	.171
J.R. Richard, 1978	.171
Rich Gossage, 1978	.171

SINGLE-SEASON OPP. BATTING AVERAGE IN HOME GAMES

Min. 500 PA

Floyd Youmans	.182
Sid Fernandez	.188
Dwight Gooden	.189
Nolan Ryan	.196
J.R. Richard	.197
Mike Armstrong	.198
Scott Garrelts	.206
Jose DeLeon	.206
Joe Cowley	.206
Roger McDowell	.206
Bill Dawley	.212
Bert Roberge	.212
Orel Hershiser	.213
Mario Soto	.213
Rich Gossage	.215
Skip Lockwood	.217
Al Holland	.218
Dave Righetti	.219
Mark Littell	.220
Bob Apodaca	.221
Sammy Stewart	.221
Joe Sambito	.221
Victor Cruz	.223
Craig Lefferts	.223
Jeff Lahti	.223

SINGLE-SEASON OPP. BATTING AVERAGE IN ROAD GAMES

Min. 500 PA

Jesse Orosco	.197
Mark Littell	.203
Floyd Youmans	.204
John Fulgham	.208
Rich Gossage	.215
Bruce Sutter	.216
Roger Clemens	.219
Mario Soto	.220
Jeff Reardon	.221
Lee Smith	.221
Tom Niedenfuer	.222
Jose DeLeon	.222
Steve Bedrosian	.222
John Martin	.222
J.R. Richard	.223
Sid Fernandez	.223
Dwight Gooden	.223
Dan Warthen	.224
Rod Scurry	.224
Nolan Ryan	.225
Cecilio Guante	.226
Andy Messersmith	.226
Greg Harris	.226
Luis DeLeon	.226
Joe Hesketh	.226

CAREER OPP. BATTING AVERAGE ON GRASS SURFACES

Min. 500 PA

J.R. Richard	.195
Danny Frisella	.199
Dwight Gooden	.202
Sid Fernandez	.203
Jose DeLeon	.208
Mark Littell	.211
Nolan Ryan	.211
Dan Warthen	.213
Frank Williams	.213
Rod Scurry	.215
Ed Correa	.217
Orel Hershiser	.218
Mario Soto	.218
Rich Gossage	.220
Greg Harris	.220
Andy Messersmith	.221
Roger McDowell	.222
Jeff Reardon	.222
Dave Righetti	.222
Bill Laxton	.222
Tom Gorman	.223
Joe Cowley	.223
Brent Strom	.223
Craig Lefferts	.224
Tom Waddell	.225

CAREER OPP. BATTING AVERAGE ON ARTIFICIAL TURF

Min. 500 PA

Jesse Orosco	.163
Floyd Youmans	.183
Mike Norris	.194
Rich Gossage	.203
Nolan Ryan	.207
Mark Littell	.212
Steve Bedrosian	.213
Jose DeLeon	.214
J.R. Richard	.215
Sid Fernandez	.215
Mario Soto	.216
Jim Kern	.216
Dwight Gooden	.217
Mark Eichhorn	.218
Don Carman	.218
Lee Smith	.220
Al Holland	.220
Fernando Valenzuela	.220
Bill Dawley	.222
Frank LaCorte	.222
Andy McGaffigan	.223
Eric Show	.223
Joe Sambito	.226
Bruce Sutter	.226
Jeff Reardon	.226

CAREER OPP. BATTING AVERAGE IN DAY GAMES

Min. 250 PA

Nolan Ryan	.198
Sid Fernandez	.202
Mario Soto	.207
Joe Cowley	.209
Tom Niedenfuer	.211
Scott Garrelts	.212
Mark Littell	.214
Dave Smith	.214
Rich Gossage	.215
Al Hrabosky	.216
Jose DeLeon	.217
Roger Clemens	.217
Jesse Orosco	.218
Steve Bedrosian	.218
David Palmer	.221
Andy Messersmith	.221
Rollie Fingers	.222
Steve Busby	.222
Craig Lefferts	.223
Bruce Berenyi	.223
Ted Higuera	.224
Tim Lollar	.225
Rod Scurry	.226
J.R. Richard	.226
Bruce Sutter	.227

CAREER OPP. BATTING AVERAGE IN NIGHT GAMES

Min. 250 PA

Dwight Gooden	.191
Floyd Youmans	.191
J.R. Richard	.205
Lance McCullers	.205
Sid Fernandez	.209
Mark Littell	.210
Jose DeLeon	.210
Jesse Orosco	.212
Mark Eichhorn	.213
Nolan Ryan	.213
Dennis Rasmussen	.213
Jeff Lahti	.215
Rich Gossage	.215
Don Carman	.216
Tom Henke	.216
Luis DeLeon	.217
Mike Norris	.218
Jeff Reardon	.219
Al Holland	.220
Bill Dawley	.221
Cecilio Guante	.221
Mario Soto	.221
Mark Clear	.222
Orel Hershiser	.222
Joe Hesketh	.223

CAREER OPP. BATTING AVERAGE IN LATE-INNING PRESSURE SITUATIONS

Min. 400 PA

Mark Davis	.198
Nolan Ryan	.200
Tom Henke	.202
Cecilio Guante	.206
J.R. Richard	.209
Bill Dawley	.212
Mike Boddicker	.212
Steve Bedrosian	.213
Dwight Gooden	.214
Mario Soto	.214
Mark Littell	.214
Jesse Orosco	.215
Rich Gossage	.216
Don Carman	.216
Sid Monge	.221
Mike Witt	.222
Don Stanhouse	.222
Todd Worrell	.223
Scott Garrelts	.224
Skip Lockwood	.224
Frank LaCorte	.224
John Candelaria	.225
Aurelio Lopez	.226
Mark Clear	.226
Dave Tobik	.226

SINGLE-SEASON OPP. BATTING AVERAGE IN LATE-INNING PRESSURE SITUATIONS

Min. 150 PA

Dave LaRoche, 1976	.142
Tom Niedenfuer, 1983	.146
Don Carman, 1985	.157
Tom Seaver, 1976	.163
Ron Davis, 1981	.166
Fernando Valenzuela, 1985	.167
Dennis Eckersley, 1977	.168
Bill Dawley, 1983	.169
Rich Gossage, 1977	.169
Tom Henke, 1986	.171
Aurelio Lopez, 1979	.173
Nolan Ryan, 1976	.174
Bill Caudill, 1982	.175
Manny Sarmiento, 1978	.176
Willie Hernandez, 1984	.176
Ed Farmer, 1979	.177
Skip Lockwood, 1976	.179
J.R. Richard, 1976	.179
Cecilio Guante, 1986	.180
Steve Bedrosian, 1982	.181
Frank Tanana, 1976	.181
Neil Allen, 1984	.182
Steve Carlton, 1979	.183
Mark Littell, 1979	.184
Jeff Reardon, 1981	.184

CAREER OPP. HOME RUN PCT. IN LATE-INNING PRESSURE SITUATIONS

Min. 400 PA

Steve Comer	0.61
Doug Sisk	0.62
Jim Todd	0.71
Jeff Lahti	0.73
Dave A. Roberts	0.75
Bill Gullickson	0.75
Fernando Valenzuela	0.77
Don Stanhouse	0.84
Don Carman	0.84
Steve Howe	0.95
Dale Murray	0.96
Dave J. Schmidt	0.96
Randy Jones	0.98
Clay Carroll	1.00
Dave Giusti	1.04
Darold Knowles	1.09
Tommy John	1.10
Roger McDowell	1.10
Pete Vuckovich	1.12
Manny Sarmiento	1.14
Vern Ruhle	1.18
Jay Howell	1.20
Woody Fryman	1.20
Frank Pastore	1.22
Gary Lavelle	1.23

CAREER OPP. STRIKEOUT PCT. IN LATE-INNING PRESSURE SITUATIONS

Min. 100 Strikeouts

Tom Henke	30.62
Dwight Gooden	27.76
Mark Davis	25.50
Ken Howell	24.79
Nolan Ryan	23.24
Mark Clear	22.95
Bill Caudill	22.90
Rich Gossage	22.64
Skip Lockwood	22.56
Steve Bedrosian	22.30
Mark Littell	22.26
Lee Smith	22.20
Rod Scurry	22.04
John Hiller	21.46
Scott Garrelts	21.42
Victor Cruz	21.13
Greg Harris	20.70
Jesse Orosco	20.45
Bruce Sutter	20.05
Ron Davis	19.83
Frank DiPino	19.63
Dave Righetti	19.62
Al Holland	19.62
Tom Niedenfuer	19.60
Dave LaRoche	19.59

CAREER OPP. BATTING AVERAGE IN LATE-INNING PRESSURE SITUATIONS WITH RUNNERS ON BASE

Min. 150 PA

Kevin Saucier	.160
Todd Worrell	.168
Mark Eichhorn	.175
Dave Tobik	.177
Cecilio Guante	.179
Dave Dravecky	.191
Don Carman	.192
Lance McCullers	.194
Steve Bedrosian	.196
Steve McCatty	.197
Ray Searage	.201
Dwight Gooden	.203
Jack Morris	.204
Jesse Orosco	.205
Nolan Ryan	.206
Sid Monge	.209
Danny Frisella	.210
Dock Ellis	.211
Randy Lerch	.211
Ernie Camacho	.212
Bud Black	.212
Bill Greif	.213
Bill Dawley	.214
Aurelio Lopez	.214
Bill Caudill	.214

SINGLE-SEASON OPP. BATTING AVERAGE IN LATE-INNING PRESSURE SITUATIONS WITH RUNNERS ON BASE

Min. 60 PA

Frank Tanana, 1976	.116
Joe Sambito, 1981	.121
Dave LaRoche, 1976	.128
Jim Kern, 1976	.128
Dave Tobik, 1979	.130
Bill Greif, 1976	.130
Bud Black, 1986	.132
Joaquin Andujar, 1978	.133
Nolan Ryan, 1978	.134
Steve Bedrosian, 1982	.136
Kevin Saucier, 1981	.140
George Frazier, 1982	.143
Mike Torrez, 1975	.143
Tug McGraw, 1980	.146
Dave Dravecky, 1984	.148
Andy Hassler, 1980	.148
George Frazier, 1983	.149
Tom Niedenfuer, 1983	.150
Jeff Reardon, 1981	.151
Jesse Orosco, 1983	.152
Cecilio Guante, 1986	.153
Richard Dotson, 1984	.153
Dave Tobik, 1982	.154
Jon Matlack, 1978	.154
Bill Dawley, 1984	.156

CAREER OPP. HOME RUN PCT. IN LATE-INNING PRESSURE SITUATIONS WITH RUNNERS ON BASE

Min. 150 PA

Steve Comer	0.00
Bill Lee	0.00
Bob Ojeda	0.00
Charlie Williams	0.00
Pat Clements	0.00
Ken Kravec	0.00
Mark Lee	0.00
Frank Williams	0.00
Mark Eichhorn	0.00
Kevin Saucier	0.00
Joaquin Andujar	0.26
Dave J. Schmidt	0.34
Dave Tomlin	0.41
Dave A. Roberts	0.45
Steve Howe	0.46
Vern Ruhle	0.47
Fernando Valenzuela	0.51
Greg Minton	0.53
Bill Gullickson	0.56
Pete Vuckovich	0.62
Doug Sisk	0.64
Don Carman	0.66
Rick Mahler	0.68
Dwight Gooden	0.68
Roy Thomas	0.69

CAREER OPP. STRIKEOUT PCT. IN LATE-INNING PRESSURE SITUATIONS WITH RUNNERS ON BASE

Min. 40 Strikeouts

Tom Henke	29.33
Dwight Gooden	27.54
Mark Clear	24.12
Bill Caudill	23.20
Ken Howell	22.38
Scott Garrelts	21.71
Skip Lockwood	21.50
Cecilio Guante	21.40
Mark Littell	21.19
Lee Smith	20.97
Nolan Ryan	20.80
Rod Scurry	20.67
John Hiller	20.00
Steve Bedrosian	19.92
Doug Bair	19.87
Dave LaRoche	19.85
Tom Niedenfuer	19.81
Victor Cruz	19.80
Rich Gossage	19.60
Tim Stoddard	19.53
Matt Young	19.52
Al Holland	19.52
Ron Davis	19.45
John Henry Johnson	18.96
Jesse Orosco	18.76

CAREER OPP. BATTING AVERAGE WITH RUNNERS ON BASE

Min. 500 PA

Jesse Orosco	.200
Dwight Gooden	.200
Sid Fernandez	.209
Jeff Reardon	.215
Ron Darling	.216
Floyd Youmans	.216
Jose DeLeon	.219
Lee Smith	.219
Bill Caudill	.220
Rod Scurry	.222
Mark Clear	.222
Mario Soto	.222
Bruce Sutter	.222
J.R. Richard	.224
Cecilio Guante	.224
Nolan Ryan	.225
Mark Littell	.225
Joe Cowley	.227
Steve Bedrosian	.227
Rich Gossage	.227
Victor Cruz	.228
Orel Hershiser	.228
Bob Apodaca	.230
Craig Lefferts	.230
Dave Dravecky	.230

SINGLE-SEASON OPP. BATTING AVERAGE WITH RUNNERS ON BASE

Min. 175 PA

John D'Acquisto, 1978	.155
Gene Garber, 1978	.160
Jesse Orosco, 1984	.167
Bill Caudill, 1980	.173
Jesse Orosco, 1983	.175
Jose DeLeon, 1986	.175
Rich Gossage, 1977	.175
Willie Hernandez, 1984	.176
Al Holland, 1983	.177
Charlie Hough, 1976	.177
Lee Smith, 1983	.178
Jim Deshaies, 1986	.180
Dwight Gooden, 1985	.180
Doug Bair, 1978	.181
Mike Scott, 1986	.181
Tippy Martinez, 1983	.181
Sid Monge, 1979	.182
Bruce Sutter, 1977	.182
Jesse Orosco, 1986	.183
Mark Eichhorn, 1986	.183
Jose DeLeon, 1983	.185
Hal Dues, 1978	.185
Todd Worrell, 1986	.185
Rich Gossage, 1975	.186
Don Sutton, 1980	.186

CAREER OPP. BATTING AVERAGE WITH RUNNERS IN SCORING POSITION

Min. 300 PA

Dwight Gooden	.179
Tim Burke	.186
Floyd Youmans	.188
Jesse Orosco	.195
Cecilio Guante	.197
Steve Bedrosian	.198
Bob Apodaca	.199
Lee Smith	.201
Sid Fernandez	.201
Ron Darling	.202
Steve Busby	.206
Rich Gossage	.207
Joe Cowley	.209
Jeff Lahti	.212
Mario Soto	.212
Stan Thomas	.213
Eric Show	.214
Tippy Martinez	.216
Mark Clear	.217
Dave Dravecky	.219
Nolan Ryan	.219
J.R. Richard	.219
Jeff Reardon	.219
Craig Lefferts	.220
Orel Hershiser	.221

SINGLE-SEASON OPP. BATTING AVERAGE WITH RUNNERS IN SCORING POSITION

Min. 125 PA

Jim Deshaies, 1986	.140
Rich Gossage, 1978	.143
Dwight Gooden, 1985	.144
Eric Show, 1986	.145
Tim Burke, 1985	.147
Joe Cowley, 1985	.148
Tom Hilgendorf, 1975	.149
John Candelaria, 1977	.149
Cecilio Guante, 1983	.151
Don Sutton, 1980	.153
Gene Garber, 1982	.156
Bob Lacey, 1977	.157
Tom Hausman, 1975	.159
Rich Gossage, 1977	.159
Mike Scott, 1986	.159
Steve McCatty, 1981	.161
Tom Seaver, 1981	.163
Steve Bedrosian, 1986	.163
Bill Campbell, 1977	.165
Joaquin Andujar, 1978	.167
Mario Soto, 1980	.167
Dwight Gooden, 1986	.167
Steve McCatty, 1982	.169
Frank Tanana, 1977	.170
Jim Kern, 1976	.171

CAREER OPP. BATTING AVERAGE WITH 2 OUTS AND RUNNERS ON BASE

Min. 250 PA

Dwight Gooden	.167
Bill Caudill	.183
Sid Fernandez	.184
Jose DeLeon	.184
Cecilio Guante	.187
Jesse Orosco	.189
Victor Cruz	.190
Pete Ladd	.190
Dave Smith	.191
Pat Dobson	.196
Ron Darling	.202
Jeff Reardon	.202
Bruce Sutter	.202
J.R. Richard	.202
Rollie Fingers	.204
Bob Welch	.204
Eric Show	.205
Ed Glynn	.205
Mario Soto	.206
Craig Lefferts	.207
Ted Higuera	.207
Dave Stewart	.207
Mark Littell	.207
Pete Filson	.208
Charlie Williams	.208

SINGLE-SEASON OPP. BATTING AVERAGE WITH 2 OUTS AND RUNNERS ON BASE

Min. 100 PA

Bill Caudill, 1980	.103
Mike Scott, 1986	.109
Pat Dobson, 1976	.115
Jerry Ujdur, 1982	.122
Eric Show, 1986	.138
John Tudor, 1984	.143
Ed Whitson, 1984	.143
Ron Darling, 1986	.143
Jose DeLeon, 1985	.144
Bob Forsch, 1978	.147
Lance McCullers, 1986	.148
Eduardo Rodriguez, 1976	.149
Sparky Lyle, 1978	.149
Dan Warthen, 1975	.149
Bill Campbell, 1977	.149
Frank Tanana, 1977	.150
Fred Norman, 1978	.152
Scott Garrelts, 1985	.152
Tom Seaver, 1981	.153
Scott Sanderson, 1980	.154
Luis Tiant, 1978	.155
Britt Burns, 1981	.155
Steve Bedrosian, 1983	.156
Gene Nelson, 1985	.156
Rick Rhoden, 1984	.157

CAREER OPP. BATTING AVERAGE WITH 2 OUTS AND RUNNERS IN SCORING POSITION

Min. 150 PA

Cecilio Guante	.153
Dwight Gooden	.154
Keith Atherton	.165
Bob Apodaca	.165
Victor Cruz	.175
Jose DeLeon	.179
Pete Ladd	.181
Sid Fernandez	.181
Ron Darling	.181
Eric Show	.181
Jesse Orosco	.181
Dave Stewart	.183
Dave Smith	.183
J.R. Richard	.185
Craig Lefferts	.185
Lee Smith	.185
Steve Busby	.186
Greg Harris	.186
Ernie Camacho	.188
Bill Caudill	.189
Tippy Martinez	.190
Bob Welch	.192
Jeff Reardon	.194
Pete Filson	.196
Scott Garrelts	.197

SINGLE-SEASON OPP. BATTING AVERAGE WITH 2 OUTS AND RUNNERS

Min. 75 PA

Dan Warthen, 1975	.100
John Tudor, 1984	.110
Luis Tiant, 1978	.113
Bill Gullickson, 1982	.118
Mike Scott, 1986	.119
Rich Gossage, 1978	.119
Ed Whitson, 1984	.119
Mike Krukow, 1986	.123
Doug Corbett, 1980	.127
Ron Darling, 1986	.129
Frank Tanana, 1977	.130
Fred Norman, 1978	.130
Dwight Gooden, 1985	.133
Pat Dobson, 1976	.133
Tim Burke, 1985	.134
Frank Tanana, 1976	.135
Bill Campbell, 1977	.136
Tom Seaver, 1981	.138
Dave Freisleben, 1976	.143
Doug Rau, 1977	.143
Rick Langford, 1977	.143
Eduardo Rodriguez, 1976	.145
Juan Eichelberger, 1981	.145
Tippy Martinez, 1984	.145
Richard Dotson, 1984	.146

SINGLE-SEASON DOUBLES ALLOWED

Dennis Leonard, 1978	62
Bruce Hurst, 1984	60
Rick Sutcliffe, 1983	58
Dennis Eckersley, 1986	58
Jim Barr, 1977	57
Jim Clancy, 1983	57
Bill Gullickson, 1983	56
Scott McGregor, 1983	55
John Montefusco, 1975	54
Dennis Leonard, 1980	54
Steve Rogers, 1983	54
Doyle Alexander, 1986	54
Wilbur Wood, 1975	53
Mike Torrez, 1983	53
Ron Guidry, 1983	53
Doyle Alexander, 1984	53
Bob Knepper, 1985	53
Charlie Leibrandt, 1986	53
Ron Reed, 1975	52
Larry Christenson, 1977	52
Steve Carlton, 1977	52
Mike Flanagan, 1978	52
Jerry Koosman, 1980	52
Dave Stieb, 1983	52
Dennis Boyd, 1985	52

SINGLE-SEASON TRIPLES ALLOWED

Larry Christenson, 1976	17
Paul Thormodsgard, 1977	16
Jim Barr, 1975	14
Jim Kaat, 1977	14
Jim Barr, 1977	14
Dave Goltz, 1977	14
Craig Swan, 1977	14
Randy Jones, 1979	14
Rick Sutcliffe, 1984	14
Ray Burris, 1976	13
Rick Reuschel, 1976	13
Luis Tiant, 1979	13
Dick Ruthven, 1980	13
Steve Carlton, 1980	13
Rich Gale, 1982	13
Tommy John, 1982	13
Mike Smithson, 1983	13
John Montefusco, 1975	12
Jim Kaat, 1976	12
Ken Holtzman, 1976	12
Ray Burris, 1978	12
Roger Erickson, 1979	12
Bob Forsch, 1979	12
Doc Medich, 1980	12
Mike Krukow, 1980	12

SINGLE-SEASON EXTRA-BASE HITS ALLOWED

Bert Blyleven, 1986	100
Phil Niekro, 1979	97
Dennis Leonard, 1978	94
Dennis Leonard, 1980	92
Rick Sutcliffe, 1983	92
LaMarr Hoyt, 1984	91
Jerry Garvin, 1977	90
Wilbur Wood, 1975	89
Jim Barr, 1977	89
Dan Petry, 1983	89
Mark Langston, 1986	89
Jim Clancy, 1983	88
Ferguson Jenkins, 1979	87
Frank Viola, 1986	87
Luis Tiant, 1975	86
Ferguson Jenkins, 1975	86
Scott McGregor, 1983	86
Bruce Hurst, 1984	86
Charlie Hough, 1984	86
Dennis Eckersley, 1986	86
Jack Morris, 1986	86
Dennis Eckersley, 1977	85
Matt Keough, 1982	85
Frank Viola, 1983	85
Mike Caldwell, 1983	85

CAREER OPP. EXTRA-BASE HIT PCT.

Min. 1,000 PA

Steve Howe	3.72
Doug Sisk	4.61
John Franco	4.93
Greg Minton	4.97
Dwight Gooden	5.00
Orel Hershiser	5.02
Scott Garrelts	5.03
Gary Lavelle	5.08
Alejandro Pena	5.10
Mark Fidrych	5.13
Jesse Orosco	5.17
J.R. Richard	5.28
Roger McDowell	5.32
Rich Gossage	5.34
Jim Kern	5.35
Nolan Ryan	5.35
Mark Littell	5.40
Kent Tekulve	5.47
Lee Smith	5.47
Dan Quisenberry	5.48
Dave Righetti	5.50
Ken Howell	5.53
Clay Carroll	5.56
David Palmer	5.59
Dave Smith	5.62

HIGHEST CAREER RATIO OF GROUND OUTS TO AIR OUTS

Min. 1,000 PA

Roger McDowell	3.31
Doug Corbett	3.01
Doug Sisk	2.75
Jeff Dedmon	2.72
Ray Fontenot	2.53
Tommy John	2.49
Greg Minton	2.41
Jim Todd	2.39
Dennis Lamp	2.35
Jaime Cocanower	2.34
Bob Stanley	2.33
Dan Quisenberry	2.31
Kent Tekulve	2.27
Zane Smith	2.25
Bill Swift	2.23
John Denny	2.21
Orel Hershiser	2.19
Bill Castro	2.17
Gene Garber	2.17
Rick Reuschel	2.15
Randy Jones	2.13
David Palmer	2.11
Jim Acker	2.11
Terry Forster	2.06
Steve Trout	2.05

LOWEST CAREER RATIO OF GROUND OUTS TO AIR OUTS

Min. 1,000 PA

Sid Fernandez	0.49
Keith Atherton	0.52
Tom Niedenfuer	0.54
Mike Armstrong	0.55
Victor Cruz	0.59
Jeff Reardon	0.59
Pete Ladd	0.60
Bill Caudill	0.61
Dave LaRoche	0.61
Chris Knapp	0.62
Juan Berenguer	0.62
Al Hrabosky	0.63
Joe Price	0.64
Al Holland	0.65
Skip Lockwood	0.66
Tim Conroy	0.67
Aurelio Lopez	0.67
Tom Browning	0.67
Luis Tiant	0.67
Dennis Rasmussen	0.68
John Henry Johnson	0.69
Catfish Hunter	0.69
Buzz Capra	0.69
Cecilio Guante	0.69
Dave Beard	0.70

CAREER GROUND OUT PCT. (PER 100 PA)

Min. 1,000 PA

Roger McDowell	44.2
Dan Quisenberry	43.1
Tommy John	41.3
Randy Jones	41.3
Doug Corbett	40.3
Doug Sisk	40.1
Bill Castro	40.0
Bob Stanley	39.7
Greg Minton	39.7
Ray Fontenot	39.2
Dennis Lamp	39.2
Kent Tekulve	38.8
Jim Todd	38.6
Paul Hartzell	38.2
Fernando Arroyo	38.0
Jeff Dedmon	37.9
Rob Dressler	37.8
Clay Carroll	37.5
Jaime Cocanower	37.4
Rick Honeycutt	37.3
Rick Matula	37.3
Dave Rozema	37.2
Mike Proly	37.1
John Denny	37.1
Jerry Reuss	37.0

CAREER AIR OUT PCT. (PER 100 PA)

Min. 1,000 PA

Gary Nolan	36.0
Catfish Hunter	35.8
Keith Atherton	35.8
John Martin	35.2
Mike Armstrong	34.9
Tom Browning	34.6
Luis Tiant	34.3
Scott McGregor	34.2
Manny Sarmiento	34.2
Tom Niedenfuer	33.9
Larry Gura	33.6
Chris Knapp	33.3
Pete Ladd	33.3
Curt Young	33.2
Grant Jackson	33.2
Bill Dawley	33.1
Steve McCatty	33.1
Joe Price	33.0
Jeff Reardon	32.9
Brian Kingman	32.9
Craig Swan	32.9
Al Hrabosky	32.8
Dan Schatzeder	32.8
Dennis Rasmussen	32.8
Pete Filson	32.8

CAREER OPP. ON-BASE AVERAGE LEADING OFF INNINGS

Min. 250 PA

Dave J. Schmidt	.246
Mike Armstrong	.248
Dan Quisenberry	.252
Brad Havens	.259
Rich Gossage	.259
John Martin	.261
Dave Tobik	.262
Tug McGraw	.269
Pete Filson	.269
Steve Howe	.269
Roger Clemens	.270
Gene Garber	.271
Joe Hesketh	.271
Gary Nolan	.272
Darold Knowles	.273
Tom Niedenfuer	.273
Gary Lucas	.274
Doug Corbett	.274
Fernando Valenzuela	.275
Don Sutton	.275
Frank Tanana	.275
Joe Sambito	.277
Rod Scurry	.278
Dwight Gooden	.278
Marty Pattin	.279

SINGLE-SEASON OPP. ON-BASE AVERAGE LEADING OFF INNINGS

Min. 100 PA

Greg Harris, 1985	.175
Dan Quisenberry, 1984	.188
Vern Ruhle, 1983	.191
Randy Martz, 1981	.202
Jeff Robinson, 1986	.212
Joe Price, 1983	.212
Dan Quisenberry, 1983	.215
Dave J. Schmidt, 1982	.217
John Tudor, 1985	.217
Rich Gossage, 1978	.219
Mike Armstrong, 1982	.220
Dan Schatzeder, 1984	.221
Don Sutton, 1975	.221
Dennis Eckersley, 1977	.223
Pat Underwood, 1982	.223
Ken Forsch, 1979	.223
Bob Forsch, 1977	.224
Marty Pattin, 1976	.224
Ron Guidry, 1981	.224
Vern Ruhle, 1981	.224
Rick Honeycutt, 1986	.225
Francisco Barrios, 1979	.225
John Martin, 1981	.229
Ron Reed, 1978	.230
Mario Soto, 1981	.231

CAREER OPP. WALK PCT. LEADING OFF INNINGS

Min. 250 PA

Dave J. Schmidt	2.01
Atlee Hammaker	2.27
Dan Quisenberry	2.29
Gary Nolan	2.49
Gene Garber	2.52
Kevin Kobel	3.02
Gary Lucas	3.51
Ron Reed	3.54
Mark Fidrych	3.55
Steve Howe	3.57
Gary Ross	3.88
Pedro Borbon	3.95
Tommy John	4.00
Dave Rozema	4.04
Jim Barr	4.05
Scott Sanderson	4.14
Roger Erickson	4.16
LaMarr Hoyt	4.25
Ferguson Jenkins	4.27
Ed Lynch	4.36
Mark Thurmond	4.37
Frank Tanana	4.38
Dennis Eckersley	4.41
Rick Reuschel	4.44
Paul Lindblad	4.47

SINGLE-SEASON OPP. WALK PCT. LEADING OFF INNINGS

Min. 100 PA

Gene Garber, 1982	0.00
Dan Quisenberry, 1983	0.00
Dan Quisenberry, 1985	0.00
Rick Langford, 1982	0.41
Jim Barr, 1982	0.78
Tom Hausman, 1980	0.82
Bob Forsch, 1980	0.89
Dave J. Schmidt, 1982	0.94
Dennis Martinez, 1986	0.95
Jeff Robinson, 1986	0.96
Ron Reed, 1978	1.00
Mike Smithson, 1983	1.29
Gaylord Perry, 1981	1.29
Ferguson Jenkins, 1976	1.38
Glenn Abbott, 1983	1.45
Roger Clemens, 1984	1.45
Ron Guidry, 1981	1.49
Bob Shirley, 1980	1.50
Rick Rhoden, 1983	1.60
Atlee Hammaker, 1982	1.62
Gary Nolan, 1976	1.64
Roger Erickson, 1982	1.67
Doyle Alexander, 1986	1.67
Atlee Hammaker, 1983	1.68
Dan Quisenberry, 1982	1.68

CAREER OPP. BATTING AVERAGE WITH BASES LOADED

Min. 50 PA

Ken Schrom	.087
Jesse Orosco	.128
Ed Figueroa	.147
Doug Rau	.152
Dave LaRoche	.159
Mike Moore	.162
Mike Smithson	.164
Keith Atherton	.167
Eric Show	.167
Dave Lemanczyk	.167
Tippy Martinez	.178
Tom House	.179
Dave J. Schmidt	.180
Bruce Berenyi	.185
Ed Halicki	.185
Butch Metzger	.188
Tom Griffin	.188
Greg Harris	.189
Craig Swan	.189
Jim Palmer	.193
Shane Rawley	.194
Dan Petry	.195
Orel Hershiser	.196
Wayne Twitchell	.196
Mike Stanton	.197

CAREER BATTERS FACED WITH BASES LOADED WITHOUT ALLOWING A GRAND-SLAM HOME RUN

Jim Kern	148
Joaquin Andujar	142
Mike Krukow	130
Pat Zachry	128
Jim Palmer	105
Danny Darwin	104
Al Hrabosky	96
Bob Welch	95
Jesse Orosco	93
Andy Hassler	93
Jesse Jefferson	91
Bruce Berenyi	84
Ted Power	83
Ed Figueroa	82
Mike Moore	81
Joe Price	77
Doug Corbett	75
Don Hood	74
Rawly Eastwick	73
Mike Stanton	73
Roger Erickson	71
Renie Martin	70
Roy Thomas	70
Luis Leal	67
Eddie Solomon	65

CAREER OPP. WALK PCT. WITH BASES LOADED

Min. 50 PA

Steve Crawford	0.00
Dave Heaverlo	0.81
Vern Ruhle	1.01
Steve McCatty	1.10
Rick Mahler	1.32
John Tudor	1.32
Matt Young	1.39
Dave Tobik	1.43
Ed Vande Berg	1.56
Mike G. Marshall	1.64
Fred Breining	1.72
John Butcher	1.75
Dennis Eckersley	1.79
Larry Christenson	1.79
Ed Lynch	1.79
Ferguson Jenkins	1.82
Mike Garman	1.82
Butch Metzger	1.82
Jim Umbarger	1.82
Ken Schrom	1.89
Will McEnaney	1.89
Mike Parrott	1.89
Steve Howe	1.92
Paul Reuschel	1.92
Paul Splittorff	2.00

CAREER OPP. STRIKEOUT PCT. WITH BASES LOADED

Min. 15 Strikeouts

Nolan Ryan	28.40
John Hiller	28.13
Bruce Berenyi	27.38
Mark Littell	26.51
Dwight Gooden	26.32
Dave LaRoche	25.20
Bill Caudill	25.00
Al Holland	25.00
Greg Harris	24.62
Keith Atherton	24.24
Steve Carlton	24.14
Sammy Stewart	24.09
Jeff Reardon	23.91
Rich Gossage	23.89
Mario Soto	23.28
Tippy Martinez	23.08
Mike Krukow	22.31
Tom Seaver	22.29
Ron Guidry	21.98
Dave Righetti	21.79
Tim Stoddard	21.78
Frank Tanana	21.59
Terry Forster	21.51
Joe Sambito	21.43
Dave Tobik	21.43

VII
Batter-Pitcher Matchups

Batter-Pitcher Matchups

The Batter-Pitcher Matchup section lists, for the selected players, their performances against every pitcher or batter they have faced for at least five at bats in their careers. These statistics include all regular season appearances since the beginning of their careers.

Earl Weaver used to keep them on index cards. Dave Johnson maintains his on a PC. But until the past few years the public was largely unaware of the importance many managers place on specific matchup statistics in setting a lineup. The stats do not even out over the long run, and the differences can be massive. In this section, we expand the "Loves to Face" and "Hates to Face" matchups listed in the Batter and Pitcher Sections to take a look at the career performances of some of the most extraordinary players in the game.

The twelve players selected here are six pitchers and six batters, six National Leaguers and six American Leaguers. Now you can see in detail just how few pitchers really give Wade Boggs trouble. Or if anyone has a book on Don Mattingly yet. Does anyone make consistent contact against Roger Clemens? And do singles hitters or power hitters have a better chance against Fernando Valenzuela? Here, at last, are the answers.

Wade Boggs

Pitcher	AB	H	2B	3B	HR	BB	SO	BA	SA	OBA
Don Aase	5	1	0	0	0	1	0	.200	.200	.333
Glenn Abbott	9	5	1	0	0	0	1	.556	.667	.556
Jim Acker	9	5	1	0	0	2	0	.556	.667	.636
Juan Agosto	6	3	1	0	0	3	1	.500	.667	.667
Doyle Alexander	30	11	5	0	0	5	2	.367	.533	.444
Bud Anderson	6	4	1	0	1	3	0	.667	1.333	.778
Joaquin Andujar	6	0	0	0	0	2	1	.000	.000	.250
Luis Aponte	5	2	0	0	1	0	0	.400	1.000	.400
Mike Armstrong	9	7	0	0	0	0	1	.778	.778	.778
Keith Atherton	11	6	2	0	1	2	1	.545	1.000	.571
Doug Bair	10	4	1	0	1	1	2	.400	.800	.455
Floyd Bannister	27	9	2	0	0	4	4	.333	.407	.419
Len Barker	8	3	0	0	0	2	0	.375	.375	.500
Rich Barnes	4	2	0	0	0	1	0	.500	.500	.600
Salome Barojas	6	2	1	0	0	1	0	.333	.500	.429
Jim Beattie	27	7	2	1	0	3	3	.259	.407	.333
Joe Beckwith	11	3	0	0	0	1	3	.273	.273	.333
Juan Berenguer	21	9	2	0	0	3	1	.429	.524	.500
Karl Best	4	2	0	0	0	1	1	.500	.500	.600
Bud Black	18	6	0	1	0	1	1	.333	.444	.368
Bert Blyleven	19	6	1	0	0	1	1	.316	.368	.350
Mike Boddicker	32	12	1	0	0	4	1	.375	.406	.459
Rich Bordi	4	0	0	0	0	1	1	.000	.000	.200
Tom Burgmeier	6	2	0	1	0	0	0	.333	.667	.333
Britt Burns	23	11	0	0	0	3	2	.478	.478	.538
Ray Burris	7	2	1	0	0	0	0	.286	.429	.286
John Butcher	28	11	1	0	0	5	0	.393	.429	.485
Marty Bystrom	6	3	1	0	0	0	0	.500	.667	.500
Mike Caldwell	10	2	1	0	0	0	1	.200	.300	.200
Ernie Camacho	6	3	0	0	0	0	0	.500	.500	.429
John Candelaria	4	2	1	0	0	1	2	.500	.750	.500
Tom Candiotti	10	5	0	0	1	1	0	.500	.800	.545
Chuck Cary	5	2	0	0	0	0	0	.400	.400	.400
Bobby Castillo	11	2	0	0	0	3	0	.182	.182	.357
Bill Castro	4	3	1	0	0	1	0	.750	1.000	.667
Bill Caudill	11	5	1	0	0	2	4	.455	.545	.538
John Cerutti	5	1	0	0	0	1	1	.200	.200	.333
Jim Clancy	23	10	1	0	0	5	0	.435	.478	.536
Bryan Clark	14	4	0	0	0	2	3	.286	.286	.375
Pat Clements	5	1	0	0	0	0	0	.200	.200	.200
Jaime Cocanower	15	3	2	0	0	5	0	.200	.333	.400
Chris Codiroli	26	11	3	0	0	5	0	.423	.538	.485
Steve Comer	5	1	0	0	0	0	0	.200	.200	.200
Tim Conroy	3	1	0	0	0	2	0	.333	.333	.600
Doug Corbett	7	3	1	0	0	0	0	.429	.571	.429
Ed Correa	9	2	1	0	0	5	0	.222	.333	.500
Joe Cowley	19	5	1	0	0	4	2	.263	.316	.360
Keith Creel	7	1	0	0	0	0	0	.143	.143	.143
Danny Darwin	27	8	2	0	1	5	2	.296	.481	.406
Ron Davis	8	5	1	0	0	2	1	.625	.750	.700
Storm Davis	25	6	2	0	0	4	5	.240	.320	.345
Jose DeLeon	5	1	0	0	0	1	1	.200	.200	.333
Ken Dixon	23	10	3	0	0	2	2	.435	.565	.480
Richard Dotson	25	7	2	0	1	6	0	.280	.480	.419
Jamie Easterly	17	9	2	0	0	0	1	.529	.647	.529
Juan Eichelberger	4	2	0	0	0	1	0	.500	.500	.600
Mark Eichhorn	4	2	0	0	0	1	0	.500	.500	.600
Steve Farr	13	5	0	0	0	2	1	.385	.385	.467
Pete Filson	8	1	1	0	0	1	1	.125	.250	.222
Mike Flanagan	15	6	1	0	0	0	1	.400	.467	.400
Ray Fontenot	9	4	0	0	0	1	0	.444	.444	.500
Ken Forsch	12	1	0	0	0	0	1	.083	.083	.083
George Frazier	12	3	1	0	0	1	1	.250	.333	.308
Bob L. Gibson	6	1	0	0	0	1	0	.167	.167	.286
Dave Goltz	3	2	0	0	0	2	0	.667	.667	.800
Jim Gott	10	2	0	0	0	2	1	.200	.200	.333
Mark Gubicza	25	8	4	0	0	10	3	.320	.480	.500
Ron Guidry	39	10	2	0	0	2	2	.256	.308	.293
Larry Gura	10	1	0	0	0	2	0	.100	.100	.250
Jose Guzman	6	1	1	0	0	2	0	.167	.333	.375
Moose Haas	34	11	3	0	0	8	1	.324	.412	.442
John Habyan	6	2	1	0	0	0	0	.333	.500	.333
Brad Havens	12	4	1	0	0	2	2	.333	.417	.429
Neal Heaton	32	8	0	1	0	5	2	.250	.406	.351
Gorman Heimueller	6	2	0	0	0	1	0	.333	.833	.429
Willie Hernandez	12	6	1	0	0	2	0	.500	.583	.571
Ted Higuera	14	5	1	0	0	2	4	.357	.429	.438
Ed Hodge	6	3	1	0	0	0	1	.500	.667	.500
Rick Honeycutt	14	4	0	0	0	1	0	.286	.286	.333
Charlie Hough	41	15	3	0	1	3	3	.366	.512	.409
Jay Howell	14	4	0	0	0	2	1	.286	.286	.375
LaMarr Hoyt	14	7	1	0	0	0	1	.500	.571	.500
Danny Jackson	12	4	1	0	0	3	1	.333	.417	.467
Roy Lee Jackson	13	6	2	0	0	1	0	.462	.615	.500
Bob James	7	2	0	0	0	1	1	.286	.286	.375
Tommy John	10	5	1	0	0	2	0	.500	.600	.583
Joe Johnson	5	1	0	0	0	0	0	.200	.200	.200
Mike Jones	10	3	0	0	0	0	0	.300	.300	.300
Odell Jones	8	4	1	0	0	3	1	.500	.625	.636
Matt Keough	11	6	2	0	1	0	0	.545	1.000	.545
Jimmy Key	21	6	2	0	0	0	4	.286	.381	.286
Bruce Kison	15	7	2	2	0	4	0	.467	.867	.579
Jerry Koosman	11	3	1	0	0	1	0	.273	.364	.333
Bill Krueger	21	4	1	0	0	1	2	.190	.238	.227
Pete Ladd	8	2	2	0	0	1	0	.250	.500	.333
Dennis Lamp	11	3	0	0	0	2	0	.273	.273	.385
Rick Langford	10	5	1	0	0	3	1	.500	.600	.615
Mark Langston	16	2	0	0	0	8	2	.125	.125	.417
Jack Lazorko	4	4	0	1	0	2	0	1.000	1.500	1.000
Luis Leal	20	10	1	1	1	2	0	.500	.800	.545
Tim Leary	16	7	1	0	0	2	2	.438	.500	.500
Charlie Leibrandt	26	10	2	0	1	3	1	.385	.577	.448
Dennis Leonard	13	3	1	0	0	1	0	.231	.308	.286
Aurelio Lopez	7	5	0	0	0	3	0	.714	.714	.800
Urbano Lugo	6	2	0	0	0	1	0	.333	.333	.429
Rick Lysander	13	7	2	0	0	1	0	.538	.692	.571
Dennis Martinez	25	9	6	0	0	1	2	.360	.600	.385
Tippy Martinez	11	1	0	0	0	1	1	.091	.091	.167
Mike Mason	13	4	1	0	1	3	1	.308	.615	.438
Jon Matlack	6	3	0	0	0	1	1	.500	.500	.571
Kirk McCaskill	17	4	0	0	1	0	1	.235	.412	.235
Steve McCatty	10	5	0	0	1	5	1	.500	.800	.667
Bob McClure	26	9	1	0	0	1	2	.346	.385	.393
Scott McGregor	18	4	0	0	0	0	1	.222	.222	.222
Doc Medich	9	0	0	0	0	2	1	.000	.000	.182
Paul Mirabella	5	2	0	0	0	2	1	.400	.400	.571
John Montefusco	6	2	0	0	0	2	0	.333	.333	.500
Bill Mooneyham	1	0	0	0	0	3	0	.000	.000	.600
Mike Moore	26	9	1	0	0	7	2	.346	.385	.471
Mike Morgan	6	4	1	0	0	4	0	.667	.833	.800
Jack Morris	40	13	3	0	0	6	9	.325	.400	.413
Dale Murray	6	3	1	0	0	2	1	.500	.667	.625
Ron Musselman	4	1	0	0	0	3	0	.250	.250	.571
Gene Nelson	11	3	0	0	1	2	0	.273	.545	.385
Phil Niekro	23	11	3	0	0	3	4	.478	.609	.538
Juan Nieves	5	2	2	0	0	0	0	.400	.800	.400
Dickie Noles	12	7	2	0	0	1	1	.583	.750	.615
Jack O'Connor	4	3	0	0	0	1	0	.750	.750	.800
Randy O'Neal	5	1	0	0	0	2	0	.200	.200	.429
Jim Palmer	5	3	0	0	0	0	0	.600	.600	.667
Gaylord Perry	16	5	0	1	0	1	0	.313	.438	.353
Dan Petry	30	6	1	0	0	12	4	.200	.233	.429
Chuck Porter	11	7	3	0	0	0	0	.636	.909	.636
Mark Portugal	14	5	2	0	0	1	1	.357	.500	.400
Dan Quisenberry	19	2	0	0	0	0	0	.105	.105	.105
Dennis Rasmussen	17	8	0	0	0	0	2	.471	.471	.471
Eric Rasmussen	6	4	0	1	0	0	0	.667	1.000	.667
Shane Rawley	14	2	0	0	0	0	0	.143	.143	.133
Jerry Reed	7	4	0	0	0	0	0	.571	.571	.571
Steve Renko	9	6	1	0	1	0	0	.667	1.111	.667
Dave Righetti	22	5	2	0	0	3	6	.227	.318	.320
Jose Rijo	8	4	1	0	0	2	0	.500	.625	.600
Ron Romanick	18	8	2	0	0	2	0	.444	.556	.500
Ramon Romero	6	1	0	0	0	2	1	.167	.167	.375
Dave Rozema	9	4	1	1	0	1	0	.444	.778	.500
Vern Ruhle	5	1	0	0	0	1	0	.200	.200	.333
Bret Saberhagen	12	6	2	1	1	2	1	.500	1.083	.571
Luis Sanchez	11	7	2	1	0	1	1	.636	1.000	.667
Bill Scherrer	5	4	0	0	0	1	0	.800	.800	.833
Dave J. Schmidt	7	2	0	0	0	1	0	.286	.286	.375

Wade Boggs continued

Pitcher	AB	H	2B	3B	HR	BB	SO	BA	SA	OBA
Ken Schrom	13	7	0	0	0	1	0	.538	.538	.571
Don Schulze	10	4	0	0	0	1	1	.400	.400	.455
Ray Searage	4	1	0	0	0	1	0	.250	.250	.400
Tom Seaver	29	9	2	0	1	3	0	.310	.483	.375
Bob Shirley	14	2	1	0	0	1	3	.143	.214	.200
Jim Slaton	26	13	5	0	1	3	1	.500	.808	.552
Roy Smith	6	2	0	0	0	2	0	.333	.333	.500
Mike Smithson	26	11	1	1	0	2	3	.423	.538	.483
Nate Snell	10	3	1	0	0	1	0	.300	.400	.364
Lary Sorensen	18	5	0	0	0	3	0	.278	.278	.381
Dan Spillner	9	3	2	0	0	2	0	.333	.556	.417
Paul Splittorff	11	2	0	0	0	1	4	.182	.182	.250
Mike Stanton	4	2	1	0	0	2	1	.500	.750	.667
Dave Stewart	13	4	2	0	0	0	3	.308	.462	.308
Sammy Stewart	14	3	0	0	0	0	0	.214	.214	.214
Dave Stieb	28	5	0	0	0	11	1	.179	.179	.410
Bob Stoddard	13	3	0	1	0	0	0	.231	.385	.231
Tim Stoddard	6	3	0	0	0	1	0	.500	.500	.571
Rick Sutcliffe	16	5	0	0	0	1	2	.313	.313	.353
Don Sutton	31	5	2	0	0	3	5	.161	.226	.235
Bill Swaggerty	8	5	0	0	0	1	0	.625	.625	.667
Bill Swift	9	5	1	0	0	0	1	.556	.667	.556
Frank Tanana	23	9	2	0	2	1	2	.391	.739	.417
Tom Tellmann	7	7	2	0	1	2	0	1.000	1.714	1.000
Walt Terrell	23	8	3	0	1	2	1	.348	.609	.400
Roy Thomas	8	4	0	0	1	0	1	.500	.875	.444
Rick Thompson	6	2	0	0	0	1	0	.333	.333	.429
Jerry Ujdur	8	4	0	0	0	0	0	.500	.500	.500
Tom Underwood	9	2	0	0	0	0	2	.222	.222	.222
Ed Vande Berg	16	5	1	0	0	3	2	.313	.375	.421
Frank Viola	36	13	0	0	0	4	2	.361	.361	.425
Pete Vuckovich	16	6	0	0	0	2	0	.375	.375	.444
Tom Waddell	5	1	1	0	0	1	0	.200	.400	.333
Curt Wardle	9	4	1	1	0	1	1	.444	.778	.545
Mike Warren	11	3	0	0	0	0	0	.273	.273	.250
Bill Wegman	7	4	0	0	0	0	0	.571	.571	.571
Ed Whitson	10	5	1	0	0	2	0	.500	.600	.583
Milt Wilcox	27	10	2	0	0	4	0	.370	.444	.452
Al Williams	15	4	0	0	0	0	0	.267	.267	.267
Frank Wills	13	5	1	0	0	1	2	.385	.462	.429
Bobby Witt	6	1	0	0	0	2	1	.167	.167	.375
Mike Witt	23	7	1	0	0	6	3	.304	.348	.448
Curt Young	10	3	1	0	0	1	1	.300	.400	.364
Matt Young	19	1	0	0	0	3	3	.053	.053	.217
Geoff Zahn	3	1	0	0	0	1	0	.333	.333	.500

Gary Carter

Pitcher	AB	H	2B	3B	HR	BB	SO	BA	SA	OBA
Doyle Alexander	9	2	0	0	0	1	2	.222	.222	.273
Neil Allen	22	8	2	0	1	1	0	.364	.591	.391
Porfi Altamirano	7	3	0	0	0	0	1	.429	.429	.429
Larry Andersen	12	4	1	0	0	1	2	.333	.417	.429
Joaquin Andujar	81	12	1	1	2	4	9	.148	.259	.207
Bob Apodaca	14	3	0	0	0	0	3	.214	.214	.250
Paul Assenmacher	5	1	0	0	0	1	2	.200	.200	.333
Doug Bair	23	4	1	0	0	5	3	.174	.217	.321
Rick Baldwin	5	2	0	0	0	2	1	.400	.400	.625
Jay Baller	5	2	0	0	1	0	1	.400	1.000	.400
Floyd Bannister	15	5	2	0	0	0	3	.333	.467	.333
Len Barker	10	1	0	0	0	2	1	.100	.100	.250
Jim Barr	34	9	2	0	1	2	2	.265	.412	.306
Steve Bedrosian	26	7	1	0	1	2	1	.269	.423	.321
Bruce Berenyi	18	4	0	0	1	2	1	.222	.389	.300
Dwight Bernard	6	4	0	0	0	0	0	.667	.667	.667
Jim Bibby	34	7	1	0	0	1	7	.206	.235	.243
Mike Bielecki	3	0	0	0	0	3	0	.000	.000	.500
Jack Billingham	15	6	0	2	2	2	2	.400	.800	.444
Doug Bird	17	7	2	1	1	0	2	.412	.824	.412
Vida Blue	28	6	4	0	1	2	6	.214	.464	.290
Bert Blyleven	42	11	5	0	1	2	7	.262	.452	.295
Tommy Boggs	7	2	0	0	0	1	0	.286	.286	.400
Mark Bomback	7	3	1	0	1	0	0	.429	1.000	.429
Bill Bonham	35	9	2	0	1	3	8	.257	.400	.316
Greg Booker	5	4	1	0	1	1	0	.800	1.600	.833
Pedro Borbon	13	3	0	0	0	2	3	.231	.231	.333
Derek Botelho	5	2	0	0	2	1	0	.400	1.600	.500
Fred Breining	12	3	0	0	1	1	2	.250	.500	.308
Tony Brizzolara	9	4	0	0	1	0	1	.444	.778	.444
Tom Browning	19	2	0	0	0	0	1	.105	.105	.105
Mike Bruhert	8	4	0	0	0	2	1	.500	.500	.600
Warren Brusstar	17	3	1	0	0	2	3	.176	.235	.286
Tim Burke	8	1	0	0	0	0	1	.125	.125	.222
Ray Burris	53	16	6	0	2	6	6	.302	.528	.373
Marty Bystrom	18	6	0	0	0	1	2	.333	.333	.368
Mike Caldwell	9	4	2	1	0	0	1	.444	.889	.444
Rick Camp	25	6	1	0	1	2	4	.240	.400	.296
Bill Campbell	16	6	1	0	0	2	4	.375	.438	.450
John Candelaria	61	15	4	0	5	9	8	.246	.557	.343
Doug Capilla	8	3	0	0	1	1	2	.375	.750	.444
Buzz Capra	6	1	1	0	0	0	3	.167	.333	.167
Steve Carlton	110	34	8	0	11	17	7	.309	.682	.398
Don Carman	8	6	1	0	1	0	0	.750	1.250	.750
Clay Carroll	6	0	0	0	0	1	3	.000	.000	.125
Bobby Castillo	5	1	1	0	0	2	1	.200	.400	.429
Bill Caudill	18	2	1	0	0	1	6	.111	.167	.158
Floyd Chiffer	4	1	1	0	0	1	0	.250	.500	.500
Larry Christenson	60	12	3	0	2	7	10	.200	.350	.290
Ralph Citarella	8	2	0	0	0	0	1	.250	.250	.250
Tim Conroy	4	1	0	0	0	2	0	.250	.250	.500
Danny Cox	28	5	2	0	0	0	2	.179	.250	.233
John Curtis	24	8	2	0	0	2	2	.333	.417	.385
John D'Acquisto	14	7	0	0	2	0	1	.500	.929	.467
Bruce DalCanton	3	1	0	0	0	2	0	.333	.333	.600
Ron Darling	8	4	0	0	2	1	0	.500	1.250	.556
Mark Davis	7	2	1	0	1	4	3	.286	.857	.545
Bill Dawley	8	3	1	0	1	0	0	.375	.875	.375
Ken Dayley	13	3	1	0	0	3	2	.231	.308	.375
Jose DeLeon	25	7	1	0	2	2	4	.280	.320	.333
Luis DeLeon	5	2	0	0	1	0	2	.400	1.000	.400
Jeff Dedmon	10	4	0	0	0	1	1	.400	.400	.455
Larry Demery	15	4	0	0	0	2	4	.267	.267	.353
John Denny	70	20	1	0	1	4	6	.286	.343	.338
Jim Deshaies	5	1	0	0	0	1	1	.200	.200	.333
Frank DiPino	12	5	1	0	0	2	1	.417	.500	.500
Carlos Diaz	7	2	0	0	0	2	0	.286	.286	.444
Larry Dierker	10	2	0	0	0	2	0	.200	.200	.333
Dave Dravecky	20	8	0	0	3	0	1	.400	.850	.429
Jamie Easterly	7	2	0	0	1	1	0	.286	.714	.286
Rawly Eastwick	17	6	0	0	1	1	2	.353	.529	.368
Dennis Eckersley	29	7	3	0	2	3	5	.241	.552	.303
Juan Eichelberger	5	2	0	0	1	1	0	.400	1.000	.500
Dock Ellis	15	7	1	0	1	2	2	.467	.733	.556
Nino Espinosa	25	6	1	0	3	5	1	.240	.640	.367
Pete Falcone	49	16	1	0	5	10	2	.327	.653	.441
Tom Filer	6	0	0	0	0	0	0	.000	.000	.000
Rollie Fingers	11	2	0	0	0	0	4	.182	.182	.250
Rich Folkers	7	1	0	0	0	0	0	.143	.143	.333
Ray Fontenot	15	7	1	1	2	2	0	.467	1.067	.556
Bob Forsch	103	30	5	2	4	6	9	.291	.495	.330
Ken Forsch	19	8	0	0	0	2	3	.421	.421	.476
Terry Forster	13	7	1	0	0	1	1	.538	.615	.571
Alan Fowlkes	7	3	0	0	1	1	1	.429	.857	.571
John Franco	7	0	0	0	0	1	1	.000	.000	.125
George Frazier	14	4	0	0	0	0	5	.286	.286	.286
Dave Freisleben	16	7	0	0	2	2	1	.438	.813	.500
Woody Fryman	6	1	0	0	1	2	0	.167	.667	.375

Gary Carter continued

Pitcher	AB	H	2B	3B	HR	BB	SO	BA	SA	OBA	Pitcher	AB	H	2B	3B	HR	BB	SO	BA	SA	OBA
John Fulgham	13	4	2	0	1	1	1	.308	.692	.357	Mark Littell	17	3	2	0	0	0	3	.176	.294	.176
Brent Gaff	6	2	0	0	0	1	0	.333	.333	.429	John Littlefield	7	3	0	0	0	0	1	.429	.429	.429
Rich Gale	6	2	0	0	0	0	1	.333	.333	.333	Skip Lockwood	18	1	0	0	0	2	4	.056	.056	.150
Gene Garber	33	6	2	0	2	3	5	.182	.424	.270	Mickey Lolich	6	0	0	0	0	0	2	.000	.000	.000
Mike Garman	10	2	0	0	1	0	3	.200	.500	.200	Tim Lollar	16	2	0	0	0	1	0	.125	.125	.167
Scott Garrelts	14	6	0	0	0	1	3	.429	.429	.412	Jim Lonborg	30	8	1	1	1	5	4	.267	.467	.371
Bob Gibson	4	2	0	0	0	2	1	.500	.500	.667	Gary Lucas	15	2	0	0	0	8	3	.133	.133	.435
Dave Giusti	7	3	0	0	0	0	1	.429	.429	.429	Sparky Lyle	5	2	1	0	1	1	0	.400	1.200	.500
Dave Goltz	4	1	0	0	0	0	0	.250	.250	.200	Ed Lynch	26	10	3	1	2	0	2	.385	.808	.385
Dwight Gooden	13	4	0	0	0	0	4	.308	.308	.308	Mickey Mahler	7	3	0	0	3	0	3	.429	.857	.600
Rich Gossage	9	1	0	0	0	1	5	.111	.111	.200	Rick Mahler	40	9	0	0	2	4	1	.225	.375	.298
Jim Gott	9	2	0	0	0	0	0	.222	.222	.222	Mike G. Marshall	5	0	0	0	0	1	1	.000	.000	.167
Bill Greif	6	1	1	0	0	0	3	.167	.333	.167	John Martin	11	3	1	0	1	2	0	.273	.636	.385
Tom Griffin	25	2	1	0	1	2	7	.080	.240	.148	Renie Martin	11	4	1	0	1	1	0	.364	.727	.417
Kevin Gross	35	8	1	0	2	3	1	.229	.429	.325	Silvio Martinez	17	5	2	0	0	0	3	.294	.412	.294
Cecilio Guante	21	6	2	0	0	1	3	.286	.381	.318	Randy Martz	16	6	2	0	1	3	1	.375	.688	.474
Don Gullett	9	3	0	0	0	0	0	.333	.333	.333	Jon Matlack	18	6	1	0	1	1	0	.333	.556	.368
Bill Gullickson	15	2	0	0	0	1	1	.133	.133	.188	Rick Matula	8	2	1	0	1	0	0	.250	.750	.250
Dave Gumpert	6	2	0	0	0	0	1	.333	.333	.333	Lance McCullers	6	2	0	0	1	0	3	.333	.833	.333
Ed Halicki	22	4	2	0	0	0	2	.182	.273	.217	Andy McGaffigan	7	3	1	0	0	0	1	.429	.571	.429
Tom Hall	3	0	0	0	0	2	1	.000	.000	.400	Lynn McGlothen	43	13	5	0	4	5	9	.302	.698	.380
Atlee Hammaker	17	9	2	0	1	0	3	.529	.824	.529	Tug McGraw	17	4	1	0	0	2	3	.235	.294	.333
Preston Hanna	16	5	1	0	1	2	5	.313	.563	.389	Joe McIntosh	6	3	0	0	0	0	0	.500	.500	.500
Alan Hargesheimer	6	2	0	0	0	0	0	.333	.333	.333	Bo McLaughlin	5	2	0	0	1	0	0	.400	1.000	.400
Greg Harris	7	1	0	0	0	0	3	.143	.143	.143	Craig McMurtry	12	2	1	0	0	1	2	.167	.250	.231
Roric Harrison	6	4	1	0	2	0	0	.667	1.833	.667	Larry McWilliams	54	20	3	0	4	11	5	.370	.648	.478
Tom Hausman	11	3	0	0	1	1	1	.273	.545	.333	Doc Medich	4	0	0	0	0	2	0	.000	.000	.333
Andy Hawkins	18	5	1	0	1	0	0	.278	.500	.278	Andy Messersmith	17	3	0	0	0	0	6	.176	.176	.176
Dave Heaverlo	6	2	0	0	0	0	0	.333	.333	.333	Butch Metzger	14	7	2	0	1	0	2	.500	.857	.500
Willie Hernandez	17	5	1	1	0	2	1	.294	.471	.368	Dyar Miller	5	1	0	0	0	0	1	.200	.200	.167
Orel Hershiser	19	5	0	0	1	1	2	.263	.421	.333	Greg Minton	27	6	0	1	0	6	1	.222	.296	.353
Joe Hesketh	8	5	0	0	1	1	1	.625	1.000	.600	Randy Moffitt	20	5	0	0	3	2	3	.250	.700	.348
Al Holland	12	3	2	0	0	3	2	.250	.417	.400	John Montefusco	42	10	2	0	2	5	10	.238	.429	.313
Rick Honeycutt	14	5	0	0	1	3	1	.357	.571	.471	Donnie Moore	14	10	2	0	1	0	0	.714	.857	.733
Burt Hooton	61	13	2	0	2	4	8	.213	.344	.254	Bob Moose	4	2	0	0	0	2	0	.500	.500	.667
Ricky Horton	15	4	0	0	0	3	2	.267	.267	.389	Carl Morton	10	3	0	0	1	0	1	.300	.600	.300
Charlie Hough	14	5	1	0	1	2	2	.357	.643	.438	Paul Moskau	13	5	0	1	2	1	0	.385	1.000	.429
Steve Howe	10	3	0	0	0	3	0	.300	.300	.462	Jamie Moyer	8	3	1	0	0	1	1	.375	.500	.400
Ken Howell	9	1	0	0	0	0	2	.111	.111	.111	Steve Mura	22	4	1	0	0	3	0	.182	.227	.269
LaMarr Hoyt	13	3	1	0	1	1	0	.231	.538	.286	Dale Murray	16	3	0	0	1	1	1	.188	.250	.235
Al Hrabosky	8	4	0	0	0	2	1	.500	.500	.600	Phil Nastu	5	1	0	0	1	0	0	.200	.800	.200
Charles Hudson	17	4	1	0	1	2	0	.235	.471	.316	Tom Niedenfuer	10	2	1	0	0	2	2	.200	.300	.333
Tom Hume	16	4	0	0	0	3	2	.250	.250	.350	Joe Niekro	58	8	2	0	1	6	8	.138	.224	.261
Roy Lee Jackson	9	4	1	0	1	1	3	.444	.889	.500	Phil Niekro	43	8	1	0	3	19	8	.186	.419	.429
Ferguson Jenkins	13	7	3	0	1	2	1	.538	1.000	.625	Randy Niemann	3	1	0	0	0	4	1	.333	.333	.714
Tommy John	16	6	0	0	0	0	4	.375	.375	.375	Gary Nolan	19	5	0	0	2	1	4	.263	.579	.300
Joe Johnson	6	2	1	0	1	0	0	.333	1.000	.333	Dickie Noles	22	6	2	0	0	3	3	.273	.364	.385
Odell Jones	7	1	0	0	0	1	3	.143	.143	.250	Fred Norman	26	5	1	0	0	1	4	.192	.231	.214
Randy Jones	44	10	1	0	2	3	3	.227	.386	.277	Jesse Orosco	13	2	0	0	0	3	3	.154	.154	.313
Jim Kaat	19	8	3	0	1	2	0	.421	.737	.476	Jim Otten	5	2	1	0	0	0	0	.400	.600	.400
Kurt Kepshire	9	1	0	0	0	1	1	.111	.111	.200	Bob Owchinko	9	4	0	0	0	1	1	.444	.444	.500
Bob Kipper	14	5	0	0	1	2	0	.357	.571	.438	Rick Ownbey	8	2	0	0	0	3	1	.250	.250	.455
Bruce Kison	41	9	0	0	2	2	6	.220	.366	.256	David Palmer	8	3	0	0	2	1	0	.375	1.125	.444
Bob Knepper	45	12	0	0	2	4	5	.267	.400	.327	Frank Pastore	31	9	1	1	2	0	8	.290	.581	.290
Darold Knowles	5	1	1	0	0	2	0	.200	.400	.429	Bob Patterson	7	2	0	0	0	1	1	.286	.286	.375
Kevin Kobel	7	1	1	0	0	2	1	.143	.286	.333	Alejandro Pena	18	6	1	0	2	0	5	.333	.722	.333
Doug Konieczny	7	2	0	0	0	0	0	.286	.286	.286	Pascual Perez	16	5	1	0	1	0	0	.313	.563	.333
Jerry Koosman	54	12	2	1	2	5	5	.222	.407	.279	Gaylord Perry	11	4	0	0	1	1	1	.364	.636	.417
Mike Krukow	53	9	0	0	1	7	9	.170	.226	.262	Pat Perry	5	2	1	0	0	1	0	.400	.600	.500
Frank LaCorte	7	2	0	0	2	3	1	.286	1.143	.500	Ted Power	12	3	2	0	0	1	3	.250	.417	.308
Mike LaCoss	40	10	3	0	0	7	7	.250	.325	.354	Joe Price	19	10	3	1	4	3	1	.526	1.421	.565
Lerrin LaGrow	6	2	0	0	0	1	0	.333	.333	.429	Mike Proly	9	2	1	0	0	2	0	.222	.333	.357
Dave LaPoint	39	11	2	0	1	2	7	.282	.410	.302	Charlie Puleo	12	5	1	0	1	3	0	.417	.750	.533
Jeff Lahti	11	3	0	0	0	2	0	.273	.273	.385	Chuck Rainey	8	3	1	0	0	0	1	.375	.500	.375
Dennis Lamp	19	5	1	0	2	3	2	.263	.632	.364	Eric Rasmussen	51	13	3	0	1	3	6	.255	.373	.291
Dan Larson	4	2	0	0	2	1	0	.500	2.000	.600	Doug Rau	25	8	4	0	1	4	2	.320	.600	.414
Bill Laskey	20	6	1	0	3	3	2	.300	.800	.391	Shane Rawley	22	4	2	0	0	3	0	.182	.273	.280
Gary Lavelle	22	4	1	0	0	4	4	.182	.227	.308	Jeff Reardon	12	3	0	0	1	0	4	.250	.500	.250
Terry Leach	5	2	0	0	0	0	0	.400	.400	.400	Ron Reed	48	14	2	0	3	7	4	.292	.521	.386
Mark Lee	7	0	0	0	0	0	0	.000	.000	.000	Steve Renko	6	1	1	0	0	0	1	.167	.333	.167
Craig Lefferts	9	2	0	0	0	2	0	.222	.222	.364	Paul Reuschel	7	1	0	0	0	4	1	.143	.143	.455
Charlie Leibrandt	4	1	0	0	0	1	0	.250	.250	.400	Rick Reuschel	91	19	2	1	2	6	18	.209	.319	.250
Mark Lemongello	12	2	0	0	0	0	3	.167	.167	.154	Jerry Reuss	59	14	1	0	4	2	7	.237	.458	.258
Max Leon	5	0	0	0	0	2	3	.000	.000	.286	Rick Rhoden	67	18	7	0	3	8	8	.269	.463	.319
Randy Lerch	26	10	3	0	4	1	0	.385	.962	.407	J.R. Richard	39	14	0	0	3	8	8	.359	.590	.458

Gary Carter continued

Pitcher	AB	H	2B	3B	HR	BB	SO	BA	SA	OBA
Andy Rincon	5	3	0	1	0	1	0	.600	1.000	.667
Allen Ripley	6	1	0	0	1	1	1	.167	.667	.286
Bert Roberge	5	0	0	0	0	1	0	.000	.000	.167
Dave A. Roberts	15	5	1	0	0	0	2	.333	.400	.333
Don Robinson	46	3	2	0	0	4	4	.065	.109	.157
Jeff Robinson	7	1	0	0	0	0	2	.143	.143	.143
Ron Robinson	5	2	0	0	0	0	2	.400	.400	.400
Enrique Romo	5	1	0	1	0	2	0	.200	.600	.429
Vicente Romo	5	1	1	0	0	0	2	.200	.400	.200
Jim Rooker	16	7	0	0	5	3	2	.438	1.375	.455
Dave Rucker	14	5	2	0	0	1	0	.357	.500	.400
Bruce Ruffin	9	1	0	0	0	1	1	.111	.111	.200
Vern Ruhle	23	7	0	0	4	1	3	.304	.826	.360
Jeff Russell	10	3	1	0	1	0	0	.300	.700	.300
Dick Ruthven	73	17	2	0	3	7	5	.233	.384	.296
Nolan Ryan	47	13	3	0	2	8	6	.277	.468	.382
Joe Sambito	5	1	1	0	0	2	2	.200	.400	.429
Scott Sanderson	13	5	1	0	2	0	1	.385	.923	.400
Manny Sarmiento	15	1	0	0	1	1	2	.067	.267	.167
Rick Sawyer	7	1	1	0	0	1	2	.143	.286	.250
Dan Schatzeder	9	3	0	0	1	2	0	.333	.667	.455
Bill Scherrer	4	1	0	0	0	1	0	.250	.250	.400
Ron Schueler	5	2	1	0	0	1	0	.400	.600	.500
Buddy Schultz	6	1	0	0	1	1	1	.167	.667	.286
Mike Scott	31	10	3	1	1	2	6	.323	.581	.353
Rod Scurry	10	2	1	0	1	0	1	.200	.600	.200
Tom Seaver	64	12	0	0	1	7	12	.188	.234	.268
Bob Sebra	11	3	1	1	0	0	2	.273	.545	.273
Bob Shirley	22	8	1	0	0	3	1	.364	.409	.423
Eric Show	25	6	0	0	2	5	2	.240	.560	.367
Doug Sisk	8	1	0	0	0	0	0	.125	.125	.125
Craig Skok	5	1	0	0	0	0	1	.200	.200	.200
Bryn Smith	17	3	0	0	0	2	2	.176	.176	.263
Dave Smith	13	1	0	0	0	0	3	.077	.077	.143
Lee Smith	23	4	1	0	0	0	6	.174	.217	.174
Zane Smith	12	3	0	0	1	4	0	.250	.500	.438
Eddie Solomon	24	7	0	1	2	4	4	.292	.625	.393
Lary Sorensen	11	3	1	0	0	0	1	.273	.364	.273
Elias Sosa	7	1	0	0	1	2	1	.143	.571	.300
Mario Soto	53	13	2	0	2	7	11	.245	.396	.333
Dan Spillner	7	1	0	0	0	0	1	.143	.143	.143
Dave Stewart	7	3	2	0	0	1	0	.429	.714	.500

Pitcher	AB	H	2B	3B	HR	BB	SO	BA	SA	OBA
Tim Stoddard	12	6	1	0	1	0	2	.500	.833	.500
George Stone	5	2	0	0	0	2	0	.400	.400	.571
Steve Stone	14	1	1	0	0	0	4	.071	.143	.071
Brent Strom	9	1	0	0	0	1	1	.111	.111	.200
John Stuper	17	2	1	0	0	0	0	.118	.176	.167
Rick Sutcliffe	27	4	0	0	1	4	3	.148	.259	.258
Bruce Sutter	43	16	1	1	3	8	6	.372	.651	.471
Don Sutton	48	11	3	0	1	7	8	.229	.354	.339
Craig Swan	58	23	5	1	3	1	3	.397	.672	.407
Randy Tate	5	2	0	0	0	2	2	.400	.400	.571
Kent Tekulve	58	14	2	0	1	2	6	.241	.328	.262
Greg Terlecky	3	0	0	0	0	2	0	.000	.000	.400
Walt Terrell	13	3	1	0	0	3	1	.231	.308	.412
Roy Thomas	5	2	1	0	0	0	0	.400	.600	.400
Mike Thompson	4	0	0	0	0	0	1	.000	.000	.000
Mark Thurmond	21	9	3	0	1	2	1	.429	.714	.478
Luis Tiant	5	2	1	0	0	1	0	.400	.400	.500
Jay Tibbs	13	3	0	0	2	3	1	.231	.692	.375
Dick Tidrow	23	5	0	0	1	1	6	.217	.348	.240
Jackson Todd	7	3	0	0	1	2	1	.429	.857	.556
Dave Tomlin	5	1	0	0	0	0	0	.200	.200	.200
Mike Torrez	9	2	1	0	1	2	0	.222	.667	.417
Steve Trout	25	9	0	0	1	2	2	.360	.480	.407
John Tudor	32	4	2	0	0	2	2	.125	.188	.176
Lee Tunnell	15	3	1	0	0	4	2	.200	.267	.368
Wayne Twitchell	4	0	0	0	0	1	0	.000	.000	.200
Tom Underwood	13	7	0	0	0	2	0	.538	.538	.563
John Urrea	22	6	1	0	0	1	5	.273	.318	.304
Fernando Valenzuela	54	13	4	0	0	7	5	.241	.315	.323
Pete Vuckovich	27	8	1	0	3	2	8	.296	.667	.345
Bob Walk	15	5	0	0	1	1	2	.333	.533	.353
Hank Webb	5	2	2	0	0	1	0	.400	.800	.500
Bob Welch	17	3	2	0	0	7	4	.176	.294	.385
Chris Welsh	14	2	0	0	0	2	0	.143	.143	.250
Ed Whitson	35	13	1	1	1	2	4	.371	.543	.405
Charlie Williams	7	3	1	0	0	2	2	.429	.571	.556
Frank Williams	6	2	0	0	0	0	1	.333	.333	.333
Jim Winn	6	2	0	0	0	2	0	.333	.333	.500
Rick Wise	7	2	0	0	1	0	0	.286	.714	.250
Todd Worrell	4	0	0	0	0	2	0	.000	.000	.333
Floyd Youmans	15	2	0	0	1	1	1	.133	.333	.188
Pat Zachry	53	17	1	1	0	8	9	.321	.377	.410

Tony Gwynn

Pitcher	AB	H	2B	3B	HR	BB	SO	BA	SA	OBA
Jim Acker	6	1	0	0	0	0	1	.167	.167	.167
Rick Aguilera	5	0	0	0	0	1	0	.000	.000	.167
Doyle Alexander	7	3	0	0	1	0	1	.429	.857	.429
Neil Allen	11	3	0	0	0	1	1	.273	.273	.333
Larry Andersen	7	3	0	0	0	0	1	.429	.429	.429
Joaquin Andujar	25	8	2	0	0	3	0	.320	.400	.393
Paul Assenmacher	4	1	0	0	0	1	0	.250	.250	.400
Len Barker	6	3	0	1	0	1	0	.500	.833	.571
Steve Bedrosian	26	7	1	0	0	1	3	.269	.308	.296
Bruce Berenyi	21	6	0	0	1	4	4	.286	.429	.400
Mike Bielecki	11	4	2	0	0	1	1	.364	.545	.417
Vida Blue	15	6	1	0	1	4	1	.400	.667	.526
Fred Breining	6	1	1	0	0	0	1	.167	.333	.167
Tom Brennan	5	2	1	0	0	0	0	.400	.600	.400
Tom Browning	32	13	0	0	2	2	1	.406	.594	.441
Tim Burke	6	2	0	0	0	0	0	.333	.333	.333
Marty Bystrom	5	1	0	0	0	2	1	.200	.200	.429
Jeff Calhoun	5	0	0	0	0	0	0	.000	.000	.000
Rick Camp	20	7	1	0	0	3	0	.350	.400	.435
Bill Campbell	5	1	0	0	1	0	0	.200	.800	.200
John Candelaria	11	3	0	0	0	0	0	.273	.273	.273
Steve Carlton	21	5	1	0	0	1	1	.238	.286	.273
Tim Conroy	5	1	0	0	0	1	0	.200	.200	.286
Danny Cox	14	3	0	0	1	0	1	.214	.429	.214

Pitcher	AB	H	2B	3B	HR	BB	SO	BA	SA	OBA
Ron Darling	24	13	1	1	0	0	3	.542	.667	.542
Mark Davis	18	6	0	0	0	5	4	.333	.333	.478
Bill Dawley	7	5	1	1	0	0	1	.714	1.143	.625
Ken Dayley	9	4	1	0	0	2	2	.444	.556	.545
Jose DeLeon	14	2	1	0	0	1	0	.143	.214	.188
Jeff Dedmon	8	1	0	0	0	1	0	.125	.125	.222
John Denny	35	15	4	0	1	3	2	.429	.629	.474
Jim Deshaies	6	0	0	0	0	1	0	.000	.000	.143
Frank DiPino	5	0	0	0	0	1	0	.000	.000	.143
Carlos Diaz	11	4	1	0	0	0	0	.364	.455	.364
Dennis Eckersley	12	4	2	0	0	0	1	.333	.500	.333
Pete Falcone	13	5	1	0	0	1	0	.385	.462	.429
Sid Fernandez	24	7	0	0	1	0	2	.292	.417	.292
Ray Fontenot	7	1	1	0	0	0	1	.143	.286	.143
Bob Forsch	14	4	0	0	0	1	0	.286	.286	.333
Terry Forster	9	1	0	0	0	3	0	.111	.111	.333
John Franco	21	5	0	0	0	0	1	.238	.238	.238
Brent Gaff	10	3	0	0	0	1	0	.300	.300	.364
Rich Gale	5	3	0	0	0	0	0	.600	.600	.600
Gene Garber	14	3	2	0	0	1	0	.214	.357	.267
Scott Garrelts	21	3	1	0	0	1	0	.143	.190	.182
Dwight Gooden	26	5	0	1	0	2	2	.192	.269	.250
Jim Gott	8	4	1	0	0	0	2	.500	.625	.500
Kevin Gross	17	5	2	0	0	0	1	.294	.412	.294

Tony Gwynn continued

Pitcher	AB	H	2B	3B	HR	BB	SO	BA	SA	OBA
Cecilio Guante	7	2	0	1	0	1	2	.286	.571	.375
Bill Gullickson	30	11	0	0	0	2	1	.367	.367	.406
Atlee Hammaker	16	5	0	1	0	0	0	.313	.438	.313
Willie Hernandez	4	0	0	0	0	0	1	.000	.000	.000
Orel Hershiser	26	7	2	0	0	1	0	.269	.346	.296
Joe Hesketh	12	3	0	0	0	3	1	.250	.250	.400
Al Holland	8	2	0	1	0	2	2	.250	.500	.400
Rick Honeycutt	34	8	1	1	0	1	2	.235	.324	.257
Burt Hooton	14	5	1	0	0	1	0	.357	.429	.400
Ricky Horton	16	6	1	0	0	0	0	.375	.438	.375
Steve Howe	4	0	0	0	0	1	0	.000	.000	.200
Ken Howell	11	5	0	0	0	3	2	.455	.455	.571
Charles Hudson	23	10	1	2	0	1	2	.435	.652	.458
Tom Hume	11	6	3	0	1	2	0	.545	1.091	.615
Joe Johnson	10	5	0	0	0	0	0	.500	.500	.583
Kurt Kepshire	9	1	0	0	0	0	0	.111	.111	.111
Charlie Kerfeld	7	3	0	0	0	0	0	.429	.429	.429
Bob Kipper	6	4	0	1	0	0	0	.667	1.000	.667
Bob Knepper	39	11	1	0	1	5	1	.282	.385	.364
Mark Knudson	5	1	0	0	0	0	1	.200	.200	.333
Jerry Koosman	9	3	0	0	0	2	1	.333	.333	.455
Mike Krukow	40	16	4	0	2	4	2	.400	.650	.444
Mike LaCoss	27	13	0	0	0	4	0	.481	.481	.548
Dave LaPoint	23	9	2	0	0	1	0	.391	.478	.391
Bill Laskey	34	14	4	0	2	0	2	.412	.706	.412
Gary Lavelle	10	4	0	0	0	1	2	.400	.400	.455
Charlie Lea	14	4	0	0	2	0	0	.286	.286	.375
Gary Lucas	6	3	1	0	0	0	0	.500	.667	.500
Ed Lynch	17	5	0	0	1	1	0	.294	.471	.333
Mike Madden	15	4	0	0	0	0	5	.267	.267	.267
Mike Maddux	7	0	0	0	0	1	0	.000	.000	.125
Rick Mahler	38	11	2	1	0	1	0	.289	.395	.308
Roger Mason	6	3	0	1	0	0	2	.500	.833	.500
Roger McDowell	8	2	0	0	0	1	1	.250	.250	.333
Andy McGaffigan	17	6	1	0	0	2	1	.353	.412	.421
Craig McMurtry	24	11	0	0	0	2	0	.458	.458	.481
Larry McWilliams	14	5	1	0	1	3	1	.357	.643	.500
Greg Minton	13	5	1	0	0	7	0	.385	.462	.600
Terry Mulholland	6	2	0	1	0	2	0	.333	.667	.500
Rob Murphy	5	0	0	0	0	0	0	.000	.000	.000
Tom Niedenfuer	11	5	1	1	0	0	1	.455	.727	.455
Joe Niekro	32	9	1	1	0	0	3	.281	.375	.281
Phil Niekro	15	3	0	0	0	1	1	.200	.200	.235
Dickie Noles	6	1	0	1	0	2	0	.167	.500	.375
Jesse Orosco	12	3	0	0	1	1	0	.250	.500	.308
Bob Owchinko	6	2	0	0	0	1	0	.333	.333	.429
David Palmer	18	5	0	1	0	0	0	.278	.389	.278
Frank Pastore	13	2	0	0	0	1	0	.154	.154	.214
Alejandro Pena	18	8	2	0	0	1	1	.444	.556	.500
Pascual Perez	30	13	1	1	0	1	0	.433	.533	.452
Dennis Powell	5	0	0	0	0	1	0	.000	.000	.167
Ted Power	13	6	0	1	1	5	2	.462	.846	.611
Joe Price	15	4	0	0	0	3	1	.267	.267	.389

Pitcher	AB	H	2B	3B	HR	BB	SO	BA	SA	OBA
Charlie Puleo	16	5	0	0	0	0	0	.313	.313	.313
Shane Rawley	13	2	0	0	0	1	0	.154	.154	.214
Jeff Reardon	6	1	0	0	0	1	0	.167	.167	.286
Rick Reuschel	17	2	0	0	0	1	0	.118	.118	.167
Jerry Reuss	15	4	1	0	0	0	0	.267	.333	.313
Rick Rhoden	30	8	2	0	0	2	0	.267	.333	.313
Bert Roberge	4	1	1	0	0	0	0	.250	.500	.400
Don Robinson	5	2	0	0	0	0	0	.400	.400	.400
Jeff Robinson	16	9	1	1	0	1	0	.563	.750	.588
Ron Robinson	9	4	1	0	0	1	0	.444	.556	.500
Steve Rogers	21	7	0	0	0	1	0	.333	.333	.364
Dave Rucker	9	2	0	0	0	1	0	.222	.222	.300
Bruce Ruffin	7	1	0	0	0	1	0	.143	.143	.250
Vern Ruhle	9	4	0	0	1	3	0	.444	.778	.583
Jeff Russell	14	7	1	0	0	1	0	.500	.571	.533
Dick Ruthven	15	4	0	0	0	0	0	.267	.267	.267
Nolan Ryan	44	10	0	0	0	2	7	.227	.227	.255
Scott Sanderson	19	7	1	0	0	0	1	.368	.421	.368
Dan Schatzeder	11	1	0	0	0	1	1	.091	.091	.167
Bill Scherrer	7	3	1	0	0	0	0	.429	.571	.429
Calvin Schiraldi	5	3	0	1	1	0	0	.600	1.600	.600
Mike Scott	47	15	2	0	0	0	0	.319	.362	.319
Rod Scurry	8	1	0	0	0	3	1	.125	.125	.364
Tom Seaver	14	3	0	0	0	0	1	.214	.214	.214
Bob Shirley	7	1	0	0	0	0	2	.143	.143	.143
Doug Sisk	4	1	0	0	0	0	2	.250	.250	.500
Bryn Smith	17	7	0	0	0	0	0	.412	.412	.412
Dave Smith	10	7	0	0	0	0	0	.700	.700	.700
Lee Smith	8	3	0	0	0	0	2	.375	.375	.375
Zane Smith	18	8	2	0	0	2	1	.444	.556	.500
Lary Sorensen	4	1	1	0	0	1	1	.250	.500	.400
Mario Soto	30	6	2	0	1	4	3	.200	.367	.294
John Stuper	6	1	0	0	0	1	0	.167	.167	.286
Rick Sutcliffe	20	6	2	0	0	2	1	.300	.400	.364
Bruce Sutter	8	3	0	0	0	0	0	.375	.375	.375
Don Sutton	6	1	1	0	0	1	1	.167	.333	.286
Craig Swan	7	3	2	0	0	0	0	.429	.714	.429
Kent Tekulve	7	2	0	0	0	1	0	.286	.286	.375
Walt Terrell	10	5	1	0	0	1	0	.500	.600	.545
Jay Tibbs	25	10	2	0	1	3	0	.400	.600	.464
Steve Trout	23	9	1	0	0	2	0	.391	.435	.462
John Tudor	26	11	2	0	2	1	4	.423	.731	.464
Lee Tunnell	9	4	0	0	0	0	0	.444	.444	.444
Fernando Valenzuela	42	12	2	0	1	0	5	.286	.405	.286
Dave Von Ohlen	5	2	1	0	0	0	0	.400	.600	.400
Bob Walk	13	3	1	0	0	1	1	.231	.308	.286
Bob Welch	34	10	2	0	0	1	3	.294	.353	.314
Chris Welsh	8	4	3	0	0	0	0	.500	.875	.500
Frank Williams	7	3	0	0	0	0	1	.429	.429	.429
Carl Willis	5	3	0	0	0	0	0	.600	.600	.600
Jim Winn	4	3	0	0	0	1	0	.750	.750	.800
Floyd Youmans	11	1	0	0	0	1	0	.091	.091	.167
Pat Zachry	5	1	0	0	0	1	0	.200	.200	.333

Don Mattingly

Pitcher	AB	H	2B	3B	HR	BB	SO	BA	SA	OBA
Don Aase	6	5	1	0	2	0	0	.833	2.000	.833
Jim Acker	11	4	0	0	0	1	0	.364	.364	.417
Juan Agosto	8	4	0	0	1	0	1	.500	.875	.556
Doyle Alexander	33	9	1	0	3	0	1	.273	.576	.273
Neil Allen	6	1	1	0	0	0	1	.167	.333	.167
Joaquin Andujar	7	1	1	0	0	0	0	.143	.286	.143
Keith Atherton	11	6	1	0	1	1	0	.545	.909	.583
Scott Bailes	5	1	0	0	0	1	0	.200	.200	.333
Scott Bankhead	4	1	0	0	0	1	0	.250	.250	.400
Floyd Bannister	26	9	2	0	3	1	1	.346	.769	.370
Salome Barojas	13	3	0	0	1	0	1	.231	.462	.231
Jim Beattie	19	6	2	0	1	1	2	.316	.579	.350
Joe Beckwith	3	2	0	0	0	2	0	.667	.667	.800

Pitcher	AB	H	2B	3B	HR	BB	SO	BA	SA	OBA
Rick Behenna	4	3	0	0	1	1	1	.750	1.500	.800
Eric Bell	7	2	0	0	0	1	0	.286	.286	.375
Juan Berenguer	6	1	0	0	0	0	0	.167	.167	.167
Karl Best	7	2	0	0	0	0	0	.286	.286	.286
Bud Black	22	5	1	0	2	1	1	.227	.545	.261
Bert Blyleven	25	8	1	1	2	2	3	.320	.680	.379
Mike Boddicker	31	9	3	0	1	1	6	.290	.484	.313
Dennis Boyd	29	10	2	0	0	0	5	.345	.414	.345
Mark Brown	6	2	1	0	0	0	0	.333	.500	.333
Mike G. Brown	5	2	0	0	1	0	0	.400	1.000	.400
Britt Burns	10	3	0	0	3	0	0	.300	1.200	.300
Ray Burris	16	4	1	0	0	3	0	.250	.313	.368
John Butcher	12	5	2	1	0	0	0	.417	.750	.385

Don Mattingly continued

Pitcher	AB	H	2B	3B	HR	BB	SO	BA	SA	OBA
Mike Caldwell	15	9	1	1	0	1	1	.600	.800	.625
Ernie Camacho	7	3	0	0	1	0	0	.429	.857	.429
John Candelaria	8	2	1	0	0	0	2	.250	.375	.250
Tom Candiotti	16	4	0	0	2	2	3	.250	.625	.333
Bill Caudill	4	4	0	0	0	3	0	1.000	1.000	1.000
John Cerutti	13	5	2	0	0	0	2	.385	.538	.357
Jim Clancy	13	5	2	0	1	0	2	.385	.769	.357
Bryan Clark	9	3	0	0	1	3	1	.333	.667	.538
Mark Clear	10	1	0	0	0	3	0	.100	.100	.308
Roger Clemens	12	4	0	0	0	0	1	.333	.333	.333
Jaime Cocanower	11	4	1	0	0	1	1	.364	.455	.417
Chris Codiroli	18	8	0	1	2	1	1	.444	.889	.474
Tim Conroy	8	3	0	0	0	1	2	.375	.375	.444
Glen Cook	6	3	2	0	0	0	0	.500	.833	.500
Doug Corbett	9	4	1	0	0	0	0	.444	.556	.444
Ed Correa	6	2	1	0	1	0	1	.333	1.000	.333
Joe Cowley	4	1	1	0	0	1	1	.250	.500	.400
Steve Crawford	17	8	1	0	0	0	0	.471	.529	.471
John Curtis	7	2	0	0	0	1	0	.286	.286	.375
Danny Darwin	19	6	2	0	1	0	0	.316	.421	.350
Ron Davis	5	2	0	0	1	2	1	.400	1.000	.571
Storm Davis	19	2	0	0	0	3	0	.105	.105	.227
Ken Dixon	12	4	2	0	1	0	1	.333	.750	.308
Richard Dotson	18	6	0	1	1	0	2	.333	.611	.333
Jamie Easterly	10	3	1	0	0	2	0	.300	.400	.417
Dennis Eckersley	7	1	0	0	0	0	0	.143	.143	.143
Steve Farr	8	2	0	0	1	0	0	.250	.625	.250
Pete Filson	17	4	0	0	1	4	1	.235	.412	.381
Rollie Fingers	6	1	1	0	0	0	0	.167	.333	.167
Mike Flanagan	15	5	2	0	0	0	2	.333	.467	.313
Ken Forsch	5	1	0	0	0	2	0	.200	.200	.429
Dave Geisel	7	2	0	0	0	0	0	.286	.286	.286
Jerry Don Gleaton	5	4	1	0	0	0	0	.800	1.000	.800
Jim Gott	5	1	0	0	0	1	0	.200	.200	.286
Mark Gubicza	19	9	2	0	2	1	1	.474	.579	.478
Jose Guzman	6	4	0	0	0	0	1	.667	.667	.667
Moose Haas	15	5	1	0	0	1	0	.333	.400	.375
Greg Harris	8	2	1	0	0	1	2	.250	.375	.400
Brad Havens	6	1	1	0	0	1	1	.167	.333	.286
Neal Heaton	26	9	3	0	2	2	3	.346	.692	.393
Tom Henke	7	3	1	0	0	1	0	.429	.571	.500
John Henry Johnson	5	2	1	0	0	0	0	.400	.600	.400
Willie Hernandez	16	6	0	0	0	1	1	.375	.375	.412
Ted Higuera	24	5	0	0	0	0	3	.208	.208	.208
Charlie Hough	22	7	0	2	3	2	2	.318	.682	.400
LaMarr Hoyt	7	2	0	0	0	1	0	.286	.286	.375
Mark Huismann	4	3	0	0	2	1	0	.750	2.250	.800
Bruce Hurst	42	8	3	0	0	3	3	.190	.262	.244
Danny Jackson	7	3	1	0	0	0	1	.429	.571	.375
Roy Lee Jackson	6	3	1	0	0	0	0	.500	.667	.500
Bob James	4	1	0	0	0	1	0	.250	.250	.400
Mike Jeffcoat	8	2	0	0	0	1	0	.250	.250	.333
Tommy John	14	4	0	0	1	1	1	.286	.500	.313
Jimmy Key	27	10	2	0	0	2	3	.370	.444	.400
Bill Krueger	11	3	1	0	0	0	0	.273	.364	.273
Pete Ladd	8	1	0	0	0	1	3	.125	.125	.222
Dennis Lamp	8	4	0	1	0	1	1	.500	.750	.556
Mark Langston	27	11	4	1	2	3	0	.407	.852	.467
Gary Lavelle	4	1	0	0	0	0	0	.250	.250	.200
Luis Leal	10	4	0	0	1	0	0	.400	.700	.400
Tim Leary	8	1	0	0	0	1	0	.125	.125	.222
Charlie Leibrandt	22	5	1	0	1	1	2	.227	.409	.292
Dennis Leonard	5	1	0	0	0	0	0	.200	.200	.200
Tim Lollar	10	3	2	0	0	2	1	.300	.500	.385
Aurelio Lopez	7	0	0	0	0	0	0	.000	.000	.000
Mickey Mahler	5	0	0	0	0	1	0	.000	.000	.143
Dennis Martinez	16	4	0	0	1	0	1	.250	.438	.235
Tippy Martinez	12	4	2	0	0	1	1	.333	.500	.385

Pitcher	AB	H	2B	3B	HR	BB	SO	BA	SA	OBA
Mike Mason	23	4	1	0	1	0	0	.174	.348	.167
Kirk McCaskill	7	0	0	0	0	1	2	.000	.000	.125
Steve McCatty	12	4	0	0	0	1	0	.333	.333	.385
Bob McClure	12	5	0	0	0	1	2	.417	.417	.462
Scott McGregor	32	16	5	0	3	4	1	.500	.938	.526
Paul Mirabella	4	2	0	0	0	0	0	.500	.500	.500
Mike Moore	13	5	0	0	2	1	1	.385	.846	.429
Mike Morgan	5	1	1	0	0	1	0	.200	.400	.286
Jack Morris	22	7	2	0	2	3	3	.318	.682	.400
Steve Mura	4	1	0	0	0	1	0	.250	.250	.400
Gene Nelson	12	6	2	0	1	0	0	.500	.917	.500
Phil Niekro	12	3	1	0	0	2	1	.250	.333	.357
Juan Nieves	5	2	0	0	0	0	0	.400	.400	.400
Al Nipper	23	10	2	0	0	1	2	.435	.522	.458
Dickie Noles	9	5	1	0	1	2	1	.556	1.000	.636
Edwin Nunez	7	3	0	0	2	1	2	.429	1.286	.500
Randy O'Neal	12	4	2	0	1	0	0	.333	.750	.385
Bob Ojeda	16	6	2	0	0	0	3	.375	.500	.353
John Pacella	3	0	0	0	0	0	0	.000	.000	.000
Dan Petry	31	14	1	1	1	1	2	.452	.645	.469
Dan Plesac	5	2	0	0	0	0	0	.400	.400	.400
Eric Plunk	5	1	0	0	0	0	1	.200	.200	.200
Chuck Porter	11	3	2	0	0	1	1	.273	.455	.333
Dan Quisenberry	13	5	1	0	0	1	0	.385	.462	.429
Ron Romanick	21	7	2	0	1	3	0	.333	.571	.417
Ramon Romero	5	2	0	0	1	1	0	.400	1.000	.500
Dave Rozema	9	5	1	0	1	0	0	.556	1.000	.556
Bret Saberhagen	23	7	2	0	0	0	1	.304	.391	.304
Joe Sambito	5	1	0	0	0	0	0	.200	.200	.200
Luis Sanchez	7	2	1	0	1	0	1	.286	.857	.286
Dave J. Schmidt	7	1	0	0	0	1	0	.143	.143	.250
Ken Schrom	18	5	0	0	1	2	0	.278	.444	.350
Don Schulze	9	1	0	0	0	0	0	.111	.111	.111
Tom Seaver	14	6	2	0	0	0	0	.429	.571	.429
Jim Slaton	16	8	2	0	1	2	0	.500	.813	.556
Roy Smith	6	4	1	0	1	1	0	.667	1.333	.625
Mike Smithson	31	8	3	0	0	0	1	.258	.355	.242
Lary Sorensen	8	3	0	0	0	0	1	.375	.375	.375
Dan Spillner	5	1	0	0	0	1	0	.200	.200	.286
Bob Stanley	19	6	0	0	1	1	1	.316	.474	.333
Dave Stewart	20	7	1	0	0	2	2	.350	.400	.409
Sammy Stewart	14	4	0	0	0	6	1	.286	.286	.500
Dave Stieb	44	18	5	1	2	0	3	.409	.705	.400
Rick Sutcliffe	5	3	0	0	1	2	0	.600	1.200	.714
Don Sutton	13	3	1	0	1	1	0	.231	.538	.286
Bill Swaggerty	9	2	0	0	0	0	0	.222	.222	.222
Bill Swift	15	4	1	0	0	0	0	.267	.333	.267
Frank Tanana	27	9	4	0	1	3	1	.333	.593	.400
Tom Tellmann	9	4	1	1	0	0	1	.444	.778	.444
Walt Terrell	17	8	0	0	2	0	0	.471	.824	.471
Roy Thomas	7	1	0	0	0	0	1	.143	.143	.143
John Tudor	9	1	0	0	0	1	1	.111	.444	.200
Ed Vande Berg	4	1	0	0	0	0	0	.250	.250	.250
Frank Viola	22	5	4	0	0	0	1	.227	.409	.227
Tom Waddell	7	1	0	0	0	0	0	.143	.143	.143
Rick Waits	8	1	0	0	0	0	0	.125	.125	.125
Curt Wardle	8	5	2	0	1	1	0	.625	1.250	.667
Mike Warren	8	4	1	0	1	2	0	.500	1.000	.600
Bill Wegman	8	1	0	0	0	1	0	.125	.125	.222
Chris Welsh	5	0	0	0	0	3	1	.000	.000	.375
Len Whitehouse	5	2	0	0	0	0	0	.400	.400	.400
Milt Wilcox	6	4	1	0	0	2	1	.667	.833	.600
Bobby Witt	5	1	1	0	0	0	1	.200	.400	.143
Mike Witt	21	6	2	0	1	4	2	.286	.524	.400
Rob Woodward	6	1	0	0	0	0	0	.167	.167	.167
Curt Young	17	5	0	0	0	0	0	.294	.294	.294
Matt Young	19	5	3	0	0	1	3	.263	.421	.300
Geoff Zahn	12	6	1	0	2	0	0	.500	1.083	.500

Tim Raines

Pitcher	AB	H	2B	3B	HR	BB	SO	BA	SA	OBA
Rick Aguilera	22	2	0	0	0	2	3	.091	.091	.167
Doyle Alexander	6	1	1	0	0	0	0	.167	.333	.167
Neil Allen	15	4	1	0	0	2	2	.267	.333	.353
Larry Andersen	6	2	0	0	1	1	2	.333	.833	.429
Joaquin Andujar	46	17	3	1	0	11	7	.370	.478	.491
Doug Bair	3	1	0	0	0	2	0	.333	.333	.600
Jay Baller	5	1	1	0	0	2	0	.200	.400	.429
Len Barker	8	2	0	0	0	4	1	.250	.250	.500
Steve Bedrosian	26	9	1	1	0	2	6	.346	.462	.414
Bruce Berenyi	30	8	2	0	0	3	11	.267	.333	.333
Jim Bibby	10	2	0	0	0	5	0	.200	.200	.467
Mike Bielecki	7	5	1	1	0	0	0	.714	1.143	.714
Doug Bird	13	5	0	0	0	0	1	.385	.385	.385
Vida Blue	20	5	0	0	0	6	3	.250	.250	.423
Tommy Boggs	5	1	0	0	0	0	0	.200	.200	.200
Rich Bordi	5	1	0	0	0	0	1	.200	.200	.200
Fred Breining	10	2	0	0	0	1	3	.200	.200	.273
Tom Browning	9	5	0	0	1	1	1	.556	.889	.600
Warren Brusstar	14	2	0	1	0	2	2	.143	.286	.250
Ray Burris	5	2	0	0	0	0	0	.400	.400	.400
Marty Bystrom	17	3	1	0	0	1	4	.176	.235	.222
Jeff Calhoun	5	3	1	0	0	0	0	.600	.800	.600
Rick Camp	25	8	1	0	0	3	1	.320	.360	.393
Bill Campbell	13	5	3	0	0	3	0	.385	.615	.500
John Candelaria	21	4	0	0	0	1	5	.190	.190	.227
Steve Carlton	57	12	1	1	0	9	10	.211	.263	.318
Don Carman	10	3	1	0	0	2	1	.300	.400	.385
Bobby Castillo	10	2	0	0	1	2	4	.200	.500	.333
Bill Caudill	5	1	1	0	0	1	1	.200	.400	.333
Floyd Chiffer	4	0	0	0	0	1	1	.000	.000	.200
Larry Christenson	27	6	1	0	0	4	1	.222	.259	.323
Ralph Citarella	5	3	1	0	0	1	1	.600	.800	.667
Tim Conroy	4	2	1	0	0	0	0	.500	.750	.400
Danny Cox	29	9	3	0	0	7	3	.310	.414	.444
Ron Darling	30	7	1	0	0	6	2	.233	.267	.361
Mark Davis	10	2	0	0	0	1	1	.200	.200	.273
Bill Dawley	6	0	0	0	0	1	2	.000	.000	.143
Ken Dayley	19	7	2	0	1	3	2	.368	.632	.455
Jose DeLeon	18	5	2	0	0	5	2	.278	.389	.435
Luis DeLeon	6	1	0	0	0	1	1	.167	.167	.286
Jeff Dedmon	8	5	2	0	1	0	0	.625	1.250	.625
John Denny	35	15	1	1	0	3	5	.429	.514	.474
Frank DiPino	7	3	1	0	0	2	0	.429	.571	.556
Carlos Diaz	9	2	0	0	0	3	1	.222	.222	.417
Kelly Downs	7	3	1	0	0	0	0	.429	.571	.429
Dave Dravecky	32	5	1	0	1	6	3	.156	.281	.289
Dennis Eckersley	43	15	3	1	0	3	4	.349	.465	.391
Juan Eichelberger	10	4	0	1	0	1	1	.400	.600	.455
Pete Falcone	17	7	2	1	0	4	1	.412	.647	.524
Ed Farmer	8	5	0	0	0	1	1	.625	.625	.667
Sid Fernandez	16	6	1	0	2	3	3	.375	.813	.474
Tom Filer	6	2	0	0	0	1	1	.333	.333	.429
Ray Fontenot	7	1	0	0	0	1	3	.143	.143	.250
Bob Forsch	63	19	6	1	0	7	3	.302	.429	.371
Terry Forster	7	2	1	0	0	0	1	.286	.429	.286
Alan Fowlkes	8	3	1	0	0	0	2	.375	.500	.375
John Franco	7	1	0	0	0	0	1	.143	.143	.143
George Frazier	11	4	2	1	0	2	2	.364	.727	.462
Brent Gaff	6	2	0	0	0	0	0	.333	.333	.333
Rich Gale	12	2	0	0	0	2	2	.167	.167	.286
Gene Garber	16	6	1	0	0	0	1	.375	.438	.375
Scott Garrelts	11	3	0	0	0	4	1	.273	.273	.467
Dwight Gooden	21	5	2	0	0	7	3	.238	.333	.429
Tom Gorman	5	1	0	0	1	1	1	.200	.800	.333
Jim Gott	11	5	0	0	0	0	1	.455	.455	.500
Tom Griffin	8	2	1	1	0	0	1	.250	.625	.250
Kevin Gross	24	6	0	1	0	4	4	.250	.333	.379
Cecilio Guante	19	7	2	0	0	0	1	.368	.474	.368
Bill Gullickson	7	3	0	0	0	2	0	.429	.429	.556
Atlee Hammaker	14	6	0	1	0	0	3	.429	.571	.400
Greg Harris	6	0	0	0	0	1	3	.000	.000	.143
Andy Hawkins	39	15	1	0	2	4	6	.385	.564	.442
Ben Hayes	5	4	1	1	0	0	0	.800	1.400	.800
Willie Hernandez	12	5	0	0	1	2	2	.417	.667	.520
Orel Hershiser	22	10	3	0	0	3	2	.455	.591	.520
Al Holland	19	9	2	0	2	3	3	.474	.895	.545
Rick Honeycutt	25	8	1	0	0	2	4	.320	.360	.370
Burt Hooton	19	9	0	0	0	5	2	.474	.474	.583
Ricky Horton	12	4	1	0	0	1	0	.333	.417	.385
Steve Howe	5	2	0	0	0	0	0	.400	.400	.571
Ken Howell	5	1	1	0	0	2	1	.200	.400	.429
LaMarr Hoyt	8	2	1	0	1	0	1	.250	.750	.250
Charles Hudson	33	13	1	0	0	2	3	.394	.424	.429
Tom Hume	14	5	3	1	0	1	1	.357	.714	.400
Ferguson Jenkins	20	4	0	1	0	0	1	.200	.300	.200
Randy Jones	4	1	0	0	0	3	0	.250	.250	.571
Jim Kaat	6	1	0	0	0	0	0	.167	.167	.143
Jeff Keener	5	2	0	1	0	3	1	.400	.800	.625
Kurt Kepshire	15	5	0	1	0	2	2	.333	.467	.389
Bob Kipper	7	0	0	0	0	0	1	.000	.000	.000
Bob Knepper	45	9	1	1	0	3	3	.200	.267	.250
Jerry Koosman	17	5	0	0	1	2	1	.294	.471	.368
Mike Krukow	30	12	1	0	0	7	5	.400	.433	.500
Frank LaCorte	4	2	0	0	0	0	0	.500	.500	.667
Mike LaCoss	29	9	1	0	0	5	1	.310	.345	.412
Dave LaPoint	37	17	2	3	2	9	5	.459	.838	.553
Jeff Lahti	11	2	0	0	0	2	1	.182	.182	.308
Bill Laskey	24	9	0	0	2	6	1	.375	.625	.500
Gary Lavelle	12	6	1	0	1	0	0	.500	.833	.500
Terry Leach	7	2	1	0	0	2	2	.286	.429	.444
Tim Leary	4	2	0	0	0	1	1	.500	.500	.600
Craig Lefferts	14	7	2	0	0	2	2	.500	.643	.563
Tim Lollar	16	6	1	0	0	6	2	.375	.438	.565
Gary Lucas	4	3	1	0	0	1	1	.750	1.000	.800
Ed Lynch	30	8	0	3	1	4	1	.267	.567	.343
Rick Mahler	31	6	1	0	0	8	4	.194	.226	.366
John Martin	9	1	1	0	0	1	0	.111	.222	.200
Renie Martin	8	4	1	0	0	2	0	.500	.625	.545
Randy Martz	19	4	1	0	0	1	1	.211	.263	.250
Greg Mathews	5	0	0	0	0	1	0	.000	.000	.167
Roger McDowell	7	1	0	0	0	2	0	.143	.143	.333
Tug McGraw	6	2	0	0	0	0	1	.333	.333	.333
Craig McMurtry	15	4	2	1	0	4	0	.267	.533	.400
Larry McWilliams	47	10	2	1	4	5	5	.213	.553	.283
Greg Minton	16	6	2	0	0	4	2	.375	.500	.476
Sid Monge	7	3	0	0	0	1	0	.429	.429	.500
John Montefusco	12	3	0	0	0	1	0	.250	.250	.357
Jamie Moyer	6	2	0	0	0	2	0	.333	.333	.500
Steve Mura	12	2	0	0	0	2	1	.167	.167	.286
Tom Niedenfuer	11	5	1	0	0	0	0	.455	.545	.455
Joe Niekro	30	7	1	0	1	4	1	.233	.367	.343
Phil Niekro	21	6	1	1	0	0	3	.286	.429	.286
Dickie Noles	21	9	1	0	0	1	1	.429	.476	.455
Bob Ojeda	9	5	0	0	0	1	0	.556	.556	.636
Jesse Orosco	20	3	0	0	0	1	10	.150	.150	.190
Rick Ownbey	8	1	0	0	0	3	1	.125	.125	.364
David Palmer	10	5	1	0	0	1	2	.500	.700	.545
Frank Pastore	28	6	1	0	0	6	4	.214	.250	.353
Alejandro Pena	19	6	1	0	1	3	4	.316	.526	.409
Pascual Perez	21	5	0	0	1	3	2	.238	.381	.333
Ted Power	16	7	3	0	0	2	2	.438	.625	.500
Joe Price	22	4	2	1	0	1	1	.182	.364	.217
Mike Proly	13	5	0	2	0	1	2	.385	.692	.467
Charlie Puleo	12	3	0	0	0	2	5	.250	.250	.357
Chuck Rainey	11	2	0	0	0	0	1	.182	.182	.250
Shane Rawley	25	5	0	0	1	1	3	.200	.320	.231
Ron Reed	10	2	0	0	0	3	1	.200	.200	.385
Rick Reuschel	38	15	0	0	0	3	3	.395	.395	.439
Jerry Reuss	31	5	0	0	0	2	2	.161	.161	.212
Rick Rhoden	79	23	6	2	2	5	6	.291	.494	.329
Allen Ripley	8	3	0	1	0	1	0	.375	.625	.444
Don Robinson	30	8	3	0	1	3	4	.267	.467	.333
Jeff Robinson	10	3	2	0	0	1	1	.300	.500	.364
Ron Robinson	10	6	3	1	0	0	1	.600	1.100	.600
Enrique Romo	6	3	0	0	0	0	1	.500	.500	.500
Vicente Romo	3	1	0	0	0	2	0	.333	.333	.600
Dave Rucker	7	4	2	0	1	1	0	.571	1.286	.625
Vern Ruhle	22	6	0	0	0	2	1	.273	.273	.333
Jeff Russell	9	2	0	0	0	1	1	.222	.222	.300
Dick Ruthven	27	8	2	1	0	4	2	.296	.444	.387

Tim Raines continued

Pitcher	AB	H	2B	3B	HR	BB	SO	BA	SA	OBA
Nolan Ryan	50	8	2	0	0	6	14	.160	.200	.250
Scott Sanderson	9	2	0	0	0	3	2	.222	.222	.417
Manny Sarmiento	7	3	1	0	0	1	0	.429	.571	.500
Bill Scherrer	8	2	0	0	0	1	1	.250	.250	.333
Mike Scott	25	11	4	1	0	3	2	.440	.680	.517
Rod Scurry	11	6	1	1	0	3	1	.545	.818	.643
Tom Seaver	27	6	1	1	0	5	3	.222	.333	.344
Bob Shirley	10	3	0	1	0	1	0	.300	.500	.364
Eric Show	29	11	3	0	1	5	1	.379	.586	.471
Doug Sisk	12	1	0	0	0	3	0	.083	.083	.267
Dave Smith	8	1	1	0	0	3	2	.125	.250	.417
Lee Smith	14	5	1	0	0	1	0	.357	.429	.400
Zane Smith	8	1	0	0	0	3	1	.125	.125	.364
Julio Solano	4	2	0	0	0	1	0	.500	.500	.600
Eddie Solomon	6	1	0	0	0	0	0	.167	.167	.286
Lary Sorensen	13	6	0	0	1	1	1	.462	.692	.500
Mario Soto	41	10	3	1	1	10	8	.244	.439	.392
Dave Stewart	6	3	1	1	1	1	2	.500	1.500	.625
Tim Stoddard	7	2	1	0	0	4	0	.286	.429	.545
John Stuper	17	11	3	0	1	4	2	.647	1.000	.714
Rick Sutcliffe	25	8	4	0	0	3	3	.320	.480	.393
Bruce Sutter	20	5	0	0	0	0	4	.250	.250	.238
Don Sutton	12	5	1	0	1	2	1	.417	.750	.500
Craig Swan	25	8	2	0	0	3	2	.320	.400	.393
Kent Tekulve	21	3	1	1	0	3	3	.143	.286	.250
Walt Terrell	18	7	1	0	1	1	1	.389	.611	.421
Mark Thurmond	14	6	2	0	1	1	1	.429	.786	.467
Jay Tibbs	8	4	0	1	0	3	0	.500	.750	.636
Dick Tidrow	10	1	0	0	1	1	0	.100	.400	.182
Mike Torrez	6	3	0	0	0	4	0	.500	.500	.700
Steve Trout	33	12	0	0	2	3	4	.364	.545	.405
John Tudor	38	13	2	0	0	2	2	.342	.395	.375
Lee Tunnell	20	9	3	0	0	2	1	.450	.600	.500
Fernando Valenzuela	46	14	1	0	0	4	6	.304	.326	.360
Bob Walk	16	6	2	0	0	4	4	.375	.500	.500
Gene Walter	8	2	1	0	0	0	2	.250	.375	.250
Bob Welch	33	13	1	1	0	3	1	.394	.485	.444
Chris Welsh	16	4	0	0	1	3	1	.250	.438	.368
Ed Whitson	16	6	1	0	0	2	4	.375	.438	.444
Frank Williams	6	2	0	0	0	2	0	.333	.333	.500
Jim Winn	9	1	0	0	0	0	1	.111	.111	.111
Todd Worrell	9	1	0	1	0	1	2	.111	.333	.200
Pat Zachry	16	5	1	0	0	1	3	.313	.375	.389

Darryl Strawberry

Pitcher	AB	H	2B	3B	HR	BB	SO	BA	SA	OBA
Neil Allen	8	2	0	0	0	1	3	.250	.250	.333
Larry Andersen	9	1	0	0	0	1	2	.111	.111	.200
Joaquin Andujar	25	5	3	0	0	2	6	.200	.320	.259
Paul Assenmacher	4	1	0	0	0	2	1	.250	.250	.500
Len Barker	9	3	0	0	2	0	4	.333	1.000	.333
Jim Barr	6	3	1	0	0	0	1	.500	.667	.500
Steve Bedrosian	14	2	0	0	1	4	5	.143	.357	.333
Bruce Berenyi	7	0	0	0	0	2	5	.000	.000	.222
Mike Bielecki	6	1	0	0	1	2	0	.167	.667	.375
Vida Blue	5	3	0	0	2	1	2	.600	1.800	.667
Derek Botelho	3	2	0	0	2	3	0	.667	2.667	.833
Fred Breining	9	1	0	0	0	0	2	.111	.111	.111
Tom Browning	18	5	1	0	0	2	7	.278	.333	.350
Warren Brusstar	7	2	0	0	1	5	3	.286	.714	.583
Tim Burke	4	1	0	0	1	1	2	.250	1.000	.333
Ray Burris	10	5	1	0	2	1	2	.500	1.200	.583
Rick Camp	7	2	1	0	0	2	2	.286	.429	.444
Bill Campbell	9	3	0	1	0	1	3	.333	.556	.400
John Candelaria	9	1	0	0	0	0	5	.111	.111	.111
Steve Carlton	19	5	0	0	1	5	5	.263	.421	.417
Don Carman	7	1	0	0	0	0	3	.143	.143	.143
Pat Clements	5	2	0	0	0	3	1	.400	.400	.667
Tim Conroy	7	1	0	0	0	1	1	.143	.143	.250
Danny Cox	25	8	2	0	1	3	3	.320	.520	.393
Mark Davis	15	1	0	0	1	1	7	.067	.267	.125
Ken Dayley	6	1	0	0	1	3	2	.167	.667	.444
Jose DeLeon	24	6	1	0	2	5	11	.250	.542	.367
Luis DeLeon	6	3	0	0	1	0	2	.500	1.000	.500
Jeff Dedmon	12	2	0	1	0	1	5	.167	.333	.231
John Denny	33	8	0	1	2	6	5	.242	.485	.375
Jim Deshaies	5	3	1	1	1	0	2	.600	1.800	.600
Frank DiPino	13	3	1	0	1	1	6	.231	.538	.267
Carlos Diaz	5	0	0	0	0	0	2	.000	.000	.000
Dave Dravecky	8	4	0	0	1	0	3	.500	.875	.500
Dennis Eckersley	13	2	1	0	0	0	3	.154	.231	.154
Ray Fontenot	12	6	1	0	2	2	2	.500	1.083	.571
Bob Forsch	18	8	2	0	5	3	2	.444	1.389	.524
Terry Forster	9	1	0	0	0	1	4	.111	.111	.273
John Franco	8	1	0	0	1	3	3	.125	.500	.417
George Frazier	4	0	0	0	0	1	3	.000	.000	.200
Gene Garber	6	1	0	0	0	0	2	.167	.167	.167
Rich Gossage	9	2	0	0	0	0	3	.222	.222	.222
Jim Gott	5	1	0	0	0	1	1	.200	.200	.333
Kevin Gross	28	6	2	0	1	1	8	.214	.286	.226
Cecilio Guante	11	2	0	0	1	3	6	.182	.455	.357
Bill Gullickson	23	8	3	0	3	3	4	.348	.870	.429
Atlee Hammaker	8	1	0	0	1	1	3	.125	.500	.222
Andy Hawkins	9	2	1	0	0	2	3	.222	.333	.364
Orel Hershiser	19	7	2	0	1	1	3	.368	.632	.400
Joe Hesketh	8	2	0	0	0	0	4	.250	.250	.250
Al Holland	6	1	0	0	1	0	2	.167	.667	.167
Rick Honeycutt	9	0	0	0	0	0	3	.000	.000	.000
Burt Hooton	6	0	0	0	0	0	3	.000	.000	.000
Ricky Horton	24	5	1	0	1	2	6	.208	.375	.269
Ken Howell	5	2	0	0	0	0	3	.400	.400	.400
Charles Hudson	18	9	1	0	3	7	4	.500	1.056	.640
Tom Hume	11	2	1	0	0	1	3	.182	.273	.250
Roy Lee Jackson	3	0	0	0	0	1	1	.000	.000	.400
Bob James	4	1	0	0	0	1	1	.250	.250	.333
Ferguson Jenkins	9	1	0	0	0	0	4	.111	.111	.111
Joe Johnson	6	3	1	0	1	0	1	.500	1.167	.500
Kurt Kepshire	9	4	1	0	2	0	0	.444	1.222	.444
Charlie Kerfeld	5	2	1	0	0	1	2	.400	.600	.500
Bob Knepper	20	2	0	0	1	1	9	.100	.250	.143
Jerry Koosman	9	4	1	0	0	1	0	.444	.556	.500
Mike Krukow	21	1	0	0	0	1	9	.048	.048	.091
Mike LaCoss	7	3	1	0	0	2	2	.429	.571	.556
Dave LaPoint	18	2	0	0	1	2	4	.111	.278	.200
Jeff Lahti	4	0	0	0	0	3	1	.000	.000	.429
Bill Laskey	8	3	2	0	0	3	1	.375	.625	.545
Gary Lavelle	9	0	0	0	0	1	4	.000	.000	.100
Charlie Lea	25	7	2	1	0	3	7	.280	.440	.357
Craig Lefferts	11	3	1	0	0	1	2	.273	.364	.333
Tim Lollar	15	5	1	0	1	0	6	.333	.600	.333
Gary Lucas	11	3	0	0	1	1	4	.273	.545	.333
Mike Madden	6	2	1	0	0	0	3	.333	.500	.333
Rick Mahler	24	11	2	0	1	3	4	.458	.667	.519
Dennis Martinez	5	2	0	0	0	1	4	.400	.400	.400
Greg Mathews	6	0	0	0	0	0	1	.000	.000	.000
Bob McClure	4	2	1	1	0	1	1	.500	1.250	.500
Lance McCullers	4	0	0	0	0	1	3	.000	.000	.200
Andy McGaffigan	11	2	1	0	0	1	5	.182	.273	.250
Tug McGraw	6	2	1	0	0	0	1	.333	.500	.333
Craig McMurtry	12	3	0	0	2	2	2	.250	.750	.357
Larry McWilliams	25	7	3	0	0	0	6	.280	.400	.280
Ron Meridith	6	2	0	0	2	1	2	.333	1.333	.429
Greg Minton	6	4	0	0	1	1	0	.667	1.167	.714
Donnie Moore	5	2	0	0	0	0	1	.400	.400	.400
Jamie Moyer	3	1	1	0	0	2	0	.333	.667	.600
Tom Niedenfuer	9	2	1	0	1	1	3	.222	.667	.300

Darryl Strawberry continued

Pitcher	AB	H	2B	3B	HR	BB	SO	BA	SA	OBA	Pitcher	AB	H	2B	3B	HR	BB	SO	BA	SA	OBA
Joe Niekro	17	6	1	0	3	4	1	.353	.941	.476	Mike Scott	19	3	0	2	0	2	4	.158	.368	.238
Phil Niekro	5	1	0	0	0	1	2	.200	.200	.333	Rod Scurry	8	1	1	0	0	3	7	.125	.250	.364
Bob Owchinko	5	2	0	0	1	1	1	.400	1.000	.500	Bob Sebra	10	1	0	0	1	0	5	.100	.400	.100
David Palmer	9	1	0	0	0	2	2	.111	.111	.333	Steve Shields	4	3	0	0	0	1	1	.750	.750	.800
Frank Pastore	6	2	0	0	0	0	2	.333	.333	.333	Eric Show	20	10	1	1	3	9	1	.500	1.100	.655
Bob Patterson	4	1	0	0	0	1	1	.250	.250	.400	Bryn Smith	27	8	0	1	3	5	4	.296	.704	.406
Alejandro Pena	6	0	0	0	0	0	1	.000	.000	.000	Dave Smith	6	1	0	0	1	0	1	.167	.667	.167
Pascual Perez	7	3	0	0	2	0	0	.429	1.286	.429	Lee Smith	12	2	0	0	0	0	3	.167	.167	.231
Pat Perry	5	1	0	0	0	0	0	.200	.200	.200	Zane Smith	11	0	0	0	0	0	5	.000	.000	.000
Ted Power	6	1	0	0	0	2	1	.167	.167	.375	Mario Soto	32	12	1	1	5	5	10	.375	.938	.447
Joe Price	16	3	0	0	2	1	5	.188	.563	.222	Tim Stoddard	5	2	0	0	0	2	1	.400	.400	.571
Charlie Puleo	4	3	1	0	0	4	0	.750	1.000	.875	John Stuper	6	1	0	0	0	4	1	.167	.167	.500
Chuck Rainey	7	4	0	0	0	1	0	.571	.571	.625	Rick Sutcliffe	17	1	0	0	1	3	8	.059	.235	.200
Shane Rawley	15	2	0	0	0	0	2	.133	.133	.133	Bruce Sutter	11	3	0	0	1	0	5	.273	.545	.273
Jeff Reardon	10	4	0	1	1	0	2	.400	.900	.400	Kent Tekulve	5	2	0	0	0	0	1	.400	.400	.400
Rick Reuschel	16	6	2	1	1	3	1	.375	.813	.450	Mark Thurmond	7	2	0	1	0	2	2	.286	.571	.444
Jerry Reuss	11	5	0	0	1	1	4	.455	.727	.500	Jay Tibbs	13	1	0	0	1	3	2	.077	.308	.250
Rick Rhoden	28	5	1	0	1	6	3	.179	.321	.306	Steve Trout	18	5	1	0	0	3	3	.278	.333	.381
Don Robinson	11	4	1	0	1	3	0	.364	.727	.500	John Tudor	19	3	0	0	1	1	9	.158	.316	.200
Jeff Robinson	9	3	2	0	0	1	1	.333	.556	.400	Lee Tunnell	17	6	0	0	3	2	2	.353	.882	.421
Ron Robinson	4	1	0	0	0	1	0	.250	.250	.400	Fernando Valenzuela	29	8	1	0	0	3	8	.276	.310	.344
Steve Rogers	5	2	2	0	0	1	0	.400	.800	.500	Bob Walk	4	2	1	0	1	1	1	.500	1.500	.600
Dave Rucker	14	2	0	0	0	1	3	.143	.143	.200	Gene Walter	4	0	0	0	0	0	2	.000	.000	.200
Bruce Ruffin	6	1	0	0	0	1	3	.167	.167	.286	Bob Welch	17	1	0	0	0	1	8	.059	.059	.111
Dick Ruthven	22	7	2	1	1	8	4	.318	.636	.500	Ed Whitson	5	2	0	0	1	1	1	.400	1.000	.500
Nolan Ryan	26	3	0	2	1	3	14	.115	.385	.194	Jim Winn	4	2	0	0	2	1	0	.500	2.000	.600
Scott Sanderson	14	1	0	0	0	2	3	.071	.071	.188	Todd Worrell	5	3	2	0	0	1	1	.600	1.000	.667
Dan Schatzeder	16	4	0	1	0	0	6	.250	.375	.250	Floyd Youmans	10	5	0	0	2	6	1	.500	1.100	.688
Bill Scherrer	10	5	1	0	0	1	2	.500	.600	.545											

Roger Clemens

Batter	AB	H	2B	3B	HR	BB	SO	BA	SA	OBA	Batter	AB	H	2B	3B	HR	BB	SO	BA	SA	OBA
Willie Aikens	6	0	0	0	0	0	4	.000	.000	.000	Scott Fletcher	11	0	0	0	0	3	3	.000	.000	.214
Harold Baines	21	5	1	0	0	2	4	.238	.286	.304	Julio Franco	13	2	1	0	0	0	4	.154	.231	.154
Steve Balboni	16	2	0	0	2	1	9	.125	.500	.176	Gary Gaetti	22	4	2	0	1	3	3	.182	.409	.280
Chris Bando	6	0	0	0	0	0	3	.000	.000	.000	Greg Gagne	10	4	0	0	1	2	2	.400	.700	.500
Jesse Barfield	13	1	0	0	0	2	5	.077	.077	.200	Jim Gantner	16	0	0	0	0	0	2	.000	.000	.000
Don Baylor	6	1	0	0	1	1	3	.167	.667	.286	Damaso Garcia	12	3	0	0	0	0	1	.250	.250	.250
George Bell	20	3	0	0	1	0	7	.150	.300	.150	Kirk Gibson	10	1	0	0	0	2	5	.100	.100	.250
Juan Beniquez	14	3	0	0	0	1	1	.214	.214	.267	Bobby Grich	5	0	0	0	0	3	3	.000	.000	.375
Tony Bernazard	9	1	1	0	0	2	3	.111	.222	.333	Ken Griffey	9	5	0	0	0	2	1	.556	.556	.636
Buddy Biancalana	6	1	0	0	0	0	3	.167	.167	.167	Alfredo Griffin	11	4	2	0	0	0	2	.364	.545	.364
Bruce Bochte	14	4	0	0	0	3	2	.286	.286	.412	Johnny Grubb	7	3	2	0	0	1	0	.429	.714	.500
Juan Bonilla	6	2	0	0	0	0	0	.333	.333	.333	Ozzie Guillen	11	3	0	0	0	0	1	.273	.273	.273
Daryl Boston	7	2	0	0	0	0	0	.286	.286	.286	Jerry Hairston	9	1	1	0	0	0	1	.111	.222	.111
Phil Bradley	12	1	0	0	0	0	7	.083	.083	.083	Mel Hall	7	1	1	0	0	1	4	.143	.286	.250
George Brett	14	2	1	0	0	3	2	.143	.214	.294	Mike Hargrove	11	3	0	0	0	0	1	.273	.273	.273
Tom Brunansky	24	7	2	0	1	3	1	.292	.500	.370	Toby Harrah	5	0	0	0	0	2	3	.000	.000	.286
Steve Buechele	5	0	0	0	0	0	2	.000	.000	.000	Ron Hassey	7	2	1	0	0	1	0	.286	.429	.375
Randy Bush	25	4	1	0	1	1	7	.160	.320	.192	Mickey Hatcher	12	3	0	0	0	1	1	.250	.250	.308
Brett Butler	13	3	0	0	0	0	2	.231	.231	.286	Mike Heath	11	1	0	0	0	0	3	.091	.091	.091
John Cangelosi	10	3	0	0	0	2	0	.300	.300	.417	Dave Henderson	9	3	1	0	0	0	4	.333	.444	.333
Jose Canseco	10	2	0	0	2	0	4	.200	.800	.200	Rickey Henderson	10	4	1	0	0	0	1	.400	.500	.400
Joe Carter	12	0	0	0	0	0	3	.000	.000	.000	Donnie Hill	6	1	0	0	0	0	1	.167	.167	.167
Darnell Coles	10	4	1	0	1	1	1	.400	.800	.455	Marc Hill	5	2	0	0	0	0	1	.400	.400	.400
Dave Collins	20	6	0	0	0	1	3	.300	.300	.333	Jack Howell	7	0	0	0	0	0	0	.000	.000	.000
Onix Concepcion	8	2	0	0	0	0	3	.250	.250	.250	Roy Howell	6	2	1	0	0	0	3	.333	.500	.333
Cecil Cooper	18	3	1	0	0	0	3	.167	.278	.158	Kent Hrbek	21	4	1	0	1	2	2	.190	.381	.240
Al Cowens	5	3	1	0	1	2	1	.600	1.400	.714	Tim Hulett	6	2	0	0	0	0	1	.333	.333	.333
Julio Cruz	3	1	0	0	0	4	0	.333	.333	.625	Dane Iorg	9	4	1	0	0	1	0	.444	.556	.500
Alvin Davis	9	3	1	0	1	0	2	.333	.778	.333	Garth Iorg	5	0	0	0	0	0	2	.000	.000	.000
Mike Davis	15	4	0	0	1	1	6	.267	.467	.313	Reggie Jackson	16	5	2	0	2	3	8	.313	.813	.421
Doug DeCinces	14	2	0	0	0	1	4	.143	.143	.200	Brook Jacoby	9	2	0	0	0	0	6	.222	.222	.300
Rob Deer	8	1	0	0	0	0	6	.125	.125	.125	Dion James	6	2	2	0	0	0	0	.333	.667	.333
Rick Dempsey	5	0	0	0	0	0	4	.000	.000	.000	Houston Jimenez	6	0	0	0	0	0	0	.000	.000	.000
Brian Downing	8	2	0	0	1	0	2	.250	.625	.300	Cliff Johnson	6	0	0	0	0	1	1	.000	.000	.143
Jim Dwyer	9	1	0	0	0	1	3	.111	.111	.200	Ruppert Jones	14	2	1	0	0	2	4	.143	.214	.250
Darrell Evans	13	2	0	0	1	1	4	.154	.385	.214	Wally Joyner	11	2	1	0	0	1	1	.182	.273	.250
Tony Fernandez	18	6	1	0	0	2	1	.333	.389	.381	Dave Kingman	18	6	0	0	3	1	5	.333	.833	.368
Carlton Fisk	16	3	0	0	2	1	2	.188	.563	.235	Ron Kittle	8	0	0	0	0	0	5	.000	.000	.000

Roger Clemens continued

Batter	AB	H	2B	3B	HR	BB	SO	BA	SA	OBA
Carney Lansford	16	4	2	0	0	0	5	.250	.375	.294
Rudy Law	14	3	1	0	0	2	4	.214	.286	.313
Vance Law	7	2	1	0	0	0	1	.286	.429	.286
Rick Leach	6	3	0	0	0	1	0	.500	.500	.571
Chet Lemon	13	5	1	0	0	0	4	.385	.462	.385
Steve Lombardozzi	10	0	0	0	0	1	6	.000	.000	.091
Greg Luzinski	5	2	0	0	0	0	2	.400	.400	.400
Fred Lynn	5	1	1	0	0	1	4	.200	.400	.429
Rick Manning	11	3	0	0	0	0	1	.273	.273	.273
Don Mattingly	12	4	0	0	0	0	1	.333	.333	.333
Oddibe McDowell	7	2	1	0	0	1	1	.286	.429	.375
Hal McRae	8	1	0	0	0	2	2	.125	.125	.300
Paul Molitor	10	4	1	0	0	0	3	.400	.500	.400
Charlie Moore	6	2	0	0	0	0	1	.333	.333	.286
Lloyd Moseby	18	2	2	0	0	2	9	.111	.222	.200
Darryl Motley	17	4	0	0	0	1	5	.235	.235	.278
Rance Mulliniks	20	5	3	0	0	2	4	.250	.400	.318
Dwayne Murphy	12	2	2	0	0	1	3	.167	.333	.231
Eddie Murray	13	6	1	0	2	3	0	.462	1.000	.563
Jerry Narron	11	4	1	0	0	1	3	.364	.455	.417
Pete O'Brien	7	1	0	0	0	4	1	.143	.143	.455
Tom O'Malley	7	1	0	0	0	1	2	.143	.143	.250
Ben Oglivie	14	6	0	0	0	0	1	.429	.429	.429
Jorge Orta	11	4	1	0	0	0	1	.364	.455	.364
Spike Owen	11	2	0	0	0	1	4	.182	.182	.250
Tom Paciorek	5	3	1	0	0	0	0	.600	.800	.600
Mike Pagliarulo	7	1	1	0	0	1	1	.143	.286	.250
Lance Parrish	6	0	0	0	0	0	0	.000	.000	.000
Larry Parrish	7	2	0	0	0	0	4	.286	.286	.286
Jack Perconte	5	1	1	0	0	1	0	.200	.400	.333
Rick Peters	5	0	0	0	0	0	2	.000	.000	.000
Gary Pettis	15	2	0	0	0	1	5	.133	.133	.188
Ken Phelps	8	2	0	0	0	0	3	.250	.250	.333
Tony Phillips	14	4	1	0	0	1	4	.286	.357	.333
Darrell Porter	7	1	0	0	1	0	1	.143	.571	.143
Jim Presley	12	4	2	0	1	1	5	.333	.750	.385
Kirby Puckett	25	5	1	0	0	1	5	.200	.240	.231
Willie Randolph	11	0	0	0	0	0	3	.000	.000	.000
Floyd Rayford	4	1	0	0	0	2	0	.250	.250	.500
Jeff Reed	6	1	1	0	0	0	2	.167	.333	.167
Ernest Riles	12	5	0	0	0	0	0	.417	.417	.385
Cal Ripken	16	5	0	0	0	0	1	.313	.313	.313
Gary Roenicke	5	2	0	0	1	0	0	.400	1.000	.400
Mark Salas	11	6	1	0	0	0	0	.545	.636	.545
Dick Schofield	12	3	0	0	0	0	2	.250	.250	.308
Donnie Scott	6	1	0	0	0	0	3	.167	.167	.167
Larry Sheets	11	4	1	0	0	0	2	.364	.455	.364
John Shelby	10	1	1	0	0	0	3	.100	.200	.100
Pat Sheridan	15	4	0	0	0	0	7	.267	.267	.267
Ted Simmons	10	2	0	0	0	1	1	.200	.200	.273
Roy Smalley	29	3	0	0	0	1	7	.103	.103	.133
Jim Sundberg	15	5	0	1	0	0	4	.333	.467	.333
Pat Tabler	14	3	0	0	0	1	4	.214	.214	.267
Danny Tartabull	5	1	0	0	0	1	1	.200	.200	.333
Tim Teufel	10	0	0	0	0	1	3	.000	.000	.083
Gorman Thomas	7	1	0	0	1	0	3	.143	.571	.143
Andre Thornton	5	2	0	0	0	4	2	.400	.400	.600
Wayne Tolleson	7	1	0	0	0	1	1	.143	.143	.250
Alan Trammell	14	4	0	0	1	1	3	.286	.500	.333
Willie Upshaw	22	6	0	1	0	0	4	.273	.364	.273
George Vukovich	12	4	1	0	0	0	5	.333	.417	.333
Greg Walker	15	4	1	0	0	2	2	.267	.333	.353
Gary Ward	5	2	0	0	1	2	1	.400	1.000	.571
John Wathan	5	1	0	0	0	0	2	.200	.200	.200
Lou Whitaker	12	5	1	0	0	2	2	.417	.500	.500
Frank White	17	1	0	0	0	1	5	.059	.059	.111
Ernie Whitt	13	1	1	0	0	0	2	.077	.154	.143
Rob Wilfong	9	2	0	0	0	0	4	.222	.222	.222
Curtis Wilkerson	6	1	0	0	0	0	1	.167	.167	.167
Jerry Willard	6	1	0	0	0	0	1	.167	.167	.167
Willie Wilson	23	5	0	1	0	0	4	.217	.304	.217
Dave Winfield	11	4	0	0	1	0	1	.364	.636	.364
George Wright	7	1	0	0	0	0	1	.143	.143	.143
Mike Young	9	1	0	0	0	0	3	.111	.111	.111
Robin Yount	16	6	0	0	2	1	3	.375	.750	.412

Jack Morris

Batter	AB	H	2B	3B	HR	BB	SO	BA	SA	OBA
Glenn Adams	24	4	1	1	1	1	1	.167	.417	.200
Willie Aikens	45	17	5	0	4	4	9	.378	.756	.412
Danny Ainge	12	1	0	0	0	2	3	.083	.083	.214
Gary Alexander	8	0	0	0	0	1	4	.000	.000	.111
Andy Allanson	5	1	0	0	0	0	0	.200	.200	.200
Jamie Allen	7	2	1	0	0	1	2	.286	.429	.375
Gary Allenson	13	3	0	0	0	1	3	.231	.231	.286
Bill Almon	19	3	1	0	0	1	5	.158	.211	.200
Jim Anderson	9	2	1	0	0	1	1	.222	.333	.300
Tony Armas	52	13	1	2	4	0	10	.250	.577	.245
Doug Ault	4	0	0	0	0	1	1	.000	.000	.333
Bob Bailor	12	2	0	0	0	1	1	.167	.167	.286
Harold Baines	56	14	0	1	1	8	8	.250	.339	.338
Steve Balboni	25	5	1	0	1	1	8	.200	.360	.231
Chris Bando	11	2	0	0	0	1	2	.182	.182	.250
Sal Bando	15	3	1	0	0	4	1	.200	.267	.364
Alan Bannister	22	3	1	0	0	1	1	.136	.182	.174
Jesse Barfield	30	8	0	1	2	3	5	.267	.533	.353
Marty Barrett	23	2	0	0	0	0	3	.087	.087	.087
Bill Bathe	4	1	0	0	0	0	2	.250	.250	.250
Don Baylor	55	15	3	1	4	5	9	.273	.582	.344
Mark Belanger	13	1	0	0	0	0	0	.077	.077	.077
Buddy Bell	46	14	1	0	2	6	5	.304	.457	.377
George Bell	32	5	1	0	2	0	1	.156	.375	.182
Kevin Bell	4	1	0	0	0	2	1	.250	.250	.500
Juan Beniquez	21	4	1	0	0	2	2	.190	.238	.261
Tony Bernazard	38	11	4	1	0	2	9	.289	.447	.325
Bruce Bochte	66	17	1	0	0	3	12	.258	.273	.290
Wade Boggs	40	13	3	0	0	6	9	.325	.400	.413
Bobby Bonds	18	5	1	0	1	1	1	.278	.500	.316
Bobby Bonilla	5	1	0	0	0	2	4	.200	.200	.429
Barry Bonnell	21	1	0	0	0	2	2	.048	.048	.130
Bob Boone	29	7	1	0	3	3	1	.241	.586	.303
Glenn Borgmann	5	0	0	0	0	3	0	.000	.000	.375
Rick Bosetti	8	3	1	0	0	1	0	.375	.500	.455
Thad Bosley	11	1	0	0	0	0	3	.091	.091	.083
Lyman Bostock	5	2	0	0	0	0	0	.400	.400	.400
Daryl Boston	5	1	0	1	0	2	2	.200	.600	.375
Phil Bradley	15	1	0	0	1	2	8	.067	.267	.176
Scott Bradley	6	2	0	0	0	0	2	.333	.333	.333
Mickey Brantley	4	0	0	0	0	1	0	.000	.000	.200
Steve Braun	5	1	0	0	0	2	2	.200	.200	.429
George Brett	45	19	3	2	3	10	3	.422	.778	.509
Jack Brohamer	10	2	0	0	0	1	0	.200	.200	.273
Mark Brouhard	12	1	0	0	0	0	0	.083	.083	.083
Bobby Brown	16	4	0	0	0	2	4	.250	.250	.333
Darrell Brown	13	3	0	0	0	0	0	.231	.231	.231
Mike C. Brown	6	1	0	0	0	0	2	.167	.167	.167
Tom Brunansky	32	5	3	0	0	4	8	.156	.250	.250
Bill Buckner	26	5	2	0	1	0	1	.192	.385	.192
Steve Buechele	12	5	0	0	1	1	1	.417	.667	.462
Al Bumbry	51	15	2	1	2	4	6	.294	.490	.339
Rick Burleson	28	6	0	0	0	3	1	.214	.214	.290
Jeff Burroughs	9	2	0	0	0	1	2	.222	.222	.300
Randy Bush	35	12	3	1	1	3	4	.343	.571	.395
Sal Butera	7	0	0	0	0	0	0	.000	.000	.000
Brett Butler	30	5	1	0	0	4	5	.167	.200	.265
Bert Campaneris	14	2	0	0	0	5	2	.143	.143	.368

Jack Morris continued

Batter	AB	H	2B	3B	HR	BB	SO	BA	SA	OBA
John Cangelosi	11	3	0	1	0	0	3	.273	.455	.273
Jose Canseco	11	1	0	0	1	3	3	.091	.364	.286
Rod Carew	39	11	4	0	1	4	5	.282	.462	.349
Joe Carter	11	4	0	0	1	2	2	.364	.636	.462
Rico Carty	7	1	0	0	0	0	1	.143	.143	.143
Carmen Castillo	5	0	0	0	0	0	1	.000	.000	.000
Manny Castillo	7	1	0	0	1	1	0	.143	.571	.250
John Castino	34	9	0	2	0	3	9	.265	.382	.324
Rick Cerone	38	4	0	0	0	0	5	.105	.105	.105
Dave Chalk	7	1	0	0	0	0	1	.143	.143	.143
Chris Chambliss	11	5	2	0	0	1	1	.455	.636	.500
Bobby Clark	11	2	0	0	0	1	5	.182	.182	.250
Darnell Coles	7	5	1	0	0	1	2	.714	.857	.750
Dave Collins	37	9	1	2	0	1	7	.243	.378	.263
Onix Concepcion	9	3	0	0	0	0	0	.333	.333	.333
Cecil Cooper	85	29	7	0	4	2	9	.341	.565	.356
Al Cowens	26	4	3	0	1	1	1	.154	.385	.185
Jeff Cox	7	1	0	0	0	0	0	.143	.143	.143
Larry Cox	12	0	0	0	0	0	3	.000	.000	.000
Ted Cox	13	5	1	0	0	0	0	.385	.462	.385
Rodney Craig	5	1	0	0	0	1	1	.200	.200	.333
Terry Crowley	17	3	1	0	1	0	2	.176	.412	.222
Julio Cruz	52	11	0	0	0	7	9	.212	.212	.300
Todd Cruz	25	6	0	0	2	0	10	.240	.480	.240
Mike Cubbage	11	0	0	0	0	6	0	.000	.000	.353
Paul Dade	6	4	0	0	0	1	0	.667	.667	.714
Rich Dauer	54	16	0	0	0	6	0	.296	.296	.367
Alvin Davis	17	4	1	0	1	2	0	.235	.471	.316
Dick Davis	10	3	0	0	1	0	2	.300	.600	.300
Mike Davis	31	11	2	0	0	5	5	.355	.419	.444
Doug DeCinces	50	14	3	0	2	4	3	.280	.460	.333
Rick Dempsey	28	6	1	0	0	7	4	.214	.250	.371
Bucky Dent	32	7	2	0	0	6	0	.219	.281	.342
Bo Diaz	6	1	0	0	0	0	2	.167	.167	.167
Miguel Dilone	13	3	1	0	0	1	0	.231	.308	.286
Brian Downing	56	15	0	0	2	5	6	.268	.375	.339
Brian Doyle	4	1	0	0	0	0	0	.250	.250	.250
Jim Dwyer	36	11	0	0	1	7	6	.306	.389	.409
Jerry Dybzinski	6	3	0	0	0	0	1	.500	.500	.500
Mike Easler	21	2	0	0	0	1	7	.095	.095	.136
Dave Edwards	3	1	1	0	0	2	1	.333	.667	.600
Marshall Edwards	6	0	0	0	0	0	3	.000	.000	.000
Jim Eisenreich	12	2	0	0	0	0	3	.167	.167	.167
Dave Engle	34	9	2	0	1	3	4	.265	.412	.324
Jim Essian	13	3	0	0	1	1	2	.231	.462	.286
Dwight Evans	61	14	3	1	5	15	15	.230	.557	.382
Lenny Faedo	17	4	1	0	0	0	2	.235	.294	.235
Tony Fernandez	22	1	0	0	0	0	4	.045	.045	.045
Mike Fischlin	15	6	2	0	0	2	5	.400	.533	.471
Carlton Fisk	45	4	2	0	1	4	10	.089	.200	.160
Scott Fletcher	22	6	4	0	0	1	1	.273	.455	.304
Doug Flynn	6	2	1	1	0	0	1	.333	.833	.333
Marvis Foley	9	3	1	0	1	1	1	.333	.778	.400
Tim Foli	11	4	1	0	1	0	1	.364	.727	.364
Barry Foote	9	1	0	0	0	0	0	.111	.111	.111
Dan Ford	16	5	1	0	0	3	1	.313	.375	.421
Julio Franco	37	10	2	0	0	5	3	.270	.324	.372
Gary Gaetti	40	10	3	0	0	2	7	.250	.325	.295
Greg Gagne	8	2	0	0	0	0	0	.250	.250	.250
Oscar Gamble	39	12	1	0	3	13	6	.308	.564	.481
Jim Gantner	60	18	3	1	0	2	7	.300	.383	.323
Damaso Garcia	43	12	2	0	1	1	4	.279	.395	.289
Kiko Garcia	8	0	0	0	0	3	4	.000	.000	.333
Ralph Garr	8	2	0	0	0	0	0	.250	.250	.250
Rich Gedman	34	6	1	0	2	2	5	.176	.382	.222
Luis Gomez	8	3	0	0	0	0	0	.375	.375	.375
Danny Goodwin	14	2	0	0	1	0	5	.143	.357	.133
Dan Graham	12	2	0	0	0	0	2	.167	.167	.167
Gary Gray	10	3	1	0	2	2	4	.300	1.000	.417
Bobby Grich	47	10	1	0	0	6	8	.213	.234	.302
Ken Griffey	39	11	3	2	1	3	7	.282	.538	.333
Alfredo Griffin	60	14	4	0	0	3	7	.233	.300	.270
Wayne Gross	51	12	0	0	2	4	7	.235	.353	.286
Johnny Grubb	9	1	0	0	0	4	2	.111	.111	.385
Mario Guerrero	11	2	0	0	0	0	2	.182	.182	.182

Batter	AB	H	2B	3B	HR	BB	SO	BA	SA	OBA
Ozzie Guillen	16	1	0	0	0	1	2	.063	.063	.118
Glenn Gulliver	5	0	0	0	0	1	1	.000	.000	.167
Jackie Gutierrez	7	2	0	0	0	0	2	.286	.286	.286
Jerry Hairston	10	3	0	0	1	2	1	.300	.600	.417
Mel Hall	18	3	1	0	0	3	3	.167	.222	.286
Garry Hancock	6	1	0	0	0	0	0	.167	.167	.167
Mike Hargrove	53	10	2	0	1	11	10	.189	.283	.318
Larry Harlow	15	6	1	0	0	2	6	.400	.467	.471
Toby Harrah	63	13	4	0	0	11	14	.206	.270	.320
Ron Hassey	38	14	2	1	2	5	7	.368	.632	.442
Mickey Hatcher	27	5	1	0	0	2	1	.185	.222	.241
Von Hayes	15	1	0	0	0	0	3	.067	.067	.067
Mike Heath	21	5	1	0	0	4	4	.238	.286	.360
Dave Henderson	30	12	4	0	0	0	5	.400	.533	.400
Rickey Henderson	57	15	3	0	1	5	6	.263	.368	.317
Steve Henderson	11	5	2	0	0	3	1	.455	.636	.571
Donnie Hill	10	3	1	0	0	0	3	.300	.400	.300
Marc Hill	7	3	1	0	0	0	1	.429	.571	.429
Butch Hobson	16	3	0	0	0	1	5	.188	.188	.235
Glenn Hoffman	24	7	2	0	1	0	4	.292	.500	.292
Willie Horton	24	6	0	0	1	0	8	.250	.375	.250
Dave Hostetler	15	4	0	0	0	0	3	.267	.267	.267
Jack Howell	11	2	0	0	0	0	3	.182	.182	.182
Roy Howell	38	12	3	0	1	2	11	.316	.474	.350
Kent Hrbek	51	12	3	1	4	4	5	.235	.569	.291
Tim Hulett	10	3	0	0	0	0	1	.300	.300	.364
Clint Hurdle	14	4	3	0	0	1	0	.286	.500	.333
Pete Incaviglia	9	2	0	0	0	1	3	.222	.222	.300
Dane Iorg	10	1	0	1	0	0	0	.100	.300	.100
Garth Iorg	16	2	0	0	0	1	2	.125	.125	.176
Reggie Jackson	52	12	4	0	2	5	19	.231	.423	.298
Ron Jackson	18	3	0	0	0	1	2	.167	.167	.211
Brook Jacoby	24	5	0	1	1	3	5	.208	.417	.286
Dion James	7	1	0	0	0	1	1	.143	.143	.250
Stan Javier	7	2	0	0	0	2	1	.286	.286	.444
Houston Jimenez	5	2	0	0	0	1	1	.400	.400	.500
Cliff Johnson	11	2	0	0	0	1	1	.182	.182	.250
Lamar Johnson	21	8	1	0	1	3	2	.381	.571	.458
Randy S. Johnson	9	1	0	0	1	2	2	.111	.444	.273
Bobby Jones	10	4	1	0	0	1	1	.400	.500	.455
Ruppert Jones	27	3	1	0	1	5	4	.111	.259	.250
Bob Kearney	15	3	0	0	0	1	3	.200	.200	.250
H. Pat Kelly	8	0	0	0	0	4	3	.000	.000	.308
Steve Kemp	15	2	1	0	0	1	2	.133	.200	.188
Dave Kingman	23	6	3	0	0	1	8	.261	.522	.269
Ron Kittle	25	5	0	0	3	2	10	.200	.560	.259
Wayne Krenchicki	6	1	0	0	0	0	1	.167	.167	.167
Duane Kuiper	18	2	0	0	0	0	1	.111	.111	.111
Pete LaCock	8	0	0	0	0	0	0	.000	.000	.000
Lee Lacy	14	5	0	0	1	1	5	.357	.571	.400
Ken Landreaux	10	2	0	1	0	0	0	.200	.400	.200
Carney Lansford	63	15	3	1	2	7	8	.238	.413	.314
Tim Laudner	14	1	1	0	0	1	4	.071	.143	.133
Rudy Law	28	6	1	0	0	3	6	.214	.250	.290
Vance Law	15	6	0	0	1	1	0	.400	.600	.438
Ron LeFlore	7	1	0	0	0	2	4	.143	.143	.333
Rick Leach	8	3	0	0	1	0	2	.375	.750	.375
Manny Lee	7	1	0	0	0	0	0	.143	.143	.143
Joe Lefebvre	4	0	0	0	0	1	0	.000	.000	.200
Chet Lemon	22	8	2	0	0	2	4	.364	.455	.417
Sixto Lezcano	15	5	1	0	0	2	1	.333	.400	.412
Bryan Little	12	1	0	0	0	0	2	.083	.083	.083
Doug Loman	8	2	0	0	0	0	1	.250	.250	.250
Steve Lombardozzi	7	3	1	0	1	0	0	.429	1.000	.429
Dave Lopes	17	6	1	0	1	1	1	.353	.588	.389
John Lowenstein	44	13	1	0	4	5	11	.295	.591	.360
Greg Luzinski	26	10	1	0	3	5	4	.385	.769	.484
Fred Lynn	42	16	2	0	2	6	11	.381	.571	.440
Steve Lyons	5	1	0	0	0	0	1	.200	.200	.200
Pete Mackanin	8	1	0	0	0	1	2	.125	.125	.222
Rick Manning	51	10	1	0	1	7	3	.196	.275	.283
Jerry Martin	5	1	0	0	0	0	2	.200	.200	.167
Buck Martinez	6	1	1	0	0	0	2	.167	.333	.143
Don Mattingly	22	7	2	0	2	3	3	.318	.682	.400
Dave May	8	3	0	0	0	0	2	.375	.375	.375

Jack Morris continued

Batter	AB	H	2B	3B	HR	BB	SO	BA	SA	OBA
Lee May	12	0	0	0	0	0	4	.000	.000	.000
John Mayberry	23	10	0	0	2	6	3	.435	.696	.516
Bake McBride	8	0	0	0	0	0	1	.000	.000	.000
Oddibe McDowell	17	2	0	0	0	0	7	.118	.118	.118
Dave McKay	12	3	1	0	1	0	3	.250	.583	.250
Hal McRae	40	9	2	0	1	5	5	.225	.350	.319
Bobby Meacham	6	0	0	0	0	4	2	.000	.000	.400
Mario Mendoza	11	2	0	0	0	0	2	.182	.182	.182
Dan Meyer	50	11	0	1	0	2	3	.220	.260	.250
Larry Milbourne	19	3	0	0	1	1	4	.158	.316	.200
Rick Miller	26	9	2	0	0	3	4	.346	.423	.400
Bob Molinaro	10	1	0	0	0	1	0	.100	.100	.182
Paul Molitor	51	9	1	0	0	6	9	.176	.196	.271
Don Money	16	3	0	0	0	3	3	.188	.188	.333
Alvin Moore	4	0	0	0	0	1	0	.000	.000	.200
Charlie Moore	36	7	2	1	1	2	6	.194	.389	.237
Omar Moreno	7	1	0	0	0	1	2	.143	.143	.250
Joe Morgan	8	2	0	0	0	0	1	.250	.250	.250
Jim Morrison	21	4	1	0	1	0	3	.190	.381	.190
Lloyd Moseby	56	12	1	0	1	6	11	.214	.286	.281
John Moses	7	2	0	1	0	0	2	.286	.571	.286
Darryl Motley	16	4	0	0	1	0	2	.250	.438	.250
Rance Mulliniks	41	9	3	0	0	5	6	.220	.293	.304
Jerry Mumphrey	22	8	1	0	1	4	2	.364	.545	.462
Thurman Munson	9	2	1	0	0	0	1	.222	.333	.222
Bobby Murcer	19	7	1	0	2	2	0	.368	.737	.429
Dwayne Murphy	50	10	0	0	1	8	12	.200	.260	.310
Eddie Murray	74	22	3	0	4	8	16	.297	.500	.361
Larry Murray	6	3	0	0	0	1	0	.500	.500	.571
Jerry Narron	12	2	0	0	0	0	2	.167	.167	.167
Graig Nettles	42	9	0	0	0	5	5	.214	.214	.298
Jeff Newman	21	5	1	0	0	0	2	.238	.286	.238
Reid Nichols	10	2	1	0	0	1	1	.200	.300	.273
Otis Nixon	10	1	0	0	0	1	1	.100	.100	.182
Joe Nolan	10	3	1	0	0	2	0	.300	.400	.417
Wayne Nordhagen	11	3	0	0	1	0	1	.273	.545	.273
Nelson Norman	5	3	1	0	0	0	0	.600	.800	.600
Jim Norris	16	4	1	0	2	0	1	.250	.688	.250
Pete O'Brien	31	7	0	0	0	2	5	.226	.226	.273
Tom O'Malley	7	2	0	0	1	0	1	.286	.714	.286
Ben Oglivie	62	13	0	0	2	6	12	.210	.306	.275
Al Oliver	23	7	1	0	0	4	4	.304	.348	.414
Jorge Orta	37	7	1	1	2	3	5	.189	.432	.268
Amos Otis	22	4	1	0	2	3	5	.182	.500	.280
Ed Ott	8	1	0	0	0	0	1	.125	.125	.125
Spike Owen	10	1	0	0	1	3	2	.100	.400	.308
Tom Paciorek	29	6	0	0	0	3	3	.207	.207	.273
Mitchell Page	12	2	0	0	0	1	3	.167	.167	.286
Mike Pagliarulo	19	3	0	0	1	3	3	.158	.316	.273
Al Pardo	5	1	0	0	0	0	3	.200	.200	.200
Larry Parrish	31	7	1	0	1	4	8	.226	.355	.306
Dan Pasqua	5	2	1	0	0	0	0	.400	.600	.400
Jack Perconte	24	5	0	0	0	1	3	.208	.208	.240
Tony Perez	9	4	0	0	1	1	0	.444	.778	.500
Broderick Perkins	5	0	0	0	0	0	2	.000	.000	.000
Rick Peters	8	1	0	0	0	1	2	.125	.125	.200
Gary Pettis	21	5	1	0	0	4	8	.238	.286	.360
Ken Phelps	20	0	0	0	0	3	12	.000	.000	.130
Tony Phillips	28	6	0	0	1	1	8	.214	.321	.241
Rob Picciolo	11	1	1	0	0	0	4	.091	.182	.091
Lou Piniella	6	0	0	0	0	1	2	.000	.000	.143
Tom Poquette	10	5	1	1	0	0	1	.500	.800	.500
Darrell Porter	8	4	0	0	0	1	2	.500	.500	.556
Hosken Powell	23	2	1	0	1	4	2	.087	.261	.222
Jim Presley	18	5	0	0	3	0	4	.278	.778	.278
Greg Pryor	19	6	0	1	0	1	3	.316	.421	.409
Kirby Puckett	23	7	1	0	1	1	3	.304	.478	.333
Pat Putnam	26	6	0	2	2	2	4	.231	.538	.286
Jamie Quirk	14	5	1	0	0	0	1	.357	.429	.357
Milt Ramirez	6	0	0	0	0	1	1	.000	.000	.143
Willie Randolph	58	17	3	0	1	10	3	.293	.397	.406
Floyd Rayford	5	0	0	0	0	1	2	.000	.000	.167
Randy Ready	4	2	1	0	0	2	1	.500	.750	.571
Jerry Remy	38	11	1	1	1	5	4	.289	.447	.372
Dave Revering	28	9	1	1	2	1	6	.321	.643	.345
Harold Reynolds	7	1	0	0	0	0	3	.143	.143	.143
Jim Rice	66	23	1	0	4	5	8	.348	.545	.389
Mike Richardt	6	2	0	0	0	0	1	.333	.333	.333
Ernest Riles	17	5	0	0	1	0	3	.294	.471	.294
Cal Ripken	41	14	2	0	3	5	8	.341	.610	.413
Mickey Rivers	40	13	1	0	1	1	3	.325	.425	.341
Leon Roberts	11	3	1	0	0	1	2	.273	.364	.333
Andre Robertson	8	2	1	0	0	0	1	.250	.375	.250
Billy Jo Robidoux	6	0	0	0	0	1	3	.000	.000	.143
Aurelio Rodriguez	7	0	0	0	0	0	4	.000	.000	.000
Gary Roenicke	15	2	1	0	0	2	5	.133	.200	.235
Ed Romero	31	7	1	0	0	0	3	.226	.258	.226
Joe Rudi	6	1	0	0	0	0	1	.167	.167	.167
Lenn Sakata	13	4	0	0	0	0	0	.308	.308	.308
Mark Salas	8	2	0	0	0	1	0	.250	.250	.333
Billy Sample	14	1	1	0	0	0	0	.071	.143	.071
Dick Schofield	13	5	0	1	1	1	3	.385	.769	.429
Bill Schroeder	10	2	0	0	0	0	0	.200	.200	.200
Daryl Sconiers	11	1	0	1	0	1	5	.091	.273	.167
Donnie Scott	5	0	0	0	0	0	2	.000	.000	.000
Paul Serna	9	3	0	0	0	0	0	.333	.333	.333
Larry Sheets	11	2	0	0	1	1	3	.182	.455	.250
John Shelby	12	1	0	0	0	0	4	.083	.083	.154
Pat Sheridan	19	4	0	0	1	0	3	.211	.368	.211
Ted Simmons	38	6	0	0	0	7	4	.158	.158	.289
Joe Simpson	39	8	1	0	1	0	4	.205	.308	.205
Ken Singleton	56	13	2	1	1	8	14	.232	.357	.328
Joel Skinner	5	1	0	0	0	0	2	.200	.200	.200
Don Slaught	26	6	1	0	0	0	5	.231	.269	.231
Roy Smalley	38	8	1	0	2	3	5	.211	.395	.268
Lonnie Smith	10	3	0	0	0	1	3	.300	.300	.364
Cory Snyder	6	2	0	0	0	0	1	.333	.333	.333
Rick Sofield	7	1	0	0	0	1	3	.143	.143	.250
Tony Solaita	4	1	0	0	0	1	1	.250	.250	.400
Jim Spencer	15	4	0	0	1	2	1	.267	.467	.353
Mike Squires	13	3	0	0	0	1	2	.231	.231	.286
Fred Stanley	5	0	0	0	0	0	0	.000	.000	.167
Lee Stanton	4	1	0	0	0	2	1	.250	.250	.500
Dave Stapleton	20	4	1	0	0	0	7	.200	.250	.200
Rusty Staub	6	2	1	0	0	1	1	.333	.500	.429
Bill Stein	19	10	2	0	1	2	0	.526	.789	.571
Bob Stinson	7	2	0	0	2	3	4	.286	1.143	.500
Jim Sundberg	42	13	1	0	1	9	9	.310	.405	.431
Leo Sutherland	4	1	0	0	0	1	0	.250	.250	.400
Rick Sweet	20	9	2	0	0	2	3	.450	.550	.500
Pat Tabler	32	8	3	0	0	3	5	.250	.344	.314
Danny Tartabull	5	2	1	0	1	2	3	.400	1.200	.571
Tim Teufel	19	3	0	1	0	0	4	.158	.263	.158
Gorman Thomas	47	9	3	0	3	8	14	.191	.447	.304
Andre Thornton	42	10	0	0	2	6	8	.238	.381	.340
Wayne Tolleson	18	3	1	0	0	3	4	.167	.222	.286
Willie Upshaw	46	10	0	1	2	10	6	.217	.391	.357
Bobby Van Mitchell	18	5	2	0	0	2	3	.278	.389	.350
Otto Velez	9	4	0	0	0	5	1	.444	.444	.643
Tom Veryzer	19	4	0	0	0	0	2	.211	.211	.211
George Vukovich	24	4	0	0	0	4	4	.167	.167	.276
Greg Walker	21	4	1	0	0	2	7	.190	.238	.261
Gary Ward	46	5	1	0	0	2	10	.109	.130	.146
Claudell Washington	13	1	0	0	0	0	3	.077	.077	.077
Ron Washington	25	6	2	0	0	0	6	.240	.320	.240
U.L. Washington	28	7	2	0	0	6	5	.250	.321	.382
John Wathan	24	6	1	0	0	1	4	.250	.292	.280
Bob Watson	13	1	0	0	0	0	0	.077	.077	.133
Frank White	60	15	4	0	2	4	11	.250	.417	.297
Roy White	6	2	0	0	1	1	0	.333	.833	.429
Ernie Whitt	55	16	1	0	6	5	7	.291	.636	.350
Alan Wiggins	4	0	0	0	0	1	0	.000	.000	.200
Rob Wilfong	44	10	1	1	0	3	5	.227	.295	.271
Curtis Wilkerson	18	5	0	1	0	1	2	.278	.389	.316
Jerry Willard	13	2	0	0	0	0	4	.154	.154	.154
Bump Wills	20	5	1	0	0	3	4	.250	.300	.333
Willie Wilson	52	13	1	4	0	3	11	.250	.423	.291
Dave Winfield	48	12	2	0	3	4	9	.250	.396	.296
Jim Wohlford	5	1	0	0	0	0	2	.200	.200	.333
Larry Wolfe	4	0	0	0	0	0	1	.000	.000	.000

Jack Morris continued

Batter	AB	H	2B	3B	HR	BB	SO	BA	SA	OBA
Al Woods	25	10	3	0	0	0	1	.400	.520	.400
George Wright	31	7	1	0	0	0	4	.226	.258	.226
Butch Wynegar	30	7	2	0	0	4	3	.233	.300	.324
Carl Yastrzemski	33	11	2	0	3	5	4	.333	.667	.400

Batter	AB	H	2B	3B	HR	BB	SO	BA	SA	OBA
Ned Yost	6	1	0	0	0	0	0	.167	.167	.167
Mike Young	10	2	0	0	1	0	2	.200	.500	.200
Robin Yount	66	18	1	1	3	6	11	.273	.455	.333
Richie Zisk	26	8	0	1	0	3	4	.308	.385	.367

Dave Righetti

Batter	AB	H	2B	3B	HR	BB	SO	BA	SA	OBA
Willie Aikens	8	2	0	0	1	2	4	.250	.625	.400
Gary Allenson	12	2	0	0	0	3	2	.167	.167	.333
Bill Almon	11	2	2	0	0	0	2	.182	.364	.182
Tony Armas	15	5	0	0	0	2	2	.333	.333	.412
Benny Ayala	7	2	0	0	1	0	2	.286	.714	.286
Harold Baines	25	5	1	0	0	2	6	.200	.240	.259
Chuck Baker	6	0	0	0	0	0	2	.000	.000	.000
Dusty Baker	6	0	0	0	0	1	1	.000	.000	.143
Steve Balboni	13	2	0	0	0	1	6	.154	.154	.214
Chris Bando	8	3	0	0	0	2	0	.375	.375	.500
Alan Bannister	22	7	3	0	0	1	1	.318	.455	.348
Jesse Barfield	20	3	0	0	1	1	7	.150	.300	.190
Marty Barrett	15	4	0	0	0	1	1	.267	.267	.313
Don Baylor	8	2	1	0	0	3	1	.250	.375	.455
Buddy Bell	25	4	0	0	0	2	1	.160	.160	.222
George Bell	14	5	1	1	1	0	3	.357	.786	.357
Juan Beniquez	21	5	0	0	0	2	3	.238	.238	.304
Tony Bernazard	16	3	1	0	0	2	3	.188	.188	.250
Bruce Bochte	5	2	1	0	0	1	0	.400	.600	.500
Wade Boggs	22	5	2	0	0	3	6	.227	.318	.320
Barry Bonnell	8	4	1	1	0	4	2	.500	.875	.667
Bob Boone	20	3	0	0	0	5	1	.150	.150	.320
Phil Bradley	4	1	0	0	0	1	2	.250	.250	.400
George Brett	30	5	1	0	1	1	9	.167	.300	.194
Tom Brookens	22	6	0	1	1	2	4	.273	.500	.333
Mark Brouhard	20	7	0	0	3	0	3	.350	.800	.381
Darrell Brown	11	3	1	0	0	0	0	.273	.364	.273
Tom Brunansky	19	3	1	0	1	2	5	.158	.368	.227
Bill Buckner	13	2	0	0	0	0	0	.154	.154	.154
Al Bumbry	9	1	1	0	0	2	4	.111	.222	.273
Rick Burleson	3	1	0	0	0	0	1	.333	.333	.250
Jeff Burroughs	8	2	0	0	0	1	3	.250	.250	.333
Sal Butera	8	3	0	0	1	0	0	.375	.375	.444
Brett Butler	7	1	1	0	0	3	1	.143	.286	.400
Enos Cabell	11	1	0	0	0	1	1	.091	.091	.167
Rod Carew	16	4	1	0	0	4	3	.250	.313	.400
Joe Carter	7	2	0	0	0	0	3	.286	.286	.286
Carmen Castillo	9	1	0	0	0	0	3	.111	.111	.111
John Castino	17	6	1	0	1	1	4	.353	.588	.389
Joe Charboneau	5	1	1	0	0	0	2	.200	.400	.167
Bobby Clark	5	0	0	0	0	1	1	.000	.000	.167
Darnell Coles	6	0	0	0	0	1	3	.000	.000	.143
Dave Collins	11	2	0	0	0	0	3	.182	.182	.182
Onix Concepcion	6	0	0	0	0	0	2	.000	.000	.000
Cecil Cooper	32	9	3	0	0	2	6	.281	.375	.324
Al Cowens	13	2	0	0	0	2	7	.154	.154	.267
Julio Cruz	16	5	0	0	0	4	2	.313	.313	.450
Todd Cruz	6	4	1	0	1	0	1	.667	1.333	.667
Rich Dauer	22	3	0	0	0	3	1	.136	.136	.240
Alvin Davis	9	2	0	0	0	3	1	.222	.222	.417
Mike Davis	3	0	0	0	0	2	2	.000	.000	.400
Doug DeCinces	29	7	2	0	2	4	5	.241	.517	.333
Rob Deer	5	1	0	0	1	1	2	.200	.800	.333
Rick Dempsey	24	7	1	0	1	4	5	.292	.458	.393
Bucky Dent	5	1	0	0	0	0	2	.200	.200	.200
Bo Diaz	8	5	4	0	0	1	0	.625	1.125	.667
Miguel Dilone	4	0	0	0	0	1	0	.000	.000	.200
Brian Downing	22	4	0	0	1	4	6	.182	.318	.308
Jerry Dybzinski	5	1	0	0	0	0	0	.200	.200	.200
Mike Easler	8	1	0	0	0	1	4	.125	.125	.222
Dave Engle	23	5	1	0	1	2	2	.217	.391	.280
Darrell Evans	7	2	0	0	0	1	0	.286	.286	.375

Batter	AB	H	2B	3B	HR	BB	SO	BA	SA	OBA
Dwight Evans	30	4	1	0	1	3	9	.133	.267	.206
Lenny Faedo	11	2	0	0	0	1	1	.182	.182	.250
Tony Fernandez	10	5	0	0	0	1	1	.500	.500	.545
Mike Fischlin	5	3	1	0	0	1	1	.600	.800	.667
Carlton Fisk	17	4	1	0	0	0	4	.235	.294	.235
Scott Fletcher	20	2	0	0	0	2	1	.100	.100	.182
Tim Foli	14	5	2	0	0	0	1	.357	.500	.357
Dan Ford	7	2	0	0	0	1	1	.286	.286	.375
Julio Franco	13	3	0	0	0	0	2	.231	.231	.231
Gary Gaetti	20	7	2	1	0	1	4	.350	.550	.381
Jim Gantner	21	6	1	0	0	5	4	.286	.333	.423
Damaso Garcia	18	6	1	0	0	0	2	.333	.389	.333
Rich Gedman	5	0	0	0	0	2	3	.000	.000	.286
Kirk Gibson	13	3	0	0	1	1	4	.231	.462	.333
Bobby Grich	18	3	1	0	0	7	3	.167	.222	.400
Alfredo Griffin	18	9	2	1	0	1	2	.500	.722	.526
Jackie Gutierrez	6	3	0	0	0	0	0	.500	.500	.500
Jerry Hairston	7	2	1	0	0	1	1	.286	.429	.375
Mike Hargrove	18	1	0	0	0	4	5	.056	.056	.227
Toby Harrah	24	2	0	0	0	3	8	.083	.083	.185
Ron Hassey	5	0	0	0	0	0	0	.000	.000	.000
Mickey Hatcher	22	5	0	0	1	2	3	.227	.364	.280
Von Hayes	6	2	0	0	0	0	1	.333	.333	.333
Mike Heath	12	2	0	0	0	1	4	.167	.167	.231
Dave Henderson	9	2	0	0	0	0	1	.222	.222	.222
Rickey Henderson	11	1	0	0	0	3	3	.091	.091	.267
Steve Henderson	10	2	1	0	0	1	5	.200	.300	.273
George Hendrick	5	1	0	0	0	0	0	.200	.200	.333
Larry Herndon	29	7	0	1	0	1	8	.241	.310	.267
Donnie Hill	5	0	0	0	0	1	0	.000	.000	.167
Marc Hill	12	0	0	0	0	1	4	.000	.000	.077
Glenn Hoffman	18	2	1	0	0	2	7	.111	.167	.238
Dave Hostetler	11	3	0	0	0	3	5	.273	.273	.429
Paul Householder	5	0	0	0	0	0	2	.000	.000	.000
Kent Hrbek	24	7	2	0	0	2	13	.292	.375	.346
Garth Iorg	21	5	0	0	0	2	2	.238	.238	.304
Reggie Jackson	18	1	0	0	0	2	8	.056	.056	.150
Ron Jackson	23	3	0	0	1	8		.130	.130	.167
Brook Jacoby	9	3	0	0	0	0	4	.333	.333	.333
Cliff Johnson	13	6	1	0	0	2	1	.462	.538	.533
Lynn Jones	9	2	0	0	0	1	0	.222	.222	.300
Ed Jurak	4	2	0	0	0	1	0	.500	.500	.500
Bob Kearney	8	3	1	0	0	0	2	.375	.500	.375
Dave Kingman	14	3	1	0	1	1	4	.214	.500	.267
Ron Kittle	15	2	0	0	1	4	8	.133	.333	.316
Rusty Kuntz	5	1	0	0	0	2	2	.200	.200	.429
Lee Lacy	6	2	0	0	0	1	2	.333	.333	.429
Carney Lansford	20	4	0	0	0	1	5	.200	.200	.238
Tim Laudner	18	2	1	0	0	2	6	.111	.167	.200
Rudy Law	5	2	0	0	0	0	1	.400	.800	.400
Vance Law	12	1	0	0	0	1	4	.083	.083	.154
Chet Lemon	20	3	0	0	0	2	3	.150	.150	.227
Dave Lopes	11	5	1	0	0	0	2	.455	.545	.500
Steve Lubratich	5	2	1	0	0	0	0	.400	.600	.400
Greg Luzinski	10	4	1	0	0	1	2	.400	.500	.500
Fred Lynn	19	3	0	0	1	3	6	.158	.316	.273
Pete Mackanin	6	1	0	0	0	0	0	.167	.333	.167
Rick Manning	28	5	0	0	0	1	9	.179	.179	.200
Jerry Martin	4	0	0	0	0	2	2	.000	.000	.333
Buck Martinez	16	3	1	0	0	3	6	.188	.250	.316
Lee May	8	3	1	0	0	1	3	.375	.500	.444
Lee Mazzilli	7	1	0	0	0	0	0	.143	.143	.143

Dave Righetti   continued

Batter	AB	H	2B	3B	HR	BB	SO	BA	SA	OBA
Bake McBride	5	3	1	0	0	1	0	.600	.800	.667
Oddibe McDowell	5	0	0	0	0	0	2	.000	.000	.000
Hal McRae	28	9	1	1	1	7	4	.321	.536	.432
Larry Milbourne	8	2	0	0	0	1	2	.250	.250	.333
Rick Miller	4	0	0	0	0	4	0	.000	.000	.500
Paul Molitor	31	12	3	1	1	2	2	.387	.645	.424
Don Money	7	0	0	0	0	0	0	.000	.000	.000
Charlie Moore	32	8	3	0	0	2	4	.250	.344	.294
Kelvin Moore	6	2	0	0	0	0	2	.333	.333	.333
Jose Morales	7	1	0	0	0	0	2	.143	.143	.143
Lloyd Moseby	23	4	0	0	1	1	11	.174	.304	.200
Darryl Motley	15	5	0	0	0	1	2	.333	.333	.353
Dwayne Murphy	21	4	1	0	1	2	8	.190	.381	.261
Eddie Murray	35	12	1	0	1	0	1	.343	.457	.343
Jeff Newman	6	0	0	0	0	1	4	.000	.000	.143
Reid Nichols	21	6	2	0	0	3	3	.286	.381	.360
Wayne Nordhagen	4	0	0	0	0	1	1	.000	.000	.200
Pete O'Brien	15	5	2	1	0	4	1	.333	.600	.474
Ben Oglivie	11	5	0	0	1	3	1	.455	.727	.571
Amos Otis	16	8	0	0	0	0	4	.500	.500	.500
Tom Paciorek	21	5	0	1	0	2	2	.238	.333	.292
Lance Parrish	23	7	1	1	1	1	6	.304	.565	.320
Larry Parrish	23	5	1	0	1	3	9	.217	.391	.333
Tony Perez	9	2	1	0	0	2	6	.222	.333	.364
Ken Phelps	3	0	0	0	0	1	1	.000	.000	.400
Tony Phillips	12	3	0	0	0	2	2	.250	.250	.357
Greg Pryor	13	3	1	0	0	0	4	.231	.308	.231
Kirby Puckett	7	3	1	0	0	0	1	.429	.571	.429
Jerry Remy	18	3	0	0	0	2	6	.167	.167	.250
Jim Rice	24	6	2	0	0	6	11	.250	.333	.400
Mike Richardt	8	1	0	0	0	1	1	.125	.125	.222
Ernest Riles	5	1	0	0	0	2	2	.200	.200	.429
Cal Ripken	23	7	1	0	2	2	6	.304	.609	.360
Leon Roberts	14	2	0	0	0	0	5	.143	.143	.143
Billy Jo Robidoux	5	2	0	0	0	1	2	.400	.400	.500
Aurelio Rodriguez	5	1	0	0	0	0	2	.200	.200	.200
Gary Roenicke	23	6	0	0	0	4	2	.261	.261	.393
Ed Romero	11	1	0	0	0	1	1	.091	.091	.167
Dave Rosello	7	2	0	0	0	0	1	.286	.286	.286
Joe Rudi	3	1	0	0	0	1	0	.333	.333	.600
Lenn Sakata	11	2	0	0	0	3	3	.182	.182	.333
Billy Sample	17	4	0	0	0	1	5	.235	.235	.278
Dick Schofield	7	1	0	0	0	1	1	.143	.143	.250
John Shelby	19	5	0	0	1	1	7	.263	.421	.300
Ted Simmons	28	7	0	1	0	0	2	.250	.321	.250
Ken Singleton	17	7	0	0	0	2	4	.412	.412	.474
Don Slaught	10	0	0	0	0	1	5	.000	.000	.091
Roy Smalley	5	1	1	0	0	0	2	.200	.400	.200
Dave Stapleton	13	1	0	0	0	1	3	.077	.077	.200
Dave Stegman	4	1	0	0	1	3	3	.250	1.000	.571
Bill Stein	13	4	2	0	0	0	3	.308	.462	.308
Jim Sundberg	20	7	1	0	0	4	1	.350	.400	.458
Pat Tabler	10	2	0	1	0	1	3	.200	.400	.250
Tim Teufel	5	1	0	0	0	1	1	.200	.200	.333
Gorman Thomas	22	6	2	0	1	1	5	.273	.500	.304
Andre Thornton	20	6	1	0	1	6	5	.300	.500	.462
Wayne Tolleson	21	7	1	0	0	2	7	.333	.381	.391
Alan Trammell	24	8	0	0	0	9	3	.333	.333	.515
Willie Upshaw	26	8	2	0	0	2	8	.308	.385	.357
Ellis Valentine	9	2	1	0	0	1	4	.222	.333	.300
Tom Veryzer	8	1	0	0	0	0	1	.125	.125	.125
Greg Walker	8	1	0	0	0	1	2	.125	.125	.222
Gary Ward	21	4	2	0	0	4	5	.190	.286	.308
Ron Washington	14	2	0	0	0	1	3	.143	.143	.200
U.L. Washington	22	4	1	0	0	1	2	.182	.227	.217
John Wathan	20	4	0	0	0	5	4	.200	.200	.360
Lou Whitaker	22	9	3	0	0	3	5	.409	.545	.462
Frank White	27	8	1	0	0	1	2	.296	.333	.310
Glenn Wilson	17	6	0	0	0	2	4	.353	.353	.421
Willie Wilson	33	5	1	0	0	0	5	.152	.182	.152
John Wockenfuss	21	3	0	0	0	3	2	.143	.143	.250
George Wright	25	6	1	0	0	2	4	.240	.280	.296
Ned Yost	14	2	1	1	0	0	3	.143	.357	.143
Mike Young	13	1	0	0	0	0	3	.077	.077	.077
Robin Yount	27	6	1	0	1	5	7	.222	.370	.344
Richie Zisk	5	1	0	0	0	0	2	.200	.200	.200

Mike Scott

Batter	AB	H	2B	3B	HR	BB	SO	BA	SA	OBA
Luis Aguayo	12	4	0	0	1	1	2	.333	.583	.385
Mike Aldrete	6	1	1	0	0	1	1	.167	.333	.286
Dave Anderson	4	0	0	0	0	3	0	.000	.000	.429
Alan Ashby	9	6	2	0	1	0	1	.667	1.222	.667
Wally Backman	20	10	1	1	0	1	2	.500	.650	.524
Dusty Baker	24	8	2	0	1	4	4	.333	.542	.400
Buddy Bell	14	5	3	0	1	0	2	.357	.786	.357
Johnny Bench	6	1	0	0	0	0	0	.167	.167	.167
Bruce Benedict	18	5	0	0	0	2	2	.278	.278	.333
Bruce Berenyi	6	2	1	0	0	0	2	.333	.500	.333
Dave Bergman	4	0	0	0	0	1	0	.000	.000	.200
Dale Berra	19	10	5	0	0	2	1	.526	.789	.522
Larry Biittner	6	2	0	0	0	1	0	.333	.333	.429
Dann Bilardello	14	2	1	0	0	0	2	.143	.214	.143
Tim Blackwell	3	0	0	0	0	2	0	.000	.000	.400
Barry Bonds	7	1	1	0	0	1	1	.143	.286	.250
Juan Bonilla	8	5	1	0	1	1	0	.625	1.125	.700
Larry Bowa	30	10	1	1	0	2	0	.333	.433	.375
Sid Bream	18	7	1	0	2	1	4	.389	.778	.421
Bob Brenly	24	3	0	0	0	2	8	.125	.125	.192
Greg Brock	25	5	1	0	0	3	4	.200	.240	.276
Lou Brock	4	1	0	0	0	1	0	.250	.250	.400
Hubie Brooks	26	5	0	0	0	1	6	.192	.192	.214
Bobby Brown	7	1	0	0	0	1	3	.143	.143	.250
Chris Brown	16	7	1	0	0	4	2	.438	.500	.550
Mike C. Brown	8	3	1	0	0	0	2	.375	.500	.375
Tom Browning	5	0	0	0	0	1	1	.000	.000	.167
Bill Buckner	26	7	0	1	2	1	1	.269	.577	.296
Brett Butler	8	1	0	0	0	1	1	.125	.125	.222
Enos Cabell	7	0	0	0	0	0	0	.000	.000	.000
Gary Carter	31	10	3	1	1	2	6	.323	.581	.353
Cesar Cedeno	18	6	1	0	1	1	2	.333	.556	.368
Ron Cey	36	12	2	0	3	7	5	.333	.639	.442
Chris Chambliss	25	9	2	0	0	5	3	.360	.440	.467
Jack Clark	22	4	0	0	0	0	4	.182	.182	.182
Will Clark	10	2	2	0	0	0	2	.200	.400	.200
Vince Coleman	14	4	2	0	0	1	1	.286	.429	.333
Dave Collins	6	2	0	0	0	2	0	.333	.333	.500
Dave Concepcion	32	10	0	1	0	4	5	.313	.375	.378
Warren Cromartie	12	2	0	0	0	5	1	.167	.167	.412
Jose Cruz	11	4	1	0	0	1	0	.364	.455	.417
John Curtis	3	1	0	0	0	0	1	.333	.333	.250
Darren Daulton	4	1	0	0	0	2	1	.250	.250	.500
Chili Davis	49	14	4	1	0	6	8	.286	.408	.364
Dick Davis	6	4	1	0	0	0	0	.667	.833	.667
Eric Davis	11	2	0	0	1	2	4	.182	.455	.308
Jody Davis	28	6	0	0	1	4	8	.214	.321	.313
Andre Dawson	27	7	1	0	0	0	7	.259	.296	.276
Ivan DeJesus	26	7	0	0	0	0	2	.269	.269	.269
Rob Deer	5	0	0	0	0	1	5	.000	.000	.167
Bob Dernier	25	7	2	0	0	2	5	.280	.360	.333
Bo Diaz	18	2	1	0	0	1	2	.111	.167	.158
Steve Dillard	11	4	0	0	0	0	1	.364	.364	.364
Miguel Dilone	10	2	0	0	0	0	0	.200	.200	.200
Dan Driessen	27	8	0	0	0	2	3	.296	.296	.355
Mariano Duncan	17	2	0	0	0	1	1	.118	.118	.167

Mike Scott continued

Batter	AB	H	2B	3B	HR	BB	SO	BA	SA	OBA
Shawon Dunston	12	4	2	1	0	0	4	.333	.667	.333
Leon Durham	50	16	2	2	2	4	10	.320	.560	.370
Len Dykstra	6	2	0	0	1	0	1	.333	.833	.333
Mike Easler	17	7	1	0	2	0	1	.412	.824	.389
Nick Esasky	21	6	1	0	1	0	6	.286	.476	.286
Barry Evans	5	1	0	0	0	0	1	.200	.200	.200
Darrell Evans	16	4	0	0	1	2	0	.250	.438	.333
Bill Fahey	4	1	0	0	1	1	0	.250	1.000	.400
Mike Fitzgerald	11	4	0	0	1	1	2	.364	.636	.385
Tim Flannery	35	7	0	0	0	8	7	.200	.200	.349
Tom Foley	17	4	1	0	0	0	1	.235	.294	.235
Tim Foli	6	0	0	0	0	0	1	.000	.000	.000
George Foster	25	7	1	0	1	2	4	.280	.440	.321
Terry Francona	10	5	2	1	0	0	1	.500	.700	.500
Doug Frobel	5	2	1	0	0	0	2	.400	1.000	.400
Phil Garner	8	3	3	0	0	0	1	.375	.750	.375
Steve Garvey	54	15	0	0	0	1	10	.278	.278	.304
Brian Giles	5	1	1	0	0	0	0	.200	.400	.200
Dan Gladden	27	7	1	0	2	0	5	.259	.519	.310
Dwight Gooden	6	1	0	0	0	0	0	.167	.400	.167
Gary Green	5	1	1	0	0	0	0	.200	.400	.200
Ken Griffey	9	2	0	0	0	0	0	.222	.222	.222
Greg Gross	13	4	0	0	0	1	0	.308	.308	.357
Pedro Guerrero	38	9	3	1	1	4	8	.237	.447	.302
Brad Gulden	5	0	0	0	0	1	0	.000	.000	.167
Tony Gwynn	47	15	2	0	0	0	0	.319	.362	.319
Mel Hall	6	1	0	0	0	1	0	.167	.167	.286
Terry Harper	10	0	0	0	0	0	3	.000	.000	.000
Andy Hawkins	5	1	0	0	0	0	2	.200	.200	.200
Von Hayes	25	11	4	1	1	4	6	.440	.800	.517
Danny Heep	13	3	2	0	0	2	2	.231	.385	.333
Steve Henderson	8	2	1	0	0	0	2	.250	.375	.250
George Hendrick	25	7	0	0	1	0	5	.280	.400	.308
Keith Hernandez	53	20	2	1	5	6	3	.377	.736	.441
Tommy Herr	39	16	3	0	0	5	3	.410	.487	.477
Ron Hodges	8	3	1	0	0	0	1	.375	.500	.375
Rick Honeycutt	5	0	0	0	0	0	0	.000	.000	.000
Bob Horner	15	3	0	0	1	3	0	.200	.400	.316
Paul Householder	8	1	1	0	0	0	1	.125	.250	.125
Art Howe	6	2	0	0	0	0	0	.333	.333	.333
Glenn Hubbard	29	8	0	0	0	3	4	.276	.276	.333
Dane Iorg	18	4	0	0	0	0	2	.222	.222	.222
Steve Jeltz	12	3	0	0	0	1	4	.250	.250	.308
Howard Johnson	6	0	0	0	0	0	0	.000	.000	.000
Jay Johnstone	3	2	0	0	0	1	0	.667	.667	.600
Ruppert Jones	13	3	1	0	0	2	3	.231	.308	.333
Mike Jorgensen	5	0	0	0	0	1	0	.000	.000	.167
Junior Kennedy	7	1	0	0	0	1	1	.143	.143	.222
Terry Kennedy	56	17	2	0	1	0	12	.304	.393	.316
Sammy Khalifa	6	3	2	0	0	1	2	.500	.833	.571
Dave Kingman	6	2	0	0	1	1	0	.333	.833	.429
Alan Knicely	4	1	0	0	1	1	2	.250	1.000	.400
Ray Knight	15	3	1	0	0	0	2	.200	.267	.200
Brad Komminsk	10	2	1	0	0	1	2	.200	.300	.273
Wayne Krenchicki	13	3	0	0	0	0	1	.231	.231	.267
John Kruk	10	4	2	1	0	1	3	.400	.800	.455
Mike Krukow	5	1	0	0	0	1	0	.200	.200	.333
Duane Kuiper	6	1	0	0	0	2	1	.167	.167	.375
Dave LaPoint	6	2	0	0	0	0	0	.333	.333	.333
Lee Lacy	14	6	1	0	0	2	4	.429	.500	.500
Ken Landreaux	36	8	3	0	0	2	8	.222	.306	.263
Tito Landrum	6	3	1	0	0	0	1	.500	.667	.500
Mike Lavalliere	5	1	0	0	0	0	0	.200	.200	.200
Vance Law	10	1	1	0	0	1	5	.100	.200	.182
Johnnie LeMaster	20	4	0	0	0	0	4	.200	.200	.190
Joe Lefebvre	13	3	0	0	1	0	2	.231	.538	.286
Jeff Leonard	28	8	0	0	1	0	4	.286	.393	.286
Sixto Lezcano	5	3	1	1	0	2	0	.600	1.200	.625
Tim Lollar	6	4	0	0	1	0	0	.667	1.167	.667
Dave Lopes	17	3	0	1	1	2	1	.176	.471	.263
Garry Maddox	7	0	0	0	0	1	1	.000	.000	.111
Bill Madlock	40	11	3	0	1	5	5	.275	.425	.370
Candy Maldonado	13	1	1	0	0	0	4	.077	.154	.077
Mike A. Marshall	30	8	0	0	0	5	10	.267	.267	.371
Carmelo Martinez	18	6	0	0	1	3	4	.333	.333	.429
Gary Matthews	22	7	1	1	1	2	6	.318	.591	.360
Len Matuszek	13	2	0	0	0	3	2	.154	.154	.313
Milt May	9	2	1	0	0	0	2	.222	.333	.222
Bake McBride	6	2	0	0	0	0	0	.333	.333	.333
Willie McGee	22	13	0	0	0	1	0	.591	.591	.609
Kevin McReynolds	27	7	2	1	1	2	5	.259	.519	.300
Bob Melvin	11	3	1	0	0	0	4	.273	.364	.273
Eddie Milner	39	9	1	2	1	3	3	.231	.436	.279
Rick Monday	10	1	0	0	1	3	0	.100	.400	.308
Jerry Morales	6	1	0	0	0	0	0	.167	.167	.167
Keith Moreland	32	8	1	0	1	3	4	.250	.375	.314
Omar Moreno	26	5	3	0	0	1	3	.192	.308	.207
Joe Morgan	12	4	0	0	0	2	0	.333	.333	.429
Jim Morrison	9	2	0	0	0	0	5	.222	.222	.222
Jerry Mumphrey	12	6	0	0	0	1	2	.500	.500	.538
Dale Murphy	37	13	0	0	3	3	11	.351	.595	.390
Graig Nettles	31	3	0	0	0	1	7	.097	.097	.125
Al Newman	6	2	0	0	0	0	1	.333	.333	.286
Steve Nicosia	13	4	0	0	1	1	1	.308	.538	.357
Joe Nolan	5	1	0	0	0	0	0	.200	.200	.200
Dickie Noles	7	0	0	0	0	1	3	.000	.000	.125
Mike O'Berry	5	2	0	0	0	2	3	.400	.400	.571
Tom O'Malley	6	2	0	0	0	1	0	.333	.333	.429
Ken Oberkfell	48	12	3	0	0	5	3	.250	.313	.333
Ron Oester	39	10	1	0	0	0	11	.256	.282	.250
Al Oliver	17	7	1	0	0	2	0	.412	.471	.474
Jose Oquendo	11	3	0	0	0	0	3	.273	.273	.273
Joe Orsulak	15	1	0	0	0	1	5	.067	.067	.125
Junior Ortiz	6	0	0	0	0	1	4	.000	.000	.143
David Palmer	9	0	0	0	0	0	5	.000	.000	.000
Dave Parker	39	13	1	2	1	4	6	.333	.538	.378
Larry Parrish	7	1	0	0	0	1	1	.143	.143	.250
Tony Pena	22	9	3	0	0	2	5	.409	.545	.440
Terry Pendleton	10	1	0	1	0	1	2	.100	.300	.182
Pascual Perez	5	1	0	0	0	0	1	.200	.200	.200
Broderick Perkins	11	5	2	0	1	0	0	.455	.909	.455
Gerald Perry	7	2	0	0	1	0	0	.286	.714	.250
Mike Phillips	5	2	0	0	0	0	0	.400	.400	.400
Darrell Porter	19	3	1	0	1	4	3	.158	.368	.304
Terry Puhl	13	3	1	0	0	0	0	.231	.308	.231
Tim Raines	25	11	4	1	0	3	2	.440	.680	.517
Gary Rajsich	4	0	0	0	0	3	2	.000	.000	.429
Rafael Ramirez	35	11	1	0	0	2	4	.314	.343	.351
Mike Ramsey	15	3	0	0	0	2	2	.200	.200	.294
Johnny Ray	37	9	2	0	0	3	3	.243	.297	.300
Gary Redus	20	5	2	1	0	2	5	.250	.450	.318
Ken Reitz	9	2	0	0	0	0	1	.222	.222	.222
Rick Reuschel	6	1	1	0	0	0	2	.167	.333	.167
Jerry Reuss	7	4	0	0	0	0	2	.571	.571	.571
Craig Reynolds	11	1	0	0	0	0	0	.091	.091	.091
R.J. Reynolds	11	2	1	1	0	2	2	.182	.455	.308
Rick Rhoden	8	1	0	0	0	0	3	.125	.125	.125
Gene Richards	18	7	1	1	0	2	1	.389	.556	.450
Ron Roenicke	9	0	0	0	0	4	3	.000	.000	.308
Pete Rose	41	15	2	1	0	2	1	.366	.463	.386
Jerry Royster	18	5	1	0	0	3	2	.278	.333	.364
Bill Russell	43	10	2	0	0	1	3	.233	.279	.244
John Russell	8	0	0	0	0	0	8	.000	.000	.000
Luis Salazar	16	2	0	0	0	0	4	.125	.125	.125
Juan Samuel	21	4	2	0	0	1	7	.190	.286	.227
Ryne Sandberg	36	11	1	0	2	2	9	.306	.500	.342
Scott Sanderson	6	1	0	0	0	0	4	.167	.167	.167
Rafael Santana	8	1	0	0	0	0	0	.125	.125	.125
Benito Santiago	6	2	1	0	1	0	2	.333	1.000	.333
Steve Sax	44	14	1	1	0	3	3	.318	.386	.362
Mike Schmidt	27	6	0	0	2	8	7	.222	.444	.389
Rick Schu	10	3	1	0	0	0	4	.300	.400	.300
Mike Scioscia	36	11	2	0	0	5	1	.306	.361	.390
Rodney Scott	6	2	0	0	0	0	1	.333	.333	.333
Tony Scott	19	7	2	0	0	1	0	.368	.474	.400
Tom Seaver	5	1	0	0	0	0	2	.200	.200	.200
Ted Simmons	13	4	0	0	0	2	0	.308	.308	.400
Lonnie Smith	14	2	0	0	0	2	1	.143	.143	.294
Ozzie Smith	27	3	0	0	0	2	3	.111	.111	.172
Mario Soto	4	1	0	0	0	0	3	.250	.250	.250

Mike Scott continued

Batter	AB	H	2B	3B	HR	BB	SO	BA	SA	OBA
Chris Speier	24	5	0	0	0	2	11	.208	.208	.269
Harry Spilman	5	0	0	0	0	0	0	.000	.000	.000
Rusty Staub	6	2	0	0	0	0	0	.333	.333	.333
Mike Stenhouse	5	3	0	0	0	0	0	.600	.600	.667
Jeff Stone	10	2	1	0	0	0	1	.200	.300	.200
Darryl Strawberry	19	3	0	2	0	2	4	.158	.368	.238
Franklin Stubbs	9	2	0	0	1	1	5	.222	.556	.300
Garry Templeton	39	6	0	1	0	2	8	.154	.205	.195
Derrel Thomas	14	2	0	1	0	0	2	.143	.286	.143
Jason Thompson	22	5	0	0	3	14	3	.227	.636	.528
Milt Thompson	7	1	1	0	0	1	2	.143	.286	.250
Rob Thompson	12	0	0	0	0	0	5	.000	.000	.000
Scot Thompson	10	5	1	0	0	1	0	.500	.600	.545
Mark Thurmond	5	0	0	0	0	0	0	.000	.000	.000
Jim Tracy	4	1	1	0	0	1	1	.250	.500	.400
Alex Trevino	8	2	0	0	1	1	2	.250	.625	.333
Manny Trillo	22	1	1	0	0	3	1	.045	.091	.154
Jose Uribe	26	3	0	0	0	2	3	.115	.115	.179
Fernando Valenzuela	15	2	0	0	0	0	4	.133	.133	.133
Andy Van Slyke	14	0	0	0	0	1	4	.000	.000	.067
Max Venable	16	5	1	1	0	1	2	.313	.500	.353
Ozzie Virgil	14	2	1	0	1	0	3	.143	.429	.143
Duane Walker	13	3	1	0	0	1	4	.231	.308	.286
Tim Wallach	27	6	3	0	2	4	5	.222	.556	.323
Claudell Washington	31	7	2	0	1	2	5	.226	.387	.273
U.L. Washington	4	0	0	0	0	2	2	.000	.000	.333
Mitch Webster	11	4	2	0	0	1	2	.364	.545	.417
Brad Wellman	10	2	0	0	0	2	0	.200	.200	.333
Jerry White	8	4	0	0	0	0	0	.500	.500	.500
Terry Whitfield	9	4	2	0	0	2	0	.444	.667	.545
Alan Wiggins	11	1	0	0	0	1	2	.091	.091	.167
Bump Wills	7	0	0	0	0	0	4	.000	.000	.000
Glenn Wilson	21	5	1	0	2	2	6	.238	.571	.320
Mookie Wilson	21	5	0	1	0	0	1	.238	.333	.238
Dave Winfield	5	0	0	0	0	0	1	.000	.000	.000
Herm Winningham	7	0	0	0	0	1	4	.000	.000	.111
Jim Wohlford	4	1	1	0	0	2	1	.250	.500	.500
Mike Woodard	6	0	0	0	0	0	0	.000	.000	.000
Gary Woods	7	3	0	0	0	0	3	.429	.429	.429
Marvell Wynne	27	7	1	0	0	0	6	.259	.296	.259
Steve Yeager	10	4	0	0	0	1	1	.400	.400	.455
Joel Youngblood	17	6	1	0	0	1	2	.353	.412	.389

Fernando Valenzuela

Batter	AB	H	2B	3B	HR	BB	SO	BA	SA	OBA
Luis Aguayo	15	2	0	0	0	1	7	.133	.133	.188
Bill Almon	16	1	1	0	0	1	4	.063	.125	.118
Alan Ashby	36	4	0	0	0	3	8	.111	.111	.179
Wally Backman	16	0	0	0	0	1	5	.000	.000	.059
Mark Bailey	7	1	0	0	0	3	4	.143	.143	.400
Bob Bailor	17	6	1	0	0	0	3	.353	.412	.353
Dusty Baker	4	1	0	0	0	1	2	.250	.250	.400
Skeeter Barnes	6	1	0	0	0	0	0	.167	.167	.167
Kevin Bass	42	6	1	0	1	3	8	.143	.238	.200
Buddy Bell	12	2	0	0	1	1	1	.167	.417	.231
Rafael Belliard	9	2	0	0	0	0	0	.222	.222	.222
Johnny Bench	21	6	3	0	0	5	4	.286	.429	.423
Bruce Benedict	61	18	1	0	1	4	4	.295	.361	.338
Dale Berra	23	2	1	0	0	1	7	.087	.130	.125
Kurt Bevacqua	38	10	2	0	0	4	7	.263	.316	.333
Dann Bilardello	11	4	1	0	0	2	1	.364	.455	.462
Bruce Bochy	7	1	0	0	0	0	2	.143	.143	.143
Tommy Boggs	6	0	0	0	0	0	1	.000	.000	.000
Juan Bonilla	23	10	0	0	0	5	2	.435	.435	.552
Larry Bowa	32	5	2	0	0	0	4	.156	.219	.156
Bob Brenly	57	13	4	0	0	11	8	.228	.298	.362
Hubie Brooks	34	12	2	1	2	3	5	.353	.647	.405
Bobby Brown	4	0	0	0	0	1	2	.000	.000	.200
Chris Brown	16	5	1	0	0	4	4	.313	.375	.450
Mike C. Brown	7	1	0	0	0	1	0	.143	.143	.250
Glenn Brummer	7	1	0	0	0	0	0	.143	.143	.143
Bill Buckner	24	11	3	0	0	0	0	.458	.583	.458
Enos Cabell	33	13	2	1	0	1	5	.394	.515	.412
Steve Carlton	5	3	0	0	1	0	1	.600	1.200	.600
Gary Carter	54	13	4	0	0	7	5	.241	.315	.323
Cesar Cedeno	47	10	3	0	2	3	9	.213	.404	.260
Ron Cey	20	4	2	0	0	3	7	.200	.300	.292
Chris Chambliss	33	3	0	0	1	1	8	.091	.182	.114
Kelvin Chapman	18	5	0	0	0	2	3	.278	.278	.350
Jack Clark	50	11	2	0	1	12	9	.220	.320	.371
Will Clark	12	5	2	0	0	1	2	.417	.583	.462
Vince Coleman	19	3	1	0	0	0	5	.158	.211	.158
Dave Collins	7	2	0	0	0	0	0	.286	.286	.286
Dave Concepcion	63	14	2	1	1	5	12	.222	.333	.279
Warren Cromartie	21	4	0	0	0	0	0	.190	.190	.190
Jose Cruz	71	20	1	0	1	2	9	.282	.338	.301
Ron Darling	5	2	1	0	0	0	0	.400	.600	.400
Darren Daulton	5	1	1	0	0	2	4	.200	.400	.429
Chili Davis	63	13	2	0	1	4	15	.206	.286	.254
Dick Davis	6	0	0	0	0	0	0	.000	.000	.000
Eric Davis	8	0	0	0	0	2	6	.000	.000	.200
Glenn Davis	30	9	1	0	1	4	9	.300	.433	.382
Jody Davis	35	11	1	1	1	1	6	.314	.486	.324
Andre Dawson	44	8	0	2	2	1	8	.182	.409	.200
Ivan DeJesus	19	3	0	1	0	5	7	.158	.263	.333
John Denny	5	2	0	0	0	1	0	.400	.400	.500
Bob Dernier	20	3	0	0	0	1	4	.150	.150	.190
Bo Diaz	17	5	3	0	0	3	1	.294	.471	.400
Mike Diaz	9	3	0	0	1	1	6	.333	.778	.400
Miguel Dilone	4	2	1	0	0	1	0	.500	.750	.600
Bill Doran	47	9	2	0	0	6	7	.191	.234	.278
Dave Dravecky	2	1	1	0	0	1	0	.500	1.000	.667
Dan Driessen	38	4	2	0	0	3	4	.105	.158	.167
Leon Durham	29	7	3	0	0	1	6	.241	.345	.290
Len Dykstra	7	2	0	0	0	0	1	.286	.286	.286
Mike Easler	12	3	1	0	0	1	6	.250	.333	.308
Dave Edwards	10	2	1	0	0	0	3	.200	.300	.200
Juan Eichelberger	6	0	0	0	0	0	2	.000	.000	.000
Nick Esasky	22	10	3	0	0	9	4	.455	.591	.613
Barry Evans	4	1	0	0	0	2	1	.250	.250	.500
Darrell Evans	32	8	0	3	1	6	5	.250	.531	.368
Sid Fernandez	6	0	0	0	0	0	2	.000	.000	.000
Mike Fitzgerald	16	2	0	0	1	2	4	.125	.313	.222
Doug Flynn	19	3	0	0	0	0	1	.158	.158	.158
Tom Foley	10	1	0	0	0	0	4	.100	.100	.100
Tim Foli	5	0	0	0	0	0	0	.000	.000	.000
Bob Forsch	6	1	0	0	0	1	1	.167	.167	.286
George Foster	50	11	0	1	3	11	11	.220	.440	.361
Andres Galarraga	7	1	0	0	0	1	0	.143	.571	.143
Kiko Garcia	8	2	1	0	0	0	0	.250	.375	.250
Ron Gardenhire	12	0	0	0	0	1	1	.000	.000	.077
Phil Garner	64	17	5	1	0	8	15	.266	.375	.342
Steve Garvey	47	11	1	0	2	4	7	.234	.383	.288
Dan Gladden	32	9	2	0	1	8	.281	.344	.303
Dwight Gooden	16	6	0	0	0	0	5	.375	.375	.375
David Green	30	5	0	0	1	1	3	.167	.267	.194
Ken Griffey	13	5	1	0	0	3	2	.385	.462	.471
Greg Gross	6	1	0	0	0	2	1	.167	.167	.375
Bill Gullickson	5	1	0	0	0	0	1	.200	.200	.200
Doug Gwosdz	9	1	0	0	0	2	3	.111	.111	.273
Tony Gwynn	42	12	2	0	1	0	5	.286	.405	.286
Albert Hall	9	1	0	0	0	1	3	.111	.111	.200
Mel Hall	8	1	0	0	0	1	3	.125	.125	.222
Brian Harper	5	1	1	0	0	0	1	.200	.400	.200
Terry Harper	32	6	1	0	1	2	7	.188	.313	.235

Fernando Valenzuela continued

Batter	AB	H	2B	3B	HR	BB	SO	BA	SA	OBA
Billy Hatcher	22	7	1	0	1	0	1	.318	.500	.318
Von Hayes	27	8	3	0	1	3	7	.296	.519	.367
Ed Hearn	6	2	0	0	1	1	3	.333	.833	.429
Mike Heath	13	1	0	0	0	1	5	.077	.077	.143
Danny Heep	3	2	2	0	0	1	0	.667	1.333	.600
Steve Henderson	10	3	1	0	0	1	1	.300	.400	.364
George Hendrick	47	13	2	0	2	2	9	.277	.447	.300
Keith Hernandez	59	20	6	1	0	10	6	.339	.475	.435
Larry Herndon	10	6	2	0	1	1	1	.600	1.100	.636
Tommy Herr	51	13	2	0	0	5	9	.255	.294	.321
Bob Horner	52	22	2	0	6	5	6	.423	.808	.474
Paul Householder	25	2	1	0	0	1	2	.080	.120	.115
Art Howe	21	2	0	0	0	2	3	.095	.095	.174
Glenn Hubbard	57	8	1	0	1	10	14	.140	.211	.265
Mike Ivie	9	0	0	0	0	0	3	.000	.000	.000
Steve Jeltz	13	0	0	0	0	1	3	.000	.000	.071
Randy G. Johnson	12	5	1	0	0	2	2	.417	.500	.500
Ruppert Jones	24	5	0	0	0	2	5	.208	.208	.269
Terry Kennedy	55	11	3	0	0	2	11	.200	.255	.228
Kurt Kepshire	6	1	0	0	0	0	4	.167	.167	.167
Dave Kingman	17	6	1	0	1	2	4	.353	.588	.421
Alan Knicely	19	4	1	0	0	3	8	.211	.263	.318
Ray Knight	53	15	3	0	2	4	8	.283	.453	.333
Brad Komminsk	27	8	1	0	0	3	7	.296	.333	.367
Mike Krukow	3	0	0	0	0	0	0	.000	.000	.250
Randy Kutcher	8	1	0	0	0	0	3	.125	.125	.125
Lee Lacy	18	7	0	0	1	3	3	.389	.556	.476
Rafael Landestoy	5	2	0	0	0	0	1	.400	.400	.400
Tito Landrum	27	3	0	0	0	0	10	.111	.111	.111
Bill Laskey	15	1	0	0	0	1	10	.067	.067	.125
Vance Law	7	2	0	0	0	0	0	.286	.286	.286
Tom Lawless	9	2	1	0	0	0	2	.222	.333	.222
Johnnie LeMaster	37	5	1	0	0	9	16	.135	.162	.304
Charlie Lea	7	2	0	0	0	0	2	.286	.286	.286
Joe Lefebvre	7	2	0	0	0	1	1	.286	.286	.286
Jeff Leonard	67	18	2	0	1	5	18	.269	.343	.319
Sixto Lezcano	37	9	2	0	0	12	10	.243	.297	.429
Rufino Linares	22	8	2	0	0	0	7	.364	.455	.364
Bryan Little	8	1	0	0	0	0	1	.125	.125	.125
Dave Lopes	14	2	0	0	1	0	3	.143	.357	.143
Garry Maddox	24	7	0	0	0	1	2	.292	.292	.308
Bill Madlock	34	6	1	0	2	0	4	.176	.382	.176
Rick Mahler	12	3	0	0	0	0	2	.250	.250	.250
Candy Maldonado	9	3	2	0	0	1	0	.333	.556	.300
Jerry Martin	10	2	0	0	0	1	6	.200	.200	.273
Carmelo Martinez	29	5	1	0	0	5	13	.172	.207	.294
Gary Matthews	24	8	2	0	0	5	5	.333	.417	.419
Len Matuszek	7	2	1	0	0	0	2	.286	.429	.286
Milt May	11	2	0	0	0	0	2	.182	.182	.182
Lee Mazzilli	7	1	0	0	0	1	2	.143	.143	.250
Willie McGee	34	8	2	0	0	1	9	.235	.294	.278
Craig McMurtry	5	2	0	0	0	0	2	.400	.400	.400
Kevin McReynolds	30	10	2	0	2	2	4	.333	.600	.375
Bob Melvin	12	1	0	0	1	1	5	.083	.333	.154
Eddie Milner	17	6	1	0	0	2	4	.353	.412	.421
Kevin Mitchell	10	2	0	0	1	1	3	.200	.500	.273
John Mizerock	4	2	0	0	0	1	1	.500	.500	.600
Jerry Morales	4	1	0	1	0	1	0	.250	.750	.400
Keith Moreland	31	13	3	1	0	5	5	.419	.581	.486
Omar Moreno	27	9	0	0	0	0	5	.333	.333	.333
Joe Morgan	19	5	0	1	1	7	3	.263	.526	.462
Jim Morrison	15	3	0	0	0	3	4	.200	.200	.316
Jerry Mumphrey	18	5	0	0	0	3	3	.278	.278	.381
Dale Murphy	78	23	5	0	5	11	17	.295	.551	.382
Graig Nettles	7	2	0	0	0	1	3	.286	.286	.375
Dan Norman	7	3	1	0	0	1	2	.429	.571	.500
Mike O'Berry	5	1	0	0	0	1	2	.200	.200	.333
Tom O'Malley	19	4	2	0	0	1	4	.211	.316	.250
Ken Oberkfell	54	14	1	0	0	5	9	.259	.278	.317
Ron Oester	51	6	0	0	0	2	13	.118	.118	.151
Al Oliver	26	7	3	0	0	2	3	.269	.385	.310
Jose Oquendo	7	3	1	0	0	3	1	.429	.571	.600
Amos Otis	4	0	0	0	0	2	0	.000	.000	.286
Tom Paciorek	9	2	0	0	0	0	1	.222	.222	.222
Jim Pankovits	13	1	0	0	0	2	8	.077	.077	.200
Kelly Paris	6	3	0	0	0	1	1	.500	.500	.571
Dave Parker	33	11	3	0	2	2	6	.333	.606	.371
Larry Parrish	5	0	0	0	0	0	3	.000	.000	.000
Tony Pena	37	8	0	0	0	2	6	.216	.216	.256
Terry Pendleton	22	6	1	0	0	2	5	.273	.318	.333
Pascual Perez	4	0	0	0	0	1	3	.000	.000	.200
Tony Perez	22	4	0	0	1	3	7	.182	.318	.280
Gerald Perry	13	3	1	0	0	3	3	.231	.308	.375
Joe Pettini	7	2	0	0	0	1	2	.286	.286	.375
Joe Pittman	12	5	0	0	0	0	2	.417	.417	.385
Darrell Porter	18	7	0	1	2	1	4	.389	.833	.455
Joe Price	7	0	0	0	0	1	3	.000	.000	.125
Terry Puhl	31	4	1	0	0	7	4	.129	.161	.282
Luis Pujols	18	5	0	0	0	0	7	.278	.278	.278
John Rabb	6	1	0	0	0	1	2	.167	.167	.286
Tim Raines	46	14	1	0	0	4	6	.304	.326	.360
Mario Ramirez	6	0	0	0	0	3	1	.000	.000	.333
Rafael Ramirez	75	15	2	1	1	4	8	.200	.293	.241
Mike Ramsey	14	4	1	0	0	1	2	.286	.357	.333
Johnny Ray	35	9	2	0	0	2	6	.257	.314	.297
Gary Redus	41	10	3	0	0	9	14	.244	.317	.380
Ken Reitz	5	1	0	0	0	0	1	.200	.200	.200
Craig Reynolds	20	5	0	0	0	0	1	.250	.250	.250
R.J. Reynolds	5	1	0	0	0	2	1	.200	.200	.429
Ronn Reynolds	10	1	0	0	0	1	0	.100	.100	.182
Rick Rhoden	5	1	1	0	0	0	0	.200	.400	.200
Gene Richards	25	7	2	0	0	0	5	.280	.360	.280
Bip Roberts	8	0	0	0	0	0	3	.000	.000	.000
Dave W. Roberts	5	0	0	0	0	0	2	.000	.000	.000
Ron Roenicke	5	1	0	0	0	0	3	.200	.200	.200
Steve Rogers	5	0	0	0	0	0	0	.000	.000	.000
Pete Rose	18	4	0	0	0	2	1	.222	.222	.300
Jerry Royster	47	9	2	0	0	2	11	.191	.234	.224
John Russell	11	3	1	0	0	1	5	.273	.364	.333
Nolan Ryan	8	0	0	0	0	0	4	.000	.000	.000
Luis Salazar	51	6	0	0	1	2	11	.118	.176	.148
Juan Samuel	37	6	2	0	1	1	12	.162	.297	.179
Ryne Sandberg	32	10	1	0	2	4	11	.313	.531	.389
Rafael Santana	26	8	0	0	0	4	6	.308	.308	.400
Mike Schmidt	43	10	1	0	3	7	9	.233	.465	.327
Rick Schu	15	3	0	0	1	0	7	.200	.400	.200
Mike Scott	13	1	0	0	0	0	8	.077	.077	.077
Rodney Scott	8	2	0	0	0	0	1	.250	.250	.250
Tony Scott	15	4	0	0	0	2	5	.267	.267	.353
Eric Show	5	1	0	0	0	0	2	.200	.200	.200
Lonnie Smith	34	9	1	0	0	2	8	.265	.294	.306
Ozzie Smith	51	8	1	0	0	3	4	.157	.176	.204
Reggie Smith	9	4	1	0	0	1	2	.444	.556	.500
Mario Soto	8	2	0	0	0	1	2	.250	.250	.333
Chris Speier	31	9	2	0	1	5	4	.290	.452	.389
John Stearns	13	1	1	0	0	1	3	.077	.154	.143
Rennie Stennett	6	0	0	0	0	0	0	.000	.000	.000
Jeff Stone	17	5	2	0	0	1	3	.294	.412	.333
Darryl Strawberry	29	8	1	0	0	3	8	.276	.310	.344
Don Sutton	4	0	0	0	0	0	1	.000	.000	.000
Steve Swisher	6	1	0	0	0	0	2	.167	.167	.167
Frank Taveras	9	1	0	0	0	1	0	.111	.111	.200
Garry Templeton	58	23	3	1	2	4	11	.397	.586	.435
Gene Tenace	11	2	0	0	1	3	5	.182	.455	.357
Tim Teufel	10	2	1	0	0	0	3	.200	.300	.200
Derrel Thomas	7	2	0	0	1	1	1	.286	.714	.375
Jason Thompson	25	5	2	0	0	7	7	.200	.280	.364
Rob Thompson	12	3	1	0	0	3	4	.250	.333	.400
Dickie Thon	54	13	2	0	0	3	11	.241	.278	.281
Mark Thurmond	8	0	0	0	0	0	3	.000	.000	.000
Tim Tolman	6	2	0	0	0	0	1	.333	.333	.333
Mike Torrez	4	1	0	0	0	0	1	.250	.250	.250
Alex Trevino	24	7	2	0	0	1	3	.292	.375	.320
Manny Trillo	30	7	1	0	0	5	7	.233	.267	.343
Jose Uribe	19	1	0	0	0	1	8	.053	.053	.100
Mike Vail	8	2	0	0	0	0	1	.250	.250	.250
Ellis Valentine	8	2	1	0	0	0	1	.250	.375	.250
Dave Van Gorder	19	2	1	0	0	0	2	.105	.158	.105
Andy Van Slyke	7	1	0	0	0	0	3	.143	.143	.143
Max Venable	4	0	0	0	0	1	2	.000	.000	.200

Fernando Valenzuela continued

Batter	AB	H	2B	3B	HR	BB	SO	BA	SA	OBA
Ozzie Virgil	17	3	0	0	0	3	7	.176	.176	.318
Tim Wallach	42	10	0	0	0	4	5	.238	.238	.298
Claudell Washington	44	13	2	0	1	0	9	.295	.409	.311
Bob Watson	15	2	1	0	0	6	0	.133	.200	.364
Mitch Webster	7	2	0	0	0	0	1	.286	.286	.286
Brad Wellman	7	0	0	0	0	0	2	.000	.000	.000
Jerry White	12	1	0	0	0	0	3	.083	.083	.083
Ed Whitson	4	0	0	0	0	0	1	.000	.000	.000

Batter	AB	H	2B	3B	HR	BB	SO	BA	SA	OBA
Alan Wiggins	34	10	2	0	0	5	1	.294	.353	.385
Bump Wills	6	1	0	0	0	1	2	.167	.167	.286
Glenn Wilson	34	6	2	0	0	2	10	.176	.235	.222
Mookie Wilson	48	16	2	0	1	5	8	.333	.438	.396
Jim Wohlford	11	3	1	0	0	2	3	.273	.364	.385
Gary Woods	9	3	1	0	0	0	5	.333	.444	.300
Marvell Wynne	12	3	0	1	0	1	1	.250	.417	.308
Joel Youngblood	35	11	4	0	0	8	11	.314	.429	.442

Mike Witt

Batter	AB	H	2B	3B	HR	BB	SO	BA	SA	OBA
Willie Aikens	17	6	2	0	1	5	3	.353	.647	.458
Gary Allenson	7	4	0	0	0	0	0	.571	.571	.571
Bill Almon	12	2	0	0	0	0	0	.167	.167	.167
Tony Armas	27	5	1	0	0	1	9	.185	.222	.214
Harold Baines	48	15	3	0	1	7	8	.313	.438	.400
Dusty Baker	8	1	0	0	0	2	0	.125	.125	.300
Steve Balboni	20	6	1	0	3	1	6	.300	.800	.318
Chris Bando	17	2	1	0	0	0	4	.118	.176	.118
Alan Bannister	8	1	0	0	1	0	3	.125	.500	.222
Jesse Barfield	19	3	1	0	0	4	6	.158	.211	.333
Marty Barrett	16	2	0	0	0	1	1	.125	.125	.167
Don Baylor	19	1	0	0	0	1	7	.053	.053	.095
Buddy Bell	22	7	1	0	0	3	3	.318	.364	.400
George Bell	20	5	1	0	0	0	4	.250	.300	.250
Juan Beniquez	9	3	0	0	0	1	2	.333	.333	.400
Dave Bergman	15	2	1	1	0	3	0	.133	.333	.316
Tony Bernazard	45	16	4	0	0	3	5	.356	.444	.396
Buddy Biancalana	9	1	0	0	0	0	4	.111	.111	.111
Bruce Bochte	39	8	0	0	1	2	4	.205	.282	.238
Wade Boggs	23	7	1	0	0	6	3	.304	.348	.448
Barry Bonnell	23	6	0	0	1	1	8	.261	.391	.292
Daryl Boston	14	4	1	0	0	1	3	.286	.357	.333
Phil Bradley	26	6	1	0	1	3	4	.231	.385	.310
George Brett	32	10	1	0	0	6	1	.313	.344	.421
Tom Brookens	14	1	0	0	0	1	2	.071	.071	.133
Tom Brunansky	24	8	1	0	2	3	3	.333	.625	.407
Bill Buckner	17	6	2	0	1	0	0	.353	.647	.353
Steve Buechele	10	4	0	0	1	0	3	.400	.700	.364
Al Bumbry	22	10	1	1	0	1	2	.455	.591	.478
Jeff Burroughs	4	1	0	0	0	1	0	.250	.250	.400
Randy Bush	16	3	0	0	0	2	6	.188	.188	.278
Brett Butler	27	8	1	1	0	6	1	.296	.407	.424
Enos Cabell	5	0	0	0	0	0	2	.000	.000	.000
Jose Canseco	13	1	0	0	1	1	5	.077	.308	.143
Joe Carter	20	3	1	0	0	1	6	.150	.200	.190
Manny Castillo	20	8	2	0	0	0	0	.400	.500	.400
Marty Castillo	6	2	0	0	1	0	1	.333	.833	.333
John Castino	10	4	1	0	1	1	2	.400	.800	.455
Rick Cerone	5	1	0	0	0	0	0	.200	.200	.200
Al Chambers	3	1	1	0	0	3	2	.333	.667	.667
Darnell Coles	9	2	1	0	0	1	1	.222	.333	.300
Dave Collins	28	6	0	1	1	2	2	.214	.393	.258
Onix Concepcion	11	4	0	0	0	0	1	.364	.364	.364
Cecil Cooper	42	14	3	2	1	2	1	.333	.571	.364
Al Cowens	38	6	2	0	0	0	12	.158	.211	.158
Julio Cruz	29	5	0	0	0	3	7	.172	.172	.250
Todd Cruz	8	4	1	0	0	1	0	.500	.625	.556
Rich Dauer	28	11	2	0	0	3	2	.393	.464	.452
Alvin Davis	32	9	2	0	1	5	3	.281	.438	.395
Mike Davis	27	8	1	0	2	1	4	.296	.556	.300
Doug DeCinces	5	3	0	0	0	1	0	.600	.600	.667
Rick Dempsey	13	1	0	0	0	3	3	.077	.077	.235
Bucky Dent	11	5	2	0	1	0	0	.455	.909	.455
Miguel Dilone	8	2	0	0	0	0	1	.250	.250	.250
Tommy Dunbar	7	0	0	0	0	0	4	.000	.000	.000
Jim Dwyer	15	4	0	0	0	5	1	.267	.267	.450
Jerry Dybzinski	6	0	0	0	0	1	1	.000	.000	.143
Mike Easler	17	10	1	1	3	2	2	.588	1.294	.650

Batter	AB	H	2B	3B	HR	BB	SO	BA	SA	OBA
Dave Engle	11	2	1	0	0	1	2	.182	.273	.250
Jim Essian	7	2	0	0	1	1	0	.286	.714	.375
Darrell Evans	28	8	0	0	0	0	4	.286	.286	.286
Dwight Evans	29	3	0	0	0	7	4	.103	.103	.278
Bill Fahey	6	2	0	0	0	1	0	.333	.333	.429
Mike Felder	5	1	0	0	0	0	0	.200	.200	.200
Tony Fernandez	22	4	0	0	0	0	3	.182	.182	.182
Mike Fischlin	13	2	0	0	0	3	2	.154	.154	.353
Carlton Fisk	42	13	0	0	2	4	6	.310	.452	.370
Scott Fletcher	20	9	3	0	0	2	5	.450	.600	.500
Julio Franco	30	8	2	0	0	5	8	.267	.333	.371
Gary Gaetti	23	4	0	0	0	1	5	.174	.174	.200
Greg Gagne	5	2	0	0	0	0	1	.400	.400	.400
Oscar Gamble	5	0	0	0	0	1	0	.000	.000	.167
Jim Gantner	36	8	2	0	0	3	2	.222	.278	.300
Damaso Garcia	29	8	0	0	1	2	3	.276	.379	.323
Rich Gedman	21	2	0	0	1	1	6	.095	.238	.136
Cesar Geronimo	6	0	0	0	0	0	1	.000	.000	.000
Kirk Gibson	33	11	1	0	0	2	6	.333	.364	.389
Ken Griffey	18	4	1	0	0	0	3	.222	.278	.222
Alfredo Griffin	45	13	1	0	0	1	8	.289	.311	.304
Wayne Gross	30	7	0	0	1	4	5	.233	.333	.314
Johnny Grubb	20	6	0	0	0	2	1	.300	.300	.364
Ozzie Guillen	13	2	0	0	0	0	2	.154	.154	.154
Jackie Gutierrez	5	0	0	0	0	1	1	.000	.000	.167
Jerry Hairston	14	0	0	0	0	1	1	.000	.000	.067
Mel Hall	15	6	0	0	2	1	3	.400	.800	.438
Mike Hargrove	31	11	2	0	0	3	1	.355	.419	.412
Toby Harrah	23	5	0	0	1	5	1	.217	.348	.379
Ron Hassey	26	10	1	0	2	1	2	.385	.654	.393
Mickey Hatcher	16	2	0	0	0	0	0	.125	.125	.118
Von Hayes	8	2	0	0	0	1	0	.250	.250	.400
Mike Heath	25	7	1	0	1	1	3	.280	.440	.308
Richie Hebner	7	2	2	0	0	1	1	.286	.571	.375
Dave Henderson	22	4	3	0	0	0	7	.182	.318	.182
Rickey Henderson	27	4	0	0	0	12	7	.148	.148	.410
Steve Henderson	3	3	1	1	0	3	0	1.000	2.000	1.000
Larry Herndon	19	3	0	0	0	0	6	.158	.158	.158
Donnie Hill	18	5	3	0	0	2	3	.278	.444	.350
Marc Hill	5	1	0	0	0	1	2	.200	.200	.333
Glenn Hoffman	18	5	1	0	0	0	4	.278	.333	.278
Dave Hostetler	5	3	0	0	0	0	2	.600	.600	.600
Roy Howell	15	2	1	0	0	0	5	.133	.200	.133
Kent Hrbek	24	7	0	0	3	3	5	.292	.667	.370
Tim Hulett	8	1	1	0	0	2	3	.125	.250	.300
Pete Incaviglia	8	1	0	0	1	1	4	.125	.500	.200
Dane Iorg	8	0	0	0	0	0	1	.000	.000	.000
Garth Iorg	9	2	0	0	0	1	0	.222	.222	.364
Mike Ivie	5	2	0	0	0	0	0	.400	.400	.400
Brook Jacoby	25	6	1	0	1	0	10	.240	.400	.240
Dion James	10	3	0	0	0	1	2	.300	.300	.364
Houston Jimenez	10	3	1	0	0	0	0	.300	.400	.300
Bobby Johnson	8	0	0	0	0	1	2	.000	.000	.111
Cliff Johnson	10	4	1	0	0	2	2	.400	.500	.500
Howard Johnson	12	3	0	0	1	1	3	.250	.500	.308
Bobby Jones	13	2	1	0	0	1	5	.154	.231	.214
Ruppert Jones	5	0	0	0	0	1	0	.000	.000	.167
Bob Kearney	26	3	0	0	0	0	7	.115	.115	.115

Mike Witt continued

Batter	AB	H	2B	3B	HR	BB	SO	BA	SA	OBA
Mick Kelleher	5	1	0	0	0	0	0	.200	.200	.200
Steve Kemp	14	4	0	0	0	1	6	.286	.286	.333
Dave Kingman	11	1	0	0	0	1	4	.091	.091	.154
Ron Kittle	26	9	3	0	0	3	6	.346	.462	.433
Wayne Krenchicki	5	2	1	0	0	0	1	.400	.600	.400
Rusty Kuntz	5	1	0	0	0	0	2	.200	.200	.200
Lee Lacy	14	4	0	0	0	4	3	.286	.286	.444
Mike Laga	5	1	1	0	0	0	1	.200	.400	.200
Carney Lansford	27	11	3	0	0	2	1	.407	.519	.467
Tim Laudner	9	0	0	0	0	1	5	.000	.000	.100
Rudy Law	39	13	3	1	0	4	3	.333	.462	.386
Vance Law	24	6	1	0	0	0	3	.250	.292	.280
Ron LeFlore	10	0	0	0	0	1	4	.000	.000	.167
Rick Leach	9	2	0	1	0	1	2	.222	.444	.273
Chet Lemon	28	10	1	0	1	6	6	.357	.500	.471
Doug Loman	6	1	1	0	0	0	2	.167	.333	.167
Steve Lombardozzi	5	2	0	0	0	0	1	.400	.400	.400
Dave Lopes	13	5	2	0	0	1	0	.385	.538	.429
John Lowenstein	16	3	1	0	0	1	3	.188	.250	.235
Dwight Lowry	4	0	0	0	0	0	0	.000	.000	.000
Greg Luzinski	31	8	0	0	1	3	8	.258	.355	.324
Fred Lynn	8	4	0	0	1	1	2	.500	.875	.556
Steve Lyons	13	2	0	0	0	1	4	.154	.154	.214
Jim Maler	6	2	0	0	0	0	1	.333	.333	.333
Rick Manning	28	5	3	0	0	1	4	.179	.286	.233
Jerry Martin	7	4	0	0	1	0	1	.571	1.000	.571
Don Mattingly	21	6	2	0	1	4	2	.286	.524	.400
John Mayberry	6	1	1	0	0	1	2	.167	.333	.286
Oddibe McDowell	20	5	0	0	0	2	3	.250	.250	.318
Dave McKay	5	0	0	0	0	1	1	.000	.000	.167
Hal McRae	15	4	3	0	0	1	3	.267	.467	.313
Bobby Meacham	12	3	0	0	0	0	5	.250	.250	.308
Dan Meyer	14	5	2	1	0	0	1	.357	.643	.357
Larry Milbourne	9	4	0	1	0	1	0	.444	.667	.500
Rick Miller	6	2	0	0	0	2	0	.333	.333	.500
Paul Molitor	29	7	1	1	0	2	6	.241	.345	.313
Charlie Moore	20	5	2	0	0	0	5	.250	.350	.250
Omar Moreno	6	0	0	0	0	0	2	.000	.000	.000
Jim Morrison	8	2	0	0	1	0	1	.250	.625	.250
Lloyd Moseby	39	12	3	0	2	6	10	.308	.538	.400
John Moses	4	2	0	0	0	0	0	.500	.500	.600
Darryl Motley	10	3	1	0	1	0	4	.300	.700	.300
Rance Mulliniks	27	5	1	0	0	2	4	.185	.222	.241
Dwayne Murphy	43	11	2	0	1	8	8	.256	.372	.373
Eddie Murray	36	12	5	1	3	11	5	.333	.778	.500
Jamie Nelson	4	2	0	0	0	0	1	.500	.500	.500
Graig Nettles	4	2	1	0	0	1	1	.500	.750	.600
Jeff Newman	4	1	0	0	0	1	0	.250	.250	.400
Reid Nichols	4	2	1	0	0	1	0	.500	.750	.600
Joe Nolan	9	1	0	0	0	0	1	.111	.111	.111
Wayne Nordhagen	5	1	0	0	0	0	2	.200	.200	.200
Pete O'Brien	33	9	2	0	1	6	6	.273	.424	.385
Ben Oglivie	39	10	0	0	2	3	5	.256	.410	.326
Al Oliver	9	3	0	0	1	0	1	.333	.667	.333
Jorge Orta	32	7	0	0	0	0	3	.219	.313	.219
Amos Otis	5	3	0	0	0	1	0	.600	.600	.667
Spike Owen	29	4	1	1	0	2	5	.138	.241	.194
Tom Paciorek	15	4	2	0	0	1	2	.267	.400	.294
Mitchell Page	10	2	0	0	0	0	2	.200	.200	.200
Mike Pagliarulo	18	3	0	0	0	0	6	.167	.167	.167
Lance Parrish	23	7	0	0	1	1	6	.304	.435	.320
Larry Parrish	30	5	1	0	1	4	6	.167	.300	.265
Dan Pasqua	15	3	0	0	0	0	5	.200	.200	.200
Jack Perconte	26	7	0	0	0	1	2	.269	.269	.296
Geno Petralli	8	2	1	0	0	0	2	.250	.375	.250
Ken Phelps	15	4	1	0	2	4	3	.267	.733	.400
Tony Phillips	16	8	1	0	0	0	5	.500	.563	.500
Tom Poquette	4	1	0	0	0	2	0	.250	.250	.500
Hosken Powell	8	1	0	0	0	1	3	.125	.125	.222
Jim Presley	23	4	0	0	0	1	9	.174	.174	.240
Greg Pryor	4	1	0	0	0	1	0	.250	.250	.400
Kirby Puckett	19	6	0	0	0	0	2	.316	.316	.316
Pat Putnam	27	10	2	0	0	0	1	.370	.444	.370
Rey Quinones	6	2	0	0	0	0	0	.333	.333	.333
Jamie Quirk	9	1	0	0	0	0	1	.111	.111	.200
Domingo Ramos	9	2	0	0	0	0	2	.222	.222	.222
Willie Randolph	22	8	0	0	0	7	4	.364	.364	.533
Floyd Rayford	12	1	0	0	0	0	4	.083	.083	.083
Randy Ready	7	1	0	1	0	0	3	.143	.429	.143
Jerry Remy	13	2	0	0	0	1	1	.154	.154	.214
Dave Revering	14	4	0	0	1	1	1	.286	.500	.333
Harold Reynolds	4	1	1	0	0	1	0	.250	.500	.400
Jim Rice	32	8	2	0	0	1	5	.250	.313	.273
Mike Richardt	6	2	0	0	0	1	1	.333	.333	.333
Ernest Riles	11	2	0	0	0	1	1	.182	.182	.250
Cal Ripken	36	10	1	0	1	8	9	.278	.389	.400
Mickey Rivers	12	2	1	0	0	1	4	.167	.250	.231
Leon Roberts	5	3	0	0	0	1	1	.600	.600	.571
Billy Jo Robidoux	5	2	1	0	0	0	0	.400	.600	.400
Aurelio Rodriguez	5	1	0	0	0	0	0	.200	.200	.200
Gary Roenicke	6	3	1	0	0	3	2	.500	.667	.667
Ron Roenicke	5	1	0	0	0	1	0	.200	.200	.333
Ed Romero	5	1	1	0	0	1	0	.200	.400	.333
Billy Sample	20	8	4	0	0	2	2	.400	.400	.455
Bill Schroeder	6	3	0	0	1	0	2	.500	1.000	.500
Donnie Scott	5	0	0	0	0	0	5	.000	.000	.000
Larry Sheets	12	2	0	0	0	1	2	.167	.167	.231
John Shelby	24	10	2	0	2	0	6	.417	.750	.417
Pat Sheridan	21	2	0	0	0	1	6	.095	.095	.136
Ruben Sierra	10	4	0	0	0	0	0	.400	.400	.400
Ted Simmons	29	8	1	0	0	3	4	.276	.310	.344
Joe Simpson	13	2	1	0	0	0	3	.154	.231	.154
Ken Singleton	10	2	0	0	0	1	3	.200	.200	.273
Joel Skinner	4	0	0	0	0	2	1	.000	.000	.333
Don Slaught	22	7	1	1	0	0	1	.318	.455	.304
Roy Smalley	20	4	0	1	1	4	2	.200	.450	.333
Lonnie Smith	20	8	3	1	0	2	3	.400	.650	.455
Cory Snyder	8	1	1	0	0	0	3	.125	.250	.125
Jim Spencer	5	2	0	0	0	2	0	.400	.400	.571
Mike Squires	16	3	0	0	1	0	2	.188	.375	.188
Fred Stanley	9	2	0	0	0	0	1	.222	.222	.222
Dave Stapleton	14	3	0	0	2	2	1	.214	.643	.313
Bill Stein	6	0	0	0	0	0	2	.000	.000	.000
Champ Summers	4	2	2	0	0	0	0	.500	1.000	.600
Jim Sundberg	31	4	0	1	0	2	8	.129	.194	.182
Pat Tabler	23	6	3	0	0	3	1	.261	.391	.346
Danny Tartabull	7	2	2	0	0	0	0	.286	.571	.286
Mickey Tettleton	10	1	0	0	0	3	2	.100	.100	.308
Tim Teufel	7	1	0	0	0	0	0	.143	.143	.143
Gorman Thomas	31	5	0	0	2	4	9	.161	.355	.250
Andre Thornton	34	10	1	0	4	7	3	.294	.676	.395
Wayne Tolleson	33	5	0	0	0	2	3	.152	.152	.200
Alan Trammell	37	9	1	0	2	1	10	.243	.432	.263
Willie Upshaw	34	7	1	0	1	4	7	.206	.324	.282
Bobby Van Mitchell	4	0	0	0	0	1	0	.000	.000	.200
Otto Velez	6	2	0	1	0	0	2	.333	.667	.429
George Vukovich	20	6	0	0	0	0	3	.300	.300	.300
Greg Walker	23	6	1	0	2	3	6	.261	.565	.346
Gary Ward	31	8	2	0	0	1	5	.258	.323	.281
Claudell Washington	5	0	0	0	0	0	1	.000	.000	.000
Ron Washington	7	2	1	0	0	0	1	.286	.429	.286
U.L. Washington	15	3	0	0	0	1	3	.200	.200	.250
John Wathan	9	1	0	0	0	1	1	.111	.111	.273
Lou Whitaker	45	13	2	1	2	2	2	.289	.511	.319
Frank White	37	11	2	1	0	0	7	.297	.405	.297
Ernie Whitt	32	6	0	0	2	3	4	.188	.375	.257
Alan Wiggins	14	2	0	0	0	2	1	.143	.143	.250
Curtis Wilkerson	19	3	0	0	0	0	9	.158	.158	.158
Jerry Willard	6	0	0	0	0	0	1	.000	.000	.000
Bump Wills	6	1	0	0	0	0	1	.167	.167	.286
Glenn Wilson	6	1	1	0	0	1	1	.167	.333	.375
Willie Wilson	49	17	4	1	0	0	12	.347	.469	.347
Dave Winfield	21	4	0	1	0	4	7	.190	.286	.308
Al Woods	6	4	0	0	1	1	0	.667	1.167	.714
George Wright	14	2	0	0	0	0	6	.143	.143	.200
Butch Wynegar	10	2	0	0	0	2	3	.200	.200	.333
Carl Yastrzemski	7	0	0	0	0	0	0	.000	.000	.000
Mike Young	26	8	2	0	1	5	4	.308	.500	.419
Robin Yount	35	7	0	0	1	8	5	.200	.286	.341
Richie Zisk	12	2	0	0	0	1	4	.167	.167	.286

VIII
Ballparks

Ballparks

The Ballparks section lists, for all twenty-six ballparks in use in the major leagues, a variety of statistics about the games played there over the past several years.

A ballpark's effect on performance has been a popular topic in recent years. Analysis that used to be limited to, "Gee, Fenway's a tough place for a lefty to pitch," has gotten increasingly sophisticated. Even the simplest conversation about an off-season trade now gets into such factors as the dimensions of a park, whether it has natural or artificial turf, the size of its foul territory, and how far it is above sea level. Our own analysis has led us to note in past editions those ballparks that promote doubles (like the Metrodome) or double plays (like Anaheim Stadium). But until this year we had not included anything systematic about the general effects of a given park.

A full page is devoted to each park. The page begins with a box containing basic statistics for the games played there, as contrasted with that home team's games on the road. The totals listed are the complete statistics *for both teams* in those games. Totals and percentage differences are listed for the 1986 season, and for the five-year period from 1982 through 1986. Since the statistics represent performance by the same players in roughly the same number of games, the differences can be attributed to the peculiarities of the park. The significance or causes of these differences are "why" questions

and are open to debate; the questions we're answering here are "what" and "how many."

The second set of tables highlights the performance of visiting players during the 1986 season. Listed are the top and bottom 10 in batting average, and the leaders in home runs and runs batted in. Qualifying for the batting average lists is based on a minimum of 3.1 plate appearances per game played by each player's team in that park.

The third set of tables lists the leaders in batting average and home run percentage among all visiting players for the past twelve seasons (since 1975). The qualifying level for ranking in batting average is ten or more hits; for home run percentage, three home runs are required. (And no, the leaders at Shea Stadium are not a misprint; Shea was an American League ballpark in 1975 while Yankee Stadium was being renovated.) Players qualify on the basis of hits and home runs rather than plate appearances to include those hitters who did so well over a short span that they would qualify even if they never got another hit in the needed at bats. (To use a Shea Stadium example, Tony Oliva is ranked on the basis of three home runs in twelve at bats. Twelve at bats may seem like a low figure, but even if Oliva went homerless in his next 38 at bats there to bring him to a reasonable qualifier of 50 at bats, his percentage of 6.00 would rank him among the leaders.)

Baltimore
Memorial Stadium

BATTING AVG. (Top 10)   HOME RUNS

	1986 SEASON			1982 – 1986		
	Home Games	Road Games	Pct. Diff.	Home Games	Road Games	Pct. Diff.
G	79	83	− 4.8	404	406	− 0.5
AB	5394	5648	− 4.5	27357	27812	− 1.6
1B	1001	1011	− 1.0	4992	5125	− 2.6
2B	201	261	− 23.0	1117	1292	− 13.5
3B	15	41	− 63.4	88	176	− 50.0
HR	189	157	20.4	839	802	4.6
HR%	3.504	2.780	26.1	3.067	2.884	6.4
R	710	758	− 6.3	3567	3743	− 4.7
BA	.261	.260	0.2	.257	.266	− 3.3
SA	.409	.404	1.0	.396	.412	− 3.7
E	118	129	− 8.5	593	602	− 1.5
SHO	6	13	− 53.8	46	47	− 2.1
R/G	8.987	9.133	− 1.6	8.829	9.219	− 4.2

BATTING AVG. (Top 10)

Phillips, OAK	.769
Harrah, TEX	.474
Kingman, OAK	.467
Boone, CAL	.438
Gibson, DET	.433
Buckner, BOS	.424
Griffin, OAK	.412
Barfield, TOR	.407
Wilson, KC	.407
2 players tied.	.400

HOME RUNS

Evans, BOS	4
Gibson, DET	4
Puckett, MIN	4
Balboni, KC	3
Barfield, TOR	3
Buckner, BOS	3
Smalley, MIN	3
15 players tied.	2

BATTING AVG. (Bottom 10)

Fisk, CHI	.048
Deer, MIL	.063
Thornton, CLE	.067
Pagliarulo, NY	.115
Davis, SEA	.125
Schofield, CAL	.125
McDowell, TEX	.130
Upshaw, TOR	.130
Hill, OAK	.154
Randolph, NY	.158

RUNS BATTED IN

Gibson, DET	12
Evans, BOS	11
Buckner, BOS	9
Balboni, KC	8
Barfield, TOR	8
Rice, BOS	8
O'Brien, TEX	7
10 players tied.	6

Career Visiting Leaders

NAME	AB	H	BA
Bill Buckner	88	38	.432
Von Hayes	34	14	.412
Tony Perez	40	16	.400
Larry Herndon	98	38	.388
Rickey Henderson	180	69	.383
Alex Johnson	43	16	.372
Dave Henderson	78	29	.372
Tim Hulett	35	13	.371
Mike Cubbage	54	20	.370
Jack Perconte	52	19	.365
Larry Hisle	96	35	.365
Bob Molinaro	33	12	.364
Bill Freehan	50	18	.360
Tony Phillips	56	20	.357
Craig Reynolds	28	10	.357
Mel Hall	40	14	.350
Willie Norwood	38	13	.342
Larry Parrish	79	27	.342
Rich Gedman	71	24	.338
Rusty Staub	110	37	.336
Mickey Rivers	179	60	.335
Marty Barrett	81	27	.333
Rod Carew	183	61	.333
Gary Gaetti	102	34	.333
Jerry Hairston	33	11	.333

NAME	AB	HR	HR%
Tony Perez	40	5	12.50
Von Hayes	34	4	11.76
Dave Hostetler	37	4	10.81
Larry Herndon	98	9	9.18
Cliff Johnson	169	13	7.69
Jesse Barfield	93	7	7.53
Tony Armas	188	14	7.45
Dave Lopes	54	4	7.41
Jim Morrison	57	4	7.02
Pat Putnam	43	3	6.98
Steve Balboni	87	6	6.90
George Bell	87	6	6.90
Graig Nettles	175	12	6.86
Kirby Puckett	59	4	6.78
Tom Brunansky	104	7	6.73
Gorman Thomas	164	11	6.71
John Wockenfuss	91	6	6.59
Craig Kusick	47	3	6.38
Larry Parrish	79	5	6.33
Greg Luzinski	81	5	6.17
Gary Ward	114	7	6.14
Wayne Nordhagen	50	3	6.00
George Brett	251	15	5.98
Bill Buckner	88	5	5.68
Wayne Gross	88	5	5.68

Boston
Fenway Park

1986 Visiting Leaders

	BATTING AVG. (Top 10)		HOME RUNS	
Whitaker, DET	.542	Balboni, KC		5
Easler, NY	.478	Kingman, OAK		4
Downing, CAL	.476	Barfield, TOR		3
Brett, KC	.474	Canseco, OAK		3
Mattingly, NY	.469	Carter, CLE		3
Collins, DET	.435	Evans, DET		3
Gaetti, MIN	.435	Parrish, TEX		3
Murray, BAL	.435	14 players tied.		2
Shelby, BAL	.421			
Gagne, MIN	.412			

BATTING AVG. (Bottom 10)		RUNS BATTED IN	
Lombardozzi, MIN	.095	Balboni, KC	10
Gibson, DET	.105	Canseco, OAK	7
Cooper, MIL	.120	Tartabull, SEA	7
Baines, CHI	.130	Young, BAL	7
Phelps, SEA	.133	7 players tied.	6
Bell, TOR	.138		
Jackson, CAL	.143		
White, KC	.160		
Lansford, OAK	.167		
Salazar, KC	.167		

	1986 SEASON			1982 – 1986		
	Home Games	Road Games	Pct. Diff.	Home Games	Road Games	Pct. Diff.
G	81	80	1.2	405	405	0.0
AB	5530	5484	0.8	28253	27857	1.4
1B	1027	999	2.8	5515	5176	6.5
2B	318	249	27.7	1618	1219	32.7
3B	24	29	– 17.2	169	145	16.6
HR	140	171	– 18.1	743	773	– 3.9
HR%	2.532	3.118	– 18.8	2.630	2.775	– 5.2
R	739	751	– 1.6	3947	3602	9.6
BA	.273	.264	3.3	.285	.263	8.5
SA	.415	.414	0.3	.433	.400	8.2
E	128	138	– 7.2	653	628	4.0
SHO	11	6	83.3	40	50	– 20.0
R/G	9.123	9.387	– 2.8	9.746	8.894	9.6

Career Visiting Leaders

NAME	AB	H	BA	NAME	AB	HR	HR%
Mike Easler	23	11	.478	Dave Kingman	76	13	17.11
Kurt Bevacqua	26	12	.462	Gene Tenace	43	6	13.95
Dion James	22	10	.455	Jose Canseco	23	3	13.04
Floyd Rayford	34	15	.441	Eric Soderholm	62	7	11.29
Lou Piniella	105	44	.419	Mitchell Page	93	9	9.68
Fred Stanley	43	18	.419	Johnny Ellis	44	4	9.09
Don Mattingly	102	41	.402	Darnell Coles	35	3	8.57
Johnny Grubb	96	38	.396	Gary Roenicke	85	7	8.24
Mel Hall	36	14	.389	Darrell Evans	63	5	7.94
Roy Howell	160	62	.387	Carlton Fisk	119	9	7.56
Johnny Ellis	44	17	.386	Steve Balboni	94	7	7.45
Mickey Klutts	26	10	.385	Joe Carter	54	4	7.41
Ron Fairly	42	16	.381	Johnny Grubb	96	7	7.29
Ken Griffey	84	32	.381	Gorman Thomas	209	15	7.18
Jim Norris	56	21	.375	Jerry Willard	42	3	7.14
Boog Powell	54	20	.370	Bobby Clark	43	3	6.98
John Castino	84	31	.369	Ron Kittle	87	6	6.90
Tom Paciorek	103	38	.369	Jeff Newman	58	4	6.90
Pete O'Brien	76	28	.368	Hal McRae	222	15	6.76
Roy White	117	43	.368	Gary Gaetti	104	7	6.73
Rod Carew	218	80	.367	Bill Almon	60	4	6.67
Rico Carty	101	37	.366	Alvin Davis	46	3	6.52
Ron Hassey	91	33	.363	George Hendrick	77	5	6.49
Jerry Remy	58	21	.362	Brian Downing	185	12	6.49
Von Joshua	47	17	.362	Jim Presley	62	4	6.45

California
Anaheim Stadium

1986 Visiting Leaders

	1986 SEASON			1982 – 1986		
	Home Games	Road Games	Pct. Diff.	Home Games	Road Games	Pct. Diff.
G	82	80	2.5	404	406	− 0.5
AB	5383	5526	− 2.6	27412	28058	− 2.3
1B	904	987	− 8.4	5002	5195	− 3.7
2B	222	242	− 8.3	1140	1314	− 13.2
3B	27	41	− 34.1	110	214	− 48.6
HR	172	148	16.2	823	708	16.2
HR%	3.195	2.678	19.3	3.002	2.523	19.0
R	706	764	− 7.6	3570	3713	− 3.9
BA	.246	.257	− 4.1	.258	.265	− 2.5
SA	.393	.396	− 0.6	.398	.403	− 1.2
E	127	132	− 3.8	640	646	− 0.9
SHO	14	8	75.0	39	56	− 30.4
R/G	8.610	9.550	− 9.8	8.837	9.145	− 3.4

BATTING AVG. (Top 10)

		HOME RUNS	
Smith, KC	.519	Balboni, KC	3
Bell, TOR	.423	Bell, TOR	3
Easler, NY	.391	Evans, DET	3
Upshaw, TOR	.391	Gedman, BOS	3
Barfield, TOR	.381	Puckett, MIN	3
Yount, MIL	.381	Shelby, BAL	3
Puckett, MIN	.375	Snyder, CLE	3
Hall, CLE	.370	14 players tied.	2
Jacoby, CLE	.360		
5 players tied.	.333		

BATTING AVG. (Bottom 10)

		RUNS BATTED IN	
Bochte, OAK	.053	Cooper, MIL	10
Kingman, OAK	.059	Bell, TOR	8
Presley, SEA	.080	Gedman, BOS	8
Canseco, OAK	.087	Puckett, MIN	8
White, KC	.087	Balboni, KC	7
Incaviglia, TEX	.100	Carter, CLE	7
McDowell, TEX	.105	Hall, CLE	7
Whitt, TOR	.111	Smith, KC	7
Young, BAL	.118	3 players tied.	6
2 players tied.	.143		

Career Visiting Leaders

NAME	AB	H	BA	NAME	AB	HR	HR%
Manny Sanguillen	30	16	.533	Lee Stanton	30	4	13.33
Jose Morales	21	10	.476	Steve Balboni	69	9	13.04
Bobby Grich	40	17	.425	Dave Hostetler	25	3	12.00
Lonnie Smith	50	21	.420	Buddy Biancalana	26	3	11.54
Gary Gray	25	10	.400	Mike Pagliarulo	45	5	11.11
Wade Boggs	103	40	.388	Cory Snyder	29	3	10.34
Joe Rudi	76	29	.382	Tim Hulett	30	3	10.00
Bobby Bonds	63	24	.381	Tony Solaita	30	3	10.00
Phil Garner	66	25	.379	John Shelby	55	5	9.09
Ted Cox	45	17	.378	Jason Thompson	79	7	8.86
Steve Henderson	30	11	.367	Mike Easler	71	6	8.45
Don Mattingly	90	33	.367	Tony Armas	175	14	8.00
Garth Iorg	71	26	.366	Bob Watson	38	3	7.89
Steve Lyons	33	12	.364	Rich Gedman	89	7	7.87
Jim Dwyer	86	31	.360	Gorman Thomas	166	13	7.83
Duane Kuiper	125	45	.360	Gary Ward	118	9	7.63
Dave Lopes	42	15	.357	Larry Parrish	93	7	7.53
Danny Thompson	48	17	.354	Lance Parrish	147	11	7.48
Lance Parrish	147	52	.354	Larry Hisle	97	7	7.22
George Vukovich	54	19	.352	Champ Summers	42	3	7.14
Phil Bradley	49	17	.347	Butch Hobson	85	6	7.06
Vance Law	49	17	.347	John Lowenstein	101	7	6.93
Kirk Gibson	104	36	.346	Tom Brunansky	116	8	6.90
Rick Miller	78	27	.346	Don Mattingly	90	6	6.67
John Shelby	55	19	.345	Darrell Evans	61	4	6.56

Chicago
Comiskey Park

1986 Visiting Leaders

	1986 SEASON			1982 – 1986		
	Home Games	Road Games	Pct. Diff.	Home Games	Road Games	Pct. Diff.
G	81	81	0.0	404	407	− 0.7
AB	5371	5459	− 1.6	27241	27688	− 1.6
1B	955	958	− 0.3	4829	4956	− 2.6
2B	215	222	− 3.2	1206	1256	− 4.0
3B	53	29	82.8	254	169	50.3
HR	114	150	− 24.0	693	725	− 4.4
HR%	2.123	2.748	− 22.8	2.544	2.618	− 2.8
R	676	667	1.3	3632	3528	2.9
BA	.249	.249	− 0.0	.256	.257	− 0.1
SA	.372	.383	− 2.7	.396	.393	0.7
E	104	130	− 20.0	666	644	3.4
SHO	8	13	− 38.5	44	49	− 10.2
R/G	8.346	8.235	1.3	8.990	8.668	3.7

BATTING AVG. (Top 10)

Collins, DET	.500
Franco, CLE	.464
Jacoby, CLE	.462
Yount, MIL	.462
Carter, CLE	.412
Brett, KC	.409
Bell, TOR	.400
Pettis, CAL	.391
Hill, OAK	.385
2 players tied.	.357

HOME RUNS

Baylor, BOS	3
Deer, MIL	3
Pagliarulo, NY	3
Brett, KC	2
Gaetti, MIN	2
Henderson, NY	2
Riles, MIL	2
Ripken, BAL	2
Sierra, TEX	2
41 players tied.	1

BATTING AVG. (Bottom 10)

Fernandez, TOR	.043
Reynolds, SEA	.056
Hrbek, MIN	.059
Balboni, KC	.083
Tabler, CLE	.105
Kingman, OAK	.120
Buckner, BOS	.125
Young, BAL	.125
Sundberg, KC	.154
2 players tied.	.167

RUNS BATTED IN

Carter, CLE	6
Jacoby, CLE	6
Rice, BOS	6
8 players tied.	5

Career Visiting Leaders

NAME	AB	H	BA
Lee Mazzilli	25	12	.480
Rich Chiles	22	10	.455
Carmen Castillo	27	11	.407
Tim Corcoran	33	13	.394
Mickey Stanley	31	12	.387
Jorge Orta	78	30	.385
Mark Salas	29	11	.379
Alan Bannister	69	26	.377
Joe Charboneau	33	12	.364
Tony Perez	33	12	.364
Ted Simmons	75	27	.360
Craig Reynolds	42	15	.357
Larry Milbourne	76	27	.355
Sandy Alomar	34	12	.353
Rodney Craig	34	12	.353
Lou Piniella	128	45	.352
Don Mattingly	83	29	.349
Randy Bush	53	18	.340
Chris Chambliss	106	36	.340
Cal Ripken	112	38	.339
Bob Bailor	71	24	.338
Lyman Bostock	101	34	.337
Brook Jacoby	66	22	.333
Sixto Lezcano	105	35	.333
Greg Pryor	33	11	.333

NAME	AB	HR	HR%
Rob Deer	19	3	15.79
Bobby Darwin	22	3	13.64
Bill Schroeder	30	4	13.33
Dave Duncan	24	3	12.50
Mike Pagliarulo	40	4	10.00
Steve Brye	46	4	8.70
Darrell Evans	38	3	7.89
Rich Gedman	65	5	7.69
George Bell	90	6	6.67
Eddie Murray	181	12	6.63
Carlton Fisk	91	6	6.59
Cal Ripken	112	7	6.25
Ben Oglivie	163	10	6.13
Gary Roenicke	99	6	6.06
Ron Hassey	67	4	5.97
Tom Brunansky	105	6	5.71
Randy Bush	53	3	5.66
Tony Armas	178	10	5.62
Kirk Gibson	89	5	5.62
Gary Allenson	54	3	5.56
Wayne Gross	133	7	5.26
Cliff Johnson	114	6	5.26
Tom Paciorek	57	3	5.26
Bobby Bonds	116	6	5.17
Willie Horton	120	6	5.00

Cleveland
Cleveland Stadium

1986 Visiting Leaders

	1986 SEASON			1982 – 1986		
	Home Games	Road Games	Pct. Diff.	Home Games	Road Games	Pct. Diff.
G	81	82	− 1.2	405	407	− 0.5
AB	5625	5739	− 2.0	27910	27995	− 0.3
1B	1147	1100	4.3	5616	5273	6.5
2B	246	286	− 14.0	1243	1285	− 3.3
3B	34	31	9.7	152	203	− 25.1
HR	160	164	− 2.4	658	653	0.8
HR%	2.844	2.858	− 0.5	2.358	2.333	1.1
R	818	854	− 4.2	3897	3812	2.2
BA	.282	.275	2.4	.275	.265	3.8
SA	.423	.422	0.3	.401	.395	1.4
E	147	164	− 10.4	694	718	− 3.3
SHO	6	5	20.0	39	41	− 4.9
R/G	10.099	10.415	− 3.0	9.622	9.366	2.7

BATTING AVG. (Top 10)

Gaetti, MIN	.571
Bochte, OAK	.500
Hrbek, MIN	.444
Murray, BAL	.440
Sveum, MIL	.435
O'Brien, TEX	.421
Fletcher, TEX	.417
Trammell, DET	.414
Fernandez, TOR	.407
DeCinces, CAL	.389

HOME RUNS

Armas, BOS	3
Baylor, BOS	3
Molitor, MIL	3
Trammell, DET	3
11 players tied.	2

BATTING AVG. (Bottom 10)

C. Johnson, TOR	.000
Grich, CAL	.071
Lynn, BAL	.095
Downing, CAL	.125
Smith, KC	.130
Coles, DET	.143
Presley, SEA	.150
Davis, OAK	.158
3 players tied.	.167

RUNS BATTED IN

Rice, BOS	10
Bell, TOR	9
Buckner, BOS	9
Baylor, BOS	8
Armas, BOS	7
Canseco, OAK	7
Trammell, DET	7
7 players tied.	6

Career Visiting Leaders

NAME	AB	H	BA
Bill Sharp	27	13	.481
Champ Summers	39	17	.436
Dale Sveum	23	10	.435
Tim Corcoran	33	14	.424
Jackie Gutierrez	44	18	.409
Dave Lopes	37	15	.405
Rod Carew	195	78	.400
Tony Fernandez	71	28	.394
Jesse Barfield	68	26	.382
Dave Bergman	29	11	.379
Thurman Munson	143	54	.378
Alan Bannister	53	20	.377
Mike Hargrove	83	31	.373
Kirby Puckett	78	29	.372
Kent Hrbek	108	40	.370
Eddie Murray	233	86	.369
Willie Aikens	95	35	.368
Joe Simpson	70	25	.357
Dave Winfield	140	50	.357
Jack Perconte	34	12	.353
Carney Lansford	174	61	.351
Al Oliver	86	30	.349
Barry Bonnell	84	29	.345
Jose Canseco	29	10	.345
Wade Boggs	122	42	.344

NAME	AB	HR	HR%
Doug Ault	24	5	20.83
Larry Sheets	30	4	13.33
Ron Kittle	62	7	11.29
Mike Young	36	4	11.11
Champ Summers	39	4	10.26
Bobby Bonds	89	9	10.11
Ken Phelps	31	3	9.68
Bill Melton	35	3	8.57
Dave Winfield	140	12	8.57
Billy E. Smith	47	4	8.51
Steve Balboni	84	7	8.33
Billy Williams	39	3	7.69
Sixto Lezcano	110	8	7.27
Otto Velez	72	5	6.94
George Bell	96	6	6.25
Mike Pagliarulo	49	3	6.12
Jim Presley	49	3	6.12
Jeff Burroughs	116	7	6.03
Gary Roenicke	83	5	6.02
Dave Kingman	50	3	6.00
Gorman Thomas	153	9	5.88
Ernie Whitt	103	6	5.83
Ben Oglivie	230	13	5.65
Kent Hrbek	108	6	5.56
Don Baylor	278	15	5.40

Detroit
Tiger Stadium

1986 Visiting Leaders

BATTING AVG. (Top 10)

		HOME RUNS	
Boggs, BOS	.452	Baines, CHI	4
Tabler, CLE	.429	Barfield, TOR	4
Gedman, BOS	.409	Kittle, NY	4
Mattingly, NY	.400	Mattingly, NY	4
Fisk, CHI	.385	Baylor, BOS	3
Fletcher, TEX	.381	Gedman, BOS	3
Schofield, CAL	.375	12 players tied.	2
Baines, CHI	.370		
Jacoby, CLE	.364		
2 players tied.	.348		

		1986 SEASON				1982 – 1986	
	Home Games	Road Games	Pct. Diff.	Home Games	Road Games	Pct. Diff.
G	81	81	0.0	406	403	0.7
AB	5476	5511	– 0.6	27575	27700	– 0.5
1B	910	977	– 6.9	4726	4927	– 4.1
2B	224	268	– 16.4	1067	1332	– 19.9
3B	27	34	– 20.6	177	197	– 10.2
HR	179	202	– 11.4	912	804	13.4
HR%	3.269	3.665	– 10.8	3.307	2.903	13.9
R	713	799	– 10.8	3565	3718	– 4.1
BA	.245	.269	– 8.9	.250	.262	– 4.8
SA	.394	.440	– 10.5	.400	.411	– 2.7
E	132	103	28.2	622	632	– 1.6
SHO	11	6	83.3	46	33	39.4
R/G	8.802	9.864	– 10.8	8.781	9.226	– 4.8

BATTING AVG. (Bottom 10)

		RUNS BATTED IN	
Smalley, MIN	.000	Barfield, TOR	9
Yount, MIL	.042	Kittle, NY	9
Shelby, BAL	.050	Fernandez, TOR	8
Ripken, BAL	.091	Baines, CHI	7
Tolleson, NY	.111	Gedman, BOS	7
Ward, TEX	.111	Rice, BOS	7
Presley, SEA	.125	Boggs, BOS	6
Gantner, MIL	.130	Joyner, CAL	6
Parrish, TEX	.136	Mattingly, NY	6
Reynolds, SEA	.136	Slaught, TEX	6

Career Visiting Leaders

NAME	AB	H	BA
Gil Flores	24	10	.417
Lonnie Smith	30	12	.400
Rico Petrocelli	38	15	.395
Thurman Munson	122	47	.385
Onix Concepcion	39	15	.385
Joe Nolan	26	10	.385
Tony Perez	34	13	.382
Tom Grieve	37	14	.378
Wade Boggs	125	47	.376
Steve Henderson	32	12	.375
Alvin Davis	58	21	.362
Jim Morrison	36	13	.361
Butch Hobson	139	50	.360
Kiko Garcia	56	20	.357
Bob Randall	45	16	.356
Wayne Nordhagen	37	13	.351
Tom Poquette	40	14	.350
Lyman Bostock	83	29	.349
Willie Horton	84	29	.345
Larry Harlow	64	22	.344
Dave Revering	79	27	.342
Eric Soderholm	106	36	.340
Richie Zisk	124	42	.339
Sandy Alomar	33	11	.333
Bobby Bonds	93	31	.333

NAME	AB	HR	HR%
Kelvin Moore	11	3	27.27
Ron Kittle	41	8	19.51
Steve Brye	22	4	18.18
Elrod Hendricks	25	3	12.00
Tom Grieve	37	4	10.81
Eric Soderholm	106	11	10.38
Bobby Bonds	93	9	9.68
Gene Tenace	31	3	9.68
Floyd Rayford	43	4	9.30
Tony Solaita	46	4	8.70
Jim Morrison	36	3	8.33
Steve Balboni	62	5	8.06
Kent Hrbek	88	7	7.95
Willie Aikens	114	9	7.89
Doug DeCinces	226	17	7.52
Don Mattingly	82	6	7.32
Gorman Thomas	196	14	7.14
Dwight Evans	242	17	7.02
Otto Velez	58	4	6.90
Lenn Sakata	44	3	6.82
Glenn Adams	74	5	6.76
Ernie Whitt	139	9	6.47
Eddie Murray	263	17	6.46
Dave Revering	79	5	6.33
Cal Ripken	127	8	6.30

Kansas City
Royals Stadium

1986 Visiting Leaders

BATTING AVG. (Top 10)		HOME RUNS	
Carter, CLE	.435	Bell, TOR	2
Davis, SEA	.417	Deer, MIL	2
Davis, OAK	.393	Hrbek, MIN	2
Mattingly, NY	.385	Lansford, OAK	2
Evans, BOS	.381	38 players tied.	1
Reynolds, SEA	.379		
Upshaw, TOR	.364		
Gedman, BOS	.350		
Guillen, CHI	.346		
Moses, SEA	.345		

BATTING AVG. (Bottom 10)		RUNS BATTED IN	
Tabler, CLE	.053	Davis, SEA	7
Evans, DET	.063	Armas, BOS	6
Incaviglia, TEX	.100	Fletcher, TEX	6
Hassey, CHI	.118	Mattingly, NY	6
Parrish, DET	.130	Phelps, SEA	6
Gaetti, MIN	.136	Presley, SEA	6
Rayford, BAL	.143	5 players tied.	5
Shelby, BAL	.143		
Franco, CLE	.150		
Buckner, BOS	.160		

	1986 SEASON			1982 – 1986		
	Home Games	Road Games	Pct. Diff.	Home Games	Road Games	Pct. Diff.
G	81	81	0.0	407	404	0.7
AB	5592	5446	2.7	28013	27518	1.8
1B	1006	961	4.7	5181	5090	1.8
2B	278	223	24.7	1373	1219	12.6
3B	55	35	57.1	284	190	49.5
HR	106	152	– 30.3	564	741	– 23.9
HR%	1.896	2.791	– 32.1	2.013	2.693	– 25.2
R	659	668	– 1.3	3502	3474	0.8
BA	.258	.252	2.6	.264	.263	0.4
SA	.385	.389	– 1.2	.394	.402	– 2.0
E	131	112	17.0	668	619	7.9
SHO	14	11	27.3	55	46	19.6
R/G	8.136	8.247	– 1.3	8.604	8.599	0.1

Career Visiting Leaders

NAME	AB	H	BA	NAME	AB	HR	HR%
Steve Buechele	26	12	.462	Bill Nahorodny	23	4	17.39
Bombo Rivera	28	12	.429	Johnny Ellis	29	3	10.34
Randy Ready	26	10	.385	Pat Putnam	58	5	8.62
Tim Hulett	34	13	.382	George Bell	78	6	7.69
Paul Householder	32	12	.375	Gary Roenicke	96	7	7.29
John Moses	48	18	.375	Willie Horton	110	7	6.36
Greg Walker	56	21	.375	Darrell Evans	49	3	6.12
Bob Bailor	70	26	.371	Don Baylor	254	15	5.91
Harold Reynolds	38	14	.368	Dwayne Murphy	138	8	5.80
Bill Schroeder	38	14	.368	Reggie Jackson	191	11	5.76
Ken Henderson	33	12	.364	Kirk Gibson	88	5	5.68
Gary Ward	143	52	.364	Don Money	143	8	5.59
Mark Brouhard	36	13	.361	Al Oliver	92	5	5.43
Chris Chambliss	106	38	.358	Dave Winfield	130	7	5.38
Jose Morales	31	11	.355	Lee May	113	6	5.31
Glenn Wilson	34	12	.353	Gorman Thomas	170	9	5.29
John Mayberry	88	31	.352	Greg Luzinski	76	4	5.26
Wade Boggs	101	35	.347	Bobby Bonds	116	6	5.17
Willie Aikens	29	10	.345	Craig Kusick	58	3	5.17
Reid Nichols	38	13	.342	Harold Baines	137	7	5.11
Leon Roberts	97	33	.340	Tony Armas	200	10	5.00
Jim Presley	50	17	.340	Cal Ripken	123	6	4.88
Alan Trammell	167	56	.335	Joe Rudi	144	7	4.86
Brett Butler	69	23	.333	Steve Henderson	63	3	4.76
Rod Carew	210	70	.333	John Wockenfuss	84	4	4.76

Milwaukee County Stadium

1986 Visiting Leaders

BATTING AVG. (Top 10)		HOME RUNS	
Boggs, BOS	.526	Baker, OAK	3
Iorg, TOR	.500	Balboni, KC	3
O'Brien, TEX	.500	Buechele, TEX	3
Gagne, MIN	.476	Carter, CLE	3
Fletcher, TEX	.450	Jacoby, CLE	3
Franco, CLE	.429	Joyner, CAL	3
Hassey, CHI	.421	O'Brien, TEX	3
Balboni, KC	.409	Snyder, CLE	3
Carter, CLE	.394	10 players tied.	2
Buechele, TEX	.389		

BATTING AVG. (Bottom 10)		RUNS BATTED IN	
Sundberg, KC	.071	O'Brien, TEX	11
Buckner, BOS	.105	Carter, CLE	10
Baylor, BOS	.111	Snyder, CLE	10
Cangelosi, CHI	.125	Joyner, CAL	9
Davis, OAK	.150	Allanson, CLE	8
Murphy, OAK	.167	Buechele, TEX	7
Pettis, CAL	.167	Murray, BAL	7
Smith, KC	.174	Tartabull, SEA	7
White, KC	.182	9 players tied.	6
Young, BAL	.185		

	1986 SEASON			1982 – 1986		
	Home Games	Road Games	Pct. Diff.	Home Games	Road Games	Pct. Diff.
G	80	81	− 1.2	404	404	0.0
AB	5505	5492	0.2	27729	28075	− 1.2
1B	1007	1020	− 1.3	5222	5439	− 4.0
2B	241	254	− 5.1	1235	1298	− 4.9
3B	35	29	20.7	203	184	10.3
HR	142	143	− 0.7	662	765	− 13.5
HR%	2.579	2.604	− 0.9	2.387	2.725	− 12.4
R	713	688	3.6	3538	3810	− 7.1
BA	.259	.263	− 1.7	.264	.274	− 3.5
SA	.393	.398	− 1.4	.395	.415	− 4.8
E	139	129	7.8	658	668	− 1.5
SHO	11	7	57.1	45	26	73.1
R/G	8.913	8.494	4.9	8.757	9.431	− 7.1

Career Visiting Leaders

NAME	AB	H	BA	NAME	AB	HR	HR%
John Moses	16	10	.625	Cory Snyder	20	3	15.00
Larry Hisle	48	24	.500	Steve Buechele	24	3	12.50
Greg Gagne	25	11	.440	Joe Carter	67	8	11.94
Carlos May	46	20	.435	Dusty Baker	29	3	10.34
Lynn Jones	36	15	.417	Dave Hostetler	29	3	10.34
Vada Pinson	24	10	.417	Wally Joyner	29	3	10.34
Lyman Bostock	56	23	.411	Gene Tenace	39	4	10.26
H. Pat Kelly	73	29	.397	Gorman Thomas	59	6	10.17
Jim Morrison	41	16	.390	Jim Spencer	76	7	9.21
Denny Doyle	59	23	.390	Oddibe McDowell	33	3	9.09
Joe Carter	67	26	.388	Andre Thornton	172	15	8.72
Jamie Quirk	31	12	.387	Darryl Motley	47	4	8.51
Paul Dade	65	25	.385	Bob Watson	48	4	8.33
Andre Robertson	34	13	.382	Willie Aikens	88	7	7.95
Cecil Cooper	58	22	.379	Reggie Jackson	247	19	7.69
Wally Joyner	29	11	.379	Alvin Davis	53	4	7.55
Ron Pruitt	52	19	.365	Brook Jacoby	67	5	7.46
Steve Henderson	36	13	.361	Billy Williams	42	3	7.14
Rudy Law	84	30	.357	Cecil Cooper	58	4	6.90
Steve Balboni	79	28	.354	Dwayne Murphy	149	10	6.71
Phil Bradley	54	19	.352	Steve Balboni	79	5	6.33
Tom Poquette	37	13	.351	Jason Thompson	112	7	6.25
Mario Guerrero	60	21	.350	Don Slaught	70	4	5.71
Jesse Barfield	78	27	.346	Gary Gaetti	108	6	5.56
Billy Sample	87	30	.345	Pete O'Brien	90	5	5.56

Minnesota
Metrodome

1986 Visiting Leaders

BATTING AVG. (Top 10)   HOME RUNS

White, KC	.565	Lynn, BAL	4
Ripken, BAL	.545	Parrish, DET	4
Boggs, BOS	.542	Carter, CLE	3
Henderson, NY	.524	Deer, MIL	3
Parrish, DET	.500	Kittle, NY	3
Rice, BOS	.480	24 players tied.	2
Whitt, TOR	.474		
P. Bradley, SEA	.462		
Joyner, CAL	.450		
Cangelosi, CHI	.429		

BATTING AVG. (Bottom 10)   RUNS BATTED IN

Young, BAL	.056	Carter, CLE	12
Tettleton, OAK	.071	Lynn, BAL	8
Wynegar, NY	.118	Parrish, DET	8
Gedman, BOS	.150	Ripken, BAL	8
Upshaw, TOR	.158	Henderson, NY	7
Canseco, OAK	.167	Moseby, TOR	7
Henderson, BOS	.167	O'Brien, TEX	7
Phillips, OAK	.174	Tartabull, SEA	7
Presley, SEA	.182	3 players tied.	6
2 players tied.	.190		

	1986 SEASON			1982 – 1986		
	Home Games	Road Games	Pct. Diff.	Home Games	Road Games	Pct. Diff.
G	81	81	0.0	408	402	1.5
AB	5746	5404	6.3	28286	27145	4.2
1B	1029	962	7.0	5116	4954	3.3
2B	316	251	25.9	1502	1174	27.9
3B	45	26	73.1	239	162	47.5
HR	223	173	28.9	855	779	9.8
HR%	3.881	3.201	21.2	3.023	2.870	5.3
R	865	715	21.0	3942	3480	13.3
BA	.281	.261	7.4	.273	.260	4.7
SA	.468	.413	13.2	.433	.402	7.9
E	125	116	7.8	588	579	1.6
SHO	7	10	– 30.0	34	54	– 37.0
R/G	10.679	8.827	21.0	9.662	8.657	11.6

Career Visiting Leaders

NAME	AB	H	BA
Andre Robertson	29	15	.517
John Cangelosi	28	12	.429
Donnie Hill	47	19	.404
Gary Roenicke	48	19	.396
Rick Leach	38	15	.395
Jim Gantner	112	44	.393
Cal Ripken	125	49	.392
Tony Armas	122	47	.385
Ken Griffey	82	31	.378
Tim Foli	53	20	.377
Wade Boggs	110	41	.373
Amos Otis	43	16	.372
Chet Lemon	108	40	.370
Phil Bradley	68	25	.368
Jim Rice	123	45	.366
Robin Yount	93	34	.366
Tom Paciorek	63	23	.365
Willie Wilson	143	52	.364
Bill Buckner	69	25	.362
Lou Whitaker	115	41	.357
Jim Dwyer	31	11	.355
Dave Lopes	51	18	.353
Cliff Johnson	54	19	.352
George Vukovich	40	14	.350
Johnny Grubb	29	10	.345

NAME	AB	HR	HR%
Rob Deer	17	3	17.65
Oscar Gamble	37	6	16.22
Don Money	21	3	14.29
Darrell Evans	68	8	11.76
Daryl Boston	26	3	11.54
Ron Kittle	89	10	11.24
John Lowenstein	38	4	10.53
Willie Aikens	46	4	8.70
Graig Nettles	35	3	8.57
Lance Parrish	105	9	8.57
Wayne Gross	59	5	8.47
Tony Armas	122	10	8.20
Jim Rice	123	10	8.13
Greg Walker	88	7	7.95
Don Baylor	104	8	7.69
Eddie Murray	120	9	7.50
George Vukovich	40	3	7.50
Ben Oglivie	96	7	7.29
Roy Smalley	55	4	7.27
Bob Kearney	57	4	7.02
Jeff Burroughs	43	3	6.98
Amos Otis	43	3	6.98
Harold Baines	103	7	6.80
Mike Pagliarulo	46	3	6.52
Reggie Jackson	93	6	6.45

New York
Yankee Stadium

1986 Visiting Leaders

BATTING AVG. (Top 10)

Tabler, CLE	.542
Grich, CAL	.529
Armas, BOS	.524
Laudner, MIN	.471
Fletcher, TEX	.440
Puckett, MIN	.429
Young, BAL	.421
Balboni, KC	.400
Schofield, CAL	.381
Baylor, BOS	.375

HOME RUNS

Barfield, TOR	4
Buckner, BOS	4
Evans, DET	3
Gaetti, MIN	3
Lacy, BAL	3
Lansford, OAK	3
Puckett, MIN	3
16 players tied.	2

BATTING AVG. (Bottom 10)

Kingman, OAK	.083
Salazar, KC	.100
Smalley, MIN	.118
Jackson, CAL	.125
Murray, BAL	.125
Evans, BOS	.136
Deer, MIL	.143
Smith, KC	.160
Franco, CLE	.161
Gedman, BOS	.167

RUNS BATTED IN

Barfield, TOR	10
Rice, BOS	10
Buckner, BOS	9
Shelby, BAL	9
Moseby, TOR	7
Motley, KC	7
Puckett, MIN	7
8 players tied.	6

	1986 SEASON			1982 – 1986		
	Home Games	Road Games	Pct. Diff.	Home Games	Road Games	Pct. Diff.
G	80	82	− 2.4	403	406	− 0.7
AB	5501	5633	− 2.3	27594	28053	− 1.6
1B	1032	1020	1.2	5142	5168	− 0.5
2B	245	255	− 3.9	1185	1361	− 12.9
3B	26	32	− 18.7	195	181	7.7
HR	189	174	8.6	709	780	− 9.1
HR%	3.436	3.089	11.2	2.569	2.780	− 7.6
R	780	755	3.3	3548	3821	− 7.1
BA	.271	.263	3.2	.262	.267	− 1.9
SA	.428	.412	3.9	.396	.412	− 3.8
E	123	123	0.0	642	670	− 4.2
SHO	7	10	− 30.0	56	40	40.0
R/G	9.750	9.207	5.9	8.804	9.411	− 6.5

Career Visiting Leaders

NAME	AB	H	BA
Bob Stinson	29	13	.448
Larry Herndon	107	43	.402
Oscar Gamble	30	12	.400
Barbaro Garbey	34	13	.382
Pat Tabler	78	29	.372
Gene Clines	27	10	.370
Bo Diaz	38	14	.368
Jose Morales	38	14	.368
Rickey Henderson	107	39	.364
Ron Fairly	33	12	.364
Ron Hassey	66	24	.364
Brett Butler	72	26	.361
Phil Mankowski	34	12	.353
Glenn Adams	43	15	.349
Willie Aikens	95	33	.347
Rudy Law	58	20	.345
Otto Velez	64	22	.344
Damaso Garcia	131	45	.344
Ernie Whitt	73	25	.342
Pete LaCock	44	15	.341
Phil Bradley	53	18	.340
Jim Rice	253	85	.336
Bob Kearney	51	17	.333
Pete Mackanin	33	11	.333
Mark Wagner	30	10	.333

NAME	AB	HR	HR%
Ron Fairly	33	4	12.12
Oscar Gamble	30	3	10.00
Wayne Gross	81	7	8.64
Jim Rice	253	21	8.30
Lee Lacy	37	3	8.11
John Mayberry	112	9	8.04
Jim Spencer	39	3	7.69
Darrell Evans	53	4	7.55
Ben Oglivie	175	12	6.86
Darrell Porter	107	7	6.54
Eric Soderholm	46	3	6.52
Jim Dwyer	47	3	6.38
Dave Hostetler	47	3	6.38
Kirk Gibson	95	6	6.32
Richie Zisk	115	7	6.09
Ron Kittle	67	4	5.97
George Brett	203	12	5.91
Larry Parrish	103	6	5.83
Carl Yastrzemski	159	9	5.66
Greg Walker	71	4	5.63
Jeff Newman	73	4	5.48
Don Slaught	55	3	5.45
Jeff Burroughs	76	4	5.26
Jesse Barfield	100	5	5.00
Bill Buckner	81	4	4.94

Oakland
Oakland-Alameda County Coliseum

1986 Visiting Leaders

	1986 SEASON			1982 – 1986		
	Home Games	Road Games	Pct. Diff.	Home Games	Road Games	Pct. Diff.
G	83	79	5.1	405	405	0.0
AB	5533	5309	4.2	27615	27623	− 0.0
1B	965	912	5.8	5031	4996	0.7
2B	183	253	− 27.7	1046	1330	− 21.4
3B	21	41	− 48.8	130	216	− 39.8
HR	156	173	− 9.8	710	841	− 15.6
HR%	2.819	3.259	− 13.5	2.571	3.045	− 15.6
R	712	779	− 8.6	3548	4021	− 11.8
BA	.239	.260	− 7.8	.250	.267	− 6.3
SA	.365	.421	− 13.3	.375	.422	− 11.2
E	136	139	− 2.2	726	701	3.6
SHO	11	3	266.7	47	24	95.8
R/G	8.578	9.861	− 13.0	8.760	9.928	− 11.8

BATTING AVG. (Top 10)

O'Brien, TEX	.450
Hrbek, MIN	.393
Gantner, MIL	.391
Hall, CLE	.381
Franco, CLE	.375
Joyner, CAL	.367
Butler, CLE	.364
Whitaker, DET	.350
5 players tied.	.348

HOME RUNS

Gibson, DET	3
Parrish, DET	3
Parrish, TEX	3
Sheets, BAL	3
Winfield, NY	3
13 players tied.	2

BATTING AVG. (Bottom 10)

Cangelosi, CHI	.000
Jones, CAL	.043
Hulett, CHI	.050
Deer, MIL	.063
Buckner, BOS	.074
Barfield, TOR	.091
Trammell, DET	.091
Buechele, TEX	.095
Tartabull, SEA	.105
Smith, KC	.111

RUNS BATTED IN

DeCinces, CAL	9
Downing, CAL	8
Winfield, NY	8
Gibson, DET	7
Incaviglia, TEX	7
6 players tied.	6

Career Visiting Leaders

NAME	AB	H	BA
Pat Sheridan	41	19	.463
Steve Brye	43	18	.419
Bernie Carbo	39	16	.410
Gene Clines	27	11	.407
Don Mattingly	86	35	.407
Bake McBride	28	11	.393
Ivan Calderon	26	10	.385
Phil Mankowski	26	10	.385
Bob Molinaro	29	11	.379
Lynn Jones	38	14	.368
Glenn Adams	68	25	.368
Wally Joyner	30	11	.367
Mel Hall	33	12	.364
Jim Essian	48	17	.354
Jerry Hairston	66	23	.348
Carney Lansford	115	40	.348
Brett Butler	72	25	.347
Vance Law	49	17	.347
Jim Gantner	179	62	.346
Jack Brohamer	55	19	.345
John Shelby	67	23	.343
Johnny Ellis	53	18	.340
U.L. Washington	112	38	.339
H. Pat Kelly	71	24	.338
Hank Aaron	30	10	.333

NAME	AB	HR	HR%
George Hendrick	50	6	12.00
Mike Pagliarulo	29	3	10.34
Larry Parrish	100	10	10.00
Ken Phelps	41	4	9.76
Dick Davis	31	3	9.68
Oscar Gamble	99	9	9.09
Mel Hall	33	3	9.09
Andre Thornton	132	11	8.33
Larry Sheets	37	3	8.11
Greg Walker	74	6	8.11
Tony Armas	62	5	8.06
Mark Brouhard	40	3	7.50
Jim Presley	44	3	6.82
Rusty Torres	44	3	6.82
Carlton Fisk	182	12	6.59
Ron Kittle	91	6	6.59
Cliff Johnson	77	5	6.49
Lance Parrish	139	9	6.47
Gorman Thomas	188	12	6.38
Reggie Jackson	206	13	6.31
Darrell Evans	65	4	6.15
Gary Roenicke	101	6	5.94
Richie Zisk	118	7	5.93
Rance Mulliniks	102	6	5.88
Eddie Murray	208	12	5.77

Seattle Kingdome

1986 Visiting Leaders

BATTING AVG. (Top 10)		HOME RUNS	
Trammell, DET	.476	Kingman, OAK	6
Hall, CLE	.471	Barfield, TOR	5
Boggs, BOS	.464	Henderson, NY	4
Paciorek, TEX	.462	Mattingly, NY	4
Guillen, CHI	.455	Puckett, MIN	3
McDowell, TEX	.455	Trammell, DET	3
Pasqua, NY	.450	14 players tied.	2
Fernandez, TOR	.440		
Phillips, OAK	.440		
Griffin, OAK	.435		

BATTING AVG. (Bottom 10)		RUNS BATTED IN	
Randolph, NY	.045	Kingman, OAK	14
Downing, CAL	.143	Barfield, TOR	10
Easler, NY	.143	Canseco, OAK	9
Collins, DET	.150	Fisk, CHI	9
Lansford, OAK	.158	Snyder, CLE	9
Riles, MIL	.158	Evans, BOS	7
Sheets, BAL	.167	Mattingly, NY	7
Hrbek, MIN	.172	Murphy, OAK	7
Joyner, CAL	.174	5 players tied.	6
Smalley, MIN	.174		

	1986 SEASON			1982 – 1986		
	Home Games	Road Games	Pct. Diff.	Home Games	Road Games	Pct. Diff.
G	82	80	2.5	408	402	1.5
AB	5703	5421	5.2	27979	27221	2.8
1B	1000	1034	− 3.3	4995	4951	0.9
2B	300	236	27.1	1343	1246	7.8
3B	44	39	12.8	170	186	− 8.6
HR	196	133	47.4	842	638	32.0
HR%	3.437	2.453	40.1	3.009	2.344	28.4
R	837	716	16.9	3731	3476	7.3
BA	.270	.266	1.5	.263	.258	1.8
SA	.441	.398	11.0	.413	.388	6.6
E	138	130	6.2	634	679	− 6.6
SHO	9	9	0.0	36	52	− 30.8
R/G	10.207	8.950	14.0	9.145	8.647	5.8

Career Visiting Leaders

NAME	AB	H	BA
Joe Charboneau	32	14	.438
Paul Dade	40	17	.425
Jerry Hairston	40	17	.425
Mike Cubbage	58	24	.414
Dan Pasqua	29	12	.414
Ron Washington	36	14	.389
Oddibe McDowell	31	12	.387
Tony Fernandez	57	22	.386
Don Mattingly	86	33	.384
Jack Brohamer	37	14	.378
Carmen Castillo	40	15	.375
Rod Carew	223	83	.372
Bombo Rivera	35	13	.371
Lyman Bostock	54	20	.370
Willie Horton	27	10	.370
Rick Leach	30	11	.367
Dave Revering	82	30	.366
Enos Cabell	33	12	.364
Roy Howell	105	38	.362
Ken Singleton	136	49	.360
Al Bumbry	131	47	.359
Tony Phillips	54	19	.352
Tom Paciorek	91	32	.352
Dave Winfield	131	46	.351
Jim Dwyer	40	14	.350

NAME	AB	HR	HR%
Mickey Klutts	17	3	17.65
George Hendrick	18	3	16.67
Joe Charboneau	32	5	15.62
Dave Kingman	79	12	15.19
Bill Schroeder	20	3	15.00
Carmen Castillo	40	5	12.50
George Scott	49	6	12.24
Dave W. Roberts	25	3	12.00
Bob Molinaro	35	4	11.43
Dave Revering	82	9	10.98
Joe Wallis	28	3	10.71
Dan Pasqua	29	3	10.34
Bob Watson	29	3	10.34
Ken Singleton	136	14	10.29
Joe Rudi	81	8	9.88
Jose Morales	41	4	9.76
Willie Aikens	105	10	9.52
John Mayberry	115	10	8.70
Benny Ayala	35	3	8.57
Don Mattingly	86	7	8.14
Reid Nichols	50	4	8.00
John Lowenstein	76	6	7.89
Aurelio Rodriguez	64	5	7.81
Dave Winfield	131	10	7.63
Reggie Jackson	178	13	7.30

Texas
Arlington Stadium

1986 Visiting Leaders

	1986 SEASON			1982 – 1986		
	Home Games	Road Games	Pct. Diff.	Home Games	Road Games	Pct. Diff.
G	81	81	0.0	403	406	− 0.7
AB	5457	5527	− 1.3	27562	27533	0.1
1B	989	958	3.2	5194	4970	4.5
2B	234	266	− 12.0	1209	1220	− 0.9
3B	29	30	− 3.3	158	201	− 21.4
HR	148	181	− 18.2	638	707	− 9.8
HR%	2.712	3.275	− 17.2	2.315	2.568	− 9.9
R	717	797	− 10.0	3402	3471	− 2.0
BA	.257	.260	− 1.2	.261	.258	1.3
SA	.391	.417	− 6.1	.386	.394	− 2.0
E	118	120	− 1.7	613	602	1.8
SHO	4	8	− 50.0	42	48	− 12.5
R/G	8.852	9.840	− 10.0	8.442	8.549	− 1.3

BATTING AVG. (Top 10)

Bell, TOR	.500
Yount, MIL	.458
Molitor, MIL	.409
Barfield, TOR	.375
Tartabull, SEA	.375
Buckner, BOS	.360
Lacy, BAL	.360
Joyner, CAL	.355
Guillen, CHI	.353
Gaetti, MIN	.350

HOME RUNS

Presley, SEA	4
Baylor, BOS	3
Parrish, DET	3
White, KC	3
Beniquez, BAL	2
Braggs, MIL	2
Canseco, OAK	2
DeCinces, CAL	2
Kingman, OAK	2
38 players tied.	1

BATTING AVG. (Bottom 10)

Thornton, CLE	.000
Owen, BOS	.083
Henderson, NY	.087
Brunansky, MIN	.091
Dempsey, BAL	.118
Balboni, KC	.130
Puckett, MIN	.130
Riles, MIL	.130
Phelps, SEA	.143
2 players tied.	.150

RUNS BATTED IN

Presley, SEA	9
Molitor, MIL	8
Bell, TOR	7
Cooper, MIL	7
Joyner, CAL	7
Parrish, DET	7
Baylor, BOS	6
Fernandez, TOR	6
Franco, CLE	6
Hall, CLE	6

Career Visiting Leaders

NAME	AB	H	BA
Elliott Maddox	18	10	.556
Andy Etchebarren	26	10	.385
Danny Tartabull	26	10	.385
George Vukovich	45	17	.378
Bob Watson	40	15	.375
Lamar Johnson	107	40	.374
Bill Stein	46	17	.370
Mike C. Brown	38	14	.368
Ed Romero	57	21	.368
Ron Hassey	93	34	.366
Jim Presley	63	23	.365
Bill Buckner	66	24	.364
Pedro Garcia	39	14	.359
George Bell	84	30	.357
Cal Ripken	129	46	.357
Wally Joyner	31	11	.355
Tony Oliva	31	11	.355
Don Mattingly	79	28	.354
Steve Henderson	48	17	.354
Ray Fosse	37	13	.351
Tony Muser	37	13	.351
Lonnie Smith	37	13	.351
Cecil Cooper	233	81	.348
Mike Hargrove	98	34	.347
Rick Sofield	29	10	.345

NAME	AB	HR	HR%
Jim Presley	63	7	11.11
Steve Balboni	72	7	9.72
Tony Oliva	31	3	9.68
John Wockenfuss	54	5	9.26
Boog Powell	33	3	9.09
Mike Pagliarulo	34	3	8.82
Dave Kingman	69	6	8.70
Lance Parrish	173	15	8.67
Billy Williams	49	4	8.16
Mike Young	38	3	7.89
Tom Brunansky	115	9	7.83
Larry Hisle	67	5	7.46
Milt May	42	3	7.14
Lee May	87	6	6.90
Ken Phelps	44	3	6.82
Bernie Carbo	45	3	6.67
Reggie Jackson	231	15	6.49
Richie Zisk	77	5	6.49
Gorman Thomas	162	10	6.17
Tony Solaita	65	4	6.15
Juan Beniquez	84	5	5.95
Ron Kittle	52	3	5.77
Sal Bando	139	8	5.76
Gary Roenicke	108	6	5.56
Don Baylor	254	14	5.51

Toronto
Exhibition Stadium

1986 Visiting Leaders

	1986 SEASON			1982 – 1986		
	Home Games	Road Games	Pct. Diff.	Home Games	Road Games	Pct. Diff.
G	81	82	– 1.2	404	407	– 0.7
AB	5560	5777	– 3.8	27724	27972	– 0.9
1B	987	1060	– 6.9	4868	5209	– 6.5
2B	297	254	16.9	1444	1182	22.2
3B	33	31	6.5	269	174	54.6
HR	176	169	4.1	783	715	9.5
HR%	3.165	2.925	8.2	2.824	2.556	10.5
R	804	738	8.9	3744	3464	8.1
BA	.269	.262	2.5	.266	.260	2.1
SA	.429	.405	6.0	.422	.392	7.7
E	114	115	– 0.9	638	647	– 1.4
SHO	4	14	– 71.4	40	43	– 7.0
R/G	9.926	9.000	10.3	9.267	8.511	8.9

BATTING AVG. (Top 10)

Mattingly, NY	.563
Easler, NY	.524
Burleson, CAL	.474
Lynn, BAL	.458
Cooper, MIL	.421
Gantner, MIL	.421
Yount, MIL	.417
Parrish, TEX	.409
Lacy, BAL	.407
Canseco, OAK	.393

HOME RUNS

Davis, OAK	4
Canseco, OAK	3
Kingman, OAK	3
12 players tied.	2

BATTING AVG. (Bottom 10)

Owen, BOS	.105
Boggs, BOS	.111
Jackson, CAL	.125
Gaetti, MIN	.130
Buechele, TEX	.136
Incaviglia, TEX	.143
Presley, SEA	.160
4 players tied.	.167

RUNS BATTED IN

Parrish, TEX	10
Davis, OAK	9
Canseco, OAK	8
Kingman, OAK	8
Easler, NY	7
Joyner, CAL	7
Gaetti, MIN	6
Ripken, BAL	6
Ward, TEX	6
11 players tied.	5

Career Visiting Leaders

NAME	AB	H	BA
Manny Sanguillen	22	11	.500
John Wockenfuss	40	19	.475
Bobby Clark	47	20	.426
Don Mattingly	112	47	.420
Jeff Burroughs	32	13	.406
Larvell Blanks	30	12	.400
Lee Lacy	35	14	.400
Rick Peters	48	19	.396
Jose Canseco	28	11	.393
Bill Almon	52	20	.385
Darrell Brown	26	10	.385
Clint Hurdle	34	13	.382
Willie Aikens	105	40	.381
Chris Bando	32	12	.375
Thurman Munson	72	27	.375
Wayne Nordhagen	32	12	.375
Mike Easler	70	26	.371
Lee May	73	27	.370
Scott Fletcher	65	24	.369
Fred Patek	63	23	.365
Ken Landreaux	55	20	.364
Lamar Johnson	58	21	.362
Bill Stein	64	23	.359
Brook Jacoby	53	19	.358
Harold Reynolds	28	10	.357

NAME	AB	HR	HR%
Kevin Bell	12	3	25.00
Larry Sheets	20	3	15.00
Jose Canseco	28	3	10.71
Cliff Johnson	91	9	9.89
Brook Jacoby	53	5	9.43
Ron Kittle	53	5	9.43
Dave Kingman	76	7	9.21
John Mayberry	34	3	8.82
Jim Dwyer	84	7	8.33
Lee May	73	6	8.22
Jerry Narron	37	3	8.11
Mike Davis	100	8	8.00
Greg Luzinski	76	6	7.89
Kirk Gibson	106	8	7.55
Milt May	40	3	7.50
Oddibe McDowell	40	3	7.50
Leon Roberts	42	3	7.14
George Scott	42	3	7.14
Jeff Newman	87	6	6.90
Dwight Evans	189	13	6.88
Lance Parrish	176	12	6.82
Jason Thompson	106	7	6.60
Bobby Bonds	62	4	6.45
Bobby Grich	155	10	6.45
Jim Rice	250	16	6.40

Atlanta
Atlanta-Fulton County Stadium

1986 Visiting Leaders

1986 SEASON			1982 – 1986		
Home Games	Road Games	Pct. Diff.	Home Games	Road Games	Pct. Diff.
G	81	80	1.2	404	405	– 0.2

	Home Games	Road Games	Pct. Diff.	Home Games	Road Games	Pct. Diff.
G	81	80	1.2	404	405	– 0.2
AB	5485	5318	3.1	27630	27114	1.9
1B	1014	982	3.3	5362	5031	6.6
2B	246	239	2.9	1154	1072	7.6
3B	24	31	– 22.6	129	167	– 22.8
HR	148	107	38.3	736	546	34.8
HR%	2.698	2.012	34.1	2.664	2.014	32.3
R	691	643	7.5	3658	3203	14.2
BA	.261	.256	2.2	.267	.251	6.3
SA	.396	.373	6.2	.398	.364	9.5
E	146	144	1.4	760	707	7.5
SHO	8	7	14.3	35	59	– 40.7
R/G	8.531	8.038	6.1	9.054	7.909	14.5

BATTING AVG. (Top 10)

Hayes, PHI	.458
Strawberry, NY	.450
Thompson, SF	.444
Dykstra, NY	.429
Diaz, CIN	.423
Wallach, MTL	.421
Brooks, MTL	.391
Samuel, PHI	.385
Dunston, CHI	.381
3 players tied.	.375

HOME RUNS

Marshall, LA	3
Parker, CIN	3
Strawberry, NY	3
9 players tied.	2

BATTING AVG. (Bottom 10)

Jeltz, PHI	.000
Carter, NY	.105
Coleman, STL	.105
Ray, PIT	.111
Dawson, MTL	.130
Sandberg, CHI	.148
Wilson, PHI	.150
Duncan, LA	.154
Law, MTL	.158
Matthews, CHI	.158

RUNS BATTED IN

Reynolds, HOU	10
Parker, CIN	9
Strawberry, NY	8
Dunston, CHI	7
Fitzgerald, MTL	7
Carter, NY	6
Hayes, PHI	6
Kruk, SD	6
Morrison, PIT	6
Schmidt, PHI	6

Career Visiting Leaders

NAME	AB	H	BA
Mike Fitzgerald	36	16	.444
Rob Thompson	36	16	.444
David Green	34	15	.441
Nick Esasky	76	32	.421
Hector Torres	27	11	.407
Pedro Guerrero	140	56	.400
Ken Oberkfell	101	40	.396
Mitch Webster	31	12	.387
Vic Harris	39	15	.385
Bud Harrelson	34	13	.382
Jerry Turner	117	44	.376
Len Dykstra	40	15	.375
Harry Spilman	41	15	.366
Ellis Valentine	115	42	.365
Ray Knight	237	86	.363
Larry Biittner	83	30	.361
Mike Anderson	28	10	.357
Candy Maldonado	45	16	.356
Reggie Smith	124	44	.355
Mike Sadek	48	17	.354
Steve Garvey	390	138	.354
Warren Cromartie	134	47	.351
Scot Thompson	60	21	.350
Wilbur Howard	46	16	.348
Greg Luzinski	101	35	.347

NAME	AB	HR	HR%
Mel Hall	16	3	18.75
Tito Landrum	18	3	16.67
Mike Lum	19	3	15.79
Nick Esasky	76	8	10.53
Willie McCovey	108	11	10.19
Darryl Strawberry	70	7	10.00
Dave Kingman	146	14	9.59
J.R. Richard	32	3	9.37
Gene Tenace	103	9	8.74
Pedro Guerrero	140	12	8.57
Sixto Lezcano	48	4	8.33
Franklin Stubbs	37	3	8.11
Reggie Smith	124	10	8.06
Mike Schmidt	250	20	8.00
Tim Wallach	114	9	7.89
Larry Parrish	127	10	7.87
Greg Brock	116	9	7.76
Rick Monday	142	11	7.75
Bill Robinson	105	8	7.62
Mike Easler	53	4	7.55
Jason Thompson	82	6	7.32
Graig Nettles	69	5	7.25
George Foster	304	22	7.24
George Hendrick	186	13	6.99
Gary Carter	232	16	6.90

Chicago
Wrigley Field

1986 Visiting Leaders

BATTING AVG. (Top 10)

Kennedy, SD	.474
Walling, HOU	.455
Wilson, NY	.429
Oberkfell, ATL	.421
Scioscia, LA	.421
Hayes, PHI	.417
Moreno, ATL	.409
Davis, CIN	.400
Raines, MTL	.400
Ray, PIT	.395

HOME RUNS

Brooks, MTL	3
Carter, NY	3
Schmidt, PHI	3
9 players tied.	2

BATTING AVG. (Bottom 10)

Kutcher, SF	.111
Bell, CIN	.143
Hubbard, ATL	.143
Van Slyke, STL	.148
Cruz, HOU	.207
Bream, PIT	.212
Backman, NY	.217
Pendleton, STL	.217
Herr, STL	.226
Virgil, ATL	.227

RUNS BATTED IN

Carter, NY	11
Hernandez, NY	9
Schmidt, PHI	9
Brock, LA	8
Sax, LA	8
Brooks, MTL	7
Knight, NY	7
Wilson, NY	7
5 players tied.	6

	1986 SEASON			1982 – 1986		
	Home Games	Road Games	Pct. Diff.	Home Games	Road Games	Pct. Diff.
G	80	80	0.0	403	404	− 0.2
AB	5673	5377	5.5	27864	27148	2.6
1B	1087	951	14.3	5218	5065	3.0
2B	282	271	4.1	1312	1261	4.0
3B	30	36	− 16.7	213	203	4.9
HR	168	130	29.2	781	542	44.1
HR%	2.961	2.418	22.5	2.803	1.996	40.4
R	793	668	18.7	3837	3264	17.6
BA	.276	.258	7.0	.270	.260	3.7
SA	.425	.394	7.8	.416	.382	9.1
E	126	120	5.0	661	616	7.3
SHO	8	8	0.0	41	48	− 14.6
R/G	9.913	8.350	18.7	9.521	8.079	17.8

Career Visiting Leaders

NAME	AB	H	BA
Wilbur Howard	23	11	.478
Tim McCarver	44	20	.455
Dick Allen	29	13	.448
Bill Doran	69	29	.420
Scot Thompson	31	13	.419
Joe Torre	24	10	.417
Mike C. Brown	25	10	.400
Marty Perez	25	10	.400
Richie Hebner	152	60	.395
Bobby Murcer	46	18	.391
Bryan Little	26	10	.385
Chris Brown	45	17	.378
Bob Boone	141	53	.376
Jim Morrison	75	28	.373
Mitch Webster	59	22	.373
Al Oliver	197	73	.371
Richie Zisk	76	28	.368
Junior Kennedy	30	11	.367
Gerald Perry	30	11	.367
Jerry Grote	41	15	.366
Candy Maldonado	36	13	.361
Bill Buckner	39	14	.359
Jerry White	56	20	.357
Vic Correll	31	11	.355
Rick Monday	62	22	.355

NAME	AB	HR	HR%
Henry Cruz	11	3	27.27
Darren Daulton	14	3	21.43
Cliff Johnson	20	4	20.00
Mike Schmidt	382	45	11.78
Greg Brock	41	4	9.76
Dave Kingman	175	15	8.57
Fernando Gonzalez	36	3	8.33
Howard Johnson	36	3	8.33
Bob Brenly	78	6	7.69
Johnny Bench	119	9	7.56
Graig Nettles	54	4	7.41
Chili Davis	98	7	7.14
Mike A. Marshall	56	4	7.14
Darryl Strawberry	84	6	7.14
Jerry Turner	57	4	7.02
Tommy Hutton	43	3	6.98
Willie Stargell	159	11	6.92
Tim McCarver	44	3	6.82
Doug Rader	44	3	6.82
Chris Brown	45	3	6.67
Richie Zisk	76	5	6.58
Kevin McReynolds	61	4	6.56
Bill Robinson	107	7	6.54
Tim Wallach	184	12	6.52
Joe Ferguson	62	4	6.45

Cincinnati
Riverfront Stadium

1986 Visiting Leaders

1986 SEASON			1982 – 1986		
Home Games	Road Games	Pct. Diff.	Home Games	Road Games	Pct. Diff.

	Home Games	Road Games	Pct. Diff.	Home Games	Road Games	Pct. Diff.
G	81	81	0.0	405	405	0.0
AB	5576	5510	1.2	27600	27121	1.8
1B	1020	1013	0.7	4979	4877	2.1
2B	263	229	14.8	1344	1078	24.7
3B	38	26	46.2	190	160	18.7
HR	157	123	27.6	602	586	2.7
HR%	2.816	2.232	26.1	2.181	2.161	0.9
R	753	696	8.2	3506	3199	9.6
BA	.265	.252	5.0	.258	.247	4.3
SA	.410	.370	10.8	.386	.363	6.1
E	130	165	− 21.2	622	696	− 10.6
SHO	7	8	− 12.5	46	48	− 4.2
R/G	9.296	8.593	8.2	8.657	7.899	9.6

BATTING AVG. (Top 10)

Raines, MTL	.577
Bass, HOU	.455
Coleman, STL	.438
Gwynn, SD	.421
Kruk, SD	.419
Backman, NY	.409
J. Davis, CHI	.400
Hernandez, NY	.400
Law, MTL	.400
Gladden, SF	.393

HOME RUNS

Wallach, MTL	4
Brock, LA	3
Garner, HOU	3
Horner, ATL	3
Maldonado, SF	3
Murphy, ATL	3
Schmidt, PHI	3
9 players tied.	2

BATTING AVG. (Bottom 10)

Orsulak, PIT	.095
Carter, NY	.125
Redus, PHI	.133
Reynolds, PIT	.136
Herr, STL	.158
Wilson, PHI	.176
Dykstra, NY	.179
T. Pena, PIT	.182
C. Davis, SF	.192
Hatcher, HOU	.207

RUNS BATTED IN

Davis, HOU	9
Maldonado, SF	9
McReynolds, SD	9
Ashby, HOU	8
Sandberg, CHI	8
Brenly, SF	7
Cruz, HOU	7
Murphy, ATL	7
Virgil, ATL	7
Wallach, MTL	7

Career Visiting Leaders

NAME	AB	H	BA
Gene Locklear	31	15	.484
Andre Thornton	26	11	.423
John Kruk	31	13	.419
Tom Nieto	24	10	.417
Sixto Lezcano	58	23	.397
Von Joshua	61	24	.393
Ed Kranepool	49	19	.388
Larry Biittner	77	29	.377
Willie McGee	83	31	.373
Tito Fuentes	54	20	.370
Dave Parker	187	68	.364
Tony Gwynn	152	55	.362
Juan Samuel	86	31	.360
Cesar Cedeno	198	70	.354
George Hendrick	182	63	.346
Mike Easler	67	23	.343
Mitch Webster	35	12	.343
Brad Komminsk	50	17	.340
Al Oliver	124	42	.339
Wally Backman	65	22	.338
Hubie Brooks	95	32	.337
Willie Davis	42	14	.333
Brian Giles	33	11	.333
Bryan Little	33	11	.333
Joe Pettini	33	11	.333

NAME	AB	HR	HR%
Sixto Lezcano	58	7	12.07
Darryl Strawberry	71	8	11.27
Willie Stargell	63	6	9.52
Mike Schmidt	254	22	8.66
Bob Horner	180	15	8.33
Willie McCovey	98	8	8.16
Andre Dawson	190	14	7.37
Richie Zisk	43	3	6.98
Greg Brock	87	6	6.90
Mike A. Marshall	118	8	6.78
Cesar Cedeno	198	13	6.57
Ellis Valentine	107	7	6.54
Mike Easler	67	4	5.97
Tony Perez	67	4	5.97
Rusty Staub	51	3	5.88
Willie Crawford	52	3	5.77
Ron Cey	278	16	5.76
Ted Simmons	123	7	5.69
Chris Brown	53	3	5.66
Bob Watson	164	9	5.49
Candy Maldonado	55	3	5.45
Joe Lefebvre	56	3	5.36
Pedro Guerrero	169	9	5.33
Mike Ivie	134	7	5.22
Greg Luzinski	115	6	5.22

Houston
Astrodome

1986 Visiting Leaders

BATTING AVG. (Top 10)		HOME RUNS	
Smith, STL	.455	McReynolds, SD	3
Herr, STL	.391	Carter, NY	2
Brown, SF	.370	Davis, CIN	2
Bream, PIT	.364	C. Davis, SF	2
McReynolds, SD	.364	J. Davis, CHI	2
Orsulak, PIT	.350	Dawson, MTL	2
Hernandez, NY	.333	Madlock, LA	2
Morrison, PIT	.333	Schmidt, PHI	2
Hayes, PHI	.318	39 players tied.	1
Ray, PIT	.318		

	1986 SEASON			1982 – 1986		
	Home Games	Road Games	Pct. Diff.	Home Games	Road Games	Pct. Diff.
G	81	81	0.0	406	404	0.5
AB	5360	5420	− 1.1	27325	27265	0.2
1B	942	869	8.4	5003	4946	1.2
2B	208	269	− 22.7	1099	1148	− 4.3
3B	30	32	− 6.3	247	178	38.8
HR	105	136	− 22.8	357	646	− 44.7
HR%	1.959	2.509	− 21.9	1.306	2.369	− 44.9
R	616	607	1.5	3044	3377	− 9.9
BA	.240	.241	− 0.5	.245	.254	− 3.3
SA	.349	.378	− 7.7	.343	.380	− 9.8
E	122	139	− 12.2	643	699	− 8.0
SHO	16	9	77.8	69	51	35.3
R/G	7.605	7.494	1.5	7.498	8.359	− 10.3

BATTING AVG. (Bottom 10)		RUNS BATTED IN	
Oester, CIN	.094	Dawson, MTL	8
Stubbs, LA	.103	C. Davis, SF	7
Roenicke, PHI	.111	Strawberry, NY	7
Uribe, SF	.120	Garvey, SD	6
Dunston, CHI	.125	Madlock, LA	6
Van Slyke, STL	.130	McReynolds, SD	6
Murphy, ATL	.143	Morrison, PIT	6
Moreland, CHI	.150	Sax, LA	6
Oberkfell, ATL	.154	Templeton, SD	6
Strawberry, NY	.154	6 players tied.	5

Career Visiting Leaders

NAME	AB	H	BA	NAME	AB	HR	HR%
Bob Watson	22	10	.455	Pepe Mangual	41	4	9.76
Bruce Boisclair	53	24	.453	Chris Brown	40	3	7.50
Von Joshua	57	24	.421	Darrell Porter	54	3	5.56
Rick Schu	27	10	.370	Willie Stargell	81	4	4.94
Teddy Martinez	30	11	.367	Nick Esasky	82	4	4.88
Tom Paciorek	28	10	.357	Willie McCovey	105	5	4.76
Dave Bergman	31	11	.355	Reggie Smith	148	7	4.73
Jerry White	31	11	.355	Pedro Guerrero	155	7	4.52
Rafael Santana	34	12	.353	Mike Schmidt	230	10	4.35
Chris Brown	40	14	.350	Tim Wallach	116	5	4.31
Jerry Grote	47	16	.340	Andre Dawson	216	9	4.17
Steve R. Ontiveros	96	32	.333	Jody Davis	99	4	4.04
Tony Gwynn	133	44	.331	Jason Thompson	75	3	4.00
Wally Backman	61	20	.328	Darryl Strawberry	77	3	3.90
Bake McBride	98	32	.327	Dale Murphy	297	11	3.70
Roger Metzger	40	13	.325	Kevin McReynolds	112	4	3.57
Larvell Blanks	34	11	.324	Dusty Baker	290	10	3.45
Jerry Mumphrey	115	37	.322	Bob Horner	186	6	3.23
Pepe Mangual	41	13	.317	Jack Clark	219	7	3.20
Steve Sax	168	53	.315	Ted Simmons	126	4	3.17
Mike Fitzgerald	51	16	.314	Gary Carter	226	7	3.10
Bruce Miller	32	10	.313	Larry Parrish	131	4	3.05
Manny Sanguillen	48	15	.313	Johnny Bench	200	6	3.00
Reggie Smith	148	46	.311	Tony Perez	167	5	2.99
Bill Madlock	251	78	.311	George Hendrick	168	5	2.98

Los Angeles
Dodger Stadium

1986 Visiting Leaders

BATTING AVG. (Top 10)

Hatcher, HOU	.444
Mumphrey, CHI	.429
Belliard, PIT	.412
Knight, NY	.412
Hernandez, NY	.393
McReynolds, SD	.389
Davis, HOU	.387
Templeton, SD	.375
Gwynn, SD	.366
3 players tied.	.333

HOME RUNS

Matthews, CHI	3
Davis, HOU	2
Foster, NY	2
Hatcher, HOU	2
Leonard, SF	2
Maldonado, SF	2
Russell, PHI	2
Walling, HOU	2
29 players tied.	1

BATTING AVG. (Bottom 10)

Law, MTL	.000
Pendleton, STL	.111
T. Pena, PIT	.118
J. Davis, CHI	.130
Smith, STL	.143
Virgil, ATL	.150
Oester, CIN	.167
Wilson, PHI	.174
Bonds, PIT	.176
Dykstra, NY	.176

RUNS BATTED IN

Hatcher, HOU	8
Maldonado, SF	8
Diaz, CIN	6
Garvey, SD	6
Strawberry, NY	6
7 players tied.	5

	1986 SEASON			1982 – 1986		
	Home Games	Road Games	Pct. Diff.	Home Games	Road Games	Pct. Diff.
G	81	81	0.0	404	407	− 0.7
AB	5467	5573	− 1.9	27515	27526	− 0.0
1B	1052	974	8.0	5323	4873	9.2
2B	195	289	− 32.5	916	1253	− 26.9
3B	16	30	− 46.7	90	178	− 49.4
HR	103	142	− 27.5	508	608	− 16.4
HR%	1.884	2.548	− 26.1	1.846	2.209	− 16.4
R	616	701	− 12.1	3008	3316	− 9.3
BA	.250	.257	− 3.0	.248	.251	− 1.0
SA	.348	.397	− 12.3	.344	.376	− 8.5
E	154	158	− 2.5	767	740	3.6
SHO	14	14	0.0	68	59	15.3
R/G	7.605	8.654	− 12.1	7.446	8.147	− 8.6

Career Visiting Leaders

NAME	AB	H	BA
Candy Maldonado	24	11	.458
Billy Hatcher	36	16	.444
Willie Davis	25	11	.440
Ron LeFlore	25	11	.440
Bump Wills	23	10	.435
Jim Pankovits	24	10	.417
Gene Locklear	29	12	.414
Manny Sanguillen	48	19	.396
Brian Asselstine	26	10	.385
Joe Nolan	60	23	.383
Pepe Frias	41	15	.366
Reggie Smith	45	16	.356
Ted Simmons	130	46	.354
Bill Buckner	171	60	.351
Larry Biittner	86	30	.349
Chris Brown	46	16	.348
Lee Lacy	72	25	.347
Andre Thornton	29	10	.345
Ralph Garr	38	13	.342
Juan Bonilla	47	16	.340
Rufino Linares	47	16	.340
Glenn Davis	53	18	.340
Greg Luzinski	133	45	.338
Dusty Baker	36	12	.333
Joe Lefebvre	45	15	.333

NAME	AB	HR	HR%
John Russell	12	3	25.00
Dave Kingman	145	18	12.41
Ron LeFlore	25	3	12.00
Mike Schmidt	227	19	8.37
Joe Ferguson	48	4	8.33
Dick Allen	37	3	8.11
Dave Winfield	185	15	8.11
Willie Stargell	77	6	7.79
George Foster	305	21	6.89
Greg Luzinski	133	9	6.77
Jeff Burroughs	90	6	6.67
Del Unser	48	3	6.25
Bobby Murcer	113	7	6.19
Jeff Leonard	196	12	6.12
Ed Ott	51	3	5.88
Glenn Davis	53	3	5.66
Darrell Evans	250	14	5.60
Claudell Washington	129	7	5.43
Bob Watson	149	7	4.70
Darrell Porter	64	3	4.69
Mike Ivie	130	6	4.62
Ted Simmons	130	6	4.62
Jack Clark	261	12	4.60
Gary Thomasson	67	3	4.48
Gary Matthews	299	13	4.35

Montreal Olympic Stadium

1986 Visiting Leaders

	1986 SEASON			1982 – 1986		
	Home Games	Road Games	Pct. Diff.	Home Games	Road Games	Pct. Diff.
G	80	81	− 1.2	404	404	0.0
AB	5421	5574	− 2.7	27207	27667	− 1.7
1B	944	984	− 4.1	4728	5071	− 6.8
2B	245	263	− 6.8	1298	1234	5.2
3B	48	38	26.3	203	197	3.0
HR	100	129	− 22.5	511	610	− 16.2
HR%	1.845	2.314	− 20.3	1.878	2.205	− 14.8
R	650	675	− 3.7	3118	3290	− 5.2
BA	.247	.254	− 2.8	.248	.257	− 3.6
SA	.365	.384	− 5.0	.367	.382	− 4.0
E	133	115	15.7	603	667	− 9.6
SHO	9	11	− 18.2	59	54	9.3
R/G	8.125	8.333	− 2.5	7.718	8.144	− 5.2

BATTING AVG. (Top 10)

Garvey, SD	.450
Parker, CIN	.409
Sax, LA	.407
Flannery, SD	.400
Bell, CIN	.368
Oberkfell, ATL	.368
Ráy, PIT	.357
Wilson, NY	.357
Aldrete, SF	.353
Backman, NY	.345

HOME RUNS

Davis, HOU	3
Garvey, SD	3
Strawberry, NY	3
8 players tied.	2

BATTING AVG. (Bottom 10)

Brenly, SF	.056
Brock, LA	.087
Reynolds, HOU	.095
Rose, CIN	.095
Dernier, CHI	.121
Anderson, LA	.143
Walling, HOU	.158
Jeltz, PHI	.160
Gwynn, SD	.167
Virgil, ATL	.167

RUNS BATTED IN

Carter, NY	8
Davis, HOU	8
Garvey, SD	8
Hernandez, NY	8
McReynolds, SD	8
Strawberry, NY	8
Schmidt, PHI	7
Wilson, PHI	7
3 players tied.	6

Career Visiting Leaders

NAME	AB	H	BA
Pedro Guerrero	91	34	.374
Ruppert Jones	49	18	.367
Jim Wohlford	28	10	.357
Kurt Bevacqua	31	11	.355
Brian Giles	34	12	.353
Rusty Staub	51	18	.353
Dave Winfield	98	34	.347
Danny Heep	78	27	.346
Juan Samuel	104	36	.346
Gene Clines	29	10	.345
Dane Iorg	93	32	.344
Alan Wiggins	65	22	.338
Brian Asselstine	45	15	.333
Thad Bosley	30	10	.333
Junior Ortiz	33	11	.333
Ron Oester	108	35	.324
Dusty Baker	153	49	.320
Kevin McReynolds	75	24	.320
Rick Rhoden	44	14	.318
Mike Vail	82	26	.317
Jeff Leonard	76	24	.316
Sid Bream	45	14	.311
Bake McBride	119	37	.311
Mookie Wilson	178	55	.309
Pete Rose	251	77	.307

NAME	AB	HR	HR%
Glenn Davis	30	4	13.33
Reggie Smith	67	7	10.45
Nick Esasky	30	3	10.00
Willie McCovey	60	6	10.00
Darryl Strawberry	99	8	8.08
Dave Kingman	118	9	7.63
Mike Schmidt	307	22	7.17
Sid Bream	45	3	6.67
Willie Stargell	77	5	6.49
Tony Pena	185	12	6.49
Gary Carter	62	4	6.45
Mike Ivie	67	4	5.97
Johnny Bench	102	6	5.88
Greg Luzinski	119	7	5.88
Greg Brock	70	4	5.71
Jerry Morales	89	5	5.62
Graig Nettles	54	3	5.56
Pedro Guerrero	91	5	5.49
Gene Tenace	73	4	5.48
Chili Davis	112	6	5.36
Kevin McReynolds	75	4	5.33
John Stearns	136	7	5.15
Ron Cey	214	11	5.14
Jack Clark	179	9	5.03
Mike Vail	82	4	4.88

New York
Shea Stadium

1986 Visiting Leaders

BATTING AVG. (Top 10)		HOME RUNS	
Webster, MTL	.382	Cey, CHI	2
Concepcion, CIN	.375	Garner, HOU	2
Thompson, SF	.360	Garvey, SD	2
Bass, HOU	.348	Hayes, PHI	2
Schmidt, PHI	.346	Sandberg, CHI	2
Samuel, PHI	.345	37 players tied.	1
Durham, CHI	.320		
Oester, CIN	.316		
C. Davis, SF	.313		
Oberkfell, ATL	.313		

BATTING AVG. (Bottom 10)		RUNS BATTED IN	
Flannery, SD	.000	Dawson, MTL	7
Kennedy, SD	.000	Hayes, PHI	7
Horner, ATL	.087	Cey, CHI	6
Sax, LA	.087	C. Davis, SF	6
J. Davis, CHI	.107	Fitzgerald, MTL	6
Pendleton, STL	.118	Concepcion, CIN	5
Doran, HOU	.120	Morris, STL	5
Dunston, CHI	.147	6 players tied.	4
Scioscia, LA	.150		
McReynolds, SD	.160		

	1986 SEASON			1982 – 1986		
	Home Games	Road Games	Pct. Diff.	Home Games	Road Games	Pct. Diff.
G	81	81	0.0	406	404	0.5
AB	5365	5712	− 6.1	27294	27620	− 1.2
1B	908	1071	− 15.2	5029	5094	− 1.3
2B	228	249	− 8.4	1078	1196	− 9.9
3B	27	32	− 15.6	122	184	− 33.7
HR	124	127	− 2.4	567	565	0.4
HR%	2.311	2.223	4.0	2.077	2.046	1.6
R	630	731	− 13.8	3184	3355	− 5.1
BA	.240	.259	− 7.4	.249	.255	− 2.3
SA	.362	.380	− 4.9	.360	.373	− 3.5
E	146	150	− 2.7	744	683	8.9
SHO	8	7	14.3	55	45	22.2
R/G	7.778	9.025	− 13.8	7.842	8.304	− 5.6

Career Visiting Leaders

NAME	AB	H	BA		NAME	AB	HR	HR%
Fred Lynn	26	12	.462		Tony Oliva	12	3	25.00
Don Baylor	33	14	.424		Dave Kingman	73	12	16.44
Joe Nolan	34	14	.412		Nate Colbert	19	3	15.79
Dave Winfield	136	53	.390		Billy Williams	21	3	14.29
Gene Richards	149	58	.389		Boog Powell	24	3	12.50
Dickie Thon	57	22	.386		Larry Christenson	26	3	11.54
Marty Perez	43	16	.372		Willie Horton	36	4	11.11
Cesar Tovar	27	10	.370		Don Baylor	33	3	9.09
Mitch Webster	46	17	.370		Bob Brenly	77	6	7.79
Jose Morales	30	11	.367		Jim Wynn	41	3	7.32
Ken Griffey	151	55	.364		George Foster	154	10	6.49
Keith Moreland	156	56	.359		Claudell Washington	126	8	6.35
Jim Wohlford	56	20	.357		John Milner	64	4	6.25
Claudell Washington	126	44	.349		Greg Brock	65	4	6.15
Ollie Brown	29	10	.345		Reggie Smith	116	7	6.03
Reggie Smith	116	40	.345		Ellis Valentine	135	8	5.93
Johnnie LeMaster	125	43	.344		Dave Winfield	136	8	5.88
Mark Bailey	35	12	.343		Mike Easler	108	6	5.56
Terry Harper	44	15	.341		Mike Schmidt	362	20	5.52
Broderick Perkins	50	17	.340		Carmelo Martinez	57	3	5.26
Larvell Blanks	33	11	.333		Dickie Thon	57	3	5.26
Willie Crawford	33	11	.333		Greg Luzinski	174	9	5.17
Willie Horton	36	12	.333		Gary Redus	58	3	5.17
Wilbur Howard	30	10	.333		Dale Murphy	157	8	5.10
Rick Manning	30	10	.333		Steve Garvey	256	13	5.08

Philadelphia
Veterans Stadium

1986 Visiting Leaders

	BATTING AVG. (Top 10)		HOME RUNS	
	Thomas, ATL	.519	Brock, LA	3
	Horner, ATL	.429	Davis, CIN	2
	Bass, HOU	.423	J. Davis, CHI	2
	Sax, LA	.423	Dykstra, NY	2
	Hubbard, ATL	.400	Harper, ATL	2
	Oester, CIN	.391	Knight, NY	2
	Brenly, SF	.389	McReynolds, SD	2
	Herr, STL	.368	Stubbs, LA	2
	Doran, HOU	.364	Winningham, MTL	2
	J. Davis, CHI	.355	30 players tied.	1

BATTING AVG. (Bottom 10)		RUNS BATTED IN	
Anderson, LA	.059	Pendleton, STL	10
Coleman, STL	.067	Carter, NY	9
Morrison, PIT	.091	J. Davis, CHI	8
Strawberry, NY	.103	Knight, NY	8
Durham, CHI	.120	Bream, PIT	7
Davis, HOU	.130	Oester, CIN	7
Bonds, PIT	.138	10 players tied.	5
Rose, CIN	.150		
Virgil, ATL	.167		
Maldonado, SF	.176		

	1986 SEASON			1982 – 1986		
	Home Games	Road Games	Pct. Diff.	Home Games	Road Games	Pct. Diff.
G	80	81	– 1.2	405	405	0.0
AB	5470	5575	– 1.9	27444	27730	– 1.0
1B	979	990	– 1.1	4873	5172	– 5.8
2B	299	234	27.8	1284	1153	11.4
3B	46	27	70.4	236	189	24.9
HR	135	149	– 9.4	613	609	0.7
HR%	2.468	2.673	– 7.7	2.234	2.196	1.7
R	757	695	8.9	3446	3405	1.2
BA	.267	.251	6.2	.255	.257	– 0.6
SA	.412	.383	7.6	.386	.378	2.2
E	140	143	– 2.1	694	714	– 2.8
SHO	10	8	25.0	56	50	12.0
R/G	9.462	8.580	10.3	8.509	8.407	1.2

Career Visiting Leaders

NAME	AB	H	BA	NAME	AB	HR	HR%
Andres Thomas	27	14	.519	Eric Davis	26	3	11.54
Herm Winningham	40	20	.500	Vic Correll	31	3	9.68
Willie Crawford	25	11	.440	Cliff Johnson	32	3	9.37
Mike Lavalliere	23	10	.435	Glenn Davis	34	3	8.82
Ken Landreaux	83	36	.434	Pedro Guerrero	108	8	7.41
Dan Gladden	51	21	.412	Rick Monday	89	6	6.74
Dane Iorg	66	27	.409	Greg Brock	61	4	6.56
Von Joshua	31	12	.387	Gary Carter	358	22	6.15
Luis Salazar	68	26	.382	Reggie Smith	134	8	5.97
Pepe Frias	42	16	.381	Bob Horner	151	9	5.96
Bobby Murcer	97	36	.371	Darryl Strawberry	101	6	5.94
Jim Wynn	30	11	.367	Nick Esasky	51	3	5.88
Alan Wiggins	64	23	.359	Jerry Turner	51	3	5.88
Wally Backman	87	31	.356	Carmelo Martinez	52	3	5.77
Mike Easler	88	31	.352	Ron Cey	250	14	5.60
Lee Lacy	176	62	.352	Darrell Evans	169	9	5.33
Rick Monday	89	31	.348	Jeff Burroughs	76	4	5.26
Terry Puhl	115	40	.348	George Hendrick	252	13	5.16
Terry Kennedy	116	40	.345	Bobby Murcer	97	5	5.15
Chris Chambliss	96	33	.344	John Milner	117	6	5.13
Bob Bailor	59	20	.339	Denny Walling	59	3	5.08
Bill Madlock	328	110	.335	Biff Pocoroba	60	3	5.00
Kevin Bass	51	17	.333	Gene Tenace	100	5	5.00
Bake McBride	36	12	.333	Dave Kingman	203	10	4.93
Mitch Webster	42	14	.333	Johnny Bench	167	8	4.79

Pittsburgh
Three Rivers Stadium

1986 Visiting Leaders

1986 SEASON			1982 – 1986		
Home Games	Road Games	Pct. Diff.	Home Games	Road Games	Pct. Diff.
G 81	81	0.0	404	405	− 0.2
AB 5503	5432	1.3	27549	27530	0.1
1B 928	974	− 4.7	5026	4982	0.9
2B 286	255	12.2	1341	1228	9.2
3B 37	34	8.8	199	178	11.8
HR 124	125	− 0.8	573	545	5.1
HR% 2.253	2.301	− 2.1	2.080	1.980	5.1
R 688	675	1.9	3350	3198	4.8
BA .250	.256	− 2.2	.259	.252	2.9
SA .383	.384	− 0.3	.385	.369	4.3
E 139	130	6.9	649	671	− 3.3
SHO 10	9	11.1	43	59	− 27.1
R/G 8.494	8.333	1.9	8.292	7.896	5.0

BATTING AVG. (Top 10)

Raines, MTL	.455
McReynolds, SD	.444
Strawberry, NY	.435
Sax, LA	.429
Brown, SF	.385
Wilson, PHI	.382
Davis, CIN	.381
Knight, NY	.357
Bass, HOU	.350
Gladden, SF	.350

HOME RUNS

Davis, CIN	4
Schmidt, PHI	4
Parker, CIN	3
Schu, PHI	3
Stubbs, LA	3
12 players tied.	2

BATTING AVG. (Bottom 10)

Hubbard, ATL	.095
Moreno, ATL	.100
Cruz, HOU	.111
Diaz, CIN	.111
Lavalliere, STL	.111
Kennedy, SD	.133
Thompson, SF	.136
Moreland, CHI	.171
Landreaux, LA	.182
Ford, STL	.185

RUNS BATTED IN

Schmidt, PHI	12
Parker, CIN	11
Davis, CIN	10
Brenly, SF	8
Harper, ATL	7
Murphy, ATL	7
Strawberry, NY	7
Wilson, PHI	7
Dawson, MTL	6
Hurdle, STL	6

Career Visiting Leaders

NAME	AB	H	BA
Mike Phillips	42	17	.405
George Hendrick	202	76	.376
Joe Lefebvre	40	15	.375
Ron Hodges	63	23	.365
Cliff Johnson	33	12	.364
Jim Wohlford	62	22	.355
Graig Nettles	48	17	.354
Milt May	76	26	.342
Lee Lacy	53	18	.340
Dan Gladden	56	19	.339
Tony Scott	133	45	.338
Jerry White	77	26	.338
Chris Brown	42	14	.333
Tom O'Malley	30	10	.333
Steve Sax	138	46	.333
Rusty Staub	72	24	.333
Enos Cabell	181	60	.331
Garry Maddox	293	97	.331
Art Howe	118	39	.331
Kevin Bass	49	16	.327
Shawon Dunston	43	14	.326
Sixto Lezcano	83	27	.325
Eric Davis	34	11	.324
Jay Johnstone	96	31	.323
Keith Moreland	177	57	.322

NAME	AB	HR	HR%
Eric Davis	34	5	14.71
Dave A. Johnson	22	3	13.64
Gene Tenace	83	10	12.05
Franklin Stubbs	26	3	11.54
Jack Clark	186	18	9.68
Dave Kingman	198	19	9.60
Darryl Strawberry	106	10	9.43
Andre Thornton	33	3	9.09
Gary Thomasson	63	5	7.94
Joe Morgan	173	13	7.51
Terry Harper	54	4	7.41
Dave Parker	69	5	7.25
Reggie Smith	129	9	6.98
Ozzie Virgil	73	5	6.85
Tony Perez	139	9	6.47
Kevin Bass	49	3	6.12
Joe Ferguson	84	5	5.95
Darrell Evans	173	10	5.78
Johnny Bench	156	9	5.77
Rick Schu	52	3	5.77
Dave Winfield	122	7	5.74
Lee Lacy	53	3	5.66
Mike A. Marshall	53	3	5.66
Dickie Thon	53	3	5.66
Dale Murphy	174	9	5.17

St. Louis
Busch Stadium

1986 Visiting Leaders

	1986 SEASON			1982 – 1986		
	Home Games	Road Games	Pct. Diff.	Home Games	Road Games	Pct. Diff.
G	81	80	1.2	405	404	0.2
AB	5462	5362	1.9	27240	27462	– 0.8
1B	954	916	4.1	5049	5189	– 2.7
2B	262	232	12.9	1268	1173	8.1
3B	45	32	40.6	283	185	53.0
HR	90	103	– 12.6	407	499	– 18.4
HR%	1.648	1.921	– 14.2	1.494	1.817	– 17.8
R	624	588	6.1	3221	3290	– 2.1
BA	.247	.239	3.4	.257	.257	0.3
SA	.361	.352	2.6	.369	.367	0.6
E	148	129	14.7	673	671	0.3
SHO	4	13	– 69.2	56	52	7.7
R/G	7.704	7.350	4.8	7.953	8.144	– 2.3

BATTING AVG. (Top 10)

Cruz, HOU	.529
Sax, LA	.481
Royster, SD	.467
Gwynn, SD	.375
Hatcher, HOU	.368
Galarraga, MTL	.357
Ray, PIT	.355
Strawberry, NY	.355
Stubbs, LA	.333
Madlock, LA	.318

HOME RUNS

12 players tied.	2

BATTING AVG. (Bottom 10)

Leonard, SF	.100
Templeton, SD	.100
Bass, HOU	.130
Horner, ATL	.143
Kennedy, SD	.143
Hayes, PHI	.147
Wilson, PHI	.147
Bream, PIT	.154
3 players tied.	.167

RUNS BATTED IN

Samuel, PHI	9
Knight, NY	8
Sandberg, CHI	8
Carter, NY	6
Moreland, CHI	6
Youngblood, SF	6
6 players tied.	5

Career Visiting Leaders

NAME	AB	H	BA
Marty Perez	24	11	.458
Rick Auerbach	22	10	.455
Denny Walling	65	26	.400
Jerry Morales	124	48	.387
Elliott Maddox	57	22	.386
Dave Collins	50	19	.380
Pedro Guerrero	118	44	.373
Steve Lake	30	11	.367
Joe Torre	30	11	.367
Mike Ivie	91	33	.363
Jack Clark	122	44	.361
Jose Oquendo	28	10	.357
Tony Scott	42	15	.357
Biff Pocoroba	29	10	.345
Andres Galarraga	32	11	.344
Andre Thornton	32	11	.344
Terry Whitfield	82	28	.341
Jose Cruz	248	84	.339
Tim Raines	195	66	.338
Chris Chambliss	98	33	.337
Mel Hall	54	18	.333
Junior Kennedy	36	12	.333
Ken Griffey	166	55	.331
Steve Sax	121	40	.331
Lenny Randle	73	24	.329

NAME	AB	HR	HR%
Bobby Bonds	15	4	26.67
Andres Galarraga	32	3	9.37
Andre Thornton	32	3	9.37
Joe Ferguson	62	5	8.06
Sid Bream	38	3	7.89
Darryl Strawberry	116	9	7.76
Johnny Bench	119	9	7.56
Del Unser	133	9	6.77
Jim Morrison	76	5	6.58
Cliff Johnson	49	3	6.12
Mitch Webster	49	3	6.12
Reggie Smith	99	6	6.06
Mel Hall	54	3	5.56
Mike Ivie	91	5	5.49
Carmelo Martinez	55	3	5.45
Rick Schu	56	3	5.36
Mike Schmidt	337	18	5.34
Jack Clark	122	6	4.92
Terry Whitfield	82	4	4.88
Bill Robinson	149	7	4.70
Dave Kingman	235	11	4.68
Gary Redus	87	4	4.60
Willie Stargell	132	6	4.55
Dave Lopes	134	6	4.48
Bob Brenly	69	3	4.35

San Diego
San Diego/Jack Murphy Stadium

1986 Visiting Leaders

	1986 SEASON			1982 – 1986		
	Home Games	Road Games	Pct. Diff.	Home Games	Road Games	Pct. Diff.
G	81	81	0.0	406	405	0.2
AB	5514	5460	1.0	27347	27646	− 1.1
1B	982	1048	− 6.3	5015	5171	− 3.0
2B	230	247	− 6.9	1012	1207	− 16.2
3B	23	32	− 28.1	162	183	− 11.5
HR	158	128	23.4	664	546	21.6
HR%	2.865	2.344	22.2	2.428	1.975	22.9
R	658	721	− 8.7	3199	3411	− 6.2
BA	.253	.266	− 5.2	.251	.257	− 2.5
SA	.389	.394	− 1.3	.372	.373	− 0.2
E	137	122	12.3	736	696	5.7
SHO	7	9	− 22.2	49	58	− 15.5
R/G	8.123	8.901	− 8.7	7.879	8.422	− 6.4

BATTING AVG. (Top 10)

Bass, HOU	.448
Santana, NY	.444
Raines, MTL	.435
Bream, PIT	.429
Orsulak, PIT	.421
Sax, LA	.407
Doran, HOU	.406
Milner, CIN	.385
Wilson, NY	.375
Ray, PIT	.370

HOME RUNS

Bass, HOU	4
Brooks, MTL	3
Murphy, ATL	3
9 players tied.	2

BATTING AVG. (Bottom 10)

Moreno, ATL	.069
Wallach, MTL	.083
Hatcher, HOU	.120
Dawson, MTL	.130
Davis, HOU	.139
Coleman, STL	.150
Morrison, PIT	.158
Oberkfell, ATL	.160
Mumphrey, CHI	.167
Thompson, SF	.171

RUNS BATTED IN

Bass, HOU	8
Duncan, LA	7
Murphy, ATL	7
Strawberry, NY	7
Brooks, MTL	6
Parker, CIN	6
Walling, HOU	6
6 players tied.	5

Career Visiting Leaders

NAME	AB	H	BA
Mike Ivie	40	17	.425
Wayne Krenchicki	50	21	.420
Jay Johnstone	67	27	.403
Rusty Staub	35	14	.400
Terry Francona	43	17	.395
Lee Lacy	161	61	.379
Tommy Hutton	32	12	.375
Rafael Santana	48	18	.375
Rick Auerbach	27	10	.370
Vic Harris	36	13	.361
Bob Watson	150	54	.360
Gene Clines	31	11	.355
Milt May	77	27	.351
Len Matuszek	29	10	.345
Johnny Ray	128	44	.344
Elliott Maddox	35	12	.343
Chili Davis	141	48	.340
Keith Hernandez	230	78	.339
Mike Tyson	68	23	.338
Junior Kennedy	51	17	.333
Joe Strain	30	10	.333
Joel Youngblood	156	51	.327
Marc Hill	74	24	.324
Randy G. Johnson	34	11	.324
Bill Doran	124	40	.323

NAME	AB	HR	HR%
Len Matuszek	29	4	13.79
Mel Hall	24	3	12.50
Pedro Guerrero	165	16	9.70
Ozzie Virgil	69	6	8.70
Jim Morrison	40	3	7.50
Dave Kingman	122	9	7.38
Johnny Bench	193	14	7.25
Jason Thompson	100	7	7.00
Mike Schmidt	264	18	6.82
Richie Zisk	44	3	6.82
Bo Diaz	94	6	6.38
Darryl Strawberry	63	4	6.35
Dave Parker	283	17	6.01
Wayne Krenchicki	50	3	6.00
Bob Watson	150	9	6.00
Gary Carter	234	14	5.98
Chili Davis	141	8	5.67
Dickie Thon	91	5	5.49
Alan Ashby	148	8	5.41
Candy Maldonado	56	3	5.36
Jeff Burroughs	113	6	5.31
Dale Murphy	284	15	5.28
Steve Yeager	190	10	5.26
Willie McCovey	80	4	5.00
Kevin Bass	101	5	4.95

San Francisco
Candlestick Park

	1986 SEASON			1982 – 1986		
	Home Games	Road Games	Pct. Diff.	Home Games	Road Games	Pct. Diff.
G	81	81	0.0	405	405	0.0
AB	5434	5417	0.3	27432	27618	− 0.7
1B	932	970	− 3.9	5018	5152	− 2.6
2B	247	214	15.4	1092	1195	− 8.6
3B	23	37	− 37.8	130	202	− 35.6
HR	111	124	− 10.5	603	620	− 2.7
HR%	2.043	2.289	− 10.8	2.198	2.245	− 2.1
R	620	696	− 10.9	3258	3521	− 7.5
BA	.242	.248	− 2.7	.249	.260	− 3.9
SA	.357	.370	− 3.6	.365	.385	− 5.2
E	149	155	− 3.9	764	756	1.1
SHO	12	10	20.0	47	41	14.6
R/G	7.654	8.593	− 10.9	8.044	8.694	− 7.5

1986 Visiting Leaders

BATTING AVG. (Top 10)

Dawson, MTL	.429
Orsulak, PIT	.423
Morrison, PIT	.409
Smith, STL	.400
Hayes, PHI	.360
Samuel, PHI	.348
Dunston, CHI	.346
Ray, PIT	.318
Hernandez, NY	.316
Strawberry, NY	.316

HOME RUNS

Bass, HOU	3
Davis, CIN	3
Brooks, MTL	2
Cey, CHI	2
Garner, HOU	2
Guerrero, LA	2
Ramirez, ATL	2
Virgil, ATL	2
Wallach, MTL	2
41 players tied.	1

BATTING AVG. (Bottom 10)

Stubbs, LA	.000
McReynolds, SD	.069
Brock, LA	.071
Davis, HOU	.094
Templeton, SD	.107
Pendleton, STL	.111
Wallach, MTL	.120
Garvey, SD	.129
Esasky, CIN	.138
Bream, PIT	.150

RUNS BATTED IN

Wallach, MTL	8
Diaz, CIN	7
Parker, CIN	7
Ray, PIT	7
Brooks, MTL	5
Dunston, CHI	5
Griffey, ATL	5
Marshall, LA	5
Murphy, ATL	5
12 players tied.	4

Career Visiting Leaders

NAME	AB	H	BA
Mike Ramsey	32	15	.469
Bill Fahey	25	11	.440
Randy G. Johnson	43	18	.419
Jack Clark	29	12	.414
David Green	52	21	.404
Tim McCarver	25	10	.400
Johnny Oates	43	17	.395
Ralph Garr	32	12	.375
Ed Kranepool	40	15	.375
Jerry Grote	33	12	.364
Tim Raines	131	47	.359
Mick Kelleher	31	11	.355
Lonnie Smith	93	33	.355
Richie Zisk	40	14	.350
Willie Crawford	66	23	.348
Manny Sanguillen	46	16	.348
Tommy Hutton	29	10	.345
Gary Thomasson	32	11	.344
Joe Nolan	44	15	.341
Mike Jorgensen	47	16	.340
Rob Andrews	56	19	.339
Luis Salazar	121	41	.339
Tony Gwynn	133	45	.338
Juan Samuel	83	28	.337
Willie Davis	42	14	.333

NAME	AB	HR	HR%
Eric Davis	54	9	16.67
Mitch Webster	24	3	12.50
Jim Pankovits	29	3	10.34
Darrell Porter	55	5	9.09
Ozzie Virgil	57	5	8.77
Ron Cey	298	23	7.72
Dale Murphy	275	21	7.64
Richie Zisk	40	3	7.50
Barry Foote	59	4	6.78
Tim Wallach	138	9	6.52
Brad Komminsk	48	3	6.25
Andre Dawson	190	11	5.79
David Green	52	3	5.77
Pedro Guerrero	160	9	5.63
George Foster	268	15	5.60
Willie Stargell	78	4	5.13
Kevin Bass	82	4	4.88
Glenn Davis	63	3	4.76
Alan Ashby	109	5	4.59
Reggie Smith	133	6	4.51
Larry Parrish	114	5	4.39
Carmelo Martinez	71	3	4.23
Bob Horner	197	8	4.06
Mike Schmidt	251	10	3.98
Ellis Valentine	101	4	3.96

Macmillan Brings You the Best in Baseball Books

The Baseball Encyclopedia, edited by Joseph L. Reichler
The complete and official record of major league baseball—every player, every record, every statistic in the history of the game. Now in its sixth edition. "I cannot imagine life without it."—Jonathan Yardley, *The Washington Post Book World*

The 1986 Baseball Encyclopedia Update
Keep your *Encyclopedia* current with the *1986 Update*. Complete career listings for everyone who played at least one game in the 1985 season, standings and leaders for the '85 season, and World Series and League Championship Series highlights.

The 1986 Elias Baseball Analyst, by Seymour Siwoff, Steve Hirdt, and Peter Hirdt
The most complete, detailed analysis of player performance ever, from the secret files of the Elias Sports Bureau. Complete batting and pitching performance at home and on the road, vs. lefties and righties, with men on base and bases empty, even with runners in scoring position in the late innings of close ball games! "The best book of baseball statistics ever created. By a multiple of about 10."—Thomas Boswell, *The Washington Post*

Baseball America, by Donald Honig
Donald Honig, our leading baseball historian, portrays the lives of the game's greatest stars: how they were shaped by their times, and how their lives and legends reflect the changes in our society over the past hundred years. *"Baseball America* is part history, part biography, part drama, and a complete pleasure."—Ira Berkow, sports columnist, *The New York Times*

Weaver on Strategy, by Earl Weaver with Terry Pluto
A guide for armchair managers, by baseball's master tactician. "Once in a lifetime, a genuine, 24-karat genius comes along, and we ought to listen. *Weaver on Strategy* is gold, burnished by the master."—Tony Kubek

A Baseball Winter: The Off-Season Life of the Summer Game,
   edited by Terry Pluto and Jeffrey Neuman
An in-depth look at the events of a baseball off-season, from the last out of the World Series to the first pitch of opening day. A unique, involving, fresh, and innovative look at the overlooked end of the year-round business of baseball. "The inside information here gives the best look I've ever seen at how a baseball team really operates."—Brooks Robinson

Voices from Cooperstown, by Anthony J. Connor
The thoughts and reminiscences of sixty-five Hall of Famers, skillfully blended to create a touching portrait of a life in the game. "Through the recollections of these old-time craftsmen, who happen to have played baseball and played it with love, we have a lively informal history of an epoch that will never come again."—Studs Terkel

The World Series, by Richard M. Cohen, David S. Neft, and Jordan A. Deutsch
Complete play-by-play of every World Series game ever, from the first Series in 1903 through the Royals' come-from-behind triumph in 1985.
(Available in August)